The SAGE Handbook of
Conflict Communication

The SAGE Handbook of
Conflict Communication

Integrating Theory, Research, and Practice

EDITORS

John G. Oetzel

University of New Mexico

Stella Ting-Toomey

California State University, Fullerton

SAGE Publications
Thousand Oaks ▪ London ▪ New Delhi

For information:

Sage Publications, Inc.
2455 Teller Road
Thousand Oaks, California 91320
E-mail: order@sagepub.com

Sage Publications Ltd.
1 Oliver's Yard
55 City Road
London EC1Y 1SP
United Kingdom

Sage Publications India Pvt. Ltd.
B-42, Panchsheel Enclave
Post Box 4109
New Delhi 110 017 India

Printed in the United States of America.

Library of Congress Cataloging-in-Publication Data

The SAGE handbook of conflict communication : integrating theory,
research, and practice / [edited by] John G. Oetzel, Stella Ting-Toomey.
   p. cm.
Includes bibliographical references and index.
ISBN 0-7619-3045-0 (cloth)
   1. Conflict management. 2. Social conflict. 3. Communication in
the social sciences. I. Oetzel, John G. II. Ting-Toomey, Stella.
HM1126.S24 2006
303.6—dc22

                            2005024648

This book is printed on acid-free paper

06 07 08 09 10   10 9 8 7 6 5 4 3 2 1

Acquiring Editor:	Todd R. Armstrong
Editorial Assistant:	Deya Saoud
Project Editor:	Astrid Virding
Copyeditor:	Kristin Bergstad
Typesetter:	C&M Digitals (P) Ltd.
Indexer:	Naomi Linzer
Cover Designer:	Michelle Lee Kenny

CONTENTS

LIST OF FIGURES AND TABLES

FIGURES

TABLES

INTRODUCTION

C onflict is a prevalent phenomenon of our lives (Thomas & Schmidt, 1976; Wilmot & Hocker, 2001). Conflict is "an expressed struggle between at least two interdependent parties who perceive incompatible goals, scarce resources, and interference from others in achieving their goals" (Wilmot & Hocker, 2001, p. 41). Turning on the news, going to work, wandering through the neighborhood, or interacting with loved ones, we witness and participate in many examples of conflict such as wars, community violence, disputes at work, and marital discord.

In addition to being frequent, conflict has certain consequences. The negative consequences get the most "press" and they—rather than positive outcomes—tend to be associated with conflict. These costs include violence/death, divorce, economic losses, dissatisfaction, discord, and trauma. On the other hand, conflict also provides such opportunities as personal growth, relational development, improved decision making, and identifying and addressing problems. Many communication scholars emphasize that the consequences of conflict are due to the way the conflict is managed (e.g., Wilmot & Hocker, 2001). If we manage conflicts constructively, then we have positive outcomes; if we manage conflicts poorly, we have negative outcomes.

What it means to manage conflict constructively or destructively is a complex issue. A simplistic answer is that constructive conflict is done cooperatively, while destructive conflict is done competitively. However, this superficial assessment belies the many factors involved in a conflict. There is a proliferation of research about conflict theory and practice. Much of this research examines the multitude of factors involved in conflict situations. The amount of research makes it difficult to synthesize key principles and practices of constructive conflict management. The chapters in this handbook aim to provide this synthesis in a variety of specific contexts.

This particular handbook emphasizes constructive conflict management from a communication perspective. This perspective places primacy in the message as the focus of conflict research and practice. The means to express conflict is through communication (verbal and nonverbal messages); likewise, the means to manage and address conflict is through communication. In this introduction, we discuss the purpose, intended audience, and organizational framework of this volume. In describing the organizational framework, we also introduce the first two chapters since these serve as general overviews for the four main sections.

PURPOSE AND AUDIENCE FOR THIS VOLUME

The general purpose of *The SAGE Handbook of Conflict Communication* is three-fold: (a) to assemble in one resource the knowledge base of the field of conflict communication; (b) to identify the best theories, ideas, and practices of conflict communication; and (c) to provide the opportunity for scholars and practitioners to link theoretical frameworks and application tools. This multi-pronged purpose grew from our focus on communication and the intended audience.

We had three primary constituencies in mind as we designed this handbook: (a) academics who will use it as a resource for their scholarship, (b) instructors who will use it as a main or supplementary text in advanced undergraduate and graduate courses in conflict communication, and (c) practitioners who are responsible for a variety of conflict management processes and systems in a variety of settings and who are interested in bridging theory and practice (e.g., organizations, political entities, mediation, counseling, courts, etc.). The multiple constituencies presented a challenge to both the structure and the authors of the *Handbook*. The authors handled this challenge brilliantly. For academics/instructors, the *Handbook* must reflect the state of the art regarding conflict communication theory and research. The content needs to advance thinking on conflict and to stimulate new ideas and guide future scholarship and research. For practitioners, the *Handbook* must be practical and applicable to the ongoing conflicts that they view and participate in on a daily basis. The application of research must promote critical reflection on existing practices as well as provide creative and innovative ideas to improve conflict practices. These goals are interdependent in that academics want innovative and heuristic ideas to benefit a variety of constituencies and practitioners want practical suggestions that are framed by current research.

Essentially, we aimed to develop a book that integrated theory, research, and practice. We asked the contributing authors to include both the latest theory and the "best known" practices in their chapters rather than having separate chapters for either practice or theory. To help integrate both research and practice (and provide some consistency in content), we provided a list of six guiding questions for each author and asked them to consider these questions in the best manner possible. The questions were as follows:

1. What organizational framework (e.g., model, theory, or schema) guides the design and the conceptual development of the chapter?

2. What lines of conflict-related research have been conducted that can be grouped under this organizational framework?

3. What are your assessments of the strengths, gaps, and/or controversies that face this line of research?

4. Does this line of research address global cross-cultural or domestic diversity conflict-related issues? Do you have any specific suggestions?

5. What do you think are the most meaningful theoretical directions or research issues that are worth pursuing in the next 10 years? Why?

6. What are the major applied or practical issues that can be derived from the review of the literature for this framework? What can you say to conflict practitioners or mediators?

You will see that certain authors emphasize research, while others emphasize practice (and some balance both). The result is a volume that does a solid job of integrating theory, research, and practice.

Finally, we also sought to expand the discourse and research beyond mainstream conflict research and practice in the United States (as evidenced by Question 4 above). We want the audience to include academics and practitioners from not only around the world, but also from diverse communities in the United States. To this end, we included a section that focuses specifically on intercultural/international conflict communication and asked some international scholars/practitioners (and U.S. scholars with international experience and backgrounds) to contribute chapters. We also asked authors to include research and practice beyond mainstream U.S. contexts where possible (or note these limitations in the literature).

ORGANIZATIONAL FRAMEWORK AND OVERVIEW OF INTRODUCTORY CHAPTERS

The *Handbook* is divided into four parts plus a general introduction and a conclusion. Two chapters are included in the introduction and provide an overview of definitional, theoretical, and methodological issues in conflict communication. In the first chapter, Putnam tracks the development of definitions and approaches to the study of conflict and communication. She reviews the early work on communication and conflict dating back to the 1970s and tracks the role that communication has played in defining conflict, developing approaches to studying it, exploring models of negotiation and mediation, and moving from quantitative to qualitative methods of research. She concludes by suggesting ways to integrate knowledge across the discipline and to investigate the ways that conflict contributes to individual, organizational, and societal growth.

In the second chapter, Fink, Cai, and Wang offer an overview of quantitative approaches for researching conflict communication. They focus on critical issues for comparing conflict communication across groups (e.g., organizations, job positions, gender, etc.), particularly cross-cultural comparisons. They consider four critical questions for making such comparisons: (a) Are the meaning of conflict and the variables representing the conflict process comparable across the cultures being investigated? (b) Are the samples comparable? (c) Do the samples use the same processes with the same variables for dealing with conflict? and (d) Are the cultures at the same place in the process under investigation? To help address these questions, they consider critical issues in types of data (qualities and quantities, levels of analysis, and time dependence), sampling, and data analysis. They also display specific approaches and instruments for observing, measuring, and interpreting conflict communication in each of the four contexts.

Both of these introductory chapters have a decidedly research flavor as they set the stage for the nature of conflict research in the four specific parts. These four parts are focused on contexts in which conflict occurs: interpersonal, organizational, community, and intercultural/international. Each section includes chapters on specific topics within the contexts and concludes with an overarching chapter focusing on "best practices" for conflict management. We describe each of these contexts, and the respective chapters, in the introductions for each part.

In the conclusion, Oetzel, Ting-Toomey, and Rinderle attempt to synthesize the chapters in this volume. The focus on specific contexts that may encourage some readers to believe that there is limited overlap in contexts. To the contrary, we believe that the contexts are layered and interdependent. We use multilevel theorizing, specifically within a social ecological framework (Rousseau & House, 1994; Stokols, 1996). Social ecological theory examines the relationship of an organism to its environment (Stokols, 1996). In this volume, the organism(s) is conflict process and/or participants and we include the four contexts as the environment. We discuss the layered nature of these contexts and identify different ways in which the contexts shape, frame, and influence conflict communication in different contexts. We also present future directions for research and practice based on the social ecological framework.

REFERENCES

Rousseau, D. M., & House, R. J. (1994). Meso organizational behavior: Avoiding three fundamental biases. In C. L. Cooper & D. M. Rousseau (Eds.), *Trends in organizational behavior* (Vol. 1, pp. 13–30). New York: John Wiley.

Stokols, D. (1996). Translating social ecological theory into guidelines for community health promotion. *American Journal of Health Promotion, 10,* 282–298.

Thomas, K., & Schmidt, W. (1976). A survey of managerial interest with respect to conflict. *Academy of Management Journal, 19,* 315–318.

Wilmot, W., & Hocker, J. (2001). *Interpersonal conflict* (6th ed). Dubuque, IA: William C. Brown.

ACKNOWLEDGMENTS

Editing *The SAGE Handbook of Conflict Communication* was a daunting and, at the same time, an exhilarating task. We are indebted to many individuals who encouraged and motivated us to bring this book to completion. First and foremost, we want to thank all the invaluable authors in the *Handbook*. Without their commitment, hard work, and focused energy, this volume would not be in your hands. They were a pure joy to work with and, as you can see from the finished product, they are an outstanding group of individuals who have dedicated their lives to researching and fine-tuning conflict communication theories and practices with passion. Thank you again to the chapter authors for journeying with us to make this handbook a reality.

Second, we express our sincere appreciation to our editorial assistant, Susana Rinderle. She did amazingly meticulous work in proofing and double-checking the citations/references in the text and helping us to coordinate with the authors in a timely fashion. Third, we want to thank Todd Armstrong, the Communication Editor at Sage, who encouraged us develop this book from the very beginning. Todd has been consistently supportive and encouraging throughout the various developmental phases of the book. Fourth, we extend our special applause to Deya Saoud, Senior Editorial Assistant to Todd, for helping us navigate the multitude of editorial steps in rounding off this book and for always being so efficient and responsive in answering our questions. Fifth, we want to thank Kristin Bergstad, Copy Editor at Sage, for her careful editing and keen eye in polishing up the collective chapters. Sixth, we express our profound gratitude and a big "thank you" to our colleagues at the University of New Mexico and the California State University at Fullerton. Our colleagues have provided us with an affirming and comfortable environment to conduct our scholarly work. We could not have asked for a more collegial and intellectually supportive group to work with. Lastly, we thank all our undergraduate and graduate students for their engaging energy, questionings, and curiosities in the classrooms and for pushing us forward in our quest to understand the connection between theory and practice issues in conflict communication.

Individually, there are several people in our personal and professional lives to whom we would like to express our special acknowledgments. *John:* I want to thank my wife and life partner, Keri, for providing me with love, personal support, intellectual stimulation, and enriching insights during this arduous editing process. I also want to thank Stella for coediting this volume with me. I value our tranquil friendship and collaborative work and look forward to continuous learning and growing as I team with you in future projects. *Stella:* I want to thank my husband, Charles, and son, Adrian, for coming along with me on this academic journey and for always providing me with light-hearted humor, affection, and a secure home space for respite and rest. I also want to thank John for inviting me to coedit the *Handbook* with him. I value your collaborative spirit, inspiring vision, dialogue, and the fortitude to see this "big, thick volume" through to the end.

To the readers, we thank you for taking the time to review each chapter in this handbook, and we encourage you to pursue your interest and goal of a deeper understanding of the rich tapestry of conflict communication in diverse arenas.

Sage Publications thanks the following reviewers; Leda Cooks, University of Massachusetts, Amherst; William Donohue, Michigan State University; Peter M. Kellett, University of North Carolina at Greensboro; Linda L. Putnam, Texas A&M University; Randall G. Rogan, Wake Forest University; and Michael E. Roloff, Northwestern University.

1

DEFINITIONS AND APPROACHES TO CONFLICT AND COMMUNICATION

LINDA L. PUTNAM

Texas A&M University

Few scholars would deny that communication is an essential feature of conflict. As Thomas and Pondy (1977) noted in their massive review of conflict in organizations, "It is communication with which we are most concerned in understanding conflict management" (p. 1100). Communication aids in the forming of issues, framing of perceptions, and enacting the conflict itself (Putnam & Poole, 1987). It functions as an impromptu code to signal intentions, exchange information, exercise influence, and coordinate outcomes. Most of all, "communication is the means by which conflict gets socially defined" (Simons, 1974b, p. 3).

Despite the importance of communication in social conflicts, early researchers often cast it as a backdrop or a taken-for-granted activity. In particular, initial studies that include communication in the Prisoner's Dilemma games often treated it simplistically, as "let the players talk or don't let them talk" or as tacit cues that conveyed preferences through moves and countermoves (Bostrom, 1968; Gergen, 1969). Disenchanted with the paucity of attention to communication in conflict studies, scholars across the discipline gathered in 1972 in Philadelphia for a conference sponsored by the Speech Communication Association. This conference and subsequent

publications that emanated from it (see Bowers, 1974b; Miller & Simons, 1974) nurtured the growth of communication and conflict studies as a distinct area that has mushroomed across the discipline. As this volume demonstrates, research on communication and conflict is alive and well.

Amid this widespread growth, communication scholars are often silent or presumptive about the relationship between communication and conflict. Scholars typically define conflict in a consensual way and then treat the elements of this definition as assumed within their research designs. Thus, characteristics and dimensions are often presumed within the operational nature and measurement instruments of conflict (Weider-Hatfield, 1993). For many scholars, communication is the manifest stage of conflict; that is, it surfaces as social interaction or as strategies and tactics. As such, communication seems bound by a set of presumed relationships between communication and conflict.

This chapter unpacks these relationships through presenting a historical overview of communication and conflict studies, including examining three seminal theories, comparing definitions and assumptions, reviewing models and approaches to conflict, and highlighting research methods. It culminates by explicating

1

the roles of communication in conflict as a variable, a process, an interpretation or meaning, and a dialectical relationship. Finally it sets forth some options for integrating research across the field and promoting theory building through future directions for communication studies.

Given the breadth of communication and conflict research, a full-scale historical treatment of each contextual arena is beyond the scope of this chapter. Moreover, each chapter in this volume offers its own historical background for conflict studies in particular domains. In like manner, this chapter is not an exhaustive state-of-the-art review, as presented in the early articles and handbook chapters (Donohue, Diez, & Stahle, 1983; Johnson, 1974; Putnam & Jones, 1982b; Putnam & Poole, 1987; Roloff, 1987; Steinfatt, 1974) or summarized in the early textbooks that now appear in multiple editions (Folger & Poole, 1984; Hocker & Wilmot, 1978). What this chapter does, however, is situate research on communication and conflict in the 1970s as a period that led to the rapid acceleration of conflict studies in family and interpersonal communication (Fitzpatrick & Winke, 1979; Millar, Rogers, & Bavelas, 1984; Sillars, 1980a, 1980b), small group interaction (Pood, 1980; Waln, 1982), negotiation and bargaining (Donohue, 1981a, 1981b; Putnam & Jones, 1982b), organizational conflict styles (Putnam & Wilson, 1982; Richmond, Wagner, & McCroskey, 1983; Riggs, 1983; Shockley-Zalabak, 1981), and intercultural conflict (Gudykunst, 1985; Ting-Toomey, 1985). This period is singled out because the conceptual and theoretical debates at that time clearly shaped the direction of future research. Although scholars have drawn heavily from conflict studies outside our field, this chapter concentrates primarily on the research and conceptual issues that have developed within communication.

HISTORICAL OVERVIEW OF COMMUNICATION AND CONFLICT STUDIES

For more than 30 years, communication scholars have studied social conflicts. Initially aligned with rhetorical scholarship, research focused on diplomacy (Oliver, 1950, 1952) and the rhetoric of confrontation and agitation

(Bowers & Ochs, 1971; Scott & Smith, 1969). Inspired by campus demonstrations, protest movements, and riots in the 1960s, communication scholars directed their attention to crisis rhetoric, persuasion in social conflicts, and rhetorical strategies of coercion (Burgess, 1973; Simons, 1969, 1972, 1974a). Specifically, Tompkins and his colleagues (Tompkins, Fisher, Infante, & Tompkins, 1974) applied Burkian concepts to an analysis of mystery and order in the administration of a public university in the midst of campus conflicts.

Also focusing on public conflicts, Bowers (1974a) compared the perceived costs, potential rewards, and probability of using different individual and institutional forms of communication during community disputes. Individuals in social conflicts differed from institutions in presenting oral and written petitions, engaging in collective actions, and escalating confrontations; institutions, in turn, were limited to avoidance, counter-persuasion, and nonviolent suppression as defensive reactions. Rhetoricians also analyzed the public discourse surrounding the Arab-Israeli conflict (Heisy, 1970) and the argumentative competence of Henry Kissinger's negotiation (Schuetz, 1978).

Amid this attention to social and political conflicts, other scholars in the field employed experimental methods to study bargaining and conflict in dyads and small groups. Communication scholars were eager to rectify the shortcomings of game theory researchers who ignored social interactions (Beisecker, 1970a; Bostrom, 1968). Their early work focused on comparing tacit nonverbal messages with explicit verbal communication (Harris & Smith, 1974). At first, researchers concluded that an increase in explicit communication between negotiators increased cooperativeness (Smith, 1969; Steinfatt, Seibold, & Frye, 1974), but additional studies revealed that in highly competitive situations, communication became distorted, leading to error and misinformation (Beisecker, 1970a). Hence, increased opportunity for communication did not necessarily lead to cooperation.

To unpack the explicit versus implicit role of communication, Johnson, McCarty, and Allen (1976) compared cooperative versus competitive bargainers in both verbal and nonverbal conditions. They observed that verbal statements of cooperation led to more agreements in less time than did the other three conditions, including nonverbal expressions of cooperation; thus, explicit cooperative messages had a strong effect on reaching a negotiated settlement. In a similar way, communication scholars contrasted bargaining outcomes in telephone, face-to-face, and written modes of interaction (Turnbull, Strickland, & Shaver, 1976). This study revealed that full, face-to-face interaction between disputants increased the number of successful payoffs and enhanced the diversity of negotiated settlements for cooperative conditions (Greenwood, 1974; Smith, 1969). Early communication researchers also examined information exchange (Smith, 1971), argumentation patterns (Reiches & Harral, 1974), cognitive complexity (Saine, 1974), and persuasive strategies that facilitated concession making (Beisecker, 1970b).

Small group researchers also began to study communication in cooperative and competitive groups. Specifically, Baird (1974) found that members of cooperative groups engaged in greater diversity of contributions, exchanged more relevant messages, and were more friendly and attentive to each other than were individuals in competitive teams. Focusing specifically on substantive, affective, and procedural conflicts, Bell (1974, 1979) observed that substantive messages were exchanged reciprocally and led to flexibility in decision making. Affective conflict seemed tied to ego involvement in that individuals who had high ego involvement were less likely to reach agreement than were dyads with minimal ego investment (Sereno & Mortensen, 1973).

In response to this growing work, Jandt (1973) assembled a collection of readings, mostly reprints from classic articles outside the field. The aim of this volume was to apply conflict research to multiple levels of communication studies—from dyads to sociopolitical conflicts. This volume also introduced the field to conflict studies in family, classroom, intraorganizational, racial, and intercultural arenas.

Thus, in the mid-1970s, the stage was set for a significant conference on communication and conflict studies that was attended by scholars throughout the discipline. Researchers both agreed and disagreed about the directions for future conflict studies. The book *Perspectives*

on Communication in Social Conflicts (Miller & Simons, 1974) embodied this controversy, particularly the diverse perspectives and ideological differences among researchers. These differences appeared in Simons's (1974b) prologue and Miller's (1974) epilogue and opened communication studies to the multiple perspectives that scholars currently see in the field today. In particular, their dissatisfaction with theories, definitions, and models for conflict research influenced the questions that scholars now pose, hybrid research designs, innovative topics and methods, and a quest to unpack the conceptual relationship between communication and conflict.

CONFLICT THEORIES AND PERSPECTIVES: CHARTING THE DISENCHANTMENT

Scholars at this landmark conference typically concurred that theories and models needed to be expanded. They recommended that research focus on "co-acting entities whose behaviors must be modeled dynamically and relationally" (Simons, 1974b, p. 3). They concurred in their critiques of game theory, but they disagreed on the viability of social exchange and systems theory as options for future studies.

Challenging Game Theory

Scholars at the conference were united in critiquing game theory and in issuing a plea for alternative models. Although pure game theory was never designed for laboratory experiments, social scientists borrowed liberally from it because it contained the basic elements of any conflict situation. Since it treated players as rational beings who aimed to maximize gains and minimize losses (Bostrom, 1968), scholars focused on how players selected moves and how these moves produced different types of rewards.

Communication scholars challenged the single-minded accounts of game theory through arguing that motives and intensions were particularly ambiguous when players could not communicate explicitly (Steinfatt & Miller, 1974). In addition, game theory's focus on payoffs and outcomes ignored a bargainer's psychological makeup, his or her relationship with the other negotiator, and concerns for face saving and self-esteem (Mortensen, 1974). This approach was also silent regarding the meanings of payoffs, utilities, and options (Simons, 1974b) and the validity of laboratory experiments (Jandt, 1974; Mortensen, 1974). Game theory also relied on static variables that failed to track changes in bargaining process, goals, and payoff schedules (Hawes & Smith, 1973; Mortensen, 1974). In effect, communication scholars concurred that pure game theory held little promise for guiding research, but they differed as to whether laboratory games per se were problematic (Miller, 1974). With this disenchantment, scholars called for the development of alternatives "to bring forth fresh perspectives and to enliven old ones" (Simons, 1974b, p. 1).

Harnessing Social Exchange

The residue of game theory surfaced in social exchange models of conflict and negotiation. Similar to game theory, social exchange emulated an economic approach in which disputants held rational motives to maximize their own self-interests. Unlike game theory, however, disputants maximized profits based on rewards minus costs that were derived from social resources. For communication scholars, social resources were symbolic (e.g., affection, status, control) and any given exchange had multiple resources involved. Social exchange, then, entailed an interaction process or a series of sequential behaviors in which disputants provided each other with resources through their interactions (Roloff & Campion, 1985).

Critical to exchange theory was the notion of reciprocity, a concept that Bell (1979) identified in small group research. Reciprocity, first explicated by Gouldner (1960), typically referred to helping those who had helped you. Communication scholars invoked this norm by examining reciprocity in a number of ways, including obligations to exchange resources of equivalent value (Roloff & Campion, 1985), symmetrical message patterns in interpersonal and marital conflicts (Bavelas, Rogers, & Millar, 1985; Sillars, 1980b; Ting-Toomey, 1983), and matching integrative or distributive strategies in negotiations (Bednar & Curington, 1983; Donohue,

1981a; Putnam & Jones, 1982a) and divorce mediations (Jones, 1989a). Thus, the decline of game theory in the 1980s led the field to adopt modified versions of social exchange theory.

Recasting System Theory

Early scholars also criticized the linear views of communication employed in conflict studies (Hawes & Smith, 1973; Miller, 1974; Ruben, 1978). Linear models situated communication as the archer's arrow shot directly into a target that would instantly impact the state of a conflict (Bowers, 1974b; Ruben 1978). This sender-oriented approach characterized much of the early conflict research. In opposition to this view, researchers called for focusing on interdependent messages that developed within the interaction process. Thus, early conflict scholars uniformly rejected the notion that communication breakdowns led to conflict and that shooting more communication at a target would resolve a dispute (Hawes & Smith, 1973; Ruben, 1978).

Moreover, they reacted negatively to the assumptions of early systems theorists that conflict deviated from harmony and normality (Gamson, 1968). At this time, the dominant view was that conflict created an imbalance in the equilibrium of a system and, thus, needed to be resolved or prevented. Conference participants were uniformly dismayed with these anti-conflict biases and challenged scholars to explore the benefits of conflict and to question conflict's role in changing rather than preserving extant systems (Miller, 1974).

Efforts to develop new models of communication and conflict grew out of these critiques. Specifically, Ruben (1978) advocated a living systems model that linked conflict to growth and change. In his view, conflict operated at the level of action and paraconflict functioned at the level of symbol to evoke a self-reflexive nature between the two constructs. This approach combined conflict action with sense-making (labeling and abstracting experiences); thus, conflict emerged as a cyclical, reflexive process in which action and sense-making crossed individual and societal levels.

Drawing from the philosophy of pragmatism, Mortensen (1974) proposed a transactional model that favored a developmental view of conflict aimed at capturing the whole process as well as the unfolding and contingent aspects of it. This approach rejected environmental determinism, severe reductionism, and obtrusive structural models. Instead, it centered on both the "knowing" and the "known" of personal reality and emphasized three conflict dimensions: orientation, intensity, and affect. Thus, this approach purported that the existence of a struggle was in itself not necessarily a conflict until someone labeled it as such. The best predictors of conflict, then, were the content, interpretations, and behaviors that emerged as transactions developed over time.

To test this model, Mortensen (1974) compared interactions from high and low intensity conflicts. His study revealed that parties in highly intense conflicts enacted self-fulfilling cycles through their use of comparative evaluations, accusatory statements, and polarized claims. In contrast, participants in low intensity conflicts talked more deliberately for longer periods of time, used fewer interruptions, more qualifiers, and fewer commitment statements than did those in the high intensity condition. By tracking the development of conflict intensity over time, the transaction model revealed how parties co-created conflict communicatively.

This effort to recast systems theory laid the groundwork for the systems-interaction views of communication that became so dominant in the 1980s. Building on small group and interpersonal communication research (Fisher, 1970; Rogers & Farace, 1975), scholars began to code interactions and track the evolution of conflict over time. This approach began with scholars who applied Bale's Interaction Process to mediation (Landsberger, 1955) and to negotiation (Theye & Seiler, 1979) and was solidified through the development of coding procedures, measurement instruments, and statistical tools that paved the way for a major shift in communication and conflict studies (Ellis & Fisher, 1975).

DEFINITIONS AND ASSUMPTIONS: IDEOLOGICAL DIFFERENCES

Definitions of conflict were also proposed at this 1972 conference. Most scholars adopted some variation of Mortensen's (1974) definition: "conflict is an expressed struggle over incompatible interests in the distribution of limited resources" (p. 93). An examination of Table 1.1 indicates considerable agreement between early and recent scholars on the definition of conflict, particularly its scope, nature of action, and relationship among parties.

Dimensions of Conflict Definitions

Specifically, conflict centers on incompatibilities, an expressed struggle, and interdependence among two or more parties (see Table 1.2). These features are similar to the ones that conflict theorists such as Fink (1968) and Mack and Snyder (1957) developed in the 1960s. Incompatibility refers to mutually exclusive or diametrically opposed goals, values, or beliefs. Most communication scholars treat incompatibilities as rooted in perceptions or located in cultures. In effect, parties may hold compatible goals, but they do not necessarily see them as congruent. Interdependence among parties typically means that individuals need each other to achieve their goals. Some scholars see interdependence as rooted in the mixed motives of cooperating and competing simultaneously (Putnam, 1985), while others treat relationships, structures, or culture as the source of this interdependence (Cahn, 1990; Canary & Cupach, 1988).

In essence, different nuances underlie the same words that scholars use in conflict definitions. Most communication scholars believe that some form of interaction is fundamental to the notion of conflict itself—as the expressed struggle, the nature of the relationship, or the strategies and tactics used. Yet, scholars differ as to whether conflict communication is a particular type of social interaction, exchanges of verbal and nonverbal messages, inconsistencies between messages, defensive communication, symbolic acts, negative interpersonal expressions, or even acts of defiance and violence (Canary, Cupach, & Messman, 1995; Miller, 1974).

Rather than define conflict, Canary et al. (1995) set forth dimensions in which interpersonal conflicts vary, particularly in terms of specific versus nonspecific behaviors and

Table 1.1   A Sample of Common Definitions of Communication and Conflict

Author	Date, Page	Definition
Mortensen	1974, p. 93	"an expressed struggle over incompatible interests in the distribution of limited resources"
Simons	1974b, p. 8	"that state of a social relationship in which incompatible interests between two or more people give rise to a struggle between them"
Hocker & Wilmot	1978, p. 9	"Conflict is an expressed struggle between at least two interdependent parties who perceive incompatible goals, scarce resources, and interference from others in achieving their goals."
Ting-Toomey	1985, p. 72	"Conflict . . . is conceptually defined as a form of intense interpersonal and /or intrapersonal dissonance (tension or antagonism) between two or more interdependent parties based on incompatible goals, needs, desires, values, beliefs/or attitudes."
Putnam & Poole	1987, p. 552	"Conflict . . . is defined as the interaction of interdependent people who perceive opposition of goals, aims, and values, and who see the other party as potentially interfering with the realization of these goals."
Pearce & Littlejohn	1997, p. 55	"Moral conflict occurs when disputants are acting within incommensurate grammars . . . or different forms of life overlap."
Ting-Toomey & Oetzel	2001, p. 17	"Intercultural conflict is defined . . . as the experience of emotional frustration in conjunction with perceived incompatibility of values, norms, face orientations, goals, scarce resources, processes, and/or outcomes between a minimum of two parties from two different cultural communities in an interactive situation."
Folger, Poole, & Stutman	2005, p. 4	"Conflict is the interaction of interdependent people who perceive incompatibility and the possibility of interference from others as a result of this incompatibility."

distinct episodes versus continual processes. Similar concerns are evident in defining moral and intractable conflicts in which episodes come and go and the management of a conflict becomes rooted in identities, relationships, and social institutions (Jameson, 2003; Pearce & Littlejohn, 1997; Putnam & Wondolleck, 2003). Thus, conflict definitions across the field are generally similar, but they also differ in types and emphasis.

Distinguishing between types of conflict. The crux of defining conflict, however, rests on differentiating it from related concepts, such as hostility, disagreement, and misunderstanding. One contribution that Keltner (1994, p. 5) made to the field was to develop a struggle spectrum in which he showed how types of conflict differed across processes, relationships, communication, intervention, and outcomes. Through this spectrum, researchers could differentiate among related concepts, such as disagreements, disputes, and wars. This conceptualization also addressed Simons's (1974a) concern that most conflict definitions center too much on rational situations and ignore nonrealistic or highly

Table 1.2   Components of Conflict Definitions

Author	Scope	Nature of Action	Relationship	Communication	Context Features
Mortensen, 1974	Incompatible interests	Expressed struggle		Distribution	Limited resources
Simons, 1974a	Incompatible interests	Struggle between them	Social relationship between two or more people	Includes symbolic acts	
Hocker & Wilmot, 1978	Incompatible goals	Expressed struggle; Interference in achieving goals	At least two interdependent parties		Scarce resources
Ting-Toomey, 1985	Incompatible goals, needs, desires, values, beliefs	Dissonance; Tension; Antagonism	Interpersonal and intrapersonal; Two or more interdependent parties	Symbolic action; Patterned sense of symbols and meanings	Regulated by culture
Putnam & Poole, 1987	Perceived opposition of goals, aims, values	Other party potentially interferes with goals	Interdependent people	Interaction	
Pearce & Littlejohn, 1997	Incommensurate grammars; Different forms of life	Acting within	Disputants		
Ting-Toomey & Oetzel, 2001	Perceived incompatibility of values, norms, face orientations, goals, processes, outcomes	Emotional frustration	Minimum of two parties		Two different cultural communities; Scarce resources
Folger, Poole, & Stutman, 2005	Perceived incompatibility	Possible interference from others	Interdependent people	Interaction; Exchange of messages	

volatile conflicts. At the level of theory, however, Keltner's (1994) model is untested, particularly in its assumption that conflict develops from mild differences to campaigns and wars. This assumption needs to be fleshed out and tested. Overall, though, researchers concur that different degrees of conflict development exist and can be arrayed on a struggle spectrum.

Distinguishing communication in conflict. Scholars have also made progress in distinguishing conflict from other types of social interaction, such as persuasion, argumentation, compliance gaining, and group decision making (Roloff, Putnam, & Anastasiou, 2003). Persuasion, defined as convincing a person to do something that he or she would not normally do, and argumentation, as the process of asserting claims and supporting them with reasoning, surface in a variety of situations that lie outside of perceived incompatibilities. Conflict communication employs persuasion and argumentation, but these terms are not synonymous with conflict itself.

Similarly, using influence tactics, such as threats, coercion, and power plays, to produce compliance may occur during conflict situations, but conflict is a broader form of social interaction than is compliance gaining. Conflicts also occur during group decision making, but groups engage in other forms of interaction in addition to conflict.

Overall, communication scholars often use the same language to define conflict. In unpacking these definitions, however, scholars differ as to which features are central to their investigations. Communication scholars also distinguish conflict communication from other types of social interaction, including persuasion, argumentation, compliance gaining, and group decision making. In effect, the field has made headway since the 1970s in identifying the scope and essential components of conflict, but more attention is needed to explain the relationships between communication and conflict.

Assumptions About Conflict

Since the 1970s, communication scholars have embraced common assumptions about the nature of conflict. These assumptions cluster into three categories: the subjective/objective basis, the normalcy of conflict, and the functional versus dysfunctional nature of it.

Subjective/objective basis of conflict. One of the key debates at the 1972 conference was whether conflict was "out there" in the real world or whether parties had to perceive or socially construct it (Miller, 1974; Simons, 1974b; Steinfatt & Miller, 1974). Not surprisingly, the empirical scholars emphasized the physical aspects of conflict, for example, scarce resources, economic and material bases of struggles, while the phenomenologists argued for subjective definitions. Other scholars believed that objective situational factors gave rise to perceived conflicts that became altered by material circumstances (Mortensen, 1974). But even scholars who embraced both perspectives had a decidedly receiver-oriented view of communication.

The growth of social construction, critical theory, and postmodernism in the field called the objective-subjective dimension into question. Specifically, scholars posited four alternative perspectives: the cognitive, systems-interactional, symbolic-interpretive, and critical perspectives (Wilson, Paulson, & Putnam, 2001). The cognitive or psychological approach advanced the belief that subjective mental processes shaped conflict behaviors, while the systems-interactional scholars focused on identifying behaviors, messages, and sequential patterns of conflict development. Interpretive/symbolic scholars centered on subjective meanings, conflict narratives, metaphors, and negotiated orders. Some critical theorists invoked both objective and subjective features through examining how conflict entered into the production and reproduction of social structures (Putnam & Poole, 1987). In effect, new approaches to communication urged scholars to avoid the objective/ subjective trap and to move away from receiver-oriented models of communication.

Normalcy of conflict. As previously noted, participants at the 1972 conference objected to the belief that conflict was an aberration that disrupted harmony. Communication scholars typically assumed that conflict was natural, inevitable, and normal. Moreover, scholars also concurred that conflicts were both rational and irrational and that they differed in intensity, disposition, frequency, and salience. Research, however, often presumed the existence of these dimensions rather than assessing what they were and how to operationalize them.

For instance, early research on conflict styles deemed confrontation or problem solving as the most effective and most satisfactory of the five styles (Burke, 1970). Yet, when researchers tested conflict dimensions, they discovered that the choice and effectiveness of a particular style depended on the perceived importance of the issue in dispute, the significance of preserving the parties' relationship, time pressures for managing the conflict, and cultural backgrounds of the participants (Folger, Poole, & Stutman, 2005). Thus, scholars concurred that conflicts were a normal and natural part of everyday life and that specific dimensions influenced how parties chose to handle them.

Conflict as functional and dysfunctional. Similarly, communication scholars believed that conflict could be functional and dysfunctional. Conflict was highly beneficial in preventing system stagnation, stimulating interest and curiosity, fostering cohesiveness within groups, operating as a safety valve to express problems, and invoking change. In contrast, it could be detrimental to relationships, produce inflexible behavior, lead to decreased communication, and result in escalated stalemates (Coser, 1956; Deutsch, 1973). While scholars adhered to both assumptions, they have rarely studied conflict's productive contributions.

Thus, communication scholars typically focused on preventing destructive or highly escalatory conflicts. Destructive conflicts were ones in which disputants ignored the original goals and, instead, aimed at hurting or annihilating each other (Deutsch, 1973). Destructive conflicts escalated through expanding the size and number of conflict issues, relying on power strategies and tactics, and increasing the costs that participants were willing to bear. In effect, communication investigators embraced the assumption that conflict was beneficial and productive, but they centered their research on preventing destructive conflict patterns.

Overall, communication scholars typically employed similar definitions, but they parted ways in highlighting different features of conflict. The field made strides in distinguishing conflict from related concepts, centering less on disagreements and more on incompatibilities, and distinguishing conflict interaction from persuasion and other types of communication. A form of unified diversity existed in which researchers differed but accepted alternative theoretical perspectives and approaches. Moreover, scholars typically concurred that conflict was normal and beneficial, yet research focused primarily on preventing destructive conflicts rather than on understanding productive ones.

Conflict Models

These definitions and assumptions underlie the conflict models that communication researchers employ. Eager to integrate interaction into the interdisciplinary domain of conflict research, early communication scholars relied on models developed outside of the field, but as conflict studies have grown, new approaches have expanded the theoretical domains of traditional research. This section provides a critical overview of three models widely used in communication and conflict research: integrative and distributive negotiation, the dual concern model, and mediation competency.

Integrative and Distributive Negotiation

Derived from Walton and McKersie's (1965) classic studies of collective bargaining, integrative and distributive negotiations refer to two of the four sub-processes that characterize conflict interaction. Prior to the 1960s, research and practice focused on distributive negotiation in which bargainers viewed their goals as fixed-sum in win-lose types of conflicts. The distributive model highlighted withholding information, learning about your opponent's resistance point, and using strategies and tactics to acquire the largest share of a "fixed pie." In contrast, integrative approaches treated bargaining as variable-sum in win-win situations. The integrative model advocated sharing information, engaging in problem solving, generating alternative solutions, making concessions, and understanding the needs and interests of the other party (Putnam & Poole, 1987).

Integrative and distributive negotiation formed the foundation for communication studies of strategies and tactics in collective bargaining (Donohue, 1978, 1981a; Donohue, Diez, & Hamilton, 1984; Donohue & Roberto, 1996; Putnam & Jones, 1982a; Putnam & Wilson, 1989; Tutzauer & Roloff, 1988), in mediation (Donohue, Allen, & Burrell (1985), and in interpersonal conflict (Sillars, 1980b; Sillars, Coletti,

Parry, & Rogers, 1982). Strategies referred to a broad plan that encompassed a series of moves while tactics were the specific messages that enacted the moves.

Communication scholarship played a pivotal role in the debates about the functions of strategies and tactics. Communication researchers observed that strategies and tactics played multiple roles, depending on how they were used during a negotiation. Even though some strategies, like flexibility and problem solving, were aligned with integrative processes and other tactics, like threats, fit with distributive processes, many strategies and tactics (e.g., information sharing, threats, arguments, and concessions) performed multiple functions (Putnam & Wilson, 1989; Roloff, Tutzauer, & Dailey, 1989). Thus, analyses of communication patterns revealed that messages can serve multiple and varying functions as conflict evolves over time. This dynamic view brought communication research into examining pre-negotiation plans and how these plans are altered during these negotiations (Jordan & Roloff, 1997; Roloff & Jordan, 1991). In effect, communication strategies and tactics played complex and interchangeable roles in integrative and distributive processes.

Dual Concern Model

Similar to studies of integrative and distributive negotiation, the dual concern model focused on styles of conflict management. Originally developed by Blake and Mouton (1964) and refined through Kilmann and Thomas's MODE (1977) instrument, this approach focused on five classic styles or predispositions for managing conflict. Shaped by two dimensions— aggressiveness or concern for self and affiliation or concern for others—these styles represented individual choices of conflict management.

The dual concern model influenced research in interpersonal, organizational, and intercultural conflict. Specifically, variations of the model shaped the development and refinement of communication-oriented conflict style scales (Nicotera, 1993, 1994; Putnam & Wilson, 1982; Riggs, 1983; Ross & DeWine, 1988). Several of these self-report measures clustered conflict tactics into three categories that paralleled integrative, distributive, and avoidance patterns (Putnam

& Wilson, 1982; Ross & DeWine, 1988; Sillars et al., 1982) and were tailored for studies of communication competencies in conflicts (Canary & Cupach, 1988; Canary & Spitzberg, 1990).

Over time, communication scholars added emotional valence to the two dimensions (Nicotera, 1993, 1994), covert and hidden tactics (Morrill & Thomas, 1992), and initial and follow-up strategies (Conrad, 1991). In intercultural settings, surveys of conflict styles provided a basis for comparing orientations to conflict across cultures (Cai & Fink, 2002; Lee & Rogan, 1991; Ting-Toomey et al., 1991) and revealed that particular styles evoked different meanings in Eastern and Western cultures.

Overall, the dual concern model and the work on conflict styles advanced research on communication and conflict. Although widely used as an index of strategies, this approach did not examine the actual ongoing interactions that were so vital to understanding conflict (Canary et al., 1995). Even though communication researchers have modified aspects of the original model, scholars have not developed full-scale alternative models to replace this approach.

Mediation Competency Models

Another basic conflict arena that early researchers explored was mediation. Mediation differed from negotiation in that a third party intervened to assist the disputants in managing conflict. Unlike arbitrators, mediators did not make decisions; instead, they employed communication skills to guide parties through substantive discussions and motivated them to reach a settlement.

Drawing from negotiation research, initial studies of communication and mediation compared strategies and tactics, phases of successful and unsuccessful mediations, and communication patterns of competent mediators. One of the earliest studies in the field focused on persuasion and wrestled with differences among bluffing, coercion, and influence in mediation (Keltner, 1965). This study also highlighted the mediator's role in framing issues for disputants, serving as a communication conduit between parties, and helping parties explore solutions.

Disenchanted with the growing list of tactics drawn from labor-management mediation,

Jones (1989b) developed a taxonomy of communication strategies and tactics used in divorce mediations, one that clustered into the general functions of facilitation, substantive direction, and procedural control. Using a systems-interaction approach, she compared the distribution of these tactics across phases of agreement and no-agreement mediations.

The role of different tactics at various stages of mediation, then, pointed to the need for competency models based on the appropriate timing of mediator interventions (Donohue, 1989, 1991). For example, to avoid conflict cycles, mediators should intervene immediately following a disputant's attack on the other party. To adjust to the disputants' emotional intensity, mediators needed to intensify framing early in the process, use structuring strategies in the middle, and decrease language intensity in the latter stages (Donohue, 1991). Continued work, particularly on peer and community mediations, incorporated perceptual and structural factors that impinged on the process (Burrell, Donohue, & Allen, 1990).

Overall, communication research has made important contributions to understanding the micro-processes of mediator interventions. Critiques of this work has led to the growth of new models that challenge problem-solving approaches to mediation. In particular, transformational mediation is an interaction-based model that treats disputes as opportunities for moral growth, empowerment, and recognition (Bush & Folger, 1994). Empowerment refers to restoring an individual's sense of value and ability to handle life's problems while recognition focuses on strengthening a person's empathy and understanding of a situation. Eschewing stage models, this approach advocates that mediators allow disputants to engage in uninterrupted dialogues, pursue diversions, reflect on the significance of events, and provide opportunities for recognition.

In a similar way, Shailor (1994) focuses on empowerment in mediation through the way that each participant structures the meaning of the situation. Also drawing on disputant's stories, he examines how participants co-construct rules and how structures of meaning are reflexively constituted and transformed. These new models situate communication and conflict in a different relationship, one that examines how they produce each other.

Models of negotiation and mediation rooted in feminist theory have emerged and challenged the dominant assumptions of exchange, reciprocity, and concession making that characterized integrative and distributive bargaining (Kolb & Putnam, 1997; Putnam & Kolb, 2000). This overview of these three models indicates that the field has clearly matured since its beginnings in the 1960s and 1970s, particularly in terms of research contexts and methods.

RESEARCH APPROACHES

Particular conflict models encourage specific research approaches to the study of conflict. Research reflects both traditional social science approaches to research, as well as those that emphasize social construction and systems theoretical perspectives. This section discusses the conflict setting and type of methods used in the study of conflict.

Conflict Settings

At the 1972 conference, participants called for studies on a wide array of contexts, including marital conflict, labor-management negotiations, international diplomacy, public conflicts, and event militant confrontations (Simons, 1974b). Researchers responded to this plea by conducting field studies of actual labor-management negotiations (Friedman, 1995), analyzing transcripts of public sector bargaining (Donohue, 1981b; Putnam, Van Hoeven, & Bullis, 1991), and examining actual and training sessions for hostage negotiations (Donohue & Roberto, 1993; Rogan & Hammer, 1994, 1995). They made audio- or videotapes of conflict interactions between marital partners (Fitzpatrick, Fallis, & Vance, 1982; Sillars et al., 1982), conducted surveys of adolescents and parents about conflict behaviors (Comstock, 1994; Comstock & Buller, 1991), and studied married and dating couples (Fitzpatrick, 1988; Witteman & Fitzpatrick, 1986). They coded transcripts of divorce mediations, community disputes, and roommate conflicts (Donohue, Allen, & Burrell, 1985; Jones, 1989b; Sillars, 1980b); developed models of intergroup and face negotiation in diplomacy conflicts (Gudykunst, 1990; Ting-Toomey & Cole, 1990), and even interviewed participants in multi-party environmental conflicts (Putnam & Peterson, 2003). Clearly, communication researchers heeded the advice of their predecessors to focus on situations in which disputants had a conflict history (Mortensen, 1974).

Although some researchers continued to use laboratory investigations, they employed buyer-seller negotiations and role-play simulations that enacted real-life experiences, such as students selling used textbooks (Jordan & Roloff, 1997). Researchers also compared communication patterns in actual negotiations with those in simulated bargaining (Donohue, Diez, & Hamilton, 1984). Thus, communication scholars have centered their research on real-world conflicts, both in their research designs and their selection of conflict settings.

Types of Methods

Communication scholars have heeded the call to conduct descriptive studies and to examine conflict interactions over time. Specifically, researchers have distributed surveys in the field, produced transcripts of naturalistic interactions, and analyzed data through a wide array of quantitative and qualitative category systems. Language and discourse analysts have examined word choices, mapped components of narratives, and tracked turn taking and topic shifts. Using ethnographic approaches, researchers have taken field notes, conducted in-depth interviews with participants, and studied relevant documents (Cobb, 1994; Putnam et al., 1991). Hostage negotiation investigators not only observed training simulations, but also talked with negotiators about their observed interactions (Hammer & Rogan, 1997; Rogan, Hammer, & Van Zandt, 1997). Scholars have also used in-depth case studies to analyze empowerment in mediations (Bush & Folger, 1994; Shailor, 1994) and to track the development of protracted conflicts (Cloud, 2005; Putnam & Peterson, 2003). These approaches illustrate the diversity of research methods that conflict scholars have employed in the past several decades.

ROLE OF COMMUNICATION IN CONFLICT RESEARCH

As this review suggests, communication scholars have embraced a type of "unified diversity" in charting the role that social interaction plays in conflict. Communication surfaces as perceived strategies, actual verbal and nonverbal messages, patterned and sequenced messages, expressions of emotions, language and word use, media, symbols, interpretations of actions-reactions, and surface and deep-level meanings. Hence, it emerges in studies as both a structural and an interaction variable, as a process that defines the essence of the conflict, and as sense-making or interpretations of the conflict. These relationships cluster into the following categories: communication as a variable, as a process, as an interpretive approach, and as a dialectical relationship.

Communication as a Variable

Early researchers in the field treated communication as one of the many variables that shaped conflict (Chatman, Putnam, & Sondak, 1991). Thus, communication directly influenced outcomes as well as mediated and moderated the effects of other variables, such as culture, gender, or orientation, on conflict management. As a mediator, communication impinged on conflict outcomes by altering the way that high and low context cultures influenced joint gains (Adair, 2003). As a moderator, such communication tactics as asking questions moderated the effects of bargainer roles on joint profits (Cai, Wilson, & Drake, 2000). Thus, as a variable, communication shaped outcomes through structuring the conflict and determining the tactics that negotiators used.

As a structural variable. As a structural variable, communication functions as or shapes the antecedent conditions in which conflict occurs; thus, it influences outcomes directly. Research on the effects of media, such as audio, written, or electronic channels, typically casts communication as a structural variable (Purdy, Nye, & Balakrishnan, 2000; Sheffield, 1995; Turnbull et al., 1976). For example, researchers study the effects of face-to-face as opposed to audio communication on cooperation or concession making. Communication media, however, are complex, both in the existence of multiple channels and in the sense-making about the media itself (Poole, Shannon, & DeSanctis, 1992). Hence, the research on media and conflict needs to move beyond treating communication as a structural variable.

Studies of conflict styles also treated communication as a structural variable that shaped conflict predispositions in particular ways. This research assessed individual preferences for handling conflicts and the links between these preferences and other structural variables, such as gender, organizational role, or type of marital relationship (Cai & Fink, 2002; Fitzpatrick & Winke, 1979; Lee & Rogan, 1991; Richmond et al., 1983). Other researchers who cast communication as a structural variable asked respondents to recall the tactics or strategies they used in a particular conflict (Canary & Cupach, 1988; Canary & Spitzberg, 1989) or the information used in planning a negotiation session (Jordan & Roloff, 1997).

As an interaction variable. Interaction variables differed from structural ones in treating communication as a system that consisted of dynamic and multi-functional messages. Communication performed particular conflict management functions. For example, researchers might code communication tactics as threats, putdowns, or commitment statements or as performing the roles of problem solving, concession making, or procedural messages (Donohue, 1981b; Putnam & Jones, 1982a; Sillars, 1980a; Sillars et al., 1982).

Interaction variables were typically linked to conflict goals and outcomes. For instance, in cooperative negotiations, disputants who exchanged messages about underlying needs and priorities enhanced their chances of reaching high joint gains (Olekalns & Smith, 2000). In a similar way, Jones's (1989b) taxonomy of mediation strategies stemmed from messages that functioned to facilitate interaction, introduce topics, and guide the disputes. Mediators also reframed disputants' comments and helped parties expand on information (Donohue, Drake, & Roberto, 1994). In agreement sessions, mediators provided intense reframing in response to a disputant's attack and used structuring and short interventions to enable both sides to speak equally (Donohue, 1991; Donohue et al., 1994).

Other lines of research that treated communication as an interaction variable included studies of concession making in negotiation, arguments in conflict management, and face management behaviors. In negotiation research, scholars deciphered how bargainers made offers and how concession-making patterns formed over time (Tutzauer, 1992). Communication researchers also coded arguments in roommate and friendship conflicts (Sillars et al., 1982; Trapp, 1986), in diplomatic disputes (Schütz, 1978), and in bargaining proposal development (Putnam & Geist, 1985; Putnam & Wilson, 1989). Face management also surfaced as a process variable when it accounted for cultural comparisons in conflict styles (Oetzel, Myers, Meares, & Lara, 2003; Ting-Toomey, 1988) and relational development in different types of hostage situations (Rogan & Hammer, 1994).

Treating communication as an interaction variable has shifted the direction of conflict studies in the field. Its growth in the early 1980s paved the way for scholars to investigate the communicative functions of conflict messages. Current scholars have moved away from equating interaction with conflict categories and functions. One problem with this approach is that messages often fit multiple categories, particularly in how they are expressed. Moreover, this approach privileges the rational, outcome-driven nature of conflict and conceals the emotional and identity dimensions that characterize many conflict situations.

Communication as a Process

Research that adopts a process perspective focuses on the development of interrelated patterns of communication and conflict over time. Thus, communication shapes the very nature of conflict through the evolution of social interaction. Rather than examining message categories as variables that shape outcomes, scholars investigate the relationships among these messages, the patterns derived from these relationships, and the role of communication in constituting conflict. Research that embraces a process approach falls into three arenas: sequential patterns, phase and stage research, and issue development.

Sequential patterns. Early scholars saw important relationships among types of messages that disputants employed and a conflict's development over time. For these researchers, action-reaction patterns or cue-response sequences formed patterns that became predictable over time and defined the nature of a conflict (Putnam, 1985). Three major types of patterns surfaced in these relationships: reciprocal, opposite, and complementary (Olekalns & Smith, 2000). Reciprocal patterns stemmed from matching the other person's tactics, potentially leading to a lengthy cycle; thus, a threat would follow a threat, a rejection would follow a rejection statement, and so on.

This pattern fostered the development of self-perpetuating cycles that could spiral out of control as a conflict gained momentum. Research across a wide array of contexts demonstrated that stalemates, no-agreement situations, and distressed interactions arose from reciprocity in contentious communication patterns that evolved into conflict cycles (Donohue, Diez, & Weider-Hatfield, 1984; Gottman, 1979; Krueger & Smith, 1982; Putnam & Jones, 1982a; Sillars, 1980b). Current studies replicated this important finding that reciprocity in contentious or competitive communication escalated conflict (Brett, Shapiro, & Lytle, 1998; Olekalns & Smith, 2000; Weingart, Prietula, Hyder, & Genovese, 1999).

In contrast, disputants also developed reciprocity in cooperative, problem-solving communication that fostered productive conflict. Specifically, couples that matched each other's use of metacommunication, statements of concern, supportive messages, or multi-issue offers developed constructive patterns of communication and conflict (Krueger & Smith, 1982; Olekalns & Smith, 2000). Scholars observed that although these patterns are hard to sustain, they are more likely to occur when disputants displayed knowledge of effective conflict management tactics or when negotiators had a cooperative orientation (Weingart et al., 1999).

Responding to the other party with an opposite move altered the development of a tight reciprocal pattern, especially an escalating one. For example, giving information or making a procedural comment in response to the other party's use of a contentious tactic could reduce the development of a conflict cycle (Donohue,

Diez, & Hamilton, 1984; Olekalns & Smith, 2000; Putnam & Jones, 1982a). Research on marital conflicts also revealed that normal couples as opposed to distressed ones responded in a variety of ways to contentious situations (Donohue, 1991; Krueger & Smith, 1982).

Another pattern that deterred the development of escalating conflict cycles was using complementary tactics. A complementary tactic balanced a partner's typical response. For example, martial couples developed complementary tactics when one of the pair asserted dominance and the other responded with a submissive reaction (Bavelas et al., 1985; Ting-Toomey, 1983). Labor-management negotiators engaged in a complementary dance through balancing each other's offensive-defensive approaches (Donohue, Diez, & Hamilton, 1984; Putnam & Jones, 1982a). Moreover, these communication patterns characterized role specializations that developed over time. However, if either party shifted to tactics that characterized the other party's role specialization, then an escalating conflict cycle could develop.

In effect, research on sequential interaction patterns revealed that communication influenced the nature of conflict. That is, reciprocal interactions could take conflict in either a constructive or a destructive direction, whereas using an opposite tactic could de-escalate a conflict spiral. Relying on complementary patterns also buffered against conflict escalation and facilitated role specialization that led to satisfactory agreements.

Phase and stage development. An extension of the work on sequential message patterns is the research on phases and stages of conflict development. Phases are lengthy constellations of sequential patterns that form coherent structures (Holmes, 1992). Studies of conflict phases reveal that particular communication patterns cluster into stages that develop over time. Research in this area initially embraces linear models of development in which the disputants pass through one stage before moving into the next one (Baxter, 1982; Tuckman, 1965). Other studies suggest that conflict is characterized by multiple, cyclical phases and that dyads and groups often skip particular phases or cycle through them multiple times (Holmes, 1992; Poole, 1981).

Communication studies of group conflict investigated stage development. Ellis and Fisher (1975), in one of the earliest studies, identified three phases—interpersonal, confrontation, and substantive. Adopting a unidimensional model, they observed that group members began their interactions with a period of favorable remarks, then moved to a confrontation stage in which disagreement prevailed, and finally into a period of coalescence around a position. Current studies reported that conflict interactions infused a group's normal activities and surfaced as members worked through problems that the group faced (see Poole & Garner, Chapter 10 in this volume).

Similarly, phase development in negotiation initially posited separate stages of conflict activity, often testing a three-phase (Douglas, 1962) or an eight-stage model (Gulliver, 1979). Initially, theorists believed that distributive and integrative processes in negotiation occurred in distinct stages (Putnam, 1990). Current research, however, suggests that bargainers moved back and forth through distributive and integrative processes and that dyads who kept both processes distinct were less likely to reach agreements than were ones who mixed them (Olekalns, Brett, & Weingart, 2003; Olekalns, Smith, & Walsh, 1996). Early scholars also observed that labor and management bargainers altered their tactics across stages, often in keeping with their role specializations (Hinkle, Stiles, & Taylor, 1988; Putnam, Wilson, & Turner, 1990).

Research on phase development in crisis negotiations employed phase mapping to examine simulated and authentic hostage negotiations. While simulated negotiations developed in patterns that resembled Gulliver's eight stages, authentic cases were less orderly and less organized (Holmes & Sykes, 1993). Events external to the negotiation, such as changing negotiators or allowing family members to talk with the suspects, influenced negotiation development in these actual situations. Using authentic negotiations, Rogan and Hammer (1995) reported that message affect increased during the initial contact stage and it generally decreased as the interaction moved into a relational development stage. In suicide and domestic cases, however, message affect became increasingly negative and erratic as the negotiation progressed.

In mediation sessions, phase patterns distinguished between successful and unsuccessful sessions. Specifically, in successful sessions mediators excelled in eliciting information, using extensive summaries, reframing the disputants' defensive arguments, maintaining control of the process, and generating proposals, especially during phases 2 and 3. In the latter stages of the mediation, successful mediators employed fewer structuring statements and rule enforcement behaviors, while mediators in no-agreement sessions increased their use of these tactics and made more process comments when they should have concentrated on solutions and agreements (Donohue, 1991; Donohue, Weider-Hatfield, Hamilton, & Diez, 1985; Jones, 1988).

Overall, communication scholars have made substantial contributions to deciphering the patterns of conflict development over time. Different studies reveal similar patterns, even across contexts, particularly as to the way reciprocal contentious tactics lead to conflict cycles and the use of opposite and complementary patterns to de-escalate these patterns. Even though phase research is primarily descriptive, it also demonstrates important findings as to the types of tactics that disputants employ early as opposed to later in a conflict's development.

Issue development. Issue development, as a variation on phase research, centered on tracking changes in conflict issues over time. Thus, it combined process analysis with disputants' interpretations of issues and showed how bargainers reframed or reevaluated the scope of their problems. This work moved beyond logrolling and compromise to explore how communication fostered proposal generation. The communicative development of proposals bridged differences and transformed the very nature of a conflict as the disputants acquired new understandings about the nature of their conflict (Felstiner, Abel, & Sarat, 1980-1981; Putnam, 1994).

Communication studies revealed that issue development occurred through reframing agenda items and shifting levels of abstraction while discussing issues (Drake & Donohue, 1996; Putnam, 2004b; Putnam & Holmer, 1992). At the beginning of a conflict, disputants defined issues through their dominant frames or worldviews. Then they searched for common framing to bridge their differences and converge on a problem definition. Reaching convergence on issue framing was directly related to obtaining agreements on substantive issues in a conflict (Drake & Donohue, 1996). Discussions that shifted levels of abstraction from literal to symbolic or from an individual fault to a system problem introduced options for reframing a conflict (Putnam, 2004b).

Process research has extended our knowledge of the micro-processes that escalate or de-escalate a conflict. Prior to this work, conflict scholars viewed escalation as primarily a perceptual concept linked to ingroup/outgroup relationships, stereotyping, and distortion (Pruitt, Rubin, & Kim, 1994). Communication scholars have demonstrated how reciprocity of contentious micro-behaviors leads to conflict spirals and how using the opposite or a complementary tactic potentially buffers the development of this cycle. Studies of conflict development over time also yield important findings about the linearity and dimensionality of these patterns. Finally, research on issue development tracks how disputants shift their framing and generate new interpretations of the conflict itself.

Communication as an Interpretive Approach

Interpretive approaches to the study of communication and conflict centered on the role of language and symbols in shaping the meaning of disputes. In keeping with the pleas of early scholars, researchers examined negotiation as a mutual exploration in which parties co-developed definitions of their experiences and images of settlements (Smith, 1983). Unlike the variable and the process approaches, the interpretive perspective introduced history and context as key factors that shaped discourse, symbolic forms, and negotiated orders.

Discourse analysis. Discourse studies treated conflict management as a particular type of conversation rather than as information exchange or strategic acts. Research examined verbal immediacy, language intensity, account giving, and conversational management in conflict situations. Verbal immediacy referred to how individuals used tacit behaviors to convey closeness or distance from the other party. Use of first-person pronouns such as *you* or *our*, short utterances, and simple sentences indicated closeness and informality, while employing third-party pronouns, long utterances, and excessive numbers of verbs conveyed distance (Donohue, 1991; Donohue, Weider-Hatfield et al., 1985). In a similar way, employing intense language, such as rude comments, excessive interruptions, and deceptive statements, strained negotiator relationships and escalated conflicts (Donohue & Diez, 1985; Donohue, Weider-Hatfield et al., 1985).

Interpretive studies also employed conversational analysis to investigate how disputants assigned blame in conflict situations and how negotiators managed turn taking (Manusov, Cody, Donohue, & Zappa, 1994; Neu, 1988). While giving accounts allowed disputants to vent and voice critical issues, patterns of aggregating account sequences spiraled into negative evaluations and thus fostered conflict escalation. Drawing from conversational management, mediators who made ample use of questions and answers controlled the topic flow, developed turn-taking norms, and made disputants' complaints less inflammatory (Garcia, 1991). Using these types of interventions, however, hinged on whether a mediator adopted a therapeutic or a bargaining style of intervention (Tracy & Spradlin, 1994).

Symbolic forms: Narratives and metaphors. Communication scholars also analyzed the symbolic use of discourse through examining conflict narratives and metaphors; that is, researchers deciphered how language functioned symbolically to create norms and social meanings. For example, a narrative analysis of teacher-administrator negotiations revealed that the opposing teams bonded with each other through chaining out vivid stories of outsiders who impeded prior negotiations (Putnam et al., 1991). Narrative analyses of social conflicts, such as labor strikes, exemplified how communities and publics played important roles in conflict performances (Fuoss, 1995) and how employees shifted from being warriors in heroic battles to victims and martyrs in reacting to management's control and material power (Cloud, 2005).

Narrative analyses also made significant contributions to the debates on mediator neutrality. Traditional problem-solving approaches cast mediators as neutral third parties who intervened on behalf of both sides. An analysis of disputants' stories, however, revealed that the most coherent and complete narratives often shaped the final agreements, thus calling into question the notion of mediator neutrality (Cobb, 1993, 1994; Cobb & Rifkin, 1991). Discourse studies confirmed these findings by showing how mediators steered disputants to particular outcomes, set up particular frames for agreements, and dismissed some suggestions as illegitimate (Dingwall & Greatbatch, 1991; Greatbatch & Dingwall, 1994). Thus, analyses of stories in mediation indicated that third parties were sometimes implicitly biased in their interactions. Recent approaches, though, encourage mediators to acknowledge dominant stories and to help disputants construct a new narrative that shifts the blame to outside parties or systems (Winslade & Monk, 2001).

Another interpretive approach centers on conflict metaphors. Metaphors expressed through disputants' language reveal the motivational, behavioral, and outcome expectations of a conflict (Beisecker, 1988). A metaphor is a way of seeing a thing as if it were something else. That is, metaphors link abstract concepts, such as a conflict, to concrete things, such as a war or a crusade. Even conflict management is a type of metaphor in which fundamental differences exist between the discourse of negotiation and that of litigation (Stutman & Putnam, 1994). First-order metaphors refer to overt behaviors or surface manifestation of a conflict while second-order metaphors capture the deep-seated meanings that are outside of a disputant's awareness. To illustrate, the use of a drama metaphor among Disney employees during a major strike underscored surface-level economic issues, while references to the family metaphor signified the deep-seated or fundamental conflict about changing relationships between management and employees (Smith & Eisenberg, 1987).

Surveys of the metaphors that organizational members hold about conflict revealed three prototypes: conflict as war/destruction, conflict as impotence/inequality, and conflict as opportunity/resolution (Burrell, Buzzanell, & McMillan, 1992). A comparison of first- and second-order symbols indicated that women adopted metaphors of powerlessness and incompetence in a bureaucratic context, but the type of conflict target moderated this finding (Buzzanell & Burrell, 1997). Specifically, disputants employed war metaphors to depict coworker conflicts, opportunity metaphors for supervisor controversies, and impotence metaphors to represent conflicts with department members.

In descriptions of interpersonal conflicts, negative metaphors surfaced more frequently than did positive ones, and disputants compared their conflicts to animals, for example, "stubborn as a mule," and to natural disasters, "a storm, hurricane, undertow of water" more frequently than to war or violence (McCorkle & Mills, 1992). Overall, metaphors reveal dominant models of conflict that individuals have and ways that people bundle their experiences to rule out some approaches to conflict management.

Negotiated orders. Other scholars, who embraced an interpretive perspective, examined how social and moral orders evolved from the enactment of conflicts. In this work, communication constituted the micro-process of social interaction as well as the context and immediate settings that impinged on the conflict. Negotiated order referred to the ways that communication shaped the social orders that enabled and constrained subsequent actions. Scholars who examined negotiated orders employed a wide array of influences, including Strauss's (1978) theory, social confrontations (Newell & Stutman, 1988), and moral order (Pearce & Littlejohn, 1997).

For example, Donohue and Roberto (1993) employed Strauss's theory of negotiated order to examine how relationship patterns became ordered within a hostage-taking context. They observed that disputants moved back and forth through cooperation and competition in relatively stable relational rhythms. In a conflict regarding organizational change, Geist and Hardesty (1992) studied the conflicts that occurred during the implementation of mandatory state and federal regulations (DRGs) in two hospitals. Specifically, organizational members negotiated new ideologies and occupational role requirements through co-constructing meanings about their situation and through establishing new social structures in the midst of their contested terrain.

In a similar way, interpersonal scholars adopted negotiated order approaches to investigate social confrontations as communication episodes (Baxter, 1982). Social confrontations surfaced when one person signaled to another party that the first person had violated a social norm or expected behavior. This confrontation, in turn, triggered a conflict as parties attributed blame in the situation and interacted with each other to negotiate a new social order (Newell & Stutman, 1988). In friendship interactions, three modes of conflict management surfaced in negotiating new orders: suggesting remedial action, confronting and comparing viewpoints, and determining which behaviors to change (Legge & Rawlins, 1992). Interviews with disputants revealed that friends distinguished between behavioral conflicts and disagreements; that is, friends agreed to disagree in idea conflicts, but they had to make decisions and changes in behavioral conflicts (Newell & Stutman, 1988).

Moreover, disputes about the proper course of action often involved value differences or conflicting moral orders (Pearce & Littlejohn, 1997). Moral orders were value-based assumptions about right, wrong, goodness, and virtue that guided individual and social actions. In social conflicts, deep-rooted moral orders emerged as natural and legitimate until a clash occurred between different subcultures and fostered intense, escalating conflicts. Communication scholars have recommended ways to transcend moral disputes through suspending judgment, creating new categories, talking across differences, and promoting dialogue.

In general, an interpretive approach supports a constitutive relationship between communication and conflict; thus communication is not an input, moderator, or mediator of outcomes; it becomes the conflict itself. Unlike the process approach, however, communication evolves from language and symbols that co-develop the conflict within a historical and contextually based set of social relationships. Discourse approaches focus on questions-answers, topic shifts, and turn taking that control conflict development. Narratives and metaphors shape conflicts through symbolically defining disputants' roles, their public performances, and the underlying meanings of events. These meanings also form social orders through shaping ideologies, occupational roles, and the moral fabric of disputes.

Communication and Conflict as Dialectics

An alternative approach to the study of communication and conflict treats the two concepts as reflecting on each other. In this way, disputants simultaneously enact both communication and conflict and their mutual constructions reflect back on the conflict itself. Researchers who embrace this view focus on dialectical tensions, paradoxes, and the push-pulls of conflict as opposite forces. In this approach, process becomes continuous change that disputants manage communicatively through making choices between perceived mutually exclusive opposites. Scholars draw inspiration from a variety of theoretical sources, including double binds in family therapy (Watzlawick, Beavin, & Jackson, 1967), dialectics (Hegel, 1968), and dialogue (Bakhtin, 1981). Research and theory building cluster into three general arenas: dialectical approaches to mediation, dialectics in organizational conflicts, and relational paradoxes in hostage negotiations.

Dialectical approaches to mediation. In a dialectical approach, patterns of mediation emerge from the tensions that both mediators and disputants face. Prescriptive approaches to mediation suggest that mediators must be detached yet proactive, empowering but asserting control, and suppressing feelings while providing emotional support (Cobb & Rifkin, 1991). These contradictions, then, set the stage for developing a reflexive relationship between communication and conflict; namely, navigating the tensions between impartiality and bias, autonomy and connectedness, and openness versus closedness (Jones, 1994).

Although mediators strive to be impartial, they often enact implicit biases, as Cobb's (1993, 1994) research on disputants' narratives illustrates. Autonomy and connectedness refer to tensions between maintaining a unique identity or being interconnected with the parties. In like manner, the tensions between openness and closedness in mediation reveal trust dilemmas that exist alongside vulnerability. That is, disputants in the mediation process are often hesitant to be open and trusting for fear of being exposed in a negative light (Jones, 1994). The management of these contradictions shapes the relational dynamics between disputants and influences the outcomes of mediation.

Managing contradictions creatively challenges the reflexive relationship between communication and conflict. A party who makes one pole dominant and ignores its opposite intensifies the push-pull tensions (Baxter, 1990). For example, feeling a bias toward one party intensifies the neutrality dialectic in mediation and increases the prospects of feeling trapped. Mediators also shift back and forth between bias and neutrality through segmenting agenda items; for example, being neutral on the monetary aspects of a divorce settlement and being biased on child custody issues, or being impartial in joint sessions and showing a bias in caucuses (Jones, 1994). Specifically, mediators may reveal a bias for protecting the children during custody discussions through raising topics that are important to the children's needs.

Mediators also chose to neutralize tensions through their indirect actions, such as allowing the disputants to avoid confrontation on the tough issues. Separating and neutralizing dialectical tensions, however, these patterns lead to problems in managing contradictions effectively. Another approach is to reframe the contradictory poles in ways that make them seem congruent. For instance, mediators can help disputants realize that refusal to be open and exchange ideas often makes a person more vulnerable than actually sharing information (Jones, 1994). If parties could see contradictory states as no longer in tension, then they could act in different ways toward each other. In effect, dialectical tensions in mediation function as a generative force to manage conflict through "both-and" as opposed to "either-or" ways of thinking. In a reflexive way, communication patterns serve as responses to dialectical tensions through shaping the discourse that imposes on the conflict itself.

Dialectics in organizational conflicts. Tensions between opposites, such as cooperation and competition, also shaped organizational conflicts (Kolb & Putnam, 1992). As organizational members worked out the nature of their interdependence, they engaged in dialectical tensions between autonomy and connectedness and control and yielding. In particular, issues of autonomy and connection characterized workgroup conflicts as members encountered incompatibilities about project priorities, task procedures, and scarce resources (Jameson, 1999, 2004). During organizational changes, these dialectics characterized informal conflicts as they surfaced in formal negotiations about authority and responsibility. In a similar way, teachers and administrators in a public sector negotiation embraced the dialectic of control and yielding through shifting the meanings of language used in a labor contract as the parties enacted a formula for reaching an agreement (Putnam, 2004a). This dialectic was also evident in a study of an airline pilots' resistance group that set up opposition tensions through discursive strategies that advocated unity while campaigning for division and upheld an elitist image of the pilots' occupation while advocating for a class system within the profession (Real & Putnam, 2005). Thus, forming dualities and pitting them against each other enabled the resistance group to construct a defense in the absence of any clear attack.

Even though most research on organizational conflict centers on public, formal, and rational disputes, these concepts simultaneously reference their opposites. To avoid making one pole of this dialectic dominant, researchers are examining private, informal, and nonrational aspects of organizational conflicts (Kolb & Putnam, 1992). Private and informal conflicts are often fused with other activities, including social events, gossip, and coalition building. These private disputes form the groundwork for public deliberations and official grievances. In contrast to the rational models of conflict, current research centers on emotional reactions and the role of emotional expressions in conflict management (Bodtker & Jameson, 2001; Jones, 2001).

Relational paradoxes in hostage negotiations. Similar to dialectics, a paradox refers to mutually exclusive injunctions that operate simultaneously and often lead to double binds. An injunction is a request or an order; for example, the command to "be spontaneous" is seen as paradoxical in that it is difficult to be spontaneous and act spontaneously at the same time. In hostage negotiations, a crisis situation prevailed in which a paradox could form within the developing relationship between the negotiator and hostage taker. This paradox stemmed from the mixed messages in verbal immediacy that signaled moving with and moving against each other (Donohue, 2001; Donohue & Roberto, 1993).

Specifically, competitive paradoxes arose from moving against each other through sending verbal immediacy messages that signaled high interdependence but low affiliation, whereas cooperative paradoxes stemmed from immediacy cues that signaled low interdependence but high affiliation or moving with each other (Donohue, Ramesh, & Borchgrevink, 1991). These relational paradoxes evolved dynamically through the incongruent messages that both parties simultaneously sent, thereby creating a double bind in which the parties felt trapped. Thus, hostage negotiations involved managing potential paradoxes to create the openness, affiliation, and interdependence necessary to form collaborative agreements.

In essence, scholars who espouse a reflexive approach to communication and conflict investigate how dualities and oppositional tensions co-develop and reflect back on each other. This approach is rooted in relational development and how relationships enable or constrain effective conflict management. In mediation, the responses to dialectical tensions shape the management of bias and neutrality and openness and closedness. In organizational conflicts, similar relational dialectics interface with control and yielding to shape responses to organizational change and to move private conflicts into the public arena. In hostage negotiations, these relational dualities intersect to form paradoxes that can entrap parties and position them in binding ways.

The key to conflict management in the reflexive approach is responding to contradictions in ways that capture the energy between opposites, generate new insights, and transform the definition of the conflict itself. Choosing one pole and ignoring the other, separating them, vacillating between them, and neutralizing them may lead to less than optimal responses. Reframing the

dualities or embracing them creatively may spawn new approaches that can engender novel solutions (Baxter & Montgomery, 1996).

CONCLUSION AND DISCUSSION

From its early game theory roots to contemporary studies on dialectical tensions, research in the field has made huge strides in understanding the complexities of conflict and conflict management. This section reviews the recommendations of early scholars to see how the field has evolved, how it depicts the communication-conflict relationship, and where it needs to move to enhance theory building and research.

Heeding the Recommendations of Early Scholars

Early communication scholars set forth four recommendations that have influenced research on conflict management. Specifically, they suggested that scholars (a) expand the theories and models of communication and conflict, (b) work from similar definitions and assumptions, (c) broaden research settings and methods, and (d) focus on conflict development over time (Miller, 1974; Mortensen, 1974; Simons, 1974b). In response to the first recommendation, communication scholars have expanded their approaches to include systems-interaction models as well as discourse, symbolic, and critical perspectives. Since its early investigations, however, the field has shifted away from social and political conflicts to focus on interpersonal, group, and organizational disputes.

During this time, the field borrowed and adapted conflict models used in other disciplines, specifically ones employed in psychology, management, and labor relations. Disenchanted with these traditional models, however, scholars introduced frameworks from discourse analysis, for example, using language intensity and verbal immediacy to study mediation and negotiation; communication competency for interpersonal disputes; and dialectics to examine hostage negotiations, interpersonal conflicts, and organizational dilemmas. Thus, the field began to develop its own theories and models for studying communication and conflict.

On the second recommendation, a general consensus exists among communication scholars regarding definitions and essential elements of conflict, even though investigators differ in their foci of conflict (i.e., incompatible relationships, incommensurate values, or scarce resources). Researchers highlight similar but diverse features of communication, including messages and interaction analyses, symbolic acts, and subjective or co-developed meanings. Moreover, most communication scholars treat conflict as normal and inevitable rather than as an aberration, thus rejecting the idea that conflict is a disruption of harmony. Research as a whole, though, focuses on successful versus unsuccessful patterns of conflict management and on ways to avoid destructive cycles rather than on the benefits of conflict. For the most part, then, communication scholars work from similar definitions and assumptions about conflict, even though they vary in how they operationalize key features of it.

Moreover, scholars have now moved away from treating conflict as something objective or outside of people's cognitive realms and social interactions, but almost to a fault. In doing so, they have removed conflict from its material manifestations. In the zeal to embrace interpretive views of social reality, communication scholars have abandoned the way that conflict cycles and symbolic meanings become rooted in material manifestations of power and control. The limited research on large-scale social conflicts and international disputes may contribute to this neglect.

In response to the third recommendation, communication scholars have clearly broadened research settings and methods. Researchers have analyzed conflicts in naturalistic settings of homes, schools, organizations, and communities; they have observed actual hostage negotiations, teacher-administrator bargaining, labor disputes, community and divorce mediations, team meetings, organizational change processes, and multiparty environmental disputes. In laboratory studies, researchers have developed creative simulations such as buying and selling used textbooks, training for intercultural interactions, and simulations of typical interpersonal conflicts.

Research methods are as diverse as these settings. Investigators have obtained transcripts of actual conflict events, used video- and audiotapes to document interactions, interviewed participants, examined documents and newspaper coverage of conflicts, and conducted ethnographies and participant observations. Systems-interaction research and discourse analyses in both laboratory and natural settings have employed laborious coding and tracking of interaction patterns—ones that privilege communication as the focal point of conflict. In addition, researchers have studied highly volatile conflicts, such as hostage negotiations, racial disputes, and multi-party intractable environmental conflicts, thus demonstrating that communication scholars do not have an aversion to uncivil and explosive disputes (Simons, 1974b). In effect, diversity in context and methods clearly adds to the contributions that communication scholars have made to the study of conflict.

In response to the fourth suggestion, communication studies have focused on conflict as a developmental process. Building from the transactional model (Mortensen, 1974), investigators have examined the functions of messages, their sequential and interdependent relationships, and their evolution over time in a variety of conflict situations. Researchers have embraced an array of quantitative and qualitative tracking techniques, including lag sequential, Markov chain analyses, phase mapping, and computer tracking of discourse patterns. Studies of conflict styles have employed scenarios that document changes in style use over time. Communication researchers, thus, have responded positively to the recommendation to focus on conflict dynamics. Overall, research in the field clearly heeded the advice of early scholars to expand theories and models, work from similar definitions of conflict, broaden research settings and methods, and focus on process and conflict development.

Relationships Between Communication and Conflict

Early scholars implied, but did not explicitly recommend, altering the ways that theorists conceived of the communication-conflict relationship. This review revealed four types of relationships that surfaced in the literature—communication as a variable, as process, as interpretive, and as a dialectical pattern. In the variable approach, communication and conflict emerged as separate constructs with conflict acting as a structural variable to shape communication or with communication serving as a structural or an interaction variable that influenced conflict. For example, studies that examined how conflict orientations affected the choice of communication strategies illustrated how conflict served as a structural variable that impinged on interaction. In reverse, research on the way different media influenced negotiated settlements cast communication as a structural variable that shaped conflict outcomes. Studies that examined how types of messages influenced conflict outcomes treated communication as an interaction variable. In each of these approaches, communication and conflict surfaced as discrete variables that impinged on each other in different ways.

In the process approach, communication produced conflict through the ways that sequences and phases of interaction determined the direction that conflict took. Patterns of action-reaction formed rhythms that became predictable over time and could influence the formation of conflict spirals. Studies of phases and stages of interaction also showed how particular communication patterns resulted in no-agreement sessions. Also, issue development scholars examined how negotiators shifted levels of abstraction during interactions to reframe issues, bridge differences, and alter conflict definitions.

Interpretive approaches nested the relationship between communication and conflict in jointly constructed meanings. In this way communication and conflict were co-developed; that is, communication constituted conflict that in turn shaped language patterns, symbolic meanings, and negotiated orders. For example, verbal immediacy patterns in hostage negotiations formed relationships that, in turn, altered conflict interactions. In the negotiated order perspective, communication functioned as both a micro-process and a way of altering the social context through changing the rules and resources that, in turn, redefined the conflict and its outcomes.

In a similar way, some researchers cast communication and conflict in a dialectical relationship, one that treated the two concepts as not only jointly constituted but also reflecting back on each other. Thus, the relationship between communication and conflict became defined through oppositional tensions that evolved from the continuous interface between conflict and communication. These dialectics infused conflict relationships in mediation, organizational conflicts, and hostage negotiations through tensions between autonomy and connectedness and high and low affiliation that both enabled and constrained the disputants and the conflict process.

Overall, communication is not simply one additional variable in conflict research. Current studies reveal sophisticated approaches to exploring alternative relationships between the two constructs, their co-development over time, and the ways that both concepts shape contexts and outcomes. Context, then, plays a critical role in thinking about the needs for future research.

Directions for Future Research

Context provides a touchstone for discussing future directions in theory development and research in the field. Specifically, studies of communication and conflict fall into highly specialized context domains that limit theory development. To this end, Simons (1974b) questioned whether researchers should aim to make generalizations and ignore subtle differences among types of conflicts or whether they should pitch their studies within context domains and avoid large-scale generalizations.

In response to this query, researchers have chosen to pitch their investigations toward context domains and avoid large-scale generalizations. In particular, scholars situate their contributions in the contexts of marital conflicts, friendship disagreements, intercultural interactions, team conflicts, labor-management negotiations, community and divorce mediations, organizational disputes, hostage negotiations, and multi-party environmental conflicts. Chapters in this volume reflect these subspecialties in the field. Given that context features directly influence communication patterns, this development seems logical as scholars acknowledge their boundaries and design their research programs to integrate within cognate areas, for example, family studies or labor-management relations.

This pattern of locating research in context domains has made communication and conflict scholarship quite fragmented and, consequently, inhibited theory development. For the most part, then, scholarship exists in isolated camps of interpersonal, group, organizational, intercultural, and media conflict studies. This isolation contributes to a problem-oriented focus that increases specialization and moves scholars away from conducting any broad-based synthesis. With the exception of this *Handbook,* very few texts in communication cross diverse conflict arenas. Thus, future studies need to bridge these isolated camps and explore types of generalizations that scholars can make for building knowledge in the field.

Two suggestions may facilitate this process. First, future studies need to integrate knowledge across different conflict dimensions. For example, research on conflict intensity across context domains could be integrated to reveal similarities and differences in communication patterns. Similar projects could focus on the salience of conflict situations, the importance of issues, and the overall emotion or affect during conflict. One finding in which communication scholars have crossed context domains is the discovery of micro-processes that foster conflict escalation and de-escalation and the role of communication in curtailing destructive conflict cycles (Cupach & Metts, 1994; Donohue, 1991; Putnam & Jones, 1982a; Sillars, 1980b). This type of synthesis in research could also occur on such topics as emotions in conflict (Bodtker & Jameson, 2001; Jones, 2001), value-based disputes (Pearce & Littlejohn, 1997), communicative framing of conflicts (Drake & Donohue, 1996; Putnam & Holmer, 1992), and apology and forgiveness in conflict situations (Bean & Johnstone, 1994; Kelley, 1998). Conflict dimensions, then, provide a lens for charting new directions for research and building on knowledge across isolated context arenas.

A second suggestion for integrating context domains across the field is to move dyadic and group research into community and institutional arenas. Studies in the field are beginning to shift in this direction, as exemplified by research on hostage negotiations (Donohue & Roberto, 1993; Rogan & Hammer, 1995), community mediations (Conrad & Sinclair-James, 1995), and moral conflicts (Pearce & Littlejohn, 1997). Yet, the majority of communication research on mediation centers on mediator-disputant interactions without attention to their court-oriented contexts, institutional pressures, and cultural processes (Conrad & Sinclair-James, 1995). Raising these issues provides a way to integrate micro-processes of mediation interaction with institutional and societal features of conflict.

Finally, communication researchers need to conduct studies on the productive aspects of conflict. Scholars in the field believe that conflict produces important benefits, including balancing power, promoting change, facilitating diversity, and correcting injustices. They acknowledge that effective conflict management serves therapeutic functions, relieves tensions, and generates creativity. Yet, investigators simply presume that these benefits accrue from successful or agreement-based outcomes.

Researchers, then, need to unpack the types of benefits that result from different conflict interactions. Specifically, how do communication patterns differ for diverse types of productive outcomes (e.g., facilitating diversity or promoting change)? Research on transformational mediation has shown that communication development differs considerably for problem-solving outcomes versus helping disputants increase recognition and empowerment (Bush & Folger, 1994). This work raises the question, Do the same interaction patterns produce benefits in substantive, relational, and identity areas or does growth in one of these domains influence benefits in the other two? Thus, communication scholars need to focus on different types of outcomes, ones that directly tie to the individual, organizational, and societal benefits of conflict.

Overall, a glimpse of the historical roots of communication and conflict reveals that scholars have adhered to the advice of their predecessors. Researchers have clearly confirmed that communication plays a vital role in shaping conflict issues and outcomes. Scholars have moved away from treating communication as a variable and have adopted complex ways that communication and conflict co-develop, constitute each other, and enable/constrain through their reflexive relationships.

REFERENCES

Adair, W. L. (2003). Integrative sequences and negotiation outcome in same- and mixed-culture negotiations. *International Journal of Conflict Management, 14,* 273–296.

Baird, J. E. (1974). A comparison of distributional and sequential structure in group discussions. *Speech Monographs, 41,* 226–232.

Bakhtin, M. (1981). *The dialogic imagination* (C. Emerson & M. Holquist, Trans.). Austin: University of Texas Press.

Bavelas, J. B., Rogers, L. E., & Millar, F. E. (1985). Interpersonal conflict. In T. H. Van Dick (Ed.), *Handbook of discourse analysis* (Vol. 4, pp. 9–25). Orlando, FL: Academic Press.

Baxter, L. A. (1982). Conflict management: An episodic approach. *Small Group Behavior, 13,* 23–42.

Baxter, L. A. (1990). Dialectical contradictions in relationship development. *Journal of Social and Personal Relationships, 7,* 69–88.

Baxter, L. A., & Montgomery, B. M. (1996). *Relating: Dialogues & dialectics.* New York: Guilford.

Bean, J. M., & Johnstone, B. (1994). Workplace reasons for saying you're sorry: Discourse task management and apology in telephone interviews. *Discourse Processes, 17,* 59–81.

Bednar, D. A., & Curington, W. P. (1983). Interaction analysis: A tool for understanding negotiations. *Industrial and Labor Relations Review, 36,* 389–401.

Beisecker, T. (1970a). Game theory in communication research: A reaction and reorientation. *Journal of Communication, 20,* 105–120.

Beisecker, T. (1970b). Verbal persuasive strategies in mixed-motive interactions. *Quarterly Journal of Speech, 56,* 149–160.

Beisecker, T. (1988). *Conflict metaphors: The importance of naming.* Unpublished manuscript, University of Kansas, Lawrence.

Bell, M. A. (1974). The effects of substantive and affective verbal conflict in problem-solving groups. *Speech Monographs, 41,* 19–23.

Bell, M. A. (1979). The effects of substantive and affective verbal conflict on the quality of decisions of small problem-solving groups. *Central States Speech Journal, 30,* 75–82.

Blake, R. R., & Mouton, J. S. (1964). *The managerial grid.* Houston, TX: Gulf.

Bodtker, A. M., & Jameson, J. K. (2001). Emotion in conflict formation and its transformation: Application to organizational conflict management. *International Journal of Conflict Management, 12,* 259–275.

Bostrom, R. N. (1968). Game theory in communication research. *Journal of Communication, 18,* 369–388.

Bowers, J. W. (1974a). Communication strategies in conflicts between institutions and their clients. In G. R. Miller & H. W. Simons (Eds.), *Perspectives on communication in social conflict* (pp. 125–152). Englewood Cliffs, NJ: Prentice Hall.

Bowers, J. W. (1974b). Guest editor's introduction: Beyond threats and promises. *Speech Monographs, 41,* ix–xi.

Bowers, J. W., & Ochs, J. (1971). *The rhetoric of agitation and control.* Reading, MA: Addison-Wesley.

Brett, J. M., Shapiro, D. L., & Lytle, A. L. (1998). Breaking the bonds of reciprocity in negotiations. *Academy of Management Journal, 41,* 410–424.

Burgess, P. G. (1973). Crisis rhetoric: Coercion versus force. *Quarterly Journal of Speech, 59,* 61–73.

Burke, R. J. (1970). Methods of resolving superior-subordinate conflict: The constructive use of subordinate differences and disagreements. *Organizational Behavior and Human Performance, 5,* 393–411.

Burrell, N. A., Buzzanell, P. M., & McMillan, J. J. (1992). Feminine tensions in conflict situations as revealed by metaphoric analyses. *Management Communication Quarterly, 6,* 115–149.

Burrell, N. A., Donohue, W. A., & Allen, M. (1990). The impact of disputants' expectations on mediation: Testing an interventionist model. *Human Communication Research, 17,* 104–139.

Bush, R. A. B., & Folger, J. P. (1994). *The promise of mediation: Responding to conflict through empowerment and recognition.* San Francisco: Jossey-Bass.

Buzzanell, P. M., & Burrell, N. A. (1997). Family and workplace conflict: Examining metaphorical conflict schemas and expressions across context and sex. *Human Communication Research, 24,* 109–146.

Cahn, D. (Ed.). (1990). *Intimates in conflict: A communication perspective.* Hillsdale, NJ: Lawrence Erlbaum.

Cai, D. A., & Fink, E. L. (2002). Conflict style differences between individualists and collectivists. *Communication Monographs, 69,* 67–87.

Cai, D. A., Wilson, S. R., & Drake, L. E. (2000). Culture in the context of intercultural negotiation: Individualism-collectivism and paths to integrative agreements. *Human Communication Research, 26,* 591–671.

Canary, D. J., & Cupach, W. R. (1988). Relational and episodic characteristics associated with conflict tactics. *Journal of Social and Personal Relationships, 5,* 305–325.

Canary, D. J., Cupach, W. R., & Messman, S. J. (1995). *Relationship conflict.* Thousand Oaks, CA: Sage.

Canary, D. J., & Spitzberg, B. H. (1989). A model of perceived competence of conflict strategies. *Human Communication Research, 15,* 630–649.

Canary, D. J., & Spitzberg, B. H. (1990). Attribution biases and associations between conflict strategies and competence outcomes. *Communication Monographs, 57,* 139–151.

Chatman, J. A., Putnam, L. L., & Sondak, H. (1991). Integrating communication and negotiation research. In M. H. Bazerman, R. J. Lewicki, & B. H. Sheppard (Eds.), *Handbook of negotiation research: Research on negotiation in organizations* (Vol. 3, pp. 139–164). Greenwich, CT: JAI.

Cloud, D. L. (2005). Fighting words: Labor and limits of communication at Staley, 1993 to 1996. *Management Communication Quarterly, 18,* 509–542.

Cobb, S. (1993). Empowerment and mediation: A narrative perspective. *Negotiation Journal, 9,* 245–260.

Cobb, S. (1994). A narrative perspective on mediation. In J. P. Folger & T. S. Jones (Eds.), *New directions in mediation: Communication research and perspectives* (pp. 48–63). Thousand Oaks, CA: Sage.

Cobb, S., & Rifkin, J. (1991). Neutrality as discursive practice: The construction and transformation of narratives in community mediation. *Studies in Law, Politics, and Society, 11,* 69–91.

Comstock, J. (1994). Parent-adolescent conflict: A developmental approach. *Western Journal of Communication, 58,* 263–282.

Comstock, J., & Buller, D. B. (1991). Conflict strategies adolescents use with their parents: Testing the cognitive communication characteristics model. *Journal of Language and Social Psychology, 10,* 47–59.

Conrad, C. (1991). Communication in conflict: Style-strategy relationships. *Communication Monographs, 58,* 135–155.

Conrad, C., & Sinclair-James, L. (1995). Institutional pressures, cultural constraints, and communication in community mediation organizations. In A. M. Nicotera (Ed.), *Conflict and organization* (pp. 63–99). Albany: State University of New York Press.

Coser, L. S. (1956). *The functions of social conflict.* New York: Free Press.

Cupach, W. R., & Metts, S. (1994). *Facework.* Thousand Oaks, CA: Sage.

Deutsch, M. (1973). *The resolution of conflict: Constructive and destructive processes.* New Haven, CT: Yale University Press.

Dingwall, R., & Greatbatch, D. (1991). Behind closed doors: A preliminary report on mediator/client interaction in England. *Family and Conciliation Courts Review, 29,* 291–303.

Donohue, W. A. (1978). An empirical framework for examining negotiation processes and outcomes. *Communication Monographs, 45,* 247–257.

Donohue, W. A. (1981a). Analyzing negotiation tactics: Development of a negotiation interact system. *Human Communication Research, 7,* 273–287.

Donohue, W. A. (1981b). Development of a model of rule use in negotiation. *Communication Monographs, 48,* 106–120.

Donohue, W. A. (1989). Communication competence in mediators. In K. Kressel, D. G. Pruitt, & Associates (Eds.), *Mediation research: The process and effectiveness of third-party intervention* (pp. 322–343). San Francisco: Jossey-Bass.

Donohue, W. A. (1991). *Communication, marital dispute, and divorce mediation.* Hillsdale, NJ: Lawrence Erlbaum.

Donohue, W. A. (2001). Resolving relational paradox: The language of conflict in relationships. In W. F. Eadie & P. E. Nelson (Eds.), *The language of conflict and resolution* (pp. 21–46). Thousand Oaks, CA: Sage.

Donohue, W. A., Allen, M., & Burrell, N. (1985). Communication strategies in mediation. *Mediation Quarterly, 10,* 75–90.

Donohue, W. A., & Diez, M. E. (1985). Directive use in negotiation interaction. *Communication Monographs, 52,* 305–318.

Donohue, W. A., Diez, M. E., & Hamilton, M. (1984). Coding naturalistic negotiation interaction. *Human Communication Research, 10,* 403–425.

Donohue, W. A., Diez, M. E., & Stahle, R. B. (1983). New directions in negotiation research. In R. Bostrom (Ed.), *Communication yearbook 7* (pp. 249–279). Beverly Hills, CA: Sage.

Donohue, W. A., Diez, M. E., & Weider-Hatfield, D. (1984). Skills for successful bargainers. In R. N. Bostrom (Ed.), *Competence in communication: A multidisciplinary approach.* Beverly Hills, CA: Sage.

Donohue, W. A., Drake, L., & Roberto, A. J. (1994). Mediator issue intervention strategies: A replication and some conclusions, *Mediation Quarterly, 11,* 261–274.

Donohue, W. A., Ramesh, C., & Borchgrevink, C. (1991). Crisis bargaining: Tracking relational paradox in hostage negotiation. *International Journal of Conflict Management, 2,* 257–274.

Donohue, W. A., & Roberto, A. J. (1993). Relational development in hostage negotiation. *Human Communication Research, 20,* 175–198.

Donohue, W. A., & Roberto, A. J. (1996). An empirical examination of three models of integrative and distributive bargaining. *International Journal of Conflict Management, 7,* 209–229.

Donohue, W. A., Weider-Hatfield, D., Hamilton, M., & Diez, M. E. (1985). Relational distance in managing conflict. *Human Communication Research, 3,* 387–405.

Douglas, A. (1962). *Industrial peacemaking.* New York: Columbia University Press.

Drake, L. E., & Donohue, W. A. (1996). Communicative framing theory in conflict resolution. *Communication Research, 23,* 297–322.

Ellis, D. G., & Fisher, B. A. (1975). Phases of conflict in small group development: A Markov analysis. *Human Communication Research, 1,* 195–212.

Felstiner, W., Abel, R., & Sarat, A. (1980–1981). "The emergence and transformation of disputes: Naming, blaming, claiming." *Law and Society Review, 15,* 631–654.

Fink, C. F. (1968). Some conceptual difficulties in the theory of social conflict. *Journal of Conflict Resolution, 12,* 412–460.

Fisher, B. A. (1970). Decision emergence: Phases in group decision-making. *Speech Monographs, 37,* 53–66.

Fitzpatrick, M. A. (1988). *Between husbands and wives: Communication in marriage.* Newbury Park, CA: Sage.

Fitzpatrick, M. A., Fallis, S., & Vance, L. (1982). Multifunctional coding of conflict resolution strategies in marital dyads. *Family Relations, 31,* 61–70.

Fitzpatrick, M. A., & Winke, T. (1979). You always hurt the one you love: Strategies and tactics in interpersonal conflict. *Communication Quarterly, 27,* 3–11.

Folger, J. P., & Poole, M. S. (1984). *Working through conflict: A communication perspective.* Glenview, IL: Scott, Foresman.

Folger, J. P., Poole, M. S., & Stutman, R. K. (2005). *Working through conflict: Strategies for relationships, groups, and organizations* (5th ed.). Boston: Pearson.

Friedman, R. A. (1995). *Front stage, back stage: The dramatic structure of labor negotiations.* Cambridge: MIT Press.

Fuoss, K. W. (1995). "Community" contested, imagined, and performed: Cultural performance, contestation, and community in an organized-labor social drama. *Text and Performance Quarterly, 15,* 79–98.

Gamson, W. A. (1968). *Power and discontent.* Homewood, IL: Dorsey Press.

Garcia, A. (1991). Dispute resolution without disputes: How the interactional organization of mediation hearings minimizes argument. *American Sociological Review, 56,* 818–835.

Geist, P., & Hardesty, M. (1992). *Negotiating the crisis: DRGs and the transformation of hospitals.* Hillsdale, NJ: Lawrence Erlbaum.

Gergen, K. J. (1969). *The psychology of behavioral exchange.* Reading, MA: Addison-Wesley.

Gottman, J. M. (1979). *Marital interaction: Experimental investigations.* New York: Academic Press.

Gouldner, A. W. (1960). The norm of reciprocity: A preliminary statement. *American Sociological Review, 25,* 161–178.

Greatbatch, D., & Dingwall, R. (1994). The interactive construction of interventions by divorce mediators. In J. P. Folger & T. S. Jones (Eds.), *New directions in mediation: Communication research and perspectives* (pp. 84–109). Thousand Oaks, CA: Sage.

Greenwood, J. G. (1974). Opportunity to communicate and social orientation in imaginary-reward bargaining. *Speech Monographs, 41,* 79–81.

Gudykunst, W. B. (1985). Normative power and conflict potential in intergroup relationships. In W. B. Gudykunst, L. P. Stewart, & S. Ting-Toomey (Eds.), *Communication, culture, and*

Definitions and Approaches • 27

organizational processes (pp. 155–173). Beverly Hills, CA: Sage.

Gudykunst, W. B. (1990). Diplomacy: A special case for intergroup communication. In F. Korzenny & S. Ting-Toomey (Eds.), *Communicating for peace: Diplomacy and negotiation* (pp. 19–39). Newbury Park, CA: Sage.

Gulliver, P. H. (1979). *Disputes and negotiations: A cross-cultural perspective.* New York: Academic Press.

Hammer, M. R., & Rogan, R. G. (1997). Negotiation models in crisis situations: The value of a communication-based approach. In R. G. Rogan, M. R. Hammer, & C. R. Van Zandt (Eds.), *Dynamic processes of crisis negotiations: Theory, research, and practice* (pp. 9–23). Westport, CT: Praeger.

Harris, T. E., & Smith, R. M. (1974). An experimental verification of Schelling's tacit communication hypothesis. *Speech Monographs, 41*, 82–84.

Hawes, L. C., & Smith, D. H. (1973). A critique of assumptions underlying the study of communication in conflict. *Quarterly Journal of Speech, 59*, 423–435.

Hegel, G. W. F. (1968). *Lectures on the history of philosophy* (Vol. 1). London: Routledge & Kegan Paul.

Heisy, D. R. (1970). The rhetoric of the Arab-Israeli conflict. *Quarterly Journal of Speech, 56*, 12–21.

Hinkle, S., Stiles, W. B., & Taylor, L. A. (1988). Verbal processes in a labour/management negotiation. *Journal of Language and Social Psychology, 7*, 123–136.

Hocker, J. L., & Wilmot, W. W. (1978). *Interpersonal conflict.* Dubuque, IA: William C. Brown.

Holmes, M. E. (1992). Phase structures in negotiation. In L. L. Putnam & M. E. Roloff (Eds.), *Communication and negotiation* (pp. 83–108). Newbury Park, CA: Sage.

Holmes, M. E., & Sykes, R. E. (1993). A test of the fit of Gulliver's phase model to hostage negotiations. *Communication Studies, 44*, 38–55.

Jameson, J. K. (1999). Toward a comprehensive model for the assessment and management of intraorganizational conflict: Developing the framework. *International Journal of Conflict Management, 10*, 268–294.

Jameson, J. K. (2003). Transcending intractable conflict in health care: An exploratory study of communication and conflict management among anesthesia providers. *Journal of Health Communication, 8*, 563–581.

Jameson, J. K. (2004). Negotiating autonomy and connection through politeness: A dialectical approach to organizational conflict management. *Western Journal of Communication, 68*, 257–277.

Jandt, F. E. (1973). *Conflict resolution through communicating.* New York: Harper & Row.

Jandt, F. E. (1974). Communication and the simulation of social conflict. In G. R. Miller & H. W. Simons (Eds.), *Perspectives on communication in social conflict* (pp. 76–89). Englewood Cliffs, NJ: Prentice Hall.

Johnson, D. W. (1974). Communication and the inducement of cooperative behavior in conflicts: A critical review. *Speech Monographs, 41*, 64–78.

Johnson, D. W., McCarty, H., & Allen, K. (1976). Congruent and contradictory verbal and non-verbal communication of cooperativeness and competitiveness in negotiations. *Communication Research, 3*, 275–292.

Jones, T. S. (1988). Phase structures in agreement and no-agreement mediation. *Communication Research, 15*, 470–495.

Jones, T. S. (1989a). Lag sequential analysis of mediator-spouse and husband-wife interaction in successful and unsuccessful divorce mediation. In M. A. Rahim (Ed.), *Managing conflict: An interdisciplinary approach* (pp. 93–107). New York: Praeger.

Jones, T. S. (1989b). A taxonomy of effective mediator strategies and tactics for nonlabor-management mediation. In M. A. Rahim (Ed.), *Managing conflict: An interdisciplinary approach* (pp. 221–229). New York: Praeger.

Jones, T. S. (1994). A dialectical reframing of the mediation process. In J. P. Folger & T. S. Jones (Eds.), *New directions in mediation: Communication research and perspectives* (pp. 26–47). Thousand Oaks, CA: Sage.

Jones, T. S. (2001). Emotional communication in conflict: Essence and impact. In W. F. Eadie & P. E. Nelson (Eds.), *The language of conflict and resolution* (pp. 81–105). Thousand Oaks, CA: Sage.

Jordan, J. M., & Roloff, M. E. (1997). Planning skills and negotiator goal accomplishment: The relationships between self-monitoring and plan generation, plan enactment, and plan consequences. *Communication Research, 24*, 31–64.

Kelley, D. (1998). The communication of forgiveness. *Communication Studies, 49*, 255–271.

Keltner, J. W. (1965). Communication and the labor-management mediation process: Some aspects and hypotheses. *Journal of Communication, 2,* 64–80.

Keltner, J. W. (1994). *The management of struggle.* Cresskill, NJ: Hampton Press.

Kilmann, R. H., & Thomas, K. W. (1977). Developing a forced-choice measure of conflict-handling behavior: The "MODE" instrument. *Educational and Psychological Measurement, 37,* 309–325.

Kolb, D. M., & Putnam, L. L. (1992). Introduction: The dialectics of disputing. In D. M. Kolb & J. M. Bartunek (Eds.), *Hidden conflicts in organizations: Uncovering behind the scenes disputes* (pp. 1–31). Newbury Park, CA: Sage.

Kolb, D. M., & Putnam, L. L. (1997). Through the looking glass: Negotiation theory refracted through the lens of gender. In S. Gleason (Ed.), *Frontiers in dispute resolution in industrial relations and human resources* (pp. 231–257). East Lansing: Michigan State University Press.

Krueger, D. L., & Smith, P. (1982). Decision-making patterns of couples: A sequential analysis. *Journal of Communication, 32,* 121–134.

Landsberger, H. A. (1955). Interaction process analysis of the mediation of labor-management disputes. *Journal of Abnormal and Social Psychology, 51,* 552–559.

Lee, H. O., & Rogan, R. G. (1991). A cross-cultural comparison of organizational conflict management behaviors. *International Journal of Conflict Management, 2,* 181–199.

Legge, N. J., & Rawlins, W. K. (1992). Managing disputes in young adult friendships: Modes of convenience, cooperation, and commitment. *Western Journal of Communication, 56,* 226–247.

Mack, R. W., & Snyder, R. C. (1957). The analysis of social conflict: Toward an overview and synthesis. *Journal of Conflict Resolution, 1,* 212–248.

Manusov, V., Cody, M. J., Donohue, W. A., & Zappa, J. (1994). Accounts in child custody mediation sessions. *Journal of Applied Communication Research, 22,* 1–15.

McCorkle, S., & Mills, J. L. (1992). Rowboat in a hurricane: Metaphors of interpersonal conflict management. *Communication Reports, 5,* 57–66.

Millar, F. E., Rogers, E., & Bavelas, J. B. (1984). Identifying patterns of verbal conflict in interpersonal dynamics. *Western Journal of Speech Communication, 48,* 231–246.

Miller, G. R. (1974). Epilogue. In G. R. Miller & H. W. Simons (Eds.), *Perspectives on communication in social conflict* (pp. 206–220). Englewood Cliffs, NJ: Prentice Hall.

Miller, G. R., & Simons, H. W. (Eds.). (1974). *Perspectives on communication in social conflict.* Englewood Cliffs, NJ: Prentice Hall.

Morrill, C., & Thomas, C. K. (1992). Organizational conflict management as disputing process: The problem of social escalation. *Human Communication Research, 18,* 400–428.

Mortensen, C. D. (1974). A transactional paradigm of social conflict. In G. R. Miller & H. W. Simons (Eds.), *Perspectives on communication in social conflict* (pp. 90–124). Englewood Cliffs, NJ: Prentice Hall.

Neu, J. (1988). Conversational structure: An explanation of bargaining behaviors in negotiations. *Management Communication Quarterly, 2,* 23–45.

Newell, S. E., & Stutman, R. K. (1988). The social confrontation episode. *Communication Monographs, 55,* 266–285.

Nicotera, A. M. (1993). Beyond two dimensions: A grounded theory model of conflict-handling behavior. *Management Communication Quarterly, 6,* 282–306.

Nicotera, A. M. (1994). The use of multiple approaches to conflict: A study of sequences. *Human Communication Research, 20,* 592–621.

Oetzel, J., Myers, K. K., Meares, M., & Lara, E. (2003). Interpersonal conflict in organizations: Explaining conflict styles via face-negotiation theory. *Communication Research Reports, 20,* 106–115.

Olekalns, M., Brett, J. M., & Weingart, L. R. (2003). Phases, transitions, and interruptions: Modeling processes in multi-party negotiations. *International Journal of Conflict Management, 14,* 191–211.

Olekalns, M., & Smith, P. L. (2000). Negotiating optimal outcomes: The role of strategic sequences in competitive negotiations. *Human Communication Research, 24,* 528–560.

Olekalns, M., Smith, P. L., & Walsh, T. (1996). The process of negotiating: Strategies, timing, and outcomes. *Organizational Behavior and Human Decision Processes, 67,* 61–77.

Oliver, R. (1950). The speech of diplomacy as a field of research. *Central States Speech Journal, 15,* 24–28.

Oliver, R. (1952). Speech in international affairs. *Quarterly Journal of Speech, 38,* 171–176.

Pearce, W. B., & Littlejohn, S. W. (1997). *Moral conflict: When social worlds collide.* Thousand Oaks, CA: Sage.

Pood, E. A. (1980). Functions of communication: An experimental study in group conflict situations. *Small Group Behavior, 11,* 76–87.

Poole, M. S. (1981). Decision development in small groups I: A comparison of two models. *Communication Monographs, 48,* 1–24.

Poole, M. S., Holmes, M., & DeSanctis, G. (1991). Conflict management in a computer supported meeting environment. *Management Science, 37,* 926–953.

Poole, M. S., Shannon, D. L., & DeSanctis, G. (1992). Communication media and negotiation processes. In L. L. Putnam & M. E. Roloff (Eds.), *Communication and negotiation* (pp. 46–66). Newbury Park, CA: Sage.

Pruitt, D. G., Rubin, J. Z., & Kim, S. H. (1994). *Social conflicts: Escalation, stalemate and settlement* (2nd ed.). New York: McGraw-Hill.

Purdy, J. M., Nye, P., & Balakrishnan, P. V. (2000). The impact of communication media on negotiated outcomes. *International Journal of Conflict Management, 11,* 162–187.

Putnam, L. L. (1985). Bargaining as organizational communication. In R. D. McPhee & P. K. Tompkins (Eds.), *Organizational communication: Traditional themes and new directions* (pp. 129–148). Beverly Hills, CA: Sage.

Putnam, L. L. (1990). Reframing integrative and distributive bargaining: A process perspective. In B. H. Sheppard, M. H. Bazerman, & R. J. Lewicki (Eds.), *Research on negotiation in organizations* (Vol. 2, pp. 3–30). Greenwich, CT: JAI.

Putnam, L. L. (1994). Challenging the assumptions of traditional approaches to negotiation. *Negotiation Journal, 10,* 337–346.

Putnam, L. L. (2004a). Dialectical tensions and rhetorical tropes in negotiations. *Organization Studies, 25,* 35–53.

Putnam, L. L. (2004b). Transformation as a critical moment in negotiations. *Negotiation Journal, 20,* 275–295.

Putnam, L. L., & Geist, P. (1985). Argument in bargaining: An analysis of the reasoning process. *Southern Speech Communication Journal, 50,* 225–245.

Putnam, L. L., & Holmer, M. (1992). Framing, reframing, and issue development. In L. L. Putnam &

M. E. Roloff (Eds.), *Communication and negotiation* (pp. 128–155). Newbury Park, CA: Sage.

Putnam, L. L., & Jones, T. S. (1982a). Reciprocity in negotiations: An analysis of bargaining interaction. *Communication Monographs, 49,* 171–191.

Putnam, L. L., & Jones, T. S. (1982b). The role of communication in bargaining. *Human Communication Research, 8,* 262–280.

Putnam, L. L., & Kolb, D. M. (2000). Rethinking negotiation: Feminist views of communication and exchange. In P. Buzzanell (Ed.), *Rethinking organizational communication from feminist perspectives* (pp. 76–104). Thousand Oaks, CA: Sage.

Putnam, L. L., & Peterson, T. (2003). The Edwards Aquifer dispute: Shifting frames in a protracted conflict. In R. J. Lewicki, B. Gray, & M. Elliott (Eds.), *Making sense of intractable environmental conflicts* (pp. 127–158). Washington, DC: Island Press.

Putnam, L. L., & Poole, M. S. (1987). Conflict and negotiation. In F. M. Jablin, L. L. Putnam, K. H. Roberts, & L. W. Porter (Eds.), *Handbook of organizational communication* (pp. 549–599). Newbury Park, CA: Sage.

Putnam, L. L., Van Hoeven, S. A., & Bullis, C. A. (1991). The role of rituals and fantasy themes in teachers' bargaining. *Western Journal of Speech Communication, 55,* 85–103.

Putnam, L. L., & Wilson, C. E. (1982). Communicative strategies in organizational conflicts: Reliability and validity of a measurement scale. In M. Burgoon (Ed.), *Communication yearbook 6* (pp. 629–652). Beverly Hills, CA: Sage.

Putnam, L. L., & Wilson, S. R. (1989). Argumentation and bargaining strategies as discriminators of integrative outcomes. In M. A. Rahim (Ed.), *Managing conflict: An interdisciplinary approach* (pp. 121–144). New York: Praeger.

Putnam, L. L., Wilson, S. R., & Turner, D. B. (1990). The evolution of policy arguments in teachers' negotiations. *Argumentation, 4,* 129–152.

Putnam, L. L., & Wondolleck, J. M. (2003). Intractability: Definitions, dimensions, and distinctions. In R. J. Lewicki, B. Gray, & M. Elliott (Eds.), *Making sense of intractable environmental conflicts* (pp. 35–59). Washington, DC: Island Press.

Real, K., & Putnam, L. L. (2005). Ironies in the discursive struggle of pilots defending the profession.

Management Communication Quarterly, 19, 91–119.

Reiches, N. A., & Harral, H. B. (1974). Argument in negotiation: A theoretical and empirical approach. *Speech Monographs, 41,* 36–48.

Richmond, V. P., Wagner, J. P., & McCroskey, J. C. (1983). The impact of perceptions of leadership style, use of power, and conflict management style on organizational outcomes. *Communication Quarterly, 31,* 27–36.

Riggs, C. J. (1983). Dimensions of organizational conflict: A functional analysis of communication tactics. In R. Bostrom (Ed.), *Communication yearbook 7* (pp. 517–531). Beverly Hills, CA: Sage.

Rogan, R. G., & Hammer, M. R. (1994). Crisis negotiations: A preliminary investigation of facework in naturalistic conflict discourse. *Journal of Applied Communication Research, 22,* 216–231.

Rogan, R. G., & Hammer, M. (1995). Assessing message affect in crisis negotiations: An exploratory study. *Human Communication Research, 21,* 553–574.

Rogan, R. G., Hammer, M. R., & Van Zandt, C. R. (Eds.). (1997). *Dynamic processes of crisis negotiation: Theory, research, and practice.* Westport, CT: Praeger.

Rogers, L. E., & Farace, R. (1975). Analysis of relationship communication in dyads: New measurement procedures. *Human Communication Research, 1,* 222–239.

Roloff, M. E. (1987). Communication and conflict. In C. R. Berger & S. H. Chaffee (Eds.), *Handbook of communication science* (pp. 484–534). Newbury Park, CA: Sage.

Roloff, M. E., & Campion, D. E. (1985). Conversational profit-seeking: Interaction as a social exchange. In R. L. Street & J. N. Cappella (Eds.), *Sequence and pattern in communication behavior* (pp. 161–189). London: Edward Arnold.

Roloff, M. E., & Jordan, J. M. (1991). The influence of effort, experience and persistence on the elements of bargaining plans. *Communication Research, 18,* 306–332.

Roloff, M. E., Putnam, L. L., & Anastasiou, L. (2003). Negotiation skills. In J. Greene & B. Burleson (Eds.), *Handbook of communication and social interaction skill* (pp. 801–833). Mahwah, NJ: Lawrence Erlbaum.

Roloff, M. E., Tutzauer, F. E., & Dailey, W. O. (1989). The role of argumentation in distributive and integrative bargaining contexts: Seeking relative advantage but at what cost? In M. A. Rahim (Ed.), *Managing conflict: An interdisciplinary approach* (pp. 109–120). New York: Praeger.

Ross, R. G., & DeWine, S. (1988). Assessing the Ross-DeWine Conflict Management Message Style (CMMS). *Management Communication Quarterly, 1,* 389–413.

Ruben, B. D. (1978). Communication and conflict: A system-theoretic perspective. *Quarterly Journal of Speech, 64,* 202–210.

Saine, T. A. (1974). Perceiving communication conflict. *Speech Monographs, 41,* 49–56.

Schütz, J. (1978). Argumentative competence and the negotiation of Henry Kissinger. *Journal of the American Forensic Association, 15,* 1–16.

Scott, R. L., & Smith, D. K. (1969). The rhetoric of confrontation. *Quarterly Journal of Speech, 55,* 1–8.

Sereno, K. K., & Mortensen, C. D. (1973). The effects of ego-involved attitudes on conflict negotiation in dyads. In F. E. Jandt (Ed.), *Conflict resolution through communication* (pp. 145–152). New York: Harper & Row.

Shailor, J. G. (1994). *Empowerment in dispute mediation: A critical analysis of communication.* Westport, CT: Praeger.

Sheffield, J. (1995). The effect of communication medium on negotiation performance. *Group Decision and Negotiation, 4,* 159–179.

Shockley-Zalabak, P. (1981). The effects of sex differences on the preference for utilization of conflict styles of managers in a work setting: An exploratory study. *Public Personnel Management, 10,* 289–295.

Sillars, A. L. (1980a). Attributions and communication in roommate conflicts. *Communication Monographs, 47,* 180–200.

Sillars, A. L. (1980b). The sequential and distributional structure of conflict interactions as a function of attributions concerning the locus of responsibility and stability of conflicts. In D. Nimmo (Ed.), *Communication yearbook 4* (pp. 217–235). New Brunswick, NJ: Transaction Publishing.

Sillars, A. L., Coletti, S. F., Parry, D., & Rogers, M. A. (1982). Coding verbal conflicts: Non-verbal and perceptual correlates of the "avoidance-distributive-integrative" distinction. *Human Communication Research, 9,* 83–95.

Simons, H. W. (1969). Confrontation as a pattern of persuasion in university settings. *Central States Speech Journal, 20,* 163–169.

Simons, H. W. (1972). Persuasion in social conflicts: A critique of the prevailing conceptions and a framework for future research. *Speech Monographs, 39,* 227–247.

Simons, H. (1974a). The carrot and stick as handmaidens of persuasion in conflict situations. In G. R. Miller & H. W. Simons (Eds.), *Perspectives on communication in social conflict* (pp. 172–205). Englewood Cliffs, NJ: Prentice Hall.

Simons, H. (1974b). Prologue. In G. R. Miller & H. W. Simons (Eds.), *Perspectives on communication in social conflict* (pp. 1–13). Englewood Cliffs, NJ: Prentice Hall.

Smith, D. H. (1969). Communication and negotiation outcome. *Journal of Communication, 19,* 248–256.

Smith, D. H. (1971). Communication, minimum disposition, and negotiation. In H. B. Pepinsky & M. J. Patton (Eds.), *The psychological experiment: A practical accomplishment.* Elmsford, NY: Pergamon.

Smith, D. H. (1983). Review of research on negotiation and bargaining: Problems with the economic model as a basis for theory and research in negotiation. In R. J. Matlon & R. J. Crawford (Eds.), *Proceedings of the Summer Conference on Communication Strategies in the Practice of Lawyering.* Annandale, VA: Speech Communication Association.

Smith, R. C., & Eisenberg, E. M. (1987). Conflict at Disneyland: A root-metaphor analysis. *Communication Monographs, 54,* 367–380.

Steinfatt, T. M. (1974). Communication and conflict: A review of new material. *Human Communication Research, 1,* 81–89.

Steinfatt, T. M., & Miller, G. R. (1974). Communication in game theoretic models of conflict. In G. R. Miller & H. W. Simons (Eds.), *Perspectives on communication in social conflict* (pp. 14–74). Englewood Cliffs, NJ: Prentice Hall.

Steinfatt, T. M., Seibold, D. R., & Frye, J. K. (1974). Communication in game simulated conflicts: Two experiments. *Speech Monographs, 41,* 24–35.

Strauss, A. (1978). *Negotiations: Varieties, contexts, processes, and social order.* San Francisco: Jossey-Bass.

Stutman, R. K., & Putnam, L. L. (1994). The consequences of language: A metaphorical look at the legalization of organizations. In S. B. Sitkin & R. J. Bies (Eds.), *The legalistic organization* (pp. 281–302). Thousand Oaks, CA: Sage.

Theye, L. D., & Seiler, W. J. (1979). Interaction analysis in collective bargaining: An alternative approach to the prediction of negotiated outcomes. In D. Nimmo (Ed.), *Communication yearbook 3* (pp. 375–392). New Brunswick, NJ: Transaction Books.

Thomas, K. W., & Pondy, L. R. (1977). Toward an "intent" model of conflict management among principal parties. *Human Relations, 30,* 1089–1102.

Ting-Toomey, S. (1983). Coding conversations between intimates: A validation study of the intimate negotiation coding system (INCS). *Communication Quarterly, 31,* 68–77.

Ting-Toomey, S. (1985). Toward a theory of conflict and culture. In W. B. Gudykunst, L. P. Stewart, & S. Ting-Toomey (Eds.), *Communication, culture, and organizational processes* (pp. 71–86). Beverly Hills, CA: Sage.

Ting-Toomey, S. (1988). Intercultural conflict styles: A face-negotiation theory. In Y. Kim & W. Gudykunst (Eds.), *Theories in intercultural communication* (pp. 213–235). Newbury Park, CA: Sage.

Ting-Toomey, S., & Cole, M. (1990). Intergroup diplomatic communication: A face-negotiation perspective. In F. Korzenny & S. Ting-Toomey (Eds.), *Communicating for peace: Diplomacy and negotiation* (pp. 77–95). Newbury Park, CA: Sage.

Ting-Toomey, S., Gao, G., Trubisky, P., Yang, Z., Liu, H. S., & Nishida, T. (1991). Culture, face maintenance, and styles of handling interpersonal conflict: A study of five cultures. *International Journal of Conflict Management, 2,* 275–296.

Ting-Toomey, S., & Oetzel, J. G. (2001). *Managing intercultural conflict effectively.* Thousand Oaks, CA: Sage.

Tompkins, P. K., Fisher, J. Y., Infante, D. A., & Tompkins, E. V. (1974). Conflict and communication within the university. In G. R. Miller & H. W. Simons (Eds.), *Perspectives on communication in social conflict* (pp. 153–171). Englewood Cliffs, NJ: Prentice Hall.

Tracy, K., & Spradlin, A. (1994). "Talking like a mediator": Conversational moves of experienced divorce mediators. In J. P. Folger & T. S. Jones (Eds.), *New directions in mediation: Communication research and perspectives* (pp. 110–132). Thousand Oaks, CA: Sage.

Trapp, R. (1986). The role of disagreement in interactional argument. *Journal of the American Forensic Association, 23,* 23–41.

Tuckman, B. (1965). Developmental sequences in small groups. *Psychological Bulletin, 63,* 384–399.

Turnbull, A. A., Strickland, L., & Shaver, K. G. (1976). Medium of communication, differential power, and phrasing of concessions: Negotiating success and attributions to the opponent. *Human Communication Research, 2,* 262–270.

Tutzauer, F. (1992). The communication of offers in dyadic bargaining. In L. L. Putnam & M. E. Roloff (Eds.), *Communication and negotiation* (pp. 67–82). Newbury Park, CA: Sage.

Tutzauer, F., & Roloff, M. E. (1988). Communication processes leading to integrative agreements: Three paths to joint benefits. *Communication Research, 15,* 360–380.

Waln, V. G. (1982). Interpersonal conflict interaction: An examination of verbal defense of self. *Central States Speech Journal, 33,* 557–566.

Walton, R. E., & McKersie, R. B. (1965). *A behavioral theory of labor negotiations: An analysis of a social interaction system.* New York: McGraw-Hill.

Watzlawick, P., Beavin, J. H., & Jackson, D. D. (1967). *Pragmatics of human communication.* New York: W. W. Norton.

Weider-Hatfield, D. (1993, November). *The role of communication in conflict: Revisiting communication scholars' assumptions about the nature of conflict.* Paper presented at the Speech Communication Association meeting, Miami, FL.

Weingart, L. R., Prietula, M. J., Hyder, E., & Genovese, C. (1999). Knowledge and the sequential processes of negotiation: A Markov chain analysis of response-in-kind. *Journal of Experimental Social Psychology, 35,* 366–393.

Wilson, S. R., Paulson, G. D., & Putnam, L. L. (2001). Negotiating. In W. P. Robinson & H. Giles (Eds.), *Handbook of language and social psychology* (2nd ed., pp. 303–315). London: Wiley.

Winslade, J., & Monk, G. (2001). *Narrative mediation: A new approach to conflict resolution.* San Francisco: Jossey-Bass.

Witteman, H., & Fitzpatrick, M. A. (1986). Compliance gaining in marital interaction: Power bases, processes, and outcomes. *Communication Monographs, 53,* 130–143.

2

Quantitative Methods for Conflict Communication Research, with Special Reference to Culture

Edward L. Fink
University of Maryland

Deborah A. Cai
University of Maryland

Qi Wang
University of Maryland

In their book on processes of social conflict, Pruitt and Carnevale (1993) noted the difficulties in studying conflict. Experimental studies provide control of extraneous variables, but in a simulated setting. On the other hand, manipulating conflict in laboratory or field experiments raises other concerns: If the manipulation is effective, the ethics of the investigation may be problematic; if the manipulation is ineffective, the lack of internal validity means that the investigation cannot inform us about conflict processes. Naturalistic studies are hard to come by, and, when available, have their own problems of internal and external validity (see Cook & Campbell, 1979). Furthermore, in everyday settings individuals and organizations are often hesitant to allow researchers to observe sensitive, confidential, or private interactions associated with conflict.

Despite these challenges, conflict research has made tremendous progress in the past 20 years. In addition to the breadth of conflict venues addressed, a variety of research methods—including quantitative, qualitative, and rhetorical methods—has been developed for studying social conflict. The purpose of this chapter is to examine the types of methods used to study conflict communication at various levels of analysis, and to suggest the types of analyses that are likely to be effective for future research.

First, we decided to focus this chapter on quantitative issues for several reasons. Qualitative methods, such as participant observation and unstructured interviews, are often used to determine the universe of meaning (i.e., the full range of connotations in addition to the denotations) of a phenomenon, the types of individuals relevant to a domain of investigation, the operative categories employed by cultural participants (i.e., the emic constructs; see Pike, 1967), and the causal attributions provided by individual participants or observers (for discussion of these methods, see Denzin & Lincoln, 2000). For this chapter, we view the goal of conflict research as the creation of general and abstract social science theory, which entails prediction as well as description. To this end, qualitative investigations, however valuable, serve as precursors to studies that explicitly take into account measurement validity, internal validity, and external validity, or, in short, quantitative investigations. Furthermore, although there exist "naïve theories" that can be well explicated by qualitative methods (see Heider, 1958), quantitative investigations are needed to check the naïve causal attributions made by cultural informants (see, e.g., Nisbett & Wilson, 1977). Finally, the literature on quantitative methods germane to conflict communication research is so extensive that even restricting our focus to these methods leaves us with little opportunity to cover them all.

Second, we chose to highlight methods that are especially relevant to cross-cultural and other group comparisons. Like many areas of investigation, the study of conflict communication began with obvious and important applied questions: How do we avoid war? Can we minimize strife within families? Can labor and management cooperate in the modern corporation? These questions lend themselves to group comparisons: warring versus non-warring countries; conflictual versus non-conflictual families; companies with cooperative labor-management relations versus those with records of labor-management clashes.

Group differences play a major role in most studies of conflict, from comparing gender differences in resolving relational conflict to cultural differences in conflict styles. As a result, a good deal of our discussion is spent examining group differences; most of this discussion considers cross-cultural comparisons, but the methods we examine apply equally well to comparing conflict in hierarchical versus nonhierarchical organizations, cross-gender versus same-gender interpersonal relationships, or people from Southern versus non-Southern U.S. states (for the latter, see Nisbett & Cohen, 1996). We hope that our discussion will alert scholars to significant considerations for research on conflict, their methodological challenges, and the needs of future research.

With increased knowledge, research that utilizes categorical independent variables (e.g., group types) is replaced by research that employs continuous independent variables that represent the distinctions embodied in the categories. Thus, during this transition, both types of independent variables (categorical and continuous) are likely to be used, with the goal of showing that the model including the continuous variables is not significantly improved by the addition of the categorical variables (e.g., Oetzel, Ting-Toomey, Yokochi, Masumoto, & Takai, 2000). The study of conflict communication is at the point of this transition, so that methods that allow group comparisons—which we highlight in this chapter—are especially valuable at this time. For example, cross-cultural research in conflict communication is especially amenable to the methods we discuss (see Kim & Leung, 2000, for a review).

Moving from categorical to continuous independent variables is a theory-construction strategy. There are other such strategies, but they are implicit in the methods we choose to discuss. The methods used in a study reflect the conceptual definitions and the generality, abstractness, parsimony, and completeness of the theory used to investigate the phenomenon of interest. We have chosen not to discuss the variety of the conceptual definitions of conflict or their appropriateness for the studies we examined in preparing this chapter (see Putnam, Chapter 1, and Nicotera & Dorsey, Chapter 11, in this volume). Instead, we have kept our focus on the issues involving types of data, sampling and data analysis, and cross-cultural and other group comparisons. We note, however, that the conceptual and theoretical issues in conflict communication research are the foundation on which investigations are constructed, and methods are useful only insofar as they provide the appropriate tools to answer questions posed by a sound theory. Furthermore, methods and theory are interdependent: Without some specific methods, some theoretical questions cannot be posed, and without some specific theory, the choice of methods is arbitrary, or, worse, irrelevant. In this chapter conceptual and theoretical issues are rarely explicated, not because they are unimportant, but rather to focus the chapter squarely on methods.

We begin by examining several issues that involve measurement and design, and then discuss sampling and analysis, the examination of group differences, and finally draw some conclusions about methods for studying conflict communication.

TYPES OF DATA I: DETERMINATION OF QUALITIES AND QUANTITIES

Measures may be differentiated based on the assumptions implicitly made regarding how the magnitude of a phenomenon is assessed. If communications or acts are to be counted, there must be a clear definition of acts. Measures resulting from these *counts* are in the form of integers (there are 5 or 6 communications, not 5.5), and in principle the frequency scale starts at 0 and has no upper bound. A study can employ counts of the number of times an individual has engaged in jealousy-inducing behaviors (e.g., Brainerd, Hunter, Moore, & Thompson, 1996), the number of multiple goals in a conflict situation (e.g., psychological data in Samp, 2000), the number of hostility and anger expressions in marital interactions (e.g., interactional data in Gordis, Margolin, & John, 2001), or the number of crimes against the person in a society (e.g., sociological data in Daly & Wilson, 1997).

Measures created by comparison to a standard (such as a yardstick) yield magnitudes of a different sort. Time and distance are prototypical *amounts,* but many measures may be constructed by defining a non-material yardstick and having respondents or coders make comparisons to it. The following examples illustrate this point:

If 0 is not feeling hostile at all, and 100 is the level of hostility you feel when you are cut off in traffic, how hostile do you feel in this negotiation? There is no highest number.

If 0 indicates no aggression, and 100 is the level of aggression in the interrogation scene shown from *Law & Order* [a particular scene is shown], how much aggression is there in this video [a hostage negotiation video is shown]? There is no highest number.

An example of amount (or magnitude) scaling in studying war and conflict is found in Sulfaro and Crislip's (1997) study on Americans' perceptions of foreign policy threats. Participants rated their perceptions of 19 countries' hostility toward the United States with two magnitude scales and one Likert-type scale (i.e., a 7-point scale varying from "least hostile" to "most hostile"; p. 110). Results indicated that the two magnitude scales were almost identical in measuring hostility across the 19 countries with an "R^2 for [the logarithmically transformed variables] . . . near . . . .987" (p. 116), whereas the Likert-type scale correlated poorly with the magnitude scales because it dealt poorly with extreme values.

By making ratios and differences, counts and amounts may be used to create derivative measures: Examples include the ratio of the number of hostile words to the total number of words expressed (ratio of a count to a count); and the acceleration of aggressiveness in interaction, as assessed by the change in the magnitude of expressed aggressiveness over time (a change in an amount divided by an amount). One study in which a ratio is derived and employed (counts over amounts) is Fuller, Murphy, Ridgley, and Ulack's (2000) research on potential conflict in Southeast Asia. Another example of such derivative measures is the use of physiological data, which tend to be amount-over-time ratios. Buss, Larsen, Westen, and Semmelroth (1992) measured the acceleration of a negative emotion, jealousy, with such physiological measurements as electrodermal activity, pulse rate, and electromyographic activity.

We argue that the methods described here (counts, amounts, and their derivatives) allow greater precision, typically evidence higher levels of reliability, and assist in the determination of the functional forms that relate our variables of interest when assessing hypotheses (Woelfel & Fink, 1980). We also realize that the typical investigator employs scales such as a 1–7 scale, with response alternatives bounded at both ends (e.g., one cannot go below 1 or above 7). Such scales are generally not examined for their many implicit assumptions: that the vectors emanating from the scale's neutral point to the end points are separated by 180°; that the distance between adjacent pairs of scale units is equal for all pairs; that the number of response alternatives is adequate for the phenomenon being scaled; and that the boundedness of the scale does not cause scale distortions due to floor or ceiling effects (see Torgerson, 1958, for a discussion of some of these issues). Conflict research, like all social science research, would benefit from greater consideration of measurement options in terms of response scales and their assumptions.

TYPES OF DATA II: LEVELS OF ANALYSIS

Conflict communication research employs data of a psychological, interactional, or sociological sort. Psychological data are descriptive of individuals, and include emotional states and traits, personality states and traits, level and type of motivation, and types and degree of knowledge. Examples of such data are measures of hostility (Buss & Durkee, 1957), propensity for abusiveness (Dutton, Landolt, Starzomski, & Bodnarchuk, 2001), and ethnocentrism (Neuliep & McCroskey, 1997a). Interactional data include attributes of verbal and nonverbal communicative behavior of people in simulated or actual interaction. Examples of such data are integrative and distributive behaviors in negotiation (Cai, Wilson, & Drake, 2000; Donohue & Roberto, 1996), emotion change between interactants (Rogan & Hammer, 1995), and coded linguistic measures (Cook-Gumperz & Szymanski, 2001; Scarry, 1985). Finally, sociological data involve attributes of groups, organizations, states, and cultures. Examples are Cashman's (1993) review of national attributes and international conflict (see also Diehl, 2004; Speer, 1986) and Doreian's (1981) analysis of network data to predict the mobilization of individuals taking sides in a conflict.

The typical methods used to gather these three types of data differ. However, all three types of data require evidence of validity. For theoretical concepts, validity is typically assessed by construct validation methods (or by related techniques, such as multi-trait multimethod matrix approaches; see Campbell & Fiske, 1959). It is quite common for measurement validity to be ignored prior to data collection, because a measure (say X) of a theoretical variable (say X^*) may be validated by finding support for a set of hypotheses in which X^* is measured by X. This strategy is risky: Without independent evidence of measurement validity, we cannot determine if failure to find support for a set of hypotheses is due to poor measurement, inadequate theory, or both.

Psychological data

For psychological variables, the typical datagathering tool is a multi-item scale completed by the respondent. For such data we generally require evidence of reliability, especially internal consistency reliability as assessed, for example, by Cronbach's α. In addition, the dimensional structure of such scales is investigated by exploratory factor analysis (e.g., Lee & Rogan's, 1991, assessment of Putnam & Wilson's, 1982, Organizational Communication Conflict Instrument [OCCI]), confirmatory factor analysis (e.g., Oetzel et al.'s, 2000, examination of a typology of facework behaviors), or a full-blown structural equation model (e.g., Reese-Weber & Bartle-Haring's, 1998, confirmation of Rubenstein & Feldman's, 1993 three-factor conflict resolution structure).

If using exploratory factor analysis, the investigator may create a set of measures, each representing a single scale dimension, or create a single factor that represents the principal construct of interest. Either of these choices may be made by (a) eliminating items that do not load on the main (first) factor of interest by some criteria, and then adding or averaging the resulting items; or (b) computing factor scores for the one or more dimensions that the researcher deems to be interpretable (see Vangelisti & Crumley's, 1998, study of underlying factors of hurtful messages).

Free-standing measurement models (i.e., measurement models that are not part of "full" structural equation models, which include relations between theoretical or latent variables) may be investigated with confirmatory factor analysis. Such an analysis can create scale composites that have advantages over the composites created via exploratory factor analysis: If the models thus created are over-identified (see Fink, 1980), full-information estimation methods to create scale composites can be used; this approach exploits the hypothesized structure that is presumed to have generated the covariances among the items. Furthermore, the measurement model that is imposed is tested as a single hypothesis (i.e., that the estimated population covariance matrix among the scale items does not differ from the estimated population covariance matrix as constrained by the measurement structure imposed by the investigator). Rejection of this hypothesis requires rethinking (and, presumably, reanalyzing) the measurement structure that was imposed. However, this procedure may have disadvantages: If our scale items or the model relating them is relatively arbitrary, it is unlikely that the data will fit a model with many constraints.

If the investigator were to test the dimensional structure of the scale items within a full structural equation model (i.e., one that incorporates both a measurement model and a theoretical model), the advantages and disadvantages would be basically the same as above. When employing a full structural equation model, investigators typically choose between what are called a one-step and a two-step approach. The two-step approach (Anderson & Gerbing, 1988) separately estimates the measurement model, as discussed above, respecifying it until the data fit. Then the respecified measurement model is incorporated within a full structural equation model. This approach differs from straightforwardly and simultaneously testing the full model, which includes the measurement component (see, e.g., Corcoran & Mallinckrodt, 2000).

Interactional data

Interactional data are typically the results of systematic observation. Coders (judges, observers, raters) are given coding rules and then code or rate the behaviors that are observed. If the behaviors are to be counted, then rules are needed to unitize the behaviors (i.e., determine

where one behavior ends and another begins). For example, in a study regarding the interaction between hostage takers and negotiators, Taylor (2002a) analyzed transcripts of nine real hostage incidents. A rhetorical structure analysis was conducted to divide each transcript into separate episodes, or dialogue movements, based on changing themes. In addition, thought units were unitized from each episode before they were coded and subjected to data analysis. Other examples of creating rules to unitize data may be found in Gordis, Margolin, and Garcia (1996) and Gordis et al. (2001); these studies examine conflict within the family.

There is a great deal of literature on the factors that affect the unitization of behavior as assessed by actors and observers, so the process of unitization should not be thought of as without difficulties (see, e.g., Girbau, 2002; Lemus, Seibold, Flanagin, & Metzger, 2004; an elaborate discussion of this issue is found in Krippendorff, 2004). In addition to creating rules for unitization, the results of the unitization must be assessed for reliability; as Krippendorff (2004, p. 251) indicated, there must be agreement not only on the total number of units, but on the actual location of the units in the behavior stream.

If observational data are quantitative ratings rather than frequency counts, reliability is typically assessed by inter-coder reliability, most commonly in the form of one or more bivariate correlations. For scores derived from multiple coders, Cronbach's alpha may also be reported: Data from multiple coders may be analyzed as if each coder variable is an item within a multi-item scale, and the consistency of these multi-coder items may be assessed like multi-item psychological scales. So, if we have three coders rating the level of conflict in a set of groups, Cronbach's alpha, representing the consistency of the coders, may be computed and reported. Further, the coder variables may be treated as congeneric measures (multi-item single-factor scales; see Loehlin, 2004, p. 95). In other words, we can assume that each coder's rating of conflict is caused by a single true (i.e., reliable) level of observed conflict, and that the ratings have random errors that are independent. Given this model, we may subject the coded ratings to assessment within a measurement model or in a full structural equation model (see Fink, 1980).

Additional examples of unitization and reliability assessment in interactional conflict data may be found in research on hostage negotiation (Donohue, Ramesh, & Borchgrevink, 1991; Donohue & Roberto, 1993, 1996; Rogan & Hammer, 1995; Taylor, 2002b), family conflict (Gottman, Levenson, & Woodin, 2001; Smetana, Yau, & Hanson, 1991), interethnic conflict (Collier, 1996), and third-party mediated conflict (Jones, 1988).

Sociological data

This type of data may be differentiated into several subtypes. To assist us in developing a vocabulary, we paraphrase Lazarsfeld and Menzel's (1961, pp. 427–433) differentiation between individual and collective properties:

> Properties of Collectives: (a) *Analytical:* properties of collectives obtained by performing some mathematical operation on some property of individuals; (b) *Structural:* properties of collectives obtained by performing some mathematical operation on data about relations of individuals to some or all of the others; and (c) *Global:* properties of collectives not based on information about individuals.

> Properties of Individuals: (a) *Absolute:* characteristics of members obtained without making use of information about the collective or of information about relationships of an individual to other individuals; (b) *Relational:* properties of individuals computed from information about relationships between the individual and other individuals; (c) *Comparative:* properties that characterize an individual by comparison between this individual's value on some absolute or relational property and the distribution of that property over the entire collective; and (d) *Contextual:* properties that describe an individual in terms of a property of the collective.

The variables identified as properties of collectives are closest to what is here referred to as sociological variables. For example, characterizing a culture as individualistic (vs. collectivistic) may be based on a content analysis of archival data or of contemporary texts (global; e.g., Castilla, 2004), on the aggregation of individual responses to survey instruments (analytical; e.g., Hofstede, 1980), or on analysis of the density of friendship networks (structural; e.g., Brass & Labianca, 1999). On the other hand, there is cross-cultural conflict research in which individuals are characterized by a property of the culture of which they are members (relational or contextual) (see Kim & Leung, 2000, for a review).

One problem in research (including conflict research) that employs sociological variables is that the reliability and dimensional structure of such variables is seldom investigated. Global variables can be assessed for inter-coder reliability, and the individual scores that enter into analytical variables may be assessed for internal-consistency reliability. Furthermore, if individuals are sampled to represent the population of interest, aggregating properties of individuals to create a societal-level variable (analytical) is like treating each individual as a random "item" for the composite variable: With some assumptions, the Spearman-Brown prophecy formula (see, e.g., Lord & Novick, 1968, chap. 4; Nunnally, 1967, chap. 6) may be used to estimate how the averaged or summed score increases in reliability as the sample size on which it is based increases.

When using variables from different levels (e.g., sociological vs. individual), researchers need to guard against the ecological fallacy (Hofstede, 1980), which occurs when relationships between variables at one level are assumed to hold at a different level. Smith (2002) provided an example of the problem by examining the predictors of happiness at the cultural and individual levels.

It is reasonable to employ measures taken from different levels of analysis. However, because the data-gathering methods and the resultant assessment of reliability and scale dimensionality are likely to differ across levels, investigators must be aware of these differences and take them into account in the creation and assessment of the measures used.

TYPES OF DATA III: TIME DEPENDENCE IN RESEARCH DESIGN

Studies can be differentiated by whether they employ cross-sectional data, such as surveys at one point in time; panel data (experimental and non-experimental) that employ at least two points in time; and time-series data, based on many points in time. (Pooled time-series cross-section studies of conflict communication are rare and need not be discussed here.) We discuss how the conception of conflict interacts with the kind of design employed. This discussion is followed by the identification of a variety of measures that have been used to study conflict.

Although some reviews of conflict communication research differentiate conflict studies based on whether the data are self-report versus observational (Canary, Cupach, & Messman, 1995) or on other differentia (e.g., Nicotera, Rodriguez, Hall, & Jackson, 1995), the distinction we wish to emphasize is the focus on conflict outcomes versus the process that leads to the outcome. Most studies of conflict examine either a sample of conflicts (e.g., Holmes & Sykes, 1993; Poole & Roth, 1989) or a sample of individuals experiencing, anticipating, imagining, or recalling conflict (e.g., Cai & Fink, 2002; Maoz & Ellis, 2001; Ting-Toomey, Oetzel, & Yee-Jung, 2001). The use of samples of individuals rather than of conflicts has been associated with outcome-oriented research rather than research oriented to the relational process between actors (e.g., individuals, groups, organizations, states, cultures) that may sometimes result in conflict. The data examined for such outcome-oriented investigations are likely to be cross-sectional, and, even when attributes of conflict are included or predicted, there is not likely to be a no-conflict control group that would enable the conflict-generating or conflict-resolving process to be understood. This kind of research (i.e., research without a no-conflict control group) helps the investigator explain the management of conflict once an interaction event has reached a threshold that justifies the label conflict.

We can contrast this approach with understanding conflict as a process, entailing a trajectory of variables indicative of conflict, disinterest, and accord between parties. Although most process-oriented conflict studies tend to focus on contexts or relationships that are conflictual, trajectories of conflict variables represent time courses of cooperation just as well as time courses of conflict (for studies over time see, e.g., Holmes, 1997; Holmes & Sykes, 1993; Poole & Roth, 1989; Rogan & Hammer, 1994, 1995). Such over-time data allow for the explanation of

conflict trajectories, whether they refer to dyads or to states. Considering conflict in this way makes conflict "normal," in the sense that we are not viewing conflict as an aberrant segment of a relationship or as a pathological event but rather as a dynamic generated by ordinary sequences and magnitudes of activity. Both Freud and Festinger exemplify scholars for whom conflict was part of the normal process of emoting, thinking, interacting, and behaving; in a word, living. A *normal conflict approach* considers conflict to be ordinary and normative (in an actuarial sense) within the vicissitudes of action of people, groups, communities, states, and cultures.

There are methodological implications of such a normal conflict approach. In this approach, conflict is likely to be examined as a continuous variable, and over-time investigations of the causes and consequences of conflict (e.g., panel and time-series investigations) are more likely. When conflict is examined experimentally, a control group is more likely to represent a state of no conflict or of cooperation rather than of a different type of conflict or of a low level of conflict.

A classic example of the normal conflict approach is the small-group interaction analysis developed by Bales (1950). Although Bales's work is not generally considered within the conflict literature, we can see how it does fit and how it reflects the normal conflict approach. Bales assigned the communicative possibilities exhibited by interactants to 12 categories. A communication by an interactant may (a) show solidarity, (b) show tension release, (c) agree, (d) give a suggestion, (e) give an opinion, (f) give orienting information, (g) ask for orienting information, (h) ask for an opinion, (i) ask for a suggestion, (j) disagree, (k) show tension, or (l) show antagonism. In any observed interaction there may be conflict, as indicated by messages of type (j), (k), or (l). However, the coding system is not restricted to interactions that necessarily involve conflict. In a similar way, negotiation research often looks at the unfolding of interaction, but the context assumes some level of conflict will arise during the interaction because of the competing goals of the interactants.

Additional interaction coding schemes were developed from the mid-1980s to the

Table 2.1   Studying Interethnic and Intercultural Conflict

Focus	Method	Measure or Instrument	Original Authors	Example of Use
Interethnic	Questionnaire	Personal report of interethnic communication apprehension	Neuliep & McCroskey (1997b)	Toale & McCroskey (2001)
	Questionnaire	General ethnocentrism scale	Neuliep & McCroskey (1997a)	Toale & McCroskey (2001)
	Questionnaire	Black metastereotypes	Sigelman & Tuch (1997)	
	Questionnaire	Ethnic/cultural identity	Ting-Toomey et al. (2000)	
	Questionnaire	Goal concerns & conflict tactics	Ohbuchi & Tedeschi (1997)	Ohbuchi, Fukushima, & Tedeschi (1999)
	Discourse analysis	Interethnic conflict	Speicher (1995)	
Intergroup	Discourse analysis	Intergroup conflict	Maoz & Ellis (2001)	
International	Coding	War: Text scoring system for historical analysis	Winter (1991)	Winter (1993)

mid-1990s, reflecting a continued interest in interaction during conflicts. For example, hostage negotiation, business negotiation, and marital mediation were studied using the methods of conversation analysis. Lag-sequential analysis was used to study interaction patterns during simulated negotiation (e.g., Cai & Donohue, 1997), and phase mapping was used to study conflict phases during interaction (e.g., Holmes, 1997). These approaches should have created opportunities for process research; however, we note that such investigations have declined over the past several years. Indeed, interaction analysis of conflict has been largely abandoned. A notable exception to this trend is a recent issue of the *International Journal of Conflict Management* (2003; also see earlier work, such as Gottman, Markman, & Notarius, 1977).

Process-oriented approaches typically do not utilize exclusively cross-sectional data, although such an approach is not impossible. For example, a structural equation model, whether recursive or nonrecursive, may use cross-sectional data to represent equilibrium values of a process; an analysis of variance or a regression model may also represent a process even though such analyses may employ exclusively cross-sectional data. However, it is typically the case that different conceptions—conflict as outcome versus conflict as process—result in different kinds of data employing different analytic methods.

TYPES OF DATA IV: MEASURES FOR THE STUDY OF CONFLICT

Although by no means exhaustive of the possible measures of conflict, Tables 2.1 through 2.3 provide examples of measures used in studying conflict in communication research for studying interethnic and intercultural conflict; interpersonal conflict, including conflict measures related to intrapersonal communication, family, marriage, and relationship conflict, and partner

Table 2.2   Studying Interpersonal Conflict

Focus	Method	Measure or Instrument	Original Authors	Example of Use
Intrapersonal	Questionnaire	Anger and distress: Interpersonal statement rating	Biglan, Rothlind, Hops, & Sherman (1989)	Kubany & Richard (1992)
	Questionnaire	5 jealousy-inducing behaviors	Brainerd, Hunter, Moore, & Thompson (1996)	
	Questionnaire	Hostility inventory	Buss & Durkee (1957)	Tangney, Wagner, Fletcher, & Gramzow (1992)
	Questionnaire	Jealousy response to relationship infidelity	Buss, Larsen, Westen, & Semmelroth (1992)	Cann, Mangum, & Wells (2001) Cramer, Abraham, Johnson, & Manning-Ryan (2001–2002)
	Questionnaire	Anger and hostility: SCL-90: Symptom checklist 90	Derogatis, Lipman, & Covi (1973)	Tangney, Wagner, Fletcher, & Gramzow (1992) Tangney, Wagner, & Gramzow (1992)
	Questionnaire	Anger expression scale	Guerrero (1992)	Guerrero (1994)
	Questionnaire	Jealousy-related goals	Guerrero & Afifi (1999)	
	Questionnaire	Communication responses to jealousy scale	Guerrero, Anderson, Jorgensen, Spitzberg, & Eloy (1995)	Anderson & Eloy (1995) Guerrero & Afifi (1999)
	Questionnaire	Criticism from ingroup vs. outgroup	Hornsey, Oppes, & Svensson (2002)	
	Questionnaire	Argumentativeness scale	Infante & Rancer (1982)	Infante, Chandler, & Rudd (1989)
	Questionnaire	Verbal aggressiveness scale	Infante & Wigley (1986)	Infante, Sabourin, Rudd, & Shannon (1990) Segrin & Fitzpatrick (1992)

(Continued)

Table 2.2 (Continued)

Focus	Method	Measure or Instrument	Original Authors	Example of Use
	Questionnaire	Interpersonal jealousy scale	Mathes & Severa (1981)	Dutton, van Ginkel, & Landolt (1996)
	Questionnaire	Cognitive and emotional jealousy	Pfeiffer & Wong (1989) Modified: Guerrero, Eloy, Jorgensen, & Anderson (1993)	Anderson & Eloy (1995) Guerrero & Afifi (1999)
	Questionnaire	Multidimensional anger inventory	Siegel (1986)	Dutton, van Ginkel, & Landolt (1996)
	Questionnaire	TAC: Trait anger scale	Spielberger, Jacobs, Russell, & Crane (1983)	Tangney, Wagner, Fletcher, & Gramzow (1992)
	Questionnaire	Interpersonal control scale for men and women	Stets (1991)	Brainerd, Hunter, Moore, & Thompson (1996)
	Questionnaire	Psychological aggression scale for men and women	Stets (1991)	Brainerd, Hunter, Moore, & Thompson (1996)
	Scenarios	4 jealousy-inducing scenarios	Fisch & Brainerd (1990)	Brainerd, Hunter, Moore, & Thompson (1996)
Family	Coding observations	Family coding system	Margolin & Gordis (1992)	Gordis, Margolin, & John (2001)
	Coding observations	Family coding scheme	Sillars (1980)	
	Physiological measures	Physiological measure of emotions involved in marital conflicts	Gottman, Levenson, & Woodin (2001)	
	Content analysis	Relational maintenance and guilt: Narratives	Baumeister, Stillwell, & Wotman (1990)	Baumeister, Stillwell, & Heartherton (1995)
	Content analysis	Mediation custody and visitation agreements	Mathis & Tanner (1998)	
	Content analysis	Mediation discourse: Language of agency	Scarry (1985)	Cobb (1997)

Focus	Method	Measure or Instrument	Original Authors	Example of Use
	Questionnaire	Family Communication Pattern instrument – Revised	Fitzpatrick & Ritchie (1994) Ritchie & Fitzpatrick (1990)	Koerner & Fitzpatrick (1997, 2002)
Marriage and Relationship	Coding	Marital coding system	Gordis, Margolin, & Garcia (1996)	Gordis, Margolin, & John (2001)
	Open-ended questions	Women's divorce and mediation	Cheung & Kwok (1999)	
	Questionnaire	Perceived helpfulness of mediation services	Cheung & Kwok (1999)	
	Questionnaire	Marital problems	Gottman (1994)	Gottman, Levenson, & Woodin (2001)
	Questionnaire	Couple's problem inventory	Gottman, Markman, & Notarius (1977)	Gottman, Levenson, & Woodin (2001)
	Questionnaire	Conflict tactics between spouses	Straus (1979)	Jenkins (2000) Swinford, DeMaris, Cernkovich, & Giordano (2000)
	Questionnaire	Marital conflict	Straus & Yodanis (1996)	
Partner Abuse and Violence	Questionnaire	Trauma symptom checklist	Briere & Runtz (1989)	Dutton, van Ginkel, & Landolt (1996)
	Questionnaire	Sources of conflict between men and women	Buss (1987)	Ellis & Malamuth (2000)
	Questionnaire	Intrusiveness	Dutton, van Ginkel, & Landolt (1996)	
	Questionnaire	PAS: Propensity of abusiveness scale	Dutton, Landolt, Starzomski, & Bodnarchuk (2001)	
	Questionnaire	Psychological maltreatment inventory	Kasian & Painter (1992)	Simonelli & Ingram (1998)
	Questionnaire	Severity of violence against women & violence against men	Marshall (1992)	Dutton, Landolt, Starzomski, & Bodnarchuk (2001)

(Continued)

Table 2.2 (Continued)

Focus	Method	Measure or Instrument	Original Authors	Example of Use
	Questionnaire	PMWI: Psychological maltreatment of women inventory	Tolman (1989)	Dutton, van Ginkel, & Landolt (1996) Dutton, Landolt, Starzomski, & Bodnarchulk (2001)
Children	Questionnaire	Self-reported delinquency scale	Elliot & Ageton (1980)	Swinford, DeMaris, Cernkovich, & Giordano (2000)
	Questionnaire	Sibling relationship questionnaire	Furman & Buhrmester (1985)	Rinaldi & Howe (2003)
	Questionnaire	Children's hostility inventory	Kazdin, Rodgers, Colbus, & Siegel (1987)	Gordis, Margolin, & John (2001)
	Questionnaire	Children's sibling relationships	Kramer & Baron (1995)	Rinaldi & Howe (2003)
Interpersonal	Coding	Constraining and enabling coding system	Maccoby & Martin (1983)	Smetana, Yau, & Hanson (1991)
	Questionnaire	Conflict issues measure	Fey (1995)	Koerner & Fitzpatrick (1997)
	Questionnaire	Conflict management survey	Hall (1969)	Evaluated: Womack (1988)
	Questionnaire	Avoidance, seeking social support, venting negative feelings	Koerner & Fitzpatrick (1997)	
	Questionnaire	Unilateral avoiding, aggressing, and resisting	Koerner & Fitzpatrick (2002)	
	Questionnaire	Conflict management message style	Ross & DeWine (1988)	Evaluated: Womack (1988)
	Questionnaire	Conflict-resolution behavior	Rubenstein & Feldman (1993)	Reese-Weber & Bartle-Haring (1998)
	Questionnaire	Concern for self or other	Sorenson, Morse, & Savage (1999)	

Focus	Method	Measure or Instrument	Original Authors	Example of Use
	Questionnaire	5-behavior conflict tactics scale to measure verbal and physical abuse	Straus (1977, 1990) Straus & Gelles (1990)	Ellis & Malamuth (2000) Straus & Yodanis (1996)
	Questionnaire	Thomas-Kilmann conflict MODE instrument	Thomas & Kilmann (1974)	Munduate, Ganaza, Peiró, & Euwema (1999) Evaluated: Womack (1988)
	Scenarios	Hypothetical conflict scenarios	Baxter (1984)	Chen, Ryan, & Chen (1999)
	Scenarios	Conflict scenario and eight resolving procedures	Leung, Bond, Carment, Krishnan, & Liebrand (1990)	Leung, Au, Fernández-Dols, & Iwawaki (1992)
	Scenarios	Conflict scenarios	Miyahara, Kim, Shin, & Yoon (1998)	

abuse and violence; and organizational and community conflict, including the study of conflict in hostage and crisis negotiation and in schools. These measures illustrate the approaches used to study conflict by observation; by qualitative measures such as those derived from interviews and open-ended questions; by coding schemes and content analysis of interactions and texts; and by questionnaires and multi-item scales of variables directly related to conflict, such as anger, depression, aggression, and conflict styles.

In their history of communication and conflict research, Nicotera et al. (1995) noted three levels of organizational conflict theory: strategy and logic (game theory), microlevel approaches (cognitive approaches), and macrolevel approaches (institutional approaches). Tables 2.1 through 2.3 show that, when studying conflict, communication researchers focus more on microlevel self-report measures of cognition and emotion and less on the strategy and macrolevel approaches (see also Canary et al., 1995, on studying relational conflict).

Observer (including peer) behavioral evaluation is used primarily to examine conflict in mediation and negotiation, and in institutional settings such as schools. Further, although researchers may observe actual conflict situations, rarely is the research conducted on the conflict as it unfolds in real time. Instead, researchers generally utilize transcripts or videos of real conflicts, as in hostage negotiations; archival data, as in international conflict negotiations; taped (video or audio) interactions, as in small-group, third-party mediated, or dyadic conflicts; or reported behaviors, either orally, as in interviews, or written, as in questionnaire responses. Nevertheless, these tables also highlight the wide range of instruments and measures that have been developed and used to study conflict.

SAMPLING AND DATA ANALYSIS

In this section we will review the issues of which conflict communication researchers should be aware regarding sampling and analysis. Although

Table 2.3   Studying Organizational and Community Conflict

Focus	Method	Measure or Instrument	Original Authors	Example of Use
Community	Case study	Environmental mediation: Longitudinal cases	Sipe (1998)	
Hostage & Crisis Negotiation	Coding	Integrative-distributive behavior coding system	Donohue & Roberto (1996)	
	Coding	Relational development	Donohue & Roberto (1993)	Donohue (1998)
	Coding	Smallest space analysis	Lingoes (1973)	Taylor (2002a)
	Coding	Thematic analysis	Orbe & Warren (2000)	
	Coding	Speech analysis	Rogan & Hammer (1995)	
	Coding	Emotion change	Rogan & Hammer (1995)	
	Coding	Immediacy coding system	Wiener & Mehrabian (1968)	Donohue, Ramesh, & Borchgrevink (1991)
	Phase mapping	Gamma analysis	Pelz (1985)	Holmes & Sykes (1993)
	Phase mapping	Interaction phase mapping	Poole & Roth (1989)	Holmes (1997) Holmes & Sykes (1993)
Organizations	Questionnaire	Negotiating style profile	Glaser & Glaser (1991)	Gabrielidis, Stephan, Ybarra, Pearson, & Villareal (1997)
	Questionnaire	Disputing process instrument	Morrill & Thomas (1992)	
	Questionnaire	OCCI: Organizational Communication Conflict Instrument	Putnam & Wilson (1982)	Lee & Rogan (1991) Evaluated: Wilson & Waltman (1988) Womack (1988)
	Questionnaire	ROCI-II: Rahim's Organizational Conflict Inventory	Rahim (1983)	Sorenson, Morse, & Savage (1999) Ting-Toomey, Oetzel, & Yee-Jung (2001) Evaluated: Cai & Fink (2002) Womack (1988)

(Continued)

Table 2.3   (Continued)

Focus	Method	Measure or Instrument	Original Authors	Example of Use
Schools	Inventory	Achenbach child behavior checklist	Achenbach (1991a)	Salzinger et al. (2002) Gordis, Margolin, & John (2001)
	Inventory	Achenbach teacher's report form	Achenbach (1991b)	Salzinger et al. (2002)
	Questionnaire	Conflict resolution scale	Smith, Daunic, Miller, & Robinson (2002)	
	Questionnaire	Disputant questionnaire	Smith, Daunic, Miller, & Robinson (2002)	
	Questionnaire	Mediator parent questionnaire	Smith, Daunic, Miller, & Robinson (2002)	
	Questionnaire	Peer mediator generalization questionnaire	Smith, Daunic, Miller, & Robinson (2002)	
	Questionnaire	School climate survey	Smith, Daunic, Miller, & Robinson (2002)	

these issues apply to all social-science research, there are particular concerns for research on conflict, and we concentrate on them.

Sampling

Sampling in conflict research poses particular challenges. At the interpersonal level, including dyadic and small-group interactions, the level of intimacy between interactants may range from low (e.g., strangers) to moderate (e.g., coworkers) to high (e.g., friends) to very high (e.g., romantic partners and family members). The predominant sampling strategy for studies at the psychological and interactional levels is nonprobability sampling, which not uncommonly uses a convenience sample of undergraduates. So what's new? Researchers implicitly rely on the notion that, although the mean levels of the variables under investigation may not be representative of the theoretical population's mean levels, the covariances among the variables—the data that inform us about process—are not biased.

To study conflict we must assume that it is possible to sample not only people, but situations

that vary in conflict (magnitude or type) as well, and that the sample of conflicts is reasonable in terms of its range on a variety of variables (e.g., intensity, duration, and theoretical cause of the conflict). This assumption is not met if the conflicts that we may need to know most about are inaccessible or have limited accessibility. For example, because of business secrets, we may not be able to sample representative negotiations between employers and employees; because of security issues, we may not be able to sample representative hostage negotiations. In these cases, we face a selection bias (Berk, 1983); if one or more variables that affect sample membership interact with any variables determinative of the conflict process under investigation, our conclusions are likely to be, at best, incomplete, or at worst, biased and misleading. For example, suppose that the only hostage negotiation transcripts that we have are those made available to us by negotiators for the government. Suppose further that this subset of transcripts is available because the government agents employed threats significantly less in them than in the other transcripts, which are unavailable to us. Finally, suppose that the presence of threats by government agents changes the effect of one or more conflict predictors significantly: Suppose threats make hostage-takers from ethnic group A more confrontational, whereas threats make hostage-takers from ethnic group B less confrontational. Then, although the sample is biased, it is more important to note that the analysis is likely to be misleading: Presence versus absence of threats interacts with ethnicity, so that the parameters for ethnicity that we estimate from this sample will be useful only if the main effect of ethnicity is relatively large and the interaction effect of ethnicity and presence versus absence of threats is relatively small.

Another example based on hostage negotiation research illustrates a different problem. Suppose we have transcripts from all or from a representative (even if not random) sample of such negotiations; we thereby avoid a selection bias. Thus, it would seem, these transcripts, although difficult to obtain, provide very useful information about high intensity conflicts. But now we face a different kind of problem: To complete the picture and create appropriate theoretical models of conflict processes that include processes that vary in intensity, we need our sample to contain a range of conflict intensities. Thus, we would need transcripts of low intensity conflict that fall within the domain being investigated, and it may be hard to imagine low intensity conflicts when we are considering hostage negotiations. Thus, even a good sample may not allow some aspects of a theory of conflict processes to be investigated adequately.

If a theory of conflict is to be developed, we may require samples that represent the universe of conflict situations, even if the sampling of such situations is a convenience sample. This is a bootstrap operation: We need a theory to sample across the types of conflict situations, and we need a representative sample of situations to generate the theory. In the absence of such theory, we can look to theories in neighboring domains to consider this sampling problem. For example, Foa and Foa (1974) described six types of resource exchanges: exchanges over love, status, information, money, services, and goods. We may identify conflict situations based on the resources primarily involved, thus generating

a "resource-exchange universe" from which to sample conflict situations. Similarly, Marwell and Hage (1970) empirically developed three dimensions descriptive of the organization of role relationships that may be useful here. Role relationships differ in terms of their intimacy, visibility, and regulation. If we are examining how individuals in different roles create, resolve, escalate, maintain, or define conflict, we can use the three role-relationship dimensions (intimacy, visibility, and regulation) to generate a $2 \times 2 \times 2$ typology of role-relationships from which we can purposively sample (see also Seeman, 1997). Thus, even in the absence of strong theory we may improve our sampling strategy so that it covers a theoretical universe and thereby enhances our ability to make theoretical discoveries.

Even if we generate an appropriate sampling strategy, we need to consider the sample size that is necessary for the proposed analyses. Sample sizes vary greatly across studies: In some of the studies reviewed for this chapter, sample sizes were inadequate for the methods used; for example, some studies attempted to estimate many parameters via ANOVA or multiple regression on samples with as few as 20 participants. The difficulty in obtaining appropriately sized samples should not be used as an excuse to do analyses that lack statistical power.

Data Analysis: Statistical Dependence

Statistical analyses make assumptions about the distribution and association between residual (error) terms. For example, significance testing of parameter estimates within regression or ANOVA assumes that population errors are homoscedastic, non-autocorrelated, and normal. Similarly, dependence among sample members (e.g., sampling pairs of husband-wife dyads rather than sampling individuals who happen to be husbands and wives, but not of each other) will likely cause correlation among error terms in the statistical model. Violations of statistical assumptions may be corrected by data transformation (Bauer & Fink, 1983) or by appropriate statistical modeling.

Many conflict situations are posed as two-sided situations: employer-employee, buyer-seller, hostage-taker and hostage, aggressor nation and target nation, violent domestic partner and violated domestic partner. Such dyadic interactions involve interdependence between agents. These samples have dependent (in the statistical sense) units, and that dependence needs to be taken into account in the analysis.

Structural equation modeling can represent the dependence in several ways. For example, Duncan's (1969) two-wave two-variable panel model can represent the interdependence between variables with correlated errors and mutual causality. In such analyses some of the variables come in pairs, one element of the pair for each partner in the dyad (see, e.g., Duncan, Haller, & Portes, 1968). So, imagine pairs of variables such as husband's level of anger and wife's level of anger, and husband's level of verbal aggression and wife's level of verbal aggression. A model that has parallel sets of variables for each interactant can be created that takes into account the dependence among the variables due to the dependence among the interactants.

One guiding rule for structural equation models is that, with well-behaved data, the sample size be a minimum of five times the number of free parameters to be estimated (Bentler & Chou, 1987). Another guiding rule is that a model should have a sample size that is 10 to 20 times the number of variables in the model (Mitchell, 1993). By either rule, the sample size for a model with more paths and more variables will need to be greater, perhaps twice as large as a sample without the paired data representing interdependent actors.

Kenny and Kashy (1991; see also Kashy & Kenny, 2000) described two types of interdependence that may exist in dyadic data sets: within-dyad interdependence and between-dyad interdependence. Within-dyad interdependence reflects systematic changes over time within a single dyad, such as the changes over time in uncertainty reduction within a dating couple. Such interdependence may appear as correlated errors over time.

Between-dyad interdependence results from cross-sectional dependence in dyads at a single point in time, such as due to omitted factors that affect both the buyer and the seller at each point in their negotiation. Such interdependence may appear as correlated errors across variables at one time. For example, suppose buyers and sellers

tend to negotiate with individuals who are similar in ethnicity, and we have a sample with many buyer-seller dyads varying in ethnicity. Suppose further that the variables used to model the buyer-seller interaction do not include variables correlated with ethnicity. Then ethnicity is an omitted factor that affects both the buyer and the seller at each point in their negotiation, causing correlated errors across variables at each time point.

Because both types of interdependence may exist, models should test for their presence. The two basic strategies, regardless of the specific analytical method employed, are to hypothesize the absence of these effects and examine model fit under this constraint, or to hypothesize the presence of these effects and to test the significance of the statistics that represent the interdependence. If the causes of interdependence are included or controlled for in such models, the effects will be "tamed"; in other words, we will have taken the interdependence into account and will thereby be able to create statistically consistent (see, e.g., Hanushek & Jackson, 1977) parameter estimates.

In studies of groups larger than dyads with multi-level sampling, the same issues appear. So, for example, in studies in which families are sampled, and within each family unit several family members are included, there is interdependence among the sampled units. Analytical methods that deal with multiple levels (with or without multiple time points within the data set) are hierarchical linear models (HLM); repeated-measures, multivariate, and other nested models in ANOVA; and multiple group (or multi-sample) analysis in structural equation models.

Of the three methods mentioned above, HLM is probably used least by scholars studying communication and conflict, but there are several exemplary studies: Julien, Chartrand, Simard, Bouthillier, and Bégin's (2003) study of positive and negative communication during conflict in heterosexual, gay, and lesbian couples (with partners nested within couples); Karney and Bradbury's (1997) analysis of trajectories of marital satisfaction; Rhoades, Arnold, and Jay's (2001) investigation of affective traits and mood on organizational conflict over time; Sanford's (2003) investigation of "topic difficulty and communication behavior across multiple problem-solving conversations" among married couples (p. 99); and Smith and Zautra's (2001) piece on the effect of spousal conflict, interpersonal sensitivity, and neuroticism on affect in a sample of older women.

Conflict communication research typically involves interdependent participants, and therefore scholars studying in this area need to be aware of the statistical problems—and, once understood, the statistical opportunities—that such data provide. Using a sophisticated analytic method such as structural equation modeling or hierarchical linear modeling encourages the researcher to think about the ways that units interact, and to represent this interdependence in the statistical models employed.

CROSS-CULTURAL CONFLICT RESEARCH, WITH APPLICATIONS TO OTHER GROUP DIFFERENCES

Conflict studies incorporating culture differ in whether the individual is the unit of analysis and culture is a contextual variable versus those in which the unit of analysis is culture (or nation) and the sample includes a set number of cultures. Almost all conflict communication studies use the former approach. (Some quantitative studies and mathematical models of the causes of war are exceptions; see Cashman, 1993, and Diehl, 2004.) Because of the way culture enters into conflict communication research, it is treated as static by necessity: It is an exogenous variable that varies over people or over space but not over time. However, culture does change over time, sometimes even over relatively short periods. Effects due to cultural change are almost always excluded from conflict communication research.

Many studies examine such static cultural differences in conflict styles (for reviews of these studies, see Oetzel & Ting-Toomey, 2003; Wilson, Cai, Campbell, Donohue, & Drake, 1995). These studies are mixed in their results, some finding members of East Asian cultures to be more avoidant or yielding and people from the United States to be more dominating (e.g., Lee & Rogan, 1991; Trubisky, Ting-Toomey, & Lin, 1991). Other studies find members of both

cultural groups to prefer integrating styles (e.g., Cai & Fink, 2002). The typical method used to investigate conflict styles across cultures is to provide a hypothetical conflict scenario, ask participants to consider a conflict with someone (e.g., a friend, colleague, or stranger), and, based on that imagined conflict, to complete instruments such as either the Rahim Organizational Conflict Inventory II (ROCI-II; Rahim, 1983) or OCCI (Putnam & Wilson, 1982) to measure the individual's approach to the conflict. To draw conclusions about how cultures compare in conflict behavior, however, researchers need to answer four questions about the sample and the conflict. First, are the meaning of conflict and the variables representing the conflict process comparable across the cultures being investigated? Second, are the samples comparable? Third, do the samples use the same processes with the same variables (the same equation or equations with the same functional forms and parameter values) for dealing with conflict? And fourth, are the cultures at the same place in the process under investigation? (Note that the discussion that follows can be made for comparing conflict across organizations or any other categorical variable, as well as across cultures.)

Are the Meaning of Conflict and the Variables Representing the Conflict Process Comparable Across the Cultures Being Investigated?

Let us consider the example of conflict styles for this question. The etic approach seeks to determine theoretical factors based on a scientific (here, transcultural or universal) analysis of variables (see Pike, 1967). Based on the etic research of Blake and Mouton (1964), Pruitt and Rubin (1987), and Thomas (1976), five basic conflict styles have been generated. That the ROCI-II and OCCI measures were derived from Western theories and imposed on Eastern cultures exemplifies the typical approach to cross-cultural conflict research, which depends on imposed rather than derived etic analysis (Berry, 1989). As a result, we do not know whether other (non-Western) styles exist for managing and resolving conflict. For example, Wall and Blum's (1991) idea of third parties having a role in dealing with conflict is not reflected in these measures, yet these researchers found the use of third parties to be a socially appropriate means for managing some conflicts among Chinese.

An imposed etic approach involves taking theories or hypotheses applicable to one culture and imposing them on another culture without knowing if the theory or the related measures are appropriate for the other cultures studied. In the area of conflict research, an imposed etic (Berry, 1989) is often relied on, assuming that the meaning of conflict is similar across cultures. A derived etic approach reflects careful observation and analysis of a variety of cultures to determine all the relevant variables that should be considered when studying a phenomenon across an even broader variety of cultures. A derived etic approach is needed to determine the meaning of conflict and conflict situations within each culture so that comparable situations within the cultures, ones that have similar meaning to the participants and that involve similar relationships and levels of emotion, can be employed in testing theory.

In studies that ask participants to recall a conflict situation, participants from different cultures are rarely asked to describe the recalled situation in sufficient depth to allow comparability across the cultures to be determined; the participants are also unlikely to be asked about the relevant state variables that define the situation, such as the level of emotion among the participants. As a result, conflict may involve qualities of anger and confrontation in one culture, whereas, in another culture, conflict may involve a rift in the relationships such that participants avoid rather than confront or communicate with each other; emotional salience may differ between the cultures because of the level of contact between the parties.

To determine whether the meaning of conflict and the variables representing the conflict process are comparable across the cultures, we need to do more than back-translate scales (see van de Vijver & Leung, 1997). The process of back-translation often involves having one party translate versions of a questionnaire from English, the language in which the original study was prepared, into the language of the target culture, then having a second person retranslate the new version back into English. Even careful translation and back-translation result in distortion of meaning (see Barnett, Palmer, & Al-Deen,

1984). Under the rubrics of bias and equivalency, van de Vijver and Leung (1997) discuss the issues involved in reducing distortion in translation. To do this task well requires more effort, more resources, and more time than most scholars anticipate, and even this extensive process does not guarantee comparability in meaning.

An alternative way of considering the problem of comparability in meaning is to use variables of sufficient abstraction so that they conceivably may apply cross-culturally. Then and only then can we examine whether there are cross-cultural process differences. In other words, the research task requires bootstrapping, cycling from theory couched in abstract variables to in-depth interviews with cultural informants to creation of measures that may involve culturally specific operationalizations to statistical analyses to revamping theory. Thus, the issues discussed below follow, and also precede, the issues discussed above.

Are the Samples Comparable?

Between-culture samples involve considerations that are different from those of within-culture samples. Convenience samples, consisting, for example, of university students, or snowball samples, consisting, for example, of friends and friends of friends, do not necessarily generate comparable samples across cultures. Any good article or book on intercultural research will raise this issue (see, e.g., Johnson & Tuttle, 1989; Tafoya, 1984; van de Vijver & Leung, 1997). Certainly social class, ethnicity, and other demographic differences are likely to affect the social norms people use for managing conflicts. Research among ethnic and cultural groups should measure and then attempt to control for socioeconomic differences, including education level, income relative to the per capita income of the nation the sample is from, occupational prestige, and the like (see, e.g., Massett, 1999). Controlling for these factors allows researchers to at least attempt to differentiate cross-cultural from (within culture) sociological factors, thereby being able to make more valid claims about how cultures compare. Without such measures, claims about culture are likely to be masking the influence of class, population density, education, and so on.

This methodological discussion has tremendous implications for theoretical development. If we are concerned with the belief and behavior systems of a population (e.g., the norms for handling conflict in the workplace, in the family, or among friends; the sanctions for transgressors of these norms; the conditions under which specific requests are appropriate), then sociological factors make a difference, but do we classify this difference as "cultural"? Because developmental effects (e.g., worldwide urbanization; increased participation in formal education) modify cultures, any differentiation between cultural and non-cultural factors is a snapshot of one point in time. We try to get a handle on this differentiation by two methods: using comparable samples, which are difficult to obtain, or relying on statistical controls. The former involves using samples that may be unrepresentative of the larger population, but similar in some characteristics to the other culture to which its members are compared. The latter is likely to "overcontrol" by removing effects that are or will be tied to cultural differences. This conundrum requires not better methods, but better theory to investigate processes and attribute effects to their appropriate sources.

Do the Samples Use the Same Processes With the Same Variables for Dealing With Conflict?

Once conflict situations are determined to be comparable across cultures in terms of the severity of the conflict, the relationship between the parties, and the level of emotion involved, then researchers can begin to determine whether the processes involved in managing the conflict are comparable. Having relatively equal means on a set of variables does not suggest that the processes that generated these means are the same, or that the means reflect the same point in the process, or that the process has equilibrated. Rather, the ability to make claims about processes involves determining the functional form of relationships between variables. In doing so, two central questions about functional forms emerge.

The first question is whether the same functional form relating a set of variables applies across the cultures under consideration. The same functional form means the same equation (statistical or mathematical), with the same variables, with (for statistical models) the error term entering into the equation in the same way (e.g., additively vs. multiplicatively), and, finally, with the same estimated parameter values.

Suppose conflict and dissatisfaction are both amount scales (see above). And suppose that, for one group, unit increases in the level of conflict at time-0 cause 2-unit increases in dissatisfaction one time unit later (i.e., at time-1):

$$\text{DISSATISFACTION}_{t1} = 2 \times (\text{CONFLICT}_{t0}).$$

For another group, dissatisfaction at time-1 increases as the square of the level of conflict at time-0:

$$\text{DISSATISFACTION}_{t1} = (\text{CONFLICT}_{t0})^2.$$

In this case, although the variables that are included in the two equations are the same, the process that relates them is different.

Differences in functional form may be approached as a theoretical question, a measurement question, or an analytic question. The first treatment of this issue, as a theoretical problem, concerns whether the variables being used in the analyses are sufficiently general and can be thought of as meaningfully tied to a process in the same way. For example, if one were assessing the level of conflict across cultures, one might use relatively concrete operationalizations that differ by culture or are even idiosyncratic to particular cultures. However, these particular operationalizations may hide important theoretical differences. For example, conflict in one group may be operationalized by the amount of anger (a psychological variable) exhibited by an individual. In another group, conflict may be operationalized by the level of language intensity employed in interaction (an interactional variable). These measures are theoretically distinct—they are at different levels of analysis. Thus, they enter into the conflict→ dissatisfaction equation differently, by definition resulting in different functional forms. Theoretical considerations suggest that the variables descriptive of the conflict process should be at the same level of analysis and should be at the locus within a network of relationships.

Second, finding that different functional forms apply to different cultures may reflect issues of measurement. As an example, consider the following situation. Researcher A and Researcher B both study the effects of level of anger (A) and level of conflict (C) on retaliation (y). Researcher A proposes and finds that the two independent variables relate in a power-law fashion (i.e., the independent variables, each raised to a power, form a product that determines the level of the dependent variable). Specifically, ignoring the error term, Researcher A finds

$$\hat{y} = b_0 (A^{b_1} * C^{b_2}). \tag{2.1}$$

Researcher B, using different measures (indicated with asterisks), proposes and finds that the effects of these independent variables are additive:

$$\hat{y}^* = b_0^* + b_1 A^* + b_2 C^*. \tag{2.2}$$

It would seem that these different functional forms reflect different processes. However, without understanding how the researchers' different measures relate, the differences may be more apparent than real. Logarithmically transforming a product converts it to a sum:

$$\ln(X_1 * X_2) = \ln(X_1) + \ln(X_2).$$

So, we are able to transform Equation 2.1 by taking the natural logarithm of both sides (again, ignoring the error terms):

$$\ln(\hat{y}) = \ln(b_0) + b_1 \ln(A) + b_2 \ln(C). \tag{2.3}$$

If $\hat{y}^* = \ln(\hat{y})$, $b_0^* = \ln(b_0)$, $A^* = \ln(A)$, and $C^* = \ln(C)$, the two seemingly different equations (Equations 2.1 and 2.2) are the same.

The moral of this story is that, if we were unaware of the different scaling rules employed by different researchers (Researcher A and Researcher B), we may believe that the researchers found support for different processes. After all, one researcher found a multiplicative relation between anger and conflict in predicting retaliation, whereas the other found an additive relation. However, transforming the measures demonstrates that the apparent differences were merely scaling artifacts: The differences in the measurements resulted in apparent differences in functional form. To deal with this issue, either all researchers need to use the same measures (unlikely in the social sciences), or researchers need to provide the rules that relate (translate) their measures to standard ones. In this way, the measures may be calibrated against the standard, and thus, to each other. As a result, debates over differences in functional form may devolve into differences in measurement rules. If the two researchers in the hypothetical example above graphed the relation between A^* and A, they would see that these two measures of anger were perfectly, though nonlinearly, correlated. In a fundamental sense, the measures are the same.

In the physical sciences, investigators employ fundamental measures for variables such as time, distance, angle, and mass. However, most other measures are derivative (i.e., they are ratios and differences) of fundamental standard measures. In human communication research, different investigators typically employ their own measures, which are not calibrated against any standard. As a result, it is very difficult to determine if process differences are merely scaling differences.

The third way of considering differences in functional forms is to treat these differences as an analytic issue. Using the above example, we can enter the two predictors and the dependent variable into a program like SHAZAM (White & Bui, 1988), which performs a Box-Cox analysis (see Bauer & Fink, 1983). Using maximum-likelihood estimates under the assumption that the population regression residuals are normal and homoscedastic, the program finds the optimal power transformations for the variables. With this analytic approach, Equation 2.1 and Equation 2.2 could be shown to represent equivalent functional forms.

Given a specified functional form relating a set of variables, is the process revealed by this functional form the same across the cultures under consideration? This question is whether the parameters relevant to the functional form are the same in different groups. Quantitative data may be analyzed within the general linear model. Time-series analysis and various forms of panel analysis and cross-sectional analysis require assumptions about process to be informative; when these assumptions are met, each method can provide comparable information about the parameters of the process (Coleman, 1968). (Other methods, such as the analysis of categorical data using a Markov chain and its variants and log-linear analysis, can also be used to provide parameter estimates for theoretical processes; due to space limitations such methods will not be discussed here.)

Process differences across groups appear as differences in the relationship of inputs to outcomes. (This appearance is a necessary but not sufficient condition; we show in the next section that differences in the relationship of inputs to outcomes can indicate that the same process is at different stages in different groups.) Suppose we are looking at the process that relates relational distance between members of a dyad (X, the independent variable) and conflict avoidance (y, the dependent variable). What do process differences look like? First, conduct separate regressions, one for each group. If the slopes relating the variables are different (ignoring differences due to differential reliability between groups and assuming statistical or substantive significance of the difference), then the processes are different. Second, if one were to use "group" as a categorical variable (with two groups, assume a single dichotomous variable coded as a dummy $\{0, 1\}$ variable, G), process differences appear as an interaction of group with the independent variable ($X * G$), because that interaction term indicates slope differences:

$$\hat{y} = b_0 + b_1 X + b_2(X * G) + b_3 G$$
$$= b_0 + (b_1 + b_2 G)X + b_3 G.$$

So, when $G = 0$, the slope relating X to $y = b_1$, whereas when $G = 1$, the slope becomes $b_1 + b_2$. (This analysis can be extended easily to multiple groups and multiple independent variables.)

Finally, if the researcher happened to ignore possible process differences between groups, a single regression might have been performed, without entering group as an independent (dummy) variable (or as a set of dummy variables). In that case the process differences will appear as a non-normal (here, with two groups, bimodal) distribution of errors around the regression line, and the errors will also have unequal variances around the line (i.e., there will be signs of heteroscedasticity). To demonstrate this idea, we have created simulated data with the following characteristics: X goes from 1–100, G is a dichotomous variable that $= 0$ if X is even and $= 1$ if X is odd, and $\hat{y} = .50 X + .25(X * G)$. Thus, the process for the two groups (i.e., the group represented by $G = 0$ and the group represented by $G = 1$) is different: When $G = 0$, the slope for $X = .50$, and when $G = 1$, the slope $= .75$. Conducting a single regression that includes both groups, the (single) slope for $X = .625$. Figure 2.1 shows that the single regression line (with slope $= .625$) goes through the middle of the scattergram, and the residuals from this single line (the points above and below the regression line) have a bimodal distribution and their spread increases as X increases. Note that other patterns of heteroscedasticity are possible.

Unfortunately, the results of most culture and conflict studies do not provide enough information to reveal whether the slopes differ as discussed above. In general, the ability to detect slope differences and other differences in functional form is optimized when (a) the scales for the continuous independent variable(s) and dependent variable have many possible values (recall that count and amount scales have, in principle, an infinite number of values); (b) there is a broad range of scores on the continuous independent variable(s); (c) there is a broad range of scores on the dependent variable; (d) the measures are reliable; and (e) we have a large sample. Determining the existence of interactions between group variables and (continuous) predictors is a job both for the methodologist (Allison, 1977) as well as the theorist (Blalock, 1965). If we are comparing cultures and they are at different temporal locations in the conflict process, we may find parameter differences that do not reflect "true" process differences. We now discuss this issue.

Are the Cultures at the Same Place in the Process Under Investigation?

Finding slope differences would seem to make a prima facie case for process differences between groups. However, in most of the studies on culture and conflict, we do not know if

Figure 2.1   Hypothetical relationship between relational distance (*X*) and conflict avoidance (*Y*) when group membership is a dichotomous dummy variable and group (*G*) interacts with *X*. $\hat{y} = .50\,X + .25(X * G)$.

different groups are at the same place in the trajectory of the conflict process.

To analyze where a group is in a process, we must first establish that the process is stable. Statistical analysis of any process must assume that there is stability to the process, either in terms of the original variables and time points being used, or in terms of transformations of those variables or time points. Such assumptions are labeled differently in different analytic techniques, with terms like *stationarity* and *invertibility* in time-series models or the term *equilibrium* as used more generally. But it should be noted that a system whose variables do not appear to be in equilibrium (and whose trajectory appears to be unbounded) may, with appropriate treatment, be used to represent a system in equilibrium. For example, suppose conflict as measured appears to have an exploding trajectory. Over time the level of conflict appears to move as follows:

1, 4, 9, 16, 25, 36, 49, 64, 81, 100, ...

(This series obviously consists of the squares of the positive integers, but it will serve to make our point.)

How can we, with appropriate treatment of these "data," represent the process as one that is in equilibrium? If we take differences of adjacent values in the series, we get:

3, 5, 7, 9, 11, 13, 15, 17, 19, . . .

and if we take differences a second time, we get:

2, 2, 2, 2, 2, 2, 2, 2, ...

This example shows that a system that appears explosive may be represented as a corresponding system that is in equilibrium. Although this is an obviously contrived example, the point is that we can evaluate processes assuming that they have stability in some representation, and not necessarily in terms of the original variables.

If different cultures have parameter values that are time (or, more precisely, time-in-process) dependent, and the processes within the cultures can be aligned, we may conclude that the cultures are at different points in the same process. (To be clear, we are discussing the conflict process over time. We do not mean that the conflict gets worse; rather, we mean that the conflict process is continuing over time.) If this were the case, perhaps the relation between conflict and dissatisfaction would look like the following:

$$\text{DISSATISFACTION}_t = b_1[1 - \exp(-b_2 t)] \cdot \text{CONFLICT}_t,$$

where "exp" is the exponential function and $b_2 > 0$. Note that when $t = 0$ (at the start), the coefficient $b_1[1 - \exp(-b_2 t)] = 0$, but as $t \to \infty$, $b_1[1 - \exp(-b_2 t)] \to b_1$. In other words, the effect of conflict on dissatisfaction is initially 0, but increases over time, approaching the value b_1.

Cultures may be assumed to manage conflict differently merely because the conflict system is at a different point in the process in different cultures. Thus, we may see that, in one culture, the coefficient relating conflict to dissatisfaction is about 0, whereas in another culture it is close to b_1. But the assumption that the process is different in these two cultures ignores the time dependence in the coefficient: It just may be that the process is identical.

"Aligning" the trajectories might reveal that a particular process is cross-culturally valid. To assess possible phase differences, we almost always require data at many points in time to create equilibrium among the variables of interest (by, e.g., differencing time-series data; see Hibbs, 1974). If the points in time are equally spaced but reveal cross-cultural differences in process parameters, we may still be able to determine if the processes are the same (Coleman, 1968), assuming that the points are sufficiently frequent in time to avoid the problem of aliasing (i.e., the spurious finding of a low frequency wave that arises because the original data are not sampled at a sufficient number of time points [Croft, 2005]; Arundale, 1980, applies this concept to communication).

CONCLUSION

This chapter is a very focused presentation of issues that we believe are critical for studying conflict and for understanding the extant literature. We have focused on various issues related to types of data, sampling issues, and specific issues related to cross-cultural conflict research. We are aware of the many issues not dealt with here; most important, we have not discussed research ethics, either in terms of internal matters (e.g., deception and potential harm to participants) or external matters (e.g., the sponsors and beneficiaries of the knowledge garnered from the research). For these matters we suggest Lewis (1975) and Sjoberg (1967). We expect that we can elaborate the comments we made here in the next *Sage Handbook of Conflict Communication*. Nevertheless, we hope the issues addressed in this chapter will stimulate careful thinking about research design and sampling that will result in research that contributes sound theoretical insights about conflict and communication.

REFERENCES

*References included only in Tables 2.1 to 2.3.
†References cited in both text and tables.
Unmarked references included only in text.

*Achenbach, T. M. (1991a). *Manual for the Child Behavior Checklist/4–18 and 1991 profile.* Burlington: University of Vermont, Department of Psychiatry.

*Achenbach, T. M. (1991b). *Manual for the teacher's report form and 1991 profile.* Burlington: University of Vermont, Department of Psychiatry.

Allison, P. D. (1977). Testing for interaction in multiple regression. *American Journal of Sociology, 83,* 144–153.

Anderson, J. C., & Gerbing, D. W. (1988). Structural equation modeling in practice: A review and recommended two-step approach. *Psychological Bulletin, 103,* 411–423.

*Anderson, P. A., & Eloy, S. V. (1995). Romantic jealousy and relational satisfaction: A look at the impact of jealousy experience and expression. *Communication Reports, 8,* 77–85.

Arundale, R. B. (1980). Studying change over time: Criteria for sampling from continuous variables. *Communication Research, 7,* 227–263.

Bales, R. F. (1950). *Interaction process analysis.* Cambridge, MA: Addison-Wesley.

Barnett, G. A., Palmer, M. T., & Al-Deen, H. N. (1984). Translation accuracy: Using multidimensional scaling. In R. N. Bostrom (Ed.),

Communication yearbook 8 (pp. 659–677). Beverly Hills, CA: Sage.

Bauer, C. L., & Fink, E. L. (1983). Fitting equations with power transformations: Examining variables with error. In R. N. Bostrom (Ed.), *Communication yearbook 7* (pp. 146–199). Beverly Hills, CA: Sage.

*Baumeister, R. F., Stillwell, A. M., & Heatherton, T. F. (1995). Personal narratives about guilt: Role in action control and interpersonal relationships. *Basic and Applied Social Psychology, 17,* 173–198.

*Baumeister, R. F., Stillwell, A. M., & Wotman, S. R. (1990). Victim and perpetrator accounts of interpersonal conflict: Autobiographical narratives about anger. *Journal of Personality and Social Psychology, 59,* 994–1005.

*Baxter, L. A. (1984). An investigation of compliance-gaining as politeness. *Human Communication Research, 10,* 427–456.

Bentler, P. M., & Chou, C.-P. (1987). Practical issues in structural modeling. *Sociological Methods & Research, 16,* 78–117.

Berk, R. A. (1983). An introduction to sample selection bias in sociological data. *American Sociological Review, 48,* 386–398.

Berry, J. W. (1989). Imposed etics-emics-derived etics: The operationalization of a compelling idea. *International Journal of Psychology, 24,* 721–735.

*Biglan, A., Rothlind, J., Hops, H., & Sherman, L. (1989). Impact of distressed and aggressive behavior. *Journal of Abnormal Psychology, 98,* 218–228.

Blake, R. R., & Mouton, J. S. (1964). *The managerial grid.* Houston, TX: Gulf.

Blalock, H. B., Jr. (1965). Theory building and the statistical concept of interaction. *American Sociological Review, 30,* 374–380.

†Brainerd, E. G., Jr., Hunter, P. A., Moore, D., & Thompson, T. R. (1996). Jealousy induction as a predictor of power and the use of other control methods in heterosexual relationships. *Psychological Reports, 79,* 1319–1325.

Brass, D. J., & Labianca, G. (1999). Social capital, social liabilities, and social resources management. In S. Gabbay & R. Leenders (Eds.), *Corporate social capital and liability* (pp. 323–340). Boston: Kluwer Academic.

*Briere, J., & Runtz, M. (1989). The Trauma Symptom Checklist (TSC-33): Early data on a new scale. *Journal of Interpersonal Violence, 4,* 151–163.

†Buss, A. H., & Durkee, A. (1957). An inventory for assessing different kinds of hostility. *Journal of Consulting Psychology, 21,* 343–349.

*Buss, D. M. (1987). Love acts: The evolutionary biology of love. In R. J. Sternberg & M. L. Barnes (Eds.), *The psychology of love* (pp. 100–118). New Haven, CT: Yale University Press.

†Buss, D. M., Larsen, R. J., Westen, D., & Semmelroth, J. (1992). Sex differences in jealousy: Evolution, physiology, and psychology. *Psychological Science, 3,* 251–255.

Cai, D. A., & Donohue, W. A. (1997). Determinants of facework in intercultural negotiation. *Asian Journal of Communication, 7,* 85–110.

†Cai, D. A., & Fink, E. L. (2002). Conflict style differences between individualists and collectivists. *Communication Monographs, 69,* 67–87.

Cai, D. A., Wilson, S. R., & Drake, L. E. (2000). Culture in the context of intercultural negotiation: Individualism-collectivism and paths to integrative agreements. *Human Communication Research, 26,* 591–617.

Campbell, D. T., & Fiske, D. W. (1959). Convergent and discriminant validation by the multitrait-multimethod matrix. *Psychological Bulletin, 56,* 81–105.

Canary, D. J., Cupach, W. R., & Messman, S. J. (1995). *Relationship conflict: Conflict in parent-child, friendship, and romantic relationships.* Thousand Oaks, CA: Sage.

*Cann, A., Mangum, J. L., & Wells, M. (2001). Distress in response to relationship infidelity: The roles of gender and attitudes about relationships. *Journal of Sex Research, 38,* 185–190.

Cashman, G. (1993). *What causes war? An introduction to theories of international conflict.* New York: Lexington Books.

Castilla, E. J. (2004). Organizing health care: A comparative analysis of national institutions and inequality over time. *International Sociology, 19,* 403–435.

*Chen, G. M., Ryan, K., & Chen, C. (1999). The determinants of conflict management among Chinese and Americans. *International Communication Studies, 9,* 163–175.

*Cheung, S.-K., & Kwok, S. Y. C. (1999). Predictors of divorcing women's use of divorce mediation. *Journal of Divorce and Remarriage, 31*(3/4), 37–52.

*Cobb, S. (1997). The domestication of violence in mediation. *Law & Society Review, 31,* 397–440.

Coleman, J. S. (1968). The mathematical study of change. In H. M. Blalock, Jr., & A. B. Blalock (Eds.), *Methodology in social research* (pp. 428–478). New York: McGraw-Hill.

*Collier, M. J. (1996). Communication competence problematics in ethnic friendships. *Communication Monographs, 63,* 314–336.

Cook, T. D., & Campbell, D. T. (1979). *Quasi-experimentation: Design and analysis issues for field settings.* Chicago: Rand McNally College Publishing.

Cook-Gumperz, J., & Szymanski, M. (2001). Classroom "families": Cooperating or competing—Girls' and boys' interactional styles in a bilingual classroom. *Research on Language & Social Interaction, 34,* 107–131.

Corcoran, K. O., & Mallinckrodt, B. (2000). Adult attachment, self-efficacy, perspective taking, and conflict resolution. *Journal of Counseling & Development, 78,* 473–483.

*Cramer, R. E., Abraham, W. T., Johnson, L. M., & Manning-Ryan, B. (2001–2002). Gender differences in subjective distress to emotional and sexual infidelity: Evolutionary or logical inference explanation? *Current Psychology: Development, Learning, Personality, Social, 20,* 327–336.

Croft, A. (2005). *Using MathCAD to help engineering students understand aliasing.* Retrieved March 12, 2005, from http://www.bham.ac.uk/ctimath/reviews/nov95/mathcad.pdf

Daly, M., & Wilson, M. (1997). Crime and conflict: Homicide in evolutionary psychological perspective. *Crime and Justice, 22,* 51–100.

Denzin, N. K., & Lincoln, Y. S. (Eds.). (2000). *Handbook of qualitative research* (2nd ed.). Thousand Oaks, CA: Sage.

*Derogatis, L. R., Lipman, R. S., & Covi, L. (1973). SCL-90: An outpatient psychiatric ratings scale—Preliminary report. *Psychopharmacology Bulletin, 9,* 13–28.

Diehl, P. F. (Ed.). (2004). *The scourge of war: New extensions on an old problem.* Ann Arbor: University of Michigan.

*Donohue, W. A. (1998). Managing equivocality and relational paradox in the Oslo peace negotiations. *Journal of Language and Social Psychology, 17,* 72–96.

†Donohue, W. A., Ramesh, C., & Borchgrevink, C. (1991). Crisis bargaining: Tracking relational paradox in hostage negotiation. *International Journal of Conflict Management, 2,* 257–274.

†Donohue, W. A., & Roberto, A. J. (1993). Relational development as negotiated order in hostage negotiation. *Human Communication Research, 20,* 175–198.

†Donohue, W. A., & Roberto, A. J. (1996). An empirical examination of three models of integrative and distributive bargaining. *International Journal of Conflict Management, 7,* 209–229.

Doreian, P. (1981). Polyhedral dynamics and conflict mobilization in social networks. *Social Networks, 3,* 107–116.

Duncan, O. D. (1969). Some linear models for two-wave, two-variable panel analysis. *Psychological Bulletin, 72,* 177–182.

Duncan, O. D., Haller, A. O., & Portes, A. (1968). Peer influences on aspirations: A reinterpretation. *American Journal of Sociology, 74,* 119–137.

†Dutton, D. G., Landolt, M. A., Starzomski, A., & Bodnarchuk, M. (2001). Validation of the Propensity for Abusiveness Scale in diverse male populations. *Journal of Family Violence, 16,* 59–73.

*Dutton, D. G., van Ginkel, C., & Landolt, M. A. (1996). Jealousy, intimate abusiveness, and intrusiveness. *Journal of Family Violence, 11,* 411–423.

*Elliot, D. S., & Ageton, S. S. (1980). Reconciling race and class differences in self-reported and official estimates of delinquency. *American Sociological Review, 45,* 95–110.

*Ellis, B. J., & Malamuth, N. M. (2000). Love and anger in romantic relationships: A discrete systems model. *Journal of Personality, 68,* 525–556.

*Fey, J. (1995). *Coping responses in family interaction.* Unpublished manuscript, University of Wisconsin–Madison.

Fink, E. L. (1980). Unobserved variables within structural equation models. In P. R. Monge & J. N. Cappella (Eds.), *Multivariate techniques in human communication research* (pp. 111–141). New York: Academic Press.

*Fisch, S., & Brainerd, E. G., Jr. (1990). *Jealousy as a method of control in romantic relationships.* Poster session presented at the annual meeting of the Southern Psychological Association, New Orleans.

*Fitzpatrick, M. A., & Ritchie, L. D. (1994). Communication schemata within the family:

Multiple perspectives on family interaction. *Human Communication Research, 20,* 275–301.

Foa, U. G., & Foa, E. B. (1974). *Societal structures of the mind.* Springfield, IL: Charles C Thomas.

Fuller, G. A., Murphy, A. B., Ridgley, M. A., & Ulack, R. (2000). Measuring potential ethnic conflict in Southeast Asia. *Growth and Change, 31,* 305–331.

*Furman, W., & Buhrmester, D. (1985). Children's perceptions of the personal relationships in their social networks. *Developmental Psychology, 21,* 1016–1024.

*Gabrielidis, C., Stephan, W. G., Ybarra, O., Pearson, V. M. D., & Villareal, L. (1997). Preferred styles of conflict resolution: Mexico and the United States. *Journal of Cross-Cultural Psychology, 28,* 661–677.

Girbau, D. (2002). A sequential analysis of private and social speech in children's dyadic communication. *Spanish Journal of Psychology, 5,* 110–118.

*Glaser, R., & Glaser, C. (1991). *Negotiating style profile.* King of Prussia, PA: Organization Design and Development.

†Gordis, E. B., Margolin, G., & Garcia, H. J. (1996). *Marital coding system.* Unpublished manual, University of Southern California.

†Gordis, E. B., Margolin, G., & John, R. S. (2001). Parents' hostility in dyadic marital and triadic family settings and children's behavior problems. *Journal of Consulting and Clinical Psychology, 69,* 727–734.

*Gottman, J. M. (1994). *What predicts divorce?: The relationship between marital processes and marital outcomes.* Hillsdale, NJ: Lawrence Erlbaum.

†Gottman, J. M., Levenson, R., & Woodin, E. (2001). Facial expressions during marital conflict. *Journal of Family Communication, 1,* 37–57.

†Gottman, J. M., Markman, H., & Notarius, C. (1977). The topography of marital conflict: A sequential analysis of verbal and nonverbal behavior. *Journal of Marriage and the Family, 39,* 461–477.

*Guerrero, L. K. (1992, November). *Expressing anger: Implications for perceived relational satisfaction and communication competence.* Paper presented at the annual meeting of the Speech Communication Association, Chicago.

*Guerrero, L. K. (1994). "I'm so mad I could scream": The effects of anger expression on relational satisfaction and communication competence. *Southern Communication Journal, 59,* 125–141.

*Guerrero, L. K., & Afifi, W. A. (1999). Toward a goal-oriented approach for understanding communicative responses to jealousy. *Western Journal of Communication, 63,* 216–248.

*Guerrero, L. K., Anderson, P. A., Jorgensen, P. F., Spitzberg, B. H., & Eloy, S. V. (1995). Coping with the green-eyed monster: Conceptualizing and measuring communicative responses to romantic jealousy. *Western Journal of Communication, 59,* 270–304.

*Guerrero, L. K., Eloy, S. V., Jorgensen, P. F., & Anderson, P. A. (1993). Hers or his? Sex differences in the experience and communication of jealousy in close relationships. In P. J. Kalbfleisch (Ed.), *Interpersonal communication: Evolving interpersonal relationships* (pp. 109–131). Hillsdale, NJ: Lawrence Erlbaum.

*Hall, J. (1969). *Conflict Management Survey: A survey on one's characteristic reactions to and handling of conflicts between himself and others.* Conroe, TX: Teleometrics International.

Hanushek, E. A., & Jackson, J. E. (1977). *Statistical methods for social scientists.* New York: Academic Press.

Heider, F. (1958). *The psychology of interpersonal relations.* New York: John Wiley.

Hibbs, D. A., Jr. (1974). Problems of statistical estimation and causal inference in time-series regression models. In H. L. Costner (Ed.), *Sociological methodology 1973–1974* (pp. 252–308). San Francisco: Jossey-Bass.

Hofstede, G. (1980). *Culture's consequences: International differences in work-related values.* Beverly Hills, CA: Sage.

†Holmes, M. E. (1997). Optimal matching analysis of negotiation phase sequences in simulated and authentic hostage negotiation. *Communication Reports, 10,* 1–8.

†Holmes, M. E., & Sykes, R. E. (1993). A test of fit of Gulliver's phase model to hostage negotiations. *Communication Studies, 44,* 38–55.

*Hornsey, M. J., Oppes, T., & Svensson, A. (2002). "It's OK if we say it, but you can't": Responses to intergroup and intragroup criticism. *European Journal of Social Psychology, 32,* 293–307.

*Infante, D. A., Chandler, T. A., & Rudd, J. E. (1989). Test of an argumentative skill deficiency model of interspousal violence. *Communication Monographs, 56,* 163–177.

*Infante, D. A., & Rancer, A. S. (1982). A conceptualization and measure of argumentativeness. *Journal of Personality Assessment, 46,* 72–80.

*Infante, D. A., Sabourin, T. C., Rudd, J. E., & Shannon, E. A. (1990). Verbal aggression in violent and nonviolent marital disputes. *Communication Quarterly, 38,* 361–371.

*Infante, D. A., & Wigley, C. J., III. (1986). Verbal aggressiveness: An interpersonal model and measure. *Communication Monographs, 53,* 61–69.

International Journal of Conflict Management. (2003). *14*(3/4).

*Jenkins, J. M. (2000). Marital conflict and children's emotions: The development of an anger organization. *Journal of Marriage and the Family, 62,* 723-736.

Johnson, J. D., & Tuttle, F. (1989). Problems in intercultural research. In M. K. Asante & W. B. Gudykunst (Eds.), *Handbook of international and intercultural communication* (pp. 461–483). Newbury Park, CA: Sage.

Jones, T. S. (1988). Phase structures in agreement and no-agreement mediation. *Communication Research, 15,* 470–495.

Julien, D., Chartrand, E., Simard, M.-C., Bouthillier, D., & Bégin, J. (2003). Conflict, social support, and relationship quality: An observational study of heterosexual, gay male, and lesbian couples' communication. *Journal of Family Psychology, 17,* 419–428.

Karney, B. R., & Bradbury, T. N. (1997). Neuroticism, marital interaction, and the trajectory of marital satisfaction. *Journal of Personality and Social Psychology, 72,* 1075–1092.

Kashy, D. A., & Kenny, D. A. (2000). The analysis of data from dyads and groups. In H. T. Reis & C. M. Rudd (Eds.), *The handbook of research methods in social and personality psychology* (pp. 451–477). New York: Cambridge University Press.

*Kasian, M., & Painter, S. L. (1992). Frequency and severity of psychological abuse in a dating population. *Journal of Interpersonal Violence, 7,* 350–364.

*Kazdin, A. E., Rodgers, A., Colbus, D., & Siegel, T. (1987). Children's hostility inventory: Measurement of aggression and hostility in psychiatric inpatient children. *Journal of Clinical Child Psychology, 16,* 320–328.

Kenny, D. A., & Kashy, D. A. (1991). Analyzing interdependence in dyads. In B. M. Montgomery & S. Duck (Eds.), *Studying interpersonal interaction* (pp. 275–285). New York: Guilford.

Kim, M. S., & Leung, T. (2000). A multicultural view of conflict management styles: Review and critical synthesis. In M. Roloff (Ed.), *Communication yearbook 23* (pp. 227–269). Thousand Oaks, CA: Sage.

*Koerner, A. F., & Fitzpatrick, M. A. (1997). Family type and conflict: The impact of conversation orientation and conformity orientation on conflict in the family. *Communication Studies, 48,* 59–75.

*Koerner, A. F., & Fitzpatrick, M. A. (2002). You never leave your family in a fight: The impact of family of origin on conflict-behavior in romantic relationships. *Communication Studies, 53,* 234–251.

*Kramer, L., & Baron, L. A. (1995). Parental perceptions of children's sibling relationships. *Family Relations, 44,* 95–103.

Krippendorff, K. (2004). *Content analysis: An introduction to its methodology* (2nd ed.). Thousand Oaks, CA: Sage.

*Kubany, E. S., & Richard, D. C. (1992). Verbalized anger and accusatory "you" messages as cues for anger and antagonism among adolescents. *Adolescence, 27,* 505–516.

Lazarsfeld, P., & Menzel, H. (1961). On the relation between individual and collective properties. In A. Etzioni (Ed.), *Complex organizations: A sociological reader* (pp. 420–440). New York: Holt, Rinehart & Winston.

†Lee, H. O., & Rogan, R. G. (1991). A cross-cultural comparison of organizational conflict management behaviors. *International Journal of Conflict Management, 2,* 181–199.

Lemus, D. R., Seibold, D. R., Flanagin, A. J., & Metzger, M. J. (2004). Argument and decision making in computer mediated groups. *Journal of Communication, 54,* 302–320.

*Leung K., Au, Y.-F., Fernández-Dols, J. M., & Iwawaki, S. (1992). Preference for methods of conflict processing in two collectivist cultures. *International Journal of Psychology, 27,* 195–209.

*Leung, K., Bond, M. H., Carment, D. W., Krishnan, L., & Liebrand, W. B. G. (1990). Effects of cultural femininity on preference for methods of conflict processing: A cross-cultural study. *Journal of Experimental Social Psychology, 26,* 373–388.

Lewis, G. H. (1975). *Fist-fights in the kitchen: Manners and methods in social research.* Santa Monica, CA: Goodyear.

*Lingoes, J. (1973). *The Guttman-Lingoes nonmetric program series.* Unpublished master's thesis, University of Michigan, Ann Arbor.

Loehlin, J. C. (2004). *Latent variable models: An introduction to factor, path, and structural equation analysis* (4th ed.). Mahwah, NJ: Lawrence Erlbaum.

Lord, F. M., & Novick, M. R. (1968). *Statistical theories of mental test scores.* Reading, MA: Addison-Wesley.

*Maccoby, E. E., & Martin, J. A. (1983). Socialization in the context of the family: Parent-child interaction. In P. H. Mussen (Series Ed.) & E. M. Hetherington (Vol. Ed.), *Handbook of child psychology: Vol. 4. Socialization, personality, and social development* (4th ed., pp. 1–101). New York: John Wiley.

†Maoz, I., & Ellis, D. G. (2001). Going to ground: Argument in Israeli-Jewish and Palestinian encounter groups. *Research on Language & Social Interaction, 34,* 399–419.

*Margolin, G., & Gordis, E. B. (1992). *Family coding system.* Unpublished manual, University of Southern California.

*Marshall, L. L. (1992). Development of the Severity of Violence Against Women Scales. *Journal of Family Violence, 7,* 103–121.

Marwell, G., & Hage, J. (1970). The organization of role-relationships: A systematic description. *American Sociological Review, 35,* 884–900.

Massett, H. A. (1999). The effects of culture and other-orientation on personal communication networks and behavioral intentions: A comparison of the United States and Mexico (Doctoral dissertation, University of Maryland at College Park, 1999). *Dissertation Abstracts International, 61* (01), 27A.

*Mathes, E. W., & Severa, N. (1981). Jealousy, romantic love, and liking: Theoretical considerations and preliminary scale development. *Psychological Reports, 49,* 23–31.

*Mathis, R. D., & Tanner, Z. (1998). Effects of unscreened spouse violence on mediated agreements. *American Journal of Family Therapy, 26,* 251–260.

Mitchell, R. J. (1993). Path analysis: Pollination. In S. M. Scheiner & J. Gurevitch (Eds.), *Design and analysis of ecological experiments* (pp. 211–231). New York: Chapman & Hall.

*Miyahara, A., Kim, M.-S., Shin, H.-C., & Yoon, K. (1998). Conflict resolution styles among "collectivist" cultures: A comparison between Japanese and Koreans. *International Journal of Intercultural Relations, 22,* 505–525.

*Morrill, C., & Thomas, C. K. (1992). Organizational conflict management as disputing process: The problem of social escalation. *Human Communication Research, 18,* 400–428.

*Munduate, L., Ganaza, J., Peiró, J. M., & Euwema, M. (1999). Patterns of styles in conflict management and effectiveness. *International Journal of Conflict Management, 10,* 5–24.

†Neuliep, J. W., & McCroskey, J. C. (1997a). The development of a U.S. and generalized ethnocentrism scale. *Communication Research Reports, 14,* 385–398.

*Neuliep, J. W., & McCroskey, J. C. (1997b). The development of intercultural and interethnic communication apprehension scales. *Communication Research Reports, 14,* 145–156.

Nicotera, A. M., Rodriguez, A. J., Hall, M., & Jackson, R. L., II. (1995). A history of the study of communication and conflict. In A. M. Nicotera (Ed.), *Conflict and organizations: Communicative processes* (pp. 17–41). Albany: State University of New York Press.

Nisbett, R. E., & Cohen, D. (1996). *Culture of honor: The psychology of violence in the South.* Boulder, CO: Westview.

Nisbett, R. E., & Wilson, T. D. (1977). Telling more than we can know: Verbal reports on mental processes. *Psychological Review, 84,* 231–259.

Nunnally, J. C. (1967). *Psychometric theory.* New York: McGraw-Hill.

Oetzel, J. G., & Ting-Toomey, S. (2003). Face concerns in interpersonal conflict: A cross-cultural empirical test of the face negotiation theory. *Communication Research, 30,* 599–624.

Oetzel, J. G., Ting-Toomey, S., Yokochi, Y., Masumoto, T., & Takai, J. (2000). A typology of facework behaviors in conflicts with best friends and relative strangers. *Communication Quarterly, 48,* 397–419.

*Ohbuchi, K.-I., Fukushima, O., & Tedeschi, J. T. (1999). Cultural values in conflict management: Goal orientation, goal attainment, and tactical decision. *Journal of Cross-Cultural Psychology, 30,* 51–71.

*Ohbuchi, K.-I., & Tedeschi, J. T. (1997). Multiple goals and tactical behaviors in social conflicts.

Journal of Applied Social Psychology, 27, 2177–2199.

*Orbe, M. P., & Warren, K. T. (2000). Different standpoints, different realities: Race, gender, and perceptions of intercultural conflict. *Qualitative Research Reports in Communication, 48*(3), 51–57.

*Pelz, D. C. (1985). Innovation complexity and the sequence of innovating stages. *Knowledge: Creation, Diffusion, Utilization, 6,* 261–291.

*Pfeiffer, S. M., & Wong, P. T. P. (1989). Multidimensional jealousy. *Journal of Social and Personal Relationships, 6,* 181–196.

Pike, K. L. (1967). *Language in relation to a unified theory of the structure of human behavior* (2nd rev. ed.). The Hague, The Netherlands: Mouton.

†Poole, M. S., & Roth, J. (1989). Decision development in small groups, IV: A typology of group decision paths. *Human Communication Research, 15,* 323–356.

Pruitt, D. G., & Carnevale, P. J. (1993). *Negotiation in social conflict.* Pacific Grove, CA: Brooks/Cole.

Pruitt, D. G., & Rubin, J. Z. (1987). *Social conflict: Escalation, stalemate, and settlement.* New York: Random House.

†Putnam, L. L., & Wilson, C. E. (1982). Communicative strategies in organizational conflicts: Reliability and validity of a measurement scale. In M. Burgoon (Ed.), *Communication yearbook 6* (pp. 629–652). Newbury Park, CA: Sage.

†Rahim, M. A. (1983). A measure of styles of handling interpersonal conflict. *Academy of Management Journal, 26,* 368–376.

†Reese-Weber, M., & Bartle-Haring, S. (1998). Conflict resolution styles in family subsystems and adolescent romantic relationships. *Journal of Youth and Adolescence, 27,* 735–752.

Rhoades, J. A., Arnold, J., & Jay, C. (2001). The role of affective traits and affective states in disputants' motivation and behavior during episodes of organizational conflict. *Journal of Organizational Behavior, 22,* 329-345.

*Rinaldi, C. M., & Howe, N. (2003). Perceptions of constructive and destructive conflict within and across family subsystems. *Infant and Child Development, 12,* 441–459.

*Ritchie, L. D., & Fitzpatrick, M. A. (1990). Family communication patterns: Measuring interpersonal perceptions of interpersonal relationships. *Communication Research, 17,* 523–544.

Rogan, R. G., & Hammer, M. R. (1994). Crisis negotiations: A preliminary investigation of facework in naturalistic conflict discourse. *Journal of Applied Communication Research, 22,* 216–231.

†Rogan, R. G., & Hammer, M. R. (1995). Assessing message affect in crisis negotiations: An exploratory study. *Human Communication Research, 21,* 553–574.

*Ross, R. G., & DeWine, S. (1988). Assessing the Ross-Dewine conflict management message style (CMMS). *Management Communication Quarterly, 1,* 389–413.

†Rubenstein, J. L., & Feldman, S. S. (1993). Conflict-resolution behavior in adolescent boys: Antecedents and adaptational correlates. *Journal of Research on Adolescence, 3,* 41–66.

*Salzinger, S., Feldman, R. S., Ng-Mak, D. S., Mojica, E., Stockhammer, T., & Rosario, M. (2002). Effects of partner violence and physical child abuse on child behavior: A study of abused and comparison children. *Journal of Family Violence, 17,* 23–52.

Samp, J. A. (2000). Relationship and self-driven influences on goal characteristics for problematic events: Components of a cybernetic cycle. *Communication Studies, 51,* 329–351.

Sanford, K. (2003). Problem-solving conversations in marriage: Does it matter what topics couples discuss? *Personal Relationships, 10,* 97–112.

†Scarry, E. (1985). *The body in pain: The making and unmaking of the world.* New York: Oxford University Press.

Seeman, M. (1997). The elusive situation in social psychology. *Social Psychology Quarterly, 60,* 4–13.

*Segrin, C., & Fitzpatrick, M. A. (1992). Depression and verbal aggressiveness in different marital couple types. *Communication Studies, 43,* 79–91.

*Siegel, J. M. (1986). The multidimensional anger inventory. *Journal of Personality and Social Psychology, 51,* 191–200.

*Sigelman, L., & Tuch, S. A. (1997). Metastereotypes: Blacks' perceptions of Whites' stereotypes of Blacks. *Public Opinion Quarterly, 61,* 87–101.

*Sillars, A. L. (1980). The sequential and distributional structure of conflict interactions as a function of attributions concerning the locus of causality and stability of conflicts. In D. Nimmo (Ed.),

Communication yearbook 4 (pp. 217–235). New Brunswick, NJ: Transaction Books.

*Simonelli, C. J., & Ingram, K. M. (1998). Psychological distress among men experiencing physical and emotional abuse in heterosexual dating relationships. *Journal of Interpersonal Violence, 13,* 667–681.

*Sipe, N. G. (1998). An empirical analysis of environmental mediation. *Journal of the American Planning Association, 64,* 275–285.

Sjoberg, G. (Ed.). (1967). *Ethics, politics, and social research.* Cambridge, MA: Schenkman.

†Smetana, J. G., Yau, J., & Hanson, S. (1991). Conflict resolution in families with adolescents. *Journal of Research on Adolescence, 1,* 189–206.

Smith, B. W., & Zautra, A. J. (2001). Interpersonal sensitivity and reactivity to spousal conflict in healthy older women. *Personality and Individual Differences, 31,* 915–923.

Smith, P. B. (2002). Levels of analysis in cross-cultural psychology. In W. J. Lonner, D. L. Dinnel, S. A. Hayes, & D. N. Sattler (Eds.), *Online readings in psychology and culture* (Unit 2, Chapter 7). Retrieved on May 19, 2005, from http://www.ac.wwu.edu/~culture/smith.htm

*Smith, S. W., Daunic, A. P., Miller, M. D., & Robinson, T. R. (2002). Conflict resolution and peer mediation in middle schools: Extending the process and outcome knowledge base. *Journal of Social Psychology, 142,* 567–586.

*Sorenson, R. L., Morse, E. A., & Savage, G. T. (1999). A test of the motivations underlying choice of conflict strategies in the dual-concern model. *International Journal of Conflict Management, 10,* 25–44.

Speer, J. P. (1986). *World polity. Conflict and war: History, causes, consequences, cures.* Fort Bragg, CA: QED Press.

*Speicher, B. L. (1995). Interethnic conflict: Attribution and cultural ignorance. *Howard Journal of Communications, 5,* 195–213.

*Spielberger, C. D., Jacobs, G., Russell, S., & Crane, R. S. (1983). Assessment of anger: The State-Trait Anger Scale. In J. N. Butcher & C. D. Spielberger (Eds.), *Advances in personality assessment* (Vol. 2, pp. 161–189). Hillsdale, NJ: Lawrence Erlbaum.

*Stets, J. E. (1991). Psychological aggression in dating relationships: The role of interpersonal control. *Journal of Family Violence, 6,* 97–114.

*Straus, M. A. (1977). Wife beating: How common and why? *Victimology, 2,* 443–458.

*Straus, M. A. (1979). Measuring intrafamily conflict and violence: The Conflict Tactics (CT) Scales. *Journal of Marriage and the Family, 41,* 75–88.

*Straus, M. A. (1990). Measuring intrafamily conflict and violence: The Conflict Tactics (CT) Scales. In M. A. Straus & R. J. Gelles (Eds.), *Physical violence in American families: Risk factors and adaptations to violence in 8,145 families* (pp. 29–47). New Brunswick, NJ: Transaction Books.

*Straus, M. A., & Gelles, R. J. (1990). How violent are American families? Estimates from the national family violence resurvey and other studies. In M. A. Straus & R. J. Gelles (Eds.), *Physical violence in American families: Risk factors and adaptations to violence in 8,145 families* (pp. 95–112). New Brunswick, NJ: Transaction Books.

*Straus, M. A., & Yodanis, C. L. (1996). Corporal punishment in adolescence and physical assaults on spouses in later life: What accounts for the link? *Journal of Marriage and the Family, 58,* 825–841.

Sulfaro, V. A., & Crislip, M. N. (1997). How Americans perceive foreign policy threats: A magnitude scaling analysis. *Political Psychology, 18,* 103–126.

*Swinford, S. P., DeMaris, A., Cernkovich, S. A., & Giordano, P. C. (2000). Harsh physical discipline in childhood and violence in later romantic involvements: The mediating role of problem behaviors. *Journal of Marriage and the Family, 62,* 508–519.

Tafoya, D. W. (1984). Research and cultural phenomena. In W. B. Gudykunst & Y. Y. Kim (Eds.), *Methods for intercultural communication research* (pp. 47–65). Beverly Hills, CA: Sage.

*Tangney, J. P., Wagner, P., Fletcher, C., & Gramzow, R. (1992). Shamed into anger? The relation of shame and guilt to anger and self-reported aggression. *Journal of Personality and Social Psychology, 62,* 669–675.

*Tangney, J. P., Wagner, P., & Gramzow, R. (1992). Proneness to shame, proneness to guilt, and psychopathology. *Journal of Abnormal Psychology, 101,* 469–478.

†Taylor, P. J. (2002a). A cylindrical model of communication behavior in crisis negotiations. *Human Communication Research, 28,* 7–48.

Taylor, P. J. (2002b). A partial order scalogram analysis of communication behavior in crisis negotiation with the prediction of outcome. *International Journal of Conflict Management, 13,* 4–37.

Thomas, K. W. (1976). Conflict and conflict management. In M. D. Dunnette (Ed.), *Handbook of industrial and organizational psychology* (pp. 889–935). Chicago: Rand McNally.

*Thomas, K. W., & Kilmann, R. H. (1974). *Thomas-Kilmann Conflict MODE Instrument.* Tuxedo, NY: Xicom.

*Ting-Toomey, S., Oetzel, J. G., & Yee-Jung, K. K. (2001). Self-construal types and conflict management styles. *Communication Reports, 14,* 87–104.

*Ting-Toomey, S., Yee-Jung, K. K., Shapiro, R. B., Garcia, W., Wright, T. J., & Oetzel, J. G. (2000). Ethnic/cultural identity salience and conflict styles in four US ethnic groups. *International Journal of Intercultural Relations, 24,* 47–81.

*Toale, M. C., & McCroskey, J. C. (2001). Ethnocentrism and trait communication apprehension as predictors of interethnic communication apprehension and use of relational maintenance strategies in interethnic communication. *Communication Quarterly, 49,* 70–83.

*Tolman, R. M. (1989). The development of a measure of psychological maltreatment of women by their male partners. *Violence and Victims, 4,* 159–177.

Torgerson, W. S. (1958). *Theory and methods of scaling.* New York: John Wiley.

*Trubisky, P., Ting-Toomey, S., & Lin, S.-L. (1991). The influence of individualism-collectivism and self-monitoring on conflict styles. *International Journal of Intercultural Relations, 15,* 65–84.

van de Vijver, F., & Leung, K. (1997). *Methods and data analysis for cross-cultural research.* Thousand Oaks, CA: Sage.

Vangelisti, A. L., & Crumley, L. P. (1998). Reactions to messages that hurt: The influence of relational contexts. *Communication Monographs, 65,* 173–196.

Wall, J. A., Jr., & Blum, M. (1991). Community mediation in the People's Republic of China. *Journal of Conflict Resolution, 35,* 3–20.

White, K. J., & Bui, L. T. M. (1988). *Basic econometrics: A computer handbook using SHAZAM.* New York: McGraw-Hill.

*Wiener, M., & Mehrabian, A. (1968). *Language within language: Immediacy, a channel in verbal communication.* New York: Appleton-Century-Crofts.

Wilson, S. R., Cai, D. A., Campbell, D. M., Donohue, W. A., & Drake, L. E. (1995). Cultural and communication processes in international business negotiations. In A. M. Nicotera (Ed.), *Conflict and organizations: Communicative processes* (pp. 201–237). Albany: State University of New York Press.

*Wilson, S. R., & Waltman, M. S. (1988). Assessing the Putnam-Wilson Organizational Communication Conflict Instrument (OCCI). *Management Communication Quarterly, 1,* 367–388.

*Winter, D. G. (1991). Measuring personality at a distance: Development of an integrated system for scoring motives in running text. In A. J. Stewart, J. M. Healy, Jr., & D. Ozer (Series Eds.) & R. Hogan (Vol. Ed.), *Perspectives in personality: Approaches to understanding lives* (pp. 59–89). London: Jessica Kingsley.

*Winter, D. G. (1993). Power, affiliation, and war: Three tests of a motivational model. *Journal of Personality and Social Psychology, 65,* 532–545.

Woelfel, J., & Fink, E. L. (1980). *The measurement of communication processes: Galileo theory and method.* New York: Academic Press.

*Womack, D. F. (1988). A review of conflict instruments in organizational settings. *Management Communication Quarterly, 1,* 437–445.

PART I

INTERPERSONAL CONFLICT

Conflict in interpersonal relationships is often emotionally draining and exhausting. It all happens because of the social or personalized ties that we form with others. Studying conflict is already a daunting task; add the term *interpersonal* and the task becomes either broader or more specific, depending on the definition used.

We opt for a broad definition of "interpersonal" conflict in this section. We define the "interpersonal" aspect of conflict as any interpersonal conflict situation or interpersonal conflict relationship in which some of the following features exist: (a) the two or more individuals in the relational system are interdependent, (b) the mutual influencing process can be casual or meaningful in direction, (c) their relationship ties can be social or personalized in nature, (d) there exist some degrees of emotional attachment and need fulfillment in the personalized relationships, (e) the conflict relationship context can be in a public or private setting, (f) one or both conflict parties perceive that they seek different outcomes or goals and they perceive their own goals as being blocked, (g) some degree of emotional frustrations or conflict threats is experienced or felt, and (h) some subtle signals of overt interpersonal conflict messages are being exchanged or traded (see Guerrero, Andersen, & Afifi, 2001). Thus, the study of interpersonal conflict can encompass the range of conflict emotional arousals or frustrations, social cognitions or appraisals, conflict communication styles, verbal and nonverbal interaction patterns, acquaintance/friendship/dating/marital/ family context, different levels of consciousness or conflict intents, to the study of underlying conflict ideologies, meanings, and metaphors (see Knapp, Daly, Albada, & Miller, 2002).

Conflict, when managed competently, can bring about positive changes in a relationship. It allows the conflict partners to use the conflict opportunity to reassess the state of the relationship. It opens doors for the individuals in conflict to discuss in depth their wants and needs in a relationship. On the other hand, incompetent conflict management affects physical, emotional, and mental health (Cupach & Canary, 1997). Recurrent, dysfunctional conflict patterns in our personalized relationships can also have strong spillover effects in our everyday work lives and stress.

A review of the current studies in interpersonal conflict, and in particular the six chapters in this section, reveals that research on interpersonal conflict focuses on two strands. The first strand tends to be more social cognitive-driven (and to a lesser extent, emotion-based; see, however, Guerrero and La Valley's chapter) and uses a relational-general approach. For example, chapters in this section include the study of emotion and cognitive appraisal process (Guerrero & La Valley), types of social knowledge and cognitive functioning (Roloff & Waite Miller), and conflict goal assessment and strategic choice (Canary & Lakey) in general interpersonal relationships. The second strand tends to be more boundary-driven and uses a relational-specific approach. For example, Caughlin and Vangelisti analyze conflict communication in dating relationships and marriage. Koerner and Fitzpatrick investigate family socialization patterns and conflict behaviors. Donohue reviews theories and practices in diverse mediation settings.

Of course there are also overlaps across various approaches used by interpersonal conflict scholars. For example, some interpersonal researchers who are interested in studying conflict communication attempt to link either social cognition or affective processing with conflict behaviors or conflict patterns. Other researchers attempt to link the impact of conflict behaviors with relational outcome dimensions such as individual depression, dyadic dissatisfaction, relational termination, or outcome competence or incompetence issues. There is a third group of theorists who try to hold a holistic view of theorizing about the interpersonal conflict phenomenon and construct testable models that incorporate antecedent, process, outcome, and environmental-temporal concepts in their explanatory schemes.

Furthermore, many interpersonal researchers and practitioners in the field advocate the importance of understanding the broader embedded contexts that surround the interpersonal conflict event or story (see Oetzel, Ting-Toomey, & Rinderle, the concluding chapter in this *Handbook*). More recently, interpersonal conflict researchers also make a concerted effort in emphasizing the importance of studying cultural, ethnic, gender, and gay/lesbian identity lenses in processing different conflict approaches and resolution processes. Moreover, they also highlight the critical interconnections among emotion, social cognition, conflict communication, and conflict outcome from both theoretical and applied viewpoints. They also articulate the importance of using a stronger systems interdependent orientation in analyzing the various reciprocal effects between marital conflict and the "spillover effect" to family conflict, or between family conflict and workplace stress, or between parents' conflict and pre-adolescent conflict, or between gay/lesbian conflict and perceived social pressure. They also go back to some fundamentals such as probing the role of conflict intensity and conflict difficulty in shaping the various conflict strategy choices in managing longitudinal conflict development. Lastly, whether we

discuss mindful conflict or competent conflict management, practitioners are interested in how to train either mediators or laypersons to connect the wealth of knowledge in the interpersonal conflict field with handling conflict appropriately and effectively in diverse relationship arenas. This section contains six chapters on interpersonal conflict communication.

In the first chapter, Guerrero and La Valley indicate that emotion and conflict share several features. Both are related to the disruption of goals, both are characterized by an affective dimension, and both are often accompanied by physiological changes, cognitive appraisals, and action tendencies. After discussing these features, the authors summarize research on four emotions that are relevant to conflict: anger, jealousy, hurt, and guilt. Next, they overview three theoretical perspectives—Gottman's cascade model, Burgoon's expectancy violations theory, and Canary and Spitzberg's competence model of conflict. The cascade model, which many consider to be the premier theory on emotion and conflict, underscores the importance of contempt and disgust in the conflict process. Expectancy violations theory and the competence model do not specifically address the relations among conflict, emotion, and communication, yet these models have the potential to illuminate these associations. Finally, eight critical issues—from identifying joint cause of emotion and conflict to incorporating culture into conflict models—for future interpersonal conflict research are highlighted.

In the second chapter, Roloff and Waite Miller believe that because of its aversive nature, conflict often stimulates sense-making activity. Consequently, many researchers have studied conflict from a social cognition perspective. Scholarship using this perspective informs us about the different types of social knowledge that people have about conflict as well as identifying the cognitive processes that influence conflict—either directly or indirectly. More specifically, the chapter summarizes and critiques extant research and draws out practical implications. The authors also conclude that many productive research programs have been developed via a social cognition conflict lens. Based on their review, Roloff and Waite Miller, advance a general social cognition integrative framework that characterizes social cognition inquiry. They end the chapter by identifying specific challenges facing social cognition researchers and possible solutions to address the existing conflict research gaps.

Conflict in dating and married relationships has been the focus of much scholarly attention. In the third chapter of this section, Caughlin and Vangelisti summarize a number of conflict behaviors and patterns that are related to various relational outcomes like dissatisfaction and dissolution. The chapter also examines various explanations of why conflict develops in particular ways and why relational partners enact certain conflict behaviors. One conclusion of the review is that communication skills are not as powerful a cause of aversive conflict behaviors as once thought. Besides skill level, conflict behaviors are shaped by factors like individual differences (e.g., sex, attachment), partners' goals, and transient factors (e.g., a stressful day at work). The theoretical framework used in the chapter highlights a need for more research on the impact of the cultural, social, and physical environments on dyads' conflict and for conflict scholars to pay more attention to temporal issues, such as how conflicts develop and change over time.

In the fourth chapter, Koerner and Fitzpatrick review theory and research on family conflict. They summarize and synthesize the material by presenting a theoretical model of family conflict socialization that links family relationship schemas, family communication patterns, and family conflict behavior through a dynamic process of mutual interdependence and reinforcement. Specifically, the authors argue that family members form mental representations of their families and their relationships with family members via the form of family relational schemas. These schemas in turn affect how families create a shared social reality. On the behavioral level, these schemas translate into or create family communication patterns that are associated with specific conflict behaviors. Conflict behaviors, in turn, have important social and psychological consequences, including the mental representations that family members form about their families. In addition to this theoretical model, the authors also discuss other aspects of family conflict, including violence and corporal punishment.

In the fifth chapter, Canary and Lakey emphasize how individuals can gain greater control of their conflict interactions by managing them competently. Throughout the chapter, they consider ways in which people can become more competent in managing conflict. The chapter adopts a competence-based approach that emphasizes the manner in which both parties in close relationships negotiate their important personal goals. The first section of the chapter offers four persuasive reasons why one should consider adopting a competence-based conflict approach. The second section examines what is meant by "competence" in conflict management. The third section explains a model of conflict that locates events where people can be mindful or strategic in the management of conflict. The authors also articulate the core assumption that mindful conflict behavior can bring about more episodic, personal, and goal-relevant strategic control. Mindful monitoring, or control, stems from understanding the context of the current conflict, recognizing options, and being sensitive to the partner's goals and behaviors. Interactional control can lead to more competent conflict management. "Competence" as a construct that reflects "communication quality" has direct practical implications to the study of everyday interpersonal conflict.

In the last chapter in this interpersonal section, Donohue reviews relevant theories and research in the various contexts of divorce, community, peer, victim-offender, environmental, and peace-keeping mediation. As the research in the chapter will reveal, overall, mediation has been fairly effective in helping disputants reach agreement and improving their satisfaction with the process and outcome. The general conclusion in the chapter suggests that the promise of mediation has been somewhat fulfilled as a tool to address interpersonal conflict effectively. Furthermore, Donohue proposes a theory, the relational order theory, as a promising conceptual lens to analyze the different relational frames in mediation interaction process. The four relational frames reflect the various levels of affiliation and interdependence between the conflict parties in a mediation session. He also offers some specific "lessons learned," including how mediation offers a very "large and clear window" into understanding fundamental conflict communication processes. He concludes with some reflections about mediation training and mediation evaluation issues.

REFERENCES

Cupach, W., & Canary, D. (Eds.). (1997). *Competence in interpersonal conflict.* New York: McGraw-Hill.

Guerrero, L., Andersen, P., & Afifi, W. (2001). *Close encounters: Communicating in relationships.* Mountain View, CA: Mayfield.

Knapp, M., Daly, J., Albada, K., & Miller, G. (2002). Background and current trends in the study of interpersonal conflict. In M. Knapp & J. Daly (Eds.), *Handbook of interpersonal communication* (3rd ed., pp. 3–20). Thousand Oaks, CA: Sage.

3

Conflict, Emotion, and Communication

Laura K. Guerrero

Arizona State University

Angela G. La Valley

Arizona State University

Kate comes home after a long, tiring day at work to find the house messy, her daughter crying, and her son covered in mud while her husband, Kevin, is watching television. Her hopes of spending a relaxing evening at home suddenly vanish and she feels frustrated and angry. She immediately lashes out at Kevin, "What kind of father are you? Don't you hear and see your own children?" Kevin becomes defensive: "What kind of mother are you, coming home from work late every night this week?" Hurt by Kevin's comment, Kate strikes back: "Well, at least I don't sit around watching TV and ignoring my kids." When Kevin ignores her and continues to look at the screen, Kate becomes exasperated and turns the TV off to get his attention. Now Kevin is even angrier. "Hey," he exclaims, "I was only watching until the weather came on. I need to know if it's going to rain since I'm coaching tomorrow. You have to control everything, don't you?" The conversation carries on this way for a few more minutes until they realize that their daughter has stopped crying and is watching them with an anxious face, while their son has retreated to sit alone in a corner, mud and all.

As the above scenario illustrates, "to be in conflict is to be emotionally charged . . . part of the reason conflict is uncomfortable is due to its accompanying emotion" (Bodtker & Jameson, 2001, p. 260). Conflict entails an expressed struggle between two or more interdependent people who perceive they have incompatible goals (Cahn, 1992). This struggle is most likely to occur when resources are scarce, when each person attaches importance to her or his goals, and when those goals are hard to obtain (Hocker & Wilmot, 1998). Conflict episodes are often filled with emotion, both in terms of the negative affect connected to the interruption of goals, and in terms of reactions to the partner's communication. Although conflict episodes can end with satisfying results, negative emotion and destructive communication often sabotage people's chances for a successful outcome.

Surprisingly, however, communication researchers have rarely investigated the connections between emotion and behavior during conflict interaction. This chapter represents an initial attempt to fill that void by examining the role that emotion plays in interpersonal conflict. After conceptualizing emotion in relation to conflict, we discuss four emotions that are sometimes experienced during conflict situations—anger, jealousy, hurt, and guilt. The same events that cause many of these emotions can instigate conflict. In addition, when these emotions are experienced during conflict episodes, they can affect communication and the ability to manage disagreements successfully. The next part of the chapter focuses on three theoretical perspectives. The first of these—Gottman's (1994) cascade model—is perhaps the leading theory examining how emotions influence conflict communication. The other two theoretical perspectives—expectancy violations and communication competence—have the potential to explain how and why emotions impact the conflict process. Finally, the chapter ends with a description of critical issues that need exploration in future research.

CONCEPTUALIZING EMOTION IN RELATION TO CONFLICT

The term *emotion* has been conceptualized various ways. However, the following ideas appear to be central in defining emotion: (a) emotions occur in reaction to stimuli that threaten to interrupt, impede, or enhance one's goals; (b) affect is the most central component of emotional experience; (c) emotional reactions are usually accompanied by physiological changes; (d) cognition frames and helps people interpret emotional reactions; and (e) specific behavioral profiles or action tendencies are associated with various emotions (Planalp, 1999; Scherer, 1994). Conflict has been described in similar terms, as is shown in Figure 3.1 and discussed next.

Emotion and Conflict as Reactions to Precipitating Events

Emotions occur in reaction to a specific stimulus or precipitating event (Frijda, 1993; Planalp, 1999). For example, people typically feel angry when betrayed or happy when someone does something nice for them. Some researchers have contrasted emotions with moods, contending that moods tend to be longer lasting, more diffuse, and less tied to specific causes than emotions (e.g., Clore, Schwartz, & Conway, 1994; Frijda, 1987). Sometimes an individual is "in a bad mood" without really knowing why. In contrast, people can usually point to causes of anger, joy, embarrassment, jealousy, and so forth. Emotions have also been connected to stimuli or events that interrupt, prevent, or facilitate an individual's ability to reach desired goals (Berscheid, 1983; Frijda, 1987). Desired situations lead to positive emotions, whereas undesired situations lead to negative emotions. In line with this thinking, scholars have identified happiness and love as occurring in response to a goal-enhancing event (e.g., Kevin wants a baby and finds out Kate is pregnant). Negative emotions, such as anger or sadness, typically occur in response to a goal-impeding event. For example, Kate might become angry if Kevin calls her "forgetful" and "disorganized" because she wants to be seen as a capable woman.

The fact that conflict involves incompatible goals necessitates that emotions are part of the conflict process. Jones (2000) took this argument further by suggesting that the event that triggers conflict also triggers emotion. In fact, Jones contended that people do not realize they are in conflict until they react emotionally. Let us take Kate and Kevin as an example. Kate may do more than the majority of housework for several weeks without complaining. When she notices Kevin watching television all day, however, she may feel overwhelmed and frustrated because she never has any free time for herself. A conflict over the seemingly unfair division of labor may then ensue as a result of Kate's frustration. Jones (2000) also contended that both emotion and conflict are inherently relational and identity based. Emotions and conflict occur most often within interdependent relationships, and both emotions and conflict are intensified when the precipitating event revolves around one's self-identity. For Kate, having an equitable partnership with her husband and being treated with respect and fairness may be core values within her relational and self identities. When these values are threatened, negative emotion and conflict are likely to follow.

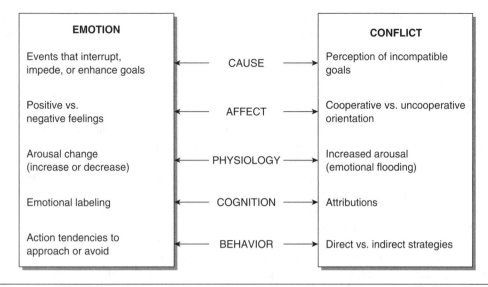

Figure 3.1   Similarities Between Components Related to Emotion and Conflict

The Affective Dimension of Emotion and Conflict

Many scholars regard affect to be the most central component defining emotion. Ortony, Clore, and Foss (1987) defined emotions as "internal mental states that are focused primarily on affect" with *affect* referring to the positive or negative valence associated with one's feelings (Clore et al., 1994; Scherer, 1994). Frijda (1986) characterized affect as the "irreducible" and "noncognitive" part of the emotional experience that is related to pure feeling states (p. 383). Thus, emotions can be thought of as affective reactions to stimuli that can be valenced positively or negatively. The specific emotion that one is experiencing (e.g., anger, disappointment) may not be evident until one interprets and labels one's feelings, so the initial affective reaction is the most fundamental component of emotional experience.

Affect may translate into a positive or negative orientation toward the partner and the conflict situation. Various scholars have described conflict behavior in terms of how cooperative (or constructive) versus uncooperative (or destructive) people act (e.g., Canary, Cupach, & Messman, 1995; Klein & Johnson, 1997; Rahim, 1986). Such behaviors may reflect an overall orientation toward the conflict situation that is influenced by the affect a person is experiencing. When intense negative affect is present, it may be more difficult to approach conflict in an optimistic, cooperative manner.

Physiological Changes

Although affect is the most central component defining emotion, most scholars agree that physiological changes also play a key role in the emotional experience. Indeed, scholars (e.g., Daly, Lancee, & Polivy, 1983; Russell, 1980) have categorized emotions based on their affective valence (e.g., pleasant vs. unpleasant), their level of arousal change or activity (e.g., low arousal vs. high arousal or passive vs. active), and their intensity level (e.g., strong vs. weak). Emotions such as anger and fear are classified as unpleasant and active; sadness is classified as unpleasant and passive; joy is classified as pleasant and active; and contentment is classified as pleasant and passive. Within each category, emotions vary in terms of intensity. For instance, depression is more intense than sadness, rage is more intense than annoyance, and elation is more intense than happiness. Emotional intensity is related positively to the degree of physiological change. Cross-cultural research has demonstrated that emotions are connected to particular types of physiological reactions. Across 37 countries, Scherer and Wallbott (1994) found the physiological profiles of joy, fear, anger, sadness, shame, and guilt to be similar. For example, joy was associated with a warm temperature and accelerated heartbeat, whereas sadness was associated with tense muscles and a lump in the throat.

Psychological changes associated with increased arousal are likely to occur during conflict episodes. Jones (2000) asserted that some level of emotional intensity is needed for partners to engage in the conflict; without emotional intensity, there is little or no motivation for confronting one's partner and dealing with the problem. On the other hand, too much emotional intensity can be counterproductive. During conflict, high emotional intensity is accompanied by strong physiological reactions, such as increased heart rate and blood pressure (Gottman, 1994). These physiological reactions can lead to defensive and irrational behavior. Jones (2000) also noted that the level of emotional intensity may be different for relational partners. One partner may be very upset about a particular situation, whereas the other partner may not be upset at all. In such cases, partners may have conflict over how important the issue is and how they are responding to the issue, rather than the issue per se. For example, Kevin may be very upset because he sat around worrying when Kate did not call to tell him she would be 90 minutes late coming home from work. Kate, in contrast, may not see her tardiness as a big issue. As a result, Kevin may want to talk about the issue whereas Kate may not. Moreover, the conflict could go off course with Kevin telling Kate that she is inconsiderate and insensitive, and Kate telling Kevin that he is possessive and worries too much.

Cognition

Cognition plays an important role in the interpretation of emotion-eliciting events (Omdahl, 1995). In articulating his appraisal theory of emotion, Lazarus (1991) asserted that people make sense of emotion-inducing events by making primary and secondary appraisals. Primary appraisals determine the affective valence of the emotional experience. When people engage in primary appraisal, they assess whether the emotion-eliciting event is personally relevant. In other words, how does the event impact one's personal goals and one's identity? Does the event make it easier or more difficult to obtain those goals? According to Lazarus (1991), negative emotions are alike in that they all arise from the disruption of a personal goal, whereas positive emotions emanate from goal facilitation or enhancement. Secondary appraisals help people label emotions and develop effective coping strategies. For example, people try to determine who is to blame for the emotion-eliciting event, how well they can manage the problem and cope with their feelings, and how likely it is that the situation will get worse or better in the future.

Similarly, people make appraisals about relevance and attributions regarding blame during conflict situations. In terms of relevance, people are unlikely to engage in conflict unless they perceive something is at stake, such as maintaining a desired relationship, protecting one's personal safety, or presenting a positive self-image. Thus, according to Jones (2000), the goal-based origin of conflict requires one to have a sense of self and to understand one's priorities. Following this reasoning, the same event could lead to conflict for one individual but not another, based on identity-related issues. For example, research has shown that people experience envy only when someone exceeds their level of competence in an area that is central to their self-esteem (Salovey & Rodin, 1989). So while a college professor might be envious of a colleague's high level of research productivity, a musician probably would not be. This is because being a skilled researcher would more likely be a part of the college professor's self-concept than the musician's.

In terms of attributions about blame, both emotions and conflicts are fundamentally evaluative (Jones, 2000). People make value-based judgments about who and what is good or bad, right or wrong, and fair or unfair. Judgments about fairness are complicated and highly emotional (Planalp, 2003). For example, anger often stems from the perception that a situation is unfair or that someone has been treated badly (Canary, Spitzberg, & Semic, 1998). Such feelings may lead people to think they are justified in engaging in aggressive or vengeful behavior, or that they are, at the very least, entitled to discuss the untoward behavior with their partner. Indeed, Sereno, Welch, and Braaten (1987) found that direct expressions of anger were evaluated the most favorably when people were perceived to be justifiably angry.

Attributions about the source of conflict and the partner's behavior also influence communication. According to Sillars (1980), people make communicative decisions during conflict based on attributions in three areas: the cause of the conflict, the intentions or personality traits of the partner, and the stability of the conflict. These attributions then influence the behaviors and strategies people enact during a conflict episode. In addition, people tend to make more positive attributions about their own behavior than their partner's behavior during conflict (Sillars, 1980; Sillars, Roberts, Leonard, & Dun, 2000), which contributes to misinterpretation and misunderstanding. Not surprisingly, people in dissatisfying relationships generally experience more misperception, misunderstanding, and negative emotion during conflict than do people in satisfying relationships (Sillars et al., 2000; Sillars & Scott, 1983). Specifically, Sillars et al. (2000) found that angry, frustrated, and blaming thoughts were more prevalent during severe conflicts and in unhappy relationships.

Behavioral Reactions

Appraisal theorists also believe that emotions are accompanied by certain action tendencies (Frijda, 1987; Lazarus, 1991; Omdahl, 1995; Scherer, 1994). Action tendencies are biologically rooted behavioral responses that help individuals cope with emotion and adapt to their environment. According to Lazarus (1991), action tendencies are based on three characteristics that underlie a particular emotional experience: (a) affect, or the positive or negative feeling state; (b) the level and type of physiological arousal change; and (c) the core theme related to the emotion-eliciting stimulus or event (e.g., relational harm stemming from discovery of a partner's betrayal; relational benefit stemming from receiving an unexpectedly nice gift). Different emotions are associated with various action tendencies. For example, the action tendency for anger is to attack, the action

tendency for fear is to move away from harm, and the action tendency for guilt is to make amends (Lazarus, 1991). To the extent that such emotions are experienced during conflict situations, various action tendencies are likely to be operative.

While action tendencies provide a blueprint for how people typically respond to particular emotions, display rules help people manage their emotions in socially acceptable ways. So although the action tendency for anger is to attack, an angry child may learn that it is more effective to address a parent calmly than aggressively. Ekman's (1978; Ekman & Friesen, 1975) work on cultural display rules describes five ways people manage emotional expressions. First, people *intensify* emotional expressions by acting as if they feel more of a particular emotion than they actually feel (e.g., Kevin is happy that Kate was promoted at work, but he acts happier than he really is). Second, people *de-intensify* emotional expressions by acting as if they feel less of a particular emotion than they actually feel (e.g., Kevin is very upset about Kate's promotion because she will have less time for him, but he acts like it will be only a minor inconvenience). Third, people can *simulate* emotions by acting as if they are experiencing an emotion that they do not actually feel (e.g., Kevin feels indifferent about Kate's promotion, but he acts happy anyway). Fourth, people can *inhibit* emotions by acting as if they do not feel any emotion when they actually feel something (e.g., Kevin is envious that Kate has been promoted, but he acts indifferent). Finally, people can *mask* emotions by acting like they feel an emotion that is very different from what they are actually experiencing (e.g., Kevin feels upset and envious but acts like he is happy for Kate). Although people use these five display rules quite regularly, during conflict situations it may be difficult for people to curb intense emotions (Gottman, 1994).

CONFLICT-RELATED EMOTIONS

A variety of emotions come into play during conflict situations. In fact, scholars have argued that people define conflict episodes based on the types of emotions they experience (Jones,

2000). Serious conflicts are characterized by high levels of emotional activation, whereas destructive conflicts are marked by both negative affect and aggressive behavior. Next, we discuss four specific emotions that are relevant to conflict: anger, jealousy, hurt, and guilt. We describe each emotion, including causes and communicative responses associated with each emotion, particularly as they relate to conflict. Although this list does not represent all of the emotions that can be implicated in the conflict process, it includes some of the most frequently mentioned. Contempt, which is another important emotion within the conflict process, is discussed subsequently when we overview Gottman's cascade model of conflict management.

Anger

When people think about the prototypical emotion associated with conflict, anger probably comes to mind. Shaver, Schwartz, Kirson, and O'Connor (1987) identified rage, irritation, exasperation, disgust/contempt, envy, and torment as specific types of emotions that people associate with anger. Research suggests that anger is a common emotion (Scherer & Tannenbaum, 1986). In fact, more than 80% of participants in a study by Carpenter and Halberstadt (1996) could think of a time they had felt angry within the past week. Although anger can range from annoyance to rage, angry individuals typically have accelerated heart rates, tense muscles, rapid breathing patterns, and feel hot or flushed (Scherer & Wallbott, 1994). If these physiological reactions are strong, angry individuals may become emotionally flooded (Gottman, 1994) and have difficulty staying calm and rational.

Causes. Anger has many causes, but consistent with our earlier definition of emotion, most scholars believe that the interruption of one's goals or plans (including the projection of a positive self-image) is a global and central cause of most anger experiences (e.g., Shaver et al., 1987). Based on a careful review of literature, Canary et al. (1998) identified seven specific sites of anger provocation: identity management, aggression, frustration, fairness, incompetence, relationship threat, and predispositions.

Identity management, which involves perceiving that "one's self-concept or public image is under attack" (Canary et al., 1998), is a common cause of anger. Retzinger (1991) argued that anger is a mechanism used to save face during conflict situations. Gottman's (1994) work (which is reviewed later in this chapter) suggests that personal criticism, teasing, insults, and blaming behavior can lead people to become angry and defensive during conflict situations. People may also become angry in response to *aggression,* such as when a partner threatens or actually causes them physical harm. *Frustrating situations,* such as having one's plans interrupted, having an expectancy violated in a negative fashion, or feeling powerless, can also lead to anger. For example, if Kevin expects Kate to do something special for him on his birthday, and she simply gets him a card, he may become angry. Thus, as Jones (2000) suggested, the interruption of goals or plans is connected to emotional experience as well as the onset of conflict.

Related to Jones's (2000) idea that conflict and emotion are both evaluative, perceptions of *unfairness or inequity* can cause anger. Individuals may perceive they do more household chores or put more effort into the relationship than their partners, or that they are being blamed or accused of something unjustly. *Incompetent behavior* can also cause anger. Canary and colleagues (1998) discussed two specific types of incompetence—a benign form of incompetence that involves acting mindlessly or out of ignorance (e.g., Kate forgets Kevin's birthday because she is absentminded and disorganized), and a selfish form of incompetence that involves acting in an egocentric fashion (e.g., Kate forgets Kevin's birthday because she is absorbed in her own life). People also display egocentric incompetence when they act like they know better than everyone else. Another site of anger is *relationship threats,* such as feeling jealous of a third party or of the time someone is spending engaged in work tasks. Finally, some people have a *predisposition* toward becoming angry, due either to personality traits or to substance abuse.

In another study on the causes of anger, Carpenter and Halberstadt (1996) asked mothers to provide descriptions of why they typically become angry at different family members (e.g., husband, child) as well as why family members become angry at them. They identified six primary causes of anger in the marital dyad: *money issues* (e.g., spending too much); *issues involving children* (e.g., disagreements about handling children, lack of participation in children's activities); *personality deficiencies* (e.g., spouse has a short temper, is impatient, jealous, or too demanding); *inadequate time* (e.g., spending time with friends instead of family; lack of time for sex/romance); *not being caring enough* (e.g., being inconsiderate, not showing affection); and *not contributing enough to household chores*. Clearly, these specific causes of marital anger could fit under some of the broader categories delineated by Canary et al. (1998). Moreover, these causes of anger correspond with research on the reasons couples engage in conflict (Canary et al., 1995) and the reasons couples break up (Guerrero, Andersen, & Afifi, 2001).

Communication. The action tendency associated with anger is to attack (Lazarus, 1991) through behaviors such as hitting or yelling at someone (Roseman, Wiest, & Swartz, 1994). As Shaver et al. (1987) put it, "Angry persons report becoming stronger . . . and more energized in order to fight or rail against the cause of anger" (p. 1078). In line with the attacking action tendency, anger has been linked to verbally and physically aggressive behaviors in romantic relationship contexts (Sugarman & Hotaling, 1989). When Shaver et al. (1987) asked people to describe the types of behaviors that are associated with anger, most of the responses concerned aggression. For example, people described *verbal attacks* (e.g., yelling, complaining, and using obscenities), *physical attacks* (e.g., clenching one's fist, making threatening gestures, and throwing things), and displays of *nonverbal disapproval* (e.g., stomping, slamming doors, and gritting one's teeth) as prototypical responses to anger.

However, Canary et al. (1998) cautioned researchers not to equate anger with aggression in all situations. As they stated: "Although people might think of a 'model' anger episode in terms of destructive and aggressive behaviors, research indicates that people also respond to

anger in constructive and less threatening ways" (p. 205). Several researchers have identified constructive means for coping with anger in relationships, including using assertive rather than aggressive communication (e.g., Guerrero, 1994; Kubany & Richard, 1992; Sereno et al., 1987). Assertive modes of anger expression involve listening to the partner's explanations and points of view; trying to discuss issues in a calm, direct, and fair manner; and taking ownership of one's feelings rather than blaming the partner for them (e.g., Kate says "I feel really mad" rather than telling Kevin "you make me so mad!").

Research suggests that it is best to express conflict assertively rather than aggressively. When people hold anger back, they may experience increased levels of physiological stress and emotional flooding (Buck, 1979; Gottman, 1994), which makes it difficult to discuss conflict issues productively. On the other hand, expressing anger aggressively is associated with relational dissatisfaction, perceptions of incompetence, and feelings of heightened distress (Kubany & Richard, 1992; Leonard & Roberts, 1998; Sereno et al., 1987). Interestingly, however, Gottman's (1993) research suggests that anger is not the main culprit in terms of predicting marital discord. Instead, "the husband's defensiveness, contempt, and stonewalling (the listener's withdrawal from the interaction) were predictive of divorce" (Gottman, 1993, p. 62). Thus, if anger does not lead to expressions of contempt and defensiveness, it is more likely to be expressed in constructive ways during conflict.

Jealousy

Scholars have defined jealousy as a unique emotion that is based on the perception that one's primary relationship is threatened by a third party (e.g., White & Mullen, 1989). Initially, jealousy is often experienced as increased arousal (Pines & Aronson, 1983) or as a jealousy flash (Ellis & Weinstein, 1986) that involves an elevated heart rate and a warm, flushed feeling. A variety of emotions can accompany the jealousy experience depending on the circumstances surrounding the jealous threat. Anger and fear appear to be central emotions in the jealousy experience, but emotions such as sadness, guilt, sexual arousal, envy, and love have also been identified as jealousy-related emotions (Guerrero, Trost, & Yoshimura, 2005; Sharpsteen, 1991; White & Mullen, 1989).

Causes. Scholars have distinguished between sexual jealousy and emotional jealousy (e.g., Buss, Larsen, Westen, & Semmelroth, 1992). People experience *sexual jealousy* when they think their partners have had (or want to have) sexual activity with a rival. In contrast, people experience *emotional jealousy* when they think their partners love or are emotionally attached to a rival. Sexual and emotional jealousy are often experienced together; people may be worried that their partner wants to have an emotionally close and sexual relationship with a rival. However, in some situations, such as finding out a partner had a one-night stand, jealousy is primarily sexual in nature. In other situations, such as finding out that a partner loves someone who is unattainable, jealousy is primarily emotional. Sexual and emotional jealousy cause people to experience considerable distress, including increased physiological arousal (Buss et al., 1992). Although both men and women get upset in response to these types of jealousy, there appears to be a sex difference in the intensity of upset feelings; men react more strongly than women when experiencing sexual jealousy, and women react more strongly than men when experiencing emotional jealousy (Buss et al., 1992; Cann, Mangum, & Wells, 2001; Cramer, Abraham, Johnson, & Manning-Ryan, 2001; see also Guerrero, Spitzberg, & Yoshimura, 2004, for a review).

Research also suggests that different behaviors prompt people to suspect that their partners are engaging in sexual versus emotional infidelity. According to Shackelford and Buss (1997), changes in sexual attitudes and behaviors, as well as unusual increases in affection, can trigger suspicion regarding sexual infidelity. For example, if one's partner does not want to have sex as much as usual, tries new positions during sex, and starts sending flowers for no apparent reason, one might surmise that he or she is having an affair and feeling guilty. In contrast, Shackelford and Buss (1997) found that distancing oneself from the partner (through actions such as suggesting they date other people or spending less time together) and using atypical communication (such as being more inconsiderate, argumentative, or anxious) may lead to the perception of emotional infidelity. Despite differences in the causes and consequences of sexual versus emotional jealousy, little if any research has examined whether jealous conflict differs based on whether the threat is sexual versus emotional. Moreover, some of the behaviors that cause suspicion of emotional infidelity, such as a partner suddenly becoming more argumentative, may also lead to negative cycles of destructive behavior.

Communication. Jealousy can be communicated in a variety of ways, with some responses to jealousy more likely to cause or exacerbate conflict than others. Guerrero and Andersen (1998) described several communicative responses to jealousy that associate positively with conflict and retaliation: *distributive communication* (i.e., direct and aggressive forms of behavior such as yelling at the partner), *active distancing* (i.e., indirect and aggressive forms of behavior such as giving the partner the "silent treatment"), *counterjealousy inductions* (i.e., attempts to make the offending partner feel jealous too), *guilt inductions* (attempts to make the partner feel guilty about her or his behavior), *violence toward the partner* (e.g., actions such as hitting, shoving, or pushing the partner), and *violence toward objects* (e.g., actions such as slamming a door or ripping up a photograph of the offending partner). These communicative responses to jealousy also associate negatively with relational satisfaction (e.g., Andersen, Eloy, Guerrero, & Spitzberg, 1995).

Jealousy is also linked to aggression and the use of particular conflict styles. Buunk (1991) argued that when people suspect their partners are interested in someone else, the tendency to be cooperative is usually replaced with a tendency to be competitive and aggressive. Indeed, research has shown jealousy to correlate with violence and aggression (e.g., Dutton, van Ginkel, & Landolt, 1996; Simonelli & Ingram, 1998), and victims of abuse often cite jealousy as a cause of violence in their relationships. In one study, 15% of participants reported that they had suffered physical aggression because their partners were jealous (Mullen & Martin, 1994). In another study, the use of jealousy-inducing behaviors was correlated moderately and positively with aggression (Brainerd, Hunter, Moore, & Thompson, 1996). Several other studies suggest that jealousy is one of the top predictors of physical aggression among couples who report using violent behavior (Hansen, 1991; Laner, 1990; Stets & Pirog-Good, 1987; Sugarman & Hotaling, 1989). These findings do not suggest that violence is a common response to jealousy. Rather, they suggest that among those couples who report violence, jealousy is a top predictor.

Nonviolent aggression, however, does appear to be a relatively common response to jealousy. Across Guerrero, Andersen, Jorgensen, Spitzberg, and Eloy's (1995) qualitative and quantitative data, responses such as distributive communication and active distancing were reported with relatively high frequency, as was integrative communication (i.e., direct, positive communication directed toward problem solving). Schaap, Buunk, and Kerkstra (1988) examined correlations between jealousy and conflict styles. Jealousy was most strongly associated with a competing or distributive conflict style ($r = .78$). There were also moderate to small significant correlations between jealousy and the compromising ($r = .42$), soothing/accommodating ($r = .40$), and avoiding ($r = .27$) conflict styles. Contrary to Guerrero et al.'s (1995) findings, the problem-solving or integrative conflict style associated negatively with jealousy ($r = -.21$). Thus, it seems safe to conclude that many jealous individuals tend to use a distributive or aggressive conflict style, although the jury is still out on the extent to which individuals take an integrative or problem-solving approach.

The type of approach individuals take when communicating (or not communicating) their jealousy is also contingent on their goals. From an emotion theory perspective, romantic jealousy is caused by the disruption of the goal to have a particular type of relationship with a valued partner. Because goal disruption is a major cause of aversive emotions such as jealousy, it makes sense that jealous individuals would engage in different communicative responses to jealousy based on their individual and relational goals. When jealous individuals have the goal of restoring equity by retaliating, they report using aggressive responses, such as distributive

communicative, active distancing, counterjealousy inductions, and guilt inductions (Guerrero & Afifi, 1999). In contrast, jealous individuals who are most concerned with maintaining their relationships report using integrative communication. Those who are driven by the goal of bolstering their self-esteem report using avoidant responses, such as denying jealous feelings and reducing communication with the partner (Guerrero & Afifi, 1999). Finally, when jealous individuals are concerned with reducing uncertainty they tend to report using integrative communication (e.g., talking about the relationship with the partner) or surveillance behavior (e.g., keeping closer tabs on the partner).

Communicative responses to jealousy are also related to different emotions. Guerrero et al. (2005) investigated the relations among communicative responses to jealousy and several jealousy-related emotions, including hostility (an intense form of anger) irritation (a mild form of anger), fear/envy, and guilt. Both forms of anger (hostility and irritation) were good predictors of distributive communication and active distancing, while irritation alone was the best predictor of integrative communication. Hostility was also a significant positive predictor of surveillance behavior, manipulation attempts (such as counterjealousy and guilt inductions), violence, and rival contacts. Jealous individuals were most likely to report making violent threats or actually using violence against their partners when they felt intense anger and a lack of guilt. Finally, fear/envy, combined with a lack of hostility, predicted compensatory restoration behavior such as trying to look more attractive or giving the partner gifts.

Hurt

Like jealousy, hurt stems from a particular type of threat and can be accompanied by a variety of emotions depending on the circumstances. Hurt is experienced as an unpleasant and often intense emotion that stems from feeling psychologically injured by another person (Folkes, 1982; Vangelisti & Sprague, 1998). Thus, hurt is an inherently interpersonal emotion. Shaver et al.'s (1987) research suggests that when people's feelings are deeply hurt they experience emotions such as agony, anger, anguish, sadness, and suffering. Although the physiological reactions associated with hurt have not been systematically studied, it is likely that hurt individuals experience physical changes similar to those found in sad or angry individuals, depending on which emotion is predominant (Shaver et al., 1987). Sadness is associated with tense muscles, crying, a lump in one's throat, and quietness, whereas anger is associated with an accelerated heartbeat, tense muscles, breathing changes, and hot temperature (Scherer & Wallbott, 1994).

Causes. Research suggests that having one's personal or relational identity attacked is the primary source of emotional hurt, as is evidenced by work on hurtful messages (Vangelisti, 1994). Vangelisti identified nine specific types of hurtful messages. *Accusations* involve making statements that show a person's faults (e.g., "you're such a snob"). *Evaluations* involve describing someone's value or worth in a negative way (e.g., "going out with you was a huge mistake"). *Advice* can be hurtful when suggesting a course of action reflects badly on one's self-image or interrupts one's plans (e.g., "I think we should take a break from each other"). *Expressed desires* are a little different in that they are statements of preference (e.g., "I'd rather be alone than with you"). *Informative statements* are hurtful when the facts disclosed reflect badly on someone (e.g., "I'm just not attracted to you anymore"). *Threats* nearly always have the potential to be hurtful because they show intent to inflict some type of punishment on someone (e.g., "If you talk to him again, I'll break up with you"). Obvious or discovered *lies* can also be hurtful because they show a lack of trust. Finally, *jokes* can be hurtful (e.g., telling an overweight individual a "fat" person joke).

Hurtful messages can be a cause or consequence of conflict. When people feel high levels of negative emotion or perceive themselves as losing an argument, they might resort to hurtful messages as a type of defensive strategy. Indeed, Infante's (1987; Infante, Chandler, & Rudd, 1989) work on argumentativeness and verbal aggressiveness suggests that hurtful messages may sometimes result from a person's inability to defend him- or herself or state a position in a competent manner. Argumentativeness involves using logical arguments to attack someone's position. In contrast, verbal aggressiveness involves personally attacking someone, often with the intent to inflict emotional hurt. Common tactics of verbal aggression include teasing, threatening, and criticizing the partner (Infante, Sabourin, Rudd, & Shannon, 1990), which are similar to the hurtful messages in Vangelisti's list. When people are in an emotionally charged conflict situation, it may be difficult to engage in problem-focused discussion, leading to an increased tendency to resort to verbal aggressiveness. Hurtful messages can also cause conflict. As noted earlier, being verbally attacked by one's partner is a cause of anger and upset in relationships (Canary et al., 1998), which can lead to conflict. The moral component of conflict is evident in such situations, with the hurt partner often feeling justified in demanding that the offending partner provide an explanation and apology.

There is also a moral component in conflict when the conflict is about relational transgressions. *Relational transgressions* are violations of implicit or explicit relational rules that are perceived as betrayals and typically lead to emotional hurt (Metts, 1994; Vangelisti & Sprague, 1998). As such, the hurt partner often feels morally justified in feeling angry. According to Metts (1994), the most common relational transgressions among college students in romantic relationships are having sex with someone outside of the primary relationship, wanting to or actually dating others, deceiving the partner, flirting with or kissing another, or being emotionally involved with someone outside of the relationship. Roscoe, Cavanaugh, and Kennedy (1988) reported similar results on the nature of betrayals in dating and marital relationships, with emotional and sexual infidelity, flirting with a rival, and lying about important matters viewed as the most common forms of betrayals. Bachman and Guerrero (2003a) found that being dumped was also frequently mentioned as a hurtful event.

Less commonly reported relational transgressions include betraying a confidence, forgetting plans or special occasions, displaying an emotional attachment with a former romantic partner, failing to trust the partner, changing important plans, threatening or actually engaging in physically abuse, and making unfair comparisons to other people (Bachman & Guerrero, 2003a; Metts, 1994). All of these transgressions can lead to emotional hurt and conflict.

Communication. Based on an analysis of both qualitative and quantitative data, Vangelisti and Crumley (1998) uncovered three main responses to hurtful messages. First, hurt individuals can use *active verbal* responses such as verbally attacking the offending partner, defending the self, making sarcastic statements, and asking for an explanation. Second, hurt individuals can engage in *acquiescent* responses, which include crying, conceding (e.g., "fine, I'll just leave then"), and apologizing. Finally, hurt individuals can use *invulnerable* responses, such as ignoring the problem, laughing it off, and becoming quiet. Vangelisti and Crumley (1998) found acquiescent responses to be reported most often when people were deeply hurt by something a close relational partner said, perhaps because their "hurt was intense enough that they were willing (or perhaps forced) to display their vulnerability and acknowledge their conversational partners' ability to hurt them" (p. 181). They also suggested that people who experience intense hurt may have a limited array of response tactics at their disposal since they are flooded with emotion. Active verbal responses, on the other hand, were most likely to be used when people were in satisfying relationships. In relation to conflict, Vangelisti and Crumley suggested that people in satisfying relationships may be more able and willing to use active verbal strategies because they believe the overall tone of their relationship will remain positive despite an occasional hurtful comment or quarrel.

In another study, Bachman and Guerrero (in press-a) identified seven distinct responses to hurtful events. *Relational repair tactics* constitute prosocial behaviors designed to mend the relationship through actions such as being affectionate, romantic, and complimentary toward the partner. Consistent with the conflict literature (e.g., Sillars, 1980), *integrative communication* involves disclosing one's feelings in a nonthreatening way and attempting to get the partner to talk about the event so an understanding can be reached. *Loyalty* involves using passive behaviors such as patiently waiting for the situation to improve (Rusbult, 1983). Another type of indirect behavior, *active distancing,* involves engaging in passive aggressive behaviors such as giving one's partner the silent treatment. *De-escalation* includes behaviors that promote the termination or de-escalation of the relationship through actions such as letting conditions get worse and threatening to break up. *Distributive communication* involves confronting the partner in a verbally aggressive manner by using behaviors such as yelling, making accusations, and blaming the partner (see also Sillars, 1980). Finally, *vengeful behavior* involves trying to get back at the partner through hurtful behaviors such as inducing guilt. People who reported responding to hurtful events with integrative communication, relational repair, and loyalty were more likely to be satisfied with their relationships and to have forgiven their partners (Bachman & Guerrero, in press-a, in press-b).

Guilt

While people experience emotional hurt when others say or do things that psychologically injure them, people experience guilt when they perceive that they have injured, unjustly hurt, or failed to help someone. Like shame and embarrassment, guilt has been classified as a "self-conscious emotion" because it is inherently social and involves self-reflection and self-evaluation (Barrett, 1995; Fischer & Tangney, 1995). Thus, like conflict itself, guilt necessarily includes an evaluative or moral component and tends to be relationally oriented. Indeed, Baumeister, Stillwell, and Heatherton (1994) maintained that a primary function of guilt is to maintain and repair positive relationships, and Shimanoff (1984) found that regret (or guilt) was one of the emotions that married couples talked about most frequently. Because guilt is self-evaluative, it is also identity based; individuals who experience guilt feel badly about their actions and typically want to make amends (Lazarus, 1991). Making amends helps repair relationships and restore self-esteem. The physiological reactions accompanying guilty feelings may also push people toward taking action to alleviate their distress. Physiological reactions to guilt include an accelerated heartbeat and irregular breathing (Barrett, 1995), as well as a lump in one's throat (Scherer & Wallbott, 1994), which are all signs of anxiety.

Causes. The same relational transgressions and cruel remarks that hurt one partner can cause the offending partner to experience guilt. Indeed, Baumeister et al. (1994) identified betraying one's partner, neglecting one's partner, and failing to live up to an interpersonal obligation as primary elicitors of guilt within relationships. Partners may also feel guilty when they hurt one another by making cruel remarks, such as unfair accusations, threats, or disclosures of negative information.

Vangelisti, Daly, and Rudnick (1991) examined conversational tactics that elicit guilt. Statements about relational obligations, the nature of things, role obligations, sacrifices, and comparisons to others were the most frequently used conversational techniques to induce guilt. Stating a *relational obligation* involves telling one's partner that he or she is not meeting relational expectations (e.g., "You need to spend more time with me and the kids than your friends"). Pointing out the *nature of things* involves implying that one should know how to think or behave properly in a given situation (e.g., "You're not going to waste your time watching that stupid show again, are you?"). Stating a *role obligation* involves telling one's partner that he or she is not fulfilling a role-related function (e.g., "As their coach you should be there on time"). Bringing up *sacrifices* involves one partner pointing out that he or she has done something for the sake of the other (e.g., "I guess I'll watch the kids today so you can go shopping with your friends"). Making *comparisons* involves contrasting the partner's behavior with one's own or a third party's behavior (e.g., "You spend more time doing what you want than I do," or "Mary's husband buys her little cards and gifts all the time"). These examples, along with Baumeister et al.'s (1994) findings, demonstrate that people are likely to feel guilty when they realize that they are not meeting their obligations or responsibilities, have betrayed their partner, or have otherwise treated the partner unfairly.

When examining the examples of guilt-inducing tactics listed above, it is easy to imagine any one of them being said during a conflict episode. Indeed, the various causes of guilt suggest that guilty feelings can emerge at various stages during a conflict situation. In some cases, one partner might enter a conflict episode feeling guilty because she or he engaged in a relational transgression that started the conflict. In other cases, people might feel guilty during the course of a conflict either because they made hurtful remarks to their partner in the heat of the moment or because their partner induces guilt in them. In yet other cases, guilt may surface after the conflict episode is over and partners have had time to reflect upon their actions.

Communication. Regardless of the cause, when people feel guilty the primary action tendency is to repair the damage (Lazarus, 1991; Tangney, Wagner, Fletcher, & Gramzow, 1992). Guerrero et al. (2001) summarized research in the areas of deception, sexual infidelity, social predicaments, and forgiveness to identify ways that people try to maintain or repair their relationships after committing a relational transgression. Their summary suggests that individuals who are feeling guilty have a number of remedial strategies at their disposal, including apologizing and conceding guilt, justifying one's behavior, trying to appease the partner, and engaging in relationship talk. For example, if Kate felt guilty because she went out to lunch with an old boyfriend without telling Kevin, she could confess and tell Kevin that she was wrong and felt badly about her actions (apology); she could tell Kevin she met her ex-boyfriend for lunch only because he sounded really depressed (justification); she could be especially nice and affectionate toward Kevin (appeasement); or she could tell Kevin that their marriage was so strong that he should not worry about her seeing an ex-boyfriend (relationship talk).

In addition to these possibilities, research suggests that individuals who commit relational transgressions sometimes use refusals or avoidance (Guerrero et al., 2001). Refusals involve failing to recognize or take responsibility for one's untoward behavior. As such, refusals are probably associated with a *lack* of guilty feelings. For instance, Kate might refuse to acknowledge that she did anything wrong, claiming that Kevin is her husband but not her "keeper," and that she has a right to see an old friend if she wants. Avoidance can occur when people feel guilty or guiltless. Talking about untoward actions sometimes makes offenders feel increasingly guilty or causes them to lose even more face, which could lead offenders to avoid conflict. On the other hand, individuals who perceive that they are guilt-free might not think it is important to talk about issues that are bothersome to their partners but not to them.

THEORETICAL PERSPECTIVES ON CONFLICT AND EMOTION

Although little research has examined how specific emotions such as anger, hurt, or guilt are evoked and communicated during conflict interaction, some theoretical perspectives give insight into how emotion generally impacts conflict communication. Gottman's (1994) cascade model is perhaps the premier relational theory linking emotion to conflict outcomes. Although less well developed than the cascade model in relation to the associations between conflict and emotion, research from expectancy violations (e.g., Burgoon, 1993) and communication competence (e.g., Spitzberg, Canary, & Cupach, 1994) perspectives also appears promising for illuminating how emotion functions in conflict interaction.

Gottman's Cascade Model

Research related to the cascade model (Gottman, 1993, 1994) illustrates the centrality of emotion in conflict, as well as the critical role that emotional experience and expression plays in determining whether conflict will be productive or damaging within the context of marital relationships. In particular, Gottman's work highlights the importance of disgust and contempt in the conflict process. Gottman's work also suggests that emotional flooding impedes constructive communication and leads to defensiveness and stonewalling.

An early study by Gottman, Markman, and Notarius (1977) laid the groundwork for the cascade model. In this study, Gottman and colleagues coded facial, vocal, and bodily cues related to positive and negative affect. For example, facial cues such as smiling, having an empathic facial expression, and nodding to show agreement were coded as nonverbal expressions

of positive affect, whereas facial cues such as frowning, sneering, crying, or looking angry were coded as expressions of negative affect. Gottman et al. (1977) found that nonverbal indicators of affect were a better discriminator of distressed versus nondistressed couples than were verbal behaviors, with distressed couples expressing more negative affect during conflict than nondistressed couples. Distressed couples were also more likely to get caught in negative cycles; when one partner experienced an increase in negative affect, so did the other partner. Importantly, this study examined general affect (in terms of the positive or negative valence of participants' emotional responses) rather than specific emotional experiences (such as disgust or anger).

In a follow-up longitudinal study, Gottman, Levenson, and Woodin (2001) investigated how the expression of discrete emotions via facial cues impacts relational outcomes. During the initial data collection, participants' facial expressions were recorded. Four years later data were collected on the following outcomes: (a) the number of months (if any) they had been separated, (b) their physical health, (c) the degree of fondness they felt for their partner, (d) the degree of negativity in the relationship, and (e) the extent to which participants identified themselves as part of a couple rather than as individuals, which Gottman and colleagues termed "we-ness."

Facial expressions of emotions were associated with relational outcomes 4 years later. Specifically, husbands who had shown facial expressions of unfelt happiness (e.g., fake smiles) and fear reported more separation from their wives over the 4-year period. In addition, husbands reported more separation when their wives had displayed facial expressions of anger, disgust, and unfelt happiness. Wives' reports of separation were also correlated positively with husbands' facial expressions of unfelt happiness as well as their own facial expressions of disgust. For physical illness, Gottman and colleagues (2001) found that only the husbands' facial expressions produced significant correlations. Husbands' reports of physical illness were correlated positively with their own expressions of fear, while wives' reports of physical illness were correlated positively with husbands' expressions of contempt, fear, and unfelt happiness. From these findings, one can speculate that wives may be more likely than husbands to react to a spouse's expressions of negative affect by becoming ill.

There were also significant correlations between facial expressions and the relational outcome measures of fondness, negativity, and we-ness. In terms of fondness, for both husbands and wives there was a negative correlation between fondness and the husband's facial expressions of sadness. For wives, fondness also correlated positively with their own facial expressions of unfelt happiness, suggesting perhaps that wives who are especially fond of their husbands will feign happiness in an effort to maintain positive relations and break or prevent negative cycles of affect and behavior. In terms of negativity, for both husbands and wives there was a positive correlation between negativity and husbands' facial expressions of fear and sadness. For wives, negativity also was associated positively with their own facial expressions of disgust. Finally, for both husbands and wives expressions of we-ness were negatively correlated with husbands' facial expressions of sadness.

Overall, Gottman et al. (2001) concluded that facial expressions of "anger, disgust, contempt, sadness, and fear, and the distinction between unfelt happiness and Duchenne [real] smiles" appear to be important in predicting relational outcomes (p. 56). Their results also suggest that men's facial expressions may have more impact on relational outcomes than women's facial expressions. More important, facial expressions of discrete emotions seem to have the power to affect outcomes over time, presumably because patterns of facial expression (and perhaps emotional experience) tend to become habitual within relationships and are repeatedly used across different conflict episodes.

The idea that patterns of behavior related to emotion become habitual in relationships is a key component of Gottman's (1994) cascade model, which is sometimes referred to as the model of the "four horsemen of the Apocalypse." There are two interrelated cascades. The first of these, the outcome cascade, involves the following sequence: becoming dissatisfied with the relationship, thinking about separation or divorce,

separating, and then divorcing. According to Gottman (1994), "there is a cascade of process variables that are related to the outcome cascade" (p. 110). These process variables include behavioral variables (such as complaining or withdrawing) as well as physiological and emotional variables. Specifically, Gottman (1994) posited that couples who are heading for divorce tend to exhibit the following patterned sequence during conflict episodes: "complaining and criticizing leads to contempt, which leads to defensiveness, which leads to listener withdrawal from interaction (stonewalling)" (p. 110). Gottman (1994) referred to these four elements as the aforementioned "four horsemen."

According to Gottman, expressions of contempt and disgust are two of the most corrosive negative behaviors. Disgust is typically communicated by "sounding fed up, sickened, and repulsed" (Gottman, 1994, p. 24). For example, Kevin might tell Kate, "I can't listen to this anymore," or Kate might tell Kevin, "You make me sick." Contempt, which implies superiority, is expressed through "any insult, mockery, or sarcasm or derision, of the other person. It includes disapproval, judgment, derision, disdain, exasperation, mockery, put downs, or communicating that the other person is absurd or incompetent" (Gottman, 1994, p. 24). Saying "you're acting psychotic," "you don't know what you are doing," or "you just don't get it" are examples of verbal expressions of contempt. Nonverbal expressions of disgust and contempt, which may involve becoming silent, looking away from someone, furrowing one's brow, and looking astonished (Scherer & Wallbott, 1994), may also be evident. Indeed, Gottman (1994) argued that even "subtle facial expressions of disgust and contempt are quite powerful" (p. 25) and can trigger a sequence leading from contempt to defensiveness and then to stonewalling. Stonewalling, which according to Gottman is an especially serious sign of relational decline, occurs when partners withdraw from the conflict and stop listening to one another. Gottman predicts that couples will divorce if stonewalling persists.

This series of negative expressions—complaining/criticizing, showing contempt, becoming defensive, and stonewalling—is often caused or exacerbated by emotional flooding. Emotional flooding occurs when people become "surprised, overwhelmed, and disorganized" by their partner's negative behavior, leading to a state of diffused physiological arousal that is often marked by increased heart rate, perspiration, warm temperature, and heightened blood pressure (Gottman, 1994, p. 21). This emotional and physiological state makes it difficult for people to listen to their partners and process information accurately. Instead, people are often focused on alleviating their negative emotions, either by attacking the partner, defending themselves, or withdrawing from the situation. Fortunately, expressions of positive emotion can act as buffers against flooding. So if Kevin tells Kate, "I'm only getting upset because I love you so much," this type of expression could prevent or alleviate emotional flooding.

Of course, not all couples engage in conflict that follows the sequence of the four horsemen of the Apocalypse. Some couples can break destructive patterns and engage in more constructive modes of conflict management. Gottman (1993) described four couple types, which are determined, in part, by the ratio of positive to negative persuasive attempts and the amount and timing of such persuasive attempts. According to Gottman (1993), three of these four couple types are stable while the fourth is unstable and likely to divorce. The three stable couple types are volatile, validating, and conflict-avoiding. Each of these types of marriages is characterized by a 5:1 ratio of positive to negative persuasion attempts. The *volatile* couple is highest in emotional expressivity. These couples are most likely to engage in conflict and try to persuade one another regarding their points of view. By contrast, the *conflict-avoiding* couple is lowest in emotional expressivity and likely to accommodate one another or avoid conflict. *Validating* couples fall between the volatile and conflict-avoiding couples—they are moderately expressive and engage in moderate amounts of conflict. From these descriptions, some might be tempted to conclude that a validating marriage is the most desirable since volatile marriages may have too much conflict while conflict-avoiding marriages may have too little. According to Gottman (1993), however, this is not the case. He notes that "each type of marriage is likely to represent a necessary adaptation that ensures a stable marriage, each

with its own rewards and costs and each with its own comfort level of emotional expression" (p. 67). In other words, the actual amount of conflict is not the determining factor in marital stability. Stability is determined by the presence of more positive than negative statements, as long as they occur in at least a 5:1 ratio.

Unstable marriages, in contrast, are marked by ratios of about 0.8:1. In other words, on average, people in unstable relationships use about as many negative expressions as positive expressions. Given that negative expressions, which may occur in the form of complaints, criticisms, contemptuous remarks, or defensiveness, can lead to emotional flooding, it is no surprise that a 0.8:1 ratio would be unhealthy in a marriage. By allowing positive expressions to outweigh negative expressions, couples can negotiate and persuade one another without risking emotional flooding and the attendant cascade of contempt, defensiveness, and stonewalling.

An Expectancy Violations Perspective

People can also break negative cycles of conflict communication by engaging in positive, compensatory behavior in response to a partner's hostility. Expectancy violations theory provides a framework for explaining sequences of communicative behavior, including reciprocity and compensation, which occur in response to unexpected events. According to Burgoon's expectancy violations theory (Burgoon & Hale, 1988; Burgoon, Stern, & Dillman, 1995), people hold both predictive and prescriptive expectancies for people's behavior. Predictive expectancies involve knowing how a person tends to act in a particular situation. For instance, based on his past behavior, Kate might expect Kevin to kiss her goodbye as they both depart for work in the morning. Prescriptive expectancies, on the other hand, involve expecting someone to conform to general rules of social appropriateness. So once at work Kate might expect to shake hands with a new business associate upon meeting her for the first time.

According to Burgoon's (1983, 1993) theory, as well as Levitt's (1991; Levitt, Coffman, Guacci-Franco, & Loveless, 1994) social expectations model, expectations help regulate both emotion and behavior. When someone's behavior is perceived to exceed expectations, positive emotions and reciprocal behavior likely follow (e.g., Kevin gives Kate an especially nice kiss; she feels positive affect and hugs him longer than usual). In contrast, when someone's behavior is perceived to fall short of expectations, negative emotions likely follow (e.g., Kate feels slighted when her new co-worker ignores her extended hand). In some cases, people compensate in response to negative expectancy violations; in other cases, they reciprocate.

Whether people compensate or reciprocate depends, at least in part, on the reward value of the person who committed the expectancy violation (e.g., how attractive, how high or low in status). If the person is unrewarding, then her or his negative behavior will likely be reciprocated (e.g., Kate's new co-worker is an intern, so she frowns and looks away when her extended hand is ignored). If the person is highly rewarding, then her or his negative behavior will likely be compensated, at least initially (e.g., Kate's new co-worker is of high status, so Kate smiles despite feeling snubbed when her attempt to shake hands fails). However, if the rewarding person persists in exhibiting negative behavior, the receiver is likely to experience increased negative affect and eventually reciprocate.

Expectancy violations theory is applicable to conflict situations. Afifi and Metts (1998) had people remember something a friend or romantic partner did that violated their expectations. People listed some positive expectancy violations, such as *relationship escalation* (e.g., saying "I love you"), *acts of devotion* (e.g., helping the partner through a crisis), and *gestures of inclusion* (e.g., extending an invitation to meet one's family). Negative expectancy violations included *criticism or accusations* (e.g., insulting someone), *relationship de-escalation* (e.g., spending less time together), *transgressions* (e.g., being unfaithful or deceitful), and *acts of disregard* (e.g., forgetting an important occasion). Obviously, these negative expectancy violations can also lead to conflict as well as emotions such as anger and guilt.

Drawing from expectancy violations theory, Bachman and Guerrero (in press-a) predicted that rewardingness and negative valence (i.e., the degree to which the event negatively violated expectancies) would associate with communicative responses to hurtful events. In line with the theory, they found that people were most likely to use integrative communication when the relationship was rewarding and the event constituted a relatively mild transgression. Conversely, when people rated their relationships as unrewarding prior to the hurtful event, they tended to report using de-escalation, distributive communication, and vengeful behavior. When people perceived the hurtful event as a severe relational transgression, they were more likely to report using de-escalation, distributive communication, and active distancing. Perhaps surprisingly, Bachman and Guerrero (in press-a) also found people report a tendency toward using constructive responses (e.g., integrative communication and loyalty) rather than destructive responses (e.g., de-escalation, vengeful behavior, and active distancing) when they were deeply hurt by the partner's actions. Similarly, Lukasik (2001) found that adolescents who were deeply hurt by something a friend said or did during conflict were more likely to forgive the friend. These findings may indicate that people tend to be the most hurt when someone they care about makes cruel remarks or engages in relational transgressions toward them; because they care about the errant partner, they may attempt to use constructive rather than destructive communication. Such an explanation is consistent with principles from expectancy violations theory, which suggest that people are more likely to respond to negative expectancy violations positively when the violator is rewarding.

Despite this tendency, the predominant pattern is to reciprocate negative behavior (Burgoon et al., 1995). This may be because of the negative emotions that ensue when someone fails to meet expectations. So if Kevin expects Kate to help entertain his friends when they come over to watch football, he will likely become angry if she goes upstairs and ignores them. In cases such as this, the same behavior that produces an expectancy violation also produces an aversive emotional response, which in turn could lead to conflict and negative behavior, such as defensiveness or accusations. Rusbult, Drigotas, and Verette (1994) claimed that it is very difficult for people to accommodate their partners and break negative cycles of behavior when they are experiencing negative emotion.

Of course, within the context of conflict interaction, the threshold for what counts as an expectancy violation may shift. Angry words and harsh vocal tones may be expected during conflict even though they are unexpected in other contexts. For couples in distressed relationships, it may become increasingly difficult to violate one another's expectations during the course of a conflict because negative spirals of behavior are expected. During conflict, behaviors such as speaking in a neutral tone, giving the partner a compliment, or failing to respond to a personal insult may sometime violate expectations more than negative behaviors. Thus, a starting point for research on conflict from an expectancy violations framework may be to determine what behaviors typically constitute positive and negative violations during conflict. Behaviors that are perceived to violate expectations positively may help stop destructive cycles of communication.

A Communication Competence Perspective

Being able to prevent or end cycles of negative behavior requires social skill. Not surprisingly, then, considerable research has investigated conflict from a communication competence or social skills perspective. For example, Canary and his colleagues advanced the competence model of conflict to help explain associations between perceptions of conflict strategies, communication competence, and relational outcomes such as satisfaction and trust (Canary & Cupach, 1988; Canary, Cupach, & Serpe, 2001; Canary & Spitzberg, 1987, 1989, 1990; Cupach, 1982; see also Canary & Lakey, Chapter 7 in this volume). Communication competence has been defined in terms of appropriateness and effectiveness (Spitzberg & Cupach, 1984). Communication is effective when problems are solved and goals are accomplished. Communication is appropriate when people adhere to situational or relational rules that dictate the proper, socially polite way of behaving. Often, there is a tension between effectiveness and appropriateness (Canary et al., 2001). Accomplishing a goal sometimes involves putting one's own needs and opinions ahead of the partner, whereas being appropriate sometimes entails accommodating the wishes of the partner even if it means losing the argument.

Conflict strategies differ in the extent to which they are judged as effective and appropriate. The integrative (or collaborating) strategy includes tactics such as agreeing with the partner, collaborating to come up with new solutions, and listening to the partner's ideas while also expressing one's own viewpoint. Research in both interpersonal and organizational contexts suggests that the integrative strategy is perceived as both effective and appropriate (e.g., Canary et al., 2001; Canary & Spitzberg, 1987; Gross & Guerrero, 2000; Gross, Guerrero, & Alberts, 2004). The distributive (or competing) strategy includes tactics such as personal attacks, yelling, refusing to consider the partner's arguments, and coercing the partner. This strategy is generally evaluated as ineffective and inappropriate in interpersonal contexts (Canary & Cupach, 1988; Canary & Spitzberg, 1987, 1989, 1990), but at least one study suggests that distributive strategies are perceived as effective but inappropriate in task-oriented contexts (e.g., Gross et al., 2004). The avoidant (or nonconfrontational) strategy, which includes tactics such as avoiding the topic or changing the subject, is often judged to be both ineffective and inappropriate (Cupach, 1982; Gross et al., 2004; Spitzberg et al., 1994). Finally, the accommodating (or obliging) strategy, which includes tactics such as giving in to the partner and playing down disagreements, has been shown to be ineffective but appropriate (Gross & Guerrero, 2000). Research has also demonstrated that perceptions of competence mediate the associations between various conflict strategies and relational outcomes such as trust and satisfaction (e.g., Canary et al., 2001). So if Kevin uses integrative tactics, Kate will judge him to be more appropriate and effective, and therefore she is likely to be more satisfied in her relationship with him.

Although the competence model does not include emotion, other research suggests that having emotional skills related to decoding and encoding enhances relational satisfaction. Gottman and Porterfield (1981) concluded that the ability to decode emotions accurately is even more important for relational satisfaction than is the ability to encode emotions. Similarly, Burleson and Denton (1997) showed a link between decoding ability and relational satisfaction for happy couples, and Sabatelli, Buck, and Kenny (1986) found wives to be less likely to have marital complaints when their husbands were skilled at decoding their emotions. In a particularly inventive study, Noller and Ruzzene (1991) videotaped distressed and happy couples engaging in conflict. Each of the relational partners then privately identified the emotions they had been experiencing during the conflict and guessed what their partners had been experiencing. The happy couples were more accurate in identifying one another's emotions than were the distressed couples. Noller's (1980) research also suggests that happy couples (and husbands in particular) are less likely to decode neutral or positive expressions as negative expressions than are distressed couples.

Interpreting neutral or positive expressions inaccurately may have a profound effect on the trajectory of a conflict episode. Gaelick, Bodenhausen, and Wyer (1985) examined patterns of reciprocity within conflict interactions. When people perceived their partners to be expressing affectionate emotion, they tended to use more positive behaviors; when people perceived their partners to be expressing hostile emotions, they tended to use more negative behaviors. The catch, however, was that people tended to decode hostile emotions more accurately than affectionate emotions, making negative spirals more likely. Thus, the interpretation of a person's facial expressions and vocal tone may be more important than the behavior itself. Being able to decode positive and neutral expressions accurately may be critical in preventing negative cycles and enhancing communication competence.

Encoding ability may also play a key role in determining the types of behaviors people use during conflict situations. People who are good at constructing logical arguments are less likely to use verbal aggression during conflict (Infante, 1987; Infante et al., 1989; Infante et al., 1990). Similarly, individuals who are unskilled in expressing emotions may resort to aggressive communication, including nonverbal displays of disapproval or contempt. Research also suggests that individuals who lack communication skills are more likely to use violence than their socially skilled counterparts (e.g., Christopher & Lloyd, 2001; Infante et al., 1990) and to find themselves in downward spirals of negative emotion and behavior during conflict situations (e.g., Burman, John, & Margolin, 1992; Margolin & Wampold, 1981).

Connecting Theory to Practice

Research related to these three theoretical frameworks provides useful information for practitioners. First, it is important for couples to understand that conflict is an emotion-laden process. Thus, partners should expect one another to display some negative affect when discussing contentious issues. Second, when emotions become intense, postponing the discussion may be a good option. As Gottman's research demonstrates, emotional flooding leads to less productive communication and more negative spirals of behavior. Third, couples should be aware of the four horsemen of the Apocalypse—criticism/complaints, disgust/contempt, defensiveness, and stonewalling. Teaching couples how to express complaints without personally attacking one another may help prevent the cascade from developing, especially because contempt and defensiveness are often reactions to insults. Fourth, Gottman's 5:1 ratio emphasizes how important it is for couples to engage in more positive than negative behavior during conflict interaction. Couples may be well advised to keep track of their behaviors mentally, and to make adjustments when their ratio is skewed toward negativity.

Fifth, work from a communication competence perspective suggests that couples can break cycles of negative behavior and increase their ratio of positive to negative expressions by engaging in integrative communication. Such communication is typically perceived as both appropriate and effective. Therefore, individuals may benefit from training focused on integrative tactics such as problem solving, validating the partner, and learning to argue one's positions without personally attacking the partner. In some cases, integrative communication may positively violate expectations during conflict situations, leading to increased positive emotion and favorable impressions. Sixth, couples may also benefit from training in decoding. Being able to decode neutral and positive emotions accurately (rather than mistaking them for negative expressions) appears to be a particularly critical skill. Gottman's (1994) work also suggests that it is imperative that partners be able to put themselves in the other's position by creating mental maps of the partner's thoughts and feelings and then verifying that the partner feels a particular way. Too often, relational partners think they know one another's thoughts and feelings when in truth they are making misattributions. A helpful exercise might be for couples to review tapes to determine when they decode each other's emotions and motives incorrectly. Such an exercise could shed light on the true underpinnings of conflict. For example, if Kevin understands that Kate is yelling because she is frustrated rather than because she thinks he is lazy, he might be less defensive and more supportive.

CRITICAL ISSUES FOR FUTURE RESEARCH

Thus far, scholars have spent considerable energy studying both conflict and emotion, but with the exception of Gottman's cascade model, little work has directly investigated the links between communication and emotion within relational conflict. Indeed, Retzinger (1991) argued that specifying the presence or absence of emotions such as contempt and anger may help "untangle the knot of protracted conflict. Both internal arousal and the communicative aspects of emotional states need to be assessed as they occur in interaction" (pp. 60–61), yet few investigations have examined moment-by-moment patterns of emotion in conflict. Jones and Bodtker (2001) also noted that the lack of attention given to emotion in research on conflict mediation is surprising. However, work on communicative responses to emotions such as anger, jealousy, hurt, and guilt, along with the three theoretical perspectives we discussed, provides a foundation for examining the role emotion plays in conflict. Next, we outline critical issues for future research.

Issue 1: Identifying Joint Causes of Emotion and Conflict

An analysis of the precipitating events that lead to emotions such as anger, jealousy, hurt,

and guilt reinforces the notion that emotions, like conflict, are rooted in issues related to fairness, identity, and relationships (Jones, 2000). Perceptions of inequity can lead to anger, feelings of jealousy or hurt can lead one to feel undervalued within a relationship, and a partner's contemptuous expression can lead to defensiveness. Since the same events that cause emotions often instigate or exacerbate conflict, it is hard to imagine relational partners engaging in an emotionless exchange during conflict. Indeed, emotions are likely a key force, if not the primary force, guiding behaviors during conflict interaction. It is essential, then, that scholars understand how various precipitating events provide different emotional starting points for conflict.

Although emotion and conflict may be precipitated by a particular event (or events), conflicts often get off track because people become emotionally flooded, preoccupied with their own thoughts, and focused on "winning" an argument at all cost. Instead of staying on the issue, couples may bring up old problems or attack one another's identities rather than one another's positions. Thus, being able to identify the precipitating event that initially caused the emotion is imperative if researchers and practitioners want to determine whether a couple has been able to stay focused on the conflict-inducing issue. If couples are to manage conflict productively, different courses of action may be required depending on the underlying cause of emotional reactions. For example, if the conflict is about a fairness issue, couples may need to discuss their perceptions and negotiate relational rules. If, on the other hand, the conflict is primarily about an identity issue, relational partners may need to engage in face-saving activities. Identifying the causes of goal interference and negative emotion may bring couples one step closer to managing the issues that cause them distress during conflict.

Issue 2: Recognizing That Conflict Communication Often Constitutes an Emotional Response

The connection between emotion and conflict is obvious when examining the types of communicative responses associated with emotions such as anger, jealousy, and hurt. Various conflict scholars have identified two major dimensions underlying conflict behavior, with

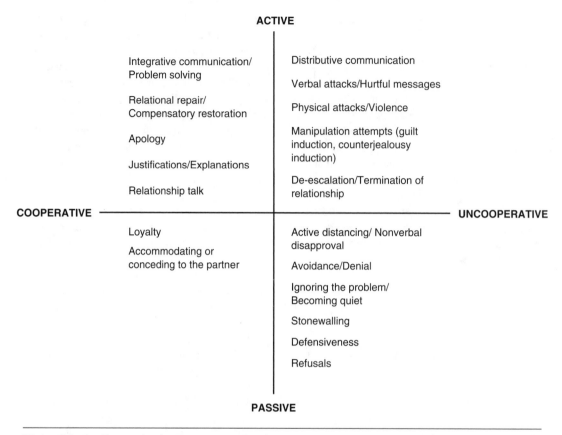

Figure 3.2   Communicative Responses to Emotion

these dimensions approximating two continua—a passive/active or direct/indirect continuum, and a cooperative/uncooperative or constructive/destructive dimension (e.g., Klein & Johnson, 1997; Rahim, 1986). Similarly, scholars studying emotions such as anger, jealousy, hurt, and guilt have identified communicative responses that fit under these quadrants (see Figure 3.2). Work on communicative responses to emotion suggests that a number of factors, including goals, emotional intensity, emotional valence, the reward value of the relationship, and uncertainty, associate with how people react to emotion-eliciting events. These same variables may help predict how people respond to conflict situations, as may the specific emotions experienced during a given conflict episode. Thus, conflict scholars would be well advised to include such variables in their studies. Practitioners may be well advised to learn more about the patterns in their clients' relationships by

determining how they act when experiencing certain emotions during conflict (e.g., Kate attacks when frustrated, whereas Kevin withdraws). Before teaching people how to avoid destructive behaviors (such as defensiveness, hurtful messages, physical attacks, and stonewalling) during conflict, it may first be necessary for clients to recognize the emotional states that lead to such behaviors.

Issue 3: Determining How Emotions Connect to Perceptions of Competence During Conflict

Research has shown that conflict strategies characterized as direct and cooperative are most likely to be perceived as communicatively competent. In addition, perceptions of appropriateness and effectiveness appear to mediate the relationships between conflict strategies and relational outcomes such as trust, liking, control mutuality (e.g., how balanced power is), and satisfaction (e.g., Canary et al., 2001). Partners who use more integrative and less distributive strategies are perceived as more effective and appropriate communicators, which in turn leads to positive relational outcomes. The role that emotion plays within this process, however, is unclear. To some extent, it is likely that conflict strategies are judged as appropriate and effective based on the emotions they elicit. Integrative strategies may produce the most positive emotions (as well as the least negative emotions), which could lead to judgments of communication competence as well as increased levels of trust, liking, and satisfaction. On the other hand, the aversive emotions elicited by distributive communication may be a key predictor of negative relational outcomes, such as distrust and dissatisfaction. At a dyadic level, emotions may also vary based on the strategies used. Integrative strategies may lead to a joint experience of positive emotion, whereas distributive strategies may lead one partner to experience more positive emotion than the other. Finally, emotional skills, including encoding and decoding ability, may influence the types of conflict strategies that people use, with highly skilled individuals most likely to use integrative tactics.

Issue 4: Identifying Hurtful Messages That Exacerbate Conflict

During the course of a conflict, couples often make hurtful remarks. These remarks can move the conflict off course by causing increased negative affect. Take Gottman's (1994) cascade model as an example. Criticism and contemptuous statements are part of a larger pattern of behavior that leads to defensiveness and stonewalling in dissatisfied couples. Vangelisti's (1994; Vangelisti & Sprague, 1998) work on hurtful messages may add specificity to the cascade model by identifying specific types of verbal messages that are perceived as especially critical or contemptuous. For example, certain types of accusations (e.g., "you are psychotic"), expressed desires (e.g. "sometimes I wish I'd never met you"), and informative statements (e.g., "you sure weighed a lot less when we got married") may be particularly hurtful because

they are perceived as intensely critical or contemptuous. These types of messages could lead to emotional flooding, cycles of negativity, and stonewalling. Identifying messages that are especially hurtful would be helpful for practitioners, who could train clients to avoid using such messages.

Issue 5: Understanding the Role of Positive Affect in Conflict Interaction

The primary focus in this chapter has been on negative emotions experienced during conflict. Yet people can experience positive emotions such as happiness and affection during conflict. Indeed, Gottman's (1993, 1994) work suggests that satisfied couples manage to make more positive than negative statements during conflict interaction. Thus, the trick to managing conflict constructively may be to alleviate negative affect, and, ideally, to experience some positive affect during the conflict episode. Conflict behaviors that are active and cooperative (such as those listed in Figure 3.2) may not only be effective because they help couples tackle issues and solve problems, they may also be effective because they detract from negative emotion and in some cases even lead to positive affect. Cooperative behaviors may also facilitate rather than impede goals, and goal facilitation has been linked to happiness and love (Ellis & Malamuth, 2000). Moreover, Isen (1993) summarized research showing that positive affect promotes openness and creativity in problem solving and conflict negotiation. It is critical, then, for researchers to understand the types of emotions that are triggered by different conflict behaviors. This information would be useful to practitioners, who could then instruct clients on the types of behaviors that can change the emotional tone of a conflict episode.

Issue 6: Exploring the Role Guilt Plays in Conflict Interaction

Little research has examined guilt within conflict episodes, yet guilt may be the emotion that best captures the evaluative or moral dimension of both conflict and emotion. When conflict is caused by a relational transgression, one person may be cast in the role of the "guilty party" while the other person may be cast as a victim. These roles may then frame the conflict interaction. Guilty feelings may cause people to make amends or, ironically, to avoid conflict if they perceive that discussing the transgression will only further harm their self-image. Individuals who feel they have been treated unfairly may induce guilt in their partners by using the types of guilt-inducing techniques that Vangelisti et al. (1991) uncovered. The effects of guilt-induction techniques, however, are unclear. Although cast as an uncooperative tactic in Figure 3.2, guilt induction may sometimes be necessary to point out inequities and solve problems. Other times, guilt-induction techniques may be perceived as contemptuous or critical remarks that imply superiority or that unfairly judge the partner. When this is the case, aggressive behavior, defensiveness, or stonewalling may follow, leading to a destructive negative cycle (Gottman, 1994; Tangney et al., 1992). Clearly, more work is necessary to understand how guilt functions within conflict interaction.

Issue 7: Focusing on Residual Emotions

Guilt, as well as other emotions, may also surface or remain after the initial conflict episode has ended. If a conflict is not managed productively, the emotions that accompanied that conflict may stay with the interactants as a kind of residual emotional effect. So if Kevin believes that Kate treated him unfairly, and the conflict interaction did little to convince him that he would be treated more fairly in the future, Kevin may walk away from the interaction feeling frustrated and angry. Kate, in contrast, may walk away feeling defensive and defiant. These residual feelings are likely to be weaker than the emotions experienced during the actual conflict situation. Nonetheless, such residual emotions provide an affective backdrop for the next conflict interaction as well as the relationship in general. So Kevin may still harbor feelings of anger at the beginning of their next conflict episode, while Kate may still feel that she needs to defend herself against the charge that she is an unfair person. The ongoing influence of residual emotion may be one reason Gottman's (1994) ratio of 5:1 positive to negative statements is so important in differentiating satisfied couples

from distressed couples. Satisfied couples may exit conflict interactions with less negative residual emotion, leading them to feel better about themselves and their relationships over time. In addition, the negative emotions experienced in one conflict may be less likely to spill over into future conflicts. The old adage that advises people not to go to bed angry may have validity when applied to various types of negative emotions that occur during conflict. Research on residual emotion following conflict interaction could test this proposition.

Issue 8: Incorporating Culture Into Emotion/Conflict Models

The vast majority of research reported in this chapter comes from U.S. samples consisting mostly of people with European American backgrounds, yet scholars recognize that people from different cultures and co-cultures express and regulate emotions differently (Planalp, 1999). Thus, culture may serve as an important variable determining the level and type of emotional expression that occurs during conflict. In general, studies suggest that people from Asian cultures tend to express less emotion than people from other cultures. For example, Rimé, Corsini, and Herbette (2002) reported a study in which people from France, Japan, Korea, Singapore, and the United States recalled their most recent experience of an unpleasant emotion. Although there were no cultural differences in felt emotional intensity, people from Asian cultures reported significantly less emotional sharing than did people from France and the United States. Similarly, research has demonstrated that people from Asian cultures avoid conflict and mask negative emotions such as shame, anger, and disgust more than their Western counterparts (Barnlund, 1989; Matsumoto, 2000). In contrast, people from Arab countries tend to approach conflict and express negative emotions more than people from the West (Almaney & Alwan, 1982; Feghali, 1997). As these studies suggest, cultural differences in emotional expression could exacerbate conflict in cross-cultural or interracial interaction.

Indeed, some studies have already shown differences in conflict patterns based on culture. Chua and Gudykunst (1987) noted that individuals from low-context cultures, such as the United States, use more solution-oriented conflict behaviors, whereas individuals from high-context cultures, such as Japan, prefer nonconfrontational behaviors. In addition, in cultures that value interdependence and group identity, people may be unlikely to confront one another or express negative emotions (Kim & Leung, 2000). In regard to Asian cultures specifically, attention needs to be focused on nonverbal communication as a means of perceiving the indirect, emotional messages conveyed during conflict (see Doi, 1973; Okabe, 1983). As cross-cultural and multi-cultural interactions become increasingly common, research on the roles that emotion and culture play in conflict could go a long way toward building scholarly understanding of conflict styles across cultures.

Summary and Conclusion

When people are engaged in conflict, their communication is as much a function of the emotion they are experiencing as the arguments they are hearing or the situation they are facing. Research on specific emotions such as anger, jealousy, hurt, and guilt provides a foundation for understanding the variables that could affect how emotions are expressed with conflict interaction. Gottman's (1994) cascade model, Burgoon's (1993) expectancy violations theory, and Spitzberg et al.'s (1994) competence model also provide invaluable starting points for understanding how emotions function in conflict. Including emotion in theories on conflict communication will give scholars more explanatory power. Indeed, emotion acts as both a cause and a consequence of conflict communication, and may ultimately guide behavior and determine outcomes. During conflict, relational partners need to do more than manage their conflict behavior; they must also be able to deal effectively with the many emotions they are experiencing.

References

Afifi, W. A., & Metts, S. (1998). Characteristics and consequences of expectation violations in close relationships. *Journal of Social and Personal Relationships, 15,* 365–392.

Almaney, A., & Alwan, A. (1982). *Communicating with the Arabs.* Prospect Heights, IL: Waveland.

Andersen, P. A., Eloy, S. V., Guerrero, L. K., & Spitzberg, B. H. (1995). Romantic jealousy and relational satisfaction: A look at the impact of jealousy experience and expression. *Communication Reports, 8,* 77–85.

Bachman, G. F., & Guerrero, L. K. (in press-a). An expectancy violations analysis of factors affecting relational outcomes and communicative responses to hurtful events in dating relationships. *Journal of Social and Personal Relationships.*

Bachman, G. F., & Guerrero, L. K. (in press-b). Relations among apology, forgiveness, and communicative responses to hurtful messages: An extension of the interpersonal forgiveness model. *Communication Reports.*

Barnlund, D. C. (1989). *Communicative styles of Japanese and Americans: Images and realities.* Belmont, CA: Wadsworth.

Barrett, K. C. (1995). A functionalist approach to shame and guilt. In J. P. Tangney & K. W. Fischer (Eds.), *Self-conscious emotions: The psychology of shame, guilt, embarrassment, and pride* (pp. 25–63). New York: Guilford.

Baumeister, R. F., Stillwell, A. M., & Heatherton, T. F. (1994). Guilt: An interpersonal approach. *Psychological Bulletin, 115,* 243–267.

Berscheid, E. (1983). Emotion. In H. H. Kelly, E. Berscheid, A. Christensen, J. H. Harvey, T. L. Huston, G. Levinger, E. McClintock, L. A. Peplau, & D. R. Peterson (Eds.), *Close relationships* (pp. 110–168). San Francisco: Freeman.

Bodtker, A. M., & Jameson, J. K. (2001). Emotion in conflict formation and its transformation: Application to organizational conflict management. *International Journal of Conflict Management, 12,* 259–275.

Brainerd, E. G., Jr., Hunter, P. A., Moore, D., & Thompson, T. R. (1996). Jealousy induction as a predictor of power and the use of other control methods in heterosexual relationships. *Psychological Reports, 79,* 1319–1325.

Buck, R. (1979). Individual differences in nonverbal sending accuracy and electrodermal responding: The externalizing-internalizing dimension. In R. Rosenthal (Ed.), *Skill in nonverbal communication: Individual differences* (pp. 139–170). Cambridge, MA: Oelgechlager, Gunn, & Hain.

Burgoon, J. K. (1983). Nonverbal violations of expectations. In J. M. Wiemann & R. P. Harrison

(Eds.), *Nonverbal interaction* (pp. 77–111). Beverly Hills, CA: Sage.

Burgoon, J. K. (1993). Interpersonal expectations, expectancy violations, and emotional communication. *Journal of Language and Social Psychology, 12,* 30–48.

Burgoon, J. K., & Hale, J. L. (1988). Nonverbal expectancy violations: Model elaboration and application to immediacy behaviors. *Communication Monographs, 55,* 58–79.

Burgoon, J. K., Stern, L. A., & Dillman, L. (1995). *Interpersonal adaptation: Dyadic interaction patterns.* New York: Cambridge University Press.

Burleson, B. R., & Denton, W. H. (1997). The relationship between communication skill and marital satisfaction: Some moderating effects. *Journal of Marriage and the Family, 59,* 884–902.

Burman, B., John, R. S., & Margolin, G. (1992). Observed patterns of conflict in violent, nonviolent, and nondistressed couples. *Behavioral Assessment, 14,* 15–37.

Buss, D. M., Larsen, R. J., Westen, D., & Semmelroth, J. (1992). Sex differences in jealousy: Evolution, physiology, and psychology. *Psychological Science, 3,* 251–255.

Buunk, B. P. (1991). Jealousy in close relationships: An exchange-theoretical perspective. In P. Salovey (Ed.), *The psychology of jealousy and envy* (pp. 148–177). New York: Guilford.

Cahn, D. D. (1992). *Conflict in intimate relationships.* New York: Guilford.

Canary, D. J., & Cupach, W. R. (1988). Relational and episodic characteristics associated with conflict tactics. *Journal of Social and Personal Relationships, 5,* 305–325.

Canary, D. J., Cupach, W. R., & Messman, S. J. (1995). *Relationship conflict: Conflict in parent-child, friendship, and romantic relationships.* Thousand Oaks, CA: Sage.

Canary, D. J., Cupach, W. R., & Serpe, R. T. (2001). A competence-based approach to interpersonal conflict—A test of a longitudinal model. *Communication Research, 28,* 79–104.

Canary, D. J., & Spitzberg, B. H. (1987). Appropriateness and effectiveness perceptions of conflict strategies. *Human Communication Research, 14,* 93–118.

Canary, D. J., & Spitzberg, B. H. (1989). A model of perceived competence of conflict strategies. *Human Communication Research, 15,* 630–649.

Canary, D. J., & Spitzberg, B. H. (1990). Attribution biases and associations between conflict strategies and competence outcomes. *Communication Monographs, 57,* 139–151.

Canary, D. J., Spitzberg, B. H., & Semic, B. A. (1998). The experience and expression of anger in interpersonal settings. In P. A. Andersen & L. K. Guerrero (Eds.), *Handbook of communication and emotion: Research, theory, applications, and contexts* (pp. 189–213). San Diego, CA: Academic Press.

Cann, A., Mangum, J. L., & Wells, M. (2001). Distress in response to relationship infidelity: The roles of gender and attitudes about relationships. *Journal of Sex Research, 38,* 185–190.

Carpenter, S., & Halberstadt, A. G. (1996). What makes people angry? Laypersons' and psychologists' categorizations of anger in the family. *Cognition and Emotion, 10,* 627–656.

Christopher, F. S., & Lloyd, S. A. (2001). Physical and sexual aggression in relationships. In C. Hendrick & S. S. Hendrick (Eds.), *Close relationships* (pp. 331-343). Thousand Oaks, CA: Sage.

Chua, E., & Gudykunst, W. B. (1987). Conflict resolution styles in low- and high-context cultures. *Communication Research Reports, 5,* 32–37.

Clore, G. L., Schwarz, N., & Conway, M. (1994). Affective causes and consequences of social information processing. In R. S. Wyer & T. K. Srull (Eds.), *Handbook of social cognition* (Vol. 1, pp. 323–417). Hillsdale, NJ: Lawrence Erlbaum.

Cramer, R. E., Abraham, W. T., Johnson, L. M., & Manning-Ryan, B. (2001). Gender differences in subjective distress to emotional and sexual infidelity: Evolutionary or logical inference explanation? *Current Psychology, 20,* 327–336.

Cupach, W. R. (1982, May). *Communication satisfaction and interpersonal solidarity as outcomes of conflict message strategy use.* Paper presented at the annual meeting of the International Communication Association, Boston.

Daly, E. M., Lancee, W. J., & Polivy, J. (1983). A conical model for the taxonomy of emotional experience. *Journal of Personality and Social Psychology, 45,* 443–457.

Doi, L. T. (1973). The Japanese patterns of communication and the concept of *amae. Quarterly Journal of Speech, 59,* 180–185.

Dutton, D. G., van Ginkel, C., & Landolt, M. A. (1996). Jealousy, intimate abusiveness, and intrusiveness. *Journal of Family Violence, 11,* 411–423.

Ekman, P. (1978). Facial expression. In A. W. Siegman & S. Feldstein (Eds.), *Nonverbal behavior and communication* (pp. 96–116). Hillsdale, NJ: Lawrence Erlbaum.

Ekman, P., & Friesen, W. V. (1975). *Unmasking the face.* Englewood Cliffs, NJ: Prentice Hall.

Ellis, B. J., & Malamuth, N. M. (2000). Love and anger in romantic relationships: A discrete systems model. *Journal of Personality, 68,* 525–556.

Ellis, C., & Weinstein, E. (1986). Jealousy and the social psychology of emotional experience. *Journal of Social and Personal Relationships, 3,* 337–357.

Feghali, E. K. (1997). Arab cultural communication patterns. *International Journal of Intercultural Relations, 21,* 345–378.

Fischer, K. W., & Tangney, J. P. (1995). Self-conscious emotions and the affect revolution: Framework and overview. In J. P. Tangney & K. W. Fischer (Eds.), *Self-conscious emotions: The psychology of shame, guilt, embarrassment, and pride* (pp. 1–24). New York: Guilford.

Folkes, V. S. (1982). Communicating the causes of social rejection. *Journal of Experimental Social Psychology, 18,* 235–252.

Frijda, N. H. (1986). *The emotions.* New York: Cambridge University Press.

Frijda, N. H. (1987). Emotion, cognitive structure, and action tendency. *Cognition and Emotion, 1,* 115–143.

Frijda, N. H. (1993). Moods, emotion episodes, and emotions. In M. Lewis & J. M. Haviland (Eds.), *Handbook of emotions* (pp. 381–403). New York: Guilford.

Gaelick, L., Bodenhausen, G. V., & Wyer, R. S., Jr. (1985). Emotional communication in close relationships. *Journal of Personality and Social Psychology, 49,* 1246–1265.

Gottman, J. M. (1993). A theory of marital dissolution and stability. *Journal of Family Psychology, 7,* 57–75.

Gottman, J. M. (1994). *What predicts divorce? The relationship between marital processes and marital outcomes.* Hillsdale, NJ: Lawrence Erlbaum.

Gottman, J. M., Levenson, R., & Woodin, E. (2001). Facial expressions during marital conflict. *Journal of Family Communication, 1,* 37–57.

Gottman, J. M., Markman, H., & Notarius, C. (1977). The topography of marital conflict: A sequential analysis of verbal and nonverbal behavior. *Journal of Marriage and the Family, 39,* 461–477.

Gottman, J. M., & Porterfield, A. L. (1981). Communicative competence in the nonverbal behavior of married couples. *Journal of Marriage and the Family, 43,* 817–824.

Gross, M. A., & Guerrero, L. K. (2000). Appropriateness and effectiveness of organizational conflict styles: An application of the competence model to Rahim's conflict inventory. *International Journal of Conflict, 11,* 200–226.

Gross, M. A., Guerrero, L. K., & Alberts, J. K. (2004). Perceptions of conflict strategies and communication competence in task-oriented dyads. *Journal of Applied Communication Research, 32,* 249–270.

Guerrero, L. K. (1994). "I'm so mad I could scream": The effects of anger expression on relational satisfaction and communication competence. *Southern Communication Journal, 59,* 125–141.

Guerrero, L. K., & Afifi, W. A. (1999). Toward a goal-oriented approach for understanding communicative responses to jealousy. *Western Journal of Communication, 63,* 216–248.

Guerrero, L. K., & Andersen, P. A. (1998). The dark side of jealousy and envy: Desire, delusion, desperation, and destructive communication. In B. H. Spitzberg & W. R. Cupach (Eds.), *The dark side of close relationships* (pp. 33–70). Mahwah, NJ: Lawrence Erlbaum.

Guerrero, L. K., Andersen, P. A., & Afifi, W. A. (2001). *Close encounters: Communicating in relationships.* Mountain View, CA: Mayfield.

Guerrero, L. K., Andersen, P. A., Jorgensen, P. F., Spitzberg, B. H., & Eloy, S. V. (1995). Coping with the green-eyed monster: Conceptualizing and measuring communicative responses to romantic jealousy. *Western Journal of Communication, 59,* 270–304.

Guerrero, L. K., Spitzberg, B. H., & Yoshimura, S. M. (2004). Sexual and emotional jealousy. In J. Harvey, A. Wenzel, & S. Sprecher (Eds.), *The handbook of sexuality in close relationships* (pp. 311–345). Thousand Oaks, CA: Sage.

Guerrero, L. K., Trost, M. L., & Yoshimura, S. M. (2005). Emotion and communication in the context of romantic jealousy. *Personal Relationships, 12,* 233–252.

Hansen, G. L. (1991). Jealousy: Its conceptualization, measurement, and integration with family stress theory. In P. Salovey (Ed.), *The psychology of jealousy and envy* (pp. 211–230). New York: Guilford.

Hocker, J. L., & Wilmot, W. W. (1998). *Interpersonal conflict* (5th ed.). Madison, WI: Brown & Benchmark.

Infante, D. A. (1987). Aggressiveness. In J. C. McCroskey & J. A. Daly (Eds.), *Personality and interpersonal communication* (pp. 157–192). Newbury Park, CA: Sage.

Infante, D. A., Chandler, T. A., & Rudd, J. E. (1989). Test of an argumentative skill deficiency model of interspousal violence. *Communication Monographs, 56,* 163–177.

Infante, D. C., Sabourin, T. C., Rudd, J. E., & Shannon, E. A. (1990). Verbal aggression in violent and nonviolent marital disputes. *Communication Quarterly, 38,* 361–371.

Isen, A. M. (1993). Positive affect and decision making. In M. Lewis & J. M. Haviland (Eds.), *Handbook of emotions* (pp. 261–277). New York: Guilford.

Jones, T. S. (2000). Emotional communication in conflict: Essence and impact. In W. Eadie & P. Nelson (Eds.), *The language of conflict and resolution* (pp. 81–104). Thousand Oaks, CA: Sage.

Jones, T. S., & Bodtker, A. (2001). Mediating with heart in mind: Addressing emotion in mediation practice. *Negotiation Journal, 17,* 217–244.

Kim, M.-S., & Leung, T. (2000). A multicultural view of conflict management styles: Review and critical synthesis. In M. E. Roloff (Ed.), *Communication yearbook 23* (pp. 227–269). Thousand Oaks, CA: Sage.

Klein, R. C. A., & Johnson, M. P. (1997). Strategies of couple conflict. In S. Duck (Ed.), *Handbook of personal relationships: Theory, research, and interventions* (2nd ed., pp. 467–486). New York: John Wiley.

Kubany, E. S., & Richard, D. C. (1992). Verbalized anger and accusatory "you" messages as cues for anger and antagonism among adolescents. *Adolescence, 27,* 505–516.

Laner, M. R. (1990). Violence or its precipitators: Which is more likely to be identified as a dating problem? *Deviant Behavior, 11,* 319–329.

Lazarus, R. S. (1991). *Emotion and adaptation.* New York: Oxford University Press.

Leonard, K. E., & Roberts, L. J. (1998). The effects of alcohol on the marital interactions of aggressive and nonaggressive husbands and their wives. *Journal of Abnormal Psychology, 107,* 602–615.

Levitt, M. J. (1991). Attachment and close relationships: A life span perspective. In J. L. Gerwitz & W. F. Kurtines (Eds.), *Intersections with attachment* (pp. 183–206). Hillsdale, NJ: Lawrence Erlbaum.

Levitt, M. J., Coffman, S., Guacci-Franco, N., & Loveless, S. C. (1994). Attachment relationships and life transitions: An expectancy model. In M. B. Sperling & W. H. Berman (Eds.), *Attachment in adults: Clinical and development perspectives* (pp. 232–255). New York: Guilford.

Lukasik, V. J. (2001). *Predictors of the willingness to use forgiveness as a coping strategy in adolescent friendships.* Unpublished doctoral dissertation, Wayne State University, Detroit, MI.

Margolin, G., & Wampold, B. (1981). Sequential analysis of conflict and accord in distressed and nondistressed marital patterns. *Journal of Consulting and Clinical Psychology, 49,* 554–567.

Matsumoto, D. (2000). *Culture and psychology: People around the world* (2nd ed.). Belmont, CA: Wadsworth/Thomson.

Metts, S. (1994). Relational transgressions. In W. R. Cupach & B. H. Spitzberg (Eds.), *The dark side of interpersonal communication* (pp. 217–239). Hillsdale, NJ: Lawrence Erlbaum.

Mullen, P. E., & Martin, J. L. (1994). Jealousy: A community study. *British Journal of Psychiatry, 164,* 35–43.

Noller, P. (1980). Misunderstanding in marital communication: A study of couples' nonverbal communication. *Journal of Personality and Social Psychology, 41,* 272–278.

Noller, P., & Ruzzene, M. (1991). The effects of cognition and affect on marital communication. In G. Fletcher & F. D. Fincham (Eds.), *Cognition in close relationships* (pp. 203–233). Hillsdale, NJ: Lawrence Erlbaum.

Okabe, R. (1983). Cultural assumptions of East and West: Japan and the United States. In W. B. Gudykunst (Ed.), *Intercultural communication theory* (pp. 21–44). Beverly Hills, CA: Sage.

Omdahl, B. L. (1995). *Cognitive appraisal, emotion, and empathy.* Hillsdale, NJ: Lawrence Erlbaum.

Ortony, A., Clore, G. L., & Foss, M. (1987). The referential structure of the affective lexicon. *Cognitive Science, 11,* 361–384.

Pines, A., & Aronson, E. (1983). Antecedents, correlates, and consequences of sexual jealousy. *Journal of Personality, 51,* 108–136.

Planalp, S. (1999). *Communicating emotion: Social, moral, and cultural processes.* New York: Cambridge University Press.

Planalp, S. (2003). The unacknowledged role of emotion in theories of close relationship: How do theories feel? *Communication Theory, 13,* 78–99.

Rahim, A. M. (1986). *Managing conflict in organizations.* New York: Praeger.

Retzinger, S. M. (1991). *Violent emotions: Shame and rage in marital quarrels.* Newbury Park, CA: Sage.

Rimé, B., Corsini, S., & Herbette, G. (2002). Emotion, verbal expression, and the social sharing of emotion. In S. R. Russell (Ed.), *The verbal communication of emotions* (pp. 185–208). Mahwah, NJ: Lawrence Erlbaum.

Roscoe, B., Cavanaugh, L. E., & Kennedy, D. R. (1988). Dating infidelity: Behaviors, reasons, and consequences. *Adolescence, 89,* 36–43.

Roseman, I. J., Wiest, C., & Swartz, T. S. (1994). Phenomenology, behaviors, and goals differentiate discrete emotions. *Journal of Personality and Social Psychology, 67,* 206–221.

Rusbult, C. E. (1983). A longitudinal test of the investment model: The development (and deterioration) of satisfaction and commitment in heterosexual involvements. *Journal of Personality and Social Psychology, 45,* 101–117.

Rusbult, C. E., Drigotas, S. E., & Verette, J. (1994). The investment model: An interdependence analysis of commitment processes and relationship maintenance phenomena. In D. J. Canary & L. Stafford (Eds.), *Communication and relational maintenance* (pp. 115–139). San Diego, CA: Academic Press.

Russell, J. A. (1980). A circumplex model of affect. *Journal of Personality and Social Psychology, 39,* 1161–1178.

Sabatelli, R., Buck, R., & Kenny, D. (1986). Nonverbal communication in married couples: A social relations analysis. *Journal of Personality, 54,* 513–527.

Salovey, P., & Rodin, J. (1989). Envy and jealousy in close relationships. In C. Hendrick (Ed.), *Close relationships* (pp. 221–246). Newbury Park, CA: Sage.

Schaap, C., Buunk, B., & Kerkstra, A. (1988). Marital conflict resolution. In P. Noller & M. A. Fitzpatrick (Eds.), *Perspectives on marital interaction* (pp. 203–244). Philadelphia: Multilingual Matters.

Scherer, K. R. (1994). Affect bursts. In S. H. M. Van Goozen, N. E. Van de Poll, & J. A. Sergeant (Eds.), *Emotions: Essays on emotion theory* (pp. 161–193). Hillsdale, NJ: Lawrence Erlbaum.

Scherer, K. R., & Tannenbaum, P. H. (1986). Emotional experiences in everyday life: A survey approach. *Motivation and Emotion, 10,* 295–314.

Scherer, K. R., & Wallbott, H. G. (1994). Evidence for universality and cultural variation of differential emotion response patterning. *Journal of Personality and Social Psychology, 66,* 310–328.

Sereno, K. K., Welch, M., & Braaten, D. (1987). Interpersonal conflict: Effects of variations in manner of expressing anger and justification for anger upon perceptions of appropriateness, competence, and satisfaction. *Journal of Applied Communication Research, 15,* 128–143.

Shackelford, T. K., & Buss, D. M. (1997). Cues to infidelity. *Personality and Social Psychology Bulletin, 23,* 1034–1045.

Sharpsteen, D. J. (1991). The organization of jealousy knowledge: Romantic jealousy as a blended emotion. In P. Salovey (Ed.), *The psychology of jealousy and envy* (pp. 31–51). New York: Guilford.

Shaver, P. R., Schwartz, J., Kirson, D., & O'Connor, C. (1987). Emotion knowledge: Further explorations of a prototype approach. *Journal of Personality and Social Psychology, 52,* 1061–1086.

Shimanoff, S. B. (1984). Commonly named emotions in everyday conversations. *Perceptual and Motor Skills, 58,* 514.

Sillars, A. L. (1980). Attributions and communication in roommate conflicts. *Communication Monographs, 47,* 180–200.

Sillars, A., Roberts, L. J., Leonard, K. E., & Dun, T. (2000). Cognition during marital conflict: The relationship of thought and talk. *Journal of Social and Personal Relationships, 17,* 479–502.

Sillars, A. L., & Scott, M. D. (1983). Interpersonal perception between intimates: An integrative review. *Human Communication Research, 10,* 153–176.

Simonelli, C. J., & Ingram, K. M. (1998). Psychological distress among men experiencing physical and emotional abuse in heterosexual dating relationships. *Journal of Interpersonal Violence, 13,* 667–681.

Spitzberg, B. H., Canary, D. J., & Cupach, W. R. (1994). A competence-based approach to the study of interpersonal conflict. In D. Cahn (Ed.), *Conflict in personal relationships* (pp. 183–202). Hillsdale, NJ: Lawrence Erlbaum.

Spitzberg, B. H., & Cupach, W. R. (1984). *Interpersonal communication competence.* Beverly Hills, CA: Sage.

Stets, J. E., & Pirog-Good, M. A. (1987). Violence in dating relationships. *Social Psychology Quarterly, 50,* 237–246.

Sugarman, D. B., & Hotaling, G. T. (1989). Dating violence: Prevalence, context, and risk markers. In M. A. Pirog-Good & J. E. Stets (Eds.), *Violence in dating relationships: Emerging social issues* (pp. 3–32). New York: Praeger.

Tangney, J. P., Wagner, P., Fletcher, C., & Gramzow, R. (1992). Shame into anger? The relation of shame and guilt to anger and self-reported aggression. *Journal of Personality and Social Psychology, 62,* 669–675.

Vangelisti, A. L. (1994). Messages that hurt. In W. R. Cupach & B. H. Spitzberg (Eds.), *The dark side of interpersonal communication* (pp. 53–82). Hillsdale, NJ: Lawrence Erlbaum.

Vangelisti, A. L., & Crumley, L. P. (1998). Reactions to messages that hurt: The influence of relational contexts. *Communication Monographs, 65,* 173–196.

Vangelisti, A. L., Daly, J. A., & Rudnick, J. R. (1991). Making people feel guilty in conversations: Techniques and correlates. *Human Communication Research, 18,* 3–39.

Vangelisti, A. L., & Sprague, R. J. (1998). Guilt and hurt: Similarities, distinctions, and conversational strategies. In P. A. Andersen & L. K. Guerrero (Eds.), *Handbook of communication and emotion: Research, theory, applications, and contexts* (pp. 123–154). San Diego, CA: Academic Press.

White, G. L., & Mullen, P. E. (1989). *Jealousy: Theory, research, and clinical strategies.* New York: Guilford.

4

SOCIAL COGNITION APPROACHES TO UNDERSTANDING INTERPERSONAL CONFLICT AND COMMUNICATION

MICHAEL E. ROLOFF

Northwestern University

COURTNEY WAITE MILLER

Elmhurst College

Conflict seems to occur in most interpersonal relationships and especially those that are intimate (Argyle & Furnham, 1983). Although scholars opine that interpersonal conflict can be functional, empirical evidence indicates that its potential is not often realized. Individuals often use negative metaphors to describe their everyday conflicts (McCorkle & Mills, 1992), and intimates frequently regret the attacks and criticisms that they express to one another (Knapp, Stafford, & Daly, 1986). Arguments account for 80% of the variance in a person's negative mood (Bolger, DeLongis, Kessler, & Schilling, 1989) and negative affectivity arising from an interpersonal conflict often leads to sleep disruption the night of the disagreement (Brissette & Cohen, 2002). Some research suggests that the emotional effects of conflict can spill over to the following day (Bolger & Zuckerman, 1995; Gable, Reis, & Elliot, 2000)

and, although an individual's emotional response to other types of everyday stressors habituates with repeated occurrences, negative moods worsen with each successive day that an argument continues (Bolger et al., 1989). Arguing also can impact the nature of a relationship. An argument can reduce relational commitment (Knee, Patrick, Vietor, & Neighbors, 2004) and McGonagle, Kessler, and Gotlib (1993) found that the frequency of spousal arguing was correlated positively with marital instability. Arguments also can adversely impact relationships with other people not directly involved in the dispute. Riggio (2004) discovered in a sample of young adults that recollections of parental arguing were correlated negatively with the emotional quality of their current relationship with their parents.

Because of the negative consequences of arguing, disagreements can stimulate cognitive activity. Relationally threatening topics are a frequent focus of daily thoughts (Klinger, Barta, & Maxeiner, 1980) and, not surprisingly, individuals often mull over their disagreements in an attempt to make sense of them (Cloven & Roloff, 1991). This sense-making activity highlights the important link between cognition and interpersonal conflict. People think about the causes and solutions for their conflicts, and the nature of this cognitive activity can influence the future course and consequences of their disputes. By understanding how individuals mentally construe their disagreements, we could gain insight into why conflict is often dysfunctional and make recommendations for how the functions of conflict might be realized.

Appropriately, many conflict researchers have adopted a social cognition perspective to guide their research, and the goal of this chapter is to review their scholarship. As noted by Fiske and Taylor (1991), the object of social cognition research "concerns how people make sense of other people and themselves" (p. 12). With regard to communication, the goal of social cognition inquiry is to study "the organized thoughts people have about human interaction" (Roloff & Berger, 1982, p. 21). There are multiple theoretical frameworks that fall within the rubric of social cognition, and researchers have used them to explore a variety of conflict-related questions. Because of its vast nature, it is not possible to identify or review all of the literature in a single chapter. Hence, we have focused on the more popular approaches with a focus on describing the key constructs, methods, and findings.

We have organized our chapter to look at overarching issues addressed by interpersonal conflict scholars who research from a social cognition perspective. Ostrom (1984) noted, "The field of social cognition is concerned with determining the nature of social knowledge and with specifying the cognitive processes that mediate social behavior" (p. 28). Therefore, we begin by reviewing research focused on the relationship between social knowledge and interpersonal conflict. Then we turn to scholarship that explores the association between cognitive processes and interpersonal conflict. We end the chapter with a summary critique of the strengths and challenges associated with research in this area.

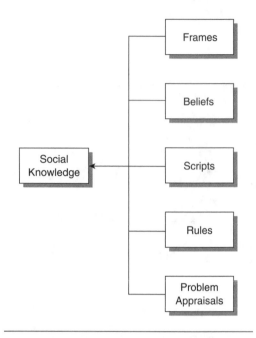

Figure 4.1   Forms of Social Knowledge

SOCIAL KNOWLEDGE AND INTERPERSONAL CONFLICT

Social cognition researchers assume that individuals have cognitive structures or organized impressions that they use to make sense of what is going on around them (Fiske & Taylor, 1991). Researchers who have investigated social knowledge about interpersonal conflict ask the following question: "What are the cognitive structures that people have regarding the features and behavioral dynamics of interpersonal conflict?" Figure 4.1 contains five forms of social knowledge that have been studied: frames, beliefs, scripts, rules, and problem appraisals. We examine the research associated with each form of cognitive structure and then provide a summary critique of this approach.

Forms of Social Knowledge About Interpersonal Conflict

By and large, scholars have focused on one form of social knowledge in isolation from the others and hence, there is not an integrative model that we could rely upon for ordering our presentation. Thus, we devised our own scheme that roughly moves from general knowledge about conflict to an analysis of the cues that people use to analyze a specific dispute. We start with frames, which are broadly focused on the characteristics of conflict, and then move to constructs that are more specifically focused on the causes and solutions of conflict, such as beliefs, scripts, and rules. We end this section by discussing research focused on how people use their knowledge to appraise a specific problem.

Frames. Pinkley (1990) argued that as a result of personal experiences, individuals have formed frames that reflect their impressions of how conflicts differ. She wrote,

> It seems likely, therefore, that conflict situations elicit a well-defined cognitive structure based on past experiences with conflict as well as present concerns and interests. These cognitive structures or interpretations of conflict (referred to here as *dimensions of conflict frame*) may then guide disputant behavior, strategy selection, outcome concerns, and evaluations of the other party. (p. 117)

Pinkley used multidimensional scaling to uncover three dimensions that ran through self-reported descriptions of everyday conflict. The first dimension was the degree to which a conflict was about issues within the relationship (e.g., relational maintenance, attitudes) or about task issues (e.g., money, property). The second dimension reflected the degree to which the conflict was emotional (e.g., anger, frustration, resentment, hatred) or intellectual (e.g., facts, thoughts). The third dimension focused on the degree to which the conflict could be resolved through compromise or required a winner-take-all solution.

By interviewing individuals currently involved in an actual conflict, Pinkley (1992) examined how the dimensions were related to other features of disagreements. Individuals using a relational, intellectual frame described their disputes as continuing for an extended time period and involving many issues. Individuals using an emotional, compromise frame reported their conflict suddenly emerged. Not surprisingly, those adopting an emotional, winner-take-all perspective described their conflict as particularly serious and intense. Finally, disputants often share the same frame with regard

to the relational/task and compromise/win dimensions but not the intellectual/emotional dimension.

Pinkley and Northcraft (1994) focused on framing during a conflict simulation. During a conflict, the disputants' frames converged. Better joint and personal outcomes resulted when disputants adopted task rather than relational frames and compromising rather than winner-take-all frames. Those who adopted an intellectual rather than emotional frame and relational rather than task frame felt that the dispute had been good for the relationship, and those with an intellectual rather than emotional frame were more satisfied with the outcome.

One of the most interesting recent developments in this area has focused on cross-cultural differences in conflict frames. Gelfand et al. (2001) examined the degree to which U.S. citizens and Japanese citizens differed in the conflict frames they used. Although members of both cultures used the compromise versus the win frame, unique dimensions emerged. In the U.S. sample an "infringement of rights" dimension emerged, and in the Japanese sample a "duty to repay obligations" dimension was discovered. This shows that members of different cultures have both shared and unique frames for understanding conflict dynamics.

Research on frames has provided useful information about the way people distinguish their disputes. From a practical viewpoint, this scholarship highlights the importance of identifying the manner in which individuals view their dispute. Because certain frames (e.g., relational and winner-take-all) seem to make conflict harder to resolve, a practitioner will need to find a way to shift the focus away from these frames.

Although initial research yielded interesting insights, limited scholarship has focused on conflict frames. Hence, a number of critical issues have not been addressed. Research does not inform as to the factors that might cause individuals to frame a conflict differently. For example, Pinkley (1990) discovered that mediators were more likely than disputants to view a conflict as involving relational issues and capable of being resolved through compromise, but it is unclear as to why. Because of their training, do mediators enter most conflicts with particular frames or, because of their experiences, are they able to discriminate among conflicts in terms of the extent to which they should be viewed as relational or task and compromise or winner-take-all? Without identifying the causes, it seems unlikely that we can predict which frames will guide behavior.

Although conflict frames have heuristic value, other researchers have identified general beliefs about conflict processes that offer different insights. We focus on that research next.

Beliefs. Some scholars have researched conflict-related beliefs. In doing so, they have focused on two categories of beliefs: assumptions and standards. We discuss each in turn.

Assumptions are "beliefs about the ways that relationships actually operate, as well as what men, women and one's partner are like" (Baucom, Epstein, Rankin, & Burnett, 1996, p. 72). The most frequent approach to studying assumptions focuses on irrational beliefs. Epstein and Eidelson (1981) noted that irrational beliefs "may create expectations (or demands) for a trouble-free relationship and decreased tolerance for the conflict inevitable in daily marital life" (p. 14). Based on the reports of marital therapists, Epstein and Eidelson initially identified three irrational beliefs. The first is "disagreement is destructive," which refers to the belief that arguing threatens a caring and loving relationship. The second belief is that "mindreading is expected" and dictates that intimates should be able to understand and address each other's needs and concerns without having to express them. The third is "the partner cannot change" belief and indicates that intimates are unable to alter their behavior to address relational problems. Not surprisingly, the degree to which couples in martial therapy held each of the beliefs was related negatively to their marital satisfaction, their estimated odds that therapy would be successful, their desire to work on their relationship rather than terminate it, and their desire to enter into marital rather than individual therapy.

In a subsequent study, Epstein, Pretzer, and Fleming (1987) examined the relationship between spouses' irrational beliefs and perceptions of their partners' problematic communication and attributions of relational problems to their partner. Consistent with their expectations,

each of the three irrational beliefs was correlated positively with husbands' and wives' perceptions that their partner is critical/defensive and with attributing relational problems to their partner's lack of love, malicious intent, behavior, and personality. For wives, perceiving their husbands as submissive was related positively to each of the three beliefs. But for husbands, the same correlations were not statistically significant. Regression analyses indicated that although irrational beliefs, perceptions of partner's communication, and attributions are correlated, they each account for unique variance in martial distress.

Eidelson and Epstein (1982) introduced two additional beliefs. "Sexual perfection" indicates that intimates should be perfect sexual partners. "The sexes are different" reflects the belief that men and women differ dramatically in their personalities and relationship needs. Using the Relational Belief Inventory (RBI) to assess all five irrational beliefs, they found that the degrees to which spouses endorsed the original three beliefs as well the two new ones were correlated negatively with marital adjustment. Some subsequent research failed to replicate this correlation for "mindreading is expected" (Bradbury & Fincham, 1993; Christian, O'Leary, & Vivian, 1994; Emmelkamp, Krol, Sanderman, & Ruphan, 1987) and "sexual perfectionism" (Bradbury & Fincham, 1993; Christian et al., 1994). Research conducted with non-U.S. samples finds that the strength of the correlations varies across cultures (Goodwin & Gaines, 2004; Moller & Van Zyl, 1991). However, when the five scales are combined into a single measure, relational beliefs are related negatively to relational satisfaction (Kurdek, 1991a, 1991b, 1993, 1999). Among wives, relational beliefs are related negatively with relational commitment (Fitzpatrick & Sollie, 1999).

Research has examined the degree to which irrational beliefs are related to conflict behavior. Metts and Cupach (1990) investigated the degree to which the association between the five relational beliefs and relational satisfaction was mediated by the manner in which a person responds to relational problems. Each of the beliefs was correlated negatively with responding to problems by voicing complaints and related positively to neglecting and exiting the relationship. A canonical correlation analysis indicated that believing that disagreement is destructive and the partner won't change were the best predictors of responses to problems. Finally, the researchers found that the relationship between irrational beliefs and relational satisfaction was mediated by problem responses.

Bradbury and Fincham (1993) examined the association between beliefs and the coded behavior of spouses discussing a marital problem. For husbands, none of the five beliefs were related to their interaction behavior. But among wives, believing their partners cannot change and that the sexes are different were correlated negatively with avoidance (e.g., denying there is a problem or shifting the topic), and believing in mindreading and the partner cannot change were correlated positively with negativity (e.g., hostility and rejection of the partner's position). Positive behaviors (e.g., being empathic) were not related to any of the beliefs among either sex. The researchers also investigated behavioral sequences. Among husbands, agreement with a composite belief measure was correlated positively with reciprocating the wife's negative actions and correlated negatively with responding to her negative action through avoidance. Among women, the composite measure was correlated negatively with the wife responding positively to the husband's negative behavior.

In a survey of gay and lesbian cohabiting couples, Kurdek (1991a) examined the degree to which a composite measure of the five beliefs was correlated with self-reported conflict behavior. He found that the belief measure was correlated negatively with positivity (e.g., focusing on the problem), correlated positively to withdrawal (e.g., refusing to talk further) and compliance (e.g., giving in), but not related to negativity (e.g., launching personal attacks).

Baucom, Epstein, Rankin, and Burnett (1996) focused on the relationship between the composite measure and self-reported functional and dysfunctional communication patterns (Sullaway & Christensen, 1983). For both men and women, endorsing relational beliefs was correlated negatively with constructive communication patterns, demand-withdrawal, and mutual avoidance/withdrawal.

Knee (1998) examined the relationship between the partner-won't-change dimension and two beliefs about relational growth (Knee,

Patrick, & Lonsbary, 2003). Growth belief entails an expectation that relational problems can be overcome and, by doing so, a relationship will grow. Destiny belief is a conviction that relational partners are inherently compatible or they are not and little can be done to change them. Not surprisingly, believing the partner will not change is correlated negatively with growth belief and correlated positively with density belief. Interestingly, growth beliefs help individuals withstand conflicts, especially when they initially have negative views of their partners and the conflicts are unresolved (Knee et al., 2004). Although not directly tested, the aforementioned could help identify why believing the partner will not change is related negatively to satisfaction.

Crohan (1992) examined the degree to which spousal consensus about three conflict beliefs predicted relational satisfaction over a 2-year period. The beliefs were similar but not identical to those identified as irrational: "(a) disagreements can always be settled if you just talk about them, (b) couples should try to avoid disagreements, and (c) disagreements in a marriage are healthy" (p. 93). The results indicated that the content of the beliefs related more strongly to marital satisfaction than the degree to which spouses shared the belief. Believing that conflict should be avoided was related negatively to long-term satisfaction, while believing that disagreements are healthy was correlated positively to satisfaction.

The second type of belief constitutes standards or "beliefs about what relationships and partners should be like" (Baucom, Epstein, Rankin, & Burnett, 1996, pp. 72–73). Whereas assumptions are thought of as statements of fact often tied to the current relationship, standards are idealized conceptions of relationships. Kurdek (1992) noted that the RBI, which is used to assess assumptions, contains items whose phrasings better suit standards rather than assumptions. To rectify this confound, he created parallel items that measured a belief as either an assumption or a standard. Composite measures of assumptions and standards were related negatively with relational satisfaction. He also found evidence that assumptions mediate the relationship between standards and relational satisfaction.

Baucom, Epstein, Rankin, and Burnett (1996) studied a different set of standards. They looked at relational standards focused on boundaries, control process, control outcomes, expressive investment, and instrumental investment. They created a composite measure that reflected the degree to which individuals endorsed relational-focused ideals (i.e., relational partners should have few boundaries, respect for each others' opinions, engage in egalitarian decision making, and have a great deal of expressive and instrumental investment). Endorsing such standards was related positively to dyadic adjustment, as was the degree to which the standards were being met in the current relationship. Hence, those who expected a great deal from their relationship were in relationships that were better adjusted. Furthermore, both variables were related positively to self-reports of constructive communication. However, they also were related positively to RBI scores and self-reports of two problematic communication patterns: demand-withdrawal and mutual avoidance/withdrawal.

In a follow-up study, Baucom, Epstein, Daiuto, et al. (1996) found that the degree to which individuals endorsed standards was less important than the number of unmet standards in their relationship and how upset they became when standards were not met. The greater the number of unmet standards and the more upset individuals were with unmet standards, the greater the likelihood that problems would be attributed to the partner or relationship, the causes of relational problems would be perceived as global and stable, and partners would respond to relational problems by exiting from the relationship.

Acitelli, Kenny, and Weiner (2001) used a much broader set of marital ideals and examined the degree to which partners rated the same ideals as being important and understood the degree to which they endorsed ideals. Similarity was correlated negatively with relational discord for men and women. Moreover, the degree to which the male understood his female partner was correlated negatively with the female's perception of negatively toned conflicts and relational tension resulting from conflict and was correlated negatively with the male's perception of the frequency of disagreements. The degree to which females understood the males' ideals was not correlated with any measure of relational discord.

Focusing on conflict beliefs provides useful insight into disagreements. They are related to other cognitive processes, a variety of conflict actions, and relational satisfaction. This literature provides useful insights into couples' therapy. Conflict beliefs reflect underlying causes for relational disputes. Hence, a couple's therapist should assess these beliefs prior to beginning therapy, and premarital counselors could use them as a predictor of future martial discord.

However, research does not provide insights into the origin of such beliefs. Are they related to one's family of origin? Individuals learn a number of lessons from their families of origin about relational commitment (Weigel, Bennett, & Ballard-Reisch, 2003) and it is possible that unrealistic beliefs could be passed on in a similar fashion. It is also possible that such beliefs are derived from actual relational experiences. A person may have encountered situations where a person of the opposite sex had different interests and views, disagreements that were destructive, or instances where a partner refused to change. In these instances, the unrealistic beliefs reflect an overgeneralization. Furthermore, it is unclear as to whether they apply to conflicts with people other than one's intimate partner. Certainly, some beliefs are phrased in a manner that suggests a general orientation toward conflict rather than a relationally specific orientation.

Although beliefs can inform as to some aspects of conflict, they do not inform as to the sequence of behaviors that people expect will occur during a dispute. Scripts attempt to do that, and we examine these next.

Scripts. Schank and Abelson (1977) described a script in the following way: "A script is a structure that describes appropriate sequences of events in a particular context. . . . Thus, a script is a predetermined, stereotyped sequence of actions that defines a well-known situation" (p. 41). The script concept seems to be an appropriate tool for understanding conflict episodes. Certainly, individuals have expectations about the kinds of verbal and nonverbal actions that typically take place during a disagreement (Resick et al., 1981) as well as the biological sex of the individuals who usually enact them (e.g.,

Kelley et al., 1978). However, the script concept carries with it more than behavioral or personal expectations; it suggests a sequence of actions. As noted by Schank and Abelson (1977), "A script is made up of slots and requirements about what can fill those slots. The structure is an interconnected whole, and what is in one slot affects what can be in another" (p. 41). Four studies have investigated the sequences of actions that individuals expect during an argument.

Although not basing their research entirely on the script concept, Harris, Gergen, and Lannamann (1986) conducted a study that has implications for it. They were interested in aggressive exchanges that escalated from an argument. They studied the response sequences that college students expected when a difference of opinion occurred between two male friends and when a husband criticized his wife's cooking. At several points in the scenario, participants were told how one of the actors responded, and at each point the response became increasingly aggressive and culminated in a physical attack. At each point, the respondents estimated the likelihood and desirability of a number of conciliatory and aggressive counter-responses by the partner. Regardless of the scenario, the data indicate that as a conflict unfolds, individuals generally see aggressive options as being more probable and desirable. Within the marital scenario, respondents felt that the wife would respond more aggressively than her husband and that her aggressive response is more desirable than his. For both scenarios, most respondents felt that the disputants would stop the physical violence before it escalated into a beating.

In a similar vein, Fehr, Baldwin, Collins, Patterson, and Benditt (1999) focused on anger scripts in close relationships. Anger scripts were characterized as "women's and men's likely reactions to various elicitors of anger as well as the kinds of response they would expect from a romantic partner" (p. 301). They asked individuals to indicate how angry they would be if their intimate partners engaged in one of several provocative actions, their responses to the provocations, and how their partners would respond to their reactions. Betrayal was the most anger-eliciting provocation, and women reported finding provocations of all types to be more anger producing than did men. Although

both genders expected that they and their partners would talk things over, women were more likely than men to expect that they would express hurt feelings and behave aggressively. Both men and women expected expressed anger would be reciprocated by the partner. However, when anger manifested itself in aggression, women were more likely to expect the partner would deny responsibility and men were more likely to expect that their partners would express hurt feelings, avoid them, or reject them.

Andrew and McMullen (2000) derived anger scripts from 109 stories provided by clients in psychotherapy. Each story was coded for the antecedents of the anger, how the anger-inducing event was construed, the expression of anger, the behavioral reactions of others to the anger expression, and the consequences. A cluster analysis of the coded behaviors yielded five scripts: (a) telling another about one's anger over a violated commitment yields a positive response and outcome; (b) another's imposition onto self causes an angry confrontation resulting in reciprocal anger; (c) another does not follow through on a commitment, which leads to the expression of anger and attributions of indifference that prompts conciliatory reactions; (d) a person does not express his or her anger; and (e) a hostile confrontation over unmet obligations initiated by verbal aggression that is reciprocated and results in long-term negative consequences.

Based on the script concept, Miller (1991) conducted two studies in which college students reported what they expected would occur in a conflict. In the first study, participants were asked to write out exactly what they expected would happen when a friend broke a promise. More than 50% of the sample expected the following actions would occur: (a) the conflict would start with an accusation rather than a promise, (b) the promise breaker would apologize rather than avoid taking responsibility, (c) the offended person would escalate the conflict rather than accept the friend's response, and (d) the conflict would be partially resolved. In the second study, respondents indicated in one of five conflict scenarios involving friends how likely a person in the scenario would be to enact a variety of conflict behaviors at the beginning, middle, and end of the scenario. Unlike participants in the first study, the majority in the second study felt that (a) the conflict would be initiated with a question, (b) apologies and excuses would be met with at least begrudging acceptance, and (c) the conflict would be completely resolved. Because the two studies used both different scenarios and methods of assessing the sequence, it is difficult to account for the difference in the findings. Few gender or scenario differences were observed in the expected sequence.

The script construct seems to offer practical insight into dealing with disagreements. Some individuals seem to have destructive expectations for how a disagreement should occur, and it is possible that these become self-fulfilling. In other words, the expectation of such behavior ensures that it will happen. In such cases, individuals may feel entrapped by the sequence, and practitioners need to convince them the sequence is indeed under their control rather than that of the script.

Intuitively, the script concept seems to be useful for understanding conflict episodes. However, it has generated little research. Hence, it is unclear whether there is a general conflict script that contains common actions and sequences or whether conflict scripts vary with particular people and relationships. Furthermore, it seems reasonable to assess whether conflict episodes conform to these expectations and, if they do, the degree to which individuals can control a sequence once it begins.

Within limits, scripts have provided insight into what people expect will occur during a disagreement. However, scripts do not address the issue of why this order is expected. Rule perspectives are focused on whether there are social conventions that might influence whether a conflict will occur and prescribe the actions that take place during a disagreement. We turn to those next.

Rules. Argyle and Henderson (1985) defined a rule as "behavior that most people, such as most members of a group, neighborhood or subculture, think or believe should be performed or should not be performed" (p. 63). In a sense, rules are a belief about normatively approved behavior. Researchers have focused on two types of conflict rules.

First, in the process of studying relational rules, researchers have uncovered rules that are specifically aimed at preventing disputes from

emerging by prohibiting undesirable behavior. Argyle, Henderson, and Furnham (1985) asked individuals to rate the importance of 33 common behavioral rules for 22 different types of relationships. Some form of conflict rules was rated as important for all 22 types of relationships and constituted 20% to 80% of the rules judged to be important for a particular relationship. The two rules most highly endorsed across the relationships focused on prohibiting behavior that could cause conflict: (a) partners should respect each other's privacy, and (b) partners should not discuss what is said in confidence with other people.

Second, other researchers have identified rules that focus on conflict once it has begun. Jones and Gallois (1989) had 16 marital couples from Australia describe rules they had followed or broken during an argument role play. This method generated a total of 145 rules that were reduced to 45 by using only those listed by at least three spouses. Another set of married couples indicated how frequently they followed each rule. Their responses were factor analyzed and five factors emerged: Consideration rules prohibit behaviors that either prevent partners from expressing themselves or that hurt the partner. Rationality rules manage the level of expressed anger. Specific self-expression rules keep the partners on topic and facilitate disclosure of specific information. Conflict-resolution rules encourage problem-solving activity. Finally, positivity rules mandate that partners should be rewarding to each other. Respondents indicated that the consideration and conflict-resolution rules were most important, followed by specific self-expression and positivity. Rationality was the least important. All of the rules but the positivity rules were judged to be more important for conflict than for other types of relational activity. Rationality rules were rated as more important in public arguments than in private. Conflict-resolution rules were more important in private contexts.

Honeycutt, Woods, and Fontenot (1993) studied the aforementioned rules with a sample of married couples from the United States. Although they used the 35 rules that had the strongest factor loadings in the study by Jones and Gallois (1989), only four factors emerged and only three were similar to those in the original.

The rationality, consideration, and specific self-expression (re-labeled conciseness) factors re-emerged, but the original conflict-resolution factor and parts of the consideration factor combined into a positive understanding factor. Positive understanding rules were rated as the most important, followed by consideration. Both rationality and conciseness were less important. Rationality was judged to be more important in public than in private contexts.

From a practical viewpoint, rules provide important insights into the social conventions associated with relational behavior and arguing. In that sense, they are prescriptions that, if obeyed, should reduce the destructive nature of some conflicts. Hence, conflict practitioners may find it useful to increase awareness of such rules as well as provide skills that will make it possible to obey them.

Research indicates that people have impressions of social rules that prescribe how an argument should unfold. Although useful, the research does not address several key issues: To what extent do individuals actually follow these rules? What specific behaviors do individuals see as conforming to or violating a given rule? Are there specific emotional results, such as guilt, that arise from violating a rule, and do individuals attempt some sort of restitution?

Thus far, the knowledge structures have been broadly cast to focus on general conflict processes. The last form is focused on the knowledge people use to appraise a specific conflict.

Problem appraisal. Witteman (1988) noted that "an interpersonal problem exists when an individual perceives a difference between a present state involving another person and a goal state involving that person" (p. 337). The existence of a problem does not always prompt a confrontation. Witteman (1992) posited that there are cognitive problem structures that are used mentally to represent the problematic situation and influence how individuals manage conflict. Witteman (1988) argued that a person's appraisal of a conflict reflects five judgments: (a) how a problem compares with previously experienced ones, (b) the nature of a problem-related goal, (c) uncertainty about the problem-related goal, (d) attribution of cause for the problem, and (e) feelings for the partner.

To test his notions, Witteman (1988) conducted two studies with undergraduate samples, one that was focused on actual interpersonal problems and a second that used a hypothetical interpersonal problem. The results were similar. The use of integrative strategies (e.g., expressing feelings) was related positively to three perceptions: the problem was unique, the goal was important and mutually shared, and the environment caused the problem. Distributive communication (e.g., insulting or threatening the partner) was related positively to negative feelings toward the partner, perceptions that the problem occurred frequently, and perceptions that the partner's actions caused the problem and were intended. Approaching the problem indirectly (e.g., waiting to confront the person until he or she is in a good mood) was correlated positively to feeling uncertain about the partner and relationship, having negative feelings toward the partner, and attributing the cause of the problem to the relationship or the partner. Finally, avoidant responses were promoted by attributing the cause to the relationship, uncertainty about the partner and relationship, and being uncertain about what to do.

In a follow-up study, Witteman (1992) focused on the relationship between the five impressions and self-reported conflict styles enacted in an ongoing conflict. Enacting a solution-oriented style was related positively to goal mutuality. Using a controlling style was correlated positively to attributing the cause of the conflict to the partner and having negative feelings toward him or her. Having a withdrawing style was related positively to uncertainty about what to do.

In some respects, Witteman's approach to problem appraisal provides a comprehensive perspective on cognition and interpersonal conflict. It incorporates a wide variety of constructs, and research generally supports the notion that problem appraisal influences conflict behaviors. From a practical view, problem appraisal research highlights the causes of constructive and destructive conflict behavior. For example, more positive approaches, such as solution-orientation, flow from perceiving shared goals whereas withdrawal is correlated positively with not knowing what to do. This finding suggests different interventions. To encourage positive responses, one should highlight areas of commonality. To avoid withdrawal, a practitioner should help identify effective responses to conflict.

However, the research does not address at least two important issues. First, it is unclear what factors influence how someone appraises a problem. Witteman's (1988, 1992) description of problem appraisals does not consider antecedents, and Witteman (1992) discovered very few statistically significant relationships between problem appraisals and conflict features (e.g., how a person found out about a relational problem and how long he or she waited to confront the partner about it). A number of possibilities seem plausible. Solomon and Samp (1998) found that the greater the power attributed to the partner, the less serious individuals perceived a problem to be and the greater the likelihood of conflict avoidance. In addition, Neff and Karney (2004) discovered that among wives, external stressors (e.g., work, school) increased their perception of the number of problems they perceived in their relationship and their tendency to blame their husbands for relational problems. Furthermore, Boon and Holmes (1999) discovered that individuals who had been primed to think about relational risks judged a relational problem as more serious and were more cautious when evaluating possible causes than those who had not been primed.

Second, research has not focused on the degree to which both disputants share the same problem appraisals. Indeed, research suggests that they may not (Kowalski, Walker, Wilkinson, Queen, & Sharpe, 2003; Schutz, 1999).

Summary. Researchers have identified a variety of knowledge structures that are focused on conflict. Some structures focus on the characteristics of conflict while others identify causes of conflict and the manner in which disagreements typically unfold or should be resolved. Because of the nature of knowledge structures, researchers rely upon self-report methods such as questionnaires, although some code personal narratives. The study of relational beliefs seems to be the best developed area. It has reasonably well-established instrumentation and a literature that links beliefs to conflict actions and relational effects.

COGNITIVE PROCESSES AND INTERPERSONAL CONFLICT

Langer (1978) argued that unexpected and negative events set off mindful activity. Because individuals expect their interactions to be positive (Kellermann, 1984), it is not surprising that researchers have found it useful to study the role of cognitive processes in conflict. Conflict researchers have studied how mental activity mediates the effect of other factors on social behavior and how cognitive processing can directly influence social behavior. Figure 4.2 contains five examples of mediating variables (expectation violation, attribution making, accommodation processes, influence goals, and sentiment override) and three direct influences (thinking, online processing, and storytelling). We examine each in turn and then provide a summary critique.

Cognitive Processes as Mediators

Research in this area is focused on the degree to which cognitive processes can account for an existing relationship between an independent and a dependent variable. As with forms of social knowledge, research in this area tends to focus on particular mediators rather than the set of all cognitive processes and, hence, there is no overarching model that discusses their interrelationship. We organize the presentation by first examining cognitive processes that affect how people perceive conflict (expectation violation) and its causes (attribution making) and then we move to perspectives that are related to how an argument will unfold (accommodation, influence goals, and sentiment override).

Expectation violation. Expectations are anticipated patterns of enduring behaviors (Burgoon, 1978). Individuals form expectations about a variety relational behaviors, including conflict management (Ebesu Hubbard, 2001), communication (Burgoon & Walther, 1990), sexual activity (Mongeau & Johnson, 1995), and parenthood (Belsky, 1985; Kach & McGhee, 1982). When individuals notice that an action falls outside the range of those that were expected, cognitive arousal results as they attempt to make sense of the situation (Burgoon, 1978). To some degree,

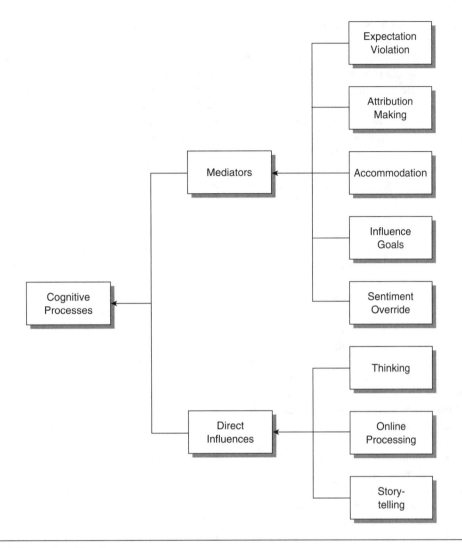

Figure 4.2   Cognitive Processes

the cognitive arousal is aimed at reducing a person's uncertainty.

Although research indicates that a variety of factors can violate relational expectations (Afifi & Metts, 1998) and cause relational uncertainty (Planalp & Honeycutt, 1985), conflict is among them. Afifi and Metts (1998) found that criticism/accusations, behavioral transgressions, and acts of disregard constitute negative relational violations. Conflict in particular is associated with frequent thought about how the partner feels about the relationship (Cate, Koval, Lloyd, & Wilson, 1995). Negative relational violations that stimulate relational uncertainty have been shown to decrease levels of interpersonal

attraction (Afifi & Burgoon, 2000), relational satisfaction, and feelings of closeness (Afifi & Metts, 1998). Furthermore, events that increase uncertainty can stimulate feelings of sadness and anger as well a desire to seek information from partners about the event (Knobloch & Solomon, 2003). However, the effects of negative expectancy violations may not be uniform. Hackel and Ruble (1992) studied women who had just given birth to their first babies and found that many reported that their husbands were doing less housework and child care than the wives had expected they would do. Violated expectations were correlated positively with negative feelings about the marriage, including greater conflict with their husbands. But these effects were confined to women who had discussed the father's role prior to giving birth, who were adaptable in assigning roles, and who were gender-role modern.

Research also suggests that behavior that conforms to or exceeds positive expectations has positive effects. Ebesu Hubbard (2001) found that intimates expect their partners will enact affiliative and non-dominating behavior during a disagreement, and she found that the degree to which they do so was related positively to martial satisfaction. Unfortunately, the study cannot shed light on whether this effect results from avoiding relational uncertainty.

Hence, research suggests that expectancy violations arising from events such as conflict can increase relational uncertainty and other negative events. From a practical view, a conflict practitioner might focus on modifying expectations so as to make them more realistic or on finding ways to increase awareness of expectations so that they are less likely to be violated.

We could not find a study that completely addressed the entire model, however. In other words, researchers need to demonstrate that violated expectations arising from a conflict stimulate relational uncertainty and, in turn, affect both behavior and relational quality. Furthermore, researchers have not investigated whether conflict behavior that conforms to expectations is related to uncertainty or if that which surpasses expectations might stimulate uncertainty but with a positive effect. Finally, because conflict is just one form of expectancy violation and one cause of relational uncertainty, it often is embedded in a questionnaire along with other forms. That makes it difficult to determine its unique effects.

In order to make sense of an expectancy violation, individuals may consider what caused the behavior, and the attributed cause could influence the course of the conflict. We consider attribution making next.

Attribution making. When encountering negative events, individuals often engage in attribution making aimed at understanding why the events occurred (Wong & Weiner, 1981). Not surprisingly, a spouse's negative behavior toward his or her partner generates more attribution activity than does positive behavior. Distressed couples are especially prone to make attributions for their partners' frequent negative behavior rather than their frequent positive behavior (Holtzworth-Munroe & Jacobson, 1985). The effect of the content of these attributions has generated a great deal of research testing what is known as the "attribution hypothesis." Fincham, Harold, and Gano-Phillips (2000) described the hypothesis as follows:

> Specifically, attributions that accentuate the impact of negative relationship events and minimize the impact of positive relationship events are associated with lower relationship satisfaction. Thus, for example, locating the cause of negative relationship events in the partner, viewing the cause as more stable and global and seeing the partner's behavior as intentional, blameworthy and reflecting selfish motivation are more likely among distressed partners than among their nondistressed counterparts. (p. 268)

There is substantial support for the hypothesis (Bradbury & Fincham, 1990), and current research suggests a bidirectional relationship between marital satisfaction and attribution making (Fincham et al., 2000).

Because of its potential for adverse consequences, conflict plays a central role in the link between attributions and relational quality. Research indicates that making maladaptive attributions promotes negative conflict behavior (Bradbury, Beach, Fincham, & Nelson, 1996; Davey, Fincham, Beach, & Brody, 2001; Fincham & Bradbury, 1992; Schweinle, Ickes, & Bernstein, 2002). Furthermore, some research suggests that this relationship is especially strong among wives in distressed marriages (Bradbury & Fincham, 1992; Miller & Bradbury, 1995). It is possible that these negative behaviors influence other perceptions that harm relationships. First, because negative conflict behaviors often lead to unsuccessful resolution (Sillars, 1980), they could decrease a couple's perception that they can effectively manage their disagreements. Indeed, Fincham et al. (2000) found in a longitudinal study of married couples that initially making maladaptive attributions reduced subsequent feelings of conflict efficacy, which predicted lowered marital satisfaction. Second, resolving a conflict often involves an element of forgiveness (Fincham, Beach, & Davila, 2004) that results from an apology (McCullough et al., 1998; McCullough, Worthington, & Rachal, 1997). When making maladaptive attributions, individuals may be prone to act negatively rather than to apologize. Furthermore, apologies may be met with skepticism rather than acceptance.

The literature on attribution is well developed. The methods, measures, and statistical analyses are sophisticated; key processes have been identified; and research has expanded into new areas. Furthermore, a number of scholars have noted the practical clinical implications of attribution making (e.g., Fincham, 1985).

However, the research has not addressed a key issue. It is unclear whether maladaptive attributions are always maladaptive. In other words, there may be instances where they are accurate reflections of a partner's role in the conflict and are necessary to prompt action. For example, McCullough, Fincham, and Tsang (2003) found that in the long term, individuals who made maladaptive attributions became more forgiving of their partners. The authors speculated that the internal attributions might have prompted a confrontation that caused the partner to become aware of the problem and to change. If so, internal attributions may stem from an individual's desire to see the partner change.

Although attribution making is focused on identifying the underlying causes of a negative behavior, when deciding a course of action individuals may also consider their commitment to the relationship. We examine accommodation processes next.

Accommodation processes. Even in the happiest relationships, partners often enact behaviors that cause each other displeasure (Birchler, Weiss, & Vincent, 1975). Some researchers have been interested in the reactions that individuals have to such negative behavior. In some cases, individuals respond in a destructive fashion and in others they seem to accommodate their partners by behaving constructively. Two approaches have been taken to studying accommodation.

First, using Kelley and Thibaut's (1978) independency theory as a frame, Rusbult, Verette, Whitney, Slovik, and Lipkus (1991) focused on the degree to which individuals accommodate their partners' destructive behavior. They defined accommodation as "an individual's willingness, when a partner has engaged in a potentially destructive behavior, to (a) inhibit tendencies to react destructively in turn and (b) instead engage in constructive behavior" (p. 53). Essentially, when encountering a partner's destructive behavior, an individual initially wishes to respond destructively by exiting or neglecting the relationship. But upon reflection, some individuals inhibit these responses and react in a constructive way by voicing their concerns or remaining loyal. Relational commitment is hypothesized to be a key predictor of accommodation. Individuals who are highly committed to their relationship are thought to consider broader issues (e.g., long-term relational objectives, past experience with the partner, and the partner's concerns) to a greater extent than those who are less committed. Hence, these individuals will shift their initial preference for self-oriented reciprocity to what is perceived to be good for the relationship.

A great deal of research has focused on accommodation. As hypothesized, after encountering a partner's negative behavior, individuals often consider responses that are more negative than their actual response. Furthermore, commitment is related positively to accommodation (Rusbult et al., 1991). It also mediates the relationship between a variety of other relational and individual difference variables and accommodation (Campbell & Foster, 2002; Rusbult et al., 1991). Moreover, commitment may stimulate relational growth through accommodative actions. An individual's commitment increases his or her accommodation. This, in turn, promotes trust and dependency in his or her partner (Wieselquist, Rusbult, Foster, & Agnew, 1999). In some cases, a person's accommodative responses are related to how empathic the partner is (Kilpatrick, Bissonnette, & Rusbult, 2002).

However, factors other than commitment may influence accommodation. The tendency to respond destructively occurs most frequently when individuals have limited time to consider a response (Yovetich & Rusbult, 1994). Finkel and Campbell (2001) found that the degree to which a person can control his or her impulses is related positively to accommodation and not related to relational commitment. Finally, individuals with an insecure attachment style respond more destructively to a partner's negative behavior than those with a secure style (Gaines et al., 1997).

Fletcher, Thomas, and Durrant (1999) advanced a somewhat different perspective on accommodation. They distinguished between cognitive and behavioral accommodation. Cognitive accommodation involves reinterpreting or re-labeling a partner's negative behavior so it is more benign. In a sense, this involves rationalizing the behavior so it is not damaging or distressing. Behavioral accommodation involves the degree to which a person avoids expressing negative reaction to the partner about his or her behavior. In this case, the person is withholding his or her thoughts rather than voicing them.

Research provides insight into how cognitive accommodation might occur. Murray and Holmes (1999) asked individuals to write essays about their partners' greatest fault and then create clusters of traits that describe their partners. Individuals attempted to embellish the virtues of their partners while minimizing their faults by (a) finding redeeming values in their faults, (b) using "yes, but" refutations aimed at minimizing the specific faults, and (c) linking virtues to faults in an integrative mental model. The degree to which they used these mechanisms allowed them to maintain positive illusions about their partners. These illusions have been shown to buffer a relationship from the conflict (Murray, Holmes, & Griffin, 1996).

However, integration may not always be effective. Showers and Zeigler-Hill (2004) focused on the process by which individuals form cognitive structures about their relational partners. They argued that some individuals compartmentalize their beliefs about their partner's attributes into categories that are largely positive or negative while others attempt to integrate positive and negative beliefs into the various categories. The researchers studied how these knowledge structures changed over time and how they were related to whether dating couples remained together. Over a year's time, individuals who initially had negative impressions of their partner but experienced infrequent conflict or individuals who initially had positive impressions of their partner but experienced frequent conflict changed their structures to be more integrative. Among individuals reporting little conflict, those whose cognitive structures became more compartmentalized were more likely to have broken up than those whose cognitive structures became more integrated. Among those experiencing frequent conflict, the reverse was true. Indeed, among individuals who initially held negative impressions of their partners, relational stability and liking for their partner increased among individuals who increasingly compartmentalized their impressions relative to those whose cognitive structures became more integrated.

Fletcher et al. (1999) investigated behavioral accommodation. They asked individuals about their negative thoughts about an instance of their partner's negative behavior and then coded the degree to which the thoughts were expressed during a confrontation. The higher the quality of their relationship (love, satisfaction, commitment), the less likely that individuals accommodated their partners by withholding their thoughts. This finding is consistent with Rusbult et al.'s (1991) perspective that relational quality should increase the likelihood of voice.

Thus, accommodation processes occur within relationships and seem to play a role in relational development. However, there are two perspectives of accommodation that make somewhat different assumptions about its nature. The concept of accommodation by Rusbult et al. (1991) includes remaining silently loyal to one's partner, which could involve the cognitive accommodation processes identified by Fletcher et al. (1999). However, Rusbult et al. (1991) argued that voicing one's opinion is also a part of accommodation, whereas Fletcher et al. (1999) posit that withholding one's opinions is accommodative. It is possible that there is an element of truth in both perspectives. Individuals who are highly committed to their relationships are generally inclined to confront their partners but choose to withhold complaints under certain conditions (Roloff & Solomon, 2002).

From a practical perspective, the key to resolving conflict in a functional manner is to maintain commitment to a relationship. To the extent that two individuals want their relationship to continue, their reactions to inevitable relational problems are constructive. This implies that practitioners need to highlight the rewards and investments that disputants have made in the relationship.

Certainly, relational commitment has an influence on how people deal with a conflict. However, researchers have also identified specific goals that impact the manner in which a confrontation occurs. We turn to that next.

Influence goals. Berger (1995) conceived of goals as "desired end states toward which persons strive" (p. 142). Scholars recognize that social influence is driven in part by goal achievement (Dillard, 1990), and conflict episodes should be no different. Stutman and Newell (1990) found that prior to a confrontation, individuals often rehearse and, in the process, develop both strategic goals (change the partner, vent frustration, maintain the relationship, seek retribution, seek information), and performance goals (present all of their arguments, be clear and organized, stand on the offensive). Not surprisingly, the most frequently reported goal was to influence the partner's behavior. Conflict researchers have taken three approaches to studying influence goals.

First, some researchers have adopted a role perspective. Two roles are inherent in the notion of an influence goal, change agent and change target. Sagrestano, Christensen, and Heavey (1998) argued that these roles imply different cognitive structures that prompt unique behaviors. Change agents often develop a scheme about relational problems that helps them understand it. The scheme contains information about the nature of the problem, its cause, their feelings, and what they want the partner to do. The information in the scheme provides information that they can use to make their case for change. At least initially, change agents may not be aware of the problem and, if so, they may not have a well-developed scheme upon which to rely. Hence, they are in a reactive state.

Some research supports this view. Canary, Cunningham, and Cody (1988) asked individuals how they would likely respond in a variety of conflict situations that differed in their goals. When individuals were attempting to change a relationship, they were less likely to criticize their partner and were more integrative (e.g.,

suggested alternative solutions, disclosed information) than when they were in a situation in which they were defending themselves from a partner's attacks.

Sagrestano et al. (1998) had spouses engage in a problem-solving discussion and examined the behaviors of individuals who were change agents or targets. When individuals confront their partners in an attempt to change them, they are more likely to describe the problem as related to the partner's behavior, attribute the problem to the partner, and suggest how the partner might change relative to what they say when the partner asks them to change. Individuals who were the target of a change attempt were more likely to seek information from the change agent about his or her perception of the problem.

It also is possible that such role effects can influence behavioral sequences. Because agents have a more developed scheme, they may be demanding during a discussion whereas their partners respond by withdrawing. Indeed, Christensen and Heavey (1990) found that when acting as change agents, spouses are demanding and partners respond by withdrawing. Johnson and Roloff (2000) found a similar pattern among daters engaged in serial arguing. Interestingly, when an issue is one in which partners want each other to change, each may enact both demanding and withdrawing behaviors (Caughlin & Vangelisti, 1999).

The second approach focuses on the degree to which individual differences predict influence goals. Rogan and La France (2003) asked individuals to recall a conflict with a friend and indicate the importance of three interaction goals: instrumental goals that focused on achieving the individual's objective, relational goals that focused on how well the friends treated each other, and face goals that focused on image. They found that verbal aggressiveness was correlated negatively with endorsing relational goals and with the likelihood of adopting a solution orientation (i.e., being collaborative and compromising) during a conflict. Because relational goals were related positively with enacting a solution orientation, it is possible that relational goals mediated the association between verbal aggressiveness and solution orientation. Also, women endorsed relational goals more than men, but there was no gender effect on adopting a solution orientation. Instead, men were more likely to be controlling than were women, but being controlling was not related to relational goals. Interestingly, endorsing instrumental goals was not related to either instrumental or face goals.

The third goal approach has focused on the degree to which relational goals impact the manner in which individuals try to achieve their influence goals. Stutman and Newell (1990) found that individuals often confront their partners with the goal to maintain or fix their relationship. As noted previously, Rogan and La France (2003) discovered that relational goals are related to conflict behaviors. Furthermore, research suggests that intimacy goals (i.e., desire to pursue self-disclosure, interdependence, and trust in a romantic relationship) influence conflict. Sanderson and Karetsky (2002) asked individuals to respond to hypothetical conflict situations in dating relationships and to describe a recent conflict episode they experienced. Endorsing intimacy goals was correlated positively to relational satisfaction, openly discussing relational problems with a partner, and expressing concern for the partner. But endorsing intimacy goals was not related to engaging in personal criticism. Importantly, the manner in which individuals dealt with their conflicts mediated the relationship between intimacy goals and relational satisfaction. Finally, intimacy goals were related positively to being able to resolve conflicts successfully.

Goal approaches have provided useful insights into conflict. For practitioners, this body of inquiry notes how the objectives that people pursue in a conflict influence behavior and outcomes. It is possible that when conflict emerges, individuals become primarily focused on achieving one goal (e.g., to influence the partner) and other goals are abandoned, given low priority, or simply not recognized. In such cases, practitioners may need to highlight multiple goals for the disputants.

However, a number of issues have not been addressed. Social influence scholars have recognized that multiple goals may be activated in a situation and that not all goals are of equal importance (e.g., Dillard, Segrin, & Harden, 1989). A primary goal drives the encounter, but secondary goals shape the manner in which it occurs. Current conflict research ignores the relative importance of goals that could provide insight into how conflict messages are constructed. In addition, researchers have not investigated the types of plans that are associated with their goals. Presumably, goals become salient during planning and should influence the actions that individuals intend to take. Furthermore, when a plan fails, individuals who remain committed to their goals must decide what to do, which may include changing the goals or elements of the plan (Berger, 1995). Afifi and Lee (2000) observed such patterns in a context involving resistance to sexual requests. Unfortunately, conflict research has not investigated plan construction or revision.

By and large, influence goals are focused on what a person wishes to achieve from the outset of the confrontation, but they offer little insight into how a person perceives what is said. The sentiment override hypothesis addresses that issue.

Sentiment override. Gottman (1994) argued that for a marriage to remain stable, spouses must enact positive behaviors at at least five times the rate of negative behaviors. This places a premium on the ability of partners to behave in a positive way toward one another. However, maintaining this ratio goes beyond behavioral enactment; individuals must take note of each other's positive behavior. Unfortunately, some spouses do not do so. Using observer judgments as a standard, distressed spouses underestimate their rate of everyday pleasurable behaviors by 50% (Robinson & Price, 1980). Weiss (1980) speculated that such discrepancies could result from individuals' allowing their global feelings about their relationship to affect their behavioral interpretations, which he labels sentiment override. Hence, among distressed couples, messages should generally be interpreted to be negative (i.e., negative sentiment override) and among nondistressed couples, messages should generally be interpreted to be positive (i.e., positive sentiment override). Such a process should influence feelings toward the partner and the marriage.

To test the sentiment override hypothesis, one must identify a standard with which to compare the subjective judgments of spouses. Researchers have used several. Some have used the judgments of trained observers. Floyd and Markman (1983) had observers rate the negativity of statements made during a marital interaction and compared them with the ratings made by the spouses. Their analysis found evidence of negative sentiment override when couples were discussing a relational problem, but only for distressed wives. Distressed wives rated their husband's behavior as more negative than observers.

Floyd (1988) used a different sample and method. He studied premarital couples that were very satisfied with their relationship and intended to marry. Couples rated the impact of their statements on each other. These ratings were compared with observer judgments of negative problem solving. In this study, observer judgments were correlated significantly with the female's impact evaluations of her male partner's statements. But observer judgments were not correlated with the male's assessments of the female partner's statements. Hence, within this sample, the interpretations of women were more congruent with observers' than those of men.

A second standard involves comparing the interpretations of one spouse's behavior with that of the partner. Gottman et al. (1976) had couples engage in problem-solving discussion and rate the intent and impact of each of their enacted messages. Consistent with sentiment override, they found that distressed and nondistressed couples did not differ in how they intended their messages to be received but that distressed couples perceived them to have less positive and to have a more negative impact than do nondistressed couples. Notarius, Benson, Sloane, Vanzetti, and Hornyak (1989) found similar patterns but only among wives and only when their husband's behavior was neutral rather than clearly positive or negative. In a recent study, Hawkins, Carrere, and Gottman (2002) found no evidence of sentiment override among husbands. Among wives, however, their marital bond (i.e., relational history) predicted how they interpreted their husband's low-intensity negative affect and positive affect; it did not predict their husband's high-intensity negative affect.

A third standard focuses on the degree to which spousal affective reactions to an interaction are due to relational quality or to behavioral patterns observed within the interaction. Flora

and Segrin (2000) found that the more generally satisfied couples were with their marriages, the less negative their affective reactions to a complaining interaction. A husband's negative affect was not correlated with his wife's behavior, but a wife's marital satisfaction and her husband's behavior influenced her negative reaction.

The sentiment override hypothesis goes directly to the issue of how individuals interpret the communication occurring within an interaction. In some respects, sentiment override presents the most difficult challenge for practitioners. Practitioners often try to modify the behavior of disputants to make it more positive. The tendency of some individuals to interpret positively intended behavior as being negative undercuts the effectiveness of that approach. In such cases, practitioners must find some way to adjust the interpretation process.

Unfortunately, although research does not clearly inform as to why sentiment override occurs, two studies indicate that distressed couples enter into disagreements expecting that their partners will enact more negative and fewer positive behaviors than do nondistressed couples (Fincham, Garnier, Gano-Phillips, & Osborne, 1995; Vanzetti, Notarius, & NeeSmith, 1992). If so, these expectations may serve as an interpretative frame for the partner's subsequent actions. Perhaps as a defensive reaction, such expectations may stimulate negative intentions toward the partner. Indeed, Denton, Burleson, and Sprenkle (1994) found that during an argument, distressed couples were more likely than nondistressed partners to perceive that their partners intended to enact negative behavior toward them and that they had similar intentions toward their partners.

Furthermore, it is unclear what effect sentiment override has on a relationship. Typically, relational quality is used to predict sentiment override, but it is unclear whether sentiment override affects relational quality. It could reinforce the current level or perhaps cause it to decay.

Summary. Researchers have identified a number of cognitive processes that mediate social behaviors, including some that focus on the onset of conflict, how conflict is managed, and how conflict behaviors are interpreted. Because these processes are treated as though they are conscious, researchers typically rely upon self-reports to assess them, and researchers in each area have established measures. Of the areas, the study of accommodation, sentiment override, and attribution making are the best developed in terms of methods and findings.

Cognitive Processing Effects

Some researchers have focused on the degree to which cognitive processing itself influences conflict. We identified three such areas of research: (a) thinking, (b) online processing, and (c) storytelling. Research on thinking focuses on cognitive activity before and after a dispute, while research on online processing investigates what people are thinking about during an argument. Storytelling examines the construction of narratives after an argument.

Thinking. At its core, sense-making involves thinking about an event. Not surprisingly, individuals report thinking about (a) their partner's provocative behavior before they initially confront him or her (Roloff, Soule, & Carey, 2001), (b) the dynamics of the initial confrontation (Roloff et al., 2001), and (c) actions performed in subsequent argumentative episodes (Johnson & Roloff, 1998). In some cases, these thoughts take the form of replaying a prior conflict as an imagined interaction and/or constructing an imagined interaction in preparation for another confrontational episode (Edwards, Honeycutt, & Zagacki, 1988). There is evidence that prolonged thinking about conflict is associated with negative outcomes. Johnson and Roloff (1998) found the degree to which individuals mulled over a conflict was correlated negatively with being optimistic that it could be resolved. Zagacki, Edwards, and Honeycutt (1992) had individuals construct an imagined interaction with their partners and found that those who imagined conflicts reported that they did not find the experiences to be satisfying. Furthermore, individuals who focus their attention on unpleasant interactions rather than distract themselves from thinking about the unpleasant interaction become more negative toward their partners (Sadler & Tesser, 1973), are more likely to act aggressively toward them (Collins & Bell,

1997), and are less likely to be forgiving (Berry, Worthington, Parrott, O'Connor, & Wade, 2001). Indeed, the more individuals ruminate about their partners' transgressions, the greater the likelihood they will adopt and maintain a vengeful motivation toward their partners (McCullough, Bellah, Kilpatrick, & Johnson, 2001).

Several perspectives attempt to shed light on the generally negative impact of prolonged thinking about a conflict. Some researchers have examined the degree to which a person who thinks about his or her feelings after being provoked has negative consequences. Several studies indicate that focusing on angry feelings rather than being distracted from thinking about them increases subsequent anger (Rusting & Nolen-Hoeksema, 1998) and the likelihood of aggression (Bushman, 2002). Other researchers have investigated a ruminative response style to depression, which is characterized as "repetitively focusing on the fact that one is depressed; on one's symptoms of depression; and on the causes, meanings and consequences of depressive symptoms" (Nolen-Hoeksema, 1991, p. 569). Unlike ruminating about anger, which seems to lead to aggression, ruminating about depressed feelings creates a sense of powerlessness that reduces the likelihood of distracting oneself from thinking about the depressing event (Lyubomirsky & Nolen-Hoeksema, 1993) or identifying effective ways to solve interpersonal problems (Lyubomirsky & Nolen-Hoeksema, 1995).

Other researchers have focused on stress-reactive rumination, which involves negative thoughts in response to stress (Alloy et al., 2000). Unlike depressive rumination, these thoughts are broadly focused on the degree to which individuals try to understand the personal meaning and significance of a stressful event. These thoughts precede, rather than result from, depressive episodes. Indeed, stress-reactive rumination is correlated with both prior occurrences of depression and the onset of depressive episodes (Alloy et al., 2000; Robinson & Alloy, 2003).

Some researchers have tied the tendency to ruminate about problems to goal completion (Martin & Tesser, 1989). Essentially, these researchers argue that when a person fails to meet a goal, cognition is activated. Some of that cognition is motivated to find ways of achieving the goal and will continue until the person is successful or abandons the goal. Consistent with this view, Lavallee and Campbell (1995) found that everyday problems that were tied to goal importance generated more negative moods and rumination than did those events that were not tied to goal importance. Moreover, Millar, Tesser, and Millar (1988) discovered that when individuals had not achieved personal goals they felt would lead to personal happiness, they ruminated more and spent more of their time unhappy. In a follow-up, McIntosh, Harlow, and Martin (1995) found that people who linked their higher-order life goals (e.g., to be happy) to the achievement of everyday goals (e.g., to lose weight) were more likely to ruminate, feel physically upset, and become depressed when they encountered everyday hassles than those who did not link those goals. This implies that rumination might not be dysfunctional to the extent that it allows individuals to identify ways of meeting their goals. Unfortunately, there is little evidence in support of this reasoning. Indeed, research suggests that individuals who are prone to ruminate create solutions in which they have little confidence, commitment, and satisfaction (Ward, Lyubomirsky, Sousa, & Nolen-Hoeksema, 2003).

Two areas of research suggest that the negative effects of prolonged thinking can be attenuated. Recently, Treynor, Gonzalez, and Nolen-Hoeksema (2003) distinguished between reflection about a problem (i.e., contemplating a problem) and brooding (i.e., moody pondering about a problem). They found that brooding had a much more negative effect on depressive symptoms than did reflection.

Cloven and Roloff (1991) focused on the degree to which individuals mulled over a conflict they had with a roommate. Generally, mulling over a conflict made individuals feel worse afterwards and did not increase their understanding of the dispute. However, communicating with the partner seemed to reduce other negative impacts of mulling. When individuals communicated frequently with their partners about a problem, mulling was less strongly related to problem seriousness and blaming the partner than when they did not discuss the problem frequently. However, the nature of the communication

with the target also played a role. When the conversation had been especially negative, mulling increased problem seriousness and blaming the partner more than when the conversation had not been negative.

In subsequent research, Cloven and Roloff (1993) investigated whether mulling in advance of talking to someone about a conflict influenced the kinds of thoughts that individuals had and their perceptions of the dispute. Regardless of whether individuals anticipated communication, those who generated self-critical thoughts while mulling over a roommate conflict were less likely to blame their partner. Among those whose roommate relationship was not satisfying, self-critical thoughts were related negatively to perceiving the conflict as serious. However, there is evidence that anticipating communication about a conflict increases the variety of thoughts individuals have about a dispute as well as thoughts focused on descriptive features of the disagreement (Cloven & Roloff, 1995).

Generally, the research suggests that prolonged thinking about aspects of a conflict is dysfunctional, although the magnitude of the harm varies. When taken to the extreme, this implies that conflict practitioners should suggest to disputants that they simply stop thinking. Research suggests, however, that this may not be an effective response. Wenzlaff and Luxton (2003) found that thought suppression is an effortful process that ultimately increases one's vulnerability to ruminative thoughts and dysphoria. Hence, research needs to investigate more thoroughly how individuals might transform their sense-making into something positive.

Although evidence indicates that the cognitive activity that occurs before, between, and after conflict episodes can have important effects, cognitive activity that occurs during an episode can also have important effects. We turn to that next.

Online processing. How individuals process information during an argument is one of the most interesting yet difficult phenomena to study. Currently, researchers cannot "read the minds" of conversationalists. Hence, they must rely on indirect indicators of online cognitive processing. However, despite this formidable problem, some researchers have focused on what happens when an argument starts.

Several researchers have focused on self-control processes. One such factor is related to emotional control. Disagreement can be arousing, and individuals often have the goal of maintaining emotional control during a conversation (Dillard et al., 1989). Richards, Butler, and Gross (2003) examine two ways of doing so. First, prior to the onset of a conflict discussion, individuals might engage in cognitive reappraisal wherein they focus on positive aspects of their partner and relationship. This could make the conflict seem less averse. Alternatively, individuals could engage in expressive suppression during the conversation by controlling their emotional displays. Richards et al.'s research indicates that individuals who used suppression during a disagreement had better recall of conversational content than did those who used emotional suppression. However, those who suppressed emotions had better recall of their emotions, primarily due to their greater self-monitoring. In effect, suppression distracts individuals from processing what is said while focusing attention on internal states. Furthermore, when one partner is engaging in emotional suppression during a discussion of an unpleasant event, the blood pressure of both interactants increases and they develop less rapport and affiliation with one another (Butler et al., 2003).

In a similar vein, some individuals attempt to reduce the relationally threatening emotional fallout from a conflict conversation by not systematically processing information. Buysse et al. (2000) argued that men are more likely to engage in such behavior than are women. To test this notion, they had individuals read transcripts of a conversation about a relationally threatening transgression or a trivial conflict. Afterward, researchers tested the ability of participants to recognize events in the conversation. Men evidenced better recognition for a trivial conflict than for a transgression, but the opposite was true for women. When participants were warned that a test would be given after they read the message, the recognition ability of males who read a relational transgression improved as did the recognition ability of females who read a trivial conflict. Although not assessing how participants process information, the research suggests that men and women might process disagreements in different ways.

Both of the aforementioned studies used memory measures to infer online processing.

Some researchers have looked at the behaviors enacted during the conversation. Sillars and Parry (1982) were interested in the degree to which stress that occurs during a conflict conversation interferes with cognitive processing. They examined the degree to which nonverbal indicators of stress (e.g., eye glances and adapters) were correlated with linguistic indicators of cognitive processes (e.g., communication complexity and speech productivity). They found that eye glances and adapters were correlated negatively with taking multiple perspectives and the length and duration of speech. Without looking directly at what information individuals are processing, this approach suggests that affect may interfere with behaviors that imply systematic, in-depth processing.

Other researchers have asked individuals to view tapes of their conversations and then report the thoughts they recalled having. Halford and Sanders (1988) had married couples discuss a problem in their relationship. After the discussion, some couples reviewed a tape of the conversation and reported their thoughts while watching the tape. Other couples simply recorded their thoughts at the end of the conversation. The thoughts were then coded for referent and tone. Both methods revealed the same patterns. Relative to nondistressed couples, distressed spouses reported more negative and fewer positive thoughts about their partners and more positive thoughts about themselves. Negative thoughts about themselves did not differ across groups. Moreover, men reported having more positive partner thoughts and fewer negative partner thoughts than did women.

Sillars, Roberts, Leonard, and Dun (2000) also asked spouses to review a videotape of their problem discussion and report their thoughts. Overall, they found that the thoughts reflected little perspective taking, but frequent attempts to understand the relational implications of the discussion and analysis of the communication process. Also, negative thoughts far exceeded positive ones, and the frequency of negative thoughts was greater than the negativity coded in the actual discussion. They also found perspective differences. Relative to husbands, wives were more focused on their partners, more sensitive to the relationship, and their thoughts were more tied to objective features of the conversation. Wives also attributed greater avoidance to their husbands than they did to themselves. Finally, distressed couples had more negative thoughts and fewer content-related thoughts than nondistressed couples.

Simpson, Orina, and Ickes (2003) asked spouses to review tapes of an earlier problem-solving discussion and recall not only their own thoughts but those of their partners. By doing so, Simpson et al. could determine the degree to which a spouse's estimate of the other spouse's thoughts matched the partner's actual thoughts and hence, whether spouses are empathically accurate. When a partner's thoughts were relationally threatening, empathic accuracy decreased feelings of closeness to the partner after the conversation. However, when the partner's thoughts were not threatening, empathic accuracy increased feelings of closeness. Exploratory analysis of the coded interaction behaviors suggested that spouses viewed each other's avoidant behaviors as a cue that the avoider was having relationally threatening thoughts.

Finally, other researchers have focused on the degree to which disputants share similar perceptions of what transpired during a disagreement. Sillars, Pike, Jones, and Murphy (1984) had couples discuss a relational problem and indicate the degree to which they and their partner felt the problem was real, important, and bothersome. Understanding was assessed by looking at the partial correlation between the spouses' estimate of their partners' responses and the partners' actual responses, while controlling for the spouses' own feelings about the problem. They found that spouses often felt that their partner agreed with their own assessment more than the spouses actually did and that understanding was correlated negatively with marital adjustment. Interestingly, among satisfied couples, the more negative they were during the conversation, the greater their understanding. Among dissatisfied couples, the behaviors enacted during the conversation were unrelated to their understanding.

Instead of looking at a specific interaction, some researchers have examined whether intimates share similar views of how they generally manage conflict. Acitelli, Douvan, and Veroff (1993) had newlyweds report about their own and their partner's use of constructive and destructive conflict management. Regardless of their behavior, both husbands and wives perceived that they had engaged in similar actions to those enacted by their partner to a greater extent than their partner reported. Furthermore, both husbands' and wives' perceptions of their partners' destructive behaviors showed closer correspondence to those reported by their partners than did their assessment of their partners' constructive behaviors. Finally, wives' accurate understanding of their husbands' behaviors was related to their own feelings of relational well-being but not to their husbands' feelings of relational well-being. The husbands' understanding was not correlated with either spouses' well-being. Instead, a husband's well-being was related negatively to the degree to which both spouses engaged in destructive behavior and related positively to his tendency to engage in constructive actions.

Hojjat (2000) asked heterosexual couples to rate the degree to which they use a number of conflict-management strategies. Relative to men, women reported that they were more negative and active during disagreements. Men reported being more positive and passive. Women, more so than men, described their partners' behaviors in a way that matched the partners' self-descriptions. Women also provided self-descriptions that were more congruent with observed judgments of their behavior than did men. Regardless of gender, accurately understanding the spouse's conflict behavior was correlated positively with satisfaction.

Gable, Reis, and Downey (2003) asked couples to record the degree to which they had enacted a set of positive, supportive, and negative behaviors (which included criticizing the partner). They then examined the degree to which the accounts matched (both partners agreed the action occurred or did not occur) or mismatched (one said it occurred and the other did not). Positive events were more frequent and more accurately perceived than were negative ones. However, negative behaviors were related more strongly to relational well-being and mood than were positive or supportive behaviors. Accurately assessing negative behaviors decreased relational well-being and positive mood while increasing negative mood. Perceiving negative actions that the partner did not report produced the same effect. Interestingly, these negative effects occurred even when the respondent's partner reported engaging in negative behaviors that the respondent did not perceive.

Scholars interested in online processing face significant methodological challenges and have employed a variety of methods to infer how individuals process information. The results are insightful and have important implications for practitioners. They imply that people do not always process their conflicts or arguments in the same manner. Some individuals may be more aware of conflict dynamics than are others. Hence, partners may not even agree on whether something happened, let alone its characteristics. Although such discrepancies could be self-serving, they could also result from differential awareness. Thus, practitioners need to assess both the degree to which there are different perceptions and their cause.

Given the inferential nature of the methods, however, it would seem useful to conduct multimethod studies to cross-validate findings and evaluate the utility of each. Only Halford and Sanders (1988) have attempted to do this, and their research not only provided useful insights into conflict but how to study it efficiently.

Thus far, we have reviewed evidence that the frequency of thinking as well as the perception of interactive behavior can have important impacts. The final area focuses on how the processing or organizing of thoughts about conflict influences individuals.

Storytelling. To help understand an event, individuals sometimes construct personal narratives that are story-like. Researchers have focused their research on the elements of conflict stories as well as the effect of constructing them.

One approach to understanding storytelling is to focus on the role played by the person in the story. A variety of studies have investigated the features of stories in which a person played either the role of an offender or a victim (Baumeister, Stillwell, & Wotman, 1990; Schutz & Baumeister, 1999). Baumeister and Catanese (2001) summarized role effects as follows:

> Relative to perpetrators, victims tell stories in which (1) victims were wholly innocent, (2) the perpetrators had no valid reason or justification for their actions, (3) severe and lasting negative consequences were caused, (4) mitigating or extenuating circumstances surrounding the perpetrator's actions are missing, (5) multiple offenses were involved, (6) the victim's reaction was either appropriate or highly restrained, and (7) the transgression is still seen as highly relevant to the present time. (p. 291)

When asked to describe stories of transgressions that were forgiven, both offenders and victims typically indicated that the issue was closed with positive outcomes, although there is evidence that some victims describe continuing problems and resentment (Zechmeister & Romero, 2002). Most important, research suggests that with consecutive telling of a transgression story, both offenders and victims distort the content of the story, typically by embellishing details that make them look good and selectively omitting those that make them look bad (Stillwell & Baumeister, 1997).

Yet, not all storytelling seems to be distorted so as to reflect negatively on the partner. Murray and Holmes (1993) argued that intimates create stories about their partners' shortcomings so as to diminish any doubts or uncertainty they have about their relationships. Indeed, intimates who become aware that their partners have traits that could threaten their relationships construct stories that refute or explain away their partners' faults and note that the partners have other traits that facilitate the relationships (Murray & Holmes, 1993, 1994). Furthermore, Cameron, Ross, and Holmes (2002) discovered that intimates who described a relational transgression they had committed were more likely to create stories that indicated the situation was improving and that they were optimistic about the future than did their partners. Hence, it appears that both offenders and victims create stories aimed at preserving their relationship. There is evidence that storytelling effects persevere over time largely because the story reflects the gist of events rather than details and that the gist is more easily recovered from memory after the event (McGregor & Holmes, 1999).

Storytelling research provides insight into how events are recalled and revised over time. From a practical perspective, it reflects a person's account of how the conflict has unfolded. Research indicates that a person's account might differ from that of his or her partner and perhaps even the actual events that transpired. Practitioners must be cognizant of such differences, particularly given that while developing the story, individuals may convince themselves that it happened in the manner they recall.

Unfortunately, storytelling research has its limits. Few studies have focused on the degree to which partners differ with regard to their stories. Furthermore, it is unclear whether storytelling differences arise from the cognitive process involved in constructing a story and/or the process of telling it to others.

Summary. A number of processing effects have been identified. Perhaps the most well developed are those focused on thinking and storytelling. In those cases, researchers have established ways to assess the relevant processes. Assessing online processing is much more difficult, although the study of online processing is advancing as researchers identify alternative means of assessment.

SUMMARY CRITIQUE

From the outset, we noted that conflict researchers who work from a social cognition perspective assume that conflict stimulates cognitive activity aimed at making sense of the conflict. Our review indicates that many productive research programs have been developed, and we noted strengths and challenges for those who adopt a social cognition approach to understanding conflict. Clearly, researchers have addressed critical issues that inform both theory and practice. Conflict has provided a useful context in which to test fundamental notions of how individuals process information as well as how the context itself influences those processes. Moreover, some research is stimulated by a concern for understanding the processes that make conflict dysfunctional for individuals and relationships and how to make these conflicts less dysfunctional. As scholarship has accumulated, methods and measures have become more diverse. In a number of areas, they are well established.

Because many social cognition researchers focus their research on particular types of cognitive activities and effects, we cannot say that there is a single accepted model that guides research. Nevertheless, trends emerged from our review that form a general framework that is reflected in Figure 4.3. This framework is based on three assumptions. First, the social knowledge and cognitive processes that are part of sense-making are related to individual factors (e.g., personality, gender) and relational factors (e.g., satisfaction, commitment). Second, both social knowledge and cognitive processes influence a variety of behaviors enacted during an argument (e.g., engagement/withdrawal, positivity/negativity, resolution/impasse). Third, these behaviors have individual (e.g., stress, depression) and relational (e.g., satisfaction, termination) outcomes. We caution the reader that the model is quite general and, as we noted earlier, not all links have been fully studied. Even so, it provides a useful means of making sense of the literature, and we hope it may have heuristic value.

Certainly, the aforementioned is good news. However, the area also faces significant challenges. First, considerable "conceptual housecleaning" is required. The reader was probably overwhelmed at times by the myriad constructs that were introduced. At times, the reader may have wondered if they were indeed distinct. Although beyond the scope of this review, scholars need to view the literature with an eye toward redundancy and integration. Can we demonstrate that the various processes are independent indicators that reflect a latent factor or are they truly separate processes? Is it possible to integrate them into a larger model? Other scholars have noticed the variety of social cognition constructs and separately reviewed the literature related to them (e.g., Baucom, Epstein, Sayers, & Sher, 1989). Like we did, they attempted to organize the literature into a model that described the research terrain. By identifying the multitude of variables, we might be better able to reduce redundancy and better explicate the key variable.

The second challenge is related to the first. As with most academic areas, research has developed within independent programs often identified with particular researchers or academic programs. Certainly, such a focus has benefits.

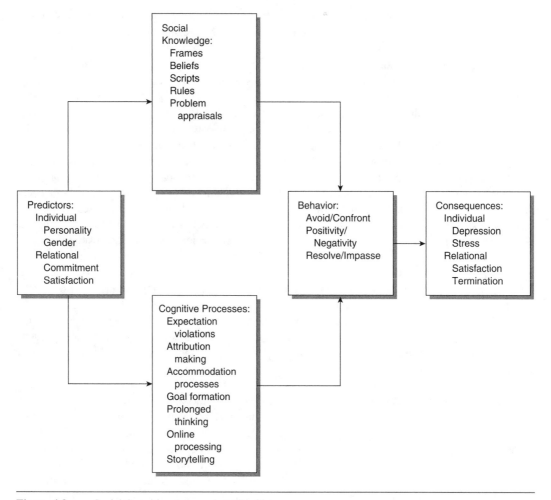

Figure 4.3   Social Cognition Approach to Conflict

For example, it often leads to refined methods and measures that are used to explore questions systematically, but such channeling could lock researchers into standard operating procedures that inhibit or actually prevent creative tests of the framework as well as the development of models that integrate constructs. This is not to say that we did not find evidence of cross-fertilization. Indeed, we did. We argue, however, that more is needed.

The third challenge is to expand the relational domain of the research. Because of the practical implications arising from conflict, research often is driven by concern for studying conflict in a given relational context, of which marriage is the most prominent. This specific focus is justified, but if the larger goal is to understand fundamental cognitive processes associated with conflict, it would be useful to test these notions in a variety of relationships. This move might provide insights into the generalizability of our findings. At the same time, it would allow us to identify how or if the nature of relationships influences cognitive processes. Kurdek's (1991a, 1992) research program has compared the conflict processes of married couples with those of homosexual partners and provides a model for future research.

The fourth challenge is to expand the cultural context into which the research is conducted. With few exceptions, most research is conducted with samples drawn from the United States, and most of that research does not explore subgroup differences. In part, this may reflect the lack of integration of cross-cultural theory with social cognition perspectives on conflict. Without a strong theoretical base from which to predict differences, researchers may assume that cultural differences are not relevant or may simply attempt to diversify their samples so as to ensure generalizability rather than test specific group differences. In our view, research conducted by Gelfand et al. (2001) should serve as a model for such inquiry.

The fifth challenge is to determine how to integrate research with practice. Because many researchers are not practitioners, they are not well equipped to translate their findings into practice. Perhaps the best illustration of meaningful application is focused on couples therapy where one can identify a number of treatments that are derived in part from cognitive approaches, and some appear to be effective (Baucom et al., 1998; Christensen et al., 2004).

The sixth challenge is methodological. The methods and measures that are employed are diverse and generally sound. However, for the most part, researchers have not used designs that would allow them to identify how or if cognition changes over the life course of a disagreement. In some cases, conflict is not effectively resolved in a single episode, and some conflicts may continue throughout a relationship. Unless longitudinal designs or retrospective analyses are employed, we cannot determine whether the sense-making process continues and conceptions change or if they remain relatively static.

The final challenge is to explore more fully the interrelationship between cognitive activity and emotional and affective responses. To their credit, many researchers who have adopted a social cognition approach have linked their constructs to conflict behavior. However, relatively little attention has been paid to the links with affective reactions, except with respect to global relational measures. Vangelisti's (1994) perspective on hurtful communication might provide a useful model for more fully identifying such linkages.

Overall, social cognition approaches to understanding conflict have provided useful insights, and there is reason to believe that, with some adjustments, they will remain useful. These seven challenges should extend this research and ensure their usefulness.

REFERENCES

Acitelli, L. K., Douvan, E., & Veroff, J. (1993). Perceptions of conflict in the first year of marriage: How important are similarity and understanding? *Journal of Social and Personal Relationships, 10,* 5–19.

Acitelli, L. K., Kenny, D. A., & Weiner, D. (2001). The importance of similarity and understanding of partners' marital ideals to relationship satisfaction. *Personal Relationships, 8,* 167–185.

Afifi, W., & Burgoon, J. K. (2000). The impact of violations on uncertainty and the consequences for attractiveness. *Human Communication Research, 26,* 203–233.

Afifi, W., & Lee, J. W. (2000). Balancing instrumental and identity goals in relationships: The role of request directness and request persistence in the selection of sexual resistance strategies. *Communication Monographs, 67,* 284–305.

Afifi, W., & Metts, S. (1998). Characteristics and consequences of expectation violations in close relationships. *Journal of Social and Personal Relationships, 15,* 365–392.

Alloy, L. B., Abramson, L. Y., Hogan, M. E., Whitehouse, W. G., Rose, D. T., Robinson, M. W., Kim, R. S., & Lapkin, J. B. (2000). The Temple-Wisconsin Cognitive Vulnerability to Depression Project: Lifetime history of Axis I psychopathology in individuals at high and low cognitive risk for depression. *Journal of Abnormal Psychology, 109,* 403–418.

Andrew, G., & McMullen, L. M. (2000). Interpersonal scripts in the anger narratives told by clients in psychotherapy. *Motivation and Emotion, 24,* 271–284.

Argyle, M., & Furnham, A. (1983). Sources of satisfaction and conflict in long-term relationships. *Journal of Marriage and the Family, 45,* 481–493.

Argyle, M., & Henderson, M. (1985). The rules of relationships. In S. Duck & D. Perlman (Eds.), *Understanding personal relationships: An interdisciplinary approach* (pp. 63–84). Thousand Oaks, CA: Sage.

Argyle, M., Henderson, M., & Furnham, A. (1985). The rules of social relationships. *British Journal of Social Psychology, 24,* 125–139.

Baucom, D. H., Epstein, N., Daiuto, A. D., Carels, R. A., Rankin, L. A., & Burnett, C. K. (1996). Cognitions in marriage: The relationship between standards and attributions. *Journal of Family Psychology, 10,* 209–222.

Baucom, D. H., Epstein, N., Rankin, L. A., & Burnett, C. K. (1996). Assessing relationship standards: The inventory of specific relationship standards. *Journal of Family Psychology, 10,* 72–88.

Baucom, D. H., Epstein, N., Sayers, S., & Sher, T. G. (1989). The role of cognitions in marital relationships: Definitional, methodological, and conceptual issues. *Journal of Consulting and Clinical Psychology, 57,* 31–38.

Baucom, D. H., Shoham, V., Mueser, K. T., Daiuto, A. D., & Stickle, T. R. (1998). Empirically supported couple and family interventions for marital distress and adult mental health problems. *Journal of Consulting and Clinical Psychology, 66,* 53–88.

Baumeister, R. F., & Catanese, K. (2001). Victims and perpetrators provide discrepant accounts: Motivated cognitive distortions about interpersonal transgressions. In J. P. Forgas, K. D. Williams, & L. Wheeler (Eds.), *The social mind: Cognitive and motivational aspects of interpersonal behavior* (pp. 274–293). Cambridge, UK: Cambridge University Press.

Baumeister, R. F., Stillwell, A. M., & Wotman, S. R. (1990). Victim and perpetrator accounts of interpersonal conflict: Autobiographical narratives about anger. *Journal of Personality and Social Psychology, 59,* 994–1005.

Belsky, J. (1985). Exploring individual differences in marital change across the transition to parenthood. *Journal of Marriage and the Family, 47,* 1037–1044.

Berger, C. R. (1995). A plan-based approach to strategic communication. In D. E. Hewes (Ed.), *The cognitive bases of interpersonal communication* (pp. 141–180). Hillsdale, NJ: Lawrence Erlbaum.

Berry, J. W., Worthington, E. L., Jr., Parrott, L., III, O'Connor, L. E., & Wade, N. (2001). Dispositional forgivingness: Development and construct validity of the Transgression Narrative Test of Forgivingness (TNTF). *Personality and Social Psychology Bulletin, 27,* 1277–1290.

Birchler, G. R., Weiss, R. L., & Vincent, J. P. (1975). Multimethod analysis of social reinforcement exchange between maritally distressed and nondistressed spouse and stranger dyads. *Journal of Personality and Social Psychology, 31,* 349–360.

Bolger, N., DeLongis, A., Kessler, R. C., & Schilling, E. A. (1989). Effects of daily stress on negative mood. *Journal of Personality and Social Psychology, 57,* 808–818.

Bolger, N., & Zuckerman, A. (1995). A framework for studying personality in the stress process. *Journal of Personality and Social Psychology, 69,* 890–902.

Boon, S. D., & Holmes, J. G. (1999). Interpersonal risk and the evaluation of transgressions in close relationships. *Personal Relationships, 6,* 151–168.

Bradbury, T. N., Beach, S. R. H., Fincham, F. D., & Nelson, G. M. (1996). Attributions and behavior in functional and dysfunctional marriages. *Journal of Consulting and Clinical Psychology, 64,* 569–576.

Bradbury, T. N., & Fincham, F. D. (1990). Attributions in marriage: Review and critique. *Psychological Bulletin, 107,* 3–33.

Bradbury, T. N., & Fincham, F. D. (1992). Attributions and behavior in marital interaction. *Journal of Personality and Social Psychology, 63,* 613–628.

Bradbury, T. N., & Fincham, F. D. (1993). Assessing dysfunctional cognition in marriage: A reconsideration of the relationship belief inventory. *Psychological Assessment, 5,* 92–101.

Brissette, I., & Cohen, S. (2002). The contribution of individual differences in hostility to the associations between daily interpersonal conflict, affect, and sleep. *Personality and Social Psychology Bulletin, 28,* 1265–1274.

Burgoon, J. K. (1978). A communication model of personal space violations: Explication and an initial test. *Human Communication Research, 4,* 129–142.

Burgoon J. K., & Walther, J. B. (1990). Nonverbal expectancies and the consequences of violations. *Human Communication Research, 17,* 232–265.

Bushman, B. J. (2002). Does venting anger feed or extinguish the flame? Catharsis, rumination, distraction, anger, and aggressive responding. *Personality and Social Psychology Bulletin, 28,* 724–731.

Butler, E. A., Egloff, B., Wihelm, F. H., Smith, N. C., Erickson, E. A., & Gross, J. J. (2003). The social consequences of expressive suppression. *Emotion, 3,* 48–67.

Buysse, A., De Clercq, A., Verhofstadt, L., Heene, E., Roeyers, H., & Van Oost, P. (2000). Dealing with relational conflict: A picture in milliseconds.

Journal of Social and Personal Relationships, 17, 574–597.

Cameron, J. J., Ross, M., & Holmes, J. G. (2002). Loving the one you hurt: Positive effects of recounting a transgression against an intimate partner. *Journal of Experimental Social Psychology, 38,* 307–314.

Campbell, W. K., & Foster, C. A. (2002). Narcissism and commitment in romantic relationships: An investment model analysis. *Personality and Social Psychology Bulletin, 28,* 484–495.

Canary, D. J., Cunningham, E. M., & Cody, M. J. (1988). Goal types, gender, and locus of control in managing interpersonal conflict. *Communication Research, 15,* 426–446.

Cate, R. M., Koval, J., Lloyd, S. A., & Wilson, G. (1995). Assessment of relationship thinking in dating relationships. *Personal Relationships, 2,* 77–95.

Caughlin, J. P., & Vangelisti, A. L. (1999). Desire for change in one's partner as a predictor of the demand/withdraw pattern of marital communication. *Communication Monographs, 66,* 66–89.

Christensen, A., Atkins, D. C., Berns, S., Wheeler, J., Baucom, D. H., & Simpson, L. E. (2004). Traditional versus integrative behavioral couple therapy for significantly and chronically distressed married couples. *Journal of Consulting and Clinical Psychology, 72,* 176–191.

Christensen, A., & Heavey, C. L. (1990). Gender and social structure in the demand/withdraw pattern of marital conflict. *Journal of Personality and Social Psychology, 59,* 73–81.

Christian, J. L., O'Leary, K. D., & Vivian, D. (1994). Depressive symptomatology in maritally discordant women and men: The role of individual and relationship variables. *Journal of Family Psychology, 8,* 32–42.

Cloven, D. H., & Roloff, M. E. (1991). Sense-making activities and interpersonal conflict: Communicative cures for the mulling blues. *Western Journal of Speech Communication, 55,* 134–158.

Cloven, D. H., & Roloff, M. E. (1993). Sense-making activities and interpersonal conflict, II: The effects of communicative intentions on internal dialogue. *Western Journal of Communication, 57,* 309–329.

Cloven, D. H., & Roloff, M. E. (1995). Cognitive tuning effects of anticipating communication on thoughts about an interpersonal conflict. *Communication Reports, 8,* 1–9.

Collins, K., & Bell, R. (1997). Personality and aggression: The Dissipation-Rumination Scale. *Personality and Individual Differences, 22,* 751–755.

Crohan, S. E. (1992). Marital happiness and spousal consensus on beliefs about marital conflict: A longitudinal investigation. *Journal of Social and Personal Relationships, 9,* 89–102.

Davey, A., Fincham, F. D., Beach, S. R. H., & Brody, G. H. (2001). Attributions in marriage: Examining the entailment model in dyadic context. *Journal of Family Psychology, 15,* 721–734.

Denton, W. H., Burleson, B. R., & Sprenkle, D. H. (1994). Motivation in marital communication: Comparison of distressed and nondistressed husbands and wives. *American Journal of Family Therapy, 22,* 17–26.

Dillard, J. P. (1990). A goal-driven model of interpersonal influence. In J. P. Dillard (Ed.), *Seeking compliance: The production of interpersonal influence messages* (pp. 41–56). Scottsdale, AZ: Gorsuch Scarisbrick.

Dillard, J. P., Segrin, C., & Harden, J. (1989). Primary and secondary goals in the interpersonal influence process. *Communication Monographs, 56,* 19–39.

Ebesu Hubbard, A. S. (2001). Conflict between relationally uncertain romantic partners: The influence of relational responsiveness and empathy. *Communication Monographs, 68,* 400–414.

Edwards, R., Honeycutt, J. M., & Zagacki, K. S. (1988). Imagined interaction as an element of social cognition. *Western Journal of Speech Communication, 52,* 23–45.

Eidelson, R. J., & Epstein, N. (1982). Cognition and relationship maladjustment: Development of a measure of dysfunctional beliefs. *Journal of Consulting and Clinical Psychology, 50,* 715–720.

Emmelkamp, P. M., Krol, B., Sanderman, R., & Ruphan, M. (1987). The assessment of relationship beliefs in a marital context. *Personality and Individual Differences, 8,* 775–780.

Epstein, N., & Eidelson, R. J. (1981). Unrealistic beliefs of clinical couples: Their relationships to expectations goals and satisfaction. *American Journal of Family Therapy, 9,* 13–22.

Epstein, N., Pretzer, J. L., & Fleming, B. (1987). The role of cognitive appraisal in self-reports of marital conflict. *Behavior Therapy, 18,* 51–69.

Fehr, B., Baldwin, M., Collins, L., Patterson, S., & Benditt, R. (1999). Anger in close relationships: An interpersonal script analysis. *Personality and Social Psychology Bullettin, 25,* 299–312.

Fincham, F. D. (1985). Attributions in close relationships. In J. H. Harvey & G. Weary (Eds.), *Attribution: Basic issues and applications* (pp. 203–234). San Diego, CA: Academic Press.

Fincham, F. D., Beach, S. R. H., & Davila, J. (2004). Forgiveness and conflict resolution in marriage. *Journal of Family Psychology, 18,* 72–81.

Fincham, F. D., & Bradbury, T. N. (1992). Assessing attributions in marriage: The Relationship Attribution Measure. *Journal of Personality and Social Psychology, 62,* 457–468.

Fincham, F. D., Garnier, P. C., Gano-Phillips, S., & Osborne, L. N. (1995). Preinteraction expectations, marital satisfaction, and accessibility: A new look at sentiment override. *Journal of Family Psychology, 9,* 3–14.

Fincham, F. D., Harold, G. T., & Gano-Phillips, S. (2000). The longitudinal association between attributions and martial satisfaction: Direction of effects and role of efficacy expectations. *Journal of Family Psychology, 14,* 267–285.

Finkel, E. J., & Campbell, W. K. (2001). Self-control and accommodation in close relationships: An interdependence analysis. *Journal of Personality and Social Psychology, 81,* 263–277.

Fiske, S. T., & Taylor, S. E. (1991). *Social cognition* (2nd ed.). New York: McGraw-Hill.

Fitzpatrick, J., & Sollie, D. L. (1999). Unrealistic gendered and relationship-specific beliefs: Contributions to investments and commitment in dating relationships. *Journal of Social and Personal Relationships, 16,* 852–867.

Fletcher, G., Thomas, G., & Durrant, R. (1999). Cognitive and behavioral accommodation in close relationships. *Journal of Social and Personal Relationships, 16,* 705–730.

Flora, J., & Segrin, C. (2000). Affect and behavioral involvement in spousal complaints and compliments. *Journal of Family Psychology, 14,* 641–657.

Floyd, F. J. (1988). Couples' cognitive/affective reactions to communication behaviors. *Journal of Marriage and the Family, 50,* 523–532.

Floyd, F. J., & Markman, H. J. (1983). Observational biases in spouse observation: Toward a cognitive/behavioral model of marriage. *Journal of Consulting and Clinical Psychology, 51,* 450–467.

Gable, S. L., Reis, H. T., & Downey, G. (2003). He said, she said: A quasi-signal detection analysis of daily interactions between close relationship partners. *Psychological Science, 14,* 100–105.

Gable, S. L., Reis, H. T., & Elliot, A. J. (2000). Behavioral activation and inhibition in everyday life. *Journal of Personality and Social Psychology, 78,* 1135–1149.

Gaines, S. O., Jr., Ries, H. T., Summers, S., Rusbult, C. E., Cox, C. L., Wexler, M. O., Marelich, W. D., & Kurland, G. J. (1997). Impact of attachment style on reactions to accommodative dilemmas in close relationships. *Personal Relationships, 4,* 93–113.

Gelfand, M. J., Nishii, L. H., Holcombe, K., Dyer, N., Ohbuchi, K., & Fukumo, M. (2001). Cultural influences on cognitive representations of conflict: Interpretations of conflict episodes in the U.S. and Japan. *Journal of Applied Psychology, 86,* 1059–1074

Goodwin, R., & Gaines, S. O., Jr. (2004). Relationship beliefs and relationship quality across cultures: Country as a moderator of dysfunctional beliefs and relationship quality in three former Communist societies. *Personal Relationships, 11,* 267–280.

Gottman, J. M. (1994). *What predicts divorce: The relationship between marital processes and divorce.* Hillsdale, NJ: Lawrence Erlbaum.

Gottman, J., Notarius, C., Markman, H., Bank, S., Yoppi, B., & Rubin, M. E. (1976). Behavior exchange theory and decision making. *Journal of Personality and Social Psychology, 34,* 14–23.

Hackel, L. S., & Ruble, D. N. (1992). Changes in the marital relationship after the first baby is born: Predicting the impact of expectancy disconfirmation. *Journal of Personality and Social Psychology, 62,* 944–957.

Halford, W. K., & Sanders, M. R. (1988). Assessment of cognitive self-statements during marital problem solving: A comparison of two methods. *Cognitive Therapy and Research, 12,* 513–530.

Harris, L. M., Gergen, K. J., & Lannamann, J. W. (1986). Aggression rituals. *Communication Monographs, 53,* 252–265.

Hawkins, M. W., Carrere, S., & Gottman, J. M. (2002). Marital sentiment override: Does it influence couples' perceptions? *Journal of Marriage and Family, 64,* 193–201.

Hojjat, M. (2000). Sex differences and perceptions of conflict in romantic relationships. *Journal of Social and Personal Relationships, 17,* 598–617.

Holtzworth-Munroe, A., & Jacobson, N. S. (1985). Causal attributions of married couples: When do they search for causes? What do they conclude when they do? *Journal of Personality and Social Psychology, 48,* 1398–1412.

Honeycutt, J. M., Woods, B. L., & Fontenot, K. (1993). The endorsement of communication conflict rules as a function of engagement, marriage and marital ideology. *Journal of Social and Personal Relationships, 10,* 285–304.

Johnson, K. L., & Roloff, M. E. (1998). Serial arguing and relational quality: Determinants and consequences of perceived resolvability. *Communication Research, 25,* 327–343.

Johnson, K. L., & Roloff, M. E. (2000). The influence of argumentative role (initiator vs. resistor) on perceptions of serial argument resolvability and relational harm. *Argumentation, 14,* 1–15.

Jones, E., & Gallois, C. (1989). Spouses' impressions of rules for communication in public and private marital conflicts. *Journal of Marriage and the Family, 51,* 957–967.

Kach, J. A., & McGhee, P. A. (1982). Adjustment of early parenthood: The role of accuracy of preparenthood experiences. *Journal of Family Issues, 3,* 375–388.

Kellermann, K. (1984). The negativity effect and its implications for initial interaction. *Communication Monographs, 51,* 37–55.

Kelley, H. H., Cunningham, J. D., Grisham, J. A., Lefebvre, L. M., Sink, C. R., & Yablon, G. (1978). Sex differences in comments made during conflict within close heterosexual pairs. *Sex Roles, 4,* 473–492.

Kelley, H. H., & Thibaut, J. W. (1978). *Interpersonal relations: A theory of interdependence.* New York: John Wiley.

Kilpatrick, S. D., Bissonnette, V. L., & Rusbult, C. E. (2002). Empathic accuracy and accommodative behavior among newly married couples. *Personal Relationships, 9,* 369–393.

Klinger, E., Barta, S. G., & Maxeiner, M. E. (1980). Motivational correlates of thought content frequency and commitment. *Journal of Personality and Social Psychology, 39,* 1222–1237.

Knapp, M. L., Stafford, L., & Daly, J. A. (1986). Regrettable messages: Things people wish they hadn't said. *Journal of Communication, 36*(4), 40–58.

Knee, C. R. (1998). Implicit theories of relationships: Assessment and prediction of romantic relationship initiation, copying and longevity. *Journal of Personality and Social Psychology, 74,* 360–370.

Knee, C. R., Patrick, H., & Lonsbary, C. (2003). Implicit theories of relationships: Orientations toward evaluation and cultivation. *Personality and Social Psychology Review, 7,* 41–55.

Knee, C. R., Patrick, H., Vietor, N. A., & Neighbors, C. (2004). Implicit theories of relationships: Moderators of the link between conflict and commitment. *Personality and Social Psychology Bulletin, 30,* 617–628.

Knobloch, L. K., & Solomon, D. H. (2003). Responses to changes in relational uncertainty within dating relationships: Emotions and communication strategies. *Communication Studies, 54,* 282–305.

Kowalski, R. M., Walker, S., Wilkinson, R., Queen, A., & Sharpe, B. (2003). Lying, cheating, complaining, and other aversive interpersonal behaviors: A narrative examination of the darker side of relationships. *Journal of Social and Personal Relationships, 20,* 471–490.

Kurdek, L. A. (1991a). Correlates of relationship satisfaction in cohabiting gay and lesbian couples: Integration of contextual, investment, and problem-solving models. *Journal of Personality and Social Psychology, 61,* 910–922.

Kurdek, L. A. (1991b). Predictors of increases in marital distress in newlywed couples: A 3-year prospective longitudinal study. *Developmental Psychology, 27,* 627–636.

Kurdek, L. A. (1992). Assumptions versus standards: The validity of two relationship cognitions in heterosexual and homosexual couples. *Journal of Family Psychology, 6,* 164–170.

Kurdek, L. A. (1993). Predicting marital dissolution: A 5-year prospective longitudinal study of newlywed couples. *Journal of Personality and Social Psychology, 64,* 221–242.

Kurdek, L. A. (1999). The nature and predictors of the trajectory of change in marital quality for husbands and wives over the first 10 years of marriage. *Developmental Psychology, 365,* 1283–1296.

Langer, E. (1978). Rethinking the role of thought in social interaction. In J. H. Harvey, W. J Ickes, & R. F. Kidd (Eds.), *New directions in attribution research* (Vol. 2, pp. 35–58). Hillsdale, NJ: Lawrence Erlbaum.

Lavallee, F., & Campbell, J. D. (1995). Impact of personal goals on self-regulation processes elicited by daily negative events. *Journal of Personality and Social Psychology, 69,* 341–352.

Lyubomirsky, S., & Nolen-Hoeksema, S. (1993). Self-perpetuating properties of dysphoric rumination. *Journal of Personality and Social Psychology, 65,* 339–349.

Lyubomirsky, S., & Nolen-Hoeksema, S. (1995). Effects of self-focused rumination on negative thinking and interpersonal problem-solving. *Journal of Personality and Social Psychology, 69,* 176–190.

Martin, L. L., & Tesser, A. (1989). Toward a motivation and structural theory of ruminative thoughts. In J. S. Uleman & J. A Bargh (Eds.), *Unintended thought* (pp. 306–326). New York: Guilford.

McCorkle, S., & Mills, J. L. (1992). Rowboat in a hurricane: Metaphors of interpersonal conflict management. *Communication Reports, 5,* 57–66.

McCullough, M. E., Bellah, C. G., Kilpatrick, S. D., & Johnson, J. L. (2001). Vengefulness: Relationships with forgiveness, rumination, well-being, and the Big Five. *Personality and Social Psychology Bulletin, 27,* 601–610.

McCullough, M. E., Fincham, F. D., & Tsang, J. A. (2003). Forgiveness, forbearance, and time: The temporal unfolding of transgression-related interpersonal motivations. *Journal of Personality and Social Psychology, 84,* 540–557.

McCullough, M. E., Rachal, K. C., Sandage, S. J., Worthington, E. L., Jr., Brown, S. W., & Hight, T. L. (1998). Interpersonal forgiving in close relationships: II. Theoretical elaboration and measurement. *Journal of Personality and Social Psychology, 75,* 1586–1603.

McCullough, M. E., Worthington, E. L., Jr., & Rachal, K. C. (1997). Interpersonal forgiving in close relationships. *Journal of Personality and Social Psychology, 73,* 321–336.

McGonagle, K. A., Kessler, R. C., & Gotlib, I. H. (1993). The effects of marital disagreement style, frequency, and outcome on marital disruption. *Journal of Social and Personal Relationships, 10,* 385–404.

McGregor, I., & Holmes, J. G. (1999). How storytelling shapes memory and impression of relationship events over time. *Journal of Personality and Social Psychology, 76,* 403–419.

McIntosh, W. D., Harlow, T. F., & Martin, L. L. (1995). Linkers and nonlinkers: Goal beliefs as a moderator of the effects of everyday hassles on rumination, depression, and physical complaints. *Journal of Applied Social Psychology, 25,* 1231–1244.

Metts, S., & Cupach, W. R. (1990). The influence of relationship beliefs and problem-solving responses on satisfaction in romantic relationships. *Human Communication Research, 17,* 170–185.

Millar, K. U., Tesser, A., & Millar, M. (1988). The effects of a threatening life event on behavior sequences and intrusive thought: A self-disruption explanation. *Cognitive Therapy and Research, 12,* 441–457.

Miller, G. E., & Bradbury, T. N. (1995). Refining the association between attributions and behavior in martial interaction. *Journal of Family Psychology, 9,* 196–208.

Miller, J. B. (1991). Women's and men's scripts for interpersonal conflict. *Psychology of Women Quarterly, 15,* 15–29.

Moller, A. T., & Van Zyl, P. D. (1991). Relationship beliefs, interpersonal perception, and marital adjustment. *Journal of Clinical Psychology, 47,* 28–33.

Mongeau, P. A., & Johnson, K. L. (1995). Predicting cross-sex first-date sexual expectations and involvement: Contextual and individual difference factors. *Personal Relationships, 2,* 301–312.

Murray, S. L., & Holmes, J. G. (1993). Seeing virtues in faults: Negativity and the transformation of interpersonal narratives in close relationships. *Journal of Personality and Social Psychology, 65,* 707–722.

Murray, S. L., & Holmes, J. G. (1994). Storytelling in close relationships: The construction of confidence. *Personality and Social Psychology Bulletin, 20,* 650–663.

Murray, S. L., & Holmes, J. G. (1999). The (mental) ties that bind: Cognitive structures that predict relationship resilience. *Journal of Personality and Social Psychology, 77,* 1228–1244.

Murray, S. L., Holmes, J. G., & Griffin, D. W. (1996). The self-fulfilling nature of positive illusions in romantic relationships: Love is not blind, but prescient. *Journal of Personality and Social Psychology, 71,* 1155–1180.

Neff, L. A., & Karney, B. R. (2004). How does context affect intimate relationships? Linking external stress and cognitive processes within marriage. *Personality and Social Psychology Bulletin, 30,* 134–148.

Nolen-Hoeksema, S. (1991). Responses to depression and their effects on the duration of depressive episodes. *Journal of Abnormal Psychology, 100,* 569–582.

Notarius, C. I., Benson, P. R., Sloane, D., Vanzetti, N. A., & Hornyak, L. M. (1989). Exploring the interface between perception and behavior: An analysis of marital interaction in distressed and nondistressed couples. *Behavioral Assessment, 11,* 39–64.

Ostrom, T. M. (1984). The sovereignty of social cognition. In R. S. Wyer, Jr., & T. K. Srull (Eds.), *Handbook of social cognition: Vol. 1* (pp. 1–38). Hillsdale, NJ: Lawrence Erlbaum.

Pinkley, R. L. (1990). Dimensions of conflict frame: Disputant interpretations of conflict. *Journal of Applied Psychology, 75,* 117–126.

Pinkley, R. L. (1992). Dimensions of conflict frame: Relation to disputant perceptions and expectations. *International Journal of Conflict Management, 3,* 95–113.

Pinkley, R. L., & Northcraft, G. B. (1994). Conflict frames of reference: Implications for dispute processes and outcomes. *Academy of Management Journal, 37,* 193–205.

Planalp, S., & Honeycutt, J. (1985). Events that increase uncertainty in personal relationships. *Human Communication Research, 11,* 593–604.

Resick, P. A., Barr, P. K., Sweet, J. J., Keiffer, D. M., Ruby, N. L., & Spiegel, D. K. (1981). Perceived and actual discriminators of conflict from accord in marital communication. *American Journal of Family Therapy, 9,* 58–68.

Richards, J. M., Butler, E. A., & Gross, J. J. (2003). Emotion regulation in romantic relationships: The cognitive consequences of concealing feelings. *Journal of Social and Personal Relationships, 20,* 599–620.

Riggio, H. R. (2004). Parental marital conflict and divorce, parent-child relationships, social support, and relationship anxiety in young adulthood. *Personal Relationships, 11,* 99–114.

Robinson, E. A., & Price, M. G. (1980). Pleasurable behavior in marital interaction: An observational study. *Journal of Consulting and Clinical Psychology, 48,* 117–118.

Robinson, M. W., & Alloy, L. B. (2003). Negative cognitive styles and stress-reactive rumination interact to predict depression: A prospective study. *Cognitive Therapy and Research, 27,* 275–292.

Rogan, R. G., & La France, B. H. (2003). An examination of the relationship between verbal aggressiveness, conflict management strategies, and conflict interaction goals. *Communication Quarterly, 51,* 458–469.

Roloff, M. E., & Berger, C. R. (1982). Social cognition and communication: An introduction. In M. E. Roloff & C. R. Berger (Eds.), *Social cognition and communication* (pp. 9–32). Thousand Oaks, CA: Sage.

Roloff, M. E., & Solomon, D. H. (2002). Conditions under which relational commitment leads to expressing relational complaints. *International Journal for Conflict Management, 13,* 276–391.

Roloff, M. E., Soule, K. P., & Carey, C. M. (2001). Reasons for remaining in a relationship and responses to relational transactions. *Journal of Social and Personal Relationships, 18,* 362–385.

Rusbult, C. E., Verette, J., Whitney, G. A., Slovik, L. F., & Lipkus, I. (1991). Accommodation processes in close relationships: Theory and preliminary empirical evidence. *Journal of Personality and Social Psychology, 60,* 53–78.

Rusting, C. L., & Nolen-Hoeksema, S. (1998). Regulating response to anger: Effects of rumination and distraction on angry mood. *Journal of Personality and Social Psychology, 74,* 790–803.

Sadler, O., & Tesser, A. (1973). Some effects of salience and time upon interpersonal hostility and attraction during social isolation. *Sociometry, 36,* 99–112.

Sagrestano, L. M., Christensen, A., & Heavey, C. L. (1998). Social influence techniques during marital conflict. *Personal Relationships, 5,* 75–89.

Sanderson, C. A., & Karetsky, K. H. (2002). Intimacy goals and strategies of conflict resolution in dating relationships: A mediational analysis. *Journal of Social and Personal Relationships, 19,* 317–337.

Schank, R., & Abelson, R. (1977). *Scripts, plans, goals and understanding: An inquiry into human knowledge structures.* Hillsdale, NJ: Lawrence Erlbaum.

Schutz, A. (1999). It was your fault! Self-serving biases in autobiographical accounts of conflicts in married couples. *Journal of Social and Personal Relationships, 16,* 193–208.

Schutz, A., & Baumeister, R. F. (1999). The language of defense: Linguistic patterns in narratives of transgression. *Journal of Language and Social Psychology, 18,* 269–286.

Schweinle, W. E., Ickes, W., & Bernstein, I. H. (2002). Empathic inaccuracy in husband to wife aggression: The overattribution bias. *Personal Relationships, 9,* 141–158.

Showers, C. J., & Zeigler-Hill, V. (2004). Organization of partner knowledge: Relationship outcomes and longitudinal change. *Personality and Social Psychology, 30,* 1198–1210.

Sillars, A. L. (1980). Attributions and communication in roommate conflicts. *Communication Monographs, 47,* 180–200.

Sillars, A. L., & Parry, D. (1982). Stress, cognition, and communication in interpersonal conflict. *Communication Research, 9,* 201–226.

Sillars, A. L., Pike, G. R., Jones, T. S., & Murphy, M. A. (1984). Communication and understanding in marriage. *Human Communication Research, 10,* 317–350.

Sillars, A. L., Roberts, L. J., Leonard, K. E., & Dun, T. (2000). Cognition during marital conflict: The relationship of thought and talk. *Journal of Social and Personal Relationships, 17,* 479–502.

Simpson, J. A., Orina, M. M., & Ickes, W. (2003). When accuracy hurts, and when it helps: A test of the empathic accuracy model in marital interactions. *Journal of Personality and Social Psychology, 85,* 881–893.

Solomon, D. H., & Samp, J. A. (1998). Power and problem appraisal: Perceptual foundations of the chilling effect in dating relationships. *Journal of Social and Personal Relationships, 15,* 191–209.

Stillwell, A. M., & Baumeister, R. F. (1997). The construction of victim and perpetrator memories: Accuracy and distortion in role-based accounts. *Personality and Social Psychology Bulletin, 11,* 1157–1173.

Stutman, R. K., & Newell, S. E. (1990). Rehearsing for confrontation. *Argumentation, 4,* 185–198.

Sullaway, M., & Christensen, A. (1983). Assessment of dysfunctional interaction patterns in couples. *Journal of Marriage and the Family, 45,* 653–660.

Treynor, W., Gonzalez, R., & Nolen-Hoeksema, S. (2003). Rumination reconsidered: A psychometric analysis. *Cognitive Therapy and Research, 27,* 247–250.

Vangelisti, A. (1994). Messages that hurt. In W. R. Cupach & B. H. Spitzberg (Eds.), *The dark side of interpersonal communication* (pp. 53–82). Hillsdale, NJ: Lawrence Erlbaum.

Vanzetti, N. A., Notarius, C. I., & NeeSmith, D. (1992). Specific and generalized expectancies in marital interaction. *Journal of Family Psychology, 6,* 171–183.

Ward, A., Lyubomirsky, S., Sousa, L., & Nolen-Hoeksema, S. (2003). Can't quite commit: Rumination and uncertainty. *Personality and Social Psychology Bulletin, 29,* 96–107.

Weigel, D. J., Bennett, K. K., & Ballard-Reisch, D. S. (2003). Family influences on commitment: Examining the family of origin correlates of relationship commitment attitudes. *Personal Relationships, 10,* 453–474.

Weiss, R. L. (1980). Strategic behavioral marital therapy: Toward a model for assessment and intervention. In J. P. Vincent (Ed.), *Advances in family intervention, assessment, and theory* (Vol. 1, pp. 229–271). New York: Guilford.

Wenzlaff, R. M., & Luxton, D. D. (2003). The role of thought suppression in depressive rumination. *Cognitive Therapy & Research, 27,* 293–308.

Wieselquist, J., Rusbult, C. E., Foster, C. A., & Agnew, C. R. (1999). Commitment, pro-relationship behavior, and trust in close relationships. *Journal of Personality and Social Psychology, 77,* 942–966.

Witteman, H. (1988). Interpersonal problem solving: Problem conceptualization and communication use. *Communication Monographs, 55,* 336–359.

Witteman, H. (1992). Analyzing interpersonal conflict: Nature of awareness, type of initiating event, situational perceptions, and management styles. *Western Journal of Communication, 56,* 248–280.

Wong, P. T. P., & Weiner, B. (1981). When people ask "why" questions, and the heuristics of attributional search. *Journal of Personality and Social Psychology, 40,* 650–663.

Yovetich, N. A., & Rusbult, C. E. (1994). Accommodative behavior in close relationships: Exploring transformation of motivation. *Journal of Experimental Social Psychology, 30,* 138–164.

Zagacki, K. S., Edwards, R., & Honeycutt, J. M. (1992). The role of mental imagery and emotion in imagined interaction. *Communication Quarterly, 40,* 56–68.

Zechmeister, J. S., & Romero, C. (2002). Victim and offender accounts of interpersonal conflict: Autobiographical narratives of forgiveness and unforgiveness. *Journal of Personality and Social Psychology, 82,* 675–686.

5

CONFLICT IN DATING AND MARITAL RELATIONSHIPS

JOHN P. CAUGHLIN
University of Illinois

ANITA L. VANGELISTI
University of Texas at Austin

With good reason, conflict in dating relationships and marriages has generated enormous scholarly and popular interest. When handled well, conflict in romantic unions can enable relational partners to learn about each other and foster a sense of cohesion and commitment (Siegert & Stamp, 1994). When not managed well, conflict can have negative implications for the relationship and for the relational partners (Fincham & Beach, 1999). Conflict in romantic relationships also has implications for individuals beyond those directly involved. Marital conflict, for instance, is an even more important predictor of negative outcomes for children than is parental divorce (Amato, Loomis, & Booth, 1995; Booth & Amato, 2001; Jekielek, 1998). Indeed, children whose parents divorce tend to benefit compared to children whose parents stay married but engage in frequent and intense marital conflict (Morrison & Coiro, 1999).

Given the significance of conflict in romantic relationships, it is not surprising that the literature in this area is enormous. By necessity, any review of this area will be selective. With the breadth and complexity of the work on this topic, it was useful to organize our review around a framework that we adapted from Huston's (2000) social ecological model for understanding marriage and similar unions (see Figure 5.1). We employed this framework because it was applicable to a wide variety of close dyadic unions, it provided a general schema for understanding conflict in romantic relationships, and it highlighted some potentially important issues and questions that appear to be understudied (e.g., the impact of the social context on relational conflict).

Following Huston (2000), we consider three interconnected levels of analysis: (a) the environment, which ranges from broad societal influences to a couple's specific social and physical context; (b) the individuals, including the enduring characteristics that people bring to their relationship and attitudes and beliefs they develop during the relationship; and (c) the relational processes, which are composed partly of relational conflict behaviors and conflict patterns. This perspective highlights the dynamic nature of the individuals and their relationship, including

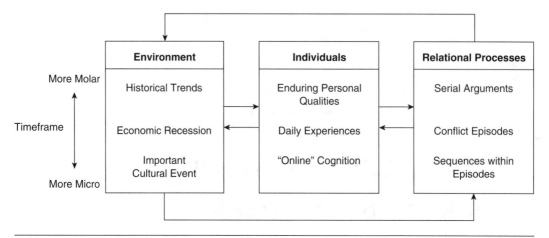

Figure 5.1   Framework for Organizing Questions About, and Research on, Conflict in Romantic Relationships

the conflict behaviors and patterns in that relationship (Huston, 2000).

The dynamic aspect of relational conflict implies that questions about conflict can reflect various timeframes. Indeed, as depicted from top to bottom in each of the boxes in Figure 5.1, all three levels of analysis can be examined over different temporal periods. In the environment, one could take a molar temporal perspective and consider the impact of historical changes on marital conflict; for example, Gadlin (1977) suggested that many issues that would now be considered private were subject to community intervention in Colonial America. One could also examine a shorter timeframe; for example, when a culture celebrates a holiday that often involves family gatherings (e.g., Thanksgiving in the U.S.), relational conflict may be affected (e.g., by highlighting an existing conflict pertaining to in-laws). Varied timeframes also can be considered when examining individuals engaging in conflict; for example, individuals' attachment styles may influence conflict over a fairly long time period (Feeney, Noller, & Roberts, 2000), but scholars may also be interested in the specific "online" thoughts that individuals have during a particular conflict (e.g., Sillars, Roberts, Dun, & Leonard, 2001; Sillars, Roberts, Leonard, & Dun, 2000). Finally, with the relational process level, one could examine relational conflicts that occur over long time periods spanning many specific encounters (Johnson & Roloff, 2000), but one could also study specific, microscopic sequences of conflict behaviors (Buysse et al., 2000).

Although the conceptual model summarized in Figure 5.1 indicates that there is interplay among the various levels, the main research foci of relational conflict researchers have been on relational behaviors and the individuals who enact them (rather than on connections to environmental factors). The largest portion of the relationship conflict literature has examined connections between conflict behaviors and relational outcomes (Bradbury, Cohan, & Karney, 1998; Karney & Bradbury, 1995; Sillars, Canary, & Tafoya, 2004). The phrase *relational outcomes* refers both to aspects of relationships (e.g., whether the dyad remains intact or breaks up) and to properties of individuals (e.g., partners' evaluations of, and satisfaction with, the relationship).

Because research on the connection between conflict behaviors and relational outcomes has been such a focus of the literature, we begin by reviewing this research. Next, we examine how individual dyad members influence the behavioral system (and particularly conflict) in a relationship. Finally, we examine how the larger environment influences conflict processes in romantic relationships.

CONFLICT BEHAVIORS AND RELATIONAL OUTCOMES

The notion of relational outcomes is a broad-based one, but the primary outcomes of interest have been individuals' satisfaction with their relationships and relational instability (i.e., break-ups among dating couples and divorce among married dyads). The prototypical studies in this genre are based on the problem-solving paradigm, which involves dyads engaging in relatively brief discussions of issues that they nominate as problematic and then researchers examining the conversations to determine if the partners' behaviors are associated with relational outcomes (e.g., Billings, 1979; Gottman, 1979). Until the early 1990s, most of this research compared the behaviors of satisfied couples to those of couples who were dissatisfied (for a review, see Robinson & Jacobson, 1987). Since then, there has been a surge in longitudinal studies examining whether conflict behaviors predict changes in relational satisfaction and relational dissolution (e.g., Gottman & Levenson, 2000; Heavey, Christensen, & Malamuth, 1995; Karney & Bradbury, 1997).

Individual Behaviors

The specific behaviors examined in studies of relational conflict are myriad (see Sillars et al., 2004). However, scholars frequently conceptualize the various behaviors in terms of two dimensions. The first is most commonly discussed in terms of positive or negative affect (Canary, Cupach, & Messman, 1995; Heavey et al., 1995; Sillars & Weisberg, 1987), but is sometimes labeled valence or cooperation versus competition (Sillars et al., 2004). The second dimension is engagement versus avoidance (Canary et al., 1995; Sillars & Weisberg, 1987) or directness (Sillars et al., 2004).

Negativity and positivity. Scholars frequently conceptualize positive and negative affect in conflict along a single dimension, but most coding systems distinguish between behaviors that are viewed as cooperative and those that are seen as competitive. Researchers using Sillars' (1986) Verbal Tactics Coding Scheme or similar measures, for example, usually make separate assessments of integrative and distributive strategies, which are viewed as having positive and negative affect, respectively (e.g., Canary & Cupach, 1988; Meeks, Hendrick, & Hendrick, 1998). Similarly, coding schemes that incorporate nonverbal assessments (e.g., Gottman, 1994; Matthews, Wickrama, & Conger, 1996) typically include categories of positivity (i.e.,

expressions of warm or positive affect) and negativity (i.e., expressions of hostile or negative affect).

Numerous studies have shown that negativity and similar constructs are associated inversely with concurrent relational satisfaction (for reviews, see Fincham & Beach, 1999; Robinson & Jacobson, 1987). This association has been found with a variety of different methods, including observations of laboratory conflict discussions (Koren, Carlton, & Shaw, 1980; Levenson & Gottman, 1983; Newton & Burgoon, 1990), retrospective reports of relational conflict (Birchler & Webb, 1977; Meeks et al., 1998), and daily diary ratings of negative behaviors that are associated with conflict (Caughlin, Huston, & Houts, 2000; Huston & Vangelisti, 1991; Wills, Weiss, & Patterson, 1974). Negativity also frequently predicts declines in relational satisfaction over time (Heyman, 2001; Huston & Vangelisti, 1991; Karney & Bradbury, 1995). There are a few studies suggesting "reversal effects" (Fincham & Beach, 1999, p. 52), in which some form of negativity is associated concurrently with dissatisfaction but predicts increases in satisfaction (Gottman & Krokoff, 1989; Heavey et al., 1995; Heavey, Layne, & Christensen, 1993). However, such effects generally have not been confirmed in attempted replications (Fincham & Beach, 1999), and due to ambiguities in the analyses, the reversal effects may reflect extremely unhappy couples becoming somewhat less unhappy— rather than couples becoming satisfied due to negativity (Caughlin, 2002; Woody & Costanzo, 1990). In short, the preponderant evidence indicates that negativity often predicts decreasing satisfaction (Fincham & Beach, 1999; Karney & Bradbury, 1995).

Compared to the findings pertaining to negativity, the connection between expressions of positive affect during conflict and satisfaction is more muted. In many studies, it is difficult to determine whether expressions of positive affection matter, because the researchers combine positive and negative affect into a single score (e.g., Karney & Bradbury, 1997; Markman, 1979; Matthews et al., 1996). When studies do distinguish between positivity and negativity, they tend to indicate that negativity is a more consistent and powerful predictor of relational satisfaction than is positivity (Gottman, 1994;

Huston & Vangelisti, 1991; Kurdek, 1995; Wills et al., 1974). However, Karney and Bradbury's (1995) meta-analysis indicated that couples' positivity predicts relative increases in satisfaction (i.e., either actual increases or at least slower declines in satisfaction), which suggests that positivity is important to marital satisfaction, even if the effect is smaller than that due to negativity.

Whereas countless studies have examined connections between expressions of affect and relational satisfaction, fairly few have examined negativity or positivity as predictors of relational stability. Those that have, indicate that negativity during conflict predicts divorce— at least over periods of a few years (Gottman, 1994; Karney & Bradbury, 1995; Lindahl, Clements, & Markman, 1998; Matthews et al., 1996). Most notably, Gottman's (1994) cascade model proposes that the trajectory toward divorce is driven by a progression of increasingly alienating conflict behaviors. Although Gottman (1994) suggested that the trajectory is related to a balance between positive and negative affect, the key predictors of the cascade involve negativity and uncooperative avoidance (i.e., stonewalling) rather than positive affect.

Engagement versus avoidance. There is a cultural bias in the United States against avoiding conflict (Parks, 1982), and some scholars are so accepting of this bias that they consider withdrawal to be a form of negativity (e.g., Lindahl et al., 1998). On the surface, such parsimony appears reasonable. Overall, there is an inverse association between relational satisfaction and various measures of conflict avoidance, including perceptions of mutual conflict avoidance (Noller, Feeney, Bonnell, & Callan, 1994; Noller & White, 1990), perceptions of the partner's avoidance (Kurdek, 1995; Meeks et al., 1998; Roberts, 2000), and perceptions of one's own avoidance (Canary & Cupach, 1988; Kurdek, 1995; Meeks et al., 1998).

However, this overall inverse association probably is modified by a number of factors. Roberts (2000) and Sillars et al. (2004), for example, argued that there are qualitatively different forms of conflict avoidance, with some forms being more hostile and other forms being more neutral or cooperative. Roberts found that

conflict avoidance that included negative affect was related more consistently to marital dissatisfaction than was neutral avoidance (e.g., husbands' angry avoidance was associated with wives' later dissatisfaction, but other conflict avoidance by husbands was not).

Moreover, Roloff and Ifert (2000) noted that conflict avoidance can occur in different circumstances. Individuals may withhold a complaint to avoid a conflict episode before it begins, suppress further discussion of an issue that has already been introduced, or agree to make a topic taboo. These various forms of avoidance may have different relational implications; for example, if one is able to avoid a conflict before it is ever discussed, the partner may remain unaware and unaffected by this avoidance (Caughlin & Golish, 2002).

In addition, Roloff and Ifert (2000) hypothesized that the success of avoiding conflict likely depends on several conditions. First, they noted that avoiding conflict can be associated with satisfaction if couples are comfortable with avoidance and tolerate differences between the partners (Sillars et al., 2004). Research with M. A. Fitzpatrick's (1988) couple types, for example, suggests that there is a positive association between conflict avoidance and relational satisfaction among people who believe conflict avoidance can be helpful for maintaining relationships. Sillars, Pike, Jones, and Redmon (1983) found that for couples classified as separates (who tend to believe that avoiding overt arguments allows problems to disappear), relational satisfaction was associated with denials of conflict and diversions from conflict topics.

Second, Roloff and Ifert (2000) suggested that various coping strategies can help couples successfully avoid conflict. Maintaining positive affect while avoiding, for instance, can diminish any negative impact of avoidance (Raush, Barry, Hertel, & Swain, 1974). Third, conflict avoidance is most likely to be successful if it is used selectively, as in cases when the issue is not considered important (Cloven & Roloff, 1993; Roloff & Ifert, 2000).

Fourth, individuals probably find conflict avoidance satisfying only if they choose to avoid without excessive pressure to do so (Roloff & Ifert, 2000). Research on the chilling effect suggests that people avoid conflicts if they fear that expressing a complaint would lead to negative consequences from their partner (Cloven & Roloff, 1993; Roloff & Cloven, 1990). Although there is a tendency for individuals experiencing a chilling effect to downplay the importance of the topic (Solomon & Samp, 1998), if they avoid due to pressure and still feel that the issue is important, they may be dissatisfied with their avoidance (Caughlin & Afifi, 2004).

Finally, conflict avoidance is most likely to be successful if the relational partners have important competencies like communication skills and perspective-taking ability (Roloff & Ifert, 2000). Gottman (1994) observed that satisfied married individuals who engaged in frequent avoidant behavior also engaged in positive behaviors and attempted to understand their partner's views. In addition, Caughlin and Afifi (2004) found that the usual inverse association between topic avoidance and relational satisfaction in dating couples was moderated by girlfriends' perceptions of their own and their boyfriend's communication competence.

Dyadic Patterns

Although most behavioral research on conflict in romantic relationships has focused on frequencies of individuals' behaviors, research influenced by a systems perspective has focused on the interdependence of relational partners' behaviors (Watzlawick, Beavin, & Jackson, 1967). This more systemic view of conflict behaviors has led some scholars to study various patterns of behaviors, including negative reciprocity and demand/withdraw (for a more complete review of conflict patterns, see Messman & Canary, 1998).

Negative reciprocity. Numerous studies, using a wide variety of coding systems and definitions, have established that exchanging negative behaviors (e.g., complaints, defensiveness, expressions of negative affect) is associated with dissatisfaction, even after controlling for the overall rates of negativity (Gottman, 1979; Margolin & Wampold, 1981). The link between negative reciprocity and dissatisfaction has been observed with measures focusing primarily on nonverbal behaviors (Krokoff, Gottman, & Roy, 1988; Levenson, & Gottman, 1983), ones focusing mainly on verbal behaviors (Alberts,

1989; Alberts & Driscoll, 1992; Ting-Toomey, 1983), and schemes mixing verbal and nonverbal assessments (Billings, 1979; Margolin & Wampold, 1981). There is some evidence that the affective aspect of negative reciprocity is more important than the verbal exchanges: Pike and Sillars (1985) replicated the usual findings pertaining to negative reciprocity with affect codes but found contrary findings with verbal codes. Overall, however, the connection between negative reciprocity and dissatisfaction is quite robust. Negative reciprocity also presages declines in satisfaction and relational dissolution (Filsinger & Thoma, 1988; Gottman, 1994).

Demand/withdraw. Demand/withdraw involves one partner nagging, complaining, or criticizing and the other partner avoiding. The label does not imply a particular order; in fact, sequential analyses have shown that withdrawal can lead to demands, just as demands can lead to withdrawal (Klinetob & Smith, 1996). Also, although some research does not explicitly note the affective component of demanding, Heavey et al. (1995) suggested that the concept of demanding involves only negative engagement tactics (e.g., criticisms) rather than more positive or neutral ones (e.g., trying to discuss a problem).

Despite variations in the specific measures of demand/withdraw, both observations and participant reports have indicated that demand/withdraw is associated inversely with concurrent relational satisfaction (Caughlin & Huston, 2002; Heavey et al., 1993; Noller et al., 1994). However, the prospective outcomes associated with demand/withdraw are less clear. Some studies indicate that demand/withdraw (especially woman-demand/man-withdraw) predicts declining satisfaction (Heavey et al., 1995) and dissolution (Gottman & Levenson, 2000). Other studies have failed to replicate such findings (Heavey et al., 1993; Noller et al., 1994) and still others suggest that demand/withdraw can foreshadow increasing relational satisfaction (Caughlin, 2002; Gottman & Krokoff, 1989; Heavey et al., 1995; Heavey et al., 1993).

Also, there is evidence that a rigid pattern of husbands' demanding while wives withdraw may be associated with spousal abuse (Eldridge & Christensen, 2002). Gottman, Driver, Yoshimoto, and Rushe (2002) suggested that violent husbands sometimes use coercive verbal tactics to gain short-term compliance, even if they cannot actually influence their wife's beliefs. Gottman et al.'s (2002) explanation is consistent with Johnson's (2001) contention that battered wives are often subjected to verbal and physical coercion that is part of a coherent pattern of control.

Critique of Research on Conflict Behaviors and Outcomes

Research in this general area has produced many impressive results. Despite huge variation in how constructs like negativity have been measured (Heyman, 2001), there is ample evidence that negativity predicts outcomes like dissatisfaction and divorce. In many cases, this general conclusion has been accompanied by detailed descriptions of conflict behaviors that have become the basis for a number of interventions to improve courting and married couples' relationships. Although one cannot assume that teaching couples to emulate satisfied couples will be an effective intervention (Stanley, Bradbury, & Markman, 2000), systematic studies of interventions based on the problem-solving paradigm demonstrate that teaching couples to enact constructive strategies and avoid excessively negative ones (e.g., criticisms of the partner's character) can prevent distress and improve strained relationships (Hahlweg, Markman, Thurmaier, Engl, & Eckert, 1998; Markman, Floyd, Stanley, & Storaasli, 1988).

In short, research on the connections between conflict resolution behaviors and relational outcomes has proved quite useful. Nevertheless, there are concerns about the research in this area. Because the extant literature is so large and varied, no particular concern applies to all the specific studies, but each is prevalent. These concerns pertain to studies that predict divorce, research on the affect dimension of conflict engagement, and some general assumptions of the problem-solving paradigm.

Research on predictors of divorce. The research demonstrating that negativity predicts divorce has been very fruitful, with some studies indicating

the ability to predict divorce at a rate greater than 90% (e.g., Gottman, 1994). Not surprisingly, such findings have generated much popular and scholarly attention, but there are also reasons for this enthusiasm to remain somewhat tempered (Bradbury, Rogge, & Lawrence, 2001). First, the statistical analyses used to predict divorce are optimized for a particular sample; unless the same prediction equations are validated with another sample, it is impossible to know how many divorces can actually be predicted. Heyman and Smith Slep (2001), for example, used half of a nationally representative sample to compute a prediction equation that correctly labeled 90% of participants as married or divorced. When they applied the same equation to the other half of the sample, however, the overall accuracy in predicting which people would divorce was only 69%, and among the individuals who had been predicted to be divorced, the equation was correct in only 29% of the cases. This suggests that previous claims of being able to predict divorce with 90% accuracy are, at best, exaggerated.

Second, even if negativity predicts relational dissolution, this does not prove a causal relationship (Glenn, 1998). Indeed, the existing evidence suggests that part of the association between negativity and divorce may be an artifact of including couples who are already moving toward dissolution. Negativity appears to be a reliable predictor of divorces in the short term but not in the longer term. Huston, Caughlin, Houts, Smith, and George (2001) found that newlywed levels of negativity were significantly higher in couples who divorced in the first 2 years of marriage than for couples who divorced after at least 2 years. Similarly, in their 14-year longitudinal study, Gottman and Levenson (2000) found that negativity predicted divorces during the first half of the study but not in the second half. Given that relational dissatisfaction predicts heightened negative conflict resolution behaviors (Noller & Feeney, 1998), it is plausible that at least part of the association between negativity and relational dissolution is a reflection of general behavioral and psychological distress rather than evidence that negativity causes divorce.

Although there is little evidence that negativity can predict divorce over more than a few years, there are behavioral predictors that do foreshadow divorces that happen later. Huston et al. (2001) found that couples who stayed married at least 7 years and then divorced before 13 years were distinct from couples who divorced earlier or who were still married after 13 years. As newlyweds, couples who divorced after at least 7 years were higher than other couples in terms of affectional expression; then, over the next 2 years, the later divorcing couples evinced greater declines in affectional expression than did other couples. Gottman and Levenson (2000) reported that expressions of positive affect during conflict did not predict divorce over a 7-year period, but the absence of positive expressions predicted divorces that happened more than 7 years after the original observation. In short, the few studies that have examined predictors of divorce over more than just a few years suggest that the predictors of short-term outcomes are different from the predictors of long-term outcomes. A prime goal of future research in this area should be to confirm and elaborate on this general conclusion.

Research on the affect dimension of conflict behaviors. A number of critiques have been made of research that focuses on the affect dimension of conflict behaviors. First, the well-documented finding that "negativity" is associated with relational dissatisfaction and relational dissolution may seem "obvious and uninteresting" (Sillars et al., 2004, p. 432). One counterargument to this point is that the general category of negativity summarizes a number of specific behaviors, some of which may be more important correlates of dissatisfaction and dissolution than are others (Gottman, 1994). Alberts (1988), for example, reported that satisfied couples were more likely than dissatisfied ones to focus on behaviors when complaining, whereas dissatisfied partners were more likely to complain about each other's personal characteristics. Also, Gottman, Coan, Carrere, and Swanson (1998) distinguished between low-intensity negativity (e.g., expressing anger) and high-intensity negativity (e.g., expressing criticism, contempt, defensiveness, or belligerence) and found that husbands' high-intensity negativity was a statistically significant predictor of divorce over a 6-year period, but husbands' low-intensity

negativity was not. Such findings suggest that it may be important for future research in this area to focus more on distinctions among types of negativity than has been common until now.

A second group of critiques regarding the affect dimension of conflict behaviors questions the appropriateness of the dimension. Erbert (2000) argued that couples' conflicts are often dialectical (i.e., the conflicts are shaped by the interaction between forces that are simultaneously unified and opposed). Erbert found that married couples viewed the contradictions of autonomy-connection and openness-closedness as important to a number of common conflict issues (e.g., personal criticisms, finances, household tasks). To the extent that such dialectics are salient in a particular conflict, conflict behaviors may function as both positive and negative at the same time. Even behaviors that often are considered negative may serve useful functions in romantic relationships; for example, although expressing a criticism may diminish connection between partners in many instances, it also may allow attention to the autonomy pole of the autonomy-connection contradiction. Similarly, given the general preference for openness in close relationships in North American culture (Parks, 1982), open criticism could be viewed as reflecting relational strength.

In addition to such theoretical arguments questioning whether conflict behaviors should be conceptualized along a positive-negative continuum, there is empirical evidence that negativity and positivity cannot be adequately described with a single dimension. Indeed, a review by Gable and Reis (2001) indicates that positive and negative behaviors in romantic relationships are "functionally independent dimensions" (p. 169). If a single dimension accounted for negativity and positivity, these behaviors would have a strong inverse correlation across all studies. However, the observed correlations are often quite small, and factor analyses support treating positive and negative behaviors separately (Huston & Vangelisti, 1991; Smith, Vivian, & O'Leary, 1990). Gottman's (1994) findings that a significant proportion of couples are high in both negativity and positivity also illustrate the lack of a strong inverse correlation. Conversely, couples can be low in both negativity and positivity. Such marriages can be described as affectively neutral or bland, and they are distinct from marriages with greater levels of negativity and positivity—even when the ratio of negative to positive affect is similar (Caughlin & Huston, in press). Moreover, positive and negative interaction behaviors often moderate each other's association with relational satisfaction (Huston & Chorost, 1994; Smith et al., 1990), a finding that would be unlikely if a single dimension adequately captured these constructs. Finally, as noted above, Gottman and Levenson (2000) and Huston et al. (2001) found that the relational outcomes associated with positive and negative interaction behaviors are distinct (i.e., negativity and positivity do not demonstrate parallelism).

In short, the empirical evidence provides a compelling case for recognizing that negativity and positivity often function as two separate dimensions. Although it may be useful for some purposes to conceptualize positive versus negative affect along a continuum, this does not mean that it is useful or appropriate to collapse behaviors with positive and negative affect into a single measure (e.g., Karney & Bradbury, 1997; Matthews et al., 1996). Because positive and negative behaviors are known to have different associations with relational outcomes, collapsing them into a single measure can create serious difficulties in interpreting findings.

Assumptions of the problem-solving paradigm. Notwithstanding the considerable methodological diversity in this area, the prototypical study of conflict and relational outcomes involves observing a single episode of problem solving (Noller & Feeney, 1998). Findings using other methods often are considered suspect unless they converge with observational research (Noller & Feeney, 2004). Obviously, there are some important advantages to observational studies; for example, biases in self-reports are well documented (Metts, Sprecher, & Cupach, 1991). Nevertheless, the problem-solving paradigm implies several questionable theoretical assumptions about relational conflict.

First, research in this area often assumes that conflict is inevitable (Beach, 2001). Whereas it may be reasonable to assume that almost all close relationships experience *some* conflict, this assumption is often taken to mean that the amount of conflict and the difficulty of the issues do not matter; for example, Clements, Cordova, Markman, and Laurenceau (1997) argued, "the number and type of conflict areas ... are less important than how couples handle these conflicts" (p. 342). The countless studies asking couples to discuss their most contentious issues implicitly assume that frequency and difficulty are unimportant. Also, using the behaviors produced in these episodes as indicative of "how couples handle" conflict presumes that couples actually discuss their disagreements and that all couples have equally troubling yet solvable conflict issues. This implies a theoretical perspective of how conflict operates in romantic relationships that is, at best, suspect.

In contrast to the assumption that managing conflict is more important than the difficulty and frequency of conflicts, experienced relationships counselors attribute the majority of couples' troubles to fundamental problems that often cause communication difficulties, rather than to problems managing conflict per se (Vangelisti, 1994). Also, Sanford (2003) showed that the difficulty of married couples' conflict issues is related positively to observations of negativity and related inversely to relational satisfaction. Thus, the observed connections between negativity and dissatisfaction may be somewhat spurious and driven by the difficulty of the conflict.

Moreover, research outside laboratories suggests that the frequency of conflict is an important predictor of relational outcomes. Diary studies of dating and married couples have suggested that, on average, conflict episodes are experienced once every few days (Ayduk, Downey, Testa, Yen, & Shoda, 1999; Caughlin & Huston, 1996) or at least several times monthly (Fitzpatrick & Sollie, 1999; McGonagle, Kessler, & Schilling, 1992). Although some scholars have suggested that the infrequent occurrence of conflict episodes means that conflict is not particularly important (Bradbury et al., 2001), variations in the frequency of conflict are associated with relational outcomes. Among dating couples, the amount of conflict is associated with dissatisfaction (Cramer, 2000) and predicts dissolution (Surra & Longstreth, 1990). Premarital conflict also foreshadows dissatisfaction after marriage (Kelly, Huston, & Cate, 1985). The amount of conflict experienced by couples is a concurrent correlate of marital dissatisfaction (Noller & Feeney, 1998; Orbuch, Veroff, Hassan, & Horrocks, 2002), and newlywed levels of conflict presage dissatisfaction 13 years later (Caughlin & Huston, 1996). The clear links between frequency of conflict and important relational outcomes highlight the theoretical importance of understanding why some couples encounter more conflicts that do others. This issue is addressed below in the section about explanations for conflict.

A second questionable theoretical assumption in the problem-solving paradigm is evident in the typical design of such studies. Most of this research, even investigations that assess other constructs longitudinally, measures conflict behaviors only once (Noller & Feeney, 1998). This is potentially problematic because behaviors in a particular episode are likely to have a greater association with judgments of a similar timeframe (e.g., satisfaction with the interaction) than with more molar judgments like overall relational satisfaction. Thus, single-episode measures must assume that the observed behaviors reflect what generally occurs in the relationship and that these behaviors are stable over time. This theoretical assumption obscures the potential importance of changes in conflicts, despite the evidence that relational conflict is linked to changes in partners' interdependence (Braiker & Kelley, 1979). The few studies that have assessed conflict at multiple points in time indicate that dissatisfaction can predict increases in negativity and the amount of conflict (Huston & Vangelisti, 1991; Noller & Feeney, 1998), suggesting that it may be best to conceptualize the connection between conflict and relational outcomes as involving reciprocal effects.

Also, in a study using both diaries and self-reports, Caughlin and Huston (1996) found that marital stability over a 13-year period was related to changes in the experiences of conflict over the first 2 years of marriage. According to daily diary reports of conflicts, dyads who divorced and those who stayed married were similar in the first 2 years in terms of the number of conflict episodes. Divorced and married couples did not differ significantly in conflict frequency, and the frequency declined over the first 2 years of marriage, regardless of whether a couple eventually divorced or not. However, retrospective reports taken first when the couples were newlyweds and again after one and 2 years indicated that couples who eventually divorced reported significant increases in conflict over time, whereas couples who stayed married reported stable levels of conflict.

Our conceptual framework (see Figure 5.1) implies one possible explanation for the discrepancy between the two assessments of conflict. The two different measures ask people to report on different timeframes, with retrospective reports reflecting a 2-month period and the diaries a single day. Although one might assume that the retrospective reports would reflect accumulated perceptions of the daily experiences, considering the different timeframes might cue individuals to count conflicts differently. Consider, for example, Johnson and Roloff's (2000; Roloff & Johnson, 2002) notion of serial arguing, which recognizes that conflict about a particular issue can extend past a single episode, with dyads revisiting an issue repeatedly. For a diary measure of conflict on a given day, participants may report only the overt conflict episodes, which means they would exclude ongoing serial arguments that were not explicitly discussed that day. When asked about the amount of conflict over the past 2 months, however, spouses likely would include ongoing serial arguments, even if they are rarely discussed on a given day. Having many (or particularly frustrating) serial arguments could explain why dyads who end up divorcing reported fewer daily episodes of conflict over time while also reporting that the amount of conflict in their relationship was increasing. Even if a couple does not discuss an issue often, the knowledge that the issue is ongoing and difficult to resolve may be just as important as overt conflict episodes (Lloyd, 1990; Roloff & Johnson, 2002). Obviously, this explanation is speculative, but it illustrates the point that theories of conflict in romantic relationships must consider more than a single episode. Patterns of conflict can develop and unfold over periods of time much longer than the typical observational study (Christensen & Heavey, 1993; Roloff & Johnson, 2002). Future research and theory should pay more attention to the broad temporal issues that are obscured in most observations of conflict episodes.

A third assumption of the problem-solving paradigm is that the sample of conflict behaviors obtained during a laboratory encounter is valid and representative. Much has been written about the external validity of typical observational studies (for review, see Heyman, 2001). The general conclusion typically is that laboratory behaviors are not as negative as conflict behaviors at home (e.g., Gottman, 1979), but given that observational methods reliably predict important outcomes like dissatisfaction and dissolution, there is some predictive validity to observational methods (Heyman, 2001).

Nevertheless, there are growing concerns about the utility of the typical observational study for addressing a number of important questions about relational conflict (Noller & Feeney, 2004). Consider, for example, the difficulties of studying conflict avoidance in a laboratory setting. Individuals are less likely to withdraw if they are directed by a researcher to discuss an issue for a preset amount of time (Kluwer, Heesink, & van de Vliert, 1997; Roberts, 2000). Moreover, much conflict avoidance occurs before an issue is even introduced (Roloff & Ifert, 2000), making it difficult to observe such avoidance.

Even if behaviors can be validly assessed in a single observational episode, there are questions about whether a single assessment is always adequate (Fincham, 2004). Retrospective reports of relational change suggest that particular conflict episodes can be critical events or turning points in a relationship (Baxter & Bullis, 1986). A couples' "first big fight," for instance, can have a large impact on the development of a relationship, leading to dissolution of some dyads and heightened interdependence in others (Siegert & Stamp, 1994). It is unlikely that a single observational period would capture episodes that happened to be the most critical ones; thus, the conflicts that most affect relationships are unlikely to be observed. Unless scholars assume that there are no behavioral differences between the most crucial conflicts and ones observed in research, laboratory studies are likely to miss some of the most important aspects of conflict.

Also, research using diary and log methods has shown that relational partners' moods influence how negatively they treat each other (Schulz, Cowan, Cowan, & Brennan, 2004). Having a negatively stressful day at work, for example, is associated with more marital conflict (Bolger, DeLongis, Kessler, & Wethington, 1989), greater expressions of anger from wives, and more withdrawn behavior from husbands (Schulz et al., 2004). Such variation in participants' moods probably adds a source of unreliability to assessments that rely on a single encounter. Given this potential for unreliability, analyses based on these measures may actually underestimate the association of conflict behaviors with relational outcomes.

In short, the aforementioned theoretical assumptions of the problem-solving paradigm may obscure important aspects of relational conflict. In the future, we need more work that (a) recognizes the importance of variations in the frequency of conflict and in the difficulties of problems that couples face, (b) examines temporal features of conflict (e.g., how conflict patterns change over time, how serial arguments are addressed over multiple episodes, and how particular conflict episodes can serve as critical turning points in relationships), and (c) attempts to document everyday experiences of conflict in relationships. It is important to emphasize that we are not just making a call for multiple methods. Instead, we suggest that a commitment to the typical observational design involves making several theoretical assumptions that are untenable and makes it impossible to address many of the questions that are important to relational conflict scholars (e.g., how do patterns of conflict unfold over long periods of time, and how do such patterns influence relationships?).

It is possible that new emphases on issues like the frequency of conflict, temporal issues surrounding conflict, and everyday experiences of conflict can help address an emerging controversy in the literature. Based primarily on data generated by the problem-solving paradigm, some scholars have argued that the longitudinal impact of conflict is exaggerated (Beach, 2001; Bradbury et al., 1998, 2001). Indeed, Bradbury et al. (2001) suggested that "conflict may play a more restricted role than is commonly believed" (p. 69). These authors' solution is to shift attention to other aspects of relationships, like social support and stressful life events (Bradbury et al.,

1998; Bradbury et al., 2001). Although more research in these areas certainly is needed, it is important not to treat the results from the problem-solving paradigm as representative of the overall impact of conflict on romantic relationships. Indeed, the aforementioned concerns about this paradigm suggest that previous studies may have underestimated the complete impact of relational conflict.

INDIVIDUALS' INFLUENCES ON RELATIONAL CONFLICT

Conflict scholars investigating how individuals shape their conflicts have sought to explain how conflicts emerge and develop, and have investigated how individuals' cognitions influence the course and outcomes of relational conflict. Again, the literature in this general area is enormous, even rivaling the research on associations between conflict behaviors and relational outcomes. Our focus here is on reviewing several common explanations for conflict and on briefly discussing the importance of interpretations of relational conflict.

Explanations of Conflict and Conflict Behaviors

Much of the work relevant to explaining conflict in romantic relationships does not refer to explicit theoretical models (Fincham & Beach, 1999), but several common explanations exist (even if sometimes implicitly). The common accounts include references to skills, gender differences, other individual differences, stressors, and goals. Each of these explanations has a number of variants; due to space considerations, we focus on general themes rather than the variations. Also, these explanations are not mutually exclusive; for example, Canary's (2003) model of strategic conflict incorporates individual differences, interpretations, and goals.

Skills. One of the most common accounts of why couples engage in communication behaviors that are associated with dissatisfaction is a skills-based one (e.g., Clements et al., 1997; Halford, Hahlweg, & Dunne, 1990; Jacobson & Margolin, 1979). The skills metaphor is implied

in the behavioral models of conflict that have been the dominant perspective on marital conflict (Fincham & Beach, 1999). In fact, the assumed connection between skills and conflict behaviors is so pervasive that many scholars treat the phrases *conflict skills* and *conflict behaviors* synonymously (e.g., Cohan & Kleinbaum, 2002; McNulty & Karney, 2004). Explaining dissatisfying conflict behaviors in terms of skills allows for a straightforward translation of research on behavioral correlates of relational distress to applied interventions. If one assumes that distressing behaviors result from a lack of skill, teaching conflict resolution skills (e.g., learning to withhold expressions of anger) seems like a reasonable remedy (Notarius, Lashley, & Sullivan, 1997).

Despite the ongoing pervasiveness of the skills explanation, there are theoretical and empirical reasons to believe that the role of communication skills as a cause of aversive relational conflict behaviors has been overstated (Canary, 2003). Sillars and Weisberg (1987) noted that communicators' goals in conflict are often "complex and ephemeral" (p. 141). This makes it difficult to judge whether a conflict behavior was effective; it is possible, for instance, that a behavior that is considered negative might be functional in a given conflict or might effectively serve a goal other than relationship enhancement (Sillars & Weisberg, 1987).

Moreover, Burleson and Denton (1997) argued that the skills deficiency approach fails to make the important conceptual distinction between ability and motivation. Burleson and Denton conducted a study in which they measured skills directly with a cognitive complexity measure and assessments of spouses' effectiveness during particular communication encounters. They found that communication skills were not reliably associated with marital distress, but expressions of negativity were. Such findings suggest that the behaviors frequently linked to dissatisfaction in relationships "may result more from ill will than poor skill" (Burleson & Denton, 1997, p. 897). Similar conclusions can be drawn from studies showing that dissatisfied spouses evince communication skills with strangers that they do not with their partner (Birchler, Weiss, & Vincent, 1975; Noller, 1984).

Gender differences. Many explanations of conflict behaviors involve research on gender differences. Two types of gender differences are potentially important: differences in the extent to which men and women enact particular behaviors and differences in terms of the associations between conflict and other constructs. Beginning with differences in behaviors, women in heterosexual dyads, as compared to their partner, exhibit more of several forms of negativity, including demands (Mikolic, Parker, & Pruitt, 1997), overt hostility (Zuroff & Duncan, 1999), criticisms (Kelley et al., 1978), and distributive tactics (Messman & Mikesell, 2000). Men tend to be more likely than women to avoid (Denton, Burleson, Hobbs, Von Stein, & Rodriguez, 2001; Gottman & Levenson, 1988; Kelley et al., 1978). Not surprisingly, woman-demand/man-withdraw occurs more frequently than does man-demand/woman-withdraw (Caughlin & Vangelisti, 1999; Christensen & Shenk, 1991; Vogel, Wester, & Heesacker, 1999).

Although less common than studies examining behavioral frequencies, some investigations have suggested that the covariance between conflict behaviors and other constructs varies by sex. Du Rocher Schudlich, Papp, and Cummings (2004), for example, reported that husbands' depression was associated more strongly with negativity than was wives' depression. Also, women's experiences in their family of origin (e.g., parental divorce) may be more strongly related to negativity during conflict discussions than are men's experiences (Levy, Wamboldt, & Fiese, 1997; Sanders, Halford, & Behrens, 1999).

Researchers and theorists have explained such gender differences in a number of different ways. One set of explanations involves enduring differences in male versus female dispositions. Some scholars have suggested that compared to men, women are socialized to focus more on relationships, which explains why women tend to approach conflicts more while men avoid them (e.g., Napier, 1978). Others have attributed sex differences to evolution (Buss, 1989) or to discrepancies in how men and women respond to arousal (Gottman & Levenson, 1988; cf. Denton et al., 2001). Another set of explanations focuses on the social structure or the power structure of heterosexual relationships, particularly marriages (for reviews, see Eldridge &

Christensen, 2002, and Klein & Johnson, 1997). This social structural model suggests that men's greater power relative to women in heterosexual relationships means that relationships tend to favor men's wishes. Women, as a consequence, often are put in a position of advocating for change while men resist change (Jacobson, 1990). A related view posits that gender differences are modified by the nature of specific conflicts; for instance, the usual gender difference in demand/withdraw is evident in discussions of issues in which women typically have the primary complaint (e.g., housework) but less so during discussions of topics that are more symmetrical in terms of who has complaints (Kluwer, Heesink, & van de Vliert, 2000; cf. Caughlin & Vangelisti, 1999). Similarly, when husbands desire more change on an issue than do wives, the tendency for wives to demand more often than do husbands disappears (Christensen & Heavey, 1990; Heavey et al., 1993), and sometimes reverses so that husband-demand/wife-withdraw is more common than wife-demand/husband-withdraw (Klinetob & Smith, 1996).

Circumstances in which usual gender patterns are reversed highlight arguments that sex differences in conflict behaviors are often exaggerated (Canary et al., 1995). Effect sizes for gender differences tend to be small, and even where there are significant sex differences, there also are similarities; for example, even though Messman and Mikesell (2000) found that women in dating dyads engaged in more distributive tactics than did men, both women and men engaged in more integrative tactics than distributive ones. Such findings are not surprising given the growing evidence that male and female communicators in relationships are more similar than they are different (e.g., Canary & Hause, 1993; Vangelisti & Daly, 1997).

Despite the evidence that gender differences in conflict sometimes are exaggerated, researchers often inadvertently perpetuate stereotypes about men and women. For example, some researchers have failed to analyze conflict behaviors that run counter to stereotypes (e.g., husbands demanding and wives withdrawing), even though attending to such behaviors can be theoretically important (see Caughlin, 2002). In the case of demand/withdraw, the pattern of wives' demanding and husbands' withdrawing is more common, but a substantial minority of couples fall into a pattern of husbands' demanding and wives' withdrawing (Denton et al., 2001; Feldman & Ridley, 2000; Vogel et al., 1999). Further, husband-demand/wife-withdraw is associated with consequential outcomes like relational dissatisfaction (Caughlin, 2002; Caughlin & Huston, 2002; Heavey et al., 1995) and relational violence (Eldridge & Christensen, 2002; Feldman & Ridley, 2000).

Given the findings suggesting that gender differences in conflict are often exaggerated, what accounts for the persistent belief that the discrepancies between men and women in conflict are large? One possible explanation is that marital conflict behaviors are usually similar but certain conditions amplify the small differences that do exist. This possibility is suggested by Schulz et al.'s (2004) diary study, which found no overall differences between husbands' and wives' expressions of anger, but found that husbands and wives responded differently to difficult workdays. Compared to their usual behavior, on stressful workdays, husbands expressed less anger and criticism but wives acted more angry and critical. This suggests that tension may amplify gender differences that are small under most conditions. Although this explanation needs confirmation, it is consistent with Allen's (1998) contention that small average sex differences can be important—and even seem large—due to salient, extreme cases.

Individual differences. The largest group of studies examining individual differences (other than sex) has linked attachment styles or dimensions to conflict behaviors (Feeney et al., 2000). According to attachment theory, experiences with important others are internalized so that individuals develop various working models or attachment orientations (Feeney et al., 2000). Individuals with secure attachment orientations (i.e., they feel comfortable in relationships) are more likely than people with other attachment styles to enact conflict behaviors such as compromises, validation, and other behaviors that are usually considered constructive (Creasey, 2002; Feeney, 1998). An avoidant orientation (i.e., the extent to which one is uncomfortable with closeness and finds it difficult to depend on

others) has been linked to low levels of warmth and supportiveness (Feeney et al., 2000; Simpson, Rholes, & Phillips, 1996) and high levels of negativity (Creasey, Kershaw, & Boston, 1999). Finally, anxious-ambivalent orientations (which involve strong desires for closeness with fears of rejection) have also been linked to negativity and to dominating and coercive tactics (Creasey et al., 1999; Simpson et al., 1996), particularly when the person is rejected during the interaction (Feeney, 1998). Although attachment orientations typically are conceptualized as having an enduring influence on relationships and behaviors in those relationships, there is evidence that the association between conflict and attachment is reciprocal. Ruvolo, Fabin, and Ruvolo (2001) found that the extent to which women reported avoiding conflicts with their dating partner was significantly related to declines in attachment security over a 5-month period.

Consistent with attachment theory's tenet that individuals' views of current relationships are rooted in prior important relationships, individuals' conduct during conflict is related to how they view their family of origin. Koerner and Fitzpatrick (2002) studied college students' perceptions of their family of origin and their reports of conflict behaviors in current romantic relationships. Having a family of origin with a conformity orientation (i.e., one that stressed homogeneous attitudes, harmony, and obedience) was associated with avoiding conflicts and with negative behaviors during conflicts. Also, reports of parental violence in the family of origin are associated with negativity during engaged couples' conflicts (Halford, Sanders, & Behrens, 2000). Such studies suggest that experiences in one's family of origin have an enduring impact on how one engages in conflict.

Also, a number of personality constructs are associated with conflict behaviors. The Big Five personality factor of agreeableness, which refers to qualities such as being likable and good-natured, is related inversely to coercive conflict tactics and expressions of negative affect (Graziano & Tobin, 2002), related negatively to demand/withdraw in marriage (Caughlin & Vangelisti, 2000), and associated positively with affectively positive strategies like affirmations and appeasements (Gonzaga, Keltner, Londahl, & Smith, 2001). The Big Five neuroticism factor, which refers to qualities like proneness to anxiety and negative moods, is correlated positively with escalating conflicts, negativity, and demand/withdraw (Bolger & Zuckerman, 1995; Caughlin et al., 2000; Caughlin & Vangelisti, 2000).

Another personality construct that has been linked to conflict is locus of control, which refers to the extent to which individuals attribute outcomes to their own internal qualities (e.g., their efforts and abilities) or external qualities (e.g., situational factors). Canary, Cunningham, and Cody (1988) developed a measure to assess locus of control pertaining to conflicts, and found that an internal conflict locus of control is associated positively with the use of integrative conflict strategies, whereas an external locus of control is associated positively with avoidance tactics and forms of negativity like sarcasm and extended denial. Along similar lines, Miller, Lefcourt, Holmes, Ware, and Saleh (1986) found that internal marriage locus of control (which concerns the locus of control regarding marital satisfaction) was related positively to open, direct conflict engagement and to judges' ratings of the effectiveness of solutions to a problem-solving exercise. Also, married partners' internal conflict locus of control is inversely related to the extent to which they engage in demand/withdraw (Caughlin & Vangelisti, 2000).

Stress. Although less common than the other explanations listed here, there is growing interest linking romantic partners' experiences of stressful circumstances to conflict. As noted above, spouses' experiences of work stress affect conflict (Bolger et al., 1989; Schulz et al., 2004). Some researchers have begun to link experiences of stress to environmental predictors of that stress. Karney and Bradbury's (1995) vulnerability-stress-adaptation (VAS) model of marriage is an example. Because the specific stressors are environmental factors, they are discussed below. However, there is evidence that the influence of such environmental factors often is mediated by individuals' experiences with stressors. For example, when Conger and his colleagues (Conger et al., 1990; Conger, Rueter, & Elder, 1999) distinguished between external economic pressures and experiences of economic strain, they found that the connection between economic pressure and conflict behaviors was mediated by subjective strain.

Goals. The notion that one's goals are associated with relational conflict has a long history (e.g., Lewin, 1948). Common definitions of interpersonal conflict refer to incompatible goals, and the relational conflict literature includes many references to related constructs (Fincham & Beach, 1999). Still, the goals explanation of conflict behaviors has been overshadowed by a focus on behavioral models, and many references to goals remain implicit (Fincham & Beach, 1999).

Prevalent explanations for the demand/withdraw pattern are a good example of how references to goals are often implied. As noted above, gender differences in demanding and withdrawing are often attributed to women wanting change while men favor the status quo (Jacobson, 1990; Klein & Johnson, 1997). Although the term *goal* usually is not used explicitly (cf. Kluwer, 1998), the clear implication is that conflict behaviors are related to one's goals.

One possible objection to an explicit goals model is that the goal construct may appear to imply that individuals in conflict always are aware of clear goals. Such an assumption would be problematic given that explicit goals probably are not a salient part individuals' cognitions during conflict (Sillars et al., 2000). Although an approach to conflict that emphasizes goals implies that people are strategic, it does not necessarily imply that people are aware of all their goals or that they define their goals clearly (Canary, 2003). Kellermann (1992) argued that the strategies involved in communication are typically automatic. Also, even if an individual is not personally concerned with a goal, many communicative episodes are inherently linked to certain types of goals. As Wilson, Aleman, and Leatham (1998) noted, the possibility of appearing nosy is pertinent when one attempts to give advice whether the advice-giver recognizes this or not. This does not mean that appearing nosy is inevitable; in fact, individuals who attend to the goal of not appearing nosy likely have a better chance of avoiding that fate than do people who remain unaware of the possibility or who do not care about that goal. Thus, the goals people do not have may be as informative about their behavior in a situation as are the goals they do pursue.

Explicit discussions of goals in relational conflict suggest that multiple goals are relevant in conflict episodes (Canary, 2003; Fincham & Beach, 1999). Although there is no single correct way to classify such goals, common types of goals include (a) instrumental or content goals, such as what outcomes or resources are desired; (b) relational goals, such as the desire to maintain or change a particular quality of a relationship; (c) identity goals, including desires to portray oneself in a positive manner and to allow one's partner to maintain a positive identity; and (d) process goals, including the desired manner of conflict management (Canary, 2003; Fincham & Beach, 1999).

Fincham and Beach (1999) argued that the relative importance of various goals can shift during an episode; for instance, identity issues may emerge during interaction. A disagreement that begins with married spouses both trying to determine how to find their destination after getting lost can shift to one in which spouses are concerned primarily with protecting their own identities by blaming each other. Based on such examples, Fincham and Beach (1999) suggested that one useful intervention would be to counsel romantic partners to recognize when a shift to identity issues is likely to lead to defensiveness and to learn to continue paying attention to more positive goals.

Similar arguments often are made about multiple goals in research on interpersonal influence (e.g., Dillard, 1990). This research suggests that dealing with multiple goals involves more than shifting goals within a conversation: Multiple goals usually operate simultaneously. Although a focus on multiple goals has not been salient in the relational conflict literature, conflict situations can be characterized by multiple goals (Canary, 2003). Newell and Stutman (1991), for example, noted that individuals' confronting somebody about a violation may have the goal of "cessation of an annoying problem, an improved relationship, and a better understanding of each other" (pp. 383–384).

A multiple goals perspective of relational conflicts may be important in two respects. First, considering multiple goals provides an opportunity for a more theoretically grounded notion of communication skills in relational conflicts. As noted above, most conflict scholars referring to skills equate expressions of negativity with a lack of skill, regardless of one's goals (cf. Burleson & Denton, 1997). In contrast, a multiple goals perspective might define skills in terms of the ability to attend to multiple goals simultaneously or in terms of the ability to reframe the situation so that the various goals are more compatible (O'Keefe, 1988).

Second, considering multiple goals can provide a more complete account of conflict behaviors than do studies that only implicitly refer to goals. Consider, for instance, the account of demand/withdraw that attributes avoidance to the goal of maintaining the status quo and demanding to the goal of changing the partner (Klein & Johnson, 1997; Kluwer, 1998). Although empirical examinations suggest that this is a partial explanation, the distinction between wanting change versus wanting the status quo cannot account for the fact that differences in desire for change do not inevitably lead to demand/withdraw. Sometimes the partner wanting change refrains from raising the issue (Roloff & Ifert, 2000), and sometimes this partner may discuss the topic without the negative affect implied by demanding (see Heavey et al., 1995). Also, why might some people who want to maintain the status quo withdraw while others defend themselves? A multiple goals perspective has the potential to address issues such as these. From the perspective of the person wanting change, for example, demanding might result not just from wanting to change the partner, but from a combination of goals that are being pursued and those that are not (e.g., because one is frustrated by the partner's avoidance; Kelley et al., 1978). In addition to the instrumental goal involving behavioral change, people who demand (compared to those who do not) may attend (a) less to relationship goals like maintaining harmony, (b) less to their own positive identity goals (e.g., one might refrain from demanding to avoid seeming overbearing), (c) less to the partner's positive identity goals (e.g., demanding might question the partner's character), (d) less to the partner's identity goals involving maintaining autonomy, and (e) more to process goals pertaining to the value of frank communication during conflict. Obviously, this list is not exhaustive and is somewhat specula-tive, but it demonstrates the potential utility of a multiple goals perspective at providing a more thorough account of conflict behaviors.

Cognition and Relational Conflict

Because there are excellent extant reviews of cognition in interpersonal conflict (e.g., Roloff & Waite Miller, Chapter 4 in this volume), our discussion is limited to three points that are par-ticularly pertinent to our framework for under-standing conflict in romantic relationships (see Figure 5.1). First, although the ample evidence of links between observable conflict behaviors and relational outcomes is impressive, it is crucial to augment such findings with an understanding of how relational partners interpret these behaviors. Individuals' perceptions of conflict behaviors mediate much of the connection between mani-fest conflict behaviors and relational outcomes (Canary, Cupach, & Serpe, 2001; Matthews et al., 1996). Also, individuals' evaluations of what they perceive during conflict depend on cognitive constructs like their values and their standards for what constitutes good communica-tion (Caughlin, 2003; Sillars et al., 1983).

Second, it is important to recognize the com-plex interconnections among cognitive elements of varying timeframes. More molar perceptions are not necessarily the simple sum of more microscopic experiences (Caughlin & Huston, 1996). In fact, once broad perceptions are formed, they probably shape more specific eval-uations, which would explain why overall rela-tional dissatisfaction predicts negative thoughts about one's partner during specific interactions (Sillars et al., 2000; Vangelisti, Corbin, Lucchetti, & Sprague, 1999).

Third, cognition is usually conceptualized in terms of how people interpret conflicts; for instance, attributions and biases concerning conflict have received considerable attention (see Roloff & Waite Miller, this volume). It is important to recognize, however, that such interpretations influence subsequent conflict interactions, although not necessarily in a straightforward manner. Consider, for example, instances when individuals perceive that their partner has been hostile in previous conflict encounters and believe that the partner will be hostile in future encounters. In some cases, the expected hostility may lead the individuals to begin conflicts in an antagonistic manner, but in other cases the expected hostility may lead the individuals to be particularly positive or to avoid conflicts altogether (see Miller & Turnbull, 1986). Many factors may influence the different reactions to expected hostility; for instance, people who lack dependence power in their rela-tionship (e.g., they are strongly committed to the relationship but perceive their partner to be only weakly committed) may consider potential conflict issues not to be important enough for a potentially risky confrontation (Solomon & Samp, 1998). Regardless of the particular reasons why people would act differently in such circum-stances, it is important to recognize that cogni-tions influence conflict behaviors in potentially complex ways.

THE ENVIRONMENT OF CONFLICT IN ROMANTIC RELATIONSHIPS

The framework depicted in Figure 5.1 suggests that is it important to consider the broader con-text of conflict in romantic relationships, but there is far less research on environmental influ-ences than there is on individuals and on dyads' behaviors. When the environment is considered, it is usually conceptualized as operating through individual differences, such as ethnicity and sexual orientation.

Ethnicity

The majority of research on conflict in romantic relationships has used samples that were mostly White. One notable exception is the Early Years of Marriage (EYM) Project (Veroff, Douvan, & Hatchett, 1995), a longitudinal study that examined both African American and White married couples. The EYM project suggested many similarities between White and Black dyads in terms of conflict, but also indicated some important differences. As newlyweds, Black and White couples report similar frequen-cies of conflict, but compared to their White counterparts, Black spouses report a signifi-cantly smaller number of areas of disagreement (Oggins, Veroff, & Leber, 1993) and significantly fewer conflict issues pertaining to their partner's family (Timmer, Veroff, & Hatchett, 1996). Also, marital discord (e.g., frequency of conflicts) is a predictor of divorce for both Black and White couples (Orbuch et al., 2002), but the connection between discord and having a shorter marriage may be stronger for Black couples than for White couples (Adelmann, Chadwick, & Baerger, 1996).

White and Black couples also differ in terms of specific conflict behaviors. Black spouses are significantly more likely to report that they withdraw from conflicts than are White spouses (Oggins et al., 1993). Furthermore, whereas wives' negativity predicts declining marital quality for White couples, Veroff et al. (1995) found no evidence of a similar association for Black dyads. Orbuch and Veroff (2002) suggested that this finding makes sense because ethnic background not only influences behavioral tendencies, but also shapes what behaviors mean in a particular conflict. Specifically, Orbuch and Veroff argued that Black spouses are more accepting of negativity than are Whites; thus, whereas White couples "might be especially put off" (p. 557) by negativity, Black couples might view negativity as a normal part of a close relationship.

Obviously, there is tremendous room for more research on the influence of ethnicity on relational conflict. Research with the EYM project demonstrates that ethnic background is important, but other groups also should be examined. The limited research on dating in Latino populations, for instance, suggests that traditional values often lead families to restrict young women's dating, which can be a source of conflict for dating dyads (Raffaelli & Ontai, 2001). Moreover, although research on interracial couples tends not to focus on conflict within the relationship, many interracial dyads face challenges like unsupportive families (McNamara, Tempenis, & Walton, 1999), which would undoubtedly influence relational conflict (see the section on the social environment, below).

Sexual Orientation

The limited research on conflict in gay male and lesbian unions suggests that conflict in these relationships often functions similarly to the way it does in heterosexual dyads (Patterson, 2000).

For instance, Kurdek (1994) found that negativity (e.g., "throwing insults and digs") was associated inversely with concurrent satisfaction and predicted declines in satisfaction for heterosexual, gay male, and lesbian relational partners. In addition, Kurdek (1994) found no differences in reported conflict behaviors among gay male, lesbian, and heterosexual dyads.

Despite such similarities, there is a need for more research in this area. As Peplau and Beals (2004) noted, "little is known about the patterns of interaction in gay and lesbian couples—the specifics of how gay and lesbian partners talk to each other and seek to resolve the conflicts of interest that inevitably arise in close relationships" (p. 240). More important, the environment for conflict is probably different for gay male and lesbian partners as compared to heterosexual ones. This environment can be a source of conflict that is probably unique for lesbian and gay couples, such as conflicts over how much to tell others about their sexual identity (Patterson, 2000). Gay male and lesbian couples may encounter prejudice from their families and others in their social network (Peplau & Beals, 2004), and compared to individuals who are married, gay male and lesbian partners feel less social pressure against dissolving their relationships (Kurdek, 1998). Given Solomon and Samp's (1998) research suggesting that perceptions about a partner's ability to leave a relationship can affect one's willingness to raise potential conflict issues, the comparatively low barriers to dissolution may affect conflict engagement in gay male and lesbian couples.

Conceptualizing the environment in terms of individual differences has yielded important findings about the influences of particular relational contexts on conflict. However, it does not provide a comprehensive understanding of conflict environments in romantic relationships. Of course, defining the environment and identifying the various ways it affects conflict is no easy task. One way to proceed is to consider the environment on five different levels: the cultural, social, dyadic, physical, and temporal levels.

The Cultural Level

Although there is a great deal of literature concerning cultural influences on conflict (see

Part III, Community Conflict, in the current volume), relatively little research addresses the effects of culture on conflict between romantic partners. Indeed, the majority of studies on conflict in romantic relationships have been conducted in the United States. Most of the remaining research had been done in Western Europe, and this work is generally consistent with research that uses U.S. samples (e.g., Bodenmann, Kaiser, Hahlweg, & Fehm-Wolfsdorf, 1998; Hahlweg, Kaiser, Christensen, Fehm-Wolfsdorf, & Groth, 2000; Halford et al., 1990).

Some studies done outside the United States and Western Europe also complement the results of investigations done in the United States. For instance, a study of married Blacks in South Africa revealed that satisfaction was related positively to reports of collaborative conflict and negatively associated with competitive conflict (Greeff & de Bruyne, 2000). Other investigations conducted with non-U.S. samples suggest that culture may shape couples' conflict in subtle ways. In one study, undergraduate students in the United States and Japan were asked to describe recent interpersonal conflicts (Ohbuchi & Takahashi, 1994). Although Japanese individuals were more likely to avoid conflicts, both groups noted that more direct strategies (e.g., bargaining, compromise) were preferable to avoidance.

The Social Level

Within any culture, the social milieu influences romantic partners' conflicts. That is, the presence or absence of other individuals, as well as interactions with those individuals, affects romantic dyads' conflicts. For example, there are sanctions against raising complaints in public settings (Alberts, 1988), and married couples report that rules barring expressions of negative affect (e.g., raising one's voice, showing anger) are more important in public than in private settings (Jones & Gallois, 1989).

When individuals who are part of the social context interact with romantic partners, they influence partners' perceptions and responses to conflict in some interesting ways. Wilson, Roloff, and Carey (1998) found that people often had some negative impressions of their friends' romantic partners and that, about half of the time, they discussed those concerns with their friends. The most common topic of these discussions was conflicts between the dating partners. Klein and Milardo (2000) further found that women perceived their positions on issues to be more legitimate to the extent that they had support from people in their social network. Such perceptions may translate into conflict behaviors as well: Women who saw their own network as supportive were less willing to compromise than were women who thought their network was comparatively unsupportive.

Families offer yet another social context for couples' conflict. Conflict between dyads within the family influences other family members. Margolin, Christensen, and John (1996) found that tensions in parent-child and sibling relationships had a tendency to "spill over" into the marital relationship and that marital tensions spilled over into the other family subsystems as well. These spillover effects were particularly salient in distressed families.

The Dyadic Level

Dyads, like social groups, develop histories and patterns of behavior that influence their conflicts. Siegert and Stamp (1994) referenced the effect of couples' shared history on their subsequent conflict behavior when they discussed romantic partners' "first big fight." These researchers found that couples who survived their first big fight distinguished it from other fights based, in part, on the lack of shared history that preceded it. Siegert and Stamp noted that prior to the first big fight, couples "don't have the knowledge base that is possessed later or the arsenal of conflictual weapons and strategies that such a knowledge base engenders" (pp. 353–354). The shared knowledge that couples develop over time influences the way they cope with and interpret conflict in their relationships.

The patterns of behavior that couples enact also create a context that may shape the meaning partners assign to conflicts. For example, romantic partners who routinely express affection to each other appear to be less susceptible to any adverse impact of negativity and demand/withdraw on relational satisfaction (Caughlin & Huston, 2002; Huston & Chorost, 1994). Thus, the meaning assigned to negative behaviors appears to be influenced by the behavioral context that couples create together.

Moreover, this behavioral context need not be limited to behaviors that are usually thought of as communication. Caughlin (2002) argued that one reason why some couples may increase their satisfaction after engaging in demand/withdraw episodes is that the person being asked to change may do so over time, which would influence the ultimate meaning of the conversation. For example, if a husband withdraws while being nagged to pick up his dirty socks, the actual interaction is likely to be unpleasant and associated with concurrent dissatisfaction. However, if this husband begins to put his dirty laundry away without being nagged (perhaps even as a strategy to avoid being nagged again), this may lead the wife to reappraise the conflict episode, downplaying its importance compared to the changed behavior. Furthermore, once the husband has demonstrated a willingness to change despite engaging in avoidance, subsequent episodes of demand/withdraw might be viewed differently (e.g., the complaining spouse may be less frustrated because she recognizes that withdrawal during a discussion does not necessarily imply that the spouse will not comply with a request for change).

The Physical Level

Conflict behavior and the interpretation of conflict behavior also are affected by various aspects of the physical environment. For instance, some studies show that aggressive acts are related positively to increases in temperature and humidity (Anderson, Bushman, & Groom, 1997). Other investigations suggest that certain variables (e.g., prior provocation, the perceived ability to leave the setting) may interact with temperature and humidity to encourage or discourage aggressive behavior (Baron & Bell, 1976). Although research has not been conducted examining the links between temperature, humidity, and aggression in dating and marital relationships, such studies could yield findings with very practical applications for couples.

Of course, the physical environment also includes architectural structures and movable objects. In their commentary on the influence of physical environments on personal relationships,

Brown, Werner, and Altman (in press) provided a very interesting comparison of people's homes during different historical time periods. For example, they note that middle-class Colonial homes might have had only two lower rooms and an upper sleeping loft. As a consequence, families inhabiting these homes shared most of their daily experiences and had very little privacy. By contrast, Victorian homes were larger and had many separate spaces for family members. Clearly, the physical access that couples living in these two types of homes had to each other, and to other family members, differed. Although Brown and her colleagues did not address the influence of these home environments on conflict, it is very likely that the way couples conducted themselves during conflict episodes (e.g., the strategies they used to avoid conflict) was affected by the physical contexts in which they lived.

The Temporal Level

The analysis offered by Brown et al. (in press) suggests that historical periods indirectly affect the way couples communicate by influencing the physical environment. Historical periods also affect social interaction in more direct ways. Hatfield and Rapson (2002) offered an analysis of passionate love during different times in history. They noted that the norms associated with love and sexual desire at different points in time (e.g., norms concerning the degree to which women should enjoy sex, the double standard for extramarital affairs) greatly influenced couples' sexual relationships. Undoubtedly, these same norms and others (e.g., those concerning decision making and the use of physical violence) also affected the way couples handled conflict.

Within any given historical period, conflict is further shaped by the temporal rhythms of couples' day-to-day activities. Several studies have demonstrated that the experiences spouses have at work predict the tone of subsequent marital interactions (Doumas, Margolin, & John, 2003). Bolger et al. (1989), for instance, found that when husbands or their wives reported having an argument at work, husbands were more likely to report having an argument with their spouse at home the following day. Similarly, Schulz et al. (2004) found that women were more likely to express anger and men were more likely to withdraw if they had negatively arousing workdays. Other researchers have found that couples are more likely to engage in conflict during particular days of the week. For instance, Halford, Gravestock, Lowe, and Scheldt (1992) found that negative marital interaction was more likely to occur on weekdays than weekends—perhaps because of the heightened stress associated with the workweek.

CONCLUSION

The literature on conflict in romantic couples is enormous and, in many respects, impressive. Considerable advances have been made in identifying conflict behaviors and patterns that are associated with outcomes like dissatisfaction and dissolution. For instance, studies have repeatedly demonstrated that partners' negativity during problem-solving interactions is associated with lower concurrent relational satisfaction, declines in satisfaction, and less relational stability. Similarly, dyadic patterns such as negative reciprocity (exchanging negative behaviors) and demand/withdraw (the pattern in which one partner nags or criticizes while the other avoids) have been linked to dissatisfaction, decreases in satisfaction, and relational dissolution.

Scholars also have made important progress in understanding why conflict develops in particular ways and why relational partners enact some conflict behaviors rather than others. Researchers have begun to recognize, for example, that the role of communication skills as a cause of aversive conflict is not as strong as was once thought. They also have found that while sex differences in conflict behaviors sometimes can be explained by distinctions in the ways men and women have been socialized, the differences also can be elicited by discrepancies in the power that men and women typically wield in their romantic relationships. Studies examining individual differences other than those associated with biological sex have revealed that enduring personality traits such as attachment orientation, agreeableness, neuroticism, and locus of control can influence conflict behaviors. Further, more transient variables including the stressors that people experience and the goals that individuals bring to conflict episodes affect the behaviors that people enact.

Although researchers have made great strides in understanding conflict behavior as well as the possible causes and consequences of conflict in romantic relationships, our review and conceptual framework suggest two particularly important foci for future study. First, the impact of conflict on close relationships probably depends on a number of temporal issues that have received scant attention. Although there have been many studies on sequences within particular conflict episodes, understanding the impact of conflict on relationships likely will require more attention to issues involving broader timeframes (e.g., the daily rhythms of conflict, how serial arguments develop over time, how changes in conflict over time affect relationships).

Second, there are sound conceptual reasons—and some empirical ones—to believe that the impact of environmental factors on conflict in romantic relationships is greater than that implied by a typical laboratory study. The ideology that a particular culture holds concerning conflict, the social milieu in which conflict occurs, and the physical environment all probably influence the conflict behaviors enacted by relational partners as well as the effects those behaviors have on their relationship. Taking a more contextual perspective on conflict in romantic dyads is likely to offer many potentially important insights.

REFERENCES

Adelmann, P. K., Chadwick, K., & Baerger, D. R. (1996). Marital quality of Black and White adults over the life course. *Journal of Social and Personal Relationships, 13,* 361–384.

Alberts, J. K. (1988). An analysis of couples' conversational complaints. *Communication Monographs, 55,* 184–197.

Alberts, J. K. (1989). Perceived effectiveness of couples' conversational complaints. *Communication Studies, 40,* 280–291.

Alberts, J. K., & Driscoll, G. (1992). Containment versus escalation: The trajectory of couples' conversational complaints. *Western Journal of Communication, 56,* 394–412.

Allen, M. (1998). Methodological considerations when examining a gendered world. In D. J. Canary & K. Dindia (Eds.), *Sex differences and similarities in communication* (pp. 427–444). Mahwah, NJ: Lawrence Erlbaum.

Amato, P. R., Loomis, L., & Booth, A. (1995). Parental divorce, marital conflict, and offspring well-being during early adulthood. *Social Forces, 73,* 895–915.

Anderson, C. A., Bushman, B. J., & Groom, R. W. (1997). Hot years and serious and deadly assault: Empirical tests of the heat hypothesis. *Journal of Personality and Social Psychology, 73,* 1213–1223.

Ayduk, O., Downey, G., Testa, A., Yen, Y., & Shoda, Y. (1999). Does rejection elicit hostility in rejection sensitive women? *Social Cognition, 17,* 245–271.

Baron, R. A., & Bell, P. A. (1976). Aggression and heat: The influence of ambient temperature, negative affect, and a cooling drink on physical aggression. *Journal of Personality and Social Psychology, 33,* 245–255.

Baxter, L. A., & Bullis, C. (1986). Turning points in developing romantic relationships. *Human Communication Research, 12,* 469–493.

Beach, S. R. H. (2001). Expanding the study of dyadic conflict: The potential role of self-evaluation maintenance processes. In A. Booth, A. C. Crouter, & M. Clements (Eds.), *Couples in conflict* (pp. 83–94). Mahwah, NJ: Lawrence Erlbaum.

Billings, A. (1979). Conflict resolution in distressed and nondistressed married couples. *Journal of Consulting and Clinical Psychology, 47,* 368–376.

Birchler, G. R., & Webb, L. J. (1977). Discriminating interaction behaviors in happy and unhappy marriage. *Journal of Consulting and Clinical Psychology, 45,* 494–495.

Birchler, G. R., Weiss, R. L., & Vincent, J. P. (1975). Multimethod analysis of social reinforcement exchange between maritally distressed and nondistressed spouse and stranger dyads. *Journal of Personality and Social Psychology, 31,* 349–360.

Bodenmann, G., Kaiser, A., Hahlweg, K., & Fehm-Wolfsdorf, G. (1998). Communication patterns during marital conflict: A cross-cultural replication. *Personal Relationships, 5,* 343–356.

Bolger, N., DeLongis, A., Kessler, R. C., & Wethington, E. (1989). The contagion of stress across multiple roles. *Journal of Marriage and the Family, 51,* 175–183.

Bolger, N., & Zuckerman, A. (1995). A framework for studying personality in the stress process. *Journal of Personality and Social Psychology, 69,* 890–902.

Booth, A., & Amato, P. R. (2001). Parental predivorce relations and offspring postdivorce well-being. *Journal of Marriage and Family, 63,* 197–212.

Bradbury, T., Rogge, R., & Lawrence, E. (2001). Reconsidering the role of conflict in marriage. In A. Booth, A. C. Crouter, & M. Clements (Eds.), *Couples in conflict* (pp. 59–81). Mahwah, NJ: Lawrence Erlbaum.

Bradbury, T. N., Cohan, C. L., & Karney, B. R. (1998). Optimizing longitudinal research for understanding and preventing marital dysfuction. In T. N. Bradbury (Ed.), *The developmental course of marital dysfunction* (pp. 279–311). New York: Cambridge University Press.

Braiker, H. B., & Kelley, H. H. (1979). Conflict in the development of close relationships. In R. L. Burgess & T. L. Huston (Eds.), *Social exchange in developing relationships* (pp. 135–168). New York: Academic Press.

Brown, B. B., Werner, C. M., & Altman, I. (in press). Relationships in home and community environments: A transactional and dialectic analysis. In A. L. Vangelisti & D. Perlman (Eds.), *The Cambridge handbook of personal relationships.* New York: Cambridge University Press.

Burleson, B. R., & Denton, W. H. (1997). The relationship between communication skills and marital satisfaction: Some moderating effects. *Journal of Marriage and the Family, 59,* 884–902.

Buss, D. M. (1989). Conflict between the sexes: Strategic interference and the evocation of anger and upset. *Journal of Personality and Social Psychology, 56,* 735–747.

Buysse, A., De Clercq, A., Verhofstadt, L., Heene, E., Roeyers, H., & Van Oost, P. (2000). Dealing with relational conflict: A picture in milliseconds. *Journal of Social and Personal Relationships, 17,* 574–597.

Canary, D. J. (2003). Managing interpersonal conflict: A model of events related to strategic choices. In J. O. Greene & B. R. Burleson (Eds.), *Handbook of communication and social interaction skills* (pp. 515–549). Mahwah, NJ: Lawrence Erlbaum.

Canary, D. J., Cunningham, E. M., & Cody, M. J. (1988). Goal types, gender, and locus of control in managing interpersonal conflict. *Communication Research, 15,* 426–446.

Canary, D. J., & Cupach, W. R. (1988). Relational and episodic characteristics associated with conflict tactics. *Journal of Social and Personal Relationships, 5,* 305–325.

Canary, D. J., Cupach, W. R., & Messman, S. J. (1995). *Relationship conflict.* Thousand Oaks, CA: Sage.

Canary, D. J., Cupach, W. R., & Serpe, R. T. (2001). A competence-based approach to examining interpersonal conflict: Test of a longitudinal model. *Communication Research, 28,* 79–104.

Canary, D. J., & Hause, K. S. (1993). Is there any reason to research sex differences in communication? *Communication Quarterly, 41,* 129–144.

Caughlin, J. P. (2002). The demand/withdraw pattern of communication as a predictor of marital satisfaction over time: Unresolved issues and future directions. *Human Communication Research, 28,* 49–85.

Caughlin, J. P. (2003). Family communication standards: What counts as excellent family communication and how are such standards associated with family satisfaction? *Human Communication Research, 29,* 5–40.

Caughlin, J. P., & Afifi, T. D. (2004). When is topic avoidance unsatisfying? Examining moderators of the association between avoidance and dissatisfaction. *Human Communication Research, 30,* 479–513.

Caughlin, J. P., & Golish, T. D. (2002). An analysis of the association between topic avoidance and dissatisfaction: Comparing perceptual and interpersonal explanations. *Communication Monographs, 69,* 275–295.

Caughlin, J. P., & Huston, T. L. (1996, November). *The development of conflict: Perception and frequency of conflict among couples with different marital outcomes.* Paper presented at the annual convention of the Speech Communication Association, San Diego, CA.

Caughlin, J. P., & Huston, T. L. (2002). A contextual analysis of the association between demand/withdraw and marital satisfaction. *Personal Relationships, 9,* 95–119.

Caughlin, J. P., & Huston, T. L. (in press). The affective structure of marriage: How and why does it change? In A. L. Vangelisti & D. Perlman (Eds.), *The Cambridge handbook of personal relationships.* New York: Cambridge University Press.

Caughlin, J. P., Huston, T. L., & Houts, R. M. (2000). How does personality matter in marriage? An examination of trait anxiety, interpersonal negativity, and marital satisfaction. *Journal of Personality and Social Psychology, 78,* 326–336.

Caughlin, J. P., & Vangelisti, A. L. (1999). Desire for change in one's partner as a predictor of the demand/withdraw pattern of marital communication. *Communication Monographs, 66,* 66–89.

Caughlin, J. P., & Vangelisti, A. L. (2000). An individual difference explanation of why married couples engage in the demand/withdraw pattern of conflict. *Journal of Social and Personal Relationships, 17,* 523–551.

Christensen, A., & Heavey, C. L. (1990). Gender and social structure in the demand/withdraw pattern of marital conflict. *Journal of Personality and Social Psychology, 59,* 73–81.

Christensen, A., & Heavey, C. L. (1993). Gender differences in marital conflict: The demand/withdraw interaction pattern. In S. Oskamp & M. Costanzo (Eds.), *Gender issues in contemporary society* (pp. 113–141). Newbury Park, CA: Sage.

Christensen, A., & Shenk, J. L. (1991). Communication, conflict, and psychological distance in nondistressed, clinic, and divorcing couples. *Journal of Consulting and Clinical Psychology, 59,* 458–463.

Clements, M. L., Cordova, A. D., Markman, H. J., & Laurenceau, J. (1997). The erosion of marital satisfaction over time and how to prevent it. In R. J. Sternberg & M. Hojjat (Eds.), *Satisfaction in close relationships* (pp. 335–355). New York: Guilford.

Cloven, D. H., & Roloff, M. E. (1993). The chilling effect of aggressive potential on the expression of complaints in intimate relationships. *Communication Monographs, 60,* 199–219.

Cohan, C. L., & Kleinbaum, S. (2002). Toward a greater understanding of the cohabitation effect: Premarital cohabitation and marital communication. *Journal of Marriage and Family, 64,* 180–192.

Conger, R. D., Elder, G. H., Jr., Lorenz, F. O., Conger, K. J., Simons, R. L., Whitbeck, L. B., et al. (1990). Linking economic hardship to marital quality and instability. *Journal of Marriage and the Family, 52,* 643–656.

Conger, R. D., Rueter, M. A., & Elder, G. H., Jr. (1999). Couple resilience to economic pressure. *Journal of Personality and Social Psychology, 76,* 54–71.

Cramer, D. (2000). Relationship satisfaction and conflict style in romantic relationships. *Journal of Psychology, 134,* 337–341.

Creasey, G. (2002). Associations between working models of attachment and conflict management behavior in romantic couples. *Journal of Counseling Psychology, 49,* 365–375.

Creasey, G., Kershaw, K., & Boston, A. (1999). Conflict management with friends and romantic partners: The role of attachment and negative mood regulation expectancies. *Journal of Youth and Adolescence, 28,* 523–543.

Denton, W. H., Burleson, B. R., Hobbs, B. V., Von Stein, M., & Rodriguez, C. P. (2001). Cardiovascular reactivity and initiate/avoid patterns of marital communication: A test of Gottman's psychophysiologic model of marital interaction. *Journal of Behavioral Medicine, 24,* 401–421.

Dillard, J. P. (1990). A goal-driven model of interpersonal influence. In J. P. Dillard (Ed.), *Seeking compliance: The production of interpersonal influence messages* (pp. 41–56). Scottsdale, AZ: Gorsuch Scarisbrick.

Doumas, D. M., Margolin, G., & John, R. S. (2003). The relationship between daily marital interaction, work, and health-promoting behaviors in dual-earner couples: An extension of the work-family spillover model. *Journal of Family Issues, 24,* 3–20.

Du Rocher Schudlich, T. D., Papp, L. M., & Cummings, E. M. (2004). Relations of husbands' and wives' dysphoria to marital conflict resolution strategies. *Journal of Family Psychology, 18,* 171–183.

Eldridge, K. A., & Christensen, A. (2002). Demand-withdraw communication during couple conflict: A review and analysis. In P. Noller & J. A. Feeney (Eds.), *Understanding marriage: Developments in the study of couple interaction* (pp. 289–322). New York: Cambridge University Press.

Erbert, L. A. (2000). Conflict and dialectics: Perceptions of dialectical contradictions in marital conflict. *Journal of Social and Personal Relationships, 17,* 638–659.

Feeney, J. A. (1998). Adult attachment and relationship-centered anxiety: Responses to physical and emotional distancing. In J. A. Simpson & W. S. Rholes (Eds.), *Attachment theory and close relationships* (pp. 189–218). New York: Guilford.

Feeney, J. A., Noller, P., & Roberts, N. (2000). Attachment and close relationships. In C. Hendrick & S. S. Hendrick (Eds.), *Close relationships: A sourcebook* (pp. 185–201). Thousand Oaks, CA: Sage.

Feldman, C. M., & Ridley, C. A. (2000). The role of conflict-based communication responses and outcomes in male domestic violence toward female partners. *Journal of Social and Personal Relationships, 17,* 552–573.

Filsinger, E. E., & Thoma, S. J. (1988). Behavioral antecedents of relationship stability and adjustment: A five-year longitudinal study. *Journal of Marriage and the Family, 50,* 785–795.

Fincham, F. D. (2004). Communication in marriage. In A. L. Vangelisti (Ed.), *Handbook of family communication* (pp. 83–103). Mahwah, NJ: Lawrence Erlbaum.

Fincham, F. D., & Beach, S. R. H. (1999). Conflict in marriage: Implications for working with couples. *Annual Review of Psychology, 50,* 47–77.

Fitzpatrick, J., & Sollie, D. L. (1999). Influence of individual and interpersonal factors on satisfaction and stability in romantic relationships. *Personal Relationships, 6,* 337–350.

Fitzpatrick, M. A. (1988). *Between husbands and wives.* Newbury Park, CA: Sage.

Gable, S. L., & Reis, H. T. (2001). Appetitive and aversive social interaction. In J. H. Harvey & A. E. Wenzel (Eds.), *Close romantic relationships: Maintenance and enhancement* (pp. 169–194). Mahwah, NJ: Lawrence Erlbaum.

Gadlin, H. (1977). Private lives and public order: A critical view of the history of intimate relations in the United States. In G. Levinger & H. L. Raush (Eds.), *Close relationships: Perspectives on the meaning of intimacy* (pp. 33–72). Amherst: University of Massachusetts Press.

Glenn, N. D. (1998). Problems and prospects in longitudinal research on marriage: A sociologist's perspective. In T. N. Bradbury (Ed.), *The developmental course of marital dysfunction* (pp. 427–440). New York: Cambridge University Press.

Gonzaga, G. C., Keltner, D., Londahl, E. A., & Smith, M. D. (2001). Love and the commitment problem in romantic relations and friendship.

Journal of Personality and Social Psychology, *81,* 247–262.

Gottman, J. M. (1979). *Marital interaction: Experimental investigations.* New York: Academic Press.

Gottman, J. M. (1994). *What predicts divorce?* Hillsdale, NJ: Lawrence Erlbaum.

Gottman, J. M., Coan, J., Carrere, S., & Swanson, C. (1998). Predicting happiness and stability from newlywed interactions. *Journal of Marriage and the Family, 60,* 5–22.

Gottman, J. M., Driver, J., Yoshimoto, D., & Rushe, R. (2002). Approaches to the study of power in violent and nonviolent marriages, and in gay male and lesbian cohabiting relationships. In P. Noller & J. A. Feeney (Eds.), *Understanding marriage: Developments in the study of couple interaction* (pp. 323–347). New York: Cambridge University Press.

Gottman, J. M., & Krokoff, L. J. (1989). Marital interaction and satisfaction: A longitudinal view. *Journal of Consulting and Clinical Psychology, 57,* 47–52.

Gottman, J. M., & Levenson, R. W. (1988). The social psychophysiology of marriage. In P. Noller & M. A. Fitzpatrick (Eds.), *Perspectives on marital interaction* (pp. 182–200). Philadelphia: Multilingual Matters.

Gottman, J. M., & Levenson, R. W. (2000). The timing of divorce: Predicting when a couple will divorce over a 14-year period. *Journal of Marriage and the Family, 62,* 737–745.

Graziano, W. G., & Tobin, R. M. (2002). Agreeableness: Dimension of personality or social desirability artifact? *Journal of Personality, 70,* 695–727.

Greeff, A. P., & de Bruyne, T. (2000). Conflict management style and marital satisfaction. *Journal of Sex and Marital Therapy, 26,* 321–334.

Hahlweg, K., Kaiser, A., Christensen, A., Fehm-Wolfsdorf, G., & Groth, T. (2000). Self-report and observational assessment of couples' conflict: The concordance between the Communication Patterns Questionnaire and the KPI observation system. *Journal of Marriage and the Family, 62,* 61–67.

Hahlweg, K., Markman, H. J., Thurmaier, F., Engl, J., & Eckert, V. (1998). Prevention of marital distress: Results of a German prospective longitudinal study. *Journal of Family Psychology, 12,* 543–556.

Halford, W. K., Gravestock, F. M., Lowe, R., & Scheldt, S. (1992). Toward a behavioral ecology of stressful marital interactions. *Behavioral Assessment, 14,* 199–217.

Halford, W. K., Hahlweg, K., & Dunne, M. (1990). The cross-cultural consistency of marital communication associated with marital distress. *Journal of Marriage and the Family, 52,* 487–500.

Halford, W. K., Sanders, M. R., & Behrens, B. C. (2000). Repeating the errors of our parents? Family-of-origin spouse violence and observed conflict management in engaged couples. *Family Process, 39,* 219–235.

Hatfield, E., & Rapson, R. L. (2002). Passionate love and sexual desire: Cultural and historical perspectives. In A. L. Vangelisti, H. T. Reis, & M. A. Fitzpatrick (Eds.), *Stability and change in relationships* (pp. 306–324). New York: Cambridge University Press.

Heavey, C. L., Christensen, A., & Malamuth, N. M. (1995). The longitudinal impact of demand and withdrawal during marital conflict. *Journal of Consulting and Clinical Psychology, 63,* 797–801.

Heavey, C. L., Layne, C., & Christensen, A. (1993). Gender and conflict structure in marital interaction: A replication and extension. *Journal of Consulting and Clinical Psychology, 61,* 16–27.

Heyman, R. E. (2001). Observation of couple conflicts: Clinical assessment applications, stubborn truths, and shaky foundations. *Psychological Assessment, 13,* 5–35.

Heyman, R. E., & Smith Slep, A. M. (2001). The hazards of predicting divorce without crossvalidation. *Journal of Marriage and Family, 63,* 473–479.

Huston, T. L. (2000). The social ecology of marriage and other intimate unions. *Journal of Marriage and the Family, 62,* 298–320.

Huston, T. L., Caughlin, J. P., Houts, R. M., Smith, S., & George, L. J. (2001). The connubial crucible: Newlywed years as predictors of marital delight, distress, and divorce. *Journal of Personality and Social Psychology, 80,* 237–252.

Huston, T. L., & Chorost, A. (1994). Behavioral buffers on the effect of negativity on marital satisfaction: A longitudinal study. *Personal Relationships, 1,* 223–239.

Huston, T. L., & Vangelisti, A. L. (1991). Socioemotional behavior and satisfaction in marital relationships: A longitudinal study. *Journal of Personality and Social Psychology, 61,* 721–733.

Jacobson, N. S. (1990). Contributions from psychology to an understanding of marriage. In F. D. Fincham & T. N. Bradbury (Eds.), *The psychology of marriage: Basic issues and applications* (pp. 258–275). New York: Guilford.

Jacobson, N. S., & Margolin, G. (1979). *Marital therapy: Strategies based on social learning and behavior exchange principles.* New York: Brunner/Mazel.

Jekielek, S. (1998). Parental conflict, marital disruption and children's emotional well-being. *Social Forces, 76,* 905–936.

Johnson, K. L., & Roloff, M. E. (2000). Correlates of the perceived resolvability and relational consequences of serial arguing in dating relationships: Argumentative features and the use of coping strategies. *Journal of Social and Personal Relationships, 17,* 677–687.

Johnson, M. P. (2001). Conflict and control: Symmetry and asymmetry in domestic violence. In A. Booth, A. C. Crouter, & M. Clements (Eds.), *Couples in conflict* (pp. 95–104). Mahwah, NJ: Lawrence Erlbaum.

Jones, E., & Gallois, C. (1989). Spouses' impressions of rules for communication in public and private marital conflicts. *Journal of Marriage and the Family, 51,* 957–967.

Karney, B. R., & Bradbury, T. N. (1995). The longitudinal course of marital quality and stability: A review of theory, method, and research. *Psychological Bulletin, 118,* 3–34.

Karney, B. R., & Bradbury, T. N. (1997). Neuroticism, marital interaction, and the trajectory of marital satisfaction. *Journal of Personality and Social Psychology, 72,* 1075–1092.

Kellermann, K. (1992). Communication: Inherently strategic and primarily automatic. *Communication Monographs, 59,* 288–300.

Kelley, H. H., Cunningham, J. D., Grisham, J. A., Lefebvre, L. M., Sink, C. R., & Yablon, G. (1978). Sex differences in comments made during conflict within close heterosexual pairs. *Sex Roles, 4,* 473–492.

Kelly, C., Huston, T. L., & Cate, R. M. (1985). Premarital relationship correlates of the erosion of satisfaction in marriage. *Journal of Social and Personal Relationships, 2,* 167–178.

Klein, R. C. A., & Johnson, M. P. (1997). Strategies of couple conflict. In S. Duck (Ed.), *Handbook of personal relationships* (2nd ed., pp. 469–486). New York: John Wiley.

Klein, R. C. A., & Milardo, R. M. (2000). The social context of couple conflict: Support and criticism from informal third parties. *Journal of Social and Personal Relationships, 17,* 618–637.

Klinetob, N. A., & Smith, D. A. (1996). Demand-withdraw communication in marital interaction: Tests of interspousal contingency and gender role hypotheses. *Journal of Marriage and the Family, 58,* 945–958.

Kluwer, E. S. (1998). Responses to gender inequality in the division of family work: The status quo effect. *Social Justice Research, 11,* 337–357.

Kluwer, E. S., Heesink, J. A. M., & Van de Vliert, E. (1997). The marital dynamics of conflict over the division of labor. *Journal of Marriage and the Family, 59,* 635–653.

Kluwer, E. S., Heesink, J. A. M., & Van de Vliert, E. (2000). The division of labor in close relationships: An asymmetrical conflict issue. *Personal Relationships, 7,* 263–282.

Koerner, A. F., & Fitzpatrick, M. A. (2002). You never leave your family in a fight: The impact of family of origin on conflict behavior in romantic relationships. *Communication Studies, 53,* 234–254.

Koren, P., Carlton, K., & Shaw, D. (1980). Marital conflict: Relations among behaviors, outcomes, and distress. *Journal of Consulting and Clinical Psychology, 48,* 460–468.

Krokoff, L. J., Gottman, J. M., & Roy, A. K. (1988). Blue-collar and white-collar marital interaction and communication orientation. *Journal of Social and Personal Relationships, 5,* 201–221.

Kurdek, L. A. (1994). Conflict resolution styles in gay, lesbian, heterosexual nonparent, and heterosexual parent couples. *Journal of Marriage and the Family, 56,* 705–722.

Kurdek, L. A. (1995). Predicting change in marital satisfaction from husbands' and wives' conflict resolution styles. *Journal of Marriage and the Family, 57,* 153–164.

Kurdek, L. A. (1998). Relationship outcomes and their predictors: Longitudinal evidence from heterosexual married, gay cohabiting, and lesbian cohabiting couples. *Journal of Marriage and the Family, 60,* 553–568.

Levenson, R. W., & Gottman, J. M. (1983). Marital interaction: Physiological linkage and affective exchange. *Journal of Personality and Social Psychology, 45,* 587–597.

Levy, S. Y., Wamboldt, F. S., & Fiese, B. H. (1997). Family-of-origin experiences and conflict resolution behaviors in young adult dating couples. *Family Process, 36,* 297–310.

Lewin, K. (1948). The background of conflict in marriage. In G. W. Lewin (Ed.), *Resolving social conflicts* (pp. 84–102). New York: Harper.

Lindahl, K., Clements, M., & Markman, H. (1998). The development of marriage: A 9-year perspective. In T. N. Bradbury (Ed.), *The developmental course of marital dysfunction* (pp. 205–236). New York: Cambridge University Press.

Lloyd, S. A. (1990). A behavioral self-report technique for assessing conflict in close relationships. *Journal of Social and Personal Relationships, 7,* 265–272.

Margolin, G., Christensen, A., & John, R. S. (1996). The continuance and spillover of everyday tensions in distressed and nondistressed families. *Journal of Family Psychology, 10,* 304–321.

Margolin, G., & Wampold, B. E. (1981). Sequential analysis of conflict and accord in distressed and nondistressed marital partners. *Journal of Consulting and Clinical Psychology, 49,* 554–567.

Markman, H. J. (1979). Application of a behavioral model of marriage in predicting relationship satisfaction of couples planning marriage. *Journal of Consulting and Clinical Psychology, 47,* 743–749.

Markman, H. J., Floyd, F., Stanley, S., & Storaasli, R. (1988). Prevention of marital distress: A longitudinal investigation. *Journal of Consulting and Clinical Psychology, 56,* 210–217.

Matthews, L. S., Wickrama, K. A. S., & Conger, R. D. (1996). Predicting marital instability from spouse and observer reports of marital interaction. *Journal of Marriage and the Family, 58,* 641–655.

McGonagle, K. A., Kessler, R. C., & Schilling, E. A. (1992). The frequency and determinants of marital disagreements in a community sample. *Journal of Social and Personal Relationships, 9,* 507–524.

McNamara, R. P., Tempenis, M., & Walton, B. (1999). *Crossing the line: Interracial couples in the South.* Westport, CT: Greenwood.

McNulty, J. K., & Karney, B. R. (2004). Positive expectations in the early years of marriage: Should couples expect the best or brace for the worst? *Journal of Personality and Social Psychology, 86,* 729–743.

Meeks, B. S., Hendrick, S. S., & Hendrick, C. (1998). Communication, love and relationship satisfaction. *Journal of Social and Personal Relationships, 15,* 755–773.

Messman, S. J., & Canary, D. J. (1998). Patterns of conflict in personal relationships. In B. H. Spitzberg & W. R. Cupach (Eds.), *The dark side of close relationships* (pp. 121–152). Mahwah, NJ: Lawrence Erlbaum.

Messman, S. J., & Mikesell, R. L. (2000). Competition and interpersonal conflict in dating relationships. *Communication Reports, 13,* 21–34.

Metts, S., Sprecher, S., & Cupach, W. R. (1991). Retrospective self-reports. In S. Duck & B. M. Montgomery (Eds.), *Studying interpersonal interaction* (pp. 162–178). New York: Guilford.

Mikolic, J. M., Parker, J. C., & Pruitt, D. G. (1997). Escalation in response to persistent annoyance: Groups versus individuals and gender effects. *Journal of Personality and Social Psychology, 72,* 151–163.

Miller, D. T., & Turnbull, W. (1986). Expectancies and interpersonal processes. *Annual Review of Psychology, 37,* 233–256.

Miller, P. C., Lefcourt, H. M., Holmes, J. G., Ware, E. E., & Saleh, W. E. (1986). Marital locus of control and marital problem solving. *Journal of Personality and Social Psychology, 51,* 161–169.

Morrison, D. R., & Coiro, M. J. (1999). Parental conflict and marital disruption: Do children benefit when high-conflict marriages are dissolved? *Journal of Marriage and the Family, 61,* 626–637.

Napier, A. Y. (1978). The rejection-intrusion pattern: A central family dynamic. *Journal of Marriage and Family Counseling, 4,* 5–12.

Newell, S. E., & Stutman, R. K. (1991). The episodic nature of social confrontation. In J. A. Anderson (Ed.), *Communication yearbook 14* (pp. 359–413). Newbury Park, CA: Sage.

Newton, D. A., & Burgoon, J. K. (1990). The use and consequences of verbal influence strategies during interpersonal disagreements. *Human Communication Research, 16,* 477–518.

Noller, P. (1984). *Nonverbal communication and marital interaction.* Elmsford, NY: Pergamon.

Noller, P., & Feeney, J. A. (1998). Communication in early marriage: Responses to conflict, nonverbal accuracy, and conversational patterns. In T. N. Bradbury (Ed.), *The developmental course of marital dysfunction* (pp. 11–43). New York: Cambridge University Press.

Noller, P., & Feeney, J. A. (2004). Studying family communication: Multiple methods and multiple sources. In A. L. Vangelisti (Ed.), *Handbook of family communication* (pp. 31–50). Mahwah, NJ: Lawrence Erlbaum.

Noller, P., Feeney, J. A., Bonnell, D., & Callan, V. J. (1994). A longitudinal study of conflict in marriage. *Journal of Social and Personal Relationships, 11,* 233–252.

Noller, P., & White, A. (1990). The validity of the Communication Patterns Questionnaire. *Psychological Assessment, 2,* 478–482.

Notarius, C. I., Lashley, S. L., & Sullivan, D. J. (1997). Angry at your partner? Think again. In R. J. Sternberg & M. Hojjat (Eds.), *Satisfaction in close relationships* (pp. 219–248). New York: Guilford.

Oggins, J., Veroff, J., & Leber, D. (1993). Perceptions of marital interaction among Black and White newlyweds. *Journal of Personality and Social Psychology, 65,* 494–511.

Ohbuchi, K., & Takahashi, Y. (1994). Cultural styles of conflict management in Japanese and Americans: Passivity, covertness, and effectiveness of strategies. *Journal of Applied Social Psychology, 24,* 1345–1366.

O'Keefe, B. J. (1988). The logic of message design: Individual differences in reasoning about communication. *Communication Monographs, 55,* 80–103.

Orbuch, T. L., & Veroff, J. (2002). A programmatic review: Building a two-way bridge between social psychology and the study of the early years of marriage. *Journal of Social and Personal Relationships, 19,* 549–568.

Orbuch, T. L., Veroff, J., Hassan, H., & Horrocks, J. (2002). Who will divorce: A 14-year longitudinal study of Black couples and White couples. *Journal of Social and Personal Relationships, 19,* 179–202.

Parks, M. R. (1982). Ideology in interpersonal communication: Off the couch and into the world. In M. Burgoon (Ed.), *Communication yearbook 6* (pp. 79–107). Beverly Hills, CA: Sage.

Patterson, C. J. (2000). Family relationships of lesbians and gay men. *Journal of Marriage and the Family, 62,* 1052–1069.

Peplau, L. A., & Beals, K. P. (2004). The family lives of lesbians and gay men. In A. L. Vangelisti (Ed.), *Handbook of family communication* (pp. 233–248). Mahwah, NJ: Lawrence Erlbaum.

Pike, G. R., & Sillars, A. L. (1985). Reciprocity of marital communication. *Journal of Social and Personal Relationships, 2,* 303–324.

Raffaelli, M., & Ontai, L. L. (2001). "She's 16 years old and there's boys calling over to the house": An exploratory study of sexual socialization in Latino families. *Culture, Health, and Sexuality, 3,* 295–310.

Raush, H. L., Barry, W. A., Hertel, R. K., & Swain, M. A. (1974). *Communication, conflict, and marriage.* San Francisco: Jossey-Bass.

Roberts, L. J. (2000). Fire and ice in marital communication: Hostile and distancing behaviors as predictors of marital distress. *Journal of Marriage and the Family, 62,* 693–707.

Robinson, E. A., & Jacobson, N. S. (1987). Social learning theory and family psychology: A Kantian model in behaviorism? In T. Jacob (Ed.), *Family interaction and psychopathology: Theory, methods, and findings* (pp. 117–162). New York: Plenum.

Roloff, M. E., & Cloven, D. E. (1990). The chilling effect in interpersonal relationships: The reluctance to speak one's mind. In D. D. Cahn (Ed.), *Intimates in conflict: A communication perspective* (pp. 49–76). Hillsdale, NJ: Lawrence Erlbaum.

Roloff, M. E., & Ifert, D. E. (2000). Conflict management through avoidance: Withholding complaints, suppressing arguments, and declaring topics taboo. In S. Petronio (Ed.), *Balancing the secrets of private disclosures* (pp. 151–163). Mahwah, NJ: Lawrence Erlbaum.

Roloff, M. E., & Johnson, K. L. (2002). Serial arguing over the relational life course: Antecedents and consequences. In A. L. Vangelisti, H. T. Reis, & M. A. Fitzpatrick (Eds.), *Stability and change in relationships* (pp. 107–128). New York: Cambridge University Press.

Ruvolo, A. P., Fabin, L. A., & Ruvolo, C. M. (2001). Relationship experiences and change in attachment characteristics of young adults: The role of relationship breakups and conflict avoidance. *Personal Relationships, 8,* 265–281.

Sanders, M. R., Halford, W. K., & Behrens, B. C. (1999). Parental divorce and premarital couple communication. *Journal of Family Psychology, 13,* 60–74.

Sanford, K. (2003). Problem-solving conversations in marriage: Does it matter what topic couples discuss? *Personal Relationships, 10,* 97–112.

Schulz, M. S., Cowan, P. A., Cowan, C. P., & Brennan, R. T. (2004). Coming home upset: Gender, marital satisfaction, and the daily spillover of workday experience into couple interactions. *Journal of Family Psychology, 18,* 250–263.

Siegert, J. R., & Stamp, G. H. (1994). "Our first big fight" as a milestone in the development of close relationships. *Communication Monographs, 61,* 345–360.

Sillars, A. L. (1986). *Procedures for coding interpersonal conflict* (Rev. manual). Missoula: University of Montana, Department of Interpersonal Communication.

Sillars, A., Canary, D. J., & Tafoya, M. (2004). Communication, conflict, and the quality of family relationships. In A. L. Vangelisti (Ed.), *Handbook of family communication* (pp. 413–446). Mahwah, NJ: Lawrence Erlbaum.

Sillars, A. L., Pike, G. R., Jones, T. S., & Redmon, K. (1983). Communication and conflict in marriage. In R. Bostrom (Ed.), *Communication yearbook 7* (pp. 414–429). Beverly Hills, CA: Sage.

Sillars, A., Roberts, L. J., Dun, T., & Leonard, K. (2001). Stepping into the stream of thought: Cognition during marital conflict. In V. Manusov & J. H. Harvey (Eds.), *Attribution, communication behavior, and close relationships* (pp. 193–210). New York: Cambridge University Press.

Sillars, A., Roberts, L. J., Leonard, K. E., & Dun, T. (2000). Cognition during marital conflict: The relationship of thought and talk. *Journal of Social and Personal Relationships, 17,* 479–502.

Sillars, A. L., & Weisberg, J. (1987). Conflict as a social skill. In M. E. Roloff & G. R. Miller, (Eds.), *Interpersonal processes: New directions in communication research* (pp. 140–171). Newbury Park, CA: Sage.

Simpson, J. A., Rholes, W. S., & Phillips, D. (1996). Conflict in close relationships: An attachment perspective. *Journal of Personality and Social Psychology, 71,* 899–914.

Smith, D. A., Vivian, D., & O'Leary, K. D. (1990). Longitudinal prediction of marital discord from premarital expressions of affect. *Journal of Consulting and Clinical Psychology, 58,* 790–798.

Solomon, D. H., & Samp, J. A. (1998). Power and problem appraisal: Perceptual foundations of the chilling effect in dating relationships. *Journal of Social and Personal Relationships, 15,* 191–210.

Stanley, S. M., Bradbury, T. N., & Markman, H. J. (2000). Structural flaws in the bridge from basic research on marriage to interventions for couples. *Journal of Marriage and the Family, 62,* 256–264.

Surra, C. A., & Longstreth, M. (1990). Similarity of outcomes, interdependence, and conflict in dating relationships. *Journal of Personality and Social Psychology, 59,* 501–516.

Timmer, S. G., Veroff, J., & Hatchett, S. (1996). Family ties and marital happiness: The different marital experiences of Black and White newlywed couples. *Journal of Social and Personal Relationships, 13,* 335–359.

Ting-Toomey, S. (1983). An analysis of verbal communication patterns in high and low marital adjustment groups. *Human Communication Research, 9,* 306–319.

Vangelisti, A. L. (1994). Couples' communication problems: The counselor's perspective. *Journal of Applied Communication Research, 22,* 106–126.

Vangelisti, A. L., Corbin, S. D., Lucchetti, A. E., & Sprague, R. J. (1999). Couples' concurrent cognitions: The influence of relational satisfaction on the thoughts couples have as they converse. *Human Communication Research, 25,* 370–398.

Vangelisti, A. L., & Daly, J. A. (1997). Gender differences in standards for romantic relationships. *Personal Relationships, 4,* 203–219.

Veroff, J., Douvan, E., & Hatchett, S. J. (1995). *Marital instability: A social and behavioral study of the early years.* Greenwich, CT: Greenwood.

Vogel, D. L., Wester, S. R., & Heesacker, M. (1999). Dating relationships and the demand/withdraw pattern of communication. *Sex Roles, 41,* 297–306.

Watzlawick, P., Beavin, J., & Jackson, D. D. (1967). *Pragmatics of human communication: A study of interactional patterns, pathologies, and paradoxes.* New York: Norton.

Wills, T. A., Weiss, R. L., & Patterson, G. R. (1974). A behavioral analysis of the determinants of marital satisfaction. *Journal of Consulting and Clinical Psychology, 42,* 802–811.

Wilson, L. L., Roloff, M. E., & Carey, C. M. (1998). Boundary rules: Factors that inhibit expressing concerns about another's romantic relationship. *Communication Research, 25,* 618–640.

Wilson, S. R., Aleman, C. G., & Leatham, G. B. (1998). Identity implications of influence goals: A revised analysis of face-threatening acts and application to seeking compliance with same-sex friends. *Human Communication Research, 25,* 64–96.

Woody, E. Z., & Constanzo, P. R. (1990). Does marital agony precede marital ecstasy? A comment on Gottman and Krokoff's "Marital interaction and satisfaction: A longitudinal view." *Journal of Consulting and Clinical Psychology, 58,* 499–501.

Zuroff, D. C., & Duncan, N. (1999). Self-criticism and conflict resolution in romantic couples. *Canadian Journal of Behavioral Science, 31,* 137–149.

6

FAMILY CONFLICT COMMUNICATION

ASCAN F. KOERNER
University of Minnesota

MARY ANNE FITZPATRICK
University of South Carolina

F amily communication is of great interest to researchers, counselors, and laypeople alike for at least three reasons. First, family is the context in which adults and children experience a great part of their most important and most intimate interpersonal relationships. Because most persons' overall life satisfaction is dependent on the quality of their interpersonal relationships, the quality of family communication has great significance for the overall quality of life for most people in our society. Second, families are children's main socialization agents (Noller, 1995). That is, the communication and relationship skills that children acquire in their families of origin, or fail to acquire, will affect the quality of their interpersonal relationships throughout their lifetime. Finally, unlike adults who are essentially free to choose with whom they associate and how they communicate with those with whom they associate, children have no choice over who is in their families and little influence on how other family members communicate. As such, they are particularly vulnerable to harmful or abusive behaviors by other family members, and society has a legitimate interest in learning about such behaviors and in protecting children from such negative influences.

All these reasons that justify an interest in family communication in general also justify an interest in family conflict communication in particular. How persons communicate during interpersonal conflict is of paramount relevance in determining the quality and stability of their close interpersonal relationships, including family relationships. In the marital context, Gottman (1991, 1994) reported that couples that manage interpersonal conflict well in their relationships report greater relationship satisfaction, more love and respect for their partners, and greater commitment to their partners. Similar findings are reported for family conflict. Families that manage their conflicts well have more satisfied parents and children, and children perform better in school and in peer relationships (Sillars, Canary, & Tafoya, 2004).

Thus, family conflict is an important determinant of relationship quality and quality of life of family members. In addition, the conflict communication behaviors socialized in families are among the most important behaviors learned in families that affect children's subsequent interpersonal relationships, further strengthening the case for studying family conflict. Finally, harmful communication and child abuse, which constitute the third reason to study family communication mentioned above, are more likely to occur during family conflict than during any other time of family communication (Anderson, Umberson, & Elliott, 2004), which makes a thorough investigation of family conflict all the more pertinent.

Despite these good reasons to study family communication in general and family conflict communication in particular, in reviewing the relevant literature, it became apparent to us that is not easy to integrate the literature on family conflict. The main reasons are inconsistent conceptualizations of both conflict and communication, as well as of the relationship between them. These problems notwithstanding, in the following pages we discuss, first, how conflict and communication have been conceptualized in various studies of family conflict. We then propose definitions of both *conflict* and *family communication* that allow us to integrate at least some of the findings on family conflict and to discuss the relevant literature utilizing these definitions. In particular, we focus on the role that conflict plays in family communication at different stages of family development and in different family types. This discussion is followed by a review of the consequences of family conflict and how family conflict affects family relationships and family members' psychological well-being and social functioning. Finally, we address issues surrounding violence in families related to conflict, including factors affecting violence and its consequences. In our conclusion, we argue that family conflict is best understood in the context of more general family communication processes, such as family communication patterns, and point to some of the lacunas in the research that warrant future investigation, including a more careful investigation of the roles of culture and ethnicity.

Defining Family Communication and Family Conflict

Defining Family Communication

In the broadest sense, family communication can be defined as all interactive behaviors of family members that establish family roles, maintain family rules, accomplish family functions, and sustain behavioral patterns in families (Vangelisti, 2004). In other words, all verbal and nonverbal behaviors by which family members affect one another and enact their interpersonal relationships with each other. The breadth of this conceptualization of family communication has the advantage that it opens for investigation by communication scholars all interpersonal behaviors. In addition, this conceptualization makes explicit the fact that interpersonal relationships are complex and that virtually any type of behavior can be interpersonally meaningful. Finally, this conceptualization highlights some of the underlying assumptions about family communication that researchers are making.

The first and probably most important of these assumptions is that family communication is a function of both psychological and interpersonal processes (Koerner & Fitzpatrick, 2002a, 2004). This means that family communication has an unequivocally empirical component in family members' behaviors that is observable by family members as well as by outsiders, such as researchers or counselors. In addition, however, family communication also has a psychological component residing within each family member's cognition that is neither observable nor controllable by anybody, except maybe the family member him- or herself. As a consequence, each family member aware of an interpersonal behavior partially determines the meaning of that interpersonal behavior individually and idiosyncratically, regardless of any intentions by the actor or any interpretations of the behaviors by others. That means that every interpersonal behavior can, and frequently does, have multiple meanings in the family context, without there being a final arbiter determining meaning for all family members. Because family members respond to behavior of others at least partially based on the meaning that they assign to it, coordinated behavior is difficult for family members unless families develop strategies to address the inherent ambiguity of meaning.

One approach families use to deal with the inherent ambiguousness of the meaning of their behaviors is to establish intersubjectivity, or a shared social reality (McLeod & Chaffee, 1972, 1973). This intersubjectivity allows them to interpret the behaviors of family members consistently and to predict how other family members interpret their own behavior. In short, intersubjectivity allows family members to assign similar meanings to their behaviors, to understand one another, and ultimately to coordinate their behaviors. Intersubjectivity, however, is never perfect—in the sense that all family members share an identical social reality. In the final analysis, each family member's social reality also is always influenced by experiences and beliefs that are uniquely the member's own and that are not shared by other family members. Thus, even in families that achieve high intersubjectivity, there is always an element of idiosyncrasy and uncertainty about meaning that may lead to misunderstandings and difficulties in enacting relationships. In other words, family communication is inherently problematic.

To say that family communication is problematic is to acknowledge at least three consequences that stem from the inherent ambiguity of meaning and that can be summarized as follows. First, any behavior enacted within the context of a family relationship may or may not be meaningful to anyone within the family who is aware of the behavior. Thus, any given behavior may or may not have meaning for the actor, may or may not have meaning for the receiver of the behavior, and may or may not have meaning for other family members aware of the behavior. Second, there can be no absolute certainty about the meaning that any given behavior has for anyone within the family. It is possible that family members agree about the meaning of a behavior, but it is also possible that different family members assign very different or even contradicting meanings to the same behavior. Finally, because family functioning requires a minimum of shared social reality (Koerner & Fitzpatrick, 2004), families spend a considerable amount of time and energy establishing a shared social reality by negotiating the meaning

of their behaviors. Because this negotiation is ongoing, one could argue that family communication is inherently conflicted.

The inherent ambiguity of meaning in families is not only problematic for families, however, but for scholars researching and theorizing about family communication as well. Simply put, to be adequate, theoretical explanations of family communication must account for both the cognitive and the behavioral aspects of family communication. In other words, theoretical models of family communication must be simultaneously anchored in the abstract and immaterial world of cognition and in the concrete and material world of behavior.

Defining Family Conflict

Like family communication, interpersonal conflict, including family conflict, has both psychological and behavioral attributes and can be defined in both terms. One example of a psychologically based definition of conflict is perceived goal incompatibility (Fincham, Bradbury, & Grych, 1990). In this definition, conflict is the perception by at least one person that another person is blocking the first person from achieving a personal, relational, or instrumental goal. That is, for there to be interpersonal conflict in this definition, the other person or persons in the relationship do not even have to be aware that the original person is perceiving an incompatibility of goals or goal blockage.

Because in this definition conflict is not necessarily expressed in interpersonal behavior, most scholars interested in interpersonal communication employ more behavioral-oriented definitions. Examples include Cahn (1992), who identified three types of conflict communication as specific disagreements, problem-solving discussions, and unhappy/dissolving relationships, respectively; Donohue and Kolt (1992), who defined conflict "as a situation in which interdependent people *express* (manifest or latent) differences in satisfying their individual needs and interests, and they experience interference from each other in accomplishing these goals" (p. 4; emphasis added); and Straus (1990), whose Conflict Tactics Scales measures behavioral manifestations of conflict such as problem solving, yelling, and pushing.

The range of behaviors covered by even such behavioral definitions, however, is still very large. In Donohue and Kolt's (1992) definition, for example, conflict behaviors range from "latent conflict" and "problem to solve" to "dispute," "help," "fight/flight," and finally to "intractable." Similarly, Straus distinguishes between three types of conflict behaviors: "reasoning," which refers to rational discussion and problem-solving behaviors; "verbal aggression," which refers to behaviors intended to hurt the other symbolically; and "violence," which refers to behaviors enacted to inflict physical pain and/or injury. Given this wide range of behaviors covered by the conceptual definitions and operationalizations of interpersonal conflict, it should be apparent that it is almost impossible to evaluate the research on family conflict in a holistic sense. Rather, it is necessary to distinguish between different types of conflict behaviors to fully assess the antecedents and consequences of family conflict.

One frequently used way to distinguish between different types of interpersonal conflict has been to focus on the relational outcomes of conflict behaviors and to label them accordingly as either functional (i.e., constructive) or as dysfunctional (i.e., destructive) (Deutsch, 1973; Donohue & Kolt, 1992). Such a distinction is meaningful as long as it can be assumed that there are conflict behaviors that fairly consistently lead to positive outcomes and conflict behaviors that fairly consistently lead to negative outcomes. This distinction is often motivated by the desire of the researchers to identify and teach "ideal" communication and relationship skills. Because of the already discussed ambiguity of meaning of behaviors, however, such an assumption can be a weak one at best. Nonetheless, research on constructive and destructive conflict communication has led to the identification of teachable conflict communication skills that often do have positive relational outcomes and that allow families to improve the quality of their problem solving and ultimately their interpersonal relationships (e.g., Christensen & Jacobson, 2000; Donohue & Kolt, 1992; Gottman, 1994).

In addition to the inherent ambiguity of conflict behaviors, another important problem in identifying constructive versus destructive conflict behaviors is that the standards by which conflict behavior is determined to be either constructive or destructive also are far from unambiguous. Whereas it is relatively easy to make theoretical distinctions that employ fairly abstract concepts such as "interest versus needs centered" and "bolstering versus compromising interdependence" (Donohue & Kolt, 1992), when labeling conflict as either constructive or destructive, judging concrete behaviors using the same abstract concepts is much more difficult. In addition, it is not entirely possible to separate the relational outcomes of conflict from its material or practical outcomes. Although process does matter, persons' relationship commitment and satisfaction is at least partially dependent on the extent to which they are able to obtain desired material or practical outcomes from their interpersonal conflicts. Thus, whether conflict is ultimately constructive also depends on whether conflict is judged using a long- or short-term perspective; whether these outcomes are psychological, behavioral, or relational; and finally, from whose perspective the outcomes are judged. As we suggested earlier, at the root of many family conflicts are incompatible goals or interests of family members, making it almost inevitable that any outcome has to be evaluated differently depending on whose perspective is used when making the evaluation.

An alternative way to distinguish between different types of conflict is based on observable qualities of behaviors rather than more abstract qualities such as psychological, behavioral, and relational outcomes. For example, Straus (1990), in his work on interpersonal conflict, distinguished between reasoning, verbal aggression, and violence as types of conflict behaviors. Although in much of his work Straus is dedicated to demonstrating different outcomes associated with these conflict behaviors, the distinction is made based on an evaluation of the behaviors themselves, not necessarily their outcomes. That is, even though Straus uses the probable outcomes of conflict behaviors to make arguments for the use of reasoning and against the use of verbal aggression and violence, his rejection of verbal aggression and physical violence is based as much on negative moral evaluations of the behaviors themselves as on the negative outcomes of the behaviors.

In this view, for example, the verbal abuse or beating of children is rejected based on the immorality of the behavior itself, independently of whether those behaviors actually harm the child's self-esteem or social functioning. Of course, how moral a behavior is always also depends on its consequences, but not exclusively so. Thus, verbal aggression against a child is immoral partially because it has negative consequences for the child, but not for that reason alone. Verbal aggression is immoral simply because it attempts to hurt a weaker person, which violates fundamental assumptions about justice and fairness.

Differentiating between reasoning, verbal aggression, and physical violence, which essentially groups behaviors into categories along an intensity dimension, is not the only way to distinguish between overt conflict communication behaviors. Sillars et al. (2004), in a recent review of family and marital conflict, classified different types of conflict behaviors identified by other researchers as falling into four types based on two underlying dimensions. In their model, the first dimension distinguishes direct from indirect communication, and the second dimension distinguishes cooperative from competitive communication. The four resulting types are *negotiation* (direct and cooperative), which includes behaviors such as agreement, analytic remarks, communication talk, description, expressing, problem solving, summarizing, and validating; *direct fighting* (direct and competitive), which includes behaviors such as blaming, coercive acts, confrontation, disagreement, invalidation, and rejecting acts; *nonconfrontation* (indirect and cooperative), which includes behaviors such as facilitation, irreverent remarks, resolving acts, and topic management; and *indirect fighting* (indirect and competitive), which includes behaviors such as denial, equivocation, dysphoric affect, and withdrawal. As in Straus's (1990) typology, conflict types are determined based on observed communication behavior and not on the perceived desirableness of the outcomes, although direct and cooperative communication is generally viewed to lead to more positive outcomes than indirect and/or competitive communication.

As this short review demonstrates, it is possible to define conflict variously in both psychological and behavioral terms. Each approach has its own distinct strengths and weaknesses, and no one definition of conflict and conflict behaviors is unequivocally superior. In the context of family communication, however, there seems to be a preference for definitions of conflict based on behavior over definitions based on psychological or otherwise unobservable outcomes. The main reason, in our estimation, is that behavioral definitions avoid having to deal with the inherent ambiguousness of meaning of communicative behaviors because their empirical nature allows them to be assessed fairly objectively from the perspective of a third-party observer rather than having to rely on the perceptions and biases of individual family members. In addition to their greater ecological validity, the clarity that results from the empirical nature of behavioral definitions makes it possible to compare research stemming from various academic disciplines, which facilitates theory building and testing and increases researchers' abilities to advance their knowledge of family conflict.

Our own inclination is to conceptualize and define conflict generally, in its broadest terms, which means including both its cognitive and behavioral aspects, because it is consistent with our similarly broad definition of family communication. Of course, at times it will be necessary to use more narrow definitions of conflict to investigate specific phenomena or test particular hypotheses. But this should not be a problem as long as such more narrow definitions and their limitations are acknowledged from the outset and taken into consideration when interpreting results from studies employing such definitions. Having defined family communication and conflict, it is now possible to assess the frequency of conflict in families and how conflict behaviors are enacted and learned in families.

CONFLICT COMMUNICATION IN FAMILY RELATIONSHIPS

Frequency and Intensity of Conflict

Of all interpersonal relationships, family relationships are arguably the most conflicted (Shantz & Hartup, 1992; Shantz & Hobart,

1989). Not only is conflict inevitable in close, interdependent relationships such as family relationships (Deutsch, 1973), conflict behavior is also more frequent in family relationships (including marital, parent-child, and sibling relationships) than in peer or work relationships (Sillars et al., 2004). In addition to being conflicted, family relationships are also among the most physically violent social relationships persons have. Despite significant changes in social norms that have made acts of severe violence (including kicking, punching, and attacks with objects) unacceptable or illegal in spousal, parent-child, and sibling relationships, severe violence occurs in at least 8% of all marital relationships, 11% of parent-child relationships, and 36% of sibling relationships (Straus & Gelles, 1990). Frequencies of less severe violence (e.g., shoving, pushing, and slapping), which is more likely to be both legal and socially acceptable, are much higher and can be observed in around 16% of marriages, in almost 100% of parent-child relationships with young children (age <3 years), in 34% of parent-child relationships with adolescents, and in 64% of sibling relationships (Straus & Gelles, 1990).

Parents and Preadolescent Children

Conflict between parents and preadolescent children most typically involves parents' attempts to regulate their children's behavior and children initially resisting these attempts but ultimately complying with the demands of their parents (Laursen, 1993). That is, conflict is a natural correlate of the socialization process that constitutes much of family communication as children move from other-regulation to self-regulation (Burleson, Delia, & Applegate, 1995). Thus, one could expect the frequency of family conflict to decrease the older, and presumably more self-regulated, children become. This expectation is certainly supported by data that show parents' use of physical punishment decreasing as children get older (Straus & Gelles, 1990). On the other hand, families often perceive an increase in the intensity of family conflict as children reach adolescence. This apparent inconsistency exists because the very nature of the parent-child relationship is changing during adolescence, which makes conflict

during adolescence more salient to family members and more relevant to the parent-child relationship (Laursen & Collins, 2004). In relationships involving younger children, both parents and children understand the parents' role in the relationship as one that provides guidance and discipline. Thus, both parents and children expect to have conflicts with one another and see it as an integral and therefore not necessarily salient aspect of their relationship. As a consequence, both parents and children may perceive their relationship to be relatively free of intense conflict, even though much of their communication consists of parents' exerting influence over their children's behavior and could objectively be defined as conflict.

Parents and Adolescent Children

Adolescents, in contrast, tend to see themselves as much more autonomous and independent in their relationships with their parents (Noller, 1995) and increasingly come to resent the regulating behavior of their parents (Smetana, You, & Hanson, 1991). For them, resistance to the parents often becomes an end in itself (Collins & Luebker, 1994), while parents try to maintain their influence over their children. Thus, the influence that parents exert over their adolescent children becomes the underlying relational issue that manifests itself in conflict about ostensibly other topics, making these conflicts more intense and both parents and adolescents more aware that they do experience conflict in their relationships.

The relative salience of conflict in the parent-adolescent relationship was recognized by Noller (1995), who argued that for adolescents, family communication serves five functions, all of which are mainly achieved through conflict communication. Specifically, she argued that family communication functions to allow adolescents to renegotiate roles, rules, and relationships; to help them to explore their identity; to enhance adolescents' self-esteem; to model and teach problem-solving behaviors; and to enable adolescents' decision making. The three functions most obviously related to conflict communication are the following: renegotiating of roles, rules, and relationships; modeling and teaching of problem-solving behaviors; and enabling decision making. Almost by definition, these functions involve intra-familial conflict communication. For example, it is hard to imagine that renegotiations of parent-adolescent relationships, and the rules that accompany them, can be accomplished without conflict. In fact, the renegotiation of roles explicitly involves a change in the power relationship from relative dependence to relative independence of the adolescents. Adolescents usually aim for greater independence, and the parents usually aim to maintain the status quo. Because both parents and children are heavily invested in their respective aims, these conflicts are not easily resolved and are often quite emotional. Similarly, for parents to teach and to model conflict behaviors and to teach decision-making skills requires them to engage in family conflict and decision making. It is an old adage that children learn more from how parents behave than from what parents say, and conflict communication is no exception.

Although ostensibly not about conflict, fulfilling the functions of helping adolescents explore their identities and enhance their self-esteem also is related to family conflict. Exploring identities almost invariably involves adolescents' taking positions and espousing opinions and values that differentiate them from other family members and particularly their parents. As Harris (1998) described in her theory of peer socialization, during adolescence children orient themselves toward their peers for their social identities precisely because this allows them to distinguish themselves from their parents. The more different adolescents are from their parents, the clearer are their identities defined for their peers and the greater the social status afforded to them by their peers. As a consequence, the process of identity formation of adolescents often involves their rejection of core values held by parents, which parents cannot help but perceive involves a rejection of them as individuals, setting the stage for often intense conflicts.

SOCIALIZATION OF CONFLICT COMMUNICATION BEHAVIORS

One of the main reasons why family conflict communication is of such interest to researchers is the assumption that families socialize children to adopt particular conflict styles in their interpersonal relationships (Koerner & Fitzpatrick, 1997; Noller, 1995; Rinaldi & Howe, 2003). That is, children learn how to communicate during interpersonal conflict from how their families of origin communicate during their conflicts. They will employ similar communication styles not only in interactions within their families, but also in relationships outside the family and in subsequent interpersonal relationships they have as adults as well. Thus, family conflict communication affects all of the children's conflict communication in current and future relationships.

Impact of Parental Conflict on Children's Conflict Behaviors

In support of a socializing influence of families on conflict styles, there is considerable evidence suggesting that children have conflict styles that are very similar to those of their parents (Koerner & Fitzpatrick, 2002c). This similarity is not only observed during intra-family conflict, but also during conflicts that children have with persons from outside the family and in the subsequent interpersonal relationships of adult children. For example, in a study by Montemayor and Hanson (1985), adolescents reported using similar conflict styles in their relationships with parents and in relationships with their siblings. Similarly, in a study of 163 families comparing the conflict styles of family members during dyadic conflict with other family members and those of adolescent children with their romantic partners, Reese-Weber and Bertle-Haring (1998) found that the conflict styles of parents and children were significantly correlated. Distinguishing among the conflict styles of compromising, attacking, and avoiding, these researchers found that inter-parental conflict style was related directly to conflict styles of parents in dyadic conflict with their children. Specifically, results showed that inter-parental use of compromising was correlated positively with adults' and children's use of compromise and correlated negatively with their use of attack and avoidance for all intra-family dyadic relationships. Use of attack and avoidance, on the other hand, were correlated positively with one another across all family dyads, and correlated negatively with use of compromise. Further, the results of the study also showed that inter-parental conflict styles were related indirectly to children's conflict style with siblings and their romantic partners. That is, these associations were mediated by parent-adolescent conflict styles. These findings suggest that parents use the same conflict styles in their relationships with one another and in relationships with their children, who in turn use similar conflict styles in their interpersonal relationships within and outside the family.

Impact of Family Conflict on Children's Conflict Behaviors and Beyond

Rinaldi and Howe (2003) also investigated similarities of conflict styles among family members. Results were similar to the Reese-Weber and Bertle-Haring (1998) study in that family members reported similar use of constructive and destructive conflict styles in all possible family dyads (parent-parent, parent-child, child-child). The researchers' interpretation of the data, however, was somewhat different. In addition to looking at reports of conflict behaviors, these authors also collected family members' perceptions of the conflict styles they employed in other family dyads and found that these perceptions also were correlated positively. From this, the authors concluded that rather than just learning conflict communication styles from one another on a behavioral level, family members also share their perceptions of family communication in general, and family conflict in particular. Thus, it is not only specific conflict behaviors that children are socialized to in families, but rather their entire perception of how families communicate with one another and the role conflict plays in family life.

Our own research (Koerner & Fitzpatrick, 1997, 2002c) on family conflict and its role in adult children's subsequent interpersonal relationship also supports the idea that conflict behaviors are not learned in isolation, but as part of the larger socialization of family communication patterns in general. Results from our research showed that the conflict behaviors adult children employ in their current romantic relationships are dependent on the family communication patterns of their families of origin.

Specifically, we found that mutually positive, mutually negative, and avoidant behaviors occur in similar frequency in families of origin and adult children's subsequent romantic relationships. In addition, our findings showed that conformity orientation of families of origin had a direct effect on determining the type of conflict behaviors of adult children. Conversation orientation of families of origin, in contrast, interacted with conformity orientation in such a way as to determine the strength of the association between conformity orientation in the family of origin and adult children's behavior in the subsequent romantic relationships. A more detailed description of these findings follows in the section on family communication patterns.

Burleson et al. (1995) also made a strong case for the assumption that children learn not only how to communicate during conflict from their families of origin, but through their experiences during family conflict also acquire beliefs and values that affect other aspects of relationships as well. Specifically, these scholars argued that how parents resolve conflicts with their children teaches children important lessons about the psychology of other persons and how to relate to them and about the social rules that apply to interpersonal relationships.

According to Burleson et al. (1995), generally parents use one of two different communication strategies to regulate their children's behaviors: a person-centered approach or a position-centered approach. In the *person-centered* approach, parents employ regulating and comforting messages that emphasize how persons are affected by the behaviors of others. In particular, person-centered regulating messages focus on the needs, values, feelings, and psychology of others and how they are affected by the child's behavior. Thus, the person-centered approach enhances children's ability to be empathetic and to take the other person's perspective. Ultimately, it leads children to develop complex and sophisticated mental representations of themselves, others, and their interpersonal relationships that are associated with flexible, supportive, and sensitive communication.

In contrast, the *position-centered* approach employs regulating and comforting messages that emphasize rules and norms that apply regardless of whether or how persons are affected by the behaviors of others. In particular, position-centered regulating messages focus on the social norms and conventions governing a particular situation and the appropriate behaviors of children. Thus, the position-centered approach leads children to focus on context and norms in relationships with others. Ultimately, it leads children to develop mental representations of relationships that are based on social rules and norms, but that do not require them to be able to take the other person's perspective into consideration. These less complex and less individuating mental representations of themselves, others, and interpersonal relationships are associated with inflexible, insensitive, and less supportive communication.

As the preceding review showed, the available evidence clearly establishes a significant role for family communication in the socialization of conflict behaviors of children in interpersonal relationships within and external to their families. This socialization, however, is not limited to the modeling of conflict behavior per se, but rather has to be understood as part of a larger socialization process. This process undoubtedly involves conflict behaviors and their mental representation, but in addition also involves communication behaviors unrelated to conflict and mental representations not only of persons in conflict, but also of persons in interpersonal and social relationships in general. Ultimately, then, we argue that the socialization of family conflict behaviors is part and parcel of a general socialization process accomplished by families that involves fundamental beliefs about family communication that are shared by family members and constitute family communication schemata (Koerner & Fitzpatrick, 2002b, 2004). Specifically, we contend that family conflict results from family members' cognitive representations of their family relationships (communication schemata) and the family communication patterns that result from these schemata.

COMMUNICATION SCHEMATA, FAMILY COMMUNICATION PATTERNS, AND FAMILY CONFLICT

Family Communication Schemata

In an earlier article (Koerner & Fitzpatrick, 2002a), we argued that family communication

schemata, like other interpersonal communication schemata, consist of declarative and procedural social knowledge and exist at three different levels of hierarchy. Knowledge that applies to all social relationships is stored in a general social schema. Knowledge that applies to all relationships of a certain type is stored in a relationship type schema, and social knowledge that applies to a specific relationship with one particular person is stored in a relationship-specific schema. During cognitive processing, these three schemata are accessed in a bottom-up process such that knowledge stored in relationship-specific schemata is accessed first, knowledge stored in relationship-type schemata is accessed second, and knowledge stored in the general social schema is accessed last. Thus, unique, individuating information that is stored in relationship-specific schemata always has precedence over typical or stereotypical information in social cognition, which are stored in relationship-type and general social schemata. Furthermore, relationship-specific schemata for persons we know well and are close to are larger and more complex than those for persons we do not know well or are not close to.

Communication schemata are developed over a lifetime and reflect knowledge based on different relationship experiences. Knowledge gained from experiences typical for all social relationships are stored in the general social schema, knowledge based on experiences representative of relationships of specific types is stored in relationship-type schemata, and knowledge from experiences unique to specific relationships with particular persons is stored in relationship-specific schemata. Social knowledge in these schemata is dynamic in that it can change to reflect new experiences (i.e., after being lied to by Tom, the personal schema for "Tom" now also includes the knowledge that Tom is not trustworthy), or knowledge can migrate from one schema to another (i.e., after repeatedly receiving social support from friends at work rather than from friends at school, knowledge designating one's primary support group could move from the "school friends schema" to the "work friends schema"). Although the precise contents of family relationship schemata at this point are not fully investigated, it appears that they contain important beliefs about family relationships and family communication that have been conceptualized as family communication patterns.

Family Communication Patterns

McLeod and Chaffee (1972) first proposed family communication patterns to explain how families process information, such as mass media messages. Family communication patterns theory (Koerner & Fitzpatrick, 2005) is based on cognitive theories explaining how families achieve a shared social environment through the process of co-orientation, which involves either a concept-orientation or a socio-orientation of family members (for a detailed description, see Koerner & Fitzpatrick, 2004). Concept-orientation of families is generally associated with an open and engaging communication style parents have with their children, whereas socio-orientation of families generally is associated with a directive and authoritarian communication style by parents. In most research on family communication, family communication patterns are measured using Fitzpatrick's and Ritchie's (1994; Ritchie, 1991; Ritchie & Fitzpatrick, 1990) Revised Family Communication Patterns (RFCP) instrument.

The RFCP is based on McLeod and Chaffee's (1972) original family communication pattern (FCP) instrument, but better labels and operationalizes the dimensions as conversation orientation (called concept-orientation by McLeod & Chaffee) and conformity orientation (called socio-orientation by McLeod & Chaffee). Although empirically often moderately negatively correlated with one another, conversation orientation and conformity orientation are conceptually orthogonal from one another and can be used to define four family types.

Conversation orientation is one of the two dimensions underlying family communication patterns. It is the degree to which families value and create a climate of open flow of communication and exchanges of ideas about attitudes, beliefs, and values (Fitzpatrick & Ritchie, 1994; Ritchie & Fitzpatrick, 1990). Families at the high end of this dimension freely, frequently, and spontaneously interact with one another about a wide variety of topics. Families at the low end of this dimension interact less openly

and less frequently with one another and limit themselves to a narrower range of topics. In regard to conflict, conversation orientation is associated with engaging rather than avoiding conflict, with using supportive communication in conflict situations (Koerner & Fitzpatrick, 1997), and with using positive (i.e., integrative) conflict strategies (Wrench & Socha-McGee, 1999). Members of families high in conversation orientation are also more likely to solicit social support in conflict situations than members of families low in conversation orientation (Koerner & Fitzpatrick, 1997).

Conformity orientation is the other dimension underlying family communication patterns. It is the degree to which families create a climate that stresses homogeneity of attitudes, values, and beliefs (Fitzpatrick & Ritchie, 1994; Ritchie & Fitzpatrick, 1990). Families at the high end of this dimension value and hold similar beliefs and attitudes and typically engage in interactions that focus on harmony and obedience to the parents. Families at the low end of this dimension value and hold more heterogeneous attitudes and beliefs and engage in interactions that focus on the uniqueness and independence of family members. Conformity orientation in families is correlated positively with conflict avoidance (Koerner & Fitzpatrick, 1997) and correlated negatively with use of positive (integrative) conflict strategies (Wrench & Socha-McGee, 1999). Families high in conformity orientation avoid conflict because they interpret it as a threat to the family system. Because conflict usually highlights differences between family members, it is perceived as undermining the harmony and conformity that these families value so much.

Conformity orientation in families is also associated with a greater frequency of verbal hostility during conflict (Koerner & Fitzpatrick, 1997). The reasons are twofold. First, in conformity-oriented families, initiating or having conflict with family members is generally regarded as a violation of family rules and norms that demand harmony and conformity, and thus leads to negative reactions by other family members. Second, because conflicts are usually avoided, family problems frequently remain unresolved and individual family members might perceive their families as unresponsive to their needs, which leads to frustration and hostility on the side of the complaining party (Segrin & Fitzpatrick, 1991).

Family Types

Families high in both conversation and conformity orientation are labeled *consensual*. Their communication is characterized by a tension between pressure to conform and an interest in open communication. Parents in these families are the ultimate decision makers, but at the same time are interested in communicating with their children. Children in these families learn to value family conversations and to adopt their parents' values and beliefs.

Families high in conversation orientation but low in conformity orientation are labeled *pluralistic*. Communication in pluralistic families is characterized by open, unconstrained discussions involving all family members. Parents in these families are willing to accept their children's opinions and to let them participate in family decision making. Children of these families learn to value family conversations and to be independent and autonomous, which fosters their communication competence in relationships outside the family and their confidence in their ability to make their own decisions.

Families low on conversation orientation but high on conformity orientation are labeled *protective*. Communication in protective families is characterized by an emphasis on obedience to parental authority and by little concern for open communication within the family. Parents in these families are the ultimate decision makers and have little interest in explaining themselves to their children. Children in protective families learn that there is little value in family conversations and to distrust their own decision-making ability. In addition, they often lack communication competence in relationships outside the family.

Families low in both conversation orientation and conformity orientation are labeled *laissez-faire*. Communication is characterized by few and usually uninvolving interactions between family members limited to a small number of topics. Parents in laissez-faire families do believe that all family members should be fairly independent, but unlike parents in pluralistic families, they have little interest in their children and do not value family conversations. Most members of laissez-faire families are emotionally divorced from their families. Children of these families learn that there is little value in family conversation and that they have to make their own decisions. Because they receive only little support from their parents, however, they question their decision-making ability and often depend on their peers for guidance.

Family Types and Conflict Communication

In an earlier study of family communication patterns and conflict, we (Koerner & Fitzpatrick, 1997) investigated the influence of conversation orientation and conformity orientation and the four resulting family types. Conversation orientation had a strong negative correlation with conflict avoidance and a strong positive correlation with seeking social support as a coping strategy during conflict. Conformity orientation was correlated positively with conflict avoidance and expressing negative affect.

In regard to family types, we found that consensual families were characterized by high incidents of the venting of negative feelings and their inclination to solicit social support, which are the result of high conformity orientation and high conversation orientation, respectively. That these families often vent their negative feelings seems counterintuitive because of the potentially harmful consequences for their interpersonal relationships. The venting of negative feelings does not fit our perception of the generally supportive and open communication of consensual families. The reason that venting of negative feelings occurs, and does not endanger the closeness of consensual families, could be that these families are also high in seeking social support. Generally, the ability to obtain social support is associated with the ability to deal positively with the negative aspects of conflict, such as being insulted or angry.

This possibility is also consistent with the observation that consensual families are in the mid-range in regard to conflict avoidance. Consensual families score high on both conformity and conversation orientation and find themselves in the somewhat peculiar situation of encouraging open expressions of conflict, while, at the same time, considering conflict to be disruptive. It seems plausible that these families are able to strike a balance between these two needs because they are able to find outside support to help them overcome the negative effects conflict has on their intra-family relationships.

Pluralistic families are characterized by their extremely low conflict avoidance, which is the result of both their high conversation and their low conformity orientation. Similar to consensual families in their inclination to seek social support, they are different from consensual families in their low expression of negative feelings. This is surprising because pluralistic families should be less constrained in expressing their negative feelings to one another than consensual families because they do not experience the same desire for harmonic relationships as consensual families. An explanation for this apparent contradiction is that pluralistic families experience less negative affect and hostility among family members because they do not avoid addressing the conflicts. That is, because addressing conflict is a precondition for solving conflict, these families experience more positive relationships than other families that are more likely to avoid conflict.

One of the most interesting patterns of conflict is that of protective families. These families are characterized by conflict avoidance paired with high incidents of venting negative feelings. This surprising pattern is much less puzzling when one considers that these families are also low in seeking social support. Thus, these families lack the mechanisms to deal productively with conflict, either by discussing and resolving conflict within their families or by obtaining social support from outsiders. As a consequence of their unresolved conflicts within their families, persons in these families develop hostility and negative feelings toward their family members that are expressed in short, but often inconsequential, emotional outbursts.

Laissez-faire families are characterized by the relative low intensity of their conflict episodes. These families experience few incidents of venting of negative feelings and tend to avoid rather than to engage in conflict. At the same time, they are low in seeking social support. This pattern is consistent with people with low investment in their family relationships and who often are emotionally divorced from their families. Although conflict is not actively avoided, it is often experienced less urgently and therefore frequently not addressed. At the same time, because the relationships are somewhat less important to family members, unresolved conflicts are not particularly taxing to them and therefore do not create the hostility expressed in protective families. Therefore, little reason exists to vent negative feelings.

Interdependence of Communication Schemata, Family Communication Patterns, and Conflict

To better understand the role of relational schemata and family communication patterns on family conflict communication, consider the following example. Kevin, a 12-year-old boy, is discussing plans for the upcoming weekend with his parents, Masha and Tom. Not present is their 10-year-old daughter, Pam, who earlier expressed her wish to go horseback riding during the weekend with the parents. The family is of the consensual type, that is, high in both conversation and conformity orientation, valuing both communication and cohesion.

Tom (to Kevin):	Well, Pam wants to go horseback riding. What do you think about that? We can do that Saturday if you like.
Kevin:	No, that's not fair. Why do we always have to do what Pam wants? I don't want to go. I don't like horses.
Tom:	That's not true. You do like horses, too. Besides, we don't always do what Pam wants. We all get to decide together.
Masha:	Your Dad is right. You just say you don't like horses because that's what Pam wants to do.
Kevin:	Not so.
Masha:	Riding doesn't take that long. Why don't you pick something for the afternoon.
Kevin:	You promise?
Masha:	Sure, I promise. You can pick something for Saturday afternoon. We won't stay longer than noon horseback riding.

Kevin:	OK. I want to go to Roboworld. You promised.
Masha:	I did. What do you think, Tom?
Tom:	Fine with me. It's horseback riding and then Roboworld. All right?
Kevin:	OK.

All three family members used their relational knowledge stored in the three different types of relational schemata to participate in this conversation. For this discussion of how relational schemata are used in cognition, however, we focus only on Kevin's cognition during this conversation. Of course, even this account of Kevin's cognition is incomplete because there are other cognitions involved that are not explicitly acknowledged. Our purpose, however, is not to explain Kevin's cognitions fully, just to illustrate how relational knowledge operates at three different levels of abstraction.

Some of the knowledge used by Kevin is stored in a general social schema. For example, the knowledge that the conversation constitutes a negotiation where all parties pursue goals and engage in strategic behaviors such as "give and take" to achieve their goals is knowledge that applies to similar situations regardless of what type of interpersonal relationship exists between partners. Similarly, the knowledge of pragmatics such that persons generally make truthful and relevant statements (Grice, 1989), that promises lead to firmer commitments about future behavior than mere expressions of intent, and that persons expect explicit responses to their offers are all part of the general social schema that applies to all interpersonal relationships. Thus, knowledge stored in the general social schema explains why, in the example interaction, Kevin opened the negotiation with the claim of unequal treatment by the parents; a move he hoped would encourage the parents to comply with his later request to establish equality. Similarly, general social knowledge explains why he was very explicit in responding to his parents' suggestions and why he reminded his mother that she made a promise to him.

Other knowledge that Kevin used in the interaction is specific to the family relationships and contained in the family relationship schema,

including knowledge of the family's beliefs and values about communication that determine their family communication patterns. Examples of this type of knowledge include knowing that in deciding what to do for the weekend, the children do have significant influence and therefore it is important what he negotiates for, because there is a good chance that he determines what the family does, and his status in the family depends on how much other family members enjoy "Kevin's activities." Other knowledge stored in the family relationship schema includes that in negotiations with his parents, what the mother says is more relevant than what the father says. Thus, knowledge stored in the family relational schema explains why, in the example interaction, Kevin pursued his goals seriously and essentially ignored the father and negotiated with the mother instead.

Finally, some knowledge Kevin used in the interaction is stored in relationship-specific schemata for his father and his mother. These schemata contain knowledge about the personalities and idiosyncrasies of his parents, memories of specific past interactions with each parent, and other knowledge that applies only to Kevin's unique relationship with each parent. Knowledge in the person-specific schema explains why, in the example interaction, Kevin did not contest his father's claim that he did like horses (he knew that he had talked to his father about his feelings about horses) and why he asked his mother to make a promise before she knew where he wanted to go (because he knew that she personally did not like Roboworld and thus was less likely to agree if she knew beforehand where he would like to go).

For individual family members, knowledge relevant to family communication is mainly stored in the family relationship schema and in the relationship-specific schemata that exist for each family member. We are not aware of empirical research that precisely establishes what type of knowledge exists at the family level, but the research that has investigated interpersonal relationship schemata suggests that it includes the following: beliefs about closeness, warmth, and intimacy; beliefs about individuality, autonomy, and interdependence; beliefs about external factors relevant to family life; and beliefs about the role of family communication

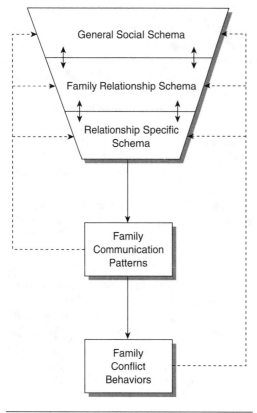

Figure 6.1   The Interdependence of Communication Schemata, Family Communication Patterns, and Family Conflict

(Koerner & Fitzpatrick, 2002a). Most relevant to family conflict are the beliefs about communication, which we have argued can best be conceptualized as family communication patterns. Family communication patterns are determined by a family's conversation orientation and conformity orientation. The interdependence of communication schemata, family communication patterns, and conflict behaviors are presented in Figure 6.1 (solid lines represent direct effects, broken lines more indirect effects).

Consequences of Family Conflict

Parents

In most discussions of family conflict, parents are usually the party thought to be mainly responsible for the occurrence, the

handling, and the consequences of family conflict. Because family conflict is regarded as inevitable, in this view parents are expected to anticipate family conflict and to be able to handle it constructively. That is, they are expected to employ constructive conflict skills themselves when in conflict with one another or with their children and thereby teach their children appropriate conflict communication skills. On the one hand, assigning parents the main responsibility for conflict and its outcomes has some merit, because, particularly in families with small children, the parents are better able to behave intentionally and with foresight, something that cannot reasonably be expected from small children. On the other hand, this view ignores that most adults are not necessarily effective in communicating during conflict either, and neither are they aware of the short- and long-term consequences of their conflict behaviors. More important, this view also ignores the bidirectionality of parent-child communication and the influence that children have on family communication (Barratt, 1995), including family conflict. Children do play an important role in determining the styles and outcomes of family communication, even if they communicate without intentions and a clear appreciation of the consequences of their behaviors.

As a consequence of the apparent culpability of parents for family conflict, there is very little research interest in parents as "victims" of family conflict; therefore our knowledge of how parents are affected by family conflict is limited. An exception is that of the battered wife, which has been extensively researched as the victim of spousal violence (for a brief discussion, see Caughlin & Vangelisti, Chapter 5 in this volume). In regard to parent-child conflict, however, we know little about the psychological and relational outcomes of family conflict for parents. We assume that frequency and negativity of family conflict lead to a similar reduction in relationship satisfaction and related psychological outcomes as conflict in the marital relationship, for example, but there is little evidence of any kind available to support that assumption. Clearly, this is an area where future research will have to provide the answers.

Children

The outcomes of family conflict for children, in contrast, are much better researched and understood. Historically, children have been cast in the role of passive victim more than in the role of active participant in, or even instigator of, family conflict. That this position is not without its problems was discussed already, but as a result of this historical bias, at least there is a large body of knowledge about the correlates of family conflict and children outcomes. Generally speaking, to the extent to which families engage in conflict communication that can be defined as destructive, hostile, or even violent, family conflict is associated with negative outcomes for children. In contrast, to the extent to which families engage in constructive conflict that can be defined as rational and focused on problem solving, family conflict is associated with positive outcomes for children in general, and for adolescents in particular.

Preadolescent children especially are affected by family conflict, both positively and negatively. Young children who are exposed to intense, destructive parental conflict experience fear, sadness, and anger (Cummings, Iannotti, & Zahn-Waxler, 1985) and feel unsafe and not secure in the home and outside the family (Gordis, Margolin, & John, 2001). In addition to negative psychological outcomes, children of families that frequently engage in destructive conflict also experience problems in their peer relationships. For example, Jenkins (2000) reported that intense parental conflict is associated with children's greater aggression and anger in relationships with teachers and peers, and Noller (1995) reported a correlation between intense parental and sibling conflict.

The processes by which parental conflict causes these negative outcomes for children are not exactly known. One possible explanation is that most of the psychological effects and some of the social effects stem from the fact that important security needs that the children have in their relationships with their parents are unmet when parents have frequent conflict. The negative psychological consequences that children exhibit are the result of these unmet needs. The social effects, by contrast, are the result of poor parental modeling of communication skills that leads children to behave poorly in their relationships outside the family. In other words, children acquire poor conflict resolution and other communication skills in their families and as a consequence have poorer relationships with others than children of families with parents' modeling effective conflict communication.

Similar causal processes are responsible for the positive outcomes children experience when exposed to constructive parental conflict behavior. These children experience both psychological and social benefits from their parents' problem-solving skills. Children of parents who exhibit positive problem-solving behaviors report more favorable psychological outcomes (Cummings et al., 1985), are generally better adjusted (Tucker, McHale, & Crouter, 2003), and experience more successful and satisfying peer relationships (Jenkins, 2000) than children of parents exhibiting less positive problem solving. Because children experience safety and security in their relationships with parents, they are psychologically better adapted, have higher self-esteem, and perceive the world to be a more friendly and less threatening place than children of families where parents model poor conflict communication. In regard to social outcomes, the conflict styles they learned from their parents help these children to manage their relationships with their siblings and peers more successfully than children of families with poor parental modeling.

Although the psychological and social benefits seem to be derived through different causal processes, in all likelihood they are very much intertwined and reinforce one another. In particular, the psychological effects of children's relationships with their parents long have been supposed to be of paramount importance for all social relationships that children have. That is, children who are secure in their relationships with their parents are also more secure in their relationships with others; children who feel unloved or even threatened in their relationship with their parents feel insecure in their relationships with others. A theoretical explanation of the effect of the parent-child relationship on children's other social relationships is provided by attachment theory (Bartholomew, 1990; Bowlby, 1973; Hazan & Shaver, 1987, 1994; Shaver & Hazan, 1988, 1994).

Originally, attachment theory, as conceived by Bowlby (1973), was a theory about parent-child relationships that was developed to explain the observation that young children react differently to being temporarily separated from their primary care givers. Children who were moderately distressed at separation and easily reconnected with their parent upon reunification were labeled "securely attached." Children who were only slightly distressed at separation and had difficulties reconnecting with their parent upon reunification were labeled "avoidant." Children who were very distressed at separation but ambivalent upon reunification were labeled "anxious-ambivalent." Bowlby theorized that the origins of attachment styles had their roots in differences in parenting behavior of primary care givers (usually mothers), particularly in how reliable primary care givers were in responding to the needs of their children. Essentially, parents who consistently meet the needs of their infants have secure children, parents who consistently fail to meet the needs of their infants have avoidant children, and parents providing inconsistent care, that is, who sometimes meet the needs of their infants and sometimes do not meet their needs, have anxious-ambivalent children.

Subsequent researchers, in particular Shaver and Hazan (1988, 1994; Hazan & Shaver, 1987), proposed that early attachment styles are influential not only in parent-child relationships, but in children's other interpersonal relationships as well, including future romantic relationships. To explain how parent-child attachment can be relevant to other interpersonal relationships, these researchers proposed that attachment styles come to represent cognitive models of relating to other people and are involved in every new relationship children form. For example, according to Bartholomew's (1990) four-category model of attachment, children develop cognitive representations of self and other that are based on interactions with their primary care givers during early childhood and that become working models for future relationships. These models incorporate fundamental beliefs about the self as loveworthy and about others as trustworthy, which is why they influence all of a child's current and future interpersonal relationships.

In Bartholomew's model, children who have a positive view of self and a positive view of other are secure in relationships with others. Children who have a positive view of self and a negative view of other are dismissive in relationships with others. Children with a negative view of self and a positive view of other are preoccupied. Children with a negative view of self and other are fearful avoidant.

A somewhat different explanation that could be regarded as a contributing factor or an altogether alternative account to attachment is that of shared family communication schemata, which are disproportionately determined by parents. For example, Reiss (1981) demonstrated that parents' perceptions of the world and their communication behavior have profound impact on how families, and in particular adolescents, perceive their social environment and their family's role in it. Specifically, he found that the extent to which families regard the world a friendly as opposed to a hostile place and are open as opposed to closed to the outside world profoundly contributes to adolescents' mental health. Similarly, Fitzpatrick and Ritchie (1994) and later Koerner and Fitzpatrick (2002a) also conceptualized the family as sharing a perception of the world and the family within it in the form of family communication schemata. Family communication schemata, in turn, not only play a role in how family members communicate with one another, but also how they solve problems, coordinate behaviors, and interact in their social relationships outside the family.

Although it is unclear at this point in time how, or if, attachment styles and family communication schemata are causally related, it is probable that both simultaneously and independently moderate or mediate the relationship between family conflict and children's mental health and social competence. Attachment styles mediate the relationship between conflict and child adjustment because when conflict undermines secure attachment of children to their parents, it leads children to develop mental models of self or others that diminish children's well-being and simultaneously their ability to relate well to others. Family communication schemata mediate the relationship between conflict and child adjustment because they affect the type of conflict behavior children are likely to employ in their relationships within and outside the family. To the extent that these behaviors are positive, they will lead to good interpersonal relationships. To the extent that these behaviors are poor, they will lead to poor interpersonal relationships.

FAMILY CONFLICT AND VIOLENCE

The Relationship Between Conflict and Violence

One important aspect of family conflict that often is overlooked is family violence. Although family conflict does not necessarily lead to family violence, the two are clearly related in that family violence is usually preceded by nonviolent family conflict. That is, in families that do experience violence, conflict is often a precursor to violence, and if the family were not to experience the initial conflict, there would be no family violence. Much like war is a continuation of politics by different means, in these families physical violence is a continuation of interpersonal conflict by different means. Not all family violence, however, is necessarily preceded by conflict. Some forms of violence, such as consistent psychological, physical, or sexual abuse, are a function of the predatory personality of a family member and/or the abusive nature of a family relationship and are more a cause of conflict than a consequence of it. Because this form of violence is qualitatively different from violence that occurs in the context of family conflict, we do not consider it further in our present discussion.

One means to formalize the relationship between nonviolent and violent family conflict is to conceptualize family conflict in general as existing along a continuum of intensity, from low-intensity problem solving at the one pole to high-intensity physical fighting at the other pole (e.g., Straus, 1990, 1994). In this conceptualization, violent family conflict can be explained as a function of the same factors that make nonviolent family conflict more intense. Factors that have been associated with increased intensity of conflict include a greater personal or relational significance of the conflict issues and

frustration resulting from the process of conflict communication itself (Donohue & Kolt, 1992). For example, conflict intensity might increase because the conflict involves a family member's needs rather than interests, where needs are defined as tied to personal and identity goals, and interests are defined as tied to instrumental goals. Alternatively, intensity can increase because one or more parties to the conflict become frustrated with the process of conflict communication or the process itself threatens important needs, such as positive and negative face (Brown & Levinson, 1987).

Fortunately, family members can avoid violence in such circumstances by learning certain communication behaviors that prevent conflict from escalating in intensity. Essentially, these are the same strategies that are recommended for communicating during interpersonal conflict in general, for example, those laid out by Donohue and Kolt (1992). First, family members can learn to avoid framing conflict issues in terms of needs and instead frame them in terms of interests. Second, family members should make conflict manifest by acknowledging differences in goals or perceived goal blockage. Third, family members should stress their interdependence by seeking solutions that enhance rather than diminish the relationship. Fourth, family members should remain flexible in their means to achieve solutions. Finally, family members should be committed to all family members achieving their goals, which is particularly important given the inherent power differences between parents and children.

Conflict and Corporal Punishment in Families

Another form of family violence that is also related to conflict but that is not always related to the intensity of the conflict is corporal punishment (Holden, Miller, & Harris, 1999). In fact, researchers reporting beneficial results of corporal punishment, such as Larzelere (2000), emphasize that nonabusive corporal punishment must be administered exclusively in a calm and deliberate manner and not during intense conflict. In other words, parents' use of corporal punishment should not be a function of the intensity of the conflict between parents and children, but of the seriousness of the behavior the corporal punishment is meant to correct.

Despite the theoretical distinction between corporal punishment and other forms of family violence, the outcomes for children are remarkably similar (but see Baumrind, Larzelere, & Cowan, 2002, for a contrasting viewpoint). In an extensive review of the existing literature on corporal punishment, Gershoff (2002) found that while corporal punishment results in the desired short-term compliance, other, less desirable outcomes of corporal punishment for children include increased aggression, delinquent and antisocial behaviors, decreased moral internalization, diminished quality of parent-child relationship, and decreased child mental health. Observed negative effects of corporal punishment that follow children into adulthood include increased risks for adult criminal and antisocial behavior and for abusing one's own children (Gershoff, 2002; Straus, 1994).

One explanation for the finding that violent family conflict and corporal punishment have similarly negative outcomes for children could be that despite parents' best intention to the opposite, the intensity of the conflict between parents and children often determines the use of corporal punishment. Ironically, this might be because parents perceive intense parent-child conflict as an indication of children's disobedience, which is exactly the type of serious behavior that they aim to correct with corporal punishment.

Another explanation for the similar outcomes of violence and corporal punishment could be that even though they are distinct theoretical concepts, behaviorally the distinction between violence and corporal punishment is less clear. Straus's (1994) definitions of both corporal punishment and violence illustrate this ambiguity. Straus defined corporal punishment as "the use of physical force with the intention of causing a child to experience pain, but not injury, for the purpose of correction or control of the child's behavior" (p. 4), whereas violence is defined as "an act carried out with the intention, or perceived intention, of causing physical pain or injury to another person" (p. 7). Thus, Straus identified parental intention as the distinction between corporal punishment and violence,

even though from the outside, and often from the children's perspective as well, these two are indistinguishable on the behavioral level. This suggests that while the parents are able to distinguish between violence and corporal punishment, the children might not be able to because they necessarily rely on their inferences and attributions when assigning intent to their parents' behaviors.

A final explanation for why the negative effects of corporal punishment mirror those of family violence in general focuses more directly on functional correlates of corporal punishment. For example, Straus and Yodanis (1996) argued that the use of corporal punishment tends to preclude the opportunity for parents to utilize other, more socially useful methods of behavior control such as reasoning and reflection and therefore results in children's truncated development of conflict resolution skills. The more parents rely on corporal punishment, the less opportunity a child has to witness, participate in, and therefore learn nonviolent modes of influencing their own and other's behavior, leaving them to rely on physically violent strategies for conflict resolution. In other words, like other types of violent family conflict, corporal punishment teaches children problem resolution and conflict skills that they either cannot use in their relationships outside the family or that negatively affect those relationships and that therefore impede their social competence and functioning.

Consequences of Family Violence

As was the case for research into the consequences of family conflict, most research investigating the outcomes of family violence has either investigated the outcomes of spousal abuse or the outcomes for children (e.g., Gershoff, 2002). Generally, children of violent families are more likely to enact violence in their peer relationships and their subsequent relationships as adolescents and adults (Carr & VanDeusen, 2002; Salzinger et al., 2002; Simons, Lin, & Gordon, 1998; Straus & Yodanis, 1996; Swinford, DeMaris, Cernkovich, & Giordano, 2000; Whitfield, Anda, Dube, & Felitti, 2003; Yexley, Borowsky, & Ireland, 2002). For example, Salzinger et al. (2002) studied the effects of partner violence and physical abuse on children's social behaviors and found that abused children exhibited significantly higher levels of meanness and fighting and were six times more likely to be rated by peers and teachers as antisocial. Similarly, Carr and VanDeusen (2002) examined inter-parental violence and parent-child aggression as risk factors for intimate partner violence in a sample of college men. They found that witnessing inter-parental violence and experiencing childhood violence predicted physical violence in subsequent dating relationships.

As is the case for family conflict in general, there are several theoretical explanations linking family violence to the negative psychological and social outcomes for children. In a recent review of research on the effects of violent parent relationships on children, Carlson (2000) identified several theoretical approaches, including Lazarus and Folkman's (1984) stress and coping perspective, Silvern and Kaersvang's (1989) trauma perspective, and the resiliency approach (e.g., Fitzpatrick & Koerner, 2005; Graham-Berman, 1998). Most researchers investigating the effects of corporal punishment and other forms of family violence, however, employ a model of intergenerational transmission of violence based on social learning theory that proposes that children who experience violence in their families come to see violence as a normal and expected aspect of interpersonal relationships. That is, family violence leads children to accept violence as normal in interpersonal relationships and to be more violent in their own interpersonal relationships (Simons et al., 1998; Straus & Yodanis, 1996; Swinford et al., 2000). Experiencing violence in families, however, not only leads children to enact more violence in their own relationships, but also to be more tolerant of violence enacted by their partner. That is, exposing children to physical violence within the family increases their risk for later victimization and perpetration of interpersonal violence. Whitfield et al. (2003) in a study of violent childhood experiences found that the risk of perpetrating interpersonal violence (for men) or being victimized by interpersonal violence (for women) increased as the number of violent childhood experiences increased.

Family Communication Patterns and Family Violence

Like conflict in general, violence in families also depends on family communication patterns. Conversation orientation of families is correlated negatively with verbal aggression (Koerner & Fitzpatrick, 1997) and the use of corporal punishment (Koerner & Maki, 2004). Parents who encourage open communication with their children are less motivated to use verbal or physical punishment to regulate the behavior of their children, even though conversation orientation is associated with more family conflict (Koerner & Fitzpatrick, 1997). Apparently, conversation orientation leads to family conflict communication that is less negative and violent and more problem focused and that allows families to come to mutually satisfying or at least acceptable solutions, without the need for the parents to punish their children to obtain their compliance.

The opposite is true for conformity orientation, which is positively associated with both verbal aggression (Koerner & Fitzpatrick, 1997) and parents' use of corporal punishment (Koerner & Maki, 2004). Families that value conformity seem to prefer outcomes to process. That is, in these families, children's compliance is more important than the reasons for their compliance, and parents consider physical punishments an effective means for gaining compliance.

CONCLUSION AND FUTURE DIRECTIONS

Family conflict is an important aspect of family communication closely associated with relational satisfaction and the psychological well-being and social functioning of all family members, and in particular that of children. Generally speaking, conflict behaviors associated with positive outcomes are those that are direct and cooperative and focus on problem solving, whereas indirect and competitive strategies associated with asserting power and authority are associated with negative outcomes. The most negative outcomes, however, are associated with violent conflict behavior, regardless of whether the violence is the result of the intensity of the conflict or whether it is deliberately used as a means of gaining compliance during conflict, as in corporal punishment. Although the causal processes linking violence to negative outcomes are not fully understood, it seems that the best advice that can be given to families is to make any form of violence, including corporal punishment, unacceptable in family relationships.

Family conflict does not occur in isolation from other communication behaviors of families. Conflict is central to family communication and plays a role in what are among the most important functions of families, including the socialization of children; the development of autonomous and more independent identities of adolescents; and the negotiation and renegotiation of family roles, rules, and relationships. At the same time, however, to focus on family conflict alone when describing these functions and developing theoretical explanations of family conflict in isolation from other communication processes is to miss important parts of the picture. Family conflict is but one part of the larger family communication process and is best understood in relationship to this process. Thus, to really understand family conflict, we need to come to a better understanding of family communication in general and how it relates to conflict. In other words, there needs to be an integration of research on family communication and research on family conflict that results in theories that make visible how these two processes are related.

In this chapter, we have argued that family communication patterns and family communication schemata are important theoretical concepts that enable researchers and practitioners alike to understand family conflict and its relationship to the larger family communication context. For example, family communication patterns suggest that conflict in conversation-oriented families is best understood as a behavior that strengthens family relationships because it helps families to establish a shared social reality. In contrast, conflict in conformity-oriented families is best understood as a behavior that undermines authority relationships and thereby prevents families from establishing a shared social reality. Scholars might disagree about whether family communication patterns are indeed the best concepts to help us understand how conflict fits in with other family communication processes. Given,

however, that family communication patterns represent one of a few full-fledged theories of family communication formulated thus far (Koerner & Fitzpatrick, 2005), we think that our focus on them in this chapter is defensible.

Although researchers and practitioners have made great strides in understanding the antecedent conditions and consequences of family conflict, there is still much to be learned about family conflict. First and foremost, we know almost nothing about the effects of family conflict on the psychological well-being and social functioning of parents. While this lacuna is understandable in its historical context that made parents the responsible and purposeful actors in family conflicts, it is clear that parents are nevertheless affected by family conflict. It would certainly be interesting to know how. Another closely related area that in our opinion is in urgent need of elaboration is how parents' conflict behaviors are influenced by the conflict behaviors of their children. This question about the interdependence of conflict behaviors is of obvious theoretical importance, but also has relevance for practitioners who have spent much of the last decades educating parents on how to conduct family conflict in ways that minimize its negative effects on children. Maybe by developing strategies to influence children's behaviors rather than that of their parents, practitioners can reach those families whose parents have either been resistant to or incapable of implementing the advice they have received.

Another important area of family conflict that is under-researched is that of the role of ethnicity and class on family conflict. Although it is well established that lower socioeconomic status is associated with poorer problem solving and greater violence in families (Straus & Gelles, 1990), the role played by ethnicity, which at least in North America is strongly correlated with social class, in this association is less well understood. In fact, it is unclear whether observed correlations between ethnicity and conflict are spurious or are indeed functions of ethnicity. Despite the significant attention paid to Kochman's (1981) seminal work on different conflict styles of African and European Americans, which was based largely on the author's observations of his own students' classroom behavior, surprisingly few researchers have tried to replicate Kochman's findings in a family context. As a result, how, or even whether, ethnicity affects family communication during conflict is largely unclear.

Similar uncertainty exists regarding any role ethnicity might play in the association between physical punishment and children's maladaptation. Recent attempts to link family and interpersonal violence more generally to genetic predispositions have been vigorously attacked as inherently racist in an intense public debate, which led many researchers either to abandon this line of inquiry or not to embark on it in the first place. As a result, we still know little about potential genetic influences on violent behaviors. Even more important, it is unclear whether such genetic influences vary along ethnic lines, or, which is more likely, are associated with genes not related to ethnicity.

Research on corporal punishment investigating different outcomes for African American and European American children also has proved inconclusive. Whereas some researchers report positive outcomes of corporal punishment for African American children (Whaley, 2000), other researchers report no substantial differences in the negative outcomes for children along ethnic lines (McLoyd & Smith, 2002). Because Whaley based his positive view of corporal punishment largely on null findings showing a lack of the typically observed positive association between corporal punishment and behavioral problems for African American samples rather than showing a positive association between corporal punishment and positive behaviors for these children, we consider Whaley's conclusions to be at best moderately supported by empirical data. Even this more conservative interpretation of the data, however, is still consistent with the idea that there are significant differences in how children of various ethnic groups respond to corporal punishment. Complicating the issue is how outcomes are defined in different ethnic contexts. For example, Kelley, Power, and Wimbush (1992) made the argument that in a racist society whose institutions endanger the lives of minority children, African American parents have to enforce discipline more forcefully than European American parents because socially deviant behavior has more negative consequences for African American children. For example, police are more likely to stop, arrest, and shoot at African American than Caucasian American adolescents. As a result, physical discipline that results in compliance has positive outcomes for African American children. Thus far, neither genetically nor sociologically oriented approaches have been able to illuminate fully the relationship between ethnicity and conflict. In fact, it is unclear whether there even is an association between ethnicity and conflict behavior that is not spurious, that is, explained by other factors that are associated correlationally but not causally with ethnicity.

Closely related to research on conflict and ethnicity and similarly in need of future exploration is the role of culture on family conflict. Although some researchers have begun to investigate how conflict is handled in different cultures, these studies focus on broad differences between cultures, such as individualism and collectivism. Although it seems fairly obvious that such fundamental cultural differences would be reflected in families, in most cultures families constitute their own, unique communication context. Consequently, knowledge of a larger cultural context does not necessarily imply knowledge of how family communication functions within that culture. For example, individualism is an important characteristic of North American culture, yet cohesion and conformity also are important characteristics of North American families. In addition, it has become increasingly clear to communication scholars that variations in communication behaviors within cultures exceed variations between cultures, making the very notion of explaining family communication through broad cultural categories even more suspect. Still, investigating how larger cultural patterns affect how families communicate is necessary to increase our understanding of family communication in general and family conflict in particular.

In summary, family conflict is of great theoretical and practical importance because of its profound effects on family communication, family relationships, and the mental and physical well-being of individual family members. In our estimation, it is best understood as intrinsically tied to broader family communication patterns that are based on cognitive structures such as relationship schemata, and cognitive processes such as co-orientation toward a shared social reality. Cognitive structures and processes alone, however, cannot fully account for family communication. Also important are social and cultural processes that affect how different families communicate during conflict. It is our hope that the continuing investigation of family conflict as one of the most important communication behaviors will add to our already impressive knowledge and ultimately result in a comprehensive theoretical model of family communication. Such a model will specify the main cognitive structures and processes involved in family communication while simultaneously accounting for the effects that culture and interacting in interdependent relationships have on these structures and processes. Beyond question, developing such a model is a tall order for any research area, but there is no doubt in our minds that through collaborative, interdisciplinary research we can and will develop precisely that.

REFERENCES

Anderson, K. L., Umberson, D., & Elliott, S. (2004). Violence and abuse in families. In A. Vangelisti (Ed.), *The handbook of family communication* (pp. 629–645). Mahwah, NJ: Lawrence Erlbaum.

Barratt, M. S. (1995). Communication in infancy. In M. A. Fitzpatrick & A. Vangelisti (Eds.), *Explaining family interactions* (pp. 5–33). Thousand Oaks, CA: Sage.

Bartholomew, K. (1990). Avoidance of intimacy: An attachment perspective. *Journal of Social & Personal Relationships, 7,* 147–178.

Baumrind, D., Larzelere, R. E., & Cowan, P. A. (2002). Ordinary physical punishment: Is it harmful? Comment on Gershoff (2002). *Psychological Bulletin, 128,* 580–589.

Bowlby, J. (1973). *Attachment and loss: Vol. 2. Separation: Anxiety and anger.* New York: Basic Books.

Brown, P., & Levinson, S. C. (1987). *Politeness: Some universals in language usage.* Cambridge, UK: Cambridge University Press.

Burleson, B. R., Delia, J. G., & Applegate, J. L. (1995). The socialization of person-centered communication: Parents' contributions to their children's social-cognitive and communication skills. In M. A. Fitzpatrick & A. Vangelisti (Eds.), *Explaining family interactions* (pp. 34–76). Thousand Oaks, CA: Sage.

Cahn, D. D. (1992). *Conflict in intimate relationships.* New York: Guilford.

Carlson, B. E. (2000). Children exposed to intimate partner violence: Research findings and implications for intervention. *Trauma, Violence, and Abuse, 1,* 321–342.

Carr, J. L., & VanDeusen, K. M. (2002). The relationship between family of origin violence and dating violence in college men. *Journal of Interpersonal Violence, 17,* 630–646.

Christensen, A., & Jacobson, N. S. (2000). *Reconcilable differences.* New York: Guilford.

Collins, W. A., & Luebker, C. (1994). Parent and adolescent expectancies: Individual and relationship significance. In J. G. Smetana (Ed.), *Beliefs about parenting: Origins and developmental implications* (New Directions for Child Development, Vol. 66, pp. 65–80). San Francisco: Jossey-Bass.

Cummings, E. M., Iannotti, R. J., & Zahn-Waxler, C. (1985). The influence of conflict between adults on the emotion and aggression in young children. *Developmental Psychology, 21,* 495–507.

Deutsch, M. (1973). *The resolution of conflict: Constructive and destructive processes.* New Haven, CT: Yale University Press.

Donohue, W. A., & Kolt, R. (1992). *Managing interpersonal conflict.* Newbury Park, CA: Sage.

Fincham, F. D., Bradbury, T. N., & Grych, J. (1990). Conflict in close relationships: The role of intrapersonal factors. In S. Graham & V. Folkes (Eds.), *Attribution theory: Applications to achievement, mental health, and interpersonal conflict* (pp. 161–184). Hillsdale, NJ: Lawrence Erlbaum.

Fitzpatrick, M. A., & Koerner, A. F. (2005). Family communication schemata: Effects in children's resiliency. In S. Dunwoody, L. B. Becker, D. McLeod, & G. Kosicki (Eds.), *The evolution of key mass communication concepts: Honoring Jack M. McLeod* (pp. 113–136). Cresskill, NJ: Hampton Press.

Fitzpatrick, M. A., & Ritchie, L. D. (1994). Communication schemata within the family: Multiple perspectives on family interaction. *Human Communication Research, 20,* 275–301.

Gershoff, E. T. (2002). Corporal punishment by parents and associated child behaviors and experiences: A meta-analytic and theoretical review. *Psychological Bulletin, 128,* 539–579.

Gordis, E. B., Margolin, G., & John, R. S. (2001). Parents' hostility in dyadic marital and triadic family settings and children's behavior problems. *Journal of Consulting and Clinical Psychology, 69,* 727–734.

Gottman, J. (1994). *Why marriages succeed or fail . . . and how you can make yours last.* New York: Simon & Schuster.

Gottman, J. M. (1991). Predicting the longitudinal course of marriages. *Journal of Marital and Family Therapy, 17,* 3–7.

Graham-Berman, S. A. (1998). The impact of woman abuse on children's social development: Research and theoretical perspectives. In G. W. Holden, R. Geffner, & E. N. Jouriles (Eds.), *Children exposed to marital violence: Theory, research and applied issues* (pp. 21–54). Washington, DC: American Psychological Association.

Grice, H. P. (1989). *Studies in the way of words.* Cambridge, MA: Harvard University Press.

Harris, J. R. (1998). *The nurture assumption: Why children turn out the way they do.* New York: Free Press.

Hazan, C., & Shaver, P. R. (1987). Romantic love conceptualized as an attachment process. *Journal of Personality and Social Psychology, 52,* 511–524.

Hazan, C., & Shaver, P. R. (1994). Attachment as an organizing framework for research on close relationships. *Psychological Inquiry, 5,* 1–22.

Holden, G. W., Miller, P. C., Harris, S. D. (1999). The instrumental side of corporal punishment: Parents' reported practices and outcome expectancies. *Journal of Marriage and the Family, 61,* 908–919.

Jenkins, J. (2000). Marital conflict and children's emotions: The development of an anger organization. *Journal of Marriage and the Family, 62,* 723–736.

Kelley, M. L., Power, T. G., & Wimbush, D. D. (1992). Determinants of disciplinary practices in low-income Black mothers. *Child Development, 63,* 573–582.

Kochman, T. (1981). *Black and white styles in conflict.* Chicago: University of Chicago Press.

Koerner, A. F., & Fitzpatrick, M. A. (1997). Family type and conflict: The impact of conversation orientation and conformity orientation on conflict in the family. *Communication Studies, 48,* 59–75.

Koerner, A. F., & Fitzpatrick, M. A. (2002a). Toward a theory of family communication. *Communication Theory, 12,* 70–91.

Koerner, A. F., & Fitzpatrick, M. A. (2002b). Understanding family communication patterns and family functioning: The roles of conversation orientation and conformity orientation. *Communication Yearbook, 26,* 37–69.

Koerner, A. F., & Fitzpatrick, M. A. (2002c). You never leave your family in a fight: The impact of family of origin on conflict behavior in romantic relationships. *Communication Studies, 53,* 234–251.

Koerner, A. F., & Fitzpatrick, M. A. (2004). Communication in intact families. In A. Vangelisti (Ed.), *The handbook of family communication* (pp. 177–195). Mahwah, NJ: Lawrence Erlbaum.

Koerner, A. F., & Fitzpatrick, M. A. (2005). Family communication patterns theory: Communication schemata and practices in family life. In L. Baxter & D. Braithwaite (Eds.), *Family communication theories* (pp. 50–65). Thousand Oaks, CA: Sage.

Koerner, A. F., & Maki, L. (2004, May). *Family communication patterns and violence in families.* Paper presented at the annual meeting of the International Communication Association, New Orleans.

Larzelere, R. E. (2000). Child outcomes of nonabusive and customary physical punishment by parents: An updated literature review. Clinical Child and Family Psychology Review, 3(4), 199–221.

Laursen, B. (1993). Conflict management among close peers. In B. Laursen (Ed.), *Close friendship in adolescents* (New Directions for Child Development, Vol. 60, pp. 39–54). San Francisco: Jossey-Bass.

Laursen, B., & Collins, W. A. (2004). Parent-child communication during adolescence. In A. Vangelisti (Ed.), *The handbook of family communication* (pp. 333–348). Mahwah, NJ: Lawrence Erlbaum.

Lazarus, R., & Folkman, S. (1984). *Stress, appraisal, and coping.* New York: Springer.

McLeod, J. M., & Chaffee, S. H. (1972). The construction of social reality. In J. Tedeschi (Ed.), *The social influence process* (pp. 50–59). Chicago: Aldine-Atherton.

McLeod, J. M., & Chaffee, S. H. (1973). Interpersonal approaches to communication research. *American Behavioral Scientist, 16,* 469–499.

McLoyd, V. C., & Smith, J. (2002). Physical discipline and behavior problems in African American, European American, and Hispanic children: Emotional support as a moderator. *Journal of Marriage and Family, 64,* 40–53.

Montemayor, R., & Hanson, E. A. (1985). A naturalistic view of conflict between adolescents and the parents and siblings. *Journal of Early Adolescents, 3,* 83–103.

Noller, P. (1995). Parent-adolescent relationships. In M. A. Fitzpatrick & A. L. Vangelisti (Eds.), *Explaining family interactions* (pp. 77–111). Thousand Oaks, CA: Sage.

Reese-Weber, M., & Bertle-Haring, S. (1998). Conflict resolution styles in family subsystems and adolescent romantic relationships. *Journal of Youth and Adolescence, 27,* 735–752.

Reiss, D. (1981). *The family's construction of social reality.* Cambridge, MA: Harvard University Press.

Rinaldi, C. M., & Howe, N. (2003). Perceptions of constructive and destructive conflict within and across family subsystems. *Infant and Child Development, 12,* 441–459.

Ritchie, L. D. (1991). Family communication patterns: An epistemic analysis and conceptual reinterpretation. *Communication Research, 18,* 548–565.

Ritchie, L. D., & Fitzpatrick, M. A. (1990). Family communication patterns: Measuring interpersonal perceptions of interpersonal relationships. *Communication Research, 17,* 523–544.

Salzinger, S., Feldman, R. S., Ng-Mak, D. S., Mojica, E., Stockhammer, T., & Rosario, M. (2002). Effects of partner violence and physical child abuse on child behavior: A study of abused and comparison children. *Journal of Family Violence, 17,* 23–52.

Segrin, C., & Fitzpatrick, M. A. (1991). Depression and verbal aggressiveness in different marital couples. *Communication Studies, 43,* 79–91.

Shantz, C. U., & Hartup, W. W. (1992). *Conflict in child and adolescent development.* New York: Cambridge University Press.

Shantz, C. U., & Hobart, C. J. (1989). Social conflict and development: Peers and siblings. In T. J. Berndt & G. W. Ladd (Eds.), *Peer relationships and child development* (pp. 71–94). New York: John Wiley.

Shaver, P. R., & Hazan, C. (1988). A biased overview of the study of love. *Journal of Social & Personal Relationships, 5,* 473–501.

Shaver, P. R., & Hazan, C. (1994). Attachment. In A. L. Weber & J. H. Harvey (Eds.), *Perspectives on close relationships* (pp. 110–130). Boston: Allyn & Bacon.

Sillars, A., Canary, D. J., & Tafoya, M. (2004). Communication, conflict, and the quality of family relationships. In A. Vangelisti (Ed.), *The handbook of family communication* (pp. 413–446). Mahwah, NJ: Lawrence Erlbaum.

Silvern, L., & Kaersvang, L. (1989). The traumatized children of violent marriages. *Child Welfare, 68,* 421–436.

Simons, R. L., Lin, K., & Gordon, L. C. (1998). Socialization in the family of origin and male dating violence: A prospective study. *Journal of Marriage and the Family, 60,* 467–478.

Smetana, J. G., You, J., & Hanson, S. (1991). Conflict resolution in families with adolescents. *Journal of Research on Adolescence, 1,* 189–206.

Straus, M. A. (1990). Measuring intrafamily conflict and violence: The Conflict Tactics (CT) Scales. In M. A. Straus & R. J. Gelles (Eds.), *Physical violence in American families: Risk factors and adaptations to violence in 8,145 families* (pp. 29–47). New Brunswick, NJ: Transaction Publishers.

Straus, M. A. (1994). *Beating the devil out of them.* New York: Lexington Books.

Straus, M. A., & Gelles, R. J. (1990). How violent are American families? Estimates from the National Family Violence Resurvey and other studies. In M. A. Straus & R. J. Gelles (Eds.), *Physical violence in American families: Risk factors and adaptations to violence in 8,145 families* (pp. 95–112). New Brunswick, NJ: Transaction Publishers.

Straus, M. A., & Yodanis, C. L. (1996). Corporal punishment in adolescence and physical assaults on spouses later in life: What accounts for the link? *Journal of Marriage and the Family, 58,* 825–841.

Swinford, S. P., DeMaris, A., Cernkovich, S. A., & Giordano, P. C. (2000). Harsh physical discipline in childhood and violence in later romantic involvements: The mediating role of problem behaviors. *Journal of Marriage and the Family, 62,* 508–519.

Tucker, C. J., McHale, S. M., & Crouter, A. C. (2003). Conflict resolution: Links with adolescents' family relationships and individual well being. *Journal of Family Issues, 24,* 715–736.

Vangelisti, A. L. (2004). Introduction. *Handbook of family communication* (pp. xiii–xx). Mahwah, NJ: Lawrence Erlbaum.

Whaley, A. L. (2000). Sociocultural differences in the development consequences of the use of physical discipline during childhood for African Americans. *Cultural Diversity and Ethnic Minority Psychology, 6,* 5–12.

Whitfield, C. L., Anda, R. F., Dube, S. R., & Felitti, V. J. (2003). Violent childhood experiences and the risk of intimate partner violence in adults. *Journal of Interpersonal Violence, 18,* 166–185.

Wrench, J. S., & Socha-McGee, D. (1999, May). *The influence of saliency and family communication patterns on adolescent perceptions of adolescent and parent conflict management strategies.* Paper presented at the meeting of the International Communication Association, New York.

Yexley, M., Borowsky, I., & Ireland, M. (2002). Correlation between different experiences of intrafamilial physical violence and violent adolescent behavior. *Journal of Interpersonal Violence, 17,* 707–720.

7

MANAGING CONFLICT IN A COMPETENT MANNER

A Mindful Look at Events That Matter

DANIEL J. CANARY

Arizona State University

SANDRA G. LAKEY

Pennsylvania College of Technology

By now, the reader has learned how important conflict management is across a variety of contexts. Our focus concerns how individuals can gain greater control of their conflict interactions by managing them competently. Throughout this chapter we consider ways in which people can become more competent in managing conflict. Our hope is that the reader can finish this chapter with a sense that it has been personally useful.

To achieve this purpose, we adopt a competence-based approach that emphasizes the manner in which both parties in close relationships negotiate their important personal goals. This approach was born from a central question: How can communicators achieve their goals that conflict with other people's goals, so

they are seen as both appropriate and effective (e.g., Canary & Spitzberg, 1987)? Ten years have passed since the research and theory on this competence-based approach to managing conflict was summarized (Spitzberg, Canary, & Cupach, 1994) and recent developments and applications continue to be published (e.g., Canary, Cupach, & Serpe, 2001; Gross & Guerrero, 2000; Lakey & Canary, 2002). This chapter reflects further development of the competence-based approach.

Of course, the reader might wonder why one would adopt a competence-based approach to begin with. Although numerous reasons warrant this approach, we offer four. Next, we examine what is meant by "competence" in conflict management, including the idea that social actors

AUTHORS' NOTE: The authors thank the editors for their thorough, thoughtful, and insightful comments on an earlier draft of this manuscript.

can become much more mindful of the manner in which they engage in conflict interaction. Following that, we rely on a model of conflict that locates events where people can be strategic in the management of conflict. Following each event, we offer implications for the competent management of conflict.

COMPETENCE IN MANAGING CONFLICT

As indicated above, we offer four reasons for adopting a competence-based approach. First, being competent implies being ethical (for a fuller treatment, see Cupach & Canary, 2000). It is imperative that people adopt a code of conduct to guide their actions when they perceive that other people oppose them. In this chapter, we focus on how people can become more adept at achieving their personal goals that conflict with another person's while meeting that person's expectations. This focus has two implications. Being competent in managing conflict most clearly reveals one's personal integrity. Remaining calm when others are angry, avoiding slander when others ridicule, and looking for ways to collaborate when others give up are only three ways that individuals can demonstrate their integrity. Also, a competence-based approach that emphasizes both people's rights to pursue their goals implies that neither person should exploit the other, harm the other, or even ignore the other. In other words, a competence-based approach suggests that people treat each other in an ethical manner.

Second, the competent management of conflict can preempt the felt need to use aggression and violence in close relationships. Approximately one quarter of all marriages and one third of all dating relationships in the United States entail episodes of violence within a year's time (for specific statistics, see Marshall, 1994; Spitzberg, 2000; Tjaden & Thoennes, 2000). Several conflict scholars have identified that a key reason for what Johnson (1995, 2001) referred to as "common couple violence" concerns how these people lack the communication skills to engage each other in a competent manner, what can be termed the *communication skill deficit* explanation (Marshall, 1994; Sabourin, Infante, & Rudd, 1993). That is, people who

lack competence in managing everyday conflict rely more on aggression to get their way than do others (Canary, Spitzberg, & Semic, 1997). For instance, people in long-term physically and verbally abusive relationships engage in withdrawing and/or hostile conflict behaviors more than do those in non-abusive relationships (e.g., Margolin, Burman, & John, 1989; Sabourin et al., 1993).

Third, and related to the last point, competence in managing conflict dramatically affects the quality of close relationships. Research shows that how partners manage conflict represents a critical factor that affects marital satisfaction and stability (e.g., Caughlin & Vangelisti, Chapter 5 in this volume; Gottman & Levenson, 2000; Huston, Caughlin, Houts, Smith, & George, 2001). Moreover, the manner in which people manage conflict dramatically affects parent-child, friendship, and sibling relationships (Canary, Cupach, & Messman, 1995; Messman & Canary, 1998).

Finally, research has shown that assessments of a person's competence in managing conflict affect desired relational characteristics. In one study, Canary and Cupach (1988) found that assessments of competence filtered the effects of cooperative and competitive strategies on trust and control mutuality (i.e., the extent to which both parties agree on who has the right to influence the other). In a longitudinal study of married couples, Canary et al. (2001) likewise found that assessments of competence filtered the effects of conflict on relational quality in terms of trust, liking, and loving. The point is that message behaviors do not directly affect outcomes; the evaluation of those messages in terms of competence criteria most directly affects outcomes. Knowing the standards that people use to judge others should help social actors learn to meet those standards. To elaborate more on our position, we discuss what we mean by competence with attention to the idea that people are not always aware of the interaction behaviors that they use.

Identifying Competence

We admit that the word *competence* sounds about as exciting as potato bread. Still, communication scholars are quite interested in the construct because of its importance for relational outcomes. Some researchers consider competence to be an ability or a capacity a person has to enact goal-directed behavior (e.g., Parks, 1994). However, other researchers view competence as a quality, an attributional judgment (Spitzberg, 1993). Confusion about the definition of the term also results because, in some circumstances, the word *competence* references minimal performance. For example, in functional communication, the word *competent* indicates the lowest level of performance (Larson, Backlund, Redmond, & Barbour, 1978). McCroskey (1984) also defines competence as minimally acceptable behavior and specifies that competent behavior includes modest levels of behavioral skill and cognitive understanding of communication processes and contextual constraints (how many people like to be referred to as only a "competent" friend or lover?). Nevertheless, in most communication research, especially that focused on the construct of communication competence, the word *competence* indicates high or even superior levels of performance (Wiemann & Bradac, 1989).

Competence occurs in degrees; it is not something that people do or do not possess. It can range from "unacceptable, to minimally functional, to adequate, to proficient, to masterful" (Spitzberg & Cupach, 1989, p. 7). Pearce and Cronin (1980) classified competence as minimal, satisfactory, and optimal. *Minimal competence* occurs when people cannot or will not consider the entire interaction, including the situation and the partner. People judged to possess this level of competence usually fail to engage in coherent, productive interactions. People who behave with *satisfactory competence* can engage in coherent interaction. They are aware of the other person and recognize the need to adapt to the situation and the partner. In addition, they follow the rules relevant to the interaction. Finally, *optimal competence* includes behavior that is flexible; optimally competent communicators enjoy options that the other two types lack. They evaluate a situation and choose the behavior they think will best serve them.

Two primary components of interpersonal communication competence, as defined by Spitzberg and Cupach (1989), are *appropriateness* (i.e., following relational and social

"norms, rules and expectations" [p. 7]) and *effectiveness* (i.e., successfully achieving one's goals). Spitzberg and Cupach noted that most current views of competence recognize the importance of these two components, but this was not always the case. Some early conceptualizations of competence equated it only with effectiveness. Rubin (1990) stated that in spite of continuing debate about some issues related to communication competence, both effectiveness and appropriateness are now generally accepted as central aspects of the concept. Of course, other dimensions for competence have emerged since Rubin's (1990) claim, including adaptability, conversational involvement, and efficiency, among others (see Ting-Toomey & Oetzel, 2001).

Including both effectiveness and appropriateness affects understandings of interpersonal communication competence, and especially the competent management of conflict, in two ways. First, it emphasizes that communication can be judged as competent only within the context of a relationship or situation because the context determines the standards of appropriateness that must be met (Canary & Cupach, 1988; Price & Bouffard, 1974; Spitzberg & Cupach, 1984, 1989). Second, as Spitzberg and Cupach (1984) noted, the inclusion of both concepts is central to the definition of interpersonal competence because communication can be appropriate without being effective and effective without being appropriate. For example, a manager might rely on his or her organizational status to intimidate a subordinate into compliance; however, it is doubtful that this supervisor's behavior would be seen as appropriate (or admirable, attractive, likeable, etc.).

Although the two concepts can occur individually, effectiveness and appropriateness are interdependent. Even in conflict, when the interactants' goals are perceived to be at odds, appropriateness and effectiveness are associated positively (Canary & Spitzberg, 1987, 1990). This paradox occurs because communication that is effective in achieving goals also tends to produce positive feelings about the interaction (Spitzberg & Cupach, 1984). Likewise, Parks (1994) explained that competent communicators are appropriate because they understand the interdependence of their goals with the goals of others. According to Parks, people realize that offending a partner or inhibiting a partner's goal achievement by behaving inappropriately would also hinder their own goal achievement.

But How Mindful Are We?

The production of communication behavior in real time challenges one assumption of the competence-based approach: To what extent are social actors aware of the repertoire of behaviors that they have at their disposal, and do they enact them in a rational manner? Conflict interactions in particular work against a rational, skills-based approach for several reasons (e.g., structure of conflict is often ambiguous; see Sillars & Weisberg, 1987). Despite the fact that conflict taxes people's ability to edit their communication behavior (Zillmann, 1990), we believe that social actors should try to improve the ways that they interact with each other. We concur with Ting-Toomey and Oetzel (2001) that being mindful of one's actions during conflict is necessary to competent conflict management. Although some people might be naturally gifted with conflict management skills, most humans need to study how to be effective and appropriate communicators.

Although not all would agree, the most useful view on this issue seems to be that consciousness represents a continuum and that people function at various points on it due to the characteristics of the immediate interaction. People make decisions about messages anywhere from deliberately conscious choice about a means to an end at one end of the continuum to intuition about what to say at the other end (Sanders, 1991). The following paragraphs elaborate this belief by focusing on how people might be conscious of their communication behavior.

Consciousness as a continuum. Howell (1982) approached the issue of communication and competence by proposing five levels that constitute a path to competence. At the lowest level of consciousness, *unconscious incompetence,* people make mistakes in their communication but are unaware of their errors. The second level, *conscious incompetence,* includes people's recognition of the problems they are having with communication. When experiencing

conscious competence, the third and middle level, people are able to modify their behavior; however, their actions may seem artificial or stilted. When communicators reach the fourth level, *unconscious competence,* they are so comfortable with their communication skills that they may become more actively involved in other communication behaviors, such as careful listening and the recognition of feedback. Finally, the fifth level is *unconscious supercompetence,* which includes all the qualities of the fourth level plus high levels of energy and optimism that help produce peak performance. This typology suggests certain conclusions: Consciousness is useful mostly during the middle level of conscious competence—wherein people recognize interaction behaviors are not working for them and make attempts to change them. In addition, this model suggests that people should avoid consciousness of mastered behaviors. For example, being mindful of one's expressiveness and conversational involvement might lead an individual to monitor and perhaps reduce those behaviors.

Andersen (1986) identified four states of consciousness (although he does not directly relate them to communication competence). *Minimal consciousness,* the lowest level, simply means wakefulness that serves as a prerequisite for the other three stages. *Perceptual consciousness* roughly equals attention and perception and requires a minimum of thoughtful awareness. *Constructual consciousness* allows planning, direction, and modeling of actions. Finally, the rarest form, *articulate consciousness,* requires that people be able to explain fully their goals and plans.

As these models indicate, people are capable of functioning at various levels of consciousness in different situations. Although Andersen's model differs from Howell's model on the premise that consciousness is linked in a linear and positive manner to competence, both scholars concur that being unaware of one's bad behaviors reflects an incompetent stance. Moreover, the step from no or minimal consciousness to more focused consciousness is necessary to remedy communication skill deficits. Of course, we concur with this assessment. In addition, we believe that moderate levels of consciousness are functional for most people most of the time. People can become too preoccupied with their own behavior, however, which can moderate the previously learned competent behaviors in a negative manner. Still, it is important to note a more likely prospect—that people have blind spots with regard to their own actions, and they rely heavily on overly learned behaviors and shortcuts to processing information when interacting with other people. The following section elaborates this point.

Mindfulness and mindlessness. The differentiation between mindfulness and mindlessness (Langer, 1989a, 1989b) helps to explain differences in levels of consciousness and their effects on behavior and communication. Langer defined *mindlessness* as minimal information processing that relies on information from past experiences to determine present action. This state of mind relies on existing categories, previously drawn distinctions, and reduced attention. According to Langer, mindless behavior is pervasive. People can mindlessly perform a variety of tasks with no harm because mindlessness does not mean the complete absence of cognitive activity (Langer, Chanowitz, & Blank, 1985). Rather, people function with reduced cognitive activity and consider the current environment based on their past experiences with similar situations. As a result, mindless behavior involves treating information and ideas as if they are context free: They are true regardless of the situation (Langer, 1989b).

According to Langer (1989a, 1989b), *mindfulness* constitutes a state of alertness and activity that relies on information from the current situation to determine behavior. Mindfulness involves active information processing, cognitive differentiation, the creation of new categories, use of multiple perspectives, and awareness of the context. Mindful thinking includes careful consideration of the context of an interaction; consequently, it emphasizes cognitive flexibility. Because people consider various ways to behave in the situation, they realize that their first thought might be just one way of reacting to the situation. They attempt to create additional options that reflect the situation, thereby demonstrating creativity, flexibility, and adaptability (Brown & Langer, 1990). People tend to be mindful when (a) an action requires more effort

than it has required in the past, (b) mindless behavior produces failure, (c) external factors interfere with completion of a behavior, or (d) behavior produces unexpected consequences. Langer (1989a, 1989b) considered mindfulness a way for people to realize their full potential. She also recognized, however, that people cannot be mindful at all times about all aspects of interaction. Rather, they can be mindful on a global level but perform certain actions mindlessly. Our assumption is that people can become more mindful of the manner in which they enter, negotiate, and exit conflict encounters.[1]

Conflict is not routine behavior and is often of some importance. Accordingly, as Langer (1989b) argued, people will pay more attention than they will in the more routine activities that they can perform mindlessly and still be successful. Several of the characteristics of mindfulness can be especially useful during conflict interactions. Creating new categories (Langer, 1989b) helps people find positive ideas that they might otherwise overlook in the conflict situation or their partners. Similarly, cognitive differentiation (Langer, 1989b) causes people to look at more specific, detailed ideas rather than to settle for global assessments that are less useful in managing the conflict. Together, these two elements of mindfulness allow people to develop a better understanding of the other person and of the situation. This active assessment of information often leads to the need for new information, which in turn may help determine a compromise that will work to manage the conflict effectively. In addition, these multiple views on the situation may lead to increased sensitivity to the needs and goals of the other person; ultimately, people may realize that the other person may have what he or she perceives to be legitimate reasons for his or her point of view. Increased information and sensitivity can help achieve compromise because people see themselves as having more choices about ways to respond to the conflict; change then becomes more possible (Langer, 1989b). Mindlessness, though, results in rigid behavior; people are less likely to go beyond their first reactions to a situation. They fail to recognize other interpretations or uses for information and continue to insist that their first reactions are correct (Langer & Piper, 1987). These people also see fewer options for managing conflict because they view conflict as resulting from simple causes. Obviously, when people use mindless behavior, they are less open to compromise (Langer, 1989b).

In sum, people in conflict assess each other in terms of appropriateness and effectiveness criteria. Being effective in conflict (i.e., achieving one's goals) is correlated positively with being appropriate (i.e., fulfilling the partner's expectations). Social actors routinely pursue instrumental, relational, and self-presentation goals both mindlessly and mindfully. They function at various points along a continuum of consciousness during different interactions; that is, they do not behave at the same level of consciousness during all their interactions. People will display higher levels of consciousness when they deal with new information, but they will function at much lower levels when dealing with information they have enacted many times before (Langer, 1989a, 1989b).

Having established a competence-based approach that emphasizes the mindful consideration of alternative actions, we now turn our attention to a model of events about which people should be mindful. These events suggest ways that people can take more control over various aspects of conflict.

STRATEGIC CHOICES CONCERNING CRITICAL EVENTS

Communication strategies and tactics are learned consciously and then become unconscious (Langer, 1989a, 1989b). Mindfulness is based on the present as people are conscious of the current situation and the need for new categories and new information as they negotiate the conflict. In contrast, mindless behavior is based in the past. People simply use what they have already experienced without evaluating its relevance or appropriateness for the current situation (Langer & Piper, 1987). Learning to become more mindful involves understanding when mindless behavior is appropriate and when it can lead to negative consequences, which include difficulty in presenting ideas, lack of judgment, defensiveness concerning other people's assessments of one's competence, and reduced self-esteem (Langer, 1989b). These

consequences themselves can negatively affect how people manage conflict.

Mindful behavior relates to people's feelings of control. Langer (1989b) argued that "control and mindfulness exist in an interactive and reciprocal relationship" (p. 144). She added that people will not experience a sense of control unless they are mindful. In conflict, mindfulness provides increased control because people perceive more options (Langer, 1989b). As we argue below, mindful behavior can bring about more episodic, personal, attributional, goal-relevant, strategic, and interactional control, which, in turn, should produce more competent conflict management.

The following material relies on a recently published model of strategic conflict that outlines how people can react at various stages to prototypical conflict to maximize their personal and relational outcomes (Canary, 2003). That model is summarized in Figure 7.1. We briefly review the components in the model and discuss their implications for the competent management of conflict (for a more elaborated discussion, see Canary, 2003).

Conflict Instigation

First, every conflict begins somewhere. *Conflict instigation* refers to the start of the problem in the actor's proximal experience. Conflicts often occur when one person is seen as frustrating another person's goal in a blameworthy fashion (e.g., not returning e–mail or telephone messages; mistreating another person's possessions). Indeed, these two elements— frustrating another person and doing so in a blameworthy manner—constitute cause for "pure" anger (Clore, Ortony, Dienes, & Fujita, 1993). According to Clore et al. (1993), pure anger involves rage, exasperation, and indignation.

Not all conflicts emerge in a clear and clean manner. As Sillars and Weisberg (1987) noted, conflicts often "hitchhike" on other events.[2] Sometimes people become angry with each other because they are under stress, or because they are uncomfortable, or because they are crowded, or simply because the air is polluted (Berkowitz, 1993). Moreover, using alcohol or other drugs promotes conflict because people have decreased ability to interpret other

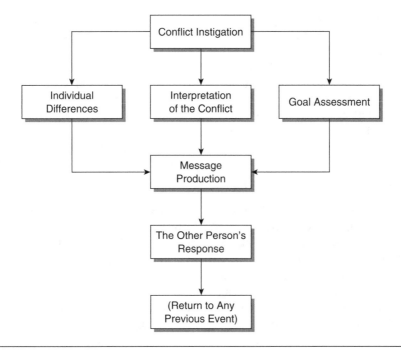

Figure 7.1   Model of Strategic Conflict

SOURCE: From Canary (2003). Copyright 2003 by Lawrence Erlbaum Associates. Reprinted by permission of the publisher.

people's behavior and limited ability to edit their own (Zillmann, 1990).

One common experience that precipitates negative interactions with others is stress. Repetti (1994) and Repetti and Wood (1997) found support for the hypothesis that daily stressors on the job lead to withdrawal from family life. Repetti (1994) examined air traffic controllers and Repetti and Wood examined working moms. Repetti and Wood found that objective ratings of mothers' interactions with their preschoolers indicated that the mothers paid less attention to their children, spoke infrequently, and offered less care and love on days when these mothers reported high work load (vs. low).

Conversely, interpersonal interactions constitute a primary source of stress. Bolger, Delongis, Kessler, and Schilling (1989) found that job stress was directly linked to interpersonal interaction. Bolger et al. asked romantic partners to report daily work and non-work stressors and mood, and found that interpersonal conflict was the most upsetting of all daily stressors. Also, Smith and Sulsky (1995) surveyed more than 600 people from three organizations and found that approximately 25% of the respondents

selected interpersonal issues as their most bothersome job stressor. Further, Repetti and Wood (1997) found evidence that negative interactions at work spill over to withdrawal from the family; negative interactions at work contribute to workload stress, which in turn affects interactions with family members.

The point of this discussion is to anticipate the potential for conflict. In a word, and when possible, people should anticipate conflict situations to exercise *episode control,* or control over situations where they can become more mindful in advance.[3] Research has shown that anticipating one's negative reactions to potential conflicts can help one limit such reactions (Zillmann, 1993). So, for example, people often arrive at work in a negative state, primed for conflict because they have spent the past hour in traffic. Following a stressful day's work, people return home in a similar state. Anticipating such negative reactions would help increase the likelihood of responding to other people in a mindful, competent manner. Taking a moment to think about the stress-producing situation before they go into the office or their homes can help people become more mindful and remain calm so they will not vent their frustrations on people who had nothing to do with the initial stressful event. People can become more aware of the immediate context and process information more actively, thereby recognizing the difference between the stress-inducing situation and the immediate context. Because they are more mindful of options and consequences, people might behave with more personal integrity.

Three Factors Affecting Strategy Choice

The model in Figure 7.1 specifies that three factors mediate the link between the onset of conflict and a person's communication behavior: *individual differences, interpretation of the conflict,* and *goal assessment.* In other words, the onset of conflict does not automatically lead to a person's message selection; rather, these three factors must be considered to predict a person's communication choices.

Individual differences. Although several individual difference factors can potentially affect the way in which people manage conflict, we emphasize locus of control. Given our objective to provide information for the mindful management of conflict, locus of control appears to be one individual difference that can be learned (as opposed to, e.g., neuroticism, Type A pattern, or biological sex). *Locus of control* refers to the extent that people take responsibility for their own successes and failures (Lefcourt, 1982). People who believe that their outcomes are due to their own ability and effort have an internal locus of control, whereas people who see their outcomes as due to chance or powerful others have an external locus of control. Moreover, locus of control is domain specific—that is, locus of control varies among different domains of life, such as health, politics, and even relationships. For example, Miller, Lefcourt, Holmes, Ware, and Saleh (1986) found that the more people had an internal locus of control for relationships, the more they worked harder at maintaining their close relationships. A general orientation toward internality or externality, however, is not as powerfully linked to maintaining relationships.

Conflict Locus of Control (CLOC) refers people's internal and external beliefs regarding

the outcomes of conflict. Research indicates that individuals who hold an internal orientation toward their interpersonal conflicts are more likely to use direct and cooperative conflict behaviors, whereas people who adopt an external orientation toward their conflicts more likely avoid the issue or engage in direct and competitive tactics (Canary, Cunningham, & Cody, 1988; Caughlin & Vangelisti, 2000). In a similar vein, Doherty (1981) argued that *efficacy* concerns the extent to which people ascertain they successfully manage their interpersonal problems. Fincham and Bradbury (1987) used Doherty's notion of efficacy to explain attributions of conflict causes. Fincham and Bradbury found that people's efficacy was related negatively to beliefs that their partner was responsible for conflict, and efficacy was associated negatively with perceived stability of conflict.

The implication of this research is that people need to have greater faith in their efforts. That is, people should exercise *personal control* by adhering to the belief that conflict can be managed in ways that bring about positive outcomes. We acknowledge that this notion of personal control might not reflect an alternative orientation toward managing conflict, which is to give up control. As the volume editors pointed out to us, people in different cultures might possess a value orientation that does not place a premium on personal control. With this caveat in mind, we offer a few ways that personal control can be achieved in managing conflict.

First, individuals need to recognize their personal roles and responsibility in the process. Admitting that they have a hand in the cause of the conflict empowers people to change the paths of the conflict. Blaming other people and acting the victim reflect a lack of personal control. Mindful behavior helps people consider more information and additional ideas related to the cause of the conflict by identifying new categories; mindless behavior causes people to remain focused on a single and simple cause (Langer, 1989b).

Second, people should be mindful of behaviors that can be used for productive outcomes, and we discuss these below (see material under Message Production). In brief, these behaviors include problem solving, information exchange, and other cooperative and direct behaviors.

Active processing of information and cognitive differentiation (Langer 1989a, 1989b) will help people because they will gain new information and new options. By thinking more mindfully about what to do, people explore options beyond their first response and often develop more effective approaches to a conflict.

Finally, people need to remind themselves throughout the process that their own outcomes are determined largely by their own abilities and actions. Believing that one can negotiate with a high probability of success is a critically important component in managing conflict effectively and appropriately. Mindless behavior can lead to a narrow self-image and learned helplessness from previous failures (Langer, 1989a). As a result, people who behave mindlessly in a conflict will not experience success and will then lack all belief that they have any potential for successfully managing a conflict. Conversely, mindful behavior focuses on the process (Langer, 1989b) and helps people become more flexible and open to alternative interpretations of the partner's behavior. In addition, people may think of new approaches and behaviors during the conflict that will help lead to a productive outcome.

Interpretation of the conflict. The theoretical perspective that we have sometimes used in this research derives from attribution theory (e.g., Canary & Spitzberg, 1990). In short, attribution theory concerns the explanations that people make for events. Moreover, attribution theory has been used by many researchers who want to examine conflict in close personal relationships.

The heart of attribution theory concerns who might be responsible for conflict, and whether the person responsible causes the conflict in an intentional manner. Research indicates that when people accept responsibility for the conflict, they tend to enact more cooperative behaviors (e.g., offering and seeking disclosure). For example, Sillars (1980) observed that college students who attributed the cause of the conflict to themselves were likely to use cooperative actions and were likely to respond to their roommate's behavior in a cooperative manner. In contrast, students who blamed the cause of the conflict on their roommates were likely to use competitive conflict behaviors and to reciprocate their roommate's competitive behaviors.

Naturally, people often hold self-serving biases. Self-serving biases function to protect self against indictment, so that one's own behavior in conflict is seen as more worthy than other people's behavior (de Dreu, Natua, & van de Vliert, 1995). More precisely, people tend to attribute competitive tactics to the internal properties of the other person in a self-serving manner and they tend to attribute cooperative behaviors to themselves (Bradbury & Fincham, 1990). Likewise, people are more likely to recount their own cooperative behavior while selectively recalling the other person's actions that were competitive or avoidant (Canary & Spitzberg, 1990). Moreover, people tend to interpret their internal reactions to the conflict largely on the basis of their *field of vision,* which is external to them (i.e., people's sensory input comes from the immediate environment; Storms, 1973). In this manner, people in conflict tend to be aware of the other person's competitive and avoidant behaviors but not their own competitive and avoidant behaviors, while simultaneously thinking that they themselves are more cooperative and competent.

Researchers have identified several dimensions that characterize the explanations that social actors construct. According to Gottman (1994), the most important dimensions regarding conflict in close relationships appear to be the following: global-specific (i.e., the cause explains many vs. few behaviors), stable-unstable (i.e., the cause continues over time), and internal-external (i.e., reside as part of the person or are separate from the person). Other relevant dimensions include intentional-unintentional, selfish-unselfish, and blameworthy-praiseworthy (e.g., Fincham, Bradbury, & Scott, 1992; Sillars, 1980). It appears that, when referring to negative conflict events, people who explain the conflict using global, stable, and internal causes appear to handicap themselves and their partners in terms of productive conflict management.

For example, one common cause of conflict in close relationships concerns the division of household labor (e.g., Kluwer, Heesink, & van de Vliert, 1997). Explaining why one's partner does not do his or her fair share can be a rigorous theoretical exercise. One explanation is that the partner is irresponsible, which also indicates why he or she does not pay the bills on time, arrives late to meetings, and forgets Mother's Day. Living with someone whom one believes is irresponsible (or selfish or neurotic) directly affects how one manages conflicts with that person, which can lead to a defensive position. Such global, stable, and internal (a.k.a. "negative") attributions have been associated with ineffective problem-solving behaviors, negative conflict management behaviors, decreased spousal support, and negative emotional expression (Fincham & Beach, 1999). Indeed, Gottman (1994) argued that adopting negative attributions reflects "an abrupt flip in the perception of [one's own] well being. . . . This is the initial catastrophic change" (p. 335) in the interpretation of behavior that leads to separation and divorce. After all, once you decide that you live with the devil, managing conflict in a cooperative fashion would appear to be a soul-threatening proposition. On the other hand, when partners try to explain conflicts using causes that are specific, unstable, and external to the partner, then more flexibility for interpretation occurs.

Given this discussion, we argue that people should engage in *attributional control*. That is, to maximize the possibility for productive outcomes, people should engage in attributions that are not self-serving and that do not blame the partner. In this light, Zillmann (1993) advised his readers to

> preattribute annoying events and information about such events—to the extent possible—to motives and circumstances that make the induction of annoyance appear unintentional and nondeliberate, and . . . to reattribute annoying events and information about such events in the same manner. (p. 382)

In addition to withholding blame, people should postpone using global, stable, and internal causes so they might find informational value in the partner's explanations for the conflict (Gottman, 1994). Mindfulness contributes to these assessments because it helps people consider more reasons to explain the partner's actions. They are not locked into attributing the conflict to a simple, seemingly obvious cause; rather, they can process information actively, create new categories of information, and use

multiple perspectives (Langer, 1989b) to help them become more sensitive to and understanding of the partner's approach to the conflict. This increased attention to the goals of the partner will also help people to behave ethically and with personal integrity. The needs and rights of both people involved in the conflict are valued and considered in the decisions made about how to conduct the conflict and what strategies and tactics to employ. People do not become self-focused and self-serving.

Goal assessment. A goal is generally defined as an idea or state that people want to achieve at some point in the future (Dillard, 1990a; Pervin, 1989). In addition, goals have cognitive and affective features that allow them to influence the activation and organization of behavior. Because of these features, goals also can be understood as the beginning point of a sequence that includes plans and actions (labeled the GPA sequence by Dillard, 1990a, 1990b). Plans, which follow from goals, determine what behaviors should be enacted to achieve the identified goal. Locke and Latham (1990) explained that understanding a goal as both the motivator of action and the outcome of that action may seem contradictory. However, a person's conception of and desire for a goal or his or her idea of the goal is what motivates the action, which is then directed toward the future and the achievement of the desired outcome (or goal).

Goals vary in their content. Clark and Delia (1979) presented a now generally recognized tripartite typology of goals based on content: *instrumental* goals, which require a response from the partner to deal with a specified problem; *identity management* (a.k.a., *self-presentation* or *face*) goals, which involve presenting a particular image to the partner; and *relational* goals, which concern defining the nature of the relationship with the partner. Moreover, Cody, Canary, and Smith (1994) found these three supraordinate goals were parsimonious in their representation of lower, basic level goals (e.g., obtain a favor from a peer, give advice to a parent).

Clark and Delia argued that some aspect of all three goals is present to some degree in all communication encounters. According to Waldron (1997), researchers dealing with cognitive properties of conversation have provided confirmation that conversational goals are "multiple and fluid" (p. 205). The instrumental, identity, and relational goals also represent the functions of strategic communication that "frame a communication event and that relationship partners expect to achieve as they negotiate definitions and understandings" (Newton & Burgoon, 1990b, p. 479). We adopt Clark and Delia's tripartite goal classification but use the more common terms *instrumental, self-presentation,* and *relational.*

Goals lead to the initiation of action, provide people with standards against which to measure the outcomes of their interactions, and give meaning to interaction. Goals also help people to understand, at least to some extent, why other people enact certain behaviors and continue to enact them (Dillard, 1990a). Berger (1997) claimed that social goals (those that involve interaction with another person) are necessary for people to conduct numerous daily activities. He adds that goals serve as the foundation for the planning and plans people must have to achieve their objectives for any interaction. Goals also influence and constrain behavioral choices (Clark & Delia, 1979; Dillard, Segrin, & Harden, 1989). According to Dillard (1990b), the primary (influence) goal predicts both cognitive and behavioral effort, whereas secondary goals provide standards of behavior that affect behavioral choices. From a communicative perspective, however, the most important impact of goals is that when people know what they want to achieve through their interactions, they are more easily able to choose relevant communication behaviors (Clark & Delia, 1979; Cody et al., 1994). For example, one study found that people who emphasized relational escalation and maintenance goals engaged in cooperative and direct conflict tactics, whereas people who were primarily concerned with defending their self-presentation more readily used competitive behaviors (Canary et al., 1988).

One implication of goals is to become more mindful of one's own goals that might be at stake. *Goal control* refers to the extent to which social actors know what they want and are sensitive to their partner's goals. People tend to be more successful if they have clear goals and standards for knowing when such goals are met versus when having only a vague idea of what they want and no clear indicates of achievement (Bandura, 1989).

Remaining clear about one's goal is not easy, because during conflict goals often shift (Sillars & Weisberg, 1987). Dillard et al. (1989) reported that people tended to pursue instrumental goals and that relational and self-presentation goals were secondary. However, as conflicts escalate, issues of relationship and self-presentation often become the focus more so than instrumental objectives (Schönbach, 1990; Zillmann, 1993). This shift in goals helps explain the common observation that a conflict can begin about one topic (e.g., paying rent on time, which is an instrumental concern) and end on a completely different matter (e.g., questioning one's responsibility and commitment, which implicates relational and self-presentation goals). In brief, the competent communicator is more likely to have a vision of his or her goals than the incompetent communicator.

Of course, it takes two to conflict, and competent communicators are mindful of their partner's goals that might be at risk. Recently, we found that being mindful of one's own goals was correlated positively with being perceived as appropriate and effective (Lakey & Canary, 2002). More critically, perceptions that the individual was sensitive to the *partner's* instrumental, relational, and self-presentation goals were strongly associated with assessments of the individual's appropriateness and effectiveness. Showing one's sensitivity to the partner's goals requires people to communicate in a cooperative manner by acknowledging one's role in the conflict, listening to the other without evaluation, and verifying one's interpretation of the partner's goals with the partner, all of which reflect the active thinking, use of multiple perspectives, increased sensitivity, and awareness of context that are characteristic of mindful thinking (Langer, 1989b). In addition, people behaving this way can use their heightened awareness of the partner to behave more ethically and with greater integrity. The choices they make are more likely to reflect their concern for both themselves and their partners. In brief, being competent in conflict means being sensitive to the partner's goals as well as having a clear idea of one's own goals, or what we refer to as *goal control.*

In sum, three factors mediate the link between conflict instigation and the enactment of conflict messages: individual differences as represented by a person's locus of control, interpreting the cause of the conflict using attributions, and ascertaining what goals are at stake. We suggest that people can become more competent to the extent they become more mindful regarding their efforts to increase personal control, attributional control, and goal control. The following section specifies how people's choices lead to conflict strategy use.

Message Production

Theory and research indicate that people make two choices regarding how they communicate to the other person in conflict: First, people must decide how direct or indirect to be; second, people decide how cooperative or competitive they will be (e.g., Hojjat, 2000; for reviews, see Sillars, Canary, & Tafoya, 2004; Sillars & Wilmot, 1994; van de Vliert & Euwema, 1994). That is, and given the preceding events, people typically rely on judgments of directness-indirectness and cooperation-competition when selecting conflict behaviors. These choices lead to the selection of various strategies (general approaches) and tactics (behaviors that institute the strategies). Table 7.1 reports the results of Sillars et al.'s (2004) classification of various conflict observational coding schemes into the four quadrants implied by the crossing of these two dimensions: Direct and Cooperative; Direct and Competitive; Indirect and Cooperative; Indirect and Competitive. The reader might wonder which of these behaviors are seen as optimally competent. The answer to that question is not obvious.

In terms of directness, people from individualistic cultures (e.g., mainstream United States) often state a preference for being direct. However, some research indicates that being indirect is more functional for people with certain self-concepts, in certain kinds of relationships, and in particular kinds of cultures. More precisely, people who have an *independent self-construal* are more likely to use directness than individuals with an *interdependent self-construal* (Kim & Leung, 2000). Interdependent people see their own identities as tied to other people, whereas independent people view themselves more as isolated agents. In addition, the use of indirectness can be functional in relationships that contain affection, though it is dysfunctional in relationships where avoidance is used to mask ongoing tensions and problems (Sillars et al., 2004). Finally, indirect communication appears to be more desired in cultures that value collectivistic versus individualistic tendencies (Ting-Toomey & Oetzel, 2001), though the research on this point has been mixed (Cai & Fink, 2002).

In terms of cooperation, most research indicates that cooperative conflict is linked positively to assessments of communication competence and that competitive messages are usually seen as both inappropriate and ineffective (e.g., Canary et al., 2001; Lakey & Canary, 2002). Some research, however, indicates that competitive communication in terms of demanding conversation and showing anger can be functional insofar as issues are dealt with and the relationship quality increases, ostensibly as a result of such confrontations (e.g., Gottman & Krokoff, 1989). Fincham and Beach (1999) speculated that a curvilinear relationship exists between conflict competitiveness and relational quality, such that too little competitive confrontation and too much competitive confrontation lead to poorer outcomes. An alternative explanation is that people learn how to balance their negative, competitive behaviors with more positive, cooperative behaviors. As a radical example, Marshall, Weston, and Honeycutt (2000) found that the use of positivity by husbands who abused their wives verbally, physically, or sexually almost entirely filtered the effects of abuse on relational satisfaction. That is, the wives of abusive husbands, who after abusive episodes showed love, stated how proud they were of their wives, were gentle, and so forth, did not experience declines in relational satisfaction as the result of being abused. Referring to non-abusive marriages, Gottman (1994) found that satisfied couples engaged in a 5:1 ratio of cooperative/competitive conflict behaviors, whereas dissatisfied couples engaged in a 1:1 ratio of cooperative/competitive behaviors.

In addition, nonverbal messages indicate one's cooperation or competition. Newton and Burgoon (1990a) found that the combination of nonverbal behaviors appears to complement verbal strategies. For example, animation,

(Text continues on page 200)

Table 7.1   Examples of Conflict Strategies and Tactics in Observational Research

Direct and Cooperative

Agreement (Gottman, 1979; Notarius, Markman, & Gottman, 1983)

Agreement involves direct agreement, acceptance of responsibility, compliance, assent, and change of opinion.

Appealing Acts (Rausch et al., 1974)

Appeals to fairness; Appeals to other's motives; Offering something else to win one's goal; Appealing to other's love; Pleading or coaxing.

Analytic Remarks (Sillars, 1986)

Descriptive Statements—nonevaluative statements about observable events related to conflict.

Disclosive Statements—nonevaluative statements about events related to conflict which the partner cannot observe, such as thoughts, feelings, intentions, etc.

Qualifying Statements—statements that explicitly qualify the nature and extent of the conflict.

Soliciting Disclosure—nonhostile questions about events related to conflict that cannot be observed.

Soliciting Criticism—nonhostile questions soliciting criticism of self.

Cognitive Acts (Rausch et al., 1974)

Conventional remarks; Opening the issue/probe; Seeking Information; Giving Information; Withholding Information; Suggesting course of action; Agreeing with Other; Giving reasons for course of action; Exploring consequences for course of action; Denying validity of other's arguments.

Communication Talk (Gottman, 1979; Notarius et al., 1983)

Concerns communication about communication as well as statements directing the discussion to the task or seeking clarification.

Conciliatory Remarks (Sillars, 1986)

Supportive Remarks—statements that refer to understanding, acceptance, support, etc. for the partner and shared interests.

Concessions—statements that express a willingness to change, show flexibility, make concessions, or consider mutually acceptable solutions to conflicts.

Acceptance of Responsibility—attributions of responsibility to self or both parties.

Description (Weiss, 1993)

Problem Description External—a statement describing a problem as external to both parties.

Problem Description Internal—describing a problem as internal to both parties.

Expressing Feelings about a Problem (Gottman, 1979; Notarius et al., 1983)

Talking about a general personal issue or the relationship in particular.

Mindreading/cooperative (Gottman, 1979; Notarius et al., 1983)

Beliefs about the partner's internal states—beliefs, emotions, attitudes, and the like—as well as explaining or predicting behaviors. Said with cooperative or neutral affect.

Problem Solving/Information Exchange (Gottman, 1979; Notarius et al., 1983)

Instances where one offers some kind of specific or nonspecific solution or one provides information about one's beliefs or relational activities.

Propose Change (Weiss, 1993)

Compromise—a negotiation of a mutual exchange of behavior.

Negative Solution—proposal for termination or decrease of some behavior.

Cooperative Solution—proposal for initiation or increase of some behavior.

Reconciling Acts (Rausch et al., 1974)

Avoiding blame or responsibility; Accepting blame or responsibility; Showing concern for other's feelings; Seeking reassurance; Attempting to make-up; Offering help or reassurance.

(Continued)

Table 7.1 (Continued)

Summarizing Self (Gottman, 1979; Notarius et al., 1983)
Statements about one's expressed opinions.

Summarizing Other (Gottman, 1979; Notarius et al., 1983)
Includes summaries of the partner or both parties' behavior.

Validation (Weiss, 1993)
Agree—statement of agreement with partner's opinion.
Approve—statement that favors couple's or partner's attributions, actions, or statements.
Accept Responsibility—statement that conveys that "I" or "we" are responsible for the problem.
Compliance—fulfills command within 10 seconds.

Direct and Competitive

Blame (Weiss, 1993)
Criticize—hostile statement of unambiguous dislike or disapproval of a specific behavior of the spouse. Non-neutral voice tone.
Mindread Negative—statement of fact which assumes a negative mindset or motivation of the partner.
Put Down—Verbal or non-verbal behavior that demeans or mocks the partner.
Threat—A verbal or non-verbal threat of physical or emotional harm.
Voice tone (indicates hostile or negative voice tone).

Coercive Acts/personal attacks (Rausch et al., 1974).
Using an external power to induce compliance; Commanding; Demanding compensation; Inducing guilt or attacking other's motives; Disparaging the other; Threatening the other.

Confrontative Remarks (Sillars, 1986)
Personal Criticism—remarks that directly criticize the personal characteristics or behaviors of the partner.
Rejection—statements in response to the partner's previous statements that imply personal antagonism toward the partner as well as disagreement.
Hostile Imperatives—requests, demands, arguments, threats, or other prescriptive statements that implicitly blame the partner and seek change in the partner's behavior.
Hostile Jokes—joking, teasing, or sarcasm at the expense of the partner.
Hostile Questions—directive or leading questions that fault the partner.
Presumptive Remarks—statements that attribute thoughts, feelings, etc. to the partner that the partner does not acknowledge.
Denial of Responsibility—statements that minimize or deny personal responsibility for the conflict.

Disagreement (Gottman, 1979; Notarius et al., 1983)
Disagreement can be explicit, involve "yes-but" answers (i.e., initial agreement stating why one disagrees), be offered with a rationale, or be stated in the form of a command or explicit non-compliance.

Invalidation (Weiss, 1993)
Disagree—statement or non-verbal gesture that indicates disagreement with spouse's opinion.
Deny Responsibility—statement that "I" or "we" are not responsible for the problem.
Excuse—denial of personal responsibility, based on implausible or weak rationale.
Interrupt—partner breaks in or attempts to break in while other is speaking.
Non Compliance—failure to fulfill command within 10 seconds.
Turn Off—nonverbal gestures that indicate displeasure, disgust, disapproval.
Withdrawal—verbal and non-verbal behavior that implies that a partner is pulling back from the interaction.

Mindreading/negative (Gottman, 1979; Notarius et al., 1983)

Beliefs about the partner's internal states—beliefs, emotions, attitudes, and the like—as well as explaining or predicting behaviors. Said with negative affect.

Rejecting Acts (Rausch et al., 1974)

Giving up or leaving the field; Recognizing other's motive as a strategy or calling the other's bluff; Rejection (of the partner).

Indirect and Cooperative

Facilitation (Weiss, 1993)

Assent—listener states "yeah," nods head to facilitate conversation.

Disengage—a statement expressing the desire not to talk about a specific issue at that time. *Neutral voice tone.*

Excuse Other—Excusing partner's behavior or statement by providing a reason for that behavior or statement.

Humor—lighthearted humor; not sarcasm.

Metacommunication—statement that attempts to direct the flow of conversation.

Cooperative Mindread—statement that implies favorable qualities of the other.

Question—any interrogative statement, including rhetorical questions.

Cooperative Physical contact—any affectionate touch, hug, kiss, etc.

Paraphrase/Reflection—statement that restates a preceding statement by the partner.

Smile/Laugh—(smile or laughter).

Irreverent Remarks (Sillars, 1986)

Friendly Joking—whenever there is friendly joking or laughter, which is not at the expense of the other person.

Noncommittal Remarks (Sillars, 1986)

Noncommittal Statements—statements that neither affirm nor deny the presence of conflict and which are not evasive replies or topic shifts.

Noncommittal Questions—include unfocused questions, rephrasing the question given by the researcher, and conflict-irrelevant information.

Abstract Remarks—abstract principles, generalizations, or hypothetical statements.

Procedural Remarks—procedural statements that supplant discussion of conflict.

Resolving Acts (Rausch et al., 1974)

Changing the subject; Using humor; Accepting the other's plans, ideas, feelings; Diversion to increase one's gain; Introduce compromise; Offer to collaborate in planning.

Indirect and Competitive

Denial and Equivocation (Sillars, 1986)

Direct Denial—statements that deny a conflict is present.

Implicit Denial—statements that imply denial by providing a rationale for a denial statement, although the denial is not explicit.

Evasive Remarks—failure to acknowledge or deny the presence of a conflict following a statement or inquiry about the conflict by the partner.

Dysphoric Affect (Weiss, 1993)

Dysphoric Affect—affect communicating depression or sadness, any self-complaint or whiny voice tone.

Topic Management (Sillars, 1986)

Topic Shifts—statements that terminate discussion of a conflict issue before each person has fully expressed an opinion or before the discussion has reached a sense of completion.

(Continued)

Table 7.1 (Continued)

Topic Avoidance—statements that explicitly terminate discussion of a conflict issue before it has been fully discussed.

Withdrawal (Weiss, 1993)

Off Topic—Comments irrelevant to the topic of discussion, including statements directed toward the experimenter, about the experimenter, or about the physical environment during the experiment.

Withdrawal—verbal and non-verbal behavior that implies that a partner is pulling back from the interaction.

SOURCE: Adapted from Sillars, Canary, & Tafoya (2004), *Handbook of Family Communication.* Copyright 2004 by Lawrence Erlbaum Associates. Reprinted by permission of the publisher.

shaking head, loud/sharp voice, and high pitch were associated positively with invalidating the other person's message content. However, the combination of animation, direct orientation, physical involvement, and physical cooperation was linked positively to supporting the other person. Also, a combination of relaxed posture, mellow and deeper voice, and behaviors that one might ordinarily associate with anxiety (e.g., self-adapters, dysfluency) was associated positively with content validation. Newton and Burgoon also reported that nonverbal expressions of physical involvement, physical cooperation, and nonverbal involvement positively affected communication satisfaction, relational satisfaction, and relational message dimensions of immediacy, similarity, equality, and the like.

In short, people make strategic choices that become manifest in conflict tactics and related nonverbal behaviors. Accordingly, individuals should exercise *strategy control*. When behaving mindfully, people consider more information, more options, and therefore obtain greater understanding of the conflict and the partner. These characteristics of mindful behavior should help people choose tactics and nonverbal behaviors that work with the partner and provide increased possibility for compromise and cooperation. If a person had to place a bet, then cooperative behaviors (direct or indirect) are clearly seen as more competent than competitive behaviors. In addition, cooperative actions are functional in limiting the negative effects of competitive behaviors.

Patterns of Communication

In terms of behavioral patterns, dissatisfied couples tend to reciprocate competitive behaviors (Gottman, 1994; Schaap, 1984). Such reciprocation can reflect symmetrical or asymmetrical exchanges. That is, people can mirror each other's behavior or complement each other's behavior. Gottman (1982) identified several patterns of negative symmetrical communication. These include the exchange of complaints (i.e., complaint-countercomplaint), reciprocation of negative metacommunication, and proposal-counterproposal without any acknowledgment of the partner's initial proposal. Other forms of symmetrical competitiveness have been reported (e.g., Raush, Barry, Hertel, & Swain, 1974; Revenstorf, Hahlweg, Schindler, & Vogel, 1984; Ting-Toomey, 1983). Consider the following example of competitive symmetry between two people living together, where the parties appear to be reflecting a mindless approach by reacting to each other in a knee-jerk fashion (data are from the set reported in Canary, Gustafson, & Mikesell, 1999). The topic concerns the man's wanting to go out, drinking with his friends, and not inviting his partner.

Turn	Speaker	Message
40	Female	Yeah, you're gonna leave me and your sister here with nothin' to do.
41	Male	Well, find something to do, and I'll take you there if you can find a ride back.
42	Female	Well, that leaves me shit out of luck 'cause . . .
43	Male	No, it doesn't because I'd be going out with my friends. And you can rent a movie, or watch TV, or go out with *your* friends.

44	Female	I'm not allowed to go out with my friends, remember?
45	Male	You can.
46	Female	You're afraid somebody's gonna molest me again. That's why I'm not allowed to go out with any of my friends.
47	Male	Well, you can go out with your friends.
48	Female	Yeah, and then you said you don't wanna hear about it when something happens to me. That's how much you care! That's what you said.
48	Male	The reason why I said that is half of your friends are all guys. *Most* of your friends are all guys!
49	Female	I get along better with guys.
50	Male	I could see it a different way if half of them were girls and half of them were guys. Go out with your *girl* friends!
51	Female	75% of your friends are female. If 75% of them want to go out . . .
52	Male	No, they are not!
53	Female	Uh huh!
54	Male	No, they're not—75% of my friends are male; 25% are female; and out of those 25% female *friends,* I don't even talk to them. So you can't say that!

On the other hand, competitive symmetry might reflect a more mindful reaction. The following example (again, from data used by Canary et al., 1999) illustrates a symmetrical disagreement-disagreement pattern that lasts approximately 15 turns. Of interest here is how the husband remains focused on the topic, working against the wife's attempts to excuse her public disapproval of her husband.

Turn	Speaker	Message
94	Husband	Well, look at what you did. Look at the scene you made!

95	Wife	Yeah, well you deserved it.
96	Husband	No, I didn't . . .
97	Wife	Everybody fights.
98	Husband	deserve that.
99	Wife	So . . .
100	Husband	No, everybody . . .
101	Wife	Yeah, everybody fights dear. 'Cause if they don't . . .
102	Husband	Yeah, but not in the presence of company. Not when, honey, we had 15 people.
103	Wife	See, I'm a very prompt [sic] person. I don't care.
104	Husband	But I do.
105	Wife	I knew everybody there.
106	Husband	Yes, but I DO.
107	Wife	And most of them was [sic] your family, and I couldn't care what they think anyway.
108	Husband	Well, I do.
109	Wife	Well, I don't!
110	Husband	Well, then I shouldn't care what your family thinks.

Reciprocation of negative behavior can also be reflected in asymmetrical negative reactivity (Margolin & Wampold, 1981), when a competitive comment is met with an asymmetrical competitive comment, as in demand-withdrawal sequences (Caughlin & Vangelisti, 2000), withdrawal-hostility sequences (Roberts & Krokoff, 1990), and attack-defend sequences (Ting-Toomey, 1983). Consider two attack-defend exchanges. In turns 225–229, the wife wants the husband not to shout at the children regarding their watching too much television, and then in turns 230–232 the husband attempts to take the offensive.

Turn	Speaker	Message
225	Wife	And you might ask nicely just as many times as you do unnicely [sic] and end up with the same results. Whether you ask them five times . . .

226	Husband	I don't agree with that, because I ask them once nicely and they don't comply, and then I bark and then they comply.
227	Wife	And you know what? You *taught* them "I don't have to comply unless dad barks at me. Until dad's voice changes and he's pissed, then I *have* to comply!" And you've trained them to do that.
228	Husband	No.
229	Wife	What you have to do is retrain them . . . we have to retrain them to show we're serious.
230	Husband	How do we do that?
231	Wife	One day at a time.
232	Husband	That is not an answer.

Such sequences can continue for some time. For example, Ting-Toomey (1983) found that maladjusted partners more frequently than expected engaged in up to 10 sequences of attack-defend patterns.

Not only do dissatisfied couples experience a higher base-rate of competitive reciprocation, they also tend to escalate the relative amount of competitive tactics as their conflicts continue. Such an increase in competitive tactics reflects an emergent pattern of negative reciprocity. For instance, Billings (1979) compared act-to-act sequences of dissatisfied married couples with those of satisfied married couples. He calculated the ratio of hostile sequences for partners as they interacted in a lab setting. Billings found that dissatisfied partners gradually escalated their sequences of hostility, and he reported these findings in point graphs, with each point indicating the ratio of hostility. Likewise, Gottman and Levenson (1992) examined couples' conflict behaviors in the lab and found a similar tendency for distressed couples to increase the relative amount of negative behaviors during the course of problem-solving conversation. In their study, the relative amount of negativity was expressed as the difference between positive and negative behaviors. Figure 7.2 illustrates the tendencies of satisfied and dissatisfied couples reported by Billings and Gottman and Levenson.[4]

How a person reacts to the partner affects not only the partner, but it affects the person as well. For instance, Siegman and Snow (1997) asked people to recall recent anger-producing episodes. Participants were assigned to one of three conditions—re-lived experience (no expression), speaking loud and fast (outward expression of anger), or speaking soft and slow (incongruous voice). Self-rated anger was reported lowest in the incongruous condition (speaking low and slow when angry) and highest in the outward expression condition (speaking loud and fast when angry). Moreover, cardiovascular reactivity (i.e., changes in pulse and blood pressure) increased for people who used the outward-expression condition more than for those in the other conditions—and the effect sizes for these differences were large. That is to say, a person's own expression of anger affected his or her physiological reactions to a large extent. To use a metaphor, in the face of emotional turbulence, people might be wise to use the strategy of airline pilots: They do not shout, "Dear God, we're about to hit turbulence!!! PLEASE return to your seats!!!" Instead, they are calm, speaking low and slow, which conveys a sense that all is right in the air.

Interaction control refers to the extent that people learn how to become aware of the patterns of conflict and their role in perpetuating them. It is certainly understandable why people reciprocate negative behavior—when faced with hostility people tend to act defensively, which then provides a warrant for the other person to continue using a competitive strategy. However, this reliance on what they have experienced in past situations is mindless behavior that, in many situations, is not productive. Yet people repeat it because it is what they know.

Perhaps the most difficult challenge for communicators is to follow this principle, which is clearly implied in the literature: *Do not perpetuate negative patterns of interaction.* Competent communicators do not rely on a strategic fallback position of simply reciprocating what the other person says. Instead, they consider their strategic options. They engage in mindful thinking and create new categories, gather new information, and develop more options than the first behavior that they would otherwise mindlessly engage in. They then focus on the process rather

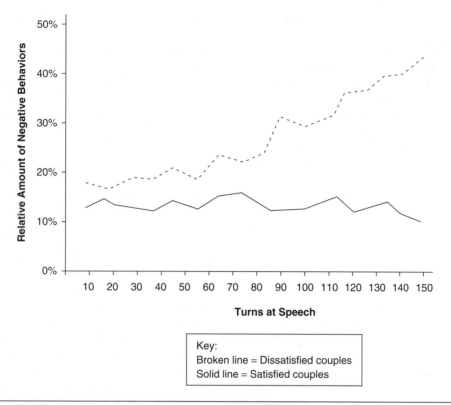

Figure 7.2   Increased Negativity Over Time

SOURCE: Based on findings from Billings (1979) and Gottman and Levenson (1992).

than the outcome and develop greater sensitivity and flexibility (Langer, 1989b). Several studies show that giving oneself time to consider options leads to a wider latitude of responses. We illustrate this point with a quick overview of one such study.

Ohbuchi, Chiba, and Fukushima (1996) examined the effects of time pressure on Japanese students' reactions to a confederate in a role play. Participants were required to respond immediately or to wait 30 seconds before responding to an unreasonable confederate who was either polite or rough/impolite. When participants had no time to consider their responses, they tended to reciprocate the confederate's behavior; but when they waited 30 seconds, participants engaged in various tactics, from appeasement (e.g., acknowledges other) to hostility (e.g., criticizes, shows anger). Ohbuchi et al. interpreted these findings as evidence that people under stress consider mostly their own immediate goals; people who can reflect more

carefully consider the self-presentation needs of their conversational partners and decide to reward or punish them in terms of face needs. Moreover, other research suggests that people simply need more time to create different, cooperative responses to a partner's competitive behavior (Yovetich & Rusbult, 1994). This research suggests that counting to ten before responding in anger is sound advice.

In sum, people can exercise *interaction control* by not reacting in an impulsive manner. By doing so, they also increase the probability that they will behave with integrity. Mindful responses consider the various characteristics of the context and include a wider range of ideas and information. They also allow time for thought and consideration of consequences, so people do not engage in automatic responses that can lead to damage to the partner and/or to the relationship.

Rather, competent communicators edit their reactions, and they rely more on a variety of cooperative tactics. In addition, they use a quiet voice, a slow speaking rate, and direct eye contact to indicate that the conflict is not going to escalate. However, if the other person is overly angry and hostile, then the best bet would be to use indirect behaviors. For instance, road rage victims often react to a person's aggressive driving with aggressive driving of their own. These behaviors often lead to very tragic consequences, including death. Incredibly, nine out of ten drivers have reported driver aggression by others, and people feel increasingly threatened by aggressive drivers (Harding, Morgan, Indermaur, Ferrante, & Blagg, 1998). Moreover, people in the United States perceive aggressive driving and road rage as bigger threats to their safety than are drunk drivers (National Highway Traffic Safety Administration, 2002). It is not an overstatement to note that reciprocating dangerous driving behavior can very well lead to one's death. When confronted with an angry and aggressive driver, the most competent option would appear to be avoidance.

The Ongoing Nature of Conflict

Finally, the model in Figure 7.1 indicates that parties in conflict will return to any previous event, from becoming more angry, to assessing goals, to reformulating strategic options, and/or deciding how to respond to one's partner. In other words, the conflict episode does not necessarily end. The goal of the model is to focus on those events where people can make unilateral strategic decisions to manage conflict more competently (i.e., effectively and appropriately).

In terms of characterizing the ongoing nature of conflict, Sillars and Wilmot (1994) examined the various properties of conflict. They proposed that five features can be used to characterize ongoing patterns of conflict: variety, continuity, symmetry, stationarity, and spontaneity. *Variety* concerns the extent to which social actors can modify their behaviors. *Continuity* refers to the range of topics that parties discuss. As discussed above, *symmetry* concerns the reciprocity of behavior. *Stationarity* concerns phases of conflict that are observed across conflict episodes; although particular couples might engage in various phases within a given encounter, their tactical patterns are similar in different conflict encounters. *Spontaneity* refers to the extent to which the parties in conflict are not being overly strategic and guarded in what they say (Sillars & Wilmot, 1994).

Sillars and Wilmot (1994) implied that the most competent management of conflict would entail both an awareness of these five characteristics of conflict and a moderate amount of each feature. For example, Sillars and Wilmot indicated that being focused on one issue or too many issues over time works against the resolution of conflict; so people in conflict should exercise moderation in continuity. About 20 years ago, a woman in Florida won a divorce case (i.e., she received the house and a large alimony). Apparently, she had an affair with her husband's brother, and for nine years her husband would constantly raise that issue. The judge who awarded the woman the huge settlement considered the husband at fault for having engaged in psychological abuse. Of course, this is an extreme example, but the structural nature of it might not be uncommon—that is, people sometimes have difficulty letting go of the past such that one issue is reincarnated in a dozen different ways.

Likewise, in terms of spontaneity, Sillars and Wilmot (1994) argued that "ideally, one would be spontaneous enough to be responsive enough to be collaborative, but strategic enough to modify destructive patterns when they arise" (p. 182). This statement implies that one might anticipate a cyclical conflict and prepare one's orientation to the problem while remaining open to the idea of altering strategic approaches midstream. For instance, one of our partners works late every Tuesday night and needs time to relax before diving into a hectic family discussion, learning about the teenager's day, or reacting to the younger child's request for help with homework. Accommodation has become the preferred strategy on Tuesday nights, though there are times when direct and cooperative tactics are needed as well.

Competent communicators know that they need to engage in the process of conflict by realizing that conflicts are often not resolved, though they are managed. Moreover, competent communicators might take a broader look at the patterns of recurring behavior to determine if they are caught in particular conversational ruts or have too much variation or not enough.

CONCLUSIONS

In this chapter, we have attempted to provide an overview of what a competence-based understanding of interpersonal conflict entails. Although the term *competence* might not generate a lot of excitement, its usefulness as a construct that represents communication quality has direct application to the study of interpersonal conflict. In addition, we noted that people can be more or less conscious of their communication behaviors but that, more often than not, being mindful of one's action is a step toward competent performance. Toward that end, we summarized a model of events to indicate where social actors might make wiser, more competent strategic choices.

We realize that in some respects, the ideas we have discussed can appear idealistic and apart from the context of the real world. However, mindfulness requires no more effort than mindlessness once people have switched from an automatic and mindless approach to a situation to a more mindful one (Langer, 1989b). Also, some people might balk at the notion that social actors can ever truly "control" such events as the onset of conflict or the patterns of interaction that come to define so many relationships. Although the control will never be complete, being mindful provides more control than people would have if they simply reacted mindlessly with the same old fallback strategy. Moreover, we argue that the model provides a useful tool for taking personal stock of what happens when one feels obstructed by another human. Control grows from understanding the context of the current conflict, recognizing options, and being sensitive to the partner's goals and behaviors. Developing this control is not easy. However, achieving what one wants in a manner that satisfies one's interaction partner is worth the effort.

Increased mindfulness can be achieved through viewing the world from a more conditional perspective. Rather than assuming they have the answers or know how something should be done, people should approach conflict situations with an eye on what they want as well as conditionally. Also, a mindful look at conflict might suggest new possibilities; in fact, mindfulness has been found to share some of the characteristics of creativity (Langer & Piper, 1987). Mindful behavior encourages people to test limits and even invites uncertainty so people will question what they encounter (Langer, 1989b). During conflict, mindfulness helps provide a way for people to deal with and even overcome old habits for handling conflict interactions; they can mindfully recognize that the old habits have not been productive and search for alternatives that will help them manage their conflicts. In this vein, we hope that the model we have provided presents occasions for becoming more mindful—a mindful look at events that matter, if you will.

We acknowledge that our model is silent with regard to psychological remedies that could very well be needed to complement the suggestions we provide. For example, once married partners fixate on negative attributions for each other's behavior, then specialized clinical treatment is warranted to help these people re-learn how to think and feel about each other. Also, some people are so depressed, anxious, and feeling out of control due to stress or other personal problems, they might need therapy and/or medical intervention.

From a communicative point of view, it is clear that the research over the past 40 years has provided a basis for making claims about what people might consider useful. We do not conclude with "Ten behaviors that we have personally discovered to improve your relationships." Rather, we conclude with the hope that the various elements of the model summarized here might help the reader become mindful of events where they can take more control, and thereby become more competent at managing interpersonal conflict.

NOTES

1. In spite of its positive connotations, mindfulness is not consistently preferable to mindless behavior. Langer and Weinman (1981) explained that both states of consciousness can have negative consequences when enacted inappropriately. Langer and Weinman's research reveals that mindlessness can have negative effects when people fail to process new information with clear attention. For example, people become less fluent when they must address a new

issue with little time to think about it. Conversely, these authors also found that mindfulness can create difficulties when someone attempts to perform an overlearned behavior with conscious attention. In separate studies, Langer and Weinman (1981) and Berger, Karol, and Jordan (1989) found that people become less fluent in their communication when they take time to think before discussing an overlearned idea.

2. Many situations occur where conflict arises without appointment. Consider this example: When writing this section a stranger called Dan's cell phone by mistake and demanded to know what Dan was doing on the stranger's wife's cell phone. The stranger was very upset and began swearing, until he realized that he misdialed. He hung up with, "I love you, brother. Peace."

3. We thank Brant Burleson for suggesting the terms *episode control*, *attribution control*, *goal control*, *strategy control*, and *interaction control*.

4. Interestingly, the reciprocation of cooperative behaviors does not appear to discriminate satisfied from dissatisfied couples. For example, Schaap (1984) reported that partners in dissatisfied couples (vs. satisfied couples) are more likely to reciprocate competitive behaviors. However, Schaap (1984) found that dissatisfied partners were *more* likely than satisfied couples to engage in reciprocations of positive, cooperative behaviors. Gottman's (1979, 1994) reviews reflect the same possibility that the reciprocation of cooperation may not necessarily reflect relational quality. Instead, the relative amount of negative to positive behaviors matters more, a point reviewed above.

References

Andersen, P. A. (1986). Consciousness, cognition, and communication. *Western Journal of Speech Communication, 50,* 87–101.

Bandura, A. (1989). Self–regulation of motivation and action through internal standards and goal systems. In L. A. Pervin (Ed.), *Goal concepts in personality and social psychology* (pp. 19–85). Hillsdale, NJ: Lawrence Erlbaum.

Berkowitz, L. (1993). Towards a general theory of anger and emotional aggression. Implications of the cognitive–neoassociationistic perspective for the analysis of anger and other emotions. In R. S. Wyer, Jr., & T. K. Srull (Eds.), *Perspectives on anger and emotion: Vol. 6. Advances in social cognition* (pp. 1–46). Hillsdale, NJ: Lawrence Erlbaum.

Berger, C. R. (1997). *Planning strategic interaction.* Hillsdale, NJ: Lawrence Erlbaum.

Berger, C. R., Karol, S. H., & Jordan, J. M. (1989). When a lot of knowledge is a dangerous thing: The debilitating effects of plan complexity on verbal fluency. *Human Communication Research, 16,* 91–119.

Billings, A. (1979). Conflict resolution in distressed and nondistressed married couples. *Journal of Consulting and Clinical Psychology, 47,* 368–376.

Bolger, N., Delongis, A., Kessler, R. C., & Schilling, E. A. (1989). Effects of daily stress on negative mood. *Journal of Personality and Social Psychology, 57,* 808–818.

Bradbury, T. N., & Fincham, F. D. (1990). Attributions in marriage: Review and critique. *Psychological Bulletin, 107,* 3–33.

Brown, J., & Langer, E. (1990). Mindfulness and intelligence: A comparison. *Educational Psychologist, 25,* 305–335.

Cai, D. A., & Fink, E. L. (2002). Conflict style differences between individualists and collectivists. *Communication Monographs, 69,* 67–87.

Canary, D. J. (2003). Managing interpersonal conflict: A model of events related to strategic choices. In J. Greene & B. Burleson (Eds.), *Handbook of communication and social interaction skills* (pp. 515–549). Mahwah, NJ: Lawrence Erlbaum.

Canary, D. J. (2004). *Handbook of communication and social interaction skills.* Mahwah, NJ: Lawrence Erlbaum.

Canary, D. J., Cunningham, E. M., & Cody, M. J. (1988). Goal types, gender, and locus of control in the management of interpersonal conflict. *Communication Research, 15,* 426–446.

Canary, D. J., & Cupach, W. R. (1988). Relational and episodic characteristics associated with conflict tactics. *Journal of Social and Personal Relationships, 5,* 305–325.

Canary, D. J., Cupach, W. R., & Messman, S. J. (1995). *Relationship conflict: Conflict in parent–child, friendship, and romantic relationships.* Thousand Oaks, CA: Sage.

Canary, D. J., Cupach, W. R., & Serpe, R. (2001). A competence–based approach to examining interpersonal conflict: Test of a longitudinal model. *Communication Research, 28,* 127–150.

Canary, D. J., Gustafson, D., & Mikesell, R. (1999, May). *Direct-indirect and cooperative-competitive conflict management behaviors: An observational analysis.* Paper presented at the International Communication Association convention, San Francisco.

Canary, D. J., & Spitzberg, B. H. (1987). Appropriateness and effectiveness perceptions of conflict strategies. *Human Communication Research, 14,* 93–118.

Canary, D. J., & Spitzberg, B. H. (1990). Attribution biases and associations between conflict strategies and competence outcomes. *Communication Monographs, 57,* 139–151.

Canary, D. J., Spitzberg, B. H., & Semic, B. A. (1997). The experience and expression of anger in interpersonal settings. In P. A. Andersen & L. K. Guerrero (Eds.), *Handbook of communication and emotion: Research, theory, applications, and contexts* (pp. 189–213). San Diego, CA: Academic Press.

Caughlin, J. P., & Vangelisti, A. L. (2000). An individual difference explanation of why married couples engage in the demand/withdraw pattern of conflict. *Journal of Social and Personal Relationships, 17,* 523–551.

Clark, R. A., & Delia, J. G. (1979). Topoi and rhetorical competence. *Quarterly Journal of Speech, 65,* 187–206.

Clore, G. L., Ortony, A., Dienes, B., & Fujita, F. (1993). Where does anger dwell? In R. S. Wyer, Jr., & T. K. Srull (Eds.), *Perspectives on anger and emotion: Advances in social cognition* (Vol. 6, pp. 57–87). Hillsdale, NJ: Lawrence Erlbaum.

Cody, M. J., Canary, D. J., & Smith, S. W. (1994). Compliance–gaining goals: An inductive analysis of actors' goal types, strategies, and successes. In J. Daly & J. Wiemann (Eds.), *Communicating strategically: Strategies in interpersonal communication* (pp. 33–90). Hillsdale, NJ: Lawrence Erlbaum.

Cupach, W. R., & Canary, D. J. (2000). *Competence in interpersonal conflict.* Prospect Heights, IL: Waveland.

de Dreu, C. K. W., Natua, A., & van de Vliert, E. (1995). Self-serving evaluations of conflict behavior and escalation of the dispute. *Journal of Applied Social Psychology, 25,* 2049–2066.

Dillard, J. P. (1990a). A goal-driven model of interpersonal influence. In J. P. Dillard (Ed.), *Seeking compliance: The production of interpersonal influence messages* (pp. 41–56). Scottsdale, AZ: Gorsuch Scarisbrick.

Dillard, J. P. (1990b). The nature and substance of goals in tactical communication. In M. J. Cody & M. L. McLaughlin (Eds.), *The psychology of tactical communication* (pp. 70–89). Philadelphia: Multilingual Matters.

Dillard, J. P., Segrin, C., & Harden, J. M. (1989). Primary and secondary goals in the production of interpersonal influence messages. *Communication Monographs, 56,* 19–37.

Doherty, W. J. (1981). Cognitive processes in intimate conflict: I. Extending attribution theory. *American Journal of Family Therapy, 9,* 3–13.

Fincham, F. D., & Beach, S. R. H. (1999). Conflict in marriage: Implications for working with couples. *Annual Review of Psychology, 50,* 47–77.

Fincham, F. D., & Bradbury, T. N. (1987). Cognitive processes and conflict in close relationships: An attribution–efficacy model. *Journal of Personality and Social Psychology, 53,* 1106–1118.

Fincham, F. D., Bradbury, T. N., & Scott, C. K. (1992). Cognition in marriage. In F. D. Fincham & T. N. Bradbury (Eds.), *The psychology of marriage: Basic issues and applications* (pp. 118–149). New York: Guilford.

Gottman, J. M. (1982). Emotional responsiveness in marital conversations. *Journal of Communication, 32,* 108–120.

Gottman, J. M. (1979). *Marital interaction: Experimental investigations.* New York: Academic Press.

Gottman, J. M. (1994). *What predicts divorce? The relationship between marital processes and marital outcomes.* Hillsdale, NJ: Lawrence Erlbaum.

Gottman, J. M., & Krokoff, L. J. (1989). Marital interaction and marital satisfaction: A longitudinal view. *Journal of Consulting and Clinical Psychology, 57,* 47–52.

Gottman, J. M., & Levenson, R. W. (1992). Marital processes predictive of later dissolution: Behavior, physiology, and health. *Journal of Personality and Social Psychology, 63,* 221–233.

Gottman, J. M., & Levenson, R. W. (2000). The timing of divorce: Predicting when a couple will divorce over a 14-year period. *Journal of Marriage and the Family, 62,* 737–745.

Gross, M. A., & Guerrero, L. K. (2000). Managing conflict appropriately and effectively: An application of the competence model to Rahim's organizational conflict styles. *International Journal of Conflict Management, 11,* 200–226.

Harding, R. W., Morgan, F. H., Indermaur, D., Ferrante, A. M., & Blagg, H. (1998). Road rage and the epidemiology of violence: Something old, something new. *Studies on Crime and Prevention, 7,* 221–238.

Hojjat, M. (2000). Sex differences and perceptions of conflict in romantic relationships. *Journal of Social and Personal Relationships, 17,* 598–617.

Howell, W. S. (1982). *The empathic communicator.* Belmont, CA: Wadsworth.

Huston, T. L., Caughlin, J. P., Houts, R. M., Smith, S. E., & George, L. J. (2001). The connubial crucible: Newlywed years as predictors of marital delight, distress, and divorce. *Journal of Personality and Social Psychology, 80,* 237–252.

Johnson, M. P. (1995). Patriarchal terrorism and common couple violence. Two forms of violence against women. *Journal of Marriage and the Family, 57,* 283–294.

Johnson, M. P. (2001). Conflict and control: Symmetry and asymmetry in domestic violence. In A. Booth, A. C. Crouter, & M. Clements (Eds.), *Couples in conflict* (pp. 95–104). Mahwah, NJ: Lawrence Erlbaum.

Kim, M.-S., & Leung, T. (2000), A multicultural view of conflict management styles: Review and critical synthesis. In M. E. Roloff (Ed.), *Communication yearbook 23* (pp. 227–269). Thousand Oaks, CA: Sage.

Kluwer, E. S., Heesink, J. A. M., & van de Vliert, E. (1997). The marital dynamics of conflict over the division of labor. *Journal of Marriage and the Family, 59,* 635–653.

Lakey, S. G., & Canary, D. J. (2002). Actor goal achievement and sensitivity to partner as critical factors in understanding interpersonal communication competence and conflict strategies. *Communication Monographs, 69,* 217–235.

Langer, E. J. (1989a). *Mindfulness.* Reading, MA: Addison-Wesley.

Langer, E. J. (1989b). Minding matters: The consequences of mindlessness–mindfulness. *Advances in Experimental Social Psychology, 22,* 137–173.

Langer, E. J., Chanowitz, B., & Blank, A. (1985). Mindlessness–mindfulness in perspective: A reply to Valerie Folkes. *Journal of Personality and Social Psychology, 48,* 605–607.

Langer, E. J., & Piper, A. (1987). The prevention of mindlessness. *Journal of Personality and Social Psychology, 53,* 280–287.

Langer, E. J., & Weinman, C. (1981). When thinking disrupts intellectual performance: Mindfulness on an overlearned task. *Personality and Social Psychology Bulletin, 7,* 240–243.

Larson, C., Backlund, P., Redmond, M., & Barbour, A. (1978). *Assessing functional communication.* Falls Church, VA: Speech Communication Association.

Lefcourt, H. M. (1982). *Locus of control: Current trends in theory and research* (2nd ed.). Hillsdale, NJ: Lawrence Erlbaum.

Locke, E. A., & Latham, G. P. (1990). *A theory of goal setting and task performance.* Englewood Cliffs, NJ: Prentice Hall.

Margolin, G., Burman, B., & John, R. S. (1989). Home observations of married couples reenacting naturalistic conflicts. *Behavioral Assessment, 11,* 101–118.

Margolin, G., & Wampold, B. E. (1981). Sequential analysis of conflict and accord in distressed and nondistressed marital partners. *Journal of Consulting and Clinical Psychology, 49,* 554–567.

Marshall, L. L. (1994). Physical and psychological abuse. In W. R. Cupach & B. H. Spitzberg (Eds.), *The dark side of interpersonal communication* (pp. 281–311). Hillsdale, NJ: Lawrence Erlbaum.

Marshall, L. L., Weston, R., & Honeycutt, T. C. (2000). Relational quality among low income women: Does men's positivity mediate their abuse? *Journal of Social and Personal Relationships, 17,* 660–675.

McCroskey, J. C. (1984). Communication competence: The elusive construct. In R. N. Bostrom (Ed.), *Competence in communication: A multidisciplinary approach* (pp. 259–268). Beverly Hills, CA: Sage.

Messman, S. J., & Canary, D. J. (1998). Patterns of conflict in personal relationships. In B. H. Spitzberg & W. R. Cupach (Eds.), *The dark side of personal relationships* (pp. 121–152). Mahwah, NJ: Lawrence Erlbaum.

Miller, P. C., Lefcourt, H. M., Holmes, J. G., Ware, E. E., & Saleh, W. E. (1986). Marital locus of control and marital problem solving. *Journal of Personality and Social Psychology, 51,* 161–169.

National Highway Traffic Safety Administration. (2002). *Strategies for aggressive driver enforcement*. Retrieved March 28, 2002, from http://www.nhtsa.dot.gov/people/injury/enforce/aggressdrivers/index.html

Newton, D. A., & Burgoon, J. K. (1990a). Nonverbal conflict behaviors: Functions, strategies, and tactics. In D. D. Cahn (Ed.), *Intimates in conflict: A communication perspective* (pp. 77–104). Hillsdale, NJ: Lawrence Erlbaum.

Newton, D. A., & Burgoon, J. K. (1990b). The use and consequences of verbal influence strategies during interpersonal disagreements. *Human Communication Research, 16,* 477–518.

Ohbuchi, K., Chiba, S., & Fukushima, O. (1996). Mitigation of interpersonal conflicts: Politeness and time pressure. *Personality and Social Psychology Bulletin, 22,* 1035–1042.

Parks, M. R. (1994). Communicative competence and interpersonal control. In M. L. Knapp & G. R. Miller (Eds.), *Handbook of interpersonal communication* (2nd ed., pp. 589–618). Thousand Oaks, CA: Sage.

Pearce, W. B., & Cronin, V. F. (1980). *Communication, action, and meaning: The creation of social reality*. New York: Praeger.

Pervin, L. A. (1989). Goals concepts: Themes, issues, and questions. In L. A. Pervin (Ed.), *Goal concepts in personality and social psychology* (pp. 473–479). Hillsdale, NJ: Lawrence Erlbaum.

Price, R. H., & Bouffard, D. L. (1974). Behavioral appropriateness and situational constraint as dimensions of social behavior. *Journal of Personality and Social Psychology, 30,* 579–586.

Raush, H. L., Barry, W. A., Hertel, R. J., & Swain, M. A. (1974). *Communication, conflict, and marriage*. San Francisco: Jossey-Bass.

Repetti, R. L. (1994). Short-term and long-term processes linking job stressors to father-child interaction. *Social Development, 3,* 1–15.

Repetti, R. L., & Wood, J. (1997). Effects of daily stress at work on mothers' interactions with preschoolers. *Journal of Family Psychology, 11,* 90–108.

Revenstorf, D., Hahlweg, K., Schindler, L., & Vogel, B. (1984). Interaction analysis of marital conflict. In K. Hahlweg & N. S. Jacobson (Eds.), *Marital interaction: Analysis and modification* (pp. 159–181). New York: Guilford.

Roberts, L. J., & Krokoff, L. J. (1990). A time series analysis of withdrawal, hostility, and displeasure in satisfied and dissatisfied marriages. *Journal of Marriage and the Family, 52,* 95–105.

Rubin, R. B. (1990). Communication competence. In G. M. Phillips & J. T. Wood (Eds.), *Speech communication: Essays to commemorate the 75th anniversary of the Speech Communication Association* (pp. 94–129). Carbondale: Southern Illinois University Press.

Sabourin, T. C., Infante, D. C., & Rudd, J. E. (1993). Verbal aggression in marriages: A comparison of violent, distressed, and nondistressed couples. *Human Communication Research, 20,* 245–267.

Sanders, R. E. (1991). The two-way relationship between talk in social interactions and actors' goals and plans. In K. Tracy (Ed.), *Understanding face-to-face interaction: Issues linking goals and discourse* (pp. 167–188). Hillsdale, NJ: Lawrence Erlbaum.

Schaap, C. (1984). A comparison of the interaction of distressed and nondistressed married couples in a laboratory situation: Literature survey, methodological issues, and an empirical investigation. In K. Hahlweg & N. S. Jacobson (Eds.), *Marital interaction: Analysis and modification* (pp. 133–158). New York: Guilford.

Schönbach, P. (1990). *Account episodes: The management or escalation of conflict*. New York: Cambridge University Press.

Siegman, A. W., & Snow, S. C. (1997). The outward expression of anger, the inward experience of anger and CVR: The role of vocal expression. *Journal of Behavioral Medicine, 20,* 29–45.

Sillars, A. L. (1980). The sequential and distributional structure of conflict interactions as a function of attributions concerning the locus of responsibility and stability of conflicts. In D. Nimmo (Ed.), *Communication yearbook 4* (pp. 217–235). New Brunswick, NJ: Transaction Books.

Sillars, A. L., Canary, D. J., & Tafoya, M. (2004). Communication, conflict, and the quality of family relationships. In A. L. Vangelisti (Ed.), *Handbook of family interaction* (pp. 413–446). Mahwah, NJ: Lawrence Erlbaum.

Sillars, A. L., & Weisberg, J. (1987). Conflict as a social skill. In M. E. Roloff & G. R. Miller (Eds.), *Interpersonal processes: New directions in communication research* (pp. 140–171). Newbury Park, CA: Sage.

Sillars, A. L., & Wilmot, W. W. (1994). Communication strategies in conflict and mediation. In J. A. Daly & J. M. Wiemann (Eds.), *Strategic interpersonal communication* (pp. 163–190). Hillsdale, NJ: Lawrence Erlbaum.

Smith, C. S., & Sulsky, L. (1995). An investigation of job-related coping strategies across multiple stressors and samples. In L. R. Murphy, J. J. Hurell, Jr., S. L. Sauter, & G. P. Keita (Eds.), *Job stress intervention* (pp. 109–123). Washington, DC: American Psychological Association.

Spitzberg, B. H. (1993). The dialectics of (in)competence. *Journal of Social and Personal Relationships, 10,* 137–158.

Spitzberg, B. H. (2000). Violence in intimate relationships. In W. R. Cupach & D. J. Canary (Eds.), *Competence in interpersonal conflict* (pp. 175–200). Prospect Heights, IL: Waveland.

Spitzberg, B. H., Canary, D. J., & Cupach, W. R. (1994). A competence-based approach to the study of interpersonal conflict. In D. D. Cahn (Ed.), *Conflict in personal relationships* (pp. 183–202). Hillsdale, NJ: Lawrence Erlbaum.

Spitzberg, B. H., & Cupach, W. R. (1984). *Interpersonal communication competence.* Beverly Hills, CA: Sage.

Spitzberg, B. H., & Cupach, W. R. (1989). *Handbook of interpersonal competence research.* New York: Springer.

Storms, M. D. (1973). Videotape and the attribution process: Reversing actors' and observers' points of view. *Journal of Personality and Social Psychology, 27,* 165–175.

Ting-Toomey, S. (1983). An analysis of verbal communication patterns in high and low marital adjustment groups. *Human Communication Research, 9,* 306–319.

Ting-Toomey, S., & Oetzel, J. G. (2001). *Managing intercultural conflict effectively.* Thousand Oaks, CA: Sage.

Tjaden, P., & Thoennes, N. (2000). Prevalence and consequences of male-to-female and female-to-male intimate partner violence as measured by the National Violence Against Women Survey. *Violence Against Women, 6,* 142–161.

van de Vliert, E., & Euwema, M. C. (1994). Agreeableness and activeness as components of conflict behaviors. *Journal of Personality and Social Psychology, 66,* 674–687.

Waldron, V. R. (1997). Toward a theory of interactive conversational planning. In J. O. Greene (Ed.), *Message production: Advances in communication theory* (pp. 195–220). Hillsdale, NJ: Lawrence Erlbaum.

Wiemann, J. M., & Bradac, J. J. (1989). Metatheoretical issues in the study of communicative competence: Structural and functional approaches. In M. Dervin & M. J. Voight (Eds.), *Progress in communication sciences* (Vol. 9, pp. 261–284). Norwood, NJ: Ablex.

Yovetich, N. A., & Rusbult, C. E. (1994). Accommodative behaviors in close relationships: Exploring transformation of motivation. *Journal of Experimental Social Psychology, 30,* 138–164.

Zillmann, D. (1990). The interplay of cognition and excitation in aggravated conflict. In D. D. Cahn (Ed.), *Intimates in conflict: A communication perspective* (pp. 187–208). Hillsdale, NJ: Lawrence Erlbaum.

Zillmann, D. (1993). Mental control of angry aggression. In D. M. Wegner & J. W. Pennebaker (Eds.), *Handbook of mental control* (pp. 370–392). Englewood Cliffs, NJ: Prentice Hall.

8

Managing Interpersonal Conflict

The Mediation Promise

William A. Donohue

Michigan State University

Managing interpersonal conflict is one of the most significant challenges facing parties involved in significant interpersonal relationships. Pioneering research by Gottman (1979) and others (Notarius & Markman, 1993) illustrates the importance of married couples' being able to manage their own differences in the course of developing a healthy, enduring relationship. Yet, this task often proves very difficult given the complexities of modern life. When parties fail in their efforts to manage their own differences, as in the course of a divorce or a neighborly dispute, they often turn to some kind of third-party intervention, the most common and well-institutionalized form of which is mediation.

The past two decades have witnessed a dramatic proliferation of mediation programs across an ever-expanding list of settings as a means of managing various kinds of interpersonal conflicts. Professionals in such areas as divorce, law, resource management, school violence prevention, community development, and international diplomacy have turned to mediation as a means of constructively managing disputes. In general, the proliferation of this strategy is a result of its perceived effectiveness in managing disputes. Recognizing its potential, the contemporary mediation movement really began in the labor field with the Federal Mediation and Conciliation Service, which established a mediation practice in 1947 to deal with labor disputes. In the 1960s, Community Justice Centers were established as mediation programs aimed at dealing with community conflict that was emerging in response to increasing urban conflict. One of the most rapidly growing mediation programs focusing on divorce was established in 1963 with the Association of Family and Conciliation Courts, which thrives today. So, mediation has been around for a long time in various forms since it appears to offer the promise of constructive conflict management.

As the research in this chapter will reveal, mediation has been fairly effective in helping parties reach agreement, improving their satisfaction with the process and outcome, and increasing their compliance with the agreements, in contrast to more traditionally adversarial ways of resolving disputes. Perhaps the most comprehensive collection of mediation research across all its major contexts is Kressel and Pruitt's (1989) volume of studies. This book clearly illustrates that mediation is no longer an "alternative dispute resolution" strategy, but is becoming a standard tool that fits into a larger dispute management scheme that often includes negotiation, conciliation, adjudication, arbitration, and perhaps other forms of conflict management. This view is confirmed in others' extensive reviews of mediation research (Lewicki, Weiss, & Lewin, 1992; Wall & Lynn, 1993).

Given that the most common third-party strategy for managing interpersonal disputes is mediation, the purpose of this chapter is to provide an overview of theory and research in mediation with an emphasis on more recent publications. What are mediation's roots, how has it proliferated into its many contexts, and what theories have emerged to account for its dispute resolution value? To answer these questions, the chapter begins by defining mediation, then turning to some of the more visible theories, followed by a review of research in its various contexts.

DEFINING MEDIATION

Berkovitch (1999) indicated that mediation is a decision-making process, activated when parties cannot solve their own problems, that involves an acceptable, neutral third party who assists disputants with their decision making. Typically, mediators do not coerce a solution or seek to modify disputants' agreements, although there are some exceptions to that practice, depending on the mediation context. Also, mediators are typically employed temporarily until the disputants make a decision. The emphasis of mediation is on problem solving as opposed to some kind of therapeutic intervention. Disputants work toward completing an agreement about substantive issues with the assistance of a neutral third party.

Donohue (1991) identified four different models that define approaches to the mediation process. The mediator-control model involves the mediator's assuming the facilitation role as long as both parties continue making progress toward a settlement. When the mediator feels that progress has broken down, the mediator becomes an arbitrator and makes the decision for the parties. This "med-arb" model, first identified by Pruitt and Rubin (1986) and later evaluated by McGillicuddy, Welton, and Pruitt (1987), is particularly effective in encouraging parties to be less contentious and more constructive in their communication since the mediator has more control. This technique is also called "muscle" mediation (Ferrick, 1986).

This med-arb or muscle mediation model is often used in contexts in which reaching an agreement is an important priority for the agency offering mediation, or for the parties using it to resolve their dispute. For example, McGillicuddy et al.'s (1987) research was conducted in a community mediation center that focused on neighbor-neighbor or small-claims kinds of disputes. Settlement is a priority here since agencies are eager to show they are "successful," and a key marker of success for community mediation agencies is settlement rates. In addition, these agencies are often staffed by volunteers, so securing one volunteer to mediate the case and another to arbitrate the case in the event of non-settlement is often not practical. Parties also hope not to drag out their cases with multiple sessions, so they are more than happy to have the mediator pull double duty just to get the case settled. Muscle mediation is also used by some family court–related agencies to manage divorce cases for many of the same reasons that it is used in community contexts: Resources are lean, and everyone wants a settlement. Of course, not all family court systems use this approach, preferring other models instead. In contexts in which resources are lean and settlement is a priority, however, muscle mediation is often used.

The second model, the disputant-control model, holds that disputants must retain total control over the outcome of the mediation session. The mediator cannot become an arbitrator if parties deadlock, and the mediator cannot "steer" parties toward certain outcomes. Early studies indicate that disputant-controlled mediation obtains high levels of cooperation and outcome satisfaction (Carnevale & Leatherwood, 1985; Welton & Pruitt, 1987). The value of this approach rests in the perceived fairness and neutrality of the mediator. If the mediator has the power to resort to arbitration, parties may not feel free to speak frankly about their issues since the mediator is also judging the value and substance of their case. The most commonly referenced guide to implementing this approach is offered by Moore (1996). He outlined in great detail how mediators can select an appropriate role and then assess disputants' needs and work with them to move their dispute along in productive ways. If some kind of additional intervention is needed after mediation, another person performing another role (e.g., a judge) will step in to process the dispute with another set of rules.

This disputant-control model is perhaps the most frequently used approach across the diverse set of mediation contexts. For example, many court-sponsored divorce mediation programs want disputants and not mediators to control outcomes. Issues such as custody and visitation must have parental buy-in, and mediation in which parents control the process is often viewed as the most effective path to achieving this goal. If parents do not agree on these issues, the courts are committed to allowing them to be heard in court and giving mediators the flexibility of allowing parents to control the process. Mediation between parents and school districts in resolving special education services disputes are also best approached from a disputant-control model. In this case, parties are assumed experts (on their children and on the school's resources) and need only facilitation to find the right combination of services to address the special education needs.

The third model is the relational development model. Perhaps the most visible advocates of this model are Bush and Folger (1994). They stress that before parties can reach a substantive agreement about issues, they need to transform their relationship through empowerment and recognition. Empowerment involves acquiring the skills and motives to problem solve, and recognition is the awareness of the dispute's impact on the other party. When individuals have acquired these resources, they can begin to build sufficient trust to bargain substantive issues. In a study relevant to this model, Jones (1987) found that mediators achieving greater levels of cooperation used more neutral nonverbal affect in their voice as opposed to more negative nonverbal affect. So, sending evaluative messages may encourage parties to become less forthright about their issues.

Bush and Folger (1994) argue that any mediation benefits from taking a more transformative approach since relational issues underlie most conflicts. In particular, when the focus of the mediation is more squarely on relationship issues, this type of mediation has the potential to be quite effective. For example, in community mediation centers that deal with many neighborhood disputes between parties with long relational histories, the focus on relational transformation as a precursor to a specific agreement seems reasonable. Or, in settings in which court-appointed mediators are trying to mediate between parents and their children in resolving run-away cases, the focus on transformation seems appropriate. It is probably less appropriate in small claims court in a typical merchant-customer mediation in which the relationship is not a core issue.

The major challenge in implementing this model of mediation is mediator training. This kind of model requires a great deal of relational-issue processing. If mediators have extensive training in this area, they may feel confident addressing recognition and empowerment issues. However, if the mediators are volunteers who struggle to learn the basics of conflict management, these skills might be more elusive.

The fourth variety of mediation is termed the interventionist model. As in the med-arb model, an interventionist mediator has a vision about how the mediation process, and perhaps part of the decision, ought to be resolved. For example, in divorce mediation, the court-appointed mediator must ensure that the agreement the parties form is in the best interests of the children. If parties stray from that path, the mediator is obliged to step in to redirect the parties because the mediator is obliged to ensure that the agreement supports the best interests of the unrepresented parties (e.g., a minor in a child custody dispute), or even the disputants themselves. In contrast to the med-arb model, the mediator does not become an arbitrator, but is somewhat more directive about enforcing a particular ideology (Bernard, Folger, Weingarten, & Zumeta, 1984).

Mediators typically come from two major professional backgrounds. Most mediators have some kind of social science training in communication, psychology, sociology, or social work. Many programs even demand that mediators have a Master of Arts degree in some kind of social science area. Sometimes marital therapists conduct mediation sessions in a divorce context, and these individuals often have advanced degrees in psychology or clinical psychology. The second background that many mediators draw upon is law. Lawyers are used in many courts as either volunteers or employees, for example. Their knowledge of the law can often be helpful in guiding disputants in some cases. This background is less desirable for cases involving extensive relational issues, however, since lawyers are typically trained to focus more on factual issues than on relational concerns (Donohue, Drake, & Roberto, 1994).

The typical career path for mediators from both backgrounds focuses primarily on the public sector. Courts or community agencies typically hire the most mediators. These individuals perform other tasks, such as child custody evaluations or case work of some kind. Then, they might spend some of their time conducting mediations. Some courts, especially in large urban areas, are very busy and employ full-time mediators, but these courts are common only in large urban areas. Typically, it is very difficult to make a living as a mediator in the private sector by conducting private mediations, for example, in divorce cases. Some individuals succeed in these roles but they also are likely to have law or counseling degrees and do other work as well. In general, being a mediator is not very profitable.

These models articulate an orientation to practice that may or may not reflect a particular theory about what makes mediation effective or gives it the best chance to work for disputants trying to manage their issues. Nevertheless, several authors have devoted a fair amount of theoretical thinking to why mediation tends to yield more effective outcomes than other forms of third-party intervention such as arbitration or adjudication. Thus, at this point it useful to review these major theoretical approaches.

THEORETICAL APPROACHES TO MEDIATION

Perhaps the most useful way of uncovering the various theoretical approaches to mediation is to provide a brief example of an actual mediation

interaction that illustrates the value of each theoretical approach. After presenting the example, four theoretical approaches are introduced and used to analyze the example: (a) narrative mediation, (b) transformative mediation, (c) strategic choice, and (d) interaction management.

Wife: Can I just explain the situation?

Mediator: Sure, I suggest you explain it to him and I'll just listen.

Wife: There is a number, he can call my attorney any time and she will take a message over visitation. IF there's an extreme emergency, I gave him the Sheriff's number.

Husband: There's no reason I should bother them. I have asked her for either a neighbor, or she can call me on Wednesday collect at 7 o'clock. But, the problem is that her boyfriend is living in her house with her and I can't come over there because he goes into a rage. So, I can't have contact with my daughter unless there is a phone. You said you were going to get a phone.

Wife: I said when I get the money. I'm still on ADC and if you would pay the installation I would get a phone.

Husband: There's just a bunch of problems with the environment you've chosen to live in.

Mediator: Well, we're kind of getting off track here and I can see that it's all pushed together.

Husband: See what she does with her life is strictly up to her. It does not matter to me. But, when it affects my children. . . . This past weekend was mine, and my lawyer called me and said that she claimed it was hers.

Wife: I told you I'm sorry.

Husband: So, my lawyer calls me on Friday and says she wants them, so I was going to let her have them. I generally don't tell David. She hasn't seen David for a year and he's really been rejected.

Wife: Oh, that's not true.

Husband: So, I agreed she could have them. I told David, "Now Mom's going to come and get you." And, then she didn't show up.

If I could have had her phone number, I could have called to see what was going on. Her situation is creating a situation in our lives too.

Narrative Mediation

In a recent book, Winslade and Monk (2000) described a process they term narrative mediation that concentrates on using disputants' stories to uncover key relational issues that prevent individuals from addressing the conflict themselves. Disputants tell many stories associated with their disputes. The narrative approach seeks to use these stories to uncover how disputants are creating their disparate realities. Identifying these individual needs and interests by deconstructing stories allows disputants to visualize the conflict better and find a path to resolution. Thus, this theoretical approach is very consistent with the disputant-control model of mediation.

Cobb (1994) also provided a perspective on narrative mediation by arguing that helping disputants to deconstruct stories allows them to highlight the paradoxical features of the mediation process (e.g., the need to be open vs. the need to control information) and of the dispute itself (e.g., the need to be flexible about parenting solutions vs. the need to be rigid about the parenting values associated with those solutions). She invoked a post-structural perspective in that the stories operate as a description of the evolving and reflexive relationship between the story content and the storytelling. For example, a story told to attribute blame and responsibility to the other party is a function of structural rules for storytelling as well as the interpretative (cultural) frames of the parties.

This perspective provides a significant break from other theories seeking to understand the forces that explain why mediation works for two reasons. First, the approach is rooted in the tradition of qualitative linguistic analysis, which allows mediators and scholars to understand how micro processes function in mediation. A story can be carefully deconstructed to reveal the full fidelity of its meaning to the disputants and to the conflict as a whole. Second, focusing on stories as windows to exposing key issues and needs is unique. Mediations are really a set of stories linked together that parties use to express a series of issues or concerns that divide them. Embracing these stories by exposing them allows the parties to see the dispute more clearly and take charge of it. The key skill for mediators is to listen carefully to the stories and work with the disputants to process the stories. Mediators who gloss over the stories and perhaps pick out only fragments may miss key elements in the dispute and key opportunities for building integrative agreements.

Notice in the interaction above that the mediator lets the parties tell their respective stories to reveal a pattern of issues that impact one another. The phone issue impacts direct communication and their ability to forge a trusting, working relationship over visitation. The issue about the wife's relationship with the son and the husband's ability to go over to the house is also a part of this communication problem. What if the mediator had made the following intervention after the husband's final utterance:

Mediator: Well, let me see if I can piece this together. It sounds like you guys are sort of stuck in a box. The phone problem causes some communication challenges to you two working directly with each other. And because you can't communicate and work directly with each other, maybe that causes some trust issues between you also.

With this comment the mediator begins to use the stories to expose the communication issues and pull them all together. The mediator exposes the paradox that the parties created for themselves and reveals its impact on other issues. By continuing on this path the mediator can begin to map the conflict for the parties to explore potential solutions to these issues. The logic of this narrative approach is that people can see the impact of their issues more clearly through the stories since the issues are made more concrete.

Transformative Mediation

Bush and Folger (1994) proposed a relational development approach to mediation in their book *The Promise of Mediation.* The key idea in their approach is that relationships drive settlements. If the mediator can successfully transform the relationship between the parties, the substantive problem solving will follow. Bush and Folger contend that the mediation process should engender moral growth toward both strength and compassion. This transformation is achieved by two processes: recognition and empowerment. Recognition involves understanding how the dispute fully impacts each party. Typically, a disputant enters mediation unaware of how the conflict impacts the other party. Each is focused on his or her own problem. Recognizing the full impact, and often the pain of the dispute for the other party, builds a sense of moral compassion that leaves open the possibility of relational repair. Empowerment involves supplying the parties with the skills they need to listen, communicate, and relate to one another. Again, individuals focused on their own issues are typically not motivated or emotionally able to reach out to the other party. Once that barrier is removed, individuals can learn to communicate more productively.

The unique and important theoretical contribution of this approach is its de-emphasis on the traditional superficial problem-solving approach to mediation, and an emphasis on the need to transform the relationship between the parties before mediation can achieve its promise. While other approaches acknowledge that relational issues are important, they do not specify the goal of transformation as the key hurdle that must be jumped before progress can be made. This same logic was employed in the South African Truth and Reconciliation Councils that were established to allow the country to heal from Apartheid. The councils offered amnesty and forgiveness if the parties demonstrated true recognition of the impact of their behavior on others, and thus remorse for their actions. This compassion and the resultant relational repair allowed the country to begin healing from very deep wounds and won Bishop Desmond Tutu a Nobel Peace Prize. While this approach has not received any major empirical support or been tested in relation to other approaches, it does offer a unique theoretical contribution to the field of dispute resolution.

In the mediation segment provided above the mediator could have attempted a transformative move following the wife's apology for the miscommunication:

Mediator: Susan (Not Wife's real name), it sounds like you have some idea about how this communication problem is affecting our discussion today. Are there other ways in which this conflict is affecting Jim (Not Husband's real name) and your daughter and son?

Pursuing this line of intervention introduces the transformative frame by encouraging this external recognition. Of course, the husband must also adopt the same frame, so the mediator would continue this intervention strategy with him, as well. Once that recognition occurs, then the mediator can pursue the substantive issues. Instead of pursuing this strategy, the mediator allows the husband to challenge the wife, which has the effect of focusing the wife on the conflict from her perspective rather than focusing externally on recognizing how the conflict impacts the husband.

Strategic Choice

Carnevale (1986; and elaborated in Carnevale, Conlon, Hanisch, & Harris, 1989) offered a strategic choice model that seeks to understand what kinds of strategies a mediator is likely to select. The model contends that a mediator's choice in selecting a general strategy for approaching the conflict is found in the intersection of two issues. The first strategic choice is the mediator's assessment of the probability that a mutually acceptable solution—or "perceived common ground"—will be found. The second choice is the value that the mediator places on the disputants' achieving their aspirations.

According to Carnevale et al. (1989), the four strategies that define the strategic choice model include integration (the ability to craft a remedy based on disputant input), pressing (establishing limits to the options available for disputant choice), compensating (providing some reward or incentive for disputants to reach a settlement), and inaction (offering no potential solutions or remedy, punishment, or incentives). The model argues that if the mediator perceives that there is little potential common ground for creating an agreement, and the mediator has low concerns for the parties' aspirations, the mediator is likely to press or coerce parties for an agreement. If the mediator has a high concern for parties' aspirations but a low or pessimistic perception of common ground, the mediator is likely to emphasize reward power or a compensation strategy that seeks to find ways of minimizing costs to parties. The model also holds that mediator inaction, or letting the disputants handle the conflict, is a function of a high perception of common ground but a low concern for parties' aspirations. Finally, integrating involves finding solutions that benefit both sides, and grows from high aspirations for disputants and a high perception of common ground.

In a study aimed at assessing disputant response to these strategies, Kimsey, Fuller, Bell, and McKinney (1994) found that mediators who employ pressing or integrating strategies are perceived as more controlling, while mediators who use inaction or compensating are perceived as less controlling. In addition, mediators who use the integration and compensation strategic choices received the most problem solving from disputants and were perceived as most competent.

The integrative and compensating strategic-choice interventions are closely related to the narrative and transformative approaches to mediation since they suggest high aspiration for parties' outcomes as the mediators work hard to use stories and transform perspectives to create valuable insights for parties. A mediator who was perhaps less concerned with the parties' aspirations might simply let the parties fight (inaction), or might force them to focus on substantive issues and ignore insights (press). More concretely, if the mediator had made the following integrative intervention after the wife's apology, it would aim at helping folks recognize common ground:

Mediator: Susan, it sounds like you and Jim agree on the issue about communication. Are there some specific ways you both might improve communication to make the visitation easier for everybody concerned?

By focusing on this common ground and translating it into a solvable issue, the mediator would be seeking some initial success to aid in identifying additional common ground later in the mediation. One of the ways that mediators can maximize disputants' understanding of common ground is to ask both parties to list key issues that they are concerned about and place them on a flip chart for all to see. Then, common perceptions can be identified and built upon in forging agreements. The other two mediation models would both endorse the idea that identifying common ground, perhaps through stories or through recognition exercises, moves the mediation along quite productively.

Interaction Management

Donohue (1991) offered an interventionist theory about what moves mediation into more productive directions. Interaction management contends that it is essential for mediators to learn to discriminate between productive and unproductive communication patterns and then direct the disputants toward more productive patterns through various interaction strategies. Mediators must recognize three kinds of patterns: relational, content, and strategic. Relational patterns consist of psychological distance (signals of trust and affiliation), social distance (signals of formality and informality), and role distance (signals associated with social power and status). Understanding content patterns requires that mediators listen to topics, issues within topics, and individual perspectives on topics. Focusing on strategic patterns requires that mediators examine disputants' position adjustment strategies (arguments, facts), compliance gaining and compliance resisting strategies, and proposal development strategies. Donohue presented a great deal of empirical evidence through the examination of actual divorce mediation transcripts that indicates which patterns discriminate between mediations that reach agreement and those that fail to reach agreement.

The challenge in implementing the interaction management model is recognizing each of the relational, content, and strategic patterns. Recall this exchange from above:

Husband: See what she does with her life is strictly up to her. It does not matter to me. But, when it affects my children. . . . This past weekend was mine, and my lawyer called me and said that she claimed it was hers.

Wife: I told you I'm sorry.

Husband: So, my lawyer calls me on Friday and says she wants them, so I was going to let her have them. I generally don't tell David. She hasn't seen David for a year and he's really been rejected.

Wife: Oh, that's not true.

From a content perspective, the mediator needs to begin recognizing the key issues that must be addressed in building a sustainable agreement. In this case, the key issues are visitation and communication. After the wife's apology the mediator could have interrupted, labeled the visitation issue, written it on a flip chart for all to see, and indicated that both seem to agree that this is an important issue. The mediator could have then spent a few more minutes developing the issue. The second issue is the husband's perception of the wife's relationship with David, the son. Though this is separate from, and unrelated to, the first issue, the mediator allows it to become confused with the visitation issue. Thus, the lack of an intervention after the wife's apology becomes particularly problematic because it results in lost opportunities both to identify a key issue and to isolate an area of agreement. Thus, from a content perspective, the interaction was not managed very effectively.

Relationally, there are some other key opportunities that are lost. The wife's apology presented the mediator with a rare opportunity to build some positive relations between the parties. Instead, the mediator allowed the husband to use the wife's apology as an opening to attack the wife on another issue. The mediation instantly becomes more negative, more formal, and the husband is clearly pulling a power play to label the wife as an incompetent parent.

Strategically, the husband is raising the topic of the communication problem perhaps in an attempt to portray the wife as incompetent or irresponsible to the mediator. Clients will often seek to portray the other negatively to curry favor with the mediator. This strategy certainly works against the client's ability to empathize with the other (needed for recognition) or to

build a positive relational foundation for the mediation. Yet, narratives often move in this direction, and the interaction management approach to mediation emphasizes the need to slow the interaction down, pull the issues apart, and discourage negative relational attacks and inappropriate strategies.

The unique theoretical contribution of this approach is the idea that success is driven by discriminating between productive and unproductive interaction patterns and then redirecting parties toward using more productive patterns. This theoretical approach differs from both the narrative and transformative approaches since it does not emphasize the need to focus on stories or to transform the relationship to drive productive mediation outcomes. While mediators use the information contained in stories to understand issues, topics, and relational assumptions, it does not limit the mediation to that particular domain or require that parties achieve a transformative experience. The concept of interaction management is driven more by empirical findings associated with what patterns seem most productive in moving parties toward settling their disputes.

Given these approaches to mediation and some of the key theoretical drivers associated with how disputes are managed, it is useful at this point to review some of the more prominent research findings across various mediation contexts. Since most mediation research is based on divorce issues, it is perhaps best to begin with this context.

Mediation Contexts

Mediation takes place in myriad contexts. In this section, I discuss six different types of mediation: (a) divorce, (b) community, (c) peer (school-based mediation), (d) victim-offender, (e) environmental, and (f) peacekeeping. For each type, I provide a brief history and then provide relevant evidence describing the mediation and noting its effectiveness.

Divorce Mediation

Brief history. As the divorce mediation process began to unfold in earnest in court systems around the United States in the early 1980s, a variety of scholars offered several insightful commentaries describing the mediation process and its features. Perhaps the most comprehensive reviews of early divorce mediation research are offered in the chapters presented by Pearson and Thoennes (1989) and Kelly and Gigy (1989) in the Kressel and Pruitt (1985) mediation research review. Most of this early work addressed the issue of how mediation might be appropriate for managing custody and visitation disputes. For example, Girdner (1985) compared child custody adjudication and mediation among divorcing parents and third parties. She found that the more traditional court-centered adjudication of the custody issue fosters conflictual and competitive interactions between parents, whereas mediation fosters cooperative and interdependent interactions. In another essay, Manocherian (1985) sought to dispel some common misconceptions about the goals of mediation by clarifying that it is not intended to be divorce counseling, legal counseling, and/or arbitration. Rather, she noted that mediation is a process by which a couple, separated or preparing to separate, meet together with a trained third party, or mediator, to discuss and decide the issues involved in a separation agreement—child and spousal support, division of marital assets and debts, and custody and visitation. In contrast to the adversarial system in which each spouse retains counsel to represent him or her, mediation allows a couple to remain in charge of the decisions affecting their lives.

Folberg and Milne (1988) offered perhaps the most comprehensive guide to understanding divorce mediation. They provided several readings that describe both the process and theory associated with divorce mediation. The most often cited guide for mediation practitioners, however, is Moore's (1996) work, which provides step-by-step instructions for managing mediated disputes. The book does not focus on any specific context, and it does not advocate a particular theoretical approach to mediation.

Relevant research. Empirically, most of the early research in divorce mediation focused on perceptions of satisfaction with the process. For example, Pearson and Thoennes (1985, 1989) evaluated several divorce mediation programs

across the country and found that between 79% and 91% of those who tried mediation expressed satisfaction with the process. Three factors appear to stimulate the satisfaction: the ability to focus on the needs of the children, the opportunity to air grievances, and the ability to focus on important issues. In a critique of early research, Kressel (1985) found that the divorce mediation process appears to be generally satisfying to the majority of participants, but that settlement rates vary dramatically depending on the study (range of 22% to 97%). In a more recent study, Jones and Bodtker (1998) conducted an evaluation of one county's custody mediation program. Data from 169 cases revealed that disputants had high rates of short-term satisfaction with the mediation process, and that satisfaction was related positively to whether disputants reached an agreement. Interestingly, the mediators were less satisfied with the mediation process than the disputants.

Other research from the field of communication focused on how disputant and mediator communication strategies influenced settlement in divorce mediation. For example, Donohue, Allen, and Burrell (1985) developed a model of mediator communication competence and tested it in a divorce mediation context. Donohue's (1991) book on communication and divorce mediation summarizes that work. Another significant body of work emerged from Jones and her colleagues. Using the same data set as in the Donohue papers, Jones (1988) examined the communication phase structures in successful and unsuccessful mediations. She learned that mediators achieving more cooperative interaction and agreements followed a more directive, involved course of action. They spent the first part of the sessions relying on process and information-exchange behaviors, followed by a focus on solutions, agreements, and process behaviors. The mediators achieving less integrative behavior waited until later phases to focus on process and information-exchange behaviors.

In a recent study reanalyzing this original data set, Taylor and Donald (2003) found that mediators who were more strategic and consistent with their interventions were more able to reduce uncertainty (from an interactional perspective). This result is consistent with

Donohue's (1991) finding that mediators who intervened more regularly and held on to those interventions were more likely to secure agreements. Combined with the Jones (1988) phase structure observations that structure is needed to move parties in more productive directions, it seems clear that strategy and consistency are key traits of effective divorce mediators.

Mediation effectiveness. In addition to these communication-focused articles, others address the issue of mediation effectiveness. For example, Jones and Bodtker (1999) conducted a study of 169 mediated cases and 61 non-mediated cases from a County Court Custody Mediation Program focusing on incidences of agreement, long-term maintenance of agreement, disputant satisfaction with process and outcome, and rates of relitigation or recidivism in mediated and non-mediated custody cases. They found that mediated cases had high rates of agreement and high rates of agreement maintenance, that disputants in mediated cases were more satisfied than disputants in non-mediated cases, and that mediated cases demonstrated lower incidents of relitigation or recidivism than non-mediated cases. However, in terms of relitigation, the data revealed that mediated cases had more general involvement with the court than non-mediated cases, although once mediation occurred there was a significant drop in relitigation.

Yet, not all studies seem to give mediation a passing grade in terms of its ability to attenuate parental conflict following mediation. In a recent article focusing on parental cooperation after divorce, Toews and McKenry (2001) surveyed divorced parents to test a model predicting parental cooperation and conflict. The predictor variables included participation in a divorce education program, participation in divorce mediation, child custody arrangement (sole vs. joint legal), and means of terminating the marital relationship (dissolution vs. divorce). Socioeconomic status and gender were statistically controlled in this study. The analyses revealed that participation in a divorce education program was related negatively to conflict with one's former spouse, whereas mediation was related positively to parental conflict after divorce. Joint custody was related positively to parental cooperation, and conflict was related negatively to parental cooperation after divorce.

In another study aimed at understanding the long-term effects of divorce mediation in the resolution of child custody disputes, Dillon and Emery (1996) surveyed divorced parents who either used or did not use mediation to deal with their custody issues after 9 years post-settlement. The results indicated that non-custodial parents who used mediation reported more frequent current contact with their children and greater involvement in current decisions about them.

To determine whether divorcing spouses experience more positive family reorganization following mediation, Mathis and Yingling (1992) tested divorcing couples before and after child custody/visitation mediation, using the Family Satisfaction Scale. The pretest family satisfaction scores of husbands as a group were significantly lower than those of the wives, but significantly improved after mediation. The family satisfaction of wives as a group did not change. Within-couple differences in family satisfaction did not change for either spousal group before and after mediation, an indication that an improvement in the family satisfaction of the husband is not necessarily at the expense of the wife.

Community Mediation

Brief history. According to Roehl and Cook (1989), the largest and best-known community mediation program in the United States is the San Francisco Community Boards Program, which began in 1977 and operates outside the court system to help neighborhoods manage their own disputes. Since that time, these programs have expanded substantially. According to the National Association for Community Mediation, there are more than 550 community programs operating in the United States, with more than 20,000 mediators. Many states fund (often through court fees) a statewide program offering community mediation services to all citizens. For example, the Michigan program has about 30 different offices scattered around the state covering all 83 counties. The programs specialize in small claims court disputes, but often handle neighbor-neighbor disputes, as well (for more detail on community mediation, see Barge, Chapter 19 in this volume).

Relevant research. Perhaps the most comprehensive community mediation evaluation program was conducted by Pruitt, Carnevale, and their associates (McGillicuddy et al., 1987; Carnevale et al., 1989). In addition to the experimental research indicating that mediators select strategies based on their perceptions of common ground and concern for disputants' aspirations, this research also sought to determine which community mediation model was most effective in securing disputant cooperation and satisfying outcomes. As indicated above, it appears that the mediation-arbitration option, in which the mediator has the option of becoming an arbitrator if the disputants end mediation in an impasse, is the most effective model. The authors speculated that it performed best because disputants were motivated to be more responsible and constructive with their comments under the threat of arbitration.

Another interesting community mediation program that has received a great deal of attention regarding the resolution of interpersonal disputes is the series of studies conducted by Jim Wall and his colleagues. In a study of mediation in the People's Republic of China, Wall and Blum (1991) described a system in which mediators were integrated informally into the fabric of urban life and were used frequently in informal settings to deal with a variety of interpersonal disputes. In a study of Malaysian community mediation, Wall and Callister (1999) found a similar pattern in which mediation was woven into the spiritual and religious fabric of the community. Mediators were often religious imams who relied on prayer, moral principles, listening, and third-party advice and called less often for concessions.

In a study of the influence of culture on negotiator behavior, Adair (2003) conducted an interesting study to determine whether high-context cultures (the information needed to interpret the message is found in the context) prefer different integrative strategies than negotiators from low-context cultures (in which the information needed to interpret the message is found in the message itself). Based on her coding of experimental negotiation interactions, Adair found that low-context negotiators rely primarily on explicit verbal messages while high-context negotiators are more skilled in inferring meaning from the context and more likely to be ambiguous when communicating, a result consistent with other studies focusing on culture and conflict. For mediators, the implication of this finding is that when mediators are interacting with clients from high-context cultures, they must be ready to slow down and check meanings with clients to avoid confusion.

In addition to dealing with the fairly typical interpersonal issues that often confront neighbors, some mediation programs deal with very difficult issues such as domestic violence. In a study of 30 community mediation sessions focusing on violence issues, Cobb (1997) used a narrative mediation perspective to focus on the kinds of violence stories that disputants used to describe the conflicts. She found that episodes of violence in these stories often become "domesticated," or tamed, as individuals learn to objectify pain, become accustomed to the loss of voice or control over their situation, and learn to eliminate or live with the pain.

Mediation effectiveness. Based on these studies it is clear that community mediation is growing quite extensively. Many states now offer programs either statewide (e.g., Michigan) or in major metropolitan areas (e.g., Ohio). It is used to address a wide variety of conflicts and services from victim-offender mediation (see below) to small claims issues that come from court referrals, to neighborhood conflicts, to school bullying education programs. A quick Internet search reveals thousands of organizations, some of which are funded by the court systems and others that are funded through other government and private resources. This proliferation suggests that these programs are becoming more popular in addressing the kinds of lower-level disputes that can often clog court systems.

Peer Mediation

Brief history. One of the most rapidly growing mediation contexts focuses on dealing with interpersonal disputes in school contexts through peer mediation in which students mediate disputes between other students. The mediation models differ by grade, with the programs at the middle and high school levels functioning at a more formal level with a designated area for discussion. The elementary programs are typically conducted on the playground at recess, or in some cases at a "peace table" in the classroom (for more detail on peer mediation, see Jones, Chapter 9 in this volume).

Relevant research. In a review of selected school-based conflict resolution and peer mediation programs in Florida, Maryland, Missouri, and North Carolina, Powell, Muir-McLain, and Halasyamani (1995) found that programs were somewhat effective in reducing such markers of violence as discipline referrals and reports of violent incidents in the schools. Typically, student mediators receive continuous training in mediation techniques, and members of the general student body are informed about the process and how to access it. Teachers and administrators often refer students to these sessions. In a more recent study, Smith, Daunic, Miller, and Robinson (2002) confirmed these findings in an analysis of peer mediation programs in three middle schools. They found that the process was effective in reducing incidents at these schools, as well.

Mediation effectiveness. One of the most significant challenges facing peer mediators is the issue of training and experience. In a study of peer mediator communication strategies in a high school setting, Hale and Nix (1997) found that mediators had a great deal of difficulty remaining neutral in disputes, given that peers are likely to know disputants. In addition, the authors found that mediators often silence disputants' stories or concerns or press them for specific outcomes. The authors recommend additional training for mediators to avoid problems associated with appearing biased or unresponsive to disputants' issues.

Victim-Offender Mediation

Brief history. A growing area of mediation that contrasts considerably with most other forms is victim-offender mediation (VOM). In all other mediation contexts the disputants are not meeting in response to criminal activity in which one party has committed an illegal act. In these sessions, however, the victim and the offender meet to discuss the crime, its impact on the victim,

and decide what kind of restitution is appropriate for the crime that has been committed. As Umbreit and Greenwood (1999) noted, in the 1970s there were only a handful of these programs in the United States. Now states boast hundreds of programs in response to the need to have greater involvement in youth development issues.

Relevant research. In a review of these programs, Umbreit and Greenwood (1999) indicated that an increasing number of them are being initiated by probation departments to deal with first-offender, relatively minor youth crimes such as vandalism. In fact, this type of program is very popular throughout Europe, New Zealand, and South Africa, as well as in the United States. Sometimes more serious crimes are mediated as well. The goal of the VOM program is to create a form of restitution that is more meaningful and impactful for the offender to deter this individual from future criminal activity.

For this process to work, the courts need an unequivocal confession of guilt by the offender. Further, this form of mediation appears to work best when both parties agree to the process, as is typically the case in mediation. Yet, it appears that may courts use the process even when the offender is unwilling to mediate with the victim driving the process. It also works best when the mediators have appropriate training. Specifically, according to Umbreit and Greenwood (1999), role play is a very important part of the mediation process since it helps in building recognition of the crime's impact for the offender. Also, this process can elicit very powerful emotions that are often equivalent to a therapy session, and mediators must be willing and able to process these feelings.

According to Wyrick and Costanzo (1999), one of the most significant challenges facing VOM is increasing client participation in the process. Their research indicates that client participation varies with the type of offense and the amount of time elapsed between the offense and the case referral. The shorter the time needed to process the property cases and the longer the delays in processing personal offense cases, the more likely it is that victims will participate in the process.

Mediation effectiveness. In an updated report on this process, van Wormer (2003) discovered that VOM is fast becoming the most common restorative justice program in the United States, with restitution and community service as the most widely used sanctions. Such programs are proliferating nationally and internationally; there are approximately 320 victim-offender mediation programs in the United States and Canada and more than 700 operating in Europe. Van Wormer reported that this form of mediation is more likely than traditional forms of dispute resolution to give effective voice to those who are traditionally disadvantaged. In Vermont, where the restorative justice model is used, preliminary studies show that over 80% of the more than 4,000 offenders who have gone through the mediation process have completed it successfully and that they are less likely to reoffend than those who go through probation.

Despite these advantages, the process has come under some criticism by those concerned about its impact on the offenders. In an analysis of several cases, Arrigo and Schehr (1998) demonstrated how VOM discourse advertently or inadvertently marginalizes juveniles by often failing to receive a full hearing of the offenders' issues. Therefore, as a policy matter, the authors argued that the goals of restorative justice should strive to achieve a more humane dialogue by advancing the transformative themes of restoration and reconciliation.

Environmental Mediation

Brief history. Environmental mediation is included in a chapter focusing on interpersonal dispute resolution because many environmental disputes are often quite personal and can often involve neighborhood water or air quality issues (Kabasek & Silverman, 1988). A typical example of an environmental dispute is an air quality issue that might involve an industrial plant or agricultural processing facility near a residential area. The rationale for mediation involves getting both parties to the table quickly to avoid expensive litigation surrounding the issue. Environmental mediation is also used in major industrial waste contexts between corporations and governmental entities charged with preserving water and air quality (for more detail

on environmental conflict, see Peterson & Franks, Chapter 15 in this volume).

Relevant research. In an early study of mediation's effectiveness, Kabasek and Silverman (1988) found that between 1974 and 1984, agreements were reached in 78% of the 133 cases they examined where the purpose of the mediation was a settlement agreement. Arguments in support of mediation as a dispute resolution alternative include its general effectiveness in reaching agreement, court overload relief, and low cost. However, they also note that problems may include the inability to protect environmental interests, the lack of possible compromise in some disputes, and inconsistent outcomes.

In another review of environmental mediation, Fiorino (1988) assessed the progress of four of the seven major cases that the Environmental Protection Agency (EPA) conducted using the regulatory negotiation process, which involves the use of mediation in advance of any dispute. Regulatory negotiation involves bringing representatives of affected interests together to reach a consensus on the content of a proposed policy. It differs from other forms of environmental mediation in two ways. First, the controversies that negotiated rule making attempts to resolve have broad applicability. Second, its purpose is to define general rules that will influence behavior rather than resolve specific disputes. The U.S. Environmental Protection Agency (EPA) began its Regulatory Negotiation Project in 1983 and has conducted several negotiations. In negotiation, the administrative agency acts as the theoretical equal of the other parties, and a decision is not made until the affected parties consent to it. The EPA's experience suggests that regulatory negotiation, within limits and with procedural safeguards, can yield rules that are superior policy products, are based on better information, and are more likely to reflect the preferences of affected groups.

Mediation effectiveness. Fiorino (1988) indicated that negotiation offers a number of advantages over the conventional rule-making process, including the parties' access to practical information that can be considered as it is needed and the opportunity to educate potential opponents and persuade them that adopting a particular provision will not harm their interests, and the ability to rank and trade off positions. To make it more effective, procedural safeguards need to be in place to ensure that parties' interests and the momentum of the process do not usurp environmental preservation.

Given these advantages, Sipe (1998) argued that the use of mediation for resolving environmental disputes has grown rapidly over the past several decades. Sipe attributed much of this growth to claims made by advocates of the mediation process that it is superior to litigation and administrative hearings for the resolution of public policy disputes. Sipe suggested, however, that there has been little empirical research to test the effectiveness of mediation over the more traditional approach of litigation. In a 5-year study of the Florida Department of Environmental Protection, Sipe's data supported the claim that mediated cases settle more frequently than do cases that use traditional legal and administrative methods (84% for mediation vs. 63% for non-mediated cases). In contrast, the claim that mediated disputes result in higher rates of compliance and implementation is not supported by the data and the model.

In a further examination of mediation/ negotiation effectiveness in an environmental context, Langbein and Kerwin (2000) surveyed participants in eight negotiated rule makings at the EPA and in six comparable conventional EPA rule makings. The authors found that, when the rule is negotiated, there is a greater satisfaction with the substance of the final rule and with the overall process. Participants in the negotiated rules also learn more, but they face higher costs. However, the level of litigation between negotiated and non-negotiated cases was about the same, leaving the authors to question the efficiency and equity of the negotiated process.

In another critique, Langbein (2002) compared negotiated and conventional rule-making processes at the EPA with respect to both responsiveness and equality. The results indicated that negotiating rules appears more responsive to concerns than the conventional rule-writing process, and that outcomes of negotiated rules may be more unequal (favor one side over another) than outcomes of conventionally written rules.

Peacekeeping Mediation

Brief history. Finally, an area that has become increasingly important is peacekeeping mediation. Wall, Stark, and Standifer (2001) defined this area as providing assistance to interacting parties in managing their conflict without any authority to impose an outcome. Many nations provide peacekeeping resources, usually in the form of troops that are stationed in a particular region to prevent local violence from spreading while viable governments have time to become established and take over their own policing efforts. These peacekeepers often do not speak the language and must either work without translators in managing local disputes, or partner with local resources to accomplish their missions. Perhaps the hallmark of this activity, and the reason it is included in this chapter on interpersonal mediation, is that the activity is both highly interpersonal and highly diverse. The peacekeepers generally get involved in a wide variety of activities, working very closely with local groups. A similar role in the United States is the community policing movement, in which officers get to know locals, manage small disputes between neighbors, and work to prevent crime by developing interpersonal relations with neighbors (for more detail on peacekeeping and peacebuilding, see Broome & Jakobsson Hatay, Chapter 23 in this volume).

Relevant research. Diehl, Druckman, and Wall (1998) provided a taxonomy of the different ways in which peacekeepers mediate. Unlike other forms of mediation, the diversity of the roles that peacekeepers might assume is emphasized. At times peacekeepers might become principals in a conflict as they implement policies, for example, to restrict movement through a particular area. At times they might focus on the causes of the conflict while at other times they might simply attempt to keep local parties from escalating a conflict into violence.

This diversity in role and in facing a number of kinds of conflicts without speaking the native language poses special challenges to the peacekeepers. In fact, Diehl et al. (1998) identified 12 categories of peacekeeping that range from simply observing (e.g., a cease-fire), to collective enforcement, to election supervision, to humanitarian assistance, to arms control verification, and more. Peacekeepers may, in fact, spend little time as neutral third parties engaged in direct facilitation of a conflict, yet their goals might be shared by other mediators who, more broadly, want to assist parties in managing their disputes. In a recent study of peacekeeper mediation practices, Wall and Druckman (2003) found that dispute severity has a strong effect on the peacekeepers' choice of techniques. When disputes are more severe, the mediators prefer to rely on gathering information and meeting separately with disputants. They are also likely to bring in an additional third party who can play a positive role in the dispute.

Mediation effectiveness. What we discover from the peacekeepers as mediators is that mediators must learn to adapt their styles and strategies to the nature of the dispute. Unlike in other contexts that are fairly well defined, peacekeepers must be able to switch gears rapidly as the parameters of the conflicts change. Several lessons emerge. The first and perhaps most important lesson is that mediators must be aware of the full range of resources available to address a conflict. All mediators face surprises as they move through a dispute. When mediators are aware of the full range of resources available to address a dispute, they become much more effective in either processing it or referring it out to others who can provide different perspectives on the dispute. The second issue is commitment. For mediators to be fully effective they must be willing to drill down into a conflict and move it along productively. All the different theoretical perspectives—narrative, transformative, and interaction management approaches—emphasize the need to probe intensively to move closer to the key drivers of the dysfunctional conflict and craft solutions that address these drivers. The third issue is flexibility. Mediators must know how to shift their language, strategies, and resources to approach a problem productively. They must take the time to understand fully what is happening and how best to craft the role that will be most productive. Thus, the peacekeeping role is a very useful context in which to understand the full range of mediation challenges.

THE PROMISE OF MEDIATION

Mediation is used in many contexts other than those mentioned in this review that are less focused on managing interpersonal relationships, such as international relations, medical risk management, real estate disputes, and the like. However, this review confirms findings in these other fields that mediation is fairly effective in assisting parties to reach agreement about issues dividing them. This general conclusion, based on decades of research on this topic, suggests that the promise of mediation has been somewhat fulfilled as a tool to address interpersonal conflict. With some important limitations mentioned in the research, mediators who are well trained in creating and facilitating a fair process that affords full issue disclosure and adequate time are effective in managing disputes that parties themselves have been unsuccessful in managing.

Yet, it is uncertain why this process is effective theoretically. The mediation theories reviewed above offer different insights into how the process drives agreement. For example, the basic idea of the narrative mediation is that deconstructing individuals' stories empowers them to see the complexity of their dispute and create options for managing it. Similarly, the transformative approach contends that the breakthrough energy contributing to mediation success is the transformation of the relationship between parties brought about by increased recognition of the impact of the dispute on the other party. Increased insight builds relational currency and encourages individuals to be more receptive to solutions.

In contrast, the other theories are more mediator centered. The strategic choice model contends that mediators must be concerned about parties' aspirations and must have a strong sense of what the common ground is that might link disputants. These insights drive a mediator's ability to direct parties toward more integrative solutions. The interaction management model also focuses on mediators, but less on their aspirations and perceptions and more on their communicative competence skills. If mediators can manage disputants' content, relational, and strategic interaction choices, they can assist disputants in building an agreement.

Perhaps there is a more fundamental process driving the ability and willingness of disputants to enter an integrative zone and a more fundamental element or process mediators must manage in helping them enter that zone than those detailed in these theories. In other words, why does relational enhancement move individuals toward agreement? What fundamental process is at work in making this transition? The final section of this chapter proposes that the fundamental process at work explaining why mediation often functions successfully is relational paradox. This process emerges through relational order theory, which is reviewed next.

Relational Order Theory

In a set of papers, Donohue and Roberto (1993), Donohue (2001), and Donohue and Hoobler (2002) outlined a theory to account for the dynamic evolution of relationships in conflict. Based on Strauss's (1978) negotiated order theory, relational order theory (ROT) contends that disputants continuously create and tacitly negotiate relational limits that serve to constrain the substantive negotiation process. In other words, as parties mediate they send relational messages to one another about how much they like and trust one another and whether or not they feel their status is higher, lower, or equal status to that of the other party. Each set of relational messages, or relational frame, both responds to the prior relational frame and proposes its own relational frame. This process evolves into a relational negotiation with proposals and counter-proposals until parties either settle on a consistent relational frame (e.g., parties both like and trust one another and assume equal status) or fail to reach an underlying consensus, which ultimately restricts their ability to find common ground on substantive issues (Donohue & Roberto, 1993).

This theoretical perspective is similar to Baxter's (1990) and Baxter and Montgomery's (1996) relational dialectics theory (RDT). That theory contends that parties negotiate a set of contradictions in managing their relationship. The contradictions include autonomy-connection and openness-closedness. Each relationship, whether it is intimate or friendship-based, must continuously manage these parameters as it

grows and changes (Rawlins, 1989, 1992). Recent research (Hoppe-Nagao & Ting-Toomey, 2002; Meyer, 2003) using the theory finds that parties use a variety of communication strategies to manage each of these dialectics. The key difference between RDT and ROT is that ROT focuses on how parties use various relational strategies to build relational frames and then use these frames to accomplish their substantive objectives. Yet, both theories also recognize that parties continuously negotiate their relationships as they communicate.

ROT contends that whenever people interact to create their frames they negotiate two key issues: *interdependence*, or how parties influence or control one another, and *affiliation*, or how parties express warmth, friendliness, intimacy, respect, trust, and cooperation toward one another. The interdependence dimension focuses on how extensively parties can influence or control one another in the context of the relationship between them (Boulding, 1990). If they engage each other frequently, share intimacy, and the like, then they are highly interdependent and able to influence one another quite extensively. The affiliation dimension, on the other hand, focuses on how parties exchange expressions of approval, liking, and trust. For example, when parties argue extensively (perhaps over dialectical issues such as openness or autonomy), they typically show disapproval, dislike, and mistrust. Notice the messages of disapproval, dislike, and mistrust in the following exchange from the segment above:

Wife: I said when I get the money. I'm still on ADC and if you would pay the installation I would get a phone.

Husband: There's just a bunch of problems with the environment you've chosen to live in.

One can almost see the scowling looks on their faces as they accuse each other of various misdeeds. In addition, notice how the parties are also expressing their interdependence here. The wife is trying to enforce prior obligations and the husband is trying to influence the wife to move. Clearly we have high interdependence and low affiliation in this exchange.

High Affiliation	Conditional Peace	Unconditional Peace
Low Affiliation	Isolationist Peace	Competition/Aggression
	Low Interdependence	High Interdependence

Figure 8.1   Relational Conditions

ROT positions interdependence and affiliation in relation to one another to define four relational frames, or contextual orientations, that negotiators create as they continually define and redefine the limits of affiliation and interdependence. These four relational frames are listed in Figure 8.1. It is important to notice that they define three kinds of peace, or conditions under which people can problem solve productively, and one condition that creates barriers to problem solving.

Unconditional peace. When parties communicate using expressions of high affiliation and interdependence, they are proposing a highly cooperative relationship. This combination challenges parties to honor their role obligations over individual rights. The focus on obligations invests parties in the needs of the relationship over the needs of the individuals. In this sense, the relationship is unconditional. Parties express mutual liking, so they accept their obligations for the sake of solidifying the relationship while paying little attention to their individual rights that might upset the relationship. Since the relationship is the focus of the interactions—not other, related issues like identity or trust— parties are free to concentrate on exchanging information, pressing proposals, offering concessions, and so forth, to create a mostly issues- or task-focused exchange. To illustrate, consider the following exchange:

Husband: I apologize. I can see now how difficult your situation is and how much support you need. You've been through a great deal and you've done the best you can. Let's figure this out and make it work.

Wife: I really appreciate your saying that. It has been tough for me, but it's also been difficult for you, too. Let's face it; we need to work together on this.

The husband is highly supportive, emphasizing his obligation to work through these problems and is proposing even greater interdependence. The wife reciprocates these moves and establishes an Unconditional frame.

Isolationist peace. When parties communicate with low levels of both affiliation and interdependence, they send isolationist messages. Parties seek to reduce their ties, push away from one another, and isolate themselves from the relationship. This is an Isolationist Peace in the sense that parties are not fighting, but they are not moving forward productively with their substantive agenda. Perhaps they both might need time to recover from some incident with the other party. Or, they might need to isolate themselves for a while to save face. Nevertheless, the goal in this condition is to create distance from role obligations, and perhaps create new role frameworks to restructure or terminate the relationship. Interaction in this condition might consist of superficial and less frequent information exchange simply to keep up appearances of adhering to old role prescriptions. Or, parties might try to distribute messages supporting their own face to maintain their credibility while they are trying to withdraw from the relationship. Unconditional Peace emphasizes constructive processes, while Isolationist Peace emphasizes withdrawal.

In the interaction sequence above in which the wife is complaining that her husband failed to pay for her phone and he responded by complaining about her living environment, the mediator was faced with the need to isolate the parties from one another. The move would involve stopping the interaction and defining and exploring each of these issues from both sides' perspectives. By allowing the parties to continue, the mediator does not contribute to a frame switch, which is needed at that moment to help the parties regroup.

Neither of these two frames is relationally paradoxical for disputants. When parties communicate in Unconditional Peace, their desire for increased interdependence is matched by their desire for increased affiliation. When they communicate using an Isolationist Peace perspective, a similar match occurs in the opposite direction; that is, parties seek to separate by decreasing both their interdependence and affiliation. Thus, communication in these two conditions is least likely to exhibit equivocal qualities. Successfully moving toward or away from someone is most easily accomplished by clearly revealing intentions to do so.

Conditional peace. In this condition of low interdependence and high affiliation, parties exchange messages that seek to retain their role autonomy, yet demonstrate approval and positive affect for one another. They assert few rights because they are not sufficiently interdependent to demand much. Yet, they remain friendly and polite, generally as an attempt to adhere to socially acceptable norms of interaction. For example, mediators have some sense of increased trust when parties start to signal some willingness to cooperate, as in the following utterance:

Wife: I am still concerned about the communication issue, but I'm willing to discuss it.

This utterance proposes a conditional frame because she is expressing some trust and, in a sense, testing the husband's interest in becoming more interdependent through the act of discussing the issue. She does not direct the husband to talk about it or assume that he wants to. She is being tentative, but trying to move forward. In this frame, individuals send increasing signals toward a desire to encumber the role obligations associated with increased interdependence, but their commitment is conditional on the other's acceptance, and thus a bit tentative. This conditional acceptance is stripped away in Unconditional Peace. In Unconditional Peace, parties have made the commitment to remain highly involved with one another and encumber those role expectations. However, in both Conditional and Unconditional Peace, the relationship is generally secondary to the substantive agenda. Under both conditions, parties generally bargain constructively in good faith.

This condition can be labeled the *cooperative paradox* because parties move in inconsistent directions at the same time. On the one hand, parties communicate a desire to increase attraction while, at the same time, remaining timid about increasing interdependence. This paradox is cooperative in the sense that it sets the stage for Unconditional Peace by providing a rationale for becoming more interdependent. However, this condition still provides some tension, albeit interesting and provocative, about the direction of the relationship.

Competition/Aggression. In this final frame, parties send unaffiliative and disapproving messages in the context of relational interdependence. The focus moves away from group or dyadic priorities and toward parties' asserting their rights aimed at achieving their own goals, while also resisting their group/alliance obligations. Since the focus is on asserting rights and resisting obligations, the communication carries almost a moral imperative and authority with it. Parties must resist with all their resources because key, central, and defining rights have been violated. This is the kind of communication that parties display during heated mediation periods or just at the onset of a deadlock.

For example, the wife and husband exchange above in which both are complaining to one another illustrates the moral imperative that often accompanies this exchange. Both are claiming their rights remain unfulfilled, and both invoke moral values. Specifically, the wife pleads for a follow-through on a prior commitment, and the husband demands a better living environment. They are facing each other toe to toe, and the mediator allows the parties to perpetuate the frame.

This condition can be labeled the *competitive paradox* because parties must move in opposite directions at the same time. To defeat their "enemy," parties must pull the opponent closer both physically and psychologically by initiating communication or aggression while also pushing the opponent away in a show of negative attraction. When parties are in this condition, they communicate the tacit message, "I want you closer to me so I can push you away." This paradox is inherently disabling since it feeds on itself. The closer the parties pull themselves together, the more they strive to push each other away, and the more frustrated and emotionally engaged they become. As in therapy, third parties are often needed to reveal both the presence of the disabling paradox and strategies for confronting it.

The Fundamental Challenge in Mediation: Resolving the Relational Paradoxes

Perhaps the most fundamental challenge for disputants and mediators is managing these paradoxes. This is a difficult task because parties come to mediation locked in the competitive paradox of a highly interdependent state with decreased affiliation resulting from years of mistrust, anger, and depression. This condition brings parties to mediation (a personal failure to manage disputes themselves) and marks the transition away from problem solving toward relational decay. As a result, parties must find a transition out of this paradoxical condition into a non-paradoxical condition.

In the case of the competitive paradox, the narrative and transformative approaches offer key strategies. Both of these perspectives ask disputants to change their frame about the conflict. In a sense, the mediator uses stories to help each party see the paradoxes or boxes he or she has erected as a result of the conflict and to develop strategies for resolving them.

In the visitation example presented earlier, the parties appear to be locked in two paradoxes that the mediator does little to relieve; in fact, the mediator allows the parties to stay locked in them. The first paradox deals with the substantive issue of visitation. The wife's communication problems coupled with the husband's ability to go over to the house for physical visitation places the parties in a difficult situation. The second paradox is clearly relational, as outlined in ROT. Both parents are highly interdependent with one another since they both are actively involved in raising the child and in the whole issue of coordinating the visits. Yet, the lack of trust demonstrated between the parties and the negative affect persists, thereby placing them in a relational paradox. Unfortunately, the mediator does little to relieve the substantive paradox and then facilitates the parties' staying in the second relational paradox by not building

on the apology that the wife offered and using it to address both the communication issue and the affiliation issue.

If the mediator had successfully altered the direction of the mediation to take advantage of the wife's apology and addressed both issues, then that kind of problem solving and positive exchange is more likely to become routine for the parties during the session and a step toward more integrative problem solving. By encouraging disputants to stay in this non-paradoxical mode for sufficient time to exchange ideas, the mediator can begin such affiliation-building activities as reaching agreements on minor points, and asking parties to reflect on positive outcomes of their relationship such as their children's well-being. This shift away from an isolationist frame begins to direct the parties toward the cooperative paradox, which encourages them to redefine their relationship and begin to create different forms of interdependence that will prove more manageable for them. Mediated agreements often seek to capture this redefined interdependence by forging very specific visitation and custody rules for parties to follow. It is hoped that with some measure of increased trust and affiliation, parties can adhere to these rules, redefine their relationship, and move on with their lives.

Each of the major approaches to mediation provides a different strategy for managing the relational paradoxes. The narrative approach focuses on stories to reveal and process the paradox. The transformative approach deals directly with the relationship between the parties and seeks to explore it in detail. The strategic choice model tries to identify the appropriate strategy or mediator approach in processing issues that lock individuals in a paradox. The interaction management approach uses more of a communication code approach by structuring the linguistic context both to model appropriate behavior and to restructure disputant interaction practices.

CONCLUSIONS

Lessons Learned

Research in mediation has yielded some important observations about managing interpersonal conflict. First, we have a fairly strong understanding of the scope and practice of mediation across its many contexts. It has become highly institutionalized in many important settings, and its value and diversity have been well documented in a number of studies. Second, we know that mediation generally affords better outcomes than other forms of dispute management that do not force the parties to confront the issues dividing them. For example, adjudication or arbitration avoids any real exchange between parties about the foundations of their dispute. Rather, it focuses on the third party's evaluation of the equity of the final solutions. Third, mediation provides a very large and clear window into understanding fundamental communication issues. Research has done an excellent job of revealing communication patterns that contribute to more and less successful outcomes. As a result, we have learned a great deal about communication's capabilities and limits.

Yet, research has generally stumbled in testing compelling theoretical explanations for mediation success. If mediation is really all about managing relational paradox, then this explanation deserves greater inquiry. ROT argues that moving out of the competitive paradox can be accomplished only if both parties use the synchronous relational frames to do so. If mediators can help parties build a frame consensus, regardless of its content, parties can establish a relational foundation for discussing their substantive issues. Propositions such as these should be tested to determine the kinds of fundamental principals at work in mediation. What work is the mediator really doing, and how can that work be expanded across contexts? These are questions for future research.

Practitioner Best Practices

I have conducted many mediation and negotiation training programs over the years and have been involved in developing many mediation programs around the country. In my observations, I have noticed some best practices that can assist both program directors and practicing mediators. First, most programs are not very effective at training mediators. In many of the cases I have observed, mediators allow disputants to walk all over them and continue to engage in highly dysfunctional communication. Mediators often fail to identify key issues and break them into smaller pieces, and they often let one party drive the agenda. Any of the perspectives identified in this review argues against this kind of inactive strategy. It continues to lock participants in a competitive paradox, it prevents the development of integrative strategies, and it certainly does not promote recognition or empowerment. Many mediators become overwhelmed by the negative energy that flows freely during many mediation sessions, and many mediators find it very difficult to deal successfully with that stress while trying to process the issues.

Second, mediation programs need more evaluation. Program managers must first evaluate mediators and their ability to perform competently. Do they have the knowledge, skills, and values to be successful? There are no standard mediation assessment tools available, but they are needed. Developing these tools would require a consensus about what effective mediation entails. There is probably substantial agreement about this issue around the edges, but mediators are very zealous about their own perspectives, something that often prevents this kind of consensus. Some of these issues could be resolved if mediation processes were evaluated more extensively. Which strategies are most effective, and what does it mean to be effective? A national consensus about these issues is needed to provide more powerful understanding of how well mediation programs are progressing.

Third, mediation is all about justice, and a big part of justice is appearance. One of the most significant barriers to justice, in my view, is allowing for only one mediator in a particular session. Some divorce mediation courts mandate a co-mediation model in which both a male and a female mediator work through the issues for both parties. However, limited resources in courts and community programs often prevent this kind of model. Co-mediation is probably needed less in small-claims disputes in which relational issues are less salient. When parties enter mediation with a long history of dysfunctional communication, large stakes, and emotional despair, however, a co-mediation model might be most effective.

Mediation has a great future. It is building rapidly. Many courts are formalizing rules about when and how mediation can be used for more traditionally adjudicated cases. Taking mediation to the next level will probably require treating it as a professional activity with proper training and evaluation. It is my hope that these best practices can be implemented to realize the full power of this process.

REFERENCES

Adair, W. L. (2003). Integrative sequences and negotiation outcomes in same- and mixed-culture negotiations. *International Journal of Conflict Management, 14,* 273–296.

Arrigo, B. A., & Schehr, R. C. (1998). Restoring justice for juveniles: A critical analysis of victim-offender mediation. *Justice Quarterly, 15,* 629–647.

Baxter, L. A. (1990). Dialectical contradictions in relationship development. *Journal of Social and Personal Relationships, 7,* 69–88.

Baxter, L. A., & Montgomery, B. M. (1996). *Relating: Dialogues & dialectics.* New York: Guilford.

Berkovitch, J. (1999). Mediation and negotiation techniques. In L. Kurtz (Ed.), *Encyclopedia of violence, peace, and conflict* (pp. 410–412). New York: Academic Press.

Bernard, S., Folger, J. P., Weingarten, H., & Zumeta, Z. (1984). The neutral mediator: Value dilemmas in divorce mediation. *Mediation Quarterly, 4,* 61–74.

Boulding, K. E. (1990). *Three faces of power.* Newbury Park, CA: Sage.

Bush, R. A. B., & Folger, J. P. (1994). *The promise of mediation.* San Francisco: Jossey-Bass.

Carnevale, P. J. (1986). Strategic choice in mediation. *Negotiation Journal, 2,* 41–56.

Carnevale, P. J., & Leatherwood, M. L. (1985, August). *Mediation and the "chilling effect" of med-arb.* Paper presented at the annual convention of the American Psychological Association, Los Angeles.

Carnevale, P. J. D., Conlon, D. E., Hanisch, K. A., & Harris, K. L. (1989). Experimental research on the strategic-choice model of mediation. In K. Kressel & D. Pruitt (Eds.), *Mediation research* (pp. 344–357). San Francisco: Jossey-Bass.

Cobb, S. (1994). A narrative perspective on mediation: Toward the materialization of the "storytelling" metaphor. In J. Folger & T. Jones (Eds.), *New directions in mediation research* (pp. 48–66). Thousand Oaks, CA: Sage.

Cobb, S. (1997). The domestication of violence in mediation. *Law & Society Review, 31,* 397–441.

Diehl, P. L., Druckman, D., & Wall, J. (1998). International peacekeeping and conflict resolution: A taxonomic analysis with implications. *Journal of Conflict Resolution, 42,* 33–55.

Dillon, P. A., & Emery, R. E. (1996). Divorce mediation and resolution of child custody disputes: Long-term effects. *American Journal of Orthopsychiatry, 66,* 131–145.

Donohue, W. A. (1991). *Communication, marital dispute and divorce mediation.* Hillsdale, NJ: Lawrence Erlbaum.

Donohue, W. A. (2001). Resolving relational paradox: The language of conflict in relationships. In W. Eadie & P. Nelson (Eds.), *The language of conflict and resolution* (pp. 21–46). Thousand Oaks, CA: Sage.

Donohue, W. A., Allen, M., & Burrell, N. (1985). Mediator communicative competence. *Mediation Quarterly, 10,* 22–32.

Donohue, W. A., Drake, L., & Roberto, A. J. (1994). Mediator issue intervention strategies: A replication and some conclusions. *Mediation Quarterly, 11,* 261–274.

Donohue, W. A., & Hoobler, G. D. (2002). Relational frames and their ethical implications in international negotiation: An analysis based on the Oslo II negotiations. *International Negotiation, 7,* 143–167.

Donohue, W. A., & Roberto, A. J. (1993). Relational development as negotiated order in hostage negotiations. *Human Communication Research, 20,* 175–198.

Ferrick, G. (1986). Three crucial questions. *Mediation Quarterly, 13,* 61–68.

Fiorino, D. J. (1988). Regulatory negotiation as a policy process. *Public Administration Review, 48,* 764–772.

Folberg, J., & Milne, A. (1988). *Divorce mediation: Theory and practice.* New York: Guilford.

Girdner, L. K. (1985). Adjudication and mediation: A comparison of custody decision-making processes involving third parties. *Journal of Divorce, 8,* 33–45.

Gottman, J. (1979). *Marital interaction.* New York: Academic Press.

Hale, C. L., & Nix, C. (1997). Achieving neutrality and impartiality: The ultimate communication challenge for peer mediators. *Mediation Quarterly, 14,* 337–352.

Hoppe-Nagao, A., & Ting-Toomey, S. (2002). Relational dialectics and management strategies in marital couples. *Southern Communication Journal, 67,* 142–159.

Jones, T. S. (1987, June). *A test of the conceptual and empirical adequacy of the Mediation Process Analysis Instrument.* Paper presented to the International Conference on Conflict, George Mason University, Fairfax, VA.

Jones, T. S. (1988). An analysis of phase structures in successful and unsuccessful child custody divorce mediation. *Communication Research, 15,* 470–495.

Jones, T. S., & Bodtker, A. (1998). Satisfaction with custody mediation: Results from the York County Custody Mediation Program. *Mediation Quarterly, 16,* 185–200.

Jones, T. S., & Bodtker, A. (1999). Agreement, maintenance, satisfaction and relitigation in mediated and non-mediated custody cases: A research note. *Journal of Divorce & Remarriage, 32,* 17–28.

Kabasek, N., & Silverman, G. (1988). Environmental mediation and regulatory negotiation. *American Business Law Journal, 26,* 533–556.

Kelly, J. B., & Gigy, L. L. (1989). Divorce mediation: Characteristics of clients and outcomes. In K. Kressel & D. Pruitt (Eds.), *Mediation research* (pp. 263–283). San Francisco: Jossey-Bass.

Kimsey, W. D., Fuller, R. M., Bell, A. J., & McKinney, B. (1994). The impact of mediator strategic choices: An experimental study. *Mediation Quarterly, 12,* 89–97.

Kressel, K. (1985). *The process of divorce.* New York: Basic Books.

Kressel, K., & Pruitt, D. G. (1985). Themes in the mediation of social conflict. *Journal of Social Issues, 41,* 11–26.

Kressel, K., & Pruitt, D. G. (1989). *Mediation research.* San Francisco: Jossey-Bass.

Langbein, L. I. (2002). Responsive bureaus, equity, and regulatory negotiation: An empirical view. *Journal of Policy Analysis and Management, 21,* 449–465.

Langbein, L. I., & Kerwin, C. M. (2000). Regulatory negotiation versus conventional rule making: Claims, counterclaims, and empirical evidence. *Journal of Public Administration Research and Theory, 10,* 599–632.

Lewicki, R. J., Weiss, S. E., & Lewin, D. (1992). Models of conflict, negotiation and third party intervention: A review and synthesis. *Journal of Organizational Behavior, 13,* 209–252.

Manocherian, J. (1985). Family mediation: A descriptive case study. *Journal of Divorce, 8,* 97–114.

Mathis, R., & Yingling, L. C. (1992). Analysis of pre and posttest gender differences in family satisfaction of divorce mediation couples. *Journal of Divorce & Remarriage, 17,* 75–89.

McGillicuddy, N. B., Welton, G. L., & Pruitt, D. G. (1987). Third-party intervention: A field experiment comparing three different models. *Journal of Personality and Social Psychology, 53,* 104–112.

Meyer, M. D. E. (2003). "It's me. I'm it.": Defining adolescent sexual identity through relational dialectics in *Dawson's Creek. Communication Quarterly, 51,* 262–276.

Moore, C. W. (1996). *The mediation process: Practical strategies for resolving conflict.* San Francisco: Jossey-Bass.

Notarius, L., & Markman, H. (1993). *We can work it out: Making sense of marital conflict.* New York: Putnam.

Pearson, J., & Thoennes, N. (1985). The preliminary portrait of client reactions to three court mediation programs. *Conciliation Courts Review, 23,* 1–15.

Pearson, J., & Thoennes, N. (1989). Divorce mediation: Reflections on a decade of research. In K. Kressel & D. Pruitt (Eds.), *Mediation research* (pp. 9–30). San Francisco: Jossey-Bass.

Powell, K. E., Muir-McLain, L., & Halasyamani, L. (1995). A review of selected school-based conflict resolution and peer mediation projects. *Journal of School Health, 65,* 426–441.

Pruitt, D. G., & Rubin, J. Z. (1986). *Social conflict: Escalation, stalemate and settlement.* New York: Random House.

Rawlins, W. K. (1989). A dialectical analysis of the tensions, functions and strategic challenges of communication in young adult friendships. In J. A. Anderson (Ed.), *Communication yearbook 12* (pp. 157–189). Newbury Park, CA: Sage.

Rawlins, W. K. (1992). *Friendship matters.* New York: Aldine de Gruyter.

Roehl, J. A., & Cook, R. F. (1989). Mediation in interpersonal disputes: Effectiveness and limitations. In K. Kressel & D. Pruitt (Eds.), *Mediation research* (pp. 31–52). San Francisco: Jossey-Bass.

Sipe, N. G. (1998). An empirical analysis of environmental mediation. *Journal of the American Planning Association, 64,* 275–285.

Smith, S. W., Daunic, A. P., Miller, M. D., & Robinson, T. R. (2002). Conflict resolution and peer mediation in middle schools: Extending the process and outcome knowledge base. *Journal of Social Psychology, 42,* 567–587.

Strauss, A. (1978). *Negotiations: Varieties, contexts, processes, and social order.* San Francisco: Jossey-Bass.

Taylor, P. J., & Donald, I. (2003). Foundations and evidence for an interaction-based approach to conflict negotiation. *International Journal of Conflict Management, 14,* 213–232.

Toews, M. L., & McKenry, P. C. (2001). Court-related predictors of parental cooperation and conflict after divorce. *Journal of Divorce & Remarriage, 35,* 57–72.

Umbreit, M. S., & Greenwood, J. (1999). National survey of victim-offender mediation programs in the United States. *Mediation Quarterly, 16,* 253–268.

van Wormer, K. (2003). Restorative justice: A model for social work practice with families. *Families in Society, 84,* 441–448.

Wall, J. A., & Blum, M. E. (1991). Community mediation in the People's Republic of China. *Journal of Conflict Resolution, 35,* 3–20.

Wall, J. A., & Callister, R. R. (1999). Malaysian community mediation. *Journal of Conflict Resolution, 43,* 343–366.

Wall, J. A., & Druckman, D. (2003). Mediation in peacekeeping missions. *Journal of Conflict Resolution, 47,* 693–705.

Wall, J. A., & Lynn, A. (1993). Mediation: A current review. *Journal of Conflict Resolution, 37,* 160–194.

Wall, J. A., Stark, J. B., & Standifer, R. L. (2001). Mediation: A current review and theory development. *Journal of Conflict Resolution, 45,* 370–391.

Welton, G. L., & Pruitt, D. G. (1987). The mediation process: The effects of mediator bias and disputant power. *Personality and Social Psychology Bulletin, 13,* 123–133.

Winslade, J., & Monk, G. (2000). *Narrative mediation: A new approach to conflict resolution.* San Francisco: Jossey-Bass

Wyrick, P. A., & Costanzo, M. A. (1999). Predictors of client participation in victim-offender mediation. *Mediation Quarterly, 16,* 253–268.

PART II

ORGANIZATIONAL CONFLICT

Unresolved and poorly managed conflict in organizations is costly. One classic study estimated that managers spend 20% of their time managing conflicts (Thomas & Schmidt, 1976). Today, there is no reason to think that conflict is less prevalent than 30 years ago, and perhaps it is even more frequent because of a fast-paced and global marketplace. In addition, poorly managed conflict is expensive for organizations. One online resource allows an individual to estimate the indirect and direct costs of a conflict (Dana, 2005). The relevant cost factors include wasted time, reduced decision quality, loss of skilled employees, restructuring, sabotage/theft/damage, lowered job motivation, lost work time, and health costs. These factors do not even include the costs of litigation, which can run into millions of dollars (Thomas, 2005). For these reasons, and the potential benefits that conflict can produce, conflict has been a popular topic of research and practice in the workplace.

Research on organizational conflict focuses on two facets. First (and by far the most popular facet), organizational conflict occurs in a particular workplace setting. The conflict can include (but is not limited to) superiors/subordinates, be among members of a work team, and between individuals from different organizations (as in a joint venture). In this sense, research focuses on conflict within an organizational container (the physical and psychological boundaries of the workplace; Deetz, 2001). Authors of chapters in this section include perspectives consistent with the container perspective. Jones discusses

conflict education in schools. Poole and Garner review literature examining the impact of conflict on group performance and work outcomes (i.e., the instrumental perspective). Nicotera and Dorsey argue that the predominant approach to understanding conflict is a focus on factors that impact conflict styles in an organizational setting. Kirby, Wieland, and McBride identify work/life conflict from a multi-level perspective, but include the importance of organizational policies and effects. Finally, Lipsky and Seeber discuss the proliferation of conflict management systems in work organizations.

The second facet is that organizational conflict occurs in the process of organizing people toward a common goal. During the process of organizing, individuals have conflict as they coordinate and arrange work patterns and practices. This process is often identified as the constitutive feature of communication (and conflict) in organizations (Deetz, 2001). The authors also include this facet in their chapters, and several emphasize this perspective more than the container perspective. While Jones focuses on the container perspective, she also recognizes that there are a number of factors that shape conflict education in schools and that these factors need to be considered in the implementation of conflict education. Poole and Garner introduce two perspectives that emphasize developmental and political factors for conflict in workgroups; both of these perspectives emphasize the constitutive quality of conflict communication. Nicotera and Dorsey urge researchers to consider conflict perspectives and research methods that emphasize the constitutive feature of conflict, including contexts, networks, and discursive methods. Kirby et al. identify relational and macrosocial levels of analyses as factors in how work/life conflicts are created, shaped, and managed. Finally, Lipsky and Seeber emphasize the container perspective, but their focus on integrative conflict management systems illustrates how conflict management needs to be a "normal" part of the work process.

In considering the organization of these chapters, we utilized the organization as container perspective and grouped like containers together. The opening chapter examines conflict in schools; this is an organization that is not often studied by organizational conflict scholars, but is critical given the focus on training people to manage conflict constructively. Jones begins by explaining the problem of violence in schools and attributes a large part of the problem to the fact that students are not taught how to deal with conflict and how to create communities in which social aggression is not acceptable. In a way, she addresses the adage, "Everything I needed to know I learned in kindergarten" by explaining that teaching conflict resolution education (CRE) to schoolchildren is an effective way to teach constructive conflict management and reduce violence in schools and society. Jones has three goals in her chapter. First, she provides an overview of CRE, including the overarching goals of these programs, the distinction between CRE and other positive youth development efforts, and a summary of typical program models. Second, she reviews contemporary research on the efficacy of CRE programs, examining both program model and educational level. Finally, she addresses what is needed for successful institutionalization of CRE. Of particular interest are initiatives for developing programs targeting pre-service educators, creating and bolstering international networks of specialists in CRE, and obtaining critical descriptive information about the current use and mandates for CRE efforts.

We then shift to the traditional focus of organizational conflict by including four chapters about conflict in work organizations. In the second chapter, Poole and Garner examine conflict in workgroups, which are the basic building blocks of today's organizations. As the authors explain, workgroups are the units in which the work of the organization (e.g., planning, design, production, sales, service delivery, etc.) is done. Poole and Garner identify three scholarly traditions for the study of workgroup conflict. Each perspective has developed independently, and for the most part researchers within each do not acknowledge or cite one another. The instrumental perspective views workgroup conflict in terms of its effects on group performance and related outcomes. The developmental perspective views conflict as a natural part of workgroup processes; conflict is treated as a phase in a group's lifecycle that offers the group and its members an opportunity for growth. The political perspective views conflict as a struggle for power in the workgroup. Poole and Garner review and critique the literature in each of the traditions, noting the nature of conflict in workgroups, the sources or causes of workgroup conflict, and the effects of conflict in workgroups from each of these perspectives. They conclude their chapter by discussing potential intersections among the three perspectives.

In the third chapter, Nicotera and Dorsey review and critique the communication literature that addresses the day-to-day informal process of interpersonal conflict management as it occurs in the workplace. The authors provide a historical overview of fundamental conceptual and definitional issues and review how well scholars have attended to these issues over time. Nicotera and Dorsey then review and critique the broad literature on conflict styles in organizations, including an emphasis on the effects of culture, gender, organizational position, and personality on conflict styles. They critique the predominant literature for being reductionistic, individualistic, and managerial focused. The authors then follow with a consideration of "fruitful directions" that identify several contexts and perspectives deserving attention from organizational conflict scholars. Finally, the authors provide theoretic and methodological recommendations for future development and discuss the challenge of practical applications of this literature to organizational communication training and development.

In the fourth chapter, Kirby et al. review the extensive literature on "conflict" between working and family/personal life. They summarize interdisciplinary and communication research on work/life conflict using four levels of analysis. For the intrapersonal level, the authors describe the construct and detail its antecedents and consequences. For the relational level, they explore supervisory and co-worker relationships as well as family and personal relationships and their intersections with work/life conflict. For the organizational level, they describe work/life policies, review their effects, and highlight the importance of organizational support in implementation. For the macrosocietal level, they discuss how economic/political and historical/cultural systems shape work/life practices. They take a structurational view, theorizing not only within levels but across levels on the premise that individual action is constitutive in (re)producing systems and structures that create work/life conflict, and yet at the same time, structures influence how individuals experience and communicate about work/life conflict.

In the final chapter, Lipsky and Seeber review the literature on the management of organizational conflicts, focusing particularly on the recent development of workplace conflict management systems by major U.S. corporations and government agencies. Beginning especially in the 1970s, a growing number of employers, concerned about the rising costs of employment litigation, began to use mediation, arbitration, and other so-called alternative dispute resolution (ADR) techniques to resolve employment disputes. By the 1990s, a growing number of organizations were moving beyond the use of ADR techniques and adopting conflict management systems. Using a system is a more comprehensive and proactive strategy for managing workplace conflict than the use of ADR. The authors discuss the various characteristics of workplace conflict management systems and assess the research on the effectiveness of the systems approach for managing organizational conflicts.

References

Dana, D. (2005). *The Dana Measure of Financial Cost of Organizational Conflict.* Retrieved April 14, 2005, from the Mediation Training Institute International Web site, http://www.mediationworks.com

Deetz, S. (2001). Conceptual foundations. In F. M. Jablin & L. L. Putnam (Eds.), *The new handbook of organizational communication: Advances in theory, research, and methods* (pp. 3–46). Thousand Oaks, CA: Sage.

Thomas, K., & Schmidt, W. (1976). A survey of managerial interest with respect to conflict. *Academy of Management Journal, 19,* 315–318.

Thomas, R. (2005). *Conflict management systems: A methodology for addressing the cost of conflict in the workplace.* Retrieved April 14, 2005, from Mediate.Com, http://www.mediate.com

9

CONFLICT RESOLUTION EDUCATION

Issues, Answers, and Directions

TRICIA S. JONES

Temple University

Over the past two decades, conflict education programs have focused on educating children about constructive approaches to managing conflict in their schools and communities. For many, conflict resolution education programs provide an answer to an increasingly troubling incidence of violence.

Teachers and administrators know that learning cannot take place unless you nurture a constructive learning environment for students (Brion-Meisels, Rendiero, & Lowenheim, 1984). Unfortunately, many students do not experience constructive learning environments in their schools and classrooms. Media often focus on incidents of aggravated assault and weapons-related violence—obviously important issues, but, there is a more pervasive problem in terms of social aggression, disrespect, and bullying. Nationally, 4.8% of teachers reported that physical fighting among students was a serious problem in their school. But 17.2% felt that students' disrespect for teachers was a serious problem, and 40.9% felt that the level of student misbehavior interferes with creating constructive learning environments (National Center for Educational Statistics, 1999–2000).

Bullying and social aggression are truly epidemic. Eighty percent of adolescents report being bullied during their school years; 90% of fourth through eighth graders report being victims of bullying at some point in their school experience; 15% of students are bullies or are long-term victims of bullies. Also, teachers are often unable or unwilling to intervene in social aggression of this type. Students reported that 71% of the teachers or other adults in the classroom ignored bullying incidents (Compton, 2003).

A large part of the problem is that students are not taught how to deal with conflict and how to create communities in which social aggression is not acceptable. Lockwood (1997) reports that reducing the initially aggressive response to an incident is critical to decreasing episodes of youth violence. In the majority of violent incidents, the initial move was a relatively minor affront (inadvertent contact in the halls) but was seen as hostile and responded to aggressively. In a study conducted by the Search Institute (1997), 41% of youth surveyed reported that when provoked they could not control anger and would fight.

Data on student misbehavior, disciplinary problems, and violence available from the

Centers for Disease Control Youth Risk Behavior Survey indicate that most school districts and especially urban districts have, at the least, moderate problems in these areas. For example, two large urban districts that have typical statistics are the Philadelphia School District and the Cleveland Municipal School District (two districts that are currently involved in a national pilot program in pre-service Conflict Resolution Education discussed later). Philadelphia, in the 2002–2003 school years, had approximately 27 serious incidents for every 1,000 students. Cleveland's 3-year average rates for suspensions for non-criminal behavior and for juvenile crime reveal that the rate for middle schools is nearly 8%, compared with about 6% at the high schools and about 3% at the elementary schools.

According to the Centers for Disease Control Youth Risk Behavior Survey Data for 1999 (the most recent data available for national trends), approximately 9% of students reported that they did not go to school because they felt unsafe at school or on their way to or from school (Centers for Disease Control, 2001). It is simply unacceptable that almost 10% of our children feel they are unsafe at school.

Educators and parents are attempting a number of reforms to address educational ills. Conflict resolution education (CRE) is one reform. The intent of this chapter is to introduce the reader to the nature and effectiveness of CRE and to advocate for future infrastructures and research to further CRE initiatives.

This chapter is divided into three sections. The first section provides an overview of CRE in three parts. The first part defines conflict resolution education and the overarching goals of these programs. The second part clarifies the distinctions between CRE and other positive youth development efforts such as violence prevention and peace education. Finally, the third part summarizes typical program models of CRE and relates them to CRE goals that are most likely to be achieved with certain program models. The second section of this chapter overviews contemporary research on the efficacy of CRE programs. The research review is presented by program model and educational level of program implementation (e.g., elementary school, middle school, or high school). The

third section addresses what is needed for successful institutionalization of CRE. Of particular interest are initiatives for developing programs targeting pre-service educators, creating and bolstering international networks of specialists in CRE, and obtaining critical descriptive information about the current use and mandates for CRE efforts.

THE NATURE OF CONFLICT RESOLUTION EDUCATION

Conflict resolution education emerged out of the social justice concerns of the 1960s and 1970s with the work of groups like the Friends Society (Quakers). In the early 1980s, Educators for Social Responsibility organized a national association that later led to the development of the National Association for Mediation in Education (NAME) in 1984. NAME subsequently merged with the National Institute for Dispute Resolution and its Conflict Resolution Education Network. Recently, the Conflict Resolution Education Network merged with the Academy of Family Mediators and the Society for Professionals in Dispute Resolution to form the Association for Conflict Resolution. As CRE has evolved, the nature and scope of these efforts has increased. Contemporary CRE can best be understood by identifying basic program goals, distinctions with related fields, and program models in use.

What Is Conflict Resolution Education?

Conflict resolution education programs focus on developing critical skills and abilities, as Bodine and Crawford (1998) have explained. They provide students with a basic understanding of the nature of conflict. Students appreciate that conflict exists whenever there is a disagreement about goals and/or methods to achieve those goals. They understand the dynamics of power and influence that operate in all conflict situations, and they become aware of the role of culture in how we see and respond to conflict.

An awareness of the nature of conflict helps students appreciate the ways people manage or respond to conflict—another program component.

Students explore a range of conflict styles (like competing, collaborating, accommodating, avoiding, and compromising) and consider the advantages and disadvantages of each. As effective conflict managers know, no approach to conflict management works all the time; the key is knowing which approach is best for the situation. However, conflict resolution education emphasizes that a violent response to conflict is almost never an appropriate response. An extremely important program component is providing students with social and emotional skills to prevent conflict and reinforce their use of pro-social strategies in conflict. Some of the skills that students are helped to develop include effective listening, perspective taking, emotional awareness, and emotional control.

GOALS OF CONFLICT RESOLUTION EDUCATION PROGRAMS

There are many possible goals for conflict resolution education programs, almost as many goals as there are permutations of the programs themselves. Below are four of the most common goals. Some CRE programs focus on only one or two of these goals, while others attempt to accomplish them all.

Create a Safe Learning Environment

In the 1990s, one of the National Education Goals stated, "all schools in America will be free of drugs, violence and the unauthorized presence of firearms and alcohol, and will offer a disciplined environment that is conducive to learning" (U.S. Department of Education, 1998). In response to that goal, Congress passed the Safe and Drug-Free Schools and Communities Act of 1994 that funded the Safe and Drug-Free Schools unit in the U.S. Department of Education. Since its inception, that office has sought to develop, implement, and monitor initiatives that can help create safe learning environments in our schools. Among those initiatives are CRE programs. Programs (e.g., bullying prevention programs, negotiation skills curricula, and peer mediation programs; for a thorough description of a range of conflict resolution education programs, see Jones & Compton, 2003) that emphasize this goal are interested in the following kinds of outcomes:

- Decrease incidents of violence
- Decrease conflicts between groups of students, particularly inter-group conflicts based on racial and ethnic differences
- Decrease suspensions, absenteeism, and drop-out rates related to unsafe learning environments

Conflict resolution education programs that emphasize creating a safe learning environment overlap with violence prevention efforts (e.g., use of school police and school resource officers, introduction of metal detectors and video surveillance equipment; for a comprehensive review of violence prevention programs, see Burstyn et al., 2001; U.S. Department of Health and Human Services, 2001). Violence prevention programs often include a CRE component, but are more likely to include increases in safety and security issues pertinent for the prevention of serious violent behaviors that are, luckily, still quite rare in schools (Greenberg et al., 2003; Zins, Weissberg, Wang, & Walberg, 2004). Violence prevention efforts seek to decrease serious risk behavior, including violence. Conflict resolution education is focused more on the development of important life skills that help students find nonviolent ways to handle their problems and, thereby, may decrease violent behavior.

It is understandable that people are concerned about school violence. In light of the tragedies in too many of our schools, we are all very aware of how senseless attacks and killings can and do occur. Yet, the vast majority of U.S. schools do not have violent incidents as common occurrences. Instead, the kinds of "safety issues" that are occurring are more appropriate for CRE programs than for metal detectors. In 1990–1991 and 1996–1997, the U.S. Department of Education surveyed principals about the violence and discipline problems in their schools (U.S. Department of Education [USDOE], 1998). The three issues most frequently rated as serious problems by principals were student tardiness, student absenteeism, and physical conflicts (without weapons) among the students.

Create a Constructive Learning Environment

Teachers and administrators know that learning cannot take place unless you nurture a constructive learning environment for students. A constructive learning environment is one in which children feel that there is a positive climate, effective classroom management, and a respectful and caring environment where children feel safe to share ideas and feelings (Jones, Johnson & Lieber, 2000; Lieber, 2003). A constructive, caring classroom community provides the foundation for the development of students' social and character development (Elias et al., 1997; Saarni, 1999; Salovey & Sluyter, 1997).

Teachers often wrestle with classroom management and classroom discipline. One of the first motivations for CRE was teachers' need to have better discipline so they could spend class time teaching content rather than correcting inappropriate behavior. Some early studies estimated that as much as 40% to 60% of class time was devoted to discipline rather than instruction (Girard & Koch, 1996).

When a CRE program creates a constructive learning environment, expected outcomes include the following:

- Improving school climate
- Improving classroom climate
- Promoting a respectful and caring environment
- Improving classroom management
- Reducing the time teachers spend on disciplinary problems in the classroom
- Increasing use of student-centered discipline

Enhance Students' Social and Emotional Development

At the heart of all conflict resolution education is the hope that we are helping our children to develop as better people—to be more socially and emotionally competent so that they can lead happier lives and contribute more positively to society. If this is achieved, it is likely that other goals of conflict resolution education will also be accomplished.

One way to think of this goal is in terms of critical abilities that students gain through their involvement in conflict resolution education.

Bodine and Crawford (1998) argued that students can gain

1. orientation abilities to develop values, beliefs, and attitudes that promote nonviolence, empathy, fairness, justice, trust, tolerance, self-respect, respect for others, and appreciation for controversy;

2. perception abilities to understand how oneself and others can have different, yet valid, perceptions of reality;

3. emotional abilities to manage and effectively communicate a range of emotions, including anger, fear, and frustration;

4. communication abilities to improve active listening skills, speaking to be understood and listening to understand;

5. creative-thinking abilities to construct cognitive models and to perceive and solve problems in new ways;

6. critical thinking abilities to contrast and compare data, predict and analyze situations, and construct and test hypotheses.

It is in the pursuit of this goal that CRE programs overlap with social and emotional learning (SEL) programs. Some people suggest that CRE encompasses social and emotional learning and adds an emphasis on understanding conflict and managing conflict. Others see social and emotional learning as the larger initiative into which conflict resolution education falls. No matter which frame you believe is more accurate, the important point is that both CRE and social and emotional learning programs support the belief that we should help students develop certain emotional, cognitive, and behavioral competencies.

It is also in this goal area that CRE overlaps with character education. Although character education is more focused on teaching students certain core values of citizenship, like CRE, character education teaches skills of cooperation, participatory decision making, and social perspective taking (Peterson & Skiba, 2001).

Overall, when CRE is effective, the benefits should include outcomes like the following:

- Increasing perspective taking
- Developing problem-solving abilities

- Improving emotional awareness and emotional management
- Reducing aggressive orientations and hostile attributions
- Increasing the students' use of constructive conflict behaviors in schools and in home and community contexts

Create a Constructive Conflict Community

As a society, we have turned more and more to our schools to help "raise" our children. Our schools are no longer "just" places of learning—they are places where students, families, and community members acquire a variety of resources. Our schools are becoming more integrated into our communities. Thus, what happens in our schools reflects the community and affects the community. The opposite is also true. It is rare to see a healthy school maintain itself over a long period when it exists in the middle of a beleaguered community.

Creating a constructive conflict community means several things. First, it means developing a sense of social justice and advocating for social justice as a cornerstone of a healthy and enriched society. Conflict resolution education is integrally linked to issues of social justice. Injustice is often the result of perceptions that the "other" is lesser or inferior in some way. Injustice and oppression go hand in hand, often accompanied by a tendency to blame the target. Through bias awareness programs, educators can help children face their biases and understand how those biases may negatively impact their interpersonal and group relationships.

A constructive conflict community is also one in which there is a shared responsibility for social ills and social accomplishments. In such a community, destructive conflict is seen as something the community needs to address. This is one of the basic assumptions underlying the notion of restorative justice approaches to conflict resolution education. William Ury (2000) talks about this idea as "the third side":

> In our societies, conflict is conventionally thought of as two-sided: husband vs. wife, union vs. employer, Arabs vs. Israelis. The introduction of a third party comes almost as an exception, an

aberration, someone meddling in someone else's business. We tend to forget what the simplest societies on earth have long known: namely that every conflict is actually three-sided. No dispute takes place in a vacuum. There are always others around—relatives, neighbors, allies, friends, or onlookers. Every conflict occurs within a community that constitutes the "third side" of any dispute. (p. 7)

Creating a constructive conflict community means actively involving parents and community members in conflict resolution education activities. Parents can and should participate actively in CRE—receiving training, modeling effective skills for their children, volunteering with program administration, and more. The school can also link with other conflict management and dispute resolution efforts in the broader community; for example, having student mediators work with community mediators to handle parent-teen conflicts in the community or to help defuse gang conflict in the community.

CONFLICT RESOLUTION EDUCATION AND RELATED FIELDS

School administrators are often a bit befuddled by the array of programming and interventions touted to help create safe and constructive learning environments. The result is a kaleidoscope of programs that cluster into fields that appear redundant to administrators. Although these fields share common foci, they are distinguishable. In this section, CRE is briefly distinguished from the most prominent related fields of peace education, violence prevention, social and emotional learning, and anti-bias education.

Conflict Resolution Education and Peace Education

CRE and peace education programs have much in common. The Peace Education Working Group at UNICEF defines peace education as

> the process of promoting the knowledge, skills, attitudes and values needed to bring about behavior

changes that will enable children, youth and adults to prevent conflict and violence, both overt and structural; to resolve conflict peacefully; and to create the conditions conducive to peace, whether at an intrapersonal, interpersonal, intergroup, national or international level. (UNESCO, 2002, p. 6)

Peace education is an activity aimed at changing the way people behave. But, as Salomon and Nevo (2002) suggested, no typical peace education curriculum exists; rather each peace education project is adapted to both local circumstances and funding requirements. Salomon (2002) stated that peace education usually includes such topics as "antiracism, conflict resolution, multiculturalism, cross-cultural training and the cultivation of a generally peaceful outlook" (p. 7). The peace education audience typically focuses on primary and secondary school-aged children—though some work is done at higher education levels and may even extend to professional development for adults.

Sommers (2003) suggested peace education is best understood in terms of the specific skills, attitudes, and knowledge imparted. Peace education programs help people develop communication skills of active listening and assertive speech; problem-solving skills of brainstorming or consensus building; and orientation skills of cultural awareness and empathy. Attitudes propagated by peace education focus on justice, respect, and democracy, though respect for democracy may be expressed indirectly through respect for individual choice. Peace education emphasizes understanding the dynamics of social conflict, warfare, and understanding conflict resolution and the dynamics of peace. In particular, participants in peace education are introduced to the distinctions of negative and positive peace. Participants may learn about different pacific methods of handling conflict, such as negotiation, mediation, or facilitation.

In his analysis of peace education in conflict-ridden societies, Williams (2004) reinforced that learners learn both more, and less, than an intended curriculum. Curriculum theorists have found it useful to distinguish between the *intended curriculum,* the one planned by curriculum developers; the *implemented curriculum,* the

curriculum as interpreted and actually taught by teachers; and the *attained curriculum,* what students actually learn (UNESCO, 2002).

A quick perusal of the definition, characteristics, and content of conflict resolution education and peace education programs suggests that the two areas overlap considerably. The basic motivations are similar, the goals for programs are similar, and the key skills and content are similar. Sommers (2001) noted that similarities are also shared between peace education and many kinds of "values education programs," such as human rights education, anti-bias training, and tolerance education. These all share a commitment to enhancing the quality of life by emphasizing the dignity of life. In all three examples, violence is rejected and participants are encouraged to find alternative ways of handling problems.

There are two primary differences between CRE and peace education. First, most U.S. practitioners see conflict resolution education as domestically applied and peace education as internationally applied. They adopt orientations like those of Gavriel Salomon (2002) that there are three basic types of peace education programs: those in intractable regions, those in regions with interethnic tensions, and those in regions of experienced tranquility. Second, many practitioners consider peace education programs to have a stronger emphasis on social justice orientations and the larger systemic issues of violence than conflict education programs.

Conflict Resolution Education and Violence Prevention

Violence prevention programs often include a CRE component, but are more likely to include increases in safety and security issues relevant to the prevention of serious violent behaviors that are, luckily, still quite rare in schools (Burstyn et al., 2001). Violence prevention efforts seek to decrease serious risk behavior, including violence toward self and others, risky sexual behavior, and substance abuse (Wilson, Gottfredson, & Najaka, 2001). Conflict resolution education is focused more on the development of important life skills, and especially communication skills, that help students find nonviolent ways to handle their problems and, thereby, may decrease violent behavior.

Conflict Resolution Education and Social and Emotional Learning

CRE and SEL programs help students develop emotional, cognitive, and behavioral competencies (Elias et al., 1997). Conflict resolution educators heartily endorse the following suggested competencies articulated by the Collaborative for Academic, Social and Emotional Learning. In the emotional domain, students should learn to identify emotions, control anger, manage frustration, and respect others' feelings. In the cognitive domain, students should develop the ability to take the other's role or perspective, problem solve, set goals, and cooperate. In the behavioral domain, students should build interpersonal skills necessary for positive social interaction, including negotiating disputes, taking responsibility for actions, managing time, respecting others' space, and appreciating social norms. The differences between CRE and SEL are becoming harder to identify as the fields truly integrate.

Conflict Resolution Education and Anti-Bias Education

Many people have argued convincingly that CRE does and should overlap with anti-bias education because prejudice is an underlying cause for conflict and we need to realize the impact of prejudice on the school and community (Lantieri & Patti, 1996; Oskamp, 2000). Most anti-bias education efforts fall into one of the following four categories: cross-cultural awareness, prejudice reduction and appreciation for diversity, hate crime prevention, and examining the systemic roots of oppression to dismantle them.

The "World" of CRE

As Jones and Compton (2003) articulated, CRE encompasses a number of programs and practices. The substantive and developmental foundation of CRE is enhanced social and emotional competencies through social and emotional learning (Elias et al., 1997), with particular emphasis on emotional awareness, empathy, and perspective taking; strategic expression; and cultural sensitivity. These competencies are often delivered through specific curricula like Second Step in early elementary years. A second foundational tier is the integration of conflict education in ongoing curricula like language arts, social studies, math, and science—a development heralded as critical to the institutionalization of CRE (Batton, 2002). Additional content-specific curricula are taught in general or in programmatic areas such as negotiation skills (Druliner & Prichard, 2003); targeted programs also address specific problems like bullying (Title, 2003), peer harassment (Juvonen & Graham, 2001), and bias-related conflicts (Prutzman, 2003; Smith & Fairman, 2004). The processes in which students and adults are educated include peer mediation (Cohen, 2003), dialogue (Johnson, Johnson, & Tjosvold, 2000), use of expressive arts (Conte, 2001), and restorative justice (Ierley & Claassen-Wilson, 2003).

Bodine and Crawford (1998), in their *Handbook of Conflict Resolution Education,* identified four program models: the mediation program approach, the process curriculum approach, the peaceable classroom approach, and the peaceable school approach. While these models are somewhat simplistic, they provide a useful framework for discussing CRE program types.

Mediation Program Approach

This model is often referred to as the peer mediation program model. These stand-alone programs are the most common form of conflict resolution education in the United States. A small group of students are trained in mediation so they can act as third parties in peer conflicts. Once students are trained, the success of the program depends upon the extent to which teachers, staff, administration, and students are willing to refer conflicts to the program.

Process Curriculum Approach

This model involves a specific curriculum of conflict content, for example something like the Workable Peace program in which students are taught a conflict and negotiation curriculum through a series of case studies and intensive role plays (Wiltenberg, 2001). While a variety of conflict curricula may be taught, most address the foundations of conflict, the principles of effective conflict resolution, and introduce some version of a problem-solving process. Depending on the school's needs, the conflict resolution curriculum may be taught as a separate course, a distinct curriculum outside of regular class time, or as a daily or weekly lesson in a related content curriculum.

Peaceable Classroom Approach

The peaceable classroom approach is a whole-classroom methodology. In this model, CRE is incorporated into the core subjects of the curriculum and into classroom management strategies. This model includes what others have termed "curriculum infusion" (Poliner, 2003). In addition, the peaceable classroom requires effective classroom management practices that create a constructive learning environment and a safe learning environment. Teachers using this approach may do it in conjunction with a larger program like cooperative learning.

Peaceable School Approach

The peaceable school approach is a comprehensive whole-school methodology that builds on the peaceable classroom approach by using conflict resolution as a system of operation for managing the school as well as the classroom. Conflict resolution principles and processes are learned and used by all members of the school (including parents). Also called "whole-school programs," they often combine peer mediation with additional training and intervention efforts to provide the "whole school" with information to improve conflict behavior and to develop key social and emotional skills. Working from the philosophy that children often model what they see, these programs attempt to improve the ways adult staff in the schools deal with their own conflicts by providing conflict skills training to staff (including teachers, non-teaching staff, and administration).

Community-Linked Programs

Although this program model was not on Bodine and Crawford's (1998) list, and is relatively rare, it deserves mention. Community-linked programs are the most ambitious of all. They are usually configured to be the logical extension of a whole-school program. However, they can involve community linkages to peer mediation cadre programs as well. In cadre-linked programs peer mediators are linked to external community groups, but other members of the school are not similarly involved. For example, the peer mediators may serve as mediation trainers or mediators in a local neighborhood mediation center. This increases the mediators' experience and exposes segments of the community to mediation by youth. However, peer mediation is not designed to institute sweeping changes in the community or school conflict culture. Peace and Safety networks involve a number of community members and organizations, linking them with the school's programs and activities. Religious, business, and governmental organizations usually work together with the school to create innovative ways to "spread the word" about mediation and constructive conflict resolution, to institute applications for mediation, and to encourage community members to take part.

RESEARCH ON CRE

In the first decade and a half of CRE programs, teachers and administrators often asked, "Does 'it' work?" There was a concerted effort to conduct and report research across CRE program models to learn which programs did work, in what ways, and with what anticipated effects.

The corpus of CRE research can be summarized in two waves—research prior to the federal mandate for research-proven practices and research after the mandate. In 2000, the U.S. Department of Education mandated that only research-proven programs would be eligible for federal Safe and Drug-Free School dollars. And, by "research proven" they meant field experimental research rather than the program evaluation and qualitative research that had predominated in the first 15 years of CRE work.

The research of the first 15 years is aptly reviewed in the volume, *Does It Work? The Case for CRE in Our Nation's Schools* (Jones & Kmitta, 2000). This volume summarizes the results of the CRE research symposia sponsored by the U.S. Department of Education and convened by the Conflict Resolution Education Network in March 2000. Teams of researchers, educators, and CRE practitioners reviewed research on five topic areas: impact on students, impact on educators/teachers, impact on diverse student populations, impact on school climate, and issues of institutionalization. CRE programs increase students' academic achievement, positive attitudes toward school, assertiveness, cooperation, communication skills, healthy interpersonal/intergroup relations, constructive CR at home and school, and self-control; and decreases students' aggressiveness, discipline referrals, drop-out rates, and suspension rates. There is little research on the effects of CRE on teachers. There is substantial evidence that CRE improves school climate (especially for elementary schools) and classroom climate. This volume attests to the woeful lack of research on CRE and diverse/nondominant populations. Measures of success do not include diversity-relevant outcomes (impact on intergroup relations or community harmony is largely ignored), and issues of class or socioeconomic status receive very little attention. Nevertheless, there is evidence that CRE programs that focus on systemic bias or include "contact theory" can improve intergroup relations (see Pettigrew & Tropp, 2000).

The research in *Does It Work* focused exclusively on K–12 populations. But, in 2000, Sandy and Cochran published a chapter in *The Handbook of Conflict Resolution* that reviewed evidence of CRE effectiveness in preschool populations as well. They summarize the Peaceful Kids ECSEL (Early Childhood Education Social and Emotional Learning) Program the authors developed and evaluated at Columbia University Teachers College. ECSEL educates teachers and parents to model and teach emotional awareness, cooperative skills, empathy/perspective taking, and problem solving to preschool children. Sandy and her colleagues reported significant increases in children's assertiveness, cooperation, and self-control and significant decreases in aggressive, withdrawn, and moody behaviors. Preschool staff was able to independently integrate the skills in the class, and parents increased in authoritative (as opposed to authoritarian) parenting practices (Sandy & Boardman, 2000).

Criteria for Reviewed Research

For individual research studies, the research reviewed and reported here met the following criteria (similar to those used in Wilson et al., 2001): (a) it evaluated a distinct intervention, program, or practice within the area of CRE as previously defined; (b) the intervention was school-based: conducted in a school building, by school staff, or under school auspices; (c) it used a comparison group evaluation methodology, including nonequivalent comparison group research designs, and the comparison group was a no-treatment or minimal-treatment condition; (d) it had adequate sample size; and (e) it measured at least one of the outcomes relevant to CRE goals discussed earlier.

Peer Mediation

Johnson and Johnson (1996) produced a very comprehensive conventional literature review that focused primarily on peer mediation programs and conflict education within a cooperative learning context. The review reported positive findings for efficacy of peer mediation and conflict education—particularly on increases in students' conflict knowledge, self-reported pro-social behavior, and negotiation skills—and positive impacts on classroom climate.

Burrell, Zirbel, and Allen (2003) conducted a meta-analysis on 43 studies (published between 1985 and 2003) of peer mediation programs that met the following criteria: (a) focused on K–12 student population, (b) used quantitative methods resulting in numerical measurable effects, and (c) involved at least one variable relating to mediation training or practices in which outcomes of the actual training or practices were measured. The results overwhelmingly support peer mediation effectiveness in terms of increasing students' conflict knowledge and skills, improving school climate, and reducing negative behavior.

Structurally, peer mediation programs differ in terms of the training delivery and the program implementation, as well as educational level and linkage with other CRE components. These models can be labeled cadre, curriculum or class linked, or mentoring. In cadre peer mediation programs, student mediators are trained outside of classes and mediate disputes in a private area designated for that purpose. In curriculum- or class-linked peer mediation, students in a classroom receive training in integrative negotiation and simple mediation process skills, rotate as mediators, and conduct mediations in class when requested by the teacher or peers in dispute. Mentoring peer mediation models involve student mediators' training younger students as peer mediators within the same school or across educational levels. While cadre peer mediation programs exist at all educational levels, curriculum- or class-linked models are most common in elementary schools, and mentoring models are most common in secondary schools (with middle school or high school mentors serving as elementary school mediators).

The following review is organized around research studies of peer mediation models (cadre, curriculum or class linked, or mentoring) in different educational levels (elementary school, middle school, and high school). As this review indicates, the vast majority of CRE research has concerned efficacy of peer mediation programs alone or in conjunction with some other CRE intervention. The overall body of evidence—as the meta-analyses suggest— proves that peer mediation has significant positive impacts on mediators, disputants, and schools.

Peer Mediation Research in Elementary Schools

Cadre models. Most peer mediation evaluation in elementary schools concerns cadre programs and concentrates on impacts of peer mediation on the mediators. Studies report that, as compared to non-mediators, mediators demonstrated increased knowledge of constructive conflict resolution (Korn, 1994; Nance, 1996), were able to mediate successfully (Johnson, Johnson, Dudley, & Ward, 1995), and demonstrated observable mediation skills (Winston, 1997). Research even suggests effectiveness for special needs students who are trained as mediators. Meyer's (1996) dissertation research examined

the impact of participation in a peer mediation program on self-perceptions and conflict styles of behaviorally at-risk students. The pretest, posttest control group design using fourth-, fifth-, and sixth-grade subjects found no impacts on perception of self-worth or conflict style, but did find reductions in disciplinary referrals for mediators as compared to non-mediators.

Several studies examined the impact of peer mediation experience in the development of social and emotional competencies of mediators. Some research confirms positive impacts of peer mediation on disciplinary referrals, but fails to find differences between mediators and non-mediators on self-concept, or on social skills as measured by the Social Skills Rating System (SSRS; Zucca-Brown, 1997). Conversely, Epstein (1996), using the same basic design and the same measure (SSRS), reported that mediators had a greater increase in social skills than disputants or control students.

Three studies investigated the impact of peer mediation on perspective taking. In his dissertation, Mankopf (2003) hypothesized that mediators would have better perspective taking, negotiation ability, attitudes toward fighting, and connectedness to school and family than non-mediators; and that mediators who mediated more would demonstrate greater developmental gains. He found partial support for these hypotheses; mediators did score higher on perspective taking and negotiation ability, although experience was not as much of an influence as anticipated. Pamela Lane-Garon (1998) studied the impact of peer mediation on cognitive and affective perspective taking of mediators and disputants. A total of 112 students (62 mediators and 50 non-mediators) in Grades 4 through 8 were administered perspective-taking measures over the course of an academic year. Both mediators and disputants showed a significant increase in cognitive and affective perspective taking, but mediators' scores were significantly higher than disputants'. In a second study, Lane-Garon (2000) examined the impact of peer mediation on cognitive perspective taking, strategy choice, and school climate. Her design compared mediators and non-mediators, by gender and ethnicity, from pretest to posttest. Eighty students in Grades 4 through 6 served as subjects. The results show significant increases in mediators' perspective taking and selection of problem-solving conflict strategy. She also found ethnic differences, with African American participants (both mediators and non-mediators) showing the greatest increase in perspective taking and Hispanic participants showing the greatest positive change in conflict strategy choice when compared to Anglo participants.

Curriculum- or class-linked models. Most of the research in class-linked peer mediation comes from the Teaching Students to be Peacemakers Program (TSPP) developed by David and Roger Johnson at the University of Minnesota. TSPP creates a cooperative learning context, instructs students in integrative negotiation and mediation skills and concepts, and uses in-class peer mediation sessions. Teachers are trained to deliver the TSPP lessons (Fitch & Marshall, 1999).

Johnson and Johnson (2001) conducted a meta-analysis of 17 evaluation studies examining TSPP effectiveness in eight schools in two countries. Students ranged from K–9 and were from urban, suburban, and rural schools. The results indicated that students learned the conflict resolution procedures taught, retained their knowledge throughout the school year, applied the knowledge to actual conflicts, transferred skills to non-classroom and non-school settings, and used the skills similarly in family and school settings. In addition, some of the studies revealed that exposure to TSPP increased academic achievement and decreased discipline referrals and classroom management problems. Although not included in the meta-analysis, two earlier TSPP studies (Johnson & Johnson, 1996; Johnson et al., 1995) showed similar results in terms of student's conflict knowledge and tendency toward integrative negotiation in hypothetical and actual conflicts.

Two other studies investigated class-linked peer mediation using the community boards model and applied in playground mediations. Hart and Gunty (1997) used a nonequivalent control group design to study fourth-through sixth-grade mediators and found that the number of student conflicts and the average time-off-teaching per conflict decreased significantly in the classroom. Miller (1995), however, examined mediators and disputants on self-concept and used teacher and parent ratings of student behavior (Behavior Dimensions Rating Scale), but found no differences on any dependent measures.

Mentoring peer mediation. A relatively recent and exciting approach to peer mediation is the mentoring model in which older students trained as mediators mentor younger students. One of the best programmatic examples of this is the Winning Against Violent Environments (WAVE) programs developed by Carole Close and institutionalized in the Cleveland Municipal School District. Bickmore (2002) evaluated 28 urban elementary schools in which WAVE high school mediators trained between 25 and 30 elementary mediators in each school, conducted follow-up visits with schools, presented at school staff meetings, and led workshops for parent groups. Data were collected on the understanding of conflict, attitudes toward conflict, and perceptions of school climate (using the Students Attitudes About Conflict survey); and attendance rate, number of suspensions, and academic achievement (in terms of Ohio Proficiency Tests of reading and citizenship). The results indicate that peer mediation has significant positive results for mediator and non-mediator attitudes about conflict, understanding of conflict, and perceptions of school climate. The mediators tended to have more significant increases on these measures than non-mediators, but this varied by experience level. In schools where the mediation program was inactive, the mediators did not score higher on these indices than non-mediators. Suspension rates were considerably reduced in the WAVE schools, and academic achievement scores increased in WAVE schools considerably more than the district average.

Lupton-Smith (1996) also examined a mentoring program using high school mentors, but focused on whether the mentoring experience affected the high school mediators' moral reasoning and ego development. The nonequivalent control group design compared mentors with other high school students involved in peer helping activities. The study found no significant differences; a finding perhaps attributable to the selection of a "helping" comparison group.

Lane-Garon and Richardson (2003) report on a cross-age mentoring mediation program in which university students served as mentors to elementary school mediators. Impacts on elementary students' cognitive and affective perspective taking, perceptions of school climate, and academic performance were assessed. The results show strong support for the impact of peer mediation on increases in mediators' cognitive and affective perspective taking and perceptions of school climate (especially in the area of perceived school safety).

Peer Mediation Research in Middle Schools

There is less research on the effectiveness of peer mediation programs in middle or high schools. This makes sense since peer mediation programs are implemented predominantly in K–6 populations. The available research reports on cadre- and class-linked programs in middle schools. No evaluations of mentoring programs were found.

Cadre models. The research on these programs reports findings consistent with those in elementary school cadre models, even though middle school students are somewhat more cynical in general about peer mediation (Robinson, Smith, & Daunic, 2000). Mediators in middle school cadre programs, when compared with non-mediators, increase their knowledge of constructive conflict and indicate they will use those approaches (Bell, Coleman, Anderson, Whelan, & Wilder, 2000; Stewart, 2000), and increase their self-esteem and self-concept— even for very aggressive students (Fast, Fanelli, & Salen, 2003).

Curriculum- or class-linked models. Once again, and as included in the TSPP meta-analysis, specific research in middle schools using the TSPP program reports that students in sixth through ninth grades benefit from this experience; they gain knowledge about conflict processes, they increase their willingness to use integrative negotiation, and they have more positive attitudes toward conflict (Dudley, 1995; Dudley, Johnson, & Johnson, 1996; Johnson & Johnson, 1997). Yet, this research does not demonstrate a positive impact of peer mediation on classroom climate.

Smith, Daunic, Miller, and Robinson (2002) conducted an evaluation of a curriculum-linked peer mediation program in three middle schools over a 4-year period. The curriculum was taught schoolwide by teachers, but not all students received mediation training. There was no evidence of improvement in students' or teachers' perceptions of school climate; this was perhaps due to implementation problems since some teachers did not complete the CR curriculum in their classes. There were no differences between mediators and non-mediators on any of the dependent measures.

Albert Farrell and his colleagues have found some impressive results from their Responding in Peaceful and Positive Ways (RIPP) program developed for urban middle schools that serve a predominantly African American student population. RIPP is a 25-session social-cognitive conflict education curriculum, with problem solving the major focus of the curriculum; and RIPP includes a peer mediation component (Farrell, Meyer, Kung, & Sullivan, 2001). In one evaluation of RIPP with classes of sixth graders at three urban middle schools, students were randomized to intervention ($N = 321$) and control groups ($N = 305$). RIPP participants had fewer disciplinary violations and in-school suspensions than control students—an impact that lasted for 12 months after program implementation (Farrell, Meyer, & White, 2001). In one middle school, RIPP-6 was implemented and outcomes were assessed using a battery of measures completed by students at pretest, posttest, and one-year follow-up. Compared with students in the comparison group, students who participated in RIPP-6 reported significantly lower approval of violent behavior, more peer support for nonviolent behaviors, less peer pressure to use drugs, and greater knowledge of the intervention at posttest. They also reported significantly lower posttest frequencies of physical aggression, drug use, and peer provocation (Farrell, Valois, & Meyer, 2002).

Peer Mediation Research in High Schools

As with middle schools, the peer mediation evaluation research in high schools concerns only cadre- or curriculum-linked programs.

Cadre models. In general, the research in this area is not supportive of peer mediation. Nelson (1997) studied the impact of mediation on self-esteem, social skills, and frequency of disciplinary referrals, but found no differences between the mediators and the control students, although these findings may be attributable to an inadequate sample size ($N = 51$). Sweeney (1996) was interested in whether mediation affected moral reasoning, orientations to others, and self-esteem; no significant differences were found between mediators and controls.

Potts's (2002) dissertation research shows more promising results. She examined the impact of mediation on interpersonal negotiation strategies (a measure of perspective taking and social problem solving) and coping styles. She compared mediators, disputants, and controls, and found that mediators demonstrated higher levels of social competence, and that more experienced mediators had the highest levels. Tolson and McDonald (1992) reported that students with high disciplinary referrals sent to mediation had significantly fewer referrals than students sent to traditional disciplinary processes.

Curriculum- or class-linked models. Stevahn and her colleagues have contributed to the research in this area, although only one study deals with U.S. schools (Stevahn, Johnson, Johnson, & Schultz, 2002). Classes were randomly assigned to receive a 5-week conflict curriculum with peer mediation (CR/PM) or act as control groups. As in similar studies in elementary and middle schools, the results strongly confirm that the training increased student knowledge of conflict and use of integrative negotiation. A very important outcome was that classes with the CR/PM training also had higher academic achievement, greater long-term retention of academic learning, and greater transfer of academic learning in social studies to language arts.

Comparative Research in Peer Mediation

Only one study has compared different models of peer mediation across educational levels on individual student and school outcomes. The Comprehensive Peer Mediation Evaluation Project (CPMEP; Jones et al., 1997) involved 27 schools in three communities (Philadelphia, Laredo, and Denver). In each community, a 3×3 field experiment compared program models (peer mediation cadre programs, peer mediation curriculum-linked [whole-school] programs, and control schools) in each of three educational levels (elementary, middle, high school). This study was guided by four research questions: (a) Does peer mediation impact students' conflict attitudes and behavior in terms of how frequently they are involved in conflict, how frequently they help others who are in conflict, their values about pro-social behavior in general, their conflict styles, their tendency toward aggressive behavior, their development of perspective taking and collaborative conflict orientations, or their ability to demonstrate or enact the skills taught in training? (b) Does peer mediation impact teachers' and students' perceptions of school climate? (c) Are cadre programs better than whole-school programs (or vice versa)? In terms of impact on students' attitudes and behaviors, school climate, and program utility, is there a difference in the efficacy of these program models? (d) Are peer mediation programs equally effective (or ineffective) for elementary, middle, and high schools?

All peer mediation schools (cadre and whole school) received peer mediation training and program implementation in the beginning of fall semester of each year. Schools receiving whole-school programs had curricular infusion training and conflict skills training by the end of fall semester. Data were collected over a 2-year period. The sample consisted of multiple responses from each of the following (approximate numbers used): For elementary schools—140 peer mediators, 1,300 control students, 400 conflict training students, and 275 teachers/administrative staff; for middle schools—140 peer mediators, 1,600 control students, 550 conflict training students, and 400 teachers/administrative staff; for high schools—150 peer mediators, 2,500 control students, 450 conflict training students, and 550 teachers/administrative staff. Thus, the overall sample consisted of 430 peer mediators, 5,400 control students, 1,400 conflict training students, and 1,225 teachers/administrative staff.

The data from the CPMEP study reveal that peer mediation programs provide significant benefit in developing constructive social and conflict behavior in children at all educational levels. It is clear that exposure to peer mediation programs, whether cadre or whole school, has a significant and lasting impact on students' conflict attitudes and behaviors. Students who are direct recipients of program training benefit more from the training, although students without direct training also benefit in terms of observing and learning social skills. The data clearly demonstrate that exposure to peer mediation reduces personal conflict and increases the tendency to help others with conflicts, increases pro-social values, decreases aggressiveness, and increases perspective taking and conflict competence. Especially for peer mediators, these impacts are significant, cumulative, and are sustained for long periods. Students trained in mediation, at all educational levels, are able to enact and utilize the behavioral skills taught in training.

The CPMEP results prove that peer mediation programs can significantly improve school climate at elementary levels, but the impact in middle and high schools is not significant, possibly due to limited diffusion capability in larger organizational environments. Similar results were obtained from a much smaller comparative study in the Dallas Public Schools (Nelson-Haynes, 1996), which found that peer mediation programs positively impact student perceptions of school climate in elementary but not secondary schools.

Process Curricula

Process curricula will be reviewed in terms of specific SEL curricula, negotiation and general conflict curricula, and bullying-prevention curricula. No research meeting the review criteria was found for bias awareness programs, dialogue programs, restorative justice, or expressive arts programs in CRE.

Social and Emotional Learning Curricula

In the area of SEL, three general literature reviews are noteworthy. Weissberg and Greenberg (1998) provided a comprehensive review of SEL programs and violence prevention programs, arguing for the efficacy of SEL programs

on the development of core emotional competencies, especially for younger children. In 2003, Greenberg and colleagues reviewed school-based intervention and youth development initiatives and concluded that programs in this area are most beneficial when they simultaneously enhance students' personal and social assets as well as improve the quality of the environments in which students are educated. They cite a meta-analysis of 161 positive youth development programs (Catalano, Berglund, Ryan, Lonczak, & Hawkins, 2002) that indicates SEL programs definitely make a difference in improvements in interpersonal skills, quality of peer and adult relationships, and academic achievement, as well as reductions in problem behaviors such as school misbehavior and truancy, violence, and aggression. Greenberg and colleagues (2003) argued that skills-building components and environmental change initiatives are critical; optimal delivery of programs is through trained teachers who integrate the concepts into their regular teaching, and do so over a longer period of time (6–9 months).

For many educators faced with "teach-to-test" pressures, questions of academic achievement are uppermost. Howard Zins and his colleagues (2004) provide valuable evidence that programs that enhance students' social-emotional competence foster better academic performance. When students are more self-aware and emotionally connected, they can focus on academics and achieve in a supportive environment.

In terms of specific studies, two SEL curricula are selected for mention in this section because they have strong overlap with CRE. The PATHS program and the Second Step program are also two of the most popular and respected programs available for elementary school populations.

PATHS. The PATHS program is a classroom-based curriculum implemented by teachers for elementary grades (Kusche & Greenberg, 1995) and is effective for regular and special needs students (i.e., learning disabled, emotionally disturbed; Greenberg & Kusche, 1996). PATHS helps children develop problem-solving, self-control, and emotional regulation skills. The program consists of 57 lessons of 20- to 30-minute duration that are taught two or three times per week. A pretest-posttest control group design with random assignment of classrooms from schools in high-risk areas across sites in the United States has been conducted with more than 6,500 students from 198 intervention classrooms and 180 matched comparison classrooms (Conduct Problems Prevention Research Group, 1999). The findings reveal PATHS decreased aggression and hyperactive-disruptive behaviors, and improved classroom atmosphere. Quality of program implementation (i.e., treatment integrity) was significantly related to decreases in teacher reports of classroom aggression and to improved classroom climate. In another investigation, 1- and 2-year longitudinal findings suggest that the PATHS curriculum may have lasting effects on emotional understanding and interpersonal social problem-solving skills (Greenberg & Kusche, 1996).

Second Step. The Second Step Program is a classwide social skills program implemented by teachers for all preschool through middle school children (Grossman et al., 1997). The objective of the program is to teach students skills related to empathy, impulse control, and anger management. The program consists of 30 classroom lessons (each is approximately 35–45 minutes in duration) typically taught one or two times per week. A recent pretest-posttest control group design with random assignment of schools to Second Step training versus control was conducted with 790 second and third graders (see Grossman et al., 1997). Students participating in Second Step were observed to exhibit less physical aggression and more pro-social behaviors than students in the control condition. Observations confirmed that treatment effects were largely maintained over a 6-month period.

Additional research suggests that target populations may respond differently to Second Step. Broadbear (2001) found that children of divorce showed more decrease in negative conflict than children from intact marriages. Further, Washburn (2002) discovered that Second Step was particularly effective with low-income urban, minority students; although Taub's (2002) research, which may have been hampered by inadequate sample size, found little positive impact on low-income, rural elementary school students.

One study compared Second Step to a class-linked peer mediation program for third- and fourth-grade students (Harris, 1999). Classes were randomly assigned to treatment and control conditions. Teachers delivered the curricula over a semester. The results indicated no difference in effectiveness of the programs, though there was a treatment-by-gender effect: Boys performed better in the peer mediation class and girls performed better in Second Step.

Negotiation and General Conflict Curricula

Other than research concerning the TSPP program, which some consider to be conflict curricula more than a peer mediation program, there is very little research on the effectiveness of general negotiation curricula. For example, Program for Young Negotiators is a popular program based on interests-based negotiation, but no studies were found that evaluated its effectiveness.

DuRant, Barkin, and Krowchuk (2001) reported on a conflict curriculum used with low-income, minority sixth graders in four middle schools; intervention schools had 292 students, and the control schools 412 students. The Peaceful Conflict Resolution and Violence Prevention Curriculum, a 13-module skills-building curriculum, taught identification of situations that could result in violence; avoidance, confrontation, problem-solving, and communication skills; conflict resolution skills; the conflict cycle; the dynamics of a fight; and how to express anger without fighting. The primary outcome variable was a 5-item scale assessing the frequency of fighting and weapon-carrying behaviors and a scale measuring intentions to use violence in 11 hypothetical situations. From pretest to posttest there was a decrease in the use of violence by students in the intervention group and an increase in the use of violence in the control group.

An innovative approach to delivering a conflict curriculum is through computer-generated lessons. Kris Bosworth and her colleagues (Bosworth, Espelage, DuBay, Daytner, & Karageorge, 2000) developed SMART Talk, a computer-based intervention containing anger-management and conflict-resolution modules. Five hundred fifty-eight middle school students were randomly assigned to treatment or control groups and were assessed on self-awareness, attitudes toward violence, and intentions to use non-violent strategies. SMART Talk was successful in diminishing students' acceptance of violence and increased their intentions to use nonviolent strategies.

Three studies of conflict education curricula focus on urban, minority populations. Heydenberk, Heydenberk, and Bailey (2003) implemented Project Peace, a teacher-delivered CRE program in fourth- and fifth-grade classes, and evaluated the impacts on students' moral reasoning and attitudes about conflict (using SAAC [Student Attitudes About Conflict Scale]). All treatment classrooms showed significant increases in moral reasoning ability and constructive conflict orientation. In a 2-year study of the impact of a conflict education curriculum in middle and high school special-needs students (in an alternative disciplinary school), researchers found that the conflict curriculum had a significant impact on students' misconduct rates, hostile attribution, and aggressive orientation (Jones & Bodtker, 1999).

Bullying Prevention Programs

In the past 5 years, many states have mandated bullying prevention programs (Title, 2003). School administrators and teachers search for effective curricula to stem the prevalence of bullying behavior (Lumsden, 2002). There is considerable research about bullying behaviors and consequences (Espelage & Swearer, 2003), and teacher orientations to bullying (Craig, Henderson, & Murphy, 2000); but only three studies in the United States examine the efficacy of bullying prevention programs (and one of those was still in progress when this chapter was written).

Instead of conducting the necessary research on these programs in U.S. contexts, educators and practitioners continue to refer to research conducted by Olweus (1991) in Norway. This large-scale evaluation looked at the efficacy of the bullying program with Norwegian children ages 8–16. The results indicate sustained (at least 2 years) reductions in school aggression (bullying was reduced by 50%), fighting, vandalism, alcohol abuse, and truancy. The effects were more pronounced the longer the program was in place. Other reports of effectiveness of the Bullying Prevention program have been forthcoming from Canada (Pepler, Craig,

Ziegler, & Charach, 1994) and England (Whitney, Rivers, Smith, & Sharp, 1994). The only obtainable study of an Olweus-based program in the United States was a process evaluation of program implementation (Price, 2003). Cunningham (2001) reported on a study in progress that will evaluate the Healthy Schools bullying prevention program in two urban middle schools, but results are pending.

Orpinas, Horne, and Staniszewski (2003) studied the application of the Peaceable Place program developed by the Mendez Foundation— a very standard conflict education curriculum to teach K–5 students conflict resolution skills, anger management, respect for self and others, and effective communication. There was a 40% reduction among younger children (K–2) in mean self-reported aggression and a 19% reduction in mean self-reported victimization. Among third through fifth graders there was a 23% reduction in mean reported victimization, but no significant differences in self-reported aggression.

In her dissertation research, Kaiser-Ulrey (2004) evaluated the BEST (Bullying Eliminated from Schools Together) program developed for middle schools. One hundred twenty-five seventh-grade students were assigned in cohort groups to either a treatment or comparison group. Teachers conducted the 12-week intervention, which consisted of four basic modules, including empathy and problem solving. The outcomes measured were (a) bullying incidence, (b) victimization incidence, (c) empathy, (d) pro-social behaviors, (e) global self-esteem, and (f) parental involvement. Results did not support any of the research hypotheses, except for an increase in social skills development of the treatment students.

Peaceable Classroom/ Curriculum Integration

The National Curriculum Integration Project (NCIP) was a 3-year study of curriculum infusion and integration in middle schools in four states (Jones & Sanford, 2003). A pretest/ posttest control group comparison design in each state examined the effect of teaching condition (NCIP experienced teaching, NCIP new teaching, and control teaching) on more than 1,000 seventh- and eighth-grade students' emotional and conflict competence (conflict orientation, emotional management, perspective taking, and hostile attribution) and classroom climate. Although the NCIP conditions did not significantly influence emotional management, they did have positive impacts on students' perspective taking and use of problem-solving strategies. NCIP has extremely strong positive impacts on classroom climate. As expected, across sites, students in NCIP classes taught by returning, experienced NCIP teachers consistently reported more positive climate (overall and in terms of the dimensions of Teacher Support, Student Support, Cohesion, Safety, and Constructive Conflict Management) than students in classes taught by new NCIP teachers. However, students in either NCIP class perceived a much more positive climate than students in control classes. NCIP impact on classroom climate increased throughout the year while perceived climate in control classes usually became notably more negative throughout the year.

In terms of Teachers' Integration of NCIP Concepts Into Curriculum, when the goals of NCIP are clearly presented, there is strong evidence that teachers are capable of integrating these concepts and practices in their ongoing curricula. There is a learning curve for teachers; it takes sustained effort for a teacher to progress to optimal levels of integration and infusion. However, teachers can effectively mentor other teachers to achieve these levels. Teachers in most sites were able to develop complex and valuable integrated lessons for use in ongoing curricula (usually in English and Language Arts). While lessons in other disciplines were developed, it was more difficult, especially for the disciplines of Math and Science.

Peaceable School/ Whole-School Programs

Few CRE efforts are truly "whole school" and fewer still have been evaluated. One excellent study addresses peaceable school models in elementary schools, and two studies evaluate peaceable school models in middle schools.

At the elementary school level, the Responding to Conflict Creatively Program (RCCP) has been the focus of an excellent evaluation (Aber,

Brown, & Jones, 2003). RCCP includes teacher training, classroom instruction and staff development, program curriculum, administrator training, peer mediation, parent training, and a targeted intervention for high-risk youth. RCCP is a complex, multiyear, multilevel CRE program. Four waves of data on features of children's social and emotional development known to forecast aggression and violence were collected in the fall and spring over 2 years for a representative sample of first to sixth graders from New York City Public Schools ($N = 11,160$). The results indicate that RCCP, when delivered by classroom teachers as designed, had significant impact on reducing attitudes and behaviors predictive of aggression and violence. Positive implications for orientation to academic achievement were also reported. Program fidelity was identified as a critical factor. Students in classes where teachers delivered some RCCP but not the amount or nature proscribed actually performed worse on dependent measures than control students.

The research at the middle school level shows mixed results. Orpinas and colleagues (2000) evaluated a multicomponent violence prevention intervention to reduce aggressive behaviors among students of eight middle schools randomly assigned to intervention or control conditions. The intervention included the formation of a School Health Promotion Council, training of peer mediators and peer helpers, training of teachers in conflict resolution, a violence-prevention curriculum, and newsletters for parents. All students were evaluated in the spring of 1994, 1995, and 1996 (approximately 9,000 students per evaluation). Sixth graders in 1994 were followed through seventh grade in 1995 or eighth grade in 1996 or both ($n = 2,246$). Cohort and cross-sectional evaluations indicated little to no intervention effect in reducing aggressive behaviors, fights at school, injuries due to fighting, or missing classes because of feeling unsafe at school or being threatened to be hurt. The Students for Peace experience suggests that interventions begin prior to middle school, explore social environmental intervention strategies, and involve parents and community members.

Shapiro, Burgoon, Welker, and Clough (2002) evaluated a middle school CRE intervention

(The Peacebuilders Program) that trains all school staff to infuse CRE through all aspects of everyday school life. The program was implemented in three middle schools and three elementary schools with one control middle school and one control elementary school. Components of the Peacemakers Program are delivered initially by teachers and remedially by school psychologists and counselors. This study sampled almost 2,000 students with pre- and postprogram assessment. There were significant, positive program effects on knowledge of psychosocial skills, self-reported aggression, and teacher-reported aggression, as well as a 41% decrease in aggression-related disciplinary incidents and a 67% reduction in suspensions for violent behavior.

WHAT WE NEED TO SUCCEED: INSTITUTIONALIZATION ISSUES FOR CRE

CRE and SEL programs have been in existence for some time, and in some cases the diffusion of innovation has been widespread. But CRE programs have traditionally been introduced into schools through external channels and treated as add-on programs rather than integrated into ongoing curricula, classroom activity, and everyday operation of the school. There are several reasons why CRE has yet to be fully institutionalized, seen as a necessary component of all education levels, and incorporated as such.

First, there is a basic issue of "ripeness"—it has been only in the past 10 years or so that we have amassed evidence of the efficacy of these programs, thus justifying their institutionalization. More important, the critical "seal of approval" for these programs was not provided by the USDOE and organizations like CASEL until 2000 at the earliest. It was essential that research demonstrate that CRE and SEL deliver promised benefits before integration into the educational canon was a possibility.

Second, CRE and SEL programs started as a means to provide students with specific knowledge and skills. As a result, the program models used were often stand-alone programs like peer mediation; intensive, short-term curricula like Program for Young Negotiators; or extensive, long-term curricula like PATHS. The basic

service delivery system was developed around CRE and SEL as "ancillary" programming. This works fairly well when resources are available. Unfortunately, when resources dwindle and pressures to "teach to the test" increase, ancillary programs are often terminated, downsized, or under-resourced. CRE and SEL educators have learned that the best means of institutionalizing these programs is to make them a part of the daily life of the school through the daily work of its teachers. This maximizes their impact and their staying power (Elias, Zins, Graczyk, & Weissberg, 2003).

Third, recent efforts at curriculum integration, like the National Curriculum Integration Project (NCIP), focused on in-service teacher education in CRE and SEL. The assumption behind these efforts was that the learning process was optimized if seasoned teachers were selected for training and implementation. While the NCIP program yielded hypothesized benefits (Jones & Sanford, 2003), the formative evaluation of NCIP identified a number of resource and administrative challenges to securing adequate support for teachers attempting to infuse and integrate CRE. Unless a school had ample resources to pay for external training, consultation, and coaching, the teachers had insufficient time to develop these skills and apply them in their classes. Basically, the in-service route seemed effective for only relatively rich and stable schools.

The culmination of these factors is that we have CRE programs that work but that have been implemented in ways that reduce their centrality and diminish the probability of their long-term survival. To overcome this, we need to focus our efforts in at least two areas: developing pre-service teacher education in CRE and SEL and forming international networks. In addition, we should engage in research that provides additional information about the efficacy, extent and current legislative and infrastructural support for CRE programs.

Pre-Service CRE

Many CRE and SEL programs exist for students, although they are often not well implemented due to lack of teacher training, and programs targeting teachers are offered almost exclusively as in-service or continuing education. Currently there are no pre-service programs in conflict education or SEL offered by colleges of education in urban environments, even though these programs have been demonstrated to deliver significant benefit. The lack of pre-service CRE is due to (a) a general lack of knowledge on the part of higher education faculty and (b) lack of a well-designed and modular curriculum that fits easily into conventional pre-service coursework.

Colleges of education are sometimes slow to change their approaches to teacher preparation, even when they see a benefit to the change. There is encouraging evidence that they are moving to embrace CRE. Over the past 7 years there has been evidence that CRE and SEL programs are being integrated into graduate level programs in colleges of education. Key examples are American University's MA in Teaching and MA in International Peace and Conflict Resolution—a dual graduate degree program in which students must take 15 credit hours of coursework in peace and conflict resolution; Lesley University's M.Ed. in Curriculum and Instruction with an emphasis in Conflict Resolution and Peaceable Schools, which prepares adults for leadership of programs that address social, emotional, and ethical development of children; and Teachers College Columbia University's International Center for Cooperation and Conflict Resolution, which offers courses for graduate students in Organizational and Social Psychology and in Education related to conflict resolution.

Motivation to incorporate CRE and SEL is increased when state standards change. For example, in Wisconsin the state requires that an applicant for an initial regular teaching license must demonstrate competency as verified by a professional education program or school district supervisor in resolving conflicts between pupils and between pupils and school staff, and assisting pupils in learning methods of resolving conflicts. As a result, the University of Wisconsin's School of Education, Teacher Certification Program has a Conflict Resolution requirement (6 hours of coursework or equivalent in outside training: http://www.dpi.state.wi.us/dpi/dlsis/tel/pi3sub2.html).

A prime motivator for colleges of education, as well as the school systems they serve, is the possibility that pre-service conflict resolution education may positively impact a problem of critical proportions—teacher attrition. The research on teacher attrition reveals that a key factor is the new teacher's inadequate preparation for dealing with the realities of managing the classroom. Unable to handle conflict among students and deal with disruptive behavior, teachers become frustrated and are more likely to leave the profession (Norton & Kelly, 1997).

New teachers complain that their education departments are not properly preparing them in classroom management. Leighfield and Trube (2005) completed a survey of faculty in 2-year and 4-year teaching institutions in Ohio during spring 2003 and reported that 89% felt completely or seriously under-prepared in their teacher preparation programs in the areas of CRE and SEL; 92% of the respondents indicated that "it is important that teacher candidates in my licensure area have knowledge and skills in conflict management."

Recently, the George Gund Foundation and the U.S. Department of Education Fund for the Improvement of Postsecondary Education funded the Conflict Resolution Education in Teacher Education project (CRETE). CRETE is designed to educate teacher candidates about CRE and SEL so they can develop these competencies through their coursework, student teaching, and initial professional practice. CRETE is designed to work with mentoring and induction processes to heighten the new teachers' abilities to apply the skills and knowledge acquired through the project. CRETE is also designed to evaluate, refine, and prepare project protocols and instructional materials for dissemination to other colleges of education throughout the nation.

The CRETE project builds on a long history of accomplishment in higher education initiatives by the Ohio Commission for Dispute Resolution and Conflict Management. The Ohio Commission on Dispute Resolution and Conflict Management has held Conflict Resolution Education Institutes for Higher Education Professional Preparation Faculty over the past 5 years. The goal of the Institute is to assist faculty in providing future educators with the conflict resolution skills they will need to be leaders in creating safer, more supportive learning environments. The Institute prepares faculty participants to achieve these objectives by (a) examining personal conflict resolution skills, (b) illustrating successful integration of conflict resolution content and skills into higher education courses, and (c) developing strategies for institutionalizing conflict resolution in the professional preparation curricula of Ohio colleges and universities.

Internationalization

CRE is becoming more prevalent around the world, with particular strongholds in European countries such as Norway, the Netherlands, the United Kingdom, France, Germany, and Northern Ireland. For example, Norway requires peer mediation and bullying prevention programs in all elementary and secondary schools—by mandate of the King of Norway. There is also considerable interest in CRE in South America (e.g., Columbia and Brazil), where programs like Responding to Conflict Creatively (sponsored by the Educators for Social Responsibility) have been widely introduced in secondary schools (Lantieri & Patti, 1996). Especially relevant for conflict-ridden societies, CRE has been increasingly used in Africa (e.g., Ghana, Sierra Leone, and South Africa). Perhaps the best example of CRE on the African continent is the reliance on restorative justice and mediation programs in schools in South Africa to enhance reconciliation and racial integration (Jones, 2004; Tihanyi & du Toit, in press). Asia (e.g., Thailand and Japan) and the Middle East (e.g., Israel, Lebanon, and Jordan) have struggled with implementing CRE programs and are making progress (van Woerkom, 2004).

There has been an expressed interest in developing an International Center to link these efforts and coordinate specific aspects of action agendas for policy with regard to the United Nations. The Global Partnership for the Prevention for Armed Conflict (GPPAC), in affiliation with the United Nations, engaged in a 3-year process of regional conferences to develop critical components of an action agenda. That agenda highlights conflict resolution education efforts as key to creating and sustaining cultures of peace (GPPAC, 2004). In July 2005, GPPAC and the United Nations will convene a worldwide conference in which CRE will be one of the topics of a working group of civil society organization and ministry of education representatives to plan strategy for the upcoming decade. Within the purview of that effort, colleagues from governments and nongovernmental organizations around the world will develop an International Center for CRE to accomplish the following:

- Development of a clearinghouse of current information on CRE programs, initiatives, and accomplishments
- Partnership with sister organizations (e.g., Peace and Justice Studies, CASEL) to facilitate support for related work and to eliminate redundancy of effort in order to present a clearer vision of CRE's role in positive youth and community development
- Creation of research and evaluation agendas that build on current knowledge and provide direction for critical work to address current "knowledge gaps"
- Development of an international youth network facilitated by communication technology to enable youth involved in school-based and community-based CRE to connect and share experiences and action plans
- Promotion of teacher and professional educator preparation in CRE through development of materials and delivery processes to address best practices
- Establishment of quality control initiatives, including standards for CRE practices and programs and possible certification for programs and initiatives meeting best practice standards
- Clarification of culturally and contextually sensitive implementation processes to enable application of CRE efforts to fit the cultural and social-political conditions of the community of use

Need for Additional Information

We can summarize several critical gaps in the current knowledge base that inhibit the development, implementation, and utility of CRE.

1. *Survey the current level of and knowledge about CRE.* There is currently no database that identifies the number and types of CRE programs in the world. We do not even have such a database strongly developed in the United States

or Europe, where the most extensive institution-alization has taken place. This survey could also be used to tap into the current level of knowl-edge about CRE, its definition and standards in the field. If educators are unaware of these issues, efforts could be targeted at increasing CRE identity and credibility.

2. *Investigate large-scale institutional-ization efforts in terms of political process and influence in related fields.* We understand relatively little about the process used to build a political initiative for a field like CRE. Examining the process used for trauma educa-tion, peace education, character education, or collaborative learning will help identify the machinery and process that helps make collabo-rative efforts and implementation happen. Examining related efforts in peace education is paramount.

3. *Determine the support mechanisms avail-able for CRE provisions in national and inter-national law or policy.* In the United States, every state has some form of legislation that requires the provision of CRE in some form (teacher pre-service, in-service, continuing edu-cation, etc.). Yet, there are only 27 states with Offices of Dispute Resolution and many of these do not attend directly to CRE efforts. There is little information available on the support mech-anisms that states assume will enable compli-ance with existing law. It would be valuable to find out about these support mechanisms and the nature of their use. On the international level, we have specific cases like Norway that have a monarchial mandate for certain CRE pro-grams, and we have policy support through international charters that broadly advocate for efforts that contribute to a culture of peace. Once again, however, we know little about the variety of mandates and supporting policy pro-visions that can be used to bolster support for CRE efforts.

CONCLUSION

Begun in the 1980s as an outgrowth of the peace movement, the alternative dispute resolution movement, and the pedagogical reform move-ment, conflict resolution education has become a complex and valuable asset to schools. CRE programs are used to develop safe learning environments, build community, and enhance students' social and emotional development. At the heart of these programs is the ability to pro-vide students with a core set of competencies; among them are foundational communication competencies linked with constructive conflict management.

The field of CRE overlaps with other fields generically labeled part of positive youth devel-opment. However, when compared to peace education, violence prevention, social and emo-tional learning, and anti-bias education, CRE is clearly the most focused on the development of skill sets coupled with ability in group and inter-personal conflict analysis.

A variety of CRE program models have been developed, with each model offering a different set of benefits and having differential success at achieving the goals of CRE. The research on CRE shows extremely strong support for the effectiveness of peer mediation programs regardless of model type or educational level. Several CRE curricula have produced impressive results, although the most touted programs—like bullying prevention—do not have a research record to match the current "hype" about the value of these efforts. In comprehensive CRE programs, some of the best research suggests significant benefit but also cautions against the dangers of poor program fidelity yielding coun-terproductive results.

CRE, once primarily if not exclusively an American phenomenon, has now spread through-out the world. Important advances in CRE are seen in Europe, Asia, Africa, North America, Latin America, and the Mid-East. For domestic and international CRE to become institutional-ized and continue to provide benefits for the world's school children, we need to turn our attention to more initiatives for pre-service CRE programs, development of networks to support international efforts, and continued research on the scope, form, and quality of CRE.

REFERENCES

Aber, J. L., Brown, J. I., & Jones, S. M. (2003). Devel-opmental trajectories toward violence in middle childhood: Course, demographic differences, and response to school-based intervention. *Developmental Psychology, 39,* 324–348.

Batton, J. (2002). Institutionalizing conflict resolution education: The Ohio model. *Conflict Resolution Quarterly, 19,* 479–494.

Bell, S. K., Coleman, J. K., Anderson, A., Whelan, J. P., & Wilder, C. (2000). The effectiveness of peer mediation in a low-SES rural elementary school. *Psychology in the Schools, 37,* 505–516.

Bickmore, K. (2002). Peer mediation training and program implementation in elementary schools: Research results. *Conflict Resolution Quarterly, 20,* 137–160.

Bodine, R. J., & Crawford, D. K. (1998). *The handbook of conflict resolution education: A guide to building quality programs in schools.* San Francisco: Jossey-Bass.

Bosworth, K., Espelage, D., DuBay, T., Daytner, G., & Karageorge, K. (2000). Preliminary evaluation of a multi-media violence prevention program for adolescents. *American Journal of Health Behavior, 24,* 268–280.

Brion-Meisels, S., Rendiero, B., & Lowenheim, G. (1984). Student decision-making: Improving school climate for all students. In S. Braaten, R. Rutherford, Jr., & C. Kardash (Eds.), *Programming for adolescents with behavioral disorders* (pp. 154–178). Reston, VA: Council for Exceptional Children.

Broadbear, B. C. (2001). Evaluation of the Second Step curriculum for conflict resolution skills in preschool children from diverse parent households (Doctoral dissertation, Indiana University, 2000). *Dissertation Abstracts International, 61 (11-A),* 4300.

Burrell, N. A., Zirbel, C. S., & Allen, M. (2003). Evaluating peer mediation outcomes in educational settings: A meta-analytic review. *Conflict Resolution Quarterly, 21,* 7–26.

Burstyn, J. N., Bender, G., Casella, R., Gordon, H. W., Guerra, D. P., Luschen, K. V., Stevens, R., & Williams, K. M. (2001). *Preventing violence in schools: A challenge to American democracy.* Mahwah, NJ: Lawrence Erlbaum.

Catalano, R. F., Berglund, M. L., Ryan, J. A. M., Lonczak, H. S., & Hawkins, J. D. (2002). Positive youth development in the United States: Research findings on evaluations of positive youth development programs. *Prevention and Treatment, 5.* Retrieved August 1, 2002, from http://journals.apa.org/prevention/volume5/pre0050015a.html

Centers for Disease Control. (2001). Youth Risk Behavior Surveillance System. Retrieved June 1, 2005, from http://www.cdc.gov/HealthyYouth/YRBS

Cohen, R. (2003). Students helping students: Peer mediation. In T. S. Jones & R. Compton (Eds.), *Kids working it out: Stories and strategies for making peace in our schools* (pp. 109–128). San Francisco: Jossey-Bass.

Compton, R. O. (2003). Kids and conflict in schools: What's it really like? In T. S. Jones & R. O. Compton (Eds.), *Kids working it out: Stories and strategies for making peace in our schools* (pp. 3–16). San Francisco: Jossey-Bass.

Conduct Problems Prevention Research Group. (1999). Initial impact of the Fast Track Prevention Trial of Conduct Problems: II. Classroom effect. *Journal of Consulting and Clinical Psychology, 67,* 648–657.

Conte, Z. (2001). The gift of the arts. In L. Lantieri (Ed.), *Schools with spirit: Nurturing the inner lives of children and teachers* (pp. 77–89). Boston: Beacon.

Craig, W., Henderson, K., & Murphy, J. (2000). Prospective teachers' attitudes toward bullying and victimization. *School Psychology International, 21*(1), 5–22.

Cunningham, P. B. (2001). Implementation of an empirically based drug and violence prevention and intervention program in public school settings. *Journal of Clinical Child Psychology, 30,* 221–233.

Druliner, J. K., & Prichard, H. (2003). "We can handle this ourselves": Learning to negotiate conflicts. In T. S. Jones & R. Compton (Eds.), *Kids working it out: Stories and strategies for making peace in our schools* (pp. 98–108). San Francisco: Jossey-Bass.

Dudley, B. S. (1995). Peer mediation and negotiation in the middle school: An investigation of training effects (Doctoral dissertation, University of Minnesota, 1994). *Dissertation Abstracts International, 56 (1-A),* 0142.

Dudley, B. S., Johnson, D. W., & Johnson, R. (1996). Conflict-resolution training and middle school students' integrative negotiation behavior. *Journal of Applied Social Psychology, 26,* 2038–2052.

DuRant, R., Barkin, S., & Krowchuk, D. (2001). Evaluation of a peaceful conflict resolution and violence prevention curriculum for sixth-grade students. *Journal of Adolescent Health, 28,* 386–393.

Elias, M. J., Zins, J., Graczyk, P. A., & Weissberg, R. P. (2003). Implementation, sustainability, and scaling up of social-emotional and academic innovations in public schools. *School Psychology Review, 32,* 303–320.

Elias, M. J., Zins, J., Weissberg, R. P., Frey, K. S., Greenberg, M. T., Haynes, N. M., Kessler, R., Schwab-Stone, M. E., & Shriver, T. P. (1997). *Promoting social and emotional learning: Guidelines for educators.* Alexandria, VA: Association for Supervision and Curriculum Development.

Epstein, E. (1996). Evaluation of an elementary school conflict resolution-peer mediation program (Doctoral dissertation, University of Memphis, 1996). *Dissertation Abstracts International, 57 (6-A),* 2370.

Espelage, D. L., & Swearer, S. (2003). Research on school bullying and victimization: What have we learned and where do we go from here? *School Psychology Review, 32,* 365–384.

Farrell, A. D., Meyer, A. L., Kung, E., & Sullivan, T. (2001). Development and evaluation of school-based violence prevention programs. *Journal of Clinical Child Psychology, 30,* 207–221.

Farrell, A. D., Meyer, A. L., & White, K. S. (2001). Evaluation of Responding in Peaceful and Positive Ways (RIPP): A school-based prevention program for reducing violence among urban adolescents. *Journal of Clinical Child Psychology, 30,* 451–464.

Farrell, A. D., Valois, R., & Meyer, A. L. (2002). Evaluations of the RIPP-6 Violence Prevention at a rural middle school. *American Journal of Health Education, 33*(3), 167–172.

Fast, J., Fanelli, F., & Salen, L. (2003). How becoming mediators affects aggressive students. *Children & Schools, 25*(3), 161–171.

Fitch, T., & Marshall, J. L. (1999). *The Teaching Students to Be Peacemakers Program: Program overview and review of the literature.* ERIC Clearinghouse, Teachers and Teacher Education (SP038908). (ERIC Document Reproduction Service No. ED436517)

Girard, K., & Koch, S. (1996). *Conflict resolution in the schools: A manual for educators.* San Francisco: Jossey-Bass.

Global Partnership for the Prevention of Armed Conflict (GPPAC). (2004). *Dublin action agenda on the prevention of violent conflict.* Utrecht, The Netherlands: European Centre for Conflict Prevention.

Greenberg, M. T., Weissberg, R., Utne-O'Brien, M., Zins, J., Fredericks, L., Resnik, H., & Elias, M. (2003). Enhancing school-based prevention and youth development through coordinated social, emotional and academic learning. *American Psychologist, 58,* 466–474.

Greenberg, M. T., & Kusche, C. A. (1996). *The PATHS project: Preventive intervention for children. Final report to the National Institutes of Health* (Grant Number R01MH42131). Seattle: University of Washington.

Grossman, D. C., Neckerman, H. J., Koepsell, T. D., Liu, P. Y., Asher, K. N., Beland, K., Frey, K., & Rivara, E. P. (1997). Effectiveness of a violence prevention curriculum among children in elementary school: A randomized controlled trial. *Journal of the American Medical Association, 277,* 1605–1611.

Harris, P. (1999). Teaching conflict resolution skills to children: A comparison between a curriculum based and a modified peer mediation program (Doctoral dissertation, University of Kansas, 1998). *Dissertation Abstracts International, 59 (9-A),* 3397.

Hart, J., & Gunty, M. (1997). The impact of a peer mediation program on an elementary school environment. *Peace & Change, 22*(1), 76–92.

Heydenberk, W. R., Heydenberk, R. A., & Bailey, S. P. (2003). Conflict resolution and moral reasoning. *Conflict Resolution Quarterly, 21,* 27–46.

Ierley, A., & Claassen-Wilson, D. (2003). Making things right: Restorative justice for school communities. In T. S. Jones & R. Compton (Eds.), *Kids working it out: Stories and strategies for making peace in our schools* (pp. 199–220). San Francisco: Jossey-Bass.

Johnson, D. W., & Johnson, R. T. (1996). Conflict resolution and peer mediation programs in elementary and secondary schools: A review of the research. *Review of Educational Research, 66,* 459–506.

Johnson, D. W., & Johnson, R. T. (1997). The impact of conflict resolution training on middle school students. *Journal of Social Psychology, 137,* 11–22.

Johnson, D. W., & Johnson, R. T. (2001, April). *Teaching students to be peacemakers: A meta-analysis.* Paper presented at the Annual Meeting of the American Educational Research Association, Seattle, WA.

Johnson, D. W., Johnson, R. T., Dudley, B., & Ward, M. (1995). The impact of peer mediation training on the management of school and home conflicts. *American Educational Research Journal, 32,* 829–844.

Johnson, D. W., Johnson, R. T., & Tjosvold, D. (2000). Constructive controversy: The value of intellectual opposition. In M. Deutsch & P. Coleman (Eds.), *The handbook of conflict resolution* (pp. 65–85). San Francisco: Jossey-Bass.

Jones, T. S. (2004). Enhancing collaborative tendencies: Extending the single identity model for youth conflict education. *New Directions in Youth Development, 102,* 11–34.

Jones, T. S., & Bodtker, A. (1999). Conflict education in a special needs population. *Mediation Quarterly, 17,* 109–125.

Jones, T. S., & Compton, R. O. (Eds.). (2003). *Kids working it out: Stories and strategies for making peace in our schools.* San Francisco: Jossey-Bass.

Jones, T. S., Johnson, D. W., & Lieber, C. M. (2000). Impact of CRE on school and classroom climate. In T. S. Jones & D. Kmitta (Eds.), *Does it work? The case for conflict education in our nation's schools* (pp. 85–102). Washington, DC: Conflict Resolution Education Network [now the Association for Conflict Resolution].

Jones, T. S., & Kmitta, D. (Eds.). (2000). *Does it work? The case for conflict education in our nation's schools.* Washington, DC: The Conflict Resolution Education Network (now the Association for Conflict Resolution). Retrieved June 1, 2005, from http://www.acrnet.org

Jones, T. S., & Sanford, R. (2003). "Building the container": Curriculum infusion and classroom climate. *Conflict Resolution Quarterly, 21,* 115–130.

Jones, T. S., Vegso, B., Jameson, J., Bodtker, A., Kusztal, I., & Kmitta, D. (1997). *Preliminary final report of the Comprehensive Peer Mediation Evaluation Project: Report for the William and Flora Hewlett Foundation.* Philadelphia: Temple University, College of Allied Health Professions.

Juvonen, J., & Graham, S. (Eds.). (2001). *Peer harassment in school: The plight of the vulnerable and victimized.* New York: Guilford.

Kaiser-Ulrey, C. L. (2004). Bullying in middle school: A study of B.E.S.T.—Bullying Eliminated from Schools Together—An anti-bullying program for seventh-grade students (Doctoral dissertation, Florida State University, 2003). *Dissertation Abstracts International, 64(7-B),* 2004.

Korn, J. (1994). *Increasing teachers' and students' skill levels of conflict resolution and peer mediation strategies through teacher and student training programs* (Ed.D. Practicum Report, Nova Southeastern University, Fort Lauderdale, FL, 1994). (ERIC Document Reproduction Services No. ED375944)

Kusche, C. A., & Greenberg, M. T. (1995). *The PATHS curriculum.* Seattle, WA: Developmental Research and Programs.

Lane-Garon, P. S. (1998). Developmental considerations: Encouraging perspective-taking in student mediators. *Mediation Quarterly, 16,* 201–217.

Lane-Garon, P. S. (2000). Practicing peace: The impact of a school-based conflict resolution program on elementary students. *Peace & Change, 25,* 467–483.

Lane-Garon, P. S., & Richardson, T. (2003). Mediator mentors: Improving school climate, nurturing student disposition. *Conflict Resolution Quarterly, 21,* 47–68.

Lantieri, L., & Patti, J. (1996). *Waging peace in our schools.* Boston: Beacon.

Leighfield, K., & Trube, B. (2005). Teacher education programs in Ohio and conflict management: Do they walk the walk? *Conflict Resolution Quarterly, 22,* 409–413.

Lieber, C. M. (2003). The building blocks of conflict resolution education: Direct instruction, adult modeling, and core practices. In T. S. Jones & R. Compton (Eds.), *Kids working it out: Stories and strategies for making peace in our schools* (pp. 35–62). San Francisco: Jossey-Bass.

Lockwood, D. (1997). *Violence among middle school and high school students: Analysis and implications for prevention. Research in Brief.* Washington, DC: U.S. Department of Justice, Office of Justice Programs, National Institute of Justice.

Lumsden, L. (2002). *Preventing bullying.* ERIC Clearinghouse on Educational Management, College of Education, University of Oregon, Eugene, OR (Contract No. R189002001). (ERIC Document Reproduction Service No. ED463563)

Lupton-Smith, H. S. (1996). The effects of a peer mediation training program on high school and elementary school students (Doctoral dissertation, North Carolina State University, 1996). *Dissertation Abstracts International, 57 (2-A),* 0589.

Mankopf, J. F. (2003). The effects of being a peer mediator on adolescents' perspective-taking and connectedness (Doctoral dissertation, University of Wisconsin-Madison, 2002). *Dissertation Abstracts International, 63 (11-A),* 3866.

Meyer, R. H. (1996). The effect of participation in a peer mediation program on the self-perceptions and conflict style of at-risk elementary students (Doctoral dissertation, Pennsylvania State University, 1995). *Dissertation Abstracts International, 56 (9-A),* 3457.

Miller, P. H. (1995). The relative effectiveness of peer mediation: Children helping each other to solve conflicts (Doctoral dissertation, University of Mississippi, 1994). *Dissertation Abstracts International, 55 (7-A),* 1880.

Nance, T. M. (1996). Impact of the peer mediation component of the New Mexico Center for Dispute Resolution Mediation in the Schools Program (Doctoral dissertation, University of Northern Colorado, 1995). *Dissertation Abstracts International, 56 (9-A),* 3512.

National Center for Educational Statistics. (1999–2000). *Teachers' perceptions about serious problems in their schools, 1999–2000.* Retrieved August 1, 2002, from http://nces.ed .gov/programs/digest/d02/dt073.asp

Nelson, K. D. (1997). The effects of peer mediation training and practice on self-esteem and social skills among peer mediators in a vocational technical high school (Doctoral dissertation, Temple University, 1997). *Dissertation Abstracts International, 58 (6-A),* 2073.

Nelson-Haynes, L. (1996). The impact of the Student Conflict Resolution Program in Dallas public schools (Doctoral dissertation, Texas Women's University, 1995). *Dissertation Abstracts International, 56 (9-A),* 3458.

Norton, M. S., & Kelly, L. K. (1997). *Resource allocation: Managing money and people.* Larchmont, NY: Eye on Education.

Olweus, D. (1991). Bully/victim problems among school children: Basic facts and effects of a school-based intervention program. In D. J. Pepler & K. H. Rubin (Eds.), *The development and treatment of childhood aggression* (pp. 411–448). Hillsdale, NJ: Lawrence Erlbaum.

Orpinas, P., & Horne, A. M., & Staniszewski, D. (2003). School bullying: Changing the problem by changing the school. *School Psychology Review, 32,* 431–445.

Orpinas, P., Kelder, S., Frankowski, R., Murray, N., Zhang, Q., & McAlister, A. (2000). Outcome evaluation of a multi-component violence prevention program for middle schools: The Students for Peace project. *Health Education Research, 15*(1), 45–58.

Oskamp, S. (Ed.). (2000). *Reducing prejudice and discrimination.* Mahwah, NJ: Lawrence Erlbaum.

Pepler, D. J., Craig, W. M., Ziegler, S., & Charach, A. (1994). An evaluation of an anti-bullying intervention in Toronto schools. *Canadian Journal of Community Mental Health, 13,* 95–110.

Peterson, R., & Skiba, R. (2001). Creating school climates that prevent school violence. *Social Studies, 92*(4), 167–175.

Pettigrew, T. F., & Tropp, L. R. (2000). Does intergroup contact reduce prejudice? Recent meta-analytic findings. In S. Oskamp (Ed.), *Reducing prejudice and discrimination* (pp. 93–114). Mahwah, NJ: Lawrence Erlbaum.

Poliner, R. (2003). Making meaningful connections: Curriculum infusion. In T. S. Jones & R. Compton (Eds.), *Kids working it out: Stories and strategies for making peace in our schools* (pp. 173–187). San Francisco: Jossey-Bass.

Potts, K. L. (2002). The relationship between the quality and number of interpersonal negotiation strategies and coping styles of high school students with and without peer mediation training (Doctoral dissertation, Temple University, 2001). *Dissertation Abstracts International, 62 (11-A),* 3692.

Price, R. H. (2003). Systems within systems: Putting program implementation in organizational context. *Prevention & Treatment, 6,* 1–14.

Prutzman, P. (2003). "R.E.S.P.E.C.T.": Appreciating and welcoming differences. In T. S. Jones & R. Compton (Eds.), *Kids working it out: Stories and strategies for making peace in our schools* (pp. 251–264). San Francisco: Jossey-Bass.

Robinson, T. R., Smith, S. W., & Daunic, A. P. (2000). Middle school students' views on the social validity of peer mediation. *Middle School Journal, 31*(5), 23–29.

Saarni, C. (1999). *The development of emotional competence.* New York: Guilford.

Salomon, G. (2002). The nature of peace education: Not all programs are created equal. In G. Salomon & B. Nevo (Eds.), *Peace education: The concept, principles and practices around the world* (pp. 3–36). London: Lawrence Erlbaum.

Salomon, G., & Nevo, B. (Eds.). (2002). *Peace education: The concept, principles and practices around the world.* London: Lawrence Erlbaum.

Salovey, P., & Sluyter, D. (Eds.). (1997). *Emotional development and emotional intelligence: Educational implications.* New York: Basic Books.

Sandy, S. V., & Boardman, S. K. (2000). The Peaceful Kids Conflict Resolution Program. *International Journal of Conflict Management, 11,* 337–357.

Sandy, S. V., & Cochran, K. (2000). The development of conflict resolution skills in children: Preschool to adolescence. In M. Deutsch & P. Coleman (Eds.), *The handbook of conflict resolution: Theory and practice* (pp. 316–342). San Francisco: Jossey-Bass.

Search Institute. (1997). *The asset approach: Giving kids what they need to succeed.* Minneapolis, MN: Search Institute.

Shapiro, J. P., Burgoon, J. D., Welker, C. J., & Clough, J. B. (2002). Evaluation of the Peacemakers Program: School-based violence prevention for students in grades four through eight. *Psychology in the Schools, 39*(1), 87–100.

Smith, S. N., & Fairman, D. (2004). Normalizing effective conflict management through academic curriculum integration: The example of Workable Peace. *New Directions for Youth Development, 102,* 47–69.

Smith, S. W., Daunic, A., Miller, M., & Robinson, T. (2002). Conflict resolution and peer mediation in middle schools: Extending the process and outcome knowledge base. *Journal of Social Psychology, 142,* 567–587.

Sommers, M. (2001). Peace education and refugee youth. In J. Crisp, C. Talbot, & D. B. Cipollone (Eds.), *Learning for a future: Refugee education in developing countries* (pp. 15–29). Geneva: United Nations Commission for Refugees.

Sommers, M. (2003, August). *Peace education: Opportunities and challenges.* Presentation at the Building Bridges to Peace and Prosperity: Education and Training for Action conference, U.S. Agency for International Development, Washington, DC.

Stevahn, L., Johnson, D. W., Johnson, R. T., & Schultz, R. (2002). Effects of conflict resolution training integrated into a high school social studies curriculum. *Journal of Social Psychology, 142,* 305–333.

Stewart, J. T. (2000). A formative evaluation of a conflict resolution program utilizing peer mediation training on the knowledge and attitudes of middle school students at a Hillsborough County, Florida, middle school (Doctoral dissertation, University of Sarasota, 2000). *Dissertation Abstracts International, 60 (12-A),* 4374.

Sweeney, B. C. (1996). Peer mediation training: Developmental effects for high school mediators (Doctoral dissertation, North Carolina State University, 1995). *Dissertation Abstracts International, 56 (11-A),* 4285.

Taub, J. (2002). Evaluation of the Second Step Violence Prevention Program at a rural elementary school. *School Psychology Review, 31,* 186–200.

Tihanyi, K., & du Toit, F. (in press). Reconciliation through integration? An examination of South Africa's reconciliation process in racially integrating high schools. *Conflict Resolution Quarterly, 23.*

Title, B. B. (2003). School bullying: Prevention and intervention. In T. S. Jones & R. Compton (Eds.), *Kids working it out: Stories and strategies for making peace in our schools* (pp. 221–250). San Francisco: Jossey-Bass.

Tolson, E. R., & McDonald, S. (1992). Peer mediation among high school students: A test of effectiveness. *Social Work in Education, 14*(2), 86–94.

UNESCO. (2002). *UNESCO: IBE education thesaurus* (6th ed.). Geneva: UNESCO, International Bureau of Education.

Ury, W. (2000). *The third side: Why we fight and how we can stop.* New York: Penguin.

U.S. Department of Education. (1998). *Violence and discipline problems in U.S. public schools 1996–1997.* Washington, DC: Author.

U.S. Department of Health and Human Services. (2001). *Youth violence: A report of the Surgeon General.* Washington, DC: Author.

van Woerkom, M. (2004). Seeds of peace: Toward a common narrative. *New Directions in Youth Development, 102,* 35–46. Retrieved December 1, 2004, from http://www.dpi.state.wi.us/dpi/dlsis/tel/pi3sub2.html

Washburn, J. J. (2002). Evaluation of a violence prevention program with low-income, urban, African-American youth (Doctoral dissertation,

DePaul University, 2001). *Dissertation Abstracts International, 62 (9-B)*, 4242.

Weissberg, R. P., & Greenberg, M. T. (1998). School and community competence enhancement and prevention programs. In I. E. Siegel & K. A. Renninger (Eds.), *Handbook of child psychology: Vol. 4. Child psychology in practice* (5th ed., pp. 877–954). New York: John Wiley.

Whitney, I., Rivers, I., Smith, P. K., & Sharp, S. (1994). The Sheffield Project: Methodology and findings. In P. K. Smith & S. Sharp, (Eds.), *School bullying: Insights and perspectives* (pp. 20–56). London: Routledge.

Williams, J. H. (2004). Civil conflict, education, and the work of schools: Twelve propositions. *Conflict Resolution Quarterly, 21,* 471–482.

Wilson, D. B., Gottfredson, D. C., & Najaka, S. S. (2001). School-based prevention of problem behaviors: A meta-analysis. *Journal of Quantitative Criminology*, 17, 247–276.

Wiltenberg, M. (2001, December 4). Peace talks. *Christian Science Monitor*, *93*(260), 13.

Winston, M. L. (1997). Assessing the effects of a peer mediation training program on skills acquisition, maintenance, and generalization (Doctoral dissertation, University of Cincinnati, 1996). *Dissertation Abstracts International, 57(7-A)*, 2863.

Zins, J. E., Weissberg, R. P., Wang, M. C., & Walberg, H. J. (Eds.). (2004). *Building school success through social and emotional learning*. New York: Columbia University, Teachers College Press.

Zucca-Brown, S. (1997). An elementary school mediation program: Its effect on student mediators and school violence (Doctoral dissertation, Temple University, 1997). *Dissertation Abstracts International, 58 (6-A)*, 2077.

10

Perspectives on Workgroup Conflict and Communication

Marshall Scott Poole

Texas A&M University

Johny T. Garner

Texas A&M University

Workgroups are the basic building blocks of today's organizations. They are the units in which the work of organization—planning, design, development, operations, production, distribution, sales, service delivery, human resources, and so on—is done. Conflict in workgroups is of interest in both its positive and negative aspects. The negative aspect of conflict in workgroups is the disruption it causes, which has the potential to break down workgroups, reduce performance, and make members dissatisfied and unhappy. This must be weighed against the positive aspects of conflict, the new ideas and procedures it often introduces or sparks, the stronger workgroup and increased trust and capabilities that result from successfully navigating a difficult conflict, and the increased participation and voice that well-managed conflicts afford members.

In conducting this review, we were surprised by the wide range of disciplines and the generations of scholars who have investigated this subject. We were also struck by the way several research traditions have pursued their particular agendas largely in isolation from each other. In sorting through the various pockets of research on workgroup conflict, we discerned three broad lines of work that this review attempts to articulate and discuss: instrumental, developmental, and political perspectives. Examining workgroup conflict from this integrative framework can help researchers to understand different points of view and increase theoretical interplay among perspectives. Such a framework can benefit practice by broadening our understanding of conflict and its effect on group processes and by suggesting novel approaches to management of workgroup conflict. This chapter begins by defining workgroup conflict before briefly introducing each of the three perspectives. Then, the chapter examines research in each of the perspectives across a range of disciplines. Finally, we attempt to show lines of intersection and potential for future research.

Defining Workgroups

A workgroup is a set of three of more people who carry out common tasks in an organization.

This definition highlights several important features of workgroups that we will briefly discuss by way of introduction.

First, the nature of their work has a strong influence on the goals, structure, and processes of workgroups (Argote & McGrath, 1993). Characteristics of work that influence the occurrence and impact of conflict include (a) term of the group—whether the group is formed for a temporary project such as a task force or for an ongoing, recurring task such as an inspection and repair team in a factory; (b) goal congruence—degree of agreement on goals of the group and standards by which its work should be evaluated; (c) means congruence—degree of agreement on how the work should be done; and (d) task interdependence—the degree to which the task requires members to coordinate their activities. Disagreement on goals and/or means is a major source of conflict in workgroups, and effective management of such conflicts is generally presumed in the literature to increase group effectiveness (e.g., Amason, 1996; de Dreu & Weingart, 2003). As we will see below, when conflict occurs in workgroups, the higher the level of task interdependence, the more serious the potential effects of conflict on the group and the less groups are able to avoid or suppress conflict. Short-term workgroups are more likely to be able to suppress or avoid confronting the conflict than long-term workgroups.

Workgroups vary considerably in terms of size. Three is the minimum size considered to be a group in this review, but typical sizes of workgroups vary widely: Amason (1996) reported an average size of about 6 in his sample; Lovelace, Shapiro, and Weingart (2001) and Kirkman, Rosen, Tesluk, and Gibson (2004) averaged 10; Panteli's (2004) virtual teams averaged 25; and one virtual team studied by Ngwenyama (1998) had 79 members.

Members of workgroups use a number of different communication channels. Most research has focused on groups that interact primarily face to face. A number of recent studies, however, have focused on virtual teams that interact via phone, e-mail, instant messaging, text- and video-conferencing, and various other types of specialized groupware. Members of virtual teams are typically dispersed across different locations, with subgroups of members co-located. The dynamics of conflict in virtual teams are somewhat different from those in co-located teams that meet mostly face to face.

Workgroups differ in significant ways from the experimental groups commonly studied in conflict research. Members of workgroups are more likely to have vested interests in the group than are members of lab groups. Laboratory groups are artificial constructions of the researcher, while workgroups originate as an outgrowth of organizational needs, and their raison d'être is grounded in consequential work and significant purpose. Most laboratory groups have no or limited history, while many workgroups have considerable history and traditions. Finally, members of most workgroups have an expectation of future interaction and experience real consequences from their behavior in the group, while members of most laboratory groups know that their time in their group is limited (even if they are not sure when the group will terminate) and that most consequences of their behavior will not stay with them once they leave the lab. For these reasons, research on workgroup conflict provides a useful reference point for the more numerous laboratory studies of conflict. It enables us to make judgments regarding the extent to which experimental findings hold in the "real world" and suggests important new questions to be explored in more controlled environments.

This review includes only studies of actual workgroups situated in private and public organizations. It does not include studies of workgroups concocted in the lab or student groups engaged in class projects.

PERSPECTIVES ON CONFLICT IN WORKGROUPS

Three scholarly traditions on workgroup conflict can be distinguished. Each advances a particular view of the nature of conflict in workgroups, the sources or causes of workgroup conflict, and the effects of conflict on group outcomes. The perspectives also differ in terms of whether they focus on public or private aspects of conflict and on whether they regard conflict as primarily based on rational or nonrational grounds (Kolb & Putnam, 1992).

The *instrumental* perspective views workgroup conflict in terms of its effects on group performance and related outcomes. This leads to a distinction between productive and destructive conflict that is fundamental to this perspective. Productive conflict originates in disagreements concerning the goals of the group (ends), how the group should go about its work (means), or over the content of the work itself. If properly managed, productive conflict promotes the group's ability to do its work effectively. Destructive conflict, which breaks down the group's capacity to work effectively, originates from relational problems among members and from members' individualistic agendas. While productive conflict deals with the group's work, destructive conflict centers on non-work aspects. Productive conflict interaction focuses on substantive issues and has as its goal a resolution of the conflict that removes blocks to group effectiveness, preserves and strengthens the group system, and meets members' individual needs. In destructive conflict interaction, on the other hand, parties are preoccupied with defeating one another and are focused on personalities and grudges.

This distinction between productive and destructive conflict runs deep in the literature on conflict in natural settings and can be traced to the thoughts of Louis Coser (1956) and Morton Deutsch (1983). More recently, Jehn (1995) distinguished task and relational conflict along these lines and presented evidence that task conflict had positive impacts on group performance, while relational conflict had negative impacts.

The instrumental perspective focuses primarily on what Kolb and Putnam (1992) termed public conflict, conflicts that are overt and visible and that have the potential to involve open confrontation among parties. It favors direct confrontation of conflicts and presumes that conflicts can be broken into issues that can then be addressed through open discussion and negotiation.

The instrumental perspective is predisposed to a rational orientation toward conflict that views conflict as a "conscious, premeditated activity guided by individual decision and choice" and "underscores the planning of maneuvers and the making of strategic choices in managing disputes" (Kolb & Putnam, 1992, p. 20). Rationality provides another ground on which productive and destructive conflicts are distinguished. For the instrumental perspective, a productive conflict is one that is dealt with through rational analysis of issues, interests, and options with the goal of attaining a resolution that satisfies members' interests as well as the master interest, group performance. In contrast, destructive conflict is viewed as nonrational or irrational. Destructive conflict does not take the needs of the group as a whole or of others into account. It sidetracks the group's attention from its instrumental goals and onto the conflict itself and fans members' emotional fires so that they can no longer conduct themselves in a civil or rational manner.

The second tradition, the *developmental* perspective, views conflict as a natural part of workgroup development. Conflict is treated as a phase or key juncture in a group's lifecycle that, properly handled, offers an opportunity for growth to the group and its members. According to the developmental perspective, conflicts arise due to commonly experienced challenges or dilemmas that members must address as they try to build an effective group. The developmental perspective, too, distinguishes constructive and destructive conflicts, but on quite different grounds from the instrumental perspective. For the developmental perspective, conflict is productive if it surfaces the problems associated with group challenges and dilemmas and enables the group to resolve them and move to a higher stage of development. Hence the productivity of a developmental conflict depends on how it is handled, which determines whether the group and its members will grow or will remain "stuck" in a conflicted state that prevents them from reaching their potential. While the development theory of productive approaches to managing group conflict includes confronting the issues, such confrontations are often neither rational nor non-emotional. The developmental perspective emphasizes the importance of surfacing feelings along with issues, on the assumption that only by dealing with both can progress truly be made.

Research in the developmental perspective does not focus on group performance, but rather on the progress of the group as a functioning entity and the growth of individual members as a result of participating in the group. An implicit assumption is that group and individual member growth are necessary conditions for positive outcomes in terms of performance, member satisfaction, and group maintenance. Whereas for the instrumental perspective the encompassing organization is a source of goals and performance demands, in the developmental perspective the broader organization is a source of problems regarding group identity and serves as a stimulus to which the group reacts as it works through problems. In some phases, members unify in opposition to perceived external enemies, which may be other groups, managers, or employees outside the group. In reacting to these external threats, the group develops its own identity and understanding of itself. It may project its own problems and fears onto external groups and individuals, embodying them as symbols or representatives of its problems. Coming to terms with or defeating these external threats enables the group to advance.

The developmental perspective privileges what Kolb and Putnam (1992) termed private conflict, conflicts that are covert and hidden, often dealt with initially by avoidance. Growth occurs through making the private public (at least within the purview of the group) and coming to terms with surfaced tensions or conflicts. In the same vein, the developmental perspective focuses on nonrational aspects of conflict. Conflicts are about needs and overcoming problems that would seem irrational and potentially counterproductive to the instrumental perspective. Conflict is more visceral in the developmental perspective than in the instrumental view.

The *political* perspective views conflict as a struggle for power in the workgroup. In some cases this struggle is conceived in terms of one social group versus another within and across workgroups, for example union versus management. In other cases the struggle is conceived in individual terms as the efforts of some individuals to control the group and of others to overcome the tyranny of a strong leader or to win consideration of minority viewpoints. The political perspective acknowledges that many conflicts in workgroups take the form of conflicts over goals and over means for reaching goals. However, it views these as covers for deeper, more fundamental conflicts over power in the group. When the dominant person or subgroup

wins, its power is affirmed and even strengthened and its dominance reproduced. When a challenging person or subgroup wins, there is a possibility that the power of the dominant will be undermined to some extent and space for other voices created. The political perspective defines productive conflict as that which surfaces and challenges dominance and that which enables alternative voices or points of view from those of the dominant group or person to be aired. A conflict that is resolved in a perfectly productive manner, according to the instrumental perspective, may well be regarded as very unproductive or even destructive from the political point of view if it reaffirms or strengthens group domination and disconfirms alternative viewpoints. For most political theorists, a good resolution is one in which all sides are accorded voice, and power is either balanced or does not enter into the equation.

The distinction between dominating and less powerful subgroups or individuals often derives from existing social categorizations. For instance, older members may dominate younger, one ethnic group may dominate a different one, one profession may dominate several others (Abrams, Hogg, Hinkle, & Otten, 2005). Dominance structures may also evolve in the group itself, however, independent of external social categories. There is a tendency in political studies of workgroups to valorize the less powerful groups at the expense of the dominating ones. Feminist studies of groups, for example, tend to presume that women's ways of handling conflict are superior to those of men and are suppressed by male domination of groups at the expense of collaboration and integrative approaches (e.g., Meyers et al., 2005). This is natural, since the dominant groups' and individuals' ideas and approaches are openly expressed, and so it is important to argue for the validity of the ideas and approaches of the less powerful. However, political theorists divide as to whether they consider the less powerful group superior to the dominant group or individual.

The political view is that conflict management first and foremost revolves around power. Hence, understanding workgroup conflict involves understanding how power dynamics play out within groups. A long tradition analyzes power in terms of the bases of power and the influence strategies and tactics these bases support (Barge & Keyton, 1994). Political approaches also look past these surface maneuvers to the deeper processes underlying them, processes in which certain positions are given presumption over others and thereby affect the effectiveness of various strategies and tactics. In a workgroup in which a single manager has traditionally made all the final decisions, rational argument will not be a particularly effective influence tactic, while appeal to previous decisions may. A workgroup that frames decisions as problems to solve will give rational argument greater weight, while appeal to previous decisions may be disparaged as uncreative. Framings are not arbitrary: They are determined by who holds power in the group. The dominant group will tend to favor framings that play to its strengths (reason or authority, in the two examples) and that sustain its legitimacy. Resistance by the less powerful group often takes the form of advocating different framings that support other types of influence. The political perspective attempts to "see past" surface appearances to the more fundamental dynamics operating within the power structures of workgroups, which are often hidden.

The political perspective focuses on private conflict, in Kolb and Putnam's (1992) terminology. It conceives of workgroup conflict as a struggle over deeper, often hidden, layers of the group, of which members are often not aware and, if aware, reluctant to acknowledge. Unlike the developmental perspective, however, the political perspective views conflict as a rational process in which different groups or individuals attempt to realize their interests. The political perspective assumes that groups and individuals can come to know their interests and can pursue them rationally. The political view of interests differs from the problems dealt with in the developmental perspective, which are often contradictory and paradoxical. The political perspective, while taking a rational approach, also acknowledges that ideologies may prevent individuals and groups from recognizing their true interests, influencing them instead to adopt and serve the interests of the dominant group. Critical analysis and education may be required to help individuals and groups become aware of their true interests. Like the developmental perspective, the political perspective often displays an emancipatory motive in that it seeks to help individuals and groups (both dominant and less powerful) grow past their preconceptions. In this case the goal is not personal growth, but development of influence skills, (sometimes) redistribution of power, and the creation of processes that ensure that all points of view can be voiced and have influence in the group.

For the most part, the instrumental, developmental, and political perspectives have developed independently of one another. Studies in the three perspectives tend to focus on different types of questions, use different designs, and appear in different journals. As a result, while each perspective obviously has insights that would be valuable to the other two, they have followed parallel paths with remarkably little dialogue or influence across perspectives. The following review summarizes and analyzes research in each perspective separately, and the final section considers possible relationships, debates, and points of cross-fertilization.

RESEARCH ON COMMUNICATION AND CONFLICT WITHIN THE INSTRUMENTAL PERSPECTIVE

Studies in this perspective have been concerned primarily with conflict-outcome relationships that contribute to organizational effectiveness. They have emphasized outcomes such as group performance, member satisfaction with the group, intent to remain in the organization, and building group capabilities to perform well in the future. Most studies have gone beyond simple conflict-outcome hypotheses to study moderators of this relationship such as task or diversity, or mediators such as conflict management style and communication processes. A major theme through these studies is that the effects of conflict on outcomes depend on how conflict is managed by the workgroup. This section illustrates the instrumental perspective by reviewing antecedents of conflict, impacts on group outcomes, conflict and diversity, and conflict in virtual teams. The section concludes by reflecting on this perspective.

Antecedents of conflict. A number of studies provide evidence on antecedents of conflict in workgroups. Amason and Sapienza (1997) found a positive association between team size and level of conflict. Stewart and Barrick (2000) reported that degree of interdependence among members was associated positively with conflict. Pelled, Eisenhardt, and Xin (1999) found that workgroups with routine tasks had higher levels of conflict than those with nonroutine tasks. Diversity among members also promotes conflict. Level of workgroup conflict has been found to be associated positively with diversity in terms of functional department (Lovelace et al., 2001; Pelled et al., 1999), knowledge base (Jehn, Northcraft, & Neale, 1999), social category such as race, gender, culture, and ethnicity (Ayoko, Hartel, & Callan, 2002; Garcia-Prieto, Bellard, & Schneider, 2003; Jehn et al., 1999; Pelled et al., 1999), and values (Jehn et al., 1999). On the darker side, Glomb and Liao (2003) found that members of group home health care teams were more likely to be aggressive if they were aggressed against. The overall level of aggression in the workgroup predicted the likelihood that individual members would engage in aggressive behavior. Glomb and Liao explained this as a function of an exchange process. Finally, Pelled et al. (1999) found that longevity of a workgroup was associated negatively with level of conflict.

Impacts of conflict on workgroup outcomes. Stimulated by Jehn's (1995) influential report, a number of recent studies have focused on the effects of conflict on workgroup outcomes. These studies demonstrate the direct effects of various types of conflict on outcomes as well as the influence of moderator variables on conflict and outcomes, moderators such as task type, internal structure, members' attitudes, and group norms. Jehn (1995) studied 79 workgroups and 26 management teams in a large freight transportation firm and found that task and relationship conflict had different associations with group outcomes. She found that both types of conflict had negative associations with member satisfaction and intent to remain with the firm, but that task conflict had a positive (slightly curvilinear) association with group performance, while relationship conflict had no significant association with performance. While task conflict had no association with members' expressed liking for one another, relationship

conflict had a significant negative association. Jehn also reported that the degree to which conflicts were resolved had a positive association with satisfaction, liking, and intent to remain with the organization. Together, these results suggest that properly managed task conflict could improve group performance while avoiding negative outcomes. Relationship conflict, on the other hand, had primarily negative impacts on workgroups, and the implication was that it should be avoided as much as possible. These results were largely replicated in a follow-up analysis (Jehn, 1997).

Several subsequent studies provide more evidence about the association of conflict with workgroup outcomes. In a study of 47 manufacturing teams, Stewart and Barrick (2000) found that the level of conflict in these teams was negatively associated with performance as rated by supervisors. Pelled et al. (1999) studied 45 process improvement teams in the electronics industry and found a positive association between task conflict and performance as rated by supervisors, but no relationship between emotional conflict and performance. A study of 43 cross-functional product development teams in the electronics industry by Lovelace et al. (2001) found that for their entire sample task disagreement was related negatively to innovativeness as rated by managers. Yet for teams that dealt with disagreements collaboratively and in which members felt free to express doubts, task disagreement was associated positively with innovativeness. This relationship did not hold for groups that met disagreement with contentious communication and whose members did not feel free to express doubts about the project. Amason (1996) studied 53 top management teams in the food processing and furniture industries and found positive associations between level of (task-related) cognitive conflict and perceived decision quality, consensus, degree of understanding of other members' positions, and affective acceptance of other members. Affective (relationship) conflict was correlated negatively with decision quality and affective acceptance of other members.

Studies have also examined the relationship between task and relational conflict. Amason and Sapienza (1997) found strong associations between affective and cognitive conflict in a study of 48 top management teams, as did Pelled et al. (1999). Simons and Peterson (2000) also reported a positive association between task and relationship conflict in their study of 91 top managers in the hotel industry. Trust moderated this relationship: For teams that had developed high levels of trust, the relationship of task and relationship conflict was nonsignificant, while it was positive for teams with lower levels of trust. A meta-analysis by de Dreu and Weingart (2003) found a mean correlation between task and relationship conflict of .54. They also found that when the task-relationship conflict correlation was high, task conflict had a more negative association with performance than when it was low.

In an attempt to sort out the results on conflict and group performance, de Dreu and Weingart (2003) conducted a meta-analysis of 30 studies through 2001. They found that overall both task and relationship conflict had an average correlation of –.22 with group performance and more substantial negative correlations with member satisfaction. As with all meta-analyses, the results give an overall assessment of effect sizes, but are hardly the final word, since they may gloss over results of specific studies that show particularly strong effects or striking insights. De Dreu and Weingart also found several moderator variables.

Several variables have been found to moderate or influence the impacts of conflict on performance. One is the nature of the group's task. Jehn (1995) found that task conflict had a positive effect on the performance of groups performing nonroutine tasks and negative effects on the performance of groups with routine tasks. She interpreted this as evidence that task conflict enhances critical evaluation of ideas, which is important to groups with nonroutine tasks. De Dreu and Weingart (2003) found that the negative effects of both task and relational conflict on performance were stronger for teams engaged in high uncertainty tasks such as decision making than in teams engaged in low uncertainty tasks such as production. Moreover, relationship conflict was more damaging than task conflict in teams with high uncertainty tasks than in those with low uncertainty tasks.

Internal structure of the group also moderates the conflict-performance relationship. Jehn (1995) found that for highly interdependent groups (a structure suited for groups with nonroutine work), the positive effects of task conflict and the negative effects of relationship conflict were heightened. Janssen, van de Vliert, and Veenstra (1999) had 102 managers recall decisions involving conflict in their management teams. They found that in teams with high levels of interdependence in goal achievement, high levels of task and personal conflict were related positively to the level of integrative behavior, which in turn was associated positively with quality and acceptance of the group decision.

Dooley and Fryxell (1999) suggested that members' attitudes toward their groups moderate the relationship of conflict to performance. Their study of 86 strategic decision-making teams in hospitals unveiled a positive relationship between dissent and decision quality in teams whose members had high levels of loyalty and commitment and who attributed competence to one another. Teams whose members had low levels of loyalty and commitment and did not perceive other members to be competent exhibited a negative association between dissent and decision quality.

Norms regarding communication and conflict management also influence the impacts of conflict on group effectiveness. Jehn (1995, 1997) found that the positive effect of task conflict and the negative effects of relationship conflict were stronger in groups with norms favoring openness than in those that did not have such norms. She also reported that groups with norms favoring avoidance of conflict did not exhibit the negative effects of relationship conflict on satisfaction and liking. Stewart and Barrick (2000) found that level of conflict and quality of communication predicted group performance, suggesting that teams with open communication systems handled differences more effectively than teams that were less open. Lovelace et al. (2001) interpreted the results of their study (summarized above) to suggest that collaborative rather than contentious communication in response to disagreements is "one way to signal norms about the consequences of disagreement and dissent" (p. 782). Of interest, they found no correlation between collaborative communication and freedom to express doubts in their new product teams, implying that some groups collaborate to confront issues while others do so to avoid conflict.

Other studies have also examined the role of group norms as a moderator of the effects of conflict on performance, focusing specifically on open, cooperative communication. Amason and Sapienza (1997) found a positive association between openness and degree of cognitive conflict in top management teams. Their research also sheds lights on norms related to teamwork: They found a negative association between mutuality—the degree to which members feel joint responsibility and share goals—and affective conflict. Teams with high mutuality and openness had the lowest levels of affective conflict. Alper, Tjosvold, and Law (2000) classified 61 self-managed teams from the production department of an electronic manufacturer into those that took a cooperative approach to conflict—characterized by an emphasis on understanding all points of view, orientation to joint benefit, and finding a solution acceptable to everyone—and those that took a competitive approach—characterized by a win-lose orientation and use of pressure and intimidation. Groups adopting a cooperative approach had higher levels of "conflict efficacy"—a belief that the team could manage conflict effectively—than competitive groups. In turn, groups with a cooperative approach received higher ratings of effectiveness from supervisors than those with a competitive approach. Milton and Westphal (2005) found that workgroups in which members expressed high levels of confirmation for each other experienced less conflict and more cooperation. Kuhn and Poole (2000) studied 10 quality improvement teams from a government agency and a large corporation. They found that teams that developed norms favoring integrative conflict management made more effective decisions than those that developed norms favoring competition or avoidance of conflict. Perhaps the most famous study of norms related to conflict and group performance is Janis's (1982) research on groupthink. The groupthink syndrome is based on norms that value consensus above all else. It is reinforced by a number of group interaction patterns, including bolstering the preferred alternative, undercutting those who raise objections, assuming the group is infallible, and yielding to the leader.

Regarding norms for dealing with conflict, Tjosvold's (1993; Tjosvold, Wedley, & Field, 1986) extensive research on constructive controversy provides a holistic model of openness in workgroups. The theory of constructive controversy posits that group performance is directly dependent on open confrontation of issues and critical discussion of different points of view on a problem or decision. In constructive controversy parties discuss differences cooperatively, consider opposing views without bias, and attempt to achieve full understanding of other members' points of view. They work for mutual benefit and try to integrate others' views and ideas. Tjosvold et al. (1986) found that while simply involving members in decisions did not necessarily improve decision making, the degree to which groups engaged in constructive controversy was associated with effective decision making, accounting for more than 40% of the variance in decision effectiveness. Alper, Tjosvold, and Law (1998) found that self-managed teams that engaged in constructive controversy were more effective than those that did not. One difficulty with the concept of constructive controversy is that it is quite complex and as a result it is difficult to determine which particular aspects of the construct are reponsible for group performance.

To summarize the studies on conflict and workgroup outcomes, there is clear evidence that conflict affects outcomes. While studies fairly consistently find a negative relationship between relationship or emotional conflict and outcomes, the record for task conflict is mixed, with some studies finding positive and some negative impacts. The impacts of process conflict have received much less attention, so it is difficult to draw clear conclusions. There is a good deal of evidence that how workgroups deal with conflict affects outcomes, and the studies reviewed here suggest that the best approach is to confront the conflict openly and promote open, cooperative communication concerning issues and options—exactly the advice given by most conflict management texts (e.g., Folger, Poole, & Stutman, 2005; Wilmot & Wilmot, 2001). This is comforting for those who have used the normatively based concepts in these texts but, as we will see below, may also be cause for concern.

Diversity and workgroup conflict. A large body of research is concerned with diversity in workgroups, and a major theme is diversity and conflict. As noted previously, diversity is a common source of conflict in workgroups, and most reviews of diversity in teams make reference to conflict or potential conflict (e.g., Larkey, 1996). In workgroup research, diversity has been conceptualized both in terms of observable characteristics such as gender, age, and race and also in terms of underlying characteristics such as beliefs, perspectives, values, functional specialty, profession, and experience (Oetzel, 2002). This review will trace the literature that explores all of these characteristics, describe how identity might be related to group diversity, and finally, consider how diversity can be practically managed.

Several studies have considered the effects of different types of diversity on workgroup conflict. Pelled et al. (1999; Pelled, 1996) studied the effects of diversity in terms of functional background, job tenure, race, gender, and age on task and emotional conflict in 45 process improvement teams from the electronics divisions of three major corporations. They found that functional diversity was related positively to task conflict and that task conflict was positively associated with group performance as rated by the team's manager. Racial and job tenure diversity were associated positively with emotional conflict, while age diversity was related negatively to emotional conflict. There was no association between emotional conflict and performance.

In a study of 90 workgroups from a moving company, Jehn et al. (1999) found that informational diversity (differences in the knowledge bases and perspectives members bring to the group) was associated positively with level of task conflict and objective team performance based on records of productivity kept by the firm. Moreover, task conflict mediated the relationship between informational diversity and performance, which suggests that conflict develops due to diversity and in turn affects performance. Social category diversity in terms of age and gender was related positively to level of relationship conflict and perceived performance, but unrelated to objective team performance. Relationship conflict mediated the association of

social category diversity and perceived performance, which again suggests that diversity gives rise to conflict, which in turn affects performance. Social category diversity also was associated positively with members' satisfaction with the team, intent to remain with the company, and organizational commitment. All three associations were mediated by level of relational conflict. Value diversity in terms of differences in member opinion of what the goal of the workgroup should be was related positively to task, relationship, and process conflict and related negatively to objective and subjective performance and to group efficiency as rated by managers. The relationships between value diversity and performance were mediated by relationship conflict. Value diversity also was related negatively to members' satisfaction with the team, intent to remain with the firm, and organizational commitment. These relationships were mediated by both relationship and process conflict.

Pelled et al. (1999) found that task moderated the impact of diversity on conflict. There was a positive association between conflict and the interaction of functional diversity and task routineness, suggesting that functional diversity was more likely to trigger task conflicts when tasks were routine than when they were nonroutine. The interaction of task routineness with racial diversity and tenure diversity had significant negative associations with emotional conflict, suggesting that racial and tenure diversity are less likely to trigger emotional conflict in groups with routine tasks than in groups with nonroutine tasks. Pelled et al. also reported that longevity of group moderated the effects of diversity on conflict. As groups exist for longer periods of time, there is a weaker association between diversity and both task and emotional conflict.

Garcia-Prieto et al. (2003) advanced a comprehensive model of diversity, conflict, and emotion in teams. They centered their analysis on members' experience of diversity in terms of subjective perceptions of diverse social identities in teams. They argued that conflicts stemming from diversity arise when members identify with different social categories that are perceived to be in opposition to one another. Garcia-Prieto et al. identified several factors that influence whether social identities that underlie diversity-related conflicts become salient. When social identity becomes salient it may influence members' cognitive appraisal of issues related to which goals are important in the situation, who is to blame for the conflict, who has control or power in the group, and which norms are perceived as important. When social identities are salient, the goals of the in-group are favored over those of other groups or personal goals, and positive events are attributed to the in-group while other groups are blamed for negative events. Amount of control or power that the in-group is perceived to have tends to be influenced by the ratio of in-group to out-group members in the workgroup and also the relative status of the in-group in relation to out-groups. Finally, when social identity is salient, people tend to conform to the norms of the in-group.

According to Garcia-Prieto et al. (2003), these four dynamics will tend to intensify conflict and make it more detrimental to group functioning when members perceive significant differences between in-group and out-group goals and interests. When goals and interests of the groups are perceived to be compatible, conflict is less likely, though the four dynamics present communication problems that may feed conflict. Conflict is least likely to occur, or to be detrimental when it does occur, when personal identity is more salient to group members than social identity or when members identify primarily with the workgroup and not with other social groups.

Several studies provide insights concerning how to manage conflicts effectively in diverse groups. Ayoko et al. (2002) observed and interviewed members of six workgroups that experienced conflicts ranging from 4 to 9 months in duration. Participants reported that more than 50% of the conflicts in their groups were rooted in cultural differences. Ayoko et al. found that the groups that handled conflict productively used discourse management strategies such as explanation and checking of own and others, talking about differences, and focusing "on the problem and not the people." Negative outcomes were related to "being loud, swearing, making threats, verbal aggression, domineering behaviors, criticism, lack of communication, and overtly paying attention to accent" (p. 177). Simons, Pelled, and Smith (1999) studied 57 top

management teams in the electronics industry and found that diversity in perceptions of environmental uncertainty and education level interacted with level of debate in the teams to affect performance of the team positively. Debate led to comprehensive consideration of the issues, which in turn improved team performance.

Von Glinow, Shapiro, and Brett (2004) offered a sobering argument regarding handling emotional conflicts due to cultural diversity. They argued that talk is not always appropriate for the management of conflict in diverse teams. Diversity of contextualization of comments and absence of word equivalents undermines effective communication, with the result that the conflict may be framed in ways that prevent constructive resolution. Moreover, cultures differ widely in their valuation of talk as a means of handling problems. Trying to talk about conflicts or differences to members of cultures that do not value talk as a means of addressing conflict may be counterproductive. Von Glinow et al. (2004) suggested that substitutes for talk such as shared activities and the use of pictures or images may be more appropriate ways to address cultural differences.

Overall, the studies on diversity and conflict suggest that diversity in terms of characteristics directly related to the work of the group, such as informational diversity and functional diversity, promote task conflict and may increase group performance. On the other hand, diversity in terms of characteristics more distally related to the group's work—racial, age, gender, value, and job tenure diversity—is associated with relational and emotional conflict and may have negative effects on performance if not managed effectively. The ultimate effects of diversity on performance, however, also depend on how the group deals with conflict. The framing of conflicts in terms of work rather than personal differences is associated with positive outcomes. Debate and confrontation of task-related aspects of conflicts are associated positively with performance and other outcomes. This, in turn, suggests that the nature of the group's work will influence impacts of diversity on workgroup conflict. Pelled et al.'s finding on the interaction of task routineness with conflict provides an interesting suggestion that deserves further investigation.

Conflict in virtual teams. Virtual teams are becoming increasingly common in knowledge-based work such as information system development, product development, and engineering design. Virtual teams (VTs) are geographically dispersed workgroups that are often composed of several co-located subgroups with different interests, work practices, and cultural backgrounds. Consequently, conflict is likely to occur in VTs. Several empirical studies have shown that VTs experience higher degrees of conflict than traditional teams (Armstrong & Cole, 1995; Cramton, 2001; Hinds & Mortensen, 2004). This section reviews conflict emergence in VTs, how such conflict may in turn affect group processes, and finally how research on conflict and VTs relates to outcome and diversity research.

Cramton (2001) explained the emergence of conflict in virtual teams as a function of inability to develop mutual understanding and shared knowledge. Members of VTs do not have access to shared local contexts, and this gives rise to misunderstandings, misinterpretations, and, subsequently, misattributions. Differences in schedules, human errors, and different technologies caused problems such as delays in responding to messages. These resulted in tension among remote partners since members tended to make relatively negative attributions regarding others' behavior. A member who did not answer e-mails, for instance, was assumed to be uncommitted to the team, and the possibility that there was a technical problem or the member was out of town was not considered. Armstrong and Cole (1995) found that team members sited in different locations labeled other members "them" versus "us." They commented, "site cultures seemed comparable to national cultures as sources of misunderstandings and conflicts" (p. 198). Other studies suggest that behavior that increases uncertainty, such as not answering e-mails or not meeting deadlines, fosters negative perceptions (Fernandez, 2004).

Research on social identity processes in computer-mediated communication (Abrams et al., 2005) suggests that computer-mediated communication may accentuate tendencies to react to others based on the social groups they belong to rather than considering them as individuals. This may result in stereotyping and

other reactions that polarize VTs. However, some studies of international VTs (Bhappu, Griffith, & Northcraft, 1997; Jarvenpaa & Leidner, 1999) suggest that the lack of nonverbal cues, fewer language errors in written messages, and the absence of accents in e-mail and other leaner communication media may foster perceptions of increased similarity among VT members and render cultural differences that might provoke social identity processes less salient.

There is also evidence that computer-mediated communication employed by many VTs may not be as conducive to consensus building and conflict resolution as face-to-face communication (Hinds & Bailey, 2003). As DeSanctis and Monge (1999) concluded, "About the only consistent finding in the empirical literature with regard to task and media is that [the tasks of] thinking convergently, resolving conflict, or reaching consensus [are] better done face-to-face than electronically" (p. 697). Conflicts in virtual contexts may be confronted as readily as in face-to-face situations, which negatively impacts the process of conflict management. Although conflicts simmer below the surface, it is often more difficult to bring them out into the open.

With regard to conflict styles, Montoya-Weiss, Massey, and Song (2001) found that competitive and collaborative conflict styles had positive effects on VT performance, whereas avoidance and compromise had negative effects. They posited that competition will not elicit negative reactions from other members of VTs, because it is perceived to be an attempt to participate actively and shape the discussion. An accommodative conflict style was not related to performance. In an insightful study that compared VTs and traditional co-located teams, Hinds and Mortensen (2004) found that while conflict was higher in VTs overall than in traditional teams, in VTs in which there were higher levels of spontaneous, informal communication and in which it was easy to coordinate work, the level of conflict was no greater than in traditional teams. This suggests that as VTs develop relationships and work out procedures over time, they will improve their conflict management capabilities. Some of the communication technologies utilized by VTs incorporate features for structuring group processes, and these may help VTs surface and manage conflict.

There are both similarities and differences between findings on conflict in VTs and those in the other two lines of research discussed in the instrumental perspective. Research on VTs strongly recapitulates two themes from research on co-located workgroups: diversity as an important source of workgroup conflict, and how the group handles the conflict influences whether it has positive or negative impacts on group outcomes. Research also indicates that conflict in VTs is driven by some of the same dynamics as in co-located groups, particularly social identity and attribution processes, but that these effects are heightened in VTs compared to co-located groups. VTs face unique challenges in managing conflict due to their channels of communication. Lean media such as e-mail, computer conferencing, and chat that are currently used by most VTs may exacerbate conflict and render conflict management more difficult than it would be in co-located workgroups.

Reflections on instrumental research on workgroup conflict and communication. Research in the instrumental perspective has advanced and substantiated a large of amount of normative and case-based research that posited that a certain style of managing conflict—marked by open communication, confrontation of the issues, recognition that conflict can be useful, participatory decision making, and confidence that the conflict can be resolved in an integrative fashion—promotes positive group outcomes. The still open question of whether certain types of conflict are more likely to lead to positive outcomes also taps a deep-seated normative strand in conflict research that posits that emotional, non-rational conflict is destructive, while substantive, rational conflict is constructive. Instrumental research on conflict is useful because it puts to the test prescriptions long held by the conflict and dispute resolution communities.

The general confirmation of these prescriptions, however, raises a troubling issue. The normative position on conflict management has been taught to several generations of employees, starting with Blake and Mouton's (1964) classic formulation of conflict styles. The research designs of most instrumental studies of workgroups have relied primarily on self-reported attitudes and behaviors. Members of teams are

asked to report their conflict behaviors and assess outcomes; managers of teams are asked to report outcomes. This raises the possibility that implicit theories about how "effective" groups handle conflict have influenced subject responses. Subjects who perceive their groups as doing well (often based on feedback from the managers who are rating team performance) may exhibit selective recall such that they remember behaviors consistent with the normative perspectives they have been taught more than behaviors inconsistent with them. Their reports of team conflict handling styles may thus be biased such that they report confrontive and open styles when they believe their team is effective and less confrontive and negative styles when they believe the team is ineffective. In short, it may be that theories of effective conflict management are reshaping data so that they are consistent with the normative theories, thus creating a self-fulfilling research design. The same may be said for studies identifying impacts of task versus relational conflicts, because the differences between them, too, have been covered in conflict management workshops and books since the days of Blake and Mouton.

Studies that observe group behavior and relate it to objective or subjective outcomes offer one way to determine whether this is, in fact, occurring. The few studies that have taken this approach (e.g., Kuhn & Poole, 2000) offer encouraging replications of the questionnaire-based studies. There is a need for more research in this area that is based on direct observation and analysis of group interaction.

A second caveat for instrumental research is that almost all studies have been cross-sectional in nature. As a result, they cannot establish causality with respect to associations among variables measuring conflict, outcomes, and mediating and moderating factors. It seems logical that behavior would be prior to outcomes, and hence that we can presume conflict management processes precede outcomes. It may also be the case that positive outcomes promote confidence in the group and therefore enable it to confront issues better than if previous outcomes were less positive. The reverse relationship may hold true for negative outcomes. Without longitudinal designs, it is impossible to determine the direction of causality. Hence, results of much of the recent instrumental research may be best considered tentative.

Finally, we might note a major gap in current instrumental research. While instrumental studies clearly indicate productive routes for dealing with task-oriented conflict, they are less definitive on what is to be done with emotion-based or relational conflicts. In view of the inevitability of such conflicts, more knowledge is needed about how best to cope with them. It is also important to realize that the distinction between the three types of conflict may be somewhat arbitrary. Janssen et al. (1999) call the separation somewhat artificial since task conflict tends to breed relational conflict and process conflict can cause both types. Some answers to these issues are suggested by research in the developmental and political perspectives.

RESEARCH ON WORKGROUP CONFLICT AND COMMUNICATION WITHIN THE DEVELOPMENTAL PERSPECTIVE

In contrast to the instrumental point of view, the developmental perspective sees conflict not in relation to group performance, but in relation to group progress. Two positions on group development see that progress as either movement from one stage of a life cycle to the next or movement between poles of an opposition, a paradox. Our review of the developmental perspective focuses on these two areas.

Long-term group development and conflict. A long tradition of research has observed the functions of conflict in long-term group development. In one of the most famous formulations, Tuckman (1965) postulated that groups pass through stages of forming, storming, norming, and performing. LaCoursiere (1980) and later Wheelan (2005) summarized studies of group development in a basic five-stage model:

Stage 1: Dependency and Inclusion. In this stage, sometimes called orientation, the group members are trying to reduce their uncertainty about what the group will be like and their place in the group. Members are very concerned with being included in the group. They are "testing the waters with regard to initial attempts to get to know each other

and to determine what the rules, roles, and structures of the group will be" (Wheelan, 2005, p. 16). They tend to be dependent on the leader for structure and guidance in this phase. If this phase is accomplished effectively, members will have a sense of the emerging structure of the group and will feel loyalty and attraction to the group.

Stage 2: Counterdependency and Fight. Once members feel they have their feet on the ground, so to speak, a stage characterized by conflict occurs. The conflict may be between a member(s) and the leader, as members seek to exert control in a situation they now are fairly comfortable in, or among members, as members seek to sort out what the direction of the group should be and establish a status structure. In this stage conflict functions to clarify the directions of the group and surfaces differences among members that could impede the group later on if not addressed at this stage. If the conflicts in this phase are managed effectively, trust increases among members and the group becomes clearer on its direction.

Stage 3: Trust and Structure. Once the conflict stage has been traversed, the members of the group feel more secure with the group and each other and begin to develop structure for their work. They define roles and work out plans and procedures. If this stage is effectively accomplished, the group will lay the foundation for effective work.

Stage 4: Work. In this stage the goals are "(1) get the job done well, (2) remain cohesive while engaging in task-related conflicts, and (3) maintain high performance over the long haul" (Wheelan, 2005, p. 18). Important to effective work are open communication, awareness of time and schedule, and prudent use of resources. If this stage is effectively accomplished, the group will carry out a great deal of work and build its own ability to work.

Stage 5: Termination. In this stage the group sometimes comes to an end, sometimes makes a transition to a different project or task, and sometimes deals with the departure of some members. The termination stage deals with transitions out of the group formed during the previous four stages. To manage this transition effectively, members must work through the meaning of their experiences and come to terms with their feelings about their fellow members and the group. Often a period of ritualistic mourning occurs, and in many cases members begin to distance themselves from the group and other members.

The various stages present the group and its members with problems they must resolve: how to deal with dependence on others; what degree of independence of member action is allowed; the purpose and direction of the group; control and power issues; organizing the group for effective work; maintaining an effective, creative work process; meeting members' individual needs; and coming to terms with the end of an important experience. If the group works through the problem effectively, it will develop and members will grow, both as group members and personally. Then the group moves on to confront its next problem in the developing sequence. If the group avoids dealing with these issues or does not address them effectively, the group may remain "stuck" in a stage and not be able to develop further. Even if the group continues to develop, the unsolved problems will come back to haunt it. A group that runs into difficulties is likely to regress to an earlier stage at some later time.

Conflict is a critical part of the developmental process. Not only does it constitute a key stage of group development, but conflict is also likely to occur in other stages as well, as members try to work through the problem(s) they encounter. Franz and Jin (1999) found that conflict was cyclical in that new conflicts would develop, be resolved, and the group would continue until the next conflict occurred. Regarding the nature of those conflicts, Franz and Jin suggested that at approximately the midpoint of group meetings, members would shift from more competitive behaviors to more collaborative efforts, a variation on Gersick's (1991) punctuated equilibrium model.

From a developmental perspective, effective conflict management depends on dealing with current issues. While constructive controversy, as described by the instrumental perspective, is one workable approach, competition and decision by a leader or oligarchy may also be effective in resolving issues (Gibbard, Hartman, & Mann, 1974). An effective outcome is one that members are satisfied with and that puts the issue to rest.

Unlike the instrumental perspective, the developmental perspective regards emotion as a necessary and potentially beneficial part of conflict. Conflict stems from existential needs and therefore inherently arouses emotions. Dealing with conflict effectively requires members to acknowledge and work through their emotional reactions to the group and to each other. Only if the group members successfully come to terms with their needs and express their emotions will a group be effective in the instrumental sense.

Much of the research behind models like Wheelan's has been conducted on educational, training, and therapy groups. Wheelan (2005) summarizes several studies that have found this pattern of long-term development in workgroups (e.g., Obert, 1983; Wheelan et al., 1994).

Tensions and conflict in workgroup development. Smith and Berg (1987) advanced a different view of the role of conflict in workgroup development. They argued that rather than following a set developmental sequence, groups develop through addressing inherent paradoxes that confront them. These paradoxes consist of "coexisting opposites"—contradictory and conflicting emotions, thoughts, and actions—that exist in groups. Smith and Berg defined three sets of paradoxes: (a) paradoxes of belonging, which represent coexisting opposites around group and individual identity, involvement, individuality, and boundaries; (b) paradoxes of engaging, which feature coexisting opposites concerned with disclosure, trust, and intimacy; and (c) paradoxes of speaking, concerned with the tensions among authority, dependency, creativity, and courage to disagree in groups. These paradoxes represent problems that continuously face groups, and groups tend to cycle within paradoxes and between them. The paradoxes are sources of conflict for groups, and groups manage conflicts through managing the paradoxes. In terms of how groups can deal effectively with paradoxes, Smith and Berg argued that attempting to eliminate the paradoxes is likely to result in the group getting stuck. Instead the group should live within the paradoxes, work to understand them and the conflicts they produce, and find links between conflicting forces and issues. Finding these links enables the group to move forward both in terms of its own effectiveness and in terms of building a stronger group.

Group dialectics is a stream of research branching off from Smith and Berg's dynamic of tensions in group development. Kramer (2004) conducted an ethnographic study of a community theatre group, arguing that group dialectics would differ from dyadic relationships because of the goal-directed nature of groups and because of group size. Kramer found four global dialectics present in his data: commitment levels to the group, ordered versus emergent group activities, inclusion versus exclusion and group boundaries, and norms for acceptable versus unacceptable behavior. In this model, a group would deal with conflict by using "a range of choices from explicitly communicating about them, such as venting or discussion, to communicating implicitly or choosing not to communicate about them through avoidance or minimization" (Kramer, 2004, p. 328).

The developmental perspective views conflict as a useful and inherent part of group life. Properly managed, conflicts can help groups resolve critical issues and become more effective. The conflicts the developmental perspective is concerned with exist at a deeper and more fundamental level than those discussed in the instrumental perspective. While some developmental models, such as Wheelan's, propose that these conflicts can be resolved, others, such as Smith and Berg's, imply that conflicts will always be with groups, continuously presenting new tensions that must be dealt with (see also Bion, 1959).

Reflections on developmental research on workgroup conflict and communication. As in the instrumental perspective, research in the developmental perspective can be questioned on the grounds that normative theory may be shaping study results. The various models of long-term development, such as Wheelan's, are normative in the sense that they present an ideal sequence of phases that—traversed properly—will result in a growth experience for both group and members. Most evidence for these models comes from interpretive case studies and from longitudinal studies that measure behavior that would be expected in the phases. By presuming patterns are present, these studies may be smoothing over other aspects of these groups that run counter to the proposed developmental

sequences. The strong presumption that there are orderly patterns of longitudinal development raises questions about the openness of this research to rejecting the null hypothesis. More studies that consciously set out to test the null are needed.

The tight connection between process and outcomes in these models also raises questions. If a group progresses through the phases in the order posited, the assumption is that it is solving the primary problems posed in the phases as it develops. If, on the other, a group "loops back" to earlier phases, the assumption is that it is regressing to previous problems that were not solved adequately. There is, then, a tendency to circular reasoning between sequence and outcome in the application of these models. It is important to assess or measure adequacy of problem solving independently of progress through phases to rigorously assess developmental models.

The developmental perspective provides a useful complement to the instrumental approach. Its long-term view of workgroups that focuses on their health has the potential to provide a useful frame for shorter-term instrumental conflict management processes.

RESEARCH ON WORKGROUP CONFLICT AND COMMUNICATION WITHIN THE POLITICAL PERSPECTIVE

Research in the political perspective regards workgroups as "contested terrain" in which individuals and subgroups vie for control of the group. This perspective focuses on power in workgroups and traces how group processes both enact and are influenced by power and the struggle for power. In instrumental studies of workgroups power is typically viewed as a characteristic or behavior of individual group members, particularly the leader. Instrumental studies focus on strategies and tactics that leaders and members use to influence other members, for example compliance-gaining tactics or argumentative strategies. Political studies of workgroup conflict, in contrast, assume that power is rooted in social groups with different interests and different social power bases, such as labor and management, male and female, experienced members and newcomers (note that these groups represent categories of social identity, as discussed above). In any particular workgroup, representatives of these interest groups constitute the power structure of the workgroup. Subgroups able to mobilize more power determine the goals and direction of the group, how resources are distributed, and the place of other subgroups in the workgroup. While the agendas and goals of the subgroups are in part defined by individuals in the subgroups, they are also powerfully shaped by the general interests of the subgroups as defined in the larger organization or society. These general interests and related conflicts among subgroups are imported into the workgroup and result in the creation of a "microcosm" that reflects more general divisions in organizations and society.

The power of individuals and subgroups is determined by a complex interplay of the resources locally available in the group and power structures in the larger society. Local power resources include the number of members in a subgroup (or the number of allies a powerful member can muster), the bases of power available to members (e.g., expertise, formal authority), and the skills with which members can utilize their coalitions or power bases. However, these local resources are deployed within the ambit of pre-existing social structures that give members of some social categories presumption over others. For example, males are generally accorded greater authority in U.S. society, the efforts of equal rights advocates notwithstanding. The power of males in a workgroup is supported by this presumption of authority, even though it is seldom mentioned explicitly within the group. A long tradition of studies grounded in status expectations theory has shown that status characteristics external to a group carry over into groups and give privileged groups a power base not available to other members (Lovaglia, Mannix, Samuelson, Sell, & Wilson, 2005).

While it acknowledges that power is often exerted openly in workgroups, the political perspective also focuses on more subtle, hidden dimensions of power. One of these is issue control, a process through which certain issues are defined as "off limits" (Folger et al., 2005). In most workgroups, for example, the legitimate right of the leader to give orders is never

questioned. That this issue is never raised reinforces the leader's power base. In turn, the leader's power gives him or her the ability to engage in issue control, setting up a self-reinforcing cycle that sustains the leader's dominance. Another aspect of hidden power is using power circumspectly within boundaries of what other members would consider acceptable behavior. Doing so limits challenges and enables power to be exercised smoothly in the course of normal activity, hence keeping its operation disguised within unquestioned activities. A third aspect of hidden power is discipline, the establishment of shared goals and premises among members that channel their behavior in the direction of the interests of the dominant members (or of managers outside the workgroup) (Barker & Cheney, 1994; Sewell, 1998; Tompkins & Cheney, 1985). Members' identification with the organization leads them to follow its premises and in so doing members exert self-control over themselves, channeling their behavior in ways consistent with the organization's interests.

According to the political perspective, conflicts of interest between different groups are the primary source of workgroup conflict. In many cases, these conflicts are played out through negotiation and alliance building among individuals and subgroups in a pluralistic political process. However, many political conflicts do not surface explicitly due to the operation of hidden power. Indeed, a hallmark of the political perspective is that it highlights the avoidance or lack of conflict as a common response to conflicts of interest. Hidden power functions to suppress or avoid conflict by defining conflicts of interest as off limits or by inculcating premises in group members that prevent conflicts or resolve them in ways consistent with dominant interests. Ironically, the political perspective argues that when conflict surfaces openly it represents a failure of the dominant individual or subgroup, because only when the power structures that normally suppress conflict have broken down or been undermined does conflict come out into the open. The remainder of this section examines control in workgroups, pluralistic examinations of political processes, the political perspective in health care teams, and a normative model for managing political conflicts.

Control and workgroup conflict. One active line of research in recent years has focused on control and conflict in workgroups (Sewell, 1998). Traditionally, workgroups have been controlled by management, which sets up the workgroup, establishes its goals, and monitors and evaluates its performance. The agent of management is the appointed team leader (foreperson, line manager), who imports and enforces the motivations of management into the group. Sewell (1998) aptly named this traditional type of arrangement "vertical control"; that is, control from the top down. A different type of control emerges in newer types of workgroups, such as self-managed teams or quality improvement teams. These teams are typically set up with the nominal goal of empowering members, and they are presented as enabling members of the team to determine their own work arrangements and have freedom to innovate. As Barker (1993) noted, however, far from equalizing power among members, these teams tend to develop systems in which members internalize organizational norms and enforce them on other members. This type of control, which Barker (following Tompkins & Cheney, 1985) termed "concertive control" and Sewell (1998) named "horizontal control," is based on teams' first negotiating arrangements and norms for attaining organizational goals and then translating them into rules and procedures that enforce member behavior. Because the members of the group willingly adopt the norms and procedures, resistance to them is met with the response "you agreed to this," which effectively short-circuits the resentment and resistance that often comes in response to rules and procedures imposed by management "from above." That the power structure is set up to reflect managerial interests is hidden by the apparent self-determination of the team members.

Barker, Melville, and Packanowsky (1993) described the role of concertive control in a conflict among members of a self-managed team in a team-based organization. One member persistently arrived late to work due to problems with child care, and members perceived this as a breach of team norms and an imposition on them. As they talked among themselves and worked out the nature of the offending member's transgression, members transformed the general guideline "we all need to be at work

at the same time" into the more precise form, "if you are more than five minutes late you will be docked a week's pay." This latter rule is clearer and easier to enforce than the more general guideline. It also reflects a more managerial orientation toward workers than the guideline. When the group confronted the late member, they used the rule to deliver an ultimatum, forestalling her attempts to ask for a reasonable accommodation. The other members confronted the latecomer with a solid front and insisted that she conform to the rule. In this action, the members inadvertently subjected themselves to further control, since they now had to conform to the tighter rule. Barker (1993) noted that in this way teams discipline themselves by replacing informal norms with rationalized behavior that serves the greater goals of the organization and its management. The promulgation of rules contributes to the suppression of conflict and enables the dominant group to prevail because members accept them as reasonable and objective. It also serves the interests of management.

Kirby and Krone's (2002) study of the enforcement of family leave policies in workgroups shows how those not taking leave developed rationalizations that pressured especially fathers, but also mothers, not to take the leaves or to take much shorter leaves than they desired. An undercurrent of conflict pervades these workplaces—conflict that is mostly hidden and serves as a pressuring mechanism. The resulting reluctance to take advantage of legally mandated leave policies serves managerial interests, but the "enforcers" who help realize managerial interests are for the most part worker proxies who believe they are acting in their own interests.

Pluralistic approaches to workgroup conflict. A more pluralistic model of politics in workgroup conflict can be found in the work of human relations and industrial organization researchers of the 1940s and 1950s. These scholars documented numerous conflicts between different formal and informal groups in work organizations in rich qualitative studies (Dalton, 1959; Sayles, 1957; Whyte, 1948). One study that epitomizes this tradition is Melville Dalton's (1959) *Men Who Manage*. Dalton described a complex set of overlapping "struggles" within and among workgroups based on differences between production and maintenance functions, staff and line, and labor and management. His analysis of these struggles found that they were often conducted via informal cliques that represent alliances based on common interests. Some of these cliques represented a single social category, such as foremen in operations, while others cut across some social categories to unify members around a common interest. The cliques and subgroups commonly struggled with one another using existing organizational rules, procedures, and resources, mobilizing and bending them to their ends.

In an ongoing process of struggle that was much more fluid than the power processes described by research on concertive control or feminist analyses, various individuals and subgroups ebbed and flowed in terms of power over one another in the firms studied by Dalton. The struggles were often conducted via indirect and hidden conflicts that were not evident to superiors or outsiders. Dalton found these conflicts beneficial to the overall organization because they helped it change to resolve operational and human problems. In his words,

> Conflict fluctuates around some balance of the constructive and disruptive. Inevitably there must be constructive conflict as responsible officers and close associates work with varying success to adapt parts of the structure to changing conditions and personnel, while others for various reasons resist corrective changes. We are currently so busy hiding conflict that we quake when we must simultaneously deal with it and pretend that it does not exist. (Dalton, 1959, p. 263)

Dalton viewed conflict in terms of power struggles, but had a much more benign attitude toward it than the control researchers.

Political conflict in health care teams. Somewhere between the managerial control and pluralistic perspectives on politics falls a large body of work on health care teams in which conflict is a persistent theme. Differences in power and status among different professions—physicians, nurses, social workers, psychologists, psychiatrists—and within each profession—among different physician specialties and different types of nurses—both foment and are involved

in the management of conflict in health care groups. The complexity of modern medical care forces health care teams to adapt constantly, often leaving room for negotiation of roles and power (Schatzman & Bucher, 1964).

The negotiations in health care teams have their share of conflict. Several factors, including the complex and pressing work, the strong authority position of the physician, and hesitancy to confront professionals outside one's own discipline, encourage avoidance or suppression of conflict (Drinka, 1996; Folger et al., 2005). Sands, Stafford, and McClelland (1990) found that conflict within interdisciplinary teams was expressed both overtly and covertly within a format that required the team to reach consensus in a short period of time. Yet conflict may also occur publicly, especially among those with similar positions in the status hierarchy. In a fascinating study of imaging groups, Simon (1999) analyzed how neurosurgeons and biophysicists jockey for professional prominence in sharp arguments over the interpretation of images. Keith (1991) described how physiologists and orthopedic surgeons contend for leadership in geriatric rehabilitation units.

Negotiations over division of labor in a group can be triggered by resistance of those whose voice was silenced by the ideology, problems with patients, or coalitions of lower status members (Schatzman & Bucher, 1964). Many of these negotiations occur "tacitly" as members work together. Abramson and Mizrahi (1996) reported that social workers (typically a lower power profession) focused more on interaction with physicians, while physicians focused more on competence of social workers, indicating that the higher status of physicians allowed them to judge the competence of social workers while social workers emphasized collaboration. The numerous articles (e.g., Fountain, 1993) advising nurses, social workers, and mental health professionals about how to interact with physicians effectively testify to the importance and potential impact of style differences in health care teams. They also indicate that resistance to the presumption of physician control and advocacy for increased input is an explicit part of the discourse of these professions.

The interdisciplinary team literature in health care emphasizes the need for mutual respect and power sharing among members of health care groups (e.g., Clark, 1997; Drinka, 1996). However, countervailing forces, including the assertiveness of professions and established status and power structures, tend to lead to the reassertion of physician dominance as teams progress (Freidson, 1970). Feiger and Schmitt (1979) found that even in teams initially committed to interdisciplinary collegiality, status differences reasserted themselves over time.

Another type of exceptional behavior, whistle-blowing, is a sensitive subject in the health care literature. Erde (1982) noted that professional norms require reporting incidents that represent negligence or harm patients, but group norms grounded in collegial decisions about care and in collegial relationships provide disincentives to do so. Erde argued that the ideology of teamwork is often used to suppress dissent and curtail or punish whistle-blowers as "uncommitted" members. The dynamics of team communication surrounding ethically driven behavior such as whistle-blowing offer an important horizon for future research.

Drinka (1996) proposed that the "maturity" of a health care team could be gauged by how it handled conflicts. She found evidence to suggest that the team "survived over time because there were leaders who were willing to try out new ideas and confront conflict" (Drinka, 1991, p. 123). Through dealing with conflict effectively, groups are often able to build stronger relationships among members based on the trust that "things will work out" and the goodwill that constructive behavior generates (Folger et al., 2005).

A normative model for management of political conflicts. Brown (1983) offered a broader normative analysis on conflict management from the political perspective. Framing his approach as "managing conflict at organizational interfaces," Brown delineated several different types of interfaces, which he defined as points of contact between different social categories in organizations: (a) department interfaces, which bring together people from different functional areas who must work together; (b) level interfaces, which bring together people with different ranks in the organizational hierarchy; (c) culture interfaces, which bring together people from different groups such as Black and White

or rich and poor; and (d) organization interfaces, which bring together people from different organizations that have different interests.

Brown's approach emphasizes the temporal development of linkages between people, often occurring in workgroups, through effective management of differences and conflicts. He posits a curvilinear relationship between conflict intensity and outcomes such that both too little and too much conflict result in negative outcomes, while a moderate level of conflict leads to positive outcomes. Brown (1983) argued, "Conflict management can require intervention to reduce conflict if there is too much or intervention to promote conflict if there is too little" (p. 9). He classifies interventions into four types: redirecting immediate behavior, reallocating relevant resources, reframing perspectives on conflict, and realigning structural forces that underlie the situation. Brown described a number of tactics for carrying out these interventions in the different types of interfaces.

Reflections on political research on workgroup conflict and communication. Research in the political perspective attempts to illuminate one of the most profound dimensions of workgroup conflict—power—and its connection to group communication and interaction. This perspective puts the most weight on communication of the three due to its emphasis on the importance of communicative interaction in influence strategies and tactics and of discourse in the constitution and maintenance of power structures.

It is something of a paradox that research in the political perspective often features conflict in terms of the absence of conflict, that is, the suppression or avoidance of conflict. The dynamics of power, however, dictate that it often can be sustained best if it remains hidden. Once the bases of power are revealed and open for discussion, they are also open to challenge. Research in this tradition thus has to delve into hidden power, trying to discern the power behind a series of influence moves or the deep-seated power structures sustained by a taken-for-granted discourse that must be deconstructed. Though it may accord the most importance to communication of the three perspectives, the political perspective also tends to regard the communication surrounding power with skepticism, as though it obscures as much as it reveals.

One shortcoming of research in the political perspective is that there are not many studies that connect pluralistic with structural conceptions of power. Pluralists tend to focus more on the surface and look for power in direct interaction (or the lack thereof). Structural views tend to focus more on deeply held, unarticulated, and unexamined premises and attempt to describe how they are communicatively constituted and sustained and how they undergird power in groups and organizations. The research approaches and basic assumptions of the two positions seem to run in different directions. Notwithstanding, the hints in structural studies such as Kirby and Krone (2002) concerning how structural power plays out in the discourse among interest groups and in studies like Dalton's (1959) concerning how positions of privilege are sustained through communicative interaction make us wish there was more articulation between the two positions.

Toward Integration and Cross-Fertilization

While research in the instrumental, developmental and political perspectives has developed in separate "silos," it is clear that the three perspectives have the potential to inform one another. The contributions each perspective can make to a more complete picture of workgroup conflict can be illuminated by comparing how they address two important questions—How can we best understand and diagnose conflict? How can we manage conflict constructively? We will also consider how synergies among the three perspectives have the potential to provide more satisfying answers to these questions than any of single perspective could by itself.

What is the nature of workgroup conflict? How should we understand and explain it? How can we diagnose it effectively? The three perspectives have different views on how workgroup conflicts typically play out that are colored by their assumptions about the causes of conflict, the role of communication in conflicts, and how best to diagnose conflicts and assess their impacts on workgroups.

The discourse of the instrumental perspective conceptualizes the typical conflict as a breakdown in the normative consensus that culminates in open arguments and clashes. This is reflected in the value instrumental research assigns to open confrontation of issues and conflict resolution and its corresponding negative opinion of avoidance or suppression of conflict. The instrumental perspective views conflict as a (possibly beneficial) departure from the normal ordered and coordinated activities of the workgroup. When conflict does occur, it is how the conflict is brought out and managed that determines whether it has constructive or destructive effects on the group. Both competitive tactics that attempt to force a solution on the group and avoidance of the conflict are likely to lower group performance and satisfaction. An open, confrontational approach that is accepting of different viewpoints, emphasizes open discussion of the problem, and searches for solutions acceptable to all promotes resolution of conflicts that increases team performance and member satisfaction. Though not always easy, diagnosing conflict seems fairly straightforward to those taking an instrumental perspective. They look for disagreements related to the group's work and to relational problems among members. They generally regard such disagreements as rooted in issues that can be stated in clear (and rational) terms. The instrumental perspective assumes that the issues are particular to the workgroup itself and are connected to the specific context of the group. It also takes a short-term view in that conflicts are assumed to have arisen during the group's history and to be resolvable within a fairly short period of time if members are willing to put in the effort.

For scholars in the political perspective, in contrast, conflict typically is hidden and indirect. It is pursued in a power struggle that often uses tactics such as agenda control to disguise the operation of power and the interests involved and redirect attention to issues unrelated to the real underlying conflict. Scholars in this perspective tend to see conflict as the basic state of the group, rather than an interruption of normal operations. Political conflict goes bubbling along in even the most placid and cooperative group and is held in check only by the forces of control and by structures of domination.

In this view, open confrontation is unlikely to resolve conflicts unless it extends beyond surface issues to address power imbalances and to foster open discussion concerning how conflicting interests may be accommodated. Diagnosing conflict requires one to look past surface appearances and discover divergent issues through careful analysis. When uncovered, these issues are often tangled and multi-layered and are usually connected to divisions within the larger organization or society. For this reason, it is difficult to define the issues as though they were discrete, local, encapsulated issues unique to the particular workgroup in question. For the political perspective, issues bring "baggage" with them from outside the group that tends to make them more difficult to address. Political scholars also tend to take a long-term view of conflict, assuming it is grounded in historical events that occurred outside the group and prior to its constitution and that resolving the conflict will take a long time.

For scholars in the developmental perspective, the typical conflict may take many forms, including open hostility, quiet competition, avoidance, accommodation, suppression, and constructive confrontation. Developmental scholars view all these manifestations as rooted in fundamental individual needs and in the "universal" problems or dilemmas groups face. For developmental scholars, the source of individual needs is member personality traits and previous life experiences. Universal problems arise from tensions between the individual and group or between the group and society. Both needs and problems are discussed as though they were "forces of nature" that are going to run their course and that cannot be suppressed or stopped without doing harm to the group and its members. This implies that the best course is to accept them and help the group and its members work through them. From a developmental standpoint, diagnosis of conflicts is a therapeutic undertaking in which we attempt to identify current needs or problems using signs garnered from careful observation of the group. A successful diagnosis depends on distinguishing the meaningful signals of authentic problems and needs from the "noise" in group communication.

The three points of view offer complementary insights into conflicts. The instrumental view

focuses our attention on the immediate give and take of conflict interaction, the surface upon which groups do their work. The political view reminds us that this interaction also reflects and plays a role in constituting the power structure that is brought to bear in conflict tactics and strategies. While the instrumental view sensitizes us to constructive and destructive patterns of conflict interaction, the political standpoint cautions us to consider factors that go beyond the immediate situation when we encounter destructive interaction patterns. The political perspective takes a long-term view that may serve goals such as group capacity building and member need fulfillment especially well, while the instrumental perspective is stronger on performance and immediate group effectiveness.

The developmental view stresses that all conflict, including that based on deep-seated interests, unfolds within an ongoing concern— the workgroup—that is developing according to its own dynamics and facing challenges that may transcend the instrumental or political dimensions. A power struggle or conflict over work means very different things and is influenced by different factors in a group just forming than in a well-established workgroup. The developmental perspective also directs our attention beyond the easy answers that conflict is concerned with immediate group activities and power to the possibility that deep-seated needs and larger aspirations are driving conflict. When this is the case, constructive responses must go beyond addressing work or structure and help the group and its members grow. Together the three perspectives remind us that multiple levels must be considered in understanding workgroup conflict. We must consider conflict as stemming from and affecting the group's work, as it reflects and shapes the power structures that make the group's work possible, and as it affects the actualization of members and the health of the group.

Provided with some understanding of the conflict and the factors that drive it, we face another question: How should conflicts be managed? Again, the three perspectives provide diverse advice. Instrumental researchers have advanced many of the most effective models for managing workgroup conflict. A long history of conflict styles research discusses the advantages and potential problems of various styles and suggests contingencies for selection of different responses (Folger et al., 2005, pp. 214–240). Several normative models for conflict management have also been advanced by instrumental scholars (e.g., Filley, 1975; Tjosvold's, 1993, work on constructive controversy). These approaches advocate dealing with conflict "in the present," that is, on immediate issues that surface during conflict interaction and in response to interventions in the conflict.

Political research has tended to focus more on describing the plight of groups with power issues and how they are controlled than to prescribe how to deal with power. Political scholars often project a sense that existing structures are so deeply embedded that it will be difficult if not impossible to change them or to use the conflict they engender for constructive purposes. This would require shifts in power relations that are often deeply rooted and reinforced by many structures in the group, the larger organization, and society. Resolving political conflicts sometimes seems more a matter of reforming society than handling things within the group. Brown's approach to managing conflict at the interfaces between groups with different interests offers the most practical take we have found on dealing with political conflict, but it is rooted also in the models of the instrumental perspective. Brown's model also tends to regard interests of different groups as "given," and does not deal with how one might undermine existing power structures.

The developmental perspective views the management of conflict as akin to psychological therapy (e.g., Gibbard et al., 1974). Like the psychoanalyst, the scholar or consultant attempts to empower members to improve the group through increasing their awareness of counterproductive interpretations and interactions. The assumption is that awareness is the first step toward change. Once aware, a group (or at least some of its members) is in a position to take the steps necessary to resolve or manage the conflict constructively. The developmental perspective emphasizes the importance of the quasi-therapeutic role. In some cases this role is filled by an outside consultant or mediator, and in others by a prominent member of the group. As occurs in psychological therapy, this person may be a facilitator who helps the group

understand itself and suggests approaches for dealing with the conflict. He or she may also become the object of rejection by the group, which projects the conflict onto the person and learns to deal with it through interacting with him or her. The developmental perspective, like the political perspective, views conflict management as broader than simply dealing with the conflict at hand. Effective conflict management involves fundamental change in the group and in its members. Unlike the political perspective, the developmental perspective views power as just one aspect of the group and, in some cases, not the most important one to address.

Combining the three perspectives has the potential to greatly enhance conflict management. The quasi-therapeutic approach of the developmental perspective offers a useful resource for resolution of political conflicts. As Jürgen Habermas (1975) noted, one useful model for critical analysis of power structures is psychoanalysis. Developmental approaches to conflict management look past the immediate conflict to deeper dynamics of the sort that drive control and domination in groups. The conflict management models advanced by instrumental scholars also have great potential in the management of political and developmental conflicts. It is difficult to deal with deeper issues if the group does not interact constructively and has to cope with outbreaks of contention and competition, and instrumental models of conflict management provide guidance and techniques for achieving civil discussion and comportment in groups. It is also difficult to deal with deeper issues if the group engages in avoidance (Bion, 1959, called this "flight") or if some members are able to keep important issues off the floor. Instrumental approaches such as constructive controversy can help groups to surface issues safely and to manage discussion so that minority voices are heard, thus increasing the probability of a successful diagnosis and change.

That conflict management means more than just handling the immediate conflict, but requires us to go beyond it to change the group and its members, is a useful addition to instrumental models of conflict management. The finding in instrumental research that groups with less open communication climates handle conflict less effectively implies that longer-term development of the group is important even for surface level conflict management.

The isolated evolution of the instrumental, developmental, and political perspectives on conflict has been beneficial because it has led to clear, well-defined views of conflict. Now the time is ripe to consider integration and cross-fertilization of the three traditions.

REFERENCES

Abrams, D., Hogg, M. A., Hinkle, S., & Otten, S. (2005). The social identity perspective on small groups. In M. S. Poole & A. B. Hollingshead (Eds.), *Theories of small groups: Interdisciplinary perspectives* (pp. 99–138). Thousand Oaks, CA: Sage.

Abramson, J. S., & Mizrahi, T. (1996). When social worker and physicians collaborate: Positive and negative interdisciplinary experiences. *Social Work, 41,* 272–281.

Alper, S., Tjosvold, D., & Law, K. S. (1998). Interdependence and controversy in group decision making: Antecedents to effective self-managing teams. *Organizational Behavior & Human Decision Processes, 74,* 33–52.

Alper, S., Tjosvold, D., & Law, K. S. (2000). Conflict management, efficacy, and performance in organizational teams. *Personnel Psychology, 53,* 625–642.

Amason, A. C. (1996). Distinguishing the effects of functional and dysfunctional conflict on strategic decision making: Resolving a paradox for top management groups. *Academy of Management Journal, 39,* 123–148.

Amason, A. C., & Sapienza, H. (1997). The effects of top management team size and interaction norms on cognitive and affective conflict. *Journal of Management, 23,* 495–516.

Argote, L., & McGrath, J. E. (1993). Group processes in organizations: Continuity and change. In C. L. Cooper & I. T. Robertson (Eds.), *International review of industrial and organizational psychology* (Vol. 8, pp. 333–389). New York: John Wiley.

Armstrong, D. J., & Cole, P. (1995). Managing distances and differences in geographically distributed work groups. In S. E. Jackson & M. N. Ruderman (Eds.), *Diversity in work teams* (pp. 187–215). Washington, DC: American Psychological Association.

Ayoko, O. B., Hartel, C. E. J., & Callan, V. J. (2002). Resolving the puzzle of productive and destructive conflict in culturally heterogeneous workgroups: A communication accommodation theory approach. *International Journal of Conflict Management, 13,* 165–195.

Barge, J. K., & Keyton, J. (1994). Contextualizing power and social influence in groups. In L. Frey (Ed.), *Group communication in context: Studies of natural groups* (pp. 85–106). Hillsdale, NJ: Lawrence Erlbaum.

Barker, J. R. (1993). Tightening the iron cage: Concertive control in self-managing teams. *Administrative Science Quarterly, 38,* 408–437.

Barker, J. R., & Cheney, G. (1994). The concept and the practices of discipline in contemporary organizational life. *Communication Monographs, 61,* 19–43.

Barker, J. R., Melville, C. W., & Packanowsky, M. E. (1993). Self-directed teams at Xel: Changes in communication practices during a program of cultural transformation. *Journal of Applied Communication, 21,* 297–312.

Bhappu, A. D., Griffith, T. L., & Northcraft, G. B. (1997). Media effects and communication bias in diverse groups. *Organizational Behavior and Human Decision Processes, 70,* 199–205.

Bion, W. R. (1959). *Experiences in groups*. New York: Basic Books.

Blake, R. R., & Mouton, J. S. (1964). *The managerial grid*. Houston, TX: Gulf.

Brown, L. D. (1983). *Managing conflict at organizational interfaces*. Reading, MA: Addison-Wesley.

Clark, P. G. (1997). Values in health care professional socialization: Implications for geriatric education in interdisciplinary teamwork. *The Gerontologist, 37,* 441–451.

Coser, L. (1956). *The functions of social conflict*. New York: Free Press.

Cramton, C. (2001). The mutual knowledge problem and its consequences for dispersed collaboration. *Organization Science, 12,* 346–371.

Dalton, M. (1959). *Men who manage*. New York: John Wiley.

de Dreu, C. K. W., & Weingart, L. R. (2003). Task versus relationship conflict, team performance, and team member satisfaction: A meta-analysis. *Journal of Applied Psychology, 88,* 741–749.

DeSanctis, G., & Monge, P. (1999). Communication processes for virtual organizations. *Organization Science, 10,* 693–703.

Deutsch, M. (1983). *The resolution of conflict.* New Haven, CT: Yale University Press.

Dooley, R. S., & Fryxell, G. E. (1999). Attaining decision quality and commitment from dissent: The moderating effects of loyalty and competence in strategic decision making teams. *Academy of Management Journal, 42,* 389–402.

Drinka, T. J. K. (1991). Development and maintenance of an interdisciplinary health care team: A case study. *Gerontology & Geriatrics Education, 12,* 111–127.

Drinka, T. J. K. (1996). Applying learning from self-directed work teams in business curriculum development for interdisciplinary geriatric teams. *Educational Gerontology, 22,* 433–450.

Erde, E. L. (1982). Logical confusions and moral dilemmas in health care teams and health care talk. In G. J. Agich (Ed.), *Responsibility in health care* (pp. 193–213). Dordrecht, The Netherlands: Reidel.

Feiger, S. M., & Schmitt, M. H. (1979). Collegiality in interdisciplinary health teams: Its measurement and its effects. *Social Science & Medicine, 13A,* 217–229.

Fernandez, W. D. (2004). Trust and the trust placement process in metateam projects. In D. J. Pauleen (Ed.), *Virtual teams: Projects, protocols, and processes* (pp. 40–69). Hershey, PA: Idea Group.

Filley, A. (1975). *Interpersonal conflict resolution.* Glenview, IL: Scott, Foresman.

Folger, J. P., Poole, M. S., & Stutman, R. (2005). *Working through conflict* (5th ed.). Boston: Pearson-Allyn Bacon.

Fountain, M. J. (1993). Key roles and issues of the multidisciplinary team. *Seminars in Oncology Nursing, 9,* 25–31.

Franz, C. R., & Jin, K. G. (1999). The structure of group conflict in a collaborative work group during information systems development. *Journal of Applied Communication Research, 23,* 108–127.

Freidson, E. (1970). *Professional dominance.* Chicago: Atherton.

Garcia-Prieto, P., Bellard, E., & Schneider, S. C. (2003). Experiencing diversity, conflict and emotions in teams. *Applied Psychology: An International Review, 52,* 413–440.

Gersick, C. J. (1991). Revolutionary change theories: A multilevel exploration of the punctuated equilibrium paradigm. *Academy of Management Review, 16,* 10–36.

Gibbard, G. S., Hartman, J. J., & Mann, R. D. (1974). *Analysis of groups.* San Francisco: Jossey-Bass.

Glomb, T. M., & Liao, H. (2003). Interpersonal aggression in workgroups: Social influence, reciprocal and individual effects. *Academy of Management Journal, 46,* 486–496.

Habermas, J. (1975). *Knowledge and human interests.* Boston: Beacon.

Hinds, P. J., & Bailey, D. E. (2003). Out of sight, out of synch: Understanding conflict in distributed teams. *Organization Science, 14,* 615–632.

Hinds, P. J., & Mortensen, M. (2004, August). *Understanding conflict in geographically distributed teams: An empirical investigation.* Paper presented at the Academy of Management Conference, New Orleans.

Janis, I. L. (1982). *Victims of groupthink* (2nd ed.). Boston: Houghton Mifflin.

Janssen, O., van de Vliert, E., & Veenstra, C. (1999). How task and person conflict shape the role of positive interdependence in management groups. *Journal of Management, 25,* 117–141.

Jarvenpaa, S. L., & Leidner, D. E. (1999). Communication and trust in global virtual teams. *Organization Science, 10,* 791–815.

Jehn, K. A. (1995). A multimethod examination of the benefits and detriments of intragroup conflict. *Administrative Science Quarterly, 40,* 256–282.

Jehn, K. A. (1997). Qualitative analysis of conflict types and dimensions in organizational groups. *Administrative Science Quarterly, 42,* 538–566.

Jehn, K. A., Northcraft, G. B., & Neale, M. A. (1999). Why differences make a difference: A field study of diversity, conflict, and performance in workgroups. *Administrative Science Quarterly, 44,* 741–763.

Keith, R. A. (1991). The comprehensive treatment team in rehabilitation. *Archives of Physical Medicine and Rehabilitation, 72,* 269–274.

Kirby, E. L., & Krone, K. J. (2002). "The policy exists but you can't really use it": Communication and the structuration of work-family policies. *Journal of Applied Communication Research, 30,* 50–77.

Kirkman, B. L., Rosen, B., Tesluk, P. E., & Gibson, C. B. (2004). The impact of team empowerment on virtual team performance: The moderating role of face-to-face interaction. *Academy of Management Journal, 47,* 175–192.

Kolb, D., & Putnam, L. L. (1992). Introduction: The dialectics of disputing. In D. Kolb & J. M. Bartunek (Eds.), *Hidden conflict in organizations: Uncovering behind-the-scenes disputes* (pp. 1–31). Newbury Park, CA: Sage.

Kramer, M. W. (2004). Toward a communication theory of group dialectics: An ethnographic study of a community theater group. *Communication Monographs, 71,* 311–332.

Kuhn, T., & Poole, M. S. (2000). Do conflict management styles affect group decision-making? Evidence from a longitudinal field study. *Human Communication Research, 26,* 558–590.

LaCoursiere, R. (1980). *The life cycle of groups.* New York: Human Sciences Press.

Larkey, L. K. (1996). Toward a theory of communicative interactions in culturally diverse workgroups. *Academy of Management Review, 21,* 463–499.

Lovaglia, M., Mannix, E. A., Samuelson, C. D., Sell, J., & Wilson, R. K. (2005). Conflict, power, and status in groups. In M. S. Poole & A. B. Hollingshead (Eds.), *Theories of small groups: Interdisciplinary perspectives* (pp. 139–184). Thousand Oaks, CA: Sage.

Lovelace, K., Shapiro, D. L., & Weingart, L. R. (2001). Maximizing cross-functional new product teams' innovativeness and constraint adherence: A conflict communications perspective. *Academy of Management Journal, 44,* 779–793.

Meyers, R. A., Berdahl, J. L., Brashers, D., Considine, J. R., Kelly, J. R., Moore, C., Peterson, J. L., & Spoor, J. R. (2005). Understanding groups from a feminist perspective. In M. S. Poole & A. B. Hollingshead (Eds.), *Theories of small groups: Interdisciplinary perspectives* (pp. 241–276). Thousand Oaks, CA: Sage.

Milton, L. P., & Westphal, J. D. (2005). Identity confirmation networks and cooperation in work groups. *Academy of Management Journal, 48,* 191–212.

Montoya-Weiss, M. M., Massey, A. P., & Song, M. (2001). Getting it together: Temporal coordination and conflict management in global virtual teams. *Academy of Management Journal, 44,* 1251–1262.

Ngwenyama, O. K. (1998). Groupware, social action and organizational emergence: On the process

dynamics of computer mediated distributed work. *Accounting, Management, and Information Technologies, 8,* 127–146.

Obert, S. L. (1983). Developmental patterns of organizational task groups: A preliminary study. *Human Relations, 36,* 37–52.

Oetzel, J. G. (2002). Effects of culture and cultural diversity on communication in work groups. In L. Frey (Ed.), *New directions in group communication* (pp. 121–137). Thousand Oaks, CA: Sage.

Panteli, N. (2004). Discursive articulation of presence in virtual organizing. *Information and Organization, 14,* 59–81.

Pelled, L. H. (1996). Demographic diversity, conflict, and work group outcomes: An intervening process theory. *Organization Science, 7,* 615–631.

Pelled, L. H., Eisenhardt, K. M., & Xin, K. R. (1999). Exploring the black box: An analysis of work group diversity, conflict, and performance. *Administrative Science Quarterly, 44,* 1–28.

Sands, R. G., Stafford, J., & McClelland, M. (1990). "I beg to differ": Conflict in the interdisciplinary team. *Social Work in Health Care, 14,* 55–73.

Sayles, L. (1957). *Research in industrial human relations.* New York: Harper & Brothers.

Schatzman, L., & Bucher, R. (1964). Negotiating a division of labor among professionals in the state mental hospital. *Psychiatry, 27,* 266–277.

Sewell, G. (1998). The discipline of teams: The control of team-based industrial work through electronic and peer surveillance. *Administrative Science Quarterly, 43,* 397–428.

Simon, C. M. (1999). Images and image: Technology and the social politics of revealing disorder in a North American hospital. *Medical Anthropology Quarterly, 13,* 141–162.

Simons, T., Pelled, L. H., & Smith, K. A. (1999). Making use of difference: Diversity, debate, and decision comprehensiveness in top management teams. *Academy of Management Journal, 42,* 663–673.

Simons, T. L., & Peterson, R. S. (2000). Task conflict and relationship conflict in top management teams: The pivotal role of intragroup trust. *Journal of Applied Psychology, 85,* 102–111.

Smith, K. K., & Berg, D. N. (1987). *Paradoxes of group life.* San Francisco: Jossey-Bass.

Stewart, G. L., & Barrick, M. R. (2000). Team structure and performance: Assessing the mediating role of intrateam process and the moderating role of task type. *Academy of Management Journal, 43,* 135–148.

Tjosvold, D. (1993). *Learning to manage conflict: Getting people to work together productively.* New York: Lexington Books.

Tjosvold, D., Wedley, W. C., & Field, R. H. G. (1986). Constructive controversy, the Vroom-Yetton model, and managerial decision making. *Journal of Occupational Behavior, 7,* 125–138.

Tompkins, P. K., & Cheney, G. (1985). Communication and unobtrusive control in contemporary organizations. In R. D. McPhee & P. K. Tompkins (Eds.), *Organizational communication: Traditional themes and new directions* (pp. 179–210). Beverly Hills, CA: Sage.

Tuckman, B. (1965). Developmental sequences in small groups. *Psychological Bulletin, 63,* 384–399.

Von Glinow, M. A., Shapiro, D. L., & Brett, J. M. (2004). Can we talk, and should we? Managing emotional conflict in multicultural teams. *Academy of Management Review, 29,* 578–592.

Wheelan, S. A. (2005). *Group processes in developmental perspective* (2nd ed.). Boston: Allyn & Bacon.

Wheelan, S. A., McKeage, R. L., Verdi, A. F., Abraham, M., Krasick, C., & Johnston, F. (1994). Communication and developmental patterns in a system of interacting groups. In L. R. Frey (Ed.), *Group communication in context: Studies of natural groups* (pp. 153–178). Hillsdale, NJ: Lawrence Erlbaum.

Whyte, W. F. (1948). *Human relations in the restaurant industry.* New York: McGraw-Hill.

Wilmot, J. H., & Wilmot, W. W. (2001). *Interpersonal conflict* (6th ed.). New York: McGraw-Hill.

11

INDIVIDUAL AND INTERACTIVE PROCESSES IN ORGANIZATIONAL CONFLICT

ANNE MAYDAN NICOTERA

Howard University

LAURA KATHLEEN DORSEY

Morgan State University

Organizational conflict is ubiquitous, as are written works about it. These written works are scattered and fragmented across disciplines, however, and most do not offer a central focus on communication. In addition, most large works about organizational conflict offer a focus on negotiation processes, often with a prescriptive bias. Following a review of conceptual issues, this chapter focuses on communication in providing a review and critique of the communication literature on organizational conflict. Although the literature from scholarly journals in the field of communication is the focus of this review, publications from other fields' journals are included when the articles have a particular communicative focus.

Many works on organizational conflict have focused primarily on negotiation and, in particular, on formal processes of dispute resolution. This chapter focuses on that literature that explores individual and interactive processes of conflict management. The underlying presumption in much of this work is the constructive nature of conflict—aiming at understanding rather than prescription. Folger, Poole, and Stutman's (2005) double entendre "working through conflict" is widely embraced. Not only do organizational members engage in communicative acts to "work through" conflicts, they also achieve task accomplishment "through conflict." Conflict, if handled appropriately, is an important vehicle through which the work of organizations gets accomplished. The focus herein is upon the day-to-day informal process of interpersonal conflict management as it occurs in the organizational setting. The literature on negotiation and bargaining is considered to be beyond the scope of this chapter as it represents the formal communication processes by which organizational members commonly deal with conflict (for formal conflict processes, see Lipsky & Seeber, Chapter 13 in this volume). We also refrain from reviewing research in areas covered by other chapters in this volume (e.g., work/family issues, workgroup conflict, culture, and intercultural conflict).

CONCEPTUALIZING CONFLICT AND COMMUNICATION

In the field of communication, we have settled on a fairly standard definition for the term *conflict,* summarized nicely by Putnam and Poole (1987): "The interaction of interdependent people who perceive the opposition of goals, aims, and (/or) values, and who see the other party as potentially interfering with the realization of these goals (aims, or values)" (p. 552). This definition has three important features that make it unique in its importance to the field of communication: *interaction, incompatibility,* and *interdependence.* Without *interaction,* we cannot study communication. Without perceived *incompatibility* of goals, there is no opposition in that interaction. Finally, without *interdependence,* perceived opposition of goals is irrelevant to the parties' ability to accomplish their organizational task(s). Although we are widely in agreement upon this definition, the extent to which our research practices remain true to it is questionable. As will be seen, our research has commonly operationalized conflict as disagreement and has relied upon self-reported recall of behavior or self-reported hypothetically "typical" behavior.

To appreciate the importance of our conceptual history fully, and to provide an organizing model for the chapter, we begin by tracing the seminal conceptual difficulties confronting early communication scholars in their attempts to conceptualize conflict as a communicative phenomenon. Here we draw heavily on seminal sources (Fink, 1968; Hawes & Smith, 1973; Ruben, 1978) to focus on conceptual issues as they were grappled with by our pioneers. We do so because in viewing our literature with a critical eye, it became quite clear that we continue to struggle with these same issues. Any treatment of organizational conflict would do well to revisit the roots of our thinking about the phenomenon, and that is the purpose of this section of the chapter.

Defining Conflict

Conflict literature is replete with conceptual and terminologic confusion. Such confusion leads to a fragmented literature with inappropriate applications of theoretic structures to particular types of social conflict (see Nicotera, 1993, 1994) and much disagreement among scholars as to what antagonistic social phenomena should even be defined as conflict (Fink, 1968). Fink accomplished what is perhaps the most cogent and comprehensive treatment of the problems inherent in defining social conflict. The problems Fink outlined have been wrestled with by several generations of scholars in the social disciplines and continue to be unresolved today.

In an exhaustive literature review, Fink (1968) argued the case for a broad "working definition" of social conflict: "any social situation or process in which two or more social entities are linked by at least one form of antagonistic psychological relation or at least one form of antagonistic interaction" (Fink, 1968, p. 456). In leading up to this broad conceptualization, Fink laid out in great detail scholarly disagreements as to levels of theoretic and definitional generality. His essay makes abundantly clear that without a conceptually consistent definition of conflict, any theorizing will be inherently flawed. Fink explored the generalist, specialist, and gradualist approaches to conflict theory. Along the way, he explicated several conceptual disagreements between the three schools.

Scholars who call for a generalist approach argue that a general theory is necessary for integrating scientific knowledge about conflict. This viewpoint necessitates a multidisciplinary approach and also implies that direct study of a specific kind of conflict cannot provide sufficient information on which to build an adequate general theory (Fink, 1968). According to this view, a special theory (e.g., of interpersonal, intraorganizational, community, interethnic, class, or international conflict) is inherently inadequate because it is not informed by comparison with other special theories or subsumed under a general theory. Fundamentally, this amounts to a positivistic stance. Scholars who have argued for a generalist approach are seeking an overarching set of generalizations or covering laws within which to make sense of the particulars of specific subdomains of the phenomenon of conflict. As we look at more current conflict literature, this call for generalization continues. One example of such recent literature is Rahim (2002), who provides an extensive theoretic analysis of conflict and argues for a broad approach to its understanding that encompasses all of its said levels (interpersonal, intragroup, intergroup, etc.). Many scholars demonstrate their quest for conflict covering laws using solely quantitative analysis (e.g., Weider-Hatfield & Hatfield, 1996).

Objections to the generalist view include the specialist or idiographic argument that each particular kind of conflict would inevitably be overlooked by general theories. Since each conflict is unique in itself, all conflicts must be treated as such theoretically (Fink, 1968). Essentially, this is an interpretivist argument. The basic assumption underlying the argument is one of the idiosyncratic nature of conflict. More recent conflict literature also continues to study the idiosyncratic nature of conflict as exemplified in Mortensen (1991), who argued that the complexity and largely qualitative nature of language plays a significant role in the evolution and understanding of communication and conflict.

Fink (1968) identified another argument against the generalist approach, the gradualist argument. Striking a balance between the generalists and the specialists, the gradualists essentially make a neo-positivist argument. They agree with the generalist approach of striving toward a general theory, but depart from the positivistic hypothetico-deductive approach. They argue that the approach to building a general theory should be nomothetic-inductive (for more information on such a neo-positivist approach, see Daniels & Frandsen, 1984). Hample and Dallinger (1995) are very representative of current communication scholars in their neo-positivist stance. In their article, they argue for the quantification of a *taking conflict personally* (TCP) scale; however they also weave into their approach a more qualitative/situational accounting for TCP based on an understanding of Lewinian theory.

Fink (1968) argued that the adequacy of the generalist argument depends most crucially on assessment of the current state of knowledge. He concluded that special theories must be advanced simultaneously to the process of gradually integrating them into a more general framework with the ultimate goal being a general theory, striking a decidedly pluralistic and synthetic stance on the advancement of scholarly knowledge. A general theory is most needed in order that we might systematically classify conflict into types, so that the domains for special theories are unambiguously defined. Until scholars can reach agreement on a classification of social units, a satisfactory categorization of conflict types is unattainable. Fink argued that terminological and conceptual confusion precludes the construction of both general and specialist theories; without a clear definition of conflict, no theorizing can be adequately conducted.

Long-standing social theories can and do influence special theories of conflict (e.g., Marxism and game theory, and, more recently for communication scholars, structuration theory). Still, special theories cannot be meaningfully integrated because they are conceptually inconsistent. Fink (1968) argued for a broad conception of social conflict, but not for one theory to account for all subsets of conflict. Hence, his definition leaves the field open for systematic classification. More important, it allows for many different kinds of psychological antagonisms and antagonistic interactions to be defined as conflict and to be discussed as part of the social phenomenon that everyone and no one seems to be able to define. It is within this rubric that communication scholars have operated, seeking to discover the role of communication in conflict. As such, communication scholars usually limit their definition of conflict to situations involving interaction. Within the study of organizational conflict, the antagonistic relationships of interest are defined in terms of interdependence and goal compatibility (Putnam & Poole, 1987).

Conflict and Communication

Early in the field of communication's history, and resting their arguments in part upon Fink (1968), Hawes and Smith (1973) attempted to sort out the answers to the conceptual-definitional question of conflict as a means of understanding the role of communication. Rooted in a system-theoretic view, Ruben (1978) argued that assumptions about the nature of communication necessarily lead to different conceptualizations of conflict. Whereas Hawes and Smith saw the definition of conflict as an essential means to understanding communication, Ruben contended that the definition of communication is an essential means to understanding conflict. Together, arguments from these two views illustrate that communication and conflict are interdependent; they simultaneously define each other. In practice, any conclusions about the nature of one carry implicit assumptions about the nature of the other. These seminal arguments by early communication theorists so greatly influenced thinking in the field that their mark continues to be seen today.

Hawes and Smith (1973) discussed the conceptualization of conflict along three dimensions or bivalued continua: *goal, strategy,* and *time.* In their discussion of goals, Hawes and Smith delineated prospective and retrospective approaches. The more common prospective approach assumes individuals have clear and direct goals and intentions. When the intentions of two or more individuals are contradictory, a state of conflict ensues. The retrospective approach (Weick, 1979) posits that goals become meaningful only after behaviors are manifest. Individuals view conflict retrospectively, and communicative behavior defines the nature of a conflict process. Hawes and Smith (1973) pointed out that most scholars define conflict somewhere on a continuum between these two extremes.

Ruben (1978) argued that the conceptualization of communication as linear or as pragmatic will lead to different decisions as to what constitutes conflict. In Ruben's analysis, the two extremes of Hawes and Smith's (1973) goals dimension can be seen as stemming from linear and pragmatic views of communication. A prospective view of goals implicitly presumes a "Sender → Message → Receiver = Effect" view of communication. This linear view presumes that the meaning of the message (communicative behavior) is the same for both interactants. Ruben's (1978) system-theoretic perspective rejects the linear view of communication, and thus the prospective view of goals. He argued for a pragmatic or transactional view of communication, which is presumed by Hawes and

Smith's (1973) retrospective view of goals. A pragmatic view defines communication as "a systemic or transactional process involving the transformation of symbols as a means by which living things organize with one another and their environment" (Ruben, 1978, p. 203). Within this view, conflict must necessarily be seen as behavioral. Using Hawes and Smith's (1973) vocabulary, the unfolding interaction makes clear to the individuals that their behaviors are the manifestation of a contradiction in their goals.

Hawes and Smith's (1973) second dimension, strategy, refers to the resolution versus the management of conflict. Typically, early scholars viewed conflict as a necessarily negative force. Hence, the *resolution* of conflict was emphasized as the preferable strategy. In the 1960s, conflict began to take on a positive and healthy aspect. In later years, conflict was seen as functional and necessary (Mathur & Sayeed, 1983) and useful to organizational goals (Mathur & Sayeed, 1983; Rahim, 1983, 1985). Conflict began to be seen as able to promote cohesiveness (Coser, 1956), maintain power balances (Blake, Shepard, & Mouton, 1964), facilitate change (Litterer, 1966), and generate creative problem solving (Hall, 1969, 1973, 1986). With these assumptions came the focus on conflict *management.* The difference lies in the assumption of conflict as destructive or constructive (Hawes & Smith, 1973).

In considering constructive versus destructive outcomes, Ruben (1978) argued for a distinction between conflict and para-conflict (conflict-as-conceived, or the experience of conflict). Conflict occurs at the level of action. Para-conflict is symbolic. All communication scholars have studied para-conflict—"the symbolic process of labeling, categorizing, and abstracting experience, and the bio-behavioral consequences of those symbolic processes" (p. 210). As a symbolic process, conflict is defined as constructive or destructive depending on *how it feels* to the participants (Ruben, 1978, citing Deutsch, 1969). Regarding conflict-as-action, Ruben (1978) argued that "determinations as to whether conflict is good or bad, functional or dysfunctional, useful or not, should be based upon . . . the extent to which conflict serves a system's (individual or social) over-time adaptive ends vis a vis its environment" (p. 209). Finally, although

> associated with feelings of stress or pain, [conflict] must nevertheless be viewed as a *sine qua non* of learning, creativity, biological and psychological growth and differentiation for the individual ... so, also, should it be regarded as the lifeblood of social change, choice, and social evolution. (p. 209)

Hawes and Smith's (1973) third dimension, time, is related to strategy. This conceptual-definitional dimension refers to the assumption of whether conflict is episodic or continuous—a temporary disruption to be eliminated or a normal, vital, and integrating aspect of human association "to be managed and maintained" (p. 425). Ruben (1978) did not allow for an episodic conceptualization; he viewed communication as continual and inevitable. Through communication, a human system *adapts* to its environment (Ruben, 1978). Conflict is defined as the discrepancies between the demands/capabilities of the system and the demands/capacities of the environment. Adaptation (communication) is constant; conflict and adaptation are inseparable. Thus, "conflict is not only essential to the growth, change and evolution of living systems, but it is, as well, a system's primary defense against stagnation, detachment, entropy, and eventual extinction" (Ruben, 1978, p. 206).

Hawes and Smith (1973) pointed out that different combinations of assumptions on their three dimensions lead to vastly different conceptualizations of conflict. They argued that the approach involving prospective goals, resolution strategies, and an episodic time frame is the most common in communication research. The opposite (retrospective goals, strategy of maintenance, and continuous time frame), they argued, is deserving of greater attention by communication scholars. Ruben's (1978) system-theoretic view embodies the retrospective, maintenance, and continuous time frame. More importantly, when taken together these two analyses of conceptual issues reveal that communication and conflict cannot be conceived of in isolation from each other. Much deeper than Hawes and Smith's (1973) analysis, an adequate conceptualization of conflict cannot rely on decisions made separately on their three dimensions. Although conceptualizations may indeed follow these dimensions, an adequate conceptualization of conflict must be grounded in a firm theoretic stance and must be considered as mutually dependent on a conceptualization of communication.

It is important to note here that Nelson's (2001) recent analysis of scholars' language (particularly in the field of communication) in the study of conflict has revealed that we have been guilty of confusion when defining conflict and have used mixed and merged diverse terminology *(conflict, competition, dispute, negotiation)* in order to define conflict simply and succinctly. Nelson challenged the field of communication to the act of self-examination when defining conflict. It seems that we continue to struggle with the conceptual issues wrestled with in the early period of our history.

Summary

All of these early theorists point to seemingly insurmountable difficulties in the definition of conflict. Hawes and Smith (1973) concluded their discussion by identifying two implicit and unwarranted assumptions that plague research in the field. First, conflict results from insufficient or ineffective communication; communication itself then becomes a panacea. Second, cooperation is inherently superior to conflict. Research conducted under one or both of these implicit assumptions is inherently biased by these tacit assumptions and cannot reveal the process or function of communication in conflict.

Ruben (1978) argued that the operation of such implicit assumptions is symptomatic of an atheoretic approach. When an atheoretic approach embodying unwarranted implicit assumptions is combined with the variety of conceptual and operational choices made (implicitly or explicitly) in research, it is no wonder that the literature on communication and conflict is fragmented, contradictory, and inconclusive. "The role of communication in conflict will not yield to easy and simple description largely because differing entering assumptions lead to different theoretical stances and different research results" (Hawes & Smith, 1973, p. 435). Ruben's (1978) article makes it clear that a theoretic stance should precede and guide entering assumptions, not vice versa.

Moreover, the phenomenon itself is so multifaceted that agreement among scholars on theoretic, conceptual, and operational issues is unlikely. Fink's (1968) treatment of the area makes this abundantly clear. Ironically, it is exactly the enigmatic nature of the phenomenon of conflict that has so fascinated generations of scholars. As producers and consumers of conflict research, we must remain vigilant to conceptual and operational issues. Producers of the research should make such issues explicit and theoretically grounded. Consumers of this research should be critical of researchers' treatments of these issues—interpreting research in light of such critical examination. With such vigilance, we may yet be able to discover the role of communication in conflict (and vice versa), which is, of course, the primary purpose of this entire volume.

The reminder of this chapter reviews and critiques the communication literature on organizational conflict. As stated above, we focus particularly on communication journals and on empirical research that addresses the day-to-day informal process of interpersonal conflict management as it occurs in the organizational setting. Research taking a conflict styles/strategies approach has been by far the most common avenue for studying organizational conflict in our field, and thus represents the lion's share of our review. Along with specific points of critique, we consider as we review research how well scholars have attended to the definitional issues above. Finally, we provide theoretic and methodological recommendations for future development.

Following the review and critique of literature, we discuss the challenge of practical applications of this literature. We distinguish the scholarly knowledge-seeking enterprise from the practical pedagogical enterprise. We then provide recommendations for applications of this literature in organizational communication training and development.

CONFLICT STYLES AND STRATEGIES

Researchers of interpersonal and relational communication have utilized a variety of approaches to study conflict, including examination of actual behavior, examination of responses to hypothetical conflict situations, and analysis of respondent reports of real past conflicts (for more details on measurement, see Fink, Cai, & Wang, Chapter 2 in this volume). Although research in the interpersonal and relational contexts has been acknowledged as part of our overall knowledge base, organizational communication researchers have traditionally approached the study of conflict from a more static perspective. Particularly in the 1970s and 1980s, the overwhelmingly dominant pattern of organizational conflict research was the explication of predispositions for conflict management styles (or tactics or modes), usually followed by an evaluation of the successfulness of each style and implications for training (Hall, 1969, 1973, 1986; Putnam & Wilson, 1982; Rahim, 1983; Ross & DeWine, 1982, 1987; Thomas & Kilmann, 1974). Although lacking a dynamic perspective, this early research was largely successful and generated a great amount of knowledge.

From the burgeoning of the field of organizational communication in the 1960s, its scholars recognized the importance of studying conflict. Research continued to underscore this value. For example, examination of successful managerial behaviors revealed that successful managers spend more time managing conflict than do unsuccessful managers (Luthans, Rosenkrantz, & Hennessy, 1985). Because organizations of various size and function have reported conflict management training to be of considerable importance to their employees (e.g., DeWine, 1994), a great demand began to grow for conflict skills training in industry. This demand prompted scholars to strive to identify successful strategies for managing conflict (e.g., Burke, 1970; Deutsch, 1973; Kilmann & Thomas, 1977; Putnam & Wilson, 1982; Renwick, 1977), and this approach led directly to the preponderance of models of organizational conflict management styles that typify the literature from the 1960s through the 1980s.

The influence of the predispositional styles/ strategies approach, largely driven by the practical concerns of training, has been enormous— so much so, that even to date most research in organizational conflict takes this approach. Later in this section of the chapter, we review, in detail, research dating back to the early 1990s. We have divided this body of most recent research into subcategories: extensions of the styles approach, superior/subordinate conflict (by far the largest—a clear indicator of the literature's managerial bias), culture and conflict styles, and gender and conflict styles. Before embarking upon this detailed review of the recent and contemporary literature in these categories, however, we provide a historical background for this more recent conflict styles research in an overview of organizational conflict management styles research through the 1980s, which was almost exclusively the approach from which conflict research was conducted in the field of organizational communication.

Overview of the Styles/Strategies Predispositional Approach

From the seminal years of this research tradition through the 1980s, a multitude of theorists and researchers conceptualized similar styles and conflict management predispositions. Blake and Mouton (1964) were the first to develop a category scheme for styles of organizational conflict management. Five conflict styles along two dimensions were posited in their Managerial Grid: *forcing, confronting, smoothing, withdrawal,* and *compromising*. Their two dimensions were labeled *Concern for Results* and *Concern for People*. *Forcing* is linked to competition and power, with little respect for the needs of others. *Confrontation* is a process of integrating and collaborating, directly facing the problem and assessing possible solutions. *Smoothing* has low concern for results but high concern for people and represents accommodating behaviors that aim to hide or ignore the conflict. *Withdrawal* is physical or psychological avoidance. Finally, *compromise* aims at simple solutions with each party acquiescing to the original demand (Putnam & Wilson, 1982).

Greatly influenced by Blake and Mouton's (1964) work, many researchers reduced the five-style taxonomy to three distinct styles: cooperative, disclosive, or integrative; competitive, antagonistic, or distributive; and avoidance (Canary & Spitzberg, 1989; Putnam & Wilson, 1982; Ross & DeWine, 1982, 1987; Sillars, 1980a, 1980b). Whether grouping conflict management styles

into five categories or reducing them to three, researchers generated a large body of knowledge about conflict from a styles approach. Blake and Mouton's (1964) theoretical framework enjoyed wide acceptance during the first three decades of conflict management research in the field of organizational communication. While researchers vary considerably in their definitions of style and in their definitions of conflict itself, several category schemes were developed based on Blake and Mouton's original five. The theoretic bases for five instruments designed to measure conflict styles (or modes or strategies) were reviewed in a special issue of *Management Communication Quarterly,* edited by Linda Putnam (1988) and titled *Communication and Conflict Styles in Organizations*. These five instruments were chosen for the special issue because, according to Putnam (1988), they were the most widely used in both research and training. Each instrument follows the theoretic structure of Blake and Mouton's Managerial Grid—thus documenting the monopoly of this approach during this period of our history.

The instruments reviewed are Hall's (1969, 1973, 1986) Conflict Management Survey (CMS), the Thomas-Kilmann MODE instrument (Kilmann & Thomas, 1977; Thomas & Kilmann, 1974), Rahim's (1983) Organizational Conflict Inventory-II (ROCI-II), Putnam and Wilson's (1982) Organizational Communication Conflict Instrument (OCCI), and Ross and DeWine's (1982, 1987) Conflict Management Message Style (CMMS) Instrument. The CMS, the MODE, and the ROCI-II maintain the two-dimensional structure with five distinct styles, although they vary in the labels for the dimensions and the style, and in their specific issues of focus. Of these, the ROCI-II remains the most widely used. The OCCI and the CMMS are similar in their focus on communicative messages and their design. Both instruments represent three styles, developed by subjecting items based on Blake and Mouton's five styles to factor analysis. The CMMS is focused on communicative messages; the OCCI is focused on strategic communication and, like the ROCI-II, remains widely used.

The collection of instrument reviews illustrates the organizational communication field's apparent inability to deal with the definitional issues spelled out by earlier scholars. As pointed out by Knapp, Putnam, and Davis (1988), despite frequent acknowledgment of a complex interactional definition of conflict (see again our review of issues raised by Fink, 1968, Hawes & Smith, 1973, and Ruben, 1978), scholars continue to simplify the operational definition of conflict to disagreement. Variability among respondents in their own definitions of conflict remained completely uncontrolled. Furthermore, all these models are reductionist; while this is not a drawback in and of itself, as it is a perfectly acceptable mode of communication research, the reductionist model does exist as the sole approach to conflict styles. The search for conflict styles does, of course, follow from the positivistic ideal of the general theory (as summarized by Fink, 1968). In fact, reductionist approaches remain overwhelmingly dominant in the study of organizational communication and conflict to date.

Although the scholars who created these instruments each acknowledge that situational constraints may lead individuals to enact various behaviors, every instrument (CMS, MODE, ROCI-II, OCCI, and CMMS) instructs respondents to report their typical behaviors or tendencies. Such measures are incapable of attending to the notions of choice and situational constraint. Thus, such measures cannot begin to sort out the communication-conflict relationship (Hawes & Smith, 1973; Ruben, 1978). In fact, the prospective view of goals espoused by each of these models leads directly to a very linear view of communication and thus a very linear view of the relationship between conflict style and communication. The reductionist methodological approach exacerbates the limitations of the linear view. Further, although many of these scholars describe a behavioral view of conflict, their methodology operationalizes conflict nonbehaviorally, through self-reported data of recalled or even hypothetically "typical" behavior. In short, even those theorists who espouse a strategic, dynamic, and behavioral view operationalize conflict management style hypothetically, psychologically, and/or statically. The interested reader is directed to examine the special issue of *Management Communication Quarterly* (Putnam, 1988) for a more detailed review and critique. It suffices our purposes here

to say that the conflict styles approach in general, and the Blake and Mouton (1964) theoretical framework specifically, has, for better or for worse, monopolized our approach to organizational communication and conflict, driving it toward static and reductionist thinking.

Explanations and Extensions of the Styles Approach

A number of studies extend the styles approach; using a variety of methodological approaches, recent studies have attempted to conceptually and operationally enrich the styles approach and to provide explanations for preferred styles. Each of these studies is reviewed in turn within three sections: (a) accounting for behavioral shifts, (b) accounting for context, and (c) accounting for personality.

Accounting for behavioral shifts. Papa and Natalle (1989) enriched the styles approach by utilizing behavioral observation to examine behavioral shifts in conflict strategy. Their guiding research questions sought to explore gender differences in conflict strategy change over time and satisfaction with conflict interaction in dyads with varying gender composition. Their sample included both superior-subordinate and co-worker dyads. Dyads were composed of individuals who differed from each other by at least 3 points on a 7-point scale in their opinion of an impending organizational change, and interactions were videotaped and coded. Oddly, strategy selection was coded with Kipnis and Schmidt's (1982) Profile of Organizational Influence Strategies rather than a system of categories specifically designed for conflict. In addition, conflict was operationalized as simple disagreement. No differences in satisfaction were found, but results revealed a significant effect on strategy for time and a significant interaction effect on strategy for time and dyad gender composition. Although the study's operationalization of conflict itself and of conflict strategy is questionable, the results do provide strong evidence for variability in an individual's communication behavior under conditions of disagreement, even within a short time span (11.42 to 18.74 minutes). This variability is undetectable by the dominant traditional conflict styles approach.

To improve conceptually upon the styles approach as well as to examine such behavioral shifts, Nicotera (1993, 1994) provided inductive analysis from open-ended recall data of actual workplace conflicts. Nicotera (1993, 1994) extended the two-dimensional styles approach in two ways. First, she developed a descriptive model of conflict-handling behavior in an inductive investigation aimed at overcoming problems of assuming two dimensions of conflict behavior. Based on a critique of the two-dimensional view and of the application of Blake and Mouton's (1964) approach, the model delineates and defines strategy categories based on actor-salient aspects of specific behavior in specific situations. Participants, who were provided with Putnam and Poole's (1987) definition of conflict (the interaction of interdependent people who perceive incompatibility in their respective goals), completed open-ended surveys of a recent interpersonal conflict that took place in their workplace, reporting on multiple behavioral approaches to a single conflict episode. Using a grounded theory approach, the data revealed three distinct themes: own view, other's view, and emotional valence (disruptiveness). These three themes were then conceptualized as dimensions. Two of the dimensions (own-view and other-view) are issue-related or content dimensions. The third dimension is relational, specifying the character of the interaction. Figure 11.1 presents the model.

Traditional models of conflict styles fail to separate issue from emotion. Nicotera (1993) provided several examples of important distinctions between her respondents' strategies that would be undetectable using the traditional two-dimensional scheme, whether those with five or three (Putnam & Wilson, 1982; Ross & DeWine, 1982, 1987) categories. Our personal favorite is, "I told him he was an asshole. . . . Then I told him we would just do it his way" (p. 299). A label such as "accommodating" or "smoothing" would clearly not fit here. This behavior was categorized as patronizing.

The orthogonal nature of the dimensions belies the still-present conceptual influence of Blake and Mouton's two dimensions, even while it moves beyond them. Nicotera (1993) suggested that other possible dimensions may yet be discovered, and that multiple dimensions may provide conceptual links between predispositions and situational or contextual constraints. Finally, she offered that coding using these three dimensions might take the form of dichotomous coding, resulting in eight categories, or of continuous ratings of intensity of the three dimensions, resulting in separate scores for each dimension of behavior. The conceptual and operational separation of issue and emotion is the model's greatest contribution. This distinction was discovered inductively, sharply revealing the limiting effect of the traditional reductionistic deductive approach.

For the second extension, Nicotera (1994) conducted an exploratory study to examine patterns of change in individuals' behavioral approaches to a single conflict episode (using the same data set as Nicotera, 1993). The episodes recalled by respondents varied in length and number of interactions that transpired during the conflict episode. Using the three-dimensional, eight-category scheme derived from the data set, Nicotera (1994) conducted a Markov analysis, which provides a summary statistic of the probability of elements within a specified set changing to other elements within the set. The analysis resulted in the conclusion that, independent of others' behavior, individuals do seem to follow particular sequences of behavior as conflict interaction progresses. The tendency was for behavior to begin and remain high on own-view, to shift to high on own-view if it started out low, to shift from high to low on other-view or start and remain low, and to shift from disruptive to nondisruptive or start and remain nondisruptive.

Accounting for context. Several studies extend conflict styles research by examining context. While scholars had frequently acknowledged that conflict style was determined in part by situational constraints without examining this relationship, Marin and Sherblom (1994) conducted an in-depth study of such constraints. In a study of professional nurses' communication with physicians, Marin and Sherblom (1994) examined responses to situations wherein interpersonal conflict is created by conflicting professional responsibilities of nurses to patients and physicians; specifically, situations where the physician has asked that certain information be

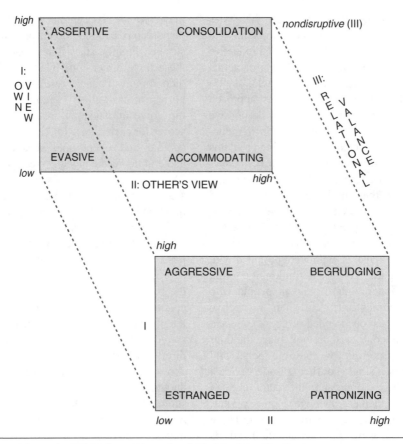

Figure 11.1   Nicotera's (1993) Three-Dimensional Model of Conflict Tactics

SOURCE: Nicotera, 1993. Reprinted with permission from Sage Publications.

withheld from the patient when the nurse's professional ethic would preclude such secrecy. A strong feature of this research is that conflict style is treated conceptually and operationally as a choice dependent on situational constraints. Discriminant analysis revealed that the contextual variables (hospital care model; action the nurse perceives as possible; anticipated support for that action; whether telling the patient the truth is beyond the scope of the nurse's professional role; perceived importance of telling the truth; dilemma seriousness; trust in the physician, head nurse, nursing, and hospital administrators; frequency with which the dilemma has occurred in the past; and how upsetting the situation is to nursing practice) together correctly predicted the conflict management strategy 73% of the time. Marin and Sherblom concluded that the respondent's perception of her or his role as a professional nurse is the primary function that

discriminates the choice of a conflict management style. This study carefully defines situational constraints and fully contextualizes the nature of the interaction, revealing a rich view of contextual influences on conflict style choice. Although conflict style itself is conceptualized and measured via the limited two-dimensional static approach, the casting of conflict style as the dependent variable represents a significant shift in thinking.

Ohbuchi and Suzuki (2003) likewise examined contextual influences on conflict strategies using self-report recall of real workplace conflicts. Furthering our understanding of how conflict strategies can be predicted by contextual factors, Ohbuchi and Suzuki, in a study of Japanese business employees, examine the underlying dimensions of conflict issues and their relationships with the concerns raised by the conflict and with the conflict strategies chosen. Conflict strategy is defined here post hoc; respondents provided recall data of their own behavior managing a recent workplace conflict. Although this study does not operationalize conflict resolution strategies according to the dual-concern model, the operationalization of strategies mirrors the typical taxonomy from the organizational communication literature. The three strategies examined are collaboration (integrative), confrontation (distributive), and avoidance/yielding. The study also serves to validate Ohbuchi's (1999) theory of the dimensional structure of conflict issues: Gain/Loss (G/L; personal interest); Right/Wrong (R/W; perceived transgression, responsibility, and blame); and Correct/Incorrect (C/I; contents and procedures of workers' tasks). The assumption is that every organizational conflict involves each of three issues to some degree.

In a carefully operationalized and methodologically sophisticated investigation, Ohbuchi and Suzuki (2003) generated a structural equation model, with interesting results. R/W issues, by activating concern for group order, prompt the use of confrontational strategies, whereas C/I issues directly prompt confrontation. C/I issues also directly prompt collaborative strategies. Finally, G/L issues activate concern for personal interest, which then prompts the use of avoidant or yielding strategies. The authors interpret these results through a rather disappointing two-dimensional consideration of organizational communication—task and relational issues. Still, a significant contribution is made by examining the underlying structure of the conflict issue itself and the ways in which the issue itself may lead to the enactment of various conflict strategies.

Friedman, Tidd, Currall, and Tsai (2000) examined the style-context relationship from the other direction, arguing that conflict style (communication) shapes the social environment, specifically the level of workplace stress. Friedman et al. also offered a more fine-tuned analysis of both task and relational conflict. Specifically, they conceptualized and operationalized conflict as ongoing and complex—they examined the ongoing organizational experience of task and relational conflict. In addition, they examined conflict style as an independent variable that has far-reaching effects

on organizational life by impacting the individual's experience of conflict as it is ongoing in the organizational context. Friedman et al. extended the impact of conflict management style beyond the immediate episode to the ongoing and far-reaching social environment of the workplace (e.g., stress and creation of social environment). To accomplish this goal, Rahim's (1983) ROCI-II and measures of the amount of task conflict (Jehn, 1997), relational conflict (Cox, 1998), and stress (Cohen, Kamarck, & Mermelstein, 1983) were administered to 82 medical personnel. A structural equation model was used to reveal that an integrating style is associated with lower levels of experienced task conflict, while dominating and avoiding styles are associated with higher levels of experienced task conflict. The model also revealed that the effects of integrating, dominating, and avoiding on relationship conflict occur through their effects on task conflict, but that there is a direct effect of obliging on relationship conflict. Overall, it was revealed that "conflict styles affect the experience of stress at work, both by affecting the level of relationship conflict experienced (indirect effects) and by providing people with resources for managing stress (direct effects)" (p. 48). Specifically, integrating and obliging styles were linked to lower stress, while dominating or avoiding styles were linked to higher stress.

The treatment of conflict as ongoing and of different types is a promising trend that does begin to conceptualize and operationalize organizational conflict as something both deeper and broader than mere disagreement. In addition, the idea that our own conflict styles impact our experience of organizational conflict and significantly impact our stress levels is an important idea. Since the sticky notion of disposition versus choice is not examined, however, it is unclear whether the impact is due to the styles themselves or to underlying dispositions that drive enactment of those styles. Furthermore, although the authors do provide a thorough literature review of conflict styles models and research, they do so uncritically, readily accepting the two-dimensional conceptual structure, and dismissing the styles-versus-strategies debate as unimportant— like others before them, they avoid the reconciliation between predisposition and choice. The only careful conceptual review is of Rahim's model. In fact, they cite other models, including those that strongly criticize and reject the two-dimensional conceptual structure, only in a passing footnote. We might be inclined to dismiss this except that they cite articles whose central point is the critical examination and conceptual rejection of the two-dimensional theoretic structure. Like so many scholars, these contemporary researchers accept so uncritically the idea of the two-dimensional structure that they ignore strong criticism in the very literature they cite.

Accounting for personality. In more decidedly psychological investigations, Antonioni (1998) and Moberg (2001) administer a variety of psychometric measures along with Rahim's ROCI-II to determine the link between personality and preferred conflict style. Antonioni (1998) attempted to link the Big Five personality factors—extraversion, agreeableness, conscientiousness, openness, and emotional stability/neuroticism (Peabody & Goldberg, 1989)—to Rahim's (1983) five styles. The Five Factor Model (FFM) is a recent theoretic development that summarizes five orthogonal dimensions that broadly encompass and organize personality theory, each composed of several specific personality variables. Although this is not a communication study per se, it does make several strong claims about interpersonal conflict. In addition, there is an attempt to explicate the link between personality and conflict style so important to earlier scholars. Rahim's ROCI-II as well as traditional self-report Likert-scaled paper-and-pencil tests of personality were administered to a student sample and a sample of managers.

The study functions as little more than a test of construct validity and is replete with conceptual and methodological confusion; however, it represents an interesting foray into the underlying explanation of conflict styles. Some of the confusion arises from the interchanging throughout the paper of the terms *emotional stability* and *neuroticism* (which are opposite expressions of a single factor) and from the lack of explanation behind the methodology. Although Antonioni (1998) states that the purpose of including a managerial sample is to provide a test of external validity, this reasoning is quickly abandoned in the face of his results, and he spends quite a bit of energy explaining the discrepancies away. The difficulty may be in the fuzzy conceptualization of conflict style—with, as usual, no reconciliation between the notions of "traits," "tendencies," "predispositions," and the like.

Moberg (2001) conducted a very similar study, but with vast conceptual and methodological improvement. FFM is used to predict conflict styles, as measured by Putnam and Wilson's OCCI. The OCCI is treated as measuring four styles (nonconfrontation, confrontation, compromise, and control), as it was originally designed. Confrontation and compromise are separated from Putnam and Wilson's "solution-oriented" style because of the conceptual distinction between them. Moberg's greatest contribution is a thorough conceptual treatment of "conflict style" as attitude. Moberg carefully distinguished attitude from intention, as well as from trait and disposition, and carefully "locates the concept of conflict style preference within a broader than nomological network" (p. 51). Moberg utilized attitude theory (e.g., Ajzen & Fishbein, 1980) to explain conflict style. Essentially, Moberg noted that conflict style preference is an attitudinal component of behavior, but that intention and beliefs are also necessary to understand conflict behavior. This is an elegant theoretical move that neatly solves many of the conceptual problems long faced by scholars in this area. Unfortunately, the conceptualization then remains untested, as the study then merely regresses conflict style onto FFM factors and then conducts some exploratory analyses of specific personality traits that comprise factors shown to be significant. Moberg's results reveal the following: Nonconfrontation is predicted positively by neuroticism and negatively by extraversion and conscientiousness; confrontation is predicted negatively by neuroticism and positively by extraversion, openness, and conscientiousness; compromise is predicted positively by openness and agreeableness; finally, control is predicted only negatively by agreeableness. Although Moberg's brilliant theoretic contribution remains untested, the careful classification of conflict style as attitude is a significant advancement in our thinking.

Summary. Utilizing a variety of methods, and with varying degrees of success, a number of scholars in the 1990s attempted to expand the conflict styles approach. Most scholars still uncritically accept Blake and Mouton's (1964) dual concern (two-dimensional) conceptual structure. The most notable directions of expansion reviewed here have included empirically based conceptual fine-tuning and expansion of the dimensional structure (Nicotera, 1993), examination of variability in conflict behavior (Nicotera, 1994; Papa & Natalle, 1989), and investigation into contextual influences on conflict style (Friedman et al., 2000; Marin & Sherblom, 1994; Ohbuchi & Suzuki, 2003) and underlying personality predictors of preferred conflict style (Antonioni, 1998; Moberg, 2001). The current state of affairs is that the styles approach is still largely the way in which organizational communication scholars conceptualize and operationalize organizational conflict management in their research. We now turn to an overview of research findings from the literature in organizational communication back to approximately 1990. As previously stated, this review is divided into three additional sections: superior/ subordinate conflict, culture and conflict styles, and, finally, gender and conflict styles.

Superior/Subordinate Conflict Styles Literature

The body of literature that examines conflict styles in superior/subordinate relations is by far the largest in organizational conflict; it demonstrates an overwhelmingly *managerial bias* and continues to grapple with conceptual and operational issues. We begin with Conrad (1991), who did make some inroads in the right direction when he approached his research from a conflict *management* stance and therefore maintains a more progressive definitional perspective, but clearly, he still takes a predictive/prescriptive approach to diagnosing communicative conflict strategies. He also challenged two implicit assumptions that lurk in the literature on superior-subordinate conflict: (a) Popular conflict styles models assume that there are no variations in the degree to which a person's diagnosed style will predict communicative strategies during a conflict, and (b) supervisors' style predisposition toward conflict will not change as a conflict persists or when the subordinate shows noncompliance. Specifically, he

examined the ways in which supervisors' predicted communicative behaviors deviate from their conflict style *(integrating, compromising,* and *avoiding)* and how supervisors further deviate from predicted communicative behaviors when a conflict persists. He included supervisor gender as another potential predictor of specific communication behavior during conflict.

Using Rahim's (1983) organizational conflict instrument, Conrad (1991) ultimately found that though conflict styles scores can predict initial communicative strategies, they do not predict what he calls "follow-up" strategies when a subordinate remains noncompliant. In addition, he found that all supervisors within his study eventually shifted their communication behavior to coercive communication with noncompliant subordinates, although female supervisors did so at a slower pace than their male counterparts. We argue that although Conrad makes an important contribution to the conflict and communication literature, he does not stray from the generalist stance (Fink, 1968) that dominates our thinking on conflict, thus continuing the implicit assumption of its necessity. Conrad did recommend observation of conflict and communication within a more naturalistic setting as well as the need to allow participants to provide their own definitions of conflict, thus beginning to argue for a more interpretive take on conflict and communication.

In another study that voices the need to focus on conflict management (as opposed to *resolution),* McCready and Roberts (1996) examined the conflict tactics of communication disorders supervisors and attempted to predict conflict style *(avoidance, competitive, collaborative)* in various supervisor-student/subordinate scenarios. They dedicated a large portion of their article to grappling with definitional issues that plague the organizational communication conflict literature and define conflict as "an expressed disagreement between people with incompatible goals" (p. 5). Results indicate that communication disorders supervisors typically use a collaborative conflict style, followed by avoidance and (least often) competitive. This work offers another communicative context within which to view conflict, but it continues the positivistic lens through which many in the field view conflict. In addition, it continues to rely upon a linear approach to conflict where certain behaviors trigger certain responses. This singular way of viewing conflict and communication is only part of the story to be told, and our field's adherence to it precludes the insight so eloquently called for by Hawes and Smith (1973) and Ruben (1978). Research in this area continues to presume a prospective and linear view of conflict, even while it focuses on a continuous view of conflict as a necessary and natural human phenomenon.

In much the same vein, Weider-Hatfield and Hatfield (1996) used a decidedly positivistic approach to study conflict as they investigated the relationship between managers' conflict management strategies (*collaborating, forcing,* and *accommodating*) and 20 potential subordinate rewards in four categories (*system, job, performance,* and *interpersonal*). Results indicate that collaborating is correlated positively with subordinate rewards, accommodating is correlated positively but weakly, and forcing is correlated strongly and negatively. This work offers an understanding of conflict management strategies by exploring the effects of these strategies on subordinates and by validating our ongoing presumption that collaboration garners the best outcome and forcing the worst. Ultimately, they provide a typology of the reactions that subordinates can have, given the manager's conflict style, but they do so through quantitative data collection methodologies and linearly predictive outcomes. This study is carefully conducted, and well-designed conceptually and methodologically, but at the end of the day, it does not add much to our basic knowledge.

In another study that neither acknowledges nor challenges positivist and linear assumptions about the relationship between conflict and communication and does not move beyond self-reports of "typical" behavior on a closed-item scale, Martin, Sirimangkala, and Anderson (1999) investigated the relationship between subordinates' socio-communicative orientations (*competent, aggressive, submissive,* and *noncompetent*) and their use of organizational conflict strategies (*nonconfrontational, collaborative, compromise,* and *control*) with their supervisors (using the OCCI divided into four subscales rather than three). After quantitative analysis of 228 questionnaires, the researchers found that noncompetent and submissive communicators used nonconfrontational strategies, while competent communicators used collaborative strategies. In addition, they found that aggressive and competent communicators used control strategies more than those that were submissive or noncompetent. These results, again, do not add much to our overall knowledge base. The study serves as little more than a construct validity test of two paper-and-pencil self-report Likert-type measures, and represents, like so many studies, the conceptual stronghold of positivism in the body of research on conflict and organizational communication.

Rahim, Magner, and Shapiro (2000) continue this trend with a strictly linear and positivistic approach. In this study, the researchers examine the relationship between employees' perceptions of three forms of organizational justice (*distributive, procedural,* and *interactional*) and the conflict styles (*integrating, obliging, dominating, avoiding, compromising*) they use with their managers. Again, as is typical, the study is based on the presumption that conflict can be constructive, and the research is conducted in an effort to help with its management. Through hierarchical regression analysis of data, the researchers found that what they call "higher interactional justice" was related to greater use of the integrating style when "distributive justice" was low and "procedural justice" was high. Similar to much of this research, this study does not focus solely on the role of communication in handling conflict, but rather on attitudinal perceptions of employees.

Tjosvold, Morishima, and Belsheim (1999) also maintain an approach that emphasizes conflict management and presume that conflict can be constructive. They apply Deutsch's (1973) theory of cooperation and competition and more recent research on open-minded interaction to explore the nature of the relationship and the flexibility of conflict management strategies between supervisors and employees on an industrial shop floor when a particular complaint must be handled. Tjosvold et al.'s work does not wholly classify as a communication study; however, it is included here because it does allude to communication through its focus on direct face-to-face discussion strategies that supervisors can use with employees to attain compliance and goal alliance when handling a complaint. It is also included in this review because it is a unique study in the organizational conflict literature in that it uses a balance between positivist and interpretative methodologies for data collection and analysis. Using Flanagan's (1954) critical incident technique, the researchers collected recalled stories from recent conflict/complaint episodes as well as administering a Likert-scale survey. Findings from the study generated the hypothesis that cooperative, compared to competitive and independent goals, promote more open-minded discussion of complaints. Although we might say that the blend of methodologies helped bring out a richer set of conclusions, the interpretive data were drawn only from recall and thus do not answer Ruben's (1978) definitional concern that conflict is seen only as a behavioral phenomenon that can and should be observed in the moment it occurs.

The final study we review in this section returns us to placing communication at the center of analysis in conflict. Powell and Hickson (2000), strangely enough however, also return us to the conceptualization of conflict as something to be *resolved*. With this assumption in place, they investigated recalled actual conflicts, examining the impact of power imbalance (*high power, low power, equal power*) on the relationship between perceived communication behaviors (Putnam & Wilson's, 1982, *nonconfrontation, solution-oriented,* and *control*) and the anticipation of conflict resolution. In conditions of perceived equal power, anticipated resolution was related to both solution-orientation and control. In conditions of power imbalance, however, solution-oriented behavior was perceived to be related to anticipated resolution—regardless of whether respondents perceived themselves as low or high powered in the situation. While these findings may be interesting, what remains more interesting to us is that the conceptual and methodological approach in our literature continues to mirror research decades older. We see this not as a criticism of Powell and Hickson (2000), so much as it is a commentary on the entire body of research examining superior-subordinate conflict communication in our field.

In summary, an important observation to be made about the state of the art of research in interpersonal conflict in the organizational setting is its managerial bias. The preponderance of studies that focus on superior-subordinate communication and conflict reveals the overwhelming importance organizational communication scholars continue to place upon this organizational relationship. In addition, few of the troublesome definitional issues lamented in the 1970s, and outlined in the introduction of this chapter, are addressed. We are left still asking the same conceptual and operational questions, while investigations of superior-subordinate communication and conflict remain positivistic in paradigm, psychometric in measurement, linear in approach, and reductionist in explanation.

Culture/Ethnicity and Styles Literature

Although the constructs "culture," "ethnicity," and "race" have recently begun to be argued as foundationally interpretive (Hall, 1990; Haney Lopez, 2000; Torres & Ngin, 1995), given that they derive their meaning from a group's communicative co-construction, the approach to culture and ethnicity in the study of conflict and organizational communication mirrors the traditionally positivistic approach to the study of superior-subordinate conflict. It must be said, however, that the sophistication with which "culture" is conceptualized has been an area of tremendous development. While a great deal of research has been conducted on culture and interpersonal conflict, and particularly conflict style, it is not until the late 1990s that attention is turned consistently to the organizational setting.

Oetzel and others' work in this area is important as it transcends both the early "cultural checklist" and more recent "collectivism/individualism" approaches of cross-cultural comparison that had been criticized in intercultural communication research. According to Oetzel (1998), self-construal is linked to cultural patterns, but has a central role in an individual's communication because it mediates the influence of cultural individualism-collectivism on an individual's behavior. Oetzel (1998) examined whether *self-construal* (independent or interdependent) or *ethnicity* predict individual self-reported conflict styles in the small group context in conditions of cooperative and competitive tasks and ingroup and outgroup relationships. This study is thus essentially a validity check on the conceptual construction of self-construal as distinct from ethnic culture. Respondents (Latinos and European Americans) read scenarios designed to manipulate the competitive/cooperative and ingroup/outgroup conditions and then completed a measure of self-construal and the ROCI-II. Oetzel concluded that self-image better predicts conflict styles than culture/ethnicity. Specifically, dominating conflict style is related positively to independent self-construal, whereas avoiding, obliging, and compromising conflict styles are related positively to interdependent self-construal. Finally, integrating conflict style is related strongly positively to interdependent self-construal but weakly positively related to independent self-construal. Neither the nature of the task nor the nature of the relationship had an effect on conflict style. While Oetzel does maintain a conflict management conceptual stance, he leads us, as do so many communication scholars, down a prescribed linear conceptual path laden with self-report hypothetical data that do not allow a close examination of the behavioral characteristics of conflict interaction. In doing so, like so many of us, he does not answer the interpretive and critical theoretical call that Fink (1968) and Ruben (1978) brought to our field more than 25 years ago.

Kozan (1999) followed the same trend. In his work, he took an important look at the influence of intracultural values on conflict management styles. Although communication is not the focus of this article, we include it here because it is the only article in the recent past that considers *intra*-cultural processes in conflict management, and we consider this an important lacuna to note within our field. Turkey was chosen as a site for research of this nature due to the intracultural variations in values present in the organizational setting presumed to be created by Westernization. With the use of the ROCI-II instrument, Kozan found that within Turkish culture, *avoidance* was most preferred by those with a strong tradition and conformity values while *forcing* was used more by those with high power values. In addition, he found that third parties were not usually invited into a conflict by those with the values of achievement and stimulation, while those with values of universalism and benevolence would indeed seek the inclusion of a third-party conflict negotiator. This research expands the overall body of conflict management literature by examining the influence of culture on conflict management not as a cross-cultural "checklist style" comparison, but by identifying and examining underlying cultural variables and values that might impact conflict management styles. Kozan (1999) does not, however, address any underlying definitional and conceptual issues of conflict. In short, this careful conceptual treatment of culture is not extended to the treatment of conflict.

Oetzel, Myers, Meares, and Lara's (2003) exploration of interpersonal conflict in organizations concludes our discussion of organizational communication research literature on culture/ethnicity and conflict. We have categorized this study here because they take an interest in how face-negotiation theory (a culturally based phenomenon) explains conflict styles. The study tests the underlying premise of face-negotiation theory that face concerns predict conflict styles. Further, the study hypothesized that face concerns would better predict conflict style than self-construal and organizational position. Conflict styles were measured with Ting-Toomey et al.'s (2000) eight-style instrument (integrating, compromising, dominating, obliging, avoiding, emotional expression, third-party help, and passive aggression). Self-face was significantly positively related to dominating and emotional expression. Other-face and mutual-face were significantly positively related to integrating, compromising, and obliging. Other-face and mutual-face were negatively associated with passive aggression, and other-face was associated negatively with the emotional expression and dominating. As predicted, face concerns better predicted conflict styles than self-construal or organizational position (manager or nonmanager) for six of the eight styles: integrating, compromising, dominating, emotional expression, obliging, and passive aggression. Ultimately, the study provides evidence that face concerns serve as a strong predictor for conflict management style, but the same critiques we have made previously about the conceptualization and operationalization of conflict management style remain relevant.

A number of studies across a number of disciplines have been accomplished that examine conflict styles across cultures (e.g., Chiu &

Kosinski, 1994; Elsayed-Ekhouly & Buda, 1996; Kozan & Ergin, 1998; Lindsley & Braithwaite, 1996; Morris et al., 1998; Smith, Dugan, Peterson, & Leung, 1998). In the interest of space, we have chosen not to review them here, selecting for review only those studies from outside the discipline that we believed to be uniquely insightful on issues of communication.

In summary, as with the vast majority of studies of conflict in the organizational setting, the positivistic approach abounds in studies of culture and organizational conflict. Because of the tremendous progress made in conceptualization and operationalization of cultural variables, the study of culture and conflict is arguably the most fruitful and progressive area. The static notion of "style" still prevails, however, precluding rich descriptions of behavior, interaction, or lived experience of interactants. We do find it somewhat bothersome that although sophisticated cultural variables have ostensibly replaced the cross-cultural checklists that typified early intercultural communication research, scholars continue to revert to generalizations about ethnic groups that function much the same to essentialize ethnicity. Moreover, in the particular arena of conflict investigations, little attention is given to how conflict is defined or conceptualized for study. In our minds, this lack of richness brings us once again to the assumptions that Hawes and Smith (1973) and Ruben (1978) asked us to question. We simply have not yet grappled with the most foundational issues facing the study of communication and conflict. Until we break the reductionist hold of positivist thinking, we may not yet do so.

Gender and Conflict Styles

With just a few exceptions, research on gender and organizational conflict has examined gender differences in conflict style. Research on gender differences and conflict style is consistent only its inconsistency. Although some studies indicate that gender and gender expectations are important factors in understanding organizational conflict behavior (e.g., Renwick, 1977; Zammuto, London, & Rowland, 1979), researchers discovered early on that men and women do not significantly differ in their conflict management communication in the workplace

(Chusmir, Koberg, & Mills, 1989; Renwick, 1977; Shockley-Zalabak & Morley, 1984; Temkin & Cummings, 1986). Still, there remains a subset of scholars who insist upon conducting conflict communication gender differences research, regardless of the fact that our research has revealed no consistent communication differences between men and women, irrespective of their organizational status. In fact, each of the studies of sex difference to be reviewed here (Brewer, Mitchell, & Weber, 2002; Gayle, 1991; Sorenson, Hawkins, & Sorenson, 1995) begins with much the same observation. These studies each seek alternative explanations for the persistent expectations for sex differences in conflict style in light of our inability to reveal consistent sex differences with empirical research.

In an investigation testing the efficacy of the structural/functional perspective, which would predict no sex differences, and the expectancy perspective, which would predict sex differences, Gayle (1991) collected both open- and closed-ended data from managers and employees representing 11 different organizations. Respondent's sex, other person's sex, and supervisor's sex were examined as predictors of conflict style. Participants were asked to write about previous disagreements with a supervisor or co-worker. These essays were then coded according to the traditional five-category scheme. Participants also completed Putnam and Wilson's (1982) OCCI, which in this study generated and was thus scored on five factors (avoid, accommodate, control/compete, collaboration, and compromise). The OCCI was conceptualized to be a measure of intent to behave in a particular way. Results revealed significant but very small, and thus meaningless, differences: "Sex differences were not salient factors affecting the selection of conflict management strategies" (p. 163). Therefore, the structural-functional perspective was supported.

In general, Gayle's (1991) description of her methodology is confusing and incomplete. For example, although she reports small significant differences for respondent's sex, it is unclear whether these differences occurred on the coded essay variable or the self-report variable. Also, it is unclear how the inherent confound between sex of other and sex of supervisor was handled when the supervisor was also the other person in the conflict. On the other hand, it is refreshing to see a study reporting no meaningful sex difference as its main point. Often, data analyses that find no significant difference languish unpublished. Studies that report significant gender difference find their way into our scholarly discourse, whereas studies that find no difference do not. In the positivistic, reductionist world of conflict styles research, what the senior author of this chapter calls in a previous work (Nicotera, 1999) "the politics of the null hypothesis" prevails. There is simply no way to know how many data analyses sit in the file cabinets of scholars, never to see the light of day, because they contain only nonsignificant data. Simply stated, finding differences between groups is privileged as "publishable knowledge"; finding no differences is not. Gayle's (1991) study does find a few significant differences; it is to her great credit that she emphasizes the point of small effect size to declare these statistically significant sex differences to be meaningless. In terms of gender research, this study's approach—to test two theoretic perspectives, one that predicts sex differences and one that does not—represents an important step in our thinking about gender and organization. It is this approach that allows for a major finding of no difference to be an important statement.

Gayle's most meaningful contribution to the conflict literature, however, has nothing to do with gender: "There was less than 17% agreement between strategies reported in the open-ended questionnaire compared to those strategies reported in the OCCI" (p. 165). Her results cast doubt upon the entire literature that uses self-report conflict styles instruments. How people reported they *actually did* behave in a conflict situation had little connection to how they reported on a set of general items about how they *typically* behave in a conflict situation. This highlights a serious validity concern for conflict styles measurements. Gayle explains it in terms of factors that may intervene between intent and action in the organizational setting.

Sorenson et al. (1995) posited that psychological type may mediate the relationship between gender and conflict style. Using the Myers-Briggs Type Inventory (Form G) (MBTI; Myers & McCaulley, 1985) to identify respondents as "feelers" or "thinkers," they hypothesized first that female managers would report higher feeling scores and that male managers would report higher thinking scores, following Myers's (1991) assertion that this dimension is the only one on which men and women significantly differ. Further, since it can be easily argued that the feeling-thinking dimension is salient to conflict style, they question how gender and psychological type may explain managers' conflict styles. Along with the MBTI, participants were asked to read a short scenario casting them as a manager in conflict with a peer over equipment purchase and cost-cutting and then to complete Rahim's (1983) ROCI-II in reference to that scenario.

Separate ANOVAs revealed sex differences for both "feeling" and "thinking," such that female managers scored significantly higher on feeling and male managers on thinking. These differences were small (less than 10% of the variance explained) and had methodological shortcomings (using parametric statistics on Myers-Briggs scores especially as dependent variables given that the "type" scores are forced-choice measures; and feeling and thinking are opposite ends of the same dimension). The analysis of the research question about conflict style inspires fewer questions of methodology, though our suspicion of the validity of the grouping variable carries through this set of analyses. Males were found to be more obliging than females, and feelers more obliging than thinkers. Like Gayle (1991), the researchers consider small effect sizes to render their statistical significance meaningless: "It is not justified to conclude that either psychological type or gender significantly influence conflict style preference" (p. 123). Once again, gender is not shown to have any impact on preferences for conflict style.

Yet, several years later, we continue to find scholars who persist in investigating what should by now be a dead issue. Brewer et al. (2002) conducted a particularly anachronistic investigation of the impact of biological sex, gender role orientation, and organizational status (managerial or nonmanagerial) on conflict style. Their rationale was based on skepticism offered by scholars in the 1970s and 1980s about the ability of women to adopt managerial roles (citing Brenner, Tomkiewitz, & Schein, 1989, and Powell & Butterfield, 1979) despite research to the contrary (citing Eagly & Johnson, 1990; Korabik, Baril, & Watson, 1993; and Powell, 1988). Their basic argument and the implications drawn from it are flawed in several ways. First, an investigation published in 2002 about gender roles in management should not be inspired by claims of skepticism about women managers published in the 1970s and 1980s. To rest a contemporary study upon the skepticism expressed as women were first entering managerial roles in great numbers while simultaneously ignoring the ensuing rise of female numbers in management is to pay no regard whatsoever to the societal context of the phenomenon. Second, the statement that such skeptical claims are made "despite" contrary findings has no ground since said contrary findings were published several years *after* the skepticism was expressed. Even worse, one such piece of contradiction comes from the very same scholar (Powell, 1988; Powell & Butterfield, 1979) who obviously explored the topic and concluded that the skepticism was unwarranted. Clearly, skepticism was expressed about women's ability to succeed in management. Scholarly investigations then followed that concluded that the skeptics were wrong. Brewer et al. (2002) missed this point.

Worse yet, Brewer et al. (2002) cited no literature on gender and conflict style newer than 1990, and the review that does exist points to the literature's inconsistency in the link between gender and conflict style. Given this opening, we remain unconvinced of the very ground the study rests upon. Conflict style is measured with the ubiquitous ROCI-II. Gender role orientation is measured with Bem's (1974) original scale. This measure separates individuals into four types: masculine, feminine, androgynous, and undifferentiated. The measure has been widely criticized on a number of levels, from its psychometric properties to its inherent reification of gender stereotypes. It is, without doubt, quite a dated instrument. By casting social behaviors as inherently "masculine" or "feminine," the scale reifies the gendered nature of certain kinds of behavior, reinforces pre-1970s stereotypes of sexed behavior, and essentializes gender. By focusing on the behavior itself, we might use more gender-neutral terms, such as "instrumental" and "expressive." Claims

that "typical" male behavior is "instrumental," and "typical" female behavior is "expressive" can then be made, but the inherent sexism of casting social behavior as inherently gendered is avoided.

Brewer et al. (2002) also made some questionable analysis decisions. The ROCI-II is administered three times, once each for two hypothetical scenarios provided and again for a recalled scenario generated by the respondent. (All scenarios are with peers, so status is operationally washed out of each conflict situation.) The ROCI-II scores used in the main analyses are averaged across the two provided scenarios. In the main analyses, rather than examining biological sex as an independent variable, they conduct a regression with biological sex as the predictor and the ROCI-II's five scores as the criterion variables. They then calculate the residuals and enter them into an ANOVA as the dependent variables with the four gender role groups as the independent variable. They do so again for organizational status. In this way, they argued, they have controlled for the effects of biological sex. However, they would have accomplished the same goal with less error by simply using biological sex as a second factor in a two-way ANOVA because the residuals have proportionally more error than the raw variable. In fact, they could also have reduced the risk of experiment-wise error by conducting a single three-way ANOVA for biological sex, gender role, and organizational status all at once.

Several rounds of follow-up analysis are conducted, analyzing the ROCI-II scores from each scenario separately, analyzing with and without "controlling" for biological sex, and then finally dropping ROCI-II scores that do not yield significance and running still more analyses. We are wary of the fact that no analysis deals with the fact that this is a repeated measure. In the end, after these several rounds of analysis, a number of conclusions are drawn. We are wary also of these conclusions given that the sheer number of statistical tests performed on this data set (in excess of 100 statistical tests including bivariate and multiple correlations, *F* tests, and *t* tests) have driven the experiment-wise error rate to the point where by-chance significance is a serious concern. In the end, the authors still find it "interesting" (p. 88) when biological sex seems to have at most a marginal impact on conflict style. Brewer et al. (2002) reported results from these independent variables (biological sex, gender role orientation, and organizational status) that explain at maximum approximately 13% of the variance in conflict style. We would caution the reader to consider the results to be even smaller given the methodological problems.

We have reviewed these studies here in such great detail to drive home a single important point: There is no *there* there. Conflict style is *not* driven by biological sex, regardless of how many studies try to find the effect; it simply is not there. Still, the fact that we continue to try to find important gender effects where clearly none exist is testimony to the fact that gender remains an important conceptual and political lens through which to examine organizational communication. However, the search for gender *differences* in organizational communication, and in conflict communication particularly, has little promise to produce any meaningful findings. In fact, such research serves more to essentialize gender and to promote and reify the implicit notion that women are not equipped for the managerial role—the notion that drives much research (e.g., Brewer et al., 2002). It is this notion and its political ramifications, both within *our* field and out in *the* field, that should be examined. That organizational scholars keep *expecting* women to be different from men communicatively, in light of the overwhelming empirical evidence that they are not, opens interesting questions about the political function of gender organizationally.

In our opinion, the most glaring false assumption underlying gender differences research in organizational communication is that the organizational context is gender-neutral. That the expectation of sex differences in organizational communication persists despite overwhelming empirical evidence that they simply do not exist seems to be a function of this very fact: Organizations are not gender-neutral (see Marshall, 1993, for an excellent treatment of this notion). A great deal of gender research recognizes the gendered nature of organization and is not about sex differences. It would seem that this might be a fruitful approach to the study of gender and organizational conflict, as well. We did find two

such studies in our literature search (Burrell, Buzzanell, & McMillan, 1992; Shuter & Turner, 1997). Inasmuch as they break the hold of the styles tradition, these are reviewed in our section titled "Fruitful Directions," to follow. We also suspect that the examination of gender identity politics in organizational conflict might be a more insightful approach, as well.

Summary

Undeniably, the predispostional styles approach to the study of communication and organizational conflict has had an overwhelming influence. Research of interpersonal conflict in the organizational setting that takes other approaches is sparse. Although early scholars called for more investigation into contextual and situational constraints, little research has done so and that which has still focuses on the explication of styles or strategies, usually using one of the fundamental two-dimensional measures (reviewed earlier) based on Blake and Mouton (1964). Rahim's (1983) ROCI-II and Putnam and Wilson's (1982) OCCI seem to be the most popular. Although interpretive and critical approaches dominate the field of organizational communication, these alternative paradigms have yet to penetrate the study of interpersonal conflict in the organizational setting in any meaningful way. In the following section, we explore the few pieces of recent research that break the hold of the styles approach in a number of ways, conceptually and methodologically.

FRUITFUL DIRECTIONS

It is our contention that the time has long since come for us to break the stranglehold of the styles approach, including the positivist, reductionist, individualistic, and managerial traditions that underlie it. Communication scholars need to move beyond this myopic unidirectional quest for understanding and broaden our approaches to the study of communication and interpersonal conflict in the organizational setting. More fruitful directions for the study of interpersonal conflict and organizational communication might include these that have begun to develop: more that stems from a broad consideration of context, including cultural context (e.g., race and gender), organizational/ professional context, and relational context; more that investigates experience of conflict and its personal and systemic ramifications; and more that takes a discursive approach.

Organizational Context

A number of recent studies have emerged that take an alternative approach to the styles tradition at the same time that they transcend the managerial individualistic bias that has governed organizational conflict research by taking a different and broad view of organizational context. These include studies that examine the following: gender and race from a feminist standpoint tradition (Burrell et al., 1992; Shuter & Turner, 1997); the professional context of the healthcare organization (Jameson, 2003); and the relational and interpersonal network of the individuals in conflict (Volkema, Bergmann, & Farquhar, 1997).

Cultural context: Gender and race. Burrell et al. (1992) combined interpretive and quantitative metaphor analyses to examine images of conflict held by women in government. Shuter and Turner (1997) enriched our understanding of gender by examining race within gender, in a study of African American and European American women's perceptions of workplace conflict. Neither study attempts to identify or predict conflict styles, but rather both attempt to understand the unique viewpoints of conflict in the workplace held by members of these gendered and racialized groups.

Burrell et al. (1992) summed up their fundamental underlying assumptions succinctly: "Central assumptions guiding this investigation are that women's conflict images offer an alternative means of examining conflict processes and then these metaphors can be analyzed to deconstruct women's multilayered realities" (Burrell et al., 1992, p. 116). As a feminist standpoint analysis, explicit assumptions also include the societal positioning of women as disempowered in a male-dominated society and thus in the workplace. That women's organizational experiences are unique from men's is

presumed. Claims of sex difference are neither pursued nor claimed.

Using metaphoric analysis, Burrell et al. (1992) sought to discover the image metaphors women in government used to depict conflict situations, the extent to which "feminine" values and tensions are exhibited in these image metaphors of conflict, and the extent to which different metaphors of conflict emerge in different professional relationships. Participants in a conflict seminar completed open-ended surveys before and after the seminar. First- and second-order analyses were carefully carried out using well-defined and established procedures for such analysis, including careful coding and assessment of coding reliability. Their results indicated that participants overwhelmingly employed war/destruction metaphors. Conflict was regarded as adversarial, with clear winners and losers. Further, "the metaphors these women selected to portray their conflict were ongoing continuous processes . . . that did not result in clear resolution or end points" (p. 134). The images revealed self-images of emotional distress, helplessness, and vulnerability. No association was found between relational context and type of metaphor.

Burrell et al. (1992) provided a rich view of the experience of organizational conflict by these women. Although warlike images of conflict prevailed, the passivity, powerlessness, and feelings of impotence "indicated that these women abhorred this confrontational approach" (p. 140). A typical "styles" approach would have missed this important point. The underlying explanation for these feelings is beyond the scope of the analysis. However, this approach that eschews the search for sex differences opens the way for pursuit of such questions. Similar studies of men's experiences would further enrich our understanding of gender as it plays out in organizational conflict. Examining ways in which women and men might experience the organizational political landscape and construct their organizational identities would be far more fruitful than looking for behavioral "sex differences."

In an open-ended survey, Shuter and Turner (1997) similarly elicited conflict metaphors from their sample of 49 African American and European American women in managerial and nonmanagerial roles. Respondents were asked to provide narratives regarding their own definition of workplace conflict and of the behaviors they believed to be indicative of conflict (verbal and nonverbal). The narratives were analyzed in terms of the value placed on directness and indirectness, because of the salience of this dimension in the literature for both conflict and racial differences in communication. Themes were then extracted from the narratives. "This analysis suggests that African American females value more direct approaches to conflict than do European American females" (pp. 86-87). It is interesting to note that African American respondents' narratives were more easily grouped thematically because they tended to be more specific. In comparison, "the European American respondents either redefined conflict in their own terms . . . or argued for contingent responses to conflict" (p. 88). Also, positive nuances about the nature of conflict were more frequently observed in the African American women's narratives.

In addition, Shuter and Turner (1997) asked respondents to typify their approaches to conflict using a system that departs from the styles approach. Using Wilmot and Wilmot's (1978) system for examining interpersonal conflict, they asked respondents to indicate which of four approaches best described their perceptions of conflict behavior in the workplace for African American women, for European American women, and for themselves personally: avoidance, maintenance, reduction, or escalation. Results indicated that perceptions about African American and European American women differed. For example, European American women were viewed as more likely to avoid conflict than African American women. In addition, as compared to European American respondents, African American respondents viewed all women as more likely to choose escalation, were more likely to see African American women as reducing workplace conflict, and were less likely to see European Americans as maintaining conflict.

No major differences were reported for self-perceptions. The size of the differences between the two groups in perceptions of others leaves no doubt that race drives perceptions of women in the workplace regarding conflict. This study also illustrates that standpoint theory and a multi-methodological approach generates far more

insight into the experience of conflict in the workplace than does the static, reductionist styles approach. It is noteworthy that these scholars do not attempt to classify behaviors and then search for "race differences," but rather examine the ways in which one's own race and the race of others might impact the perceptions and experiences of these organizational women. In this way, race is treated as a political thread in the organizational fabric that shapes our experiences.

Organizational/professional context. Jameson (2003) examined the professional context of the healthcare organization in a qualitative study of the intractable conflict (Northrup, 1989) among anesthesia providers. Like Marin and Sherblom (1994), Jameson (2003) accounted for the unique context of both the healthcare organization and the particular professional field of the participants. Jameson (2003), however, went farther because she did so without the shackles of conflict styles and reductionism. Jameson (2003) offered a rich professional context by providing a detailed analysis of the history of the practice of anesthesiology. Certified registered nurse anesthetists (CRNAs) are supervised by anesthesiologists (who are MDs). These two groups have a long and complicated political history that manifests in significant tensions in contemporary work relationships.

Jameson (2003) used qualitative interviews of 16 participants (8 CRNAs and 8 anesthesiologists) in three hospitals to trace Northrup's (1989) four stages of escalation in intractable conflict (threat, distortion, rigidification, and collusion) and extract communicative themes for each stage. "The overarching theme for the 'threat' stage was *identity*" (p. 568). For "distortion," the predominant theme was *similarity vs. dissimilarity of perceptions.* For "rigidification" there were three predominant themes: *separation* (physical or emotional); *differentiation,* or the tendency to perceive the differences between the groups; and *dominance* of the anesthesiologists over the CRNAs. It is interesting to note that this sense of dominance occurs at the institutional but not at the individual level. Finally, for "collusion," the predominant theme was *escalation vs. de-escalation.* Ongoing reliance on power-based strategies increases conflict. For example, CRNAs and anesthesiologists both reported situations where dishonesty fosters mistrust, which escalates conflict. On the other hand, strategies of collaboration transcend conflict.

Jameson (2003) was able to show that organizational and professional context are powerful forces that impinge on the occurrence, experience, and management of interpersonal conflict in the workplace. She accomplished this insight though the use of richly described qualitative data organized by a well-grounded theoretical model. Her treatment of communication is not reductionist in the positivistic sense, which is deductive; rather, she examines communicative relationships between members the two groups through the use of interpretive methodology, inductively deriving themes that emerge from the data. She also is able to show that Northrup's (1989) characterization of communication as dichotomous is oversimplified and that communication in the four stages seems to fall more on a set of continua than in dichotomous categories. This conclusion, too, is the result of an interpretive inductive rather than a quantitative deductive analysis.

The most obvious flaw in this research is the glossing over of the gender politics that obviously prevail. In the beginning of the practice of aesthesia delivery, anesthesia providers were nurses, who were exclusively female. Surgeons of the time were exclusively male. Nursing is still seen as a feminine occupation and surgery as masculine (Marin & Sherblom, 1994). Although Jameson (2003) noted the complication of gendered roles, she did not make room in her interpretation for this important dynamic. An interesting dynamic is at play here, perhaps suggesting an important empirical question as to whether the occupation of anesthesia is somehow seen by surgeons as something "less than" surgery due to its connection to the feminine. This, too, could be the explanation for early (male) physicians specializing in anesthesia seeking to bar (female) nurses from the practice—so that the practice would be more highly valued by the virtue of its masculinization. Clearly, this phenomenon is ripe for a gendered or feminist analysis.

Relational and interpersonal networks. Volkema et al. (1997) provided analysis of yet another important contextual factor: "conflict-induced third-party discussions in the workplace" (p. 185). Traditionally, our concept of *third party* has been limited to the formal process of mediation. Volkema et al. (1997) pointed out that informal third-party discussions have been overlooked, in part because of the dominance of the styles approach. They examined the factors associated with the use of informal third-party discussions with co-workers as well as external parties (family, friends, etc.) and the effect of such communication on the person's subsequent behavior in the conflict. Specifically, they studied the impact of *conflict intensity* and the respondent's *positional power, organizational tenure,* and *employment status* (part-time or full-time) on the *incidence* (number of occurrences) and *timing* (delay in use) of third-party discussions (tested with multiple regression analysis). In addition, they explored the impact of informal third-party discussion on subsequent assertive and cooperative behavior.

Nearly 400 respondents of various levels of positions from a cross-section of organizations were surveyed, using the critical incident method. Findings indicate that perceived conflict intensity is related positively to incidence of discussion with co-workers. Positional power is related negatively; those in conflict with a superior are more like to engage in third-party discussions with co-workers than those in conflict with a peer or a subordinate. For discussion with organizational outsiders, positional power likewise is related to incidence. Regarding timing, no significance was found for discussion with outsiders. However, respondents with higher positional power (in conflict with their subordinate) and those with longer tenure were found to be more likely to delay the third-party discussion with co-workers. Further, the more delayed the third-party discussion with co-workers, the more intense the conflict. Regarding the impact of informal third-party discussion on subsequent assertiveness and cooperativeness, discussion with co-workers had no effect on cooperativeness, but assertiveness decreased following discussion with co-workers, even more so when the conflict was with a peer as compared to with a subordinate. Conversely, assertiveness increased and cooperativeness decreased following discussion with outsiders. All effects sizes were in the moderate range.

This research is an excellent example of quantitative research that eschews both the styles approach and the managerial bias and enriches our understanding of communicative context. Although conceptually complex due to the sheer number of variables, the analyses are carefully conducted, with appropriate safeguards for repeated measures. The one conceptual confusion is in the treatment of conflict intensity; the distinction between this variable as independent or dependent is clouded. In the research design, conflict intensity is an independent variable with occurrence and timing of third-party discussion dependent variables. Conceptually, however, conflict intensity is treated as a dependent variable with timing of third-party discussion treated as independent. We surmise that the relationship between timing and conflict intensity is not linear and therefore not treated appropriately by this design. (The more intense the conflict, the more likely one is to seek outside counsel quickly; however, the longer one waits to do so, the more intense becomes the conflict.) Otherwise, the results are clear and reported concisely. The positivistic approach does, however, carry the deductively reductionist disadvantage of a lack of richness. Conflict behavior is operationalized as strategies chosen from a checklist with each then scored according to only two dimensions (assertiveness and cooperativeness), which is an operational throwback to conflict style models. The design and measurements thus severely limit the depth of insight generated by the results. Although we know that informal third-party discussion is common and has important effects on interpersonal conflict in the workplace, we have little sense of the particular nuances of this importance. However, this study has tremendous heuristic value. Our suggestion would be to pursue the phenomenon of informal third-party discussion multi-methodologically to explore further what leads to such communication and how such communication affects both the individual in conflict and the subsequent management of the conflict. Focus groups and in-depth interviews regarding this phenomenon would stand to produce a great deal of understanding to supplement this excellent piece of quantitative research.

Personal and Systemic Ramifications of Organizational Conflict

We turn our attention now to the subset of organizational conflict literature that deals specifically with emotions. This direction in organizational conflict research represents, in our view, a good beginning into examining personal and systemic ramifications of organizational conflict. The development of this literature coincides directly with the introduction and momentum of interest in emotional labor in organizational life, which became prominent in the latter 1990s and early 2000s (e.g., Kruml & Geddes, 2000; Shuler & Davenport Sypher, 2000; Tracy, 2000). We approach this portion of our review from a chronological standpoint, given the youth of the literature and the obvious connections of one work to another.

Gayle and Preiss (1998) posited that the presence of emotional intensity in recalled organizational conflicts can have constraining effects on organizational members' relationships. They formulated this thesis by reviewing organizational relationship, leader-member exchange, emotion management in organizations, and conflict outcomes literature. Gayle and Preiss grounded their discussion of conflict in the definitional standpoint that conflict can be managed, although their treatment of specific communication issues and outcomes is minimal. Data were collected from 174 employees and supervisors from 11 various organizations who shared their memories of a particular organizational conflict. These stories were then quantitatively coded and analyzed to determine if there was a strong relationship between emotional intensity and what they call conflict topic, status of the conflict partner, conflict management strategy used, and resolution status of the conflict. Although Gayle and Preiss (1998) rely solely on self-report data and continue to move our understanding of conflict away from the behavioral (Ruben, 1978), they do conclude that organizational members' lingering emotions from past conflict experiences can affect workplace relationships. Furthermore, they stipulated that these emotions can be more intense if the recollected conflict is perceived to be unresolved.

Gayle and Preiss (1999) continued their work with a focus on justifying the use of retrospective accounts of conflict interaction as a viable methodology to study the relationship between conflict features (resolution status, strategy selection, topic, relational status of the other) and the important construct of emotionality. The premise of their rationale for using recall data is that the use of intense language marks the hostility or aggressiveness of a conflict and indicates an individual's emotional state. Similar to their 1998 work, Gayle and Preiss (1999) used self-report recall data from 64 participants and analyzed the use of language in terms of the presence of emotional intensity. While we can say that this study, along with its predecessor, does add to the overall body of organizational conflict literature as it concerns emotions, it does not really fulfill its potential to answer any of the key definitional and methodological concerns that guide our critique, particularly as it relates to theorizing the central role of communication in conflict management.

We make the same overarching critique of the remaining two articles in this section of our literature review. Calabrese (2000) took a quantitative look at the predisposition of conflict in organizational settings based upon those who have personality traits responsible for increased sarcasm and increased anger. More specifically, he stated that one's determined "personality composition may be a significant predictor of the frequency and tolerance of sarcasm in an organizational setting" (p. 459). The variables that receive the focus in the article relate to what is determined to cause anger in the workplace and where certain personality traits correlate and predict the expression of anger and sarcasm. Calabrese used the Keirsey Temperament Sorter (Keirsey, 1998), which tests personality on four dimensions (expressive/reserved, observant/ introspective, tough-minded/friendly, scheduling/ probing) that, depending upon a person's scores, are associated with 16 characteristics of each temperament. In addition to this, he used a self-designed sarcasm survey instrument on a 39-person sample of participants. Although the study of emotion is a fruitful direction in that it breaks both the managerial and conflict styles biases, both instruments were used simply as predictor instruments that did not allow the explanation of the data to transcend the immediate.

Although Calabrese did not find significantly higher levels of sarcasm in the different personality temperaments, he did find that the temperament labeled "guardian" was a higher predictor of anger. He argued that the influence of organizational culture might encourage the guardian temperament more than the others, and he provides an extensive review of literature that supports this claim. His study, however, did not explore culture sufficiently to add to the literature that he reviews. This article's connection to the field of communication lies only in the mention of verbal speech as the vehicle by which a person can express her sarcasm and level of anger; the promise of studying communication as a central process is missed.

Bodtker and Jameson (2001) argued that there is a benefit to being what they call "emotionally activated" when in conflict and that directly addressing emotions while in conflict is central to its management. In other words, they stated that human conflict in organizational life cannot exist in the absence of emotion. Moreover, they stated that conflict has physiological and cognitive components, but is also a "socially constructed phenomena" (p. 262). Using Galtung's (1996) triadic theory of conflict transformation, they located three points of entry for conflict generation: attitude (cognitive ideas and emotions), behavior (that which is overt and has potential for hostility), and contradiction (values and interests that are not compatible). The remaining attention in the article is given to in-depth case studies that Bodtker and Jameson believe illustrate the utility of dealing with emotions in organizational life directly. Our critique of this work is twofold. First, what they do achieve is adherence to the definition of conflict as that which can and should be managed as opposed to resolved (or removed). In fact, the tone of their work is the strongest we came across when it comes to its insistence that conflict is not to be avoided, but rather embraced. What they fail to do is ever deal properly with the necessity of understanding communication (except for the mention of a few communication studies in their literature review) in their attempt to understand conflict as a process. Given their argument that conflict is a socially constructed phenomenon, the absence of communication as a central factor in the expression and understanding of emotion in conflict is obvious and weakens the overall study.

As we stated at the beginning of this section, this area of organizational conflict literature provides tremendous promise for our field. So far, the literature generally points scholars in the direction of understanding which emotional temperaments work best in organizational conflict situations (a prescriptive stance) and can potentially diffuse and *manage* those situations. Two general criticisms can then be leveled against studies of conflict and emotion. First, their positivist approach limits their insight. Emotion is a powerful individual experience with profound influences on organizational life, but a positivistic reductionist approach does not allow deep exploration of such. Second, one of our central critiques of the current organizational conflict literature overall is that although there is an implicit assumption permeating the literature that communication is a panacea for managing conflict, communication itself is rarely the intentional focus of research. This body of literature is particularly weakened by this fault.

Discursive Approaches

Discursive approaches have been utilized in the field of organizational communication for some time, yet have not been applied to the study of organizational conflict. Given the field of organizational communication's most recent theorizing of the very nature of organization as communicatively constituted (e.g., Cooren, 2000; Taylor & Van Every, 2000), it would seem a discursive approach to the study of organizational conflict is both overdue and most promising. We were unable to unearth a study of interpersonal conflict in the organizational context that takes a discursive approach, though we did identify two studies that illustrate the potential of a discursive approach for understanding organizational conflict.

Roberts (1999) examined "the conflicts, and specifically the discursive methods of solving these conflicts—faced by individuals within an organization as they negotiate competing demands" (p. 112). Roberts describes a case study of a Canadian bank during its biggest public relations crisis following a public scandal.

In particular, she examined the creation of unified identity in the face of the negotiation of multiple roles and allegiances via the production and consumption of organizational texts. Roberts studied the rhetorical strategies of the bank's response to the crisis, focusing on two particular individuals who represent the production and consumption of text. With a focus on language, she concluded that, "the ability to maintain a unified sense of self plays a pivotal role in our ability to survive amidst the complexity that surrounds us daily" (p. 115).

Burrell et al.'s (1992) feminist metaphor analysis, reviewed previously, also begins to take the discursive step, but does not examine naturalistic discourse and limits the analysis of language to the identification of metaphors. It is our contention that a naturalistic focus on language and discourse, which has so captivated the field of organizational communication in other topical areas (e.g., most recent work, Ashcraft & Mumby, 2004; Fairhurst & Putnam, 2004; Ganesh, 2003; Kuhn & Corman, 2003; Larson & Pepper, 2003; Thackaberry, 2004), would offer tremendous potential for the understanding of organizational conflict as well.

Summary

We have positioned our review of these pieces of research as "fruitful directions" because as we set out to conduct this review of the organizational conflict literature we fully expected "conflict styles" to dominate, but were dismayed at the degree of that domination. As we explored this largely reductionist and positivist body of individually and managerially biased literature, we regarded the small body of research moving beyond such thinking to be precious. Important seeds of new knowledge have been planted and must be nurtured. We remind our readers of Hawes and Smith's (1973) call for communication research on organizational conflict to break free of the implicit assumptions that ineffective communication causes all conflict and that cooperation is inherently superior to conflict. In addition, we ask the reader to consider Ruben's (1978) major challenge of the all-too-often linear approach to understanding conflict and seeing it only as behavioral. Much of the research reviewed in this section finally begins to answer these calls in ways that the bulk of organizational conflict research has not. Some discuss the role of communication in their analysis and/or move it to the center for understanding organizational conflict as a whole; some address the complexity of context and its multiple layers. We see it as our responsibility to feature this new literature in the way that we have because it provides a sign of progress within our field, sets the stage for new ways to critique this same progress, and offers new approaches to uncover more layers of the ubiquitous phenomenon of organizational conflict.

APPLICATIONS IN THE FIELD

Having reviewed and critiqued the research literature from the academic viewpoint, we turn now to the practitioner's viewpoint. Application of organizational conflict research to the field is imperative; organizational scholars cannot remain content with the pursuit of academic knowledge as its own end. We must continually bring our knowledge to the field as trainers and consultants, to facilitate improvement in organizational process and outcome. As we make a transition into our discussion of application to nonacademic contexts, a return to a discussion of conflict styles becomes necessary. This return represents the most efficacious way to bridge academic thinking to applied contexts as it represents a return to fundamentals. As such, the practitioner should take advantage of this easily explained and readily accepted approach. Although we have lamented the preponderance of the styles approach in the scholarly literature of interpersonal conflict in the organizational setting, we advocate its use in practice. The styles approach to the study of communication and conflict in organizational settings was driven largely by the demand for training in industry. It should come as no surprise, then, that the application is so direct. Although the styles approach limits a full theoretic understanding of conflict phenomena, it has generated a large body of knowledge that can be used quite successfully as a basis for communication training. Recall that the scholarly problem for the styles approach is the presumption of a linear, goal-directed view of communication—the very view that communication training depends upon.

We recommend that the styles approach be applied in the field as a set of skills within which individual ability or comfort level may vary, emphasizing to learners the importance of developing a set of communication skills (in and out of their own "comfort zones"), the adaptability to enact them, and the analytic skill to select the appropriate communication skill for any given situation. Hence, our philosophy for organizational training and development is to teach skills grounded in theory. Lest our reader cast aspersions that we are self-contradictory, we draw the parallel of the difference between teaching the skills-based freshman public speaking course and the advanced doctoral seminar in rhetorical criticism of public address. We apply pedagogic content in the former that has little use in advancing the goals of the latter, yet both rest upon the same disciplinary knowledge base.

The method that often works best in our field experience is to offer clients the metaphor of the toolbox, as opposed to the metaphor of the recipe. As we have all experienced, learners often come to the training seminar or workshop environment, or to the consultancy relationship, in search of an easy fix. They want a simple recipe: Do actions A, then B, then C, and problems X, Y, and Z will be eliminated. Our first step with a client or workshop/seminar group is to explain that such an approach is doomed to failure because of the complexity of human communication (the practitioner can use her or his own expertise to bring forth examples of the complexity of factors that bear on organizational communication). Instead, we explain, we offer a toolbox of diagnostic and problem-solving skills and enough theoretic knowledge to know what tools to try and how to analyze why they do or do not work in any given situation.

Although we believe its usefulness has been exhausted in generating academic knowledge, we recommend the Thomas-Kilmann Conflict Mode Instrument (Thomas & Kilmann, 1974) for use in the applied setting (for which it was originally designed). Updated kits are widely available; the TKI (as it is now known) remains one of the most widely used conflict assessment instruments in the field. Entering "Thomas-Kilmann" into a good internet search engine will reveal thousands of links to information on purchasing and applying the instrument. We have no affiliation with producers or distributors of the TKI. We recommend that the serious practitioner purchase the kit for several reasons. First, the issue of copyright infringement is no small matter, ethically or legally. Second, we believe that one should take full advantage of the TKI instructions and scoring guides, as well as supplementary materials. Re-inventing the wheel is never a good idea. Keep in mind that the TKI model's greatest weakness is its lack of basis in communication theory. With such a base added, the model is quite fruitful in the learning/training context.

To wit, before introducing the model and assessing personal tendencies, we strongly recommend providing a theoretic context in which to ground it. It is crucial to ground everything in a communicative definition of conflict, including the inevitability and potentially positive nature of conflict. Further, it is important to teach the communicative and noncommunicative sources of conflict. Once they have this grounding, we feel a client audience is ready to discuss their own style tendencies; we then emphasize the importance of making choices for the most effective conflict styles. It is crucial to emphasize the importance of a constructive communicative climate and teach clients how to achieve one as the first in a series of conflict management steps. Our steps are then no longer a recipe, because at this point the audience has gained a theoretic base. We also highly recommend the construction of a running case study to illustrate the concepts being taught, using information gathered from training participants about their particular organization or industry. In the extended training situation, the group can even develop the illustration. The steps we use are establishing constructive climate, checking perceptions of group members, determining the type(s) of conflict, analyzing the problem issue, selecting and enacting a strategy (using compromise as a last resort), and analyzing the ongoing situation—looping between analyzing and strategy, with frequent perception-checking.

In summary, the practitioner's setting is a quite different arena from the scholar's. As practitioners, we labor under a set of ethics distinct from our scholarly endeavors. The primary ethic, of course, is to be helpful in our interventions. As communication scholars, however, we also believe we have an obligation to teach communication theory in the field and to ground our practice in this body of theory. Our presentation here of a set of guidelines for conflict management training in organizational settings is based on the ethic of helpful intervention and the dissemination of communication theory. It is also based on a great deal of experience using this approach successfully.

CONCLUSION

As the length and breadth of this volume so clearly illustrates, the study of conflict and communication is an enormous and complex arena. Work is scattered across disciplines, and even that which offers a central focus on communication is often contradictory. In this chapter, we have focused on communication in providing a review and critique of the communication journal literature on interpersonal conflict in the organizational setting. Because of the vastness of the area, it was difficult to determine what to include. We limited our domain to the journal literature that was particularly focused on interpersonal conflict in the organizational setting. However, many other areas, most covered elsewhere in this volume, are germane to our particular topic. We have provided evidence that the underlying presumptions in much of this work are the constructive nature of conflict and the emphasis on conflict management (as opposed to resolution). Owing in large part to the demand for training in industry and in no small part to a psychological orientation, the vast preponderance of research takes the "conflict styles" approach, and revealing our managerial and individualistic biases, the largest body of this research examines the superior-subordinate relationship. In reviewing this research literature we have brought attention back to our most fundamental issues of definition (Hawes & Smith, 1973; Ruben, 1978), concluding that we have not yet resolved these basic issues. Our research remains mostly linear, positivistic, and reductionist. Our critique has been focused on advancing that which might begin to address these definitional issues: interpretive, naturalistic, and discursive approaches.

REFERENCES

Ajzen, I., & Fishbein, M. (1980). *Understanding attitudes and predicting social behavior*. Chicago: Dorsey.

Antonioni, D. (1998). Relationship between the Big Five personality factors and conflict management styles. *International Journal of Conflict Management, 9,* 336–355.

Ashcraft, K. L., & Mumby, D. K. (2004). Organizing a critical communicology of gender and work. *International Journal of the Sociology of Language, 166,* 19–43.

Bem, S. L. (1974). The measurement of psychological androgyny. *Journal of Consulting and Clinical Psychology, 42,* 155–162.

Blake, R. R., & Mouton, J. S. (1964). *The managerial grid*. Houston, TX: Gulf.

Blake, R. R., Shepard, H., & Mouton, J. S. (1964). *Managing intergroup conflict in industry*. Houston, TX: Gulf.

Bodtker, A. M., & Jameson, J. K. (2001). Emotion in conflict formation and its transformation: Application to organizational conflict management. *International Journal of Conflict Management, 12,* 259–275.

Brenner, O. C., Tomkiewitz, J., & Schein, V. E. (1989). The relationship between sex role stereotypes and requisite management characteristics revisited. *Academy of Management Journal, 32,* 662–669.

Brewer, N., Mitchell, P., & Weber, N. (2002). Gender role, organizational status and conflict management styles. *International Journal of Conflict Management, 13,* 78–94.

Burke, R. J. (1970). Methods of resolving superior-subordinate conflict: The constructive use of subordinate differences and disagreements. *Organizational Behavior and Human Performance, 5,* 393–411.

Burrell, N. A., Buzzanell, P. M., & McMillan, J. J. (1992). Feminine tensions in conflict situations as revealed by metaphoric analyses. *Management Communication Quarterly, 6,* 115–149.

Calabrese, K. R. (2000). Interpersonal conflict and sarcasm in the workplace. *Genetic, Social, and General Psychology Monographs, 126,* 459–494.

Canary, D. J., & Spitzberg, B. H. (1989). A model of the perceived competence of conflict strategies. *Human Communication Research, 15,* 630–649.

Chiu, R. K., & Kosinski, F. A. (1994). Is Chinese conflict-handling behavior influenced by Chinese values? *Social Behavior and Personality, 22,* 81–90.

Chusmir, L. H., Koberg, C. S., & Mills, J. (1989). Male-female differences in the association of managerial style and personal values. *Journal of Social Psychology, 129,* 65–78.

Cohen, S., Kamarck, T., & Mermelstein, R. (1983). A global measure of perceived stress. *Journal of Health and Social Behavior, 24,* 385–396.

Conrad, C. (1991). Communication in conflict: Style-strategy relationships. *Communication Monographs, 58,* 143–155.

Cooren, F. (2000). *The organizing property of communication*. Amsterdam, The Netherlands: John Benjamins.

Coser, L. A. (1956). *The functions of social conflict*. New York: Macmillan.

Cox, K. B. (1998). *Antecedents and effects of intergroup conflict in the nursing unit*. Unpublished doctoral dissertation, Virginia Commonwealth University, Richmond.

Daniels, T. D., & Frandsen, K. D. (1984). Conventional social science inquiry in human communication: Theory and practice. *Quarterly Journal of Speech, 70,* 223–240.

Deutsch, M. (1969). Conflicts: Productive and destructive. *Journal of Social Issues, 25,* 7–41.

Deutsch, M. (1973). *The resolution of conflict*. New Haven, CT: Yale University Press.

DeWine, S. (1994). *The consultant's craft*. New York: St. Martin's.

Eagly, A. H., & Johnson, B. T. (1990). Gender and leadership style: A meta-analysis. *Psychological Bulletin, 108,* 233–256.

Elsayed-Ekhouly, S. M., & Buda, R. (1996). Organizational conflict: A comparative analysis of conflict style across cultures. *International Journal of Conflict Management, 7,* 71–81.

Fairhurst, G. T., & Putnam, L. (2004). Organizations as discursive constructions. *Communication Theory, 14,* 5–26.

Fink, C. F. (1968). Some conceptual difficulties in the theory of social conflict. *Conflict Resolution, 12,* 412–460.

Flanagan, J. C. (1954). The critical incident technique. *Psychological Bulletin, 54,* 327–358.

Folger, J. P., Poole, M. S., & Stutman, R. K. (2005). *Working through conflict: Strategies for relationships, groups, and organizations* (5th ed.). New York: Allyn & Bacon.

Friedman, R. A., Tidd, S. T., Currall, S. C., & Tsai, J. C. (2000). What goes around comes around: The impact of personal conflict style on work conflict and stress. *International Journal of Conflict Management, 11,* 32–55.

Galtung, J. (1996). *Peace by peaceful means: Peace and conflict development and civilization.* Thousand Oaks, CA: Sage.

Ganesh, S. (2003). Organizational narcissism. *Management Communication Quarterly, 16,* 558–594.

Gayle, B. M. (1991). Sex equity in workplace conflict management. *Journal of Applied Communication Research, 19,* 152–169.

Gayle, B. M., & Preiss, R. W. (1998). Assessing emotionality in organizational conflicts. *Management Communication Quarterly, 12,* 280–302.

Gayle, B. M., & Preiss, R. W. (1999). Language intensity plus: A methodological approach to validate emotions in conflicts. *Communication Reports, 12,* 43–50.

Hall, J. (1969, 1973, 1986). *Conflict Management Survey: A survey of one's characteristic reaction to and handling of conflicts between himself and others.* Conroe, TX: Teleometrics.

Hall, S. (1990). Ethnicity, identity and difference. *Radical America, 13*(4), 9–20.

Hample, D., & Dallinger, J. M. (1995). A Lewinian perspective on taking conflict personally: Revision, refinement, and validation of the instrument. *Communication Quarterly, 43,* 297–219.

Haney Lopez, I. F. (2000). The social construction of race. In R. Delgado & J. Stefancic (Eds.), *Critical race theory: The cutting edge* (pp. 163–175). Philadelphia: Temple University Press.

Hawes, L. C., & Smith, D. H. (1973). A critique of assumptions underlying the study of communication in conflict. *Quarterly Journal of Speech, 59,* 423–435.

Jameson, J. K. (2003). Transcending intractable conflict in health care: An exploratory study of communication and conflict management among anesthesia providers. *Journal of Health Communication, 8,* 563–581.

Jehn, K. A. (1997). Affective and cognitive conflict in work groups: Increasing performance through value-based intragroup conflict. In C. K. W. de

Dreu & E. van de Vliert (Eds.), *Using conflict in organizations* (pp. 87–100). Thousand Oaks, CA: Sage.

Keirsey, D. (1998). *Please understand me II: Temperament character intelligence.* Del Mar, CA: Prometheus Nemesis.

Kilmann, R. H., & Thomas, K. W. (1977). Developing a forced-choice measure of conflict-handling behavior: The "MODE" instrument. *Educational and Psychological Measurement, 37,* 309–325.

Kipnis, D., & Schmidt, S. M. (1982). *Respondent's guide to the Kipnis-Schmidt profile of organizational influence strategies.* Beverly Hills, CA: University Associates.

Knapp, M. L., Putnam, L. L., & Davis, L. J. (1988). Measuring interpersonal conflict in organizations: Where do we go from here? *Management Communication Quarterly, 1,* 414–429.

Korabik, K., Baril, G. L., & Watson, C. (1993). Managers' conflict management style and leadership effectiveness: The moderating effects of gender. *Sex Roles, 29,* 405–420.

Kozan, M. K. (1999). The influence of intra-cultural value differences on conflict management practices. *International Journal of Conflict Management, 10,* 249–267.

Kozan, M. K., & Ergin, C. (1998). Preference for third party help in conflict management in the United States and Turkey: An experimental study. *Journal of Cross-Cultural Psychology, 29,* 525–539.

Kruml, S. M., & Geddes, D. (2000). Exploring the dimensions of emotional labor. *Management Communication Quarterly, 14,* 8–49.

Kuhn, T., & Corman, S. R. (2003). The emergence of homogeneity and heterogeneity in knowledge structures during a planned organizational change. *Communication Monographs, 70,* 198–229.

Larson, G. S., & Pepper, G. L. (2003). Strategies for managing multiple organizational identifications. *Management Communication Quarterly, 16,* 528–557.

Lindsley, S. L., & Braithwaite, C. A. (1996). "You should 'wear a mask'": Facework norms in cultural and intercultural conflict in maquiladoras. *International Journal of Intercultural Relations, 20,* 199–225.

Litterer, J. A. (1966). Conflict in organizations: A re-examination. *Academy of Management Journal, 9,* 178–186.

Luthans, F., Rosenkrantz, S. A., & Hennessy, H. W. (1985). What do successful managers really do? An observation study of managerial activities. *Journal of Applied Behavioral Science, 21,* 255–270.

Marin, M. J., & Sherblom, J. C. (1994). Contextual influences on nurses' conflict management strategies. *Western Journal of Communication, 58,* 201–228.

Marshall, J. (1993). Viewing organizational communication from a feminist perspective: A critique and some offerings. *Communication Yearbook, 16,* 122–143.

Martin, M. M., Sirimangkala, P., & Anderson, C. M. (1999). Subordinates' socio-communicative orientation and their use of conflict strategies with superiors. *Communication Research Reports, 16,* 370–376.

Mathur, H. B., & Sayeed, O. B. (1983). Conflict management in organizations: Development of a model. *Indian Journal of Social Work, 44,* 175–185.

McCready, V., & Roberts, J. E. (1996). A comparison of conflict tactics in the supervisory process. *Journal of Speech & Hearing Research, 39,* 191–199.

Moberg, P. J. (2001). Linking conflict strategy to the five-factor model: Theoretical and empirical foundations. *International Journal of Conflict Management, 12,* 47–68.

Morris, M. W., Williams, K. Y., Leung, K., Larrick, R., Mendoza, M. T., Bhatnagar, D., Li, J., Kondo, M., Luo, J.-L., & Hu, J.-C. (1998). Conflict management style: Accounting for cross-national differences. *Journal of International Business Studies, 29,* 729–748.

Mortensen, C. D. (1991). Communication, conflict, and culture. *Communication Theory, 1,* 273–293.

Myers, I. B. (1991). *Gifts differing.* Palo Alto, CA: Consulting Psychologists Press.

Myers, I. B., & McCaulley, M. H. (1985). *Manual: A guide to the development and use of the Myers-Briggs Type Indicator.* Palo Alto, CA: Consulting Psychologists Press.

Nelson, C. K. (2001). If it sounds too good to be true, it is: A Wittgensteinian approach to the conflict literature. *Language & Communication, 21,* 1–21.

Nicotera, A. M. (1993). Beyond two dimensions: A grounded theory model of conflict-handling behavior. *Management Communication Quarterly, 6,* 282–306.

Nicotera, A. M. (1994). The use of multiple approaches to conflict: A study of sequences. *Human Communication Research, 20,* 592–621.

Nicotera, A. M. (1999). The woman academic as subject/object/self: Dismantling the illusion of duality. *Communication Theory, 9,* 430–464.

Northrup, T. A. (1989). The dynamic of identity in personal and social conflict. In L. Kriesberg, T. A. Northrup, & S. J. Thorson (Eds.), *Intractable conflicts and their transformation.* Syracuse, NY: Syracuse University Press.

Oetzel, J. G. (1998). The effects of self-construals and ethnicity on self-reported conflict styles. *Communication Reports, 11,* 133–144.

Oetzel, J. G., Myers, K. K., Meares M., & Lara, E. (2003). Interpersonal conflict in organizations: Explaining conflict styles via face-negotiation theory. *Communication Research Reports, 20,* 106–115.

Ohbuchi, K. (1999). *Cross-cultural study of dispute resolution: Cases between Japan and United States* [Japanese]. Research report of Grant-in Aid for International Scientific Research by the Ministry of Education, Science, Sports, and Culture of Japan.

Ohbuchi, K., & Suzuki, M. (2003). Three dimensions of conflict issues and their effects on resolution strategies in organizational settings. *International Journal of Conflict Management, 14,* 61–73.

Papa, M. J., & Natalle, E. J. (1989). Gender, strategy selection, and satisfaction in interpersonal conflict. *Western Journal of Speech Communication, 53,* 260–272.

Peabody, D., & Goldberg, L. (1989). Some determinants of factor structures from personality-trait descriptors. *Journal of Personality and Social Psychology, 57,* 552–567.

Powell, G. N. (1988). *Women and men in management.* Newbury Park, CA: Sage

Powell, G. N., & Butterfield, D. A. (1979). The "good manager": Masculine or androgynous? *Academy of Management Journal, 22,* 395–403.

Powell, L., & Hickson, M. (2000). Power imbalance and anticipation of conflict resolution: Positive and negative attributes of perceptual recall. *Communication Research Reports, 17,* 181–190.

Putnam, L. L. (Ed.). (1988). Communication and conflict styles in organizations [Special issue]. *Management Communication Quarterly, 1*(3), 291–445.

Putnam, L. L., & Poole, M. S. (1987). Conflict and negotiation. In F. M. Jablin, L. L. Putnam,

K. H. Roberts, & L. W. Porter (Eds.), *Handbook of organizational communication* (pp. 549–599). Newbury Park, CA: Sage.

Putnam, L. L., & Wilson, C. E. (1982). Communicative strategies in organizational conflicts: Reliability and validity of a measurement scale. *Communication Yearbook, 6,* 629–652.

Rahim, M. A. (1983). A measure of styles of handling interpersonal conflict. *Academy of Management Journal, 26,* 368–376.

Rahim, M. A. (1985). A strategy for managing conflict in complex organizations. *Human Relations, 38,* 81–89.

Rahim, M. A. (2002). Toward a theory of managing organizational conflict. *International Journal of Conflict Management, 13,* 206–235.

Rahim, M. A., Magner, D. R., & Shapiro, D. L. (2000). Do justice perceptions influence styles of handling conflict with supervisors? What justice perceptions, precisely? *International Journal of Conflict Management, 11,* 9–31.

Renwick, P. A. (1977). Effects of sex differences on the perception and management of conflict: An exploratory study. *Organizational Behavior and Human Performance, 16,* 143–155.

Roberts, J. S. (1999). A rhetorical analysis of the self in an organization: The production and reception of discourse in a bank. *Business Communication Quarterly, 62*(2), 112–116.

Ross, R. G., & DeWine, S. (1982, November). *Interpersonal conflict: Measurement and validation.* Paper presented at the annual meeting of the Speech Communication Association, Louisville, KY.

Ross, R. G., & DeWine, S. (1987). *Communication messages in interpersonal conflict: Reliability and validity of an assessment tool.* Paper presented at the annual meeting of the International Communication Association, Montreal.

Ruben, B. D. (1978). Communication and conflict: A system-theoretic perspective. *Quarterly Journal of Speech, 64,* 202–210.

Shockley-Zalabak, P. S., & Morley, D. D. (1984). Sex differences in conflict style preferences. *Communication Research Reports, 1,* 28–32.

Shuler, S., & Davenport Sypher, B. (2000). Seeking emotional labor. *Management Communication Quarterly, 14,* 50–89.

Shuter, R., & Turner, L. H. (1997). African American and European American women in the workplace. *Management Communication Quarterly, 11,* 74–96.

Sillars, A. L. (1980a). Attributions and communication in roommate conflicts. *Communication Monographs, 47,* 180–200.

Sillars, A. L. (1980b). The sequential and distributional structure of conflict interactions as a function of attributions concerning the locus of responsibility and stability of conflicts. *Communication Yearbook, 4,* 218–235.

Smith, P. B., Dugan, S., Peterson, M. F., & Leung, K. (1998). Individualism, collectivism and the handling of disagreement: A 23 country study. *International Journal of Intercultural Relations, 22,* 351–367.

Sorenson, P. S., Hawkins, K., & Sorenson, R. L. (1995). Gender, psychological type and conflict style preference. *Management Communication Quarterly, 9,* 115–126.

Taylor, J. R., & Van Every, E. J. (2000). *The emergent organization: Communication as its site and surface.* Mahwah, NJ: Lawrence Erlbaum.

Temkin, T., & Cummings, H. W. (1986). The use of conflict management behaviors in voluntary organizations: An exploratory study. *Journal of Voluntary Action Research, 15,* 5–18.

Thackaberry, J. A. (2004). Discursive opening and closing in organizational self-study. *Management Communication Quarterly, 17,* 319–359.

Thomas, K. W., & Kilmann, R. H. (1974). *Thomas-Kilmann conflict MODE instrument.* Tuxedo, NY: Xicom.

Ting-Toomey, S. T., Yee-Jung, K. K., Shapiro, R. B., Garcia, W., Wright, T. J., & Oetzel, J. G. (2000). Ethnic/cultural identity salience and conflict styles in four US ethnic groups. *International Journal of Intercultural Relations, 24,* 47–81.

Tjosvold, D., Morishima, M., & Belsheim, J. A. (1999). Complaint handling on the shop floor: Cooperative relationships and open-minded strategies. *International Journal of Conflict Management, 10,* 45–68.

Torres, R. D., & Ngin, C. (1995). Racialized boundaries, class relations, and cultural politics: The Asian-American and Latino experience. In A. Darder (Ed.), *Culture and difference: Critical perspectives on the bicultural experience in the United States* (pp. 51–69). Westport, CT: Bergin & Garvey.

Tracy, S. J. (2000). Becoming a character for commerce. *Management Communication Quarterly, 14,* 90–128.

Volkema, R. J., Bergmann, T. J, & Farquhar, K. (1997). Use and impact of informal third-party discussions in interpersonal conflicts at work. *Management Communication Quarterly, 11,* 185–216.

Weick, K. E. (1979). *The social psychology of organizing* (2nd ed.). Reading, MA: Addison-Wesley.

Weider-Hatfield, D., & Hatfield, J. D. (1996). Superiors' conflict management strategies and subordinate outcomes. *Management Communication Quarterly, 10,* 189–208.

Wilmot, J. H., & Wilmot, W. W. (1978). *Interpersonal conflict*. Dubuque, IA: William C. Brown.

Zammuto, M. L., London, M., & Rowland, K. W. (1979). Effects of sex on commitment and conflict resolution. *Journal of Applied Psychology, 64,* 227–231.

12

WORK/LIFE CONFLICT

ERIKA L. KIRBY

Creighton University

STACEY M. WIELAND

University of Colorado

M. CHAD MCBRIDE

Creighton University

Numerous linguistic representations exist to describe when individuals feel conflicted about "balancing," "managing," "integrating,"[1] or otherwise accomplishing their lives both in the paid labor force and as family members and friends (e.g., work/family conflict, home/work conflict, personal/professional conflict, job/family role strain, work/family tension, family/work role incompatibility, work/life conflict). Multiple representations exist in part because this "has become a principal daily task for many employed adults" (Williams & Alliger, 1994, p. 837). In fact, flexibility and family is a major challenge facing workers at the dawn of the 21st century, gaining increased attention in light of increasing participation of (European American) women in the workforce and the resulting "norm" of dual-career couples (Orrange, 2002). Workers, especially those with children, say they are far less willing to make sacrifices in their personal and family lives than in their education, career, and jobs (Galinsky, Bond, & Friedman, 1993).

Yet conflicts between work and personal life are not *exclusively* a problem for employees with traditional family responsibilities (Grant-Vallone & Donaldson, 2001). Conflicts and initiatives that used to be framed as "work/family" have in recent years been "recast as work/life initiatives in recognition of the home and personal pressures that may conflict with work for all employees" (Greenhaus, Collins, Singh, & Parasuraman, 1997, p. 266; also see Cutcher-Gershenfeld, Kossek, & Sandling, 1997). Thus, research conducted until the late 1990s uses the terminology of "work/family" almost exclusively, and then after this point some researchers broadened their focus. As Kirby, Golden, Medved, Jorgenson, and Buzzanell (2003) suggested, expanding to "work/life" is not a trivial point in that "some researchers argue the term work-family both inadequately represents the workforce and unnecessarily restricts academic and popular discussion to concerns about balancing children's and employers' needs" (p. 34).

We agree the focus on "work/family" is discursively limiting because single workers, and to some extent "childless" workers, are not always considered to have a "family" (which creates a heterosexist discourse as well—see Kirby et al., 2003). In this chapter, we therefore adopt the spirit of this movement and use "work/life" to acknowledge that all individuals have more than just a working existence; all workers have some form of personal *life*. Concomitantly, we want to be clear that much of the work conducted to this point has used the more specific terminology of work/family. In moving forward from the construct of work/family to the broader vision of work/life, we use WLC to represent the construct of work/life conflict, and many references note whether the authors specifically limited to a focus on family. Our purpose is to provide a summary of the interdisciplinary as well as communication-based research on the topic of WLC and offer future directions for communication scholars to pursue regarding WLC.

Scholars across disciplines—including communication studies, sociology, psychology, and organizational behavior—have studied WLC in terms of (a) the impact of work characteristics on the quality and characteristics of personal and family life and (b) the impact of life characteristics on the quality and characteristics of work life. The body of research on work and life extends from micro-level analyses of individual perceptions of stress related to work/life (WL) (Greenhaus & Beutell, 1985) to macro-level, cross-cultural analyses of how work and life are treated in the United States of America and other countries. In order to theorize WLC across such multiple levels of analysis, we begin by outlining aspects of Giddens's (1984) structuration theory in relation to how it informs our project. We then review WLC literature at the intrapersonal, relational, organizational, and macrosocietal levels. Finally, we articulate directions for future research and practical applications within and across levels of analysis.

A Structurational Framing of Issues of Work/Life Conflict

A structurational perspective is a set of sensitizing concepts to study social practices ordered across space and time (Giddens, 1979, 1984).

Giddens (1984) suggested the key to understanding the reproduction of social structures lies in the routinized, day-to-day interactions of individuals in their use of rules and resources. When we apply structuration theory to WLC, the ways individuals communicate about and negotiate boundaries and conflicts in their work and family/personal lives on a daily basis influences their relationships at work and at home (see Kirby & Krone, 2002). Furthermore, such communication and enactments can even influence policy when individuals seek help "balancing" work and life from their organizations and/or their government. In other words, individual communication and action is constitutive in producing and reproducing systems and structures that create or reduce WLC. At the same time, structures influence how individuals experience and communicate about WLC. Structuration is able to theorize this link between human interaction at the micro level and social institutions at the macro level (Krone, Schrodt, & Kirby, 2006).

To illustrate, the ways in which individuals experience and talk about WLC in U.S. society has implications for whether or not the "work/life balancing act" is actually seen as a societal problem. If and when WLC is seen as a "conflict" worth addressing, the systems that are created in the family (such as spousal collaboration), the organization (such as work/life policies), and/or the government (such as the Family and Medical Leave Act of 1993) to help address the conflicts then in turn influence new experiences of (and attitudes about) WLC. Furthermore, often when systems are created to address such problems, they are "appropriated" from preexisting social institutions, such as larger political, economic, religious, or cultural institutions (Poole, Seibold, & McPhee, 1996). Overall, structuration theory offers a framework for exploring how WLC is constructed and reconstructed on a daily basis, from the stance that discourse from multiple levels can impact how individuals "manage" the interrelated realms of working life and family/personal life (see also Krone et al., 2006). Thus, in keeping with the assumption that microlevel interactions and macrolevel structures are mutually constitutive, we summarize WLC concepts in the WL literature using the organizational framework of intrapersonal, relational, organizational, and macrosocietal issues.[2]

INTRAPERSONAL ISSUES CONCERNING WORK AND LIFE

The perspective of WLC, typically attributed to Greenhaus and Beutell (1985), suggests the expectations of (a) the employing organization and (b) family/personal life are "mutually incompatible," and therefore when these domains compete for employees' time and energy, internal conflict results. This formulation has generated many models of WLC, and most have as a common conclusion that "this conflict can have an important effect on the quality of both work and family life" (Adams, King, & King, 1996, p. 411). At this level of intrapersonal issues, we describe the construct of WLC as well as detail both antecedents and consequences of WLC.

Conceptualizing WLC

Contemporary models of work/life take a bidirectional approach that gives equal emphasis to the effect of work on life and life on work (Adams et al., 1996; Cinamon & Rich, 2002; Crouter, 1984; Frone, Russell, & Cooper, 1992a; Gutek, Searle, & Klepa, 1991; Near, Rice, & Hunt, 1980; Netemeyer, Boles, & McMurrian, 1996; Williams & Alliger, 1994). The first component is life interference with work (LIW), which occurs when life-role responsibilities hinder performance at work: An example would be the illness of a child or life partner preventing attendance at work. The second component is work interference with life (WIL), which occurs when work activities impede performance of life responsibilities: An example would be when long hours in paid work prevent the performance of duties at home (Gutek et al., 1991).

When the domains of work and life interfere with one another, three different forms of conflict can arise: (a) time-based, (b) strain-based, and (c) behavior-based (Greenhaus & Beutell, 1985). Time-based conflicts arise as a consequence of competition for an individual's time by multiple role demands, and may include excessive work hours as well as schedule conflicts (Pleck, Staines, & Lang, 1980). Much research utilizes the time-squeeze/time-bind hypothesis (Hochschild, 1997); as Voydanoff (2004) noted, "work and community responsibilities make it difficult to participate in family activities" due to the limited resource of time (p. 7). Strain-based conflicts result when role stressors in one domain induce physical or psychological strain, hampering the fulfillment of the role expectations in the other. Finally, behavior-based conflicts occur when patterns of behavior appropriate to each domain are incompatible (e.g., parenting vs. managerial styles), yet individuals do not adjust across domains (Greenhaus & Beutell, 1985).

As illustrated by these types of "strain," researchers who study WLC often utilize a stress-based framework (Grant-Vallone & Donaldson, 2001). This research often employs scarcity theory, where personal resources of time, energy, and attention are considered to be finite and the devotion of greater resources to one role necessitates the devotion of lesser resources to the other role (Edwards & Rothbard, 2000). Such research has been conducted for two decades, and "there has been considerable (and often discrepant) research on the causes and consequences of conflict between work and family[life]" (Kossek & Ozeki, 1998, p. 139).

Antecedents of Work/Life Conflict

Different factors have been associated with WLC; work-related factors are assumed to interfere with life—WIL, and life-related factors are assumed to interfere with work—LIW. There is strong and consistent evidence that quantitative workload (i.e., having too many things to do and not enough time to do them) is the most relevant antecedent of WLC (Hecht, 2001). In addition, personal characteristics are also seen as a factor impacting WLC.

Work-related factors. There are numerous "work-related demands" (Jansen, Kant, Kristensen, & Nijhuis, 2003) that are antecedents to WLC. A primary area of study has been working hours—including shift schedules and overtime—because spending time at work and commuting to work precludes spending that time on personal life (Bohen & Viveros-Long, 1981; Burke, 1989; Frone, Yardley, & Markel, 1997; Fu & Shaffer, 2001; Greenhaus et al., 1997; Jansen et al., 2003; Major, Klein, & Ehrhart, 2002; Maume & Houston, 2001; Pleck et al., 1980).

Once "on the job," aspects of work design are also antecedents to WLC, including (a) autonomy, task challenge, and work load (Boles, Howard, & Donofrio, 2001; Burke, 1989); (b) travel (Boles et al., 2001; Greenhaus & Kopelman, 1981; Kirby & Krone, 2002); (c) team structures (Appelbaum, Berg, & Kalleberg, 2000; Boles et al., 2001; Kirby & Krone, 2002); and (d) physical demands of the work itself (Jansen et al., 2003). Whether individuals are self-employed or organizationally employed also seems to make a difference: Self-employed persons enjoy greater autonomy and schedule flexibility at work but concomitantly experience higher levels of WLC than those employed in organizations (Parasuraman & Simmers, 2001).

Relationships with individuals in the organizational environment can also impact WLC, including (a) workgroup composition (Maume & Houston, 2001), (b) conflicts with coworkers and supervisors (Jansen et al., 2003; Kirby & Krone, 2002), and (c) supervisor support (Allen, 2001; Burke, 1989; Kirby, 2000b; O'Driscoll et al., 2003). As a research example, Warren and Johnson (1995) studied 116 employed mothers with preschool-aged children and found the more supportive the organizational culture was perceived to be of employees with family responsibilities, the less WLC was perceived.

Life-related factors. Factors in the family and personal life are also antecedents to WLC. A basic area of study has been the size and developmental stage of family (e.g., Greenhaus & Kopelman, 1981). There are differences in WLC for individuals in two-parent and single-parent families, as well as between single-provider and dual-income families (Mortimer & London, 1984). Parental demands (Frone et al., 1992a; Fu & Shaffer, 2001) are a central area of interest—not only in terms of having dependent children (Jansen et al., 2003; Voydanoff, 1988) but also having young children (Crouter, 1984; Frone et al., 1997; Greenhaus & Kopelman, 1981; Higgins, Duxbury, & Lee, 1994; Kinnunen &

Mauno, 1998) and how the children behave (Frone et al., 1992a). These findings reflect the life cycle approach: Conflicts increase as one's obligations to life increase through marriage and the arrival of children, and many of these conflicts will decrease as the age of the youngest child increases (e.g., Eckman, 2002). The spousal relationship can also serve as an antecedent to WLC conflict (Frone et al., 1992a; Hochschild & Machung, 1990), including spousal or partner working hours (Geurts, Rutte, & Peeters, 1999). Researchers have also found domestic responsibilities can serve as antecedents to WLC in terms of the hours spent on household work and whether individuals must perform a "second shift" (Fu & Shaffer, 2001; Hochschild & Machung, 1990; Jansen et al., 2003).

Personal characteristics. Research has illustrated the level of importance assigned to work roles (Cinamon & Rich, 2002; Frone, Russell, & Cooper, 1992b; Greenhaus & Kopelman, 1981; Greenhaus & Parasuraman, 1986) and life roles (Greenhaus & Parasuraman, 1986) is an important antecedent to WLC. As Rothbard and Edwards (2003) discovered, identification with a role is related positively to time invested in that role—and individuals not only seek pleasure from roles, but they also invest time coping with role displeasure. Thus, more general role conflict and role overload also have been found to be antecedents of WLC (Fu & Shaffer, 2001). In the past few years, there has also been a movement to study how personality characteristics impact WLC (perhaps as moderators), including (a) "agreeableness" and emotional stability (Kinnunen, Vermulst, Gerris, & Makikangas, 2003), (b) internal career orientations (Carlson, Derr, & Wadsworth, 2003), (c) negative affectivity (Stoeva, Chiu, & Greenhaus, 2002), and (d) the Big Five personality traits (Wayne, Musisca, & Fleeson, 2004).

Consequences of Work/Life Conflict

Given this background on the causes of WLC, we now move to research that details its consequences. Consequences of WLC have been studied for family/personal life satisfaction and relationships as well as for job satisfaction and work relationships. Within this research, emphasis is often given to individual differences in consequences.

Consequences for life satisfaction and relationships. In their meta-analysis of 26 correlations between life satisfaction and WLC, Kossek and Ozeki (1998) found that regardless of type of measure used, a consistent negative relationship exists between WLC and life satisfaction. As Geurts, Kompier, Roxburgh, and Houtman (2003) explained, WIL may compromise opportunities to recover (both qualitatively and quantitatively) from work demands, which in turn increases the chances that work demands erode affective well-being and subjective health. Individual consequences resulting from work-family conflict include (a) increased health risks for employed parents (Duxbury & Higgins, 1991), (b) reported psychosomatic symptoms (Williams & Alliger, 1994), (c) poor performance of the parenting role (Pleck et al., 1980), (d) reduced life satisfaction (Burke, 1989; Frone et al., 1992a; Near et al., 1980, Williams & Alliger, 1994), (e) psychological burnout (Ray & Miller, 1994), (f) lower mental health to include clinical depression (Frone et al., 1992a), (g) increased likelihood of sleeping disorders (Burke, 1989; Geurts et al., 1999), (h) decreased marital satisfaction (Adams et al., 1996; Crouter, Perry-Jenkins, Huston, & Crawford, 1989), and (i) decreased family well-being (Perrewe & Hochwarter, 1999).

Consequences for job satisfaction and work relationships. In their meta-analysis of 46 correlations between job satisfaction and WLC, Kossek and Ozeki (1998) found that regardless of type of measure used, a consistent negative relationship exists between WLC and job satisfaction. WLC influences individuals' attitudes toward work (Loscocco & Roschelle, 1991), and the strain of "balancing" work and life can lead to (a) depression (Burke, 1989; Frone et al., 1992b; Greenhaus & Beutell, 1985; Near et al., 1980), (b) work alienation (Burke, 1989; Frone et al., 1992b; Greenhaus & Beutell, 1985; Near et al., 1980), (c) poor morale (Adams et al. 1996), (d) reduced job satisfaction (Adams et al. 1996; Eckman, 2002; Perrewe & Hochwarter, 1999), and (e) job stress and burnout (Eckman, 2002; Frone et al., 1992b; Ray & Miller, 1994).

Individual differences in consequences. Across these generalized consequences, there are individual differences. Women consistently experience higher levels of WLC than men (Duxbury & Higgins, 1991; Greenglass, Pantony, & Burke, 1989; Gutek et al., 1991; Higgins et al., 1994). Rothbard and Edwards (2003) rationalized that men may have greater reserves of time from roles other than work and life that make it unnecessary for them to draw from work time to meet increasing life demands. Yet as Pleck (1993) is careful to note, while men's behavioral reactions to WLC may differ from women's, men experience considerable pressure to balance life and work. WLC also appears to cross hierarchical boundaries, with frontline, blue-collar employees, professionals, and managers all reporting negative effects stemming from WLC (see Boles et al., 2001; Grant-Vallone & Donaldson, 2001). In addition, research has found that some personality characteristics can "buffer" these effects; in a study of Dutch fathers, Kinnunen and colleagues (2003) found that emotionally stable fathers were protected from the negative effects of WLC on job exhaustion and on depression.

To conclude this section, while we have talked about causes and consequences of WLC separately, research indicates these processes are more complex: After studying 831 employees in the Netherlands, Demerouti, Bakker, and Bulters (2004) found that work pressure, WLC, and exhaustion *predict each other* over time so that none of these constructs can be considered as only a cause or only a consequence. Instead, there are reciprocal relationships that can start a process of "loss spirals" in working and personal life. In review, intrapersonal issues concerning work and life largely surround WLC as well as its antecedents and its consequences. Given this background, we now move on to how WLC emerges in relationships.

RELATIONAL ISSUES CONCERNING WORK AND LIFE

As previously discussed, WIL and LIW are interrelated constructs. It is often the *relationships* within each of these domains of work and life that impact the relationships in the other as well as WLC in general. At this level of relational issues, we first highlight the impact of work relationships on WLC by focusing on supervisors and coworkers. We then discuss spousal/partner and dependent familial relationships that impact WLC and highlight ways in which the family as a unit both impacts and is impacted by issues in the workplace.

Workplace Relationships

Supportive relationships in the workplace are critical social resources in dealing with work/life issues (Frone et al., 1992a; Greenhaus & Parasuraman, 1986; Roehling, Roehling, & Moen, 2001). When supervisors or coworkers are not supportive of an individual's efforts to combine work and life, WLC is increased. Research has demonstrated that work/life policies are ineffective if supervisors do not support them (Galinsky & Stein, 1990; Kirby, 2000b). On the other hand, several studies have found that for employees who have supervisor support, job satisfaction is higher and work-family conflict is lower (Carlson & Perrewe, 1999; Thomas & Ganster, 1995). As noted by Cramer and Pearce (1990), "workplace policies are important, but over and above policy is the workplace supervisor's role in terms of understanding and supportiveness" (p. 43). Similarly, Kirby and Krone (2002) articulated how coworkers can also deter policy utilization. Therefore, we discuss how relationships with supervisors and coworkers can both facilitate and buffer WLC.

Supervisor/supervisee relationships. Research indicates that having a supportive supervisor moderates WLC and stress levels for both men and women (Cramer & Pearce, 1990; Frone et al., 1997; Goff, Mount, & Jamison, 1990; O'Driscoll et al., 2003; Ray & Miller, 1994; Warren & Johnson, 1995). Two dimensions of supervisory support can affect employees' perceived ability to combine work and family roles: (a) supervisor sensitivity to employees' family responsibilities and (b) supervisor flexibility in times of family needs (Warren & Johnson, 1995). Supervisors who are aware of their workers' life situations and accommodate these issues are among the powerful predictors of employee well-being (Galinsky & Stein, 1990). For employed parents, having a supportive supervisor results in lower levels of stress

(Galinsky & Stein, 1990; Ray & Miller, 1994), decreased burnout (Ray & Miller, 1994), and reduced role conflict (Greenglass et al., 1989). Of course, these benefits are more likely to occur when employees trust their supervisor and her or his intentions (Harvey, Kelloway, & Duncan-Leiper, 2003).

Friedman and Lobel (2003) also found "authenticity" to be essential in a supervisor's buffering WLC from their series of 100 interviews in 25 organizations over a 4-year period. Such an approach resulted in employees who were more able to balance effective business and personal lives. Interestingly, these authentic supervisors took two forms: "poster children for balance" and "happy workaholics." Even though some supervisors were workaholics, characterized by long working hours (see also Kirby, 2000b), these supervisors still helped buffer WLC in their employees because they encouraged employee actions to reflect their own core values (whether that was family and/or work) through respecting diverse choices, talking to employees about what matters most (aligning values and actions), helping employees take responsibility for their choices, and fostering trust (Friedman & Lobel, 2003).

Unfortunately, not all supervisors serve as WL facilitators. Morgan and Milliken (1992) reported a common cycle where individuals are uncomfortable with talking about personal needs with their supervisors, and so "managers often assume that their employees have no childcare or eldercare problems, and that their companies are not suffering from the effects of work-family[life] conflict" (p. 243; see also Galinsky & Stein, 1990). In a study of governmental employees, supervisor attitudes created the most significant difference between user and nonuser groups concerning the utilization of flextime benefits (Bohen & Viveros-Long, 1981).

A "gap" between policy and practice often arises because, while WL policies are designed and administered by human resources, managers are often the "interpreters and implementers" of policy (Cramer & Pearce, 1990; Rapoport & Bailyn, 1996; Swiss, 1998). A growing body of research has disclosed that formal policies do not always equate with corresponding practices (Cramer & Pearce, 1990; Kirby, 2000b; Kirby & Krone, 2002; Raabe & Gessner, 1988; Rapoport & Bailyn, 1996; Swiss, 1998).

Since some supervisors may be more supportive than others, and supervisors implement policy, this can result in variation in the implementation of work-family policies even within an organization (Perlow, 1997; Raabe & Gessner, 1988; Rapoport & Bailyn, 1996).

Kirby (2000b) found supervisors who did not apply WL policy consistently used a philosophy of "always fair if not always consistent" when making decisions. She further explained "mixed messages" in supervisory discourse. Specifically, while supervisors tell employees that WL policies are available, concomitantly, they may not want people to utilize these benefits (such as family leave or part-time work) so the work will get done. In such cases, they may send employees mixed messages in direct verbal/written forms as well as more indirect forms of communication such as organizational role models and "counteractive" policies.

Coworker relationships. Obviously, supervisory relationships impact WLC, but other work relationships can also assist in or impede WLC. Nippert-Eng (1996) illustrated that if organizational norms surrounding work-life issues are unclear, the work group is where they are most likely interpreted. In this process, coworkers may operate in ways that reduce WLC. For example, social support at work has been found to be correlated negatively with anxiety and depression (Barnett & Hyde, 2001), and a positive correlation has been established between team collaboration and the ability to balance WL (Appelbaum et al., 2000).

Talking with coworkers about family and personal life has been shown to lead to greater work satisfaction and higher work functioning as well as higher satisfaction with family activities (Clark, 2002). While WL issues may rarely be openly talked about in the workplace, they "simmer under the surface and [a]re frequently the topic of informal discussions" (Rapoport & Bailyn, 1996, p. 28). As an example of such research, Nippert-Eng (1996) described how workplace conversations about home and family may be habitually reserved for lunchrooms, bathrooms, and places altogether outside office buildings; she discovered that people tend to talk less about home and family while at work than vice versa.

But in these processes of interaction, coworkers can also discourage each other from taking advantage of WL policies to reduce WLC. Just as managers are reluctant to grant flexibility, coworkers may fear having to take on more work as a result of individuals' taking advantage of policies such as family leave and consequently might communicate negatively about WL policies (Kirby & Krone, 2002). WL policies may generate resentment rather than support from employees who have no need for them; there are emerging issues of equity where individuals without families feel burdened by policies because of the increased workloads they are facing (Kirby & Krone, 2002; Rapoport & Bailyn, 1996). In a study of 56 bank examiners, Kirby and Krone (2002) found employees frequently communicated a perception that WL policies granted preferential treatment based on demographics, including whether the employee (a) had children or not, (b) was male or female, and (c) had part-time or full-time status. Consequently, they found "the single examiners . . . talked about 'banding together' to share their perceptions of inequity, which translated to feelings of resentment toward those who were using the policies" (p. 63). This resentment fostered an environment of peer pressure where many bank examiners felt they could not utilize their available benefits.

There are gendered implications to these processes. For men, taking advantage of policies to reduce WLC challenges traditional notions of masculinity and work commitment (Pleck, 1993). While women may desire to communicate with coworkers about WLC, they will often "edit out" family involvements in conversations so as not to invite questions of commitment and professionalism (Jorgenson, 2000) in what can be interpreted as a strategy to manage WLC. Indeed, talking with coworkers (and supervisors) about family issues may cause the perception that one is not a serious organizational member (e.g., Jorgenson, 2000). In sum, workplace relationships with supervisors and coworkers can either buffer or further contribute to WLC. We now discuss the other side of the WL interface—family relationships.

Family Relationships

Much like workplace relationships, the interpersonal relationships within families and social support networks impact and are impacted by WLC. We discuss how specific familial relationships (with spouses/partner and dependents) and general familial relationships (viewing "family" as a unit) both contribute to and buffer WLC.

Spousal/partner relationships. Researchers have noted a variety of ways that spousal relationships in the life domain are impacted by workplace issues. For example, Crouter, Bumpus, Head, and McHale (2001) found high levels of role overload consistently predicted less positive marital relationships. Conversely, they also discussed how increased amounts of time at work by men lead to less couple time, but that these increased work hours were not related to wife's love, perspective-taking between the couple, or conflict. However, women who were still in their primary career reported higher marital conflict once their husband retired (Moen, Kim, & Hofmeister, 2001), suggesting that increased time at work for women might have more impact on spousal relationships than for men.

While WLC can certainly impact the spousal relationship, spouses can also help buffer some of the issues associated with WLC. For example, "encouraging wives" provided emotional and esteem support to buffer their husbands' self-esteem from threats stemming from events at work (Willis, 1985), and full-time employed men in dual-career families are protected from the psychological distress associated with poor job quality if they have positive relationships with their wives (Barnett, Marshall, & Pleck, 1992). Greenberger and O'Neil (1993) also found men's well-being was associated with social support from their wives. Yet women's well-being was not limited to spousal support but also impacted by neighbors, supervisors, and coworkers.

Spouses can also help each other communicatively reconstruct the seemingly competing roles of worker and parent/spouse. Kinnier, Katz, and Berry (1991) illustrated when couples were resolved about decisions regarding work/ life, they had more satisfaction and worried less because they could refer to ideologies such as "my family comes first" as a touchstone for making decisions. Golden (2001, 2002) highlighted the construction of identities/roles between worker-parents in the processes of "co-arranging" the management of work and life through spousal collaboration. Using discursive analysis of parental accounts, she informs the question of "what we talk about when we talk about work and family" (Golden, 2000). The ways working parents account for their WL arrangements reveals (and constructs) self-identity (Golden, 2001).

Dependent relationships. Like spousal relationships, dependent relationships with children and elderly parents can both contribute to and buffer WLC. Researchers have clearly demonstrated the impact of children on WLC (e.g., Kinnunen & Mauno, 1998; Voydanoff, 1988). In addition, WLC impacts the parent-child relationship and how much knowledge working parents have of their children's experiences (Bumpus, Crouter, & McHale, 2001). Crouter and colleagues (2001) found that a combination of long hours and high work overload was consistently associated with less positive father-adolescent relationships among both younger and older adolescent sons and daughters. Conversely, mothers' shorter work hours are related positively to increased activities with their adolescents (Voydanoff, 2004). While these findings highlight increases in WLC due to children, other researchers have noted that, like spouses, children can act as a buffer to WLC (e.g., Barnett et al., 1992).

Additional research has explored other dependent familial relationships that also impact WLC, and caregiving (of both children and others) has been referred to as an "unexpected career" (Aneshensel, Pearlin, Mullan, Zarit, & Whitlach, 1995). Kossek, Colquitt, and Noe (2001) found caregiving decisions had more impact when based on elderly family members rather than children; specifically, individuals who care for an elderly family member in their own home see detrimental effects on work performance as well as their well-being. Similarly, while social support from networks typically serves as a buffer to WLC, Belle (1982) found that larger social networks of low-income women lead to increased distress due to having to care for more people who were in need of support.

Family units. While some researchers have focused on specific familial relationships and how they contribute to or buffer WLC, other researchers have looked at the family as a unit in relation to both WIL and LIW. While families are made up of a nexus of various relationships, the family unit itself can be studied as a relational entity. We discuss how family is influenced by WIL, how family impacts LIW, and how both work and family contribute to and buffer WLC.

First, researchers have found that work hours and stress at work can impact the family unit's cohesiveness, functionality, and integration (e.g., Boyar, Maertz, Pearson, & Keough, 2003; Clark, 2002; Voydanoff, 2004). As previously discussed, mothers' shorter paid work hours and fathers' lower participation in professional organizations are related positively to activities with adolescents (Voydanoff, 2004). Voydanoff (2004) found such moderate levels of participation in youth activities (which occur when parental work demands are less) are related positively with family integration. Further, subjective demands (such as job satisfaction, demands of work/community roles, psychological conditions, etc.) are related to family cohesion. Boyar and colleagues (2003) noted WLC is more likely to spill over into the life domain, and argued the family unit is impacted because "employees make adjustments in their home lives rather than their work lives since the immediate effect is less damaging to one's livelihood" (p. 185).

Additional research has examined how life issues can both contribute to and buffer WLC (or its outcomes) in the workplace (e.g., Caligiuri, Hyland, Joshi, & Bross, 1998; Clark, 2002; Kossek et al., 2001; La Rocco, House, & French, 1980; Thoits, 1982; Voydanoff, 1988). For example, stress and social support from familial roles can reduce the strain experienced by individuals (Thoits, 1982) and moderate the impact of work-related stressors (La Rocco et al., 1980). Caligiuri and colleagues (1998) found that adjustment to work was significantly better when family communication was good, which was operationalized as the family members' sensitivity to each other, their ability to pick up on verbal and nonverbal cues, and the parents' ability to notice how a child is feeling and respond appropriately. Similarly, family climates that were open and conducive to sharing concerns were directly related to well-being, work performance, and WLC (Kossek et al., 2001).

Of course, work and life climates can interact together to contribute to and buffer WLC in each. While Kossek et al. (2001) found family climates open to sharing concerns had a positive impact on workplace issues, they also found that if either family *or* work climates were not open to sharing WL concerns (especially regarding the care of elderly dependents), general well-being and work performance of the caregiver was particularly damaged. In addition, Clark (2002) found talking with family about work and talking with coworkers/supervisors about life impacted both the work and life domains, leading to greater work satisfaction, higher work functioning, higher satisfaction with home and family activities, and resulting in more functional families. In this section, we have examined how relationships in the organization and in life impact WLC. We now concentrate more specifically on the organization as an entity and its influence on WLC.

ORGANIZATIONAL ISSUES CONCERNING WORK AND LIFE

To this point, we have examined the consequences of WLC on individuals, their work relationships, and their families. But what are the effects of WLC on *organizational outcomes*? As Casper and Martin (2002) noted, when organizational practices interfere with life, "employees may not quit because of such practices, they may stay because they feel they have no choice . . . [and] are likely to exhibit weaker job performance" (p. 106). When WLC is linked to reduced work performance (Frone et al., 1997), absenteeism and tardiness rates are often used as proxies for productivity measurement (Burke, 1989; Duxbury & Higgins, 1991; Goff et al., 1990; Greenhaus & Beutell, 1985; Near et al., 1980; Pleck et al., 1980).

A substantial body of research has found WLC is related negatively to organizational commitment (e.g., Casper & Martin, 2002; Greenberger & O'Neil, 1993; Netemeyer et al., 1996). Mixed results have been found as to whether WLC impacts turnover; Good, Page, and Young (1996) found support for direct effects of WLC on turnover, while Greenhaus and colleagues (1997) reported only indirect effects. WLC is associated positively with intentions to withdraw from work (Kelloway, Gottlieb, & Barham, 1999; Netemeyer et al., 1996; Shaffer, Harrison, Gilley, & Luk, 2001) and this relationship is stronger for individuals who are relatively uninvolved in their careers (Greenhaus, Parasuraman, & Collins, 2001). Given the organizational implications of WLC, companies have begun to take steps to help employees "balance" their working and personal lives. At the level of organizational issues, we describe the evolution of WL policies, review the organizational effects of WL policies, and highlight the importance of organizational support in implementing WL policy.

WL Policies

Today, many organizations have WL policies (Cutcher-Gershenfeld et al., 1997); *Working Mother* magazine even publishes "The Top Companies for Working Mothers." Since employers offer WL benefits on a voluntary basis, availability is very uneven. More benefits are received by higher income rather than lower income workers, by employees of medium and large rather than small firms, by white-collar rather than blue-collar workers, by unionized rather than non-unionized workers, and by those who hold full-time rather than part-time jobs (Nippert-Eng, 1996). Reasons companies cite for committing to WL policies include: (a) to improve recruitment and retention, (b) to increase morale and quality of life, (c) to reduce burnout and stress, and (d) to keep up with competitors (Galinsky & Stein, 1990; Goodstein, 1994; Morgan & Milliken, 1992). Of course, there is also a desire that such programs will impact the "bottom line" in terms of financial benefits, although the business case for these benefits is unclear (Christensen & Staines, 1990; Friedman & Johnson, 1991; Galinsky & Stein, 1990; Gonyea & Googins, 1992; Morgan & Milliken, 1992).

There are three primary types of WL benefits: leave policies, flexible work options, and dependent-care benefits (Morgan & Milliken, 1992). Types of leave policies include: (a) maternity leave, (b) parental and paternity leave, (c) adoptive leave, and (d) leave for elder care or other family emergencies (Morgan & Milliken, 1992). Flexible work options/alternate work arrangements are one of the most frequently used ways for companies to address WLC (Kemske, 1998) and include: (a) flextime (e.g., compressed workweeks, adjusted starting times, and fewer breaks to shorten the working day), (b) permanent and temporary part-time work, (c) job sharing, (d) flexplace or telecommuting, and (e) flexible use of vacation time and personal days (Morgan & Milliken, 1992; Rodgers, 1992; Swiss, 1998). While part-time options are typically of lower status with less pay and fewer career opportunities (Barnett & Gareis, 2002; Kirby & Krone, 2002), this may be changing; what has been called "new-concept part time" is a high-status, career-oriented, reduced-hours option that conserves prorated professional salaries and benefits (Barnett & Gareis, 2002; Hill, Martinson, Ferris, & Baker, 2004). Finally, the most recognizable dependent-care benefits are childcare and eldercare services—including on-site centers (Magid & Fleming, 1987; Morgan & Milliken, 1992; Zedeck & Mosier, 1990). Given the potential array of WL (and other) benefits, some companies have instituted a "cafeteria plan" for benefit selection (Magid & Fleming, 1987), and others offer "personal" rather than specifically parental benefits. But do these policies work to reduce WLC?

Organizational Effects of WL Policies

Research on the organizational effects of WL policies has been criticized in terms of both quantity and quality (Christensen & Staines, 1990; Gonyea & Googins, 1992; Rodgers, 1992). In their meta-analysis, Kossek and Ozeki (1998) asserted the human resources research on "policy is less theoretically developed, more descriptive, and 'best practices' oriented, and has often focused on ramifications of work-family[life] policies for work attitudes" (p. 140). They further argued such research often uses demographics as a proxy for WLC (rather than measuring the construct). Evidence regarding the benefits of WL policies often comes from testimonials rather than from scientific studies (Friedman, 1987).

Yet employers and supervisors consistently cite improvement in worker morale and job satisfaction after introducing life-sensitive benefits or programs (Gonyea & Googins, 1992; Rapoport & Bailyn, 1996). MacDermid,

Williams, and Marks (1994) found the availability and accessibility of WL benefits had a significant negative relationship with WLC; women reported less difficulty managing the demands of work and family life when they perceived benefits as available and accessible. Additional benefits of WL policies include (see Lobel, 1999, for extended review): (a) increased "organizational attractiveness" for applicants (Rau & Hyland, 2002), (b) increased satisfaction with WL balance (Bohen & Viveros-Long, 1981), (c) reduced turnover intention (Grover & Crooker, 1995), (d) higher levels of perceived organizational performance (Perry-Smith & Blum, 2000), and (e) increased productivity (Konrad & Mangel, 2000; Rapoport & Bailyn, 1996).

Lambert (2000) found workers who considered the WL benefits available to them to be *useful* were more likely to view their organization as supportive. Yet the outcome that seems to receive the most attention is organizational commitment. Results suggest an organization that accommodates the life concerns of employees is able to sustain a higher level of work commitment among its labor force (Grover & Crooker, 1995). As Grover and Crooker (1995) argued, "people are more attached to organizations that offer family-friendly policies, regardless of the extent to which people might personally benefit from the policies" (p. 283).

Behson (2002b) reported contradictory findings, asserting "organizational policies, programs, and attitudes that specifically address the topic of work-family balance may be of limited salience to 'non-familied' employees" (p. 67). Additional studies also suggest WL policy availability is less important than policy usage (O'Driscoll et al., 2003). Batt and Valcour (2003) have further questioned the validity of WL policy findings. They studied human resource incentives designed to induce attachment to the firm (e.g., salary, job security, career development program) and found these explain the most variance in WLC and turnover intentions, beyond WL policies. Although WL policies are associated with lower turnover intentions, so are flexible scheduling practices, supportive supervisors, job security, and high relative pay. Behson (2002b) also found that WL context failed to explain unique variance in

job satisfaction and affective commitment when studied alongside broader indicants of general organizational context. Other studies have also found limited or no support for the relationship between flexible scheduling practices and turnover or organizational commitment (Christensen & Staines, 1990; Thomas & Ganster, 1995). In addition, research has generally not supported the contention that WL policies reduce absenteeism (Hill et al., 2004).

These outcomes also depend on the WL benefit. Batt and Valcour (2003) asserted there is no credible research linking employer-sponsored childcare to lower WLC, absenteeism, turnover, or higher productivity (see also Goff et al., 1990; Thomas & Ganster, 1995). The benefit of part-time work, however, *has* been shown to result in significantly greater WL balance (Hill et al., 2004). Research has also examined outcomes associated with flexible work arrangements and documented significant positive outcomes for employees (Roehling et al., 2001). For example, Baltes, Briggs, Huff, Wright, and Neumann (1999) conducted a meta-analysis of 31 studies of flexible scheduling practices and reported a significant relationship between flexible scheduling and employee outcomes (job satisfaction, satisfaction with scheduling) in 18 studies of flextime and eight studies of compressed workweeks. Some researchers assert these findings may not be a direct effect of flexible scheduling, but rather of the perceived control over work schedules that these policies provide (Tausig & Fenwick, 2001; Thomas & Ganster, 1995).

WL Policy Implementation and Organizational Culture

As illustrated, the outcomes of WL policies are unclear. Perhaps this can be partially attributed to a problem linked to WL policies (and their ability to reduce WLC): the "double-edged sword" of perceived career repercussions for individuals who take advantage of them (Grover & Crooker, 1995; Perlow, 1995; Rapoport & Bailyn, 1996). In a study conducted by the Ford Foundation, employees who used such benefits as flextime, job-sharing, telecommuting, and part-time work suffered career consequences, although they were typically more efficient and productive than their colleagues (Rapoport & Bailyn, 1996). Organizational researchers have found employers often place a greater premium on "face time" and the number of hours worked as an indication of productivity rather than on actual productivity, and that these cultural norms are often difficult to change (Bailyn, 1992, 1993; Perlow, 1995, 1997; Rapoport & Bailyn, 1996; Thompson, Beauvais, & Lyness, 1999).

Several scholars have therefore noted the need for organizations to expand their conception of what it takes to be a "successful" employee (Bailyn, 1992, 1993; Bailyn, Fletcher, & Kolb, 1997; Perlow, 1995, 1997). As Perlow (1995) illustrated, current notions of success embed an assumption of "presence," and three assumptions about presence prevent WL policies from effectively reducing WLC: (a) one has to be at work, (b) one has to be there for long hours, and (c) one has to continually commit to work as a top priority—the ideal worker is "career primary" (p. 233). Thus, employees who take advantage of a flexible work option to work at home are penalized if the company rewards employees based on "face time" (Rapoport & Bailyn, 1996). Definitions of *commitment* go beyond work performance: "commitment to work—an abstracted notion, sanctified by tradition—must supersede other commitments" (Bailyn, 1993, p. 106).

Since employees may fear the consequences of using WL policies, many companies find that a lower-than-expected number of employees take advantage of these benefits; in particular, benefits are "underutilized" by men, single workers, and career-oriented mothers (Bailyn et al., 1997).[3] Thus, researchers advocate changing taken-for-granted procedures and underlying assumptions for organizations to succeed in this new environment (Bailyn, 1993; Perlow, 1995, 1997; Rodgers, 1992): Recent studies have shown organizations must create a corporate culture that supports work/life for WL policies to be effective (Grover & Crooker, 1995; Thompson et al., 1999). In the past, WL policies were often merely "added on" to the existing system of employee benefits without changing the culture and daily work practices (Bailyn, 1992, 1993; Cutcher-Gershenfeld et al., 1997; Perlow, 1995, 1997; Rapoport & Bailyn, 1996). Along with prompting "mixed messages" about

utilization (Kirby, 2000b), such "adding on" of benefits also created perceptions of unfairness among single or childless workers who are either precluded from taking advantage of flexible benefits, or burdened with a heavier workload because colleagues take parental leave or reduce their schedules (Kirby & Krone, 2002; Rapoport & Bailyn, 1996).

To review, we have considered organizational outcomes of WLC and explored how (and if) WL policies assist in buffering such conflict. We illustrated organizational norms of presence that often prevent WL policies from being effective, and the resulting push toward changing organizational culture. However, these organizational norms still need context. For example, the U.S. Protestant work ethic and related notions of meritocracy create the potential for "face time" to be expected: These notions imply people need to be seen working hard in order for supervisors to know they merit rewards. This leads to our final level of discussion, macrosocietal issues surrounding WLC.

MACROSOCIETAL ISSUES CONCERNING WORK AND LIFE

Considering the intersections between WLC and macrosocietal issues acknowledges the ways intrapersonal, relational, and organizational experiences of WLC are shaped by the macrocontexts within which they occur. In this section, we consider the macrosocietal level of WLC by discussing two categories of systems that shape work/life norms and practices: (a) economic and political, and (b) historical and cultural. While these four systems are admittedly intertwined, we argue the latter pair has received much more attention by WL scholars in the context of the United States than the former, although both are important for contextualizing our understandings of possibilities for navigating WLC. After discussing how U.S. American WL scholars have studied such systems, we also consider scholarship that focuses on WLC in other national contexts. We conclude that contextualizing WLC within macrosocietal structures is crucial not only for understanding how WL possibilities are constructed, but also for imagining other possible constructions.

Economic and Political Contexts

Economic and political contexts have been largely ignored in studying WLC. In fact, economic and political systems are taken into account in relation to WLC mainly when they are considered from a comparative perspective (Den Dulk, 2001; Gornick, Meyers, & Ross, 1997). In other nations, the economic and political context is more of a focal point because of ways other governments (e.g., Sweden) have taken a more proactive role in shaping their citizens' quality of working life. However, just because the United States is a context where government takes a "hands-off" approach to WLC does not mean that economic and political contexts are of less consequence; on the contrary, this hands-off approach has major implications for ways WLC is conceptualized and navigated by those living in the United States. Googins (1997) argued that because of the U.S. government's minimalist position in relation to issues such as parental leave and childcare, such public policy issues became the purview of corporations (see Organizational Issues). This "corporate colonization" (Deetz, 1992) of issues surrounding parenting and childcare is directly tied to the less active role that the U.S. government has taken in comparison to other countries in pursuing issues related to WLC (Googins, 1997).

Gross (2001) argued similarly that scholars in the United States should broaden their understanding of the ways policy issues directly affect issues and experiences of work and life. Gross described the ways American academics have considered mainly what she calls "piecemeal solutions" (p. 188) that resolve only particular tensions rather than leading to "more fundamental and wholesale change" (p. 189). She argued that political and economic forces actively limit what is considered to be part of WLC. She rebuked work/life scholars for forgetting that "having a job and being able to afford a family in the first place is a fundamental work/family[life] issue" (p. 191) and called for them to give up their "narrow (i.e., privatized) view of relevant 'family policies' to address a broad range of political issues and possibilities for redress" (p. 197). Connecting WLC research to policy issues is crucial not only for understanding how the political context shapes work/life practices but also for considering how scholars might be able to work with others to shape policies that enable different WL practices.

The concerns of Googins (1997) and Gross (2001) about the importance of economic and political systems in understanding work/life issues are consistent with critiques that work/life scholars have been quick to focus on certain groups of people (specifically White, middle-class women) in their studies while ignoring others (Kirby et al., 2003). The conceptualization of WLC oftentimes presumes ideals of "choice" and "balance" that in reality are tied to certain positions of economic or political privilege while precluding others—it is a classist discourse. Presumptions of positionality within economic and political systems that enable certain WL choices become evident when we further investigate WLC in other contexts.

Historical and Cultural Contexts

WL scholars have devoted much attention to the broader historical and cultural context within which WLC is experienced. At different points in time (and in different cultures) work and life are understood and valued differently (Ciulla, 2000). Looking back to see the evolution of concepts of work and life across time helps to situate WLC studies in meaningful ways. Most of the literature historically and culturally situating work and life spans far beyond the bounds of the WL literature to encompass broader concerns that have implications for WL. Situating WLC within these broader literatures entails thinking about how changing structures such as globalization, technology, the social contract between employers and employees, distinctions between public and private, and concepts of what it means to be masculine and feminine influence WLC. In this section, we discuss the different ways WLC has been situated historically and culturally in relation to these aspects in the United States.

The trends of globalization, the increase in communication technologies, and changes in the social contract between employers and employees go hand in hand, resulting in major changes in how people work and live. One shift that has accompanied the rise of globalizing and communication technologies is what is described as a shift from Fordist to post-Fordist work. Post-Fordism is marked by the rise of knowledge workers, the flattening of organizational hierarchies, a rise in the amount of flexible labor, and the feminization of labor (Holmer Nadesan, 2001). We see in these trends some basic changes in the social contract between employers and employees (Buzzanell, 2000). This new social contract is marked by an environment in which organizations are less accountable in terms of what they offer to employees by way of benefits and job security. Buzzanell (2000) described a major aspect of this new contract as the temporary nature of exchange between employees and employers. While this redefinition of the social contract can be seen across industries and types of jobs (Buzzanell, 2000), the rise in temporary work is a stark example (Krasas Rogers, 1995; Smith, 2001).

While most of these global trends have been largely ignored by WL scholars, the effects of technology have been given some attention. At a theoretical level, Kirby and colleagues (2003) argued technology can be both exploitative and empowering—exploitative because new information technologies increasingly intrude across "boundaries" of home and work, and yet empowering because they simultaneously allow workers to exercise increased control over where and when they do their work. Thus, technology allows individuals to either set up or cross boundaries between work and life (Nippert-Eng, 1996).

When WL scholars have considered the impacts of technology on WLC, it is most often in the context of considering the ways broad technological changes facilitate new flexible work practices such as telework. The major question this literature addresses is whether work arrangements such as telework facilitate more WLC or less (e.g., Sullivan & Lewis, 2001). There are mixed conclusions—for example, while Madsen (2003) concluded teleworkers experience less WLC, Hill, Miller, Weiner, and Colihan (1998) failed to demonstrate a consistent relationship between telecommuting and WL balance. Mallia and Ferris (2000) further stressed that many different factors (the individual, organization, and other circumstances) influence how telework affects WLC. Thus, scholars have focused on telework as a specific phenomenon enabled by

macrosocietal changes in technology; this broader shift toward more flexibility in work practices is seen as enabling different local enactments of WLC. Often such shifts hinge on changes in the ways that organizations and individuals orient to time at work (Hylmö & Buzzanell, 2003) and whether "face time" is important.

The other major historical and cultural context shaping experiences of WLC is gender—as Kirby and colleagues (2003) illustrated, gender is a macrodiscourse within which WL practices and processes are embedded. As relevant, we have already discussed issues of gender on the intrapersonal, relational, and organizational levels. However, gendered notions and experiences of WLC are ultimately shaped by macrosocietal values and beliefs about men and women, and the ways gendered expectations have developed in relation to WL is largely tied to the historical development of the distinction between the public (work) and private (home) spheres. The distinction between public and private formed during the period of early industrialization in the 19th century, where job site and household fractured into separate spheres and a two-sphere ideology emerged, with men in the public (occupational) sphere and women in the private (family/domestic) sphere (Gerstel & Gross, 1987). Today, this separation is reflected in the myth of separate worlds, where work life and family life supposedly constitute two separate and non-overlapping worlds (Deetz, 1992; Kanter, 1977).

This "separation" between work and home is being renegotiated because of the ways that (socially constructed) "boundaries" (for a review of this, see Kirby et al., 2003) are being blurred through practices such as telework. However, the influence that the public/private distinction has exercised historically in setting up distinct roles and expectations for men and women remains influential even as the distinction between public and private begins to be unmasked. Consistent with the myth of separate spheres, WLC and the need to "juggle" career and life demands is often narrowly considered as a "woman's issue" (Bailyn, 1993; Friedman, 1987; Haas & Hwang, 1995; Higgins et al., 1994). Research suggests, however, that when men take on more family responsibilities they experience the same strains as women (Friedman, 1987; Higgins et al., 1994; Raabe & Gessner, 1988). Unfortunately, because it is still often seen as a women's issue, much WL research focuses on the "difference question" and establishing equal opportunities for men and women rather than challenging the ways we "do gender" in relation to WL (Ashcraft & Mumby, 2004).

International Contexts

A final concern at the macrosocietal level is to provide international context for understanding WLC. Broadening the study of WLC to include national contexts other than the United States can be helpful for several reasons. Not only does such work provide perspectives of how historical, cultural, economic, and political systems shape WLC in other nations, but it also has the potential to stimulate reflection about how such systems shape WLC in the United States. Further, studying WLC in multiple national contexts can provide a deeper understanding of how navigating WLC at intrapersonal, relational, and organizational levels can (re)shape these broader systemic contexts.

Those studying WLC in national contexts other than the United States have taken interest in Scandinavia. Sweden, in particular, has been heralded as an ideal model in terms of WL. As Nasman (1999) commented, "the problems of reconciling work and family in Sweden are, to a large extent, treated as public rather than private issues" (p. 131). Consistent with its reputation for using "direct political measures and universalistic public programs" to accomplish specific goals (Persson, 1990, p. 27), Sweden's policies focus on providing gender equity and care for children (Haas & Hwang, 2000). Childcare and parental leave policies have been especially influential on the ways Swedish citizens experience WLC (Bjornberg, 2000). In 1974, Sweden was the first country to make it possible for parents to earn a large percentage of their usual wage (90%) for 6 months of parental leave (Sundstrom & Duvander, 2002). As of 1998, Swedish parental leave policy provides a full year of leave with 80% pay, which can be used over the course of the first 8 years of the child's life; further, the "daddy month" requires the male partner to take at least one month of the leave or it is forfeited (Haas & Hwang, 2000). There is some empirical research (Bjornberg, 2000; Haas & Hwang, 1995, 2000) that considers how these parental leave policies construct WLC in Sweden; however, much of the work that has been published in this area (in English) is primarily descriptive of Swedish WL policies and the economic outcomes.

While Scandinavia in general and Sweden in particular have been considered to be models for understanding WLC in a unique context, other nations have been studied as well. Nations in the following regions are some that have been considered: (a) Asia (Chuang & Lee, 2003; Kim & Ling, 2001; Lan, 2003; Ling & Powell, 2001; Lo, 2003; Moon, 2003), (b) North America (non-U.S.) (Janzen & Muhajarine, 2003), (c) the Middle East (Kulik, 2003), (d) Africa (Natdoo & Jano, 2003; Walters, Avotri, & Charles, 2003), and (e) Europe (Lahelma, Arber, Kivela, & Roos, 2002; Romito, Saurel-Cuizolles, & Escriba-Aguir, 2002). In considering WLC in these contexts scholars have acknowledged the importance of taking a macrosocietal perspective; this broader systemic perspective includes considering factors related to the economy (e.g., income), policy (e.g., welfare and health), history (e.g., immigration), and culture (e.g., values and attitudes). For example, in a comparative study of 15 countries in the Anglo world, Asia, and Latin America, Spector et al. (2004) found a stronger correlation between the number of working hours and WL stress in Anglo countries than in the other regions. They conclude that cultural differences in terms of individualism and collectivism directly impact the ways people experience WLC in Anglo cultures, Asia, and Latin America. Certainly further such research considering how macrosocietal contexts connect with experiences of WLC is a worthwhile and important direction for WLC research.

WLC: DIRECTIONS FOR RESEARCH AND IMPLICATIONS FOR PRACTICE

Throughout this chapter, we have outlined the construct of WLC and described related literature at the intrapersonal, relational, organizational, and macrosocietal levels. At this point, within each level and across levels, we outline some theoretical directions for research as well as practical applications of available findings.

The Intrapersonal Level and Work/Life Conflict

Directions for research. At an empirical level, we reiterate Kossek and Ozeki's (1998) suggestions for the future of WLC research: (a) to strive for greater consistency in measurement, using measures clearly specifying the direction of role conflict (i.e., WIL or LIW) since these perform better than general measures (also see Shaffer et al., 2001); (b) to examine how sample composition influences findings; and (c) to examine WLC and policies concomitantly. Jansen and colleagues (2003) further argued for more longitudinal research; most research has been cross-sectional in nature. Such moves would help clarify the more outcomes-related research that typifies WLC. But perhaps more important, we echo the notions of some researchers that along with looking at the WLC construct, scholars should also examine the "positive side" of the WL interface, because relationships between work and life are characterized by both conflict and support (Adams et al., 1996; Barnett & Hyde, 2001; Wayne et al., 2004). Most research has operated from a scarcity perspective (Wayne et al., 2004) and failed to recognize that "work and family [life] roles can have positive or enriching effects on one another" (Greenhaus & Parasuraman, 1999, p. 395). Recent research has advanced such concepts as *work-family facilitation* (WLF; Wayne et al., 2004), *work-family compatibility* (Barnett & Hyde, 2001), and *work-family enhancement* (Greenhaus & Parasuraman, 1999) to represent the benefits that occur when individuals combine work and (family)life (Grzywacz & Bass, 2003). Moving to consider WLF as well as WLC will provide a more holistic picture of WL relationships.

A more sophisticated theoretical direction for WLC is established by Kirby and colleagues (2003)—that work/life research should move from roles, conflicts, and outcomes to more subtle processes of identity construction. They argued such an emphasis "shows that what individuals are trying to accomplish is not merely the

avoidance of conflict but the positive accomplishment of personhood" (p. 14). Researchers of WLC who adopted this perspective would not only focus on "what individuals do but who they are" (p. 16). If and when individuals operate from this frame, they "can see themselves not as *victims of conflict and stress,* but as agents of selfhood" (Kirby et al., 2003, p. 16, emphasis added). Any of these theoretical directions should help deepen current understandings of WLC.

Implications for practice. So what can practitioners of conflict communication (and those impacted by WLC) learn from intrapersonal research on WLC? Several researchers suggest that an important first step in reducing WLC is to clarify one's own values (Friedman & Greenhaus, 2000; Friedman & Lobel, 2003)— that *psychological interference* between work and life is a more subtle and pervasive problem than a lack of time. Friedman and Greenhaus (2000) argued the first principle of creating allies of work and (family)life is to "clarify what's important" in terms of "understanding our values, our life role priorities. From that understanding, we can see how the choices we make in the work and family domains have consequences across the divide" (p. 146). Thus, practitioners who are helping individuals deal with WLC should first help them through this process of clarification.

Then, once an individual has clarified what is important, she or he needs to manage these boundaries by (re)assessing needs at work and in personal life—not only in terms of time but also psychological attention. Individuals need to strive to make the "boundaries" between work and their personal life "less permeable" and protect them in attempting to reduce their WLC (Friedman & Greenhaus, 2000). Practitioners can help individuals become more aware of how seemingly innocuous choices can impact WLC. For example, in an age of technology, individuals often bring home laptop computers and may even utilize wireless technology so they can work anywhere in their homes. This will likely create psychological interference between work and personal life, and the practical implications of such choices should be considered.

When WLC does occur, some research provides advice on coping strategies individuals can use. Rotondo, Carlson, and Kincaid (2003) examined four styles of work and family coping (taking direct action, seeking help, positive thinking, and avoidance) and found that taking direct action and seeking help at home were associated with lower LIW conflict levels. Being able to seek help is especially important in a society where the "superwoman" myth often makes women think they need to do it all. Overall, individuals need to be mindful of the ways they can reduce WLC, and practitioner training on these coping strategies through organizational development programs as well as teaching these strategies in parenting and time management classes offered more broadly in the community would be helpful.

Further, while there are many sources of WLC that must be considered, there are also multiple sources of facilitation. Individuals must be mindful of looking for support from various sources to help mitigate the effects of WLC—and those who want to be supportive of WL "balance" must find ways to outwardly show they are allies. For example, if a coworker is struggling with whether or not it is acceptable to leave work for a family emergency, reassuring her or him with a simple "your family is important and you have a life outside of work—you should go" would be an enactment of WLF that reinforces people are "agents of selfhood." Such an outward showing of social support manifests the intrapersonal decision to be an ally of work/life and bridges to the relational level.

The Relational Level and WLC

Directions for research. As evidenced, relationships within both the work (supervisor and coworker) and life (spouse/partner, dependent, and family unit) domains can contribute to and buffer WLC. In addition, these relationships can influence the relationships in the other domain. Research outside of the communication discipline has greatly contributed to our knowledge of the antecedents and consequences of these various relationships on each other and WLC in general. But as Kirby and colleagues (2003) noted, a common theme throughout this research (not based in communication) is a concern with outcomes rather

than with social construction. Thus, future work needs to examine the constructive process of co-managing WLC in these various relationships (Golden, 2001, 2002; Medved, 2004; Nippert-Eng, 1996).

Clark (2002) specifically concerned herself with the social construction of the WL experience. She was interested in how individuals "enacted" balance between work and personal life, noting that much of it was "done through our conversations and the stories we tell" (p. 24). She then used communication in each domain as both a dependent and an independent variable to understand its relationship with other situational variables. While her findings shed light on some of the issues surrounding WLC and suggest some ways that communication or "enactment" may influence aspects of the situation, the dynamic process of communication should be valued for its constitutive nature. The exemplar of Clark (2002) illustrates that while some interdisciplinary scholars have alluded to the importance of communication in WL relationships, it is often treated as a quantitative outcome variable (see Morgan & Milliken, 1992) or a tool to be used by management to communicate policies to employees (e.g., Friedman & Johnson, 1991).

Relationships, and the management of them (including the WLC that arises), are constructed through dialogue (Baxter, 2004), which is difficult to describe when communication is reduced to a variable. We argue this level is where communication scholars in work/life can most centrally make a contribution to understanding the management of WLC because communication provides a link between experiences within and outside of the workplace (Stohl, 1995). Kirby et al. (2003) provide a review of such research centered in communication; even more recently, Medved (2004) argued that, "Doing work and family must be explained as *doing relationships,* not just taken-for-granted as a function of time management or organizational policies" (p. 140, emphasis added). Thus, scholars should explore the extent to which WLC is related to communicative interactions individuals engage in with significant others from their home and work environments.

As a final area for theoretical development at the relational level, with all the research that has been reported on WLC, we still often fail to hear the voice of an important constituent— "the children" (Galinsky, 1999). What role (if any) do they have in the ways their parents or caretakers manage WLC? Do they experience WLC of their own (or do they pretend to when they play, etc.)? Some researchers even argue that current conditions of WLC for working parents have created a new type of child who matures at an early age— the "kinderdult" (e.g., Ehrensaft, 2001). Furthermore, when we hear of eldercare issues, we know how the adult children feel about these arrangements—but how do these elders feel? How are they impacted by WLC? Family scholars of WL, in particular, have a unique niche to fill in bringing these voices to the fore (also see Krone et al., 2006).

Implications for practice. So what can practitioners of conflict communication (and those impacted by WLC) learn from relational research on WLC? To begin, individuals should be mindful that communicative exchanges with spouses, friends, managers, and coworkers can both create and alleviate WLC. As McNamee and Gergen (1999) argued, we have "relational responsibilities." The way one individual communicates has an influence on the identity and self-concept of her relational partner; the relational partner then takes that influence on to the next person with whom she communicates. Thus, when individuals are dealing with WLC and its related potential to "spill over" into other domains, they should consider their "relational responsibility" before communicating. This is particularly important when communicating with children, but relevant when communicating with partners, coworkers, and supervisors.

In addition, since personal life is supposed to be a haven from the pressures of work, it is important to establish a network of social support of both family and friends (Friedman & Greenhaus, 2000). Medved (2004) gives some concrete examples of supportive behaviors between partners and larger network members. One category of behaviors is routinizing actions, which are those that "are part of carrying out daily or reoccurring household, paid work, and childcare duties" (p. 133) and include connecting, alternating, prepping, and reciprocating behaviors. An example of prepping

behavior is when a partner packs lunches and sets out children's clothes the night before. A second category of behaviors is improvising actions, which are when short-term interruptions to a routine occur that must be figured out, and include requesting assistance, trading off, and evading. Trading off happens when partners alternate who takes off work during a child care emergency. The final category of behaviors is (re)structuring actions, which is a process leading to a new set of routinized behaviors. For example, these can be performed through negotiating routinized structures.

Practitioners of WLC who counsel families might even be able to help individuals learn and label these behaviors as an additional way to cope with WLC; if a couple were familiar with these terms, and one partner felt like he was doing more than his share of WL responsibilities, a simple "I have been doing a lot of the *prepping* lately; isn't it about time to *alternate?*" would convey a concrete WLC message in the relationship. This is also echoed in other research; Friedman and Greenhaus (2000) asserted a first step for relationships in the home is to evaluate, and then perhaps to redistribute, the division of labor so that one partner is not performing a "second shift" (e.g., Hochschild & Machung, 1990).

Just as it is important for individuals to establish networks of social support at home, it is also important to establish them at work (Friedman & Greenhaus, 2000). In forming these networks, an irony emerges—listening to a coworker expressing feelings of guilt that her child is home alone sick has the potential to increase an individual's own feelings of WLC. Especially in the workplace, human resource professionals who have a goal of creating WL balance for employees should educate coworkers and supervisors on their power to contribute to or alleviate the WLC of others. As Kirby and Krone (2003) explained, "Coworkers have a large influence through how they talk about [WL] policies, so 'water-cooler' chat matters and should not be blown off as mere gossip" (p. 4). In keeping with this observation, those who want to show they are allies in addressing WLC should articulate their concerns. There are often occasions when WL policies are characterized as inequitable, and yet "the whole story" remains untold. For example, if an individual is complaining about the favorable schedule of a part-time employee and a manager or coworker "gives a gentle reminder about their proportionate reduction in salary and benefits, perhaps this would diffuse some resentment and reduce some of the negative discourse" about WL policy (Kirby & Krone, 2003, p. 4). Thus, when practitioners train on WL balance, it is important to consider not only what individuals can do for themselves but how they can facilitate work/life for others by fulfilling relational responsibilities.

The Organizational Level and WLC

Directions for research. Research continually emphasizes that truly to enact change, organizations need to go beyond simply creating written policies to developing supportive supervisors and "open supportive cultures." However, few studies lay out any specific communicative behaviors and/or messages that create such conditions where WL policies can be effective for both employees and the organization. In addition, the more informal accommodations to WLC (outside of formal policy) warrant additional investigation from a communication-centered standpoint. Allen (2001) began to do this—she introduced the concept of family supportive organizational perceptions (FSOP) to explore how emotional, practical, and social support by supervisors and coworkers reduce WLC. Allen and others argued it is not formal policies by themselves that make a critical difference in reducing WLC, but rather the practical support received from the organization and management in daily operations (Behson, 2002a; Galinsky & Stein, 1990; O'Driscoll et al., 2003; Thompson et al., 1999).

Employees who perceived their organizations as "supportive" made greater use of available WL benefits and experienced less WLC, greater job satisfaction, greater organizational commitment, and less turnover intentions than did employees who perceived the organization as less life supportive (Allen, 2001). Furthermore, when informal support is not available, parents find informal ways to cope when WLC emerges, including: (a) leaving work to attend a family matter but making

up for the work later that weekend (Behson, 2002a); (b) taking work home with them; and (c) "taking a day of vacation to stay home with a sick child and going to a child's school program while out on a sales call" so their supervisor would not assume they were with their families (Berry & Rao, 1997, p. 399). These forms of informal support—especially those that hint at organizational resistance—are a fruitful direction for communication scholars.

Implications for practice. So what can practitioners of conflict communication (and those impacted by WLC) learn from organizational research on WLC? Overall, results suggest the most effective organizational responses to WLC are those that combine WL policies with other human resource practices, including work redesign and commitment-enhancing incentives (Batt & Valcour, 2003). As illustrated, different types of benefits also have different levels of effectiveness and differing levels of attractiveness to applicants, so organizations should consider the needs of their applicant pool and carefully consider recruitment implications of work arrangements when analyzing costs associated with those policies (Rau & Hyland, 2002). In addition, the resentment that (strictly) work-family policies receive (vs. those broadened to WL) is also instructive from a communicative standpoint on WLC. Boles et al. (2001) illustrated WLC can occur for all employees, and if individuals are single they may still have important personal obligations to friends and family members. Thus, organizational members should remember that just because a person has less obvious WLC does not mean that individual should be expected to work all of the unpleasant and/or unwanted assignments involving weekends, holidays, special events, overtime, and so on.

When WL policies have been decided upon and implemented, human resource practitioners should endeavor to make sure these are well communicated and well understood. There is a need to continually "market" WL programs, even after their implementation (Friedman & Johnson, 1991; Kirby & Krone, 2003). In particular, Rodgers (1992) advocated that "success stories" in implementing programs must be disseminated throughout the organization. Galinsky and Stein (1990) found that communication about WL policies has been shown to be related positively to creating life-supportive work cultures (also see Clark, 2002) and higher WL balance among employees. Further, since a supportive WL culture is seen as important to recruit and retain employees (Galinsky & Stein, 1990), companies can demonstrate the value of investing in family friendliness (Friedman & Greenhaus, 2000) by announcing such benefits to shareholders and other important stakeholders.

Kirby and Krone (2003) emphasized the importance of communicating the "spirit" or philosophy of WL policies to all organizational members; they explained that since policies are often changed in practice, when individuals understand their intent, such changes will be more likely to preserve the policy's spirit. Building on this suggestion, they make some very practical recommendations:

> We suggest having training for ALL organizational members about WF[L] programs when they are introduced. Such training would illustrate not only the expectations for the programs, but also the philosophy, the positive aspects of work-family programs (such as increased commitment and retention, productivity, reduced absenteeism), while providing a realistic overview of their potential limitations . . . such training should also clarify that they [WL benefits] are not intended to be just "women's benefits." (p. 4)

Yet as O'Driscoll and colleagues (2003) noted, "organizational change agents *should not just focus on policy development and communication* but should also focus on the actual change of organizational norms and values" (p. 9, emphasis added). For successful implementation of initiatives, (a) WL needs to be seen as relevant to organizational mission, (b) WL efforts need a champion in the upper echelons, (c) WL policies and initiatives need a specific person responsible for addressing issues, and (d) WL policies need to be frequently reviewed and assessed (Galinsky & Stein, 1990). Managers may need to be trained to take a new look at work processes and realize that much work can be accomplished on alternate schedules and even at home, breaking away from the myth of face time (Friedman & Greenhaus, 2000; Galinsky & Stein, 1990). Finally, Friedman and Greenhaus (2000) also emphasized the importance of creating a work environment that values employees as whole people—what Jesuit educators would call "cura personalis."

The Macrosocietal Level and WLC

Directions for research. At a general theoretical level, this discussion of historical, cultural, economic, and political systems shows that such broader structures are crucial to consider when studying WLC. Only by contextualizing the intrapersonal, relational, and organizational levels of WLC within this broader frame can we understand the ways those levels have been shaped by the bigger picture. For example, Kirby and Krone (2002) contextualized their study of WLC and WL benefit utilization using several macrosocietal contexts. The ideology of separate spheres became apparent when individuals' use of leave or a part-time schedule was perceived as time away from "real" (read: public sphere) work. Meritocratic principles emerged when individuals perceived WL benefits rewarded people for *not* being at work (inconsistent with a meritocracy). Finally, sex-role stereotypes in U.S. society emerged in that "an underlying expectation existed (and was somewhat articulated) that it was the responsibility of the female examiners to take a primary caregiving role" (p. 69). Such research illustrates how macrosocietal contexts impact organizations and the relationships therein.

In the research we reviewed, with the exception of exploring telework, the implications of the global and technological environment in which WLC is now situated have been under-theorized and under-studied. Gross (2001) argued the "analysis of the work/family relationship must be grounded in today's socioeconomic reality—a globalizing economy with profound implications for working families" (p. 199). This global environment, in which work is increasingly technologized and employer-employee social contracts are increasingly fragile, certainly has important implications for the ways people experience and enact WLC.

An important direction is to develop more local studies that consider how individuals navigate

WLC in different macrocontexts. Ironically, much empirical work exploring how contextually situated policies (such as Swedish WL initiatives) structure individual experiences is primarily quantitative in nature (e.g., Haas & Hwang, 1995, 2000). Thus, there is a great opportunity for ethnographic scholars to consider how culturally diverse WL policies and values are enacted locally. Exploring differences across cultures unveils discursive closures, the ways that micropractices cause certain ways of living to seem natural and neutral and in turn preclude alternative possibilities (Deetz, 1992). Comparing WL norms and practices across cultures can provide practical insights into how individuals in these cultures might live and work differently.

Currently, however, the theoretical and empirical frameworks for considering macrosocietal systems in relation to other levels are underdeveloped. Most scholars have focused on either the micro or macro levels, but not both simultaneously (Korabik, Lero, & Ayman, 2003). Developing both theoretical and empirical frameworks that better enable scholars to look at how the macrosocietal contexts interact with one another and also with other levels of WLC might help us conceive of ways to navigate WLC by initiating change at multiple levels.

Implications for practice. So what can practitioners of conflict communication (and those impacted by WLC) learn from macrosocietal research on WLC? We argue these issues do not translate as readily to the practitioner level, except in a comparative policy sense. However, it is individuals that make up societies, and so people who are striving to find balance between work and personal life should be lobbying those in government who can do something about such conflicts at a policy level. Kirby and colleagues (2003) point out the importance of individuals' taking a more communal orientation; as they note, "there has not been an organized push for widespread change because in an individualistic, achieving society, balance between work and personal life is not always seen as a high priority goal" (p. 32).

Friedman and Greenhaus (2000) argued that to change the societal view of work and life, children need to be educated on outdated gender role stereotypes and how both men and women can thrive in public and private spheres, breaking through the "separate spheres" ideology as a macrosocietal context for future generations. This is important, because often scholarship—and indeed, our everyday enactments of work/life—reproduce this ideology by conceptualizing what counts as (public) "work" and what counts as (private) "life" in specific (and often narrow) ways. For example, "work" generally means paid work and does not include childcare, eldercare, housework, or volunteer work, although these are certainly forms of labor. Scholars and individuals need to be mindful that stay-at-home parents do indeed *work* (Medved & Kirby, 2005)—yet this labor is not recognized in current notions of work and life.

Further, what we have in this chapter referred to as "life" is often labeled more narrowly as "family," which usually insinuates the presence of children and/or "home." These conceptualizations of what stands in contrast to work are limited in that they preclude experiences of certain individuals (single adults and married people without children) and experiences in certain locations (outside of work or home). It also has a heterosexist implication/bias. It is crucial that we continue to broaden the range of what is considered to be "work" and what is considered to be "life." By incorporating broader definitions of these central organizing terms, we open up not only the possibility that other aspects of being human might be important, but also the possibility of learning from those who have typically been outside of the purview of work/life studies.

Connecting Across Intrapersonal, Relational, Organizational, and Macrosocietal Levels

Directions for research. In this review, we have adopted a structurational perspective, operating on the assumption that micro-issues can have macrolevel consequences (and vice versa). We close this chapter by linking across these levels in suggesting future research. To begin, there are communicative implications of WLC linking the intrapersonal and relational levels. Many endorsed "coping strategies" for dealing with WLC fall within the intrapersonal level, including increased role behavior and cognitive restructuring (Elman & Gilbert, 1984). Additional coping strategies may be relational in nature, such as communicating the need for social support when tensions between work and life arise (e.g., Rotondo et al., 2003). Once such help is sought, little research has explored potential "advice giving" (and taking) strategies, such as a group of coworkers (friends, sisters, brothers, etc.) conversing about how they integrate work and personal life. A further area of interest is how individuals communicate about their WLC with others—employees may differ in *whom* they are comfortable talking with about work/life issues. Beyond this, within the realm of work/life there may also be differences in *what* organizational members are comfortable talking about: For example, a child's illness may be appropriate, but a spouse's alcoholism may not.

There are also avenues for research between the intrapersonal and organizational level. Warren and Johnson (1995) found "work environment" was a significant predictor of WLC. However, this research used a generalized measure of employee perceptions of work environment, which creates a need "to investigate the meaning that employed parents attach to a 'family[life] friendly' work environment" (p. 168). In other words, what communicative conditions influence whether individuals perceive their organizational climate as being supportive of personal life? Another way communication may be involved between intrapersonal and organizational levels relates to organizational commitment. Grover and Crooker (1995) found that company sponsorship of (family)life-supportive policies may symbolize corporate concern. This needs further rhetorical examination—how do such policies function symbolically for employees? Kirby, Pawlowski, and Dressel (2000) studied the rhetorical positioning of work/life policies in the recruiting materials of the (then) Big Five accounting firms. They found organizations positioned themselves as helper, enabler, competitor, business, and community. Which of these strategies has the most "symbolic power" to foster organizational commitment?

Communicative implications also exist between the relational and organizational levels. For example, employees may prefer to interact only with individuals at certain organizational levels concerning issues of WLC. They may feel comfortable talking to their coworkers, but not their supervisors. Conversely, they may prefer to talk directly to their supervisors, since these individuals are perceived to have more decision-making power to change working conditions in response to WLC (Warren & Johnson, 1995). In such situations, what communicative behaviors influence individuals' perceptions of supervisory support? While some research has indicated that organizations can change the level of supervisory support (Thomas & Ganster, 1995), no research "prescribes" any specific supportive behaviors. The impact of relationships outside the workplace on employee understandings of work/life also brings up communicative dimensions between interpersonal and organizational levels. For example, if friends in other organizations also have WL policies, do they communicate about these? How does talking to one's spouse, children, extended family, and friends about WL policies influence an individual's attitudes about those programs?

Beyond implications for individuals, the literature also has communicative and political implications for organizations. These are most visible between the organizational and macrosocietal levels. To illustrate, how does the treatment of "work" and "life" *within* the organization influence how employees see these constructs at the societal level? For example, the way WL policies are written and communicated about within the organization affect broader conceptions of the "proper role" of men and women—not only in the workplace, but in society as a whole (Kirby, 2002). As Kirby and Krone (2002) contended, when women are accepted in taking maternity leave and using leave to spend time with children "but men were discouraged from paternity and parental leave, this sends a message about gender stereotypes that extends beyond the confines of the organization" (p. 71). Of course, this relationship can be examined from the reverse perspective as well, lending insight into how cultural conceptions of men and women as parents and workers are communicated about, and the implications when generalized stereotypes constrain how organizations view WL.

Concerning these links between the various levels, one shared characteristic is the importance of *everyday interactions* in creating the environment within which individuals communicate about WLC, WL issues, and the use of WL policies. As an example, it is beneficial to examine how a policy such as flextime is enacted on a day-to-day basis. Communicative interactions surrounding the creation of a flexible schedule between an employee and his or her supervisor impact future scheduling arrangements for other workers. While the outcomes of the current negotiation can set constraints on future negotiations and perhaps increase WLC, they could also "enable" future negotiations when the policies are negotiated and utilized in a positive manner and encourage work/life facilitation. Such instances of communication, with their resulting ability to enable or constrain future interactions, reflect Giddens's (1984) theory of structuration as applied to the (re)production of work/life conflicts.

Implications for practice. There are some practical implications that cut across levels as well. As noted, when individuals go from reflecting on the importance of balancing work and life to facilitating such balance for others and providing social support, we have transitioned from the intrapersonal level to the relational level. Then, if individuals are talking about WL issues and decide to organize to do something about these issues in the organization and/or in broader governmental and societal contexts, we have transitioned from the relational level to the organizational and macrosocietal levels. To illustrate such transitions, Friedman and Greenhaus (2000) emphasized the importance of educating young people early about choosing to prioritize what is important to them so that they can enact their work/life relationships in ways that fit with their value systems and to work in organizations that support their vision of WL balance.

This notion of prioritizing "what's important" can happen at the organizational level as well; many organizations have decided to honor employee needs for WL balance even though they are not legally required to. For example, while companies are not required by the government to provide benefits to part-time workers, some choose to out of a sense of corporate responsibility, blending the levels between organizational and macrosocietal. When companies do this, others may feel pressured to follow (institutional theory; see Goodstein, 1994), which increases the likelihood that these trends will spread.

A final application that a structurational perspective on work/life offers across levels is this: that just because structures exist does not mean people always live by them. In organizations where WLC is not addressed through policy, individuals can make informal accommodations to meet their needs for balance. When existing WL policies are not working, individuals may modify or appropriate them. Individuals can choose to have egalitarian relationships where domestic responsibilities are shared equally—even though this may not be the societal norm. Since structures are both produced and reproduced through interaction, individual actions across levels can have systemic consequences for WLC (Giddens, 1984).

CONCLUSION

Our purpose in this chapter was to provide a summary of the interdisciplinary as well as communication-based research on WLC. Literature was reviewed surrounding how WLC is impacted at intrapersonal, relational, organizational, and macrosocietal levels, and future directions for scholarship on WLC as well as practical applications for WLC were offered within and between levels. A central conclusion that can be taken from this review is that while the body of interdisciplinary research on WLC is extensive, it is also often narrowly defined. A shortcoming of WLC research is a lack of theoretical "richness," and so an important direction for work/life scholars in communication is to develop theories that provide adequate grounding for the study of work/life practices. While emerging scholarship in organizational communication has begun to address some of these limitations, scholars of conflict communication and family communication also have unique contributions to make in extending current understandings of work/life conflict— and, hopefully, in helping to elucidate communicative behaviors that encourage work/life facilitation.

NOTES

1. As a construct, work-family integration "is similar to that of work-family balance but does not imply the equality of spheres implicit in the concept of balance" (Grant-Vallone & Donaldson, 2001, p. 191).

2. In selecting WLC literature, relevant sources were included as follows: the first author's dissertation (Kirby, 2000a) served as a basis for literature until 2000. For more recent literature, a search was conducted through the Sloan Electronic Researchers Work-Family Literature Database (Sloan Foundation, n.d.) for the keywords "work family conflict" and "work life conflict," which yielded 186 interdisciplinary articles. Finally, the inclusion of relevant sources in communication studies was guided by Kirby et al.'s (2003) review.

3. Granted, there are additional reasons for "underutilizing" WL benefits: Golden (2000) found a potential mismatch exists between these accommodations and working parents' ideology of individualism, and Hochschild (1997) argued many parents would just rather be at work than at home—it is the new "haven."

REFERENCES

Adams, G. A., King, L. A., & King, D. W. (1996). Relationships of job and family involvement, family social support, and work-family conflict with job and life satisfaction. *Journal of Applied Psychology, 81*, 411–420.

Allen, T. D. (2001). Family-supportive work environments: The role of organizational perceptions. *Journal of Vocational Behavior, 58*, 414–435.

Aneshensel, J. S., Pearlin, L., Mullan, J., Zarit, S., & Whitlach, C. (1995). *Profiles in caregiving: The unexpected career.* Boston: Academic Press.

Appelbaum, E., Berg, P., & Kalleberg, A. L. (2000). *Balancing work and family: Effects of high-performance work systems and high-commitment workplaces.* Report to the U.S. Department of Labor, Washington.

Ashcraft, K., & Mumby, D. K. (2004). *Reworking gender: A feminist communicology of gender.* Thousand Oaks, CA: Sage.

Bailyn, L. (1992). Issues of work and family in different national contexts: How the United States, Britain, and Sweden respond. *Human Resource Management, 31,* 201–208.

Bailyn, L. (1993). *Breaking the mold: Women, men, and time in the new corporate world.* New York: Free Press.

Bailyn, L., Fletcher, J. K., & Kolb, D. (1997). Unexpected connections: Considering employees' personal lives can revitalize your business. *Sloan Management Review, 38*, 11–19.

Baltes, B. B., Briggs, T. E., Huff, J. W., Wright, J. A., & Neumann, G. A. (1999). Flexible and compressed workweek schedules: A meta-analysis of their effects on work-related criteria. *Journal of Applied Psychology, 84*, 496–513.

Barnett, R. C., & Gareis, K. C. (2002). Full-time and reduced-hours work schedules and marital quality: A study of female physicians with young children. *Work and Occupations, 29,* 364–379.

Barnett, R. C., & Hyde, J. S. (2001). Women, men, work, and family: An expansionist theory. *American Psychologist, 56*, 781–796.

Barnett, R., Marshall, N., & Pleck, J. (1992). Men's multiple roles and their relationship to men's psychological distress. *Journal of Marriage and the Family, 54*, 358–367.

Batt, R., & Valcour, P. M. (2003). Human resource practices as predictors of work-family outcomes and employee turnover. *Industrial Relations, 42*, 189–220.

Baxter, L. (2004). Relationships as dialogues. *Personal Relationships, 11*, 1–22.

Behson, S. J. (2002a). Coping with family-to-work conflict: The role of informal work accommodations to family. *Journal of Occupational Health Psychology, 7*, 324–341.

Behson, S. J. (2002b). Which dominates? The relative importance of work-family organizational support and general organizational context on employee outcomes. *Journal of Vocational Behavior, 61,* 53–72.

Belle, D. (1982). The stress of caring: Women as providers of social support. In L. Goldberger & S. Breznitz (Eds.), *Handbook of stress: Theoretical and clinical aspects* (pp. 496–505). New York: Free Press.

Berry, J. O., & Rao, J. M. (1997). Balancing employment and fatherhood. *Journal of Family Issues, 18,* 386–202.

Bjornberg, U. (2000). Equality and backlash: Family, gender and social policy in Sweden. In L. Haas, P. Hwang, & G. Russell (Eds.), *Organizational change and gender equity:*

International perspectives on fathers and mothers at the workplace (pp. 57–76). Thousand Oaks, CA: Sage.

Bohen, H., & Viveros-Long, A. M. (1981). *Balancing jobs and family life: Do flexible working schedules help?* Philadelphia: Temple University Press.

Boles, J. S., Howard, W. G., & Donofrio, H. H. (2001). An investigation into the inter-relationships of work-family conflict, family-work conflict and work satisfaction. *Journal of Managerial Issues, 13*, 376–390.

Boyar, S. L., Maertz, C. P., Jr., Pearson, A. W., & Keough, S. (2003). Work-family conflict: A model of linkages between work and family domain variables and turnover intentions. *Journal of Managerial Issues, 15*, 175–191.

Bumpus, M. F., Crouter, A. C., & McHale, S. M. (2001). Parental autonomy granting adolescence: Exploring gender differences in context. *Developmental Psychology, 37*, 163–173.

Burke, R. J. (1989). Some antecedents and consequences of work-family conflict. In E. B. Goldsmith (Ed.), *Work and family: Theory, research, and applications* (pp. 287–302). Newbury Park, CA: Sage.

Buzzanell, P. M. (2000). The promise and practice of the new career and social contract: Illusions exposed and suggestions for reform. In P. M. Buzzanell (Ed.), *Rethinking organizational and managerial communication from feminist perspectives* (pp. 209–235). Thousand Oaks, CA: Sage.

Caligiuri, P. M., Hyland, M. M., Joshi, A., & Bross, A. S. (1998). Testing a theoretical model for examining the relationship between family adjustment and expatriates' work adjustment. *Journal of Applied Psychology, 83*, 598–614.

Carlson, D. S., Derr, C. B., & Wadsworth, L. L. (2003). The effects of internal career orientation on multiple dimensions of work-family conflict. *Journal of Family and Economic Issues, 24*, 99–116.

Carlson, D. S., & Perrewe, P. L. (1999). The role of social support in the stressor-strain relationship: An examination of work-family conflict. *Journal of Management, 25*, 513–540.

Casper, W. J., & Martin, J. A. (2002). Work-family conflict, perceived organizational support, and organizational commitment among employed mothers. *Journal of Occupational Health Psychology, 7*, 99–108.

Christensen, K. E., & Staines, G. L. (1990). Flextime: A viable solution to work/family conflict? *Journal of Family Issues, 11*, 455–476.

Chuang, H. L., & Lee, H. Y. (2003). The return on women's human capital and the role of male attitudes toward working wives: Gender roles, work interruption, and women's earnings in Taiwan. *American Journal of Economics & Sociology, 62*, 435–460.

Cinamon, R. G., & Rich, Y. (2002). Profiles of attribution of importance to life roles and their implications for the work-family conflict. *Journal of Counseling Psychology, 49*, 212–220.

Ciulla, J. B. (2000). *The working life: The promise and betrayal of modern work*. New York: Three Rivers Press.

Clark, S. C. (2002). Communicating across the work/home border. *Community, Work, & Family, 5*, 23–48.

Cramer, K., & Pearce, J. (1990). Work and family policies become productivity tools. *Management Review, 79*(11), 42–44.

Crouter, A. C. (1984). Spillover from family to work: The neglected side of the work-family interface. *Human Relations, 37*, 425–442.

Crouter, A. C., Bumpus, M. F., Head, M. R., & McHale, S. M. (2001). Implications of overwork and overload for the quality of men's family relationships. *Journal of Marriage and Family, 62*, 404–416.

Crouter, A. C., Perry-Jenkins, M., Huston, T. L., & Crawford, D. W. (1989). The influence of work-induced psychological states on behavior at home. *Basic and Applied Social Psychology, 10*, 273–292.

Cutcher-Gershenfeld, J., Kossek, E. E., & Sandling, H. (1997). Managing concurrent change initiatives: Integrating total quality and work/family strategies. *Organizational Dynamics, 25*, 21–37.

Deetz, S. A. (1992). *Democracy in an age of corporate colonization*. Albany: State University of New York Press.

Demerouti, E., & Bakker, A. B., & Bulters, A. (2004). The loss spiral of work pressure, work-home interference and exhaustion: Reciprocal relations in a three-wave study. *Journal of Vocational Behavior, 64*, 131–149.

Den Dulk, L. (2001). Work-family arrangements in organizations: An international comparison. In T. Van Der Lippe & L. S. Van Dijk (Eds.),

Women's employment in a comparative perspective (pp. 59–84). New York: Aldine de Gruyter.

Duxbury, L. E., & Higgins, C. A. (1991). Gender differences in work-family conflict. *Journal of Applied Psychology, 76*, 60–74.

Eckman, E. W. (2002). Woman high school principals: Perspectives on role conflict, role commitment, and job satisfaction. *Journal of School Leadership, 12*, 57–77.

Edwards, J. R., & Rothbard, N. P. (2000). Mechanisms linking work and family: Clarifying the relationship between work and family constructs. *Academy of Management Review, 25*, 178–199.

Ehrensaft, D. (2001). The Kinderdult: The new child born to conflict between work and family. In R. Hertz & N. L. Marshall (Eds.), *Working families: The transformation of the American home* (pp. 304–322). Berkeley: University of California Press.

Elman, M. R., & Gilbert, L. A. (1984). Coping strategies for role conflict in married professional women with children. *Family Relations, 33*, 317–327.

Friedman, D. E. (1987). *Family supportive policies: The corporate decision making process.* New York: The Conference Board.

Friedman, D. E., & Greenhaus, J. H. (2000). *Work and family—Allies or enemies? What happens when business professionals confront life choices?* New York: Oxford University Press.

Friedman, D. E., & Johnson, A. A. (1991). *Strategies for promoting a work-family agenda.* New York: The Conference Board.

Friedman, S., & Lobel, S. (2003). The happy workaholic: A role model for employees. *Academy of Management Executive, 17*, 87–98.

Frone, M. R., Russell, M., & Cooper, M. L. (1992a). Antecedents and outcomes of work-family conflict: Testing a model of the work-family interface. *Journal of Applied Psychology, 77*, 65–78.

Frone, M. R., Russell, M., & Cooper, M. L. (1992b). Prevalence of work-family conflict: Are work and family boundaries asymmetrically permeable? *Journal of Organizational Behaviour, 13*, 723–729.

Frone, M. R., Yardley, J. U., & Markel, K. S. (1997). Developing and testing an integrative model of the work-family interface. *Journal of Vocational Behavior, 50*, 145–167.

Fu, C. K., & Shaffer, M. A. (2001). The tug of work and family: Direct and indirect domain-specific determinants of work-family conflict. *Personnel Review, 30*, 502–522.

Galinsky, E. (1999). *Ask the children: What America's children really think about working parents.* New York: Morrow.

Galinsky, E., Bond, J. T., & Friedman, D. E. (1993). *The changing workforce: Highlights of the national study.* New York: Families and Work Institute.

Galinsky, E., & Stein, P. J. (1990). The impact of human resource policies on employees: Balancing work-family life. *Journal of Family Issues, 11*, 368–383.

Gerstel, N., & Gross, H. E. (Eds.). (1987). *Families and work.* Philadelphia: Temple University Press.

Geurts, S. A., Kompier, M. A., Roxburgh, S., & Houtman, I. L. D. (2003). Does work-home interference mediate the relationship between workload and well-being? *Journal of Vocational Behavior, 63*, 532–559.

Geurts, S., Rutte, C., & Peeters, M. (1999). Antecedents and consequences of work-home interference among medical students. *Social Scientific Medicine, 48*, 1135–1148.

Giddens, A. (1979). *Central problems in social theory.* Berkeley: University of California Press.

Giddens, A. (1984). *The constitution of society: Outline of the theory of structuration.* Cambridge, MA: Polity Press.

Goff, S. J., Mount, M. K., & Jamison, R. L. (1990). Employer supported childcare, work/family conflict, and absenteeism: A field study. *Personnel Psychology, 43*, 793–809.

Golden, A. G. (2000). What we talk about when we talk about work and family: A discourse analysis of parental accounts. *The Electronic Journal of Communication, 10*(3). Retrieved June 15, 2000, from http://www.cios.org/www/ejc/v10n3400 .htm

Golden, A. G. (2001). Modernity and the communicative management of multiple role-identities: The case of the worker-parent. *The Journal of Family Communication, 1*, 233–264.

Golden, A. G. (2002). Speaking of work and family: Spousal collaboration on defining role-identities and developing shared meanings. *Southern Communication Journal, 67*, 122–141.

Gonyea, J. G., & Googins, B. K. (1992). Linking the worlds of work and family: Beyond the productivity trap. *Human Resource Management, 31*, 209–226.

Good, L. K., Page T. J., Jr., & Young, C. E. (1996). Assessing hierarchical differences in job-related attitudes and turnover among retail managers. *Journal of the Academy of Marketing Science, 24*, 148–156.

Goodstein, J. D. (1994). Institutional pressures and strategic responsiveness: Employer involvement in work-family issues. *Academy of Management Journal, 37*, 350–382.

Googins, B. K. (1997). Shared responsibility for managing work and family relationships: A community perspective. In S. Parasuraman & J. H. Greenhaus (Eds.), *Integrating work and family: Challenges and choices for a changing world* (pp. 220–231). Westport, CT: Quorum Books.

Gornick, J. C., Meyers, M. K., & Ross, K. E. (1997). Supporting the employment of mothers: Policy variation across fourteen welfare states. *Journal of European Social Policy, 7*, 45–70.

Grant-Vallone, E. J., & Donaldson, S. I. (2001). Consequences of work-family conflict on employee well-being over time. *Work & Stress, 15*, 214–226.

Greenberger, E., & O'Neil, R. (1993). Spouse, parent, worker: Role commitments and role-related experiences in the construction of well-being. *Developmental Psychology, 29*, 181–197.

Greenglass, E. R., Pantony, K. L., & Burke, R. J. (1989). A gender-role perspective on role conflict. In E. B. Goldsmith (Ed.), *Work and family: Theory, research, and applications* (pp. 159–174). Newbury Park, CA: Sage.

Greenhaus, J. H., & Beutell, N. J. (1985). Sources of conflict between work and family roles. *Academy of Management Review, 10*, 76–88.

Greenhaus, J. H., Collins, K., Singh, R., & Parasuraman, S. (1997). Work and family influence on departure from public accounting. *Journal of Vocational Behavior, 50*, 249–270.

Greenhaus, J. H., & Kopelman, S. (1981). Conflict between work and non-work roles: Implications for the career planning process. *Human Resources Planning, 4*, 1–10.

Greenhaus, J. H., & Parasuraman, S. (1986). A work-nonwork interactive perspective of stress and its consequences. *Journal of Organizational Behavior Management, 8*, 37–60.

Greenhaus, J. H., & Parasuraman, S. (1999). Research on work, family, and gender: Current status and future directions. In G. N. Powell (Ed.), *Handbook of gender and work* (pp. 391–412). Newbury Park, CA: Sage.

Greenhaus, J. H., Parasuraman, S., & Collins, K. M. (2001). Career involvement and family involvement as moderators of relationships between work-family conflict and withdrawal from a profession. *Journal of Occupational Health Psychology, 6*, 91–100.

Gross, H. E. (2001). Work, family, and globalization: Broadening the scope of policy analysis. In R. Hertz & N. L. Marshall (Eds.), *Working families: The transformation of the American home* (pp. 187–203). Berkeley: University of California Press.

Grover, S. L., & Crooker, K. J. (1995). Who appreciates family-responsive human resource policies: The impact of family-friendly policies on the organizational attachment of parents and non-parents. *Personnel Psychology, 48*, 271–288.

Grzywacz, J. G., & Bass, B. L. (2003). Work, family, and mental health: Testing different models of work-family fit. *Journal of Marriage and Family, 65*, 248–262.

Gutek, B. A., Searle, S., & Klepa, L. (1991). Rational versus gender role explanations for work-family conflict. *Journal of Applied Psychology, 76*, 560–568.

Haas, L., & Hwang, P. (1995). Company culture and men's usage of family leave benefits in Sweden. *Family Relations, 44*, 28–36.

Haas, L., & Hwang, P. (2000). Programs and policies promoting women's economic equality and men's sharing of child care in Sweden. In L. Haas, P. Hwang, & G. Russell (Eds.), *Organizational change and gender equity: International perspectives on fathers and mothers at the workplace* (pp. 133–162). Thousand Oaks, CA: Sage.

Harvey, S., Kelloway, E. K., & Duncan-Leiper, L. (2003). Trust in management as a buffer of the relationships between overload and strain. *Journal of Occupational Health Psychology, 8*, 306–315.

Hecht, L. M. (2001). Role conflict and role overload: Different concepts, different consequences. *Sociological Inquiry, 71*, 111–121.

Higgins, C., Duxbury, L., & Lee, C. (1994). Impact of life-cycle stage and gender on the ability to balance work and family responsibilities. *Family Relations, 43*, 144–150.

Hill, E. J., Martinson, V. K., Ferris, M., & Baker, R. Z. (2004). Beyond the mommy track: The influence of new-concept part-time work for professional women on work and family. *Journal of Family and Economic Issues, 25*, 121–136.

Hill, E. J., Miller, B. C., Weiner, S. P., & Colihan, J. (1998). Influences of the virtual office on aspects of work and work/life. *Personnel Psychology, 51,* 667–683.

Hochschild, A. (1997). *The time bind: When work becomes home and home becomes work.* New York: Metropolitan Books.

Hochschild, A. R., & Machung, A. (1990). *The second shift.* New York: Avon Books.

Holmer Nadesan, M. (2001). Post-Fordism, political economy, and critical organization communication studies. *Management Communication Quarterly, 15,* 259–267.

Hylmö, A., & Buzzanell, P. M. (2003). Telecommuting as viewed through cultural lenses: An empirical investigation of the discourses of utopia, identity, and mystery. *Communication Monographs, 69,* 329–356.

Jansen, N. W. H., Kant, I., Kristensen, T. S., & Nijhuis, T. S. (2003). Antecedents and consequences of work-family conflict: A prospective cohort study. *Journal of Occupational and Environmental Medicine, 45,* 479–491.

Janzen, B. L., & Muhajarine, N. (2003). Social role occupancy, gender, income adequacy, and health: A longitudinal study of employed Canadian men and women. *Social Science & Medicine, 57,* 1492–1503.

Jorgenson, J. (2000). Interpreting the intersections of work and family: Frame conflicts in women's work. *The Electronic Journal of Communication/La Revue Electronique de Communication, 10.* Retrieved June 15, 2000, from http://www.cios.org/www/ejc/v10n3400.htm

Kanter, R. M. (1977). *Work and family in the U. S.: A critical review and agenda for research and policy.* Newbury Park, CA: Sage.

Kelloway, E. K., Gottlieb, B. H., & Barham, L. (1999). The source, nature, and direction of work and family conflict: A longitudinal investigation. *Journal of Occupational Health Psychology, 4,* 337–346.

Kemske, F. (1998). *HR 2008. Workforce, 77*(1), 46–54.

Kim, J. L. S., & Ling, C. S. (2001). Work-family conflict of women entrepreneurs in Singapore. *Women in Management Review, 16,* 204–221.

Kinnier, R. T., Katz, E. C., & Berry, M. A. (1991). Successful resolutions to the career-versus-family conflict. *Journal of Counseling & Development, 69,* 439–444.

Kinnunen, U., & Mauno, S. (1998). Antecedents and outcomes of work-family conflict among employed women and men in Finland. *Human Relations, 51,* 157–178.

Kinnunen, U., Vermulst, A., Gerris, J., & Makikangas, A. (2003). Work-family conflict and its relation to well-being: The role of personality as a moderating factor. *Personality & Individual Differences, 35,* 1669–1693.

Kirby, E. L. (2000a). *Communicating organizational tension: Balancing work and family.* Unpublished doctoral dissertation, University of Nebraska–Lincoln.

Kirby, E. L. (2000b). Should I do as you say, or do as you do? Mixed messages about work and family. *The Electronic Journal of Communication/La Revue Electronique de Communication, 10*(3). Retrieved June 15, 2000, from http://www.cios.org/www/ejc/v10n3400.htm

Kirby, E. L. (2002, March). *"Gendering" careers: Discourses about work versus family at Regulators.* Paper presented at the annual meeting of the Western States Communication Association, Long Beach, CA.

Kirby, E. L., Golden, A. G., Medved, C. E., Jorgenson, J., & Buzzanell, P. M. (2003). An organizational communication challenge to the discourse of work and family research: From problematics to empowerment. In P. Kalbfleisch (Ed.), *Communication Yearbook, 27* (pp. 1–43). Mahwah, NJ: Lawrence Erlbaum.

Kirby, E. L., & Krone, K. J. (2002). "The policy exists but you can't really use it": Communication and the structuration of work-family policies. *Journal of Applied Communication Research, 30,* 50–77.

Kirby, E. L., & Krone, K. J. (2003). *For the community.* Suggestions for practitioners based on E. L. Kirby & K. J. Krone (2002) approved by the National Communication Association Legislative Council to pilot an online journal.

Kirby, E. L., Pawlowski, D. R., & Dressel, C. (2000, April). *To promote or not to promote? Work-family programs as corporate discourse.* Paper presented at the annual meeting of the Organizational and Professional Division of the Central States Communication Association, Detroit, MI.

Konrad, A. M., & Mangel, R. (2000). The impact of work-life programs on firm productivity. *Strategic Management Journal, 21,* 1225–1237.

Korabik, K., Lero, D. S., & Ayman, R. (2003). A multilevel approach to cross-cultural work-family research: A micro and macro perspective. *International Journal of Cross Cultural Management, 3*, 289–303.

Kossek, E. E., Colquitt, J. A., & Noe, R. A. (2001). Caregiving decisions, well-being, and performance: The effects of place and provider as a function of dependent type and work-family climates. *Academy of Management Journal, 44*, 29–44.

Kossek, E. E., & Ozeki, C. (1998). Work-family conflict, policies, and the job-life satisfaction relationship: A review and directions for organizational behavior-human resources research. *Journal of Applied Psychology, 83*, 139–149.

Krasas Rogers, J. (1995). Just a temp: Experience and structure of alienation in temporary clerical employment. *Work and Occupations, 22*, 137–166.

Krone, K. J., Schrodt, P., & Kirby, E. L. (2006). Structuration theory: Promising directions for family communication research. In D. O. Braithwaite & L. Baxter (Eds.), *Family communication theories* (pp. 293–308). Thousand Oaks, CA: Sage.

Kulik, L. (2003). Morning passages from home to work among mangers in Israel: Intergender differences. *Sex Roles, 48*, 205–215.

Lahelma, E., Arber, S., Kivela, K., & Roos, E. (2002). Multiple roles and health among British and Finnish women: The influence of socioeconomic circumstances. *Social Science & Medicine, 54*, 727–740.

Lambert, S. J. (2000). Added benefits: The link between work-life benefits and organizational citizenship behavior. *Academy of Management Journal, 43*, 801–815.

Lan, P. C. (2003). Maid or madam? Filipina migrant workers and the continuity of domestic labor. *Gender & Society, 17*, 187–208.

La Rocco, J. M., House, J. S., & French, J. R. P. (1980). Social support, occupational stress, and health. *Journal of Health and Social Behavior, 21*, 202–218.

Ling, Y., & Powell, G. N. (2001). Work-family conflict in contemporary China: Beyond an American-based model. *International Journal of Cross-Cultural Management, 1*, 357–373.

Lo, S. (2003). Perceptions of work-family conflict among married female professionals in Hong Kong. *Personnel Review, 32*, 376–390.

Lobel, S. A. (1999). Impacts of diversity and work-life initiatives in organizations. In G. N. Powell (Ed.), *Handbook of gender and work* (pp. 453–474). Thousand Oaks, CA: Sage.

Loscocco, K. A., & Roschelle, A. R. (1991). Influences on the quality of work and nonwork life: Two decades in review. *Journal of Vocational Behavior, 39*, 182–225.

MacDermid, S. M., Williams, M., & Marks, S. (1994). Is small beautiful? Work family tension, work conditions, and organizational size. *Family Relations, 43*, 159–167.

Madsen, S. R. (2003). The effects of home-based teleworking on work-family conflict. *Human Resource Development Quarterly, 14*, 35–58.

Magid, R. Y., & Fleming, N. E. (1987). *When mothers and fathers work: Creative strategies for balancing career and family.* New York: American Management Association.

Major, V. S., Klein, K. S., & Ehrhart, M. G. (2002). Work time, work interference, and family and psychological distress. *Journal of Applied Psychology, 87,* 427–436.

Mallia, K. L., & Ferris, S. P. (2000). Telework: A consideration of its impact on individuals and organizations. *The Electronic Journal of Communication/La Revue Electronique de Communication, 10*(3). Retrieved June 15, 2000, from http://www.cios.org/www/ejc/v10n3400 .htm

Maume, D. J., & Houston, P. (2001). Job segregation and gender differences in work-family spillover among white-collar workers. *Journal of Family and Economic Issues, 22*, 171–189.

McNamee, S., & Gergen, K. J. (1999). *Relational responsibility: Resources for sustainable dialogue.* Thousand Oaks, CA: Sage.

Medved, C. E. (2004). The everyday accomplishment of work and family: Exploring practical actions in daily routines. *Communication Studies, 55*, 128–145.

Medved, C. E., & Kirby, E. L. (2005). Family CEOs: A feminist analysis of corporate mothering discourses. *Management Communication Quarterly, 18*, 435–478.

Moen, P., Kim, J. E., & Hofmeister, H. (2001). Couples' work/retirement transitions, gender, and marital quality. *Social Psychology Quarterly, 64*, 55–71.

Moon, S. (2003). Immigration and mothering: Case studies from two generations of Korean immigrant women. *Gender & Society, 17*, 840–860.

Morgan, H., & Milliken, F. J. (1992). Keys to action: Understanding differences in organizations' responsiveness to work-and-family issues. *Human Resource Management, 31*, 227–248.

Mortimer, J. T., & London, J. (1984). The varying linkages of work and family. In P. Voydanoff (Ed.), *Work and family: Changing roles of men and women* (pp. 20–35). Palo Alto, CA: Mayfield.

Nasman, E. (1999). Sweden and the reconciliation of work and family life. In L. den Dulk, A. van Doorne-Huiskes, & J. Schippers (Eds.), *Work-family arrangements in Europe* (pp. 131–149). Amsterdam: Thela Thesis.

Natdoo, A. V., & Jano, R. (2003). Role conflict of South African women in dual-career families. *Psychological Reports, 93,* 693–697.

Near, J. P., Rice, R. W., & Hunt, R. G. (1980). The relationship between work and nonwork domains: A review of empirical research. *Academy of Management Review, 5,* 415–429.

Netemeyer, R. G., Boles, J. S., & McMurrian, R. (1996). Development and validation of work-family conflict and family-work conflict scales. *Journal of Applied Psychology, 81,* 400–410.

Nippert-Eng, C. E. (1996). *Home and work: Negotiating boundaries through everyday life.* Chicago: University of Chicago Press.

O'Driscoll, M. P., Poelmans, S., Spector, P. E., Kalliah, T., Allen, T. D., Cooper, C. L., et al. (2003). Family responsive interventions, perceived organizational and supervisor support, work-family conflict, and psychological strain. *International Journal of Stress Management, 10,* 326–317.

Orrange, R. (2002). Aspiring law and business professionals' orientations to work and family life. *Journal of Family Issues, 23,* 287–317.

Parasuraman, S., & Simmers, C. A. (2001). Type of employment, work-family conflict and well being: A comparative study. *Journal of Organizational Behavior, 22,* 552–568.

Perlow, L. A. (1995). Putting the work back into work/family. *Group & Organization Management, 20,* 227–239.

Perlow, L. A. (1997). *Finding time: How corporations, individuals and families can benefit from new work practices.* Ithaca, NY: ILR Press.

Perrewe, P. L., & Hochwarter, W. A. (1999). Value attainment: An explanation for the negative effects of work-family conflict on job and life satisfaction. *Journal of Occupational Health Psychology, 4,* 318–326.

Perry-Smith, J. E., & Blum, T. C. (2000). Work-family human resource bundles and perceived organizational preference. *Academy of Management Journal, 43,* 1107–1117.

Persson, I. (Ed.). (1990). *Generating equality in the welfare state: The Swedish experience.* Oslo: Norwegian University Press.

Pleck, J. H. (1993). Are family-supportive employer policies relevant to men? In J. C. Hood (Ed.), *Men, work, and family* (pp. 217–237). Newbury Park: Sage.

Pleck, J. H., Staines, G. L., & Lang, L. (1980). Conflicts between work and family life. *Monthly Labor Review, 103,* 29–32.

Poole, M. S., Seibold, D. R., & McPhee, R. D. (1996). The structuration of group decisions. In R. Y. Hirokawa & M. S. Poole (Eds.), *Communication and group decision-making* (2nd ed., pp. 114–146). Newbury Park, CA: Sage.

Raabe, P., & Gessner, J. (1988). Employer family-supportive policies: Diverse variations on a theme. *Family Relations, 37,* 196–202.

Rapoport, R., & Bailyn, L. (1996). *Relinking life and work: Toward a better future.* New York: Ford Foundation.

Rau, B. L., & Hyland, M. A. M. (2002). Role conflict and flexible work arrangements: The effects on applicant attraction. *Personnel Psychology, 55,* 111–136.

Ray, E. B., & Miller, K. I. (1994). Social support, home/work stress, and burnout: Who can help? *The Journal of Applied Behavioral Science, 30,* 357–373.

Rodgers, C. S. (1992). The flexible workplace: What have we learned? *Human Resource Management, 31,* 83–199.

Roehling, P. V., Roehling, M. V., & Moen, P. (2001). The relationship between work-life policies and practices and employee loyalty: A life course perspective. *Journal of Family and Economic Issues, 22,* 141–170.

Romito, P., Saurel-Cuizolles, M. J., & Escriba-Aguir, V. (2002). Maternity rights, work, and health in France and Italy. *Journal of the American Medical Women's Association, 57,* 47–56.

Rothbard, N. P., & Edwards, J. R. (2003). Investment in work and family roles: A test of identity and utilitarian motives. *Personnel Psychology, 56,* 699–730.

Rotondo, D. M., Carlson, D. S., & Kincaid, J. F. (2003). Coping with multiple dimensions of work-family conflict. *Personnel Review, 32,* 275–296.

Shaffer, M. A., Harrison, D. A., Gilley, K. M., & Luk, D. M. (2001). Struggling for balance amid turbulence on international assignments: Work-family, support, and commitment. *Journal of Management, 27,* 99–121.

Sloan Foundation. (n.d.). Work-family researchers' electronic network. Retrieved April 1, 2004, from http://www.bc.edu/bc_org/avp/wfnetwork/

Smith, V. (2001). *Crossing the great divide: Worker risk and opportunity in the new economy.* Ithaca, NY: Cornell University Press.

Spector, P. E., Cooper, C. L., Poelmans, S., Allen, T. D., O'Driscoll, M., & Sanchez, J. I. (2004). A cross-national comparative study of work-family stressors, working hours, and well-being: China and Latin America versus the Anglo world. *Personnel Psychology, 57,* 119–142.

Stoeva, A. Z., Chiu, R. K., & Greenhaus, J. H. (2002). Negativity affectivity, role stress, and work-family conflict. *Journal of Vocational Behavior, 60,* 1–16.

Stohl, C. (1995). *Organizational communication: Connectedness in action.* Thousand Oaks, CA: Sage.

Sullivan, C., & Lewis, S. (2001). Home-based telework, gender, and the synchronization of work and family: Perspectives of teleworkers and their co-residents. *Gender, Work and Organization, 8,* 123–145.

Sundstrom, M., & Duvander, A. E. (2002). Gender division of childcare and the sharing of leave among new parents in Sweden. *European Sociological Review, 18,* 433–447.

Swiss, D. J. (1998). Good worker or good parent: The conflict between policy and practice. In M. G. Mackavey & R. L. Levin (Eds.), *Shared purpose: Working together to build strong families and high-performance companies* (pp. 87–104). New York: AMACOM.

Tausig, M., & Fenwick, R. (2001). Unbinding time: Alternative work schedules and work-life balance. *Journal of Family and Economic Issues, 22,* 101–119.

Thoits, P. A. (1982). Identity structures and psychological well-being: Gender and marital status comparisons. *Social Psychology Quarterly, 55,* 236–256.

Thomas, L. T., & Ganster, D. C. (1995). Impact of family-supportive work variables on work-family conflict and strain: A control perspective. *Journal of Applied Psychology, 80,* 6–15.

Thompson, C. A., Beauvais, L. L., & Lyness, K. S. (1999). When work-family benefits are not enough: The influence of work-family culture on benefit utilization, organizational attachment, and work-family conflict. *Journal of Vocational Behavior, 54,* 392–415.

Voydanoff, P. (1988). Work role characteristics, family structure demands and work/family conflict. *Journal of Marriage and the Family, 50,* 749–761.

Voydanoff, P. (2004). The effects of work and community resources and demands on family integration. *Journal of Family and Economic Issues, 25,* 7–23.

Walters, V., Avotri, J. Y., & Charles, N. (2003). "Your heart is never free": Women in Wales and Ghana talking about distress. In J. M. Stoppard & L. M. McMullen (Eds.), *Situating sadness: Women and depression in social context* (pp. 183–206). New York: New York University Press.

Warren, J. A., & Johnson, P. J. (1995). The impact of workplace support on work-family role strain. *Family Relations, 44,* 163–169.

Wayne, J. H., Musisca, N., & Fleeson, W. (2004). Considering the role of personality in the work-family experience: Relationships of the big five to work-family conflict and facilitation. *Journal of Vocational Behavior, 64,* 108–130.

Williams, K. J., & Alliger, G. M. (1994). Role stressors, mood spillover, and perceptions of work-family conflict in employed parents. *Academy of Management Journal, 37,* 837–868.

Willis, T. A. (1985). Supportive functions of interpersonal relationships. In S. Cohen & S. L. Syme (Eds.), *Social support and health* (pp. 61–82). New York: Academic Press.

Zedeck, S., & Mosier, K. L. (1990). Work in the family and employing organization. *American Psychologist, 45,* 240–251.

13

Managing Organizational Conflicts

David B. Lipsky

Cornell University

Ronald L. Seeber

Cornell University

The Prudential Insurance Company of America ranks as the number one provider of life insurance in the United States. Over the years, Prudential developed not only a complete line of insurance products but also began to offer a diversity of financial services, such as asset management and investment banking. Its annual sales of nearly $30 billion place it squarely in the middle of the *Fortune* 100. In the 1990s, however, Prudential's reputation was seriously damaged by scandals involving improper sales practices by its insurance agents. In 1998, the company recorded a pretax charge of more than $1.6 billion to cover restitution payments resulting from a series of lawsuits (Scism, 1998, p. 3). This charge reduced Prudential's profits in the previous year by 43%. In all, the lawsuits cost Prudential well over $2 billion in the 1990s (Lohse, 1998, p. 4).

The company, which uses the Rock of Gibraltar as its logo, always took considerable pride in its reputation for integrity and high ethical standards. Top management, understandably alarmed by the effect of the scandals on the company's good name and success, took several steps to address the crisis. For example, the company put renewed emphasis on compliance with its code of ethics, establishing an independent ethics office to help ensure that all Prudential employees understood their obligation to adhere to the high standards of behavior required by the code. In addition, top managers came to realize that promoting ethical behavior by Prudential's employees required the establishment of a comprehensive and fair dispute resolution system. The company hired Ernst & Young to conduct a yearlong benchmarking study of workplace dispute resolution systems used by major U.S. corporations and organizations. The study identified "best practices" in workplace conflict management and recommended that Prudential adopt a system that combined these best practices. In 1999, after careful consideration of the Ernst & Young study, Prudential established the "Roads to Resolution"® program and hired a new vice president to manage both the ethics office and the new comprehensive conflict management system (Lipsky, Seeber, & Fincher, 2003).

The Prudential story was one of more than 50 we examined in conducting research (with Richard D. Fincher) on conflict management systems (Lipsky et al., 2003). Since publishing the book, we have stayed in contact with the Prudential vice president and members of his staff, and all indications suggest that the Roads to Resolution program has been a great success. But Prudential is far from the only company to adopt a sophisticated conflict management system in recent years. General Electric, Nestlé U.S.A., Johnson & Johnson, Alcoa, Chevron, Raytheon, and many other U.S. corporations have also adopted, in one form or another, workplace conflict management systems (Lipsky et al., 2003). In the federal sector, Congress passed the Administrative Dispute Resolution Act (ADRA) in 1990, authorizing and encouraging federal agencies to use alternative dispute resolution (ADR; Dunlop & Zack, 1997).[1] By 1996, the Government Accounting Office (GAO) estimated that about half of the federal agencies were using some form of ADR to resolve employee complaints (U.S. General Accounting Office, 1997). By the turn of the new century several executive-level agencies had designed and implemented conflict management systems, including the Equal Employment Opportunity Commission, the Department of the Interior, the Air Force, and several others (Senger, 2003).[2] Some of these systems are designed to deal not only with complaints by the agency's employees but also with complaints by users of its services. Increasingly, state and local governments as well as nonprofit organizations are also designing and implementing systems for managing organizational conflicts. For example, the U.S. Postal Service is well known for its REDRESS program (Bingham, 2001; Bingham et al., 2001), and we were personally involved in the development of a workplace dispute resolution system for the employees of the New York State courts, assisting court administrators and representatives from 14 unions in designing and implementing a workplace system that covers 17,000 employees.[3]

There is abundant evidence that managing organizational conflicts is receiving increasing attention by top managers, attorneys, policy makers, and consultants. Major corporations, public sector agencies, and nonprofit organizations are

more inclined now than ever before to adopt a proactive, strategic approach to managing organizational conflicts. This trend is particularly pronounced in large organizations, but there is evidence that the trend is now reaching even smaller companies (American Arbitration Association, 2003). Many of the practices, if not the strategies, adopted by large U.S. corporations have been diffusing to smaller companies and other types of organizations. In a bygone era, most managers assumed that conflict was not a phenomenon that could be easily managed. Almost all organizations took a reactive or passive approach to conflict. They would wait for conflicts to arise before taking action. But the growing costs of disputes as well as dissatisfaction with the traditional means of managing and resolving conflict have motivated many organizations to embark on a new approach to conflict management.

This chapter provides a review of the literature on the management of organizational conflicts (for earlier reviews of the literature, see Brett, 1984; Brown, 1983; Derr, 1978; Pneuman & Bruehl, 1982). A substantial part of the research on this topic is descriptive and is based on the knowledge and experience of researchers and practitioners working in the field; some of the descriptive research is based on case studies. Another part of the literature is prescriptive: Practitioners and professionals, usually on the basis of their own experiences, have attempted to provide guidance on "best practice" in conflict management. Embedded in both the descriptive and prescriptive literatures are implicit theories about the management of organizational conflict. In this chapter, we attempt to coax out of the literature several theories that seem to underlie much of the writing on the topic. Because the law has played such an important role in the development of practice in this field, a significant portion of the research has consisted of doctrinal analysis by legal scholars. Although we assess some of the legal research on employment dispute resolution, our principal focus is on the literature that deals with how and why organizations have adopted alternative approaches to the management of conflict. Lastly, there is a growing body of data-based empirical research on various aspects of dispute resolution in organizations, and we provide an assessment of this research.

CONCEPTUAL FRAMEWORK

The conceptual framework that guided the design and development of this chapter is drawn from several theories of management and organizational behavior. First, we apply the concept of *transformation,* which has provided the underpinning for a considerable amount of research on the management of organizations in recent years (see, e.g., Kochan, Katz, & McKersie, 1986). Specifically, we discuss the transformation that has occurred in U.S. organizations over the past decade or so in their methods of managing workplace conflicts. By workplace conflict, we mean conflicts that can arise in relationships between supervisors and employees, managers and employees, employees and employees, and within work teams, including managerial or supervisory teams. In other words, we focus on *intraorganizational,* and not *interorganizational,* conflicts. We are not concerned here, for example, with business-to-business, business-to-government, or government-to-government conflicts. Also, we do not deal with conflicts that may arise between an organization and external stakeholders or constituents, such as customers, clients, suppliers, and vendors. We do indeed approach the topic from an *organizational* perspective, focusing on both the nature of the new strategies and systems being adopted by many organizations and on conflict management at the *individual* level. We particularly are concerned with how and why decision makers have moved from reactive or passive processes for handling disputes to proactive or anticipative strategies for managing conflict.

Second, we draw on theories of decision making in organizations, particularly by top managers. We have been especially influenced by conventional theories of *rational decision making* that dominate much of the thinking in economics, game theory, and other social sciences. In these models, managers of organizations are capable of weighing the expected costs and benefits of alternative courses of action and choosing a course of action that efficiently and effectively achieves the organization's objectives (see, e.g., Dixit & Nalebuff,

1991; Eisenhardt & Zbaracki, 1992). One important form of the conventional model of decision making is contained in the literature on *risk management.* In risk management models managers must take account of uncertainty in making their decisions, and managers' decisions are affected by their risk preferences (see, e.g., Doherty, 2000; Marrison, 2002). We maintain that risk management is an especially useful tool in understanding the management of organizational conflict. Of course, we understand the limitations on rational models of decision making, but we will not have the opportunity in this chapter to discuss the psychological, emotional, and cognitive limitations on rational decision making (see Hastie & Dawes, 2001, and Kahneman, Slovic, & Tversky, 1982, for more on rational decision making).

Third, we distinguish alternative conceptions of management *strategy* and *strategic thinking.* In the past decade there has been an intense debate in the management literature over the meaning and relevance of strategic thinking in an age of globalization, rapid technological change, and other forces of transformation (see, e.g., Hammonds, 2001; Porter, 1980, 1985, 2002). In our own research, we discovered that most organizations do not consciously adopt strategies for managing conflict, but an increasing number are doing so (Lipsky et al., 2003). There remains an open question as to whether an organization should adopt relatively long-term conflict management strategies or, instead, nurture a more flexible and agile approach that stresses the development of organizational capabilities and capacities for dealing with conflict.

Fourth, we discuss the utility of a *systems* approach to conflict management. We maintain that the term *system* is often used indiscriminately in conflict resolution as it is in other contexts. Both scholars and practitioners frequently use the term *system* when they actually mean "policy," "procedure," or "practice." It is probably too late in the day to eliminate the imprecision that affects common parlance, but we will try to distinguish a genuine *conflict management system* from conflict resolution policies, procedures, and practices. The concept of a system, as initially developed by Bertalanffy (1951), Boulding (1956), and others, requires elements such as inputs, outputs, and feedback loops. There are organizations that have adopted conflict management systems that include such elements, but most have not. Understanding the difference between the establishment and operation of an authentic *integrated conflict management system* and a policy of routinely using mediation (or any other dispute resolution technique) to resolve workplace disputes is, we maintain, critical to understanding the contemporary management of organizational conflicts (Gosline et al., 2001; Lipsky et al., 2003).

Distinguishing the Management of Disputes From the Management of Conflict

Organizational conflicts manifest themselves in three forms: (a) latent (unexpressed) or manifest (expressed) *disagreements* among and between members of the organization; (b) *disputes*, including formal grievances and complaints; and (c) *litigation,* including not only lawsuits but charges filed with regulatory agencies. We discovered in our research on large U.S. corporations that a typical organization waits for conflicts to evolve into disputes and then for disputes to evolve into litigation, and only then begins to manage "conflict." We also observed that an organization's approach to managing these three types of conflict differs with respect to who is primarily responsible for handling the conflict, what techniques are used to prevent or resolve the conflict, the extent to which third parties are involved in the conflict, and other dimensions (Lipsky et al., 2003). Understanding how organizations manage these three types of conflicts requires elaboration.

Managing Workplace Conflict: Latent and Manifest Disagreements

Differences in goals, objectives, values, and opinions between two or more members of the organization are an everyday occurrence in most organizations. We have described these disagreements as "any organizational friction that produces a mismatch in expectations of the proper course of action for an employee or group of employees" (Lipsky et al., 2003, p. 8). These differences or frictions can be latent or manifest. By latent, we mean disagreements that are not directly expressed and do not necessarily surface in the day-to-day operation of the workplace. Latent or unexpressed conflict, however, can clearly have an effect (usually negative) on the performance, productivity, and climate of the workplace (Kolb & Putnam, 1992; Mechanic, 1962; Pondy, 1967). By manifest, we mean disagreements that are expressed by the members of the organization or work unit. Employees can express disagreement with their supervisors or fellow employees, for example, on how a job should be performed, who should perform it, and when it should be performed. As Dunlop (1958) noted more than 40 years ago, the relationship between employers and employees is governed by a complex "web of rules" that deals with every facet of the workplace: the rate of pay; the method of payment; the scheduling, assignment, and pace of work; standards of performance; and numerous other matters. Each of these facets is a potential source of conflict. We also know, of course, that interpersonal relationships on the job are another source of conflict. Unhappiness with these relationships can lead to disagreements, complaints, gripes, accusations, recriminations, and other forms of negative behavior. But these frictions need not and usually do not become formal complaints or grievances.

Most organizations expect (or at least hope) that the exercise of *formal authority* by a supervisor (sometimes called *forcing*) will be sufficient to resolve these types of workplace conflicts, but both scholars and practitioners have observed that *avoiding* or ignoring workplace disagreements is a common practice in many organizations. Still another approach used by some managers and supervisors is the technique of *accommodating* workplace disagreements by yielding to the wishes of the employees. In some organizations *compromising* is the approach used to resolve many conflicts; it is expected that differences of opinion and disagreements will be resolved through negotiation, in which each of the parties is expected to compromise in order to reach an agreement. Lastly, some organizations favor *collaborating* as an approach to resolving disagreements; they foster a problem-solving approach to achieving a mutually satisfactory solution to workplace conflicts (Aldag & Kuzuhara, 2002; Fairhurst, Green, & Snavely, 1984; Hellriegel et al., 2003; Rahim, 1983).

Many organizations do not have clear policies or procedures for managing routine workplace disagreements. Top managers expect that first-line supervisors will have primary responsibility for resolving these disagreements. They do not attempt to manage directly or systematically such disagreements but assume a laissez-faire attitude, hoping that the supervisors and employees involved in such conflicts will resolve their differences on their own or learn to live with them. Our research suggests, however, that a growing number of organizations are more actively managing conflict at this level because they have come to believe that the potential costs to the organization that can result from a laissez-faire attitude to workplace disagreements can become too large to tolerate. They have concluded that unresolved and unmanaged conflicts at the workgroup level too often mature into serious disputes and expensive lawsuits.

Accordingly, many organizations have recognized that they need to manage the disagreements that affect the performance of their supervisors and employees. A major factor explaining the trend toward active management of workplace conflicts is the development of so-called high-performance or high-commitment work systems. Globalization, rapid technological change, a more educated workforce, and other factors have led to a significant reorganization in the way work is performed in many U.S. companies. In many organizations the hierarchical, bureaucratic organization of work has been replaced by the use of teams (Lipsky et al., 2003). Disagreements among members of an organization become much more critical in a workplace where participation, empowerment, and teamwork are valued. The decline of hierarchy in U.S. organizations helps explain the rise of a more proactive approach to managing conflicts (Batt, Colvin, & Keefe, 2002; Colvin, 1999, 2003; Lipsky et al., 2003; Stone, 2004).

A vanguard of organizations has adopted comprehensive policies, or systems, designed to address the roots of organizational conflict. In a later section, we discuss the recent development of so-called integrated conflict management systems, which are expressly intended to allow an organization to deal with the fundamental causes of conflicts and to prevent disagreements from growing into serious disputes.

Managing Workplace Disputes

We define *disputes* as conflicts that ripen into formal *complaints, grievances,* and *charges.* Some unsettled disputes can become the basis for legal action—a complaint filed by an employee with a regulatory agency, such as the Equal Employment Opportunity Commission, a lawsuit by one or more employees against the organization, or a charge alleging an unlawful act by the employer. We also need to distinguish dispute resolution in a unionized setting from dispute resolution in a nonunion workplace.

Dispute resolution in unionized settings. Traditionally, in U.S. labor-management relations, a distinction has been made between disputes over "interests" and disputes over "rights" (Kheel, 1999). In collective bargaining, *disputes over interests* are usually resolved by negotiations between the employer and the union that result in a written collective bargaining agreement or contract. Disputes over interests emerge from the parties' attempt to *form and shape their relationship,* particularly their effort at contract formation. The failure of the parties in collective bargaining to agree on a new contract can result in a strike or lockout. In the United States, nonbinding techniques, especially mediation, are used to prevent or resolve interest disputes. Binding arbitration is almost never used to resolve interest disputes, with the notable exception of certain states that use arbitration to resolve labor disputes in the public sector, particularly those involving police officers and firefighters (Katz & Kochan, 2004).

By contrast, *disputes over rights* are disagreements over *the interpretation or application of the collective bargaining contract.* The term *grievance* has a special meaning in U.S. American labor relations. A *grievance* is defined as a dispute involving the interpretation of a collective bargaining contract. To handle such disputes, virtually all collective bargaining contracts in the United States contain *grievance procedures.* The precise design of a grievance procedure is subject to negotiation by the parties in collective bargaining but almost always requires the use of binding arbitration to resolve unsettled grievances. The first issue the union and the employer must decide is the *scope* of the grievance procedure, namely, what is grievable and what is not grievable. For example, a typical scope clause may stipulate that every provision in the collective bargaining agreement is subject to the grievance procedure. But the parties do not necessarily need to define the scope of the grievance procedure as the "four corners of the contract," but can agree to either a broader or narrower definition of what is grievable.

Every grievance procedure contains *steps*. Each step prescribes what action a grievant (usually an employee or a union) can take to have his or her complaint addressed and what response the employer is required to make. For example, step one in a grievance procedure usually requires that an employee discuss his or her grievance with his or her supervisor and attempt to resolve the matter informally. If a grievance is not resolved at step one, step two may require that the employee submit the grievance in writing to his or her supervisor, who in turn is required to give the employee a written response within certain time limits (e.g., 3 working days). Step three may require a meeting between the employee, his or her union representative, and managers responsible for labor relations. Other steps can be elaborated, but as noted, the last step almost always requires that an unresolved grievance be submitted to a neutral third-party arbitrator who is given the authority by the parties to make a final and binding decision in the case (Ruben, 2003; Slichter, Healy, & Livernash, 1960). The use of grievance procedures and arbitration to resolve rights disputes developed rapidly in U.S. collective bargaining after World War II (Katz & Lipsky, 1998).

Dispute resolution in nonunion settings. Although associated with collective bargaining, nevertheless throughout most of the 20th century there were some nonunion employers who used grievance procedures to handle employee disputes (Jacoby, 1997; Lewin, 1987). There is an obvious and highly significant distinction between dispute resolution in unionized and nonunion settings. In a unionized setting, the dispute resolution process is jointly controlled by the employer and the union, and the two parties negotiate the procedures used to resolve their disputes. In a nonunionized setting, the employer unilaterally decides what, if any, dispute resolution procedures will be used to handle workplace disputes. The employer may choose to confer with employees about such procedures, but the authority to devise and implement dispute resolution policies and procedures rests with the employer alone (provided, of course, the employer abides by statutory requirements).

Several scholars have documented the extent to which nonunion employers have established grievance procedures and the circumstances governing their use (Foulkes, 1980; Lewin, 1987; McCabe, 1989). We discovered in our research that about a third of the *Fortune* 1000 corporations had established in-house grievance procedures for nonunion employees, although the majority did not use final and binding arbitration as the final step of the procedure. In the absence of a collective bargaining agreement, it is the employer who must decide the scope of the grievance procedure. An employer, for example, can allow an employee to file a grievance alleging a violation of any policy contained in the employer's personnel handbook. Alternatively, an employer can restrict the scope of the grievance procedure to a relatively narrow range of human resource policies (e.g., a grievance over an employee's performance appraisal, merit pay adjustment, job assignment, etc.). In a majority of nonunion grievance procedures, management reserves the right to make a final decision regarding an unsettled grievance.

Most industrial relations scholars view the development of grievance procedures as an early form of *alternative dispute resolution* (ADR). In the absence of a grievance procedure in a collective bargaining contract, the major recourse for a union that believes its employer has violated the contract is to file a lawsuit alleging breach of contract.[4] After World War II the vast majority of unions and employers realized that using grievance procedures and arbitration, rather than litigation or concerted activity, to handle rights disputes would save both parties time and money. Similarly, some nonunion employers established grievance procedures in the belief that allowing employees to have some means of appealing the employer's decisions would deter them from resorting to the courts. Beginning especially in the 1970s an increasing number of nonunion employers began to use binding third-party arbitration as a means of resolving disputes with their employees. For many years the question of whether the courts would consider nonunion arbitration to be a substitute for an employee's right to sue remained unsettled. In recent years, however, the Supreme Court has made it clear that it is perfectly lawful for an employer to require that an employee waive his or her right to sue the employer and use arbitration to resolve the employee's complaint.[5]

The rise of ADR in U.S. employment relations over the past 25 years has been such a significant development that it requires special attention. After discussing litigation management we will return to a fuller discussion of ADR in employment relations.

Managing Litigation

Litigation management is a downstream activity, often far removed from the actual sources and causes of organizational conflict, and seldom involves the direct participation of employees, supervisors, and managers unless they are the parties in the litigation. Even top managers are not usually involved in litigation management unless the litigation centers on an important matter of principle to the organization or involves the possibility of large awards, settlements, or costs.

Litigation management is a form of *risk management* (Doherty, 2000; Marrison, 2002). Attorneys handling lawsuits are constantly weighing the costs, financial and otherwise, of settling a lawsuit quickly (usually through negotiation) against the risk of not settling but proceeding to the next stage of the suit. Attorneys are obliged to consult with their clients, of course, but the actual management of a lawsuit is in their hands. In a large corporation the chief counsel has overall responsibility for managing litigation and will, in a typical organization, regularly consult with the CEO and other top managers (e.g., the COO, the CFO, etc.) on the litigation strategy the corporation ought to pursue. The traditional approach to "managing

organizational conflict" is for top managers to play an active role only in litigation management and to play no more than a very minimal role in the management of workplace disagreements, trusting supervisors to discharge that responsibility. But in many organizations the traditional approach has proved to be increasingly unsatisfactory to managers and stakeholders. Most stakeholders have concluded that confining proactive conflict management to litigation management is tantamount to dealing with only the tip of the conflict iceberg. In the longer term, many corporations have concluded, an organizational strategy of focusing on the management of litigation, while largely ignoring the proactive management of disagreements and disputes, is a penny-wise and pound-foolish strategy.

In our research, we interviewed hundreds of corporate attorneys, and many of them discussed their initial attitudes about moving away from the traditional approach to managing organizational conflict. They told us they had been trained as litigators and were skeptical about alternative approaches to managing conflict. These attorneys, and other managers we interviewed, seemed to view conflict as a zero-sum game. They tended to think of every conflict as a contest in which there was a winner and a loser. Given this mind-set, their objective was to win these contests: Victory was the goal, rather than problem solving. They were reluctant to abandon an adversarial approach to conflict and to adopt a more cooperative strategy. These attorneys frequently set the tone for the entire organization. In our 1997 survey, we discovered that nearly 30% of the corporate attorneys we interviewed said that the policy of their organization in managing disputes was to "always litigate" or "litigate first, then move to ADR when appropriate" (Lipsky & Seeber, 1998, p. 11).

By the 1990s, globalization, increasing competition, and market pressures had forced many companies to take a different view of conflict management. The companies that were particularly exposed to competitive pressures could no longer afford to think of conflict in zero-sum terms. Experience had taught them that such an approach was too costly, and to remain competitive their companies had to adopt an alternative strategy. Other factors (the changing nature of

Table 13.1   Managing Three Types of Workplace Conflict

	Managing Disagreements	Managing Disputes	Managing Litigation
Who is responsible?	First-line supervisors and managers	HR managers, middle-managers, and attorneys	Corporate counsel, counsel's office, outside counsel
Type of conflict	Latent or expressed disagreements, differences of opinion, frictions	Complaints, grievances, charges (usually written)	Lawsuits, allegations of statutory infractions, formal charges
What techniques are used?	Exercise of supervisory authority, discussion, problem solving, negotiation	Discussion, negotiation, mediation, arbitration, other ADR techniques	Risk assessment, risk management, negotiation, advocacy in legal proceedings
Nature of outcome	Compliance with supervisory decision, mutual consent, informal agreement, no resolution	Negotiated or mediated agreement, complaint withdrawn or dismissed, arbitrated award, no resolution	Lawsuit or charge withdrawn or dismissed, negotiated agreement, jury trial and decision, bench trial and decision
Third-party involvement	Seldom but occasional use of consultants, facilitators, ombudspersons, etc.	Facilitators, mediators, ombudspersons, arbitrators, etc.	Court-appointed mediators, administrative law judges, magistrates, judges, etc.

the workforce, technological change, the decline of the union movement) also contributed to the change in the mind-set of corporate attorneys and managers.

The growing importance of government regulation and litigation in the life of the organization justified the inclusion of the chief counsel on the company's top management team. But when a top attorney became a so-called business partner of the organization's top managers, his or her view of the best strategy for managing conflict was likely to change. Participation in the formulation of the organization's basic business strategies tended to enlarge the attorneys' perspective from a relatively narrow focus on legal matters to a larger focus on overall business goals and objectives. We noted in our earlier work that the elevation of the status of corporate counsel, along with the restructuring of the legal function in many organizations, partly explains the transition from a reactive strategy of managing litigation to a more active strategy of managing disputes and, ultimately,

to a proactive strategy of managing conflict (Lipsky & Seeber, 1998).

In recent years, a growing number of attorneys and other decision makers in organizations have come to think of conflict as a variable-sum game. They no longer believe that every conflict is a contest with a winner and a loser. Rather, they have come to believe that in most conflicts so-called win-win solutions are possible: Both or all parties in the conflict may end up better off after a conflict is resolved than they were before. Victory, for these individuals, is no longer the important objective. Achieving resolutions that serve the organization's best interests became the goal (Lipsky et al., 2003).

Table 13.1 provides a summary of the preceding discussion. It recognizes the principal differences in managing the three types of workplace conflict described in this section. Obviously, there is overlap across the three types of conflict, but we believe the distinctions far exceed the similarities. The well of disagreements and frictions, whether hidden or revealed, that exists in almost all workplaces is the source of most organizational conflicts. Out of the day-to-day disagreements emerge the serious conflicts that can result in costly lawsuits. "Managing disputes" has always been a major responsibility of all organizations, but in many organizations it assumed a critical new dimension with the rise of ADR.

EXPLAINING THE RISE OF ADR

Most scholars attribute the growing use of ADR over the past quarter century to a combination of factors, including the growing federal regulation of business and employment, the concomitant growth of business and employment litigation, the changing nature of the workforce, and the strong support of ADR provided by a series of key Supreme Court decisions.

Frustration With the Legal System

There is a widespread perception, particularly among managers and corporate attorneys, that litigation has become increasingly costly and time-consuming. The dockets of federal, state, and local courts became crowded with a backlog of unresolved disputes after the passage of new workplace legislation in the 1960s and 1970s. Between 1970 and 1989, employment discrimination case filings increased by 2,166% (Ford, 2000). By the 1990s, the courts were attempting to manage 30 million civil cases per year. It has been estimated that the cost of civil litigation in the United States is now in the range of $200 to $300 billion annually (American Arbitration Association, 2003).

The business community's dissatisfaction with the legal system caused it to search for measures that would alleviate the growing burden of litigation. For example, it began to lobby for tort reforms that would place limitations on civil lawsuits. The movement for tort reform, however, had only piecemeal success in the 1990s, which probably strengthened the business community's resolve to use ADR (Lipsky et al., 2003).

The Changing Nature of the Workforce

As the proportion of professional, technical, high-skilled, and other white-collar employees in the U.S. workforce grew, employers began to realize that traditional methods of resolving disputes were not sufficient to meet the expectations of the individuals holding these types of jobs. To recruit and retain high-skilled employees, employers needed to establish dispute resolution procedures that these employees perceived to be fair and impartial. Many nonunion employers realized it was in their best interest to establish dispute resolution procedures that were, in some sense, a substitute for collectively bargained procedures. In our interviews with corporate managers and attorneys, several freely admitted that their companies' use of ADR was motivated by a desire to avoid unionization. Indeed, many unions believe that ADR procedures were consciously adopted by some employers as part of a union-avoidance strategy (Lipsky et al., 2003).

Legal Precedents

In 1991, the U.S. Supreme Court in the case of *Gilmer v. Interstate/Johnson Lane Corp.* (500 U.S. 20) held that a stock broker who had been discharged by his employer could not bring a claim of discrimination under the Age Discrimination in Employment Act in federal court because he was subject to regulations in the securities industry requiring the use of binding arbitration to resolve employment complaints. The Court's endorsement of binding arbitration set the stage for the widespread development of employer-promulgated private arbitration systems for statutory disputes. After *Gilmer,* many employers began to require that employees, as a condition of their hiring by the organization, sign an agreement waiving their access to judicial forums in favor of the employer's private system of arbitration (Stone, 1996).

Gilmer did not actually deal with an employment contract but rather with a requirement that was part of the agreement all new brokers signed when they registered with the New York Stock Exchange. Whether an employer could require a new employee to sign an *employment contract* requiring arbitration of statutory disputes remained an open issue until the Supreme Court's 2001 decision in *Circuit City Stores, Inc. v. Saint Clair Adams* (121 S.Ct. 1302). In this case, the Court ruled that an employee who had signed a mandatory pre-dispute arbitration agreement could not sue his employer on a claim that the employer had violated Title VII of the Civil Rights Act but rather was required to submit his claim to arbitration.

There has been a considerable amount of controversy over the wisdom of the *Gilmer* and *Circuit City* decisions (see, e.g., Stone, 1996). Nevertheless, it now appears that the employer's use of mandatory arbitration to settle statutory disputes is settled law. The legal battleground has shifted to the question of whether the mandatory arbitration procedures used by employers provide adequate due process protections for employees (see, e.g., *Hooters of America, Inc. v. Annette R. Phillips,* 173 F.3d 933 [1999]). Eventually the Supreme Court will deal with due process protections in employment arbitration. In the meantime, while lower courts sift through these issues, the use of mandatory pre-dispute arbitration in employment relations continues to grow.

The Evaluation of ADR Programs and Techniques

Most of the research on dispute resolution in individual organizations is case-study research, but a handful of studies have evaluated systematically the effectiveness and efficiency of ADR programs in a single organization. This section evaluates the use of ADR and employment arbitration, as well as discusses the extent of the use of ADR in corporations.

The Evaluation of ADR in Individual Organizations

The major example of the systematic evaluation of ADR in one organization is the research on dispute resolution in the United States Postal Service (USPS). The USPS is an organization that is almost entirely unionized. Its labor-management relations have been typical of a mature organization, but perhaps a bit more contentious than most. Postal workers do not have the right to strike, and by all accounts the USPS and its unions have high grievance and arbitration rates. Many of the employment disputes that occur in the USPS are statutory disputes, particularly disputes over race and gender discrimination. Some well-publicized incidents in the 1990s gave the impression that workplace violence was a serious problem in the postal system (and caused the term "going postal" to come into vogue), although objective evidence suggests that violence in the USPS had not necessarily been a more serious problem than it had been in many other organizations.

Nevertheless, workplace conflict was serious enough to prompt the USPS to undertake a variety of experiments designed to resolve disputes locally and reduce the number that proceeded to external public forums for resolution. After conducting a pilot program in Florida, the USPS initiated the REDRESS program in 1998 (Bingham et al., 2001b). The REDRESS program sought to reduce the number of discrimination complaints filed by postal workers, resolve conflicts at low levels, and transform the workplace culture. A prominent feature of the REDRESS program is its use of so-called transformative mediation to resolve disputes (Bush & Folger, 1994). Evaluations of the REDRESS program have produced strong evidence that this systematic change in conflict management resulted in high settlement rates at lower levels of the organization. Evidence that REDRESS brought about cultural change in the USPS, however, is weak (Bingham et al., 2001).

The USPS story is, in our experience, similar to that of many other organizations. Changes in the external environment as well as dissatisfaction with the existing system for resolving disputes led the organization to attempt wholesale change in its approach to conflict management. The reliance on transformative mediation is a distinctive feature of the USPS's system. Nevertheless, the USPS's objectives of saving time and money are the same objectives the vast majority of organizations have had for adopting new approaches to dispute resolution (Lipsky & Seeber, 1998).

There have been several surveys of participant satisfaction with private mediation and arbitration forums (Lipsky et al., 2003; McDermott, Obar, Jose, & Bowers, 2000; Seeber, Schmidle, & Smith, 2001). These surveys generally show high levels of participant satisfaction, but there are obvious difficulties in comparing levels of participant satisfaction across different types of forums—it is the classic problem of comparing apples and oranges. Nevertheless, we believe it is possible to draw some general conclusions about participant satisfaction with ADR procedures and outcomes. On the one hand, participants are generally satisfied with various characteristics of such procedures, including their fairness. On the other hand, participant satisfaction with the outcomes of such processes has been measured less frequently (McDermott et al., 2000; Seeber et al., 2001). When it has been measured, however, it compares favorably with measures of participant satisfaction with outcomes in judicial forums.

The Evaluation of Employment Arbitration

There have been a number of studies that have analyzed "win" rates or "loss" rates of the parties in arbitration cases. Determining which party wins or loses an arbitration case can be a difficult task for a researcher. Nonetheless, in practice the parties frequently do make judgments about who wins and loses such cases, and these perceptions can influence the parties' attitudes about the fairness of arbitration and whether it should be used to resolve future disputes.

Several studies have analyzed American Arbitration Association (AAA) data for employment arbitration cases. Bingham conducted two of these studies, reporting that employees won 73% of these cases in 1992 (Bingham, 1995) and 63% of such cases in 1993-1995 (Bingham, 1997). Maltby (2002) examined employment arbitration cases decided in 2000 and found that employees won 66% of these cases. Eisenberg and Hill (2003) analyzed a random sample of cases from 1999-2000 and found that employees won 43% of the cases.

Some studies compare win rates in arbitration with win rates in the courts and other adjudicative forums (Eisenberg & Hill, 2003). Unless a study contains appropriate controls for the substantive issues in the cases and for other factors, it is difficult to attach much credence to the comparison of win rates across forums. If it is difficult to conduct an empirical evaluation of outcomes in arbitration cases, it is nearly impossible to do so in mediation cases. No accepted model of evaluation has emerged for assessing

settlements in mediation cases. Much of the research on mediation has, instead, focused on individual participants' perceptions of procedural, rather than distributive, justice (Bingham, 2004). In the end, of course, it is the stakeholders' perceptions of procedural and distributive fairness that influence their willingness to accept and use these various techniques.

Surveys on the Corporate Use of ADR

In the 1990s, there was growing recognition in both the research and practitioner communities that, although the use of ADR techniques had expanded dramatically, there were virtually no hard data on the extent of their use, the satisfaction of the parties who had used them, or their effectiveness. To fill the gap in our knowledge, several surveys were conducted, and they have shown that the growth of ADR in employment disputes over the past 20 or 30 years has truly been astounding (American Arbitration Association, 2003; Deloitte Touche Tohmatsu International, 1993; U.S. General Accounting Office, 1997). They also demonstrate that many organizations have found that using ADR techniques to resolve employment disputes is an effective means of reducing the costly and time-consuming aspects of conventional litigation. For example, a 1993 survey by Deloitte Touche Tohmatsu International provided estimates of the use of arbitration and mediation in a wide variety of corporate disputes and revealed that large private sector corporations had serious concerns with the costs of disputes and were seeking more systematic approaches to managing conflict (Deloitte Touche Tohmatsu International, 1993).

In 1997, we conducted a survey of the general counsel of the Fortune 1000 corporations; interviews were completed with 606 of these corporate lawyers. We had two principal objectives when we conducted our 1997 survey. First, we wanted to document the extent to which major U.S. corporations used various dispute resolution techniques and whether these organizations were satisfied with such techniques. Second, we wanted to obtain an understanding of the factors influencing corporations in their development of policies on conflict and dispute resolution (Lipsky & Seeber, 1998). Our survey demonstrated that the vast majority of the largest U.S. corporations relied heavily on a variety of ADR techniques (arbitration, mediation, fact-finding, facilitation, peer review, early neutral evaluation, etc.) to resolve employment and business disputes (Lipsky & Seeber, 1998).

In 2003, the American Arbitration Association (AAA) surveyed the *Fortune* 1000 companies using virtually the same survey instrument the authors had used in 1997. The AAA reported,

> In broad terms, the current study confirms the findings of the Cornell study with respect to the ongoing use of both mediation and arbitration by legal departments of Fortune 1000 companies, and it records increases in the use of ADR procedures along with improvement in the perceived qualifications of mediators and arbitrators. (American Arbitration Association, 2003, p. 26)

In 1997 we found, for example, that 62% of the *Fortune* 1000 firms had used arbitration in employment cases at least once in the preceding 3 years and 79% had used mediation. In commercial (business-to-business) disputes, the comparable figures were 85% and 78%. We also found that the median use of arbitration or mediation in employment disputes by a *Fortune* 1000 company was about five or six cases a year (Lipsky & Seeber, 1998). The AAA found modest but steady growth in ADR usage over the intervening 6 years.

Both our study and the AAA's documented the reasons major companies had used ADR. The rank order of these reasons in the 1997 and 2003 surveys was remarkably similar. Here we report the percentage of the respondents in the AAA survey that said one of the listed factors was the reason their organization had used ADR: saves money (90%), provides a more satisfactory process (84%), saves time (83%), allows parties to resolve disputes themselves (82%), is court mandated (73%), has limited discovery (70%), preserves good relationships between disputing parties (65%), uses expertise of mediators/arbitrators (63%), gives more satisfactory settlements (60%), and is required by contract (57%) (American Arbitration Association, 2003).

The AAA survey, however, sampled not only *Fortune* 1000 companies but also a set of medium-size corporations and some privately held companies. The AAA discovered that the use of ADR by these smaller companies almost matched the use of ADR by the *Fortune* 1000, a finding that contradicts the conventional wisdom (American Arbitration Association, 2003).

A consistent finding across all these surveys is that many corporations and other organizations have been moving beyond the use of ADR techniques and toward the adoption of a more strategic view of conflict management. As we said in 1998, "ADR practice is not haphazard or incidental, but rather seems to be integral to a systematic, long-term change in the way corporations resolve disputes. Many corporations see it as a strategic tool for use in all conflicts" (Lipsky & Seeber, 1998, p. 8).

CONFLICT MANAGEMENT: STRATEGIES AND SYSTEMS

Does the concept of "strategy" apply to the management of organizational conflict? Scholars disagree on this matter, but most acknowledge that a company cannot have a conflict management strategy independent of its business strategy (Porter, 1985). Central to the traditional concept of strategy is the notion of a *goal* or *objective,* but a strategy is much more than an enumeration of goals and objectives: A strategy also includes a *plan* to achieve them. For some scholars, however, the idea that a strategy is essentially a plan to achieve certain objectives is inadequate. Particularly in the 1990s, it became fashionable to claim that, in the face of globalization, the rise of the Internet, and other dramatic changes, the environment was so volatile the idea that an organization should have a strategy, at least in the traditional sense, was wrongheaded. In an Internet age, some people argued, long-term strategic planning made little sense; rather, the strategic process had to focus on enhancing the organization's capacity to manage change (Khanna & Palepu, 1999; Mintzberg, 1994).

Applying Strategic Concepts to Conflict Management

How do we apply these basic strategic concepts to conflict management? In the United States, following World War II, employment relations enjoyed a lengthy period of relative stability. Kochan et al. (1986) argued that the American workplace, during the 30 years that followed the end of World War II, operated under relatively fixed conditions they called the "New Deal system of industrial relations" (Kochan et al., 1986, p. 29). They acknowledged that the employment relations system during this 30-year period was not immune to change and modification. They maintained, however, that "a critical aspect of the operation of the New Deal system was the long history of incremental change and resistance to more fundamental modification. This incremental adjustment orientation was apparent in government policy, managerial practice, and union bargaining objectives" (Kochan et al., 1986, p. 45). By the 1970s, they pointed out, "pressures that challenged the traditional system began to build up" (Kochan et al., 1986, p. 46). These pressures included most notably the growing globalization of the U.S. economy, which resulted in more intense competitive pressures for most employers. A principal consequence of these pressures was the erosion of the strength of the union movement (Lipsky et al., 2003).

The relative stability that characterized employment relations for nearly three decades after World War II was replaced by significantly more volatility in the workplace environment. The conflict management strategies that had worked for most employers during the postwar period were no longer viable. Beginning in the 1970s, employers who had become accustomed to a static and orderly means of handling workplace disputes began to realize they were playing a different, significantly more dynamic game (Lipsky et al., 2003). The destabilization of employment relations over the past quarter of a century caused many employers to search for new approaches for managing workplace conflict. Many employers who had not previously conceived of conflict management in strategic terms (nor in many cases had even thought of conflict as a phenomenon that needed proactive management) began to understand the imperative for thinking strategically about the management of conflict.

In our research on conflict management, we concluded that, to the extent that major U.S. corporations had consciously adopted a conflict

management strategy, they had chosen one of three possibilities that we labeled *contend, settle,* and *prevent* (Lipsky et al., 2003). Our focus was on the choice of a strategy at the macro or organizational level rather than at the micro or workplace level, and we were principally concerned with the company's choice between pursuing a traditional approach, relying heavily on litigation, or adopting a more contemporary approach, relying on the use of ADR or, possibly, a conflict management system. In the *contend* category are the corporations that clearly prefer litigation to ADR. They never or rarely use any ADR technique to resolve a workplace dispute, and many of them reject the use of ADR as a matter of policy. We estimated that currently less than 9% of the *Fortune* 1000 fell into the *contend* category, and the number was probably shrinking. In the *settle* category, we placed all the corporations that were routinely using ADR techniques to settle workplace disputes, some as a matter of predetermined policy and some on an ad hoc basis. Our data suggested that the vast majority of U.S. corporations— approximately 74%—fell into this category. In the *prevent* category, we placed the corporations that had established a workplace *conflict management system*. Rather than merely using a particular dispute resolution technique as a matter of practice or even policy, as the organizations in the *settle* category did, these corporations had developed a comprehensive set of policies designed to manage workplace conflict and (if possible) prevent workplace conflict from blossoming into serious disputes (Lipsky et al., 2003).

Integrated Conflict Management Systems

By the 1990s practitioners and scholars recognized that a growing number of organizations were moving beyond the use of ADR techniques and adopting conflict management systems (CMS). Based on our 1997 survey of the *Fortune* 1000, we estimated that approximately 17% of these companies had adopted some form of a CMS (Lipsky et al., 2003). There has been, however, considerable imprecision in the use of the term *conflict management system*. How does one distinguish an authentic "system" from a "policy," "procedure," or "practice"? What precisely distinguishes an organization's use of ADR policies and techniques from an organization's establishment of a CMS? Several influential books have attempted to define the nature of a CMS but there has been no consensus on a definition (Costantino & Merchant, 1996; Slaikeu & Hasson, 1998; Stitt, 1998; Ury, Brett, & Goldberg, 1993).

Costantino and Merchant (1996), for example, closely followed standard systems theory (Bertalanffy, 1951; Boulding, 1956) in defining a CMS. They listed several characteristics of a CMS: (a) *Boundaries*—Boundaries separate one system (e.g., human resources) from another (e.g., legal); (b) *Purpose*—All systems have a goal or purpose, such as the resolution of various types of disputes; (c) *Inputs*—A system uses resources (raw materials, human resources, and financial resources) to achieve its purpose; (d) *Transformation*—A system transforms inputs into outputs that achieve the system's purpose (i.e., transforming conflict and disputes into solutions); (e) *Outputs*—Conflict management systems produce outputs (decisions, agreements, and settlements of disputes) that affect the external environment; (f) *Feedback*—Conflict management systems receive feedback from clients (customers, constituents, employees) that organizations use to improve or change the system.

Phillips (2004) also enumerated the elements of a CMS based on his synthesis of several company case studies. He discussed "the classic challenges" of systems design, focusing on some of the common elements of design faced by all companies that adopt a CMS. Phillips's version of these elements included the following: (a) *Scope* precisely defines the employees and claims that fall within each phase of the system; (b) *Cost* specifies whether and to what extent an employee needs to pay for the use of a dispute resolution procedure; (c) *Incentives* refer to the effect that the allocation of the costs of the program have on the parties' inclination to use the program; imposing a significant proportion of the costs on employees, for example, may significantly diminish their incentive to use the program; (d) *Attributes* refer to which options (mediation, arbitration, the ombuds function, etc.) are available to employees, whether an employee has access to one option if he or she has not exhausted the use of another, and (if arbitration is an option) whether it is mandatory or voluntary; and (e) *Implementation* refers to getting the support of all levels of management and the participation of the workforce in the system; implementation also requires the development of a communication strategy by the organization. Phillips concluded, "The essential prerequisite to any successful employment dispute resolution program is an attitudinal adjustment: a recognition that managing employment disputes is a legitimate, ongoing task of management, rather than an unexpected and intrusive interruption" (p. 255).

The Society of Professionals in Dispute Resolution (SPIDR) believed that many organizations were seeking authoritative guidance on "best practice" in the design and implementation of a CMS but could find only conflicting points of view in the professional literature. (In 2001, SPIDR merged with two other organizations to become the Association for Conflict Resolution.) It launched an initiative to develop a consensus on the nature and design of a CMS. A committee was appointed to identify the critical elements of a CMS and to provide guidance to organizations considering the adoption of such a system. After 3 years of deliberation, the committee published its report in 2001 (Gosline et al., 2001)[6].

The committee stated in its report, "The current trend is toward the introduction of 'integrated conflict management systems.' An integrated conflict management system introduces a systematic approach to preventing, managing, and resolving conflict that focuses on the causes of conflict within the organization" (Gosline et al., 2001, p. 8). It should be noted that the concept of an *integrated conflict management system* (ICMS) is different from that of a CMS in the sense that an ICMS is a more comprehensive version of a CMS. In the committee's opinion, an authentic ICMS was a more effective means of managing organizational conflict than the use of ADR techniques.

> [W]hile the more formal dispute resolution processes such as grievance procedures and mediation are necessary, they are insufficient because

they usually address only the symptoms of conflict, not the sources. . . . An integrated conflict management system addresses the sources of conflict and provides a method for promoting competence in dealing with conflict throughout the organization. (Gosline et al., 2001, p. 8)

The committee identified five essential characteristics of an ICMS: (a) an ICMS provides "options for all types of problems and all people in the workplace"; (b) it creates "a culture that welcomes dissent and encourages resolution of conflict at the lower level through direct negotiation"; (c) it provides "multiple access points"; (d) it provides "multiple options—both rights based and interest based—for addressing conflict"; and (e) it provides "systemic support and structures . . . that integrate effective conflict management into the organization's daily operations" (Gosline et al., 2001, p. 9). Below is a discussion of each of these key characteristics.

Scope. The committee's recommendation that an ICMS should provide "options for all types of problems" in effect addresses the *scope* of the system. An ICMS should have the broadest feasible scope, giving employees the opportunity to voice complaints about any workplace-related issue. This recommendation can be contrasted with the scope of the grievance procedure contained in a typical collective bargaining contract: Ordinarily only an employee has the right to grieve an alleged infraction of one or more of the provisions contained in the contract. In a nonunion setting, an employer maintaining a CMS may allow an employee to file a complaint on any matter covered in the employer's personnel handbook. But in an authentic ICMS, the SPIDR committee maintained, employees should be able to pursue any workplace-related issue, even if the matter is not covered by a collective bargaining agreement or the personnel handbook. Accordingly, under an ICMS an employee may pursue a complaint that pertains not only to the terms and conditions of the employee's job (wage, salary, hours of work, performance appraisal, etc.) or to an employee's allegation of a statutory violation by the employer (discrimination, sexual harassment, etc.), but also to an employee's complaint about so-called quality-of-work life issues (including the

employee's relationships with supervisors and other employees, the resources and tools the employee has available on the job, etc.). In the SPIDR committee's view, a true ICMS can accommodate a complaint by a so-called whistle-blower (an employee who believes there is a need to complain about the unethical or illegal behavior of a manager), a problem faced by an employee who has an emotional or psychological problem and needs counseling, or a situation created by an employee who abuses drugs and alcohol and needs treatment.[7]

Culture. The SPIDR committee maintained that to manage conflict effectively, "an organization must accept conflict as inevitable" (Gosline et al., 2001, p. 10). Many organizations hinder effective conflict management by discouraging employees from raising concerns or voicing complaints. Effective conflict management requires that managers communicate to employees not merely their tolerance for but their active encouragement of employees' expressing their concerns. To encourage the expression of dissent, the organization must guarantee that an employee can voice a concern or file a complaint without fear of retaliation. The committee cited an example of a "conflict competent culture": The Polaroid Corporation maintains a policy that "stresses a commitment to create an environment that recognizes disputes as a natural cultural process and communicates to employees that they can expect to air their issues with full assurance of 'safe harbor' and without adverse repercussions" (Gosline et al., 2001, p. 10).

The culture of an organization consists of the norms, standards, customs, and practices that govern the behavior of the members of the organization. "At the core of the definition of culture is 'the way people treat each other'" (Gosline et al., 2001, p. 20). The culture of an organization also is a manifestation of the organization's values—"those principles intended to guide both employee conduct and business strategy" (Lipsky et al., 2003, p. 324). An ICMS needs to be integrated with the core values of an organization. If an organization does not value voluntariness, open communication, dissent, and protections against retaliation, any attempt to establish an ICMS is likely to fail. An ICMS is not a stand-alone feature of an organization, but must be carefully aligned not only with the organization's values but also with other organizational processes and systems. For example, an ICMS and the organization's human resource strategies and processes must be in proper alignment. An ICMS is not a substitute for an organization's policies on performance standards, discipline, rewards, and incentives, but must be integrated with such policies. For an organization adopting an ICMS, "this is a difficult task, and not all organizations will find this integration to be a smooth transition" (Lipsky et al., 2003, p. 325).

Multiple access points. The proposition that a system should have multiple access points can be contrasted with the design of more traditional grievance procedures. As noted earlier, a grievance procedure has "steps," and the first step usually requires an employee to take a grievance to his or her immediate supervisor and attempt to resolve it informally. The employee has one access point, or portal, for dealing with grievances, which is usually his or her supervisor. By contrast, in an ICMS an employee would not be restricted to dealing with his or her supervisor but could take a complaint to one of several access points, depending on the nature of the complaint. For example, in the Prudential CMS an employee can discuss a complaint with his or her immediate supervisor, but also has the choice of contacting any one of several offices, including human resources, the law department, the audit office, the office of investigation, the company's compliance officers, as well as higher-level managers (Lipsky et al., 2003). If an employee's complaint is against a frontline supervisor, then restricting that employee's point of access to the supervisor who may be the source of the problem seriously erodes the effectiveness of the complaint procedure.

Multiple options. An ICMS should have both *rights-based options* and *interest-based options.* Ury et al. (1993) pointed out that there are three methods of resolving disputes: The parties in a dispute may (a) reconcile their underlying interests, (b) decide who is right, or (c) allow the more powerful party to determine the outcome.[8] They also noted that there are procedures (or

options) associated with each of these three methods. Interest-based methods include negotiation, facilitation, mediation, and consultation. Rights-based options include litigation and various forms of arbitration, including conventional, expedited, final-offer, and the like. The essential difference between an interest-based option and a rights-based option is that an interest-based option allows the parties to reach agreement voluntarily, whereas a rights-based option involves the possibility of a solution being imposed on the parties in the dispute. Power-based methods involve the use of wars, strikes, picketing, and other forms of coercive behavior, including violence (Ury et al., 1993; see also Costantino & Merchant, 1996).

Under collective bargaining, certain power-based methods, such as strikes and picketing, are sanctioned and regulated by law, but we do not know of an organizational CMS that permits the use of power-based methods. An ICMS, according to the SPIDR committee, should allow employees to use both rights-based and interest-based options. Another important distinction is between conflict resolution options that use internal processes and resources and those that use external processes and resources. Internal processes involve people and resources within the organization, whereas external processes involve people and resources outside the organization (Slaikeu & Hasson, 1998). Thus, for example, an ICMS may give employees access to both *internal mediation* and *external mediation.* Most authorities in the field recommend that systems be designed to channel complainants progressively from interest-based options to rights-based options and from internal processes to external processes. This recommendation is based on at least two premises: (a) Interest-based options encourage voluntary settlement, and parties derive greater satisfaction from voluntarily settling a dispute; and (b) Internal processes are almost always less expensive and time-consuming than external processes, and similarly interest-based options are less expensive and time-consuming than rights-based options (Ury et al., 1993).

In Table 13.2, we classify various common options in an ICMS on two dimensions: whether the option is rights-based or interest-based and whether it is internal or external (Lipsky et al.,

Table 13.2   Conflict Management System Options

	Internal Processes	*External Processes*
Interest-based options	Negotiation	Third-party facilitation
	Hot lines	Conciliation
	The open door	Early neutral evaluation
	Consultation	External mediation
	Counseling	Fact-finding
	Internal facilitation	Advisory arbitration
	Peer mediation	Minitrial without binding decision
	Managerial mediation	
	Ombudspersons	
Rights-based options	Peer review	Mediation-arbitration (med-arb)
	Employee appeals board	Minitrial with binding decision
	Executive panels	Conventional arbitration
		Expedited arbitration
		Final-offer arbitration
		Voluntary arbitration
		Mandatory arbitration
		Adjudication

2003; see also Costantino & Merchant, 1996; Ury et al., 1993). The options listed in Table 13.2 constitute essentially a menu of choices for those designing a CMS. Although the SPIDR committee recommended that an ICMS have "multiple options," we have not encountered a system that offers all the options listed in Table 13.2. For example, the ICMS used by PECO, a large utility company, specifies that a disputant can use the following options: open door, a "resolution facilitator," internal mediation, external mediation, peer review, and voluntary binding arbitration (Lipsky et al., 2003).[9]

Support structures. According to the SPIDR committee, "to develop an effective [ICMS], an organization must provide necessary systemic support and structures that coordinate access to [the ICMS]" (Gosline et al., 2001, p. 14). Essential to the success of an ICMS is the commitment of top management (and in unionized settings, the commitment of top union leaders). The organization must also undertake ongoing training programs for managers, supervisors, and employees, designed to equip them with the skills necessary to operate a successful ICMS. A partial list of some of these skills includes problem solving, negotiation, coaching, mediation, and a range of skills needed for

individuals to be "conflict competent" (Gosline et al., 2001; see also Lipsky et al., 2003).

All authorities agree that if a conflict management system is to be successful, the organization must dedicate people and resources to the system. Slaikeu and Hasson (1998) maintained that "best practice" in strengthening support structures in an organization consists of four components: (a) *Build on existing resources*—In most organizations, support and assistance for a CMS can be found in the law department, the human resource function, or an employee assistance program (EAP); (b) *Provide a source of independent and confidential assistance*—In many organizations that independent source may be an ombuds office; in other organizations it may be a semiautonomous office that serves as a source of information and referral for employees filing complaints; (c) *Provide human supports that reflect the preferred path*—Every organization should have individuals who will assist parties in disputes; for example, expert staff is needed to assist parties in mediation, in processing appeals, and in investigative functions; and (d) *Provide supporting physical resources and ensure that they work for all*—The physical resources that are needed in a CMS range from toll-free hot lines to conference rooms allowing privacy and confidentiality

(Slaikeu & Hasson, 1998; see also Gosline et al., 2001).

Occasionally jurisdictional issues affect the relationship between the office or personnel responsible for a CMS and other offices in the organization. In our own research, we heard many stories about these so-called turf battles. In many organizations an internal champion pushes for the adoption of a conflict management system, frequently against the opposition of other stakeholders in the organization. As Ulrich (1997) noted, a champion is a change agent who seeks the "cultural transformation" of the organization. "Champions are trailblazers, who build an integrated conflict management system piece by piece—never losing sight of the difficulty of creating change" (Gosline et al., 2001, p. 14; see also Westin & Feliu, 1998). Needless to say, changing the culture of an organization is difficult work; often a champion prevails, but sometimes even the most zealous champion fails and the organization maintains the status quo. The successful establishment of an ICMS requires that top management incorporates the system as part of the organization's overall strategy and communicates that commitment clearly to all the stakeholders in the organization (see Gosline et al., 2001; Lipsky et al., 2003).

Fairness and Due Process in Conflict Management Systems

The question of fairness and due process must also be considered in the design and operation of any system, particularly an ICMS. An organization may have a well-articulated conflict management strategy and that strategy may be operationalized in the form of a conflict management system, but nonetheless the system may or may not provide due process protections for those who use it. Indeed, the evidence suggests there is wide variation in the extent to which workplace systems promulgated by private employers provide due process protections (Lipsky et al., 2003). The SPIDR committee deliberated at length on this question and concluded there were eight essential elements of a fair CMS: (a) voluntary participation; (b) protection of privacy and confidentiality; (c) truly neutral and impartial third parties; (d) adequately

trained and qualified neutrals; (e) a diverse roster of neutrals; (f) policies prohibiting reprisal and retaliation; (g) consistency with collective bargaining contracts; and (h) protection of the statutory and constitutional rights of disputants (Gosline et al., 2001; Lipsky et al., 2003).

Several other professional organizations and groups have also offered recommendations on the elements essential to a fair workplace system. For example, the Due Process Protocol was developed by a task force consisting of representatives from seven major professional organizations (Dunlop & Zack, 1997).[10] The Protocol focuses on the use of external mediation and arbitration and not on a CMS, and therefore the list of protections developed by the task force differs from the list developed by the SPIDR committee. The Due Process Protocol sets out the following standards: (a) *Representation*—Employees using mediation or arbitration should have the right to be represented by an attorney or an advocate of their own choosing; (b) *Fees for representation*—The employer should reimburse some or all of the costs of an employee's representation, especially if the employee is low paid; (c) *Access to information*—Employees should have access to all the information that is relevant to their claims; (d) *Roster membership*—Mediators and arbitrators should have the skill necessary to conduct a fair hearing and should have knowledge of the statutory issues in the dispute. Moreover, the roster of neutrals should be diverse with respect to gender, ethnicity, background, and experience. Neutrals should be jointly selected by the parties in the dispute; (e) *Training of neutrals*—Rosters should consist of mediators and arbitrators trained in substantive, procedural, and remedial issues likely to arise in disputes; (f) *Panel selection*—The parties in a dispute should use a procedure for selecting a neutral that assures the impartiality of the neutral; (g) *Conflicts of interest*—A mediator or arbitrator in a dispute has a duty to disclose any relationship that might constitute or be perceived as a conflict of interest; (h) *The authority of the arbitrator*—When arbitration is used to resolve a dispute, the arbitrator should have the authority to award whatever relief would be available under the law. The arbitrator should issue a written opinion that includes a summary of the issues and a clear declaration of the damages or relief, if any, awarded in the case; and (i) *Compensation of the neutral*—The Due Process Protocol maintains that impartiality is strengthened if the parties share the neutral's fees and expenses. It recognizes, however, that if one of the parties in a dispute lacks the ability to pay, then sharing the expenses equally may not be feasible. In such instances the Protocol advises the parties to make alternative arrangements. If the parties cannot make such arrangements, the Protocol recommends that the neutral determine the allocation of fees.

There was one important matter on which the members of the Due Process task force were unable to agree, namely, the question of the propriety of mandatory pre-dispute arbitration in employment relations. Should an employer have the right to insist that employees agree, as a condition of their hiring or continued employment, to waive their right to sue the employer for breaching an employment statute and agree instead to have such claims decided by an arbitrator? About half of the companies we studied that have a workplace system use some form of external arbitration, and most of those companies require mandatory pre-dispute arbitration (Lipsky et al., 2003). Although the Supreme Court has sanctioned the use of such agreements, in recent years no subject in employment relations has been more intensely debated. One critic has called the practice the "yellow-dog contract" of contemporary employment relations (Stone, 1996). Cohen and Domagalski (1988) argued that mandatory employment arbitration can have adverse effects on claimants' perceptions of both procedural and distributive justice. On the other hand, advocates of mandatory arbitration contend that, if the process is properly designed, it provides a means of resolving disputes that is less cumbersome, less costly, and less time-consuming than court proceedings (Bedman, 2004; Taussig, 2004). The Due Process task force acknowledged that "it did not achieve consensus on this difficult issue.... The Task Force takes no position on the timing of agreements to mediate [or] arbitrate statutory employment disputes, though it agrees that such agreements be knowingly made" (Dunlop & Zack, 1997, pp. 172–173).[11]

The AAA and JAMS (originally Judicial, Arbitration, and Mediation Services), two of the major "providers" of mediators and arbitrators in the United States, both pledged to abide by the Due Process Protocol in their administration of cases (Dunlop & Zack, 1997). By 2000, the AAA reported that it was administering employment arbitration programs that covered "more than five hundred employers and five million employees" (LeRoy & Feuille, 2004, p. 524). The growth of mandatory employment arbitration has been so dramatic that one of the co-chairs of the Due Process task force now claims there are more employees covered by the Protocol than are covered by collective bargaining agreements.[12]

Case Studies of Conflict Management Systems

The literature contains numerous case studies of the development of conflict management strategies and systems. Although there are many case studies of how individual organizations manage conflict, the majority are written by attorneys or managers associated with those organizations and do not provide data on the operation of the organization's conflict management program. It is also difficult, in many of these studies, to determine whether the program has achieved its goals (e.g., see Bedman, 2004; Clark, 2004; Kartman, 2004; Malin, 2004; Millard, 2004; Nordstrom, 2004; Perdue, 2004; Taussig, 2004). Each organization has its own special motivations for adopting a conflict management system, but research suggests that the similarity of their motives far outweighs their differences. Each company encountered an increasingly difficult litigation environment, sought a means of avoiding the costs and delays of litigation, and established a workplace conflict management system.

Phillips (2004), on the basis of case studies of several organizations, identifies common themes across several "model" organizations that have adopted a CMS. On the one hand, he noted that successful systems promote the resolution of disputes at the lowest level of the organization. The vast majority of disputes are resolved quickly and efficiently, and it is not uncommon to encounter a system in which arbitration, if it is an option, is rarely if ever used. For example, Halliburton, General

Electric, and Shell all report that the vast proportion of their disputes were resolved well before any of them needed to be submitted to arbitration (Phillips, 2004). On the other hand, Phillips pointed out the difficulties that organizations face in building and maintaining credibility not only with the general employee population but also with line management. Employees often fear that a system created by their employer will not serve their best interests, but only those of the employer. Even though a system may prohibit retaliation against an employee who uses it, many employees believe the company will be unable to prevent retaliation by supervisors on the shop floor. Many line managers believe a system undermines their authority and constrains their ability "to respond creatively and intelligently in the first instance to problems that employees bring" (Phillips, 2004, p. 254). Also, some managers recognize that they lack and will need to obtain the conflict resolution skills necessary to participate effectively in a CMS.

Finally, Phillips (2004) noted that although there have been numerous case studies of conflict management systems, there have been very few systematic evaluations of such systems.

> [F]ew programs have a strong emphasis on building in the capturing of data, cost savings, and quality experiences that are needed in order to quantify and enhance program effectiveness. . . . Systems limited to methods of addressing the disputes themselves do not always reflect built-in evaluative processes. (Phillips, 2004, pp. 254–255)

The evaluation of conflict management systems is a task that has been undertaken only by large government agencies (e.g., the Air Force) or very large private corporations (e.g., GE and Shell Oil) (Lipsky et al., 2003). Cost-benefit analysis is clearly one tool that can be used to justify a system's economic value, but there are others. A barrier to evaluating conflict management systems, according to many of our interviewees, is the fact that it is relatively easy for organizations to identify the *costs* associated with the use of a CMS, but it is much more difficult to identify the *benefits*. As long as it remains difficult to gauge accurately the benefits of a CMS, then, at least for the foreseeable

future, the use of a CMS will continue to be based more on faith than on evidence.

The conflict management system at General Electric (GE) illustrates many of the points made by Phillips and other authors. GE is one of the largest corporations in the world and has a dozen different business units, ranging from refrigerators and other appliances to aircraft engines to the National Broadcasting Company (NBC). For many years GE's CEO was Jack Welch, a dynamic business leader. At the height of Welch's reign at GE, in the 1990s, the company's strategic objective was for each of its business units to be either number one or number two in the market in which it operated ("How Jack Welch Runs GE," 1998; Slater, 1998). GE developed a reputation for innovative management practices, so it is not surprising that the company turned to the use of a conflict management system. In the mid-1990s the company faced substantial litigation, principally because significant downsizing had led many laid-off employees to bring suit against the corporation. Fearing the "attendant costs, drain on management time, and unfavorable publicity" of these employee lawsuits, management adopted a four-step ADR process known as the "Dispute Resolution Procedure," or "DRP" (Nordstrom, 2004, p. 198).

Mandatory pre-dispute arbitration was the ultimate step in the DRP. In the period following implementation of the DRP, GE's litigation costs fell dramatically even though the coverage of the program was limited to exempt employees at a specific location (Nordstrom, 2004). GE management, impressed by the success of the DRP, decided to develop an authentic conflict management system, which it calls "Resolve." In 1998 management required all of its business units to adopt either the DRP or the new Resolve program. Some of GE's business units adopted the original version of the DRP, some adopted a revised version of the DRP that did not require mandatory arbitration, and most adopted the Resolve program.

Resolve has all the features of a CMS discussed earlier in this chapter. For example, it features multiple access points and multiple options, including both interest-based and rights-based options. Employees using the Resolve program can choose informal problem solving, mediation, or arbitration to resolve a dispute. The corporation also established an ombudsperson's office, but the ombudsperson is only empowered to assist employees with integrity-related concerns. In the rollout (or implementation) of the program, GE—as it always does in the rollout of a new program—developed an elaborate communications strategy designed to make all employees covered by Resolve fully aware of their rights and options under the program. Nordstrom summarizes the effectiveness of GE's DRP and Resolve programs as follows:

> The various ADR programs adopted by GE have proved to be effective in responding quickly to a broad range of labor and employment issues. They permit employees to give voice to their concerns early, before they grow in number and severity. They offer management relief from the cost and contentiousness of litigation. In the period between 1996 and 1999, GE . . . experienced a nineteen percent decline in labor and employment litigation, at a time when the general employment litigation trend was substantially upward. (Nordstrom, 2004, p. 204)

Conclusion: Assessing the Research on Managing Organizational Conflict

By the beginning of the 21st century, it was becoming increasingly evident that the use of ADR and conflict management systems was having a significant effect on the U.S. system of justice. The resolution of many types of disputes had shifted from public forums to private ones. Some observers claimed that this shift represented the de facto privatization of our system of justice. One index of this transformation is the declining use of trials to resolve disputes. Samborn (2002), for example, reported a significant decrease in federal trials over the period 1970–2001: 30 years ago 10% of the civil and criminal cases filed in federal courts were resolved after a jury or a bench trial; in 2001, although the number of federal cases had increased by nearly 150%, the proportion resolved by trial had declined to 2.2%. A major reason for the declining trend in the use of trials, Samborn noted, was the increasing reliance of the courts and the disputants on ADR.

To assess the research on managing organizational conflict, one must imagine a patchwork quilt in which many of the squares in the quilt are blank. As we have demonstrated in this chapter, choosing a theoretical framework for viewing conflict in organizations is neither easy nor obvious, and the choice of a conflict management strategy by an organization does not necessarily dictate the methods it uses to process disputes. We have learned why some organizations use ADR and some do not, and why some organizations have adopted a CMS and many have not (Lipsky et al., 2003; see also Colvin, 2004). But there is a relatively small number of empirical studies that assess either the effectiveness or the efficiency of an organization's choice of strategies and methods (the most recent review of these studies is Bingham, 2004). As a consequence, we cannot with certainty draw many conclusions about the ultimate utility of managing organizational conflict on the basis of research conducted to date. Our assessment of this research is further complicated by the variety of disciplinary perspectives and methodologies used by researchers to conduct their studies. Nonetheless, a rather substantial body of research on managing conflict within organizations has been published in recent years.

Three Categories of Research

The research on managing organizational conflict reviewed in this chapter can be grouped into three broad categories. In the first category are studies that examine *the effect of change external to the organization on conflict management within the organization*. Such studies might be termed "extra organizational" in their level of analysis. In this category, we include scholarship dealing with changes in statutes, court decisions, and other shifts in the legal system that have affected conflict resolution within organizations. We also include research that evaluates experiments and pilot programs instigated by public agencies. In the second category are studies that use the organization itself as the unit of analysis and examine *the influence of organizational variables on conflict management*. Such studies might be termed "macro organizational" in their level of analysis. We

Table 13.3   Three Types of Research on Managing Organizational Conflict

Level of Analysis	Unit of Analysis	Purpose	Methodology
Extra-organizational	Mediation, arbitration, and court cases; grievances and complaints; comparative public policies; comparative system performance; trends in court cases	To assess the effect of external or exogenous factors (statutes, court cases, policy changes, market factors, etc.) on conflict management; to compare outcomes across organizations and systems; to evaluate the efficiency and effectiveness of alternative methods of conflict resolution	Legal scholarship; statistical (including multivariate) analysis; historical analysis; comparative case studies
Macro-organizational	Organization; units within an organization; specific public policies; pilot programs and experiments	To assess the effect of organizational-level variables (management commitment, culture, cost, etc.) on conflict management within the organization; to assess the efficiency and effectiveness of alternative conflict management strategies	Case studies; statistical analysis; historical and ethnographic analyses
Micro-organizational	Mediation and arbitration cases; complaints and grievances; other disputes	To assess the effect of procedural and process variables on the outcomes of disputes; to evaluate the effectiveness of dispute resolution procedures and participant satisfaction with them	Statistical analysis, surveys of participants

include in this category case studies of conflict management in particular organizations, including those that deal with the development of conflict management strategies and systems as well as those that analyze the effectiveness or efficiency of conflict management within an organization. In the third category are studies that use individual disputes as the unit of analysis and attempt to analyze *the effects of using a particular dispute resolution technique on the outcome of the dispute*. Such studies might be termed "micro organizational" in their level of analysis. In this category we include studies that analyze "win rates" in arbitration cases, research on the effectiveness of mediation in settling disputes (such as Bingham's [2001] evaluation of transformative mediation in the USPS), and surveys of participants' satisfaction with particular dispute resolution techniques. These studies often draw implications from an analysis of the outcomes of disputes for the

management of organizational conflict. In Table 13.3, for each of the three categories of research we summarize the unit of analysis used, the purpose of the research, and the methodologies generally employed by researchers.

The Equity and Efficiency of Conflict Management Systems

Most researchers, regardless of the type of research they are conducting, are concerned with either the *equity* or *efficiency* of dispute resolution procedures and conflict management systems. By equity, we refer to studies that attempt to assess the fairness of procedures and systems, and the extent to which they provide adequate due process protections for the parties who use them. By efficiency, we refer to studies that attempt to assess the relationship between the outcomes produced by alternative approaches

Table 13.4   The Equity of Conflict Management Systems Within Organizations Compared to Litigation and Collective Bargaining

Measure	Hypothesized Effect	Confirmed
Access to system	Much easier than litigation; equal to collective bargaining	Yes
Satisfaction: Procedural	Higher than litigation; equal to collective bargaining	Yes
Satisfaction: Outcome	At least equal to both alternatives	No
Due process standards	Lower than both alternatives	No
Impartiality of neutrals	Equal to both alternatives	No
Costs	Higher than collective bargaining; lower than litigation	No

SOURCE: Adapted from Lipsky, Seeber, and Fincher, 2003.

Table 13.5   The Efficiency of Conflict Management Systems Within Organizations Compared to Litigation and Collective Bargaining

Measure	Hypothesized Effect	Confirmed
Time from complaint to resolution	Quicker than litigation; equal to collective bargaining	Yes
Amount of awards or settlements	Equal to both alternatives	No
Costs to disputants of procedures	Lower than both alternatives	No
Costs to employers of maintenance: operation, training, neutrals	Higher than both alternatives	No
Avoidance of adversarial proceedings	Higher than both alternatives	No
Usage rates	Higher than litigation; equal to collective bargaining	No

SOURCE: Adapted from Lipsky, Seeber, and Fincher, 2003.

to managing conflict and the time, money, and other resources invested by participants in achieving those outcomes. Cost-benefit analysis is one methodology for assessing efficiency but there are others.

In Tables 13.4 and 13.5, we present hypotheses regarding the equity and efficiency effects of using conflict management systems compared to the alternatives of using either collective bargaining or litigation to resolve employment disputes (these tables are adaptations of tables used in Lipsky et al., 2003). In these exhibits, we focus on the hypothetical effects of systems,

rather than the ad hoc use of ADR procedures or processes, and the hypotheses are most suitable to the macro-organizational evaluation of a CMS in a single organization, rather than the analysis of conflict management at either an extra-organizational or micro-organizational level. The hypotheses in the two tables are based on our understanding of both the conceptual and empirical research reviewed in this chapter.

In Table 13.4, the measures of equity represent some (but certainly not all) of the features of a CMS that are generally considered to be critical dimensions of a fair system. By definition, a CMS is designed to provide ease of access for employees. Although there are no contrafactual experiments that actually test this hypothesis, by all accounts conflict management systems are easier to access than either public forums or collective bargaining procedures. Almost all of the evaluation studies show that participant satisfaction with conflict management systems is significantly higher than the participants' satisfaction with litigation (Bingham, 2001; McDermott et al., 2000). Most scholars and practitioners have also claimed that participant satisfaction with the outcomes produced by systems should not be significantly different from (and might even be higher than) the disputants' satisfaction with the outcomes produced by either collective bargaining or litigation (Bingham, 2004). There has not been sufficient research to date that either confirms or refutes such claims.

Are the due process standards in conflict management systems lower than the due process standards ordinarily found in collective bargaining and in the courts? Most observers seem to think so, and there are certainly court cases suggesting that standards in systems are lower. But there is very little systematic evidence on whether due process standards in general are higher or lower than they are in the two alternative forums. Similarly, advocates of systems assert that the arbitrators, mediators, and other neutrals used in these systems are no more or less impartial than neutrals used in collective bargaining or judges who hear court cases. Again, however, systematic evidence on this hypothesis is lacking. Lastly, the costs of using a system, for both employers and employees, are assumed to be higher than the costs of using collective bargaining but lower than the costs of litigation.[13] Again, however, there is only fragmentary evidence on these hypotheses.

In Table 13.5, we show some of the key measures needed to judge the efficiency of a CMS along with the hypothesized effects of using a CMS on each of the measures. Virtually all scholars and practitioners believe that using a CMS, compared to using either litigation or collective bargaining, should reduce the time that elapses between the filing of a complaint and its resolution. Hypothetically, processing complaints under collective bargaining should not be

more time-consuming than doing so in a CMS, but over time the growing legalism of collective bargaining has lengthened the time needed to resolve complaints. Also, in theory the method used to settle or resolve a dispute should not influence the monetary award or settlement reached in the dispute, but again systematic evidence on this hypothesis is missing (but see, e.g., Eisenberg & Hill, 2003; Hill, 2003).

A major motivation, discussed in this chapter, for adopting a CMS is the belief that *using* a system will be much less costly than resolving disputes through collective bargaining or by litigation. On the other hand, the costs to an employer of *maintaining* a system can be significantly higher than the costs to the employer of "maintaining" either collective bargaining or the court system. Once again, however, hard evidence on the costs associated with either the use or the maintenance of a system is virtually absent. One of the bedrock principles of every CMS is the desire to deal with conflict at the earliest possible stage, preferably before mere disagreements become formal disputes. Many organizations, however, fear that if they establish a CMS they will promote the filing of complaints by their employees. Most of the managers and attorneys we interviewed told us that the introduction of a CMS in their organization did not result in higher levels of complaints and disputes. The evidence on this hypothesis is not yet strong enough to allow us to say that it has either been confirmed or denied.

Strengths of Existing Research on the Management of Organizational Conflict

In the realm of *extra-organizational* research, legal scholars have been extraordinarily helpful in clarifying murky areas of law and policy. Whether ADR is or is not a viable alternative to litigation has been debated vigorously in law reviews (see, e.g., Stone, 1996). In employment relations, the question of whether the Federal Arbitration Act of 1925 (Federal Arbitration Act, 1994) covered employment contracts requiring the use of arbitration was also heatedly debated by legal scholars. But these scholarly debates were effectively terminated by the U.S. Supreme Court's seminal decision in *Circuit City Stores, Inc. v. Saint Clair Adams*

(2001), in which the Court ruled that employment contracts were covered by the 1925 statute. Now the ground has shifted to the question of the adequacy of due process protections in employment dispute procedures (Bingham, 2004; Stone, 2004).

At the *macro-organizational* level, research has shed considerable light on the environmental and organizational variables that lead organizations to adopt ADR procedures and conflict management systems. We know some of the fundamental correlates of organizational choice: for example, large organizations operating in global markets are more likely to have a CMS than small organizations operating in wholly domestic markets. Establishing a system also requires a high level of management commitment and a supportive organizational culture (Lipsky et al., 2003). Moreover, systems are seldom established unless the organization has faced a crisis (or, as we call it elsewhere, a "precipitating event"; Lipsky et al., 2003). We have learned much about management decision making in this arena, usually by researchers conducting case studies and interviewing managers and attorneys and from practitioners who publish accounts of their organization's experiences.

At the *micro-organizational* level, researchers have made considerable progress in assessing how particular procedures and processes affect the outcomes of disputes. For example, we have learned that the effectiveness of a given procedure (e.g., mediation) depends upon the timing of the intervention by the third party, the degree of voluntarism permitted by the procedure, and the precise approach the third party takes to resolving the dispute (see, e.g., Bingham, 2004). The use of descriptive statistics and univariate analysis has been sufficient to teach us useful lessons about matters such as mediation settlement rates in various settings and the satisfaction of the disputants with such processes.

Weaknesses of Existing Research on the Management of Organizational Conflict

Lack of data. As an emerging area of study, it is not surprising that there are significant weaknesses in the research conducted to date. One of

the principal handicaps scholars have faced is the lack of accessible data. No government agency collects data on employment mediation and arbitration cases, for example. We have asked corporations about the availability of data on their conflict management systems, but we have been unsuccessful in obtaining such data. Most corporations consider the data to be proprietary, partly because of the confidentiality requirements in dispute resolution systems and more generally because of the sensitive nature of the issues handled in these systems. We have also discovered that many corporations simply do not have the kind of data a researcher would find useful. Some researchers have gained access to data maintained by a public agency about its own program (e.g., the EEOC's mediation program) or by organizations that administer arbitration and mediation cases (e.g., AAA and National Association of Securities Dealers—NASD), but the availability of secondary data is very limited. Some researchers have relied on primary data, devising their own survey instruments and administering such instruments to participants in dispute resolution programs. Collecting primary data can be expensive, of course, and most government agencies and foundations have not been willing to support such endeavors.

Lack of rigorous methodologies. The legal scholarship on employment dispute resolution has been highly sophisticated, but social scientists have lagged behind the legal scholars. There are very few studies on employment dispute resolution that use sophisticated social science methodologies: a well-developed model based on sound theory, clearly defined hypotheses, and multivariate statistical analysis. Some of the research we have summarized by Bingham (1995, 1997, 2001), Eisenberg and Hill (2003), Hill (2003), Lewin (1987), and others is the exception to this general proposition. The lack of data, of course, constrains researchers in the use of rigorous methodologies, which is not unusual in an emerging field of study. Nevertheless, in the future researchers will have to do a much better job of applying standard social science methodologies to the study of conflict management and dispute resolution.

Weaknesses at the extra-organizational level. Our review of the literature should make it apparent that there is much useful research that might be undertaken. Very few of the hypotheses described in Tables 13.4 and 13.5, for example, have been tested adequately. Although we know that most organizations in the United States now rely heavily on ADR and a growing number are using conflict management systems, we have very little systematic evidence on the factors that have led so many organizations to move in this direction. We have written that a "tipping point" was reached in the use of ADR in employment relations at some point in the past decade or so (Lipsky et al., 2003). Gladwell (2002) described the factors that bring about a tipping point in the spread of social innovations, but scholars have only a partial understanding of the factors that brought about the diffusion of ADR over the past 25 years. In the absence of a full understanding, no one can safely predict whether ADR and the transformation of conflict management described here will become institutionalized in most organizations or will simply be another passing fad, tossed into the management dustbin that also contains quality circles, reengineering, and other voguish programs.

Accordingly, we need additional studies that examine carefully how and why organizations make strategic choices in managing conflict. Case studies of management decision making have been useful, but more rigorous studies using empirical data are required. Given the newness of conflict management systems, studying the factors motivating managers to establish them is a timely topic. We only hope the window of opportunity will not soon close, preventing researchers from capturing perishable information on the factors motivating managers to adopt systems.

The conventional wisdom suggests that two of the important factors motivating organizations to adopt ADR and conflict management systems are (a) the so-called litigation explosion, which led to higher costs and longer delays in the court system; and (b) the lower cost and greater speed associated with using a CMS and various ADR techniques. Surprisingly there is very little hard evidence on either factor. On the one hand, survey data have shown that most people believe litigation has become costlier and more time-consuming. In our survey of the *Fortune* 1000, about 80% of the respondents said his or her company used mediation because it saved time and money (Lipsky & Seeber, 1998). These findings, however, represent only the respondents' perceptions. On the other hand, on the basis of a rigorous study of federal litigation, Dunworth and Rogers (1996) concluded that the litigation explosion is largely a myth. Is it possible that the ADR movement has been based on faulty perceptions and a mythical phenomenon? Although research shows that most managers and attorneys believe that using mediation, arbitration, and other ADR techniques is cheaper and less time-consuming than relying on litigation, there are very few rigorous, controlled studies that confirm this belief. Only careful research can determine whether commonly held perceptions are confirmed by hard realities.

Weaknesses at the macro-organizational level. Another critical need is for research on the costs and benefits of conflict management systems. It has been very difficult for researchers to undertake cost-benefit analyses of systems primarily because the establishment of these systems has occurred so recently. The most effective means of conducting a cost-benefit analysis of a system is for a researcher to gain access to an organization when it is designing and implementing such a system. Under ideal circumstances, the researcher can collaborate with the parties during the design phase to set up a system for collecting data that will be useful in conducting a rigorous evaluation. Another difficulty in conducting cost-benefit analyses is the fact there are no accepted standards for the measurement of the benefits of alternative methods of managing organizational conflict. Many organizations do an adequate job of tracking the costs of conflict resolution methods, but have not developed a methodology for tracking benefits. Benefits are difficult to track in part because to a significant degree they are not financial in nature or easily quantifiable. Also, the benefits of managing organizational conflict clearly depend on the goals and strategies of the organization, and since there is considerable variation in these goals and strategies across organizations, it is difficult to devise a standard set of metrics to measure benefits.

Experts agree that there is a close correspondence between the successful adoption of a conflict management system and a supportive organizational culture. Earlier we noted the significance the SPIDR committee attached to a "conflict competent culture," a belief confirmed by our own research on the use of workplace systems by U.S. corporations (Gosline et al., 2001, p. 10; Lipsky et al., 2003). Researchers, however, have not yet explored systematically the precise nature of the relationship between culture and conflict management systems. For example, we do not yet know with certainty which factor is the cause and which is the effect. Case studies illustrate that the successful use of a CMS invariably is associated with significant cultural change within the organization. But we do not know whether changing the culture of the organization is a prerequisite for establishing a CMS or, inversely, whether establishing a successful CMS is feasible even when the organization does not have a supportive culture. A CMS, with appropriate incentives, may be capable of changing the behavior of the members of an organization, and behavioral change may lead to cultural change. Some social scientists believe that changing behavior ultimately brings about a change in attitudes, but others believe that changing attitudes is necessary to bring about a change in behavior. Understanding the relationship between a CMS and culture represents another version of this time-honored debate.

Weaknesses at the micro-organizational level. An additional weakness lies in the overreliance in micro-organizational research on settlement rates and win-loss rates for assessing the effectiveness of particular dispute resolution procedures. The success of mediation cannot always be measured by whether a settlement has or has not been achieved, and the success of arbitration cannot be measured by which party has won or lost the case. These types of measures are often useful, but their limitations need to be recognized. Researchers need to develop a more holistic framework for analyzing ADR outcomes, and they need more rigorous multivariate models that include extra-organizational (or exogenous) variables, macro-organizational (or endogenous) variables, and micro-organizational (or procedural) variables as independent variables that are likely to explain outcomes.

Finally, in the micro-organizational realm very little is known about the effects of dispute resolution procedures on the perceptions and behaviors of employees and supervisors. As we have noted, some studies show that employees and other participants have had favorable perceptions about particular ADR programs. Nevertheless, much more work is needed to understand the relationship between the particular characteristics of a dispute resolution program (e.g., its due process protections) and the attitudes of employees and supervisors. Also, we know almost nothing about the long-term effects of dispute resolution programs on employee and supervisor attitudes. After the novelty of the program has faded, are employees and supervisors still satisfied with its operation? Or do they become alienated or cynical about the operation of the program? We need to understand not only the factors that bring about the institutionalization of a conflict management program but also the factors that keep the program vibrant and effective.

Is There a Need for a New Research Paradigm?

Thomas Kuhn argued that in any era there was a dominant paradigm that guided the research in a given field. He maintained that "normal science" is devoted to explaining phenomena in a given field on the basis of the dominant paradigm. Over time, however, normal science uncovers "anomalies" that subvert the existing paradigm. When enough anomalies have accumulated, it becomes clear to researchers that the dominant paradigm is obsolete. Eventually, an alternative paradigm emerges that does a better job of explaining the phenomena of interest, including the existing anomalies. The replacement of one research paradigm by another, Kuhn (1962) asserted, was a "scientific revolution."

We have argued here that there has been a transformation in the management of organizational conflict over the past quarter century—that is, a paradigm shift in the practice of conflict management. But there has not been a paradigm shift in the framework guiding research on this topic. Researchers have relied on the dominant paradigm in their discipline to guide their research. Increasingly, however, researchers on conflict management have uncovered anomalies that cannot be explained adequately by their disciplinary paradigm. Ironically, perhaps, the use of a new paradigm for practice has not been followed by the use of a new paradigm for research. We cannot predict if or when a new research paradigm will emerge. We merely want to point out, in closing, that the preconditions specified by Kuhn for the emergence of a new research paradigm have been met by the research on managing organizational conflict summarized in this chapter.

NOTES

1. PL 101-552, as amended by PL 102-354. The statute expired on October 1, 1995, but a successor statute was signed into law on October 19, 1996, PL 104-320 (Dunlop & Zack, 1997, pp. 119–121).

2. We have worked with the U.S. Department of Labor, U.S. Department of the Interior, and the Equal Employment Opportunity Commission in the development of their ADR programs.

3. A team of Cornell University faculty assisted the New York State Office of Court Administration and 14 unions representing court employees in developing a conflict management system during the period 1999–2003. The project was funded by an appropriation from the New York State Legislature.

4. Section 301 of the Taft-Hartley Act, 73 Stat. 519. Another possibility is for the parties to use some form of collective action, such as a strike or lockout, to resolve an unsettled grievance. In Europe, work stoppages resulting from unsettled grievances were a common occurrence throughout most of the post–World War II period, but in the United States, unions and employers incorporated no strike/no lockout clauses in their collective bargaining agreements as a necessary complement to their grievance and arbitration provisions (Ruben, 2003, pp. 8–11).

5. *Gilmer v. Interstate/Johnson Lane Corp.* 500 U.S. 20 (1991); *Circuit City Stores v. Saint Clair Adams.* 121 S.Ct. 1302 (2001).

6. The SPIDR committee was co-chaired by Ann Gosline and Lamont Stallworth. The senior author of this chapter was a member of the 11-person committee. Shortly after the completion of the committee's report, SPIDR merged with the Academy of Family Mediators and CRENet (Conflict Resolution Education Network) to become the Association for Conflict Resolution (ACR). The committee's report, therefore, is frequently referred to as the "ACR Report."

7. Not all organizations, of course, have the human and financial resources necessary to deal with all of these employee problems and complaints. It has been argued that only the very largest organizations (e.g., *Fortune* 1000 corporations) can afford to maintain an ICMS. Members of the SPIDR committee vigorously debated the committee's recommendation on scope. A minority believed "the broadest feasible scope" was an impractical recommendation for most organizations. For a discussion of these issues, see Lipsky et al., 2003, pp. 155–161.

8. Ury et al. define interests as "needs, desires, concerns, fears—the things one cares about or wants. They underlie people's positions—the tangible items they *say* they want" (Ury et al., 1993, p. 5). This definition is drawn from Fisher and Ury (1991), particularly pp. 40–55. It is worth noting that the distinction between interest-based methods and rights-based methods does not necessarily correspond to the distinction between disputes over interests and disputes over rights. For example, an interest-based method such as mediation can be used to resolve a dispute over rights, such as a grievance. By the same token, a rights-based method such as arbitration can be used to resolve a dispute over interests, such as an impasse in the negotiation of a new collective bargaining agreement.

9. A resolution facilitator is an employee who is specially trained to give advice and guidance to employees with complaints that do not involve a statutory claim. In other words, a resolution facilitator is essentially a peer who serves as a coach for employees with complaints.

10. The task force consisted of representatives from the American Bar Association, the American Arbitration Association, the National Academy of Arbitrators, the Society of Professionals in Dispute Resolution, the Federal Mediation and Conciliation Service, the National Employment Lawyers' Association, and the American Civil Liberties Union. For the text of the Due Process Protocol, see Dunlop and Zack, 1997, pp. 171-178; see also Dunlop and Zack, pp. 93–118. The work of the task force was motivated in large part by the Supreme Court's landmark *Gilmer* decision.

11. A score of books and articles has discussed the pros and cons of mandatory pre-dispute arbitration

(sometimes called compulsory arbitration). For a thorough treatment of the subject, see Bales, 1997.

12. The claim has been made in private conversations the authors have had with Arnold Zack.

13. The costs to employers and employees of using a system should be higher than the costs of using collective bargaining processes because the costs of processing a single dispute in a unionized organization are spread over all the members of the international union. Although the average cost to an international union of handling disputes may be high, the marginal cost of handling a single dispute in one organization is virtually zero. Both the employer and the employees in a single organization benefit from the absorption of the costs of dispute handling by an external organization. In effect, an international union provides so-called public goods that benefit all employees represented by the union. But public goods create a classic "free-rider" problem. The mismatch between the collective interests of all the union members and the interests of a single member (or the member's employer) allow individuals to take advantage of services that appear to be costless to them but in fact are significant for the external organization. See especially Olson 1965; see also Hardin, 1982.

REFERENCES

Aldag, R. J., & Kuzuhara, L. W. (2002). *Organizational behavior and management: An integrated skills approach*. Cincinnati, OH: South-Western Thomson Learning.

American Arbitration Association. (2003). *Disputewise management: Improving economic and noneconomic outcomes in managing business conflicts*. New York: American Arbitration. Available online at http://www.businessweek.com/1998/23/b3581001.htm

Bales, R. A. (1997). *Compulsory arbitration: The grand experiment in employment*. Ithaca, NY: Cornell University Press.

Batt, R., Colvin, J. S., & Keefe, J. (2002). Employee voice, human resource practices, and quit rates: Evidence from the telecommunications industry. *Industrial and Labor Relations Review, 55,* 573–594.

Bedman, W. (2004). Alternative dispute resolution: The Halliburton experience. In S. Estreicher & D. Sherwyn (Eds.), *Alternative dispute resolution in the employment arena: Proceedings of the New York University 53rd Annual Conference on Law* (pp. 155–169). New York: Kluwer Law International.

Bertalanffy, L. (1951). General system theory: A new approach to the unity of science. *Human Biology, 23,* 301–361.

Bingham, L. B. (1995). Is there a bias in arbitration of nonunion employment disputes? An analysis of actual cases and outcomes. *International Journal of Conflict Management, 6*(4), 369–386.

Bingham, L. B. (1997). Employment arbitration: The repeat player effect. *Employee Rights and Employment Policy Journal, 1*(1), 189–220.

Bingham, L. B. (2001). Mediating employment disputes: Perceptions of redress at the United States Postal Service. *Review of Public Personnel Administration, 17,* 20–30.

Bingham, L. B. (2004). Employment dispute resolution: The case for mediation. *Conflict Resolution Quarterly, 22,* 145–174.

Bingham, L. B., Kim, K., Moon, Y., Nabatchi, T., Napoli, L. M., Novac, M. C., & Raines, S. S. (2001). *Mediation at work: The report of the National REDRESS Evaluation Project of the United States Postal Service*. Bloomington: Indiana Conflict Resolution Institute.

Boulding, K. E. (1956). General systems—The skeleton of science. *Management Science, 2,* 197–208.

Brett, J. M. (1984). Managing organizational conflict. *Professional Psychology: Research and Practice, 15*(5), 664–678.

Brown, L. D. (1983). *Managing conflict at organizational interfaces*. Reading, MA: Addison-Wesley.

Bush, R. A. B., & Folger, J. P. (1994). *The promise of mediation: Responding to conflict through empowerment and recognition*. San Francisco: Jossey-Bass.

Circuit City Stores, Inc. v. Saint Clair Adams (2001). 121 S.Ct. 1302.

Clark, E. (2004). The Citigroup corporate and investment bank's dispute resolution procedure. In S. Estreicher & D. Sherwyn (Eds.), *Alternative dispute resolution in the employment arena: Proceedings of the New York University 53rd Annual Conference on Law* (pp. 185–196). New York: Kluwer Law International.

Cohen, C. F., & Domagalski, T. (1998). The effects of mandatory arbitration of employment discrimination claims: Perceptions of justice and suggestions for change. *Employee Responsibilities and Rights Journal, 11*(1), 27–40.

Colvin, A. J. (1999). *Citizens and citadels: Dispute resolution and the governance of employment relations.* Unpublished doctoral dissertation, Cornell University.

Colvin, A. J. S. (2003). Institutional pressures, human resource strategies, and the rise of nonunion dispute resolution procedures. *Industrial and Labor Relations Review, 56,* 375–391.

Colvin, A. J. S. (2004). The relationship between employment arbitration and workplace dispute resolution procedures. In S. Estreicher & D. Sherwyn (Eds.), *Alternative dispute resolution in the employment arena: Proceedings of the New York University 53rd Annual Conference on Law* (pp. 587–615). New York: Kluwer Law International.

Costantino, C. A., & Merchant, C. S. (1996). *Designing conflict management systems.* San Francisco: Jossey-Bass.

Deloitte Touche Tohmatsu International. (1993). *DeLoitte and Touche Litigation Services 1993 Survey of General and Outside Counsels: Alternative dispute resolution (ADR).* Chicago: Deloitte Touche Tohmatsu International.

Derr, C. B. (1978). Managing organizational conflict: Collaboration, bargaining, and power approaches. *California Management Review, 21*(2), 76–83.

Dixit, A. K., & Nalebuff, B. J. (1991). *Thinking strategically: The competitive edge in business, policies, and everyday life.* New York: W. W. Norton.

Doherty, N. A. (2000). *Integrated risk management: Techniques and strategies for managing corporate risk.* New York: McGraw-Hill.

Dunlop, J. T. (1958). *Industrial relations systems.* New York: Holt.

Dunlop, J. T., & Zack, A. M. (1997). *Mediation and arbitration of employment disputes.* San Francisco: Jossey-Bass.

Dunworth, T., & Rogers, J. (1996). Corporations in court: Big business litigation in U.S. federal courts, 1971–1991. *Law and Social Inquiry, 21,* 497–592.

Eisenberg, T., & Hill, E. (2003). *Employment arbitration and litigation: An empirical comparison* (New York University School of Law, Public Law and Legal Theory Research Paper Series No. 65). Retrieved April 29, 2004, from http://ssrn.com/abstract

Eisenhardt, K. M., & Zbaracki, M. J. (1992). Strategic decision making. *Strategic Management Journal, 13,* 17–37.

Fairhurst, G. T., Green, S. G., & Snavely, B. (1984). Face support in controlling poor performance. *Human Communication Research, 11,* 272–295.

Federal Arbitration Act. (1994 and Supp. 2000). 9 U.S.C. Sec. 1.

Fisher, R., & Ury, W. (1991). *Getting to yes: Negotiating agreement without giving in.* New York: Penguin (2nd ed., with B. Patton, Ed.).

Ford, J. (2000). Workplace conflict: Facts and figures. *Mediate.com.* Retrieved November 29, 2001, from http://mediate.com/articles/Ford1.cfm

Foulkes, F. K. (1980). *Personnel policies in large nonunion companies.* Englewood Cliffs, NJ: Prentice Hall.

Gilmer v. Interstate/Johnson Lane Corp. (1991). 500 U.S. 20.

Gladwell, M. (2002). *The tipping point.* Boston: Little, Brown.

Gosline, A., Stallworth, L., Adams, M. C., Brand, N., Hallberlin, C. J., Houk, C. S., et al. (2001). *Designing integrated conflict management systems: Guidelines for practitioners and decision makers in organizations.* Ithaca, NY: Cornell University, Institute on Conflict Resolution.

Hammonds, K. H. (2001). *Michael Porter's big ideas.* Retrieved March 8, 2004, from the Fast Company Web site: http://www.fastcompany.com/online/44/porter.html

Hardin, R. (1982). *Collective action.* Baltimore: Johns Hopkins University Press.

Hastie, R., & Dawes, R. M. (2001). *Rational choice in an uncertain world: The psychology of judgment and decision making.* Thousand Oaks, CA: Sage.

Hellriegel, D., Slocum, J. W., & Woodman, R. W. (2003). *Organizational behavior* (10th ed.). Cincinnati, OH: South-Western Thomson Learning.

Hill, E. (2003). Due process at low cost: An empirical study of employment arbitration under the auspices of the American Arbitration Association. *Ohio State Journal on Dispute Resolution, 18,* 777–828.

Hooters of America, Inc. v. Annette R. Phillips. (1999). 173 F.3d 933.

How Jack Welch runs GE. (1998, June 8). *Business Week.* Retrieved May 8, 2004 from the *Business*

Week Web site: http://www.businessweek.com/ 1998/23/b3581001.htm

Jacoby, S. M. (1997). *Modern manors: Welfare capitalism since the New Deal.* Princeton, NJ: Princeton University Press

Kahneman, D., Slovic, P., & Tversky, A. (Eds.). (1982). *Judgment under uncertainty: Heuristics and biases.* Cambridge, UK: Cambridge University Press.

Kartman, M. G. (2004). Arbitration/peer review of statutory employment claims: The experience at Rockwell. In S. Estreicher & D. Sherwyn (Eds.), *Alternative dispute resolution in the employment arena: Proceedings of the New York University 53rd Annual Conference on Law* (pp. 227–232). New York: Kluwer Law International.

Katz, H. C., & Kochan, T. A. (2004). *An introduction to collective bargaining and industrial relations.* New York: McGraw-Hill Irwin.

Katz, H. C., & Lipsky, D. B. (1998). The collective bargaining system in the United States: The legacy and the lessons. In M. F. Neufeld & J. T. McKelvey (Eds.), *Industrial relations at the dawn of the new millennium* (pp. 145–161). Ithaca, NY: Cornell University, New York State School of Industrial and Labor Relations.

Khanna, T., & Palepu, K. (1999). Why focused strategies may be wrong for emerging markets. In *Harvard Business Review on corporate strategy* (pp. 147–170). Cambridge, MA: Harvard Business School Press.

Kheel, T. W. (1999). *The keys to conflict resolution: Proven methods of resolving disputes voluntarily.* New York: Four Walls Eight Windows.

Kochan, T., Katz, H. C., & McKersie, R. B. (1986). *The transformation of American industrial relations.* New York: Basic Books.

Kolb, D. M., & Putnam, L. L. (1992). Introduction: The dialectics of disputing. In D. M. Kolb & J. M. Bartunek (Eds.), *Hidden conflict in organizations: Uncovering behind-the-scenes disputes.* Newbury Park, CA: Sage.

Kuhn, T. S. (1962). *The structure of scientific revolutions.* Chicago: University of Chicago Press.

LeRoy, M., & Feuille, P. (2004). When is cost an unlawful barrier to alternative dispute resolution: The ever *green tree* of mandatory employment arbitration. In S. Estreicher & D. Sherwyn (Eds.), *Alternative dispute resolution in the employment arena: Proceedings of the New York University 53rd Annual Conference on Law*

(pp. 511–586). New York: Kluwer Law International.

Lewin, D. (1987). Dispute resolution in the nonunion firm: A theoretical and empirical analysis. *Journal of Conflict Resolution, 13*(3), 465–502.

Lipsky, D. B., & Seeber, R. L. (1998). *The appropriate resolution of corporate disputes: A report on the growing use of ADR by U.S. corporations.* Ithaca, NY: Cornell University, Institute on Conflict Resolution.

Lipsky, D. B., Seeber, R. L., & Fincher, R. D. (2003). *Emerging systems for managing workplace conflict: Lessons from American corporations for managers and dispute resolution professionals.* San Francisco: Jossey-Bass.

Lohse, D. (1998, December 11). Corporate focus: Uncertainty clouds Prudential's settlement process. *Wall Street Journal,* Section B, p. 4.

Malin, D. M. (2004). Johnson & Johnson's dispute resolution program: A new formula for achieving common ground. In S. Estreicher & D. Sherwyn (Eds.), *Alternative dispute resolution in the employment arena: Proceedings of the New York University 53rd Annual Conference on Law* (pp. 235–242). New York: Kluwer Law International.

Maltby, L. L. (2002). The myth of second class justice: Resolving employment disputes in arbitration. In N. Brand (Ed.), *How ADR works* (pp. 915–921). Washington, DC: BNA Books.

Marrison, C. (2002). *The fundamentals of risk management.* New York: McGraw-Hill.

McCabe, D. M. (1989). *Corporate nonunion complaint procedures and systems: A strategic human resources management analysis.* New York: Praeger.

McDermott, E. P., Obar, R., Jose, A., & Bowers, M. (2000). *An evaluation of the Equal Employment Opportunity Commission mediation program.* Retrieved December 20, 2002, from http://www .eeoc.gov/mediate/report/index/html

Mechanic, D. (1962). Sources of power of lower participants in complex organizations. *Administrative Science Quarterly, 7,* 349–364.

Millard, E. W. (2004). Credit Suisse First Boston employment dispute resolution program. In S. Estreicher & D. Sherwyn (Eds.), *Alternative dispute resolution in the employment arena: Proceedings of the New York University 53rd Annual Conference on Law* (pp. 181–183). New York: Kluwer Law International.

Mintzberg, H. (1994). *The rise and fall of strategic planning.* Englewood Cliffs, NJ: Prentice Hall.

Nordstrom, M. (2004). General Electric's experience with ADR. In S. Estreicher & D. Sherwyn (Eds.), *Alternative dispute resolution in the employment arena: Proceedings of the New York University 53rd Annual Conference on Law* (pp. 197–226). New York: Kluwer Law International.

Olson, M., Jr. (1965). *The logic of collective action.* Cambridge, MA: Harvard University Press.

Perdue, D. C. (2004). Employment dispute: Resolve it! Alcoa at the forefront of alternative dispute resolution. In S. Estreicher & D. Sherwyn (Eds.), *Alternative dispute resolution in the employment arena: Proceedings of the New York University 53rd Annual Conference on Law* (pp. 233–234). New York: Kluwer Law International.

Phillips, F. P. (2004). Employment dispute resolution systems: An empirical survey and tentative conclusions. In S. Estreicher & D. Sherwyn (Eds.), *Alternative dispute resolution in the employment arena: Proceedings of the New York University 53rd Annual conference on law* (pp. 245–256). New York: Kluwer Law International.

Pneuman, R. W., & Bruehl, M. E. (1982). *Managing conflict.* Englewood Cliffs, NJ: Prentice Hall.

Pondy, L. R. (1967). Organizational conflict: Concepts and models. *Administrative Science Quarterly, 17,* 296–320.

Porter, M. E. (1980). *Competitive strategy: Techniques for analyzing industries and competitors.* New York: Free Press.

Porter, M. E. (1985). *Competitive advantage: Creating and sustaining superior performance.* New York: Free Press.

Porter, M. E. (2002). Strategy and the Internet. *Harvard Business Review on advances in strategy* (pp. 1–50). Cambridge, MA: Harvard Business School Press.

Rahim, M. A. (1983). A measure of styles of handling interpersonal conflict. *Academy of Management Journal, 26,* 368–376.

Ruben, A. M. (Ed.). (2003). *Elkouri & Elkouri: How arbitration works* (6th ed.). Washington, DC: Bureau of National Affairs.

Samborn, H. V. (2002, October). The vanishing trial. *ABA Journal,* pp. 24–27.

Scism, L. (1998, March 3). Profit falls 43% amid $1.64 billion restitution charge. *Wall Street Journal,* Section A, p. 3.

Seeber, R. L., Schmidle, T. B., & Smith, R. S. (2001). *An evaluation of the New York State Workers' Compensation Pilot Program for Alternative Dispute Resolution.* Albany: New York State Workers' Compensation Board.

Senger, J. M. (2003). *Federal dispute resolution: Using ADR with the United States government.* San Francisco: Jossey-Bass.

Slaikeu, K. A., & Hasson, R. H. (1998). *Controlling the costs of conflict.* San Francisco: Jossey-Bass.

Slater, R. (1998). *Jack Welch and the GE way: Management insights and leadership secrets of the legendary CEO.* New York: McGraw-Hill.

Slichter, S. H., Healy, J. J., & Livernash, R. E. (1960). *The impact of collective bargaining on management.* Washington, DC: Brookings Institution.

Stitt, A. J. (1998). *Alternative dispute resolution: How to design a system for effective conflict resolution.* Toronto, Canada: Wiley.

Stone, K. V. W. (1996). Mandatory arbitration of individual employment rights: The yellow dog contract of the 1990s. *Denver University Law Review, 73,* 1017–1050.

Stone, K. V. W. (2004). Dispute resolution in the boundaryless workplace. In S. Estreicher & D. Sherwyn (Eds.), *Alternative dispute resolution in the employment arena: Proceedings of the New York University 53rd Annual Conference on Law* (pp. 653–679). New York: Kluwer Law International.

Taussig, E. (2004). Predispute arbitration agreements: The Philip Morris program. In S. Estreicher & D. Sherwyn (Eds.), *Alternative dispute resolution in the employment arena: Proceedings of the New York University 53rd Annual Conference on Law* (pp. 171–180). New York: Kluwer Law International.

Ulrich, D. (1997). *Human resource champions: The next agenda for adding value and delivering results.* Boston: Harvard Business School Press.

Ury, W. L., Brett, J. M., & Goldberg, S. B. (1993). *Getting disputes resolved: Designing systems to cut the costs of conflict.* Cambridge, MA: Harvard Law School, Program on Negotiation.

U.S. General Accounting Office. (1997). *Alternative dispute resolution: Employers' experiences with ADR in the workplace* (GAO/GGD-97-157). Washington, DC: Government Printing Office.

Westin, A. F., & Feliu, A. G. (1998). *Resolving employment disputes without litigation.* Washington, DC: Bureau of National Affairs.

PART III

COMMUNITY CONFLICT

Conflicts in the community have the potential to divide members, but also the potential to bring people closer so they can work together. In some situations, community conflict can do both—uniting people of a similar perspective in the face of a perceived common enemy. The consequences of community conflict appear to polarize individuals more than in the previous two contexts (interpersonal and organizational). One of the reasons is that conflict over resources and values typifies many community conflicts (see Chapter 15, Peterson & Franks, and Chapter 14, Littlejohn); these conflicts often result in "us-versus-them" scenarios because the parties involved perceive lack of intimacy (in the case of interpersonal conflict) or lack of coordinated activity (in the case of organizational conflict). Violence becomes more justifiable in the face of an other who is less than "us" (and perhaps less than human) and someone we are not dependent on. The dilemma, however, is that the "us" live and work near "them" and conflict communication becomes an everyday activity.

The authors in this part do not advocate trying to minimize or avoid conflict, because the underlying causes are deeply held and embedded in history. Rather, they emphasize the effective management of conflict, which may reduce the negative consequences and facilitate growth and opportunity from conflict. Littlejohn examines moral conflicts, which result from incommensurate assumptions. He encourages the use of dialogue as a form of transcending, rather than resolving, these differences. Peterson and Franks discuss the inevitability of environmental conflict and

in fact note that this conflict is beneficial for environmental policy. Their focus is on strategies and forums that will encourage public participation in the process, which they feel is key to managing these conflicts. Rogan and Hammer introduce crisis negotiation, particularly around hostage situations. In fact, this is one situation that community conflict researchers would like to eliminate because of the potential for death and injury. Rogan and Hammer describe the communication approaches for best negotiating these situations. Warfield illustrates the antecedents and consequences of racial/ethnic conflict in communities and describes approaches to addressing these situations when they arise. Kandath examines conflict in developing communities in India from a cultural studies perspective, which emphasizes that conflict is a normal facet of life and that effective conflict management will include various types of mediation. Finally, Barge addresses three important movements from managing community conflict in a manner that fosters democratic practice.

The concept of community has been defined in many ways and used in many contexts. Community can refer to a psychological sense of community (Glynn, 1981; Parker et al., 2001), an aggregate of physically co-located individuals (McLeroy, Bibeau, Steckler, & Glanz, 1988), individuals who share a pattern of interaction (Hunter, 1974), social capital and social networks (Kawachi, Kennedy, Lochner, & Prothrow-Stith, 1997), or a political entity (Long, 1986). The common definition is to consider individuals who live in a physical neighborhood as constituting a community. However, there are communities of people who interact only on the Internet (e.g., cancer support groups or hand-weavers' listservs). The chapters in this section focus predominantly on face-to-face interaction and emphasize the physical collocation aspect of community, while also including other components. Littlejohn considers community from the psychological sense since people with moral conflicts do not need to share the same physical space (e.g., the moral conflict can be played out in the media). Peterson and Franks consider individuals with a shared psychological sense of community, but include co-location because environmental conflicts are usually physically situated (e.g., around grazing rights in a particular setting). Rogan and Hammer discuss crisis negotiations that involve a physical location. Warfield emphasizes racial conflicts in neighborhoods within a city. Kandath focuses on co-located individuals, but emphasizes political entities. Finally, Barge notes dialogic tools that can be used for co-located and other types of community conflicts.

We organize this section by first considering five specific types of community conflict, including moral conflict, environmental conflict, crisis negotiation, racial/ethnic group conflict, and conflict in developing communities. We then conclude with the final chapter, which introduces three different types of conflict management techniques for addressing community conflict, but emphasizes dialogic perspectives.

In the first chapter, Littlejohn introduces the concept of moral conflict, which is a clash between groups or individuals based on incommensurate philosophical assumptions. Communication in such situations can be strident and destructive, but with conscious intent and a creative approach, civil, even productive, discourse can take place in the face of moral difference. Littlejohn reviews case studies and action research projects to provide insights into the nature of moral conflict and forms of discourse that can transcend it. He argues that dialogue, as a paradigm case of transcendent communication, affords the greatest potential for transforming destructive patterns of communication in complex and difficult conflict situations. Such communication creates new frames in which to understand difference, transforms relationships, and allows

parties to explore and reflect on the powers and limits of multiple worldviews. Dialogue can be created by careful attention to process, the creation of joining places, and shifting contexts of meaning.

In the second chapter, Peterson and Franks address public participation in environmental conflict. In many nations, legal requirements to include the public in environmental decision making render environmental conflict increasingly difficult to ignore. Yet, even when public participation is mandated, environmental conflicts continue to escalate. The authors provide an overview of legal requirements for public participation in environmental issues, emphasizing the influential National Environmental Policy Act of 1969 in the United States. Second, they review research on the social demand for public participation in environmental policy making, providing an overview of approaches that have gained significant public currency. They summarize critiques of the public hearing, which is the most commonly used method of public participation. The authors also provide a summary of more recently emerging research critiquing consensus-based processes. Finally, they discuss especially promising research on the topics of framing, critical/cultural studies, and systems thinking and include suggestions for how this research might impact practice.

In the third chapter, Rogan and Hammer introduce crisis negotiation as a unique context for community conflict; one in which knowledge about the communicative dynamics of conflict are highlighted by the potential for injury or death of the parties involved. Over the years, crisis negotiation has grown into a field of practice and inquiry for practitioners and scholars alike, with a sizable body of accompanying literature. The authors organize and summarize the publications that comprise the essential domains of knowledge for this context of conflict communication. The chapter is framed around the core publications that inform the field, including practitioner how-to guides, surveys, and concluding with publications of original communication-based research. The latter type of publication is the principal focus of this chapter as the authors provide in-depth reviews of the research programs of a handful of communication scholars in terms of how their work has shaped contemporary theory, research, and practice of crisis negotiation.

In the fourth chapter, Warfield addresses community conflict around racial and ethnic issues. Due in large part to heightened patterns of social stratification and a rise in ethnic identity in the post–Cold War era, the author examines community conflicts driven by friction between local law enforcement and minority groups, racial hate incidents, and intercommunal ethnic conflicts occurring in the United States and selected international venues. Of particular interest are various approaches taken by internal and external so-called third parties to manage or mitigate these conflicts, the kinds of outcomes resulting from these interventions, and how these outcomes lend themselves to community building. Based on these observations, the author comments on the status of theory and research in community conflicts and what gaps need to be filled.

In the fifth chapter, Kandath discusses community conflict in developing communities from a cultural studies perspective. He explains that conflict is a defining feature of all social systems and that conflict involves threat to identities. He defines culture as the site of conflict, over meaning making in a complex and constantly changing sign system and over various interests—material, social, economic, and political. Kandath argues that focusing on India provides the opportunity to understand conflict from the vantage point of community ties, incorporating the perspectives of nondominant groups. He examines several types of community-related conflicts in India, including border disputes, ethnic conflicts, environmental conflict, and relational and family conflict. He discusses the cultural perspective of mediation in India as a tool to manage these various types of conflicts. The chapter ends with a discussion of future directions and practical applications.

In the final chapter, Barge continues the discussion on dialogue introduced by several other authors (e.g., Littlejohn), but expands it by emphasizing how dialogue represents an important form of communication that allows community members to work through important conflicts and foster democratic practice. He summarizes the relationships among dialogue, conflict, and democratic practice within community settings and highlights three important movements that take these sets of interrelationships seriously: (a) community mediation, (b) public participation and dialogue, and (c) appreciative inquiry. In this sense, this chapter provides "best practices" for managing community conflict. The tensions of inclusion-exclusion, deliberative-relational, and macro-micro practices represent dilemmas in dialogical democratic practice that merit future theorizing and research. Practitioners are encouraged to articulate their sensibility for dialogical practice as both a means to make wise choices that manage these tensions in specific situations and to ensure coherence within their practice.

REFERENCES

Glynn, T. J. (1981). Psychological sense of community: Measurement and application. *Human Relations, 34,* 789–818.

Hunter, A. (1974). *Symbolic communities: The persistence and change of Chicago's local communities.* Chicago: University of Chicago Press.

Kawachi, I., Kennedy, B. P., Lochner, K., & Prothrow-Stith, D. (1997). Social capital, income inequality, and mortality. *American Journal of Public Health, 87,* 1491–1498.

Long, N. E. (1986). The city as a political community. *Journal of Community Psychology, 14,* 72–80.

McLeroy, K. R., Bibeau, D., Steckler, A., & Glanz, K. (1988). An ecological perspective on health promotion programs. *Health Education Quarterly, 15,* 351–377.

Parker, E., Lichtenstein, R. L., Schulz, A. J., Israel, B. A., Schork, M. A., Steinman, K. J., & James, S. A. (2001). Disentangling measures of individual perceptions of community social dynamics: Results of a community survey. *Health Education and Behavior, 28,* 462–486.

14

MORAL CONFLICT

STEPHEN W. LITTLEJOHN
Domenici Littlejohn, Inc.

On every occasion over the past 20 years that my fingers have met the keyboard on the subject of this chapter, some persistent moral clash has been in the news. Right now, the validity and morality of same-sex marriage is making headlines. This controversy joins many others such as abortion, women's rights, environmental protection, gun control, and war as vital issues that are seemingly impossible to manage. Resolutions to such conflicts are temporary at best, as moral issues keep cycling back in various forms.

Moral conflict is a clash between opposing parties based on differences in deeply held philosophical assumptions about being, knowledge, and the world. The existence of moral difference is neither surprising nor problematic in itself, but how we respond to such clash can create disturbing conditions that warrant careful attention, creative intervention, and scholarly study. Moral conflict, although a compelling challenge in society, opens rich opportunities for interpersonal learning, improved relationships, and creative collaboration.

My task in this chapter is to summarize the literature on moral conflict and suggest possibilities for transcending these types of conflicts. I address this purpose through the following sections: (a) description of the problem of moral conflict; (b) review of transcendent communication,

including theoretical foundations and three discourses of conflict; (c) discussion of dialogue as transcendent communication, including practical guidelines; and (d) summary of challenges and future directions.

MORAL DIFFERENCE AND MORAL CONFLICT

Personal action is always embedded within a moral order, or set of assumptions about what is real, how we know reality, and what is right. The moral order is a set of ideas on which we rely (Wong, 1984). As such, it is a kind of common sense (Lakoff, 1996; Wentworth, 1989), a tradition of thought (Stout, 1988), or a grammar of rules (Wittgenstein, 1972). Largely cultural, the moral order is infused with symbols and ways of seeing the world (Carbaugh, 1985; Pearce & Littlejohn, 1997). The moral order is a kind of knowledge base, or epistemic field, complete with a system for judging the truth of claims (Willard, 1996).

The Basis of Moral Difference

The observation that human communities differ in how they see the world is a truism bordering on the trite, but the consequence of this state of affairs can be profound when moral orders come to clash. Pro-life and pro-choice forces may disagree on whether abortion should be legal, but their respective positions on this issue rest on very different moral orders. Thus, arguing abortion is useless when the two sides share no common way of resolving the issue. Herein lies the essential problem of moral conflict: The parties have *incommensurate* moral orders.

I take the term *incommensurate* from Thomas Kuhn (1970), who applied the term to competing scientific paradigms, the logics of which cannot be mapped onto each other. The vocabulary, categories, and logical relations of one paradigm do not permit straight-across translation to those of the other. The two systems of thought cannot be compared point by point. Richard Bernstein (1985) applied the term to philosophy and social theory, noting that incommensurate systems can be compared, but only by moving to larger, transcendent categories that require understanding each moral order on a deeper level.

For example, most divorces are strictly interest based. In other words, the husband and wife differ on custody, real estate, money, personal property, and so forth. In such cases, you can actually compare the demands and interests of the parties right down the line, issue by issue. In contrast to this typical case, my colleagues and I once conducted a case study of a divorce mediation in which the parties had deep moral differences (Littlejohn, Shailor, & Pearce, 1994). The wife was arguing from a basis of personal empowerment and choice, while the husband was arguing from conservative family values. We could make sense of the difference only by creating new categories that enabled us to compare moral orders. I will say more about this fascinating case later in the chapter.

There seems to be a reflexive relationship between culture and moral order, though neither can be reduced to the other. Because cultures are determined in part by underlying belief systems, moral differences among cultures are often salient and can lead to conflict. Where cultural groups—ethnic or otherwise—clash, moral differences may be part of the problem. When the moral orders of various cultures are incommensurate, moral conflict can result. Some groups, for example, understand honor as prevailing in physical confrontation, where speech has little place (e.g., Philipsen, 1975), while other groups find honor in resolving disputes through collaboration and talk. Shailor (1988), for example, found significant differences in cultural ways of managing conflict in a survey of some 15 cultural groups worldwide. Foeman and Pressley (1987) offered an example: "In addition to the perceived chasm between white and black Americans, a real gap exists between their divergent perspectives regarding the nature of the world and the ways of surviving in it" (p. 295). Hispanic-Anglo differences provide another example, as Hispanics tend to be oriented more to relationships and communities, while Anglos tend to be more task oriented and to emphasize independence (Triandis & Albert, 1987).

Characteristics of Moral Conflict

My colleagues and I were not the first to discover moral conflict and, indeed, we join a large group of concerned scholars and practitioners. Hunter (1991) referred to such conflicts as *culture wars,* or "political and social hostility rooted in different systems of moral understanding" (p. 42). Docherty (2001) showed that such conflicts arise not merely from different views on materiality and social life, but from our deepest symbols and meanings.

When moral orders come to open clash, several things are likely to happen (Pearce & Littlejohn, 1997). The language of the two sides will differ, and where similar terms are used, they will probably have quite different meanings. The parties will seem locked into the dispute and may even say that they have no choice but to fight. Attempts to resolve the dispute by one side may end up actually fueling the conflict. Neither side can explain the moral order of the other in any satisfactory way. The disputants fail to see why the other party rejects their case, which seems so compellingly clear to them, leading each to describe the other as ignorant, misguided, evil, or sick. Creativity is nil, as the conflicting parties can think of no solution other than capitulation or elimination.

This pattern of mutual frustration and entrenchment leads to conflicts that are intractable, morally attenuated, and rhetorically ineloquent (Pearce & Littlejohn, 1997). They are intractable because there seems to be no way to resolve them, and they continue, often in many guises, over the years (Kriesberg, Northrup, & Thorson, 1989). They are morally attenuated because the disputants often violate their own principles of good behavior, and they are rhetorically ineloquent as they rely on the least sophisticated rhetorical strategies. Christians, for example, believing fundamentally in the principle of love, can become rather hateful when they are involved in moral conflicts. Peace advocates have been known to aggress, radical environmentalists have been known to destroy, and prolife advocates have been known to kill in response to moral difference. When their best and most eloquent arguments are rejected, parties to moral conflict will tend to reduce their rhetorical strategies to chants, slogans, signs, and reciprocated diatribe. As Willard (1996) described it,

> Challenged speakers go to ground. . . . They assume this is not from fear of criticism but from a kind of self-righteousness born of competence: I'm right; my opponent is wrong. This closure thwarts discourse with outsiders. It precludes agreement . . . but its worst political effect is that it obstructs disagreement: It makes argument untenable by undercutting its necessary conditions. (p. 128)

An Illustrative Case of Moral Conflict

An extreme case that illustrates just how harmful moral conflict can be is the violent confrontation between Federal agents and a religious group, the Branch Davidians, at Mount Carmel near Waco, Texas, in 1993. Believing that the Davidians, led by their prophet David Koresh, were preparing for armed conflict, the FBI and the Bureau of Alcohol, Tobacco, and Firearms (ATF) raided the group's property, which led to a stand-off lasting 51 days. After several individuals were killed or wounded on both sides, the agents gassed and burned the complex, killing almost all of the occupants, including 21 children. The incident led to numerous Congressional hearings, agency reviews, inquiries, and lawsuits.

On the face, this was clearly an incident involving crisis negotiation gone wrong. In an astute study of this case, Jayne Docherty (2001) claimed that it is much more than a crisis negotiation. Referring to the incident as a *worldview conflict*, she outlined the differences that led to misunderstanding, miscalculation, and a tragic ending. The incident did have all of the elements of a barricade situation, in which authorities surround and negotiate with an ensconced group that could be a danger to themselves and others. The first goal of such situations is to save lives, the second goal is to save property, and the third is to bring the perpetrators to justice. None of these goals was met in the case of the Davidians. The considerable negotiations during this period were marred by many elements of moral conflict.

Docherty (2001) analyzed the worldviews of the two sides in terms of *ontology*, or what is believed to be true; *logic*, or how reality is believed to be organized; *epistemology*, or how we believe knowledge to arise; *axiology*, or what is believed valuable or important; and *ethics*, or beliefs about proper action. Although there was some overlap among the worldviews of the two sides in this dispute, the moral differences were palpable. The ontology of the FBI classified human beings as normal or abnormal, and barricaded situations always involved the "bad guys" on the inside and the "good guys" on the outside. This ontology further divided the world of emotion from the world of reason, such that negotiators were forced to separate the two. These ontological features revealed a dualistic logic, or an either-or type of reasoning. A manifestation of this ontology and logic was that the police turned to clinicians, who were ready to psychoanalyze the perpetuator, a standard procedure in crisis negotiations.

Although the Davidians also used a dualistic logic, their ontology was actually quite different. Believing in the apocalypse, the Davidians divided their world into good and evil, those who are saved and those who are damned, the believers and the non-believers. People are not inherently good or bad, but can be saved, which explains why the Davidians encouraged negotiators to choose God's way, which the FBI took as inappropriate, irrational behavior.

As for epistemology, the Federal agents used science as a basis for knowledge, relying especially on psychology. Consequently, they understood barricade situations in terms of diagnostic categories, believing that appropriate response should be based on psychological knowledge. In contrast to this view, the Davidians gained knowledge only through the word of God as revealed in scripture. You know what is right by listening to God.

Questions of axiology and ethics revolve around action, or what one should actually do. If your epistemology is based on psychological knowledge, as was the case for the agents, then proper action will be counseling strategies designed to calm subjects down and to move from emotion to reason. The Davidians, however, valued faith, prophecy, and obedience to God. They eschewed things valued by ordinary society as materialistic and anti-godly. At one point the FBI sent the Davidians a video of the children who had been released to show that they were being well cared for. Unfortunately, what the group saw was their children eating sweets and watching television, which was not particularly reassuring to their worldview. The proper course of action for the Davidians was to obey God's law, which meant to resist the materialistic values such as those perceived to be part of the FBI's childcare practices.

As another example, the FBI negotiators never really understood the Davidians' attempts to engage them in Bible study. The group would swing back and forth between negotiation on the issues and attempts to convert the negotiators, which the FBI finally ascribed to irrationality and bad faith. The authorities responded to this perception by an abrupt change in approach, which involved changing negotiators, agenda, and process. The new hard-line position of the negotiators, which involved leveling criminal charges at the Davidians, merely served to reinforce the Davidians' apocalyptic view.

The negotiations came down to a clash of language—instrumental bargaining versus life narratives. The agents were perfectly willing to try to establish a connection with Koresh by talking about personal things like hobbies and children, but they were clearly uncomfortable talking about God and the meaning of life. The FBI negotiators wanted to frame the negotiations as bargaining, which Koresh resisted. For example, the FBI essentially ignored Davidian concerns about equity and justice, believing that such issues should be handled only in the courts. Specifically, the Davidians wanted fair treatment; they expressed a desire for the ATF agents to be held accountable for earlier killings, and they wanted an investigation by a neutral organization.

There was also a fascinating difference in the time scales of the two sides. The Davidians saw the episode as one small part of God's long plan, in contrast with the agents' short-term view of the incident as a single event. This meant getting everyone out safely, while for the Davidians, safety, though important, was subordinate to an equitable outcome approved by God. In the end, frustrated by their perceived lack of progress, the authorities forced the issue by demanding that everyone leave the compound, and when they did not, tanks breached the building, igniting the fatal fire. Not all moral conflicts end this tragically, but frequently do lead to considerable "collateral damage," long-term resentment, frustration, and paralysis of action.

An Evolving Inquiry

In the 20 years that my colleagues and I have been studying this subject, our program has taken some intriguing turns. In this section, I provide a bit of background and history on the project. Our inquiry started as an elucidation of the problem of moral conflict and has evolved into an exploration of processes that can transcend difficult differences, including moral conflict. In this section, I outline four dimensions of this inquiry: (a) theoretical and methodological influences, (b) case studies, (c) conceptualizing the discourse of conflict, and (d) exploring transcendent communication.

Theoretical and Methodological Influences

Since our first studies of moral conflict (Freeman, Littlejohn, & Pearce, 1992; Pearce & Littlejohn, 1997), our inquiry has developed and moved in directions we could not have anticipated in those early years. Consistently over the years, however, this work has been guided by a set of four related academic traditions—system theory, social constructionism, practical theory, and action research.

System theory. This broad tradition draws attention from individual attributes to relationships and connections, in which communication processes are emphasized over personality and individual behavior. From system theory, we learn that the "whole" is created through interaction among parts and that processes of interaction produce outcomes (Littlejohn & Domenici, 2001; Littlejohn & Foss, 2005). Systems are organized sets of components that act on one another to create something more than a mere accumulation of characteristics. When you take a systems approach, you look at the dynamic forces among parts in terms of some kind of energy or information. Control and self-regulation are also important, as the system forces lead to homeostasis as well as adaptation and change. In addition, systems cannot be understood apart from their environments, because the system itself always interacts within a network of shifting relationships.

Our work has been especially influenced by a line of systems inquiry known as *second order cybernetics,* primarily attributable to such thinkers as Gregory Bateson (1972) and Heinz von Foerster (1981). Observing always means interacting with the system itself. Automatically, the system widens to include the observer, who both influences and is influenced by the system. The implication of this point is that one can never observe a system purely and objectively, but must take his or her own role into account. Thus we become part of the system we observe.

In all of our work, then, we want to concentrate on what happens between parties in conflict, how they communicate with one another, and how this communication impacts and is affected by larger systems. Much of our work is interventionist in nature. In other words, we become involved with actual communities and learn from this experience. Our "knowledge" about moral conflict and transcendent discourse develops over time as a result of this engaged practice, which I discuss in more detail below. *Our key learning from system theory is that moral conflict is a dynamic relational state arising in certain forms of interaction.*

Social constructionism. The second influence on our work hails originally from two movements

in sociology—symbolic interactionism (Lal, 1995) and the "social construction of reality" (Berger & Luckmann, 1966)—and from the philosophy of language (e.g., Schutz, 1967; Wittgenstein, 1953). This work expanded to a movement throughout the social sciences that Kenneth Gergen (1985, 1999) aptly named *constructionism* (Littlejohn & Domenici, 2001). In the communication field, this school of thought forms an important part of what has been called *the social approach* (e.g., Leeds Hurwitz, 1995; Littlejohn & Foss, 2005), which is based on the ideas that human beings always make their realities socially, through interaction, and that language and other symbolic forms shape what we experience. The focus of attention in constructionist research is *what gets made* in a social situation and *how social worlds come into being* through communication (Pearce, 1995). In other words, humans "make" or "construct" social worlds through the forms of communication they employ. Though the process of social construction is not normally conscious, we have learned that it can become deliberate if participants think about the consequences of their interactional patterns within the situations they face.

Constructionism is really an application of system theory to human social life, acknowledging that interactional patterns create understandings that give meaning to human experience. Individuals come to understand their experience through interaction within social groups. Language and other symbol systems assume great importance in establishing social realities, as human beings can never have pure, unfiltered experience. Because reality is created socially, it will shift from situation to situation. Something that assumes great importance at one time will fade at other moments, and the actual meaning of experiences shifts from one group to another. Our work, then, is based on situated practice, understanding that human beings must come to some sort of understanding of what is happening in various situations and then to respond in a way that makes sense to them from the perspective of some set of social worlds.

Even when one has the experience of "acting alone," one still acts from within social meanings salient at the moment—meanings created and reproduced in many interactions of the past. As people communicate in new situations with new conversational partners in new communities across time, their repertoire of meanings and actions can develop in new and unpredictable ways. Many aspects of a person's social realities remain relatively stable over time, as they are repeatedly reinforced, while other aspects can undergo considerable change.

In the realm of moral conflict and transcendent discourse, then, we can look at (a) how moral conflict involves certain patterns of interaction, the use of certain kinds of language and action; (b) what is created in moral conflict situations; and (c) what could get made if the language and process of communication were to change. *Our key learning from constructionism is that moral conflicts are made in human interaction, and they can be transcended when communicators shift their patterns of talk.*

Practical theory. A practical theory establishes a set of principles by which an actor can make difficult situational decisions (Littlejohn & Foss, 2005). Instead of predicting outcomes from causal models, practical theory provides a basis for achieving goals in complex situations where many solutions and outcomes may be possible. Following this tradition, our work is designed to provide practical guides for action. According to Craig and Tracy (1995), practical theories "construct a tentative, revisable, but still rationally warranted normative model that is relevant to a broad range of practical situations" (p. 252). Cronen (2001) wrote that practical theory "offers principles informed by engagement in the details of lived experience that facilitate joining with others to produce change" (p. 14). According to Cronen, practical theories provide a basis for understanding the uniqueness of situations in order to learn from experience and to weigh alternative courses of action for achieving positive outcomes. Our emerging theory of transcendent communication (Littlejohn, 2004), summarized later in this chapter, is itself an example of practical theory.

An example—indeed, an exemplar—of practical theory, is the *coordinated management of meaning,* or CMM (Pearce & Cronen, 1980; Pearce & Kearney, 2004; Pearce & Pearce, 1999). Especially influential in our work, CMM looks at the ways in which action, particularly interaction, is embedded in socially constructed contexts of meaning. CMM provides a basis for understanding how people connect their actions with meaning, the logics that drive interaction, and the ways in which shifting contexts can bring about changes in meaning and action (Littlejohn & Domenici, 2001; Littlejohn & Foss, 2005).

CMM has expanded considerably since its original formulation. Some of the many extensions through research, application, and conceptual development are discussed in a special edition of *Human Systems* (Pearce & Kearney, 2004). In reflecting on this work, Pearce (2004) mentioned several themes he believes important in the theory. These include (a) multiple contextuality, or the idea that all experience is understood in a web or in dynamic contexts that give meaning to action; (b) connected stories, or the relationship between the interactions that people live and the stories they tell; (c) coordination, or the challenges of organizing and understanding actions within a system; (d) mystery, or openness where firm answers cannot be found; and (e) continuing creation, or the dynamic, constantly created nature of our social worlds. *Our key learning from practical theory and CMM is that responses to moral difference are coordinated practices by which communicators manage actual situations in their lives.*

Action research. As a final influence on our work, action research involves inquiry accomplished through engagement in actual communities (e.g., Stringer, 1996). Action research is learning by doing. We work in communities with real people facing normal conditions of life, experience and learn from this work, codify and write our observations, and continually refine our ideas about how to work in communities. Spano (2001) outlined three characteristics of action research. First, it is participative, working collaboratively with members of actual communities. Rather than treating people as "subjects" to be "observed," action research relies on partnerships and relationships in real situations. Second, researchers take the role of facilitators and invite participants into new forms of communication that will help them reflect on the system and make decisions about how to orient and respond to the situations they face. These processes are never invented out of context and imported into the situation, but are tested and developed collaboratively over time so that they become "owned" by and "meaningful" to the participants themselves. Third, action research produces practical knowledge that allows participants and facilitators to gain insight into the situation, desired changes, and new forms of action that can lead to salutary outcomes. For the researcher/facilitators, these insights grow over time to enable the development of evolving practical theories that provide frameworks for (a) understanding important dynamics of situations, (b) identifying potential community visions, and (c) making decisions about how to act in complex and potentially problematic situations. *Thus our key learning from action research is that understanding grows as we engage actual communities facing real situations.*

In summary, the four influences on our evolving inquiry are system theory, social constructionism, practical theory, and action research. These traditions have influenced our work in many ways. Spano (2001) provided useful discussion of the methodology that my colleagues and I have used over the years in our studies of moral conflict and transcendent discourse and show the practical application of the four traditions discussed in this section. These are outlined in Table 14.1.

Our inquiry into moral conflict began with a series of case studies. From these, we began to conceptualize patterns of communication in moral conflict situations, and we explored new forms of interaction that can transcend moral differences. In the following sections, I outline these dimensions of our work—case studies, conceptualizing the discourse of conflict, and exploring transcendent communication.

Case Studies

Moral orders are never just things-in-themselves, but are always reflected in, and reproduced by, the discourses that the parties use in discussing actual issues such as abortion,

women's rights, and prayer in the schools. Our case studies, then, looked at the discourse used by groups to speak to their own constituents and the logics and categories used to "make the case." We also looked at how groups characterize and address opponents (Pearce & Littlejohn, 1997). Two large case studies—the Religious Right and conflict mediation—in combination with our readings and unpublished studies on gay and lesbian rights, abortion, and the Persian Gulf War (Freeman et al., 1992), formed the corpus of our initial studies of moral conflict.

The Religious Right. Our first major study concentrated on the conflict between the New Christian Right and its critics. In the early 1980s, certain fundamentalist Christians became active in politics and, indeed, quite powerful in those years. Under the leadership of Jerry Falwell and others, such organizations as the Moral Majority and the Christian Roundtable came into being. This effort became a movement known as the New Christian Right, or, more generically, the Religious Right. Liberal critics of this movement immediately emerged. Less organized than their conservative counterparts, many liberals spoke out against the movement. Perhaps the most visible oppositional organization was People for the American Way, led by Norman Lear. The struggle between these two opposing voices continued in different forms well into the 1990s (Yoachum & Tuller, 1993). Our studies concentrated on the pattern of interaction in public discourse between these two broad groups (Pearce & Littlejohn, 1997).

In our early studies of the Religious Right (Pearce, Littlejohn, & Alexander, 1989), we began to hypothesize that groups in moral conflict would be unable to understand one another's ideas within a common moral order. We observed a pattern there in which the discourse within each tradition would inflame the other party and lead to frustration and reciprocated diatribe. We noticed an important difference between the discourse used within groups, which seemed intelligible and eloquent, and that between groups, which appeared strident and ineloquent. Intermural discourse, as opposed to intramural communication, departed from civil attempts to make the case and

Table 14.1   Elements of a Way of Working

Aspect of the Work	Tools Employed	Purpose or Impact
Communication practices	Neutrality and a not-knowing position	Empowers participants to tell their stories. Puts researcher/facilitator in a listening/learning position.
	Dialogic listening	Embodies an attitude of openness and curiosity. Shows engagement. Brings participants in as collaborators.
	Eliciting experiences and stories	Encourages participants to speak from personal experience. Enhances the "data" by including rich personal detail.
	Appreciative inquiry	Focuses on the positive resources within the system. Allows futures to be built on past successes. Opens up the possibility of fresh new ideas and pathways. Calls participants' attention to connections and relationships.
	Systemic questioning	Highlights difference and change. Builds a systemic view.
	Reflecting	Expands participants' perspectives on the system. Helps the community "see itself." Helps participants see the powers and limits of their current social realities.
Connecting theory and practice	Constructionist attitude	Highlights the creative potential of various communication forms. Invites participants to think about the kinds of social worlds they wish to co-construct. Emphasizes that all forms of communication have consequences.
	Social intervention model	Builds principles for practical action.
	Orientation to public communication	Acknowledges that every form of public communication has both powers and limits. Builds a willingness to engage, not avoid, important issues. Shows that healthy, positive, and affirming public relationships around difficult public issues are possible. Empowers citizens to become constructively involved in civic life.
Community-based action research	Ideal of democratic participation	Aims to involve all community stakeholders. Initiates work by and for the community.
	Use of skilled facilitators	Provides process, not content, expertise. Helps guide the forms of communication used to address public issues.

(Continued)

Table 14.1 (Continued)

Aspect of the Work	Tools Employed	Purpose or Impact
		Provides forums whereby the researcher/facilitators and participants can listen to the concerns, visions, and stories of the community.
	Emphasis on practical outcomes	Leads to practical actions plans for the benefit of the community.
		Increases the sophistication of communication practices used within the community.
		Builds the capacity and skill of the researcher/facilitator in continuing this kind of work.
		Builds momentum for continued dialogue within communities.

SOURCE: Adapted from Spano, 2001.

moved toward attempts to obstruct or disempower the other group.

It was clear to us that this conflict—reflecting other disputes on such issues as gay rights (Gattis, 2003), abortion (Tribe, 1990), and environmental conflict (Smith, 1998)—was based not so much on surface issues as deeply held philosophical and moral tenets, which Hunter (1991) referred to as a culture war between the orthodox and progressive. Lipset and Raab (1970) presented a fair description of the moral differences lying behind the clash between these two: (a) *simplism,* or reduction of choices to a few clear options, versus *complexity* and situational decision making; (b) *moralism,* or defining all action as morally right or wrong, versus *nonjudgmentalism;* (c) *monism,* or the establishment of a clear, unified set of criteria and authority for judging action, versus *situational ethics;* and (d) *preservationism,* or the conservation of perceived traditional values, versus *change.*

These value differences are striking in many moral conflicts. They held up very well, for example, in our analysis of the anti-abortion commercials of the Arthur S. DeMoss Foundation, aired in the early 1990s (Pearce & Littlejohn, 1997). This campaign consisted of about seven 30-second spots described by one observer as "Hallmark card ads" (Ames, Leonard, Lewis, & Annin, 1992). Each celebrated the birth and life of children who might otherwise have been aborted, and each ended with the slogan, "Life. What a beautiful choice." These were highly emotional ads featuring happy scenes and lovely backgrounds over music. Each of Lipset and Raab's (1970) orthodox ideals were depicted clearly in the series—simplism, moralism, monism, and preservationism.

When faced with deep differences such as those outlined by Lipset and Raab (1970), communicating across a moral divide may look futile; yet even in our study of the Religious Right, we began to see seeds of transcendence, raising hope that new forms of interaction are possible in these very difficult situations. It seems that archliberal Edward Kennedy received a Moral Majority membership card by mistake. Upon informing the national office of this error, he was encouraged to keep the card and was in fact invited to speak at Jerry Falwell's institution, Liberty Baptist College. Kennedy accepted this invitation and there proposed a kind of contract of civility that led to a cooperative relationship and joint speaking engagements for Kennedy and Falwell. In their study of Kennedy's speech and its outcomes,

Branham and Pearce (1985) noted that Kennedy and Falwell initiated "a new form of public discourse about religion and politics" (p. 438).

Mediation. The second piece of work within the Moral Conflict Project involved a series of eight case studies of mediation conducted at the University of Massachusetts in the mid-1980s (Littlejohn et al., 1994; Pearce & Littlejohn, 1997). Videotaped, with permission, from behind a one-way mirror, these mediations included a family dispute, a consumer case, two roommate conflicts, an assault case, a deteriorating romantic relationship, a property-division case, and a divorce case. Our observations and interviews with the mediators revealed an interesting set of patterns. First, the meaning of essential moral terms such as *fairness* tended to shift from one party to another. Second, the structure and process of mediation itself reflected a certain moral order that may or may not have matched that of the disputants, and mediators sometimes became unwittingly aligned with the party that most shared the mediation-process ideal. In other words, moral similarity and difference did play an important part in these cases.

Not all of the cases we observed were moral conflicts, but where significant philosophical and moral principles were at stake, we found that patterns of communication were similar in many ways to those of more public moral conflicts such as those involving the New Christian Right. One case involving a divorce in particular reinforced this view (Littlejohn et al., 1994). This case involved a dispute between a divorced couple regarding custody and property issues. To help understand this case, we constructed an interpretive model consisting of three dimensions: (a) moral reality, (b) conflict reality, and (c) justice reality. The *moral reality* included deeply held ideas about proper conduct. Using the work of Bellah and his colleagues (Bellah, Madsen, Sullivan, Swidler, & Tipton, 1985), we identified four moral ideals—the authoritarian, based on scriptural or divine authority; the republican, based on civic duty; the utilitarian, based on individual interests; and the expressivist, which is based on individual freedom. These "realities" are not necessarily incommensurate,

though elements of them may be. In the divorce mediation, for example, we found that the husband was very much driven by a traditional, authoritarian moral vision, while the wife based her actions on a highly expressivist one. This difference led to very different styles that frustrated both parties.

The second dimension, *conflict reality,* involves assumptions about the meaning of conflict and how it should be managed. Using Zartman (1978) and Kilmann and Thomas (1975) we identified three approaches: (a) reliance on outside parties, (b) conflict "management," and (c) avoidance and prevention. The first of these—*reliance on outside parties*—defers to adjudication and cultural authorities to settle conflicts. The second—*conflict management*—involves negotiation, fighting, competition, and coalition building. The third—*avoidance and prevention*—tends to be libertarian, or "live-and-let-live." In our divorce case, the husband had a strong avoidance, or libertarian, set of assumptions, which led him to want to be left alone. The wife, on the other hand, held a conflict management model that drove her motivation to "be creative" and to negotiate solutions.

The third dimension, *justice reality,* consists of principles for decision making in conflict situations—criteria for what constitutes a just and right solution. Based largely on the theory of Tedeschi and Rosenfeld (1980), we posited three types of justice. The first, *retributive justice,* involves punishing wrongdoers. The second, *competitive justice,* involves moving to maximize gains and minimize losses. The third, *distributive justice,* involves distributing resources fairly according to a defined principle such as entitlement, equality, equity, or social welfare. In the divorce case, the husband operated out of a strong sense of social welfare, in which he argued for a settlement in the best interests of the children. The wife, in contrast, worked out of a sense of justice based on equality, or equal division.

It was clear to us that the husband and wife in this case were experiencing a moral conflict. Their apparent moral realities did clash, this frustrated them, and their interaction conformed to a typical moral conflict pattern. We saw also in this case that the mediators' moral view conformed largely to that of the wife, and they became unconscious collaborators with her, further alienating the husband. Needless to say, this mediation was not successful. Because of this and our other case studies, we became intensely curious about the patterns of interaction commonly found in conflict situations and began to codify our observations in this regard (Pearce & Littlejohn, 1997).

Conceptualizing the Discourse of Conflict

We have organized forms of conflict communication in several ways over the years (e.g., Pearce & Littlejohn, 1997), but I now prefer to think in terms of three types of discourse, each responding to a particular challenge (Littlejohn, 2004). The first is *advocacy,* which is a response to the *challenge of confrontation.* The second is *negotiation,* which is a response to the *challenge of peacemaking.* The third form of communication is *redefinition,* which responds to the *challenge of transcendence.*

The discourse of advocacy. The discourse of advocacy is a response to the challenge of confrontation. Recognizing the radical meaning of the term, I am using *confrontation* more broadly to mean any form of direct pressure for resistance or change. The most typical means of advocacy in democratic societies involve persuasion, which aims to influence the thoughts and behavior of others. Indeed, the art of persuasion is the oldest and most studied communication form (Foss, Foss, & Trapp, 2002). On matters of public policy, persuasion and debate are the chief instruments by which differences are settled (Gouinlock, 1986). Traditional debate is especially effective and appropriate when parties agree to the standards of good argument and the means by which decisions should be made. For example, legislation and election usually work in democracies, because the stakeholders agree that decisions will be made by vote or by fiat. The process may seem to take forever, but the issue will eventually get settled, or at least the mythology teaches us that this is the case.

The discourse of advocacy serves important functions in society. For one, it is a way of constructing community (Pearce, 1993). A community is built on identification along some set of dimensions important to a group. As people identify with others who share their interests, concerns, visions, and ideas, they begin to draw symbolic boundaries between themselves and other groups. Communities are defined through the discourse of identification and division (Burke, 1969). Over time, the tenets of belief and action are constructed jointly through a series of turns in an ongoing conversation about what is right and good, what should be promoted and won, and what should be attacked and defeated. Whether the discourse of advocacy is based on reasoned argument, diatribe, or violence, it functions to create moral orders and define communities.

Too often, however, advocacy falters when differences are moral. What seems to happen is that the failure to persuade leads to frustration, diatribe, or even violence (Pearce & Littlejohn, 1997). Moral principle and the will to prevail can make confrontation harsh, as advocates "hit the streets" to force results. Yet, open clash is unsettling because of the collateral damage that can occur; the perceived overconfidence of the disputants, whose cause belies the complexity of a multi-valued world; and the incivility of the communication between the combatants. Such conditions lead many to search for a way to make peace, which is the second challenge, addressed by the discourse of negotiation.

The discourse of negotiation. Peacemaking can take many forms. In international affairs, the term *diplomacy* best captures this genre of action. Bargaining, mediation, even collaboration among conflicting parties are typical. I am using the term *negotiation* generically to capture many discursive forms associated with the challenge of peacemaking (Folger & Jones, 1994; Putnam & Roloff, 1992). In general, the goal of these types of communication is to work out compromises or consensual solutions that will settle the dispute (e.g., Fisher & Ury, 1991). The discourse of negotiation is vital. It can help to reduce tensions and even resolve conflicts in many cases. It can stimulate creative thinking and collaborative problem solving. Erstwhile enemies can even find a common ground in working through a difficult situation, which can in turn create a basis for future collaboration.

And negotiation, once it actually gets going, can return a feeling of civility into an otherwise hostile environment.

The discourses of advocacy and negotiation aim to achieve first-order change, or movement on the issue of contention (Watzlawick, Weakland, & Fisch, 1974). In the discourse of advocacy, the aim is to achieve a goal by having others move toward the desired end; in the discourse of negotiation, the goal is to achieve resolution by having one or more parties move toward an acceptable solution. The point of contention does not change, though positions can.

For this reason, the discourses of both advocacy and negotiation encapsulate the conflict. By arguing, forcing, bargaining, even collaborating, communicators participate in the mutual construction of their respective identities as conflicting parties. The idea of encapsulation comes from the theory of dialectics (Handelman, 1984; Rawlins, 1988). In managing a contradiction or opposition, the solution further reproduces the opposition itself. Any attempt to promote or select one option over another or mediate between them merely perpetuates the distinction between choices. For example, selecting policy A over policy B reinforces the idea that we have only two policies. Even a compromise policy includes a little of A and a little of B, making these the only starting points. Consequently, the discourses of advocacy and negotiation construct a reality of durable categories. This is paradoxical: As we struggle to overcome a conflict, we reproduce the very categories that made the conflict in the first place. Often attempts to negotiate solutions are successful, especially in interest-based conflicts, but they often fail because the conflicting parties, positions, and interests get hardened in the process of resolution, a tendency exacerbated in moral conflicts. This outcome leads to the third challenge—transcendence—and the discourse of redefinition.

The discourse of redefinition. The discourse of redefinition is a search for ways to transform the conversation from encapsulating contradiction to productive dialogue. This discourse is a kind of "negation of the negation" (Rawlins, 1988), a new set of organizing principles that leads participants to think differently about what they are doing as they work through their differences and to help them achieve unimagined outcomes. In the Cupertino Community Project, for example, the "undiscussable" issue of racial tension was transformed by reframing the issue in citywide dialogue groups from "racial difference" to "cultural richness" (Spano, 2001). The Cupertino Community Project is a decade-long dialogue project with many facets within the city of Cupertino, California. Cupertino has afforded me and my colleagues the opportunity to develop a number of dialogue tools and to learn a great deal about what can happen when care is taken about how to frame issues and structure conversations (see Barge, Chapter 19 in this volume, for a more detailed description of dialogue tools and Cupertino).

Successful discourse of the third type will achieve second-order change (Watzlawick et al., 1974). If first-order change is movement on the content issues of a dispute, second-order change aims to switch the definition of what we are doing as we work through our differences. It involves a change in the meaning of winning. Where once it meant prevailing on the issue, winning now means communicating in a way that leads to humane outcomes for all. Such discourse may not, perhaps should not, change anybody's position on the issue; but it can profoundly change their ideas about communication and human relationships. When communicators successfully redefine their issues, their points of difference, and their relationship, they are able to *transcend* old patterns that held them in frustrating and negative patterns of interaction. They are, in other words, able to engage in *transcendent communication.*

EXPLORING TRANSCENDENT COMMUNICATION

The Transcendent Communication Project

From the beginning of the Moral Conflict Project, we imagined better forms of communication between parties with significant moral differences, and our work soon began to explore creative methods for managing significant differences. The Transcendent Communication Project is an ongoing exploration of methods for helping communities manage potentially complex and difficult conflict situations humanely, effectively, and appropriately (Littlejohn, 2004). I use the term *transcendence* to mean moving above or beyond typical patterns of communication found in difficult conflict situations. My colleagues and I have maintained an intense interest in ways in which communicators can transcend negative patterns in which they are caught in situations where difference matters. This work is based on our own research and practice along with what we have learned from other groups such as the Public Conversations Project (Chasin et al., 1996).

Kaleidoscope Project. The early Kaleidoscope Project, a collaboration between the University of Massachusetts and the National Council of Christians and Jews, marked a clear transition from studying moral conflict to looking at alternative forms of discourse. An experiment in public discourse, Kaleidoscope invited spokespersons with different worldviews to discuss a difficult issue in a new way (Pearce & Littlejohn, 1997). At the University of Massachusetts, we held Kaleidoscope sessions on such issues as animal rights, U.S. policy in Central America, gay rights, and more. A later version of Kaleidoscope, on the topic of affirmative action, led to the establishment of the Public Dialogue Consortium and the now decade-long Cupertino Community Project, a series of dialogues in Cupertino, California (Spano, 2001). Kaleidoscope was designed to enable people to talk constructively about difficult and undiscussable public issues—issues that were so hot that proponents refused to talk to one another, issues on which participants were terrified that a discussion might explode into an uncontrollable conflict, or issues on which discussion might imply capitulation of some sort. The idea behind Kaleidoscope was to create a public-event format that would make constructive communication possible where moral difference stood in the way.

The initial Kaleidoscope format included opening statements by opponents on the issue followed by a public interview of each side and then both sides together on the stage. The interview was designed to have the speakers reflect on their interaction and on the limits of their respective worldviews. The audience was then taught to ask questions of the same nature, not to spark debate, but to invite mutual reflection. This format was clearly experimental. Participants tended to find it odd, but they "played" and, in most cases, constructive conversation was made possible.

The Kaleidoscope Project was probably our first piece of action research on conflict. Since then, we have been involved in many projects with actual communities aimed at transcending important and potentially moral differences. As the limitations of traditional discourse become increasingly apparent, many organizations have worked on methods that, like Kaleidoscope, aim to transcend and transform communication in the most difficult cases of conflict. We have learned a great deal from our own work and that of others and have expanded our repertoire of ways of working in the management of difference (Littlejohn & Domenici, 2001; Pearce & Littlejohn, 1997; Spano, 2001).

Characteristics of transcendent communication. We have found that transcendent communication tends to embody three characteristics. First, it creates new frames that transcend differences. Using the metaphor of Wittgenstein (1953), this kind of dialogue establishes a new "grammar" that enables parties to reconceptualize their differences and even find common ground. The new categories of conversation constitute a creole of sorts, making it possible for parties to have a coherent dialogue across otherwise incommensurate worldviews (Stout, 1988). In his book *The Soul of Politics,* Jim Wallis (1994) championed a new set of topics that could bridge liberal and conservative ways of thinking. Instead of pitting opposing economic, political, and social categories against one another, Wallis proposed that new conversations address transcendent topics such as compassion, community, reverence, diversity, justice, and courage.

Second, transcendent communication transforms relationships. Abandoning the discourses of confrontation and negotiation that privilege arguments, positions, interests, and solutions, dialogue features personal stories, new contexts of meaning, and relationship building. The Public Conversations Project, for example, had amazing success in some 20 dialogues on abortion, where participants were invited into a safe environment to talk about their lives (Chasin et al., 1996). Using strong facilitation and ground rules, these dialogues encouraged participants to share stories, to listen well to the experiences of others, to ask questions based on curiosity, and to explore the complexity of their own and others' positions on this intractable issue. The outcomes of the abortion dialogues were remarkable. No one really changed their opinions on the issues, but they changed their perceptions of themselves and those who held opposing views.

Third, transcendent communication creates opportunities to explore the powers and limits of multiple worldviews. In addition to exploring common ground, the discourse of redefinition allows participants to explore differences, but to do so in a way that helps group members learn significant new things, make new distinctions, and realize that every perspective is limited in what it can do. Transcendent communication allows participants to explore complexity in ways often not permitted by advocacy and negotiation. In contrast, when we have the opportunity to go beyond simplistic categories and have a more nuanced discussion, we can learn a great deal about ourselves, others, and the issues at hand. For example, in a fascinating dissertation on the struggle over homosexuality in the United Methodist Church, William Gattis (2003) provided dialogue groups with a set of guidelines designed to change the nature of the discussion. Specifically, he encouraged participants to,

> Learn all you can from others about the points of view with which you disagree . . . compare and contrast your own point of view with the viewpoint of others . . . [and] compare and contrast the strengths and weaknesses of each point of view. (pp. 184–185)

Meeting the challenge of transcendence cannot rely on established methods. Engaging in discourses of redefinition is a foray into new territory and is inherently creative, which is why there is no canon of transformative methods. They are worked out anew whenever and wherever the challenge is experienced. Sometimes traditional approaches such as mediation are adapted to meet transformative goals. The publication of Bernard Baruch Bush and Joseph Folger's book *The Promise of Mediation* (1994),

for example, sparked something of a movement aiming to make mediation more transformative. Many new methods of conflict communication are truly innovative. Transformative discourse frequently proceeds by trial and error, and in this act of creation, we can learn a great deal about both content and process. We use the term *dialogue* to capture these transformative aspects of transcendent communication. Chapter 19 (Barge) of this volume summarizes much of the growing literature on dialogue, especially as it relates to communities. For this reason, I will limit my discussion to the transcendent qualities of dialogue with special attention to its application in public and private situations, where important differences become a factor.

Dialogue as Transcendence

If persuasion is the paradigm case of advocacy and negotiation is the paradigm case of peacemaking, then dialogue is surely the form of communication most associated with redefinition. For me, the term *dialogue* usefully designates a certain communication practice, which aims to *redefine* issues, conflicts, and relationships, thereby enabling participants to *transcend* hopeless patterns of interaction. The terms *dialogue, redefinition,* and *transcendence* are not exactly synonyms, but each term does capture a particular dimension of the same process. In general this process has several characteristics:

- It embodies a relationship in which parties treat one another as fully formed, whole, and complex human beings, whose life experiences provide a basis for their moral orders, positions on issues, and actions in the world.
- It allows communicators to say what is important to them, be assured that their stories will be heard, and allow others the same privilege.
- It permits participants to move from a place of being stuck to new territory where joining places may be found.
- It is multi-voiced and non-polarized.
- It includes fresh, constructive questions that demand critical, creative thinking.
- It is educative and allows participants to learn important new things, including how to look at the problem in new ways.

- It leads communicators to see the powers and limits of a variety of points of view.
- It builds relationships of respect.

Dialogue is designed to "keep the conversation going" (Rorty, 1979, p. 378) in ways that open up, rather than close down, possibilities (Arnett & Arneson, 1999). Unlike persuasion and negotiation, dialogue does not necessarily aim to settle issues, though it can lead to consensual decisions in some cases. More importantly, it allows people to live in a world in which difference is seen as a positive resource that does not have to be resolved. This new orientation provides a basis for managing, if not resolving, such differences. This orientation is a change leading to mutual respect, or "a favorable attitude toward, and constructive interaction with, the persons with whom one disagrees" (Gutmann & Thompson, 1996, p. 79). Such change gives us pause to stew a bit about our position and remain open to the powers of other points of view, even when we disagree with them. We can allow democratic processes to work and live with decisions we disagree with when we come to understand the basis for prevailing decisions. In other words, "the principles and values with which we live are provisional, formed and continually revised in the process of making and responding to moral claims in public life" (Gutmann & Thompson, 1996, p. 26).

Willard (1996) referred to this kind of discourse as epistemic, meaning that it is a form of mutual inquiry. We can learn more about ourselves including the basis of our beliefs, we can learn more about others and how life experience leads to moral action, we can learn about complexity, and we can learn about difference itself and how to manage it productively. It is a shift of commitment to what Robert Kegan (1994) calls in his remarkable study *In Over Our Heads: The Mental Demands of Modern Life* the "new curriculum" of "reconstructive postmodernism" (p. 324).

Dialogue allows us to go to a new place, to reframe our differences, to find or construct a joining spot (Littlejohn, 2004; Littlejohn & Domenici, 2001; Pearce & Pearce, 1999). If old patterns merely encapsulate old categories, can new patterns be found? If familiar forms of interaction serve to perpetuate, even enflame, a conflict without a positive result, can the participants find a new form of communication that might change their relationship?

Although there are many traditions of dialogue, I find the work of Martin Buber especially helpful. In his book *I and Thou* (1958), he showed how important it is to treat others as subjects whose legitimate experience can impact our own lives. Persons in an I-Thou relationship together open up new vistas. There is an interesting irony in I-Thou dialogue. It is a place where you stay in the tension between "standing your own ground" and being "profoundly open to the other." Pearce and Pearce (1999) called this ability *dialogic virtuosity*. My own view is that dialogue should move beyond the tension of difference to find a place for constructive conversation and to create a context for shared meaning and action (Littlejohn, 2004). In this section, I outline three keys for the practice of dialogue. These are (a) working with process, (b) creating joining places, and (c) changing the context of the conversation.

Working With Process

In new realms of discourse, the question of *how* we talk to one another is as important as the question of *what* we talk about. The dialogue literature is infused with discussions of process. Indeed, the transcendent communication project itself is process-driven (Littlejohn, 2004). A key to the success of the Public Conversations Project's abortion dialogues was the fact that they invited participants into a "new kind of conversation" on the issue and paid very careful attention to the way in which the dialogue was actually conducted. Two dimensions of process talk are important. The first is really a design question that facilitators and sponsors may address: What form should the dialogue take? The second dimension is an invitation for participants themselves to transcend the issue on which they are stuck by talking explicitly about how they might be able to have a good conversation.

As an example of process, Mary Alice Speke Ferdig (2001) used a set of five sensibilities as a guide for dialogue. The first is the *spirit of freedom,* or the desire to empower everyone to engage in discussion of issues of importance.

The second is the *spirit of inclusion,* which means acknowledging the necessity of hearing others and valuing differences. Ferdig's third sensibility is the *spirit of inquiry,* or the willingness to learn and discover new things within the process of dialogue. The fourth, the *spirit of spontaneity,* allows the conversation to develop turn by turn and permits participants to change. Finally, *the spirit of possibility* acknowledges that transformative dialogue can lead to unexpected outcomes. Ferdig, then, asked how we can create a process that encourages the spirit of freedom, inclusion, inquiry, spontaneity, and possibility. Dialogue participants themselves can address these questions: "How can we talk in this spirit about a hard issue?"

Kathy Domenici and I have worked with another set of criteria that can be useful in making process decisions (Littlejohn & Domenici, 2001). These are collaborative communication, power management, process management, facework, and a safe environment. *Collaborative communication* means that participants are working with, rather than against, one another. They perceive that they have a common stake and must cooperate to achieve a set of supraordinate goals. They work creatively to develop solutions that are workable for everyone. *Power management* means empowering each person to use the individual and collective resources he or she has for the benefit of the whole community. It means helping individuals to express what is most important to them, to hear what is important to others, and to work to bring a diversity of perspectives and interests together. *Process management* means keeping process issues at the fore, bringing the importance of process into awareness, and collaborating on process methods as well as content issues. *Facework* means building honor and dignity. It means treating others with respect and present the self respectably. Finally, *a safe environment* simply refers to creating ways in which people can explore ideas without threat of harm. In other words, how can we make constructive and creative dialogue possible?

The point here is that the "how" question itself can be transformative, as participants must think beyond the issue to the process of communication that will be employed. The question, *How shall we talk?* sets a new ground or place where the disputants can come together. An illustrative case occurred in Catron County in rural southwestern New Mexico in the 1990s (Smith, 1998). Located amid beautiful national forest land, the community of only 2,500 people found itself in distress. The economy was depressed because of declines in the two major industries—lumber and ranching—caused at least in part by environmental protection policies. This state of affairs led to a severe conflict among environmentalists, ranchers and timber workers, and Forest Service personnel. The conflict was strident, it was moral, and it seemed intractable. Alarmed by the amount of stress-related illness, the area's only doctor felt that the community itself was sick and arranged to bring in the New Mexico Center for Dispute Resolution (NMCDR) to initiate a community-wide dialogue process.

The key question for the NMCDR and local participants was how to have a new kind of conversation, one that could take them beyond hateful slogans, threats of violence, flashing guns, and frightening displays. A small group agreed to meet and take up this question. Indeed, much of the initial talk centered on ground rules. One initial decision was to allow all of the perspectives to be heard and to concentrate on listening respectfully to various points of view. Soon the initial group grew to as many as 50 and the discussion moved from various opinions on the issues at hand to a vision for the community. Over the course of several years, a variety of processes was used, including dialogue groups, planning committees, field-trip discussions, mediation and negotiation, community visioning meetings, and youth meetings. Although the community did experience setbacks, concrete solutions were created and, most important, continued conversation was made possible. Community members were able to find areas that could be discussed in ways that built positive relationships.

Creating Joining Places

Process talk addresses the question of *how* we communicate with one another and seeks an answer to *what* can we talk about? Areas where constructive conversation can occur constitute the joining place. Nola Heidlebaugh (2001) used the term *commonplacing* to identify the ground where people engaged in moral conflict can meet. She likened commonplacing to weaving together two pieces of cloth. In moral conflict, the weaves in the separate tapestries are too tight, so we must find a way to loosen them to make a joining place possible. Notice that the metaphor is not "sewing." Indeed, stitching the pieces together would be like what we see too often in moral conflicts today—some kind of a forced seam that does not work for either piece of fabric. Instead, the metaphor calls for loosening threads and actually weaving them together at some point without threatening the integrity of either tapestry. This is the joining point. In the vein of social construction, the joining point is not "found," but "created." Where can insights be coordinated in some meaningful way? In essence, we are saying, "Let's be creative and see what we can do."

Between 1999 and 2003, the provinces of Maluku in Indonesia were involved in a terrible conflict, as Muslims and Christians bombed one another's homes, mosques, churches, schools, and public buildings, resulting in some 6,000 deaths and many thousands of displaced persons. As part of a restoration process, the International Catholic Migration Commission (2004) put together a dialogue institute for village and religious leaders in Central Maluku. Tired of war and ready to rebuild their communities, 40 participants came together for 4 days to explore their differences and find a way to build a foundation for restoration. During the institute, the participants created a number of joining places. Despite their many differences, they were able to talk very productively about their common culture and shared religious values and to discuss how to use these as resources for restoration. They did not spend time on old conflict issues, but instead built a vision for a unified community in which mental, physical, and economic well-being could be achieved. One place where tapestries could be woven was *pela gandong,* a cultural practice akin to blood brotherhood. Recognizing that their ancestors had created a blood bond that made them like family, the dialogue participants found a common place and bond for future work together (Lowry & Littlejohn, in press).

Changing the Context of the Conversation

A powerful way to create joining places is to shift the context of the conversation. I like to use the metaphor of *scoping* to capture this idea. The frame limits what you see in a scope, but you can change the frame by "scoping out," which leads to a broader context, or "scoping in," which leads to a narrower one. In many conflicts, especially moral conflicts, the parties are stuck at one lens length. Debates on abortion, for example, focus right on the issue of abortion itself; but the Public Conversations Project (Chasin et al., 1996) has learned that productive dialogue can occur by asking participants to reflect on their life experiences, which is a kind of scoping in. In the Catron County conflict described above (Smith, 1998), the dialogue groups found it useful to scope out to explore a common vision for the community. We can also change the context by moving the scope around to look at different spots. In good dialogue, then, we may want to continually shift the context by scoping and pointing.

Ferdig (2001) explained the power of questions in shifting the context of the discussion. She outlined several ways in which questions can focus on different contexts. To focus on *contexts of identity,* for example, the group may ask, "Who am I?" "What is important to me?" "Who are we together?" "What do we both care about?" To focus on *contexts of principle,* we might ask, "What do I stand for?" "What do we jointly stand for?" "How do our choices and actions reflect our individual and collective values?" *Contexts of intention* can be revealed in discussions on questions such as, "Where am I going?" "What do I want to see happen here?" "What are we up to in this conversation?" To focus on *contexts of assumption,* we ask questions like these: "What aren't we thinking about here?" "What is our logic for these conclusions?" Finally, a focus on *contexts of possibility* would require such questions as, "What are the things you value most about yourself and the self-organizing experience of which you are a part?" "What are the core factors that give 'life' and 'energy' to the self-organizing process of which you are a part?" "What are the possibilities of that which we can create together based on the best of who we are?"

The power of good questions is illustrated by a remarkable set of dialogues on Vietnam sponsored by Robert McNamara (McNamara, Blight, & Brigham, 1999), the U.S. Secretary of Defense during the Vietnam era. Between 1995 and 1998, McNamara assembled a group of scholars and former government officials from both countries for a series of six dialogue sessions held in Hanoi and Bellagio, Italy. The dialogue was made possible by focusing on a single well-crafted question, which set the context for discussion. The group did not ask who was to blame, how it happened, or who was right. Such questions would have reproduced the differences dividing the two countries in the first place. Instead, the question was this: "In light of what now can be learned from the historical record, what U.S. and Vietnamese decisions might have been different and what difference would they have made in the course of the war—*if each side had judged the other side's intentions and capabilities more accurately*" (p. 17)? Once the participants worked out their misgivings about dialogue, they were able to have a productive conversation and, indeed, did identify a number of mistakes made on both sides in judging one another and explored what might have happened if they had more accurately judged one another. Most notably, Vietnamese participants learned that the United States had not been motivated by colonialism, as they had believed during the war, but a fear of the spread of international Communism. The U.S. participants learned that the North Vietnamese had not been motivated by Chinese influence, as they had once assumed, but by a strong desire to win what they considered a civil war motivated by nationalism.

Practical Guidelines

Over the years, we have learned several lessons that have informed our practice (Littlejohn & Domenici, 2001). The following is a synopsis—(a) Create the right conditions; (b) manage safety; (c) provide a process that encourages constructive conversation; and (d) maintain ends-in-view and think about possibilities for outcomes of the conversation.

Create the right conditions. Dialogue is rarely possible in the heat of conflict. Timing is a critical factor of success, and opportunities for dialogue must be made, either by intervention agents or concerned stakeholders. Several points can be helpful here:

- Don't wait until conflict breaks out. Engage stakeholders in conversations early on.
- If open conflict has already happened, look for the right moment, often when participants are tired of fighting or become desperate for new solutions.
- Work initially in small, private groups.
- Be careful about the role of "leaders" and other powerful persons. Allow all of the voices to be heard from the start.
- Build on prior success. Avoid single-shot interventions, and use a grow-as-it-goes process.
- Be creative about process. Think about what will work best, now, under the conditions currently experienced.

Manage safety. Safety is crucial and must be managed well. People will not experiment with new forms of talk when they feel unsafe. Here are a few points for guidance:

- Think consciously about time and place.
- Provide appropriate structure.
- Solicit agreements on process.
- Promote good facework.
- Respond to willingness and felt need.
- Find a shared level of comfort.
- Leave an out.
- Use an impartial facilitator.

Provide a process that encourages constructive conversation. Encourage participants to treat people as people, not as representatives of positions. Several principles can help:

- Take sufficient time to explore.
- Encourage listening, and build listening into the process.
- Help participants to listen beyond mere content. Listen deeply to lived experience, stories told, values, shared concerns, and differences.
- Ask good questions designed to open the conversation, not close it down.
- Frame issues carefully to capture a context that will create a joining place.
- Be appreciative. Look for positive resources, and look for the vision behind negative comments.

- When speaking, aim to be understood rather than to prevail in a contest.
- Base positions in personal experience, and help others to understand your life's experiences.
- Maintain a multi-valued, rather than bi-polar, purview. Listen for all the voices.

Maintain ends-in-view and think about possibilities for outcomes of the conversation. Several ends are possible:

- Discovering the heart of the matter, or learning what is most important to all participants
- Building respect by looking for the ways in which others are experienced, complex, concerned, intelligent, healthy, and rational
- Learning about complexity and developing a healthy suspicion of a two-valued framing of any issue
- Building a context for collaboration

CHALLENGES AND NEW DIRECTIONS

As I look back at the ways in which our ideas and practices have developed, I see a number of challenges facing this line of work in the future.

What conditions create the possibility for transcendence? When are people ready for dialogue? What makes them ready to engage in new forms of discourse? So far, our studies have concentrated on the nature of moral conflict, methods of conflict intervention, and forms of communication that can promote dialogue in conflict and non-conflict situations. We have not looked particularly closely at the situations in which people seem ready for these methods and forms. It would be interesting to generate a series of case studies of moments of readiness and non-readiness to identify some of the factors at play. Here are some potential places to look for answers to this question: (a) moments of frustration and fatigue when participants realize that old forms of communication are leading to dead ends; (b) cases of forced alliances, when erstwhile enemies must come together to provide mutual support; (c) upstream opportunities in which important issues can be explored before open conflict arises; (d) downstream

opportunities when the reality of destruction is most salient; and (e) times when larger contextual factors create new opportunities to transcend old patterns of interaction.

What settings and situations provide opportunities for transcendent communication? This question is similar to the one above, but it looks more specifically at times and places in which transcendent communication sometimes occurs naturally. What is it about these times and places that seems to create an environment in which participants find themselves engaging in a new type of communication? Most of our studies so far have dealt with problem situations in which the need for dialogue is apparent and with good dialogue situations in which intervention agents were able to establish it. But something lies between these two points, places where individuals come together in new ways because of the force of the setting and situation. A series of case studies of this type would be beneficial. Here are some settings and situations that might create opportunities for transcendence: (a) the experience of mutual adversity; (b) the presence of powerful models and leaders; (c) moments of strong lessons learned from previously failed communication; and (d) a heightened sense of humanity that overrides moral differences.

How can parties to a dispute respond constructively when others are unwilling to engage in dialogue? This is a perennial question in conflict-resolution circles. How can people go on when significant stakeholders refuse to talk? In interest-based negotiations, this state of affairs is common when one stakeholder group has effective power and perceives nothing to gain from dialogue. A different form of non-participation occurs in situations in which the moral order of one group precludes dialogue. In our experience, this condition does not mean that dialogue is impossible—indeed, we have seen that it can happen—though not as easily. I feel that there are creative responses to such situations that could permit willing participants to cope if not create conditions for effective processes and salutary conclusions in the future. For example, one might treat non-participation as an act in and of itself, which has meaning and can be understood as a legitimate move. As a

Table 14.2   Lessons Learned

Project	Focus	Lessons Learned
Case studies	Religious Right	Moral conflict is created in patterns of interaction between parties with incommensurate moral orders. Initially civil discourse leads to frustration and reciprocated diatribe. With conscious intent, civil discourse is possible in the presence of moral difference.
	Mediation	Moral conflict can be private as well as public, where similar patterns occur. Intervention agents can be co-opted into the moral order of one side over that of the other.
Discourse	Discourse of advocacy	Moral difference cannot be managed easily or effectively with advocacy. When differences are moral, advocacy will usually lead to frustration and lost eloquence.
	Discourse of negotiation	Moral conflicts are rarely resolved through negotiation because disputants do not share ideas about what constitutes proper process or fair settlement.
	Discourse of redefinition	The discourse of redefinition affords the greatest potential for transforming destructive patterns of communication in complex and difficult conflict situations.
Transcendent communication	Kaleidoscope Project	Innovations in public communication about moral difference are possible and potentially effective.
	Identifying characteristics	Transcendent communication creates new frames that transcend difference. Transcendent communication transforms relationships. Transcendent communication creates opportunities to explore the powers and limits of multiple worldviews.
Dialogue	Working with process	How people talk about their issues is as important as what they talk about.
	Creating joining spaces	People who have serious differences can find joining places, or some ground, on which to have a productive conversation.
	Changing the context of the conversation	If an issue is undiscussable on one level, changing the context of the conversation may be a way to make discussion possible.
	Generating practical guidelines	You can help people achieve dialogue by (a) creating the right conditions, (b) managing safety, (c) providing a process that encourages constructive conversation, and (d) maintaining ends-in-view.

response, one might acknowledge the desire not to participate, be open to this possibility, ask for advice and clarification, and open discussions of when and how dialogue might begin.

What defines a transformative moment in dialogue, and what makes such moments transformative? Professionals in the dialogue field have experienced transformative moments, but I think we need to know much more about these. In pursuing this question, we need to look for three kinds of things. The first are markers of change, or interactional features common at such moments when the group moves to a new plane. This might be a moment of collective excitement; it might be a time of clear shift or change on the part of certain participants; or it might be a change in tone or mood. Second, we need to interpret the meanings of participants for such moments. What did they see happening? What did it mean to them at that time? Finally, we need to identify some of the interactional events leading up to and following from these moments.

CONCLUSION

We have now a sufficient body of work on difficult conflict and forms of transcendence to provide some understanding of problems and solutions. This line of work is immensely heuristic as it continues to offer opportunities for additional inquiry and the further development of practice. Table 14.2 outlines the lessons we have learned from our own work and that of others within this realm.

We live in a world where surface disagreements belie the complexity of the true differences that divide us. In a world of many voices, our very ways of thinking and knowing create chasms on issues that will shape the human condition—issues like war and peace, the environment, poverty and prosperity, the role of science and religion, forms of government, cultural preservation and change, biology and genetics, and education and human development. We need to create meeting places where we can explore the moral orders that lie at the heart of our actions, where we can learn important things about ourselves and others, where we can join in a common endeavor, and where we can create futures of mutual benefit.

REFERENCES

Ames, K., Leonard, E. A., Lewis, S. D., & Annin, P. (1992, April 6). A hymn to adoption—or is it? *Newsweek, 119,* 52.

Arnett, R. C., & Arneson, P. (1999). *Dialogic civility in a cynical age: Community, hope, and interpersonal relationships.* Albany: State University of New York Press.

Bateson, G. (1972). *Steps to an ecology of mind.* New York: Ballantine.

Bellah, R. N., Madsen, R., Sullivan, W. M., Swidler, A., & Tipton, S. M. (1985). *Habits of the heart: Individualism and commitment in American life.* Berkeley: University of California Press.

Berger, P., & Luckmann, T. (1966). *The social construction of reality: A treatise in the sociology of knowledge.* Garden City, NY: Doubleday.

Bernstein, R. J. (1985). *Beyond objectivism and relativism.* Philadelphia: University of Pennsylvania Press.

Branham, R. J., & Pearce, W. B. (1985). Between text and context: Toward a rhetoric of contextual reconstruction. *Quarterly Journal of Speech, 71,* 19–36.

Buber, M. (1958). *I and thou.* New York: Scribner.

Burke, K. (1969). *A rhetoric of motives.* Berkeley: University of California Press.

Bush, R. A. B., & Folger, J. P. (1994). *The promise of mediation: Responding to conflict through empowerment and recognition.* San Francisco: Jossey-Bass.

Carbaugh, D. (1985). Cultural communication and organizing. In W. B. Gudykunst, L. P. Stewart, & S. Ting-Toomey (Eds.), *Communication, culture, and organizational processes* (pp. 30–47). Beverly Hills, CA: Sage.

Chasin, R., Herzig, M., Roth, S., Chasin, L., Becker, C., & Stains, R. R. (1996). From diatribe to dialogue on divisive public issues: Approaches drawn from family therapy. *Mediation Quarterly, 13,* 323–344.

Craig, R. T., & Tracy, K. (1995). Grounded practical theory: The case of intellectual discussion. *Communication Theory, 5,* 248–272.

Cronen, V. E. (2001). Practical theory, practical art, and the pragmatic-systemic account of inquiry. *Communication Theory, 11,* 14–35.

Docherty, J. S. (2001). *Learning lessons from Waco: When the parties bring their gods to the negotiation table.* Syracuse, NY: Syracuse University Press.

Ferdig, M. A. S. (2001). *Exploring the social construction of complex self-organizing change: A study of emerging change in the regulation of nuclear power.* Unpublished doctoral dissertation, Organizational Development, Benedictine University, Lisle, IL.

Fisher, R., & Ury, W. (1991). *Getting to yes: Negotiating agreement without giving in.* Boston: Houghton Mifflin.

Foeman, A. K., & Pressley, G. (1987). Ethnic culture and corporate culture: Using Black styles in organizations. *Communication Quarterly*, 35, 293–307.

Folger, J. P., & Jones, T. S. (Eds.). (1994). *New directions in mediation: Communication research and perspectives.* Thousand Oaks, CA: Sage.

Foss, S. K., Foss, K. A., & Trapp, R. (2002). *Contemporary perspectives on rhetoric.* Prospects Heights, IL: Waveland.

Freeman, S. A., Littlejohn, S. W., & Pearce, W. B. (1992). Communication and moral conflict. *Western Journal of Communication, 56,* 311–329.

Gattis, W. A. (2003). *Transcendent discourse and moral conflict: The use of dialogue groups to improve communication in long-standing moral struggles.* Unpublished doctoral dissertation, University of Kansas.

Gergen, K. J. (1985). The social constructionist movement in modern psychology. *American Psychologist, 40,* 266–275.

Gergen, K. J. (1999). *An invitation to social construction.* Thousand Oaks, CA: Sage.

Gouinlock, J. (1986). *Excellence in public discourse: John Stuart Mill, John Dewey, and social intelligence.* New York: Teachers College Press.

Gutmann, A., & Thompson, D. (1996). *Democracy and disagreement: Why moral conflict cannot be avoided in politics, and what should be done about it.* Cambridge, MA: Harvard University Press.

Handelman, D. (1984). Inside-out, outside in: Concealment and revelation in Newfoundland Christmas mumming. In E. M. Bruner (Ed.), *Text, play, and story: The construction and reconstruction of self and society: 1983 Proceedings of the American Ethnological Society* (pp. 247–277). Washington, DC: American Ethnological Society.

Heidlebaugh, N. J. (2001). *Judgment, rhetoric, and the problem of incommensurability.* Columbia: University of South Carolina Press.

Hunter, J. D. (1991). *Culture wars: The struggle to define America.* New York: HarperCollins.

International Catholic Migration Commission. (2004). *The Interfaith Peacebuilding Institute Maluku Tengah District Indonesia.* Jakarta, Indonesia: Author.

Kegan, R. (1994). *In over our heads: The mental demands of modern life.* Cambridge, MA: Harvard University Press.

Kilmann, R., & Thomas, K. (1975). Interpersonal conflict handling behavior as reflections of Jungian personality dimensions. *Psychological Reports, 37,* 971–980.

Kriesberg, L., Northrup, T. A., & Thorson, S. J. (Eds.). (1989). *Intractable conflicts and their transformation.* Syracuse, NY: Syracuse University Press.

Kuhn, T. S. (1970). *The structure of scientific revolutions.* Chicago: University of Chicago Press.

Lakoff, G. (1996). *Moral politics: What conservatives know that liberals don't.* Chicago: University of Chicago Press.

Lal, B. B. (1995). Symbolic interaction theories. *American Behavioral Scientist, 38,* 421–441.

Leeds Hurwitz, W. (Ed.). (1995). *Social approaches to communication.* New York: Guilford.

Lipset, S. M., & Raab, E. (1970). *The politics of unreason.* New York: Harper & Row.

Littlejohn, S. W. (2004). The Transcendent Communication Project: Searching for a praxis of dialogue. *Conflict Resolution Quarterly, 21,* 337–360.

Littlejohn, S. W., & Domenici, K. (2001). *Engaging communication in conflict: Systemic practice.* Thousand Oaks, CA: Sage.

Littlejohn, S. W., & Foss, K. A. (2005). *Theories of human communication* (8th ed.). Belmont, CA: Wadsworth.

Littlejohn, S. W., Shailor, J., & Pearce, W. B. (1994). The deep structure of reality in mediation. In J. Folger & T. S. Jones (Eds.), *New directions in mediation: Communication research and perspectives* (pp. 67–83). Thousand Oaks, CA: Sage.

Lowry, C., & Littlejohn, S. W. (in press). Dialogue and the discourse of peacebuilding in Maluku, Indonesia. *Conflict Resolution Quarterly.*

McNamara, R. S., Blight, J. G., & Brigham, R. K. (1999). *Argument without end: In search of answers to the Vietnam tragedy.* New York: Public Affairs.

Pearce, W. B. (1993). Achieving dialogue with "the other" in the postmodern world. In P. Gaunt (Ed.), *Beyond agendas: New directions in communication research* (pp. 59–74). Westport, CT: Greenwood.

Pearce, W. B. (1995). A sailing guide for social constructionists. In W. Leeds-Hurwitz (Ed.), *Social approaches to communication* (pp. 88–113). New York: Guilford.

Pearce, W. B. (2004). Some personal reflections. *Human Systems, 15,* 205–208.

Pearce, W. B., & Cronen, V. E. (1980). *Communication, action, and meaning.* New York: Praeger.

Pearce, W. B., & Kearney, J. (Eds.). (2004). Coordinated management of meaning: Extensions and applications [Special issue]. *Human Systems, 15,* 1–207.

Pearce, W. B., & Littlejohn, S. W. (1997). *Moral conflict: When social worlds collide.* Thousand Oaks, CA: Sage.

Pearce, W. B., Littlejohn, S. W., & Alexander, A. A. (1987). The new Christian Right and the humanist response: Reciprocated diatribe. *Communication Quarterly, 35,* 171–192.

Pearce, W. B., Littlejohn, S. W., & Alexander, A. A. (1989). The quixotic quest for civility: Patterns of interaction between the new Christian Right and secular humanists. In J. K. Hadden & A. Shupe (Eds.), *Secularization and fundamentalism reconsidered: Religion and the political order* (Vol. 3, pp. 152–177). New York: Paragon.

Pearce, W. B., & Pearce, K. A. (1999). Combining passions and abilities: Toward dialogic virtuosity. *Southern Communication Journal, 65,* 161–175.

Philipsen, G. (1975). Speaking "like a man" in Teamsterville: Culture patterns of role enactment in an urban neighborhood. *Quarterly Journal of Speech, 61,* 13-22

Putnam, L. L., & Roloff, M. E. (Eds.). (1992). *Communication and negotiation.* Newbury Park, CA: Sage.

Rawlins, W. K. (1988). A dialectical analysis of the tensions, functions and strategic challenges of communication in young adult friendships. In J. A. Anderson (Ed.), *Communication yearbook 12* (pp. 157–189). Newbury Park, CA: Sage.

Rorty, R. (1979). *Philosophy and the mirror of nature.* Princeton, NJ: Princeton University Press.

Schütz, A. (1967). *The phenomenology of the social world* (G. Walsh & F. Lehnert, Trans.). Evanston, IL: Northwestern University Press.

Shailor, J. G. (1988). *Conflict, communication, and culture: A review and analysis of 15 case studies.* Unpublished master's thesis. University of Massachusetts, Amherst.

Smith, M. (1998). *The Catron County citizens group: A case study.* Albuquerque: New Mexico Center for Dispute Resolution.

Spano, S. (2001). *Public dialogue and participatory democracy: The Cupertino Community Project.* Cresskill, NJ: Hampton Press.

Stout, J. (1988). *Ethics after Babel: The languages of morals and their discontents.* Boston: Beacon.

Stringer, E. T. (1996). *Action research: A handbook for practitioners.* Thousand Oaks, CA: Sage.

Tedeschi, J. T., & Rosenfeld, P. (1980). Communication in bargaining and negotiation. In M. E. Roloff & G. R. Miller (Eds.), *Persuasion: New directions in theory and research* (pp. 225–248). Beverly Hills, CA: Sage.

Triandis, H. C., & Albert, R. D. (1987). Cross-cultural perspectives. In F. M. Jablin, L. L. Putnam, K. H. Roberts, & L. W. Porter (Eds.), *Handbook of organizational communication: An interdisciplinary perspective* (pp. 264–296). Newbury Park, CA: Sage.

Tribe, L. H. (1990). *Abortion: The clash of absolutes.* New York: W. W. Norton.

Von Foerster, H. (1981). *Observing systems: Selected papers of Heinz von Foerster.* Seaside, CA: Intersystems Publications.

Wallis, J. (1994). *The soul of politics: A practical and prophetic vision for change.* New York: New Press.

Watzlawick, P., Weakland, J. H., & Fisch, R. (1974). *Change: Principles of problem formation and problem resolution.* New York: W. W. Norton.

Willard, C. A. (1996). *Liberalism and the problem of knowledge: A new rhetoric for modern democracy.* Chicago: University of Chicago Press.

Wittgenstein, L. (1953). *Philosophical investigations.* Oxford, UK: Basil Blackwell.

Wittgenstein, L. (1972). *On certainty* (D. Paul & G. E. M. Anscombe, Trans.). New York: Harper Torchbook.

Wong, D. B. (1984). *Moral relativity.* Berkeley: University of California Press.

Yoachum, S., & Tuller, D. (1993, September 13). Born-again political movement. *San Francisco Chronicle,* p. A1.

Zartman, I. W. (1978). Negotiation as a joint decision-making process. In I. W. Zartman (Ed.), *The negotiation process: Theories and applications* (pp. 67–86). Beverly Hills, CA: Sage.

15

Environmental Conflict Communication

Tarla Rai Peterson

University of Utah

Rebecca Royer Franks

University of Utah

We live in a world relatively filled with human activity, to the extent that humans are capable of irreversibly altering ecological systems on a global scale (Costanza, d'Arge et al., 1997; Daly & Cobb, 1989). In addition, the temporal and spatial scales at which environmental changes occur are rarely synchronized with institutional structures and political cycles (Grant, Peterson, & Peterson, 2002; T. R. Peterson, Peterson, & Grant, 2004). This mismatch is not surprising, given the relatively short window of time and narrow confines of space experienced by the human organism, and the related fact that political and legal frameworks favor linear causal explanations rather than dynamic perspectives (Ehrlich, 2000). The lack of incentives to close these gaps is predictable, yet problematic (Costanza, Cumberland, Daly, Goodland, & Norgaard, 1997).

This phenomenon is especially relevant to conflict studies because human and natural systems are linked in complex ways that result in interdependency. Worldwide human population expansion, coupled with increased awareness of drastic disparities in the standard of living experienced by people in different places, has brought environmental conflict to the attention of international institutions ranging from the United Nations to Amnesty International. Conflicts rage over the relative risks and benefits associated with industrial processes, with exposure to toxins taking a central position. The increasing human population also puts pressure on wildlife (both plant and animal) and its habitats. Even access to natural resources required to sustain life (such as relatively clean air and water) is insecure. For example, natural resource economists are fond of stating that "water does not run downhill; it runs toward

AUTHORS' NOTE: The authors wish to acknowledge the assistance of Markus J. Peterson in preparation of this manuscript.

419

money." Environmental conflict is among the greatest challenges facing humanity in the 21st century. Although these conflicts sometimes can be characterized as simple problems of distribution, they also implicate communication.

In many nations, legal requirements to include the public in environmental decision making render environmental conflict increasingly difficult to ignore. Yet, even when public participation is mandated, technical experts continue to accumulate disciplinarily bounded knowledge, leaving stakeholders out of the decision-making loop. This causes environmental conflicts to escalate. Because communication in environmental conflict is tied closely to public participation, we use the concept of public participation as a central organizing construct in this chapter. We first provide an overview of legal requirements for public participation in environmental issues, with an emphasis on the influential National Environmental Policy Act (NEPA) of 1969 in the United States. Second, we review research on the social demand for public participation in environmental policy making, providing an overview of common approaches. Within this section, we include a brief summary of *sustainable development,* which has been instrumental in shaping practices for managing environmental conflict since at least 1987. Third, we review critical research on two models that have gained significant public currency. Here we summarize critiques of the public hearing, which is the most commonly used method of public participation. We also provide a summary of the more recently emerging research critiquing consensus-based processes. Finally, we discuss especially promising research directions, including suggestions for how they might impact practice. We follow most research on communication and environmental conflict in its emphasis on the United States and other industrialized, nominally democratic nations. Within this framework we also attempt to highlight research that explores global cross-cultural and domestic diversity issues.

LEGAL MANDATE FOR PUBLIC PARTICIPATION

Numerous nations have laws requiring stakeholder identification and invitation for involvement in planning addressing significant environmental issues. Most of these laws, however, do not specify how to structure public participation in such conflicts, nor do they provide guidelines on how information gathered from the public should be incorporated into management decisions made by regulatory agencies. As society has become increasingly aware of environmental issues and has expressed a desire to participate in the regulatory process, the problems of structuring appropriate public participation opportunities, identifying appropriate stakeholders, and constructively incorporating public interests has become a central concern for many natural resource agencies, industries, interest groups, and individual members of the public.

NEPA probably is the most significant national law requiring public participation. Although its legal jurisdiction is limited to the United States, "NEPA's influence has been far-reaching, with its progeny in the statute books of 19 states and over 130 of the world's nations" (Salzman & Thompson, 2003, p. 275). NEPA was preceded by the Administrative Procedures Act (APA) of 1946, which required agencies to allow public comment on draft rules. The APA also allowed citizens access to the courts to request judicial review of actions taken by federal agencies, generally referred to as the citizen suit provision of the APA (Doremus, 1999).

In his study of the evolution of U.S. environmental policy, Hays (1987) argued that economic growth and lifestyle changes following World War II created the conditions for intensified environmental conflict in the United States. He claimed that, between 1957 and 1965, increased concern for recreation, wetlands, parklands, and other aesthetic pleasures of the natural environment led to the first phase of federal legislation addressing environmental conflict. In the midst of this phase, concern also began to increase regarding adverse effects of industrial development, especially air and water pollution. These concerns marked the beginning of a second phase in environmental policy development, between 1965 and 1972, in which the focus shifted to the relationship between ecological integrity and human health and safety.

NEPA was signed into law on January 1, 1970, creating the White House Council on Environmental Quality (CEQ). President

Richard Nixon stated in his first State of the Union Address (January 22, 1970) that the environment, "next to our desire for peace, may well become the major concern of the American people in the decade of the seventies." On February 10, 1970, he delivered a special message to the Congress on environmental quality in which he asserted the goal of fighting pollution and touted the CEQ as "the keeper of our environmental conscience and a goad to our ingenuity." Then, the White House transmitted Reorganization Plan 3 of 1970 to Congress in the summer of the same year, calling for the creation of the Environmental Protection Agency (EPA), which would demonstrate "a profound commitment to the rescue of our natural environment, and the preservation of the Earth as a place both habitable by and hospitable to man" (Nixon, 1970). As President Nixon approached the end of his second full year in office, NEPA had been passed, the White House CEQ had been established and had presented its first report to the Congress, the EPA was almost a year old, and the president had used his first State of Union address to mark the environment as a centerpiece of his administration's domestic agenda.

NEPA dictates that "every recommendation or report on proposals for legislation and other major federal actions significantly affecting the quality of the human environment" must prepare detailed statements regarding the "environmental impacts of proposed action" (42 U.S.C. § 4332c). These detailed statements, called draft environmental impact statements (EIS), are to be provided to the public for comment, whether through a public meeting or a solicitation of written public comments (Steelman & Ascher, 1997). While the earlier APA had required that citizens take the initiative to become involved in public participation, NEPA requires that agencies actively solicit input from the public on any federal decisions that might significantly affect the environment. Both industrialized and developing nations have used NEPA as a model for public participation in the development of environmental policy.

Members of the public vary in their interest and willingness to participate in environmental policy making, though all members of the public are assumed to provide valuable information pertinent to the decision-making process. Yosie and Herbst (1998) categorized citizen-stakeholders into four groups: those who are directly affected by a decision; those who are interested in the issue at hand and wish to become involved and provide input; those who seek information on the issue from a general interest; and those who are directly impacted by a decision and are unaware of, or choose not to participate in, any public participation process. The challenge to federal agencies, as required by NEPA, is to identify this last group of stakeholders and actively solicit their input.

Agencies also are required to respond formally to any concerns and comments submitted by the public on a draft EIS (Doremus, 1999). NEPA requires

> publication of a notice of intent, a scoping process, publication of a draft document identifying alternatives and impacts, a public hearing, preparation of a formal record, a record of decision specifying what had been decided and on what basis, and adequate notice for all the above. (Creighton, 1999, p. 250)

Though the law is prescriptive in requiring agencies to solicit and respond to public comment, NEPA-type processes have failed to satisfy public demands for a variety of reasons. Members of the public complain that the documents required by NEPA are too technical, that agencies have frequently determined the outcome of the situation before the public is allowed access to the process, and that agencies do not make sufficient effort to identify and involve affected stakeholders. The initial scoping stage of the NEPA process is the point at which potential environmental impacts are determined by the relevant agency, and many members of the public argue that by the conclusion of this phase agencies already have made their decision regarding outcomes. Involving the public in scoping activities before creating the draft EIS could provide more meaningful opportunities for stakeholders to influence the process and help to prevent "premature agency decisions" (Spyke, 1999, p. 278). Public involvement, however, often begins with an opportunity to comment on the draft EIS. The NEPA process also lacks specification regarding how much weight public comment should be given in the decision-making process. Essentially, public involvement still spans a broad gulf ranging from the right to know what information was used to arrive at a decision, to direct participation in the decision-making process itself.

Regulatory agencies in the U.S., Canada, and the European Union are now required in most cases to identify and invite impacted stakeholders and other members of the interested public to provide comment on significant actions that will modify the environment. How these public participation processes should be structured and how the information gathered from the public should be incorporated into the management decisions regulatory agencies are mandated to make has been at the center of environmental controversies since long before public participation was mandated.

SOCIAL DEMAND FOR PUBLIC PARTICIPATION

Cvetkovich and Earle (1994) defined public participation as "direct involvement of individual citizens and citizen groups in the seeking of information about decision making related to and the management planning regarding land issues" (p. 163). One reason public participation is so central to environmental conflict is that it is considered a critical component of democratic society, "an unassailable good" (Steelman & Ascher, 1997, p. 73). Arnstein (1969) posited that public participation is essentially a redistribution of power, from government to citizen. Supporters of broad public participation posit that the public can best judge and represent its own interests and that participation will further enhance the public's ability to participate in the democratic system of government, reduce public feelings of powerlessness and alienation, and increase the legitimacy of the governing body (Fiorino, 1990). Public participation and deliberation can benefit society by creating public policy that is reflective of public values and opinions and that nurtures social, psychological, and political empowerment of the public. Conflict over how public participation should be constructed occurs on a regular basis, however. Steelman and Ascher (1997) noted that

"the general public may not be particularly competent, interested or knowledgeable participants . . . the preferences expressed by the public can be inconsistent and may lead to conflict, leaving decision makers with confusing data on which to base their policies" (p. 73).

Given the regulatory context for environmental conflicts and the expectation for civic participation, government agencies are tasked with gathering data from diverse groups and individuals and incorporating that data into policy decisions. These data often are internally conflicting, with competing claims of validity dependent upon multiple goals for participating in the process, as well as multiple ideologies for resource management. Dustin, Schneider, McAvoy, and Frakt (2002) used the controversy between rock climbers and American Indians at Devils Tower National Monument in Wyoming (USA) to point out that conflict over something so apparently mundane as outdoor recreation pits people with fundamentally different worldviews against each other. A special section of *American Indian Quarterly* (Martin & Piper, 2001) provides an extended description of current environmental conflicts between American Indians and other land users, and also argues that public participation processes must improve opportunities for self-representation among American Indians. Gericke and Sullivan (1994) noted that if the public does not feel its concerns have been adequately addressed in the resulting decisions, the attempt to reduce conflict through public participation will have been for naught. Yet, it is nearly impossible for agencies to address all public concerns and create decisions that align with the ideologies of all stakeholders.

Yosie and Herbst (1998) identified the impetus for increased public participation in environmental conflict as (a) a lack of public confidence in government and lack of trust in its ability to manage resources effectively, (b) increased public demand for improved environmental quality, (c) increased public interest in participating in environmental issues, (d) increased regulatory requirements to provide environmental performance information to the public, (e) failure of governmental organizations to consider the values and opinions of stakeholders, and (f) increased commitment by governmental agencies to include public participation in their environmental management decisions. Walters, Aydelotte, and Miller (2000) argued that the public expects elected and appointed decision makers within government to represent the public interest and to protect the public good when addressing environmental resource issues. When the public perceives that environmental policy has not addressed the public interest, dissatisfaction arises.

Public expectations for participation in environmental policy deliberations, then, suggest that it should provide an opportunity to examine scientific and technical information and result in well-informed governmental decisions that are accepted by most stakeholders. Public participation could set up a collaborative dialogue among stakeholders to achieve understanding of perspectives and jointly constructed public policies. As it applies to environmental policy, however, public participation is much more likely to be competitive than collaborative. The existence of scarce, and sometimes fragile, nonrenewable resources and the distributive negotiation structure of most public participation processes results in disputes "centered around the distributive allocation of a fairly fixed set of resources" rather than the pursuit of mutually beneficial and satisfactory decisions for all stakeholders (Walker & Daniels, 1996, p. 80). Communication researchers and practitioners, then, are challenged to develop processes that enhance collaborative potential without ignoring material realities such as correlations between childhood asthma and air pollution, the rates of human population increase and species extinction, and low-income neighborhoods and toxic waste facilities. In this section, we discuss types of participation processes available to the public and the theoretical constructs used to evaluate the participative nature of these processes.

Venues

Various methods have emerged to engage stakeholders in the public participation process. The most common are written public comment periods, public hearings, listening sessions, workshops, negotiated rule making, and consensus-based decision making. The degree of involvement may range from providing a spontaneous

reaction to specific questions, such as to a telephone survey, to engaging in extended consideration and study of an issue over time with direct power and influence over the final decision.

The least interactive participation methods are the written public comment period and listening sessions. *Written public comment periods* are mandated under NEPA and provide the public an opportunity to review draft EISs and give written comment that must be formally addressed by the regulatory agency in the final record of decision. The written public comment period does not allow dialogue between the agency and public, and the agency can simply indicate, "we disagree," in the final decision, without offering further detail (Ratliff, 1998). *Public hearings* are more formal opportunities for the public to address their comments on draft decisions verbally to agency officials; this method has been heavily used and has been subjected to extensive critique. *Listening sessions* are less formal opportunities for the public to voice their concerns and opinions to agency officials. The officials are obligated to listen, but are not obligated to respond to the public or to engage in dialogue regarding the issues and concerns.

Workshops, negotiated rule making, and consensus-based decision making engage the public in more interactive, sustained communication and provide members of the public potentially greater influence over the final decision. *Workshops* of various kinds involve small groups of stakeholders engaged in working sessions designed to complete a task such as identifying problems to be addressed by a study or action, developing alternatives from which the agency will choose, evaluating alternative action plans, or identifying the potential impacts of action plans (Creighton, 1981). In *negotiated rule making,* an agency solicits representatives from diverse stakeholder communities and forms a panel that is tasked with collaboratively defining an acceptable industry standard for an environmental issue (e.g., air quality levels for certain chemical compounds). The premise is that if diverse representatives can agree, it is highly probable that the agency would agree with the standard as well. Their agreement becomes the draft regulation that is presented to the public for comment (Creighton, 1999). *Consensus-based decision making* is a process whereby stakeholders and agency officials negotiate a consensual agreement for the management of an environmental issue. As such processes have become more popular, the definition of consensus has become increasingly vague (Peterson, Peterson, & Peterson, 2005). Walker and Daniels (1996) argued that, at best, all of these approaches are based on joint learning and fact finding, exploring underlying value differences, encouraging constructive dialogue, and direct communication among stakeholders to address issues, concerns, and interests openly. In the next section, we evaluate the participative nature of these processes according to various theoretical models of citizen participation and the issue of legitimacy.

Legitimacy

Several researchers have used legitimacy as a unifying construct for evaluating public participation. Mascarenhas and Scarce (2004) drew on the concept of legitimacy, as articulated in alternative dispute resolution (ADR) theory, to study natural resource planning in British Columbia and found that successful public processes must have fair representation, appropriate government resources, and be consensus driven. They stated that the most fundamental criterion for a successful public process was legitimacy. This does not necessarily translate into broad agreement on how to achieve legitimacy. Webler, Tuler, and Krueger (2001) found that residents in northern New England and New York emphasized a diverse and internally conflicted set of factors as essential to legitimacy. Different respondents indicated that a public participation process was legitimate if it (a) was popular, (b) facilitated an ideological discussion across interest groups, (c) highlighted the reality of power struggle, or (d) provided strong leadership leading toward compromise. Drawing from decades of process work in environmental conflicts throughout the state of New York, Senecah (2004) argued that a legitimate conflict management process must provide all stakeholders with access, standing, and influence, requiring that conflict resolution practitioners have a broad expertise in ADR principles (see Lipsky & Seeber, Chapter 13 in this volume).

Arnstein (1969) developed a model of citizen participation based on the analogy of a ladder.

As citizens climb the ladder, their participation gains increased legitimacy as it empowers them to determine the outcome of policy deliberation. At the bottom of the ladder are methods of *nonparticipation* for educating stakeholders in order to cure them of their misconceptions. One rung up the ladder is *tokenism,* which allows participants to speak, though without power to ensure their voice will have any impact. Cvetkovich and Earle (1994) referred to tokenism as simple voice. Examples of this level of participation are written public comment periods and listening sessions. *Placation* allows stakeholders to advise decision makers but does not provide any power to enforce their advice. Stakeholder workshops often exemplify this advisory role. Arnstein's ladder then moves into *degrees of citizen power.* At these levels, stakeholders have the authority to negotiate with those in power and may even move into the position of a powerful majority where they take full managerial control of the issue. Some types of negotiated rule making and consensus-based decision making allow this level of participation.

Waddell (1996) took a different approach to categorizing public participation modes. He defined four models, differentiating among them by their approach to information transfer and their attitude toward values and emotions evidenced by participating experts and the public. The *technocratic* model allows environmental decisions to remain under the full authority of the experts in science, engineering, industry, and government without providing any formal opportunity for the public to monitor implementation of the decisions. Under this model, the only information that must be transferred between the experts and the public is the final decision. The experts must inform the public of their decision so the public can follow the rules. The *one-way Jeffersonian* model allows the public to participate in decision making by listening when experts provide them with technical information. Within this model, the purpose of public participation is to educate the public so that it will agree with decisions reached by experts. Public hearings generally exemplify the one-way Jeffersonian model. The *interactive Jeffersonian* model requires that experts provide technical information to the public, and allows members of the public to share their opinions, values, and emotions with the experts. Thus, resulting decisions should integrate technical information drawn from the experts with opinions, values, and emotions drawn from the public. Workshops where members of the public have an opportunity both to learn technical information from the experts and to share their opinions with those experts exemplify the interactive Jeffersonian model. Most public participation processes fall someplace along a continuum between the one-way and interactive Jeffersonian models.

The fourth possibility elaborated by Waddell (1996), the *social constructionist* model, recognizes that both technical experts and members of the general public have access to technical information that may be valuable in making decisions. Further, it assumes that technical experts, as well as members of the public, are influenced by opinions, values, and emotions and allows "an interactive exchange of information during which *all participants* also communicate, appeal to, and engage values, beliefs, and emotions" (p. 142). The approach results in policy that is jointly constructed by all participants. Although the social constructionist model is rarely practiced, it is more likely to occur in negotiated rule making and consensus-based decision-making efforts where stakeholders are viewed as equals with agency officials (Fiorino, 1990).

Sustainable Development

No term associated with environmental conflict has enjoyed more widespread public legitimacy than *sustainable development. Our Common Future* (World Commission on Environment and Development, 1987), which linked sustainability to development and intergenerational and international equity, suggested sustainable development as a concept that could resolve environmental conflict (M. J. Peterson et al., 2004; T. R. Peterson, 1997). This capitalized on the famous definition of sustainable development as that "meeting the needs of the present without compromising the ability of future generations to meet their own needs" (World Commission on Environment and Development, 1987, p. 43). It was further legitimated by the fact that conservation biologists had long advocated sustained use of natural resources (Allen & Hoekstra, 1993; Leopold, 1949). Perhaps

because its definition allows proponents to simultaneously endorse both environmental protection and economic development, governments, private industries, natural resource agencies, conflict resolution professionals, and many environmental advocacy groups wholeheartedly embraced sustainable development. Mazmanian and Craft (1999) argued that sustainable development enables people to move beyond the conventional focus on biological well-being, to the inclusion of psychological, sociological, economic, political, and cultural well-being. Its potential to build a sense of community among disputants makes sustainable development especially attractive to ADR professionals.

Organizations ranging from the World Wildlife Fund to the World Bank have embraced the term. One of its most attractive features is that each community can create its own reality for the concept (T. R. Peterson, 1997). Initially, academics, public policy makers, and industry vigorously endorsed sustainable development (Aguirre, 2002). As supporters vociferously petitioned for interpretations complementary with their own ethical perspectives, multiple meanings evolved (M. N. Peterson, Peterson, & Peterson, 2005). Following the widespread acceptance of sustainable development, these diverse groups attempted to co-opt the meaning of the concept for their idiosyncratic purposes. For example, the concept became popular with advocates for indigenous groups, some of whom argued that because such groups have always used their natural resources in a sustainable way, they should not be denied access to them in the name of protecting wilderness or pristine nature (Nabhan, 1995), while others argued that such groups should not be denied the right to protect nature in the name of economic development (Amnesty International and Sierra Club, 2000). Business interests used sustainable development in marketing campaigns designed to persuade the public that purchasing green merchandise (ranging from electric cars to organic salad mixes) would do away with environmental conflicts associated with consumerism (Stauber, 1994; Woollard & Ostry, 2000). This melee led to an array of perspectives on sustainable development rooted in vastly different values and beliefs.

The failure of sustainable development to meet the expectations of conflicting interest groups generated at least as much conflict as it promised to resolve (M. N. Peterson et al., 2005). Many advocates discarded the concept when the conflicting value-based assumptions of competing views of sustainable development became apparent (Aguirre, 2002; Jacob, 1994; Lélé & Norgaard, 1996). Environmental ethicists such as Callicott and Mumford (1997) rejected anthropocentric versions of sustainable development in favor of "ecosystem sustainability." Faced with the surge in green marketing, many environmentalists determined that sustainable development was "code for perpetual growth . . . force-fed to the world community by the global corporate-political-media network" (Willers, 1994, p. 1146) and repudiated the term.

Critical evaluation of sustainable development as a foundational concept for managing environmental conflict can be summed up in the claim that, at best, it is an unproven concept and, at worst, it has failed to slow the inexorable shrinkage of the habitats needed to preserve environmental health. No one has yet figured out how best to reconcile environmental protection with temporally and spatially immediate human preferences. Successful strategies will require far more commitment and far more difficult choices than have been made to date. Those who would manage environmental conflict must discover and implement social processes that enable humans to overcome our current inability to make many small consistent decisions that lead to a broad sustainable outcome.

As these frameworks illustrate, various approaches to public participation provide diverse combinations of opportunities to voice opinions, participate in dialogue with decision makers, and influence the outcome of environmental dilemmas. Moreover, multiple communication processes can be present in a single public participation venue. For example, a public workshop may involve soliciting and gathering information, consulting with stakeholders, and direct negotiation leading to a final decision.

CRITIQUES OF PUBLIC HEARING AND CONSENSUS-BASED PROCESSES

The most commonly used approaches to public involvement in disputes over environmental policy are public hearings of various sorts and consensus-based processes. Despite the fact that public hearings produce almost universally negative public reaction, they are the regulatory agencies' method of choice for nearly every environmental issue requiring public involvement. We use the terms *public hearing* and *public meeting* interchangeably in this chapter to describe a formal gathering of regulatory agency officials and members of the public to address an environmental policy concern. Consensus-based processes have emerged in response to negative reactions among both the general public and technical experts to public hearings. While not so ubiquitous as public hearings, consensus-based processes are enjoying a wave of popularity among both natural resource management agencies and ADR practitioners. In this section, we review critiques of public hearings and consensus processes from the perspectives of communication functions, conflict dynamics, and (social and ecological) effectiveness.

Public Hearings

Ideally, the public hearing represents "such democratic principles as the rights of assembly, free speech and representation . . . [and] seem[s] to provide ideal opportunities for people to gather, confront issues, and work toward finding solutions" (McComas, 2001a, p. 135). In practice, however, the public hearing rarely achieves this ideal (Arnstein, 1969; Fiorino, 1990; Heberlein, 1976; Kasperson, 1986; McComas, 2001a, 2001b; T. R. Peterson, 1997; Rosener, 1981). Despite having the lowest outcome acceptance and process satisfaction ratings of any regularly used public participation method (Rowe & Frewer, 2000), public hearings remain the most frequently used approach to public involvement in environmental policy formation (McComas, 2001a, 2001b).

The typical public meeting involves a technical presentation by agency officials, limited opportunity for the members of the public to ask questions for clarification, and then a formal comment period. During the formal comment period, members of the public are given a certain amount of time to present their comments and concerns to agency officials. Their comments and concerns are recorded so that agency officials may formally respond on the record in the final decision (Ratliff, 1998). A fundamental problem with the use of public hearings is that agency officials and citizen stakeholders attending the meetings often have different goals and use different forms of discourse to present their ideas and concerns—thus often exacerbating rather than ameliorating conflicts.

All stakeholders involved in public participatory processes have goals for their involvement. Broad goals shared by most stakeholders include improvement of government, sharing power among relevant stakeholders, increased positive regard for the government by the public, enhanced public policy, and incorporation of multiple perspectives into environmental policy decisions. Community-based goals include empowering the citizenry to take action and have a voice in public policy, strengthening community relationships, and fostering local leadership in environmental issues. The primary goal of most citizen stakeholders is to handle the immediate concern affecting their interests. Stakeholders also may attempt to persuade decision makers to adopt their perspective toward the issues or to increase the public's share of control in democratic government (Spyke, 1999). According to NEPA, governmental decision makers are mandated to enter this process with several goals. They are to use the meetings to improve the decision-making processes, share information with stakeholders, reach diverse communities, respond to public concerns, and lobby for public acceptance of their decisions. From the perspective of all stakeholders, the success of public hearings typically is defined by whether participant goals are achieved.

Chess and Purcell's (1999) synopsis of studies evaluating the success of public hearings reported that standards for evaluating public participation focus on the efficacy of the process itself and on satisfaction with the outcome based on theoretical values imposed by the researcher and/or the goals of the agencies and stakeholders. Fiorino (1990) identified four criteria for evaluating public participation processes based on democratic principles. He argued that participation processes should (a) allow amateurs (nonexperts) to participate directly in decision making, (b) allow the public to work collaboratively with agency officials to determine policy, (c) provide a means for direct interaction over an extended period of time, and (d) allow the public to participate in the process with standing equal to agency officials. Fiorino found that, in public hearings, members of the public typically are permitted only limited and indirect participation in discussion and are subordinated to agency officials.

Cvetkovich and Earle (1994) found that even when a public participation process meets Fiorino's (1990) democratic principles, the public remains dissatisfied with public meetings if the outcome (or final decision) fails to protect their individual interests or is incompatible with personal values. T. R. Peterson's (1997) analysis of discourse and political outcomes from hearings over whether Agricultural Canada should destroy all bison in an area where most human residents were members of Cree or Dene Metis bands indicated that public participants found the hearings satisfactory only to the degree the public was able to subvert the hearing process. Dispute resolution professionals are challenged to find a process that will allow the public to participate meaningfully in a self-determinate manner, yet also create a sense of legitimacy for the process and the outcome—so that a broad range of outcomes will be accepted by most stakeholders—even when the decision fails to meet their interests completely.

Given the research indicating that public hearings rarely help agencies accomplish their public involvement goals, and often create further conflict, it is puzzling that they remain the most widely used method of public participation in environmental decision making. Checkoway (1981) suggested this occurs because public meetings serve various needs for the agency in addition to allowing public involvement in the final decision. Checkoway argued that natural resource agencies use public hearings to satisfy the minimum legal requirements for public participation under NEPA, to prove that information was disseminated, and to demonstrate that required public participation occurred, without focusing on the process or outcomes of that participation. Heberlein (1976) described this purpose as the informational function of public meetings, where information is disseminated and public opinion is gathered without any plans to incorporate it into the final decision. Another reason to use public meetings is to build support for agency decisions. Public meetings often are sites for persuasive communication designed to influence the public to support the plan recommended by the agency and industries that stand to benefit from the preferred alternative (Kaminstein, 1996; Ratliff, 1998). Checkoway argued that public meetings are also used to defuse community antagonism through a controlled, orderly display of concern for the public interest. This display of concern is intended to legitimate a priori decisions.

Heberlein (1976) claimed that public meetings serve a co-optation function when "the goal of the hearing is to let irate citizens and interest groups let off steam and complain about the project" (p. 200). In such cases, agency officials use the hearing to indicate that they are concerned about the needs of the public; however, they remain in control of the final decision. Though the agency decision may not be influenced by public comments, allowing the public to voice their concerns in a formal setting negates the public's ability to win a lawsuit against the agency for not allowing public participation. Cvetkovich and Earle (1994) noted that by allowing the public to have its say, those in power are avoiding possible claims of injustice, and thus maintaining the power imbalance between agency officials and members of the public. Conversely, Heberlein asserted that public meetings could serve the beneficial function of encouraging meaningful interaction if agency officials used them as opportunities to genuinely listen to, and understand, the needs and concerns represented by the public, particularly if they then attempted to incorporate those concerns into the final decision. Heberlein did not indicate how such an interaction could be facilitated, however. In fact, in most studies the communication and conflict dynamics of public hearings are not specifically identified, let alone discussed.

A review of the literature addressing public hearings suggests that such meetings often exacerbate the very conflicts they attempt to resolve and do not encourage meaningful dialogue between regulatory agency officials and members of the public. Citizens perceive a significant power imbalance between agency personnel and expert consultants on the one hand, and members of the public on the other (Kaminstein, 1996; Ratliff, 1998). This is evidenced by the scientific language and other jargon used by agency personnel and their expert consultants, agency control over the agenda—including definition of relevant issues, the formal atmosphere established and maintained by agency officials, and the retention by the convening agency of sole determination of the final decision or outcome. Though public hearings may be referenced as opportunities for dialogue between agency officials and members of the public, empirical research on public meetings indicates that rather than realizing these opportunities, public meetings typically inhibit dialogue and reinforce existing positions and competition among stakeholders. The following sections address the ways power imbalances between the public and agency officials are established and maintained.

Scientific knowledge and language. Pearce and Littlejohn (1997) noted that one of the stressors acting upon public discourse is the "hegemony of experts and an increasing gap between expert/technical discourse and the discourse of the electorate" (p. 96). In the case of public meetings, two forms of discourse typically occur, technical/scientific discourse and emotional/personal rights discourse. Agency officials and expert consultants open the meeting with a formal presentation about the environmental issue couched in a barrage of technical language, including scientific facts, chemical names, and statistics, that can overwhelm the public (Kaminstein, 1996). Kaminstein also noted that although scientists are required to support any assertion with data, the form in which these data are presented often is confusing.

In environmental conflicts, science often is portrayed as the neutral authority within the political fray. Ozawa (1996) noted that, because of the authority given to the scientific method, scientific results often are presented as indisputable facts. These results typically are characterized as having been discovered in a manner free from research biases and as forming the appropriate foundation for decisions. This leads to the presumption in the minds of some that, by advocating results supported by science, decision makers are able to step out of the political milieu and render value-free judgments. Science is thus used to shield decision makers from criticism because science is portrayed as the arbiter among multiple perspectives. Ozawa emphasized that, because Western culture tends to accept scientific fact as immutable and unquestionable, the fact that science also is used as a tool of persuasion to support and attack positions is masked. Kaminstein (1996) also noted that agency officials and scientists present technical information as though it were unarguable. When members of the public attempt to question the science of experts, the responses generally are in the same technically complex language that sparked the question in the first place, thus shedding no more light on the subject than the initial presentation. The use of complex, technical, and scientific language by convening agencies and their consultants effectively discourages participants from asking apparently naïve questions.

In addition to the jargon used by experts, members of the lay public often are blocked from understanding the technical and scientific content of the meetings because they lack access to critical data (Wondolleck, Manring, & Crowfoot, 1996). Kaminstein (1996) noted that participants often remain silent because they feel they do "not have the technical background to question, contest or disagree with the scientists as they presented their battery of facts" (p. 460). Often, participants simply fear they will be ridiculed. Ratliff (1998) observed a Department of Energy representative tell a public hearing participant that the information the participant requested could be found in any health physics textbook, "insinuating that the information either is, can or could be, easily available to anybody, as though anyone can understand a health physics text, or have one laying around to consult whenever a question comes up" (p. 12). Ratliff asserted that, though members of the public should try to inform themselves before coming to public meetings, they also should be able to expect respectful answers to questions about confusing technical material presented by agency officials and scientists.

The language disparity between agency officials and their consulting scientists, and members of the public discourages questions

and comments from the public and limits the appropriate discourse for the meeting. Members of the public often speak a discourse of rights, emotions, concerns, and personal interests. Tauxe (1995) noted that when members of the public use local rhetorical conventions to address planning issues, they are at a significant disadvantage as compared to those who speak within the bureaucratic, rationalistic conventions of the decision makers. Kaminstein (1996) suggested that, because the language of scientific discourse does not leave room for the language of emotions, members of the public are unable to express themselves fully in public hearings. This inability to communicate results in frustration and anger that, when expressed, is even more inappropriate within the scientifically rationalized discursive environment of the public hearing. Pearce and Littlejohn (1997) asserted that if conflicts of this sort are to be resolved, the parties must use a common discourse to express and settle differences. Agency officials establish the dominant scientific discourse, however, which effectively silences most members of the public.

Agenda setting and definitional hegemony. Wondolleck et al. (1996) asserted that public meetings reinforce power imbalances between agency officials and members of the public in that the public has no influence or control over the agenda or structure of the meeting. Chess and Purcell (1999) claimed that scheduling public meetings toward the end of the planning process places members of the public in a reactive mode rather than allowing them to contribute ideas to the development of the draft plan. Agency officials also exert control over the participation process by structuring the meeting and setting the agenda. Participants in public meetings often are required to register their request to comment prior to the beginning of the meeting and are given a preset amount of time (e.g., 3 minutes) in which to present their comments (Ratliff, 1998). Often, agency officials retain the right to change the structure of the meeting or the agenda at any point. For example, Ratliff (1998) observed officials instructing a meeting participant that he was barred from asking any more questions in the question-and-answer session before the formal comment period of the meeting. These officials also decided to end the session early without explanation to the participants.

In addition to structural control, agency officials control the scope of pertinent issues for discussion and how those issues are defined. They use a rhetorical device that Dionisopoulos and Crable (1988) termed *definitional hegemony*, where parties in power establish the definition of issues and then obtain influence over the outcomes by the very fact that they established the definitions in the first place. Chess and Purcell (1999) found that agency officials limit the scope of discussion in public meetings so that non-technical topics, including social issues and concerns, are outside the scope of discussion and therefore do not warrant comment from agency officials. Kaminstein (1996) observed that "how a problem is defined by public officials, and what public officials are willing and unwilling to talk about, drastically shapes the ensuing dialogue at public meetings" (p. 462). Once a problem or issue is defined, that definition establishes boundaries for what can and cannot be included in discussion, thus ruling out topics that others might see as pertinent. For example, Ratliff (1998) recounted how agency officials announced in their technical presentation that the scope of the discussion included only how nuclear waste would be contained and transported to an area, not whether the area should be chosen as a dumpsite. Subsequently, members of the public were not able to voice their concerns over having a toxic dump in their backyard to the agency officials—that was outside the scope of discussion.

Kaminstein (1996) asserted that what is left unsaid in public meetings often is of great concern to participants. Agency officials seem to operate from the notion that to avoid conflict, they must avoid discussing controversial issues with the public. Suppressing environmental conflict through avoidance strategies, however, tends to produce deeper intractability (M. N. Peterson, Peterson, Peterson, Lopez, & Silvy, 2002; T. R. Peterson & Horton, 1995). Members of the public may feel that the agency is withholding crucial information, or that they are being "pushed aside and patronized" (Kaminstein, 1996, p. 463). Chess and Purcell (1999) found that when agencies used a public meeting to avoid responding to public concerns and worries, those same agencies often found themselves faced with bitter opposition and conflict.

Formal atmosphere. The atmosphere of the public hearing itself is set by the physical arrangements of the meeting room, the formality of the event, and the ground rules for participating in the public comment period. The typical public meeting is arranged with a panel of agency officials and experts at the front of the room, a lectern and microphone facing the panel at which members of the public may speak, and auditorium-style seating for the public behind the lectern. Presentations by agency officials generally are calm and rational, with responses to questions offered in the same tone even if the questions are hostile and emotional. This communication style establishes an atmosphere in which it is inappropriate to respond to the presentations in an emotional manner or to admit that the issue causes emotional trauma. The formal atmosphere and apparent rationality of agency-sponsored presentations interact to discourage open discussion of personal opposition to preferred alternatives. It can inhibit discussion of deeply felt concerns and issues between agency officials and members of the public. Kaminstein (1996) observed that it is "difficult for residents to gripe, complain, disagree, or dispute [the information presented], since they [are] treated in such an ostensibly kind and respectful way by the government officials" (p. 461).

Final determination. Regardless of the majority opinion expressed by the public in a hearing, the agency retains the right and responsibility to make the final decision. The NEPA process requires only that they respond formally to each of the comments offered during the public comment period. Kaminstein (1996) offered an illustration when describing a situation where the EPA continued to follow existing protocol for cleaning up a Superfund site even though there was overwhelming public opposition expressed in public meetings. Agencies leading the public meetings studied by Cvetkovich and Earle (1994) and Ratliff (1998) also decided against public opinion and continued with the plans they had originally offered for public comment. Ignoring public opinion that has been clearly expressed in hearings perpetuates the notion that public participation is futile and that agencies conduct public hearings simply to avoid lawsuits, to gauge public support for predetermined projects, or to legitimate previously made decisions.

Through the NEPA process, agencies determine policy, either making use of public comment or ignoring it. As Ratliff (1998) noted, "assessing comments as meaningless" sends a message that public participation is mere window dressing (p. 14). Kaminstein (1996) asserted that "public officials not only have the power to define problems, but they also have the legal power to decide solutions, regardless of citizens' reservations and concerns" (p. 462). Research on social justice has shown that giving people the opportunity to voice their concerns, whether or not their concerns have any significant effect on the outcome, will lead to greater perceived fairness in the process (Lind, Kray, & Thompson, 1998). Cvetkovich and Earle (1994) argued, however, that the salience of fair process is severely minimized if the outcome of the public participation process appears to ignore the public interest.

Summary. These four characteristics of public hearings (emphasis on scientific jargon, agency control of the agenda and scope of issues, formal meeting atmosphere, and agency authority to determine outcomes without adhering to public opinion) all combine to discourage effective dialogue. Littlejohn and Domenici (2001) laid out the requirements for creating dialogue as constructive conversation. They asserted that dialogue does not occur without "treating people like people" (p. 33), or taking their concerns seriously. Even though agency officials may treat members of the public with formalized respect, failure to address their personal concerns and worries, ignoring their opinions, and bombarding them with technical information does not constitute treating them "like people" (p. 33). Instead, this behavior objectifies the public and makes it easier to ignore personal concerns and opinions. The question-and-answer format of the public meeting, rigid scheduling of the public comment period, and control over the scope of the issues to be discussed all work against meaningful opportunities

for dialogue to occur within the traditional public hearing format.

Public meetings generally treat communication as a mere conduit through which discrete packets of preexisting information can flow—technical information from experts to members of the public, and opinions and values from members of the public to the experts. Technical experts have information they believe would help make the public more tractable if members of the public could just learn it. Agency officials also believe that, by understanding public opinion and values, they can explain agency policy in a way that will encourage greater public acceptance. Public hearings occur within a system that combines severe power imbalances among parties, a constrained environment for dialogue, and a strong likelihood that interdependence among parties will be ignored. All these factors combine to yield a public participation process that fails to realize significant dialogic potential. Still, public hearings are a common, though generally ineffective, means for managing environmental conflict.

Consensus Building

Media attention and public outcry over environmental issues have occurred since at least the beginning of the 20th century (Neuzil & Kovarik, 1996), and environmental policy and regulations have been rooted in conflict and argumentation (M. N. Peterson et al., 2005). Public hearings, which are common in North America and Western Europe, offer the potential for increased dialogue, but that potential has not been realized. Rather, hearings have largely excluded legitimate discussion of non-technical dimensions of environmental disputes. Consensus-based processes have emerged as an alternative to the acrimonious exchanges constructed with zero-sum outcomes that have led increasingly to gridlock and citizen outrage. In the following sections, we discuss the rationale for, and challenges to, consensus-building processes.

Rationale for consensus building. The search for alternative approaches to environmental decision making and regulation has led governments at all levels and in multiple nations to involve citizens in ways other than voting, contacting representatives, and participating in the formal public hearings encouraged by legislation such as the APA and NEPA. This trend emphasizes facilitation of diverse sets of individuals in long-term relationships, where they establish mutually agreed upon goals and seek solutions to complex problems. These approaches promise to enrich the overall quality of democracy by endowing governments and their regulatory agencies with additional legitimacy and providing communication channels for generating agreement on environmental policies.

Susskind, McKearnan, and Thomas-Larmer (1999) argued that addressing today's complex environmental conflicts requires a greater sharing of information across time, space, and institutional jurisdictions, or consensus building in a broad sense. They pointed out that consensus building is important in all environmental domains, from local to regional to global, and ultimately to developing a clear vision of what a sustainable future encompasses for all humans.

The shift to consensus-based models as a foundation for environmental decision making gained rapid momentum during the late 1980s (M. N. Peterson et al., 2005). This change was facilitated by the meteoric rise of sustainable development. Sustainable development's focus on local conditions, diversity, participation, and locally produced development strengthened this link (de la Court, 1992; Kothari, 1990; T. R. Peterson, 1997), particularly because consensus is more readily attainable at smaller, local scales (T. R. Peterson et al., 2004).

Bingham (1985) noted that although environmental controversy was not a new phenomenon, the fact that "consensus-building processes show considerable promise for resolving environmental disputes," was (p. 291). She identified consensus-building processes as especially useful for situations where parties needed to maintain a "continuing relationship" to "solve future problems with one another" (p. 291). Bingham cautioned, however, that general discomfort with controversy evidenced in the "enthusiasm for the word nonadversarial" should not be allowed to overshadow awareness of the basic assumptions on which consensus processes are based, "in particular, how the issues are defined, and how well all parties are represented" (p. 291).

Consensus models usually are linked to some type of community building. Although the process often inspires initial conflict involving the diverse interests that make up a community, it can lead to greater support for environmental policies (Lin, 1996; Turner & Rylander, 1998). Greater support within the local community carries benefits, including lower enforcement costs, higher compliance rates, less conflict, and higher community satisfaction. Consensus-based approaches to environmental conflict promise to reduce implementation costs through the creation and use of social capital and more efficient use of natural and human capital (Costanza & Ruth, 1998; Farley & Costanza, 2002). Social capital is "the aggregate of the actual or potential resources which are linked to possession of a durable network of more or less institutionalized relationships of mutual acquaintance or recognition" (Bourdieu, 1985, p. 248). The ability to secure benefits through membership in communities and other social structures (social capital) motivates observance of group norms. Community-based approaches promise to reduce administrative costs by paying for management at least in part with social capital (Kollock, 1998; Ostrom, 1990).

The transition to consensus-based resolution of environmental conflict has been facilitated in the United States by presidential support of Community-Based Conservation Planning (CBCP) for the purpose of developing Habitat Conservation Plans (HCP) (M. N. Peterson et al., 2004). To enable landowners to protect property rights when their land is identified as critical habitat for endangered and threatened species, a 1982 amendment to the Endangered Species Act (ESA) of 1973 made it possible to apply for a permit that allows incidental taking of a listed species on private lands. To obtain this permit, an HCP must be submitted to the Secretary of the Interior for approval. The plan must show how incidental takings will be minimized and that actions taken by the applicant will not significantly reduce the likelihood of species survival (Allison, 2002; Salzman & Thompson, 2003). Communities sharing space with endangered species have recognized that community-based HCPs can benefit the entire community by pooling resources, including money, land, scientific information, and time. As a result, CBCP has become increasingly popular (Chase, Schusler, & Decker, 2000; Lin, 1996; Reilly, 1998; Tuler & Webler, 1999). Although CBCP often encounters initial resistance, it increases the chances that the final management decision will be accepted by those involved in the process and the rest of the community (Laird, 1993). This acceptance occurs because programs that develop local consensus gain broad support and therefore result in more effective conservation plans (Turner & Rylander, 1998). The ideal result of CBCP is an acceptable decision for all parties, including the endangered species (Lin, 1996).

The possible creation of economic and social capital by CBCP "engaged the attention of administrators and managers—extending to U.S. presidents—who sought less costly alternatives to traditional privatization, command and control, and subsidy-based approaches to" management of environmental conflicts (M. N. Peterson et al., 2005, p. 263). In the 1992 presidential race, George W. H. Bush called for amending the ESA to give more weight to economic concerns. He suggested that species endangerment should be jointly determined by natural and social sciences, rather than primarily by natural sciences. For example, even if a certain plant had become extremely rare, if preservation of the habitat needed for its recovery was economically detrimental, that plant should not be listed as endangered. Bill Clinton countered by claiming Bush posed a false choice between environmental protection and economic growth, and promised to move the country beyond that dichotomous thinking. The ensuing Clinton administration attempted to use the HCP process to achieve the necessary flexibility to fulfill this pledge (Doremus, 1999). Reconciliation of the fundamental schism between property rights and environmental protection on private lands was implicit in the Clinton administration's attempts to enhance public participation (Cox, 2004; T. R. Peterson et al., 2004). The HCP process was used "selectively" and "experimentally" for the first 10 years of its existence (Schoenbaum & Rosenburg, 1996, p. 564), but its potential to transcend the environmental protection versus economic growth dichotomy encouraged overuse in recent years. While only 14 permits were issued prior to the 1992 U.S. presidential race, 425 had been approved as of July 2003 (U.S. Fish and Wildlife Service, 2003).

Gwartney, Fessenden, and Landt (2002) found that the positive relationships developed through a consensus-building process used to resolve a dispute over human population growth and sustainable development in an Oregon community disseminated beyond actual participants and remained in existence over time. They concluded that the enhanced working relationships among previous adversaries were largely the result of the consensus-building process. Appelstrand (2002) argued that the fundamental purpose of public participation is to build consensus. He claimed that, by engaging in consensus-building processes with members of the public, agencies responsible for managing natural resources should be able to produce more sustainable environmental policy. Singleton (2002) examined several community-level consensus-building processes and concluded that the increased regulatory flexibility and decentralization, coupled with broadly based accountability, offers opportunities to enhance democratic practice as well as to improve the quality of environmental decision making.

Consensus-building approaches to environmental conservation also have become more common in developing countries known for their biodiversity and unique landscapes, such as Costa Rica, Nepal, Belize, and parts of Africa (Donovan, 1994; Fabricius, Koch, & Magome, 2001; Few, 2000; Gbadegisin & Ayileka, 2000; Metha & Heinen, 2001; Wells, 1994). Case studies suggest that community-based attempts to build consensus have led to relatively more effective environmental conservation policies than those dictated by either national or international bodies. Fabricius et al. (2001) found the increase in locally based environmental decision making was especially pronounced in southern Africa following a wave of democracy in the late 1980s and early 1990s. Working relationships between national governments, industry, and local communities improved; participants identified common goals; and conflict management tactics became less violent.

As is typical for fashionable notions experiencing a collective surge, consensus models are loosely defined (T. R. Peterson et al., 2004). They generally purport to engender win-win outcomes, educate participants, and foster a sense of community. They also have a variety of labels, including community-based conservation (Western & Wright, 1994), co-management (Chase et al., 2000), collaborative resource management (Wondolleck & Yaffee, 2000), and community-based initiatives (Brunner, Colburn, Cromley, Klein, & Olson, 2002). Although each consensus model defines success somewhat differently, all share varying degrees of commitment to mutual agreement as an end goal and the assumption that resolution lies someplace in between the positions taken by disputants (Dahl, 2003; T. R. Peterson et al., 2004).

Challenges to consensus building. Ironically, about the time consensus was gaining momentum among environmental practitioners, its theoretical weaknesses were being thoroughly deconstructed by social theorists (Hikins, 1989; Russman, 1987; Tukey, 1988). The theoretical debate over consensus theory and its philosophical antecedents is by no means over, but its implications are decidedly unfavorable for environmental conservation. Consensus processes are philosophically rooted in social constructionism. From a radical constructionist perspective, no reality constrains decision making other than consensus among community members (Hikins, 1989). An approach to environmental decision making rooted in this epistemology seems intuitively irresponsible and has been used to legitimize existing patterns of environmental degradation. For instance, the dubious claim that sustainable development can occur indefinitely alongside current economic growth patterns (Czeck, 2000; Gowdy, 2000) is valid only if reality is socially constructed so as to ignore ecological research (T. R. Peterson et al., 2004). The fundamental premise of HCPs—that current development patterns can continue without impairing biodiversity conservation—relies on similarly unsubstantiated assumptions (Redford & Richter, 1999).

Peters (1999) and Ivie (1998, 2002, 2004) argued that communication is most productive when it enables humans to respect others without reducing them to ourselves. Ivie (2002) stated, "The illusion of consensus and unanimity is fatal to democracy because a healthy democratic process requires the vibrant clash of political positions and an open conflict of interests" (p. 277). He advocated that public participation should celebrate the diversity of participants, languages, types of reasoning, and evidence involved in public debate. His analyses of political rhetoric (1998, 2002, 2004) have demonstrated how the absence of argument allows elites to control deliberative processes, leading to his claim that the existence of vociferous debate is not a "sign of hostility, alienation, misbehavior, inefficiency, or even impending chaos and ruin" (2002, p. 278) but rather a sign of a healthy, pluralistic democracy. Ivie's (2004) claim that "democratic dissent . . . is as alarming to the purveyors of prevailing opinion as it is critical to a nation's political welfare" (p. 21) is particularly relevant to environmental groups seeking to change existing patterns of development (Blumberg & Knuffke, 1998; Lange, 1990).

Toker (2004) argued that the pursuit of an ideal public sphere grounded in consensus has encouraged uncritical acceptance of models that promise facilitation of open and free public deliberation according to principles of equality, representation, openness, and consensus. In these forums, stakeholders from all walks of life theoretically come together and engage in open and free deliberation. Through such deliberation, individuals overcome differences to unite in the spirit of the common good and reach a rationally determined consensus. Because decision making occurs through an open exchange between interests, the results will be legitimate and fair. Critics of consensus-based processes claim that management by consensus is dangerous because the attempt to placate everyone risks the attenuation of any impetus for change and reifies the status quo (Mouffe, 2000; M. N. Peterson et al., 2005; T. R. Peterson et al., 2004). Further, although many consensus conveners and facilitators affirmatively attempt to expand the diversity of people involved in public processes and create an atmosphere that promotes egalitarian participation, such processes necessarily occur within existing political structures where some groups have more power than others (Ivie, 2004; Mouffe, 2000). These groups have the advantage in shaping group consensus so as to favor continuation of existing hierarchical relationships. For this reason dominant elites generally prefer consensus building to debate. The emphasis on civility and reason in consensus-based models is problematic in part because the illusion of objectivity and universal reason requires bracketing or masking conflicts among participating groups and individuals. We thus treat as truth that which could just as easily be understood as hegemony.

Given the strong social preference for agreement noted by Bingham (1985, 1987), it is difficult to prevent consensus processes from degenerating into the hyper-rationalized atmosphere of the public hearing. Singleton (2002) argued that consensus-building processes aimed at enhancing public participation in environmental decision making are limited by failure to confront core conflicts over equity, distribution, and valuation of nature. This difficulty is further exacerbated because natural resources such as air, land, and water do not start and stop at political boundaries, whether those boundaries surround a private residence or a nation. Because environmental disputes rarely sort out according to political boundaries, it is difficult to procure sufficient institutional support to stabilize consensus-based environmental agreements.

Toker's (2004) analysis of a stakeholder group created by the Georgia Port Authority documented a consensus process that held members of the public hostage while allowing powerful institutions to use legal and legislative channels with little disruption. She found the implicit goal of agreement made the stakeholder process especially vulnerable to stalemate by veto of a single powerful group. She argued that public participation would be better served through an exploration of rhetorical strategies that disenfranchised groups can use to redefine situations, disassociate dysfunctional relationships, and introduce new perspectives.

Gregory, McDaniels, and Fields (2001) argued that the focus on consensus building impedes critical thinking and leads to the development of inferior policy. Poncelet (2001), who studied environmental partnerships in Europe and the United States, found that all were characterized by conflict avoidance and diffusion of difference. His analysis of the partnerships' sociohistoric contexts indicated that this proclivity grew out of a prominent cultural model that conceptualizes the partnership process as fundamentally consensual. Detailed analysis of one partnership, a European Union initiative aimed toward encouraging sustainable development throughout member states, led to the conclusion that consensus-based environmental partnerships inadvertently engender a retreat from radical thinking and innovative environmental solutions.

When scientific information regarding an environmental issue has high predictive power, and infrastructure needed for implementation is well developed and thoroughly integrated into the community, consensus-based approaches may be appropriate. Daniels and Walker (2001), however, suggested that these conditions rarely exist in environmental conflicts; and acting as though they do simply increases apathy and cynicism among the public. Stakeholders who enter a public participation process believing that consensus will emerge generally come away disenchanted by the inexplicably contrary behavior of those with opposing views (M. N. Peterson et al., 2005; T. R. Peterson et al., 2004). This leads to increased cynicism regarding participation in efforts designed to improve the quality of environmental decisions and further minimizes possibilities for progressive environmental policy (Ehrlich, 2003; Freyfogle, 2003; Orr, 2003).

Margerum (1999) noted that, in the United States and Australia, stakeholders often reach consensus on environmental problems and objectives but then fail to implement that consensus because they lack strategic direction, a limited set of the public participates, and stakeholders lack commitment to implementation. Participants then experience dissonance between an apparently successful process and a failed outcome. T. R. Peterson et al. (2004) used an ethnographic approach to critically review the consensus-building processes used in partnerships formed to develop regional HCPs that would enable cooperation between community development needs and habitat needs for the endangered Houston toad (Texas, U.S.) and the Florida Key deer (U.S.). In both cases, they found the process was framed as a search for the optimum solution through consensus building; and in neither case was the solution achieved. Failure to find the optimal solution led to disillusionment and pessimism among participants. Based on their analysis, they suggest that, within democratic political contexts, approaches to conservation planning that encourage vigorous debate are more likely to produce satisfactory environmental policy than are consensus-building approaches.

Fabricius et al. (2001) cautioned that consensus-based processes are not a panacea for environmental conflict in developing nations. Political instability in these locations means it is difficult to predict changes in political regimes, which can spawn new power struggles, many of which threaten the stability of environmental agreements reached through consensus. They noted that citizens who had participated in these consensus-building processes in southern African nations during the early 1990s are deeply invested in the resulting environmental policies and felt betrayed by the threat of change. The high expectations that consensus-based approaches will yield significant benefits for the community are a further cause for concern. Fabricius et al. argued that the conventional wisdom that devolution of power to the smallest local group will inevitably result in good governance and sustainable resource management is flawed. To be effective, devolution of power must be accompanied by appropriate strategies such as mediation services at the local level, the creation of locally developed and enforced rules, and training in monitoring environmental outcomes. Gbadegisin and Ayileka (2000) also cautioned against overgeneralization of positive results in community-based environmental management in developing countries, suggesting past successes may have resulted from the community's direct reliance on natural resources for food, shelter, and clothing—a relationship that is undergoing rapid change.

Summary. Environmental managers and dispute resolution professionals are embracing consensus-based approaches in an attempt to enhance public participation and facilitate the potentially incompatible goals of environmental protection and economic growth. Although such approaches may produce positive results in immediate spatial and temporal contexts and under some forms of governance, their overuse could have potentially dangerous implications for conservation. This critique suggests that consensus often is purchased at the cost of legitimizing current power hegemonies rooted in unsustainable social constructions of reality. Despite increased awareness of the direct link between human society and nature, environmental policy makers appear curiously unaware of the uneasy political atmosphere within which their decisions are accepted or rejected, implemented or ignored. A model for managing environmental conflict rooted in debate rather than consensus may facilitate both positive working relationships and progressive environmental policy by placing the environmental agenda on firmer epistemological ground and legitimizing challenges to current power hegemonies.

Over-reliance on consensus processes jeopardizes both democracy in general and conservation specifically by legitimizing existing hegemonic configurations of power and precluding resistance against dominant elites. It artificially reduces power relationships to conflicts of interest, presumably reconcilable through mutual good will. Public cynicism increases when positive expectations created through consensus-building processes are not met. In the absence of debate, existing hierarchies become naturalized as uncontested reality, closing off consideration of their implications for sustainable environmental policy. Precipitous reliance on consensus precludes essential debate over the sustainability of any environmental practice.

PROMISING LINKS BETWEEN RESEARCH AND PRACTICE

Although general principles of dispute resolution are applicable to environmental conflict, we focus on research related directly to environmental conflict. Bingham (1985) noted that ADR models were drawn largely from labor-management conflict, which differs significantly from environmental conflict. Most significantly, "the rules of the game and who gets to play are clear" in labor-management disputes, but not in environmental disputes (p. 291). Walker and Daniels (2004) and Senecah (2004) added that environmental conflicts are necessarily multidimensional, with numerous interconnections between multiple parties and across multiple jurisdictions.

One of the earliest applications of dispute resolution constructs to the environmental context was Creighton's (1981) basic manual for those who were required to develop and implement public involvement venues. Others offered suggestions for specific approaches. Mernitz (1980) provided straightforward direction for mediating environmental disputes. Buckle and Thomas-Buckle's (1986) analysis of failed mediations indicated that environmental mediation might be more complex than Mernitz's presentation suggested. Blackburn and Bruce (1995) presented a more nuanced description that did a better job of integrating mediation theory and practice. Susskind, Levy, and Thomas-Larmer (2000) produced a thoroughly documented handbook where they applied many of the consensus-building concepts detailed in earlier work (Susskind et al., 1999). Selin and Chaves (1995) offered straightforward suggestions on how to develop a collaborative approach to environmental conflict. Dukes and Firehock (2001) produced a user-friendly guidebook for environmental advocates who want to shift from an adversarial to a collaborative approach. Wondolleck (1988) and Brick, Snow, and Van de Wetering (2001) described applications of this approach in the western United States, with its vast public lands.

It is clear that, over the past two decades, researchers and practitioners have heeded the call for attention to environmental conflict. We highlight here three especially promising research directions that seem likely to enhance our understanding of how environmental conflicts are delineated, who has a stake in that process, and how conflict interveners can improve the situation.

Frame Analysis

Dingwall (2002) suggested that, unless it directly confronts the frames parties bring to a conflict, environmental dispute resolution research threatens to be irrelevant. Frame theory contends that parties or negotiators bring experiences with them that shape their respective frames for conflict. These experiences include, but are not limited to, previous negotiations of any kind, past interactions with other participants in the dispute, and attitudes toward the issue under negotiation (Drake & Donohue, 1996; Putnam & Holmer, 1992; Tannen, 1995).

Since past experience helps determine what is important and shapes future expectations, participants are likely predisposed to consider certain elements of the conflict as more important than others. By analyzing communication interactions of dispute participants, third-party interveners can discover the operative frames parties bring to a negotiation (Tannen, 1993) and can use that knowledge to encourage more productive relations among stakeholders (Gray, 2003). Pinkley (1990) and Pinkley and Northcraft (1994) identified the following dominant frames parties tend to bring to conflict interactions: (a) *substantive* frames, or what the conflict is about; (b) *loss/gain* frames, or how the parties view the risks associated with particular outcomes; (c) *characterization* frames, or how the parties view other stakeholders; (d) *outcome* frames, or what goals the parties bring so far as achieving a specific result or outcome from the negotiation; (e) *aspiration* frames, or what predispositions the parties have toward satisfying a set of interests or needs that extend beyond the current negotiation; (f) *process* frames, or strategies and techniques the parties expect to use for resolving the dispute; and (g) *evidentiary* frames, or facts and evidence that parties offer in support of claims they use to justify arguments for or against the legitimacy of a particular outcome or loss-gain frame.

Many parties come into environmental disputes with a sense of their own moral rectitude that is not amenable to negotiation (Dingwall, 2002). Killingsworth and Palmer (1992) argued that *ecospeak*, which they defined as "a way of framing arguments that stops thinking and inhibits social cooperation rather than extending thinking and promoting cooperation through communication," compounds environmental conflict by oversimplifying issues and polarizing communities (p. 9). Killingsworth and Palmer argued further that ecospeak controls an audience by discouraging its members from perceiving commonalities among perspectives. Driedger and Eyles (2003) used frame analysis to examine a debate over chloroform and human health risks. They focused on how participants framed acceptability of scientific claims that were used in a U.S. Court of Appeals. They argued that understanding how disputants frame scientific knowledge is valuable because it has important implications for science policy agendas not only in the United States, but also in other, similar jurisdictions such as Canada and Western Europe.

Riemer (2004) demonstrated how frame analysis can help make sense of intercultural conflict. Reimer interviewed 55 participants in a conflict over Chippewa spearfishing in northern Wisconsin to discover the primary frames used by disputants and offered suggestions for how to begin the reframing process. Much of the conflict centered around the increasing scarcity of the walleye (a fish sought by sports fishers). Non-native people framed spearfishing as a fundamentally selfish activity that causes depletion of a natural resource (walleye). They argued that by continuing this practice, the Chippewa are failing to fulfill stewardship responsibilities that should be a condition of receiving the privilege of spearfishing. The Chippewa, on the other hand, view spearfishing as a sacred activity that should continue whether or not there are any walleye. From their frame, walleye depletion is an angler problem. Without significant reframing, this conflict remains intractable. Reimer noted that legitimization of multiple possibilities for framing the situation is a basic component of any reframing strategy.

Lewicki, Gray, and Elliot (2003) offered framing as an especially promising approach to apparently intractable environmental conflict. Their rationale is that, since frame analysis opens possibilities for more complete understanding of the interaction dynamics involved in conflicts, it can pave the way for frame shifts. Framing research demonstrates how an understanding of "framing dynamics can provide a richer understanding of the reasons why many environmental disputes become so polarized and difficult to resolve" (Davis & Lewicki, 2003, p. 205). In better understanding these dynamics, third-party interveners can provide disputants with opportunities to reframe conflicts in more productive ways and provide space for the design of intervention techniques especially formulated for each situation.

Practical application. Frame analysis suggests that conflict interveners should plan on devoting relatively more time and other resources to assisting parties to conceptualize alternative frames and relatively less resources to developing other dispute resolution strategies and techniques. Putnam, Burgess, and Royer (2003) pointed out that intractable conflicts require reframing. They suggest that environmental practitioners can encourage reframing by helping disputants develop more realistic expectations, identify potential shifts within the conflict, and identify potential shifts outside of, yet related to, the conflict. As they learn to interpret their situations differently, disputants become more open to possibilities for resolution. T. R. Peterson (2003) added that practitioners need to develop a deep understanding of conflict participants' social control frames before they suggest possibilities for improving the situation. For example, it is counterproductive to extol a conflict management approach that relies primarily on federal regulation to people whose social control frame indicates a strong preference for low interdependence among members of society and requires strong opportunities for individual voice. Conflict participants who prefer high social interdependence, and do not require strong opportunities for individual voice, however, may find such an approach appealing.

Critical-Cultural Analysis

The language of critical, cultural, and rhetorical analysis provides a rich basis for examining questions about the sources and social dynamics of reflexivity with which we might transform environmental conflict. For example, Lange's (1993) and Moore's (1993) analyses of a dispute over old-growth forests and spotted owl habitat in the Pacific Northwest illustrated how rhetorical and cultural criticism can provide complementary understandings of the complex dynamics involved in environmental conflict.

Hamilton (2003) analyzed the rhetorical strategies participants in the Fernald (Ohio, U.S.) radium debate used to articulate tensions between technical and cultural understandings of risk. She used a concept of framing similar to that described earlier to structure her analysis of public meetings designed to enable local residents and technical experts to discuss alternative possibilities for managing nuclear waste. Hamilton's analysis revealed that individual frames of acceptance shaped both technical and cultural rationality, which then acted as competing sources of rhetorical invention. As such, they influenced participants' interpretation of the situation, the strategies they used to develop persuasive messages, and their receptivity of persuasive messages developed by other participants. She found that residents not only framed the case as a local issue (while technical experts framed it as a global situation) but also exhibited a social constructionist frame for public participation (while technical experts exhibited a one-way Jeffersonian frame). Hamilton's analysis suggests that, prior to attempting facilitation of public participation processes designed to resolve environmental conflicts, interveners should critically examine the fundamental process assumptions of all participants, taking nothing for granted.

Moore (2004) expanded upon this claim when he identified multiple incongruities in a Pacific Northwest timber controversy in the United States. He argued that President Clinton's campaign promise to resolve the issue probably stemmed from the optimistic belief that, as with other political problems, all that was lacking was a sense of community. The presidential candidate assumed that if someone (and who better than a newly elected president) provided an opportunity for key disputants to come together, they would develop a consensus enabling a rational compromise. Following his election, Clinton devoted valuable time and energy to an activity that eventually alienated him from both timber and environmental interests, at the same time it solidified existing hostilities. Moore pointed out the irony associated with the timber companies' dire warnings that environmentally motivated stoppages of logging on public lands would destroy the economy of the region, environmentalists' predictions of total ecological devastation, and loggers' self-righteous paranoia. By ignoring the cultural complexity of the controversy, Clinton ensured disastrous results. Similarly, M. N. Peterson et al. (2002) used critical ethnography to explore how moral culture (see Littlejohn, Chapter 14 in this volume) applies to environmental conflict. They found that temporary solutions to superficial problems that were maladapted to the moralized nature of the conflict exacerbated it. These analyses highlight the danger of precipitously attempting to reach consensus and suggest the utility of cultural analysis of environmental conflicts prior to designing management strategies.

Prelli (2004) examined the largely unrealized potential of rhetorical analysis for environmental conflict. He examined the rhetoric of the New Hampshire Forest Sustainability Standards Work Team, a group of stakeholders charged to implement sustainable forestry on 26 million acres across Maine, New Hampshire, Vermont, and New York. His analysis demonstrated how rhetorical analysis can clarify general structures of decision making that constrain judgments. Prelli called attention to three discursive moves that structured the group's decision points: (a) appeal to a foundational standard, (b) bifurcation, and (c) interdependence. He emphasized that these discursive moves yield possibilities for arguments that may or may not prove useful in other circumstances. Rather than argue that effective public processes enable people to replace personal preferences with community goals, Prelli suggested using rhetorical constructs to enhance practical environmental communication and advocacy and to contribute to a more sophisticated understanding of public processes—one that enhances participants' abilities to transcend personal preferences through collaborative action. Toward this goal, he explained how an awareness of discursive moves could be incorporated into training to complement the standard education currently provided to environmental managers.

Hellström (2001) extended critical analysis beyond national borders by conducting comparative analysis of conflict cultures manifested in environmental conflicts in Finland, France, Minnesota (U.S.), Norway, the Pacific Northwest (U.S.), Sweden, and Germany. She used observation and in-depth interviews with participants at all of these locations to identify culturally grounded frames for producing and managing environmental conflicts in forestry that were associated with social, political, economic, and resource characteristics. Using an interpretive analytical framework, she constructed models of conflict cultures characterized by mild versus intense conflicts, individualistic versus cooperative relationships among participants, and preference for stability versus change in natural resource policy. She also identified preferences for distinct conflict management strategies characterized by the relative emphasis on conflicting subcultures within the society versus the society's overall conflict culture and interactive versus institutional management of conflict.

Critical analyses such as these remind us that public participation in the environmental policy context is intensely political and always linked to power relationships and value conflicts (Depoe, Delicath, & Elsenbeer, 2004; Linnros & Hallin, 2001). The conditions of public participation always privilege some interests over others. This makes them necessarily incomplete rather than fully representative. They call our attention to the disturbing reality that, rather than creating a safe space for genuine public deliberation, third-party interveners could inadvertently create a dangerous space where participants expend their energy articulating public ideals of freedom, equality, and openness while decisions are made elsewhere.

Practical application. Given that management of natural resources increasingly depends on securing cooperation of culturally diverse groups of people, it is essential to develop cultural understanding. Toward this end, environmental conflict practitioners can use critical/cultural analyses to develop frameworks within which to design responses to the conflicts that emerge out of concern for how to prevent, minimize, dramatize, or focus the risks and hazards systematically produced as part of modernization. Conflict management practitioners should not look to this approach for formal algorithms, however, so much as for guiding principles. Critical inquiry addresses challenges disputants confront as they deliberate about the plurality of goods and the most efficacious means to their attainment within complex and disputed situations. Their attention to the cultural milieu responds to the practical necessity of working to minimize polarization and establish a collaborative pursuit of acceptable (and necessarily) temporary resolution to environmental disputes.

Systems Analysis

Systems analysis offers a promising approach to integrating the study of biophysical processes and social practices that converge in environmental conflict (Grant et al., 2002;

T. R. Peterson et al., 2004). Despite increasing awareness of the complexity inherent to environmental conflict, environmental policy (and the underlying research and decisions leading up to it) is often accomplished through compartmentalization. Since the values assigned to cultural, environmental, economic, and other activities may have different conceptual and empirical bases, weighing one against the other results in a competitive win-lose situation. In an attempt to avoid hostility, decision making is often compartmentalized and fragmented into economic versus environmental versus social and cultural spheres. The bigger, integrated picture gets lost, and potential tradeoffs are difficult to discover.

Responses to these challenges include the development of public participation processes that incorporate integrated assessment, ecosystem management, and adaptive environmental management (van den Belt, 2004). Adaptive management, which evolved from the research at the Institute of Applied Systems Analysis in Austria, emphasizes how policies can be designed to cope with uncertainty in environmental decision making and management (Holling, 1978; Lee, 1993; Walters, 1986; Walters & Holling, 1990). Policy is viewed as a hypothesis-driven experiment that is informed by learning. One of the most important assumptions of the approach is that understanding system-level behavior is essential for designing better policy. The stress on taking a system-wide perspective leads to consideration of ecological, social, economic, and cultural factors early in environmental decision making and the management process. In addition, constant interaction between scientists, managers, and other stakeholders is encouraged as a form of social learning that improves the policy-making process and builds robust consensus (Costanza & Ruth, 1998). By way of illustration, we now explain two distinct yet closely related approaches to managing environmental conflict through systems analysis.

Computer models, especially systems simulation models, are an important technique for comparing the potential effects of policies and for including the input of stakeholders into the decision-making process (Walters, 1986; Walters & Holling, 1990). Mediated modeling, which is based on dynamic systems thinking, has grown out of an increasing awareness that humans are a part of the ecosystem and are capable of irreversibly damaging it (Costanza & Jorgenson, 2002; van den Belt, 2004). Van den Belt (2004) described mediated modeling as a tool for overcoming problems inherent in linear thinking and compartmentalized, non-participatory decision making. It provides a structured process for including the most important aspects of a problem in a coherent system simulation model. This structure enhances management of complex environmental conflicts by integrating culture, ecology, economics, politics, and any other relevant dimensions. It enables participants to envision the system as more multidimensional, dynamic, and interactive. Rather than experts' dispensing answers or a discussion about the perceptions of a group of stakeholders, mediated modeling aims for a collaborative team learning experience to raise the shared level of understanding in a group as well as fostering a robust consensus. Dynamic systems thinking and supporting software is used to construct computer-based simulation models at a scoping level. The model construction process is used to structure the discussion and the thinking of stakeholder groups and foster team learning. This structure enables participants to avoid some of the pitfalls associated with consensus-building processes.

Yearley, Cinderby, Forrester, Bailey, and Rosen's (2003) empirical analysis of public processes in three cities in the United Kingdom demonstrates how mediated modeling can be used as an effective means of obtaining and interpreting this information. Participation in mediated modeling enabled local residents to evaluate their individual perspectives against those of their neighbors and led to an integrated assessment of the problem. In all three cities, the modeling activity provided a structure within which high-quality public contributions to local governance of air quality were produced. Maguire's (2003) evaluation of stakeholder interactions with water quality models and modelers in the Neuse River total maximum daily load (TMDL) process clarified the limitations of the current TMDL process, identified which limitations were most problematic, and suggested structural improvements that could enable a facilitator to respond more effectively to stakeholder interests.

Van den Belt (van den Belt, 2004; van den Belt, Deutch, & Jansson, 1998) has conducted extensive mediated modeling activities and has found that it enhances public involvement in controversial and complex environmental policy issues. Van den Belt et al. (1998) analyzed a mediated modeling process in Patagonia; and van den Belt (2004) analyzed similar processes in five sites: coastal zone management in the Ria Formosa (Portugal), futures planning in Banff National Park (Canada), decision support for watershed management in Wisconsin (U.S.), watershed restoration for a TMDL process in Texas (U.S.), and managing sage grouse populations in Idaho (U.S.). In all cases, building and manipulating simulation models enabled stakeholders to (a) perceive interconnections across sectors; (b) connect their own past, present, and future actions; and (c) respond systemically to the intrinsic complexity of environmental management. In all of these projects, mediated modeling helped stakeholder groups reframe their understanding of controversies and suggested multiple options for achieving a new course that promised benefits to all stakeholders.

Systemic approaches to environmental conflict are not limited to quantitative modeling (Checkland & Scholes, 1990). Fiorino (2001) suggested it could be valuable to reframe public participation in environmental conflict as an opportunity for systemic learning. As articulated by Daniels and Walker (2001), *soft systems* approaches to environmental conflict refer to combining multiple ideas, without reducing them to a single disciplinary perspective, to enable a public process with the emergent properties required for effective management of most environmental conflicts. They emphasized that useful insights into complex problems require numerous perspectives and various fields of expertise and articulate their claims in terms of basic communication principles. Brogden and Greenberg (2003) argued that apparently intractable environmental conflicts might actually be emergent properties of complex systems. They analyzed conflicts between grazing and urban growth in Arizona (U.S.) to illustrate this claim. Their analysis suggests that conflict management professionals should develop conflict resolution processes that systemically incorporate integrated assessment into existing decision-making structures. To be successful, such processes should foster collaboration and knowledge sharing between disputing stakeholders.

Community-based adaptive management integrates social and ecological suitability to achieve conservation outcomes by providing landowners the flexibility to use a diverse set of conservation practices to achieve desired ecological outcomes, instead of imposing regulations or specific practices. Daniels and Walker (2001) suggested soft systems as a means to involve communities in adaptive environmental management. They synthesized theory from systems thinking, adult learning, and ADR to derive principles and strategies for creating a social climate that enables participants to learn from each other and cooperate across divergent perspectives. Their emphasis on debate among diverse viewpoints responds directly to the critiques of consensus approaches. Through case studies drawn from several locations in the United States, they demonstrated that collaborative learning enables stakeholders to achieve measurable improvements in both biological processes and social practices involved in natural resource management. Their analysis included a conceptual explanation, a strategic guide for designing public process, and a set of learning activities adapted specifically for enhancing participants' ability to work systematically through environmental conflict.

Whether using formal modeling or soft systems (Senge, 1990), systemic analysis of, and intervention in, environmental conflict should communicate the linkage between decision making, environmental impacts, and planning. Blumenthal and Jannink (2000) classified collaborative systems approaches to environmental conflict, using the criteria of participation, institutional analysis, simplification of natural resource, and scale of application. Their most interesting finding was the strong degree of similarity among the approaches. Key elements for success include integration of ecology, economics, and social and cultural aspects (Costanza & Daly, 1992); effective stakeholder participation at the appropriate scales (Chambers, 1997); and a linked understanding of past, present, and future relationships (Senge, 1990).

Practical applications. Habron (2003) suggested the systemic use of adaptive management for addressing entrenched tensions within both community-level and watershed-level approaches to natural resource management. He maintained that agencies could encourage public cooperation by understanding and working within landowners' preferred cultural system. For example, by conceptualizing watershed policy within the constructs supported by landowners, agencies could capitalize on landowners' belief in environmental resilience and acceptance of experimentation. They could then construct a framework for environmental policy that honors landowners' independence and fear of government intrusion, acknowledges the benefits of community cooperation through watershed councils, and enables ecological assessment of landowner-preferred practices.

CONCLUSIONS

People involved in environmental conflicts invariably face difficult problems concerning the complex interactions between human systems and ecosystems (Costanza & Jorgenson, 2002; Walker & Daniels, 2004). Environmental managers, dispute resolution professionals, industry leaders, and concerned citizens regularly deal with existing or anticipated conflicts over alternative uses for natural resources, their economic implications, and the distribution of social impacts over the medium and long term. Although many people's preferred visions of the future include sustainability of both natural and economic systems, few approaches to environmental conflict facilitate integration of these diverse preferences into a holistic vision. There is neither a single, simple answer nor a single discipline capable of adequately addressing these complex problems. However unwillingly, those who study biophysical processes both influence and are influenced by environmental conflict, just as those who study environmental conflict both influence and are influenced by biophysical processes.

Traditional organizational command-and-control strategies are not necessarily well suited for the interdependence within environmental conflicts. Interdependence implies that the parties in conflict need each other in some way, that they have interlocking goals, and that everyone's actions affect everyone else. The public needs natural resource agencies to protect its interests. This need is interlocked with the goals of environmental agencies to manage natural resources effectively. Agencies need the public to provide input on projects so they satisfy their legal requirements. Beyond this minimal level of interdependence, an agency's ability to manage natural resources effectively depends on public cooperation and support. The public can create such intense opposition to a regulation or even an entire project that an agency may be forced, at immense cost, to change its plans.

The widespread requirement for public participation in environmental decision making has developed out of an expanded awareness that environmental policy cannot achieve legitimacy (and therefore success) without broad public involvement. Awareness of the need to involve the public in decision making does not necessarily translate into successful process, however. Public hearings, the most common method for involving the public in environmental issues, have not proven successful. Faced with open hostility, environmental managers have turned to consensus-building processes, often facilitated by conflict resolution professionals. Research pointing out potential pitfalls associated with overuse of consensus-building processes has led some to differentiate collaborative from consensus-building approaches. Promising approaches to environmental conflict have come from a variety of research and practice traditions. Frame analysis, cultural analysis, and systems analysis offer innovative ideas for the practice of environmental conflict resolution.

Environmental conflict is woven into human society. These disputes have the potential to tear communities apart or draw them together. The three research trajectories identified in the last section of this chapter all indicate how concepts drawn from ADR can be used to enhance our ability to manage these conflicts more effectively. This juxtaposition offers numerous untapped opportunities for assisting in the creation of a more just society. We are not suggesting that communication can resolve all environmental conflicts. Unfortunately, unsustainable development practices and severe inequities are only too

real (Amnesty International and Sierra Club, 2000; Payne, 1998). Effective conflict management can, however, minimize the damage that destructive environmental conflicts cause both individuals and communities.

By their very nature, environmental conflicts pit people against strangers—the northern hemisphere versus the southern, east against west, urban against rural. Within this milieu, research and practice in environmental conflict communication would do well to recall Peters's (1999) recommendation that "instead of being terrorized by the quest for communication with aliens, we should recognize its ordinariness"; indeed, "there is no other kind of communication" (p. 257). Littlejohn and Domenici (2001) listed three requirements for developing healthy dialogue among people united only by their diversity: (a) taking time to explore experiences, ideas, concerns, and doubts; (b) listening for both differences and commonalities in the experiences and stories, as well as values expressed by all parties; and (c) asking open, nonjudgmental, and curious questions to learn more about the other. If public participation in the management of environmental conflict is to contribute to an increasingly sustainable and just world, it must be transformed into a joint social construction of policies, as noted by Waddell (1996), where the knowledge of stakeholders and experts is integrated into the development, implementation, and continued monitoring of environmental policy.

REFERENCES

Administrative Procedures Act, 5 U.S.C. § 551 *et seq.* (1946).

Aguirre, B. E. (2002). "Sustainable development" as collective surge. *Social Science Quarterly, 83,* 101–118.

Allen, T. F. H., & Hoekstra, T. W. (1993). Toward a definition of sustainability. In W. W. Covington & L. F. Debano (Eds.), *Sustainable ecological systems: Implementing an ecological approach to land management* (pp. 98–107). Fort Collins, CO: Rocky Mountain Forest and Range Experiment Station.

Allison, S. A. (2002). *Community-based conservation planning: The case of the endangered*

Houston toad in Bastrop County, Texas. Unpublished master's thesis, Texas A&M University, College Station.

Amnesty International and Sierra Club. (2000). *Environmentalists under fire: 10 urgent cases of human rights abuses.* Retrieved May 28, 2004, from http://www.sierraclub.org/human-rights/amnesty/report.pdf

Appelstrand, M. (2002). Participation and societal values: The challenge for lawmakers and policy practitioners. *Forest Policy and Economics, 4,* 281–290.

Arnstein, S. R. (1969). A ladder of citizen participation. *Journal of the American Institute of Planners, 25,* 216–224.

Bingham, G. (1985). A note of hope for resolving environmental conflict. *Environmental Science & Technology, 19,* 291.

Bingham, G. (1987). Resolving environmental disputes: A decade of experience. In R. W. Lake (Ed.), *Resolving locational conflict* (pp. 314–323). New Brunswick, NJ: Rutgers, Center for Urban Policy Research.

Blackburn, J. W., & Bruce, W. M. (1995). *Mediating environmental conflicts: Theory and practice.* Westport, CT: Quorum Books.

Blumberg, L., & Knuffke, D. (1998). Count us out: Why the Wilderness Society opposed the Quincy Library Group legislation. *Chronicle of Community, 2,* 41–44.

Blumenthal, D., & Jannink, J. L. (2000). A classification of collaborative management methods. *Conservation Ecology, 4,* 13. Retrieved November 9, 2004, from http://www.consecol.org/vol4/iss2/art13

Bourdieu, P. (1985). The forms of capital. In J. G. Richardson (Ed.), *Handbook of theory and research for the sociology of education* (pp. 241–258). New York: Greenwood.

Brick, P., Snow, D., & Van de Wetering, S. (Eds.). (2001). *Across the Great Divide: Explorations in collaborative conservation in the American West.* Washington, DC: Island Press.

Brogden, M. J., & Greenberg, J. B. (2003). The fight for the west: A political ecology of land use conflicts in Arizona. *Human Organization, 62,* 289–298.

Brunner, R. D., Colburn, C. H., Cromley, C. M., Klein, C. M., & Olson, E. A. (2002). *Finding common ground: Governance and natural*

resources in the American West. New Haven, CT: Yale University Press.

Buckle, L. G., & Thomas-Buckle, S. R. (1986). Placing environmental mediation in context: Lessons from "failed" mediations. *Environmental Impact Assessment Review, 6,* 55–70.

Callicott, J. B., & Mumford, K. (1997). Ecological sustainability as a conservation concept. *Conservation Biology, 11,* 32–40.

Chambers, R. (1997). *Whose reality counts? Putting the first last.* London: Intermediate Technology Publishers.

Chase, L. C., Schusler, T. M., & Decker, D. J. (2000). Innovations in stakeholder involvement: What's the next step? *Wildlife Society Bulletin, 28,* 208–217.

Checkland, P., & Scholes, J. (1990). *Soft systems methodology in action.* New York: John Wiley.

Checkoway, B. (1981). The politics of public hearings. *Journal of Applied Behavioral Science, 17,* 566–582.

Chess, C., & Purcell, K. (1999). Public participation and the environment: Do we know what works? *Environmental Science & Technology, 33,* 2685–2692.

Costanza, R., Cumberland, J., Daly, H., Goodland, R., & Norgaard, R. (1997). *An introduction to ecological economics.* Boca Raton, FL: St. Lucie Press.

Costanza, J., & Daly, H. (1992). Natural capital and sustainable development. *Conservation Biology, 6,* 37–47.

Costanza, R., d'Arge, R., de Groot, R., Farber, S., Grasso, M., Hannon, B., et al. (1997). The value of the world's ecosystem services and natural capital. *Nature, 387,* 253–260.

Costanza, R., & Jorgenson, S. E. (2002). *Understanding and solving environmental problems in the 21st century: Toward a new, integrated hard problem science.* Amsterdam: Elsevier.

Costanza, R., & Ruth, M. (1998). Using dynamic modeling to scope environmental problems and build consensus. *Environmental Management, 22,* 183–195.

Cox, J. R. (2004). The re/making of the "environmental president": Clinton/Gore and the rhetoric of U.S. environmental politics, 1992–1996. In T. R. Peterson (Ed.), *Green talk in the White House: The rhetorical presidency encounters ecology* (pp. 157–180). College Station: Texas A&M University Press.

Creighton, J. L. (1981). *The public involvement manual*. Cambridge, MA: Abt Books.

Creighton, J. L. (1999). Public participation in federal agencies' decision making in the 1990's. *National Civic Review, 88*, 249–258.

Cvetkovich, G., & Earle, T. C. (1994). The construction of justice: A case study of public participation in land management. *Journal of Social Issues, 50*, 161–178.

Czeck, B. (2000). Economic growth as the limiting factor for wildlife conservation. *Wildlife Society Bulletin, 28*, 4–15.

Dahl, R. (2003). Finding middle ground: Environmental conflict resolution. *Environmental Health Perspectives, 111*, 650–652.

Daly, H. E., & Cobb, J. (1989). *For the common good: Redirecting the economy towards community, the environment, and a sustainable future*. Boston: Beacon.

Daniels, S. E., & Walker, G. B. (1996). Collaborative learning: Improving public deliberation in ecosystem-based management. *Environmental Impact Assessment Review, 16*, 71–102.

Daniels, S. E., & Walker, G. B. (2001). *Working through environmental conflict: The collaborative learning approach*. Westport, CT: Praeger.

Davis, C. B., & Lewicki, R. J. (2003). Introduction to special issue: Environmental conflict resolution: Framing and intractability—An introduction. *Environmental Practice, 5*, 200–272.

de la Court, T. (1992). Critique of the dominant development paradigm. *Development, 2*, 42–46.

Depoe, S. P., Delicath, J. W., & Elsenbeer, M. A. (Eds.). (2004). *Communication and public participation in environmental decision making*. Albany: State University of New York Press.

Dingwall, R. (2002). What makes conflict resolution possible? *Negotiation Journal—On the Process of Dispute Settlement, 18*, 321–326.

Dionisopoulos, G. N., & Crable, R. E. (1988). Definitional hegemony as a public relations strategy: The rhetoric of the nuclear power industry after Three Mile Island. *Central States Speech Journal, 39*, 134–145.

Donovan, R. (1994). BOSCOSA: Forest conservation and management through local institutions (Costa Rica). In D. Western & M. Wright (Eds.), *Natural connections: Perspectives in community-based conservation* (pp. 215–233). Washington, DC: Island Press.

Doremus, H. (1999). Preserving citizen participation in the era of reinvention: The Endangered Species Act example. *Ecology Law Quarterly, 25*, 707–717.

Drake, L., & Donohue, W. (1996). Communicative framing theory in conflict resolution. *Communication Research, 23*, 297–322.

Driedger, S. M., & Eyles, J. (2003). Drawing the battle lines: Tracing the "science war" in the construction of the chloroform and human health risks debate. *Environmental Management, 31*, 476–488.

Dukes, E., & Firehock, K. (2001). *Collaboration: A guide for environmental advocates*. Charlottesville: University of Virginia Press.

Dustin, D. L., Schneider, I. E., McAvoy, L. H., & Frakt, A. N. (2002). Cross-cultural claims on Devils Tower National Monument: A case study. *Leisure Sciences, 24*, 79–88.

Ehrlich, P. R. (2000). *Human natures: Genes, cultures, and the human prospect*. Washington, DC: Island Press.

Ehrlich, P. R. (2003). Get off the train and walk. *Conservation Biology, 17*, 352–353.

Endangered Species Act, 16 U.S.C. § 1531 *et seq.* (1973).

Fabricius, C., Koch, E., & Magome, H. (2001). Towards strengthening collaborative ecosystem management: Lessons from environmental conflict and political change in southern Africa. *Journal of the Royal Society of New Zealand, 31*, 831–844.

Farley, J., & Costanza, R. (2002). Envisioning shared goals for humanity: A detailed, shared vision of a sustainable and desirable USA in 2100. *Ecological Economics, 43*, 245–259.

Few, R. (2000). Conservation, participation, and power: Protected-area planning in the coastal zone of Belize. *Journal of Planning Education and Research, 19*, 401–408.

Fiorino, D. J. (1990). Citizen participation and environmental risk: A survey of institutional mechanisms. *Science, Technology, and Human Values, 15*, 226–243.

Fiorino, D. J. (2001). Environmental policy as learning: A new view of an old landscape. *Public Administration Review, 61*, 322–334.

Freyfogle, E. T. (2003). Conservation and the culture war. *Conservation Biology, 17*, 354–355.

Gbadegisin, A., & Ayileka, O. (2000). Avoiding mistakes of the past: Towards a community-oriented management strategy for the proposed National Park in Abuja-Nigeria. *Land Use Policy, 17,* 89–100.

Gericke, K. L., & Sullivan, J. (1994). Public participation and appeals of Forest Service plans: An empirical examination. *Society and Natural Resources, 7,* 125–135.

Gowdy, J. M. (2000). Terms and concepts in ecological economics. *Wildlife Society Bulletin, 28,* 26–33.

Grant, W. E., Peterson, T. R., & Peterson, M. J. (2002). Quantitative modeling of coupled natural/human systems: Simulation of societal constraints on environmental action drawing on Luhmann's social theory. *Ecological Modeling, 158,* 143–165.

Gray, B. (2003). Framing of environmental disputes. In R. Lewicki, B. Gray, & M. Elliot (Eds.), *Making sense of intractable environmental conflicts: Concepts and cases* (pp. 11–34). Washington, DC: Island Press.

Gregory, R., McDaniels, T., & Fields, D. (2001). Decision aiding, not dispute resolution: Creating insights through structured environmental decisions. *Journal of Policy Analysis and Management, 20,* 415–432.

Gwartney, P. A., Fessenden, L., & Landt, G. (2002). Measuring the long-term impact of a community conflict resolution process: A case study using content analysis of public documents. *Negotiation Journal—On the Process of Dispute Settlement, 18,* 51–74.

Habron, G. (2003). Role of adaptive management for watershed councils. *Environmental Management, 31,* 29–41.

Hamilton, J. D. (2003). Exploring technical and cultural appeals in strategic risk communication: The Fernald radium case. *Risk Analysis, 23,* 291–302.

Hays, S. P. (1987). *Beauty, health, and permanence: Environmental politics in the United States, 1955–1985.* Cambridge, UK: Cambridge University Press.

Heberlein, T. A. (1976). Some observations on alternative mechanisms for public involvement: The hearing, public opinion poll, the workshop, and the quasi-experiment. *Natural Resources Journal, 16,* 197–212.

Hellström, E. (2001). Conflict cultures: Qualitative comparative analysis of environmental conflicts in forestry. *Silva Fennica Monographs, 2.* Finnish Society of Forest Science.

Hikins, A. (1989). Through the rhetorical looking-glass: Consensus theory and fairy tales in the epistemology of communication. *Communication Studies, 40,* 161–171.

Holling, C. S. (1978). *Adaptive environmental assessment and management.* London: Wiley.

Ivie, R. L. (1998). Democratic deliberation in a rhetorical republic. *Quarterly Journal of Speech, 84,* 419–505.

Ivie, R. L. (2002). Rhetorical deliberation and democratic politics in the here and now. *Rhetoric and Public Affairs, 5,* 277–285.

Ivie, R. L. (2004). Prologue to democratic dissent in America. *Javnost, The Public: Journal of the European Institute for Communication and Culture, 11,* 19–35.

Jacob, M. (1994). Sustainable development and deep ecology: An analysis of competing traditions. *Environmental Management, 18,* 477–488.

Kaminstein, D. S. (1996). Persuasion in a toxic community: Rhetorical aspects of public meetings. *Human Organization, 55,* 458–464.

Kasperson, R. E. (1986). Six propositions on public participation and their relevance for risk communication. *Risk Analysis, 6,* 275–281.

Killingsworth, J. M., & Palmer, J. S. (1992). *Ecospeak: Rhetoric and environmental politics in America.* Carbondale: Southern Illinois University Press.

Kollock, P. (1998). Social dilemmas: The anatomy of cooperation. *Annual Review of Sociology, 24,* 183–214.

Kothari, R. (1990). Environment, technology and ethics. In J. R. Engels & J. G. Engels (Eds.), *Ethics of the environment and development* (pp. 27–35). Tucson: University of Arizona Press.

Laird, F. (1993). Participatory analysis, democracy, and technological decision making. *Science, Technology, and Human Values, 18,* 341–361.

Lange, J. (1990). Refusal to compromise: The case of Earth First! *Western Journal of Speech Communication, 54,* 473–494.

Lange, J. (1993). The logic of competing information campaigns: Conflict over old growth and the spotted owl. *Communication Monographs, 60,* 239–257.

Lee, K. (1993). *Compass and gyroscope.* Washington, DC: Island Press.

Lélé, S., & Norgaard, R. B. (1996). Sustainability and the scientist's burden. *Conservation Biology, 10,* 354–365.

Leopold, A. (1949). *A Sand County almanac and sketches here and there*. London: Oxford University Press.

Lewicki, R., Gray, B., & Elliot, M. (Eds.). (2003). *Making sense of intractable environmental conflicts: Concepts and cases*. Washington, DC: Island Press.

Lin, A. C. (1996). Participants' experiences with habitat conservation plans and suggestions for streamlining the process. *Ecology Law Quarterly, 23*, 369–446.

Lind, E. A., Kray, L., & Thompson, L. (1998). The social construction of injustice: Fairness judgments in response to own and others' unfair treatment by authorities. *Organizational Behavior and Human Decision Processes, 75*, 1–22.

Linnros, H. D., & Hallin, P. O. (2001). The discursive nature of environmental conflicts: The case of the Oresund link. *Area, 33*, 391–403.

Littlejohn, S. W., & Domenici, K. (2001). *Engaging communication in conflict: Systemic practice*. Thousand Oaks, CA: Sage.

Maguire, L. A. (2003). Interplay of science and stakeholder values in Neuse River total maximum daily load process. *Journal of Water Resources Planning and Management-A, 1299*, 261–270.

Margerum, R. D. (1999). Getting past yes: From capital creation to action. *Journal of the American Planning Association, 65*, 181–192.

Martin, R., & Piper, J.-E. (Eds.). (2001). Native voices: An informal collection of papers presented at the AAA Meeting, November 2000. *American Indian Quarterly, 25*(1), 1–40.

Mascarenhas, M., & Scarce, R. (2004). "The intention was good": Legitimacy, consensus-based decision making, and the case of forest planning in British Columbia, Canada. *Society & Natural Resources, 17*, 17–38.

Mazmanian, D. A., & Craft, M. E. (1999). *Toward sustainable communities: Transition and transformations in environmental policy*. Cambridge: MIT Press.

McComas, K. A. (2001a). Public meetings about local waste management problems: Comparing participants to nonparticipants. *Environmental Management, 27*, 135–147.

McComas, K. A. (2001b). Theory and practice of public meetings. *Communication Theory, 11*, 36–55.

Mernitz, S. (1980). *Mediation of environmental disputes: A sourcebook*. New York: Praeger.

Metha, J. N., & Heinen, J. T. (2001). Does community-based conservation shape favorable attitudes among locals? An empirical study from Nepal. *Environmental Management, 28*, 165–177.

Moore, M. (1993). Constructing irreconcilable conflict: The function of synecdoche in the spotted owl controversy. *Communication Monographs, 60*, 258–274.

Moore, M. (2004). Colliding ironies and Clinton's salvage rider rhetoric in the Northwest timber controversy. In T. R. Peterson (Ed.), *Green talk in the White House: The rhetorical presidency encounters ecology* (pp. 181–206). College Station: Texas A&M University Press.

Mouffe, C. (2000). *The democratic paradox*. New York: Verso.

Nabhan, G. P. (1995). Cultural parallax in viewing North American habitats. In M. E. Soule & G. Lease (Eds.), *Reinventing nature: Responses to postmodern deconstruction* (pp. 87–101). Washington, DC: Island Press.

National Environmental Policy Act, 42 U.S.C. § 4321 *et seq.* (1969).

Neuzil, M., & Kovarik, W. (1996). *Mass media and environmental conflict: America's green crusades*. Thousand Oaks, CA: Sage.

Nixon, R. M. (1970). Annual message to the Congress on the state of the union, January 22; Special message to the Congress on environmental quality, February 10; Special message to Congress about reorganization plans to establish the Environmental Protection Agency and the National Oceanic and Atmospheric Administration, July 9. *The American Presidency Project*. Retrieved November 9, 2004, from http://www.presidency.uscb.edu/ws/

Orr, D. W. (2003). Walking north on a southbound train. *Conservation Biology, 17*, 348–351.

Ostrom, E. (1990). *Governing the commons: The evolution of institutions for collective action*. New York: Cambridge University Press.

Ozawa, C. P. (1996). Science in environmental conflicts. *Sociological Perspectives, 39*, 219–230.

Payne, R. A. (1998). The limits and promise of environmental conflict prevention: The case of the GEF. *Journal of Peace Research, 35*, 363–380.

Pearce, W. B., & Littlejohn, S. W. (1997). *Moral conflict: When social worlds collide*. Thousand Oaks, CA: Sage.

Peters, J. D. (1999). *Speaking into the air: A history of the idea of communication*. Chicago: University of Chicago Press.

Peterson, M. N., Peterson, M. J., & Peterson, T. R. (2005). Conservation and the myth of consensus. *Conservation Biology, 19,* 762–767.

Peterson, M. N., Peterson, T. R., Peterson, M. J., Lopez, R. R., & Silvy, N. J. (2002). Cultural conflict and the endangered Florida Key deer. *Journal of Wildlife Management, 66,* 947–968.

Peterson, T. R. (1997). *Sharing the earth: The rhetoric of sustainable development.* Columbia: University of South Carolina Press.

Peterson, T. R. (2003). Social control frames: Opportunities or constraints. *Environmental Practice, 5,* 232–238.

Peterson, T. R., & Horton, C. C. (1995). Rooted in the soil: How understanding the perspectives of landowners can enhance the management of environmental disputes. *Quarterly Journal of Speech, 81,* 139–166.

Peterson, T. R., Peterson, M. J., & Grant, W. E. (2004). Social practice and biophysical process. In S. L. Senecah (Ed.), *Environmental communication yearbook, 1* (pp. 15–32). Mahwah, NJ: Lawrence Erlbaum.

Pinkley, R. (1990). Dimensions of conflict frame: Disputant interpretations of conflict. *Journal of Applied Psychology, 75,* 117–126.

Pinkley, R., & Northcraft, G. (1994). Conflict frames of reference: Implications for dispute processes and outcomes. *Academy of Management Journal, 37,* 193–205.

Poncelet, E. C. (2001). "A kiss here and a kiss there": Conflict and collaboration in environmental partnerships. *Environmental Management, 27,* 13–25.

Prelli, L. (2004). Sustainable forestry in New Hampshire. In T. R. Peterson (Ed.), *Green talk in the White House: The rhetorical presidency encounters ecology* (pp. 233–257). College Station: Texas A&M University Press.

Putnam, L. L., Burgess, G., & Royer, R. (2003). We can't go on like this: Frame changes in intractable conflicts. *Environmental Practice, 5,* 247–255.

Putnam, L. L., & Holmer, M. (1992). Framing, reframing, and issue development. In L. Putnam & M. Roloff (Eds.), *Communication & negotiation* (pp. 128–155). Thousand Oaks, CA: Sage.

Ratliff, J. N. (1998). The politics of nuclear waste: An analysis of a public hearing on the proposed Yucca Mountain Nuclear Waste Repository.

Electronic Journal of Communication, 8. Retrieved May 28, 2004, from http://www.cios.org/getfile/Ratliff_V8N198

Redford, K. H., & Richter, B. D. (1999). Conservation of biodiversity in a world of use. *Conservation Biology, 13,* 1246–1256.

Reilly, T. (1998). Communities in conflict: Resolving difference through collaborative efforts in environmental planning and human service delivery. *Journal of Sociology and Social Welfare, 25,* 115–142.

Riemer, J. W. (2004). Chippewa spearfishing, lake property owners/anglers, and tourism: A case study of environmental social conflict. *Sociological Spectrum, 24,* 43–70.

Rosener, J. B. (1981). User-oriented evaluation: A new way to view citizen participation. *Journal of Applied Behavioral Science, 17,* 583–596.

Rowe, G., & Frewer, L. J. (2000). Public participation methods: A framework for evaluation. *Science, Technology, and Human Values, 25,* 3–29.

Russman, T. A. (1987). *A prospectus for the triumph of realism.* Macon, GA: Mercer University Press.

Salzman, J., & Thompson, B. H. (2003). *Environmental law and policy.* New York: Foundation Press.

Schoenbaum, T. J., & Rosenburg, R. H. (1996). *Environmental policy law: Problems, cases, and readings.* Westbury, NY: Foundation Press.

Selin, S., & Chaves, D. (1995). Developing a collaborative model for environmental planning and management. *Environmental Management, 19,* 189–195.

Senecah, S. L. (2004). The process trinity of access, standing, and influence: The role of practical theory in planning and evaluating the effectiveness of environmental participatory processes. In S. P. Depoe, J. W. Delicath, & M. A. Elsenbeer (Eds.), *Communication and public participation in environmental decision making* (pp. 13–33). Albany: State University of New York Press.

Senge, P. M. (1990). *The fifth discipline.* Garden City, NY: Doubleday.

Singleton, S. (2002). Collaborative environmental planning in the American West: The good, the bad and the ugly. *Environmental Politics, 11,* 54–75.

Spyke, N. P. (1999). Public participation in environmental decisionmaking at the new millennium: Structuring new spheres of public influence. *Boston College Environmental Affairs Law Review, 26,* 263–313.

Stauber, J. C. (1994). Going . . . going . . . green! *PR Watch, 1,* 1–3.

Steelman, T. A., & Ascher, W. (1997). Public involvement methods in natural resource policy making: Advantages, disadvantages and trade-offs. *Policy Sciences, 30,* 71–90.

Susskind, L., Levy, P. F., & Thomas-Larmer, J. (2000). *Negotiating environmental agreements: How to avoid escalating confrontation, needless costs, and unnecessary litigation.* Washington, DC: Island Press.

Susskind, L., McKearnan, S., & Thomas-Larmer, J. (1999). *The consensus building handbook: A comprehensive guide to reaching agreement.* Thousand Oaks, CA: Sage.

Tannen, D. (1993). *Framing in discourse.* New York: Oxford University Press.

Tannen, D. (1995). Framing and reframing. In R. Lewicki, D. Saunders, & J. Minton (Eds.), *Negotiation: Readings, exercises, and cases* (pp. 68–80). New York: McGraw-Hill.

Tauxe, C. S. (1995). Marginalizing public participation in local planning: An ethnographic account. *Journal of the American Planning Association, 61,* 471–481.

Toker, C. W. (2004). Public participation or stakeholder frustration: An analysis of consensus-based participation in the Georgia Port Authority's stakeholder evaluation group. In S. P. Depoe, J. W. Delicath, & M. A. Elsenbeer (Eds.), *Communication and public participation in environmental decision making* (pp. 175–199). Albany: State University of New York Press.

Tukey, D. (1988). Toward a spiritual critique of inter-subjectivist rhetoric. *Journal of Communication and Religion, 10,* 1–8.

Tuler, S., & Webler, T. (1999). Voices from the forest: What participants expect of a public participation process. *Society & Natural Resources, 12,* 437–453.

Turner, J. F., & Rylander, J. C. (1998). The private lands challenge: Integrating biodiversity conservation and private property. In J. F. Shogren (Ed.), *Private property and the Endangered Species Act* (pp. 92–137). Austin: University of Texas Press.

U.S. Fish and Wildlife Service. (2003). *Conservation plans and agreements database.* Retrieved July 15, 2003, from http://ecos.fws.gov/conserv_plans/public.jsp

van den Belt, M. J. (2004). *Mediated modeling: A system dynamics approach to environmental consensus building.* Washington, DC: Island Press.

van den Belt, M. J., Deutch, L., & Jansson, Å. (1998). A consensus-based simulation model for management in the Patagonia coastal zone. *Ecological Modeling, 110,* 79–103.

Waddell, C. (1996). Saving the Great Lakes: Public participation in environmental policy. In C. G. Herndl & S. C. Brown (Eds.), *Green culture: Environmental rhetoric in contemporary America* (pp. 141–165). Madison: University of Wisconsin Press.

Walker, G. B., & Daniels, S. E. (2004). Dialogue and deliberation in environmental conflict: Enacting civic science. In S. L. Senecah (Ed.), *Environmental communication yearbook, 1* (pp. 135–152). Mahwah, NJ: Lawrence Erlbaum.

Walters, C. J. (1986). *Adaptive management of renewable resources.* New York: Macmillan.

Walters, C. J., & Holling, C. S. (1990). Large-scale management experiments and learning by doing. *Ecology, 71,* 2060–2068.

Walters, L. C., Aydelotte, J., & Miller, J. (2000). Putting more public in policy analysis. *Public Administration Review, 60,* 349–359.

Webler, T., Tuler, S., & Krueger, R. (2001). What is a good public participation process? Five perspectives from the public. *Environmental Management, 27,* 435–450.

Wells, M. P. (1994). A profile and interim assessment of the Annapurna Conservation Area Project, Nepal. In D. Western & R. M. Wright (Eds.), *Natural connections: Perspectives in community-based conservation* (pp. 261–281). Washington, DC: Island Press.

Western, D., & Wright, R. M. (1994). *Natural connections: Perspectives in community-based conservation.* Washington, DC: Island Press.

Willers, B. (1994). Sustainable development: A new world deception. *Conservation Biology, 8,* 1146–1148.

Wondolleck, J. M. (1988). *Public lands conflict and resolution.* New York: Plenum.

Wondolleck, J. M., Manring, N. J., & Crowfoot, J. E. (1996). Teetering at the top of the ladder: The experience of citizen group participants in alternative dispute resolution processes. *Sociological Perspectives, 39,* 249–262.

Wondolleck, J. M., & Yaffee, S. L. (2000). *Making collaboration work: Lessons from innovation in natural resource management*. Washington, DC: Island Press.

Woollard, R. G., & Ostry, A. S. (2000). *Fatal consumption: Rethinking sustainable development*. Vancouver: University of British Columbia Press.

World Commission on Environment and Development. (1987). *Our common future*. Oxford, UK: Oxford University Press.

Yearley, S., Cinderby, S., Forrester, J., Bailey, P., & Rosen, P. (2003). Participatory modeling and the local governance of the politics of UK air pollution: A three-city case study. *Environmental Values, 12*, 247–262.

Yosie, T. F., & Herbst, T. D. (1998). *Using stakeholder processes in environmental decisionmaking: An evaluation of lessons learned, key issues, and future challenges*. Washington, DC: Rudder Finn Washington and ICF Incorporated.

16

THE EMERGING FIELD OF CRISIS/HOSTAGE NEGOTIATION

A Communication-Based Perspective

RANDALL G. ROGAN

Wake Forest University

MITCHELL R. HAMMER

American University

It has been a little more than 30 years since the New York City Police Department (NYPD) began implementing its strategy of negotiating barricade standoff incidents (Louden, 1998), yet the act of taking hostages is an ancient tactic for exercising geo-political and relational power. In fact, it has been argued that in Genesis 14 of the Old Testament book of the Bible, one can read what may be the first recorded hostage taking and rescue operation. According to this account, a nephew of Abraham is taken captive by an opposing army, to which Abraham responds by assembling a force to rescue Lot from his captors (McMains & Mullins, 2001; Soskis & Van Zandt, 1986). Rogan and Hammer (2002) contended that with some general modifications to equipment, tactics, and training, the strategy employed by Abraham has been the standard operating procedure for more than 2,000 years. Events of the 1970s, however, would challenge this centuries-old paradigm.

The Attica prison riot of 1971 and the Munich Olympic Games of 1972 are two incidents with which students of crisis negotiation are universally familiar. On September 9, 1971, inmates at the New York State Prison in Attica, New York, took control of the prison, taking 42 guards and prison personnel as hostages. Following 3 days of ill-conceived efforts of deal-brokering between prisoners and prison officials, a tactical assault was made to retake the prison. In the ensuing siege, lasting only 15 minutes, more than 80 people were wounded and 39 killed. Eleven of the dead and 33 of the wounded were hostages and prison personnel. Comparatively, during the 3-day standoff, rioting prisoners killed 3 of their fellow inmates and only one prison guard (Bolz & Hershey, 1979; Poland & McCrystle, 1999).

In 1972, members of the terrorist group Black September forced their way into the Israeli athletes' apartments of the Olympic Village, killing two Israelis and taking 11 athletes hostage.

Similar to the Attica prison riot, attempts to bargain with the terrorists were poorly conceived and managed. After several hours of tense standoff, both the terrorists and their Israeli hostages were transported to the Munich airport where they were ostensibly to board an airplane bound for Egypt. It was at this point, however, that German authorities attempted a tactical rescue effort. Unfortunately, while three of the terrorists were ultimately arrested, all 11 of the hostages, 10 terrorists, and 1 German police officer were killed (Antokol & Nudell, 1990; Aston, 1982; L. B. Taylor, 1989).

It was shortly after these two watershed events that psychologist Harvey Schlossberg, who was serving with NYPD, began to question the efficacy of tactical resolution—a practice in which police would employ their general strategy of surrounding the suspect with overbearing and overwhelming force in an effort to convince him or her to surrender, or to be forcibly apprehended. Schlossberg was granted permission to implement an alternative "negotiate first" policy. Although he met some initial resistance from traditional "beat cops" and commanders, the success of what he termed "dynamic inactivity," the process of engaging the subject in effective communication became evident (Bolz & Hershey, 1979; Louden, 1998). Ultimately, what became known as the New York Plan gained popularity and was adopted by many metropolitan police departments throughout the United States. Within a few years, and with some refinement to basic principles and practices, the Federal Bureau of Investigation (FBI) had commenced its own hostage negotiation training program at the FBI Academy in Quantico, Virginia. Today, crisis negotiation is firmly established as a central approach to resolving barricade and hostage taking incidents.

Based on a survey of more than 1,000 law enforcement agencies, Butler (1991) found that 72% of recorded situations were resolved through a negotiated surrender, compared with the 18% that ended by means of a tactical assault. More recent data obtained from the FBI's HOBAS (Hostage, Barricade, and Suicide) database of 4,067 incidents suggest that negotiation continues to be a highly effective strategy, with 58% of all reported incidents resolved through negotiations and 11% resolved by means of an integrated negotiation and tactical approach. In only 20% of the incidents recorded was tactical action employed to resolve the crisis event. The remaining incidents were resolved by the suspect's escape (2.7%), suspect's suicide/attempted suicide (8.2%), or police disengagement from the incident (0.5%). Perhaps the most telling finding that the HOBAS data reveal, however, is that in 80% of all incidents no injuries or deaths were reported for bystanders, law enforcement officers, or hostage takers (Crisis Negotiation Unit, 2004).

Given its ubiquitous proliferation and undeniable effectiveness, crisis negotiation has become a highly specialized area of practice within the law enforcement community. Since its initial development in the 1970s, much has been written and published by practitioners and academic scholars on crisis negotiation. The purpose of this chapter is to review the general development of crisis/hostage negotiation as a specialized field of practice and scholarly investigation as reflected in myriad papers, articles, and books published on the topic. Given the general nascency of crisis negotiation as a context of scholarly inquiry, the chapter is framed around the core publications that inform the field, ranging from seminal introductory books, articles, and book chapters, to practitioner "how-to" guides, and concluding with publications of original research. Publications of the latter type will be the principal focus of this chapter, with an indepth review of the various research publications as they have come to shape contemporary crisis negotiation theory, research, and practice. We begin by reviewing some extant definitional perspectives of hostage negotiation and advancing a contemporary conceptualization that is grounded in a communication and conflict theoretic framework.

CONCEPTUALIZING CRISIS/HOSTAGE NEGOTIATION

While there exist myriad publications devoted to the topic of crisis/hostage negotiation, much of this literature takes for granted a presumed shared understanding concerning what constitutes a crisis negotiation event. Thus, it is essential that we provide a clear definition of how we are conceptualizing this phenomenon prior to embarking on our review of the literature.

Some of the earliest definitions of crisis/hostage negotiation reflect a traditional bargaining orientation focused largely on resolving terrorist incidents (e.g., Bolz, Dudonis, & Schulz, 1990; MacWillson, 1992; Maher, 1977; Miller, 1980; Miron & Goldstein, 1979; Ochberg & Soskis, 1982). For example, Cooper (1981) defined hostage taking as "a way of setting up a bargaining position that cannot be as conveniently or as well achieved by other means . . . (it) is a naked power play" (p. 1). Such conceptualizations presumed a general commonality among hostage-takings that was grounded in positional bargaining and in which hostages served as commodities to be exchanged and actions were rationally framed. In other words, early definitions tended not to differentiate hostage negotiation from other more traditional forms of negotiation (e.g., labor and contract negotiation) wherein the underlying presumption is one of quid pro quo bargaining and emotion-free decision making.

More contemporary conceptualizations generally retain an element of forced detainment, yet broaden the view beyond rational bargaining and terrorist events. For example, McMains and Mullins (2001) defined hostage taking as "any incident in which people are being held by another person or persons against their will, usually by force or coercion, and demands are being made by the hostage taker" (p. 35). Rogan and Hammer (1994, 2002) pointed out that the term *hostage negotiation* has historically denoted various types of incidents, including hostage takings, suicides, and barricade standoffs, in which a suspect acts to create an extortionate transaction with police. Donohue, Ramesh, and Borchgrevink (1991) posited that the term *crisis negotiations* more accurately captures the nature of such interactions as police strive to manage a crisis situation, transitioning from crisis bargaining to more normative incident management. Lanceley (2003) described hostage negotiation as a combination of crisis intervention and bargaining. He differentiated, however, between crisis intervention, in which a possible hostage is of no substantive value to the hostage taker, and hostage negotiations, where a hostage is held in order to force the fulfillment of

substantive demands. Hammer (2001) noted that crisis negotiation inherently involves a conflict dynamic that includes both incompatibilities and interference by one or more of the parties, which gives rise to perceptions of threat and negative emotions. Hammer and Weaver (1994) and Hammer (1997) emphasized the importance of the cultural characteristics of the parties involved as well as the cultural context within which negotiation strategies were employed.

As evidenced in these conceptualizations, we see the developmental progression in defining crisis/hostage negotiation, with an initial focus on the act of taking hostages, to the suspect's motives for engaging in hostage taking, and the type of incident. Building upon these initial definitions, more contemporary thinking shifts attention to crisis incident management, concern for the functional value of the hostages and the inherent cultural dynamics of the various individuals involved, to recognition of the essential interactional interdependencies and the consequent communicative dynamics. In an effort to synthesize the essential elements of extant definitions, Rogan and Hammer (2002) advanced the following conceptualization of crisis negotiation:

> a unique form of conflict interaction in which law enforcement officers attempt to facilitate a (peaceful) resolution to an incident where an individual barricades him/herself, sometimes with a number of hostages, in an effort to elicit some desired want or to communicate anger and frustration about a personal or social concern. (pp. 229–230)

Such a conceptualization captures the broad-based nature of crisis/hostage negotiation without artificially bifurcating it as either crisis intervention or substantive bargaining. This definition also identifies a class of crisis incidents beyond the terrorist event, including barricade situations and suicides, as well as intergroup (e.g., cult) standoffs. Further, this definition serves as a viable heuristic, capturing the integrative nature of crisis/hostage negotiation in which police employ crisis intervention in substantive hostage incidents as well as instrumental bargaining in non-hostage crisis situations. Finally, this definition directly positions hostage taking as a form of conflict interaction that is framed as a communicative event. Yet as will be gleaned in the next section, the development of an overarching definition for crisis negotiation has not been an easy objective. The practice of crisis negotiation has tended to dictate the conceptual parameters, while scholarly inquiry is still in its infancy.

THE EMERGENCE OF CRISIS/HOSTAGE NEGOTIATION AS A FIELD OF INQUIRY

Crisis/hostage negotiation emerged as a specialized form of police response to hostage takings or barricade standoffs that were either part of a terrorist tactic or the consequence of a non-terrorist criminal act. Given the diffuse and dramatic nature of international terrorism, early publications on crisis negotiation tended to focus on the terrorist hostage taker. This emphasis was often accompanied by a profiling of the terrorist's motives. Many such publications were written by cognitive psychologists and reflected their bias for cognitive and clinical factors in defining the hostage standoff and advancing a protocol for its resolution. In addition, the dominance of clinical psychology likewise focused attention on the effect of hostage taking on the hostage, such as the Stockholm syndrome (Fuselier, 1999; Gachnochi & Skurnik, 1992; Strentz, 1982).

Yet, early in its development, domestic law enforcement personnel realized that not all hostage taking and barricade standoffs involved terrorists. In fact, the vast majority of incidents that police were confronting did not involve any form of terrorism (Miller, 1980). Thus, there arose a need to differentiate the nature of hostage-taking incidents. The bulk of early publications on crisis negotiation focused on this differentiation as manifest in the proliferation of incident typologies.

Incident Typologies

Most attempts at differentiating hostage/barricade situations have relied on relatively simple descriptive categorizations that are based upon the ostensive practical motivation of the hostage taker, his or her psychological characteristics, specific features of the context in which the incident occurred, or a combination of these various features. For example, Middendorf (1975) developed one of the first such classification schemes in which he differentiated between hostage takings as political, escape, or for personal gain. Hacker (1976) advanced an alternative tripartite classification of incidents based upon a differentiation between hostage takers as criminals, crusaders, and crazies. Schlossberg (1979) likewise developed a three-part classification consisting of professional criminals, groups, and psychos.

While an essential basis of distinction between incident types in these three typologies is the suspect's presumed motivation for engaging in the act of taking hostages, an additional critical determinant is the suspect's mental health, thereby reflecting the dominant influence of clinical and cognitive psychologists in defining hostage-taking events. While such typologies are highly parsimonious in their simplicity and number of categories, they tend to lack sufficient clarity between incident type, resulting in confusion of proper classification due to overlap among types. For example, it could be possible to have a group of professional criminals who may be argued to manifest particular psychotic disorders engaging in hostage taking (e.g., the Simbianese Liberation Army or Charles Manson). Thus, greater clarity is necessary in order to more accurately capture the types of hostage-taking incidents that occur.

Cooper's (1981) categorization system provides further differentiation of incidents according to the functional motivation of the perpetrator and certain contextual conditions. Briefly, Cooper identified seven types of incidents, including political extremists, fleeing criminals, institutionalized persons, estranged persons, wronged persons, religious fanatics, and mentally disturbed persons. Focusing specifically on the motivation and mental condition of the perpetrator, Goldaber (1979) identified three overarching incident categories, into which he fit more precise sub-categories. The first broad category is the psychological, which is characterized by a hostage taker who is unpredictable and prone to violence. Sub-categories include the suicidal person, the mentally disturbed suspect, and the vengeance seeker. The second broad category is the criminal suspect. This type of perpetrator is generally regarded as a rational thinker who will surrender to police if there is no other option for achieving resolution. Sub-categories within this grouping are the cornered perpetrator, aggrieved inmate, and extortionist. The third and final category is the political perpetrator who acts to fulfill a particular political cause. This is composed of the more specific sub-categories of social protestor, militant ideological zealot, and terrorist. Continuing in this mode of distinguishing incidents according to presumed motivation, context of the incident, and the suspect's psychological condition, the FBI has, for many years, relied upon a four-part classification of hostage takings, including criminal hostage takings (e.g., bank robbery), hostage takings by mentally/emotionally disturbed individuals, terrorist hostage takings, and prison hostage takings (Borum & Strentz, 1992; DiVasto, Lanceley, & Gruys, 1992; Friedland, 1986; Fuselier, 1986; Fuselier & Noesner, 1990; McMains & Mullins, 2001; Soskis & Van Zandt, 1986).

Generally speaking, the benefit of such classification typologies is their utility in helping law enforcement to better understand the types of incidents that they encounter and some of the essential conditions associated with these incidents. Yet, early schemes, such as Hacker's (1976) typology, were overly simplistic, while later schemes (e.g., Cooper, 1981) tended to be overly complex with too many points of differentiation. Additional problems have arisen as negotiators have attempted to employ these typologies as structures for developing negotiation guidelines for each incident type. One basic variable common to all typologies has been the presumed functional motivation of the hostage taker. Still, the core deficiency of most typologies is the absence of any theoretically constructed conceptual framework that accounts for suspect motivation and that transcends all barricaded standoffs with police.

Interestingly, however, one of the most significant incident-type conceptualizations advanced was Miron and Goldstein's (1979) two-part instrumental-expressive scheme, which is grounded in a social psychological interpretation of a perpetrator's presumed motives. An instrumental orientation denotes a primary concern for satisfying some recognizable goal that is constructively beneficial to the perpetrator (e.g., obtaining money).

Comparatively, an expressive orientation by a suspect refers to

> those acts which serve only to display the power or significance of the perpetrator—acts which appear to be senseless in that there is no obvious way in which the perpetrator can stand to gain anything or in which the act is clearly self-destructive. (Miron & Goldstein, 1979, p. 10)

Miron and Goldstein concluded that while a suspect's behavior may be either instrumental or expressive, it often tends to be simultaneously both instrumental and expressive. With this two-part model of suspect motivation, Miron and Goldstein successfully advanced a theoretically grounded mechanism for analyzing hostage-taking incidents.

Unfortunately, however, most practitioners have not fully appreciated the parsimonious and heuristic value of Miron and Goldstein's (1979) model. Most, if not all subsequent classifications have tended to bifurcate their classification scheme, defining a suspect's motivation as either instrumentally or expressively motivated (e.g., Noesner & Webster, 1997). For example, Schlossberg (1979) argued that in an expressive-based hostage incident hostages do not have any instrumental value to the perpetrator. Rather, the taking of hostages is done for the purpose of drawing attention to the needs or plight of the suspect. Likewise, he argued that an expressively motivated perpetrator will have little interest or need to deal with instrumental issues or concerns.

The FBI's (Noesner, 1999) most recent hostage–non-hostage typology further reflects this bifurcated thinking, thus effectively negating an essential melding of instrumentality and expressiveness. Specifically, the FBI has modified its four-part classification to a two-part scheme made up of hostage and non-hostage incidents (Noesner, 1999). According to Noesner, an actual hostage situation is characterized by a suspect engaging in purposeful behavior for the attainment of some concrete outcome that denotes substantive value for the suspect, where hostages function as commodities for bargaining. Comparatively, non-hostage incidents are marked by a suspect whose behavior and whose demands are pragmatically unrealistic and where hostages serve no functional value (Noesner, 1999). This two-part instrumental/expressive (hostage/non-hostage) conceptualization now serves as the foundation upon which negotiators determine the type of incident to which they are responding and the appropriate strategy for managing the situation (Biggs, 1987; Botting, Lanceley, & Noesner, 1995; DiVasto et al., 1992; Fuselier, 1986; Noesner & Dolan, 1992; Van Zandt & Fuselier, 1989; Wind, 1995).

For the most part, the development of the various incident typologies provided preliminary definitions for understanding the nature of hostage negotiation incidents. Most notably, these schemes offered significant operational definitions that helped dictate the particular strategies that negotiators should use to resolve the standoff. With the preponderance of classifications derived from a psychological profiling of the perpetrator, most of the consequent guidelines were constructed around how to negotiate with a suspect manifesting particular psychological traits. It is to a review of those publications that emphasize the "how-to" of crisis negotiation that we now turn our attention.

Guidelines for Managing a Barricade Standoff

The majority of publications on crisis/hostage negotiation are how-to books and articles. These include publications in which the authors, who are frequently law enforcement personnel, outline and describe various critical aspects of crisis negotiation and offer recommendations for dealing with them. The authors typically present select psychological and behavioral concepts as central themes in their discussion, thereby conceptualizing crisis negotiation within a psychological framework. While the majority of such publications draw upon cognitive and abnormal psychology as their conceptual foundation, a small handful attempt to integrate concepts from other disciplines (e.g., counseling and business negotiation).

Generally speaking, these presentations are derived from the practitioners' personal experience as a crisis/hostage negotiator, or from the experience of other negotiators, and are devoid of substantive social or behavioral science research methodology. The absence of a dedicated base of social and behavioral science

research of crisis negotiations was a specific deficiency noted by Heymann (1993) in his report following the FBI's standoff with the Branch Davidians in Waco, Texas. Topics covered in these publications include such issues as general negotiation guidelines (Bolz & Hershey, 1979; Dalfonzo & Romano, 2003; Davidson, 2002; DiVasto, 1996; Fagan & Van Zandt, 1993; Fuselier, 1981a, 1981b; Fuselier & Noesner, 1990; Fuselier, Van Zandt, & Lanceley, 1991; Kobetz & Cooper, 1979; Noesner & Dolan, 1992; Smith & Kaufmann, 1988; Soskis & Van Zandt, 1986; R. W. Taylor, 1983; Vecchi, 2002; Wind, 1995), the use of third-party intermediaries (TPIs) during negotiation (Romano, 1998), integration of tactical and negotiation units, along with guidelines for on-scene commanders (Fuselier, 1986; Greenstone, 1995a, 1995b; Noesner, 1999; Vecchi, 2002), team training and team dynamics (Bahn & Louden, 1999; Geiger, Holmes, Goergen, & Skomra, 1990; Greenstone, 1995a, 1995b), negotiator selection and training (Regini, 2002; Soskis & Van Zandt, 1986), and delineation of the risk factors associated with potentially violent incidents (Fuselier et al., 1991; Strentz, 1991). Most of these publications present skill-oriented recommendations for how to actually negotiate with a suspect and over the years have evolved with an emphasis on the negotiators' use of therapeutic communication and active listening (Noesner & Webster, 1997; Slatkin, 1996).

For example, in one of the FBI's earliest presentations of guidelines for managing hostage-taking incidents, Fuselier (1981a) delineated five responses for achieving incident resolution, including: contain and negotiate, contain and demand surrender, use of chemical agents to obtain a surrender, use of snipers and sharpshooters, and the use of a tactical assault team. Fuselier admonished would-be negotiators always to start at the most basic level of contain and negotiate, warning readers that it is next to impossible to move from assault to negotiation. Since the publication of Fuselier's early article, countless other publications have presented specific guidelines for incident management. Davidson (2002) offered a summarization of some of the most basic guidelines that have prevailed over the years.

The first action that police need to take is to contain the situation and establish physical parameters around the geographic location of the hostage taking (Davidson, 2002). Containment affords law enforcement control of the physical environment and reduces the likelihood of other persons' becoming hostages or fatalities. Once containment is achieved, contact must be made with the suspect. While various communicative modes exist for making contact (e.g., throw phone, bullhorn, face to face), the preferred approach is the telephone as it tends to be the most reliable and least dangerous for negotiators, who should be trained law enforcement personnel. Davidson contends that the most basic factor at this point is a willingness on the part of the suspect to engage in meaningful communication with police. Absent this dynamic, actual negotiation toward a peaceful resolution will prove unlikely. It is also at this initial point of contact that the negotiator needs to evaluate the suspect's mental and emotional condition, as well as the potential influence of alcohol and drugs as precipitators of the suspect's behavior.

In terms of general operating guidelines, Davidson (2002) argued that negotiators should slow the interaction down by acting as a calming agent for the suspect. This will require the negotiator to build rapport with the suspect by using such techniques as stalling for time, engaging in self-disclosure, demonstrating empathy, minimizing the suspect's crimes, communicating warmth for the suspect by one's paralinguistic behavior, and utilizing active listening skills. In order to sustain the new-found relational affiliation, negotiators are warned to avoid lying to the suspect or saying "no" to their demands. Toward this end, negotiators are encouraged to "talk around" the issue and to strive to be as honest as possible throughout the duration of the siege, as trust for the negotiator will likely be the key reason for an ultimate surrender. Additional recommendations include talking through deadlines for demands (as few hostages are ever killed on deadline), viewing the passage of time as an ally for it strengthens the position of police and weakens the resolve of the suspect, letting the suspect state demands rather than seeking them out, continually assessing the suspect's mental and emotional condition, and calmly working toward resolution (Davidson, 2002).

Noesner (1999) offered recommended strategies according to the bifurcation of incidents into hostage (where the suspect holds a hostage to achieve some sort of substantive demand) and non-hostage (in which no substantive demand is made and where hostages are held with the intent of harming them). In actual hostage incidents, Noesner argued that law enforcement should employ highly visible containment, use delay tactics, make subjects work for everything they receive, lower the suspects' expectations about what they can achieve, contrast the benefits of surrender with the risks of a tactical assault, and offer suspects surrender with dignity. Comparatively, police should employ low visibility containment, demonstrate patience and empathy, make minor concessions, employ active listening skills, and provide nonviolent resolution options when dealing with a non-hostage incident. In general, however, Noesner asserted that negotiators, regardless of the precise nature of the incident, should always employ active listening skills to build rapport, be patient and use restraint in initiating any action, use force only when it is necessary, and carefully coordinate all actions with the various responding units (e.g., tactical assault team).

In addition to those publications that advance general incident guidelines, other how-to materials focus on managing and negotiating specific types of incidents, such as prison riots (Useem, Camp, & Camp, 1996), terrorist hostage takings (Fuselier & Noesner, 1990), and interacting with cults (Szubin, Jensen, & Gregg, 2000; Van Zandt, 1997). Further, a small group of publications have been devoted to explaining the impact of hostage taking on the hostage (i.e., Stockholm syndrome; Fuselier, 1999; Gachnochi & Skurnik, 1992; Giebels, Noelanders, & Vervaeke, in press; Strentz, 1982) as well as its effect on the police negotiator (Bohl, 1991, 1992, 1995, 1997; Carson, 1982).

Yet, the greatest number of publications are those that advance recommendations for negotiating with persons possessing various personality or psychological disorders and/or suicidal tendencies (e.g., Borum & Strentz, 1992; Bower & Pettit, 2001; Davidson, 1981; DiVasto et al., 1992; Fuselier et al., 1991; Lanceley, 1981, 2003; Lanceley, Ruple, & Moss, 1985; Mohandie & Duffy, 1999; Romano, 1990; Slatkin, 2003;

Strentz, 1983, 1986; Van Zandt, 1993). For example, Fuselier (1981a) proposed that mentally disturbed hostage takers could be differentiated into four basic types, including paranoid schizophrenic, manic-depressive, the inadequate personality, and the anti-social personality. A suspect who is an inadequate personality manifests ineffective and inappropriate responses to various social, physical, and emotional pressures; is often a high school dropout; and has generally failed at most efforts to succeed and thus views himself as a failure (Fuselier, 1981a). The taking of hostages is often the suspect's last attempt to demonstrate competency and success. When responding to an incident with such a perpetrator, Fuselier recommended that negotiators convey sympathy, understanding, and uncritical acceptance of the suspect. The goal should be to help the individual find a means to end the situation without feeling like he has failed yet again. Negotiators should avoid using TPIs (e.g., family, parents) as they may elicit strong negative emotions and hostile reactions.

Strentz (1983) concurred with Fuselier's recommendations, advocating that police provide ego support and a means to end the incident that will enhance the suspect's sense of self. Toward this end, Strentz argued that negotiators should allow the suspect to vent his or her emotions, work to build trust, provide for basic needs (food and drink), and stall for time. By comparison, such tactics are not wholly encouraged when dealing with the antisocial personality. This type of suspect typically fails to demonstrate conscience or guilt for his actions and is often regarded as either a sociopath or psychopath. The antisocial personality individual is concerned only about himself and fulfilling his desires. Thus, when confronted with this type of suspect, negotiators are admonished to avoid deceptive tactics and to guard against being tricked by the suspect (Fuselier, 1981a). Family and friends will not typically elicit heightened arousal from the suspect, but rather disdain, as such relationships are generally meaningless to the suspect. Strentz also argued that such individuals require frequent stimulation, which makes stalling for time an ill-advised strategy as the suspect may turn to the hostages when bored (Lancelely, 2003). While there are some general commonalities for how

to interact with these two types of suspects, it is also evident that subtle differences do in fact exist, and that the tactics advocated for one personality type may be detrimental when inappropriately used with the other.

Further, such difficulties are also found when examining the relationship of hostages to their captors. Specifically, recent work by Giebels et al. (in press) documents differences in the experience of being taken hostage in kidnapping versus siege situations. Their work suggests that feelings of uncertainty and isolation were strong for victims of kidnappings and not particularly present for victims in sieges. Further, their analysis suggests caution in labeling the positive bond that can develop between hostages and their captors as a psychological, abnormal artifact or syndrome. Rather, they suggest it may be more fruitful to view this relationship from the perspective of more normal, social interaction dynamics.

Taken together, these recommendations are the direct consequence of the early influence of cognitive and abnormal psychologists in crisis negotiation activities, which itself was a result of the early incident typologies that emphasized the cognitive and abnormal psychological characteristics of hostage takers. Furthermore, this focus is the result of a claim by the FBI that approximately 52% of all hostage incidents involved persons who were "mentally disturbed" (Fuselier, 1981a). Unfortunately, incident typologies and the accompanying guidelines that limit attention to the suspect's psychological condition provide little useful insight into the actual interaction dynamics involved in crisis negotiation. Significant confusion arises due to the lack of conceptual clarity in the *relationship* between the various categories, wherein psychological disorder categories are mixed with incident situational features. For example, Hacker (1976) included the category *criminal,* which is defined legally (i.e., someone is caught breaking the law); *crusader,* defined politically; and *crazies,* defined presumably through a psychological diagnosis of a mental disorder. No clear conceptual distinctiveness exists among these proposed categories. If police respond to a robbery alarm at a store, confronting an individual who was recently released from a psychiatric institution and who has stopped taking his medication for the diagnosed mental disorder of paranoid schizophrenia, and the individual now "holds" the cashier hostage, are they dealing with a "criminal" or a "crazy"? In addition, is this a hostage or a non-hostage situation? Will the suspect "use" the hostage for instrumental or expressive ends?

Moreover, serious questions arise about the ability of negotiators, who are not trained professional abnormal or cognitive psychologists and who do not employ standardized testing coupled with interview procedures, to effectively and accurately diagnose a suspect's mental state or personality. Failing to diagnose a suspect properly as either inadequate personality or antisocial personality, and the consequent misapplication of recommended tactics could fatally undermine efforts to achieve a peaceful resolution. Further, the unique conditions associated with a crisis negotiation incident not only cast doubt on anyone's ability to make an accurate psychological diagnosis of a perpetrator but also undermine the presumed static quality of such trait profiles.

Finally, because of the conceptual confusion associated with the various classification schemes, coupled with the absence of any coherent analysis of hostage-taking incidents on a broad-based scale via social and behavioral science methodology, recommendations on how to negotiate effectively with the various types of hostage takers have generally been advanced based on single cases and the anecdotal "data" of the practicing negotiator (see Fuselier, 1988, for an early, cogent analysis of some these contradictions). For example, while Fuselier (1981a) recommended against the use of TPIs, Romano (1998) argued that TPIs can be usefully engaged when negotiating with suspects. Taken together, the various categorical and psychological approaches to understanding crisis situations provided a preliminary effort at bringing coherence to the emerging practice of crisis negotiation and therefore serve an important function in increasing scholarly attention in this neglected area of study. Their usefulness, however, is constrained due to the inherent conceptual confusion among the categories as well as their limited praxis for developing theoretically grounded, consistent, behavioral science insights for negotiating these types of high stress events.

In sum, most negotiation guidelines to this point had principally been derived from the single incident experience of individual negotiators, with the consequent guidelines for incident management derived from select cases, accompanied by attempts to transfer clinical and cognitive psychology concepts and practices to a unique and potentially deadly form of conflict interaction. As early as the late 1980s, Fuselier (1988) was commenting on the fact that no systematic federal database existed for the collection, review, or scientific analysis of hostage negotiation events from which law enforcement could improve their effectiveness. Heymann (1993) likewise cited the absence of any significant social and behavioral science research of crisis negotiations as a specific criticism subsequent to the FBI's fateful management of its siege of David Koresh. Yet, both law enforcement practitioners and academic scholars were beginning to conduct scientifically grounded research of hostage negotiations. We now focus our attention on these efforts.

CRISIS HOSTAGE NEGOTIATION RESEARCH

Since the late 1980s, two general lines of original research have tended to evolve. The first program area has focused principally on data gathering and analysis of the various facets of hostage negotiation teams, including the types of incidents to which law enforcement respond and the psychological traits of suspects. Such information has been useful in the subsequent development of negotiator training programs, along with a national database of hostage and barricade incidents managed by the FBI. The second line of research has come primarily from a small cadre of communication scholars who have conducted a number of investigations into the communicative dynamics of crisis/hostage negotiation using authentic negotiation incidents. The effort of these scholars has facilitated the application and testing of various social and behavioral science theories of conflict interaction as they become manifest in crisis negotiation. We now review and discuss these two research tracts.

Survey Research

Over the years, a number of surveys have been administered to law enforcement agencies that profiled hostage negotiation efforts. These surveys have explored largely demographic aspects of hostage negotiation, including use of trained hostage negotiators, negotiator training, the use of mental health consultants, types of incidents managed, and the mental health of the perpetrator. The bulk of these surveys have been administered within the United States (e.g., Butler, 1991; Butler, Leitenberg, & Fuselier, 1993; Delprino & Bahn, 1988; Fuselier, 1988; Gettys, 1983; Hammer, Van Zandt, & Rogan, 1994; Rogan, Hammer, & Van Zandt, 1994; Strentz, 1985). One exception is Giebels (1999), who surveyed national and regional law enforcement coordinators among European Member States concerning existing hostage negotiation policies and practices prior to the first European Conference on Hostage Negotiations held in Doorwerth, Holland.

The most complete demographic survey of crisis/hostage incidents is that compiled by the FBI Crisis Negotiation Unit. Since 1997, this unit has been collecting information about domestic crisis incidents through HOBAS. To date, in-depth information has been catalogued and analyzed on more than 4,000 incidents, producing the most current and comprehensive databases on hostage/crisis incidents in the United States (Crisis Negotiation Unit, 2004).

Information is gathered through HOBAS by obtaining responses from local police negotiators to a set of close-ended questions regarding various aspects of a crisis incident in which they negotiated. This information is submitted by the incident negotiator to a central database maintained by the FBI, and summaries of the demographic information are made available to law enforcement agencies and crisis negotiation teams for review. Information is organized into three primary categories: demographic information concerning the incident, information regarding the subjects (perpetrators), and information on the victims (e.g., hostages). Below is presented a summary of current data on selected factors.

HOBAS data incident characteristics. Based on a total of 4,067 submitted incident reports through July 2004, 71% were identified as unplanned, 24% planned, and 5% unknown. Of these incidents, 5% are classified as hostage, 58% as barricade, 7% as suicide, and 29% as attempted suicide. The majority of incident (37%) events lasted 1 to 2 hours, while 31% lasted 2 to 4 hours. Existing phone service was used in the majority of the situations (29%), followed by a bullhorn (19%), voice contact from cover (18%), face to face (15%), cell phone (8%), and hostage/rescue phone system (9%). Finally, a TPI was used in only 17% of the incidents to communicate with the subject. When used, the TPI was most commonly either a family member or a friend. A mental health consultant was rarely used to negotiate with the subject (9%). English was the predominant language used in negotiation (87%), followed by Spanish (1.6%). In 58% of the cases, the incident was peacefully resolved through negotiation, 11% through a combination of negotiation and tactical actions, 20% through tactical intervention, and 8% by the subject committing suicide. Finally, in 97% of the incidents, no bystanders or law enforcement personnel were injured or killed during a hostage situation.

HOBAS subject characteristics. Of a total number of 4,342 subjects (perpetrators, hostage takers), almost half were between the ages of 30 and 45 (43%) or between the ages of 18 and 29 (28%). The vast majority were male (90%), with the following ethnic characteristics: European American (57%), African American (19%), and Hispanic (8%). Almost all subjects (90%) were fluent in English. Only about 10% of the subjects had a diagnosable mental illness evidenced by either commitment in the past to a mental facility (7%) or a residential treatment facility (1%). In 83% of the cases, the incident ended with no injury to the subject. In 6% of the situations, the subject committed suicide, and in a small number of incidents the subject was either injured (10%) or killed (1%).

HOBAS victim/hostage characteristics. A total of 1,080 individuals were held against their will by the subject(s). The victims were generally younger than the subjects, either under 18 years of age (25%) or between 18 and 29 years old (16%). Approximately 20% were 30 to 45 years of age. The majority of victims were female (56%). In terms of ethnic background, most of victims were European American (50%), African American (17%), or Hispanic (8%). In one third of the cases, the victim was not mistreated by the subject, while in other incidents victims were verbally abused (20%), physically abused (17%), or sexually abused (3%). The victim had no prior relationship with the subject in 37% of the cases. In those cases where there was a prior relationship, the victim was a family member (24%), spouse/ex-spouse (10%), or significant other (11%). Overall, in 80% of the situations, the victim was not injured, while in 14% of the cases the victim was injured and in 6% of the incidents the victim was killed by the subject.

While these data can be useful in capturing some general trends, the methodology employed to gather the information suggests caution in interpretation of at least some of the identified demographic trends. First, the information is submitted presumably by a negotiator who actually participated in the stated incident. However, this assumption is not clearly demonstrated. Second, there are definitional difficulties with some of the questions and/or response options. For example, it is not clear how to consistently distinguish "incident type" among the following response options: hostage, barricade, suicide, attempted suicide, and combination. It is quite possible, for example, that an incident can begin as a barricade situation whereupon some tactical action is then undertaken such that the fear and perhaps anger of the subject dramatically increases to the point where the subject either attempts suicide or completes a suicide act. In this case, is the incident type categorized as a barricade, a suicide, or perhaps even a police precipitated suicide, a category missing from the response options?

Similar problems exist regarding questions focusing on the mental health of both the subject and the victim. To what extent does the responder to the HOBAS questionnaire obtain accurate information with which to answer a question concerning the subject's mental health? The response options include commitment in the past to a state mental facility, no known current problems, no known prior problems, receiving counseling/therapy, and presumable prior commitment to a resident treatment facility. What, for instance, does receiving counseling/therapy actually mean? Does this indicate general mental health difficulties, a diagnosable mental disorder, or simply relational conflict? Might the

counseling be attended because one of the subject's children has substance abuse problems and the subject is attending counseling to help his or her child? Does attendance at a residential treatment facility indicate mood disorder issues, substance abuse issues, or some other disorder? While, clearly, the negotiator respondent may be well intentioned in providing such information, the lack of a more rigorous reporting protocol coupled with inconsistent verification methods suggest caution with such survey gathered information on crisis incidents.

Communication-Based Research of Crisis/Hostage Negotiation

It has been only since the late 1980s that communication scholars began researching the communicative dynamics of crisis negotiation (see Hammer, 2001, and Rogan, Hammer, & Van Zandt, 1997b, for a recent summary of some of this work). While it has been nearly a decade and a half since the first series of research-based conference papers were presented and subsequently published, it must be acknowledged that communication-based research of crisis/hostage negotiation is still in its early development. To date, there is a relatively small cadre of scholars who have actually published research specifically examining crisis/hostage negotiation dynamics. Most of this research involves discourse/content analysis of transcribed recordings of authentic hostage-taking incidents. Table 16.1 provides an overview of the central elements of these principal programs of research. Generally speaking, this research can be grouped into three broad categories of (a) relational interdependence, (b) phase modeling, and (c) behavioral model development and testing.

Relational interdependence. William Donohue and his colleagues have been the primary investigators of relational interdependence within crisis negotiation. Drawing on the work of Snyder and Diesing (1977) in international relations, Donohue and colleagues (Donohue, Ramesh, & Borchgrevink, 1991; Donohue, Ramesh, Kaufmann, & Smith, 1991) conceptualized hostage negotiation as crisis bargaining and differentiate crisis negotiation from normative bargaining interactions (e.g., labor negotiations).

Table 16.1 Communication-Based Programs of Research of Crisis/Hostage Negotiation Dynamics

Communication Approach	Domain of Inquiry	Research View of Negotiation	Theoretic Feature	Key Premise	Communication Focus	Key Question of Interest
Donohue and Colleagues	Relational development	Crisis bargaining transformed into normative bargaining	Relational/ negotiated order	Relational paradox created as a result of tension over relational control and distance	Verbal immediacy: spatial and implicit	How do participants negotiate relational dimensions of affiliation and interdependence?
Holmes	Phase structures	Integration of static incident properties and dynamic contextual and interactive forces	Phasic modeling	Crisis negotiation is a progression of ordered periods of interaction	Participant interaction, dynamics, incident structural factors, and environmental forces	What are essential core elements of negotiation, the shared dynamics, and the dissimilarities that mark developmental progression of negotiation?
Taylor	Participant motivation and communication dynamics	Multi-dimensional communication-based interaction	Negotiation behavior	Negotiation involves dynamic interaction among three essential behavioral dimensions	Linguistic cues as markers for dispositional motivation, interaction goals, and affective state	What is the interplay of three behavioral dynamics and how do they vary by incident and outcome?
Rogan and Hammer	Communication affective dynamics of participants	Multi-dimensional communication-based conflict interaction	Framing and behavioral goals	Linguistic cues frame speaker's goal concern and affective condition	Linguistic cues as markers for three core interaction goals and speaker message affect	What is the dynamic interplay among three interaction goals, message affect, and incident outcome?

Donohue and colleagues contended that the crisis features of hostage negotiation (emotional intensity) create particularly unique pressures on police negotiators as they strive to facilitate relational development with a suspect. Specifically, Donohue, Ramesh, and Borchgrevink (1991) argued that the core relational issues of control and distance combine to create a relational paradox for negotiators and suspects as they verbally joust to sustain either a coercive interdependence or transition to a more cooperative and normative bargaining relationship.

Donohue, Ramesh, and Borchgrevink (1991) explored this double bind by focusing on negotiators' and suspects' verbal immediacy behaviors, where *immediacy* was defined as the directness and intensity of communication. For the purpose of this study, the researchers differentiated between implicit immediacy and spatial immediacy. The former denotes the extent to which the parties communicate candidly and openly about their thoughts, feelings, and needs, while the latter denotes the extent to which negotiators' and suspects' language conveys physical and psychological closeness. Employing a set of nine authentic hostage negotiations, Donohue and colleagues coded individual speaker thought units for each of the two immediacy forms.

Their findings indicate that fairly distinct relational development trends exist between different types of hostage negotiations, marked by varying levels of competition and cooperation. For example, incidents involving mentally ill suspects began as cooperative and became competitive over time, while criminal incidents became cooperative over time, and domestic incidents remained competitive throughout. The authors concluded that an increased presence of the relational paradox undermines the ability of negotiators to achieve a nonviolent resolution. Of particular importance, they surmised that problems associated with facilitating trust may be more a consequence of indirect rather than direct negotiation strategies.

Donohue and Roberto (1993) continued this line of inquiry with their investigation of relational development as negotiated order. Employing negotiated order theory as their framework, Donohue and Roberto argued that the process of relational development is an implicit negotiation embedded within the explicit negotiation dynamic in which negotiators accept and reject definitions of the relational limits of their interaction. Drawing upon research of the dimensions of relational communication, they identified four relational limits that are derived from the interaction of relational affiliation and relational interdependence, including moving toward the other party, moving with the other party, moving away from the other party, and moving against the other party. Linguistic manifestations of spatial and implicit verbal immediacy were coded as representations of these limits. In addition, Donohue and Roberto employed a phase mapping analysis in their investigation in an effort to identify the potential phases, or contexts of patterns of verbal immediacy.

Their findings indicate that parties to hostage negotiation develop fairly stable relational dynamics early in the negotiation and tend to adhere to this pattern throughout the interaction. These stable patterns revealed a general consistency around the affiliation dimension with a greater level of implicit negotiation centering on interdependence. More specifically, cycles of "moving away" or "moving against" were marked by a diminished capacity to build relational understanding, while patterns marked by cycles of "moving with" and "moving toward" were associated with enhanced relational consensus. Taken together, these results suggest that negotiated order theory provides a valuable heuristic for understanding the implicit communication dynamics that negotiators and suspects engage in as they strive to determine the limits of their relationship, and thereby impact the ultimate outcome of the explicit negotiation.

Finally, Donohue and Roberto (1996) examined relational interdependence as manifest in integrative and distributive negotiation processes. They sought to test the applicability of three different models of negotiation: independent (integrative and distributive behaviors as orthogonal), stage (integrative and distributive behaviors cluster during the evolution of a negotiation), and interdependent (integrative and distributive behaviors are mutually dependent and intertwined within discourse). Employing a number of authentic and simulated hostage negotiations, Donohue and Roberto coded speakers' utterances for their relational and strategic value according to a 10-point scheme reflecting an integrative-distributive continuum.

Their findings indicate that an interdependence model best fits simulated negotiations, while authentic negotiations display patterns more consistent with the independent and stage models. Further, they report that the authentic incidents were characterized by a more diverse set of integrative-distributive strategies than the simulations. Donohue and Roberto surmised that this is due to the extreme variability associated with authentic negotiations and the need to employ a wider range of behaviors when compared with simulated incidents. Of particular noteworthiness, the authors commented that in practically all simulated interactions, the actor-hostage taker commenced the negotiation from a more distributive posture and tended to maintain this level of behavior throughout the interaction, while negotiators were more integrative. Comparatively, participants in the authentic cases tended to "match" each other more consistently. These results suggest that simulated training negotiations are marked by higher levels of distributiveness and patterns of behavioral consistency than are authentic incidents.

Phase analysis. Michael Holmes is one of the leading investigators of phase structures in crisis/hostage negotiations. In his 1993 collaboration with Sykes (Holmes & Sykes, 1993), Holmes sought to elucidate the coherent periods of communicative activity that characterize a negotiation's progression from initiation to conclusion. In this study, Holmes and Sykes conducted an exploratory investigation into the goodness-of-fit of Gulliver's (1979) phase model (a relatively general model of negotiation as opposed to more specific hostage negotiation practitioner models) to the developmental trajectories of authentic and simulated hostage negotiations. Briefly, Gulliver's model comprises the following eight phases: search for an arena, agenda and issue identification, exploring the range, narrowing the range, preliminaries to final bargaining, final bargaining, ritualization, and execution. The researchers coded each of their 16 incidents according to a scheme based on Gulliver's phases. These coded interactions were then transformed into phase markers and subsequently mapped.

Their findings indicate that simulations most closely match the phase structure detailed in Gulliver's model, while authentic negotiations are characterized by a more disorderly and disorganized progression. Holmes and Sykes posited that the training demands present in simulations seem to create an order and conformity to negotiation dynamics not present in authentic incidents. In fact, they contend that factors external to the actual negotiation discourse appear to influence the longitudinal structure of the interaction in ways not accounted for in what the parties say to one another. As such, they caution practitioners about relying on simulations for understanding the actual dynamics of authentic negotiations.

In a subsequent publication, Holmes and Fletcher-Bergland (1995) presented a conceptual framework consisting of five theoretic propositions concerning the developmental processes of crisis negotiation. Cautioning that normative bargaining models fail to account for the unique situational qualities of crisis bargaining, Holmes and Fletcher-Bergland argued that such interactions are not wholly chaotic or unpredictable, but rather may be characterized by structured patterns. In their first proposition, they stated that agenda setting and issue identification will occur during the initial stages of actual negotiation as opposed to a pre-negotiation stage. They contended that crisis negotiations will be most disruptive at the conclusion of conflict initiation. This leads to their second proposition: that crisis negotiations will move toward increased escalation following initiation, as opposed to problem solving. Such escalation will likely entail increased used of coercive and threatening behavior in the ultimate problem-solving stages, particularly if both parties are in crisis, which is their third proposition. Holmes and Fletcher-Bergland's fourth proposition was that the party not in crisis will employ various therapeutic strategies to attempt a more normative bargaining dynamic. Finally, any involvement of TPIs will cause a cycling back to earlier stages of negotiation in order to establish the necessary relational developmental patterns.

Holmes and Fletcher-Bergland argued that because of the unique stressors associated with crisis negotiations, developmental processes to realize incident resolution will be negatively affected by conflict escalation at the outset of the interaction, thereby hampering movement toward problem solving. As such, the application of normative bargaining guidelines will fail to accurately define or explain the structural nature of crisis interactions.

Holmes (1997a, 1997b) elaborated upon his position that crisis negotiation is not a wholly chaotic and unpredictable phenomenon, but rather is characterized by particular orderliness and predictability. Toward this end, Holmes contrasted static and dynamic conceptualizations of hostage negotiations, concluding with an integrated model that captures a number of factors that influence the organizational development of such incidents. According to Holmes, most traditional and practitioner models of hostage negotiation are grounded in a static model. Such a perspective seeks to identify the various relevant ingredients of hostage negotiation, thereby facilitating a delineation of the components into separate domains and sub-domains to create prescriptive models. This process seeks to inventory the relevant recurrent similarities in order to establish coherency, while dismissing inconsistencies as the result of the myriad permutations possible as a confluence of the primary domains. Traditional categories and typologies are reflective of this static view. Alternatively, a dynamic view focuses on the sequential and dynamic nature of negotiation. According to Holmes (1997a), this dynamic perspective seeks to clarify the shared commonalities in negotiation processes across incidents, as well as the dissimilarities that are created by the various forces that impact on the negotiation event, and the interactive dynamic of those processes. As such, a dynamic view focuses on negotiation as a series of events constitutive of the negotiation process.

In an effort to meld the static and dynamic perspectives, Holmes advanced an integrated model of crisis negotiation. His presumption was that hostage negotiation is more than the conversational dynamics of relational development, bargaining, and information exchange. Holmes conceptualizes hostage negotiation as situated in a contextual framework consisting of internal negotiation dynamics, structural features, and external environmental forces. Taken together, these forces combine to create the conditions associated with crisis negotiations. According to Holmes (1997b), such an integrated perspective more accurately captures the fluidity present in hostage negotiations and provides a valuable alternative for moving beyond static and prescriptive interpretations that presume that orderly progression is the result of a negotiator's ability to impose an agenda to the interaction, to a more dynamic view in which myriad forces combine to affect the longitudinal structure of the interaction, of which negotiator efforts are only one variable.

Behavioral models of crisis negotiation. Recently, Paul Taylor, a U.K. scholar, advanced a cylindrical model of the communication in crisis negotiations. In his first publication (Taylor, 2002a) Taylor advanced a tripartite model of communication that integrates several of the existing theoretical perspectives concerning the linguistic cues and motivational definitions for suspects and police negotiators. Drawing on extant negotiation literature, and crisis negotiation research specifically, Taylor proposed a model that melds negotiator behavior on two levels with behavioral intensity. The first level is in terms of a party's general dispositional orientation toward a threefold behavioral scheme of avoidance, integrative, and distributive behavior. The second level is in terms of individuals' motivational goal orientations according to a second threefold distinction, comprising instrumental goals, relational goals, and identity goals. Finally, Taylor proposed a third dimension of behavioral intensity, in which a negotiator's and subject's affective state is marked by manifestations of intense language. Taylor sought to test this model when applied to authentic crisis negotiations.

Using a data set of nine actual incidents, Taylor coded each of the parties' linguistic cues at the thought unit level, according to a coding scheme reflective of the three-part model. The results offered support for the three-part model, with negotiator and subject communication revolving around confluent expressions of integrative, distributive, and avoidance, mixed with goal-oriented expressions for instrumental, relational, and identity concerns, and varying by level of intensity. On a more specific level, the results suggest that negotiators and perpetrators move among the three broad levels of behavioral orientation as they seek to pursue their specific goals, which are affected by participants' linguistic intensity. According to P. J. Taylor (2002a), a major strength and contribution of the model is its recognition of the multidimensionality of actual crisis negotiations and the interrelationship of various communication behaviors, as opposed to traditional categorical or taxonomic conceptualizations.

In a subsequent article, P. J. Taylor (2002b) published results from a test of his three-part model in predicting incident outcome. He employed the same data set and coding procedure used in his first study, including incident resolution status. According to Taylor, participants' behavior could be plotted along a scale of competitiveness, as marked by distributive-expressive and integrative-instrumental behavior. Findings also indicate that success of incident resolution varied by movement along the competitiveness dimension, with unsuccessful outcomes characterized by extreme competition. This investigation lends additional support to the heuristic value of employing a multivariate behavioral model in capturing and explaining the communicative dynamics of crisis negotiation. But more important, Taylor's research highlights the critical value that an integrated communication-based model of crisis negotiation can provide in helping to predict the outcome trajectories of actual negotiation incidents. Taylor has continued this general line of research in his recent publications (P. J. Taylor, 2003, 2004).

Over the past decade, Hammer and Rogan have published a number of communication-based pieces exploring the communicative dynamics of crisis negotiation (Hammer, 1997, 2001; Hammer & Rogan, 1997; Hammer & Weaver, 1994; Rogan, 1997, 1999; Rogan & Hammer, 1994, 1995, 2002; Rogan, Hammer, & Van Zandt, 1997a, 1997b). Their most recent publications are a synthesis of their prior research, culminating in a four-part behavioral model known in its most contemporary form as the S.A.F.E. model. The S.A.F.E. model identifies four core interactive frames that are related to conflict escalation and de-escalation. These four interpretive frames are: (a) Substantive demands/wants, (b) Attunement, (c) Face, and (d) Emotional distress.

The S.A.F.E. model is based in the social constructivist paradigm in that it focuses on the functional meaning of communicative symbols manifest during the conflict interaction, and grounded in pragmatics theory of human communication (Hammer, 2001; Hammer & Rogan, 2002). Central to the model is the theoretic distinction between a report (content) and command (relational and metacommunicative) level of meaning in communication (Cissna & Sieburg, 1981; Watzlawick, Bavelas, & Jackson, 1967). Drawing on this conceptualization, Hammer and Rogan (2002) contended that the (command) function of communication serves as a framing device by which negotiators and subjects make sense of and define their interaction.

Hammer and Rogan (1997) posited that a pivotal means by which to understand conflict frames is in terms of the goals individuals are said to pursue during conflict. According to Putnam and Holmer (1992), the act of framing is a communicative process whereby individuals create verbal descriptions and/or representations of an issue or relationship. Namely, the three goals noted by various conflict scholars (e.g., Roloff & Jordan, 1992; Wilson & Putnam, 1990) include face (identity), substantive/instrumental interests, and relational concerns. Recent conceptualizations of conflict posit emotion to be a central element to conflict interaction (e.g., Adler, Rosen, & Silverstein, 1998; Barry & Oliver, 1994; Jones, 2001), and it is thus included as a fourth frame in their model.

Consistent with instrumentally focused conceptualizations, a substantive frame denotes individual concern for generally objective and tangible wants and demands (Roloff & Jordan, 1992; Wilson & Putnam, 1990). Within the context of crisis negotiation, two fundamental types of substantive goals have been identified: central substantive interests/demands and peripheral substantive interests/demands (Hammer & Rogan, 1997; McMains & Mullins, 1996; Rogan & Hammer, 2002). Briefly, central substantive interests and demands deal with situationally related wants, while peripheral interests and demands are wants that are not directly dependent upon the specific situation. For example, a subject who requests a car to flee the scene of an attempted robbery with hostages is communicating a central substantive demand. On the other hand, if this same individual requests food and drink, he or she would be communicating a peripheral, substantive demand.

According to Hammer (2001), the number and type of interests and demands communicated during a crisis negotiation are related to conflict escalation and de-escalation. Briefly, increased expression of peripheral demands and greater expressed commitment to previously communicated central demands tends to be associated with conflict escalation. Hammer further contended that an increased expression of peripheral demands may be associated with escalating relational conflict dynamics involving power issues and trust between the negotiator and perpetrator. Comparatively, increased flexibility toward central, substantive wants and a reduction in the number of peripheral demands is related to conflict de-escalation. It may be the case that a perpetrator's substantive demands reflect the level of relational attunement between the negotiator and subject.

Rogan and Hammer (2002) posited that attunement is concerned with the negotiation of relational dynamics between the negotiator and subject. Trust, power, affiliation, and understanding are all facets of personal relationships. Within crisis negotiation these qualities are typically absent at the outset of contact between the subject and police. In striving to deal with the relational dynamics of crisis negotiation, police must often overcome a suspect's general distrust for law enforcement. The importance for negotiators to attend to such issues and to develop a positive relationship with the perpetrator has been acknowledged as essential to incident resolution (Miron & Goldstein, 1979; Womack & Walsh, 1997).

Research by Donohue and associates further delineates the importance of attunement to crisis escalation and de-escalation dynamics. According to Donohue (1998), affiliation denotes the extent to which individuals communicate attraction, liking, respect, trust, and a willingness to cooperate with one another. In other words, affiliation is defined as the level of relational distance (attunement) between interactants. As previously reported, Donohue and Roberto (1993) found that relational patterns established early in a negotiation tend to remain fairly constant throughout the negotiation.

Further, they found that in low affiliation conditions parties were less able to establish any consistent relational consensus (attunement) upon which to resolve substantive concerns; whereas in cases of high affiliation, communicators were more readily able to focus on instrumental issues rather than on relational definitions.

There exists general agreement among scholars that the concept of face denotes individual concern for self and others' image, reputation, and/or identity as presented during a social interaction (Hammer & Rogan, 1997; Northrup, 1989; Ting-Toomey, 1988; Ting-Toomey & Kurogi, 1998). Rogan and Hammer (1994) suggested that within the context of crisis negotiation, facework strategies vary along three dimensions: (a) locus of concern: self or other directed; (b) face valence: defend, maintain, attack, or honor facework; and (c) temporality: proactive attempts to protect against face loss/retroactive efforts to restore lost face. Combining these dimensions produces six types of facework: (a) Defend Self Face, (b) Attack Self Face, (c) Restore Self Face, (d) Defend Other's Face, (e) Attack Other's Face, and (f) Restore Other's Face. Rogan and Hammer (1994) employed this face scheme to code a set of three authentic negotiation incidents. Results from their investigation indicate that Restore Other's Face was the primary behavior used by negotiators while Restore Self Face was the principal strategy for suspects. Attack Self Face was also commonly used by suspects, particularly in the suicide incident investigated.

Hammer and Rogan (1997) argued that two additional types of face that seem to be particularly important to crisis negotiation are group identity and individual identity. According to Hammer and Rogan (1997), "Personal identity is based on an individual's unique perceptions of his/her own attributes (e.g., strong, weak, intelligent) while social identity consists of those characteristics and their emotional significance that is attached to one's membership in social group(s)" (pp. 15–16). The importance of these two types of face can vary from incident to incident as well as over time within an incident. For example, Rogan and Hammer (1994) concluded that personal identity may be most salient in negotiations involving a suicidal person, while social identity is of greater concern in incidents involving members of certain groups, cults, or national organizations.

With increased attention devoted to the expressive motivation of the perpetrator, the subject's emotional state was recognized to be a crucial ingredient in determining the success or failure of a negotiated outcome (Miron & Goldstein, 1979). Attending to emotional distress requires that negotiators learn appropriate effective listening and interaction skills in order to deal with perpetrator emotion as a means for reducing the potential for negative and violent (fight/flight) reactions on the part of the perpetrator (Cannon, 1929; Hammer, 2001). The premise of this approach is that by reducing the subject's emotion, the negotiator will facilitate increased rationality and normative bargaining in the interaction. In addition to focusing on the motivation of the suspect, concern for the emotional impact of intense negotiations on the police negotiator, in the form of post-traumatic stress, has also been an area of focus (Bohl, 1991, 1992, 1995, 1997).

In one study, Rogan and Hammer (1995) explored the verbal expression of emotion in a select sample of crisis negotiation incidents. Focusing on the communicative dimensions of language (emotional) intensity and emotional valence (affect), they coded the message behavior of perpetrators and negotiators. They discovered that across all incidents the perpetrators' level of emotional expression was negative and intense at the outset of the interactions. This is the point at which the subject is first confronted and forced to come to terms with the situation. Subsequent to this initial period of emotional excitation, the perpetrators' emotional expression tended to become more positively intense, resulting in a peaceful surrender. This, however, was not the case in the suicide incident analyzed. In this incident, the suspect's emotional expressiveness cycled between positive intensity and negative intensity culminating in extreme negative intensity during the final stages of the incident and his ultimate suicide. These results suggest that verbal cues of language intensity and message affect may differ between incidents that end in suicide and those that do not.

This line of research offers preliminary insight into the interactive dynamics of emotion and emotional expression during crisis negotiation and also highlights the potential benefit of attending to verbal message behavior to understand more fully the emotional state of the suspect as it forecasts future behavior. Yet, our understanding of the role of emotion in crisis negotiation and how we interact with the subject in an attempt to manage emotion-based communicative dynamics is still in its infancy. Consequently, it is imperative that we develop a more complete understanding of emotion and how it impacts conflict interaction in general and crisis/hostage negotiation specifically.

Overall, the S.A.F.E. model offers an emerging theoretical structure within which to examine further the complex interactional dynamics involved in crisis negotiations. This model identifies preliminary propositions concerning the relationship between central and peripheral substantive demands, level of attunement (relational cooperation), degree to which face attack/honor messages are sent and grounded around individual or group face dimensions, and level of emotional distress in terms of interactively influencing conflict escalation and de-escalation in crisis incidents.

DIRECTIONS FOR FUTURE RESEARCH

Admittedly, there exists much opportunity and many possible avenues for future research. Three research topics, however, represent areas in which significant attention is warranted.

Emotion and Emotional Expression

Identification of a suspect's emotional state is of central concern to police negotiators because they realize that the perpetrator's emotional condition is a significant determinant for how the incident is concluded (Rogan, 1997). It is for this reason that essentially all practitioner guidelines for negotiating with a hostage taker include suggestions for identifying the suspect's emotion. Yet, such strategies as mirroring, paraphrasing, and emotion labeling do little more than provide police with a sense of the suspect's gestalt-level emotional condition. In fact, one does not really even need to engage in such tactics to predict that the suspect will be angry, upset, frightened, or confused. These are merely the emotional parameters within which most crisis/hostage-taking events normally occur. What is more critical is that negotiators gain an increased understanding of a suspect's transitory emotional states while they shift during the course of a barricaded siege.

While there exist diverse theoretical and conceptual opinions about emotion, most scholars of emotion generally agree that emotion is a complex triadic event involving physiological, cognitive, and behavioral processes (Lazarus, 1984; Metts & Bowers, 1994). While it is beyond the scope of this chapter to review the myriad research on this topic and to parse through the extant debate concerning the social construction of emotion, it is safe to conclude that current thinking postulates emotion as the consequence of cognitive appraisal processes, which are socially influenced, and linked to both discrete and indiscriminant physiological experiences, which combine to determine a person's emotional experience and his or her consequent emotional expression (Averill, 1992; Izard, 1990). In addition, scholars agree that there exist numerous types of distinct and complex emotions that vary in intensity, and that people can experience multiple emotions simultaneously (Jones, 2001). Finally, researchers distinguish between feelings, moods, and emotions, such that feelings are defined as sensations that are generally devoid of cognition and moods as existing in longer duration but less intensity than emotions (Batson, Shaw, & Oleson, 1992). As such, the simple, albeit admirable effort of negotiators to "label the suspect's emotion" by focusing on the person's gestalt emotional state negates the complexity of emotions at play in such incidents and the transitory nature of an emotional experience. Research needs to provide practitioners with procedures for increasing their understanding and discernment of a perpetrator's emotional condition.

To date, only limited research has been initiated in this area. Briefly, as reported previously, Rogan and Hammer (1995) conducted a language-based investigation of message affect employing a quantitative metric for coding a suspect's verbal communication. Their findings offered preliminary insight into the dynamic nature of emotion by highlighting certain linguistic patterns associated with a suspect's violent and suicidal behavior. Subsequently, Bilsky, Muller, Voss, and Von Groote (in press) tested Rogan and Hammer's message affect metric on a single corpus of negotiation, comparing it with the Gottshalk-Gleser hostility scale, and found support for the mutual validity, reliability, and utility of the two metrics. Additional research needs to further refine the efficaciousness of such metrics so that they might be employed to help provide insight into the dynamics of emotion and emotional expression as they impact incident management and outcome. Such research should likewise seek to investigate linguistic and paralinguistic expressions of emotion as potential correlates of threatening behavior and the potentiality of threat enactment.

Communication and Incident Outcome

Given the centrality of communication to crisis/hostage negotiation, much more research needs to investigate the effect of various communicative variables, strategies, and tactics on incident outcome. To date, communication-based research of crisis negotiation has tended to be primarily descriptive in nature. For example, the work of Donohue and his colleagues (e.g., Donohue & Roberto, 1993) has focused principally on describing expressions and patterns of relational interdependence and affiliation between perpetrator and negotiator; Holmes (e.g., Holmes & Sykes, 1993) has focused on explicating the dynamic processes involved in the developmental progression of incidents, comparing actual situations with training simulations; P. J. Taylor's (2002a, 2002b) research has sought to test some of the proffered core variables and bargaining strategies delineated in existing models of negotiation in general, and crisis negotiation specifically, focusing on their interrelationship; and Rogan and Hammer's research (e.g., Hammer, 1997; Hammer & Rogan, 2002; Rogan & Hammer, 1994, 2002) has provided generally descriptive insights into the dynamics of facework, culture, and message affect, culminating in their S.A.F.E. model. While such descriptive investigations are an essential step in social science research in helping to explain the dynamics of such conflict incidents, scholars need to proceed with investigations that seek to offer predictive knowledge by actively testing specific research hypotheses that employ outcome as a key dependent variable.

For example, scholars should test for the effect of general negotiation strategies (i.e., integrative, distributive, avoidance), as explicated by P. J. Taylor (2002b), for their association with incident outcome. Similarly, more research needs to explore the manner in which negotiators and suspects manage frames, shift between frames, and ultimately achieve incident resolution. Additional research efforts should delve into the effect of negotiator problem reformulation on suspect frame shifting and incident resolution. Research could also seek to determine if there are particular communicative "frame markers" associated with different types of perpetrator frames (e.g., a suicidal perpetrator). Such research should seek to examine patterns of incident escalation and de-escalation, as well as incident outcome.

In addition to focusing on the interaction between perpetrator and negotiator, researchers should also investigate the communicative dynamics among the various law enforcement units (e.g., negotiators, tactical team, on-scene commander) and various other community agencies that respond to such incidents. According to Vecchi (2002), the interaction among such police units is potentially rife with conflict as they strive to collaborate toward a common outcome yet approach it from ostensibly competing paradigms about how to facilitate the resolution. While several practitioners have written recommendations for on-scene commanders for managing these dynamics (Noesner, 1999; Vecchi, 2002), there exists scant research into the actual interactions and their impact on incident outcome.

Cultural Dynamics of Crisis Negotiation

Both within the United States and globally, cultural diversity is increasing—not decreasing. Culturally based patterns of difference are emerging today as critical aspects of crisis incidents. Yet while a large number of studies have examined patterns of cultural difference in negotiation more broadly (e.g., Augsburger, 1992; Moran & Stripp, 1991), this work has not focused specifically on the unique dynamics

involved in crisis and hostage situations. Also, of the numerous articles and books written on crisis negotiation, very few discuss cultural variability. Yet under conditions of stress and threat, people revert to their primary cultural patterns as they attempt to cope with the demands of the crisis event (Hammer, 1997), thus portending a key aspect that may be present in crisis negotiations. Perhaps one of the most important directions for future work in crisis negotiations, therefore, examines the impact of cultural differences in negotiating peaceful resolution of crisis incidents. We believe one promising approach focuses on the conflict resolution style individuals from different cultural communities use in crisis situations.

At a general level, interaction style is concerned with the patterns of behavior that constitute the way individuals communicate (Norton, 1983), or "the root sense of a way or mode of doing something" (Hymes, 1974, p. 434). When applied to conflictual interaction, conflict style refers to "patterned responses to conflict in a variety of situations" (Ting-Toomey et al., 2000, p. 48) and is identified as one of the central dimensions that escalate conflict between contending parties (Ting-Toomey et al., 2000). As such, conflict style differences across cultures represent one important, though unexplored, area of future crisis negotiation research.

A variety of taxonomic models has been proposed in conceptualizing conflict style (see van de Vliert, 1997, for a comprehensive review). These taxonomies have included flight/fight (Cannon, 1929); cooperation-competition (Deutsch, 1973); moving away, moving with, moving toward, and moving against (Horney, 1945); and withdrawing, yielding, problem solving, or inaction (Rubin, Pruitt, & Kim, 1994). One of the more common typologies is based on the early work of Blake and Mouton (1964), who viewed conflict style as emerging from an individual's concern for self-interests versus concern for the interests of the other. Rahim (1983), for instance, identified five conflict styles based on the individual's concern for self or other, including dominating style (high self/low other concern), obliging style (low self/high other concern), avoiding style (low self/other concern), integrating style (high self/other concern), and compromising style (moderate self/other concern).

Difficulties arise, however, when current conceptualizations of conflict style are applied across cultures. First, current models of conflict style have been developed within Western-based, individualistic cultural settings (Ting-Toomey et al., 2000). For example, Ting-Toomey (1994) argues that an avoiding approach reflects a low concern for self-interests and a low concern for other interests only in Western cultures. In contrast, an avoiding strategy reflects a high concern for self and other goals in Asian cultures because of their more collectivistic (as opposed to individualistic) value orientations. Second, these taxonomies have not been developed to assess *intercultural* conflict styles insofar as the underlying conceptual frameworks are not focused on culturally based patterns of differences (Hammer, in press). Therefore, while it is important to examine cultural differences in conflict style and their impact on crisis negotiation outcomes, current conceptual models and assessment measures are not sufficiently "intercultural" in scope to warrant uncritical application to the cross-cultural crisis arena.

One approach, recently developed by Hammer (in press), may be useful in examining the impact of conflict style differences across cultures in the crisis/hostage taking event. Specifically, Hammer presents a model and assessment tool of intercultural conflict resolution style. This model is grounded in the pragmatics and interactional theoretical framework advanced by Watzlawick et al. (1967) wherein communication "not only conveys information, but that at the same time imposes behavior" (p. 51). Within this framework conflict style is conceptualized as "the manner in which contending parties communicate with one another around substantive disagreements and their emotional or affective reaction to one another" (Hammer, in press). When extended interculturally, how individuals negotiate substantive disagreements reflects more Direct versus Indirect approaches and how individuals communicate their affective state to one another reflects more Emotionally Expressive versus Emotionally Restrained patterns. Research conducted largely under the rubric of individualism/collectivism (e.g., Pearson & Stratton, 1998; Ting-Toomey, 1999; Trubisky, Ting-Toomey, & Lin, 1991) and high/low context (e.g., Augsburger, 1992;

Hammer, 1997; Ting-Toomey, 1985) identifies the core cultural dimension of Direct/Indirect approaches as central for dealing with disagreements across cultures and Emotional Expressiveness/Restraint (Hammer & Rogan, 2002; Ting-Toomey, 1988, 1999; Trompenaars & Hampden-Turner, 1998) as central to how emotional experiences are communicated across cultural boundaries (see Hammer, in press, for a comprehensive review of related literature in this area).

The model of conflict resolution style proposed by Hammer (in press) identifies four core approaches: (a) A Discussion style describes an approach that emphasizes more verbally direct strategies for dealing with disagreements and a more emotionally restrained or controlled manner for dealing with each party's emotional state, (b) an Engagement style emphasizes a more verbally direct approach infused with an emotionally expressive demeanor, (c) an Accommodation style describes an approach to conflict resolution that is grounded in more indirect strategies for dealing with disagreements and more emotionally restrained or controlled approaches for dealing with each party's emotional response to conflict, and (d) a Dynamic style involves more indirect approaches for negotiating substantive disagreements coupled with more emotionally intense expression. This model serves as a valuable heuristic for investigating and explicating the culturally based patterns in conflict styles as they occur within crisis/hostage negotiation; researchers should devote increased attention to this critical communicative dynamic.

MANAGING CRISIS INCIDENTS

While research examining the effect of general negotiation strategies and tactics, as well as specific communication dynamics and culturally based patterns of difference on incident outcome, is essentially nonexistent at this time, some tentative recommendations for managing crisis conflicts can, nonetheless, be gleaned from existing crisis negotiation guidelines and extant communication-based research. To begin, dealing with the heightened level of emotional arousal associated with crisis incidents is perhaps the most demanding and challenging dynamic. Conflict is inherently an emotional event, such that parties to conflict interaction need to understand how emotion morally frames conflict, affecting the manner by which parties define the conflict and thus the means for managing the situation (Jones, 2001). Crisis negotiation guidelines recommend that negotiators strive to understand their opponent's emotional state by enacting empathic communication and active listening in order to define, label, and express comprehension of the other's emotions. In this way, negotiators work to calm the suspect in order to reduce the potential for violent behavior. For the negotiators, this typically requires exemplary self-control of their own emotional state and visceral responses to the suspect's communication toward them. Such is also the recommendation of most basic communication and conflict textbooks (Folger, Poole, & Stutman, 2001; Wilmot & Hocker, 2001).

Time management is also a significant factor in crisis negotiation. Generally speaking, negotiators are encouraged to stall for time, as time constitutes an ally for law enforcement in effectuating a peaceful resolution (Lanceley, 2003; Strentz, 1983). More specifically, during the course of a siege, suspects usually experience a reduction in emotional excitation, increased deliberative decision making, and increased fatigue, all of which serve to facilitate the efforts of law enforcement. Time management and timing of conflict engagement are likewise essential elements of interpersonal conflict management (Folger et al., 2001). Knowing when to engage another party about a grievance and understanding that resolutions need not be rushed can enable individuals to achieve more meaningful and mutually agreeable outcomes (Hocker & Wilmot, 2001).

From a communication goals perspective, conflict managers can be well served by understanding that parties to conflict pursue multiple functional and intentional goals, including relational, face, and instrumental needs (Cupach & Canary, 1997). Communication functions to frame these concerns, thereby providing negotiators with insight into their opponent's primary need(s) at any particular point in time (Rogan & Hammer, 2002). Of particular value is knowing that a suspect's instrumental needs can be distinguished as either substantive or nonsubstantive to the particular interaction, thereby enabling negotiators to fulfill certain nonsubstantive needs without surrendering instrumental needs of significant importance to the episode but that can enhance relational affiliation with the suspect. Furthermore, knowing that relational and face needs often overshadow and outweigh a suspect's actual instrumental needs (Head, 1988) enables negotiators to be less reliant on traditional quid pro quo bargaining strategies. Such insight arms negotiators with knowledge that allows them to be dynamic and flexible in their management of crisis conflict interactions.

CONCLUSION

The emerging field of crisis/hostage negotiation represents one of the most complex yet critically important facets of human interaction—where lives are saved or lost based largely on the interactive dynamics that arise between the negotiator and the subject. Previous efforts at capturing this complexity have been either conceptually inconsistent or limited in focus. Early typologies of the crisis incident tended to be categorical rather than interactively grounded. Further, these typologies mixed demographic characteristics with psychological and motivational assessments of the subject, resulting in theoretically confused frameworks and, more important, inconsistent and at times inaccurate recommendations for practice.

While early and continued emphasis on psychological disorders and the mental health of the subject is clearly important, these more clinical or abnormal psychological frameworks do not lend themselves easily to capturing the fluidity and interactive influence that arises in and governs negotiator and subject communication dynamics. Further, the crisis situation itself rarely lends itself as a context within which an accurate psychological assessment can be made of a subject insofar as standardized testing and interviewing protocols are not possible.

A communication-based approach to crisis negotiation represents one promising effort at examining the complexity of the interaction that arises in crisis events. Promising work in relational interdependence, phase analysis, and behavioral models represents initial theoretically grounded approaches that deserve additional exploration. Further, the discourse-analytic methods many of these studies employ offer a strong methodological approach for generating impactful research results that both advance theory as well as improve practice. In this regard, the various communication-oriented theoretical formulations coupled with discourse-analytic methods offer hope that the theory that is developed is, indeed, practical insofar as it contributes to saving lives and de-escalating and peacefully resolving violent situations through negotiation.

REFERENCES

Adler, R. S., Rosen, B., & Silverstein, E. M. (1998). Emotions in negotiation: How to manage fear and anger. *Negotiation Journal, 14,* 161–179.

Antokol, N., & Nudell, M. (1990). *No one a neutral: Political hostage-taking in the modern world.* Medina, OH: Alpha Publications.

Aston, C. C. (1982). *A contemporary crisis: Political hostage-taking and the experience of Western Europe.* Westport, CT: Greenwood.

Augsburger, D. W. (1992). *Conflict mediation across cultures.* Louisville, KY: Westminster/John Knox.

Averill, J. R. (1992). The structural bases of emotional behavior: A metatheoretical analysis. In M. S. Clark (Ed.), *Emotion* (pp. 1–23). Newbury Park, CA: Sage.

Bahn, C., & Louden, R. J. (1999). Hostage negotiation as a team enterprise. *Group, 23,* 77–85.

Barry, B., & Oliver, R. L. (1994). *Affect in negotiation: A model and propositions.* Paper presented at the meeting of the International Association for Conflict Management, Eugene, OR.

Batson, C. D., Shaw, L. L., & Oleson, K. C. (1992). Defining affect, mood, and emotion: Toward functionally based conceptual distinctions. In M. S. Clark (Ed.), *Emotion* (pp. 294–326). Newbury Park, CA: Sage.

Biggs, J. R. (1987, May). Defusing hostage situations. *Police Chief,* pp. 33–34.

Bilsky, W., Muller, J., Voss, A., & Von Groote, E. (in press). Affect assessment in crisis negotiation: An exploratory case study using two distinct indicators. *Psychology, Crime, and Law.*

Blake, R. R., & Mouton, J. S. (1964). *The managerial grid.* Houston, TX: Gulf.

Bohl, N. K. (1991). The effectiveness of brief psychological interventions in police officers after critical incidents. In J. T. Reese & M. M. Horn (Eds.), *Critical incidents in policing* (Rev. ed., pp. 31–38). Washington, DC: U.S. Department of Justice, Federal Bureau of Investigation.

Bohl, N. K. (1992). Hostage negotiator stress. *FBI Law Enforcement Bulletin, 61*(8), 23–26.

Bohl, N. K. (1995). Professionally-administered critical incident debriefing for police officers. In M. I. Kurke & E. M. Scrivner (Eds.), *Police psychology into the 21st century* (pp. 149–188). Hillsdale, NJ: Lawrence Erlbaum.

Bohl, N. K. (1997). Postincident crisis counseling for hostage negotiators. In R. G. Rogan, M. R. Hammer, & C. R. Van Zandt (Eds.), *Dynamic processes of crisis negotiation: Theory, research, and practice* (pp. 45–56). Westport, CT: Praeger.

Bolz, F., Dudonis, K. J., & Schulz, D. P. (1990). *The counter-terrorism handbook: Tactics, procedures, and techniques.* New York: Elsevier Science.

Bolz, F., & Hershey, E. (1979). *Hostage cop.* New York: Rawson Wade.

Borum, R., & Strentz, T. (1992). The borderline personality. *FBI Law Enforcement Bulletin, 61*(8), 6–10.

Botting, J. M., Lanceley, F. J., & Noesner, G. W. (1995). The FBI's critical incident negotiation team. *FBI Law Enforcement Bulletin, 61*(4), 12–15.

Bower, D. L., & Pettit, W. G. (2001). The Albuquerque Police Department's crisis intervention team: A report card. *FBI Law Enforcement Bulletin, 70*(2), 1–9.

Butler, W. M. (1991). *Hostage taking and barricade incidents in the United States: A nationwide survey and analysis.* Unpublished doctoral dissertation, University of Vermont, Storrs.

Butler, W. M., Leitenberg, H., & Fuselier, G. D. (1993). The use of mental health professional consultants to police hostage negotiation teams. *Behavioral Sciences and the Law, 11,* 213–221.

Cannon, W. B. (1929). *Bodily changes in pain, hunger, fear and rage.* New York: Appleton-Century.

Carson, S. (1982, October). Post-shooting stress reaction. *Police Chief*, pp. 66–68.

Cissna, K. N. L., & Sieburg, E. (1981). Patterns of interaction confirmation and disconfirmation. In C. Wilder & J. H. Weakland (Eds.), *Rigor and imagination: Essays from the legacy of Gregory Bateson* (pp. 253–282). New York: Praeger.

Cooper, H. H. A. (1981). *The hostage-takers*. Boulder, CO: Paladin Press.

Crisis Negotiation Unit. (2004, January). *HOBAS: Statistical report of incidents*. Quantico, VA: FBI Academy.

Cupach, W. R., & Canary, D. J. (1997). *Competence in interpersonal conflict*. Prospect Heights, IL: Waveland.

Dalfonzo, V. A., & Romano, S. J. (2003). Negotiation position papers: A tool for crisis negotiators. *FBI Law Enforcement Bulletin, 72*(10), 27–31.

Davidson, G. P. (1981). Anxiety and authority: Psychological aspects in hostage negotiation situations. *Journal of Police Science and Administration, 9*(1), 35–38.

Davidson, T. N. (2002). *To preserve life: Hostage-crisis management*. Indianapolis, IN: CIMACOM.

Delprino, R. P., & Bahn, C. (1988). National survey of the extent and nature of psychological services in police departments. *Professional Psychology: Research and Practice, 19,* 421–425.

Deutsch, M. (1973). Conflicts: Productive and destructive. In F. E. Jandt (Ed.), *Conflict resolution through communication*. New York: Harper & Row.

DiVasto, P. (1996, June). Negotiating with foreign language–speaking subjects. *FBI Law Enforcement Bulletin, 65,* 11–15.

DiVasto, P., Lanceley, F. J., & Gruys, A. (1992). Critical issues in suicide intervention. *FBI Law Enforcement Bulletin, 61*(8), 13–26.

Donohue, W. A. (1998). Managing equivocality and relational paradox in the Oslo peace negotiations. *Journal of Language and Social Psychology, 17*(1), 72–96.

Donohue, W. A., Ramesh, C., & Borchgrevink, C. (1991). Crisis bargaining: Tracking relational paradox in hostage negotiation. *International Journal of Conflict Management, 2,* 257–274.

Donohue, W. A., Ramesh, C., Kaufmann, G., & Smith, R. (1991). Crisis bargaining in hostage negotiations. *International Journal of Group Tensions, 21,* 133–154.

Donohue, W. A., & Roberto, A. J. (1993). Relational development in hostage negotiation. *Human Communication Research, 20,* 175–198.

Donohue, W. A., & Roberto, A. J. (1996). An empirical examination of three models of integrative and distributive bargaining. *International Journal of Conflict Management, 7,* 209–229.

Fagan, T. J., & Van Zandt, C. R. (1993). Even in non-negotiable situations, negotiation plays a critical role. *Corrections Today, 55,* 132–141.

Feldman, T. B. (2001). Characteristics of hostage and barricade incidents: Implications for negotiation strategies and training. *Journal of Police Crisis Negotiations, 1*(1), 3–33.

Folger, J. P., Poole, M. S., & Stutman, R. K. (2001). *Working through conflict* (4th ed.). New York: Longman.

Friedland, N. (1986, January). Hostage negotiations: Types, processes, outcomes. *Negotiation Journal,* pp. 57–72.

Fuselier, G. D. (1981a). A practical overview of hostage negotiations (Part I). *FBI Law Enforcement Bulletin, 50*(6), 2–6.

Fuselier, G. D. (1981b). A practical overview of hostage negotiations (Part II). *FBI Law Enforcement Bulletin, 50*(6), 10–15.

Fuselier, G. D. (1986). What every negotiator would like his chief to know. *FBI Law Enforcement Bulletin, 55*(3), 1–4.

Fuselier, G. D. (1988). Hostage negotiation consultant: Emerging role for the clinical psychologist. *Professional Psychology: Research and Practice, 19,* 175–179.

Fuselier, G. D. (1999). Placing the Stockholm syndrome in perspective. *FBI Law Enforcement Bulletin, 68*(7), 22–25.

Fuselier, G. D., & Noesner, G. W. (1990). Confronting the terrorist hostage taker. *FBI Law Enforcement Bulletin, 59*(7), 6–11.

Fuselier, G. D., Van Zandt, C. R., & Lanceley, F. J. (1991). Hostage/barricade incidents: High risk factors and the action criteria. *FBI Law Enforcement Bulletin, 60*(1), 6–12.

Gachnochi, G., & Skurnik, N. (1992). The paradoxical effects of hostage-taking. *International Social Science Journal, 44,* 235–246.

Geiger, S., Holmes, M. E., Goergen, M., & Skomra, W. (1990, November). Hostage negotiation. *Police Chief*, pp. 52–57.

Gettys, V. S. (1983). *National survey-negotiator selection and hostage negotiation activity*. Paper presented at the meeting of the American Psychological Association, Anaheim, CA.

Giebels, E. (1999). A comparison of crisis negotiation across Europe. In O. Adang & E. Giebels (Eds.), *To save lives: Proceedings of the First European Conference on Hostage Negotiations* (pp. 17–27). Amsterdam: Elsevier.

Giebels, E., Noelanders, S., & Vervaeke, G. (in press). The hostage experience: Implications for negotiation strategies. *Clinical Psychology and Psychotherapy.*

Goldaber, I. (1979, June). A typology of hostage-takers. *Police Chief,* pp. 21–23.

Greenstone, J. L. (1995a). Hostage negotiations team training for small police departments. In M. I. Kurke & E. M. Scrivner (Eds.), *Police psychology into the 21st century* (pp. 279–296). Hillsdale, NJ: Lawrence Erlbaum.

Greenstone, J. L. (1995b). Tactics and negotiating techniques (TNT): The way of the past and the way of the future. In M. I. Kurke & E. M. Scrivner (Eds.), *Police psychology into the 21st century* (pp. 357–372). Hillsdale, NJ: Lawrence Erlbaum.

Gulliver, P. H. (1979). *Disputes and negotiations: A cross-cultural perspective.* Orlando, FL: Academic Press.

Hacker, F. (1976). *Crusaders, criminals and crazies.* New York: W. W. Norton.

Hammer, M. R. (1997). Negotiating across the cultural divide: Intercultural dynamics in crisis incidents. In R. G. Rogan, M. R. Hammer, & C. R. Van Zandt (Eds.), *Dynamic processes of crisis negotiations: Theory, research and practice* (pp. 105–114). Westport, CT: Praeger.

Hammer, M. R. (2001). Conflict negotiation under crisis conditions. In W. F. Eadie & P. E. Nelson (Eds.), *The language of conflict resolution* (pp. 57–80). Thousand Oaks, CA: Sage.

Hammer, M. R. (in press). The Intercultural Conflict Style Inventory: A conceptual framework and measure of intercultural conflict resolution practices. *Conflict Resolution Quarterly.*

Hammer, M. R., & Rogan, R. G. (1997). Negotiation models in crisis situations: The value of a communication-based approach. In R. G. Rogan, M. R. Hammer, & C. R. Van Zandt (Eds.), *Dynamic processes of crisis negotiations: Theory, research, and practice* (pp. 9–23). Westport, CT: Praeger.

Hammer, M. R., & Rogan, R. G. (2002). Latino and Indochinese interpretive frames in negotiating conflict with law enforcement: A focus group analysis. *International Journal of Intercultural Relations, 26*(5), 551–576.

Hammer, M. R., Van Zandt, C. R., & Rogan, R. G. (1994). Crisis/hostage negotiation team profile of demographic and functional characteristics. *FBI Law Enforcement Bulletin, 63*(3), 8–11.

Hammer, M. R., & Weaver, G. R. (1994). Cultural considerations in hostage negotiations. In G. R. Weaver (Ed.), *Culture, communication and conflict: Readings in intercultural relations* (pp. 499–510). Needham Heights, MA: Ginn Press.

Head, W. B. (1988). *The hostage response.* Unpublished doctoral dissertation, State University of New York, Albany.

Heymann, P. B. (1993). *Lessons of Waco: Proposed changes in federal law enforcement.* Washington, DC: U.S. Department of Justice.

Holmes, M. E. (1997a). Optimal matching analysis of negotiation phase sequences in simulated and authentic hostage negotiation. *Communication Reports, 10*(1), 1–8.

Holmes, M. E. (1997b). Processes and patterns in hostage negotiations. In R. G. Rogan, M. R. Hammer, & C. R. Van Zandt (Eds.), *Dynamic processes of crisis negotiation: Theory, research, and practice* (pp. 77–94). Westport, CT: Praeger.

Holmes, M. E., & Fletcher-Bergland, T. (1995). Negotiations in crisis. In A. Nicotera (Ed.), *Conflict and organizations: Communicative processes* (pp. 239–256). Albany: State University of New York Press.

Holmes, M. E., & Sykes, R. E. (1993). A test of the fit of Gulliver's phase model to hostage negotiations. *Communication Studies, 44*(1), 38–55.

Horney, K. (1945). *Our inner conflicts.* New York: W. W. Norton.

Hymes, D. (1974). Ways of speaking. In R. Bauman & J. Sherzer (Eds.), *Explorations in ethnography of speaking* (pp. 433–451). London: Cambridge University Press.

Izard, C. E. (1990). Facial expressions and the regulation of emotions. *Journal of Personality and Social Psychology, 58,* 87–98.

Jones, T. S. (2001). Emotional communication in conflict: Essence and impact. In W. Eadie & P. Nelson (Eds.), *The language of conflict resolution* (pp. 81–104). Thousand Oaks, CA: Sage.

Kobetz, R. W., & Cooper, H. H. A. (1979, June). Hostage rescue operations: Teaching the unteachable. *Police Chief,* pp. 24–27.

Lanceley, F. J. (1981). The antisocial personality as hostage-taker. *Journal of Police Science and Administration, 9*(1), 28–34.

Lanceley, F. J. (2003). *On-scene guide for crisis negotiations* (2nd ed.). Boca Raton, FL: CRC Press.

Lanceley, F. J., Ruple, S. W., & Moss, C. G. (1985). *Crisis and suicide intervention* (Unpublished report, Operations and Research Unit). FBI Academy, Quantico, VA.

Lazarus, R. S. (1984). Thoughts on the relationship between emotion and cognition. In K. R. Scherer & P. Ekman (Eds.), *Approaches to emotion* (pp. 247–258). Hillsdale, NJ: Lawrence Erlbaum.

Louden, R. (1998). The development of hostage negotiation by the NYPD. In A. Karmen (Ed.), *Crime and justice in New York City* (pp. 148–157). New York: McGraw-Hill.

MacWillson, A. C. (1992). *Hostage-taking terrorism: Incident-response strategy.* New York: St. Martin's.

Maher, G. F. (1977). *Hostage: A police approach to a contemporary crisis.* Springfield, IL: Charles C Thomas.

McMains, M. J., & Mullins, W. C. (1996). *Crisis negotiations: Managing critical incidents and hostage situations in law enforcement and corrections.* Cincinnati, OH: Anderson.

McMains, M. J., & Mullins, W. C. (2001). *Crisis negotiations: Managing critical incidents and hostage situations in law enforcement and corrections* (2nd ed.). Cincinnati, OH: Anderson.

Metts, S., & Bowers, J. W. (1994). Emotion in interpersonal communication. In M. L. Knapp & G. R. Miller (Eds.), *Handbook of interpersonal communication* (pp. 87–103). Thousand Oaks, CA: Sage.

Middendorf, W. (1975). *New developments in the taking of hostages and kidnapping: A summary* (National Criminal Justice Reference Service). Washington, DC: Government Printing Office.

Miller, A. H. (1980). *Terrorism and hostage negotiations.* Boulder, CO: Westview.

Miron, M. S., & Goldstein, A. P. (1979). *Hostage.* Elmsford, NY: Pergamon.

Mohandie, K., & Duffy, J. E. (1999). Understanding subjects with paranoid schizophrenia. *FBI Law Enforcement Bulletin, 68*(12), 8–17.

Moran, R. T., & Stripp, W. G. (1991). *Dynamics of successful international business negotiations.* Houston, TX: Gulf.

Noesner, G. W. (1999). Negotiation concepts for commanders. *FBI Law Enforcement Bulletin, 68*(1), 6–18.

Noesner, G. W., & Dolan, J. T. (1992). First responder negotiation training. *FBI Law Enforcement Bulletin, 61*(8), 1–4.

Noesner, G. W., & Webster, M. (1997). Crisis intervention: Using active listening skills in negotiations. *FBI Law Enforcement Bulletin, 66*(8), 13–19.

Northrup, T. A. (1989). The dynamic of identity in personal and social conflict. In L. Kriesberg, T. Northrup, & S. J. Thorson (Eds.), *Intractable conflicts and their transformation* (pp. 55–82). Syracuse, NY: Syracuse University Press.

Norton, B. (1983). *Communicator style.* Beverly Hills, CA: Sage.

Ochberg, F. M., & Soskis, D. A. (Eds.). (1982). *Victims of terrorism.* Boulder, CO: Westview.

Pearson, V. M. S., & Stratton, J. G. (1998). Preferences for styles of negotiation: A comparison of Brazil and the U.S. *International Journal of Intercultural Relations, 22,* 67–83.

Poland, J. M., & McCrystle, M. J. (1999). *Practical, tactical, and legal perspectives of terrorism and hostage-taking.* New York: Edwin Mellen.

Putnam, L. L., & Holmer, M. (1992). Framing, reframing, and issue development. In L. L. Putnam & M. E. Roloff (Eds.), *Communication and negotiation* (pp. 128–155). Newbury Park, CA: Sage.

Rahim, M. A. (1983). A measure of styles of handling interpersonal conflict. *Academy of Management Journal, 26,* 368–376.

Regini, C. (2002). Crisis negotiation teams: Selection and training. *FBI Law Enforcement Bulletin, 71*(11), 1–5.

Rogan, R. G. (1997). Emotion and emotional expression in crisis negotiation. In R. G. Rogan, M. R. Hammer, & C.R. Van Zandt (Eds.), *Dynamic processes of crisis negotiation: Theory, research, and practice* (pp. 25–44). Westport, CT: Praeger.

Rogan, R. G. (1999). F.I.R.E.: A communication-based approach for understanding crisis negotiation. In O. Adang & E. Giebels (Eds.), *To save lives* (pp. 29–45). Amsterdam: Elsevier.

Rogan, R. G., & Hammer, M. R. (1994). Crisis negotiations: A preliminary investigation of facework in naturalistic conflict. *Journal of Applied Communication Research, 22,* 216–231.

Rogan, R. G., & Hammer, M. R. (1995). Assessing message affect in crisis negotiations: An exploratory study. *Human Communication Research, 21,* 553–574.

Rogan, R. G., & Hammer, M. R. (2002). Crisis/hostage negotiations: Conceptualization of a communication-based approach. In H. Giles (Ed.), *Law enforcement, communication, and community* (pp. 229–254). Amsterdam: John Benjamins.

Rogan, R. G., Hammer, M. R., & Van Zandt, C. R. (1994, November). Profiling crisis negotiation teams. *Police Chief, 61,* 14–18.

Rogan, R. G., & Hammer, M. R., & Van Zandt, C. R. (Eds.). (1997a). *Dynamic processes of crisis negotiation: Theory, research and practice.* Westport, CT: Praeger.

Rogan, R. G., Hammer, M. R., & Van Zandt, C. R. (1997b). Dynamic processes of crisis negotiations: An overview. In R. G. Rogan, M. R. Hammer, & C. R. Van Zandt (Eds.), *Dynamic processes of crisis negotiation: Theory, research and practice* (pp. 1–8). Westport, CT: Praeger.

Roloff, M. E., & Jordan, J. M. (1992). Achieving negotiation goals: The "fruits and foibles" of planning ahead. In L. L. Putnam & M. E. Roloff (Eds.), *Communication and negotiation* (pp. 21–45). Newbury Park, CA: Sage.

Romano, A. T. (1990). *Taking charge: Crisis intervention in criminal justice.* New York: Greenwood.

Romano, S. J. (1998). Third-party intermediaries and crisis negotiations. *FBI Law Enforcement Bulletin, 67*(10), 20–24.

Rubin, J. Z., Pruitt, D. G., & Kim, S. H. (1994). *Social conflict.* New York: McGraw-Hill.

Schlossberg, H. (1979). Police response to hostage situations. In J. T. O'Brien & M. Marcus (Eds.), *Crime and justice in America* (pp. 209–220). Elmsford, NY: Pergamon.

Slatkin, A. (1996). Enhancing negotiator training: Therapeutic communication. *FBI Law Enforcement Bulletin, 65*(5), 1–11.

Slatkin, A. (2003). Suicide risk and hostage/barricade situations involving older persons. *FBI Law Enforcement Bulletin, 72*(4), 26–32.

Smith, R. G., & Kaufmann, G. M. (1988). *Stages in hostage/barricaded gunman negotiations* (Unpublished manuscript). Lansing: Michigan State Police.

Snyder, G. H., & Diesing, P. (1977). *Conflict among nations.* Princeton, NJ: Princeton University Press.

Soskis, D. A., & Van Zandt, C. R. (1986). Hostage negotiation: Law enforcement's most effective nonlethal weapon. *Behavioral Sciences & the Law, 4,* 423–435.

Strentz, T. (1982). The Stockholm syndrome: Law enforcement policy and hostage behavior. In F. M. Ochberg & D. A. Soskis (Eds.), *Victims of terrorism* (pp. 149–164). Boulder, CO: Westview.

Strentz, T. (1983). The inadequate personality as hostage taker. *Journal of Police Science and Administration, 11,* 363–368.

Strentz, T. (1985). *A statistical analysis of American hostage situations.* Quantico, VA: FBI Academy, Special Operations and Research Unit.

Strentz, T. (1986). Negotiating with the hostage taker exhibiting paranoid schizophrenic symptoms. *Journal of Police Science and Administration, 14*(1), 12–16.

Strentz, T. (1991, September). Indicators of volatile negotiations. *Law and Order,* pp. 135–139.

Szubin, A., Jensen, C. J., & Gregg, R. (2000). Interacting with cults: A policing model. *FBI Law Enforcement Bulletin, 69*(9), 16–25.

Taylor, L. B. (1989). *Hostage! Kidnapping and terrorism in our time.* New York: Franklin Watts.

Taylor, P. J. (2002a). A cylindrical model of communication behavior in crisis negotiations. *Human Communication Research, 28*(1), 7–48.

Taylor, P. J. (2002b). A partial order scalogram analysis of communication behavior in crisis negotiation with the prediction of outcome. *International Journal of Conflict Management, 13*(1), 4–37.

Taylor, P. J. (2003). Foundations and evidence for an interaction-based approach to conflict. *International Journal of Conflict Management, 14,* 213, 232.

Taylor, P. J. (2004). The structure of communication behavior in simulated and actual crisis negotiations. *Human Communication Research, 30,* 443–478.

Taylor, R. W. (1983, March). Hostage and crisis negotiation procedures: Assessing police liability. *Trial, 19,* 64–69, 100.

Ting-Toomey, S. (1985). Toward a theory of conflict and culture. In W. Gudykunst, L. Stewart, & S. Ting-Toomey (Eds.), *Communication, culture, and organizational processes* (pp. 71–86). Beverly Hills, CA: Sage.

Ting-Toomey, S. (1988). Intercultural conflict styles: A face-negotiation theory. In Y. Y. Kim &

W. B. Gudykunst (Eds.), *Theories in intercultural communication* (pp. 213–235). Newbury Park, CA: Sage.

Ting-Toomey, S. (1994). Managing intercultural conflicts effectively. In L. Samovar & R. Porter (Eds.), *Intercultural communication: A reader* (pp. 360–372). Belmont, CA: Wadsworth.

Ting-Toomey, S. (1999). *Communicating across cultures*. New York: Guilford.

Ting-Toomey, S., & Kurogi, A. (1998). Facework competence in intercultural conflict: An updated face-negotiation theory. *International Journal of Intercultural Relations, 22,* 187–225.

Ting-Toomey, S., Yee-Jung, K. K., Shapiro, R. B., Garcia, W., Wright, R. J., & Oetzel, J. G. (2000). Ethnic/cultural identity salience and conflict styles in four US ethnic groups. *International Journal of Intercultural Relations, 24,* 47–82.

Trompenaars, F., & Hampden-Turner, C. (1998). *Riding the waves of culture*. New York: McGraw-Hill.

Trubisky, P., Ting-Toomey, S., & Lin, S. L. (1991). The influence of individualism-collectivism and self-monitoring on conflict styles. *International Journal of Intercultural Relations, 15,* 65–84.

Useem, B., Camp, C. G., & Camp, G. M. (1996). *Resolution of prison riots: Strategies and polices*. New York: Oxford University Press.

van de Vliert, E. (1997). *Complex interpersonal conflict behavior: Theoretical frontiers*. East Sussex, UK: Psychology Press.

Van Zandt, C. R. (1993, July). Suicide by cop. *Police Chief, 60,* 24–30.

Van Zandt, C. R. (1997). Negotiating with cults. In R. G. Rogan, M. R. Hammer, & C. R. Van Zandt (Eds.), *Dynamic processes of crisis negotiation: Theory, research, and practice* (pp. 143–150). Westport, CT: Praeger.

Van Zandt, C. R., & Fuselier, G. D. (1989, July). Nine days of crisis negotiations: The Oakdale siege. *Corrections Today,* pp. 16–24.

Vecchi, G. M. (2002). Hostage/barricade management: A hidden conflict within law enforcement. *FBI Law Enforcement Bulletin, 71*(5), 1–13.

Watzlawick, P., Bavelas, J. B., & Jackson, D. D. (1967). *Pragmatics of human communication: A study of interactional patterns, pathologies, and paradoxes*. New York: W. W. Norton.

Wilmot, W. W., & Hocker, J. E. (2001). *Interpersonal conflict* (6th ed.). New York: McGraw-Hill.

Wilson, S., & Putnam, L. L. (1990). Interaction goals in negotiation. In J. Anderson (Ed.), *Communication yearbook 13* (pp. 374–406). Newbury Park, CA: Sage.

Wind, B. (1995). A guide to crisis negotiations. *FBI Law Enforcement Bulletin, 64*(10), 8–11.

Womack, D. F., & Walsh, K. (1997). A three-dimensional model of relationship development in hostage negotiations. In R. G. Rogan, M. R. Hammer, & C. R. Van Zandt (Eds.), *Dynamic processes of crisis negotiation: Theory, research, and practice* (pp. 57–76). Westport, CT: Praeger.

17

MANAGING RACIAL/ETHNIC CONFLICT FOR COMMUNITY BUILDING

WALLACE WARFIELD

George Mason University

Any discussion of community conflict and its management begins with a number of recognitions. First, as Coleman (1957) noted, "Controversies within communities are as old as civilization itself" (p. 2). Interestingly, the early literature on the subject (see Coleman, 1957; Laue & Cormick, 1978; Whyte, 1943) had a distinctly American flavor. Now however, modernization (Appadurai, 1996; C. E. Black, 1966) brings with it heightened patterns of social stratification and a post–Cold War rise in ethnic identity, and thus has placed community conflict on a worldwide landscape.

A second consideration is the kind of community the conflict takes place in. G. Black (1974) argued there was an over-concentration of study and emphasis on large urban areas experiencing violent conflict, "ignoring important contributions that smaller communities can make to the understanding of community conflict" (p. 1245). This can be partially attributed to the proliferation of U.S. urban riots from the late 1960s through early 1980s and the 1968 study conducted by the National Advisory Commission on Civil Disorders (often referred to as the Kerner Commission), which tended to focus on large urban areas.

A third consideration is that with the advent of the environmental movement, a certain amount of community conflict has lost its class flavor. The implications of this can be seen in two dimensions. First, while many environmental conflicts taking place around the world continue to pit a disenfranchised peasantry or indigenous group against a landed and wealth-holding "upper class" (in Latin America, for example), or people-of-color minorities versus industrialists and majority policy interests in the United States (raising the cry of environmental justice), a number of these conflicts see middle-class community groups confronting local policy regimes around some issue of public policy (Berry, Portney, & Thompson, 1993). In fact, most public conflicts (at least in the U.S.) are community conflicts in one form or another. Also, on the international level, but in the United States as well, many community conflicts seem to place less of an emphasis on class cleavages, and more on *intra* class power struggles between identity groups (Thom, 2002).

The ambiguity is further compounded when we see that a shift to a more international understanding of community conflict brings a recognition that the nature of statism and political culture in many countries outside the United States results in a blurring of the definitional boundaries between community and national conflicts. I will expand on this shortly. On the opposite end, there is the classic "barking dog" conflict; while admittedly salient for neighbor-to-neighbor peace, is a bit too *diminimis* for this study.

Having taken some pains to probe standard assumptions about community conflict, we could try on Coser's (1956) definition to see if it retains a good fit. Coser described community conflict as

> a struggle over values and claims to scarce status, power, and resources in which the aims of the opponents are to neutralize, injure or eliminate their rivals. Such conflict may take place between individuals, between collectivities or between individuals and collectivities. (p. 232)

Coser's definition continues to be relevant for many contemporary conflicts that involve competing community groups, but gives the impression that the conflict takes place between groups with rough symmetries of power. It tends to underexplain conflicts that involve entities of unequal strength, particularly where one of the parties is a low power community group opposed by a more powerful local government. I want to examine a range of community conflicts to see how this may inform a more embracing definition.

The purpose of this chapter is to throw light on the status of theory, practice, and research in community conflict. I attempt to determine the various ways that community conflict is managed (some might prefer *mitigated*[1]) and how this management lends itself to actual or potential community capacity building. This chapter will take a closer look at where these conflicts are occurring and develop an informal typology. A description of these conflicts will address conflict roles and provide a descriptive overview of intervention practice such as conciliation, mediation, community dialogues, and problem-solving workshops. I examine the role of diversity in community building and explore processes that can manage diversity as a positive resource in a community. I conclude by examining and commenting on the status of theory and research in community conflicts and what gaps need to be filled.

DESCRIPTIONS OF COMMUNITY CONFLICT

Because the range of community conflicts is so broad, it would be impossible to do justice descriptively and analytically to a full complement within the constraints of this chapter. Rather, the focus is on conflicts generated by racial/ethnic hatred, friction between local law enforcement and minority groups, and ethnic identity. These conflicts tend to be marked by high levels of violence, reflect the dynamic changes taking place within societies, are potentially rich in theory application, and pose the greatest challenges for intervention practice and community capacity building. Despite earnest attempts to minimize ambiguity, there is not always a bright line between these conflicts. Some community conflicts may reflect elements of two or more of these characteristics.

Further, it was decided not to include conflicts where the political boundaries between local and State overlapped, particularly where the State regime was an active participant. For example, Brazilian rain forest conflicts involve indigenous Indian communities and oligarchic land owners, where the State frequently intervenes in the form of legislative, policy, and physical force in support of landowners in what is perceived to be the national interest (Balduino, 2001). Or in Bolivia and other parts of Latin America, indigenous Indian communities have staged protests in reaction to various governments' intent to allow globalized industrial forces to exploit natural resources (Slack, 2003).

These conflicts and others like them could fit within Coser's definition. Coleman (1957), however, offered three criteria for conflict to emerge in communities: (a) the issue must relate to important facets of community members' lives, (b) the issue must have a differential impact on different members of the community, and (c) community members must feel they have sufficient agency to change a condition caused by the issue. Certainly, the first and the third could apply to a wide range of multiparty conflicts including the two just mentioned. The third condition in particular reflects a middle-class ideology that privileged a narrow stratum of civil society that was in existence at the time of Coleman's writing. In fact, much of the civil unrest that produces violent community conflict is directly attributable to a segment of society that feels it does *not* have the agency to bring about demanded changes. It is the second condition—*the issue must have a differential impact on different members of the community*—that supplies a critical distinction between amorphously bounded conflicts that affect a particular demography but whose outcome is controlled by a national agenda, and those that tear at the fabric of community harmony. This explication suggests a fourth criterion: that while deep-rooted causal factors may lie outside the domain of the local community, the conflict responses and outcomes (where they are known) must reflect a dynamic that takes place within the community.

Here, Lederach's (1997) levels of leadership model is helpful in disentangling the aspects of a conflict that can be said to be "community" from those that are controlled (or significantly influenced) by external actors. Lederach's model is derived from his extensive work as a scholar-practitioner at the international level and depicts leadership arrangements in severe intra-state conflict. Still, it lends analytical clarity to community conflicts that take place outside the United States. Lederach envisions three levels of leadership. At Level One we find the top leadership in a conflict setting. It would comprise the highest level of political, military, and religious leaders whose high level negotiations take place under the bright lights of public scrutiny. Often the agreements reached (outcomes) are short-term and symbolic. Level Two is occupied by mid-range leadership that tends to be highly respected members of civil society such as academics, NGO leaders, and religious leaders as well. These individuals have access to and often play key broker roles between the top-level leaders and the grass roots. Finally, at Level Three is where the grassroots leadership is located. Here we may find indigenous NGO leaders, political leaders who represent constituencies at the district level, religious figures, and even gang leaders may figure prominently at this level.

In community conflicts that take place outside the United States, thin levels of constitutional arrangements will produce, at certain points, an intermingling of all three levels of leadership. Given this interdependency, it is still possible to discern conflict management dynamics occurring at Levels Two and Three that function independently of Level One and whose are outcomes are community based.

ORGANIZING MODEL FOR COMMUNITY CONFLICT

Gwartney-Gibbs and Lach's (1991) model provides an organizational framework for this chapter. They organize conflicts around three generic attributes: *origins* (alternatively described as sources), *processes* (which can be thought of as responses by affected parties singularly or in combination with intervention involving third parties), and *outcomes*. Origins are not the incidents that draw conflicting parties together in their confrontational stance and usually headlined in news stories. Rather, conflict origins are the deep-rooted causal factors, usually needs-driven, that stimulate responses in the form of confrontational actions undertaken by stakeholder parties who want to produce a certain outcome. Processes are a combination of unassisted forms of negotiations engaged by parties and, when the opportunity presents itself, so-called third parties who are intervening between conflicting stakeholders to manage, mitigate, or help resolve the conflict. A confluence of processes, in turn, produces outcomes.

Outcomes themselves can take many forms. For example, CDR Associates (2004) identified three aspects to the satisfactory resolution of a conflict. The resolution must provide parties with a measure of *relational* satisfaction. This would be an important factor in community conflict where there are ongoing relationships and where the potential for conflict renewal is always present. The agreement must reflect *procedural* satisfaction (sometimes thought of as procedural justice). This deals with how the agreement will be implemented and, where local policy is involved, can get quite complicated, particularly when the accustomed way of doing things has to be altered. There must be some form of *substantive* satisfaction in that the tangible or structural issues in the conflict have to reflect the needs of the conflicting parties.

The outcomes of community conflict will rarely, if ever, reflect a balance between the three aspects of satisfactory resolution. In fact, there is much masking going on in the discourse of community conflict where the protesting party will initially articulate the issue in one form, for example, a change in procedure (because this is what is thought will gain the attention of the more powerful opposing party), but what is really wanted is a change in relationships. It is the task of the third-party intervener to be able to ferret out these distinctions. The framework assumes that most community conflicts are identity based and that these identities are based on race, ethnicity, gender, or other social constructions. Using this model, I review literature about three types of community conflicts: (a) local law enforcement and minorities, (b) racial/ethnic hatred conflicts, and (c) ethnic identity conflicts.

LOCAL LAW ENFORCEMENT AND MINORITIES

Origins

This form of community conflict involves a pattern of hostile interactions between racial and/or ethnic minorities and law enforcement officers in a particular locale. These interactions have often produced a triggering incident involving an act of alleged police use of excessive force, resulting in injury and death to a minority member, that led to violent reactions (riots or severe public disorder) by a significant mass of the affected minority community. While the triggering incident ignites the violent response in a segment of the minority community, the origins of the conflict lie in a condition of needs deprivation, producing feelings of insecurity, lack of recognition, and political disenfranchisement. These factors were present in the racial disturbances in Miami, Dade County, Florida, in the early 1980s;[2] the Los Angeles, California, riot of 1992 as a reaction to the beating of Rodney King and subsequent dismissal of charges against defendant police officers; and the more recent rioting in Cincinnati, Ohio, in the 2000s.

Conflict Processes

Racial conflict initiated by acts of police use of excessive force has produced responses ranging from agitated protest to physical violence including rioting. In these circumstances, conflict management or mitigation by third parties has varied. One exemplar of intervention in these kinds of conflicts has been the activity carried out by the U.S. Justice Department's Community Relations Service (CRS), an organization that was created out of Title X of the 1964 Civil Rights Act.[3] The basic conflict management approach undertaken by CRS field staff responding to these conflicts is conciliation. The intervener goes into the affected community either by invitation or own volition and identifies relevant stakeholders who could be part of a process to reach an agreement to end violent confrontations.

For example, in the mid-1970s, the author was a member of a CRS team that intervened in a conflict involving several days of racial disturbances in Jamaica, New York. The conflict was initiated over allegations that White police officers used excessive force in the shooting death of an African American youth allegedly fleeing the scene of a crime. There was no "invitation" extended to CRS from either local officials or protest leadership. Rather, CRS staff made extensive contacts with relevant parties prior to entry and while on the ground that established the basis for the conciliation work that was conducted.

At this point, the epistemology of praxis for CRS interveners has been historically framed by a rather colloquial theorem called "Two Tap Roots and a Triggering Incident."[4] At its most foundational level, Tap Root (TR) One is a general perception by low-power members of society that the system, as shaped by more powerful and dominant members, is inherently oppressive and discriminatory. TR One, then, has seeds lodged firmly in Galtung's (1969) notion of structural violence. Resting on this foundation is TR Two, a lack of confidence by low-power groups in the interests and capabilities of public and private institutions to provide adequate redress for their grievances. Finally, at the uppermost level, there is invariably a triggering incident involving an act of alleged police abuse.

Partly because of limited resources and partly due to ideology, CRS intervention in this form of community conflict is, more often than not, reactive rather than preventive. Further, when a CRS intervener comes into a community on an own-volition basis, prudence dictates that the first people to be contacted are law enforcement and other high-ranking public officials: individuals who are primarily interested in quelling violence. This means that whatever recognition the CRS intervener may have of causal factors embedded in TR foundations such as structural violence or the unequal distribution of scarce public resources, choice strategies are constrained by the above factors. Intervention, therefore, is contingent, aimed at the triggering incident, which is usually symptomatic of deep-rooted causal factors.

CRS is not sui generis in the likelihood that intervention will encounter factors that constrain the management of racial conflict to issues surrounding the triggering incident. Most conflict resolvers, poised to intervene, would be faced with the same situation. Given the organization and leadership culture of many locales, the attributions are not mysterious. While the conflict is in a stage of escalation, manifestations of tension are often ascribed to other factors, denied, or simply do not fit the cognitive schema of responsible public officials (Nagel, 1990). Under these circumstances, it is difficult to bring all the necessary parties "to the table" to begin an intervention process. The incident that triggers the civil disturbance acts as a wake-up call, and it is at this point that public and private sector leaders are most amenable to an external third-party role.

The challenge for the intervener acting from a TR perspective is to avoid being seduced into a conciliation mode that circumscribes the practice to the treatment of symptomatic issues. How can the intervention process be used to probe underlying causal factors that, if addressed in the appropriate forum, could lead to a more sustained resolution? Evidence of this can be seen in data reviewed for this chapter and in the author's experience.

In some interventions, experienced CRS field workers in meetings with local law enforcement have been able to use these occasions to convey that leadership in the minority community has an agenda pertaining to police-community relations of which police use of excessive force is only one of many interrelated issues (M. Walsh, 2002). In Cincinnati, Ohio, a series of excessive force incidents taking place in the same minority community and stretching back over a period of 5 years, culminated in a shooting death of an African American male in 2000. The court-ordered intervention involved the ARIA Group, Inc., a conflict resolution organization, as Special Master, facilitating a collaborative process involving a broad section of public and private leadership in a six-stage process over approximately a year (Rothman, 2003). The workshops allowed participants to identify a number of issues pertaining to police-community friction that were relational, substantive, and procedural in nature. In Roanoke, Virginia, several years ago, a local chapter of the NAACP and other minority leaders protested an alleged incident of police use of excessive force involving a popular African American high school coach. The coach had sought to intervene in a fracas involving several African American youth outside of a convenience store. The alarmed store owner, meanwhile, called the police, who when arriving on the scene, did not discern the role the coach was attempting to play and in the process of arresting him, were accused by witnesses of using excessive force. While the incident was the precipitating event, the facilitated problem-solving workshops revealed that the minority-led community coalition was really concerned about inclusion in a range of public policy decision making (Warfield, 1996).

In summary, these interventions suggest at least two conflict management approaches designed to move the process beyond symptomatic issues. One is to devise the conflict management forums so that traditionally demotic voices can be heard with the same agency as those emanating from the more dominant community, essentially democratizing the discourse. Another, as in the case of the CRS and Cincinnati interventions, is to use the power of the intervener's platform to affect a more activist (and less iconoclastically neutral) role.

Outcomes and Community Capacity Building

I spoke earlier in this chapter of outcomes as a reflection of parties' substantive, relational, and procedural needs and interests and noted that they are not necessarily balanced. For example, one or more parties may consider the nature of ongoing relationships more important than the substance of an agreement. Complicating satisfaction preferences is the realization that interests articulated as non-negotiable positions, often disguise underlying needs. In the case of Roanoke, Virginia, the positional demand was the firing of the police chief and more representation of minority police officers. These issues could be characterized as relational interests. The facilitated workshops revealed, however, that what the minority community *really* wanted was greater participation in policy decision making in many areas that had little to do with police-community relations (Warfield, 1996). This spoke to underlying needs of development and participation, which share an association with all three outcome categories. Responding to underlying needs or sources of a conflict does not mean that the issues precipitating the conflict are ignored or unimportant. The argument is that it is the responsiveness to TR needs that lends itself to community capacity building and the emergence of a vibrant civil society. In Roanoke, 7 years after the initial problem-solving workshops were conducted, the author learned the leadership group was continuing to meet and consult with the mayor, city manager, and other local officials across a range of issues.

What is possible to draw from these interventions is the importance of a critical mass of community leadership that has the capacity to go beyond protest to carry out proposed implementation resulting from an agreement; more than the critical mass in and of itself is the diversity of this body. While, undoubtedly, public policy is at the seat of changes that need to be undertaken to mitigate a repetition of excessive force incidents, in many communities the private sector (which tends to reflect a greater proportion of the majority White community) has points of intersection with the policy regime that are critical to implementation capacity.

The key to implementation capacity is governmental responsiveness. Governmental responsiveness (or policy responsiveness) is twofold: First, the item of concern (police abuse) has to get on the policy agenda. The protest activity initiated by the affected minority community will frequently assure this will happen, but emergence on the policy agenda is no guarantee the regime will respond in accordance with the community's interests or needs (Berry et al., 1993). If the issue is not deemed important to the interests and needs of the majority-dominated private sector, it will simply die on the vine, hardening the frustration-aggression of the minority community and setting the stage for more incidents and violent responses. In Gurr's (1970) seminal work, the principal thesis is that for many groups in society, there is a gap between that group's value expectations and value capabilities. If this is not relieved, it can lead to frustration, which can result in aggression—often in the form of violence. This may well have been the case with the succession of riots in the Miami-Dade area of Florida in the early 1980s.

The second component of government responsiveness is that agenda setting (and from it, implementation) is biased in favor of those who have the most resources (Berry et al., 1993). While it is true that local governments have legislative and budgetary authority, it is the private sector that has access to responding public officials. In all but the largest urban communities, private sector individuals, government leaders, and legislators often live in the same neighborhoods and interact in the same social circles. In fact, in many small to medium-sized communities that have part-time legislators and business leaders, they are one and the same. Therefore, the more broadly inclusive the community coalition, the more likely the issues of concern will get on the agenda and will be implemented. In looking at these kinds of conflicts, what we see is a variety of intervention techniques designed to increase community capacity building (for the most part). "Successful" outcomes are linked to the ability of cross-sectional leadership to go beyond protest and, where possible, expand implementation resulting from an agreement.

RACIAL/ETHNIC HATRED CONFLICTS

Racial/ethnic hatred conflicts[5] in the United States have a long history of antagonistic attitudes of Whites toward African Americans, with antecedents dating back to the era of Jim Crow. With increased immigration from Latin America and Southeast Asia from the mid-1970s to the present time, hate incidents have become no stranger to Hispanic and Asian identity groups as well. Nonetheless, community conflicts driven by race or ethnic hatred, arguably up to the late 1980s, were associated strongly with the United States. However, we now know this once uniquely American experience can be found throughout Eastern Europe, particularly in states that house a significant Roma population (e.g., the Czech Republic, Slovakia, Hungary, and Romania). Great Britain and other Western European countries like France and Germany, having experienced their own waves of immigration from the Caribbean, South Asia, and North Africa, have seen significant increases in these kinds of conflicts.

In several instances, racial/ethnic hate acts never reach beyond the level of incidents to become community conflicts. They are often isolated attacks, like a graveyard desecration or a graffiti-scarred church associated with a particular racial or ethnic group. Here, the anonymity of the attacker, coupled with a vocal disassociation of the majority community from the incident, is sufficient to dampen mobilization of the victim's identity group. Such incidents are not addressed in this study. I focus on this form of conflict where there is an appearance of majority community support (if not active engagement) for the hate behavior and where the minority community has gained a degree of political agency that allows it to mobilize and generate a response from within its own ranks conducive to an intercessional response by a third party. I elaborate with the aid of a few examples from the United States, Great Britain, and Eastern Europe. Each example includes origins and processes, and then outcomes are collectively discussed in a separate segment.

The United States

Origins. Racial/ethnic hate activity that has stimulated community conflict has taken varied forms in recent years and has manifested regional patterns. In the Northwest, community unrest has been generated by White hate groups such as the Aryan Nation and affiliated organizations in the form of cross-burning and sundry harassments directed at racial and ethnic minorities. In the late 1970s and early 1980s, in the aftermath of the Vietnam War, several thousand Southeast Asians settled along the Texas Gulf Coast and took up shrimp fishing. Their entry into the market (which they eventually dominated) was resented by local, mostly White fishing people and their cause was articulated by the local KKK (Ku Klux Klan). In the Southeastern region of the United States, a spate of Black church burnings in the early to mid-1990s drew a vociferous response from local civil rights organizations. In Midwestern cities like Chicago and in Northeastern metropolitan areas like New York and Boston, hate incidents that matriculated into community conflicts have typically been triggered by minorities who have "trespassed" boundaries of traditional White ethnic neighborhoods either accidentally or as the result of public policies like school desegregation. More recently, attention has been given to hate incidents post the September 11, 2001, attacks on the World Trade Center and the Pentagon ("9/11"), which has drawn responses from human rights and ethnic advocacy organizations representing Arab immigrant groups.

Conflict response processes. Once again, the CRS role in responding to these kinds of conflicts is instructive. In a number of instances, the CRS conciliator, recognizing the limitations even a non-investigatory federal representative could play, acted as a catalyst for community mobilization, and devolved the conciliation role to a local coalition. For example, in the Northwest, the CRS conciliator was instrumental in convening a fledging response group in Coeur d'Alene, Idaho, composed of law enforcement chiefs, church leadership, a member of the bar association, and the state human rights commission. The group began to track hate group activity more formally and formed a Human Rights Observance Day to coincide with the hate groups' annual get-togethers (Hughs, 2002).

Responding to Texas Gulf Coast conflict, a CRS conciliator played a catalytic role by consulting in the formation of anti-Klan protest group rallies, encouraging the use of self-marshalling techniques to reduce the potential for violence. There was a stratagem to his intervention as well, in that he sought to expand the anti-Klan "voice" in communities that were vulnerable to Klan agitation and propagandistic organizing (Martinez, 2002).

In Chicago in 1997 an African American youth riding a bicycle on the perimeter of the Bridgeport neighborhood, a White ethnic stronghold, was beaten into a coma by four White youth. The resultant local and national media attention mobilized the African American community, stripped the White community of its tacit support for racial hate activity, and shook the complacency of local officials (E. Walsh, 1997). Perhaps because Chicago retains remnants of its political machine culture, the conflict management response was internally driven by the mayor, who played a "mediator-with-clout" role (Moore, 1996). The mayor created a strategic alliance with a major African American civil rights leader from that city (but who enjoys a national reputation) and together they forged a biracial coalition of interracial and interfaith religious leaders. This group then led a series of dialogues involving representation from both communities in an attempt to bridge differences.

The post 9/11 hate incidents directed at Arab minorities required a period of self-reflection and adjustment for CRS staff. Outside of ethnic tensions that have existed between Arab Americans, Arab immigrants, and other racial and ethnic groups in the Dearborn, Michigan, area, there was not much experience working with what was for many conciliators an unfamiliar ethnic group. Staff underwent cultural awareness training before providing intervention service to these communities. Even so, conflict management appears to have been limited to arranging meetings between these groups and the U.S. Attorney General's office, creating conflict assessment instruments for local police chiefs and school superintendents to enhance conflict response, and providing on-site assessments and other forms of conciliation to hate crime incidents involving attacks on mosques and neighborhood stores owned by Arabs.

The spate of church burnings received a fair amount of media attention, enough to cause CRS to organize a task force out of its headquarters in Washington, D.C. The agency even hired temporary conciliators to augment the overstretched regional staff. Again, the role was largely catalytic—attempting to build coalitions of coherent voices that could demonstrate that affected communities would not accept these incidents passively.

Interestingly, CRS conciliators often find themselves in paradoxical situations where they feel compelled to balance social justice inclinations with intervention pragmatism. Many agency field staff come from a civil rights background. It is that background, honed by TR theory, that operationalizes the paradigm of righting unjust circumstances for traditionally disempowered groups. At the same time, the conciliator recognizes that community conflicts are complex and ambiguous, that disempowerment is subjectively perceived across a spectrum of alienated groups. Regardless of the vantage point held by conciliators, they recognize that if the conflict is to be mitigated, they will have to understand how the other side sees the issue. For example, one conciliator arranged and facilitated a meeting between the Klan Grand Dragon and the head of a Vietnamese fishing group so they could air mutual grievances and, it was hoped, collaborate in contingency planning and implementation.

Great Britain

Origins. In Great Britain, racial and ethnic riots that took place in the Brixton section of London in 1980 and 1981 and the Tottenham section of London in 1983[6] seem to have sprung from a mixture of excessive force police practices and hate group activity in the form of attacks by White skinhead groups against Asian and African immigrants. The combination of precipitating factors demonstrates the elusiveness of developing neat typologies for community conflicts. The stimuli for many forms of conflict flow turbulently through a community like logs in a swiftly moving current. They can entwine and become the catalyst for an explosion. However, it appears that while the police abuse was a constant irritant, it was the skinhead attacks that became the triggering incident.

The origins or sources of the conflict were not vastly dissimilar from those that existed for minorities in the U.S. communities where high rates of unemployment, substandard housing, and other poverty factors (Marshall, 1992) created a needs-driven relative deprivation. Further, these factors were aggravated by a political culture's rhetoric of "we are all British" (Youngh, 2002), but with practices that functionally isolated immigrant groups (Yassine, 2001). Or as one Muslim put it in an article in the *Guardian* newspaper, "Even if we had desperately wanted to integrate—and a great many did—we could not have done it without a welcoming hand from our new compatriots" (Kabbani, 2002, p. 1). Although no new racial and ethnic conflicts of this scale have taken place in Great Britain in the past 10 years or so, if A. H. Richmond (as cited in Yassine, 2001) is correct in proposing that social changes in the United States will appear about 8 years later in Great Britain, the time is ripe for more upheavals along these lines. In fact, hate incidents against Muslim immigrants increased after the September 11th attacks, but it remains to be seen if a continuation of these incidents will eventuate into community conflicts in the fuller sense I am working with in this chapter.

Conflict response processes. As commented on above, the fact that the civil disturbances in Britain sprang from a confluence of factors (hate acts appearing to be the triggering incident) complicates the task of parsing the processes used to respond to the conflicts. Thus, while a hate incident involving skinheads against members of the minority population may have been the triggering incident, once police became involved attempting to quell the rioting, attention shifted to allegations of police use of excessive force and, to a certain extent, reshaped the problem definition.

During the disturbances, the bulk of the response came from law enforcement, and third-party intervention was minimal and sidelined. Post-conflict reflection by police and community social workers created the opportunity for a more open dialogue between police and community residents in the form of a series of facilitated workshops designed to improve police-community relations (Craig, 1992). There is no sense that TR issues, while understood, were dealt with in a prescriptive way.

Eastern Europe

Origins. Eastern Europe has been the locale for this kind of community conflict as well. In Slovakia and Hungary, the Roma population has been the target of attacks by skinheads and victimized by police use of excessive force. The Roma (more commonly known as gypsies) are believed to have immigrated to Europe from India sometime between the 9th and 14th centuries (Olson, 2000). In Hungary, the Roma are divided into three distinct identity groups with their own culture and language and ability to assimilate into mainstream society. The *Romungro,* at about 75%, are by far the largest group of the Roma population and are the most assimilated, having forsaken Roma traditions. The *Olah* are the second largest Roma group, constituting approximately 20% of that population. As with the Romungro, the Olah are also an immigrant group, but of a more recent vintage, having arrived in Hungary about 250 years ago. The Olah tend to be a more close-knit sub-ethnic community and live quite separately from the indigenous Hungarian community. At around 50,000, the *Beash* are the smallest of three Roma communities and reflect a life pattern similar to the Olah (Olson, 2000). The lack of cohesive lifestyles of the Roma ethnic communities has diluted their ability to mobilize and muted their responses to conflict. Observers note, however, that if national economic conditions do not improve in Hungary, a relatively passive Roma population could explode into more focused violence as the gap between value expectations and value capabilities increases (Olson, 2000).

Conflict response processes. Three conflict response processes are relevant for Eastern Europe: (a) mobilization, (b) third-party role shift, and (c) forecasting values. I commented earlier that for racial/ethnic hate incidents to become a community conflict, the victimized minority must gain a measure of political agency that stimulates mobilization. Similar to conflicts involving police use of excessive force, mobilization to counteract racial/ethnic hate activities has the potential to create an awareness of some level of interdependency in the majority community and its leadership. Mobilization, however, does not always spring forth innately from low-power minority communities, particularly when the minority community has been politically, economically, and socially disenfranchised. In these circumstances, external third-party advocates stimulate agency through conflict escalation. In Hungary, national human rights lawyers and international NGOs played this role through the use of national and international media, educating Roma about their rights and taking high-profile cases to court (Olson, 2000).

The conflict escalation role undertaken by advocates at the national level has the potential for creating a climate of ripeness (Pruitt & Kim, 2004)[7] for a more neutral third party to engage in conflict management in local communities. In Hungary this assistance was provided by Partners Hungary (PH), the forerunner of 10 national centers established by the U.S.-based Partners for Democratic Change (PDC). Focusing on the town of Nagykanizsa in Zala County, Hungarian PH facilitators worked with county authorities and the leadership of a Roma ethnic group to approve education, housing, and employment possibilities for the affected population (Olson, 2000). Although PH interveners were trained in a range of intervention techniques, they soon discovered that the concept of mediation in a political culture was not fully free of the mind-set of the old Soviet cordon sanitaire; it implied an imposed solution from an external source and was, therefore, unacceptable. Moreover, mediation in circumstances of extreme power asymmetry can result in a problem-solving dependency, and PH was interested in building long-term capacity in the Roma leadership. For these reasons, PH changed its conflict management style to a form of facilitation called "cooperative planning" that engaged a wide range of local stakeholders to work on complex problems (Olson, 2000), allowing for more control of the process by participants. However, PH found that mediation *techniques* used in contingent situations and as a culturally relevant construct were still useful.

Still another process learning was that while the epistemological approach was normatively geared toward building better relations in a severely divided community, "it was the kiss of death to tell communities that you want to help improve their ethnic relations" (Olson, 2000, p. 11). The better approach was to focus on the more pragmatic substantive or procedural issues. In addition to facilitation and mediation in specific situations, PH helped stakeholders to develop conflict diagnostic tools, provided training, and taught conflict management courses at local universities.

Outcomes and Community Capacity Building

Much of the conflict management conducted by interveners in the United States and Great Britain in racial hate conflict was pragmatically focused. While some attention was paid to changing a pattern of negative interaction between opposing groups and one or more of these groups and law enforcement, outcomes were mainly procedural in that interventions frequently resulted in changing the way law enforcement personnel conducted their activities in affected communities, or how opposing groups conducted protest behavior to minimize the opportunity for violence. On the other hand, Chicago offers an example of community capacity building that has the potential to go beyond conflict management to conflict resolution (if not transformation in outcome). This could be seen in reconciliatory behavior such as the cross visits between African American and White ethnic church congregations and mutual acknowledgment of pain and suffering by families of the victim and perpetrators.

In these examples (Chicago notwithstanding), to the extent third-party intervention looked at relationships, it was primarily in the short term. For example, bringing the leader of the Vietnamese fishing delegation together with the Texas Gulf Coast Grand Dragon of the Klan was not in recognition of a need for an ongoing relationship, but rather a short-term mutual interest in avoiding further conflict; in other words, changing behavior to better manage the conflict and mitigate the possibility of further violence. Attitudinal change is not undertaken, either because interveners assumed there was no interest on the part of opposing groups to transform their relationship (there may not have been) or an ontological perspective was adopted that attitudes were unchangeable and segregated lifestyles was the normative relational status between groups.

Similarly, the intervention work between minority Roma communities and majority populations conducted in Hungary and other parts of Eastern Europe produced procedural and to some extent substantive outcomes. Here, opposing groups were quite clear they were interested in, at best, a minimalist approach to changing relationships, tolerating a shift in direction from a segregated state to a limited form of pluralism, but not going so far as integration (Schellenberg, 1996). In some instances, it appears relationships were enhanced *within* anti-hate coalitions rather than between opposing groups, as was the case in the Northwestern part of the United States where, prior to the intervention, there were concerned individuals who, for the most part, were working alone.

ETHNIC GROUP CONFLICT

Ethnic group conflict enjoys a rich literature (e.g., P. W. Black, 2003; Horowitz, 1985; Kaufman, 2001; Smith, 1993), most of which focuses on competing *ethnies* (Smith, 1993) attempting to shape or reshape a national landscape. Once again, I feel compelled to acknowledge the difficulty in parsing the difference between a community conflict and a national conflict that is being played out in a local community—a particularly ambiguous distinction in settings where constitutional democracy with devolved governmental responsibility is thin or non-existent. To the degree that ethnic group conflict can be determined to be a community phenomenon, one wonders that it is not even more prolific. Ethnic divisions exist in every society even if only subtly. Further, where there are these divisions, there is always a degree of friction if not outright conflict.

While most of the theory generation pertaining to ethnic group conflict deals with these relations at the nation-state level, many of the assumptions can be applied to local manifestations. For example, Smith (1993) identifies five traits such groups must share in common. First, the group has to have a name, one that has symbolic meaning members can rally around. Second, members must have a belief in a common descent; that they come from a certain lineage occupying a place in time and space. It matters little if this is true, only that group members *believe* it to be true. Third, the group typically shares common historical memories

that get told and retold throughout the generations of the group. Fourth, group members would have a shared culture. Finally, group members share a specific territory; a neighborhood or site where most if not all the members live. If these traits (or characteristics) can be distinctively applied to two groups who share geographical space, social relations tend to become crystallized around "we/they" interpretations and form the basis for conflict. A sample of community ethnic conflict follows that hopefully lends descriptive and explanatory weight to how these conflicts originate, what processes are used to manage them, and how outcomes (to the extent that they can be determined) lend themselves to community capacity building. Specifically, the origins and processes from cases in the United States, South Africa, and Northern Ireland are introduced, and then outcomes from each of these cases are reviewed.

United States

Origins. Ethnic group conflict in its various manifestations has existed in the United States for quite some time. Certainly from the mid-1850s to arguably the early part of the 20th century, conflict between White ethnic groups was rife in burgeoning urban areas as waves of Irish, Italian, Polish, and Jewish immigrants battled over the distribution of scarce resources and political power (Erie, 1988; Rakove, 1975). In a more contemporary period, new immigration patterns have sparked a renewal of ethnic conflict, but this time involving Asians, Hispanics from Mexico and Central America, Middle Easterners, and groups of Afro-Caribbean descent. There are times when these conflicts occur between one or more immigrant groups and indigenous African Americans. Finally, we should not overlook recurrent conflict between historically embedded *ethnies,* as is the case with American Blacks and Hassidic Jews in the Crown Heights section of Brooklyn, New York.

Conflict response processes. Where conflicts have involved Southeast Asians and African Americans, interveners like the CRS and Federal Mediation and Conciliation Service field staff have employed short-term conciliation techniques such as facilitating meetings between ethnic group leaders, arranging meetings between these groups and local law enforcement, and engaging in cross-cultural awareness training. Conciliators have used innovative approaches when going on site was problematic. For example, one CRS conciliator guided a local high school principal through a conflict involving Samoan and African American youth via a week-long series of telephone conversations when he realized on-site intervention was not possible because of scheduling conflicts and budgetary concerns. This approach effectively reframed the principal's role from enforcer-disciplinarian to process facilitator (Thom, 2002).

Not all intervention processes involving ethnic conflict have required (or even welcomed) assistance from external third-party sources. More often than not, a local politician's response to ethnic conflict has been avoidance, but on occasion effective conflict management roles have been played by "insider partials"[8] such as local politicians. In Crown Heights, the borough president and local city council members were effective in building interracial and interethnic coalitions because of their strong social network capabilities with Blacks and Hassidic Jewish groups who formed the basis of their political support.

South Africa

Origins. The apartheid system of governance in South Africa, which began in 1950 with the Population Registration Act and did not end until the Nationalist Party unbanned Black political parties in 1990 (Arnold, 1994), established a legacy of particularly violent community conflict that took place primarily in ghetto townships surrounding the major metropolitan areas and in hostels that housed workers who labored in the gold and diamond mines. Complicating the analysis and resolution of these conflicts is the realization that in a number of instances, ethnic factions were (and still are, although to a lesser degree) stimulated by the major Black political parties vying for power. The Inkatha Freedom Party (IFP), whose core constituency is Zulu, and the African National Congress (ANC), which draws its strength from the Xhosa ethnic group, deserve mention in this regard.

Hostel worker conflict generated by poor working conditions, inadequate pay, the removal of the male population from families, and frequently exacerbated by rival political parties, produced subsidiary conflicts. As noted above, hostels are located in townships that are themselves desperately poor. One secondary manifestation is between residents of these townships who are squatters and who view migrant workers as competition for jobs and other resources (Arnold, 1994). Another ancillary conflict stems from rival taxicab companies that have sprung up to service the worker population. In some cases, these companies are backed by warring political factions and have been extremely violent, resulting in serious injuries and deaths to passengers and drivers (Barrow, 1999; McIntyre, 2000).

Conflict response processes. A number of South Africa–based conflict management organizations have intervened in these conflicts over the years, utilizing a combination of mediation and conciliation techniques. These interventions have been mainly contingency focused and aimed at mitigation of further violence, but some initiatives have the potential for building more sustained collaborations.

One such intervention in the taxicab conflict was undertaken by the Centre for Conflict Resolution (CCR) located in Cape Town. Over a period of several months in the summer and fall of 2000, CCR mediators convened a series of facilitated negotiations in that city between several warring cab companies, public transportation officials, and police to assist parties to find ways to end the violence (Centre for Conflict Resolution, 2000). Some of the key issues were the allocation of taxi permits, impoundment of taxis by local authorities, and the prosecution of bus drivers.

CCR's ideology of practice distinguishes between impartiality (maintaining equidistance between parties) and neutrality. Mediators make clear to parties they are not neutral about violence and, therefore, will not be a part of negotiations that attempt to set conditions under which violence is permitted. In other words, CCR makes its ethics of intervention clear from the beginning. Even so, a level of violence continued while parties were in negotiations and threatened to wreck the process. Fortunately, the parties recommitted themselves to a peaceful resolution. While the mediation did not result in substantive agreement, CCR reports there was some reduction in violence and parties reached a few agreements on procedure, principally that they would continue to use a dialogical forum to try to reach agreements on remaining issues.

Northern Ireland

Origins. The history of the Northern Ireland conflict, particularly in Belfast, has been detailed extensively (Fitzduff, 2002) and will not be re-documented here. It is sufficient to recognize that it is a complex conflict, deeply embedded in sectarian identities that have been formed over centuries of chosen traumas and chosen glories (Volkan, 1998), clung to by Protestant Loyalists who favor maintaining the current political relationship with Britain and Catholic Nationalists who want the North to become a part of the Irish Republic: the former backed by the Ulster Defense Force (UDF) loyalist paramilitaries and the latter by the Provisional Irish Republican Army (IRA). Continuing the observations made about other forms of community conflicts that take place outside the United States, Northern Ireland community conflicts often are played out with devastating effects in ethnically entrenched neighborhoods, but their implications carry weight at the national and international level.

Conflict response processes. There has been an array of interventions woven into the history of "the Troubles" designed to manage that conflict. Employing Lederach's (1997) model, we can see that some interventions have functioned at Level One for the purposes of engaging the formal political leadership. Former U.S. Senator George Mitchell's mediation that produced a tentative peace has been well publicized in news media and other forums. Other conflict management initiatives have taken place at Levels Two (mid-level) and Three (grass roots) and it is at these levels we will focus our attention.

Fitzduff (2002) reported on a variety of conflict management interventions in the form of conciliation, mediation, problem-solving workshops, and training that have been employed at one point or another to end conflict in Northern Ireland. Much of this work has been undertaken by the Initiative on Conflict Resolution and Ethnicity (INCORE)[9] and, as the former director, Fitzduff drew from this organization's experience a number of principles of practice, some of which are reviewed here. One principle is the importance of integrating contingency responses of law enforcement to deal with triggering incidents with longer term problem-solving initiatives. In high-intensity conflict, the tendency (and the temptation) is to limit response to procedural issues designed to mitigate violence. The focus is on *containment,* ignoring the substantive and structural causes that lie beneath. The risk, of course, is that the conflict will resurface when the next triggering incident occurs. A second principle is the importance of carrying on talks at all levels of community and leadership, not concentrating negotiations and decision making in the ranks of the political leaders at Level One. Finally, talks must not be limited to gender stereotypes of conflict resolution, but reflect the important roles that women play in conflict management and peace building.

The literature about conflict resolution practice gives great attention to the roles and techniques of the external and professional mediator (Moore, 1996; Pruitt & Kim, 2004), but largely ignores the activities played by informal insider partials (for an exception see Lederach, 1997). Yet in many identity-based community conflicts, the external mediator is viewed with suspicion and mistrust. A unique initiative in conflict management was undertaken by the Community Development Centre (CDC), a multi-service NGO, to respond to the high scale of violence that took place in North Belfast in the mid-1990s. There were, of course, the ever-present TR conditions based on differentiation of needs fulfillment between Catholics and Protestants. The triggering incident was an amalgam of factors including police abuse, rumors, media hype, and a breakdown in communication between sectarian leadership and local authorities. At the height of the violence, 110 families abandoned their homes and neighborhoods that had painstakingly become dual identity, and now reverted back to single identity status.

The CDC was instrumental in setting up an interagency task force to respond to increased levels of violence anticipated as a result of the upcoming marching season, when Protestant Loyalists march provocatively through selected Catholic neighborhoods to celebrate the victory of Protestant William of Orange over King James II at the Battle of the Boyne in 1690. Rather than taking on all the conflict management roles themselves, the task force equipped a small, balanced contingent of Catholic and Protestant community leaders with mobile phones. This group went out in sectarian communities and used the phones as rumor control mechanisms and to hasten response by appropriate local authorities to emergent violence.

Outcomes and Community Capacity Building

Certainly, one could reach a conclusion when looking at U.S.-based conflict management processes that these were closely held roles carried out by mediators with clout (at least in the case of local politicians) for status-preserving ends or by well-meaning but socially astigmatic external third parties. Perhaps it would be more charitable to acknowledge a certain unfairness in this observation since I take an admittedly small slice of the ethnic community conflict landscape. A closer examination suggests that the telephone conciliation, for example, is a form of community capacity building in that the school principal discussed earlier now knows a process that can work and possibly be transferable to other conflict settings. The Crown Heights, Brooklyn, initiatives lend themselves to community capacity building because while it may be true that local politicians have an almost Darwinian need to survive, their efforts have resulted in a leadership network that is now functioning on its own.

The Northern Ireland conflict and the South African taxi wars demonstrate the limitations of community capacity building in situations of extreme and protracted violence. Leadership at the mid- and grassroots level become traumatized and, in effect, leave communities rudderless. Both examples suggest that when community conflicts are nested within structural issues at the state level, external third parties are needed to jump-start the management process. It may be that the best that can be hoped for with respect to community capacity building is the ability to contain the violence until such time as a pathway toward resolution is constructed at the state level. Certainly, the South African taxi wars demonstrate the difficulty of managing (much less resolving) conflict that is embedded in a system of structural violence left in place by apartheid. The relative deprivation experienced by taxi drivers as a result of economic disparity results in a form of displacement (Dougherty & Pfaltzgraff, 1990), turning frustration-aggression inward, away from a system that causes the condition toward a relatively "safe" target—other taxi drivers and their associations.

THEORY, PRACTICE, AND FUTURE RESEARCH DIRECTIONS

In this section, the intent is to bring into sharper focus the relationship between theory, practice, and research and how these disciplines inform interventions designed to build sustainable and conflict-mitigated communities. In doing so, I hope to tease out and make more explicit the synergy that exists between often competing bodies of knowledge—a synergy that can be the basis for a more reflective practice. To better understand this synergy, I will discuss ethical consideration and future research directions.

Theoretical Implications for Practice

A number of theoretical concepts and principles (some more explicitly than others) have been woven throughout the discussion of community conflict and its management. The following are ones that I feel are notably important for intervention in community conflicts.

Worldviews. I briefly looked at group identities with an emphasis on how these groups memorialize conflict through chosen traumas and chosen glories; those generational events that give a group a sense of "weness"—a worldview of who they are in relation to others they may be in conflict with. This worldview, having its origins in TRs of structural violence, will often be ignited by some triggering event, such as an act of police abuse or a predatory attack undertaken by a more powerful opposing group.

Status change. Communities exist in a dynamic continuum ranging from cooperation to conflict and even crisis (Laue & Cormick, 1978). As relationships between groups or between groups and local government move from a state of harmony to one that is unharmonious, the condition of relative deprivation becomes more stratified and, as we noted earlier, sets the stage for pronounced frustration, leading to aggression, not infrequently in the form of violence.

The utility of conflict. From the vantage point of practice, theorizing about the nature of groups in conflict would seem to give impetus to initiating an intervention before conflict emerges (i.e., taking a preventive approach). But Coser (1956) reminded us that (if we believe groups are integral components in a functioning society) a certain amount of conflict is necessary to maintain group boundaries and cohesiveness. Further, while postmodernists might consider Marx theoretically unfashionable, if community conflict is stimulated by an imbalance in the distribution of scarce resources, can real change take place without conflict?

The inter-relationship of mobilization and escalation. Cormick (1992) underscored the importance of mobilization to low-power community groups for the purposes of articulating nested grievances and developing symmetries of negotiating power. In fact, the history of community conflict suggests that poorly mobilized groups have difficulty getting to the table or, once there, having their demands taken seriously. This brings us to awareness that there is a dynamic cause-and-effect relationship between mobilization and escalation. Pruitt and Kim (2004) observed that "escalation occurs when Party's contentious tactics become heavier, putting more pressure on Other and often inflicting greater suffering" (p. 151). Mobilization acts to escalate conflict, but escalation in turn stimulates mobilization.

The issue for conflict management is at what point does the escalation of conflict from a "healthy" state become one that is unhealthy and disruptive? It would seem to me that "healthy/unhealthy" are social constructions with contingent meaning depending on culture, degree, and interpretation of relative deprivation and the form the aggressiveness takes. As this applies to Cincinnati or Los Angeles civil disturbances, could there have been a form of mobilization that would have produced an "acceptable" level of disruption and confrontation?

Ethical Considerations

Mobilization leading to conflict escalation, particularly where it involves the use of contentious tactics, raises troubling ethical dilemmas for the conflict manager. If the intervention initiated by the conflict manager has the effect of stimulating mobilization, does this violate professional icons of neutrality and impartiality? For example, the conflict manager in assessing the protest parties who should be "at the table" might conclude that more militant elements have not been given a voice and seek to include them in a resolution process. However, the inclusion, while energizing the mobilization, could also escalate the conflict. On the other hand, is there not a risk that encouraging parties to negotiate before a sufficient mobilization has been undertaken co-opts the negotiating equilibrium?

An approach to dealing with this dilemma might begin with the conflict manager's recognizing that if the purpose of the intervention is to help build healthy, more inclusive communities, then process cannot be divorced from outcome. That is, an intervention designed to create this kind of community is not a neutral process, but rather a form of advocacy for a conceptual outcome, one in which the particular dimensions will be shaped by *all* the affected parties. A critical task for the conflict manager is twofold: One is to convince the more powerful party to accept the full spectrum of potential parties affected by the conflict even if past behavior of some of those individuals or groups has not fallen within the norms of the more powerful party. Second, the intervener has to convince the insufficiently mobilized party that if it agrees to enter a negotiations process with the intention of having a viable role in the outcome, then some constraints will have to be placed on the "tools" of mobilization. Acts of extreme violence, for example, would not be acceptable. Accordingly, there is an acknowledgment by all that this may escalate the conflict, but in the end produce a more holistic and sustainable outcome.

In community conflicts where there is a disenfranchised, low-power group confronting more powerful public and private entities, a prescriptive approach would be to diversify intervention roles, such as was the case with the Hungarian Roma conflict. International and national NGOs acted as advocates that escalated the conflict, creating a sense of ripeness, laying the foundation for more neutral third-party conflict management. Indeed, Mitchell (1993) argued that some conflicts call for as many as 13 intervention roles. But as was noted when commenting on this example, some Roma rights activists were concerned that external and internal advocates focused on conflict escalation could worsen relations with the majority community, increasing the possibility of retaliation rather than negotiation.

Responding to this kind of ethical dilemma through the diversification of conflict management roles is clearer in community conflicts where there are asymmetries of power. It is somewhat murkier when the conflict is driven by contesting groups of relatively equal power, as we have seen with the South African taxi wars and Northern Ireland. In these instances, on-the-ground violence is inextricably caught up with underlying structural sources. Diversified intervention roles are important here as well, but the likelihood that ongoing community violence could derail negotiations around structural issues requires that both levels be worked on simultaneously by multiple actors.

Given the relational, procedural, and structural complexity of community conflict, how, then, to articulate the ethical dilemmas permeating intervention? One view invites the conflict resolver into a paradox. The Society for Professionals in Dispute Resolution (SPIDR, 1989), noted that it was the conflict resolver's responsibility "as a disinterested third party" (p. 6) to be neutral in his or her conduct with the parties. Shortly thereafter, however, it instructs this individual that if he or she determines one of the parties in a negotiation is at a functional disadvantage, the conflict resolver has a responsibility to address this. How one addresses this situation while at the same time maintaining a posture of disinterest is left up to the imagination.

Another view draws the conflict resolver into a reflective mode in relationship to an ethical dilemma and can be assessed by potential intervenors from two perspectives. In the first, an ethical dilemma can be construed as one in which the practitioner is faced with a doubt about how to act in relation to personal and professional values, norms, and obligations (Conrad, 1988). This suggests a dual epistemology, the personal and professional, and represents a tension between them. The conflict resolver brings his or her own values and worldviews into a conflict, and whether this individual is conscious of them or not they imprint the dynamic of the conflict. This may clash with a professional code of ethics and take on added significance if we consider that these worldviews have cultural frames that carry a different logic about what is the rightness or wrongness of a practitioner's behavior.

The above duality clarifies the intra-personal dilemma confronting the conflict resolver but leaves untouched another dilemma that is present in complex community conflicts; that is, the relationship between the conflict resolver and the parties and the relationship *between* the parties (the second perspective). Adding to the first perspective, I argue that a critical point is where the choice of action (of the conflict resolver) has consequences for the relationships between the conflict resolver and the parties, between the parties, and the objectives to which the intervention is being applied. This acknowledges the complex set of relationships in multiparty community conflicts and the recognition that these relationships are interdependent.

When a conflict manager is engaged in a complex, multiparty community conflict where events on the ground are changing rapidly, this individual may not always have the luxury of determining ethical implications in advance. One technique an intervener can use to get out of the ethical maze is called *model building:*

> Model building is the process of constructing frames of reference that will allow the conflict manager to develop multiple rationales for what is occurring or what could occur. The process encourages the conflict manager to move from an

over-reliance on short term, contingent observa-tions to a deeper understanding of anticipated or unfolding events. (Warfield, 2002, p. 218)

In my model, I envision four stages where a conflict manager may contemplate and respond to an ethical dilemma—*pause, reflect, share, and determine options and select*—that mirror a sequence in conflict dynamics.

Stage 1: Pause. Often when conflict managers are planning an intervention or are even in the midst of one, they experience a sense of dis-comfort; a feeling that something is not quite right. Rather than ignoring this "inner tug" and plunging ahead, conflict managers should find a quiet space to identify what they are feeling. They may have uncovered an ethical dilemma.

Stage 2: Reflect. The intent of reflection is to give meaning to an observed act or pattern of activity. Here conflict managers try to determine the implications for their commonsense ethics and whether these ethics have changed.

Stage 3: Share. Teams conduct many commu-nity conflict interventions. Intervention teams form complex sets of relationships that, like any other relationship, are fraught with para-doxes of cooperation and competition. If during an intervention one or more members of the team encounter the first two stages of an ethical dilemma, they may not communicate their con-cerns to other team members out of fear of dis-rupting a delicate set of relationships. One of the team members has to have the courage to bring his or her concerns to colleagues for the greater good of the intervention and the outcomes.

Stage 4: Determine Options and Select. Having carried out the first three stages, conflict man-agers are now engaged in a determination of what options are available to prevent the ethical dilemma from worsening. Choice is informed by three factors: (a) the core values conflict managers bring with them as implicit compo-nents of the intervention and how these values interact with the ethical dilemma; (b) how these values diverge from the values held by the profes-sion the conflict managers associate themselves

with; and (c) conflict managers' understanding of what others have done in similar situations and the esteem in which these individuals are held.

Future Research Directions

This modest review of community conflict management and community capacity building does yield a few areas for research to delve into. A first area to examine is understudied communi-ties such as non-industrial societies and Native American/First Nation communities. A few prior studies provide insights into the depth of issues for conflict resolution in these communities. Merry (1989) discussed methods used for dispute and conflict resolution in non-industrial (traditional) societies. Merry reported on the studies conducted in four societies: the *Nuer,* pastoral nomads who inhabit areas of Ethiopia and Sudan; the *Ifugao* of the Philippines; the *Waigali,* a tribal society from the mountainous areas of Afghanistan; and the *Zinacantecos,* a Mayan Indian community that lives in the Chiapas area in southern Mexico. Conflicts in these societies tend to be *intra* com-munal rather than *inter* communal in that they involve factions or families living in close or over-lapping physical arrangements rather than distinct and segregated geographies. While some conflicts can involve small groups engaged in activities such as cattle theft, by and large the conflicts were interpersonal and covered such acts as theft, adul-tery, assault, and homicide. There are significant implications for escalation into community con-flicts because of the close-knit kinship patterns that exist in these societies. Third-party intervention, then, conducted by respected insider partials, has a larger purpose of maintaining a level of harmony in that community.

In addition, a small but important body of research has begun to emerge that addresses con-flicts involving Native American and (in Canada) First Nation peoples that brings emphasis to cultural differences. Often, these conflicts are intra-tribal, and even where they involve external, non-native communities, they tend not to reflect the high level of violence manifested in the conflicts discussed earlier in this chapter. Nevertheless, these conflicts do involve deeply embedded cultural issues. For example, Chataway (1994) looked at a conflict involving two competing governing bodies in the Kahnawake Mohawk community in Canada: the traditional Longhouse system of governance and the band council system. The band council designed by non-aboriginal Canadians replaced the traditionalist form around the turn of the 20th century and was designed to administer programs and policies of the state and surrounding jurisdictions. The traditionalists resurfaced in 1979, and the conflict was engaged when both systems of governance began to compete over which system could best represent the internal interests of the Kahnawake community. Chataway found, ironically, that while the community felt the traditional Longhouse provided the more authentic cultural image of inclusiveness, the leadership acted to exclude the community in many of its decision-making processes; whereas the band council, which many in the community were not disposed to accept ideologically, was actually more responsive to the community's needs. Both systems of governance claimed the mantle of cultural legitimacy for the Kahnawake Mohawks. The conflict placed the community in a cognitive dilemma since it was felt that coherence concerning culture and its representation was of critical importance in the interface with the Canadian government.

A second area where research is needed is in the application of relative deprivation and frustration-aggression theories to propensity toward violence in community conflict. For example, why is it that some communities embroiled in issues of police use of excessive force will translate frustration-aggression into violence while communities in another city with similar variables will not? This could be important because a better understanding of this might enable us to construct more focused conflict management interventions that could lend themselves to sustained conflict resolution outcomes.

A third area for future research is examining the process of community conflict. Even a casual perusal of the conflicts discussed in this chapter would reveal that community conflicts are dynamic events subject to change. What, then, is the relationship between community conflict and change? For example, who defines the conflict and what events act to change how the conflict is defined? How does a change in conflict dynamics shift roles of stakeholders in conflict and the capacity to be cooperative or competitive?

Another direction that research might take in relation to managing community conflict is role negotiation by the third-party intervener. In some of the interventions undertaken by CRS conciliators there are strong inferences of role negotiation. For example, a CRS conciliator I worked with noted that she considered a case in the initial assessment as ripe for formal table mediation, but realized once she was into conflict management that a more informal conciliation style was called for. We need to know more about shift points in community conflicts that signal to the intervener a need for a role change and what the actual negotiations look like.

Finally, a meta-research question should inquire about the relationship of community conflict management to the development of civil society and participatory democracy. Assuming this is even a desirable goal for research, what conditions need to be in place for conflict management to become a catalyst for these outcomes? The work by PH with regards to the Roma-majority community conflict is informative but paradoxical. There does seem to be a relationship between the PH intervention and the indication that the Roma profile in municipal electoral politics has been raised somewhat. As well, there appears to have been increased participation of one Roma ethnic group in the community planning process. At the same time, there seems to be little change in attitudes by the majority community toward the Romas.

In sum, a modest body of ethnographic research has emerged that examines *inter* and *intra* community conflict engaged in by identity groups of one sort or another. However, little has been done that focuses on intervention roles either by external or internal third parties. We need to know more about how communities interpret triggering events and link them (or not) to causal factors that then determine a level of response. Finally, more research in this area should help us determine if a normative outcome of a community conflict intervention is co-existence (as appears to be the case with the Romas) or if a reconciliatory and transformative relationship is possible.

CONCLUSION

I have attempted to examine a deliberately small variety of community conflicts that is underreported in theory development, research, and the popular literature. The idea was to bring an international perspective to community conflict and its management, and to learn to what extent intervention lent itself to community capacity building. Patterns of some forms of community conflict such as that generated by police use of excessive force, whether it takes place in the U.S. or abroad, have similar dynamics. The work of conflict managers, not unexpectedly, is reactive, pointing to the difficulty of designing and conducting an intervention into the causal factors in which triggering incidents are nested.

While interventions seem dependent on a triggering incident (or series of incidents) to initiate an intervention, in some instances conflict managers, using a variety of third-party consensual techniques, provided a catalyst for stakeholders to go deeper into causal factors. Where this occurred, a key element appeared to be the diversification of the stakeholder base. Broadening the stakeholder base beyond the original protest group to include individuals who could influence policy decisions provides some assurance that structural issues will be addressed and agreements will be sustained for longer periods.

The work of PH highlights the importance of tandem third-party intervention roles; in this case, a complementarity between advocates who can stimulate mobilization and so-called neutrals who can follow in their wake to do the more balanced conflict management. Indeed, the notion of "complementarity" and "tandem" raises the question of whether there really is such a thing as neutrality in these kinds of community conflicts, suggesting ethical dilemmas not typically faced in other forms of conflict management.

Finally, from what was sampled in this chapter we can see there is no small amount of theory that can be applied to the understanding of these forms of conflict. What we lack is empirical research that can help us better understand how these conflicts are formed and what conditions cause them to change. Given the apparently unrelenting march of globalization, we are likely to have more complex community conflicts than ever before. The more we know about them, the more likely conflict interveners will know how to manage them and transfer this capacity to communities in the true participatory model.

NOTES

1. Community conflicts, along with other multi-party, complex conflicts, engage the debate as to whether such events can be managed, mitigated, or resolved. The debate speaks to the ideological hubris between the realist camp that believes these kinds of conflicts can at best be kept at less destructive or less harsh levels and the resolutionists who believe that intervention must address underlying causes and lead ultimately to the ending of the conflict.

2. For a discussion of this conflict, see Warfield (1993).

3. I was a member of this agency, serving in a number of field and administrative positions.

4. The "Tap Root" theory, as it became commonly known, was first articulated by Bertram Levine, an associate director with CRS, as an ontological worldview of many disenfranchised minority communities in the United States and to suggest choice points for intervention. Moira Dugan (1996) developed a similar concept.

5. For the purposes of this chapter, a distinction is made between interethnic conflicts and conflicts driven by racial hatred. I acknowledge a certain artificiality in this distinction. For example, both forms of conflict are stimulated by social identity where individuals and groups use "cultural markers to claim, achieve, or ascribe group membership" (P. W. Black, 2003, p. 121). However, ethnic conflict is inclined to be more episodic, where periods of tranquility can be shattered by bursts of violence. As well, ethnic conflict seems to take place between groups who share the same social space and have rough (although at times interchangeable) symmetries of power (see Horowitz, 1985, for an excellent treatment of features of ethnic conflict). Racial conflict as examined in this chapter is exemplified by social constructions based on beliefs about biological differences of skin color enhanced by historical circumstances built

around the slave trade (P. W. Black, 2003, p. 129). It is the latter I am dealing with in this section. The former will be explicated and treated as a separate category.

6. For a discussion and comparison of the Great Britain and U.S. racial disturbances, see Marshall (1992).

7. There is a risk factor associated with this role if there is too great a lag time before a more neutral third party can become involved. Some Roma rights activists were concerned that advocacy conflict escalation would actually worsen relations with the majority community and leave them vulnerable to increased attacks (Olson, 2000).

8. The term *insider partial* is associated with the intervention work conducted by John Paul Lederach in Latin America in the 1970s. He found that *confianza* (trust) was more important than external third-party neutrality and that this role could often be played by an individual who came from inside the culture. For a fuller description, see Lederach (1995).

9. INCORE is a United Nations University program within the University of Ulster to examine conflict resolution through research, training, and policy development.

References

Appadurai, A. (1996). *Modernity at large.* Minneapolis: University of Minnesota Press.

Balduino, D. T. (2001, March). *Land conflicts in Brazil.* Paper presented at the Access to Land conference, Bonn, Germany.

Barrow, G. (1999). *World: African opposition shootings continue in Cape Town.* BBC News online network. Retrieved May 16, 2004, from http://news.bbc.co.uk/hi/english/world/africa/newsid_293000/293932.stm

Berry, M. J., Portney, K. E., & Thompson, K. (1993). *The rebirth of urban democracy.* Washington, DC: Brookings Institution.

Black, C. E. (1966). *The dynamics of modernization.* Harper & Row.

Black, G. S. (1974). Conflicts in community: A theory of the effects of community size. *American Political Science Review, 68,* 1245–1261.

Black, P. W. (2003). Identities. In S. Cheldelin, D. Druckman, & L. Fast (Eds.), *Conflict from analysis to intervention* (pp. 120–139). New York: Continuum.

CDR Associates. (2004). *The CDR mediation process training manual.* Boulder, CO: Center for Dispute Resolution Associates.

Centre for Conflict Resolution. (2000). *Western Cape transport conflict: Progress report.* Retrieved May 16, 2004, from http://ccrweb.cct.uct.ac.za

Chataway, C. (1994). *Challenges to aboriginal self-government.* Retrieved May 15, 2004, from http://www.kahonwes.com/iroquois/s94chata.htm

Coleman, J. A. (1957). *Community conflict.* New York: Free Press.

Conrad, A. P. (1988). Ethical considerations in the psychological process. *Social Casework, 69,* 603–610.

Cormick, G. W. (1992). Environmental conflict, community mobilization, and the "public good." In S. S. Silbey & A. Sarat (Eds.), *Studies in law, politics, and society* (Vol. 12, pp. 309–329). Greenwich, CT: JAI.

Coser, L. A. (1956). *The functions of social conflict.* New York: Free Press.

Craig, Y. (1992). Policing the poor: Conciliation or confrontation? In T. F. Marshall (Ed.), *Community disorder and policing: Conflict management in action* (pp. 77–86). London: Whiting & Birch.

Dougherty, J. E., & Pfaltzgraff, R. L., Jr. (1990). *Contending theories of international relations* (3rd ed.). New York: Harper & Row.

Dugan, M. A. (1996). A nested theory of conflict. *Women in Leadership: Sharing the Vision, 1,* 9–20.

Erie, S. P. (1988). *Rainbow's end: Irish Americans and the dilemma of urban machine politics, 1840-1985.* Berkeley: University of California Press.

Fitzduff, M. (2002). *Conflict resolution processes in Northern Ireland.* New York: United Nations Press.

Galtung, J. (1969). Violence, peace and peace research. *Journal of Peace Research, 6,* 167–191.

Gurr, T. R. (1970). *Why men rebel.* Princeton, NJ: Princeton University Press.

Gwartney-Gibbs, P. A., & Lach, D. H. (1991). Research report: Workplace dispute resolution and gender inequality. *Negotiation Journal, 7,* 1–9.

Hocker, J. L., & Wilmot, W. W. (1995). *Interpersonal conflict* (4th ed.) Dubuque, IA: Brown & Benchmark.

Horowitz, D. L. (1985). *Ethnic groups in conflict.* Berkeley: University of California Press.

Hughs, R. (2002). *Interview for CRS Oral History Project.* Retrieved May 15, 2004, from the University of Colorado's Conflict Research Consortium Web site: http://www.colorado.edu/conflict/civil_rights/notes_med.html

Kabbani, R. (2002). *Dislocation and neglect in Muslim Britain's ghettos.* Retrieved May 15, 2004, from the Guardian Unlimited Web site: http://www.guardian.co.uk/religion/Story/0,276 3,738861,00.html

Kaufman, S. J. (2001). *Modern hatreds: The symbolic politics of ethnic war.* Ithaca, NY: Cornell University Press.

Laue, J., & Cormick, G. (1978). The ethics of intervention in community disputes. In G. Bermant, H. C. Kelman, & D. P. Warwick (Eds.), *The ethics of social intervention* (pp. 205–232). Washington, DC: Halstead Press.

Lederach, J. P. (1995). *Preparing for peace: Conflict transformation across cultures.* Syracuse, NY: Syracuse University Press.

Lederach, J. P. (1997). *Building peace: Sustainable reconciliation in divided societies.* Washington, DC: U.S. Institute of Peace Press.

Marshall, T. F. (Ed.). (1992). *Community disorders and policing: Conflict management in action.* London: Whiting & Birch.

Martinez, E. (2002). *Interview for CRS Oral History Project.* Retrieved May 15, 2004, from the University of Colorado's Conflict Research Consortium Web site: http://www.colorado.edu/conflict/civil_rights/notes_med.html

McIntyre, J. (2000). *Police seal off taxi war township.* BBC News online network. Retrieved May 16, 2004, from http://news.bbc.co.uk/hi/english/world/africa/newsid_864000/86 4116.stm

Merry, S. E. (1989). Mediation in nonindustrial societies. In K. Kressel & D. G. Pruitt (Eds.), *Mediation research* (pp. 68–90). San Francisco: Jossey-Bass.

Mitchell, C. (1993). The process and stages of mediation: Two Sudanese cases. In D. R. Smock (Ed.), *Making war and waging peace: Foreign intervention in Africa* (pp. 139–159). Washington, DC: U.S. Institute of Peace Press.

Moore, C. W. (1996). *The mediation process: Practical strategies for resolving conflict* (2nd ed.). San Francisco: Jossey-Bass.

Nagel, J. H. (1990). Psychological obstacles to administrative responsibility: Lessons of the MOVE disaster. *Journal of Policy Analysis and Management, 10,* 1–23.

National Advisory Commission on Civil Disorders. (1968). *The American dream does not yet exist for all our citizens: Kerner Commission members discuss civil unrest.* Retrieved January 12, 2005, from History Matters Web site: http://historymatters.gmu.edu/d/6465

Olson, L. (2000). *Managing conflict through cooperative planning: Partners Hungary's work on majority-minority (Roma) tensions.* A Reflecting on Peace Practice Project case study. Cambridge, MA: Collaborative for Development Action.

Pruitt, D. G., & Kim, S. H. (2004). *Social conflict: Escalation, stalemate, and settlement* (3rd ed.). New York: McGraw-Hill.

Rakove, M. L. (1975). Reflections on the machine. In M. G. Holli & P. M. Green (Eds.), *The making of the mayor: Chicago, 1983* (pp. 127–143). Grand Rapids, MI: Wm. G. Erdsman.

Rothman, J. (2003). *The Cincinnati Collaborative executive summary.* Retrieved May 15, 2004, from the ARIA Group, Inc. Web site: http://www.ariagroup.com/cinti.html

Schellenberg, J. A. (1996). *Conflict resolution: Theory, research, and practice.* New York: Sate University of New York Press.

Slack, K. (2003, October 19). Poor vs. profit in Bolivian revolt. *Los Angeles Times,* p. M5.

Smith, A. D. (1993). The ethnic sources of nationalism. *Survival, 35,* 48–62.

Society for Professionals in Dispute Resolution. (1989). *Making the tough calls: Ethical exercises for neutral dispute resolvers.* Washington, DC: SPIDR.

Thom, S. (2002). *Interview for CRS Oral History Project.* Retrieved May 15, 2004, from the University of Colorado's Conflict Research Consortium Web site: http://www.colorado.edu/conflict/civil_rights/index.html

Volkan, V. (1998). *Bloodlines: From ethnic pride to ethnic terrorism.* Boulder, CO: Westview.

Walsh, E. (1997, March 27). Chicago establishment condemns latest episode in ugly history of race relations. *Washington Post,* p. A13.

Walsh, M. (2002). *Interview for CRS Oral History Project.* Retrieved May 15, 2004, from the University of Colorado's Conflict Research Consortium Web site: http://www.colorado.edu/conflict/civil_rights/index.html

Warfield, W. (1993). Public policy conflict resolution: The nexus between culture and process. In D. J. D. Sandole & H. van der Merwe (Eds.), *Conflict resolution theory and practice: Integration and application* (pp. 176–193). Manchester, UK: Manchester University Press.

Warfield, W. (1996). Building consensus for racial harmony in American cities: A case model approach. *Missouri Journal of Dispute Resolution, 1996*(1), 151–176.

Warfield, W. (2002). Is this the right thing to do? A practical framework for ethical decisions. In J. P. Lederach & J. M. Jenner (Eds.), *Into the eye of the storm: A handbook on international peacebuilding* (pp. 213–223). San Francisco: Jossey-Bass.

Whyte, W. F. (1943). *Street corner society: The social structure of an Italian slum.* Chicago: University of Chicago Press.

Yassine, H.-Q. (2001). *Causes of racism in Britain.* Retrieved May 15, 2004, from the Immigrant Institute Web site: http://www.Immi.se/ir/ir2001/yassine.htm

Youngh, G. (2002). *No place like home: A Black Briton's journey through the American South.* London: Pickadore.

18

CRITICAL APPROACHES TO COMMUNITY CONFLICT IN DEVELOPING COUNTRIES

A Case Study of India

KRISHNA KANDATH

University of New Mexico

Conflict is a defining feature of all social systems. It is even reasonable to suggest that what best identifies us as humans is our propensity for conflict. To make such an observation is to adopt a critical perspective on conflict. Dominant perspectives tend to attach negative connotations to conflict, often indicative of a kind of disruption to the assumed normality of social and personal relations (see, e.g., Wilmot & Hocker, 2001). In general, Western cultures do not value conflict. Conflicts are targeted for resolution or sometimes even ignored. There is not much room in the social discourse to talk openly about conflict. Some workplaces even have codes of conduct that prevent the expression of conflicting emotions (Sass, 2000; Tracy, 2004).

A critical perspective situates conflict as a common and necessary occurrence in daily life; an inevitable condition of the human existence. Here, my focus is on humans as people having interests and seeking to carve out stakes in various situations. Where interests are involved, conflicts are a necessary condition, a key assumption that shapes this chapter. Burke's (1950) ideas on communication remain extremely relevant to frame the foundational idea on conflict and communication that is developed in this chapter. Burke wrote that communication becomes a necessary practice because of our innate need to transcend differences and to identify with the other. Conflicts, in this perspective, become the ground for conversation. Conflict is a necessary condition for dialogue. We may have differences but never have the opportunity to engage them and even appreciate them without some disturbance to the normality that everyday life assumes.

The approach I take in this chapter is one shaped by cultural studies. Specifically, I define culture as the site of conflict, over meaning making in a complex and constantly changing sign system that we all inhibit, and over various interests—material, social, economic, and political—that we have as humans. The cultural studies approach is a theoretical intervention into the largely structural functionalist theorizing common to conflict communication literature in the United States. The primary limitations with existing theoretical streams in the conflict literature are twofold: (a) the extensive reliance on the spoken word for analysis and understanding, such as in "The Coordinated Management of Meaning" (Pearce, 2005); and (b) the compilation of recorded or collected data into pre-labeled categories for purposes of statistical computation and analysis, such as in research informed by face-negotiation theory (e.g., Oetzel & Ting-Toomey, 2003).

This chapter focuses on conflict in developing countries, specifically using India as a case study. The particularity of a country like India is that we have the benefit of examining conflicts in two Indias: before the liberalization program was initiated and during and after the liberalization had occurred. The economic liberalization program started in the 1990s, before which time India's economy was a protected one. With the onset of liberalization, markets were opened to foreign investments in phases, leading to more opportunities for outsourced jobs in the cities and increased purchasing power for people in general. To privilege the economic liberalization program is to point clearly toward the role of power and material interests in shaping conflict. In addition, it is important to realize that literature on conflict in India, from a communication perspective, does not exist. Most studies may have a traditional sociological focus. At best, commentaries and occasional studies have addressed the issue of mass-mediated sensationalism during conflicts involving differences premised on caste and religion (e.g., Pandey, 1990; Varshney, 1997). The literature on conflict tends to be biased toward dominant group perspectives, specifically of religion, caste, and class. This chapter emphasizes the relationship of conflicts and their management to community ties, but also seeks to relate nondominant group systems and nondominant perspectives. Given the limitations of literature, I provide numerous first person accounts, derived from my own experiences growing up in India until 1995 and then following up with regular visits and maintaining contacts with friends and family members.

This chapter starts with an elaboration of the assumptions framing the discussion of conflict, followed by a description of India, specifically the Indian context, using a sociocultural lens. Different types of conflict are examined. Subsequently, the various practices of mediation and conflict management are examined. The chapter ends with a discussion of future directions and practical applications.

ASSUMPTIONS

Four assumptions shape my understanding of conflict and communication. First, communication is constitutive of conflict and vice versa. This assumption is what I call a constructionist position. Human communication is conflictual; our communication with another person occurs despite the conflicting circumstances of language and meaning-making systems. Influenced in part by Derrida's (1994) ideas about language, this conflictual aspect of human communication processes is less emphasized in the scholarly study of human communication. Similarly, all conflict is communicative and communicated. The first notion expresses the idea that communication constructs conflict. Being a semiotic position, the emphasis here is that signs generate more meanings than what exists in the content. A related idea, the second notion, emphasizes the fact that our understanding and knowledge of conflict derives from what is communicated about it. Consider the case of an environmental conflict between a multinational corporation (MNC) and a local community. MNCs are in the business of generating profits and will work, to a large extent, to engage in public relations that seek to communicate their perspective as accurate and justified. Similarly, the local community, often with fewer resources, will seek to provide their story to articulate the case for the conflict. Here, the mixed (and conflicting) messages will generate unintended and unexpected meanings about the conflict. In combination, the two notions entail all conflicts as comprising both "facts" and "representations," a postmodern condition that makes conflict a meta-condition of communication. In the traditions of conflict research, both within and outside communication, we are witness to knowledge that derives from statistical manipulations of recalls of actual and imaginary conflict situations, basically from what gets communicated about conflict.

Second, there exists a material, social basis for all conflict. Culture, understood as a way of life, is determined by the logic of material interests. Such material interests often exist due to a basic need for survival, not necessarily to accumulate wealth. This argument has ties to traces of materialists' positions explicated by Harris (1979) and Williams (1977). The materialist position does not negate the constructionist position on meaning. We need this perspective as a way to engage social change processes. As Foucault (1965/1973, 1975/1979) argued, language and social interaction are both material practices; they produce and position us as subjects, specifically discursive subjects. However, such a position does not seek to deny the distinctions between materiality and discourse; instead it subscribes to the view that social structures do obtain from relations of power based in material interests (see Cloud, 1994). Basically, discourse practices are responses to our material circumstances, even though we will never find a language of absolute truth to reflect some absolute human condition.

Third, conflict is a site of identity construction, management, and performance. This assumption is informed by traces of theoretical perspectives such as symbolic interactionism (Blumer, 1969; Mead, 1934) and dramaturgy (Goffman, 1959). One such trace emphasizes the role that symbols play in shaping our sense of who we are, especially as they occur through our perceptions of how others perceive us. Missing in this articulation is the notion that we come to know who we are in the context of who is present during our performances. Through these performances we reveal who we are as we learn who we are not. We do not reveal our identities all at once; often we may conceal parts of our identity that we consider others may perceive negatively or as threatening. However, conflicts engage the hidden dimensions of our identity and, therefore, may even provide us with the opportunity to repair or revive the sides to our identity that we do not often reveal in our routinized performances.

Finally, conflicts materialize from our actual lived experiences. In the Western understanding of conflict, there is some erasure of such social formations that shape our lived experiences as class, race, caste, gender, sexuality, nationality, and age, to name some. The mainstream literature on interpersonal conflict looks a lot like the story of White America (see, e.g., Wilmot & Hocker, 2001). In addition, a limited perspective is offered by scholarship that addresses intercultural conflict without attempting to feel the complexity that characterizes understanding conflict from the framework of our different positionalities in society (see Orbe & Everett, Chapter 22 in this volume). Most dangerous is the erasure of any discussion of how class may determine what becomes of conflict and its mediation or management, because of the faith in such theses as the end of ideology or even in Hall's (1980) closure to culturalist streams of cultural studies that were based on empirical examinations of people's lived experiences, often tied to their class positions. In the Indian context, class is still an important feature of society; in this case the reference being to economic/material bases of persons and what they are able to accomplish in the realm of social and political discourse.

In conclusion, these assumptions combine a constructionist and cultural materialist perspective, a perspective that continues to hinge on some aspect of Marxist explanations of social life but privileging the discursive view of conflict, insofar as what best defines conflict communication is the "miscommunication." Such a position implicates language and emphasizes the "impossibility" of communication, in the process subscribing to a view of conflict as "communication work" in progress. We perform identities as we engage in conflict and yet these performances are based in the different social formations of our discursivity.

INDIA: A PROFILE

Historically, India is among the few civilizations in the world that have withstood the stress of numerous forced occupations, attempted conquests, wars, and colonization. However, all these external interruptions have also made India a strong multicultural and secular mosaic, comprising peoples that subscribe to various cultures, traditions, thousands of languages and dialects, and numerous finer nuances of experience that are far too complex to capture in any simplistic way. India comprises a vast array of persons belonging to different religions, castes, classes, and more.

The complex secular fabric of which India is woven has also been a problematic for India. Multiple castes, religious, and ethnic groups have coexisted in large part by consenting to the Hindu social order. Being a Hindu majority nation, India has struggled through the challenges of having minority Muslim and Christian populations (and a small population of Sikhs). The Buddhist presence has provided succor and hope to a constantly rising global tourist population in search of spirituality and the nonmaterial solace. While Christianity has a history of missionary and church presence in India, especially for the positive role played in accomplishing India's social development programs, more recently the religion and its priests and missionaries have been targeted by ordinary Hindus and politicians alike for perceived religious conversions of people under the guise of social work. The minority Muslim populations, comprising a mix of small numbers of the rich and the intelligentsia and large numbers of the poor and uneducated, have often been positioned as a challenge to India's status as a Hindu majority nation.

The caste system has always posed a challenge to India. The received view on caste is different from the practices that define the caste system (see Charsley, 1996; Dirks, 2001). Even to this day, upward mobility poses numerous dialectical tensions for persons belonging to lower castes (Mallick, 1997). However, developing any understanding of culture from a purely caste standpoint is unproductive. Persons belonging to castes also belong to classes and religions, not to mention their geographic and community ties. Today, in India, religion tends to play a more dominant role than caste, thanks to the wave of religious national fundamentalism in place during the past two decades.

People enveloped in various faiths and religions have always lived together, certainly with the attendant tensions that may be expected of living, engaging, and relating through difference (Pandey, 1990). The meta-narrative of a country deeply entrenched in ethnic or communal conflict, particularly Hindu-Muslim conflict, originated as a colonial discourse. Varshney (1997) wrote,

There is no "scientific knowledge" about the origins, rise, and spread of Hindu-Muslim antagonisms; rather, there have only been "discourses" or "narratives." In the hands of the British, a primordial antagonism between Hindus and Muslims dating back centuries became the "master narrative," even though there was enough evidence of Hindu-Muslim coexistence. Primordial antagonism was not the "truth" about Hindus and Muslims. It was constructed and promoted as such by the British, partly because it suited them to divide India into communities and partly because the "natives," the British argued, could not constitute a "modern" nation. They could think only in terms of premodern religious communities. (pp. 1–2)

A key aspect of this coexistence is that individuals belonging to different communities have always borrowed and adapted from other communities. Cultures are dynamic and have always borrowed and adapted from other cultures, in part, for their own survival. So-called indigenous Native cultures, such as the Zia and Hopi, have also borrowed from other tribal communities for their own ingenuity in survival and appeal. Even though we identify India with three main religions, namely Hinduism, Islam, and Christianity, there are hundreds of variations in practices, as they manifest through varying beliefs, faiths, and value systems.

Most often what is defined as "Indian" culture is based on received narratives of Hinduism or derives from streams of cultural consciousness articulated by urban and educated persons. Mallick (1997) wrote, "As Indian culture is primarily linguistically and religiously based, rather than national, there is no Indian culture that can be defined as universal to virtually all Indians" (p. 361). However, if there is an Indian culture it resides outside of the urban complex. Sprawling cities and urban towns have more in common with New York and London than they do with rural India. There is an occasional sprinkle of rural India in the urban centers, more as a combination of nostalgia for the rural and the commercial value for the esoteric, exotic rural than as a sincere engagement with the romanticized rural "other."

Literature in intercultural communication cannot describe adequately the complexity and contradictions of cultural values or orientations because India is a nation of states and peoples. Most social scientific research that addresses the so-called Indian culture is (a) simplistic at best and (b) based on self-reports or accounts of middle- and upper-class students or organizational members from the cities (e.g., Bradford et al., 2003; Brislin, 1993; Chandra, Griffith, & Ryans, 2002). Writing on fieldwork based research, Mallick (1997) noted: "India can be doubly obscured, both by the perceptions westerners bring to the field, and the perspectives of usually upper-caste informants" (p. 362). Countries such as China, Japan, and Israel may be amenable to simplistic description in value-orientations because of their size and commonalities of language, although this is debatable given transitions and changes in cultures. In addition, their systems of governance have ensured the sustenance of common beliefs and values, certainly with minimal attendant subversions and resistances. Despite the onslaught of capitalism and the mediascapes that define contemporary lived experiences, the forced focus of social scientific lenses makes it possible to capture the commonality of value orientations. In the case of India, the complex layers of society, the numerous finer nuances, the numerous faiths and beliefs of subscription, all complicate and challenge any effort to establish standardized codes of cultural orientation, especially for purposes of categorization and comparison. A good example is Hofstede's (1980) four dimensions of cultural variability that has achieved the status of master narrative in intercultural communication. Based on interviews with a sample of IBM employees in different countries, this cultural script of Western social science continues to be used to examine various cultural dimensions of communication in countries. Clearly, the employees working for IBM in India are in no measure a representative sample or even a token of the cultural landscape of India.

Conflict Types

Various types of community conflicts prevail in India just as they do in other countries. Here, I focus on conflicts that are productive for our understanding, considering them from the perspective of a diverse country like India as well given the assumptions that inform this chapter.

These conflicts range from those that impact a large number of people to those that impact relatively few. Each has an impact on the social relations within the community, either from a top-down or bottom-up perspective (Klein, Tosi, & Cannella, 1999; Rousseau & House, 1994). The top-down perspective focuses on broad conflicts that impact everyday interpersonal interaction, while the bottom-up perspective focuses on interpersonal conflicts that shape broader community conflict.

The kind of conflict that provides for immediate recall is the one mass mediated every day, either through television, the Internet, or political discourse—border disputes. Border conflicts anywhere in the world provide much fodder for uninformed discussion. Next, ethnic conflicts are discussed, more from the perspective of incitement rather than as being generated by necessarily natural and disturbing differences. The next key arena of conflict, one that increases every day, is the natural environment. This section also examines family and relational conflict as more micro-level foci. The primary characteristic emphasized and important to understand in discussing these various conflicts is the role of identities in conflict communication, both how communication is conflicted and conflict is communicated.

Border Conflicts

Borders and boundaries are politically motivated barriers and produce "national" imaginations for the people surrounded by them. They are an invention of Europe and the United States.

Historically, the Indian subcontinent was made up of kingdoms. Kingdoms were protected territories whose borders were fluid, and the identities of people were tied to both sides of the border. The organization, rather arbitrary, of the subcontinent into nations and states is the accomplishment of colonial Britain and its "divide and rule" policy. Quite a surprise, if one visited Britain, to find out that such a small island nation ruled so much of the world for so long. India and Pakistan, with which India is now locked in a bitter border dispute, gained independence in 1947 from the British Empire in India.

Going against the wishes of Mahatma Gandhi, two separate India-Pakistan frontiers were created for religious reasons: one on the west and one on the east; East Pakistan became Bangladesh in 1971, and the western border remains disputed today. The two countries were identified as Hindu India and Muslim Pakistan. Some of the remote areas of the subcontinent, such as Kashmir, were feudal systems, having very little connection to a national government. Monarchs (locally identified as Maharajas) ruled these places, a situation common to present-day Afghanistan with its tribal governments. At the time of the creation of India and Pakistan, the status of Kashmir (a predominantly Muslim area) was left uncertain. Two months after the countries were created, the Maharaja of Kashmir, a Hindu ruler, wanted to retain Kashmir's independence but, faced with an invasion by Muslim tribesmen from Pakistan, hastily acceded control to India in October 1947 in return for help against the "invaders."

These new neighbors fought their first war, from 1947 to 1948, over the control of Kashmir, which, to this day, remains a disputed territory. Eventually a ceasefire was agreed upon via United Nations mediation and the war ended in January 1949 with a promise to Kashmiris that they would choose their own future. Pakistan gained one third of Kashmir's territory, and the agreement allowed for the remaining two thirds to remain under India's control, with a status of near independence. Despite this arrangement, India formally annexed Kashmir as a state in 1956, which provoked rioting among the Muslim population. War resumed briefly in the region in 1965; in 1971, India and Pakistan fought their third war—over the independence of Bangladesh.

These border disputes, including India's border dispute with China (after its freedom and partition from the British Empire), are indicative of a political struggle for identity at the global/national level and a cultural struggle for identity at the local/regional level. The political argument for the accession or even independence of Kashmir, in the name of independence for the people of Kashmir, has always echoed with feelings of religious sympathy. Historically, however, Kashmir comprises a mixed religious population. To consider Kashmir a Muslim state is symptomatic of both ignorance and arrogance. Nonetheless, for the people native to Kashmir, especially survivors of the freedom

and partition, the struggle is tied to resuscitating and reconstructing their lost identity, less about being on the side of Pakistan or India. On the contrary, the political conflict, nationally and often portrayed internationally, involves two countries whose identities are in conflict over a disputed border.

Border conflicts are painful because they involve contestation of identities and sociocultural environmental markers. There are the identities of a large mass of people living within the borders, but at greater risk are the identities of persons living close to the borders for whom the borders are imaginary and are politically motivated. Mass media and even social discourse often communicate distortions about borders, thereby impacting on our understanding of border conflicts.

Ethnic Conflict

India is one of the oldest and boldest experiments in multiculturalism. Multiculturalism in the United States or the now-defunct Soviet Union is not as strongly rooted as in the sociocultural mosaic of India. Ancient India consisted of provinces and kingdoms; independent India was reconstituted from princely states into a nation of political states, with linguistic regionality shaping the state boundaries. Indians have multilayered and multidimensional identities that are dynamic and marked by their situatedness in various social formations such as caste, class, religion, and tribe (Parameswaran, 2002; Varshney, 2003). Even language and region shape how one knows and speaks of oneself, not to mention how one is labeled and spoken about. Individual identities have no known boundaries (despite the linguistic markings that determined state boundaries), and persons with similar identities can be found in two or more states. Consequently, conflicts between members of two ethnic groups can have different origins depending on the time frame and the place of occurrence. Lake and Rothchild (1996) noted that,

Ethnic conflict is most often caused by collective fears of the future. As groups begin to fear for their safety, dangerous and difficult-to-resolve strategic dilemmas arise that contain within them the potential for tremendous violence. As information failures, problems of credible commitment, and the security dilemma take hold, groups become apprehensive, the state weakens, and conflict becomes more likely. Ethnic activists and political entrepreneurs, operating within groups, build upon these fears of insecurity and polarize society. Political memories and emotions also magnify these anxieties, driving groups further apart. (p. 41)

Ethnic identities are very dynamic and are themselves not symptomatic of the fragility of the sociocultural fabric of a country like India. Yet interested persons, almost always for purposes of political mobilization and discourse formation, will galvanize the boundaries of their ethnic groups, creating awareness and politicization of ethnic identities. The new awareness may create opportunities for enhanced appreciation of their identities and for redefinition as well. However, the conflicts arise with the politicization of ethnic identities. The process involves constructing discourse for political and material gains, but with the active enlistment of support from members of the ethnic group. Conflicts among Hindus and Muslims have a cyclical pattern; during the past two decades, to recall recent history, these conflicts have occurred in Bangalore, Mumbai, and Gujarat. Most often the incitement for the communal violence, which results in deaths and destruction to property, is political. The political forces, clearly, accomplish their goals with support of the local police forces. Hindus and Muslims have always lived together. Minority ethnic groups have always found the need to protect their boundaries and interests. As a minority ethnic group, Muslims are often socioeconomically below the national average. In addition, a key factor for Hindu-Muslim conflicts is nonavailability of networks of civic engagement. The towns, cities, and states where numerous opportunities are available to work together, to engage in activities together, are also the places least likely to see communal violence (Varshney, 2003).

The processes of political mobilization of ethnic groups can take on the dimensions of social movements, whereby the government and even the judiciary is forced to take notice and even make legal amendments, the Mandal Commission report and its aftermath being one

such example. One of the divisions, partly discursive, that characterizes India's existence is the caste system. Persons belonging to lower castes have a long history of being oppressed by members of higher castes. The Constitution provided for affirmative action by ensuring that 22.5% of jobs in government services and public undertakings are reserved for persons belonging to the Scheduled Castes (read *dalits* or "untouchables") and Scheduled Tribes. The Janata government (1977–1979) constituted the Mandal Commission to make recommendations on the reservation system. The committee tabled its report in December 1980, recommending that 27% of jobs in government services and public undertakings be reserved for persons belonging to the Backward Castes (not covered in the 22.5% ensured by the Constitution), taking the total reservations to 50%. Nothing was done about the report for more than 10 years. Prime Minister Vishwanath Pratap Singh, during his brief tenure from December 1989 to November 1990, implemented the recommendations. The decision created widespread dismay and anger, inciting protests and violence around the country.

The Mandal decision was socially divisive; it pitted caste against caste in the name of social justice and made no effort to convince those who would stand to lose that they should accept it in the larger interest of society. The Mandal decision, with the support of committed political leaders who were from lower castes themselves, encouraged the potential beneficiaries to treat all those who opposed the decision as representing upper-caste interests, and re-introduced caste as a concept and identity even in those sectors of society from which it had virtually disappeared. Even though the report and the implementation of its recommendations may eradicate the evils of the caste system, it cannot erase the prejudices that accompany caste positions for many. Even to this day, intercaste marriage is a very difficult experience for the few that practice it because of the ostracism the person from the upper caste will face within the family and the immediate community. This is especially true in rural contexts or in caste conscious communities in the urban areas.

Historically, caste conflicts were the most prevalent of the ethnic conflicts. More recently, during the past few decades or so, religious and linguistic conflicts have increased in size and number. Communal (read religious) violence is a modern phenomenon. Linguistic violence has a longer history. When the new Indian Constitution went into effect on January 26, 1950, Hindi was declared the official language of India, relegating the other languages to a secondary status. Hindi is a language spoken in northern states such as Uttar Pradesh that also had a major presence in shaping governance and decision making in newly independent India. Hindi and English are now the national languages of India. In addition, each state has its own regional majority language (e.g., Tamil is the regional language of the state of Tamil Nadu).

The declaration of Hindi as a national language has remained unpalatable for individuals considering themselves natives of Tamil Nadu and who have a strong love and following for their language. Tamilians believe that Hindi was imposed upon the nation, although mainstream political discourse portrays the picture as one deriving from majority consensus. The "imposition" of Hindi upon Tamil Nadu started even before British rule ended. During the last decade of their rule over the Indian subcontinent, the British rulers allowed elected local provincial governments under the British Government of India. In 1937, the Congress Party formed the Government of Madras Presidency (Province), consisting of most of today's Tamil Nadu and parts of Andhra Pradesh and Karnataka. This Congress Government under C. Rajagopalachari (Rajaji) was the first to impose Hindi on the Tamil people. This immediately started protests in Tamil Nadu. Anti-Hindi agitation has had a long history. When Hindi was declared a national language, the government noted that Hindi would become the only official language on January 26, 1965; English was allowed to serve as an official language during the interim 15-year period. After several hundred protests and agitations and numerous self-immolations, in 1960 the first Indian Prime Minister, Jawaharlal Nehru, provided assurance that Hindi would not be imposed on Tamil Nadu. He also assured that English would continue as an official language of India as long as non–Hindi-speaking persons wanted it.

Ethnic conflicts originate when identities are threatened. The threat may be real or perceived.

Nevertheless, ethnic conflicts have consequences for identities in that persons involved develop a stronger sense of the aspects of their identities under threat and, sometimes, do not emphasize the aspects that are not as much in contention. For example, the language conflict between Tamil Nadu and the government of India has led to the people of Tamil Nadu making Tamil Nadu one of the states in India with the greatest demonstrated love for their language. Despite Chennai, the capital of Tamil Nadu, being a metropolitan city and one of the intellectual capitals of the country, one cannot miss the strong presence of Tamil everywhere.

Ethnic conflicts often involve issues of self-determination, and thus I have defined them more broadly than other scholars. For example, Basu (1997) clearly articulated distinctions between caste, religious, and ethnic conflicts. This distinction does serve an important purpose in understanding how power mediates conflicts and conflicts construct power for involved communities. Basu wrote,

> By broadening the definition of community conflicts to comprise caste, ethnic, and religious nationalist movements, their very different implications for democracy become evident. Religious nationalist movements employ methods and seek objectives that are most inimical to democracy; although caste conflicts may generate violence, lower-caste struggles to achieve greater power and representation may contribute to creating a more democratic society. The methods and objectives of ethnic movements are diverse, particularly in recent years when they have taken on religious shadings, but ethnic self-determination movements have contributed to democracy by enhancing cultural pluralism and strengthening provincial governments. (p. 395)

Ethnic conflict, like the struggle over the Tamil language, is tied to self-determination more than it is to maintaining democracies of the status quo that serve the interests of dominant and political groups.

Environmental Conflict

Environmental conflicts in India vary depending on where the communities are located (urban and rural) and the size of the communities; it might be a neighborhood in a city or a village in the rural landscape. Conflicts more often arise from issues of access to natural resources and common property management, and so are most common and noteworthy in rural areas. Environmental conflicts occur over mega-development projects such as dam building that lead to displacement of indigenous persons from their native lands or even forced occupation of land belonging to indigenous persons. Indigenous communities, also referred to as tribes, are most threatened by development (concomitantly, also by encroachment) projects. Seen from their perspective, environmental occupation and/or destruction is the cause of conflict.

A developing country like India is faced with many challenges, caught in the continuing temptations of the modernization project, of the demands of new-liberal economics (that crosses political party ideologies), and of opening up markets to foreign investment. The biggest price developing countries pay come in the form of massive need for water and land. The next world war will likely be fought over access to good, clean drinking water (for a discussion of the importance of culture in water disputes, see Faure & Rubin, 1993). Access to land, while not as critical as water, becomes important when understood from the perspective of the landowners. Around the world, and within India, indigenous people, mostly belonging to various tribes and lower castes, are waging battles over ownership of native lands where ancestors are buried and where prayers are conducted, over access to good drinking water, and over control of local resources.

Conflicts arise when people are asked to give up what they have owned and considered sacred or when their lands are forcibly occupied. Indigenous people have a strong distrust of politicians and political parties because of their association with greed and self-interest. The legal system does not offer indigenous people much hope, either, because of the elitism and pro-development bias the courts have maintained. The media are also biased in favor of development (some combination of capital-intensive modernization and globalization) to the extent that environmental conflicts make for human-interest stories or environmental news fillers.

Recently, multinational corporations have been at the center of environmental conflicts. Consider the case of Pepsico. Pepsico India, the Indian subsidiary of Pepsico, runs a bottling plant in Kanjikode in Palakkad district of Kerala state. The local villagers of Pudussery protested for several days against what they claimed was extensive depletion of ground water resources, resulting in the village government's canceling the water-use license of the plant on May 16, 2003. Pepsico filed a petition in the State High Court and obtained a stay on the cancellation of its bottling plant license, although the court demanded that Pepsico stop production until further notice.

Similarly, the village government of Perumatty shut down a plant belonging to the Indian subsidiary of Coca Cola (Coke), based in Plachimada, also in Palakkad. The plant has been shut down since March 21, 2004. Residents from the villages surrounding Coke's bottling factory noted that the indiscriminate mining of groundwater had dried up many wells and contaminated adjacent wells. Extremely poor people inhabit Plachimada and Pudussery. The state government, in its move to please neo-liberalists and multinational corporations, further revoked the suspension of licenses. At present the local government of Perumatty has filed a Special Leave Petition in the Supreme Court, challenging the High Court's judgment permitting Coca Cola's bottling plant at Plachimada in Palakkad district to draw ground water.

In both instances villagers protested over several months, demanding access to clean drinking water. The conflict was always constructed as being uninformed and motivated by political interests. What is particularly surprising is that indigenous persons who inhabit these villages do not have the monetary resources to muster support (until NGOs came to their rescue) or the resources to construct and transmit discourse that puts forward their viewpoints. More important, the struggle over water is also tied to the struggle over identity. The relationship tribal persons have with land and water has also shaped who they are and how they want to be known.

In most environmental conflicts, the onus is placed on the courts because political parties in power do not want to appear as conflicting in values and ideas with MNCs. Environmental conflicts, in this case, are not exactly moral conflicts either (Littlejohn, Chapter 14 in this volume; Pearce & Littlejohn, 1997). Politicians and courts are notorious for using scientific data, as if science were the lasting home of truth and neutrality (for more on environmental conflict see Peterson & Franks, Chapter 15 in this volume). Environmental conflicts have to do with the struggle for survival, for meeting basic needs, in the face of larger national interest of gaining access to foreign capital and staying the course with globalization and its demands. Addressing environmental conflict involves more than the legitimization of science; it demands compassion and political willpower. The struggle for survival is also a struggle over one's identity. Identity maintenance or management, here, emphasizes the need to have access to the prized possessions of native peoples, namely the natural resources that are their only inheritance in a world filled with material possessions.

Relational and Family Conflict

Relational and family conflicts have various connections to the community. Entering a new relationship is also a passport to forming ties with new communities. Relationships and families derive from and move into communities. These may be communities that shape the social formation of persons in relationships or in families, such as caste, religion, class, and language, to name some. The communities may be also be defined by location, by material interests, and by political interests. Relational and family conflicts, therefore, almost always impact various communities of affiliation and membership.

By relational conflict, I refer to conflicts that occur in the lives of newly married couples. Two common reasons for conflict are (a) differential financial statuses and (b) increasing opportunities for education and financial independence for women. The first kind of conflict often results from perceived inadequacies in financial compensation vis-à-vis dowry from the bride's family to the groom. Stories of dowry deaths are common in the newspapers. Conflicts over dowry from the bride's family are more common to people from lower socioeconomic communities in both rural and urban India, although

there are instances of such conflicts among upper socioeconomic communities that often go unreported in the media. Dowry is a continuing evil that is kept in place by economically upper-class families and practiced religiously by middle- and lower-class families aspiring to gain access to families from classes higher than theirs. Recently, one of the daughters of a middle-class family I knew was getting married. When asked, the soon-to-be-groom's family did not state their "demands" (common parlance for dowry), instead used a new discourse: "Give what you consider is decent." At use here is "strategic ambiguity," which involves the deliberate use of ambiguity in one's communication in order to create a "space" in which multiple interpretations by stakeholders are enabled and to which many responses are possible (Eisenberg, 1984). Nonetheless, what one considers decent in most cases ends up being a whole life's savings (to pay for gold jewelry and marriage). In addition, the decency often involves giving the house, land, and sometimes a car. The price of a groom increases depending on the duration the bride's family has searched for one, the education of the groom and bride, the job of the groom (the most sought after are doctors, engineers, based in the U.S., and government employed), and the worth of the groom's family, with rough estimates of wealth that would accrue to the groom in the event of death of his parents.

Dowry-related conflicts are drawn out, often involving family members of the groom, and leading either to the suicide of the bride (and her children if she has any, although they often are very young) or her murder either by the husband or with the assistance of one or more of his family members and/or their friends. These conflicts involve extensive verbal duels, but the secrecy of the situation, given the prevalence of laws barring the giving and accepting of dowry, makes it extremely difficult to mediate in these types of conflict. Despite numerous information campaigns in the mass media and social intervention programs by nonprofit organizations and the government, the alarming numbers of dowry deaths speaks to the issue of prevailing conditions of patriarchy, gender relations, the social stigma of remaining an unmarried woman, and the continuing limitations in both the primary and secondary education system for female children.

Interestingly, among newly married couples in urban India, where women have realized their goal for higher education and have access to financial independence, there are numerous reported incidents of marital conflicts. These conflicts are more common in couples working in the field of information technology, where the employment opportunities have been excellent for a country like India. In many of these conflicts, women frown upon the idea of putting up with the traditional expectations that men have for a relationship. In some cases, women pursue the need to be in control of the relationship. In either situation, their extended work hours make it difficult for both partners to make the time to talk. In addition, their lack of knowledge or their egos deny them the opportunity to seek mediation. Clearly, most of these couples are without children and therefore turn to divorce as the first and last option. Divorce cases in India are conducted in family courts. Ten years ago, Bangalore, the Silicon Valley of India, had one family court; today there are three courts, each with numerous outstanding cases (Poonacha, personal communication, 2004). Common in the Indian legal system, when a divorce case goes to court, the judge appoints a third-party mediator to work with both partners for about 6 months. Despite the prevalence of mediation facilities, the number of successful mediations is rather slim.

A key dimension of relational conflicts is that differences arise over personalities and identities, more than from the lack of communication, especially given the limited opportunities for interaction. In addition, relational interaction demands an environment different from the workplace. If all one has to relate to are friends from work, topics from work, and problems from work, clearly there is a dimension missing to make relationships happen, and if necessary, to start a family.

Four types of conflict common to the family are (a) between parents, (b) between parents and children, (c) among children, and (d) between daughters-in-law and mothers-in-law. Conflicts between parents may occur for several reasons. Traditionally, conflicts result from the struggle to navigate conventional roles within the relationship, especially as husband and wife.

More recently, conflicts occur due to changing needs and interests of parents. Conflicts between parents and children differ at the various stages of life. When children are younger, especially as they approach their teens, conflicts result from differences in the worldviews of parents and children. Parents and children, belonging to different generations, are bound to have differences in values and meanings for what is of interest to them. As parents age, however, differences arise over the responsibilities of the children in caring for the parent(s) and over access to material and financial assets of the parent(s). These conflicts are better understood from a cultural standpoint, especially the Indian contexts.

Parental conflict is common in India. Among more traditional couples, the conflict can be seen as a struggle for control by the male partner and for autonomy by the female partner. Although decreasing in urban India, but still prevalent in rural India, such conflicts are common in single-income families where women's work as homemakers often goes unrecognized; the resulting lack of financial independence denies women the ability to walk out of a relationship or to negotiate different terms in their relationship. From a cultural standpoint, under the aegis of patriarchy and cultural norms, parental conflict is not necessarily seen negatively. However, most of such conflicts result in both reported and unreported instances of spousal abuse, especially with men exerting physical and sexual control over women.

In more recent instances of parental conflict, especially among younger generations, both partners may have similar financial independence and so may experiment with newer needs and interests. Partners are more comfortable walking out of the relationship and, in some cases, experimenting with nonmarital relationships. In some cases, the partner with the custody of the child will even lead the life of a single parent. Although not common in a country like India, these scenarios are important for analysis and future understanding.

Conflicts between parents and children, before the children are grown—what might be called intergenerational conflict—is not uncommon or unheard of, especially considering that at all ages parents and children belong to different generations. Over the past three decades or so, however, there have been rising incidents of intergenerational conflict. These conflicts point to the diminishing role of cultural values as a mediator of conflict and the increasing exposure to and opportunities teenagers have in matters of personal or relational independence. The need for personal or relational independence is more commonly exhibited when children express a desire to marry someone of their own choosing, often outside of the community, class position, caste, or religion, and to the displeasure of the parents.

On the other hand, intergenerational conflicts that occur between parents and children in their later years relate to matters of estate and wealth. In countries like India there is an expectation, not always expressed, that children will care for their parents as the parents age. Also, preserved through oral narratives is expectation that the parents' estate and wealth will pass to the children on the parents' death. The exceptions to these are in the cases of matrilineal and patrilineal families.

Conflict among children, also called sibling rivalry, prevails to a considerable extent. Sibling rivalry is more common as adults and grown-ups. Sibling rivalries have their basis in differences among siblings, in miscommunication among siblings, and sometimes in larger family issues. In the first scenario, siblings may have differences of opinion on matters of lifestyle choices. In the second case, one sibling might have said something, unintentionally, that hurt the feelings of the other. The third type is more common, where one sibling is in conflict with the family over issues of marriage or life choices and other sibling(s) in a show of solidarity with parents choose to close lines of communication.

The first two types of family conflict involve material factors. In the first case, teenagers exhibit the need for financial independence where parents may consider such a desire as challenging the traditional norms of the parent-child relationship where parents retained some control of matters financial and there was a sense of children's obligation toward their parents since parents make large investments in education in children's formative years. In the latter scenario, there is an unwritten code that when parents die their estates and assets will pass to the children, in different measure depending on the religious/community codes that prevail over such transfer of estate/ wealth. In many situations children, grown up and establishing their own families, start expressing the desire for wealth, sometimes leading to bitter disputes and in other cases to parents' choosing to part with some wealth as a goodwill gesture and to express their love for their children.

Conflicts between daughters-in-law and mothers-in-law have their origins in the joint family system. Although modernization has altered the nuclear family system, conflicts between daughters-in-law and mothers-in-law continue. Historically, especially where the joint family system or its values are pursued, mothers-in-law tend to be dominant and daughters-in-law are expected to be submissive. Recently, daughters-in-law, with changing social and economic circumstances, have been found to inverse the traditional relationship in their favor (see Vera-Sanso, 1999). In either relational order, conflicts are common, most often over struggles for control of the relationship. Conflicts also arise in many families, especially in rural areas and in urban areas among families belonging to lower socioeconomic classes, when daughters-in-law are unable or unwilling to reproduce. Among all classes, conflicts can arise between a woman and her in-laws when she fails to produce a son. Female infanticide is a common practice because of the conflicts that the birth of girl children cause in families. A high premium is placed on boys, partly because boys are seen as having more potential to be wage earners (in some cases to continue the family's line of commercial enterprise) and support the parents, and partly because girls are considered more expensive when it comes to marriage, with the attendant practices of dowry. In India the sex ratio is very lopsided in some states; Kerala is one of the few states with more females than males.

Relational and family conflicts arise over resources, interests, and identities, and are all tied to one's current standing and image within the community. Understanding these conflicts involves understanding the social discourses that shape individual ideas and perceptions. However, conflicting ideologies lead to conflicting messages, making it difficult in some cases for persons in conflict to understand one another. Most relational and family conflicts have their roots in social and economic conditions and, therefore, necessitate extensive critique of the prevailing social order, more focused on political underpinnings in some cases and material consequences in others.

MEDIATION AS A STRATEGY TO MANAGE CONFLICT

This section addresses different types of mediation and provides a cultural perspective on mediation. Attempts at addressing conflict involve questions of individual identity and various personality issues such as ego and face. A common strategy adopted to manage conflict is mediation. Various types of mediation include involving (a) a third party, (b) respected elders, (c) religious authority figures, (d) political authority figures, and (e) corporate authority figures. When conflicts reach the courts, the courts may appoint mediators or negotiators, but the failure to arrive at a mutually acceptable solution may lead the judges to arbitrate. Mention must also be made of an increasing coterie of law schools that run clinics in rural parts of the country where students, with supervision, work for the poor and illiterate people caught in various conflict situations.

A cultural perspective emphasizes the importance of allowing for persons in conflict to air their differences (if possible, without involving physical or material resources), to allow for a cooling off time, to engage with respective parties in their versions of the problem, and then to provide suggestions and solutions to the conflict. Such an approach emphasizes the involvement of "respected" elders (in the case of family and community), and respected leaders and citizens otherwise. Involving respected elders is common to mediation within joint families.

India has a long history of joint families, a tradition that likely will be lost once the demands of modernization and the status of nuclear families become deeply entrenched. When conflict occurs in joint families, the parties resort to advice and solutions from elders. In the case of nuclear families, the marketplace and courts are sought for mediation and resolution.

The problem with the latter option is the cumbersome nature of the process and the extensive time involved in relaying the life context of the conflict, something available to elders in joint families. The notion of resolving conflict is often a meaningless one. To arrive at a state of resolution means more than coming to an agreement on meanings and understanding. Ultimate resolution involves (a) addressing the conditions that led to the conflict; and (b) complete erasure of conflict from our memory, something very difficult and challenging that we experience as human beings. We may at best be able to talk about managing the conditions/causes of conflict.

Modernization produced the idea of privacy and its concomitant values, such as individual accumulation of wealth, ideas not in line with the life of joint families. In joint families, resources are shared, interests revolve around the whole family (sometimes articulated by the elder head of the family), and primacy is placed on the identity of the "family." Mediation, in this scenario, emphasizes the family's needs first. Where joint families are not the norm, conflicts emerge because resources, interests, and identities are always in contestation.

In any mediation situation, the issues of resources, interests, and identities cannot be handled separately. Issues of identity are most difficult to handle. Conflicts emerge when identities are under threat or frustrations arise over existing identities. The conflict, if mediation is involved, can actually forge new identities. To summarize, the key to a cultural perspective of mediation involves (a) the trust placed in elders and (b) an emphasis on addressing identity needs.

CONCLUSION: PRACTICAL APPLICATIONS AND FUTURE DIRECTIONS

The critical/cultural perspective on conflict focuses on power and on struggles over resources, interests, and identities. To understand conflict from this perspective is also to recognize that issues of resources, interests, and identities are tied to prevailing social discourses, sometimes at the local level and sometimes at higher levels. The immediate application of this perspective is to focus on the conditions that led to the conflict and to examine identity needs of persons involved in the conflict. Social mediation processes in the West assume a neutrality that in the case of countries like India is very threatening. Third-party mediators are often not trusted, especially where the claim is made of being and remaining neutral. To be a proactive mediator means to understand the discursive conditions that gave rise to the conflict and also to make efforts to restore or repair fractured identities of the persons involved. Sometimes the suggestions provided to manage the conflict may end up building new identities for the parties.

Scholarship on conflict from the critical/cultural perspective needs to focus on the social, economic, cultural, and political conditions that give rise to conflict. These very conditions shape the discourses to which individuals subscribe for their identities. Extensive analyses and critiques of these conditions may provide more opportunities for understanding conflict, but to also reflect on the human condition. In the end, every attempt at addressing conflict will provide new lenses to the same conflict as well as open avenues where the problematic introduces newer conflicts. This is the nature and structure of the human condition, the premise that shapes this chapter. At the least, it is important that we make the case for talking about conflict and for provide for a social discourse that remains truthful to our condition.

REFERENCES

Basu, A. (1997). Reflections on community conflicts and the state in India. *Journal of Asian Studies, 56,* 391–397.

Blumer, H. (1969). *Symbolic interactionism: Perspective and method.* Englewood Cliffs, NJ: Prentice Hall.

Bradford, K., Barber, B. K., Olsen, J. A., Maughan, S. L., Erickson, L. D., Ward, D., & Stolz, H. E. (2003). A multi-national study of interparental conflict, parenting, and adolescent functioning: South Africa, Bangladesh, China, India, Bosnia, Germany, Palestine, Colombia, and the United States. *Marriage & Family Review, 35,* 107–137.

Brislin, R. (1993). *Understanding culture's influence on behavior.* Forth Worth, TX: Harcourt Brace Jovanovich.

Burke, K. (1950). *A rhetoric of motives.* Englewood Cliffs, NJ: Prentice Hall.

Chandra, A., Griffith, D. A., & Ryans, J. K. (2002). Advertising standardisation in India: U.S. multinational experience. *International Journal of Advertising, 21,* 47–66.

Charsley, S. (1996). "Untouchable": What is in a name? *Journal of the Royal Anthropological Institute, 2*(1), 1–23.

Cloud, D. L. (1994). The materiality of discourse as oxymoron: A challenge to critical rhetoric. *Western Journal of Communication, 58,* 141–163.

Derrida, J. (1994). *Of grammatology* (G. Spivak, Trans.). Delhi: Motilal Banarsidass. (Original work published 1976)

Dirks, N. B. (2001). *Castes of mind: Colonialism and the making of modern India.* Princeton, NJ: Princeton University Press.

Eisenberg, E. (1984). Ambiguity as strategy in organizational communication. *Communication Monographs, 51,* 227–242.

Faure, G. O., & Rubin, J. Z. (Eds.). (1993). *Culture and negotiation: The resolution of water disputes.* Newbury Park, CA: Sage.

Foucault, M. (1973). *Madness & civilization: A history of insanity in the age of reason* (R. Howard, Trans.). New York: Vintage. (Original work published 1965)

Foucault, M. (1979). *Discipline & punish: The birth of the prison* (A. Sheridan, Trans.). New York: Vintage. (Original work published 1975)

Goffman, E. (1959). *The presentation of self in everyday life.* Garden City, NY: Doubleday.

Hall, S. (1980). Cultural studies: Two paradigms. *Media, Culture and Society, 2,* 57–72.

Harris, M. (1979). *Cultural materialism: The struggle for a science of culture.* New York: Random House.

Hofstede, G. (1980). *Culture's consequences: International differences in work-related values.* Beverly Hills, CA: Sage.

Klein, K. J., Tosi, H., & Cannella, A. A. (1999). Multilevel theory building: Benefits, barriers, and new developments. *Academy of Management Review, 24,* 243–248.

Lake, D. A., & Rothchild, D. (1996). Containing fear: The origins and management of ethnic conflict. *International Security, 21*(2), 41–75.

Mallick, R. (1997). Affirmative action and elite formation: An untouchable family history. *Ethnohistory, 44,* 345–374.

Mead, G. H. (1934). *Mind, self, and society.* Chicago: University of Chicago Press.

Oetzel, J. G., & Ting-Toomey, S. (2003). Face concerns and facework during conflict: A test of the face-negotiation theory. *Communication Research, 30,* 599–624.

Pandey, G. (1990). *The construction of communalism in colonial North India.* New Delhi: Oxford University Press.

Parameswaran, R. (2002). Reading fictions of romance: Gender, sexuality, and nationalism in postcolonial India. *Journal of Communication, 52,* 832–851.

Pearce, W. B. (2005). The coordinated management of meaning (CMM). In W. B. Gudykunst (Ed.), *Theorizing about intercultural communication* (pp. 35–54). Thousand Oaks, CA: Sage.

Pearce, W. B., & Littlejohn, S. (1997). *Moral conflict: When social worlds collide.* Thousand Oaks, CA: Sage.

Rousseau, D. M., & House, R. J. (1994). Meso organizational behavior: Avoiding three fundamental biases. In C. L. Cooper & D. M. Rousseau (Eds.), *Trends in organizational behavior* (Vol. 1, pp. 13–30). New York: John Wiley.

Sass, J. S. (2000). Emotional labor as cultural performance: The communication of caregiving in a nonprofit nursing home. *Western Journal of Communication, 64,* 330–358.

Tracy, S. J. (2004). Dialectic, contradiction, or double-bind? Analyzing and theorizing employee reactions to organizational tensions. *Journal of Applied Communication Research, 32,* 119–145.

Varshney, A. (1997). Postmodernism, civic engagement and ethnic conflict: A passage to India. *Comparative Politics, 30*(1), 1–20.

Varshney, A. (2003). *Ethnic conflict and civic life: Hindus and Muslims in India* (2nd ed.). New Haven, CT: Yale University Press.

Vera-Sanso, P. (1999). Dominant daughters-in-law and submissive mothers-in-law? Cooperation and conflict in South India. *Journal of the Royal Anthropological Institute, 5,* 577–593.

Williams, R. (1977). *Marxism and literature.* Oxford, UK: Oxford University Press.

Wilmot, W. W., & Hocker, J. L. (2001). *Interpersonal conflict* (6th ed.). Boston, MA: McGraw-Hill.

19

DIALOGUE, CONFLICT, AND COMMUNITY

J. KEVIN BARGE

The University of Georgia

There is a growing recognition that our communities have a pluralistic flavor, reflected by the wide variety of individuals and groups who have competing interests; some of which dovetail nicely with one another while others collide with one another in dramatic fashion. It is not surprising, therefore, that conflict scholars and practitioners have turned their attention to the ways that citizens in communities ranging from small towns, to large cities, to regions manage conflicts over important social, cultural, and environmental issues. Barge (2001) observed that many of the conflicts communities grapple with are inherently moral in nature whereby the individuals and groups locked in conflict have incommensurate moral orders that move them to articulate the conflict in different ways because they have distinct value orientations toward what is important. Working through moral conflicts within communities is particularly challenging because changing one's position involves more than a shift in the actions or policies that one is willing to support; it simultaneously involves a change in identity, as the deeply and passionately felt commitments that people make regarding how they enact and understand their experience are radically changed.

From a communication perspective, managing moral conflicts is challenging because the normal communication tactics that we use, such as explaining, persuading, and compromising, do not work. As Pearce and Littlejohn (1997) observe, when people use "the same language and symbols in incompatible ways" and when "each side is compelled by its highest and best motive to act in ways that are repugnant to the other" (p. 7), making one's point clearer, successfully persuading people to join the other side, or compromising one's own values and virtues is unlikely. As a result, managing moral conflicts in communities requires us to adopt a form of discourse that allows citizens to listen deeply to each other's moral orders, to explore the particular rationality that each uses, and to create new categories that allow the competing moral orders to be compared and weighed. This form of discourse has been called dialogue.

The practice of dialogue within communities has at least two important consequences. First, it helps people build community by having them collaboratively work through conflict. Chasin and colleagues (1996) clearly demonstrate how dialogue can bring together community members who strongly oppose one another on moral issues like abortion to develop more

517

humane and respectful ways of working together. As they point out, their dialogue sessions between pro-life and pro-choice advocates were not aimed at developing a consensus on this moral conflict, but designed to make the conversations between the two sides less polarizing and more collaborative. Second, dialogue fosters democratic practice within communities. Spano (2001) observed that the performance of participatory democracy, or what others have called deliberative democracy (Cooke, 2000) or citizen politics (Mathews, 1994), depends on dialogue. Dialogue, with its focus on including all the voices of the public within the conversation and its emphasis on the free, open expression and discussion of different points of view, is crucial for citizens to participate fully in the political decision-making process.

While there is an emerging consensus that dialogue is helpful for managing community conflict and fostering democracy, it is unclear what obstacles citizens and practitioners confront when creating dialogue for democratic purposes. The focus of this chapter is to explore the relationships among dialogue, conflict, and democracy. In order to explore the challenges that communities confront when engaging in dialogue to manage conflict and foster democracy, I have selected three important movements in the conflict management literature that emphasize dialogical practice: (a) community mediation, (b) public participation and dialogue, and (c) appreciative inquiry. For each movement, I summarize its focus and the associated tensions and dilemmas that must be managed when fostering democracy. I conclude with a discussion of possible future research involving dialogue, conflict, and democracy and highlight some important sensibilities that citizens and practitioners need to cultivate in order to facilitate dialogue.

Democracy, Deliberation, and Dialogue

[T]he most compelling vision of an ideal democracy is one in which there are ongoing, structured opportunities for everyone to meet as citizens, across different backgrounds and affiliations, and not just as members of a group with similar interests and ideas. In these face-to-face settings, not only does everyone have a voice, but each person also has a way to use that voice in inclusive, diverse, problem-solving conversations that connect directly to action and change. (McCoy & Scully, 2002, p. 119)

Two distinct traditions toward democratic practice and communication exist in the U.S. American experience. Representative democracy embodies one tradition of democratic practice within the United States. The early founders, to a great extent, recognized that a dedication to the public good was paramount for the establishment of the republic (Murphy, 1994). Pursuing the common good was difficult, however, given the post-revolutionary political landscape was constituted by a variety of political factions, each pursuing distinct and self-interested goals. Moreover, the United States' public posed a significant challenge as they were viewed as lacking the self-discipline to focus on the common good, leading to a fear by political elites that they would make unwise and intemperate choices based on heated emotions and passion rather than impartial reason (Jasinski, 1992, 1993). Representative democracy exemplified one way to address the factious nature of political life and ensure justice through the use of sound reason.

Representative democracy is based on two important ideas. First, competitive elections are the best way to elect representative leadership. Representative democracy presumes that the individuals who are elected to local, state, and national offices will be fit and wise, ready to pronounce the public good. While the people may be incapable of governing society directly, they are capable of choosing and holding accountable a small number of elected leaders to govern society. As Matthews (1994) observed,

Officials see their role and relationship to the public in almost precisely the way the theory of representative government says they should: as guardians of the public interest. They believe that the public has an opportunity to vote them out of office if people don't like the job they are doing. (p. 66)

Second, a procedural system of checks and balances is required to ensure reasonable deliberation. Jasinski (1992) explained Federalists, such as James Madison, emphasized the role of checks and balances in the refinement of individual interests for the common good:

> Madison argued that the electoral process outlined in the Constitution provided a system of elections that refined impure virtue and the inchoate public good. In the proposed electoral system, citizens would vote for state legislators, representatives, and presidential electors. Madison explained that these groups would, in turn, refine the public's vision by eliminating local or partial views through their deliberations. (pp. 204–205)

The refinement of individual to public interest moves through two distinct phases: the election of wise officials committed to the public good, and their subsequent deliberation over important issues and problems. For communication scholars, it is this latter phase that is particularly important. The metaphor of refinement evokes the image of a refiner's fire burning away impurities, and when used as a lens for viewing the relationship between democracy and communication the impurities associated with factional self-interest can be burned away only through rational deliberation.

Persuasive rational forms of communication such as argument, advocacy, and debate dominate representative democracy as they allow elected officials to articulate the common good. Factional interests are pitted against one another, and through argument, advocacy, and debate, conflicting views and interests are articulated and eventually managed in a way that serves the public interest. The importance of persuasive communication is not limited to the conversations among elected officials; it also carries over to the kinds of conversations between elected officials and the public. Yankelovich (1991, 1999) observed that representative democracy is informed by a culture of technical control that begins with the assumption that elected officials know the views of the electorate and are able to represent them well. When coupled with the belief that policy decisions are best rendered by experts who possess specialized knowledge and skills and that the public is largely apathetic about issues that do not directly affect their pocketbook, the experts share their information with the public and attempt to convince the public about the validity of their positions in an attempt to win consent. He calls this form of communication public education, which positions members of the public in a subordinate secondary position to elected officials.

A second tradition of democratic practice in the U.S. American experience is participatory democracy (Barber, 1984), or what others have referred to as deliberative democracy (Cooke, 2000) or citizen politics (Mathews, 1994). Emerging from the early U.S. American habit of town hall meetings, participatory democracy emphasizes the participation and contribution of everyday citizens in making important decisions that affect their lives and common destiny. As Spano (2001) observed,

> In participatory democracy citizens are actively engaged in public decision-making processes. This means that they are involved in shaping the issues that confront them, deciding among various policy options and developing concrete projects that allow them to achieve common goals. (pp. 22–23)

Participatory democracy emphasizes citizens in conversation with one another deliberating over what choices might be pursued to address public problems and interests. Participatory democracy shares a family resemblance to Habermas's (1984) notion of the public sphere where citizens freely come together and have political conversations over what matters most to the public. The public sphere is not limited to already existing definitions and frames of problems as determined by the state; rather, Benhabib (1992) noted "the effect of collective action in concert will be to put ever new and unexpected items on the agenda of public debate" (p. 95). By engaging with one another in conversation, new possibilities for articulating issues, problems, and solutions emerge.

Participative democracy, however, does not displace the need for elected leaders; rather it brings elected leaders into a different kind of relationship with citizens. Citizens are positioned as equal partners in the deliberative process as opposed to a subordinate secondary player. Daniels and Walker's (2001) multistakeholder approach toward addressing environmental and land-use issues is illustrative of elected and appointed state officials acting as equal partners with citizens. They observed that the U.S. Forest Service historically had its technical experts analyze potential land-use policies for national parks and lands and develop a plan that then was subjected to a series of public hearings to collect public opinion. Citizens typically viewed such hearings as adversarial because the technical experts of the government agency were viewed as imposing their views on the public: more concerned about persuading citizens about the correctness of their views than listening to the deeply felt concerns of citizens. Daniels and Walker (2001) demonstrated how multi-stakeholder dialogues with environmentalists, hikers and campers, land developers, homeowners, business owners, and the like can be used collaboratively to frame land-use issues and jointly develop solutions. Rather than view their role as educating the public over a particular issue and persuading the public to accept their expert analysis, elected officials and technical experts engage in dialogue with their constituents and collaboratively frame issues and problems.

Participatory democracy emphasizes more collaborative and inclusive forms of communication. Matthews (1994) pointed out several differences between representative and participatory democracy, or what he calls conventional and citizen politics:

> While conventional politics uses a language of advocacy and "winning," citizen politics uses a language of practical problem solving and relationship building. Conventional politics is more about having diversity; citizen politics is more about using diversity and getting diverse groups to work together. Conventional politics looks on the public as a source of accountability; citizen politics looks to the public for direction. Conventional politics gives citizens information; citizen politics teaches the skills of effective public action. Conventional politics is about coordinated action; citizen politics is about complementary or collaborative action. Conventional politics creates public events; citizen politics creates public space. (p. 137)

If citizen politics is about fostering citizens' participation in the democratic process in their community, then communicative practices must help citizens build relationships, use their diversity to address important issues, articulate a common direction, and foster collaboration. Dialogue represents one form of communication that helps participatory democracy achieve its potential by emphasizing the importance of listening and understanding one another while using critical thinking and argument to facilitate citizen decision making (McCoy & Scully, 2002).

The practice of dialogue within participatory democracy efforts has taken different forms. Pearce and Pearce (2004) noted that many participatory democracy practitioners in communities focus on dialogue such as the National Issues Forum (Gastil & Dillard, 1999a, 1999b; Mathews, 1994), Study Circles (2005), and the Public Dialogue Consortium (Spano, 2001). While each of these practitioner groups describes what they do in different ways, they share several common commitments that emphasize developing collective thinking and fostering respectful relationships:

a. Multiple voices, perspectives, and points of view constitute communities. Dialogue provides a space for this multivocality to emerge and be respected.

b. Otherness and alterity are valued. It is important to honor, engage, and understand different citizens and groups within a community, particularly if they articulate a position you oppose.

c. Dialogue involves a richer understanding of the complexity of a situation, issue, or problem. Dialogue helps citizens see the connections among differing positions and interests.

d. New possibilities for meaning and action are generated through dialogue. Dialogue allows for the emergence of new possibilities that may be totally different than the original ideas and positions that existed prior to dialogue.

e. Dialogue transcends polarization by moving beyond antagonistic realities to a seeking of the commonplaces that link people together.

The practice of dialogue does not guarantee the accomplishment of participatory democracy in the form of consensually agreed upon policy decisions. But it does provides a way of being and living together that recognizes the differences that exist among members of a community and highlights possibilities for collaboration.

LOCATING SPACE FOR DIALOGUE AND COMMUNITY

The idea that dialogue can help communities manage conflict and foster democracy has grown dramatically since the turbulence of the 1960s. An exhaustive review of emerging dialogic practice would encompass several literatures, including environmental disputes (Peterson & Franks, Chapter 15 in this volume; Depoe, Delicath, & Elsenbeer, 2004), planning processes (Forester, 1999), public participation research (Delli Carpini, Cook, & Jacobs, 2004), stakeholder theory (Deetz, 1995), public dialogue (Spano, 2001), and community building (Mathie & Cunningham, 2003). For purposes of this review, I focus on three community-based movements: (a) community mediation, (b) public participation and dialogue, and (c) appreciative inquiry. Table 19.1 compares the three movements regarding the commitments each makes and the challenges each confronts when fostering democracy, dialogue, and conflict management. These three approaches were selected because they explicitly linked dialogue, democracy, and conflict and have increasingly been the focus of communication theorists and researchers. For each movement, I describe the process, explain how it is dialogic, and highlight challenges to dialogue.

Community Mediation

Mediation is typically defined as assistance to two or more disputants by third-party neutrals that typically do not have the authority to impose an outcome on the disputant (Wall, Stark, & Standifer, 2001). Community mediation is characterized by the use of volunteers from differing backgrounds who begin mediating after receiving a relatively short amount of training. This emphasis on volunteerism directly places "the responsibility of neighborly relations and the civil duty of peacemaking on the citizenry" (Tan, 2002, p. 289). Community

mediation encompasses a variety of mediation activities, including interventions in judicial systems, family disputes, and public arguments over the environment and land-use management (see Donohue, Chapter 8, and Peterson & Franks, Chapter 15, both in this volume). Community mediation has grown dramatically during the past 25 years as the National Association for Community Mediation (2005) estimated that more than 550 community mediation programs exist, more than 19,500 volunteers serve as community mediators, over 76,000 citizens have been trained by community mediation programs, more than 97,500 cases are referred to community mediation centers on an annual basis, and over 45,500 cases are mediated annually.

Community mediation, democratic practice, and dialogue. Community mediation programs have developed along two different paths. According to Bradley and Smith (2000), one path evolved from an initial effort to reform the justice systems or what Shonholtz (2000) calls the justice center model. Court reform advocates viewed community mediation as a way to lessen the court caseload by diverting appropriate cases such as victim-offender mediation and small claims to community mediation. The benefits to the judicial systems were both economic and substantive as community mediation helped the judicial system reduce its case processing costs and citizens were given more efficient and accessible services that led them to be more satisfied with their judicial system experience. While community mediation centers are not limited to performing court-related mediations, a large proportion of the caseload and financing for most local community mediation centers still comes from the judicial system.

The other path of community mediation was a response to the urban turmoil and social justice issues of the 1960s. Historically, many of the disputes that surfaced within our communities were managed by societal and community institutions, not by the courts. The Department of Justice Report in the 1980s pointed out that several institutions such as the family, church, and informal community leaders would settle disputes before they got to the courts:

Table 19.1 Comparing Three Approaches to Democracy, Conflict Management, and Dialogue

	Community Mediation	Public Participation and Dialogue	Appreciative Inquiry
What is the approach's commitment to democratic practice?	Community mediation promotes local democracy by creating a space outside of the legal system to manage disputes and by strengthening the capacity of citizens to manage disputes.	Public participation and dialogue emphasize the importance of bringing multiple stakeholders together to deliberate about important community issues. Public participation and dialogue processes typically lead to new actions and policy initiatives taken by individuals and groups in the community.	Multiple stakeholders comprise a community and community transformation can occur if they are engaged in meaningful dialogue with one another. Dialogue emphasizes stakeholders having a voice in the process by engaging in affirmative discourse that stresses the positive core of the community—its values, best practices, peak moments, hopes, and dreams.
What is the approach's perspective on conflict management?	Conflict is best managed by having citizens mediate conflicts among citizens. Managing conflict depends on developing structures for citizens to have voice, typically through processes such as venting or storytelling, and to invent mutually satisfying options for reaching agreement.	Conflict is managed by creating forums that foster learning among stakeholders. Creating safe space where stakeholders can explore their own and others' positions and interests from a position of curiosity is important.	Conflicts are best managed by using affirmative linguistic practice. Language, stories, and metaphors used to manage conflict should emphasize past successes, core values, and future hopes and dreams. Deficit language that solicits voices of vulnerability, critique, hurt, shame, and anger should be avoided.
What are the challenges associated with fostering democracy and dialogue and managing conflict?	*Overreliance on Judicial Funding:* Community mediation centers heavily rely on judicial-system funding. This may decrease centers' autonomy as their ability to refuse inappropriate case referrals is decreased in order maintain funding. This may also lead mediators to pressure disputants toward reaching settlement.	*Representation:* Ensuring representation of key stakeholders during dialogue is difficult due to large numbers of stakeholders as well as time and economic constraints. *Fairness:* Maintaining fairness during dialogue poses a challenge as practitioners must balance competing	*Suppressing Voices:* "Negative" stories and voices may be suppressed during dialogue. The result is that certain voices go unrecognized and unheard.

Community Mediation	Public Participation and Dialogue	Appreciative Inquiry
	goals, such as the need to be inclusive by including a large numbers of stakeholders but exclusive in order to have a manageable number of people to explore an issue in depth.	
Lack of State Accountability: The state's responsibility and contribution to community conflicts is minimized as the state is positioned as a dispute processor rather than a party in disputes.		
Cultural Pressure: Cultural differences may challenge dialogic process as a particular culture may privilege the mediator's voice over those of the disputants.	*Overemphasis on Deliverables:* Dialogue processes may over-emphasize action orientation and creating deliverables in the form of new programs and policies at the expense of relationship building.	

The courts have not actively sought to become the central institution for dispute resolution; rather the task has fallen to them by default as the significance and influence of other institutions has waned over the years. . . . Many of the disputes which are presently brought to the courts would have been settled in the past by the family, the church, or the informal community leadership. Although the current role of these societal institutions in resolving interpersonal disputes is in doubt, many citizens take their cases to the courts. (Cook, Roehl, & Sheppard, 1980, p. 2, as cited in Hedeen & Coy, 2000, p. 353)

Community conciliation mechanisms, such as neighborhood justice centers, were created to give citizens an alternative to the court system and allowed them to participate in the prevention and early intervention of community conflicts. Citizens within neighborhoods were placed at the center of the conciliation process as the "principles of democratic participation, drawing on citizen rights and responsibilities and the involvement of networks of community organizations" was emphasized (Bradley & Smith, 2000, p. 316).

The point of community mediation was local democracy building and to create a truly alternative system that would keep many disputants from seeing the inside of the courtroom.

Community mediation programs shared many of the goals of court reform programs but also elaborated them in the following ways:

Address disputes before they entered the formal legal system.

Prevent and deescalate conflicts.

Use conciliatory mechanisms as a vehicle for addressing the relationship between disputing parties.

Strengthen the capacity of neighborhood, church, school, and social service organizations to address conflict effectively.

Strengthen the role of citizens in the exercise of their democratic responsibilities.

Use community support to recruit volunteers as diverse as the neighborhoods served and to solicit appropriate conflicts and issues. (Shonholtz, 2000, p. 332)

Challenges to dialogical communication in community mediation. The conduct of community mediation emphasizes a democratic process where each party's voice is heard and all parties work collaboratively to accomplish a mutually desirable outcome. The importance of democratic process and dialogic practice within mediation episodes is particularly pronounced given the transformative turn in mediation (Bush & Folger, 1994) with its dual emphasis on empowerment and recognition—being able to articulate your interests and positions in ways that others will be able to hear, understand, and appreciate while simultaneously recognizing the interests, perspectives, and views of others. Rather than focus on the way dialogue functions within mediation, I want to focus on the pressures that community mediation centers face and how these pressures influence the possibility to foster dialogue.

First, there is a concern that the judicial system exercises undue influence over the mediation process, diminishing the possibility for democratic process to emerge. Some argue the close ties to judicial systems do not make community mediation a genuine alternative, but a supplement to judicial systems (Mulcahy, 2000). Since roughly half of the community mediation centers associated with the National Association for Community Mediation receive more than 50% of their case referrals from the court systems (Bradley & Smith, 2000) and "form often follows funding" (Davis, 1986, p. 35), the close tie to judicial systems may influence the types of cases that are accepted and the way they are mediated by community mediation centers.

Hedeen and Coy (2000) contended the close relationship between the courts and community mediation centers might undermine democratic process due to a loss of autonomy to turn back inappropriate referrals, the appearance of coerced participation by disputants, and a pressure to achieve agreement. They noted that community mediation centers may not be able to turn back inappropriate referrals because they fear upsetting their major funder. Disputants may also perceive little choice but to participate in mediation because many states in the United States have created statutes that mandate their participation (Thoennes, Salem, & Pearson, 1995; Winston, 1996). Finally, disputants and mediators are pressured to achieve agreement because community mediations that fail to produce written agreements are viewed as "unsuccessful." For example, in a 1998 profile of a North Carolina program, McGillis (1998) observed, "Referral letters from the district attorney's office have a stronger tone and are sent by the Center on official stationery from the district attorney's office" with the warning, "If you choose not to appear at the Dispute Settlement Center *or if mediation is not successful, you must be in Criminal Court at* [specific time and place]" (italics added, in Hedeen & Coy, 2000, p. 359). Such language pressures disputants to achieve agreement, even if it is not in their best interest, for fear of going to court, and also influences mediators to apply pressure on disputants to achieve agreement. This pressure toward agreement is not surprising given that the success of community mediation programs is typically measured by dispute settlement rates (Wall et al., 2001). However, as Hedeen and Coy (2000) argued, written settlements are a by-product of mediation, and community mediation's more important advantages include "its ability to address conflicts constructively, respect each party's perspective, empower individuals to take personal responsibility for conflicted relations, establish mutually beneficial dialogue, and reduce violence" (p. 356).

Second, the state emerges as a dispute processor rather than being implicated as one of the parties in dispute. Mulcahy (2000) observed that many times neighborhood disputes are constructed as conflicts between neighbors such as tenants and landlords, which ignores the role of the state or government as a party in the conflict. For example, Mulcahy (2000) described two tenants in a public housing unit who were in conflict with one another over noise due to poor insulation. When remanded to mediation, such disputants would typically engage in "confessional discourse" (Pavlich, 1996) with each other, reporting their transgressions to one another and locating the blame for the conflict in either one or both parties. What this mode of "confessional discourse" ignores is the role of the state in constructing public housing units with poor insulation in the first place. In this actual dispute, the mediators depersonalized the conflict by pointing out that the disputants were in conflict with each other through no fault of their own, which created the space for them to work through the issue and become aware of how the state contributed to the problem by providing substandard housing. Moreover, the mediators were able to collect instances of such conflicts and report them to the local housing authorities. Mulcahy's (2000) research not only highlights how the state shifts its position from a potential disputant to a dispute processor, but how the confidentiality of the mediation process may prevent important issues from becoming public. In this instance, the mediators were able to collect information and share it with the public housing managers, but mediation is typically viewed as a private and confidential matter, and settlements are not discussed publicly. As a result, important community issues may go unnoticed given the private nature of community mediation.

Third, differing cultural expectations regarding peacemaking can undermine dialogic practice within mediation. Cloke (1994) characterized mediation as an inherently democratic practice because elites do not dictate the outcome and disputants achieve their outcomes through a neutral process. Such processes typically view the mediator as employing facilitative versus directive techniques (i.e., not telling the disputants what to do). However, in some cultures, directive facilitation by a mediator may be needed. Tudy-Jackson (cited in Smith, 2000) acknowledged when establishing a mediation program in Chinatown in New York that the Chinese community expected the mediator to "tell them what to do," and when the mediator did not, felt highly dissatisfied with the process. While mediators from Eastern cultures tend to utilize techniques that emphasize harmony and save the face of disputants (e.g., Baine & Sawatzky, 1991), mediators from Eastern cultures also are likely to employ pressure tactics by threatening and criticizing disputants, as well as demanding concessions from them (Abu-Nimer, 1996; Callister & Wall, 2004). The ability to use pressure tactics in Eastern cultures may be due to the disputant's respect for elders' viewpoints. Given that mediators are often trusted, elder spokespersons in the neighborhood and Eastern culture views elders' viewpoints with honor and respect, the opportunity to use pressure tactics is enhanced.

The key issue in the intersection between mediation and culture is how to balance the democratic tendency rooted in the dominant model of mediation in U.S. culture when disputants from other cultures may not share that impulse. Historically, co-mediation, a process where two mediators representing the culture of each disputant, has been recommended as one way to manage cultural differences (Weinstein, 2001). Co-mediation allows disputants to be heard fully and their cultural background to be taken seriously. However, it does not assume that the fundamental model for mediation that emphasizes disputants collaboratively working out their differences and mediators adopting a facilitative approach changes. For example, consider the typical skills mediators need to develop in order to be effective: active listening, restating, summarizing, asking questions, reframing, reflecting, acknowledging, issue framing, agenda setting, option generation, and deliberation (Domenici & Littlejohn, 2001). While these skills may be adapted depending on the cultural background of the disputants, the overall model does not allow for the development of skills such as pressuring, criticizing, and demanding. Given that some cultures may grant the mediator the authority to perform such communicative acts, it becomes important to see how such forms of communication alter, subvert, or enhance the practice of democracy in mediation.

Public Participation and Dialogue

Public participation and dialogue refer to those processes that solicit citizens' opinions and engage them in conversation regarding community conflicts and issues (Rowe, Marsh, & Frewer, 2004). Given that multiple stakeholders exist within communities, each with differing interests, it becomes important to work with assorted stakeholders in order to manage community conflicts and disputes. This recognition has led practitioners to emphasize more democratic processes that emphasize collaborative and dialogic forms of communication to mediate community conflicts. The community planning literature provides a good example of the shift from expert monological forms of communication where elites dictate solutions to community conflicts to collaborative dialogical forms of communication where various stakeholders jointly craft solutions to community conflicts (see Forester, 1989, 1993, 1999; Healey, 1996, 1997). Community planners traditionally have adopted a rational-scientific planning model, which emphasizes technical rationality. This means that ends must be clearly articulated and the most efficient means to achieve ends identified. The rational-scientific planning model privileges expert opinion because only those individuals with the appropriate technical and scientific training are in a position to make important judgments for a community. Though community planners solicited public opinion, they typically structured meetings in ways that valued expert voices and dismissed citizen voices as being uniformed (Ratliff, 1997). Community planning theory and research has now taken a communicative turn that emphasizes the importance of dialogical communication where a diverse set of voices from within the community is invited to participate in conversation and stakeholder collaboration is underscored (Lidskog, 1997).

A variety of rationales have been offered for the importance of public participation and dialogue for democratic practice (Campbell & Marshall, 2000; Ryfe, 2002; Spano, 2001). These rationales range from creating a more informed and knowledgeable public, to fostering cooperation among stakeholders, to developing effective public policy. Assessing the validity of these rationales requires us to examine the empirical evidence regarding who takes part in public participation and dialogue, what conversational formats are used to foster such discourse, and the consequences of engaging in public participation and dialogue.

Antecedents of participation. Numerous factors have been linked to citizens' participation in dialogues over community issues. Citizens who participate in community dialogues tend to be higher in socio-economic status (Ryfe, 2002), White (Laurian, 2004), longer term residents of a community (Greenberg & Lewis, 2000), and occupy centralized positions in social networks (Verba, Schlozman, & Brady, 1995). Laurian (2004) provided perhaps the most comprehensive model to predict citizen participation. Building on Hirschman's (1970) and Lyons and

Lowery's (1986) model of exit, voice, loyalty, and neglect as responses to stress, Laurian (2004) explored the comparative influence of sociodemographic characteristics, individual motivations, local social context, and trust in government agencies on participation (voice) and nonparticipation (exit, loyalty, neglect) in environmental issues.

Laurian (2004) found that individual motivations in the form of knowledge, perceptions of environmental risks, and attachment to the community were the main predictors of participation. She also found that length of residency and distrust of the governmental agency in charge of addressing the issue was correlated positively with participation. Nonparticipation in local politics was predicted best by trust and resignation. Citizens did not participate in community action over environmental issues if they trusted the agency in charge of the environmental remediation or if they were resigned to the fact that the unsatisfactory situation would not be addressed. The finding on trust is particularly interesting in light of the mixed research on the role trust plays in public participation. Some researchers have contended that trust fosters higher levels of participation (Docherty, Goodlad, & Paddison, 2001; Gopalan, 1997), while other researchers suggested that political mobilization is more likely when trust in government is low and people believe their participation will make a difference (Gamson, 1968). Laurian's (2004) finding suggests that public participation is negatively correlated with trust.

Public participation and dialogue practices. A wide variety of public participation and dialogue models and practices have been developed at both a macro and micro level. A full review of the various models and practices is not possible in this chapter and the reader is referred to several studies that compare and contrast different public participation and dialogue programs (Pearce & Littlejohn, 1997; Ryfe, 2002). For purposes of this chapter, the common themes that characterize participation and dialogue processes at a macro and a micro level are presented. At a macro level, a number of models for structuring citizen conversations have been articulated. Such models include the National Issues Forum (Gastil & Dillard, 1999a, 1999b),

the Appreciative Inquiry Summit (Powley, Fry, Barrett, & Bright, 2004), Future Search (Weisbord & Janoff, 1995), Study Circles (Study Circles, 2005), deliberative polling (Fishkin, 1995), Open Space (Owen, 1997), citizen juries (Coote & Lenaghan, 1997; Crosby, 1995), the SHEDD model (Pearce & Pearce, 2001), design charrettes (Tyler, 2003), and dialogue sessions (Chasin et al., 1996). Each model articulates a set of practices for structuring dialogue, and these are typically applied to a wide range of community issues. Table 19.2 briefly summarizes each model's approach. Despite the diversity of models, "Common to all ... is the deliberative component where participants are provided with information about the issue being considered, encouraged to discuss and challenge the information and consider each others' views before making a final decision or recommendation for action" (Abelson et al., 2003, p. 242).

Take, for example, the study circles process developed by the National Issues Forum (NIF) and the SHEDD model articulated by the Public Dialogue Consortium (Pearce & Pearce, 2001). The NIF model emphasizes the importance of study circles as a way for citizens to familiarize themselves with issues and have input into the political process. A typical NIF process includes the following steps: (a) the distribution of an issue booklet prior to the meeting to participants that focuses on an important topic of interest such as the environment, (b) the completion of a pre-forum ballot on the issue to focus people's position on the issue, (c) a review of NIF's goals and philosophy at the beginning of the forum, (d) the sharing of participants' stories of personal experience with the topic to the group, (e) participant deliberation on the pros and cons on alternative choices that can address the problem, and (f) the use of harvesting—where differences and common ground in regard to the values and any shared values can be communicated to the policy makers (Pearce & Littlejohn, 1997).

The Public Dialogue Consortium developed a five-phase model called the SHEDD model to foster dialogue over important issues within school settings (Pearce & Pearce, 2001). The five phases include (a) Getting *S*tarted—enlisting support from key decision makers and training student facilitators; (b) *H*earing All the

Table 19.2   Macro-Level Models for Structuring Citizen Conversations

National Issues Forum (http://www.nifi.org). Sponsored by the Kettering Foundation, the National Issues Forum (NIF) creates a number of issue booklets on important community and society issues such as the environment. The issue booklets contain general information on the topic as well as the pros and cons for three possible solutions that may be selected to manage the issue. Small groups of citizens are invited to read the issue booklet and have a facilitated discussion on the topic where they engage in choice work (selecting among the three choices) and harvesting (the articulation of shared common ground and potential values that may be shared with policy makers).

The Appreciative Inquiry Summit (http://appreciativeinquiry.cwru.edu/). The Appreciative Inquiry (AI) Summit is a four-phase process designed to elicit best practices, core values, highpoints, and peak moments in community and leverage these resources for positive change. Paralleling the original 4-D model articulated in the initial theoretical explication of AI, the four phases of the AI Summit include (a) Discover, (b) Dream, (c) Dialogue, and (d) Destiny. The importance of affirmative linguistic practice in terms of topic framing and dialogue is emphasized.

Future Search (http://www.futuresearch.net). Future Search is a conferencing technique that emphasizes whole system change by getting all key stakeholders in the room and focusing on the future versus problems. The process is organized chronologically with participants initially focusing on the past, then discussing the present where they develop mind maps of the trends affecting the discussion topic and describe what they are currently doing and are proud of, to articulating future scenarios. The conference concludes with participants confirming common ground and action planning.

Study Circles Resource Center (http://www.studycircles.org). Study Circles emphasize communitywide participation in deliberative democracy. A coalition representing the diverse interests in a community organizes the process and involves people from different parts of the community. Trained facilitators run several study circles concurrently over a period of 2 months. During the study circles, easy-to-read non-partisan materials on the issue in question are provided to participants and participants seek to understand the complexity of the issue and develop community-based solutions. A large community meeting is held at the end of the study circles, to pull together the action items emerging from all the study circles.

Deliberative Polling (http://www.la.utexas.edu/research/delpol/cdpindex.html). Deliberative Polling® begins by conducting a scientific poll using a random representative sample of citizens to survey public opinion on an issue. Members of the sample then attend a 2–3 day meeting where they participate in a facilitated discussion to generate questions regarding the issue. Prior to the meeting, they receive briefing materials outlining the issue that represent differing viewpoints. They then dialogue with experts and political leaders based on the questions they develop. A post-meeting survey is sent following the deliberation that mirrors the questions asked in the initial survey to assess what changes, if any, occurred as a result of participating in the event.

Open Space (http://www.openspaceworld.org). Developed by Owen Harrison (1997), Open Space is a self-organizing deliberative conference. People are invited to discuss a topical theme and come to a venue where they are initially seated in a large circle. Participants are asked to come before the group and volunteer to lead a breakout session on an issue related to the topical theme that they find to be significant. The agenda is completely open, with the walls of the meeting room simply covered with a grid of meeting times with room assignments. Participants create the agenda by writing down the topic they will be discussing during their breakout session in one of the spaces. Open Space is iterative as participants work in breakout groups, come back to the large group to report the results, alter the agenda in light of the large-group discussion that takes place, and return to breakout sessions. Facilitators are charged with taking notes, and during a closing ceremony the notes from the entire process are typically given to the people, who will continue the process.

Citizen Juries (http://www.jefferson-center.org). Public policy makers and government officials may use citizen juries to gauge informed citizen opinion regarding an issue. Citizen juries use scientific polling techniques to create a representative sample of citizens, typically 18–24, that will deliberate on an issue for a number of days and make recommendations on the best way to manage it. Witnesses offer testimony on the specific issue, and the testimony is balanced to represent all sides to an issue. After becoming informed about the topic through testimony, citizens deliberate and make recommendations.

Public Dialogue Consortium's SHEDD Model (http://www.publicdiaglogue.org). Developed in the context of fostering school dialogues, the SHEDD model emphasizes the importance of engaging students as facilitators of the dialogue process (*Getting Started*). Once trained, the student facilitators work at making sure all student, teacher, and administrative voices are heard (*Hearing All the Voices*) and, as differing voices are heard, work at framing issues in ways that foster constructive dialogue (*Enriching the Conversation*). As the process unfolds, action plan scenarios are developed and discussed (*Deliberating the Options*). The results of the dialogue are then reported back to the participants and a new round of student facilitators is trained (*Deciding and Moving Together*). The SHEDD model is grounded in several traditions such as deliberative democracy, systemic thinking, and Appreciative Inquiry.

Design charettes. Design charettes are short, intensive design and planning activities. They typically take the form of group meetings convened by designers such as urban planners to bring key stakeholders and designers together to talk about development projects (Tyler, 2003). Though the actual form of the charettes may vary, they emphasize collaborative work among key stakeholders in a design project. For an example of the charette process, see the National Charette Institute (http://www.charretteinstitute.org/).

Public Conversations Project (http://www.publicconversations.org). The Public Conversations Project (PCP) is guided by a model of facilitation that emphasizes transparency, an openness to participants about the assumptions and beliefs the PCP works from, and developing a set of deliberative methods that foster ownership in the process by participants. A 13-phase model of PCP's Collaborative Dialogue Process has been developed that includes the initial request and establishment of the contract, provisional meeting design, pre-meeting facilitation in the form of engaging participants in a conversation about the topic and the ground rules that will inform the discussion, the structure of the meeting among participants, and follow-up reflections and reports. One distinctive characteristic of PCP's work is its creation of safe space for dialogue by setting conversational ground-rules.

Voices—identifying the topic for the dialogue process and reflecting on the selection process; (c) *E*nriching the Conversation—engaging in dialogue and issue framing; (d) *D*eliberating the Options—discussing the pros and cons of action plan scenarios and moving toward a decision; and (e) *D*eciding and Moving Together—reporting the results of the dialogue back to the participants and having the current student facilitators train a new group of student facilitators. Though these two models vary in their number of phases and their labels for each phase, they share a common commitment to inclusivity—making sure that different perspectives, voices, and positions are honored and heard in regard to an issue, information accessibility—providing participants timely and relevant information, and deliberation—the careful weighing of different possible solutions.

At a micro level, a number of communication practices that foster dialogue have been identified elsewhere in more detail (see Littlejohn, Chapter 14 in this volume). They include creating safe space (Chasin et al., 1996; Isaacs, 1993); developing effective facilitation skills such as active listening, questioning, topic framing, and reflecting (Pearce & Pearce, 2001); and increasing personal capacities such as listening, respecting, suspending, and voicing (Isaacs, 1999). Though a variety of communication micro practices have emerged that are associated with dialogue, two key themes characterize these micro practices. First, micro practices such as active listening, questioning, and suspending reflect a commitment to effective deliberation. Echoing the micro practices associated with action research, they emphasize the ability of persons to inquire into their own and others' positions and interests as well as advocate for their own and others' positions (Argyris, 1993). From a dialogic perspective, the key is to maintain a constructive tension between these two processes (Senge, 1990). Second, micro practices such as creating safe space, topic framing, and respecting emphasize the relational elements of dialogue. Dialogic practice is more than simply collective thinking; it simultaneously emphasizes developing collaborative working relationships among participants. While differing typologies of dialogic micro practices exist, there is a shared commitment to managing tensions during dialogue—both between advocacy and inquiry as well as deliberation and relational management.

Consequences of public participation and dialogue. Public participation and dialogue processes contribute to the transformation of both individuals and communities. Public participation and dialogue processes have been linked to a variety of individual outcomes. The research suggested when people participate in dialogue they altered their beliefs and perceived the sponsoring government agency of the dialogue as being more responsive to their needs (Halvorsen, 2003), were more likely to become involved in other forms of civic engagement such as voting (Delli Carpini et al., 2004; Gastil, Deess, & Weiser, 2002), and became more knowledgeable about the topic and better able to generate more sophisticated opinions regarding policy choices (Gastil & Dillard, 1999a, 1999b). The results suggested that participating in dialogue facilitated persons becoming better citizens as they became more likely to engage with civic life and more educated about issues.

Engagement with public participation and dialogue not only transforms individuals but communities as well. Most of the research that explores how participation and dialogue processes connect to community outcomes is anecdotal. Gastil (2000) provided an illustrative summary of differing sample projects that led to large-scale community transformation. The Chattanooga Venture involved a group of 50 citizens deliberating more than 20 weeks in 1984 over the problems and issues confronting Chattanooga, Tennessee. They identified a set of priorities and solutions such as a shelter for abused women and encouraged a variety of organizations such as neighborhood associations and nonprofit organizations to reach their goals. By the early 1990s, they had accomplished most of their goals. Similarly, a group of 30 community volunteers organized a series of neighborhood forums to discuss health care rationing in Oregon during the early 1980s. Over the next decade, they convened hundreds of forums over this issue with the state ultimately adopting this process using the Health Services Commission, which was developed in 1990. In 1991, the commission used these forums to develop a list of health care priorities. Finally, the Cupertino Project developed by the Public Dialogue Consortium hosted a series of meetings focusing on the issue of cultural richness and community safety in Cupertino, California. The project began in 1996 with a series of focus groups, followed by a town-hall meeting, and a 2½-day training and deliberation with citizens. The project led to a number of initiatives, including a consortium of concerned citizens who work with cultural issues in the city (Spano, 2001) and the development of dialogue programs in the schools (Pearce & Pearce, 2001). The case studies that examine the relationship between public participation and dialogue and community transformation tended to highlight new policies and programs that were developed and lessons learned from the process (Ryfe, 2002).

Challenges to dialogical democratic practice. Several different challenges exist for individuals, groups, and organizations that wish to foster democratic practice through public participation and dialogue. First, representation becomes a dilemma to be managed during the process. The issue of representation becomes important given that certain types of citizens are more likely to engage in public participation and dialogue than others. The research on antecedents of participation and dialogue documents who participated in public conversations about community issues but neglects the issue of who should participate. Ryfe (2002) pointed out that most organizations that foster deliberation and organization addressed the issue of representation by allowing individuals and groups to self-select. The question becomes whether self-selected individuals or groups are representative of the various stakeholder groups within a community. If we presume that fair representation is accomplished by having those people and groups that have a stake in the issue participate, using self-selection as a way of including people and groups in dialogue may have the effect of underrepresenting the diverse set of interests that constitutes a community.

As a result, some deliberative organizations and processes such as Fishkin's (1995) deliberative polling emphasize the importance of constructing a representative sample of those individuals and groups from within a community to participate in public dialogues. Constructing a representative sample for deliberative activities may lessen the impact of "interest capture," which is a function of who gets invited to participate in the consultation process (Harrison, Munton, & Collins, 2004). McKinney and Harmon (2002) noted that citizens frequently complained that economic interests captured public participation exercises because the term *stakeholder* was narrowly conceptualized as persons or groups who had an economic interest in the issue. As a result, Harrison et al. (2004) suggested that better public participation could be gained by setting "out criteria for inclusion, how representative groups are, systematic feedback mechanisms, and outcome targets" (p. 915). Still, it may be difficult and unrealistic to create fair representation given the large number of persons who have a stake in the issue (Rowe et al., 2004). While this may be managed by designing public participation and dialogue exercises that have breakout sessions or having follow-up conferences that involve the different stakeholders, representativeness may not be possible, thus limiting the democratic flavor of the process.

The concern over representation is directly tied to the second issue, maintaining fairness in the process. The ability to create a fair process has implications for the acceptance of the suggested policy outcomes by stakeholders (Rowe & Frewer, 2000) as well as their ability to collaborate in the future (Tuler & Webler, 1999). From a communication perspective, fairness focuses our attention on the process criteria used to evaluate public participation and dialogue processes. Renn, Webler, and Wiedemann (1995) articulated a model that assessed the

quality of discourse in terms of the fairness and competence of the process. They called this a normative theory of public participation that was based on Habermas's (1984) notions regarding the ideal speech situation and communicative competence. They suggested that two meta-principles, fairness and competence, can be used to assess the quality of discourse. The fairness meta-principle "refers to the opportunity for all interested or affected parties to assume any legitimate role in the decision-making process" (Webler & Tuler, 2000, p. 568). This means stakeholders are engaged and present during the process, able to initiate discourse by making statements; take part in the discussion by asking for clarification as well as challenging, answering, and arguing about the information; and participate in decision making. The way they conceptualized the fairness meta-principle closely corresponded to Smith and McDonough's (2001) research that solicited participant perceptions of the fairness of public participation experiences. Smith and McDonough found that citizen evaluations of fairness involved ensuring representativeness so that broad involvement by stakeholders was encouraged, facilitating stakeholder voice and participation in decision making, and the displaying of consideration to citizens and citizen groups by agencies genuinely hearing and responding to their viewpoints and concerns.

Competence "refers to the ability of the process to reach the best decision possible given what was recently knowable under the present conditions" (Webler & Tuler, 2000, p. 568). This means that all participants should have access to information and its interpretations and that stakeholders use the best available procedures for knowledge selection. Rowe and Frewer (2000) offered a similar view of competence by arguing that good process must include resource accessibility (representatives have the necessary resources to complete their task), task definition (the range of task activities is clearly defined), and structured decision making (appropriate tools and techniques are used that facilitate and display the decision-making process). In two studies, Tuler and Webler (1999) and Webler and Tuler (2000) found that the theoretically derived categories from Habermas partially matched the criteria that citizens use to evaluate the quality of the discourse.

The central dilemma for public participation and dialogue practitioners is how to manage competing concerns and trade-offs among differing process criteria when designing a process. Abelson et al. (2003) argued that trade-offs among competing goals are inevitable:

> For example, emphasis on the design of procedurally fair and legitimate processes that provide opportunities for meaningful involvement, shared learning and the consideration of a range of views—the pillars of deliberative methods—are, by design, exclusive processes that involve only a small group of citizens. Furthermore, the outcomes (i.e., decisions) may not be held accountable to or by the broader community. (p. 245)

In order to achieve competence through rigorous deliberation, the goal of achieving fairness as marked by representativeness may be sacrificed, which could lead to lower acceptance of decisions by the larger community. The challenge for public participation and dialogue practitioners is to create public conversations that honor the democratic commitments to representativeness and voice. Addressing this challenge is difficult because even if practitioners consciously design processes that are representative and fair, factors such as different levels of expertise may still diminish the performance of democratic process. For example, Campbell and Marshall (2000) suggested that it is important to design processes that honor all voices by valuing nonexpert sentiments as much as expert analyses. Abelson et al. (2003) observed, however, that even with involvement by citizens in selecting experts and information to participate in the process, they still defer to the knowledge of the "experts" because they do not have the theoretical background to make decisions. Even though the process honored the democratic commitment to ensure that all voices are heard, power differences could not be overcome.

Third, public participation and dialogue practitioners need to guard against a bias toward action and creating deliverables. Ryfe (2002) suggested two different modes of deliberation exist—rational and relational. Rational deliberation emphasized the marshalling of evidence, the construction of arguments, and the manufacturing of counterarguments. Relational deliberation stressed emotion and relationship building during deliberation. Relational deliberation emphasizes "equality, respect for difference, participation, and community" (p. 360). This same distinction can be seen in the dialogue literature that differentiates between dialogue as a form of collective thinking as reflected in the work by David Bohm (1990) and the MIT Dialogue Project (Isaacs, 1999; Senge, 1990) and dialogue as a form of relational practice reflected in the work of Bakhtin (Bakhtin, 1981, 1929/1984, 1986, 1993; Barge & Little, 2002) and Buber (Buber, 1958; Pearce & Pearce, 2000). Ryfe (2002) observed that as deliberative organizations stressed outcomes, they emphasized more rational than relational forms of deliberation. This is not surprising as the discourse of citizens and funders of public participation and dialogue projects is concerned about the "deliverables"; talk that leads to action is more highly valued than talk without direct policy implications. The assumption is that talk that leads to relationship building does not generate concrete action in the form of deliverables such as new plans, programs, and projects.

This duality is problematic, however, because dialogue is a systemic practice, which necessitates that we examine how rationality and emotionality intersect at particular moments in time. It is nonsensical to say that a particular conversation is either rational or emotional; it is both simultaneously, and the issue is how this tension is managed (Barge & Little, 2002). Wenger (1998) concurred, suggesting that such oppositions are not separate, but function as an interacting duality where each defines the other. This requires public participation and dialogue practitioners to determine how best to manage the need for rationality and the expression of emotionality within participation and dialogue exercises. Rather than view rationality and emotionality in a fragmented way, it is important for practitioners to view public participation and dialogue practices holistically and determine how best to manage the connection between rationality and emotionality at different moments during the interaction.

Appreciative Inquiry

The community-building literature recently has emphasized the importance of an asset-based approach to community development and the power of affirmative linguistic practice. Mathie and Cunningham (2003) suggested that the traditional language of community building has been needs based, which places great emphasis on articulating the needs of a community, identifying its deficits or problems, and then proposing solutions to meet those needs. From their perspective, the needs-based approach has generated three negative consequences. First, needs-based approaches denigrate the community. In order to locate the needed resources to solve the community's problems, community leaders must portray the community's problems as severe and its members as incapable of solving them. Second, community members begin to believe their leader's rhetoric, and as a result, feel disempowered and unable to act. They no longer view themselves as citizens who have agency to improve their condition, but become clients who depend on outside groups to provide them services. Third, community members and leaders focus their energy on working with groups and institutions outside their community to help solve their problems as opposed to key stakeholders within their community. Intracommunity links become weakened.

Asset-based community development shifts from an approach grounded in deficit language to affirmative linguistic practice. Barge (2001) observed that community builders who operate from an asset-based approach work are committed to affirmative linguistic practice. Affirmative linguistic practice emphasizes the importance of community members articulating assets, possibilities, and resources as opposed to deficits, constraints, and problems. Affirmative linguistic practice starts by examining what works well within a community and invites community members to bring into language their community's assets, capacities, and strengths. The language of affirmation and assets moves citizens toward articulating and creating resources that give life and energy to the community. Several researchers have suggested that affirmative linguistic practice fosters hope and possibility

within communities and expands their capacity for managing community conflicts, disputes, and problems (Barge, 2003; Ludema, 2000; Ludema, Wilmot, & Srivastva, 1997). A dominant asset-based community development approach that emerged in the mid-1980s, which emphasized affirmative linguistic practice and dialogue, was appreciative inquiry.

Appreciative inquiry, dialogue, and democratic practice. Appreciative inquiry (AI) is a social constructionist perspective toward community development that emphasizes the positive core of community life. AI differs from other social constructionist approaches with its emphasis on creating a positive linguistic universe that crowds out the negative stories, enabling community members to carry the best parts about the past into the future. AI practitioners believe that in every living system there are moments and areas of excellence, and these areas of excellence serve as the basis for creating possible futures (Zemke, 1999). Community development should be based on "recognizing the best in people or the world around us; affirming past and present strengths, successes, and potentials; [and] to perceive those things that give life (health, vitality, excellence) to living systems" (Cooperrider, 1998, p. 3). AI provides a grounded basis for community transformation by starting with embodied moments of excellence that have actually been performed within the community. Since such moments are indeed possible, as they have been performed in the past, the question becomes how particular moments of excellence can be re-created and elaborated within the community. For example, when community members are in conflict with one another, focusing on times when they have collaborated well can serve as the basis for transforming the conflict (Cooperrider & Whitney, 1999).

The 4-D model has been developed as a conversational structure to shape the type and progression of communication toward creating the future and is frequently used in community settings (Browne, 1998; Foster, 1998; Pinto & Curran, 1998; Stewart & Royal, 1998). The 4-D model organizes appreciative conversations according to a four-stage process:

1. Discover: Community members appreciate and value the best of "what is." Appreciative interviews are conducted with community members centering on and valuing the positive core of community life—the best of what is in the community—by focusing on moments of excellence, high points, core values, proud moments, and life-giving forces.

2. Dream: Community members envision "what might be." Provocative propositions or affirmative statements that simultaneously describe the present as well as an idealized future are generated from the interview data.

3. Dialogue: Community members discuss "what should be." Community members talk about what should occur within their community in light of the information gained from the appreciative interviews and provocative propositions.

4. Destiny: Community members determine "what will be" by deliberating on what next steps need to be taken to create the kind of desired future that is articulated in the provocative propositions.

Powley et al. (2004) contended AI is a democratic process (also see Ludema, Whitney, Mohr, & Griffin, 2003). In their study of dialogical democracy in organization, they argued that the AI Summit, which is based on the 4-D model, represented one form of dialogical democracy. The AI Summit brings together stakeholders from across differing levels of the organization and creates a setting in which each has voice. The summit allows people to engage in dialogue about key issues within the organization, deliberate on possible solutions, and determine future policy actions. Unlike traditional command and control structures within organizations, the AI Summit equalizes power among participants and gives them the space to have voice. Though articulated in an organizational context, the same democratic principles that inform the AI Summit also inform the way AI is used in community settings. For example, Bliss Browne's pioneering work in Imagine Chicago, an international community-building initiative designed to foster the economic imagination of citizens, reflects the same democratic principles of equality, voice, and

affirmation that are emphasized in the AI Summit (Barge, 2003).

Challenges to dialogical democracy. The underpinnings of AI are democratic with an emphasis on including all relevant stakeholders in the dialogue and honoring their voices. The challenge to democratic practice in AI is what to do with voices that are nonappreciative, hostile, or critical. AI explicitly adopts the "Positive Principle," which emphasizes the need to create a "positive outlook" by inquiring into the hopes, dreams, moments of excellence, high points, inspirational moments, and best practices of communities (Cooperrider & Whitney, 1999; Hammond, 1998; Hammond & Royal, 1998). Some practitioners and theorists contend that potentially "negative" stories or life-draining experiences should not be discussed during AI, given the "positive" focus of the approach (see Kelm, 1998). As a result, being appreciative in dialogue has become associated with being positive, which has meant that voices of vulnerability, critique, hurt, shame, and anger are often dismissed. Barge and Oliver (2003) observed that the silencing of certain voices in the dialogue simultaneously prohibits particular forms of emotionality and rationality from entering the conversation.

Excising particular voices from dialogue and their attendant emotionalities and rationalities is problematic in two ways. First, excluding particular voices from the dialogue, even with the best of intentions, goes against democratic practice. If democracy is rooted in citizen participation and hearing all the voices, then differing voices, including those that are "negative," must be honored. The challenge, of course, is to work with those voices in such a way that fosters forward movement within a community as opposed to creating roadblocks and generating a sense of stuckness. Second, the adaptability of the community is decreased when particular points of view and emotionalities are not given voice. One of the reasons that democratic practice works well is that by hearing all the voices, alternatives can be rigorously assessed and new ideas be generated. Similar to the literature in group decision making, hearing conflicting, opposing, and minority views leads to the enhanced evaluation of alternatives and the generation of creative innovative alternatives (Janis, 1989). Similarly, from a communication perspective, if a human system's ability to adapt to complex situations depends on the system's ability to construct more complex forms of communication (Weick, 1995), then engaging in more monologic forms of communication that limit the kinds of voices and emotionalities that can be expressed, as opposed to engaging in dialogue with its emphasis on multivocality, diminishes the capacity of the human system to adapt. AI's emphasis on positive language contains the possibility of excluding particular voices from the democratic process, which, in turn, can limit a community's ability to manage conflicts.

FUTURE DIRECTIONS AND PRACTICAL APPLICATIONS

The centrality of dialogic communication for managing community conflicts and fostering democracy is clear. Through dialogic communication, citizens are able to listen to one another's positions and interests deeply and to work collaboratively in ways that address a community's conflicts and disputes. Dialogic communication's emphasis on inclusivity, being responsive to the needs of self and other, hearing all the voices in a dispute, and giving stakeholders a chance to determine their own destiny reflects participative democracy's impulse to engage citizens in decision making over issues that matter most to them. Dialogue, conflict management, and democracy are interwoven practices where each influences how the other is performed.

While each approach to dialogue reviewed in this chapter is unique and invites differing research opportunities, I would like to highlight cross-cutting areas for possible research and practice. Stewart, Zediker, and Black (2004) observed that even though dialogue emanates from several different philosophical bases, all approaches to dialogue share two underlying themes. First, dialogue is systemic, meaning that theorists and researchers approach communication holistically. Rather than emphasizing fragmentation, dialogue theorists and researchers are concerned with exploring the relationships among different parts within a human linguistic system. Second, dialogue is a

tensional practice. Stewart et al. (2004) argued that dialogue is marked by tensionality, "the sense that the whole . . . is marked by both a complementary and contradictory quality that renders it inherently fluid and dynamic" (p. 27). What this suggests is that one way to articulate future research areas is by identifying the tensions that constitute dialogical processes and distinguishing those conversational moves that manage them. Though the contexts for dialogue and the strategies that citizens and practitioners use for managing tensions may vary, the tensions associated with the process of dialogical communication should remain relatively stable.

Dialogical communication involves persons managing a variety of tensions such as who to include or exclude in the dialogue, what conversational topics to foreground or background, what elements of the system to connect or separate, and whether to deliberate over ideational issues or develop relationships. Given the current research, I suggest that there are at least three tensions that dialogue researchers and practitioners should address in future research and practice: (a) inclusion-exclusion, (b) deliberative-relational, and (c) micro-macro practices. I begin by highlighting the importance of these tensions for academic research and conclude by articulating one approach that may assist practitioners in managing these tensions.

Inclusion-Exclusion

One area for future research regards how to manage inclusion-exclusion within dialogical practice—who is invited and not invited to participate in the conversation. The tension of inclusion-exclusion emerges across the different approaches as community mediation wrestles with the issue of what role the state plays in the mediation process, public participation and dialogue grapples with the issue of representation, and AI struggles with the appropriateness of enabling positive voices while limiting negative voices. Future research needs to give attention more closely to how participation is managed given various economic, time, and social pressures and how various forms of participation generate different kinds of outcomes. Moreover, most studies take participation as a constant where the same group of individuals who began the dialogue process remains until it is finished. However, during long-term community projects citizens and various stakeholder groups migrate in and out of the dialogue. This suggests that future research should also explore how transitions within dialogical communication are negotiated and performed when existing voices exit and new voices enter the process.

Deliberative-Relational

There is a distinction in the literature between deliberative and relational forms of dialogue with the former emphasizing collective thinking and the latter focusing on relational processes. However, dialogical processes are infused with both deliberative and relational flavors; they co-occur within dialogical communication. As a result, future research needs to focus on the interconnection between deliberative and relational aspects of dialogue. When do forms of deliberative practice facilitate or harm relational development? When do the relational aspects of dialogue add to or detract from its deliberative elements? For example, one criticism that has been leveled against AI is that it silences voices of dissent in order to build positive relationships. Yet, as Golembiewski (1998) argued, the inability to focus on deficits and problems may limit people's ability to fully grasp a situation and deliberate over future actions.

The tension between deliberative and relational forms of dialogue also occurs when assessing the outcomes of dialogue. Deliberative forms of dialogue tend to be assessed by task outcomes such as enhanced citizen knowledge, information processing, and participation in political activities while relational forms of dialogue tend to be marked by relational outcomes such as the ability for future collaboration. Most dialogue studies appear to emphasize task versus relational outcomes. For example, the dominant outcome variable for evaluating community mediation is whether disputants reach agreement. In public participation and dialogue as well as AI research, the typical assessed outcomes for judgments regarding effectiveness are the development of new policies and programs. These typical outcomes reflect the consequences of effective deliberation; for example, we have reached an agreement on the best way

to move forward. What is neglected in most studies is the assessment of dialogical communication processes on relational outcomes. This neglect of relational outcomes is ironic given that Hackman (1990) contended that one key criterion for evaluating decision-making effectiveness is the ability of group members to work collaboratively in the future. Particularly in the case of intractable moral conflicts where agreement on an issue may never be reached, it would be appropriate to include the ability for future collaboration as a key relational outcome. As a result, future research needs to track simultaneously both the task and relational consequences generated by dialogue and how dialogue constitutes task and relational outcomes and their interrelationship.

Macro-Micro Levels of Practice

Most of the research on dialogue has occurred at a macro-level, in the form of articulating dialogue models that can be used to structure public meetings and deliberations. Little research has explored episodes of dialogical communication with an emphasis on the message-by-message generation of dialogue. As Pearce and Pearce (2000) observed, little research has examined the texts of dialogue because few texts are available. For dialogue practitioners, it is important to achieve a consistency between the macro-design of a dialogue event and the actual communication that constitutes it. We need to have a better understanding of the connection between macro-structures, the conversational architectures that guide how we structure dialogue episodes, and the micro-practices of dialogue. For example, there is good evidence that participating in National Issues Forums leads to good individual outcomes such as enhanced topic knowledge and the ability to make more sophisticated political judgments (Gastil & Dillard, 1999a, 1999b). However, we know very little about what specific micro-processes in the forums lead to greater knowledge and sophistication about political issues. Moreover, we know very little about how these micro-processes lead to larger macro-outcomes such as community transformation. In order to understand the dynamics of micro- and macro-practices in dialogue, we need to develop research projects that look at the connections among macro- and micro-practices and their relationship to individual and community outcomes.

Managing the Tensions

Viewing dialogue as a tension-filled process also has implications for dialogue practitioners concerned with managing community disputes and fostering democracy. As Ashcraft and Trethewey (2004) argued, the process of managing tensions is ongoing; tensions are never completely resolved, they can only be managed as communication unfolds. Moreover, given the uniqueness of situations, practitioners not only must be able to discern the unique tensions constituting the situation, but also make practical judgments of how best to foster dialogue in light of those tensions, whether it is in community mediation centers, citizens' forums, or AI Summits. Though several different models for fostering dialogical processes have been created, such as the NIF (Gastil & Dillard, 1999a, 1999b), the SHEDD model (Pearce & Pearce, 2001), and the AI Summit (Powley et al., 2004), preexisting models for fostering dialogue cannot simply be applied in a wholesale fashion to situations. Rather, practitioners need to make judgments of how best to adapt, alter, and modify their model of dialogical communication to the particulars of situations. This may mean altering the dominant model that they use to create dialogue, such as making minor modifications to the sequence of phases in the SHEDD model, or finding ways to blend differing models such as the SHEDD model with AI. Practitioners find themselves constantly tacking between the principles that inform their practice and the models they use to foster dialogue and the unique particulars of situations.

Consider the following two examples that illustrate how practitioners tack back and forth between their principles and the dialogue models they employ. First, dialogue practitioners must make situated judgments about how best to implement a particular model within specific situations. For example, we know that culture has the potential to influence and alter our patterns of communication and that practitioners should take into account the importance of culture when designing dialogical forums. Nevertheless, most empirical studies of public participation and AI diminish the role that culture plays in the design and implementation of dialogical forums. For example, in the public participation literature, most research examines how public participation occurs within a specific country or region and is more concerned with explaining how a particular process works as opposed to exploring how the culture influences the design of the process or drawing critical cross-cultural comparisons and the resulting implications for practice (e.g., Alfasi, 2003; Aprioku, 1998; Rogers, 2003; Smith & Vawda, 2003; Tabara, Sauri, & Cerdan, 2003; Vari, 2002; Vasconcelos, Hamilton, & Barrett, 2000; Wiseman, Mooney, Berry, & Tang, 2003). Nevertheless, practitioners need to take into account how the specific model they employ may be adapted to the unique cultural constraints within a given situation. For example, Barge, Lee, Maddux, Nabring, and Townsend (2004) examined how dialogical communication was structured in a change process that was designed to elaborate the information technology infrastructure at tribal colleges and universities and elaborate Native Americans' technological capacity. Operating from an appreciative perspective, the process designers faced the following question: "What does it mean to act appreciatively within a Native American cultural context?" One of the responses they developed was to open each event with a Native American ceremony or prayer to affirm Indian people's values and beliefs. The particular response they created was not described in any of the existing literature; rather, it emerged from being committed to the importance of fostering appreciation and drawing on the resources of the culture to create an opening for meetings that was appreciative and culturally appropriate.

Second, dialogue practitioners may need to make situated judgments about how best to blend differing dialogue models within specific situations. Assume that you are a dialogical practitioner who is committed to the principles of inclusivity (hearing all the voices), authenticity (people should be transparent in their communication), and ownership (people should feel that they are able to shape the process). When you facilitate dialogue processes in school settings, you normally use the SHEDD model. However, you sense from the participants in the school that you currently are working with that many key stakeholders—students, parents, and teachers—do not feel that their voices are being heard. As a result, you feel that when it comes to the phase of "Deliberating the Options," you need to do more than simply have the facilitator present the action scenarios and begin deliberation. Instead, you borrow from the NIF process and create an issues booklet that summarizes three different solutions to the problem, each emphasizing a different voice, such as the student, parent, or teacher. Your intent is to facilitate the participants' taking differing voices into account during their deliberation. However, as the deliberation phase unfolds, you sense that new issues and voices are emerging in the conversation that you had not planned for. You then decide to honor these voices by doing an impromptu version of open space to make sure these issues and voices are heard (Owen, 1997). You have participants volunteer to lead small group discussions on an issue that they find to be important. At the close of the small group discussions, each facilitator reports back to the entire group on their recommendations. Even though the dialogic practitioner began with the SHEDD model, the practitioner integrated other elements such as issues booklets and open space from other models in order to ensure that all voices were heard and respected. In so doing, the practitioner honored the commitments of inclusivity and ownership while modifying the model given the particulars of the situation.

Practitioners, as a result, need to develop the ability to make wise choices in situations for the best way to foster dialogue and democratic process. There is a growing literature that emphasizes the importance of practitioners being reflective (Schon, 1983, 1987) or deliberative (Forester, 1999), which means they must be able to make situated judgments about how best to move the conversation among stakeholders forward. Barge (2003) contended that practitioners develop sensibilities that allow them to make situated judgments regarding how to act within a conversation and manage competing tensions. Sensibilities are the moral-aesthetic commitments practitioners make regarding how best to work with human systems made up of multiple stakeholders. In a sense, they are guiding principles or sensitizing concepts that

practitioners rely on when they make judgments about how to structure dialogue. They are moral in the sense that they point to what practitioners should give attention to when they make decisions, and they are aesthetic in the sense that they inform what the practitioner views as beautiful or elegant practice. Barge (2003) argued community-building practitioners should cultivate four sensibilities that allow them to make wise choices:

1. Affirmative sensibility: A sensibility for what generates life and needs to be appreciated in the moment. Community builders should develop communication frameworks that notice and inquire into the life-generating moments of excellence within community life.

2. Relational sensibility: A sensibility for the unique historical and social circumstances that have informed this moment in community life and how people, situations, and actions fit together. Rather than view a community as a set of independent parts, community builders need to engage communities as systems of persons-in-conversations that have a history and share possible futures.

3. Generative sensibility: A sensibility for creating transformation within a community through practical action. Community programs and interventions should emphasize an action orientation that builds the capacity of individuals and institutions to develop initiatives and actions for creating change.

4. Imaginative sensibility: A sensibility for creating programs and interventions that are fun, novel, and engaging. Community transformation depends on capturing the imagination of participants, which involves creating events that inspire one's imaginative abilities. (p. 79)

These sensibilities are particularly helpful for dialogical practitioners. Practitioners are always making choices of how to manage participation in dialogue, how to deal with the sometimes opposing demands of deliberation and relational management, and how to ensure a coherency between the macro- and micro-structures that constitute dialogic practice. The way these tensions show themselves in differing situations will vary, and if practitioners wish to maintain a coherency in their practice within and across dialogical episodes, they need to make wise choices that reflect their sensibilities. Do the decisions I make to structure the conversation in this way take into account the unique socio-historical contexts we are acting from? Is the choice I am making likely to generate life and transformation? Will my judgment enable persons to act with agency and become engaged in and inspired by the process? The specific ways that practitioners structure dialogical communication to manage conflict and foster democracy will be unique to the emerging situation, but they will be grounded in a set of commitments that cut across differing contexts.

These four sensibilities are offered for their heuristic value and should not be considered as definitive or exhaustive. Rather, the point I wish to make is that it is critical for practitioners to articulate their sensibility toward dialogic practice. Their sensibility provides a way for them to reflect on the appropriateness of particular ways of structuring the conversation when making decisions and also provides a way to ensure coherency within their practice. Even though the specific way they engage and structure dialogical communication will be uniquely tailored to the uniqueness of the situation, there should be a sense of "family resemblance" (Wittgenstein, 1953) regarding their practice within and across dialogical episodes, which can be traced to their sensibility toward dialogue. From an academic perspective, future research needs to explore the kinds of dialogical sensibilities that practitioners develop to guide their practice.

A Beginning and an Ending

Mikhail Bakhtin (1929/1984) observed, "The single adequate form for verbally expressing authentic human life is the open-ended dialogue. Life by its very nature is dialogic. To live means to participate in dialogue" (p. 293). Dialogue is a continually emerging phenomenon that never ends, with each utterance simultaneously being a response to what has transpired previously and an invitation to take the conversation in a new direction. The focus of this chapter has been to highlight the intersections

among democratic practice, dialogue, conflict, and community. As a result, this chapter is partially a response to what has transpired previously in deliberative democracy, community mediation, public participation and dialogue, and appreciative inquiry. It draws together seemingly disparate approaches to dialogue and articulates some of the common tensions that merit the attention of dialogic theorists and practitioners: (a) inclusion-exclusion, (b) deliberative-relational, and (c) micro-macro levels of practice. The chapter concludes by inviting readers to think about the role that tension management and sensibility play in persons' ability to create and sustain dialogue. The hope is that the concepts of tension management and sensibility may help us elaborate our conversation about dialogue in useful ways.

Dialogue is crucial to our ability to work through our disputes and conflicts and build a healthy democracy. As Mathews (1994) argued,

> New thinking concentrates on bringing together all the parts of a community, in all of their differences. Creating a majority is not enough. No one today has made this point better than Mary Parker Follett: "Our rate of progress . . . depend[s] upon our understanding that man . . . gets . . . power through his capacity to join with others to form a real whole, a living group. Give your difference, welcome my difference, unify all difference in the larger whole, such is the law of growth." (p. 146)

Dialogue represents a form of communicative practice that helps us surface and manage our differences constructively and form a democratic society. When we honor the voices of different stakeholders, we learn from another, and this learning allows us to grow our collective capacity to collaborate and work together.

References

Abelson, J., Forest, P., Eyles, J., Smith, P., Martin, E., & Gauvin, F. (2003). Deliberations about deliberative methods: Issues in the design and evaluation of public participation processes. *Social Science and Medicine, 57,* 239–251.

Abu-Nimer, M. (1996). Conflict resolution approaches: Western and Middle Eastern lessons and possibilities. *American Journal of Economics and Sociology, 55,* 35–52.

Alfasi, N. (2003). Is public participation making urban planning more democratic? The Israeli experience. *Planning Theory and Practice, 4,* 185–202.

Aprioku, I. M. (1998). Local planning and public participation: The case of waterfront redevelopment in Port Harcourt, Nigeria. *Planning Perspectives, 13,* 69–88.

Argyris, C. (1993). *Knowledge for action: A guide to overcoming barriers to organizational change.* San Francisco: Jossey-Bass.

Ashcraft, K. L., & Trethewey, A. (2004). Developing tension: An agenda for applied research on the organization of irrationality. *Journal of Applied Communication Research, 32,* 171–181.

Baine, D., & Sawatzky, D. (1991). Mediation methods as an adjunct to counseling couples. *International Journal for the Advancement of Counseling, 14,* 237–284.

Bakhtin, M. M. (1981). *The dialogic imagination.* Austin: University of Texas Press.

Bakhtin, M. M. (1984). *Problems of Dostoevsky's poetics* (C. Emerson, Ed. & Trans.). Minneapolis: University of Minnesota Press. (Original work published 1929)

Bakhtin, M. M. (1986). *Speech genres and other late essays.* Austin: University of Texas Press.

Bakhtin, M. M. (1993). *Toward a philosophy of the act.* Austin: University of Texas Press.

Barber, B. (1984). *Strong democracy: Participatory politics for a new age.* Berkeley: University of California Press.

Barge, J. K. (2001). Creating healthy communities through affirmative conflict communication. *Conflict Resolution Quarterly, 19,* 89–102.

Barge, J. K. (2003). Hope, communication, and community building. *Southern Communication Journal, 69,* 63–81.

Barge, J. K., Lee, M., Maddux, K., Nabring, R., & Townsend, B. (2004, November). *Dialogical communication, tension, and organizational change.* Paper presented at the annual meeting of the National Communication Association, Chicago.

Barge, J. K., & Little, M. (2002). Dialogical wisdom, communicative practice, and organizational life. *Communication Theory, 12,* 365–397.

Barge, J. K., & Oliver, C. (2003). Working with appreciation in managerial practice. *Academy of Management Review, 28,* 124–142.

Benhabib, S. (1992). *Situating the self: Gender, community, and postmodernism in contemporary ethics.* New York: Routledge.

Bohm, D. (1990). *David Bohm: On dialogue.* Ojai, CA: David Bohm Seminars.

Bradley, S., & Smith, M. (2000). Community mediation: Reflections on a quarter century of practice. *Mediation Quarterly, 17,* 315–320.

Browne, B. (1998). Imagine Chicago: A study in intergenerational appreciative inquiry. In S. A. Hammond & C. Royal (Eds.), *Lessons from the field: Applying appreciative inquiry* (pp. 76–89). Plano, TX: Practical Press.

Buber, M. (1958). *I and thou* (2nd ed.; R. G. Smith, Trans.). New York: Scribner.

Bush, R. A. B., & Folger, J. P. (1994). *The promise of mediation: Responding to conflict through empowerment and recognition.* San Francisco: Jossey-Bass.

Callister, R. R., & Wall, J. A., Jr. (2004). Thai and U.S. community mediation. *Journal of Conflict Resolution, 48,* 573–598.

Campbell, H., & Marshall, R. (2000). Public involvement and planning: Looking beyond the one to the many. *International Planning Studies, 5,* 321–344.

Chasin, R., Herzig, M., Roth, S., Chasin, L., Becker, C., & Stains, R. R., Jr. (1996). From diatribe to dialogue on divisive public issues: Approaches drawn from family therapy. *Mediation Quarterly, 13,* 323–344.

Cloke, K. (1994). *Mediation: Revenge and the magic of forgiveness.* Santa Monica, CA: Center for Dispute Resolution.

Cook, R. F., Roehl, J. A., & Sheppard, D. I. (1980). *Neighborhood justice centers field test: Final evaluation report.* Washington, DC: U.S. Department of Justice.

Cooke, M. (2000). Five arguments for deliberative democracy. *Political Studies, 48,* 947–969.

Cooperrider, D. (1998). Foreword: What is appreciative inquiry. In S. A. Hammond & C. Royal (Eds.), *Lessons from the field: Applying appreciative inquiry* (p. 3). Plano, TX: Practical Press.

Cooperrider, D. L., & Whitney, D. (1999). *Appreciative inquiry.* San Francisco: Berrett-Koehler.

Coote, A., & Lenaghan, J. (1997). *Citizens' juries: Theory into practice.* London: Institute for Public Policy Research.

Crosby, N. (1995). Citizens' juries: One solution for difficult environmental questions. In O. Renn, T. Webler, & P. Wiedelmann (Eds.), *Fairness and competence in citizen participation: Evaluating models for environmental discourse* (pp. 157–174). Boston: Kluwer Academic.

Daniels, S. E., & Walker, G. B. (2001). *Working through environmental conflict: The collaborative learning approach*. New York: Praeger.

Davis, A. (1986). *Community mediation in Massachusetts: A decade of development, 1975–1986*. Salem, MA: Administrative Office of the District Court.

Deetz, S. (1995). *Transforming communication, transforming business*. Cresskill, NJ: Hampton Press.

Delli Carpini, M. X., Cook, F. L., & Jacobs, L. R. (2004). Public deliberation, discursive participation, and citizen engagement: A review of the empirical literature. *Annual Review of Political Science, 7,* 315–344.

Depoe, S. P., Delicath, J. W., & Elsenbeer, M. F. A. (2004). *Communication and public participation in environmental decision making*. Albany: State University of New York Press.

Docherty, I., Goodlad, R., & Paddison, R. (2001). Civic culture, community and citizen participation in contrasting neighborhoods. *Urban Studies, 38,* 2225–2250.

Domenici, K., & Littlejohn, S. W. (2001). *Mediation: Empowerment in conflict management*. Prospect Heights, IL: Waveland.

Fishkin, J. (1995). *The voice of the people*. New Haven, CT: Yale University Press.

Forester, J. (1989). *Planning in the face of power*. Berkeley: University of California Press.

Forester, J. (1993). *Critical theory, public policy, and planning practice*. Albany: State University of New York Press.

Forester, J. (1999). *The deliberative practitioner: Encouraging participatory planning processes*. Cambridge: MIT Press.

Foster, M. S. (1998). Imagine Dallas: Appreciative inquiry for a community. In S. A. Hammond & C. Royal (Eds.), *Lessons from the field: Applying appreciative inquiry* (pp. 90–99). Plano, TX: Practical Press.

Gamson, W. A. (1968). *Power and discontent*. Homewood, IL: Dorsey.

Gastil, J. (2000). *By popular demand*. Berkeley: University of California Press.

Gastil, J., Deess, E. P., & Weiser, P. (2002). Civic awakening in the jury room: A test of the connection between jury deliberation and political participation. *Journal of Politics, 64,* 585–595.

Gastil, J., & Dillard, J. P. (1999a). The aims, methods, and effects of deliberative civic education through the National Issues Forums. *Communication Education, 48,* 179–192.

Gastil, J., & Dillard, J. P. (1999b). Increasing political sophistication through public deliberation. *Political Communication, 16,* 3–23.

Golembiewski, R. T. (1998). Appreciating appreciative inquiry: Diagnosis and perspectives on how to do better. In W. A. Pasmore & R. W. Woodman (Eds.), *Research in organizational change and development* (Vol. 11, pp. 1–45). Greenwich, CT: JAI.

Gopalan, P. (1997). The trust factor in participation and social education. *Annals of the American Academy of Political and Social Science, 554,* 179–192.

Greenberg, M., & Lewis, J. (2000). Brownfield redevelopment, preferences and public involvement: A case study of an ethnically mixed neighborhood. *Urban Studies, 37,* 2501–2514.

Habermas, J. (1984). *The theory of communicative action I: Reason and the rationalization of society*. Boston: Beacon.

Hackman, J. R. (Ed.). (1990). *Groups that work (and those that don't.)*. San Francisco: Jossey-Bass.

Halvorsen, K. E. (2003). Assessing the effects of public participation. *Public Administration Review, 63,* 535–543.

Hammond, S. A. (1998). *The thin book of appreciative inquiry* (2nd ed.). Plano, TX: Thin Book.

Hammond, S. A., & Royal, C. (1998). *Lessons from the field: Applying appreciative inquiry*. Plano, TX: Practical Press.

Harrison, C. M., Munton, R. J. C., & Collins, K. (2004). Experimental discursive spaces: Policy processes, public participation and the Greater London Authority. *Urban Studies, 41,* 903–917.

Harrison, O. (1997). *Open space technology: A user's guide* (2nd ed.). San Francisco: Berrett-Koehler.

Healey, P. (1996). The communicative turn in planning theory and its implication for spatial strategy formation. *Environment and Planning B: Planning and Design B, 23,* 207–234.

Healey, P. (1997). *Collaborative planning: Making frameworks in fragmented societies*. London: Macmillan.

Hedeen, T., & Coy, P. G. (2000). Community mediation and the court system: The ties that bind. *Mediation Quarterly, 17,* 351–367.

Hirschman, A. O. (1970). *Exit, voice, and loyalty: Responses to decline in firms, organizations, and states.* Cambridge, MA: Harvard University Press.

Isaacs, W. (1999). *Dialogue and the art of thinking together.* New York: Currency.

Isaacs, W. N. (1993). Taking flight: Dialogue, collective thinking, and organizational learning. *Organizational Dynamics, 22,* 24–39.

Janis, I. (1989). *Crucial decisions.* New York: Harper.

Jasinski, J. (1992). Rhetoric and judgment in the constitutional ratification debate of 1787–1788: An exploration in the relationship between theory and critical practice. *Quarterly Journal of Speech, 78,* 197–218.

Jasinski, J. (1993). The feminization of liberty, domesticated virtue, and the reconstitution of power and authority in early American political discourse. *Quarterly Journal of Speech, 79,* 146–164.

Kelm, J. (1998). Introducing the appreciative inquiry philosophy. In S. A. Hammond & C. Royal (Eds.), *Lessons from the field: Applying appreciative inquiry* (pp. 158–171). Plano, TX: Practical Press.

Laurian, L. (2004). Public participation in decision making. *Journal of the American Planning Association, 70,* 53–65.

Lidskog, R. (1997). From conflict to communication? Public participation and critical communication as a solution to siting conflicts in planning for hazardous waste. *Planning Practice & Research, 12,* 239–249.

Ludema, J. D. (2000). From deficit discourse to vocabularies of hope: The power of appreciation. In D. L. Cooperrider, P. F. Sorensen, Jr., D. Whitney, & T. F. Yaeger (Eds.), *Appreciative inquiry: Rethinking human organization toward a positive theory of change* (pp. 265–287). Champaign, IL: Stipes.

Ludema, J. D., Whitney, D., Mohr, B. J., & Griffin, T. J. (2003). *The Appreciative Inquiry Summit.* San Francisco: Berrett-Koehler.

Ludema, J. D., Wilmot, T. R., & Srivastva, S. (1997). Organizational hope: Reaffirming the constructive task of social and organizational inquiry. *Human Relations, 50,* 1015–1052.

Lyons, W. E., & Lowery, D. (1986). The organization of political space and citizen responses to dissatisfaction in urban communities: An integrative model. *Journal of Politics, 48,* 321–346.

Mathews, D. (1994). *Politics for people: Finding a responsible public voice.* Urbana: University of Illinois Press.

Mathie, A., & Cunningham, G. (2003). From clients to citizens: Asset-based community development as a strategy for community-driven development. *Development in Practice, 13,* 474–486.

McCoy, M. L., & Scully, P. L. (2002). Deliberative dialogue to expand civic engagement: What kind of talk does democracy need? *National Civic Review, 91,* 117–135.

McGillis, D. (1998). *Resolving community conflict: The dispute settlement center of Durham, North Carolina.* Washington, DC: National Institute of Justice.

McKinney, M., & Harmon, W. (2002). Public participation in environmental decision making: Is it working? *National Civic Review, 91,* 149–170.

Mulcahy, L. (2000). The devil and the deep blue sea? A critique of the ability of communication mediation to suppress and facilitate participation in civil life. *Journal of Law & Society, 27,* 133–150.

Murphy, J. M. (1994). Civic republicanism in the modern age: Adlai Stevenson in the 1952 presidential campaign. *Quarterly Journal of Speech, 80,* 313–328.

National Association for Community Mediation. (2005). *Community mediation program statistics.* Retrieved February 15, 2005, from http://www.nafcm.org/

Owen, H. (1997). *Open space technology: A user's guide* (2nd ed.). San Francisco: Berrett-Koehler.

Pavlich, G. (1996). The power of community mediation: Government and formation of self-identity. *Law & Society Review, 30,* 707–733.

Pearce, K. A., & Pearce, W. B. (2001). The Public Dialogue Consortium's school-wide dialogue process: A communication approach to develop citizenship skills and enhance school climate. *Communication Theory, 11,* 105–123.

Pearce, W. B., & Littlejohn, S. W. (1997). *Moral conflict.* Thousand Oaks, CA: Sage.

Pearce, W. B., & Pearce, K. A. (2000). Combining passions and abilities: Toward dialogic virtuosity. *Southern Communication Journal, 65,* 161–175.

Pearce, W. B., & Pearce, K. A. (2004). Taking a communication perspective on dialogue. In R. Anderson, L. A. Baxter, & K. N. Cissna (Eds.), *Dialogue: Theorizing difference in communication studies* (pp. 39–56). Thousand Oaks, CA: Sage.

Pinto, M., & Curran, M. (1998). The Laguna Beach Education Foundation, Schoolpower. In S. A. Hammond & C. Royal (Eds.), *Lessons from the field: Applying appreciative inquiry* (pp. 16–47). Plano, TX: Practical Press.

Powley, E. H., Fry, R. E., Barrett, F. J., & Bright, D. S. (2004). Dialogic democracy meets command and control: Transformation through the Appreciative Inquiry Summit. *Academy of Management Executive, 18,* 67–80.

Ratliff, J. N. (1997). The politics of nuclear waste: An analysis of a public hearing on the proposed Yucca Mountain Nuclear Waste Repository. *Communication Studies, 48,* 359–380.

Renn, O., Webler, T., & Wiedemann, P. (Eds.). (1995). *Fairness and competence in citizen participation: Evaluating models for environmental discourse.* Boston: Kluwer.

Rogers, R. (2003). Public participation in the 1970s channel tunnel debate part I: The defeat of a "traffic tunnel." *Science & Culture, 12,* 189–237.

Rowe, G., & Frewer, L. J. (2000). Public participation methods: A framework for evaluation. *Science, Technology, & Human Values, 25,* 3–29.

Rowe, G., Marsh, R., & Frewer, L. J. (2004). Evaluation of a deliberative conference. *Science, Technology, & Values, 29,* 88–121.

Ryfe, D. M. (2002). The practice of deliberative democracy: A study of 16 deliberative organizations. *Political Communication, 19,* 359–377.

Schon, D. A. (1983). *The reflective practitioner.* New York: Basic Books.

Schon, D. A. (1987). *Educating the reflective practitioner.* San Francisco: Jossey-Bass.

Senge, P. M. (1990). *The fifth discipline: The art and practice of the learning organization.* Garden City, NY: Doubleday.

Shonholtz, R. (2000). Community mediation centers: Renewing the civic mission for the twenty-first century. *Mediation Quarterly, 17,* 331–340.

Smith, L., & Vawda, A. (2003). Citizen vs. customer: Different approaches to public participation in service delivery in Cape Town. *Urban Forum, 14,* 26–52.

Smith, M. (2000). Diversity in community mediation: A conversation with Janice Tudy-Jackson and Roberto Chene. *Mediation Quarterly, 17,* 369–377.

Smith, P. D., & McDonough, M. H. (2001). Beyond public participation: Fairness in natural resource decision making. *Society & Natural Resources, 14,* 239–249.

Spano, S. (2001). *Public dialogue and participatory democracy: The Cupertino Community Project.* Cresskill, NJ: Hampton Press.

Stewart, A. K., & Royal, C. (1998). Imagine South Carolina: A citizen's summit and public dialogue. In S. A. Hammond & C. Royal (Eds.), *Lessons from the field: Applying appreciative inquiry* (pp. 100–111). Plano, TX: Practical Press.

Stewart, J., Zediker, K. E., & Black, L. (2004). Relationships among philosophies of dialogue. In R. Anderson, L. A. Baxter, & K. N. Cissna (Eds.), *Dialogue: Theorizing difference in communication studies* (pp. 21–38). Thousand Oaks, CA: Sage.

Study Circles. (2005). *Who we are.* Retrieved February 15, 2005, from http://www.studycircles .org/pages/who.html

Tabara, D., Sauri, D., & Cerdan, R. (2003). Forest fire risk management and public participation in changing socioenvironmental conditions: A case study in a Mediterranean region. *Risk Analysis, 23,* 249–260.

Tan, N. (2002). Community mediation in Singapore: Principles for community conflict resolution. *Conflict Resolution Quarterly, 19,* 289–301.

Thoennes, N. P., Salem, P., & Pearson, J. (1995). Mediation and domestic violence: Current policies and practices. *Family and Conciliation Courts Review, 33,* 6–28.

Tuler, S., & Webler, T. (1999). Voices from the forest: What participants expect of a public participation process. *Society & Natural Resources, 12,* 437–453.

Tyler, N. (2003). Practical experience of public participation: Evidence from methodological experiments. *Innovation, 16,* 253–270.

Vari, A. (2002). Public involvement in flood risk management in Hungary. *Journal of Risk Research, 5,* 211–224.

Vasconcelos, C., Hamilton, A., & Barrett, P. (2000). Public participation in EIA: A study from a Portuguese perspective. *Journal of Environmental Assessment Policy and Management, 2,* 561–582.

Verba, S., Schlozman, K. L., & Brady, H. E. (1995). *Voice and equality: Civic voluntarism in American politics.* Cambridge, MA: Harvard University Press.

Wall, J. A., Jr., Stark, J. B., & Standifer, R. L. (2001). Mediation: A current review and theory development. *Journal of Conflict Resolution, 45,* 370–391.

Webler, T., & Tuler, S. (2000). Fairness and competence in citizen participation: Theoretical reflections from a case study. *Administration and Society, 32,* 566–595.

Weick, K. (1995). *Sensemaking in organizations.* Thousand Oaks, CA: Sage.

Weinstein, M. (2001). Community mediation: Providing justice and promoting transformation. *Conflict Resolution Quarterly, 19,* 251–259.

Weisbord, M. R., & Janoff, S. (1995). *Future search.* San Francisco: Berrett-Koehler.

Wenger, E. (1998). *Communities of practice: Learning, meaning, and identity.* Cambridge, UK: Cambridge University Press.

Winston, D. W. (1996). Participation standards in mandatory mediation statutes: "You can lead a horse to water ..." *Ohio State Journal on Dispute Resolution, 11,* 187–206.

Wiseman, V., Mooney, G., Berry, G., & Tang, K. C. (2003). Involving the general public in priority setting: Experience from Australia. *Social Science & Medicine, 56,* 1001–1012.

Wittgenstein, L. (1953). *Philosophical investigations.* Oxford, UK: Blackwell.

Yankelovich, D. (1991). *Coming to public judgment: Making democracy work in a complex world.* Syracuse, NY: Syracuse University Press.

Yankelovich, D. (1999). *The magic of dialogue: Transforming conflict into cooperation.* New York: Simon & Schuster.

Zemke, R. (1999). Don't fix that company! Maybe problem-solving is the problem. *Training, 36,* 26–33.

PART IV

INTERCULTURAL/INTERNATIONAL CONFLICT

Intercultural conflict is broadly defined in this section as the experience of emotional frustration and/or antagonistic struggle between a minimum of two different cultural parties (or identity groups) in conjunction with perceived or actual incompatibility of values, norms, face orientations, goals, scarce resources, processes, and/or outcomes in a face-to-face or mediated context (Ting-Toomey & Oetzel, 2001). Intercultural conflict revolves around the diverse cultural approaches people bring with them in expressing their different cultural or ethnic values, identity issues, interaction norms, face-saving orientations, power resource transactions, divergent goal emphasis, and contrastive conflict styles in a conflict episode or protracted conflict episodes.

In conjunction with steeply held sociocultural roots and historical grievances and other macro-level differences (e.g., political system differences, spiritual belief differences, or identity/power struggle issues; see Oetzel et al., and Broome & Jakobsson Hatay), the more divergent the two cultural conflict approaches, the wider the conflict schism between members of the two or more cultures. In "intercultural" conflict, scholars and practitioners are often interested in studying the layered factors, assumptions, meanings, processes, and/or outcomes of conflicts that impact face-to-face or mediated (e.g., via e-mails) interactions that involve individuals from diverse identity groups. Specific theories and programs of research have been developed

following the broad label of "intercultural communication" (see Gudykunst, 2005). The unit of analysis focuses on the individual level of conflict management and resolution more than group-based systems' entity conflicts. Comparatively, in "international" conflict, researchers and practitioners are often interested in the study of "heterophilous mass-mediated communication between two or more countries with different backgrounds. . . . The primary unit of analysis in INC [international communication] is the interaction of two or more societies/nations that are linked by mass media communication" (Rogers & Hart, 2002, p. 5).

By our inclusion of chapters on both intercultural/interethnic (e.g., Orbe & Everett) and international conflict (e.g., Gilboa) levels, our choice reflects the importance of understanding intercultural and international conflict from an integrative ecological perspective (see Oetzel, Ting-Toomey, & Rinderle, Chapter 26). Moreover, concepts in several chapters (e.g., Oetzel et al., Broome & Jakobsson Hatay; Coleman & Raider) in this section integrate ideas from both the intercultural and international/macro arenas. Oftentimes, authors do use the two terms "intercultural" and "international" conflict loosely and flexibly in their writings. Thus, we also take an inclusive, multidisciplinary definition of a broad intercultural/international conflict perspective in presenting the chapters in this section to you. Scholars and practitioners in this section indeed draw their inspirations and conflict ideas from multiple disciplines such as conflict studies, cross-cultural psychology, ethnic and racial studies, human communication, intergroup relations, international relations/negotiation, peace studies, political science, international business and management, and intercultural training and development.

The six chapters in the section provide readers with both macro-level and micro-level lenses for analyzing global to specific interpersonal/intercultural conflict modalities in distinctive identity groups, nations, and cultures. Taken together, the chapters offer illuminating insights, fresh ideas, and unique viewpoints in understanding intercultural and international conflict either from a scholarly, applied, or a scholarly applied angle. Several common themes emerge as we review the different chapters in this intercultural and international conflict section.

Theme 1: Intercultural conflict involves emotional frustrations or mismatched expectations that stem, in part, from cultural group membership differences. When we experience conflict, we experience emotional vulnerabilities, fears, and frustrations. Part of the emotional frustration or fragile insecurity and fear often stems, in part, from cultural difference, mismatched expectation, or ignorance (see, e.g., Coleman & Raider, and Ting-Toomey & Takai).

Theme 2: Intercultural conflict involves different types of group-based or individual-based identity struggle or identity "push-and-pull" issues. Broome and Jakobsson Hatay discuss how the incongruous views of Cyprus history, differing religious beliefs, contrastive identity belongings, and polarized opinions of how to settle the conflict between Greek Cypriots and Turkish Cypriots create an intractable conflict situation. In the context of the U.S. communication setting, Orbe and Everett critique the perpetual dominance of the Eurocentric model in researching interracial/interethnic conflict concepts. They discuss the urgent need for bringing in the muted voices of co-culture or minority group perspectives in theorizing about and researching racial and interethnic conflict tensions.

Theme 3: Intercultural conflict involves biased intergroup attribution processes and biased perceptual and representation images. Intergroup-biased perceptions involve ethnocentric evaluations and prejudiced mind-sets in evaluating a conflict situation. In addition, other exo-level factors such as the media can present either a functional or dysfunctional image of a war-torn nation or community that further impacts the role of international intervention or the peacebuilding agenda-setting process (see Gilboa).

Theme 4: Intercultural conflict involves different face-loss and face-saving behaviors. Conflict is an emotionally laden face-threatening phenomenon. Face refers to a claimed sense of desired social self-image in a relational or international setting (Ting-Toomey, 2004, 2005; see also Ting-Toomey and Takai). Face loss occurs when we are being treated in a way that our identity claims are either challenged or ignored. Face-loss can occur on the individual level or the identity group level, or both. Repeated face-loss and face-threat often lead to escalatory conflict spirals or an impasse in the conflict negotiation process.

Theme 5: Intercultural conflict involves multiple goals, and the development of competitive versus collaborative goals depends on multiple factors. These multiple factors can include the conflict parties involved; their relationship; their specific intentions, wants, and needs; the negotiation climate; third-party facilitation skills; and the anticipated outcomes of the conflict situation (see Deutsch & Coleman, 2000). Conflict parties often seek different conflict outcomes and these conflict outcomes are often influenced by the negotiation climate in a conflict interaction session. A competitive negotiation climate breeds mistrust, while a collaborative negotiation climate cultivates and nurtures trust (see Coleman & Raider).

Theme 6: Intercultural conflict competence or peacebuilding effort involves divergent methods and culturally inclusive communication skills. To engage in an inclusive conflict competence approach, the international community needs to adopt a paradigm shift in its usual conflict management practice. As Lederach (1997) noted, conflict mediators need to focus their attention on "discovering and empowering the resources, modalities, and mechanisms for building peace that exist *within* the cultural context" (p. 95). LeBaron (2003) also concluded, "Conflict fluency means cultivating a repertoire of ways to engage conflict constructively and productively, with respect for a range of cultural starting points" (p. 134). Many examples of divergent conflict management and reconciliation paths can be identified (see the specific suggestions in each chapter in this section). While the roads to peace are diverse and the conflict modalities are rich across cultural and ethnic lines, the ultimate goal of universal peace without violence in international and intercultural conflict remains a common humanistic vision. We begin the section by highlighting the key ideas in each chapter.

In the first chapter, Oetzel, Arcos, Mabizela, Weinman, and Zhang examine perspectives and conceptualizations of culture and conflict in four understudied cultures: the Muslim world, China, Colombia, and South Africa. The chapter's objective is to provide an insider lens or emic perspective that moves beyond traditional etic viewpoints. In reviewing conflict practices within each culture, the authors (a) present the socio-historical roots and movements that shape evolving conflict worldviews; (b) explore core conflict symbols that are deemed important from the cultural insider's viewpoint; and (c) understand conflict management/resolution from a cultural indigenous perspective. After reviewing these aspects, the authors discuss future directions—especially paying close attention to the historical, political, and spiritual roots that help to understand unique conflict perspectives and to examine culture and conflict in transformation. Finally, they translate key concepts such as understanding the socio-historical roots of conflict, core symbols, and constructive conflict into practical applications for the practitioners. They end their discussion of the chapter with a call for skillful facework management in upholding self-face and other-face in all four cultures—with special recognition of the distinctive meanings and enactment of facework in each particular cultural system.

The second chapter, by Orbe and Everett, focuses on interracial and interethnic conflict communication in the United States. In particular,

the authors review existing research that has explored the issues of race, ethnicity, and conflict communication. Following a systematic review of the literature, the authors present a discussion of several limitations of this growing body of conflict literature: a tradition steeped in empirical emphasis, a Eurocentric/ethnocentric bias, a micro-level practice orientation, an assumption of and focus on difference, and a perpetuation of essentializing generalizations. The concluding section of the chapter presents co-cultural theory as a viable framework to conceptualize potential directions for future research. They advocate for the importance of developing trusting relationships between the scholars-practitioners and community conflict resolution programs through which marginalized voices can be heard and the concerns of communities of color can be included and validated.

In the third chapter, on media and international conflict, Gilboa examines basic and applied research on media coverage and intervention in international conflicts. The chapter explores normative theories of media role, identifies strengths and weaknesses, and offers an alternative functional framework for analyzing the relationship between media and international conflict. He argues that international conflict—as a dynamic, developmental process—moves through four phases: prevention, management, resolution, and reconciliation. Gilboa further comments that research has focused more on the management and resolution phases, but not enough attention has been paid to the prevention and reconciliation phases. He observes that the media often operate as both a tool in the hands of politicians and policy makers and as independent actors pursuing their own agenda. The author concludes that a functional perspective on media coverage and international conflict can bolster public confidence in international peacemaking efforts and actual reconciliation outcomes.

In the fourth chapter, Broome and Jakobsson Hatay examine some of the dialogic approaches that have emerged in response to the challenge of building peace in protracted intergroup conflict situations, in particular, in Cyprus. From a scholar-practitioner lens, the authors examine the diversity of dialogic approaches to peacebuilding as well as their strengths and limitations. The authors believe that in order for a peacebuilding process to be successful, the initiative needs to involve multi-level effort—from the parties' respective leaderships to the collective society at large. They conceptualize a systematic peacebuilding program as a multi-track dialogue process that integrates an inclusive process of citizenship involvement and peacebuilding and the exclusive process of elite peacemaking and peace negotiation efforts. They end the chapter with some concrete recommendations for both research and practice concerning diverse dialogic approaches to peace.

In commenting on specific issues in international/intercultural conflict resolution training, Coleman and Raider, in the fifth chapter, share their wealth of training experience in designing and delivering conflict resolution programs. They identify key insights, activities, and specific training lessons learned concerning the intersection between conflict negotiation and culture. While understanding cultural differences is paramount in analyzing conflict clashes, the authors believe that learning and mastering collaborative negotiation skills is the most important conflict resolution task. They further comment that many cultural or identity group differences become exacerbated in a competitive negotiation climate. Indeed, for the authors, it is the "culture" of collaboration that is, ultimately, the premium factor in promoting intercultural conflict resolution. They conclude with the vision of developing more global and inclusive conflict training materials that are reflective of different cultural worldviews and practices.

In the last chapter in the section, Ting-Toomey and Takai provide a synopsis review of theories that hold promise for explaining intercultural and intergroup conflict communication process. They then review some relevant research findings related to the conflict face-negotiation theory. They further discuss the importance of perceived face threats, self-construal activation, relational distance, and status difference features, and propose an initial situational appraisal model for future researching effort to explain the relationship among self-construals, face concerns, and conflict styles. Finally, they provide specific recommendations and directions for future theorizing attempts to understand the complex, multidimensional phenomenon of intercultural conflict communication.

REFERENCES

Deutsch, M., & Coleman, P. (Eds.). (2000). *The handbook of conflict resolution: Theory and practice.* San Francisco: Jossey-Bass.

Gudykunst, W. (Ed.). (2005). *Theorizing about intercultural communication.* Thousand Oaks, CA: Sage.

LeBaron, M. (2003). *Bridging cultural conflicts: A new approach for a changing world.* San Francisco: Jossey-Bass.

Lederach, J. (1997). *Building peace: Sustainable reconciliation in divided societies.* Washington, DC: United States Institute of Peace Press.

Rogers, E., & Hart, W. (2002). The histories of intercultural, international, and development communication. In W. Gudykunst & B. Mody (Eds.), *Handbook of international & intercultural communication* (2nd ed., pp. 1–23). Thousand Oaks, CA: Sage.

Ting-Toomey, S. (2004). Translating conflict face-negotiation theory into practice. In D. Landis, J. Bennett, & M. Bennett (Eds.), *Handbook of intercultural training* (3rd ed., pp. 217–248). Thousand Oaks, CA: Sage.

Ting-Toomey, S. (2005). The matrix of face: An updated face-negotiation theory. In W. Gudykunst (Ed.), *Theorizing about intercultural communication* (pp. 71–92). Thousand Oaks, CA: Sage.

Ting-Toomey, S., & Oetzel, J. (2001). *Managing intercultural conflict effectively.* Thousand Oaks, CA: Sage.

20

HISTORICAL, POLITICAL, AND SPIRITUAL FACTORS OF CONFLICT

Understanding Conflict Perspectives and Communication in the Muslim World, China, Colombia, and South Africa

JOHN G. OETZEL

University of New Mexico

BIBIANA ARCOS

University of New Mexico

PHOLA MABIZELA

University of New Mexico

A. MICHAEL WEINMAN

University of New Mexico

QIN ZHANG[1]

University of New Mexico

The majority of research investigations on intercultural conflict and cross-cultural comparisons of conflict behavior utilize Western/individualistic conceptualizations of conflict and conflict styles in an etic manner (e.g., Elsayed-Ekhouly & Buda, 1996; Gabrielidis, Stephan, Ybarra, Dos Santos Pearson, & Villareal, 1997; Oetzel et al., 2001; Ohbuchi, Fukushima, & Tedeschi, 1999; for a review of this line of research see Ting-Toomey & Oetzel,

2003). The purpose of these types of studies is to understand how members of various cultures communicate during conflict so that conflict participants and practitioners can effectively manage conflict. While this research has laudable goals and has produced important findings, the etic approach glosses over unique cultural differences in conceptualizations of conflict communication. In addition, the use of Western conceptualizations privileges these perspectives in determining what the effective and appropriate conflict behaviors are. In contrast, an emic approach examines conflict approaches from a cultural insider's point of view. This approach examines unique cultural features, socio-historical frameworks, and spiritual and cultural institutions to understand definitions, symbols, and perspectives for conflict communication (Shuter, 1990). The emic approach is important to understand nuances of culture and why members of cultural groups communicate as they do (Shuter, 1990).

In this chapter, we present the emic conceptualizations of conflict in four different and often understudied cultures (understudied in the Western conflict literature): the Muslim world, China, Colombia, and South Africa. These four cultures were chosen because each of these cultures comes from a different region of the world (with the Muslim world spread across the globe); they have important historical, political, and business implications for other countries/ cultures in the world (e.g., the Muslim world is frequently viewed as a mysterious and contrasting perspective to the Western world; China is the most populous country, with a strong effect on business and politics; Colombia is often viewed as a country perpetually in civil turmoil and the center of drug trafficking; and South Africa was held up as an exemplar of racial hatred because of apartheid); and they are all traditionally classified as being collectivistic cultures (Hofstede, 1991; Triandis, 1995), thus providing some contrast to the predominant individualistic, Western perspective. *Individualism* is a social pattern that consists of loosely linked individuals who view themselves as independent of collectives, while *collectivism* is a social pattern consisting of closely linked individuals who see themselves as part of one or more collectives and are willing to give priority to the goals of these collectives over their own personal goals (Triandis, 1995).

While each of the cultures reviewed in this study is collectivistic, each has a different socio-historical framework for understanding conflict. History, social institutions, philosophy, spirituality, and other macro features provide a foundation that shapes individuals' conflict communication (Ting-Toomey & Oetzel, 2001). These macro features are rarely examined in the context of interpersonal conflict, but rather are usually the focus of geo-political conflict (see Gilboa, Chapter 22 Broome & Jakobsson, Chapter 23 in this volume). Our purpose in this chapter is threefold: (a) to present the socio-historical roots and movements that shape evolving conflict worldviews; (b) to explore core conflict symbols that are deemed important from the cultural insider's point of view; and (c) to understand conflict management/resolution from a culturally indigenous perspective. We address these objectives for each culture and then conclude by synthesizing the review, noting future directions and practical implications.[2] We order the review of the four cultures (Muslim, China, Colombia, and South Africa) because of two reasons: (a) Muslim and Chinese cultures have common features such as spiritual values, social order, face-sensitive cultures, and positional roles; and (b) Colombia and South Africa have commonalities, including colonial and violent histories. In this review, we emphasize the spiritual value framework with the Muslim and Chinese cultures and a socio-historical framework with the Colombian and South African cultures.

THE MUSLIM LENS FOR CONFLICT COMMUNICATION: INTEGRATING RELIGION AND CULTURE

The distorted image of a strange, primitive, and dark Muslim world somewhere "out there," as projected by orientalists (Said, 1978, 1994) and the mass media (Said, 1981), should be challenged. The Muslim world is a complex multinational and multi-cultural global phenomenon with roots in the Middle East. The Muslim supra-culture, or *'ummah,* is global in its cultural diversity, geography, and size (about one fifth of the world population). The organizing principle of the *'ummah* is the Muslim religion (Islam) and the Muslim way of life (*ad-din*).

Less than 20% of Muslims are "Arabs" (Feghali, 1997), while the rest belong to diverse cultures and subcultures whose first languages are not Arabic. Nevertheless, Arabic is the language of Islam since it is the language of the Qur'anic revelation, of the collections of *hadith* (the recorded teachings and examples of the Prophet Muhammed), of the prescribed Islamic prayers, and of traditional Muslim scholarship.

Islamization is a historical process of creative integration between local and tribal cultural contexts (*'urf*) and the universal message of Islam (von Grunebaum, 1955). Adherence to Islam is therefore a decentralized phenomenon embedded in local cultural realities that are in transformation. Cultural integration is a dynamic balance of the relative power between cultures. Integration can manifest either as an additive or a transformative process or both, and is unique to the power-relationship between the universality of Islam and a particular *'urf*. Whether the relationship between the two takes the form of conflict, coexistence, or interaction, the eventual specific outcome of Islamization manifests different qualities according to the compatibility and the integrity of a specific *'urf*. The dynamic balance of power between Islamic principles and local cultures is further complicated by repeated colonial penetrations and domination of *dar al-Islam* (the Muslim regions) by the West. Current conflict perspectives in various parts of the Muslim world reflect these post-colonial realities, which manifest as humiliation, anger, and frustration experienced by Muslims. Western colonialism affected the Muslim world in yet another way. Muslims from all parts of the multicultural *dar al-Islam* began emigrating in large numbers to Europe and America. Also, in the United States, many native-born citizens, mostly African Americans, converted to Islam. The Muslim world has extended its boundaries into the "West" in the form of local, multi-cultural Muslim communities in which intercultural conflict has become a major challenge.

The basic premise underlying this section is that a process of cultural transformation takes place when local cultures come in contact with Islam. Thus, the way in which Muslims experience and negotiate conflict in their lives is shaped by the integration between their specific local cultural conflict perspectives and universal Islamic principles. An illustration of this point is how the advent of Islam affected conflict perspectives among Arab cultures—the first cultures to encounter and convert to Islam.

Socio-Historical and Religious Roots Shaping the Muslim Conflict Lens

Conflict in Arabia. The first example of a local culture transformed by the message of Islam is that of the tribes of the Arabian Peninsula. The prophetic message of Islam, an Arabic Qur'an, introduced novel transformative principles into the violent *jahiliyya* (time of ignorance and revenge) culture of the pagan Arabs. Von Grunebaum (1955) classified these Islamic principles into three major categories: (a) the goal of life is the other-world; (b) the individual is continuously responsible for making an effort toward salvation; and (c) the unified political organization of the *'ummah* is the concern of each Muslim. The newly transformed Arab Muslims experienced their prophet living among them, teaching and demonstrating how to live these principles. In order to better understand this process of transformative integration of the Arabs, one must first examine their pre-Islamic culture.

Conflict perspectives of the desert Arabs prior to Islam. Conflict in pre-Islamic Arabia (prior to 622 CE) often resulted in prolonged fighting and violence between warring tribes and between extended families (*hama'il*) (Abu-Nimer, 2003). Rigid patriarchal social structures emphasized the connection of the individual to the collective "based on criteria such as age, gender, clan, tribe, religion, ethnicity, race, and region" (p. 116). Other major cultural values that influenced conflict behavior among Arab groups were face-saving concerns (*karama*), preventing shame, and restoring respect. Face represents an individual's claimed sense of positive image in the context of social interaction and includes cognitive, emotional, and behavioral components (Ting-Toomey & Kurogi, 1998). Conflict between individuals automatically became conflict between larger groups, and even marital conflicts could quickly escalate into conflicts between families or even between tribes. Personal power was relevant only in relationship to one's group affiliation and position. Issues of tribal and family honor (*sharaf*) (e.g., seeking revenge for past violence) tended to escalate out of proportion and continued for long periods or indefinitely. Warring tribes and large clans engaged in the practice of taking the women of the enemy as loot, which would further fuel the conflict. Consequently, the major Arabic terms to describe conflict—*mushkila* (difficulty), *ikhtilaf* (disagreement), *tanaqudh* (dispute), *fitna* (test), *niza'un* (moral or very intense conflict)—all have negative connotations for the Arabs.

The traditional tribal structure for dispute resolution, which is practiced even today, allows both victim and offender to attempt exiting the vicious circle of violent retribution and revenge (Abu-Nimer, 2003). A first step is for the offender's family to offer a sum of money (*atwah*) to the victim's family as guarantee of seeking resolution. If the *atwah* is accepted, revenge subsides for a truce (*hudnah*) to allow mediation and investigation to take place. A process of reconciliation between the feuding families (*sulh*) ensues and agreements for payment take place. The *sulh* culminates with a public ceremony (*sulhah*) in which the parties to the conflict share food together and make public their declarations of communal harmony and peace.

The Arabs also use the traditional practice of *musayara* when negotiating conflict (Griefat & Katriel, 1989). *Musayara* uses empathy to reduce the intensity of interpersonal conflict by expressing self-humiliation and by not asserting one's position of power. Literally, *musayara* means to go along with the other or to travel together and is "designed to enhance commonalities rather than differences, cooperation rather than conflict, and mutuality rather than self-assertion" (p. 123). Examples of *musayara* can be verbally praising and elevating the status of the other, bringing gifts, and extending favors or service to an adversary. The Prophet Muhammad himself recommended such practices.

Core Conflict Symbols Indigenous to the Muslim Culture

As the Arabs accepted the Qur'anic message of Islam, principles of the new religion began to transform Arab culture and the way Arabs approached conflict. The Qur'anic revelation

was a 23-year process that gradually enhanced the integration between the local Arab culture of the 6th century and the universal principles of monotheistic Islam. The Muslim *'ummah* was a brotherhood[3] that surpassed tribal and family affiliations. The new religion taught the Arabian tribes the message of the universality of humanity and about the special status of humankind in God's creation (Abu-Nimer, 2003). Humankind is created as one community that encompasses different nations, different tribes, different races, different languages, and different cultural codes (Qur'an,[4] 49:13 & 5:48). At the same time, the Arab cultural context was not abrogated but rather transformed and endowed with new meanings. For example, the Qur'an affirmed the tribal rule that murder can be avenged by equal and opposing retribution, but also emphasized that, in truth, forgiveness and mercy are better and more beneficial (Qur'an, 2:178). Several principles reflect these values: shame-orientation, forgiveness, patience, peace, commanding right and forbidding wrong, and jihad.

Shame-orientation. Relationships between individuals within the Muslim society are defined by a set of duties (or obligations) to, and rights over, others. For example: A man as the head of his family has the obligation to support his wife and his children; a wife must obey her husband; and sons must obey their mothers during their entire life. The same is true in other social structures. Rulers have recognized rights over and obligations to their citizens while citizens must be loyal to their government. The deeply embedded tribal-cultural mechanism that maintains this system of duties and rights is that of shame-orientation, where issues of "preventing shame, restoring respect, and saving face" are central (Abu-Nimer, 2003, p. 98). A main concern in the culture is not to bring shame on one's family or clan but rather to maintain the honor of all concerned. Islam introduced into this existing equation of shame-orientation a shame of another kind. It is the shame and awe that a believing individual experiences in front of an all-seeing and aware God. The Prophet taught the Muslims very specifically not to expose and make public the fault of another or of oneself.

Conflict will usually erupt due to action or actions perceived disruptive to the balance of honor between parties (Abu-Nimer, 2003). There are two options to address loss of honor. One party may take the "warpath" to victory in an effort to regain lost honor. The preferred option, however, is to have a third party convince the disputants "that harmony is better than victory" (p. 96). Islam proposes two values in particular, forgiveness and patience (*sabr*), in guiding the conflicting parties to engage in that second option.

Forgiveness. Forgiveness as an approach to conflict is a highly valued Islamic principle (Abu-Nimer, 2003). Forgiveness, which is one of the attributes of God (The Forgiver), implies the possibility of restoring social relationships and returning to a more harmonious coexistence. For a Muslim, to forgive another is to accept and allow rectification of relationships. In fact, Islam celebrates forgiveness as a higher virtue than justice and punishment. Traditionally, the advice of the Prophet was for people to be like trees; when a stone is thrown at them, fruit descends. The important Arab custom of hospitality is also related to forgiveness through the symbolic sharing of food and drink. The ritualized guest-host relationship and eating together transforms conflict and restores honor. Forgiveness can be exercised only from a position of power, and therefore, again, the balance of honor is restored. A public ritual as a demonstration of forgiveness is an important aspect of resolving conflict. For example, in North Africa

> there is a special ritual for cases of murder. The offender agrees to surrender and lie on the ground beside a sheep. A member of the victim's family approaches the offender and has the choice of killing him or the sheep. Obviously, the victim's family representative will choose the sheep. However, the fact that the victim has had the opportunity to take revenge restores the respect, dignity, and the honor of the victim's family. (Abu-Nimer, 2003, p. 108)

Patience. Patience (*sabr*) has subtly varied meanings, most of them related to difficulty and to the attitude one must adopt in a difficult situation (Abu-Nimer, 2003). The Qur'anic guidance is, "O you who believe, seek help through patience and prayer, surely God is with the patient ones" (2:153). In a conflict situation, the virtue of *sabr* may imply not to react but rather to trust in the wisdom of God's overall plan. Through patience one may transform a situation of conflict into an inner process of growth and self-control. When applied to conflict, *sabr* allows time for a peaceful process to take place, to allow healing through negotiation and reflection, and to allow time for forgiving and forgetting. Exercising *sabr* in conflict could include praying for God's help and for guidance, teaching and preaching to the conflicting parties the relevant religious values, allowing time for people of authority within the families and a neutral third party to get involved, separating the parties for a time, and/or engaging in dialogue.

Peace. The Islamic understanding of peace (*as-Salaam*) relates less to the absence of conflict than to the positive affirmation of a state of peace. Peace, which is again one of the attributes of God (who is the source of all peace), includes the meaning of submission—to surrender to God's order. It implies the ideal of personal and social harmony and the justice that is possible within that order. So, in the human realm, the concepts of social justice and peace are closely related.

Commanding right and forbidding wrong. An important Islamic principle that can shed additional light on conflict perspectives in the Muslim world and that has some aspects that may be foreign to Western thinking is the Qur'anic directive of "commanding right and forbidding wrong" (Cook, 2000). Simply put, a Muslim is directed to take action to correct another Muslim who is engaged in doing something wrong. This can take the form of giving sincere advice (*nasiha*) to the wrongdoer or by getting the wrongdoer to stop through legal means. If one has the actual power to forbid a wrong, one must do so. If not, one must speak out against a wrong action or at least resist it inwardly. Here, one is allowed to engage in conflict only for the sake of God. In contrast to most Western ethical conception, the Islamic commanding right and forbidding wrong includes situations in which there is no victim per se but where a moral code was broken or a sin has been committed.

Jihad. Jihad (conflict as struggle) is an important concept for every Muslim and unfortunately is highly misrepresented and misinterpreted in the West and by its media (Armstrong, 2002; El-Fadl, 2002). In the Qur'an, the word *jihad* is most frequently used in the verbal form meaning to struggle, to strive, or to make an effort—inwardly or outwardly. The idea of jihad emphasizes the inherent possibilities in conflict and always has a positive connotation; in contrast to the basic assumption of the Arabs that conflict is negative and destructive. When the Muslims returned victorious from their last battle against the Meccans, the Prophet proclaimed: "we are returning from the lesser *jihad* [the struggle of war] and to the greater *jihad* [the struggle in time of peace]" (Armstrong, 2002, p. 29). To the Muslims, the greater jihad is both, the struggle to build and maintain an *'ummah* of believers and also the inner struggle with the "self" (*nafs*) to perfect one's faith and to grow spiritually. Jihad when it pertains to war is narrowly restricted in the Qur'an and is not favored as an option in resolving conflict (Esposito, 2003).

Cultural Attitudes Toward Constructive Conflict Management

In the Arab social context, "loyalty to one's extended family and larger 'in groups' take precedence over individual needs and goals" (Feghali, 1997, p. 352). Therefore, conflict will naturally tend to depart from the individual realm and to become a public dispute. The cultural assumption of conflict is that it is negative and destructive to the community and therefore must be avoided and resolved (Abu-Nimer, 2003). The integration of Islamic principles and Arab cultural values results in two preferred ways to approach and resolve conflict: third-party arbitration and the Muslim judicial system.

Third-party arbitration. Traditional dispute resolution among the Arabs depends heavily on third-party arbitration, which may consist of one arbitrator or a whole arbitration committee (Abu-Nimer, 2003). Dispute resolution through third-party intervention was already practiced in pre-Islamic Arabia. The Prophet Muhammad arbitrated in intertribal disputes even before receiving prophethood. The qualifications and the functions of the arbitrators may vary. An arbitrator must possess the necessary Islamic knowledge to support the arbitration process and give sound advice that can be respected. An arbitrator may be required to have the correct family and tribal affiliation either to ensure objectivity and trustworthiness by belonging to a neutral group or by being related to a disputant so as to exert influence toward resolving the conflict. Arbitrators may choose not to rely on face-to-face negotiations during part or all of the dispute resolution process in order to avoid excessive emotional and confrontational displays, which may cloud sound reason.

The use of witnesses, testimonies, and oaths are important parts of the third-party arbitration process since the fear and awe of God (*taqwa*) in this world and the next is a strong element of the Muslim worldview (Abu-Nimer, 2003). Truthfulness is highly valued in Islam and swearing by the Qur'an or by the name of God is viewed with great reverence. "A false oath is believed to affect the person himself as well as his relatives, which may have catastrophic consequences for the person and his social network" (Abu-Nimer, p. 93) in this world and in the next.

The Muslim judge. Unlike an arbitrator who functions as an advisor and a negotiator, the position of the Muslim judge (*qadi*) carries with it the authority to rule according to the knowledge of the Qur'an and the Sunna law (the legitimate tradition of the prophet) (Kamali, 1991; Schacht, 1955). The *qadi* is traditionally a jurist and scholar who is trained as a judge and could be a government official. The distinction between arbitration and judgment is demonstrated in the Qur'an when God informs the Prophet, "people will not believe until they make you an arbitrator over what they are disputing among themselves and after that they find no hesitation within themselves to accept your judgment with complete submission" (4:65). Submission to God's law and to the ruling of the Prophet as a judge over disputes and conflicts is a measure of a Muslim's faith and adherence to the religion. Muslims practice the overlap between arbitration and judgment in conflict resolution even today. Each Muslim is ultimately responsible before God for his or her own actions, words, and thoughts as reflected in the following *hadith:*

The Prophet heard people in dispute by the door to his house, so he came to them and said: I am just a human being so when disputants come to me for judgment, it might be that one is more eloquent in presenting his case than the other so then I may assume [incorrectly] that he is right and judge in his favor. In such a case, when I judge for him and give him his right as a Muslim, in actuality he is receiving a portion of the [Hell] fire. So that person has the option to accept the judgment or [better for him] to reject it [for what he knows to be the truth]. (Al-Bukhari, n.d., as cited in Khan, 1994, p. 154)

The Muslim ideal is that justice should be self-administered and that conflict resolution should be voluntary. According to another *hadith* (Khalid, 1986), Umar bin-Khattab (who later became the second *khalif*) asked to resign from his post as the *qadi* of Medina, a job to which he was appointed by the first *khalif,* Abu-Bakr a-Sadiq. He reasoned that he was made a judge over angels living on earth because no one came to his court for a year from his appointment. The way Islam was practiced in Medina has been the model to emulate for Muslims throughout the ages. Later, the history of the Muslim world encompassed a variety of cultures, which changed over time due to influences imposed locally or externally. Yet by integrating the same Islamic principles, these diverse cultures share common spiritual goals to constitute the global Muslim *'ummah* (von Grunebaum, 1955). Later Muslim rulers established the *qadis* as paid officials, which introduced a possible conflict of interest due to the government-controlled justice system (Schacht, 1955). The original responsibility of the *qadi* as a Muslim scholar was to provide knowledge-based legal rulings according to the Qur'an and the *Sunna* in order to support the believers in their ultimate goal of obeying God's law. That responsibility was now compromised. History provides numerous reports about conflicts between a Muslim ruler and an admonishing Muslim scholar, and about cases in which a *qadi* was imprisoned, exiled, or even executed by an unjust ruler. As an alternative, many jurists refrained from government affiliation and supported themselves by means of other trades. Even today there is a widespread phenomenon of grassroots-based *qadis* and jurist-scholars who

serve their communities throughout the Muslim *'ummah.*

In sum, this section illustrates a general Islamic approach to conflict as reflected in some Arab cultures. Two divergent conflict characteristics emerge. In its negative aspect, conflict is perceived as a destructive force in the community to be managed and eliminated in order to restore peace. In its positive aspect, conflict and struggle contain the potential for spiritual transformation and the pursuit of justice. The balance between the two aspects is realized through Islamic scholarship and jurisprudence.

CHINESE LENS FOR CONFLICT COMMUNICATION: SPIRITUAL AND POLITICAL INFLUENCES

The Chinese and Muslim lenses share certain perspectives. Specifically, both lenses emphasize social hierarchical structures, face-sensitive perspectives, and spiritual/philosophical foundations. In addition, both cultures affect billions of people over a large region. There are differences, however, in that China is a single geopolitical unit, ruled by a Communist political regime, but has embraced a market economy. Similar to the Muslim world, Chinese spiritual and philosophical roots can be traced back centuries. These roots provide a strong foundation for core symbols and conflict communication in Chinese culture.

Philosophical Roots Shaping the Chinese Conflict Lens

The examination of communication and conflict should go inextricably with the exploration of its philosophical underpinnings since philosophy serves as a content, context, and method of communication (Cheng, 1987). Despite the richness and diversity in traditional Chinese philosophy and ideology, Confucianism, Buddhism, and Daoism (Taoism) are generally regarded as the three most influential and dominant philosophies in Chinese culture, whose doctrines and teachings, without slightest exaggeration, have touched the heart of every Chinese person, permeated every facet of Chinese civilization, affected every aspect of Chinese life, and inevitably impacted Chinese conflict management and resolution. The Confucian notion of *hexie* (harmony) and *guanxi* (relationship), the Buddhist concept of *yuan* and enlightenment, and the Daoist (Taoist) idea of the *Dao* (the Way) and *wuwei* (nonaction) all have helped shape Chinese conflict worldviews, attitudes, and expectations.

Although the study of conflict management and resolution should focus on the interplay of cultural, situational, and individual variables (Chen & Starosta, 1997; Gudykunst et al., 1996; Kim & Leung, 2000; Ting-Toomey & Kurogi, 1998; Ting-Toomey & Oetzel, 2001; Triandis, 1988), by and large, culture exerts the strongest influence on people's selection and preference of conflict styles. Accordingly, to explore Chinese conflict management, indigenous Chinese philosophical and religious concepts and ideas have been examined from an emic perspective and these findings have shed light on a better understanding of Chinese conflict management and resolution (Yu, 2002).

Comparatively, Confucianism has captivated most attention of communication scholars interested in Chinese and even East Asian conflict research. Among the conflict-related Confucian cultural constructs, *hexie* (harmony), *mianzi* (face), *guanxi* (interrelationship), and *quanli* (power) are the most widely investigated, since they play a vital role in the smooth functioning of the wheel of Chinese conflict management and resolution, in which *hexie* is the axis, *mianzi* and *guanxi* are the supporting spokes (in which *mianzi* functions as the operational mechanism connecting social network and *guanxi* as the structural pattern of the social fabric), and *quanli* the internal contingency working with the spokes and axis (Chen & Starosta, 1997; Hwang, 1997).

Philosophically, *hexie* is the foundation of major Chinese schools of thought, including Confucianism and Daoism (Chen, 2002). Harmony subsumes the human relationship, the dialectic balance between the *yin* ("feminine energy") and the *yang* ("masculine energy") forces, and the oneness between human and nature (*tian ren he yi*). Harmony is the ends rather than means of human communication, as it is a cardinal value guiding human relationships in Chinese culture (Chen, 2002; Chen & Starosta, 1997). The wheel of harmony, being sustained by the axis of *zhong* (equilibrium) and

three spokes of *ren* (benevolence), *yi* (righteousness), and *li* (propriety or rite), has run continuously through Chinese history, modeling the Chinese people's mentality toward conflict and directing their conflict behaviors (Chen, 2002). To pursue a harmonious human relationship and an ideal conflict-free society, conflict should, first of all, be avoided, which could be achieved with five conflict-handling core rules stemming from the tenets of *zhong, ren, yi,* and *li*, which include self-restraint/self-discipline, indirect expression of disapproval, saving/making face for others, reciprocity, and emphasis on particularistic relationships (Chen, 2002).

The concept of *mianzi* traces at least 2,000 years back to the Confucian root in ancient China (Hu, 1944; Jia, 1997, 2001), which embodies two conceptually distinctive dimensions: *lian* (face) and *mian* (image) (Hu, 1944; Gao, 1998; Gao & Ting-Toomey, 1998). *Lian* involves the integrity and moral character of an individual, the loss of which usually brings shame and disgrace to the individual and his or her family and relational network, whereas *mian* is the projection of one's public image, representing one's social position and prestige gained from the performance of one's social roles (Hu, 1944). Chinese *mianzi* includes four major characteristics: relational (connoting harmony, interdependence, and trust), moral (primary carrier of moral codes and reputation), communal/social (public censure for any deviation from the community norms), and hierarchical (emphasizing the relational hierarchy by age, power, and blood ties, etc.; Jia, 1997).

The Chinese concept of *mianzi* is distinct from the Western concept of facework in that the former is largely relational and moral, but the latter is mostly rational and transactional (Jia, 1997). As a power game in which people earn face, give face, and enhance face, Chinese *mianzi* typically functions as a conflict-preventive mechanism, a substitute for strict legislation regarding rights, obligations, and punishments, as well as a primary means of cultivating Confucian *junzi* (gentlemanhood) (Chen, Ryan, & Chen, 1999; Hwang, 1997; Jia, 1997). In a nutshell, *mianzi* serves both as an ultimate goal and an effective means to prevent conflict and to establish, maintain, and strengthen harmonious human relationships (Jia, 1997).

Guanxi is the relationship between the parties involved. Human relationships under Confucianism are governed by *Wu Lun* (the Five Codes of Ethics), which is based on five unequal and complementary relationships: ruler (supervisor)/subject (subordinator), father/son, husband/wife, older brother/younger brother, and between friends, in which each party has its own commitments and obligations (Chen & Chung, 1994). Specifically, the juniors owe their seniors respect and obedience, and the seniors owe their juniors protection and consideration (Chen & Chung, 1994; Chen & Starosta, 1997; Yum, 1997). The emphasis on particularistic relationships and the ingroup/outgroup distinction in Chinese culture (which regulate people's communication behaviors to avoid or resolve conflict and to strengthen harmony among people) is derived from *Wu Lun* (Chen & Chung, 1994). To achieve harmony and avoid conflict, the Chinese usually endeavor to establish *guanxi* with others and save face for each other, which gives rise to an indirect communication pattern and the use of an intermediary in case of conflict (Chen & Starosta, 1997).

Quanli is the control of resources valued by others, which is embedded and manifested in seniority and authority in Chinese society (Chen et al., 1999; Chen & Starosta, 1997). Seniority is an important variable affecting Chinese conflict management and decision-making processes because cultures under Confucianism pay great respect to the elderly, who enjoy a variety of privileges, power, and prerogatives (Chen & Starosta, 1997). In addition, seniority contributes to trust and credibility and, as a result, individuals might adopt a different conflict style depending on their own degree of seniority and credibility (Chen & Starosta, 1997). Authority plays an important role in Chinese conflict resolution because of its inherent hierarchical social structure. Socially superiors are assumed to have larger control or power over their inferiors and, hence, carry more weight in conflict management (Yu, 2002).

The Buddhist concept of *yuan,* dependent origination, also provides a philosophical underpinning for conflict styles (Chang, 2002; Chang & Holt, 1991; Chuang, 2002). Buddhists believe that *yuan* is predetermined by one's previous deeds, so one should focus on the self, rather than the other, in seeking the causes for conflict. *Yuan* also provides an alternative explanation to the observation that Chinese tend to be less aggressive and confrontational, but more consensual and obliging in approaching conflict because they cherish the precious "predetermined" opportunities to meet relational others (Chang, 2002; Chang & Holt, 1991; Chuang, 2002).

Scholars have also explored Daoist (Taoist) teachings and their effect on Chinese conflict styles (Chuang, 2002; Crawford, 1997, 2002). Dao (Tao) is viewed as "vacuity characterized by namelessness, elusiveness, fathomlessness, pervasiveness, profundity, and shapelessness" (Chen & Holt, 2002, p. 167). Daoists believe that everything extreme will swing to the opposite end, and Dao is the harmonious mutual transformation between the *yin* (the negative) and the *yang* (the positive) forces. Thus, "conflict is a natural process and to lose something in an adversarial situation is to gain something in return" (Chuang, 2002, pp. 29-30), so the best way to approach conflict is *wuwei* (nonaction), and just let Dao go on its own course. Based on the Daoist philosophy, Crawford (1997) proposed four approaches to manage conflict:

> Do not fight. . . . Recognize conflict as merely part of a larger whole. . . . Realize that fighting to get closer is a conceivable way of creating solidarity with another person or within the context of a group . . . and acknowledge exhausting the *yang* to return to the *yin* as a viable frame of reference for construing conflict. (p. 367)

Core Conflict Symbols
Indigenous to the Chinese Culture

Of the Chinese concepts that convey meanings similar to conflict, such as *chongtu* (clash), *maodun* (contradiction), *jiufen* (dispute), *fenqi* (difference), *wenti* (problem), and *yijian* (disagreement), *maodun* is most frequently used by Chinese people to describe conflict (Yu, 1997). *Maodun* is made up of two Chinese characters: *mao* (spear) and *dun* (shield). The idiom *zi xiang maodun* (contradicting oneself) originated in an ancient Chinese story. A man in the Kingdom of Chu (1100-223 BCE) had a spear and a shield for sale. After he boasted to the crowds around that his shield was so strong that nothing could pierce it, he boasted that his spear was strong enough to pierce anything. "What will happen," one person in the crowds asked, "if your spear is used to pierce your shield?" Clearly, it is logically incompatible to simultaneously have an impenetrable shield and a spear that finds nothing impenetrable. The original meaning of *maodun* emphasizes logical incompatibility or mutual contradiction (Yu, 1997).

The meaning of *maodun* evolved and expanded over time and was particularly influenced by Mao Zedong's (Mao Tse-tung, 1960) *On Maodun,* in which he examined *maodun* in three distinct yet related contexts: natural, social, and personal. Mao claimed that *maodun* in the social context is the most important because it referred to the dynamic relationship of interaction between different or even opposed groups (Yu, 1997). What was noticeable was that he shifted the focus of meaning of *maodun* from the original logical contradiction to the dynamic relationship of interaction in terms of differences, problems, and antagonism (Soo, 1981; Yu, 1997).

Interestingly, two seemingly contradictory factors frame Chinese people's attitudes toward conflict. On the one hand, the accentuation of harmony, face, and relationship in interpersonal relationships in traditional Chinese culture might inevitably engender a negative attitude toward conflict, in which conflict is perceived as something bad and destructive. On the other hand, the influence of Mao's doctrine on *maodun* and the Chinese Communist Party's propagandizing power over the Chinese people should not be underestimated. Mao urged the Chinese people to view *maodun* in a positive light, asserting that *maodun* is a catalyst for change and a denial of *maodun* is a denial of everything since *maodun* is everywhere (Yu, 1997). Yu (1997) found that most Chinese agreed in words that *maodun* is something positive, but adhered to the traditional Chinese view of conflict in deeds. Thus, he concluded that most Chinese perceive conflict as primarily negative and destructive.

Cultural Attitudes Toward Constructive Conflict Resolution

In light of the emphasis on harmony, face, and relationship in Chinese culture, unsurprisingly,

huibi (evading) is usually the preferred approach in managing conflict, especially when the conflict involves family members, relatives, friends, or other ingroup members (Yu, 1997). During such conflict, the Chinese tend to *da shi hua xiao, xiao shi hua liao* (make big conflict small, and small conflict nothing). The connotation of Chinese *huibi* is different from the Western conceptualizations of the avoiding style, however, because *huibi* from the Chinese perspective is high in self and other concern, which also lends support to the assertion that the avoiding style is understood differently across cultures (Kim & Leung, 2000; Ting-Toomey & Oetzel, 2001).

The preference of *huibi* does not rule out the use of confrontation, which is often used either in conflict with strangers and outgroups or in conflict with ingroups to fight for principles (Leung, 1988; Yu, 1997). Hwang (1997) developed a theoretical framework for illuminating Chinese conflict management in a number of contexts from the Confucian perspective. He incorporated three categories of Chinese interpersonal relationship (vertical ingroup, horizontal ingroup, and horizontal outgroup) with four aspects of Chinese conflict behaviors (harmony maintenance, personal goal attainment, coordination strategies, and dominant responses), and generated a total of 12 Chinese conflict resolution styles: forbearance, endurance, indirect communication, confrontation, caring about other's face in a perfunctory manner, taking care of other's face, obeying publicly and defying privately for the vertical ingroup, giving face, fighting overtly for the horizontal ingroup, struggling covertly for the horizontal ingroup, confrontation for the horizontal outgroup, and mediation for the horizontal outgroup. Although he did not use *huibi* as a specific style, the meaning of *huibi* was subsumed in several styles including endurance, giving face, and taking care of other's face. This model offers invaluable insight into the understanding of Chinese conflict management and resolution, particularly the confrontational aspects of Chinese conflict resolution contrary to the stereotypical views of nonconfrontation (Yu, 2002).

In addition, third-party mediation or the use of intermediaries is also a common practice in conflict resolution; "since Chinese culture does not encourage strong expressions of personal feelings, discussion through an intermediary will reduce the need for direct, emotional responses" (Hsu, 1970, p. 47). Unofficial mediators tend to be mutual close friends, family members, close relatives, elderly people high in social status, or other ingroup members trusted and respected by the conflicting parties primarily for two reasons: (a) *jia chou bu ke wai yang* (family disgrace should not be made public), so "the entitlement of mediation in Chinese culture is usually reserved for insiders" (Ma, 1992, p. 276); and (b) seniority represents more prestige and persuasive power in mediation, so a senior member is often sought after to mediate (Ma, 1992; Yu, 1997).

In contemporary China under the Communist political regime it is not uncommon for conflicting parties, especially those who are relatively old, to go to *danwei lingdao* (supervisors in working units) for arbitration, but young people seem to be reluctant to approach *lingdao* to resolve conflict (Yu, 1997). One possible explanation is that before China's open-door policy and economic reform, especially during the Great Cultural Revolution, *lingdao* had absolute authority and power over everything, including political issues, work problems, and personal matters, but after China adopted a market economy, *lingdao* are no longer authoritative over everything, and they have begun to lose their prestige and power over certain issues, like personal problems.

In summary, *maodun,* the Chinese equivalent of the Western notion of conflict, has shifted its meaning from incompatible contradiction to the dynamic relationship of interaction between different groups (Yu, 1997). *Hexie, guanxi, mianzi,* and *quanli* are the most important determinants of Chinese conflict management and resolution, in which *hexie* functions as an axis, working together with the spokes of *guanxi* and *mianzi* and the internal contingency of *quanli* to guarantee the smooth running of the wheel of Chinese conflict management and resolution (Chen & Starosta, 1997). *Maodun* is generally perceived as harmful and destructive, thus, *huibi* is the preferred approach to conflict management in the Chinese culture (Yu, 1997). Finally, spiritual principles also reinforce the use of *huibi,* but situational features encourage the use of confrontational strategies.

COLOMBIAN LENS FOR CONFLICT COMMUNICATION: A CULTURE UNDER VIOLENCE

Colombia presents a contrasting image to the Chinese conflict lens. Colombia is a democratic society with a colonial history. Colonization, and the resulting social institutions, had a strong impact in shaping the Colombian conflict lens. As with most Central and South American countries, socio-economic inequalities, cultural and ethnic differences, and political interests have been sources of conflict within Colombian society. Colombia holds a history of violent, destructive, and unresolved conflict that has deeply permeated its cultural structure.

In order to understand how Colombians perceive and address conflict, it is necessary to consider a complex set of factors. With more than 30,000 homicides a year, Colombia has one of the highest rates in the world, but it is not officially at war (Schneider, 2000). Colombia has a democratic political system, but corruption and state absenteeism has been rampant. Colombia owns important natural resources and a unique cultural diversity, but holds among the highest rates of unemployment and poverty. Conflict, in its many different forms, has been the axis of Colombian history, and violence has been the most common mechanism to deal with conflict at all levels. "The Colombian society has learned to coexist with a chronic, endemic, and permanent violence. . . . For the Colombians, violence is also a way of social relations" (Blair Trujillo, 1999, p. xvii). Moreover, within a culture where "interpersonal ideology of connectedness to people is a powerful symbolic resource for dealing with difficulties" (Fitch, 1998, p. 18), violence has permeated the structure of social relationships. Violence in forms of interpersonal intimidation, verbal aggression, and physical attacks are practiced ways to resolve conflicts within a strong system of interdependent family relationships. It is also present in schools and it is reproduced in the street (Salm & Gomez, 2000). Richani (1997) stated that violence tends not only to be maintained in Colombia, but it continues to increase, in a ceaseless, ever increasing spiral. This section emphasizes a historical perspective to understand the development of this "spiral of destructive conflict" that has created a culture of intolerance and violence in Colombia.[5] The development of repetitive, permanent, and cyclical unresolved conflicts in Colombia is in fact the result of the country's social, economical, political, and cultural structure.

Historical, Religious, and Socio-Cultural Roots Shaping the Colombian Conflict Lens

Colonial roots. When the conquerors from Spain arrived in Colombia in the early 1500s in search of El Dorado's treasure, they did not face any centralized vast indigenous empire in this country like the Aztecs in Mexico or the Inca in Peru. Yet as in many Latin American countries, the process of conquest and the imposition of the arriving Spanish socio-economic structure was largely a violent process. The Spaniards easily weakened the largest Colombian native group, the Muisca, after eliminating its regional leaders.

After the conquest (17th–18th century), indigenous people were subjected to violence in order to maintain the structure of domination within the colonial society. This population became the most important labor force of the new system, and the basis for a new mixed race, *mestizos*. Only some unconquered indigenous groups resisted this process, opting to live in the most isolated jungles or mountains of the country. Some of these groups still survive today, albeit at the bottom of the social hierarchy. As a consequence of the process of conquest, violence during the colonial period was spurred by inter-class conflicts (Oquist, 1980). The complex social hierarchy of dominance and the paternalistic economic system was the cause of strong conflicts that would continue through Colombian history.

Religious influences. Even though the Muiscas's descendents found hidden ways of keeping cultural and religious practices, most of them quickly assimilated to the imposed Catholicism in order to survive. In several cases, priests accepted people practicing old traditions and, at the same time, mixed them with the new imposed celebrations. This *sincretismo* (the process of fusion of the precolonial spiritual practices and the new imposed Catholic tradition) was evident in the process of assimilation and establishment of Catholicism, which became the principal axis of spiritual Colombian life in the colonial period (Haddox, 1965). In a country of regions, religion was the basis for the national unity. In fact, political, moral, and social Colombian values, as well as the educational system, were developed under the light of the Catholic Church. Everybody had to be baptized in order to appear in the birth register books of the state. A politically conservative and economically paternalistic system was highly supported by the leaders of the Catholic clergy. Values of continuity, submission, and obedience were implanted through its control of education. As a result, the Church approved and supported the growing social inequality, and simultaneously laid the groundwork for social conflicts (Blair Trujillo, 1999).

Socio-cultural roots. Columbia's political system has also developed through a chain of violent acts and processes. After struggles with the Spanish crown to obtain political independence, the Creole oligarchy (natives who were born in the new Spanish vice-royalty of Nueva Granada with direct and demonstrable descendants from Spaniards or Europeans) created a new state, strongly linked with the Church as its moral bastion. The first century of independence was characterized by a weak state within a strong structure of social domination. When the traditional structure began to weaken due to the impact of industrialization, social movements began to appear among the minority groups. These movements were violently repressed, and multiple civil wars took place in Colombia in the 19th century.

The earlier exclusionist and authoritarian character of the state was perpetuated through the founding and maintaining of two official parties that divided the country in two in the early years of the 20th century. Under conditions of socio-economic inequalities and the hegemony of the oligarchy, the democratic system of elections began to resemble vendettas in which strong and highly destructive violent practices came to be used. Political confrontation was, as a result, an internal socio-economic conflict where religion, land, and political power were involved. This confrontation ended in the 20-year period known as *La Violencia* (The Violence: 1946–1966). During this period at least 200,000 people died; it would constitute an important historical referent for future generations (Oquist, 1980). This internal war resulted in the two oligarchies' negotiating to share the government during the second half of the 20th century, but this pact did not end the conflict. On the contrary, it increasingly excluded minority representation and legitimated the repression of any alternative political group. As a result, this exclusionism favored the formation of guerrilla movements, and increased the internal conflict between these groups and the armed forces of the state. In addition to the internal conflict, the fact that the state and its representatives were increasingly absent began to weaken its legitimacy among the citizens. The gap between a changing society and a conservative state that could not satisfy its necessities opened the door to a culture of non-tolerance and the private resolution of conflicts.

The culture of interpersonal violence is also the result socio-economic development. As in other Latin American countries, economic modernization came to Colombia with industrialization. This process of modernization was one of exclusion due to the existing social hierarchy and strong conservative principles of the society. Only the elite of the country, owners of the productive land, benefited from the production of capital, and the promises of democratization and secularization of the modernization were never fulfilled. This lack of social change increased the gap between the conservative oligarchy and the rest of the population. Even though Colombia gained a relatively stable economic system, social contradictions matured into acute conflicts. With time, these deep social conflicts became potential sources of violent response within an exclusionist and authoritarian political environment. Illegal activities, such as contraband and drug trafficking, resulted and became the base of an underground economy that helped to prevent the consolidation of democracy and weakened, even further, the administrative capacity of the state (Galan Sarmiento, 1997).

With the arrival of new actors in the Colombian conflict scenarios, new forms of legitimacies also appeared. Guerrillas argued about the narrowness of the political system, the military defended the institutions, the paramilitaries evoked the incompetence of the state against the guerrillas, the *sicarios* (paid assassins) defended their right to earn money to live, and the popular militias supported the communities threatened by the *sicarios*. These situations led to the annihilation of collective interests and the individualization of values (Blair Trujillo, 1999).

Core Conflict Symbols Indigenous to the Colombian Culture

These historical roots provide a frame of reference for understanding conflict perspectives in Colombia. Further, the specific symbols illustrate how conflict is viewed. While the words *conflicto* (conflict) or *discusión* (discussion) are terms used within more formal-official environments to designate *desacuerdos* (disagreements), *pelea* (fight) is perhaps the most popular term when talking about and within daily conflictive situations. Because it is a word that can be used both as a noun and as a verb, *pelea* became useful to describe a situation where two or more actors were involved, but at the same time to connect the specific event in time and context. *Estamos de pelea* (we are in a fight), *tuviste una pelea?* (did you have a fight?), *estamos peliando* (we are fighting), *ayer nos peliamos* (we fought yesterday), *ya dejamos de pelear* (we already stopped fighting), are all common expressions to describe and locate conflicts at all levels within particular frames. *Pelea* also reflects and reinforces the negative meaning of conflict.

In general, Colombians view conflict as a negative confrontation to win at all cost. Resolutions are strategic in order to obtain the highest personal benefit. Within situations of conflict, Colombians see themselves as victims and others as aggressors. Lies, deception, intimidation, coercion, physical elimination of the other, and private justice show the absence of a collective normative-symbolic order (Blair Trujillo, 1999).

Even though the structural conditions of the Colombian society can explain the causes of the crises that evoke violent responses, these objective conditions need subjective actors that reproduce and perpetuate this dynamic. Randall Salm, a U.S. American conflict resolution expert and professor in several universities in Colombia, has explained that these actors internalized the evident effectiveness of individual methods to resolve conflicts and reproduced and increased the practice of violence at all levels of action (Salm, personal communication, September 9, 2003). The justification for using these strategic behaviors to address conflict comes from individuals' being "prisoners" of the state: "If the visible heads of the state like politicians and judges fall into inconsistencies and injustices, it is fine if I, an individual immersed within the system, do the same" (Gutierrez, 1998, p. 188). Under this assumption, men can justify deceiving their wives, social leaders can justify corruption, and fathers can justify the aggressive behaviors of their children.

The study of violence in Colombia emphasizes the perpetuation of violence from a symbolic level. In the search for collective referents, Colombians legitimate violence as a collective practice, and look at the common image of the enemy as a symbolic referent (Blair Trujillo, 1999). At this level, Colombians have given violence a ritual characteristic. There is limited space for communication of differences. As a consequence, the practice of excluding relationships is being reproduced, because the other represents a threat within the new collective referent of the enemy.

The intensive representation and symbolization of the Colombian spiral of violence in all forms of art gives an idea of the deep impact of this phenomenon in the collective memory of its actors and the alternative ways to face it. Salm (personal communication, September 9, 2003) explained how the sense of frustration, fear, and resentment can be seen in the communication habits of Colombians. From persuasion, he observed, it is very easy to fall into aggression and then into violent acts because all of these strategies are justified by the society. The reproduction of a culture of intolerance makes Colombians look at conflict as a competition to win at all cost, and most of the time as a destructive process. Maria Arcos (personal communication, September 7, 2003), a clinical psychologist and professor of conflict resolution at several universities in Colombia, argued that conflict situations are viewed as obstacles for both parties. If the obstacle is minor, we attack it. If it is major, we eliminate it, and then we get what we want. When Mockus (2003), the mayor of

Bogotá, was asked about the way Colombians behave, he said most of us respect the rules, but prefer the shortcut, the fast way, and the most convenient way for us.

(New) Cultural Attitudes Toward Constructive Conflict Resolution

The study of conflict and the phenomenon of violence has become one of the most important topics for Colombian academic research. Even though it has focused primarily on the political and military spheres, the study of violence as a reproduced way to solve conflict among all citizens and its impact over all the society is a key issue for Colombian academics, the Catholic Church, and a new generation of politicians. Recently, governmental and non-governmental organizations have given some attention to the use of conciliation, negotiation, and mediation as alternative strategies to resolve conflicts within the community.

As a consequence of congestion, low effectiveness, high costs, and the corruption of the justice system, conciliation began to gain importance as a conflict resolution strategy. In Colombia, conciliation is a formal process where two or more parties seek to solve their differences with the help of a neutral third party called a conciliator. Although it occurs within the structure of the judicial system, conciliation is considered a tacit agreement that should be equitable and of mutual benefit to all the parties. The conciliator can be a civil or official functionary, but needs to be empowered by the law to administer justice (Trujillo, 2002).

The conciliator intercedes, helping to solve the conflict by facilitating communication and constructive dialogue among the parties. He or she conducts the process to foster negotiation, so that the parties are responsible for finding the best solution (Trujillo, 2002). The figure of the private conciliator has always existed within some Colombian communities, but only now it is officially recognized. Within some indigenous *Guajira* communities of the north of Colombia, for example, this figure is well known as *el palabrero:* the man who has the words, or the man who helps to speak. These people, who are not necessarily lawyers, know their communities in depth and are honored, recognized, and respected by the community (Maria Arcos, personal communication, November 23, 2004).

This figure began to be reproduced within the cities by lawyers and law students who are accredited as conciliators using official centers of conciliation. Since 1991, these new "centers of conciliation and arbitration" have been supported by the state and can be found in urban areas to resolve domestic conflicts before resorting to trial. During 1999, Colombians solicited 13,509 audiences to these centers around the country. Almost 54% of these conciliation processes reached agreements, demonstrating an increasing popularity among the population and effective practical application of this mechanism (Trujillo, 2002). This process is relevant considering that the agreement achieved implies both sides in the conflict have agreed to give up part of their own interests.

Similarly, although less formal, the process of mediation is another alternative to solve domestic or civil conflicts outside of the regular justice process. Within this process, there is a first attempt to negotiate directly among the parties involved in the conflict. If this first step fails, a third party or mediator is involved. He or she could be a neighbor, a family member, or a friend who is recognized by all parties as being impartial. Unlike conciliation, at the end of this process there is no legal documentation or judicial act. This process, called a mediated negotiation, can be found within small rural communities or urban organized neighborhoods (Maria Arcos, personal communication, November 23, 2004).

In summary, conflict is a daily component of Colombian society. It is as complex as its history. The roots of the spiral of unresolved conflicts that made Colombians lose faith in institutions are deep and will not be reduced easily. Although the informal processes of conciliation and mediation have been increasingly recognized by communities to solve civil conflicts, there is still a long way to go before Colombian people believe in justice and legal processes. These mechanisms need time to be legitimized and to generate a deep cultural change that goes from a confrontational, bipolar, and passive attitude to a more conciliatory, participatory, and active perspective of resolving conflicts in Colombia. Perhaps this urgent need to deeply analyze and understand the causes of the reproduction of violence as the rooted way to face and resolve conflicts will lead Colombians to find a way to reinterpret conflict as a positive and constructive social tool for facing differences.

SOUTH AFRICAN LENS FOR CONFLICT COMMUNICATION: SOCIAL HISTORICAL FRAMING

The South African lens has many similarities with the Colombian lens. Both countries share a colonial history resulting in deep power inequities, conflict, and violence. In contrast, South Africa has attempted to move beyond the violence and is focused on peace-building. An examination of conflict management in the South African context must necessarily incorporate a socio-economic, political, and historical perspective. The section considers three eras that have shaped differing conflict management perspectives: the precolonial era (pre-1652); the colonial/apartheid era (1652–early 1990s); and contemporary, post-apartheid democratic South Africa (1994–present). Conflict was primarily characterized by prevention, confrontation, and resolution, respectively, in these three eras. The focus of this section is to illuminate how approaches to conflict evolved and altered significantly as a consequence of socio-economic and political changes, particularly between Blacks and Whites.

Socio-Historical/Political Roots Shaping the South African Conflict Lens

Precolonial era: Traditional norms and customs. During the precolonial era, traditional norms and customs were applied primarily to prevent conflict, which, if and when it did arise, was frowned upon.[6] Although some variations might be found from tribe to tribe, the Nguni people of southern Africa are representative of the norms and values that applied generally throughout the region. The Nguni strived to exist in harmony, particularly respectful of recognized hierarchies and adhering to the confines of established traditional norms and values. Within this social structure, different types of disputes arose that required a specific type of intervention. Depending on the severity of a dispute, a matter might be addressed at one of three levels; the family level, the community level, or the level of royal intervention (intertribal). The resolution of a family feud would involve family elders; failing that, the dispute would be taken to a community council. A regular community meeting, *imbizo,* was held at which community members presented items for discussion. This monthly gathering consisted of all male tribal elders and was presided over by the chief. If the *imbizo* could not resolve the matter satisfactorily, the dispute would then be taken before the king, as a very last resort. Preventive measures were usually applied before a matter required intervention at the community or royal level.

When parties engaged in dispute were unable to reach a peaceful agreement on their own, the next step would be to approach family or community elders. These individuals would then take into account the relevant mitigating factors and arrive at a decision that served not only the interests of the parties involved but also the interests of the larger community. Harmony was prized, and as such the needs of the individual became secondary to those of the collective. Generally, communities used recognized dispute resolution practices to encourage and maintain harmony. The advent of colonialism would alter these practices and lead to a less community-driven approach to conflict resolution.

Colonial/apartheid era: Modern law and judicial process. The advent of colonialism and the institution of modern laws, such as "antivagrancy laws," the Poll Tax (late 18th and early 19th centuries), and later, Pass Laws (mid-20th century), took precedence over the powers of the chiefs and kings, disrupting entrenched social systems and culminating in myriad disparities that were blamed on European authorities (Feit, 1965; Turner, 1978). The socio-economic disparities engendered by European immigrants and settlers initially related to land and stock theft, which dispossessed the indigenous nations (Turner, 1978). These inequities led to disputes that quickly escalated into conflict. Later, these disputes acquired racial and political dimensions as conflict heightened between Blacks and Whites.

Conflict management during the colonial and apartheid periods was defined by the imposition of Roman-Dutch Law and an ethos based on Judeo-Christian norms and values (de Gruchy, 1997). Traditional councils presided over by *indunas* (chiefs or headman) represented communities in these ruling systems. The *indunas,* co-opted into the colonial structures and judicial system, were forced to bring indigenous communities under the rule of customary law and colonial rule. A discernible shift in conflict management occurred as a result of these measures. Increasingly, the power to resolve disputes came to rest within a legal system that removed the authority of traditional leaders and imposed a subordinate status on native communities.

In 1927, the Black Administration Act #38 inserted legal councils into the colonial judicial system. Indigenous peoples were divided according to ethnicity, and separate laws were enacted for Blacks and Whites. Kings and chiefs now fell under the jurisdiction of the customary law courts, and all matters of civil and petty criminal cases were adjudicated at the magistrates' courts. In terms of hierarchy, the native affairs commissioner now took precedence over the traditional structures (Koyana, 1980).

Conflict management at this time began to include more punitive measures in the form of jail time. In much the same way as in precolonial South Africa, disputing parties adhered to a certain protocol. Those engaged in disagreements would first seek a mutually agreeable solution on their own. If the process continued to be impossible to reconcile, the matter was then taken before a headman who was invested with civil and criminal jurisdiction by the (South African) Minister of Justice and who could, in turn, take it to the customary law court. The major difference here lies in the absence of communal consensus that, at this stage of dispute resolution in precolonial times, would have been summarily handed down by the chief and adhered to by opposing parties. Instead, individuals found to be in violation of a law would be summarily punished as warranted by the severity of the matter in dispute. While the focus on Roman-Dutch law continues today, conflict management and resolution in postapartheid South Africa has become characterized by a greater ethos of compromise, compassion, and a focus on nation building.

Contemporary era: Consensus-driven conflict resolution. During the mid-1980s, scholars had begun to ask how to ensure a future for both Blacks and Whites in the region. Intergroup conflict had, by this time, escalated into incessant violence. Rotberg (1980) stated that any shared future needed to focus on a system wherein conflict could be diminished and conciliation and harmony maximized. The culmination of resistance and negotiation that came out of this period of South African history was an end to apartheid in 1990, and, after the first democratic elections of 1994, revised approaches to conflict management focusing on negotiation, compromise, and resolution.

The contemporary view on conflict in post-apartheid South Africa is that it is antithetical to the process of establishing a democratic state. Contemporary South Africa is also characterized by derivation of agreement by consensus rather than coercion. This is a noteworthy departure from the centuries of conflict that Ngubane (1979) stated were due to mutually exclusive attitudes in Africa and Europe toward the person. The latter formerly assigned and evaluated value of the person through investment and profit margins, whereas the former functioned on the basis of mutual respect and cooperation, irrespective of race. More recently, these attitudes have shifted toward a middle ground, discernible in contemporary socio-political discourse (Makgoba, 1999).

Core Conflict Symbols of South African Culture

During the precolonial era, the prevalent ethos was the philosophy of *ubuntu,* a way of life that advocated mutual respect, dignity, and humaneness. Tutu (1999) defined this philosophy as an acknowledgment that the individual humanity of all persons is closely wedded to and inextricably bound with the humanity of their fellow humans. Conflict was therefore regarded as a failure to uphold this ethos and was regarded as unconstructive. Disagreements were usually treated as or *impikiswano* (disputes). Only when these disagreements escalated were they regarded as *ungquzulwano* (conflict), which was extremely negative.

Because of this perspective, the focus was on preventive measures. Kings ruled benevolently

and compassionately, with little involvement in the daily community life of their people. Communities revolved on cooperative living, which, although far from utopic, was invariably practical. Notably, the prevention and resolution of conflict was strictly the domain of male elders in the community, a distinctive feature of the tribal, patriarchal, and hierarchical precolonial societies in South Africa.

By the time a disagreement warranted resolution by a chief or a king, it would have become quite egregious in nature, such as inter-tribal conflicts or livestock theft. The latter, especially if it occurred between tribes as a result of a raid, was a very serious offense because livestock were inextricably linked to ways of life in rural communities. The resolution of this type of conflict involved representations to the offending tribe's king. If amicable settlement proved impossible and successive representations failed, the tribes engaged in physical combat to decide the matter. The emergent victor was entitled to claim not only his own livestock but also some from the offending tribe, as a punitive measure, and conflict was thus summarily concluded.

In the colonial/apartheid era, conflict management moved from prevention to confrontation, especially between Blacks and Whites. During this era, South Africa was divided into several *Bantustans* (homelands), areas where each Black tribe was enclosed within specific boundaries. For example, the Zulu inhabited Zululand, and the Xhosa were confined to the Transkei and the Ciskei and the Tswana to Bophuthatswana. Each homeland had a judicial system that was presided over by, in descending order of status, the native affairs commissioner, a headman (chief), and a sub-headman (head of the ward—a subunit of the homeland). In both civil and petty criminal cases, the onus rested with a defendant to prove innocence, based on the assumption that *kungaqhuma kubasiwe* (there is no fire without smoke; Koyana, 1980). These proceedings, held in formal courtrooms, added a new dimension to conflict management and resolution that differed significantly from the indigenous communal approach. This period in South African history was also similarly characterized by an absence of women in dispute resolution. Koyana (1980) stated that this dearth of women in legal proceedings was due to the inferior position to which women were relegated, both in tribal structures and under customary law. Appearances by women in court were expected only if a woman was directly related to the case at hand.

In the 1900s, urban Blacks fell under separate "native" administration and laws within the socio-culturally premised system of apartheid (Ngubane, 1979; Turner 1978). The 20th century bore witness to high levels of resistance to discriminatory laws that were arbitrarily applied. Feit (1965) stated that limits on economic mobility constituted a significant part of the impetus for Black-White political and social antagonism. Increasingly, conflict revolved primarily around economic and political confrontation of apartheid and its concomitant inequalities. This era witnessed unrestrained conflict (*ungquzulwano*) wherein parties actively sought to destabilize the perceived opponent. In 1948, when the Nationalist Party came to power, apartheid was instituted as official state policy. This saw the beginning of state-sanctioned segregation as the country was effectively divided into administrative systems that catered separately for Blacks, Whites, Coloreds, and Indians. All native tribes, encapsulated under the single label Black, were relegated to the lowest rung of the social ladder and systematically disenfranchised, leading to a desperate struggle for survival. Resistance to apartheid policies therefore surged most strongly in Black communities. Initially, this resistance took the form of nonviolent protests prior to the 1960s, but escalated to an armed struggle and guerrilla warfare that lasted until the late 1980s. The result was an impasse between the parties engaged in conflict, eventually leading to negotiations for peaceful political settlement. The beginning of the 1990s evidenced the lifting the bans against liberation movements, an end to apartheid policies, and the beginning of reconciliatory measures.

In the contemporary era, core symbols toward conflict have returned to a manner similar to the guidelines of *ubuntu*. Conflict is positive if it is *impikiswano,* but *ungquzulwano* is extremely negative. The focus on minimizing conflict and reconciling the problems of apartheid and on the continent (results from colonialism) led to two new approaches to conflict management and resolution: (a) the socio-political process of the Truth and Reconciliation Commission (TRC); and (b) the political and consensus-driven approach that incorporates a national, regional, and continent-wide perspective. We discuss these processes in the next subsection.

Cultural Attitudes Toward Constructive Conflict Resolution

Examining the state of conflict resolution in post-apartheid South Africa, Nathan (1994, 1995) argued that conflict management was an indispensable component of everyday governance. This point is intrinsic to understanding the rationale for the institution of the Truth and Reconciliation Commission (TRC), a process that aimed to make South Africa more governable by facilitating the resolution of conflict ensuing from old wounds, particularly in a politically, socially, and economically volatile context. The process of finding common ground between all South Africans presented two options. The first was to achieve reconciliation through the punishment of past wrongdoing. The second, more favored, alternative was to find ways to forgive the deeds of the past across the political spectrum (Lodge, 2002). The TRC was an indicator of a new, reconciliatory national ethos, one that attempted to recall aspects of *ubuntu* in that it called for compromise and collaboration by all citizens in this fledgling democracy. The public hearings, televised on a daily basis, were vaunted as a therapeutic process for the country, and for southern Africa too as the region had been similarly affected by apartheid. These truth-telling proceedings sought to build a bridge between Blacks, Whites, and other ethnic groups as political conflicts continued to dominate the national landscape (Tutu, 1999). Supplementing this process, leaders of political parties were also engaged in fervent diplomacy and ardent negotiations to achieve a politically acceptable resolution to the raging political conflicts of that tenuous time.

The merits of this public approach to conflict resolution continue to be debated (Krog, 2000; Tutu, 1999). Lodge (2002) stated that the public's ambiguous response to the TRC process makes it difficult to evaluate just how effective it was as a tool of reconciliation, particularly as the list of recommendations in the final report have largely been ignored. There have, however, been some efforts at restitution to affected parties such as financial reparation, and obtaining answers to questions related to finding out about political activists who either disappeared or were killed and buried in unmarked graves. In addition, the TRC raised the level of social awareness, particularly among White South Africans, about the most awful materialization of apartheid (Krog, 2000; Tutu, 1999). These negotiated successes and the TRC process have highlighted, among other factors, one salient point: namely, the political and social motivation for the cessation of conflict is adamantly focused on the creation of a single, unified South African nation. This move toward cultural/national homogeneity indicated that conflict was once again viewed as undesirable, and efforts at prevention increasingly became the norm, especially in urban and semi-urban areas. National partners in brokering conflict resolution included chiefs and kings, now constitutionally recognized but with limited spheres of influence. Other peace-building partnerships involved community-based organizations (largely made up of volunteer members of local communities with limited resources) and non-governmental organizations (many of which were foreign-based and received external funding).

The political role of the newly democratic South African state expanded post-1994 focusing on addressing social problems resulting from colonialism and apartheid. Working closely with its neighbors, South Africa's approaches to conflict prevention and management have increasingly become premised on early intervention, diplomatic mediation, and negotiation. Nathan (1994) outlined specific steps in contemporary approaches to conflict management that focused on addressing causes rather than symptoms. These steps included the following: (a) focusing on structural causes; (b) allowing for lengthy intra-state crisis resolution; (c) understanding that cessation of warfare is not an indicator of an end to crisis; (d) increasing peace-building mechanisms; (e) increasing the efficiency and effectiveness of state institutions; (f) focusing on uniting and accommodating politically, culturally, and ethnically diverse populations; (g) making peace-building the work of Africans rather than foreigners; (h) insisting foreigners follow the guidelines of African sensibilities in intervention proceedings; and (i) holding international partners accountable. These measures or steps in conflict prevention, management, and resolution are indicative of the complexity of the process both on the subcontinent and on the continent as a whole.

A critical component in the prevention and negotiation of conflict is the acceptance of political, religious, and ethnic diversity (Nathan, 1994). Breytenbach (1999) emphasized this acceptance, alluding to the "dehumanized boundaries" (p. 97) that are an outcome of colonialism. He stated that part of the solution to the major challenge to unity and peace on the continent would be a careful reconsideration of the artificial boundaries imposed on Africans that had rendered inexplicable divisions among indigenous nations and peoples, effectively separating entire cultures. The acceptance of diversity would be part of the path toward restitution and enduring cooperative peace on the continent. In this vein, African leaders, both past and present, continuously emphasize the need for tolerance at all levels. For example, President Obasanjo in Nigeria encourages mutuality between the majority Christian population and the expanding Muslim populations in cities such as Jos in central Nigeria (Herman, 2001). Similarly, in strife-torn Mozambique and Angola, greater tolerance between ethnic groups is encouraged by leaders, given the history of civil war that frequently pitted tribes against one another in service to political and economic gain.

In conclusion, there is a lingering understanding among African intellectuals that the path of reconciliation is hampered by the enduring legacy of more than 500 years of colonialism and inequity. According to Mandaza (1999), southern Africa (and the entire continent of Africa) is a hybrid that has resulted from the complex interaction between historical extraneous entities and internal dynamics that are evidenced by the contemporary politics of reconciliation. Against this backdrop, the path toward change is, not unexpectedly, defined by contemporary uneasy socio-political relations with former colonial powers. Africa's reality is that neocolonialism is very much a part of the continent (Mandaza, 1999). The renewal of the continent and the cessation of conflicts thus hinges, to a great extent, on the success of contemporary social movements such as the African Renaissance, which emphasize social, political, and economic regeneration as the assurance for the revival of Africa. This social movement emphasizes the spirit of *ubuntu* in the focus on preventing conflict and fostering harmony, cooperation, and negotiation as essential tools for the successful development of South Africa and the continent.

INTEGRATING PERSPECTIVES ON CONFLICT: FUTURE DIRECTIONS AND PRACTICAL APPLICATIONS

In the extant literature, the predominant approach to understanding conflict perspectives and conflict management style is to utilize a model of cultural- and individual-level components. Specifically, researchers argue that the influence of cultural-level variables and conflict styles is mediated by individual-level factors (Gudykunst et al., 1996; Oetzel & Ting-Toomey, 2003; Ting-Toomey & Oetzel, 2001). Conflict behavior is learned within the primary socialization process of one's cultural or ethnic group. Individuals learn the norms and scripts for appropriate and effective conflict conduct in their immediate cultural environment. Essentially, cultural values have a direct effect on conflict behaviors and an indirect effect that is mediated through individual-level factors (Gudykunst et al., 1996; Oetzel & Ting-Toomey, 2003).

While the cultural- and individual-level model for explaining conflict behavior has led to important and practical findings, this approach ignores macro factors that may be important considerations. Thus, we compare the four cultures to illustrate how historical, political, and spiritual roots shape core symbols and cultural attitudes toward conflict management. With this comparison, we identify future directions and practical applications.

Comparison of Conflict Perspectives and Future Directions

The perspective taken in each culture demonstrates that conflict perspectives and communication in each of the cultures has transformed over time. The changes occurred because of spiritual and political influences within the culture that, in turn, created different perspectives on conflict. In addition, while each of the cultures reviewed in this study is collectivistic, the predominant conflict behaviors vary from culture to culture, suggesting different notions of collectivism as a result of the spiritual, historical, and political influences.

Social-cultural roots. Spirituality is a key factor for the conflict perspectives in these cultures. Confucianism, Daoism, and Buddhism have long been integrated into conflict practices in China. These spiritual notions help to reinforce the existing social relations and preference for harmony. In Colombia, the introduction of the Catholic Church provided an institution that helped to create social inequalities, but at the same time provided a model for interacting with one another in a respectful manner. The spiritual values of *ubuntu* provide a historical foundation and a goal for increasing harmony in South Africa. Finally, Islam helped to transform the tribal emphasis of honor and shame in Arab cultures by encouraging the use of third-party advisors and judges to resolve conflict peacefully and justly. The integration of spiritual values, along with other historical and political factors, demonstrates that these cultures are constantly in a state of transformation.

Political forces also shaped conflict perspectives and behaviors in these cultures. In China, political influences were apparent with the impact of Mao Zedong's perspectives on conflict and society. In the other three cultures, the collective memories are strongly shaped by colonization and post-colonial perspectives (Said, 1978, 1981). Colonization instituted foreign and incompatible structures that directly impacted the nature and amount of conflict, as well as influencing the manner in which conflict was managed. These structures created social inequities that encouraged greater confrontation in an attempt to address inequities and restore honor and justice.

Political and spiritual factors are not often discussed in the intercultural and cross-cultural literatures on conflict. This review, however, demonstrates the importance of historical, political, spiritual, contextual, and cultural factors for conflict perspectives and communicative behaviors. Future research should attempt to integrate these factors, as well as individual-level factors, into models of cross-cultural and intercultural conflict. Further, this review suggests a critical question for future research: What are the combinations of spiritual, political, and cultural factors that shape individuals' conflict communication?

Core conflict symbols. These four cultures have similarities and differences in perspectives about conflict. The conflict symbols illustrate varying conceptualizations of conflict ranging in meaning from minor disagreement to intense fighting. An important implication for researchers is to ensure that meanings are equivalent when comparing conflict across cultures.

Further, all four cultures have a perspective that conflict, in general, is bad and should be avoided if possible. There is a strong sense of encouraging harmony within each of the cultures (it appears to be an ideal state in Colombia). This general overview is consistent with views about conflict in collectivistic cultures (Ting-Toomey, 1988), but is an incomplete view. In China, conflict also has the connotation of opportunity and thus confrontation is appropriate in certain situations. In the Arab culture framed by Islam, conflict impacts honor and thus an appropriate response can be to seek retribution in the restoration of justice and honor. In Colombia, conflict is so commonplace and violence is so accepted that people adopt a competitive stance to make sure that their needs (and their family's) are taken care of. Perhaps it is only in South Africa, where conflict and apartheid caused so much damage, that people seek predominantly harmonious resolutions to conflict.

Closely related to the concern for harmony is the emphasis on face and facework. All four cultures emphasize the importance of face as a relational construct rather than the rational and transactional conceptualization of face in the West (Jia, 1997). Yet, differences exist in the process of restoring and maintaining face. In the Arab world, with the influence of Islam, the restoration of justice and honor is of primary importance and rituals exist to restore face and also preserve harmony. In China, face is a critical facet of everyday life and face is given to others

to prevent conflict (Gao & Ting-Toomey, 1998). In Colombia, facework is used to facilitate daily interaction (Fitch, 1998), but the restoration of face loss due to social inequalities often results in verbal aggressiveness and physical violence. Finally, in South Africa, the restoration of face (along with resources and opportunities) is an important component of the TRC.

The similar emphasis on harmony and face is likely related to the importance of collectivism in each of these cultures. Different cultural components and socio-cultural roots, however, shaped the processes for restoring and maintaining harmony and face. Important future directions include gaining a better understanding of the culturally appropriate facework strategies within these cultures—both intraculturally and when individuals from these cultures interact with members of different cultural groups.

Cultural attitudes toward conflict management. While the core conflict symbols have some overlap, the approaches to conflict management differ across the cultures. In both the Muslim-Arab culture and Colombia, violence and revenge have a level of acceptability to restore face loss and right wrongs. The long-lasting social equalities in these cultures strongly influence the frequency of violent resolutions to conflict. However, the religious influence in both cultures emphasizes the importance of forgiveness and peaceful solutions as appropriate alternatives to violence. In the Muslim-Arab culture, in particular, the use of religious leaders as third-party arbitrators and judges is critical to the peaceful and culturally appropriate management of conflict. In South Africa, conflict management has taken a strong preventive approach. Because of the past violence, proactive approaches are utilized to foster understanding and acceptance of cultural differences, as well as to provide economic development in post-colonial Africa. China also emphasizes preventive approaches to interpersonal conflict, but confrontation and competition are appropriate under certain conditions (especially with outgroup members and in the context of a market economy).

The differences in conflict management spark important questions for future research. The histories of South Africa, the Arab Muslim world, and Colombia share a colonial past, yet one of these cultures has moved beyond violence whereas the other two have violence still a part of the culture. An important question is why have these differences arisen? Social inequalities have not been completely addressed in South Africa, so why is violence not the answer there? The important point is to understand when and why dialogue is appropriate to manage conflict.

Practical Applications

This review also has implications for practitioners working specifically with members of these cultures, but also for practitioners working in the field of intercultural conflict in general. Similar to the previous sections, we organize these suggestions around roots, core symbols, and constructive conflict.

There are two critical applications regarding socio-cultural roots. First, the information in this review helps to illustrate how conflict perspectives are shaped by history, politics, and spiritual components. An important first step for a conflict practitioner is to study these macro features in order to have a sense of their foundations. This review helps to show some of the roots of conflict behaviors in these four cultures, but certainly is not complete because of space limitations. The historical and cultural frame is particularly important to illuminate the colonization process, which created social inequalities in Colombia, the Muslim world, and South Africa (as well as many other cultures). Illuminating the result of colonization helps potential practitioners to see beyond the "strong West and weak East/third world" imageries. These imageries open the door to understand conflict dynamics in situations with deep unequal power relationships.

The second application for practitioners is to move beyond binary imageries of power, which can help practitioners balance power without adopting a paternalistic stance. Colonization produced social inequalities that help to shape many conflict behaviors in these cultures. Thus, there are power imbalances that need to be addressed during conflict management, which should be done without the conflict practitioner adopting a paternalistic approach to balancing the power. A paternalistic approach would be characteristic of a practitioner who wants to take care of the "poor" disadvantaged conflict participants

and to give them a voice to be heard. This approach will shift power to the practitioner, but not to the conflict participants. Thus, practitioners are met with a challenge to provide dynamic opportunities and spaces for conflict participants to balance power on their own.

For the core symbols, a key practical application is to understand subtle variations in harmony and facework. Many intercultural conflict trainers utilize cultural values, particularly individualism-collectivism, to understand conflict communication (see Coleman & Raider and Ting-Toomey & Takai, Chapters 24 and 25, respectively, in this volume). This approach is a useful foundation, but also misses some subtle nuances about collectivism. An overly simplistic view of collectivism may lead a practitioner to emphasize harmony in each of these cultures. Harmony is only part of the story, however. In the Muslim world, appropriate responses to conflict include both peaceful resolution by using a third party and retribution to restore honor. Further, harmony must be emphasized within the religious context. In South Africa, in contrast, there is a strong push to emphasize harmony to move away from the destructive past. In Colombia, interpersonal bonds and harmony are important, but social inequality has encouraged a violent approach in many disputes. Harmony and opportunity mark the conflict perspectives in China.

Finally, the cultural attitudes toward constructive conflict illustrate that dialogue is a useful approach. The components of dialogue are discussed in depth elsewhere in this volume (see Barge, Chapter 19, and Littlejohn, Chapter 14, in this volume) and therefore are not reviewed here. Dialogue is a tool that can be used effectively so long as it is adapted to fit each of the cultural specifics. For example, one key component is to make sure that appropriate constituents are involved in the dialogue process. Each of these cultures has individuals who have a high social standing and thus can be important to shaping the conflict management process. In the Muslim-Arab world, if the participation of religious leaders serving as judges and arbitrators is not included, the dialogue process can be rendered useless. In Colombia, priests are respected members whose perspectives should be included. In South Africa, depending on the specific participants, tribal and governmental leaders have an important place in the process. Finally, in China, respected elders are critical to success. In addition to important parties who need to be included, specific cultural values should be emphasized, or at least respected, for a peaceful and satisfactory resolution. These values include forgiveness, shame, and justice (Muslim-Arab culture); social relationships and reducing inequalities (Colombia); *ubuntu* (South Africa); and *mianzi, guanxi, hexie,* and *quanli* (China).

While culture perspectives should not be ascribed to all individuals within these cultures (i.e., it is important to keep in mind that each of these cultures—particularly the Muslim world—is not monolithic and there is within-culture variation), understanding these differences provides a challenge and opportunity for conflict practitioners operating in these cultures (or working with members from these cultures) to uphold or maintain the face of the participants (Ting-Toomey & Oetzel, 2001). Maintaining face is an important skill for conflict practitioners (Domenici & Littlejohn, 2001). Helping participants maintain honor, stand for their social rights, and achieve goals are self-face concerns that are consistent with the conflict perspectives in these cultures. Harmony and relational maintenance are other-face or mutual-face concerns that are consistent with some of the traditional collectivistic notions toward conflict in these cultures. Helping participants maintain and support self- and other-face encourages participants to choose peaceful and collaborative management communication.

In summary, this chapter reviewed four different collectivistic cultures to challenge predominant Western perspectives about conflict. In so doing, the review suggests alternative perspectives about conflict, as well as identifies political, spiritual, and historical factors shaping conflict communication. These factors provide important insights into cross-cultural and intercultural conflict, suggesting future research and applications for practitioners.

NOTES

1. The second through fifth authors are listed alphabetically.

2. We do not wish to suggest that the reviews of literature for each culture are complete. They are meant to be overviews of key points. Space constraints make complete coverage impossible. A member of the specific culture predominantly constructed each section and thus it is important for the reader to understand that the review is shaped by personal bias and should not be taken as a treatise of what the "true" culture is like.

3. The Arabic word for brotherhood includes both genders.

4. Qur'an references in this section are based on the original Arabic text with consultation with various English translations of the Qur'an.

5. A historical perspective is used to address the complexity of several cultural factors that have constructed the conceptualization of conflict in Colombia. Other perspectives (e.g., social psychological and communication) have explained causes and management styles within a system of interdependent relationships that exist in Colombia. For example, Fitch (1998) focused on the way Colombians manage conflict through an ideology of connectedness and maintaining strong interpersonal communication patterns. She argued that "to survive in the complexity that is Bogotá—indeed, to be truly a 'person' in the Colombian sense of the word—interpersonal bonds *must* be accorded primordial importance" (p. 18). Our purpose is not to contradict the importance of strong interpersonal bonds, but rather to offer an alternative (and perhaps complementary) explanation grounded in the historical perspective.

6. We wish to acknowledge Glenrose Thembisa Mabizela for her insights about tribal conflict patterns for the Nguni. She is a South African woman of Xhosa descent and grew up in rural Eastern Cape (then Transkei) among people who lived according to traditional ways and norms.

REFERENCES

Abu-Nimer, M. (2003). *Nonviolence and peace building in Islam.* Gainesville: University Press of Florida.

Armstrong, K. (2002). Is Islam violent? In M. Wolfe (Ed.), *Taking back Islam* (pp. 27–32). Emmaus, PA: Rodale.

Blair Trujillo, E. (1999). *Conflicto armado y militares en Colombia* [Armed conflict and the military in Colombia]. Medellin, Colombia: Universidad de Antioquia Editores.

Breytenbach, W. (1999). The history and destiny of national minorities in the African renaissance: The case for better boundaries. In M. W. Makgoba (Ed.),

African renaissance (pp. 91–100). Johannesburg, South Africa: Mafube Publishers, & Cape Town, South Africa: Tafelberg Publishers.

Chang, H. C. (2002). The concept of *yuan* and Chinese conflict resolution. In G. M. Chen & R. Ma (Eds.), *Chinese conflict management and resolution* (pp. 19–38). Westport, CT: Ablex.

Chang, H. C., & Holt, G. R. (1991). The concept of *yuan* and Chinese interpersonal relationships. In S. Ting-Toomey & F. Korzenny (Eds.), *Cross-cultural interpersonal communication* (pp. 28–57). Newbury Park, CA: Sage.

Chen, G. M. (2002). The impact of harmony on Chinese conflict management. In G. M. Chen & R. Ma (Eds.), *Chinese conflict management and resolution* (pp. 3–17). Westport, CT: Ablex.

Chen, G. M., & Chung, J. (1994). The impact of Confucianism on organizational communication. *Communication Quarterly, 42,* 93–105.

Chen, G. M., & Holt, G. R. (2002). Persuasion through the water metaphor in Dao De Jing. *Intercultural Communication Studies, 11,* 153–171.

Chen, G. M., Ryan, K., & Chen, C. (1999). The determinants of conflict management among Chinese and Americans. *Intercultural Communication Studies, 9,* 163–175.

Chen, G. M., & Starosta, W. J. (1997). Chinese conflict management and resolution: Overview and implications. *Intercultural Communication Studies, 7,* 1–16.

Cheng, C.-Y. (1987). Chinese philosophy and contemporary human communication theory. In D. L. Kincaid (Ed.), *Communication theory: Eastern and Western perspectives* (pp. 23–43). San Diego, CA: Academic Press.

Chuang, R. (2002). An examination of Taoist and Buddhist perspectives on interpersonal conflicts, emotions, and adversities. *Intercultural Communication Studies, 11,* 23–40.

Cook, M. (2000). *Commanding right and forbidding wrong in Islamic thought.* New York: Cambridge University Press.

Crawford, L. (1997). Conflict and Tao. *Howard Journal of Communications, 8,* 357–370.

Crawford, L. (2002). Six ideas, interpersonal conflict, and philosophical Taoism. In G. M. Chen & R. Ma (Eds.), *Chinese conflict management and resolution* (pp. 117–126). Westport, CT: Ablex.

de Gruchy, J. W. (1997). Christian witness at a time of African Renaissance. *Ecumenical Review, 49,* 476–481.

Domenici, K., & Littlejohn, S. W. (2001). *Mediation: Empowerment in conflict manage*ment. Prospect Heights, IL: Waveland.

El-Fadl, K. A. (2002). Peaceful jihad. In M. Wolfe (Ed.), *Taking back Islam* (pp. 33–39). Emmaus, PA: Rodale.

Elsayed-Ekhouly, S. M., & Buda, R. (1996). Organizational conflict: A comparative analysis of conflict style across cultures. *International Journal of Conflict Management, 7,* 71–81.

Esposito, J. L. (2003). *The Oxford dictionary of Islam.* Oxford, UK: Oxford University Press.

Feghali, E. (1997). Arab cultural communication patterns. *International Journal of Intercultural Relations, 21,* 345–378.

Feit, E. (1965). *Conflict and communication: An analysis of the "Western areas" and "Bantu-Education" campaigns of the African National Congress of South Africa based on communication and conflict theories.* Unpublished doctoral dissertation, University of Michigan.

Fitch, K. (1998). *Speaking relationally: Culture, communication, and interpersonal connection.* New York: Guilford.

Gabrielidis, C., Stephan, W. G., Ybarra, O., Dos Santos Pearson, V. M., & Villareal, L. (1997). Preferred styles of conflict resolution: Mexico and the United States. *Journal of Cross-Cultural Psychology, 28,* 661–677.

Galan Sarmiento, A. (1997). A turbulent history: Violence and Colombia's efforts to reform. *Harvard International Review, 19*(4), 28–33.

Gao, G. (1998). An initial analysis of the effects of face and concern for "other" in Chinese interpersonal communication. *International Journal of Intercultural Relations, 22,* 467–482.

Gao, G., & Ting-Toomey, S. (1998). *Communicating effectively with the Chinese.* Thousand Oaks, CA: Sage.

Griefat, Y., & Katriel, T. (1989). Life demands *Musayara:* Communication and culture among Arabs in Israel. In S. Ting-Toomey & Korzenny (Eds.), *Language, communication, & culture* (pp. 187–225). Newbury Park, CA: Sage.

Gudykunst, W. B., Matsumoto, Y., Ting-Toomey, S., Nishida, T., Kim, K., & Heyman, S. (1996). The influence of cultural individualism-collectivism, self-construals, and individual values on communication styles across cultures. *Human Communication Research, 22,* 510–543.

Gutierrez, F. (1998). *La ciudad representada: Política y conflicto en Bogotá* [The represented city: Politics and conflict in Bogotá]. Bogotá, Colombia: Tercer Mundo Editores.

Haddox, B. (1965). *Sociedad y religión en Colombia* [Society and religion in Colombia]. Bogotá, Colombia: Universidad Nacional.

Herman, J. (2001). *A divided Nigeria.* Paper delivered at the Institute for Global Engagement. Retrieved October 2, 2004, from http://www.gobalengagement.org

Hofstede, G. (1991). *Cultures and organizations: Software of the mind.* London: McGraw-Hill.

Hsu, F. L. K. (1970). *Americans and Chinese: Purpose and fulfillment in great civilizations.* Garden City, NY: Natural History Press.

Hu, H. C. (1944). The Chinese concept of "face." *American Anthropologist, 46,* 45–64.

Hwang, K. K. (1997). *Guanxi* and *Mientze:* Conflict resolution in Chinese society. *Intercultural Communication Studies, 7,* 17–42.

Jia, W. (1997). Facework as a Chinese conflict-preventive mechanism: A cultural/discourse analysis. *Intercultural Communication Studies, 7,* 43–61.

Jia, W. (2001). *The remaking of the Chinese character and identity in the 21st century.* Westport, CT: Ablex.

Kamali, M. H. (1991). *Principles of Islamic jurisprudence.* Cambridge, UK: Islamic Text Society.

Khalid, K. M. (1986). *Khulafa al-rasul* [Successors of the messenger]. Cairo, Egypt: Dar Thabit Publications.

Khan, M. (1994). *Summarized sahih Al Bukhari: Arabic-English.* Riyadh, Saudi Arabia: Dar-us-Salam Publications.

Kim, M. S., & Leung, T. (2000). A multicultural view of conflict management styles: Review and critical synthesis. In M. Roloff (Ed.), *Communication yearbook 23* (pp. 227–269). Thousand Oaks, CA: Sage.

Koyana, D. S. (1980). *Customary law in tomorrow's society.* Cape Town, South Africa: Juta Publishers.

Krog, A. (2000). *Country of my skull: Guilt, sorrow, and the limits of forgiveness in the new South Africa.* New York: Random House.

Leung, K. (1988). Some determinants of conflict avoidance. *Journal of Cross-Cultural Psychology, 16,* 125–136.

Lodge, T. (2002). *Politics in South Africa: From Mandela to Mbeki.* Bloomington: Indiana University Press.

Ma, R. (1992). The role of unofficial intermediaries in interpersonal conflicts in the Chinese culture. *Communication Quarterly, 40,* 269–278.

Makgoba, M. W. (Ed.). (1999). *African Renaissance.* Johannesburg, South Africa: Mafube Publishers, & Cape Town, South Africa: Tafelberg Publishers.

Mandaza, I. (1999). Reconciliation and social justice in Southern Africa: The Zimbabwe experience. In M. W. Makgoba (Ed.), *African Renaissance* (pp. 77–90). Johannesburg, South Africa: Mafube Publishers and Cape Town, South Africa: Tafelberg Publishers.

Mao, T.-T. (1960). *Selected works of Mao Tse-tung.* Beijing, China: People's Publishing House.

Mockus, A. (2003, May). Untitled presentation to the graduation ceremony for conciliators of the Universidad de Javeriana, Bogotá, Colombia.

Nathan, L. (1994). *Crisis resolution and conflict management in Africa.* Paper presented at the Consultation on the Nexus Between Economic Management and the Restoration of Social Capital in Southern Africa, World Bank and Center for Conflict Resolution. Retrieved September 12, 2003, from http://ccrweb.ccr.uct.ac.za/archive/staff_papers/laurie_bank.html

Nathan, L. (1995). *"Let us gather by the river": Conflict resolution and security in Southern Africa.* Paper presented at the Seminar on Conflict Resolution in Southern Africa, United Nations Development Programme, Lesotho. Retrieved September 12, 2003, from http://ccrweb.ccr.uct.ac.za/archive/staff_papers/laurie_river.html

Ngubane, J. K. (1979). *Conflict of minds: Changing power dispositions in South Africa.* New York: Books in Focus.

Oetzel, J. G., & Ting-Toomey, S. (2003). Face concerns and facework during conflict: A test of the face-negotiation theory. *Communication Research, 30,* 599–624.

Oetzel, J. G., Ting-Toomey, S., Masumoto, T., Yokochi, Y., Pan, X., Takai, J., & Wilcox, R. (2001). Face and facework in conflict: A cross-cultural comparison of China, Germany, Japan, and the United States. *Communication Monographs, 68,* 235–258.

Ohbuchi, K., Fukushima, O., & Tedeschi, J. T. (1999). Cultural values in conflict management: Goal orientation, goal attainment, and tactical decision. *Journal of Cross-Cultural Psychology, 30,* 51–71.

Oquist, P. (1980). *Studies in social discontinuity.* New York: Academic Press.

Richani, N. (1997). The political economy of violence: The war-system in Colombia. *Journal of Interamerican Studies & World Affairs, 39,* 37–92.

Rotberg, R. (1980). Creating a more harmonious South Africa. In R. Rotberg & J. Barratt (Eds.), *Conflict and compromise in South Africa* (pp. 3–14). Boston: World Peace Foundation.

Said, E. W. (1978). *Orientalism.* New York: Pantheon.

Said, E. W. (1981). *Covering Islam.* New York: Pantheon.

Said, E. W. (1994). Orientalism. In P. Williams & L. Chrisman (Eds.), *Colonial discourse and postcolonial theory: A reader* (pp. 132–149). New York: Colombia University Press.

Salm, R., & Gomez, E. (2000). *Un estudio de conflictos estudiantiles en Colombia* [A study of conflict among students in Colombia]. Bogotá, Colombia: Universidad del Bosque.

Schacht, J. (1955). The law. In G. E. von Grunebaum (Ed.), *Unity and variety in Muslim civilization* (pp. 65–86). Chicago: University of Chicago Press.

Schneider, C. (2000). Violence, identity and spaces of contention in Chile, Argentina and Colombia. *Social Research, 67,* 773–803.

Shuter, R. (1990). The centrality of culture. *Southern Communication Journal, 55,* 237–249.

Soo, F. Y. K. (1981). *Mao Tse-tung's theory of dialectic.* Boston: D. Reidel.

Ting-Toomey, S. (1988). Intercultural conflict styles: A face-negotiation theory. In Y. Y. Kim & W. Gudykunst (Eds.), *Theories in intercultural communication* (pp. 213–235). Newbury Park, CA: Sage.

Ting-Toomey, S., & Kurogi, A. (1998). Facework competence in intercultural conflict: An updated face-negotiation theory. *International Journal of Intercultural Relations, 22,* 187–225.

Ting-Toomey, S., & Oetzel, J. (2001). *Managing intercultural conflict effectively.* Thousand Oaks, CA: Sage.

Ting-Toomey, S., & Oetzel, J. G. (2003). Cross-cultural face concerns, conflict styles, and facework behaviors: Current status and future directions. In W. B. Gudykunst (Ed.), *Cross-cultural and intercultural communication* (pp. 127–147). Thousand Oaks, CA: Sage.

Triandis, H. C. (1988). Collectivism vs. individualism: A reconceptualization of a basic concept in cross-cultural psychology. In C. Bagley & G. K. Verma (Eds.), *Cross-cultural studies of personality, attitudes, and cognition* (pp. 60–95). London: Macmillan.

Triandis, H. C. (1995). *Individualism and collectivism.* Boulder, CO: Westview.

Trujillo, E. (2002). *La conciliación como requisito de procedibilidad en la jurisdicción civil Colombiana* [Conciliation as a required procedure within the civil Colombian jurisdiction]. Paper presented at the Seminar of Judicial Reforms, University of Los Andes. Retrieved November 2, 2004, from http://derecho.uniandes.edu.co

Turner, R. (1978). *The eye of the needle: Toward participatory democracy in South Africa.* Maryknoll, NY: Orbis Books.

Tutu, D. (1999). *No future without forgiveness.* Garden City, NY: Doubleday.

von Grunebaum, G. E. (Ed.). (1955). *Unity and variety in Muslim civilization.* Chicago: University of Chicago Press.

Yu, X. (1997). The Chinese "native" perspective on *mao-dun* (conflict) and *mao-dun* resolution strategies: A qualitative investigation. *Intercultural Communication Studies, 7,* 63–82.

Yu, X. (2002). Conflict resolution strategies in state-owned enterprises in China. In G. M. Chen & R. Ma (Eds.), *Chinese conflict management and resolution* (pp. 183–202). Westport, CT: Ablex.

Yum, J. O. (1997). The impact of Confucianism on interpersonal relationships and communication patterns in East Asia. In L. A. Samovar & R. E. Porter (Eds.), *Intercultural communication: A reader* (pp. 78–88). Belmont, CA: Wadsworth.

21

Interracial and Interethnic Conflict and Communication in the United States

Mark P. Orbe

Western Michigan University

Melodi A. Everett

Western Michigan University

Conflict is an inevitable part of the human experience (Roloff, 1987). Consequently, people in relationships find themselves in conflict on a regular basis (Collier, 1991). When in conflict, individuals often demonstrate preferences for certain communication styles (Roloff, 1987), a cognitive process that cannot be separated from the cultural context in which it resides (Kitayama, Markus, Matsumoto, & Norasakkunkit, 1997; Orbe, 1998a). As part of an individual's ethnic background, he or she is taught how to deal with conflict through his or her family and friends (Collier, 1991). In this regard, ethnicity and culture are the frames through which we view, experience, and perceive conflict (Ribeau, 1995).

This chapter focuses on interracial and interethnic conflict. We adopted the definition of intercultural conflict conceptualized by Ting-Toomey (1994): "the perceived and/or actual incompatibility of values, expectations, processes, or outcomes between two or more parties ... over substantive and/or relational issues" (p. 360) to apply specifically to individuals from different racial and ethnic groups within the United States. As such, we differentiate between interracial conflict (conflict between members of different races, i.e., African African/Asian American) and interethnic conflict (conflict between members of different ethnic groups, i.e., Cuban Americans/ Puerto Rican Americans; see Orbe & Harris, 2001). Our objective in this chapter is threefold. First, we summarize existing research that addresses issues of race, ethnicity, and conflict. Second, we identify several limitations inherent in existing lines of research. Third, and finally, we utilize a co-cultural theoretical framework to outline what we suggest are important avenues for both future studies and practical applications of interracial/ethnic conflict research.

SUMMARY OF EXISTING RESEARCH ON INTERRACIAL/INTERETHNIC CONFLICT

Research on intercultural conflict generally, and interracial and interethnic conflict specifically, is a rapidly growing area of study. The vast majority of research on culture and conflict, however, has focused on comparison studies of conflict styles among people from different national cultures (Kim & Leung, 2000). In other words, the focus has been on differences in styles used by members of different countries (Kim & Leung, 2000). The same could be said for research on interracial or interethnic conflict (Houston, 2002). Yet, a significantly smaller amount of intercultural conflict research exists that focuses on race and ethnicity.

At times, it is the different cultural styles of individuals, and not necessarily the context of the conflict itself, that create problems within the conflict episode (Ting-Toomey, 1988). Not surprisingly, much of the existing research on interracial/ethnic conflict focuses on these differences. This section summarizes existing research studies on race, ethnicity, and conflict. Specifically, our review is organized into two main areas of research: (a) sources of conflict and (b) conflict styles.

Sources of Conflict

A significant amount of existing research on race, ethnicity, and conflict has focused on identifying various sources of conflict. Despite these attempts to identity specific sources of interracial/ethnic conflict, interracial/ethnic conflict is a dynamic process; any one episode is typically the result of multiple sources of conflict (Waters, 1992). However, in order to delineate these in a coherent manner, we separate various sources of interracial/ethnic conflict as if they exist in a unilateral manner.

Present-day social inequality. While ingroup/ outgroup tensions may be grounded in a historical context, another source of interracial and interethnic conflict is seen within present-day social inequality between different groups (Stephan & Stephan, 2001). As described earlier, some of this current racial differentiation— especially as it relates to acceptability by the

European American dominant group—can be traced to historical conceptualizations of a racial hierarchy (Blumenbach, 1865/1973). According to Kim (1994), another reason for interracial/ ethnic conflict lies within the fact that the status quo is the focal point, and those racial/ethnic groups closer to the European norms are more accepted into existing value systems. What is especially frustrating for those perceived as most divergent from the dominant group are recent attempts to deny racial and ethnic differences and work toward colorblind communication (Tierney & Jackson, 2002).

Yet, despite the attempts to mend a history of oppression, African Americans continue to suffer from oppression in employment, housing, and health care (Rudman, Ashmore, & Melvin, 2001). African Americans do not have equal opportunity in the area of the justice system or police protection, and although they have equal access to public education, the quality of education is highly unequal (Rudman et al., 2001). In research on face-to-face interactions between Korean immigrant retailers and African American customers, Bailey (2000) concluded that social inequality in the United States shapes the local context in which interracial encounters occur. Specifically, he found that social inequality fueled social assumptions that storekeepers and customers brought to the stores, the result of which were interracial episodes grounded in misunderstanding and mistrust.

Similar social inequalities are at the root of tensions between African Americans and Latinos/Latinas. According to Shah and Thornton (1994), and explicated by Orbe and Harris (2001), Latinos/Latinas are considered higher on the social hierarchy because their morals and values are more similar to those of European Americans. This only adds to the feelings of resentment by African Americans because, despite the portrayals of Latinos/ Latinas as experiencing more severe injustice and hardships than do African Americans, African Americans have also been portrayed as victims of Latino/Latina immigration (Shah & Thornton, 1994). In this context, African Americans are shown as unsympathetic victims who complain about Latino/Latina success despite their continued struggles (Shah & Thornton, 1994). The end result is that the racialized social hierarchy, where certain racial and ethnic groups are positioned higher than others, is perpetuated. Consequently, the social inequality that stems from such a rigid racial classification system remains a salient source of conflict in the United States.

Ingroup/outgroup tensions. Within a historical context of domination, slavery, colonization, and military conquests, it is no surprise that ingroup/outgroup tensions exist among different racial and ethnic groups (Kim, 1994). At times, individual knowledge of the history of mistreatment of one group at the hands of another enhances negativity between racial and ethnic groups (Gallois, 2003). Given this history, community conflict is often triggered by an influx of new racial and ethnic groups (Oliver & Wong, 2003) that are perceived by residents as a threat (Ross, 2000). Within this context, the majority group may feel that its economic and social privilege is threatened; such, reportedly, has been the case for some European Americans and African Americans who have felt threatened by the economic power of Asian Americans (Oliver & Wong, 2003). The end result is an increased ingroup/outgroup tension, one that typically results in increased communication apprehension (Toale & McCroskey, 2001). According to Hornsey, Oppes, and Svensson (2002), any criticism from the outgroup can be seen as a threat to the ingroup, and consequently can aggravate intergroup tensions, heighten intergroup differences, and result in defensiveness and hostility. To make matters worse, ingroup members believe that the motives behind the criticisms of the outgroup are discriminatory and that outgroup members are not qualified to cast judgment on the ingroup (Hornsey et al., 2002).

Historically, much of the literature on race, ethnicity, and conflict has focused on tensions between European Americans and different racial/ethnic groups. However, according to Shah and Thornton (1994), one of the most tense relationships between different racial and ethnic groups exists between African Americans and Latinos/Latinas. Because of the political inroads that have been gained by the Latin community, and the new Latin immigrants taking low-paying jobs, African Americans believe that Latino/Latina success has come at their expense

(Shah & Thornton, 1994). Latinos/Latinas counter the African Americans' argument, stating that African Americans are insensitive to Latino/Latina needs and that African Americans do not want to share their resources with other minorities (Shah & Thornton, 1994).

Another form of ingroup/outgroup tension currently exists between some Korean Americans and African Americans in urban areas across the United States. According to Jo (1992), the tension began when Korean Americans moved into the African American communities and established residences and businesses in the area. African Americans accuse Korean Americans of overcharging, rudeness, taking over African Americans' businesses, and taking money out of the community without putting it back in (Jo, 1992). Korean Americans argue that the African Americans are wrong, and that the misunderstanding comes from conflicting cultures and miscommunication. For instance, Jo explained that the reason Korean Americans are less likely to exchange pleasantries is because of their unfamiliarity of the English language, not rudeness. Also, Korean Americans are less likely to hire African Americans in their stores because they cannot afford to pay well, so they employ their own families, who will work for a lot less than the average employee. In the end, Cho (1995) argued that Korean Americans, like their African American counterparts, face ingroup/outgroup tensions with different racial and ethnic groups on varying levels (e.g., Korean American/European American).

Perceptual differences. Members of different racial and ethnic groups define and perceive conflict differently (Collier, 1991). From a person of color's standpoint, it is not always clear if the conflict is a function of race or some other variable (e.g., personality differences; Waters, 1992). In addition, when conflict arises, people of color are left wondering if the conflict was malicious (reflective of racial bias) or more indicative of naïveté, miscommunication, or misperceptions (Waters, 1992). European Americans, in comparison, often misunderstand the degree of offense that often accompanies unintentional, subtle forms of racially biased statements and questions (Warren, Orbe, & Greer-Williams,

2003). Perceptual differences also exist in terms of expectations of what constitutes appropriate conflict behavior, something that can facilitate a polarized conflict situation where trust and respect are lacking (Buttny & Williams, 2000) and further distorted perceptions emerge (Ting-Toomey & Oetzel, 2001).

Communicating styles and values can be misinterpreted by individuals who are not a part of the same race (Houston & Wood, 1996). For example, certain common practices that are valued within the African American community (e.g., verbal dueling) can be misperceived as attacking by members of other racial groups (Kochman, 1990). Another example involves instances when European Americans view African American styles of communicating as rude and African Americans see European American styles as cold and unfeeling (Houston & Wood, 1996). African Americans have a tendency to be very expressive with their feelings, while European Americans tend to be more reserved and believe that emotions should be more contained (Speicher, 1995). Accordingly, when interethnic encounters do occur in the context of differing interests, values, and norms, there is a sense of psychological distance, which inhibits the ability for different races to reach common goals (Kim, 1994). Furthermore, interracial/ethnic interactions generate different meanings, which may fuel a conflict (Habke & Sept, 1993; Speicher, 1995).

In addition to different perceptions toward one another, racial and ethnic groups may view the same communication episode in contrasting ways (Orbe & Warren, 2000; Speicher, 1995). For example, Warren et al. (2003) conducted a study in which a videotape of an interaction between an European American woman and an African American man was shown to separate groups of African American men, African American women, European American men, European American women, Latinos, and Latinas. The participants were then asked to discuss the conflict and analyze what they felt the source of the conflict was. Interestingly, European American women responded that they viewed the primary source of the conflict to be about gender. European American men determined that personality differences were at the core of the disagreement. The other groups of

people of color defined the conflict in terms of race albeit to varying degrees (Warren et al., 2003). African American women saw race as the most salient issue, whereas African American men, Latinos, and Latinas identified race, gender, age, and socioeconomic differences as influential to the interaction. This research concluded that perceptions of conflict are informed by racial and gendered standpoints (Orbe & Warren, 2000).

Stereotyping/lack of exposure. Although the United States is attempting to move toward an ideology of a racially integrated nation, most races tend to live apart rather than together (Oliver & Wong, 2003). Racial segregation in neighborhood communities, worship centers, educational institutions, and social organizations increases the likelihood of misunderstanding (Kim, 1994). One of the primary reasons is that racial segregation facilitates the perpetuation of stereotypes and false generalizations that make interracial/ethnic interactions potentially volatile (Oliver & Wong, 2003). At the least, it results in great caution on the part of diverse individuals (Allen, 1995). At worst, it creates a history of relational inequality that makes effective intercultural encounters difficult (Gallois, 2003).

Kim (1994) recognized stereotyping and a lack of interest in communicating with other ethnic groups as a source of conflict. When different races are trying to uplift their own race while other races hold stereotypes against them, it can cause serious conflict between the two races (Habke & Sept, 1993). For example, according to Oliver and Wong (2003), in some contexts Asian Americans are likely to view Latinos/Latinas as having a lack of intelligence and being welfare dependent. Alternatively, Blacks and Latinos both may view Asian Americans as difficult to get along with. Both stereotypes, given the competition for limited resources, typically result in pseudo-conflicts between these racial and ethnic groups (Lee & Rogan, 1991). Romer, Jamieson, Riegner, and Rouson (1997) noted that ethnic tension may also be ongoing because many Latino/Latinas still have negative feelings and hold negative stereotypes toward African Americans. Interestingly, meta-stereotypes—the perceptions that racial and ethnic groups have concerning the stereotypes that others have for them—appear to be more prevalent than the actual stereotypes themselves (Sigelman & Tuch, 1997). Hence, their perceptions of outgroup stereotypes by racial and ethnic group members may actually exacerbate tensions that are not as salient as assumed (Stephan & Stephan, 2001).

Media also play a role in accelerating stereotypical images of racialized others (e.g., Orbe, Warren, & Cornwell, 2001), especially when people have little or no contact with individuals from that particular race (Bramlett-Solomon & Hernandez, 2003). Shah and Thornton (1994) found that African American and Latino/Latina communities were represented as inner-city Black ghettos and Hispanic districts, and positioned as isolated from other communities. The neighborhoods of African Americans, for example, were portrayed in the media as neighborhoods of destruction and danger (Shah & Thornton, 1994). Naming the neighborhoods in this manner created a symbolic distance from the European American community (Shah & Thornton, 1994). Not surprisingly, journalists who report to mainly European American audiences frame minority stories as interracial conflicts to make the stories more newsworthy (Romer, Jamieson, & de Coteau, 1998). When negative images are constantly placed in the media, individuals who have not had contact with the different racial and ethnic groups may either have the stereotypes that they hold against these ethnic groups reinforced, or new stereotypes and negative feelings may emerge (Oliver & Wong, 2003). In either case, the result is a public image that perpetuates interracial and interethnic conflict as normative (Viswanath & Arora, 2000).

Conflict Styles

Styles themselves can be regarded as a source of conflict (Ting-Toomey, 1988). However, in order to review the wealth of existing literature in this area, we treat it as a separate area of research. In this regard, we summarize research on the ways in which individuals from different racial and ethnic groups "do" conflict (see Chapter 1 in this volume for definitions of the conflict styles), not necessarily how divergent styles themselves lead to interracial/ethnic conflict.

Racial/ethnic conflict styles. As alluded to earlier, intercultural conflict researchers have primarily focused on the conflict styles of U.S. and non-U.S. cultures (Ting-Toomey et al., 2000). This significant body of research has largely utilized traditional conflict frameworks and measures of individualism/collectivism as a means to identify patterns of conflict strategies (Kim & Leung, 2000). In similar ways, interpersonal conflict researchers in the United States have tended to use similar constructs to inform their research on race, ethnicity, and conflict. The result has been research that stems from individualistic and collectivistic value systems regarding communication generally, and conflict specifically.

According to Ting-Toomey et al. (2000), the assumption is that European Americans are individualistic, while Latinos/Latinas, Asians, and African Americans are collectivistic. Consequently, research has explored how these cultural values affect the ways in which these racial and ethnic groups regard conflict. Trubisky, Ting-Toomey, and Lin (1991) found evidence that during conflict with acquaintances, Asians tend to use higher degrees of obliging and avoiding conflict styles than European Americans. Asians also tend to use a third party more often than other racial groups (Leung, Au, Fernandez-Dols, & Iwawaki, 1992). In comparison, European Americans tend to use upfront, solution-oriented styles, such as integrating and compromising, in dealing with conflict problems (Leung et al., 1992). Mexican Americans, according to Kagan, Knight, and Martinez-Romero (1982), utilize avoiding conflict styles as a means to preserve relational harmony when conflict arises among close Mexican American friends. Given their high degree of collectivism, conflict styles that privilege tactfulness and consideration of others' feelings appear logical (Garcia, 1996). Research on African Americans has concluded that they tend to use more emotionally expressive and involving modes of conflict (Ting-Toomey, 1986).

While this line of research reflects the dominant frame of traditional research on race/ethnicity and conflict, research has begun to advance conceptual assumptions beyond a simple individualistic-collectivistic dichotomy. As early as the mid-1980s, researchers began to study intragroup differences, like those related to gender. For example, Ting-Toomey (1986) found that African American women tend to use more emotionally expressive conflict styles than African American men, European American men, and European American women. Other research has also utilized self-construals—one's conception of oneself as either independent or interdependent (Markus & Kitayama, 1991)—to explore additional factors predicting conflict style patterns. In a study of Latinos/Latinas and European Americans, self-construals were a better predicator of conflict styles than racial/ethnic background (Oetzel, 1998). While some have criticized the dichotomous nature of self-construals (Kim & Leung, 2000), they represent an advance in research beyond unilateral assumptions between race, ethnicity, and conflict styles (Gudykunst et al., 1996).

A smaller, but significant, body of research exists alongside that which is situated within social scientific examinations of cultural variables and conflict behavior. Much of this research has utilized culturally based qualitative research designs to uncover conceptualizations of conflict that were traditionally difficult to obtain through recall data via written surveys. For example, ethnographic studies involving various Native American nations have pointed to the importance of recognizing varying cultural values and the ways in which they explicitly and implicitly are manifested through communication (Sanchez, 2001). Such research has been invaluable in recognizing that dominant interpretations of other racial and ethnic group behavior often missed the mark in terms of the rationale/intention of conflict strategies. For example, Basso (1990) reported that, in times of conflict or negotiation, non-Native Americans often can misinterpret the silence of Native Americans—like that which occurs within the Western Apache culture—as disinterest, a reluctance to speak, or lack of personal warmth. What cultural outsiders fail to recognize in this context is that silence itself carries multiple meanings (see also Braithwaite, 1990).

Gaining the perspectives of traditionally marginalized racial and ethnic groups—outside of comparisons with European Americans as the normative group—represents an important advance in existing conflict research. As such, additional research has focused on accessing ingroup racial and ethnic normative assumptions of communication behaviors. Of particular note is the work of Hecht and colleagues on African American (e.g., Hecht, Ribeau, & Alberts, 1989) and Mexican American (e.g., Hecht, Ribeau, & Sedano, 1990) perspectives on interethnic communication. This research does not focus solely on conflict, but instead what each racial/ethnic group regards as satisfying interaction, a framework that is useful when looking at conflict (Ribeau, 1995). While this line of research appears especially useful in advancing existing understanding of how different racial and ethnic groups conceptualize conflict, the dominant pattern of research has been that of intergroup comparisons (Houston, 2002).

Racial/ethnic comparisons. From the outset of scholarship in the area of race, ethnicity, and conflict, researchers have compared the conflict styles of different groups (Donohue, 1985). For instance, in his seminal research on Black and White styles in conflict, Kochman (1981) focused on direct comparisons: "Black mode of conflicts is high-keyed, animated, interpersonal and confrontational; the white mode of conflict is relatively low-keyed, dispassionate, impersonal, and non-challenging" (Kochman, 1981, p. 18). Contrasting African American and European American conflict styles was adopted by other interethnic communication researchers (e.g., Hecht, Larkey, & Johnson, 1992; Ting-Toomey, 1986) and continues to frame current work (e.g., Hecht, Jackson, & Ribeau, 2003).

Such research has provided insight into various points of particular comparison. For example, Martin, Hecht, and Larkey (1994) explored the concepts of realism and honesty. African Americans view realism as telling it like it is whether you are being positive or negative (Martin et al., 1994). According to Martin et al., European Americans' conceptualization of realism is slightly different. European Americans use the term *honesty* in the place of realism (Martin et al., 1994). Honesty can be honest but unrealistic, and can become problematic when disclosing positive and negatives. For example, if an African American is too honest to a European American, the European American may become offended; similarly, if a European

American is not "real" with an African American, it can produce the same results (Martin et al., 1994).

This line of research has generated additional racial comparisons between African Americans and European Americans within particular situational contexts, like organizations. Shuter and Turner (1997), for example, focused on the different perceptions of organizational conflict between African American and European American women. While both groups perceived their own attempts to reduce conflict as most effective, each enacted different strategies toward the same objective. African American women, interested in getting the conflict out on the table so it could be readily addressed and moved beyond, reported that a direct approach to conflict is most effective (Shuter & Turner, 1997). In comparison, European American women used more of an avoidance strategy and felt fear or anxiety when having to approach conflict directly (Shuter & Turner, 1997).

In a study conducted by Collier (1991), three ethnic groups (Mexican, African, and Anglo American) were examined to analyze conflict differences within friendships. Participants were asked to describe their definitions of friendship and conflict, and whether or not they felt that their friends handled conflict effectively or ineffectively in a recalled interaction. Collier found that the different races defined conflict differently. The Anglo American males defined conflict as a difference of opinion, attack on a person's beliefs and opinions, an unresolved situation, and an inability to compromise; African American men saw conflict as a disagreement, different views, and misunderstandings; Mexican Americans described conflict in a more relational manner. The study also examined how each racial/ethnic group perceived competent communication during conflict episodes. Anglo Americans valued taking responsibility for behaviors, directness, equality, rational decision making, concern for others, and shared control. African Americans found that information should be given, opinions should be credible, criticism is not appropriate, and assertiveness is important. Mexican Americans' answers were similar to European Americans' in the sense of being concerned about the other person, but unlike European Americans, Mexican Americans believed confrontation was appropriate in some situations (Collier, 1991).

The research of Ting-Toomey et al. (2000), which compared the conflict styles of multiple racial and ethnic groups (Latinos/Latinas, African, Asian, and European Americans), is significant for three reasons. First, it studied conflict styles of all racial and ethnic groups without privileging any one as normative. Second, it did not assume that racial/ethnic identity was the strongest predicator of conflict style. Instead it examined the relationship between ethnic identity salience (how important is ethnicity to an individual), larger U.S. cultural identity (how important is belonging to the larger culture), and conflict management styles in the four different racial/ethnic groups. Third, the research focused on acquaintance relationships, a relational context where racial/ethnic conflict styles are largely maintained.

According to Ting-Toomey et al. (2000), strong identification with one's racial/ethnic group increases the likelihood of culturally orientated conflict behaviors. African Americans were found to identify strongly with their own racial/ethnic group; Latinos/Latinas and Asian Americans identified both with their racial/ethnic group and U.S. culture; European Americans identified primarily with the larger U.S. culture. Some of Ting-Toomey et al.'s findings reaffirmed earlier research (e.g., Asian Americans use more avoiding than European Americans, and Latino/Latinas use more third-party conflict styles than African Americans). However, the study did make significant contributions to existing research on race, ethnicity, and conflict by providing insight into the complex ways that multiple aspects of a person's identity influence conflict styles.

Limitations of Existing Research

As illustrated through our summary in the previous section, existing research on interracial and interethnic conflict has established a strong base of foundational knowledge. While earlier studies explored the conflict styles of different racial/ethnic groups, more recent scholarship has advanced this research by examining the saliency of other variables (e.g., gender and national identity). In similar ways, researchers have explored various sources of conflict. Despite its strengths, existing research is limited in a number of different ways. Within this section, we highlight five of the most salient limitations.

Traditional empirical approaches. One limitation of the existing research on interracial/ethnic conflict is that the vast majority of research is situated within a traditional empirical methodological framework. While existing quantitative work has generated an important foundation for culture and communication scholarship, it lacks the ability to provide descriptive insight into how individuals *experience* interracial/ethnic conflict. It also has failed to adequately capture the intricate ways in which interracial/ethnic conflict episodes are influenced by multiple factors simultaneously. Consequently, contemporary scholars have called for more methodological diversity in research exploring the dynamics of race, ethnicity, and communication. Specifically, Hecht et al. (2003), in their review of African American communication research, called for "more direct observations in addition to self-reports . . . more observations, oral narratives, auto-ethnographies, and textual-archival research . . . [this needs] to be initiated to get at the varied subtleties in lived African American experiences" (p. 253). Without question, qualitative research, such as that described by Hecht et al. (2003), can collaboratively advance existing conceptual understandings of interracial/ethnic conflict.

Earlier we discussed the value of recent research by Ting-Toomey et al. (2000), who sought to explore the saliency of factors beyond racial/ethnic identity. While they found correlations between larger national (U.S.) identity and conflict styles among different cultural groups (an important contribution to the study of interracial/ethnic conflict), the study remains limited because it fails to consider the differences among these cultural groups. In this regard, racial differences (e.g., European American and Asian American) are privileged over ethnic differences (e.g., Italian Americans, German Americans, Chinese Americans, Filipino Americans, Korean Americans, Asian Indians). As established by Miyahara, Kim, Shin, and Yoon (1998), assumptions that all members of one racial group (e.g., Asian) share common cultural values

(e.g., individualism/collectivism) are problematic. Additional empirical research suggests that using self-construals (Markus & Wurf, 1987) offers a better lens for predicting racial/ethnic conflict styles (Oetzel, 1998). However, we argue that even this line of research is limited because it fails to capture the complex essence of racial/ethnic conflict styles (see also Kim & Leung, 2000).

Eurocentric/ethnocentric bias. Much of the existing research on interracial/ethnic conflict is limited in that European Americans have been situated as the normative group. That is, the norms and rules of the European American group have been the focus of study while other racial and ethnic groups have been neglected (Ting-Toomey et al., 2000). As such, the vast majority of research reviewed earlier situates interracial/ethnic conflict around the experiences of the dominant group (e.g., European American/African American conflict, European American/Latino-Latina conflict, etc.). What is largely absent from the literature are studies that focus on intraracial and intraethnic conflict—or any studies that do not involve European Americans—as a legitimate area of study in its own right (Houston, 2002).

Existing research is also limited in the ways in which the conflict styles of people of color are situated, both explicitly and implicitly, in comparison to European Americans (see, e.g., Orbe, 1995). Traditionally, European American conflict styles have been situated as the norm (Donohue, 1985); divergent styles were misinterpreted as strange, deviant, incompetent, and unproductive (see, e.g., descriptions from Kochman, 1981). More recently, several scholars have revealed how historical conceptualizations of conflict styles reflect Eurocentric values; the most notable examples involve the conflict strategies of Asian and Native Americans. Specifically, Kim and Leung (2000) critiqued widely accepted conflict management styles that define avoidance style as reflecting a low concern for self and other. They argued that a Eurocentric bias failed to conceptualize the strategy, when enacted by Asians, as positively related to one's desire to preserve relational harmony (high concern for self and other). Similar insights have been offered regarding the use of silence by Native Americans—not as avoidance but as a means to communicate uncertainty, ambiguity, or a respect for the unknown power of others (Braithwaite, 1990).

Essentializing generalizations. A significant limitation of existing research on race, ethnicity, and conflict are the ways in which studies have contributed to the creation of preferred conflict styles of prototypical "culture-typed" persons (Kim & Leung, 2000). In other words, much of the research has contributed to a universal iconography (Orbe, 1995) of racial/ethnic conflict styles that gives little, if any, attention to intragroup differences. Instead, stylized forms for each racial/ethnic group have been perpetuated without much scholarly critique (Hecht, Andersen, & Ribeau, 1989).

Studies have pointed to the importance of considering ethnic, gender, and class differences alongside racial lines (Cook-Gumperz & Szymanski, 2001; Houston & Wood, 1996; Miyahara et al., 1998). However, the majority of research continues to promote racialized conflict styles as normative. A good example of this can be seen within the work of Kochman (1981). His often-cited book, *Black and White Styles in Conflict,* has served as the foundation reference for research on African Americans and European Americans. While his findings are applied generally across contexts, he specified the particular circumstances of Blacks and Whites described in his work: "Middle-class whites, the white group I have been writing about, and Blacks whose social network exists almost entirely within the Black community" (p. 165). Research often fails to recognize that conflict is experienced differently by racial/ethnic group members based on factors such as class, gender, age, and spirituality. This point is driven home by Houston (2002), who provided the following caution, and guidance, to researchers:

> While researchers may choose to emphasize one aspect of African Americans' complex, intersecting identities in a particular study, no single aspect should be conceived as universally "more important" than the others. Black research participants, particularly those in one-shot surveys or interviews, may not automatically articulate the ways in which gender, class, and sexuality matter in their communicative lives. . . . [instead] . . . Researchers

should take responsibility for finding productive ways of breaking the silences and demonstrating how African Americans construct and perform complex, heterogeneous communicative lives. (Houston, 2002, p. 37)

Assumption of/focus on difference. The essentializing generalizations of racial/ethnic conflict strategies have been grounded in and, in turn, been limited by historical conceptualizations of racial and ethnic groups. In large part, this has meant a focus on, and assumption of, racial/ethnic differences. This is not to say that differences among cultural groups do not exist. Yet, existing research is limited in that it pays little, if any, attention to seeking similarities between different racial and ethnic groups. In this regard, few researchers have studied the interpersonal *and* intercultural nature of intergroup encounters (Gallois, 2003). While some studies have reported on both similarities and differences in communication patterns within intraethnic and interethnic relationships (e.g., Collier, 1996), empirical research has generally hypothesized differences as the primary means of examination. Quite simply put, "racial/ethnic 'difference' has been the dominant story in research" (Houston, 2002, p. 37).

The assumption of, and focus on, racial/ethnic differences can be traced to the work of Blumenbach (1865/1973), the first to incorporate a hierarchical ordering mechanism into classifications of race. In his own words, he described the process of creating a social hierarchy:

> I have allotted the first place to the Caucasian . . . which makes me esteem it the primeval one. This diverges in both directions into two, most remote and very different from each other; one the one side, namely the Ethiopian, and on the other the Mongolian. (p. 131)

Existing research on race, ethnicity, and conflict, for the most part reflects Blumenbach's social hierarchy in several different ways. First, it maintains European-based conflict styles as a primordial position. Second, it has focused on attending to the differences among racial and ethnic groups as distinct, separate entities. Third, and finally, interracial/ethnic conflict research has embraced the assumption that groups the farthest away from one another in the social hierarchy will experience the greatest amount of conflict due to divergent cultural styles. Giving privilege to racial and ethnic differences, while ignoring how individuals are similar in other ways, "presents an incomplete picture" (Collier, 1996, p. 334) of how people ultimately communicate.

Focus on micro-level practices. The final limitation described here relates to the focus on micro-level practices, namely how existing research has concentrated primarily on two areas: (a) the sources of interracial/ethnic conflict and (b) conflict style differences. While these lines of research have produced multiple studies providing significant insight, they have been criticized as doing so through an "evaded analysis of how interpersonal practices connect to larger cultural, historical, and political systems" (Houston, 2002, p. 31). Communication generally, and the ways in which individuals engage in conflict specifically, is an essential aspect of one's culture. Yet, simply focusing on communication micro-practices without recognizing how they are shaped by larger macro-level frameworks does little to advance understanding of these particular forms of communication (Ribeau, 1995). Contemporary scholars, in fact, have called for research that attends to historical power structures within society (Stephan & Stephan, 2001) that inform present-day hostile cultural distances between different racial and ethnic groups (Gallois, 2003).

Research by Stanback and Pearce (1981) on subordinate communication strategies illustrates the importance of recognizing macro-level structural influences on the interpretation of micro-level, everyday behaviors. Within their research, Stanback and Pearce (1981) examined four strategies used by African Americans to survive within oppressive circumstances. Their research describes these strategies—tomming, passing, shucking, and dissembling—from the perspectives of the marginalized person; in doing so, they give voice to the strategic meaning behind practices that were often misinterpreted by dominant group members. For instance, shucking, according to Stanback and Pearce (1981), "behaviorally conforms to stereotypes while cognitively rejecting the meanings

associated with those behaviors/stereotypes" (p. 25). This interpretation is especially relevant given that shucking—and other communicative behaviors of oppressed individuals—was misunderstood by individuals who simply focused on the practice itself. Recognizing that the practice is situated within the larger political, economic, and social systems of oppression enhances our understanding considerably (Stephan & Stephan, 2001). In short, existing research has failed to adequately address issues of power in interracial and interethnic conflict.

Given the limitations described here, research on race, ethnicity, and conflict can be advanced through multiple avenues of scholarly activities. In the next section, we utilize a co-cultural theoretical framework to describe what we argue are important considerations for future research and theorizing.

CO-CULTURAL THEORY: A FRAMEWORK FOR FUTURE RESEARCH AND PRACTICAL APPLICATIONS

Co-cultural theory, as described by Orbe (1998a), assists in understanding the ways that people who are traditionally marginalized in dominant societal structures communicate in their everyday lives. It assumes that communicative behavior is inextricably linked to both cultural standpoints and societal power dynamics. Grounded in muted group (e.g., Kramarae, 1981) and standpoint theories (e.g., Smith, 1987), co-cultural theory is derived from the lived experiences of a variety of "nondominant" groups, including people of color, women, persons with disabilities, gays/lesbians/bisexuals, and those from a lower socioeconomic background. Two epistemological assumptions ground the theory: (a) although representing a widely diverse array of lived experiences, co-cultural group members will share a similar positioning that renders them marginalized within society; and (b) in order to negotiate oppressive dominant forces and achieve any measure of success, co-cultural group members adopt certain communication practices and orientations in their everyday interactions (Orbe, 1998a). While the theory purports to address marginalized group members generally, it has depended largely on the lived experiences of people of color in the United States (e.g., Orbe, 1996).

According to co-cultural theory, six factors influence the strategic selection of different communication practices: field of experience, perceived costs and rewards, abilities, preferred outcomes, communication approaches, and situational context. The core concept of the theory incorporates these factors, and is best summarized as:

> Situated within a particular field of experience that governs their perceptions of the costs and rewards associated with, as well as their ability to engage in, various communicative practices, co-cultural group members will adopt certain communication orientations—based on their preferred outcomes and communication approaches—to fit the circumstances of a specific situation. (Orbe, 1998a, p. 13)

According to the theory, no one particular communication style or set of strategies exists for any particular co-cultural group. Instead, co-cultural theory explores the various ways in which all individuals enact certain strategies depending on the negotiation of the six co-cultural factors.

Since its inception, communication researchers have utilized co-cultural theory to study the communication of different co-cultural groups based on race/ethnicity (e.g., Buzzanell, 1999; Gates, 2003; Miura, 2001; Orbe, 1996, 1998b; Phillips-Gott, 1999; Spellers, Sanders, & Orbe, 2003). In different contexts, the theory lends insight into the process by which co-cultural group members negotiate their "cultural differentness" with others (with others both like, and unlike, themselves). Such a framework appears especially relevant to the study of interracial/ethnic conflict for several reasons. First, co-cultural theory provides a mechanism to gain insight into how racial/ethnic minority group members perceive interracial/ethnic conflict. It also presents the opportunity to situate majority group members (e.g., European Americans) as co-cultural group members in certain settings. Second, the theoretical framework allows researchers and practitioners to explore how power, explicitly and implicitly, is manifested within interracial and interethnic

conflict situations. Power, in this regard, can be situated as both a negative and positive power force (Hammond, Anderson, & Cissna, 2003). Third, and most important given the existing work on interracial/ethnic conflict, co-cultural theory represents a holistic theoretical framework that captures how the selection of certain communicative practices (i.e., strategies) is negotiated around six different factors. Unlike much of the current literature, it does not presume a unidimensional relationship between race/ethnicity and conflict style. Instead, it purports to understand the multiple factors that potentially have the greatest saliency during interracial/ethnic conflict episodes without ignoring the larger societal structures that frame them.

In short, in light of the critique of existing research on interracial/ethnic conflict outlined earlier, co-cultural theory provides a productive framework for outlining theoretical directions and research ideas that are worth pursuing in the 21st century. In this regard, we argue that the theory represents a valuable lens through which challenges for culturally centered research studies can be met. As explicated in the next section, the six factors associated with co-cultural theory provide a clear framework for outlining the direction of future research regarding race, ethnicity, and conflict.

FUTURE RESEARCH

As described earlier, existing research on interracial and interethnic conflict is limited by traditional empirical approaches that largely have reflected a Eurocentric bias and produced findings that essentialize culture-typed micro-level communicative practices of individuals from different racial and ethnic groups. The challenge for future research, then, is to address these limitations through innovative studies that make contributions beyond what currently exists. Within this larger context is also the need to determine relevant intervening variables that assist in understanding the complexities of the influence of culture on conflict behavior (Kim & Leung, 2000). While these potential variables are countless, we situate co-cultural theory as a productive framework to outline potential lines of research on race, ethnicity, and conflict. In this section, we specifically discuss future research as it relates to situational context, field of experience, communication approach, abilities, perceived costs and rewards, and preferred outcome. Throughout each description we also highlight the ways in which this research can be applied in various contexts.

Situational context. In all communication interactions, considerations of situational context are important. Some scholars argue that conflict styles are not static patterns of behavior but are influenced by the situation (Stephan & Stephan, 2001); individuals are flexible and change their behavior during conflict (Folger, Poole, & Stutman, 1993). Within co-cultural theory, "different practices are considered the most appropriate and effective depending on the specific situational circumstances" (Orbe, 1998a, p. 98). In other words, conflict styles can be strategically selected in order to meet the needs of any particular situation. Existing research on race/ethnicity and conflict has concentrated primarily on that which occurs during interactions between people of different racial and ethnic groups. Additional research is warranted that examines both intragroup and intergroup conflict across a variety of contexts. Only through multiple studies, across diverse settings, will existing findings be understood contextually.

How conflict is negotiated by various racial and ethnic group members can be studied by diversifying both relational and situational contexts. By relational contexts, we are referring to studies that look at conflict within coworkers, family, acquaintances, strangers, and close friends (e.g., Collier, 1996; Houston, 2002; Ting-Toomey et al., 2000; Way, Cowal, Gingold, Pahl, & Bissessar, 2001). This line of research can explore conflict within the context of positive relationships (Kim & Leung, 2000). Future research can also include a variety of situational contexts in which to study race/ethnicity and conflict: spiritual centers, athletic teams, various organizations, online computer exchanges, and the like (Shuter & Turner, 1997; Vance, 2002/2003). Both positive and negative ingroup/outgroup situations (Tzeng & Jackson, 1994) as well as task/social contexts (Bradford, Meyers, & Kane, 1999) can also be investigated (Tzeng & Jackson, 1994). Ultimately, scholars can explore "the combined effects of context" (Kim & Leung, 2000, p. 259) within both intra- and intergroup conflict. Results that demonstrate divergent conflict strategies for different contexts should be viewed, not as "waffling, hypocritical, or pathological" (Kim & Leung, 2000, p. 249), but as responsive, flexible, and effective.

Field of experience. Field of experience, according to co-cultural theory, is the sum total of a person's life occurrences (Orbe, 1998a). This factor encourages the exploration of past socialization on current conflict behaviors, something that could facilitate countless studies on race, ethnicity, and conflict. For instance, as a means to build upon existing research on any one racial/ethnic group, scholars can explore how particular experiences related to gender, age, socioeconomic status, spirituality, sexuality, nation of origin, family type, and the like also influence how conflict is conceptualized and negotiated (Houston, 2002). In addition, research can begin to explore the effect of particular experiences (e.g., media exposure, integrated schooling, spiritual teachings) on current conflict practices. In this regard, exploring the field of experiences of different individuals' essentializing generalizations can be problematized by identifying intragroup differences.

Culture traditionally has been studied as if it were a static variable; a more effective means to capture its dynamic nature is to describe it as "culturing" (Rodriguez, 2003/2004). A similar perspective should be advanced in terms of studies exploring the field of experiences of individuals. Within this line of research, scholars can study how recent/current conflict experience—including the ways in which conflict styles are maintained or adapted—affect future preferences (Kim & Leung, 2000). For example, research studies can attempt to discern whether participation in a study on conflict influences individual awareness, or use, of alternative styles of conflict. In other words, does the experience of participation affect future preferences and behaviors? In a similar vein, conflict resolution practitioners can explore what lessons, exercises, or activities have the greatest influence toward reducing the negative consequences of interracial and interethnic conflict.

Communication approach. Within co-cultural theory, "communication approach" refers to specific co-cultural practices that are regarded as nonassertive, assertive, or aggressive behaviors by the persons who enact them (Orbe, 1998a). Within a larger context, however, it can also be seen as a synonym for communication style. Of each of the co-cultural factors discussed in this section, communication approach/ style is the one that has attracted the greatest attention from interracial and interethnic conflict scholars thus far. As described in our review of existing literature, a large body of work has been completed that delineates the particular communication approaches of different racial and ethnic groups. Future research, consequently, can continue to generate an understanding of how conflict styles are developed, challenged, and/or ultimately extended.

One potential avenue for research in this area is to investigate the complex ways in which intragroup and intergroup conflict can be seen as a site of identity negotiation (Hecht et al., 2003). According to Hecht's (1993) communication theory of identity, identity is co-created through four different frames (personal, enacted, relational, and communal). Existing research on communication approaches has typically focused on what occurs within the enacted frame (i.e., how identity is communicated to others). Additional research can begin to explore the negotiation of multiple frames simultaneously, or the "interpenetration of frames" (Hecht, 1993, p. 80), something that can enhance our understanding of race, ethnicity, and conflict on multiple levels (Golden, Niles, & Hecht, 2002). In particular, research can explore how identification with larger groups affects communication approaches to conflict situations (e.g., Ting-Toomey et al., 2000), or how intergroup interactions are negotiated around multiple dimensions of ingroup/ outgroup positioning (e.g., Orbe, 2004). Existing research on racial and ethnic communication approaches to conflict is highly regarded in terms of its depth and breadth, but more information is needed in terms of how conflict styles are a reflection of larger identity issues. As Hecht et al. (2003) stated, "if identities are negotiated in everyday conversations and if identity negotiation is a process, then we need much

more information about the negotiation process itself" (pp. 253–254).

Abilities. According to co-cultural theory, another factor that influences the selection of communicative practices, including those enacted during conflict, are the abilities of individuals (Orbe, 1998b). Existing research has done some work to establish what is appropriate, expected, and satisfying within different cultures (Hecht et al., 1992; Hecht, Ribeau, & Alberts, 1989; Martin et al., 1994). Additional research is needed, however, in terms of the abilities of different racial and ethnic group members to enact specific strategies. For instance, research can explore the range of abilities within and across different groups (Orbe, 1998a), as well as individuals' capability to enact conflict strategies that seemingly contradict ingroup cultural norms. Existing studies on code-switching (e.g., Seymour & Seymour, 1979) could be used as a foundation for these efforts. Yet the focus, according to Ribeau (1995), should not be on universal, generalized definitions of what constitutes competence or incompetence, but instead on the ongoing abilities to manage interracial/ ethnic conversations effectively in diverse settings. In this regard, what is seen as appropriate behavior should be consistent with intra- and interracial/ethnic norms, situational demands, and individual responses (Hecht et al., 2003; Ribeau, 1995).

A particularly interesting line of research within this topical focus could involve individuals who are bicultural or multicultural. According to Kim and Leung (2000), "whether through immigration, sojourning, marriage, adoption, or birth, a wide range of people are actively carrying the frames of reference of two or more cultures" (p. 253). Adler (1987; see also Bennett, 1993) suggested that multicultural people can embrace all aspects of their multiple cultural experiences; such individuals may be capable of reconciling the conflicts posed by competing styles and, ultimately, achieve high levels of communication competence within different cultural contexts. Hence, future research can explore how the ability to enhance one's effectiveness during conflict situations is informed by a multicultural identity. For instance, Lindsley and Braithwaite (1996), in their research on U.S. managers in *maquiladoras*

(U.S. American-owned assembly plants in Mexico), presented some evidence that continuous and everyday interracial/ethnic interactions can lead to a multicultural identity (Adler, 1987). In a similar vein, Hamby (2003/2004) explored the communication of biracial (Black/White) individuals in the African American community. Her assertion was that a fully integrated biracial identity, in this context, incorporated conflict styles traditionally associated with both European Americans and African Americans. While such research could look at the abilities of such persons, other potential studies could explore how individuals conceptualize varying perceived costs and rewards of interracial/ethnic interactions.

Perceived costs and rewards. Every communicative behavior, including those used during times of conflict, has potential costs and rewards. According to co-cultural theory, individuals who are marginalized in terms of societal power (e.g., people of color in the United States) give consciousness to the consequences of behaviors prior to enactment (Orbe, 1998a). Other scholars (Todd-Mancillas, 2000) have argued that the process of co-cultural communication applies to all persons, including those in the dominant group (e.g., European Americans). Research that examines the strategic selection of conflict strategies is important to advance existing research that primarily has relied on the assumption that culture and communicative behaviors during conflict are inextricably linked. A relevant line of research within this topical area is the identification of what, if any, correlations can be found between the perceived costs and rewards associated with different conflict strategies. In addition, scholars can explore the process by which different racial and ethnic group members negotiate these costs and rewards in different settings (see, e.g., social exchange theory research: Cox & Kramer, 1995; Welch-Cline, 1987).

In addition to exploring the perceived costs and rewards associated with different conflict strategies, future research can also focus on the positive and negative outcomes of conflict episodes themselves. A significant amount of literature has concentrated on the sources of conflict and the ways in which divergent styles have exacerbated interracial and interethnic conflict. Yet, equal attention needs to be paid to the positive effects of conflict, especially those that appear to be unlikely in the absence of conflict (Hammond et al., 2003). For example, Hoffman (1990), in her research on Iranian immigrants in California, found that cultural conflicts between immigrants and U.S. Americans were seen as a significant source of learning. She concluded that "the dominant research orientation of the intercultural field, characterizable by a concern with culture differences and culture conflict, has often obscured consideration for the dimensions of cultural learning that transcend the experience of conflict" (Hoffman, 1990, p. 275). Additional studies are needed that examine conflict within the context of intercultural learning.

Preferred outcome. A major contribution of co-cultural theory to existing theoretical work on culture and communication is the recognition that traditionally marginalized group members do not all strive toward assimilation into dominant group norms; other alternatives like accommodation and separation also exist (Orbe, 1996). Applying co-cultural theory to interracial and interethnic conflict facilitates an understanding that people of color can consciously choose conflict behaviors that lead to desired outcomes. In this regard, some consciousness is given to how particular communication practices during conflict affect immediate and ultimate relationships with others. While qualitative evidence exists on the association of different co-cultural practices with specific preferred outcomes (Orbe, 1998a), additional research can demonstrate correlations via empirical studies (e.g., Lapinski & Orbe, 2002). In addition, scholars can begin to explore how preferred outcome may have greater saliency than racial/ethnic identity when it comes to conflict strategies (see, e.g., Ting-Toomey et al., 2000).

A contact hypothesis suggests that increased exposure to diverse groups will, over time, lead to better intergroup relations (Stephan & Stephan, 2001). Several necessary conditions are necessary for this to occur, however, including equal-status interactions, common goals, and commitment to humanity. Given this, it is no surprise that existing research has established that when individuals have contact without these conditions, the result is increased negative perceptions of those from different racial and ethnic groups (Tzeng & Jackson, 1994). Cocultural theory suggests that preferred outcome is informed by past experiences, direct or indirect, with those who are racially/ethnically different (Orbe, 1998a). Future research can explore the sense-making processes that result in rigid or flexible preferred outcomes for various contexts of interracial/ethnic conflict. In addition, it can also explore how particular conflict episodes affect the future preferred outcomes of different individuals (Kim & Leung, 2000). In other words, what conflict or harmonious interactions with others ultimately can facilitate a shift in preferred outcome?

PRACTICAL IMPLICATIONS

Given current and future demographic shifts of racially and ethnically diverse groups in the United States, the topic of interracial/ethnic conflict undoubtedly will continue to gain importance for both researchers and practitioners. While such conflict managed effectively can have positive effects on long-term interracial and interethnic relations (e.g., Hoffman, 1990), this is not the case when issues regarding race are not adequately addressed (Allen, 1995; Donohue, 1985). According to Waters (1992), "race-based conflicts undermine organizational unity, sap energy and motivation, create tensions, and, if not handled properly, lead to further feelings of hostility and resentment" (p. 439). Successfully negotiating racial and ethnic conflict and establishing peace in interracial encounters can be very challenging (Ross, 2000). This is especially the case when educational training approaches do not meet the needs of the population that is being served (see Stephan & Stephan, 2001, for a conceptualization of programmatic approaches). Within this final section we discuss how this challenge can best be met by understanding the inseparable overlap between research and practice.

The most effective research informs, and is informed by, everyday practice (Orbe, 2003/2004). To avoid privileging research over practice, we must also acknowledge that the most

effective everyday practices inform, and are informed by, research. In this regard, an important implication for the future of studies on race, ethnicity, and conflict revolves around the creation, implementation, and evaluation of projects that make a difference in communities outside of the academy. This concept is not a new one, as race and communication scholars have advocated for community-cognizant (Houston, 2000) and action-sensitive research (Orbe, 1995). An important consideration in these efforts is realizing that the lines between researcher and practitioner are blurred. According to Trujillo (2002/2003),

> there is only a barely discernible demarcation between researcher and practitioner. Sometimes the distinction may lie only in the eyes of the one doing the defining. In truth, the worlds of the practitioner-scholar and the research-scholar mutually reinforce and sustain each other. (p. 3)

The most effective means to address conflict steeped in racial and ethnic tensions is at the grassroots level (Ross, 2000). Research consistently reveals that a sure avenue toward reducing interracial/ethnic conflict is through continuous, meaningful contact (Habke & Sept, 1993). This contact can lead to the breakdown of negative images and stereotypes that may be held by different racial and ethnic groups (Ross, 2000). Once authentic relationships can be formed, both parties need to be flexible in their communication along with realizing and acknowledging that there are differences, as well as similarities, between the two racial groups (Habke & Sept, 1993; Orbe, 2004). Recognizing that you might not understand characteristics of a certain ethnic group, resisting the tendency to impose your standards on another racial/ethnic group, respecting how others may interpret things, and not overemphasizing differences are all ways to improve interracial interaction (Houston & Wood, 1996).

The challenge for scholars-practitioners, then, is to create avenues whereby research on interracial and interethnic conflict can be used to increase awareness and communication effectiveness. According to Ross (2000), a logical place to begin is establishing partnerships with local organizations through which marginalized voices and concerns can be heard. Community-based conflict resolution programs (e.g., Pearce & Pearce, 2001) represent one example where research and practice can be united; Stephan and Stephan (2001) discuss other approaches. While such efforts can reap tremendous benefits, scholars-practitioners should be prepared to negotiate the distrust and suspicions of local communities, especially communities of color (Jackson, 2002/2003), that describe existing structures as culturally insensitive (Donohue, 1985). Trujillo (2002/2003) described the source of mistrust as follows:

> The historic mistrust between scholars and practitioners is rooted in notions of who is qualified to contribute to the Academy, as well as what is worthy of study. Scholars have traditionally been trained to discount folk wisdom or common experience, unless it could be operationalized in the laboratory, translated into formal academic language, and published in academic journals. "Ordinary" folks tended to view the academic arena as "irrelevant" and dismissed theory as "mind games" or worse. (p. 3)

Conclusion

In closing, we acknowledge that many individuals—both within and outside the academy—may regard the challenges inherent in both interracial/ethnic conflict and existing tensions between scholars and practitioners as insurmountable. While we recognize such is the case for some of the barriers that must be overcome in the work that we advocate for within this chapter, we do so with three points in mind. First, conflict situated within racial and ethnic tensions will increase unless proactive, informed efforts are introduced at the community level. Second, the most effective means to address the issue of interracial and interethnic conflict is through the collaborative efforts of scholars and practitioners. Third, the base of knowledge cultivated through the field of human communication holds significant potential to assist in the transformation of our society. In order to meet our potential, we must recognize and address limitations within our own work, and in doing so, generate tremendous opportunities for all.

Houston and Wood (1996) capture the essence of this idea when they state,

> As long as we avoid or condemn communication that differs from our own, we can't prosper from diversity and we can't create a society hospitable to all who compose it. If instead we explore the opportunities for relationships with people of different races and classes, we heighten insight into ourselves, and the range of human experience. (p. 54)

References

Adler, P. S. (1987). Beyond cultural identity: Reflections on cultural and multicultural man. In L. A. Samovar & R. E. Porter (Eds.), *Intercultural communication: A reader* (5th ed., pp. 55–76). Belmont, CA: Wadsworth.

Allen, B. J. (1995). "Diversity" and organizational communication. *Journal of Applied Communication Research, 23,* 143–155.

Bailey, B. (2000). Communicative behavior and conflict between African American customers and Korean immigrant retailers in Los Angeles. *Discourse and Society, 11,* 86–108.

Basso, K. (1990). "To give up on words": Silence in Western Apache culture. In D. C. Carbaugh (Ed.), *Cultural communication and intercultural contact* (pp. 303–320). Hillsdale, NJ: Lawrence Erlbaum.

Bennett, J. M. (1993). Cultural marginality: Identity issues in intercultural training. In M. Paige (Ed.), *Education for the intercultural experience* (pp. 109–135). Yarmouth, ME: Intercultural Press.

Blumenbach, J. F. (1973). *The anthropological treatises of Johann Friedrich Blumenbach.* Boston: Milford House. (Original work published 1865)

Bradford, L., Meyers, R., & Kane, K. A. (1999). Latino expectations of communicative competence: A focus group interview study. *Communication Quarterly, 47,* 98–117.

Braithwaite, C. A. (1990). Communicative silence: A cross-cultural study of Basso's hypothesis. In D. C. Carbaugh (Ed.), *Cultural communication and intercultural contact* (pp. 321–328). Hillsdale, NJ: Lawrence Erlbaum.

Bramlett-Solomon, S., & Hernandez, P. (2003). Photo coverage of Hispanics and Blacks in a southwestern daily newspaper. In D. I. Rios &

A. N. Mohamed (Eds.), *Brown and black communication: Latino and African American conflict and convergence in mass media.* (pp. 71–79). Westport, CT: Praeger.

Buttny, R., & Williams, P. L. (2000). Demanding respect: The uses of reported speech in discursive constructions of interracial contact. *Discourse & Society, 11,* 109–133.

Buzzanell, P. M. (1999). Tensions and burdens in employment interviewing processes: Perspectives of non-dominant group members. *Journal of Business Communication, 36*(2), 143–162.

Cho, S. K. (1995). Korean Americans vs. African Americans: Conflict and construction. In M. L. Andersen & P. H. Collins (Eds.), *Race, class, and gender: An anthology* (pp. 461–469). Belmont, CA: Wadsworth.

Collier, M. J. (1991). Conflict competence within African, Mexican, and Anglo American friendships. In S. Ting-Toomey & F. Korzenny (Eds.), *Cross-cultural interpersonal communication* (pp. 132–154). Newbury Park, CA: Sage.

Collier, M. J. (1996). Communication competence problematics in ethnic friendships. *Communication Monographs, 63,* 314–336.

Cook-Gumperz, J., & Szymanski, M. (2001). Classroom "families": Cooperating or competing—Girls' and boys' interactional styles in a bilingual classroom. *Research on Language and Social Interaction, 34,* 107–130.

Cox, S. A., & Kramer, M. W. (1995). Communication during employee dismissals: Social exchange principles and group influences on employee exit. *Management Communication Quarterly, 9,* 156–190.

Donohue, W. A. (1985). Ethnicity and mediation. In W. B. Gudykunst, L. P. Stewart, & S. Ting-Toomey (Eds.), *Communication, culture, and organizational processes* (pp. 134–154). Beverly Hills, CA: Sage.

Folger, J. P., Poole, M. S., & Stutman, R. K. (1993). *Working through conflict: Strategies for relationships, groups, and organizations* (2nd ed.). New York: HarperCollins.

Gallois, C. (2003). Reconciliation through communication in intercultural encounters: Potential or peril? *Journal of Communication, 53,* 5–15.

Garcia, W. R. (1996). Respeto: A Mexican base for interpersonal relationships. In W. Gudykunst, S. Ting-Toomey, & T. Nishida (Eds.), *Communication in personal relationships across cultures* (pp. 55–76). Thousand Oaks, CA: Sage.

Gates, D. (2003). Learning to play the game: An exploratory study of how African American women and men interact with others in organizations. *Electronic Journal of Communication, 13*(2/3).

Golden, D. R., Niles, T. A., & Hecht, M. L. (2002). Jewish American identity. In J. N. Martin, T. K. Nakayama, & L. A. Flores (Eds.), *Readings in intercultural communication: Experiences and contexts* (pp. 44–52). New York: McGraw-Hill.

Gudykunst, W. B., Matsumoto, Y., Ting-Toomey, S., Nishida, T., Kim, K., & Heyman, S. (1996). The influence of cultural individualism-collectivism, self construals, and individual values on communication styles across cultures. *Human Communication Research, 22,* 510–543.

Habke, A., & Sept, R. (1993). Distinguishing group and cultural influences in inter-ethnic conflict: A diagnostic model. *Canadian Journal of Communication, 18,* 415–436.

Hamby, C. E. (2003/2004). Biracial communication in the African American community: A preliminary study. *Journal of Intergroup Relations, 30*(4), 62–74.

Hammond, S. C., Anderson, R., & Cissna, K. N. (2003). The problematics of dialogue and power. *Communication Yearbook, 27,* 125–157.

Hecht, M. L. (1993). 2002—A research odyssey: Toward the development of a communication theory of identity. *Communication Monographs, 60,* 76–81.

Hecht, M. L., Andersen, P. A., & Ribeau, S. A. (1989). The cultural dimensions of nonverbal communication. In M. K. Asante & W. B. Gudykunst (Eds.), *Handbook of international and intercultural communication* (pp. 163–185). Newbury Park, CA: Sage.

Hecht, M. L., Jackson, R. L., & Ribeau, S. A. (2003). *African American communication: Exploring identity and culture* (2nd ed.). Mahwah, NJ: Lawrence Erlbaum.

Hecht, M. L., Larkey, L. K., & Johnson, J. N. (1992). African American and European American perceptions of problematic issues in interethnic communication effectiveness. *Human Communication Research, 19,* 209–236.

Hecht, M. L., Ribeau, S. A., & Alberts, J. K. (1989). An Afro-American perspective on interethnic communication. *Communication Monographs, 56,* 385–410.

Hecht, M. L., Ribeau, S. A., & Sedano, M. V. (1990). A Mexican American perspective on interethnic communication. *International Journal of Intercultural Relations, 14,* 31–55.

Hoffman, D. M. (1990). Beyond conflict: Culture, self, and intercultural learning among Iranians in the U.S. *International Journal of Intercultural Relations, 14,* 275–299.

Hornsey, M. J., Oppes, T., & Svensson, A. (2002). "It's OK if we say it, but you can't": Responses to intergroup and intragroup criticism. *European Journal of Social Psychology, 32,* 293–307.

Houston, M. (2000). Writing for my life: Community-cognizant scholarship on African American women and communication. *International Journal of Intercultural Relations, 24,* 673–686.

Houston, M. (2002). Seeking difference: African Americans in interpersonal communication research, 1975–2000. *Howard Journal of Communications, 13,* 25–41.

Houston, M., & Wood, J. T. (1996). Difficult dialogues, expanded horizons: Communicating across race and class. In J. T. Wood (Ed.), *Gendered relationships* (pp. 39–56). Mountain View, CA: Mayfield.

Jackson, J. M. (2002/2003). Conflict resolution and mediation in the African American community. *Journal of Intergroup Relations, 29*(4), 97–101.

Jo, M. H. (1992). Korean merchants in the black community: Prejudice among the victims of prejudice. *Ethnic and Racial Studies, 15,* 395–411.

Kagan, S., Knight, G., & Martinez-Romero, S. (1982). Culture and the development of conflict resolution style. *Journal of Cross-Cultural Psychology, 13,* 43–59.

Kim, M.-S., & Leung, T. (2000). A multicultural view of conflict management styles: Review and critical synthesis. *Communication Yearbook, 23,* 227–269.

Kim, Y. Y. (1994). Interethnic communication: The context and the behavior. *Communication Yearbook, 17,* 511–538.

Kitayama, S., Markus, H. R., Matsumoto, H., & Norasakkunkit, V. (1997). Individual and collective processes in the construction of self: Self-enhancement in the United States and self-criticism in Japan. *Journal of Personality and Social Psychology, 72,* 1245–1267.

Kochman, T. (1981). *Black and white styles in conflict.* Chicago: University of Chicago Press.

Kochman, T. (1990). Cultural pluralism: Black and white styles. In D. Carbaugh (Ed.), *Cultural communication and intercultural contact* (pp. 219–224). Hillsdale, NJ: Lawrence Erlbaum.

Kramarae, C. (1981). *Women and men speaking.* Rowley, MA: Newbury House.

Lapinski, M. K., & Orbe, M. P. (2002, July). *Evidence for the construct validity and reliability of the co-cultural theory scales.* Paper presented at the annual meeting of the International Communication Association, Seoul, Korea.

Lee, H., & Rogan, R. (1991). A cross-cultural comparison of organizational conflict management behaviors. *International Journal of Conflict Management, 2,* 181–199.

Leung, K., Au, Y.-F., Fernandez-Dols, J. M., & Iwawaki, S. (1992). Preference for methods of conflict processing in two collectivistic cultures. *International Journal of Psychology, 27,* 195–209.

Lindsley, S. L., & Braithwaite, C. A. (1996). "You should 'wear a mask'": Facework norms in cultural and intercultural conflict in maquiladoras. *International Journal of Intercultural Relations, 20,* 199–225.

Markus, H., & Kitayama, S. (1991). Culture and the self: Implications for cognition, emotion, and motivation. *Psychological Review, 98,* 224–252.

Markus, H., & Wurf, E. (1987). The dynamic of self-concept: A social psychological perspective. *Annual Review of Psychology, 38,* 299–337.

Martin, J. N., Hecht, M. L., & Larkey, L. K. (1994). Conversational improvement strategies for interethnic communication: African American and European American perspectives. *Communication Monographs, 61,* 236–255.

Miura, S. Y. (2001). New identity, new rhetoric: The Native Hawaiian quest for independence. *Journal of Intergroup Relations, 28*(2), 3–16.

Miyahara, A., Kim, M. S., Shin, H. C., & Yoon, K. (1998). Conflict resolution styles among "collectivist" cultures: A comparison between Japanese and Koreans. *International Journal of Intercultural Relations, 22,* 505–525.

Oetzel, J. G. (1998). The effects of self-construals and ethnicity on self-reported conflict styles. *Communication Reports, 11,* 133–144.

Oliver, J. E., & Wong, J. (2003). Intergroup prejudice in multiethnic settings. *American Journal of Political Science, 47,* 567–582.

Orbe, M. P. (1995). African American communication research: Toward a deeper understanding of interethnic communication. *Western Journal of Communication, 59,* 61–78.

Orbe, M. P. (1996). Laying the foundation for co-cultural communication theory: An inductive approach to studying the non-dominant communication strategies and the factors that influence them. *Communication Studies, 47,* 157–176.

Orbe, M. P. (1998a). *Constructing co-cultural theory: An explication of culture, power, and communication.* Thousand Oaks, CA: Sage.

Orbe, M. P. (1998b). An outsider within perspective to organizational communication: Explicating the communication practices of co-cultural group members. *Management Communication Quarterly, 12,* 230–279.

Orbe, M. P. (2003/2004). The importance of recognizing multiple identities in human rights research and practice. *Journal of Intergroup Relations, 30*(4), 3–7.

Orbe, M. P. (2004). Negotiating multiple identities within multiple frames: An analysis of first generation college students. *Communication Education, 53,* 131–149.

Orbe, M. P., & Harris, T. M. (2001). *Interracial communication: Theory into practice.* Belmont, CA: Wadsworth.

Orbe, M. P., & Warren, K. T. (2000). Different standpoints, different realities: Race, gender, and perceptions of intercultural conflict. *Communication Quarterly, 48,* 51–57.

Orbe, M. P., Warren, K. T., & Cornwell, N. C. (2001). Negotiating societal stereotypes: Analyzing *The real world* discourse by and about African American men. In M. J. Collier (Ed.), *Constituting cultural difference through discourse* (pp. 107–134). Thousand Oaks, CA: Sage.

Pearce, K. A., & Pearce, W. B. (2001). The Public Dialogue Consortium's school-wide dialogue process: A communication approach to develop citizen skills and enhance school climate. *Communication Theory, 1,* 105–123.

Phillips-Gott, P. C. (1999, November). *African American communication, organizations, and assimilation: A co-cultural perspective.* Paper presented at the annual meeting of the National Communication Association, Chicago.

Ribeau, S. A. (1995, October). *African American communication and conflict resolution: A new dialogue.* B. Aubrey Fisher Memorial Lecture, University of Utah, Salt Lake City.

Rodriguez, A. (2003/2004). Searching for new models of identity in Spanglish. *Journal of Intergroup Relations, 30*(4), 8–22.

Roloff, M. E. (1987). Communication and conflict. In C. R. Berger & S. H. Chaffee (Eds.), *Handbook of communication science* (pp. 484–534). Newbury Park, CA: Sage.

Romer, D., Jamieson, K. H., & de Coteau, N. J. (1998). The treatment of persons of color in local television news: Ethnic blame discourse or realistic group conflict? *Communication Research, 25,* 286–305.

Romer, D., Jamieson, K. H., Riegner, C., & Rouson, B. (1997). Blame discourse versus realistic conflict as explanations of ethnic tension in urban neighborhoods. *Political Communication, 14,* 273–291.

Ross, M. H. (2000). Creating conditions for peacemaking: Theories of practice in ethnic conflict resolution. *Ethnic and Racial Studies, 23,* 1002–1034.

Rudman, L. A., Ashmore, R. D., & Melvin, L. (2001). "Unlearning" automatic biases: The malleability of implicit prejudice and stereotypes. *Journal of Personality and Social Psychology, 81,* 856–868.

Sanchez, V. E. (2001). Intertribal dance and cross cultural communication. Traditional powwows in Ohio. *Communication Studies, 51*(1), 51–69.

Seymour, H. N., & Seymour, C. M. (1979). The symbolism of Ebonics: I'd rather switch than fight. *Journal of Black Studies, 9,* 397–410.

Shah, H., & Thornton, M. C. (1994). Racial ideology in U.S. mainstream news magazine coverage of Black-Latino interaction, 1980–1992. *Critical Studies in Mass Communication, 11*(2), 141–161.

Shuter, R., & Turner, L. H. (1997). African American and European American women in the workplace: Perceptions of conflict communication. *Management Communication Quarterly, 11*(1), 74–96.

Sigelman, L., & Tuch, S. A. (1997). Metastereotypes: Blacks' perceptions of Whites' stereotypes of Blacks. *Public Opinion Quarterly, 61,* 87–101.

Smith, D. E. (1987). *The everyday world as problematic: A feminist sociology of knowledge.* Boston: Northeastern University Press.

Speicher, B. L. (1995). Interethnic conflict: Attribution and cultural ignorance. *Howard Journal of Communications, 5,* 195–213.

Spellers, R. E., Sanders, F. L., & Orbe, M. P. (2003, November). *The business of Black hair/body politics: A co-cultural analysis of Black professional women's aesthetic representations in a contested site of workplace culture.* Paper presented at the annual meeting of the National Communication Association, Miami, FL.

Stanback, M. H., & Pearce, W. B. (1981). Talking to "the man": Some communication strategies used by members of "subordinate" social groups. *Quarterly Journal of Speech, 67,* 21–30.

Stephan, W. G., & Stephan, C. W. (2001). *Improving intergroup relations.* Thousand Oaks, CA: Sage.

Tierney, S., & Jackson, R. L. (2002). Deconstructing whiteness ideology as a set of rhetorical fantasy themes: Implications for interracial alliance building in the United States. *International and Intercultural Communication Annual, 25,* 81–107.

Ting-Toomey, S. (1986). Conflict communication styles in Black and White subjective cultures. In Y. Y. Kim (Ed.), *Interethnic communication: Current research* (pp. 75–88). Newbury Park, CA: Sage.

Ting-Toomey, S. (1988). Intercultural conflict styles: A face negotiation theory. In Y. Y. Kim & W. B. Gudykunst (Eds.), *Theories in intercultural communication* (pp. 213–235). Newbury Park, CA: Sage.

Ting-Toomey, S. (1994). Managing intercultural conflicts effectively. In L. A. Samovar & R. E. Porter (Eds.), *Intercultural communication: A reader* (pp. 360–372). Belmont, CA: Wadsworth.

Ting-Toomey, S., & Oetzel, J. G. (2001). *Managing intercultural conflict effectively.* Thousand Oaks, CA: Sage.

Ting-Toomey, S., Yee-Jung, K. K., Shapiro, R. B., Garcia, W., Wright, T. J., & Oetzel, J. G. (2000). Ethnic/cultural identity salience and conflict styles in four US ethnic groups. *International Journal of Intercultural Relations, 24,* 47–81.

Toale, M. C., & McCroskey, J. C. (2001). Ethnocentrism and trait communication apprehension as predictors of interethnic communication apprehension and use of relational maintenance strategies in interethnic communication. *Communication Quarterly, 49,* 70–83.

Todd-Mancillas, W. (2000). [Review of *Constructing Co-cultural Theory* by M. Orbe and *Communication and Identity Across Cultures* edited D. V. Tanno and A. Gonzalez]. *Communication Theory, 10,* 475–480.

Trubisky, P., Ting-Toomey, S., & Lin, S.-L. (1991). The influence of individualism-collectivism and self-monitoring on conflict styles. *International Journal of Intercultural Relations, 15,* 65–84.

Trujillo, M. A. (2002/2003). Intergroup conflict: Practical and scholarly considerations. *Journal of Intergroup Relations, 29*(4), 3–5.

Tzeng, O. C. S., & Jackson, J. W. (1994). Effects of contact, conflict, and social identity on interethnic group hostilities. *International Journal of Intercultural Relations, 18,* 259–276.

Vance, D. C. (2002/2003). The same yet different: Creating unity among the diverse members of the Baha'i faith. *Journal of Intergroup Relations, 29*(4), 64–88.

Viswanath, K., & Arora, P. (2000). Ethnic media in the United States: An essay on their role in integration, assimilation, and social control. *Mass Communication and Society, 3,* 39–56.

Warren, K. T., Orbe, M., & Greer-Williams, N. (2003). Perceiving conflict: Similarities and differences between and among Latino/as, African Americans, and European Americans. In D. I. Rios & A. N. Mohamed (Eds.), *Brown and Black communication: Latino and African American conflict and convergence in mass media* (pp. 13–26). Westport, CT: Praeger.

Waters, H., Jr. (1992). Race, culture, and interpersonal conflict. *International Journal of Intercultural Relations, 16,* 437–454.

Way, N., Cowal, K., Gingold, R., Pahl, K., & Bissessar, N. (2001). Friendship patterns among African American, Asian American, and Latino adolescents from low-income families. *Journal of Social and Personal Relationships, 18,* 29–53.

Welch-Cline, R. J. (1987). The politics of intimacy: Costs and benefits determining disclosure intimacy in male-female dyads. *Journal of Social and Personal Relationships, 6,* 5–20.

22

MEDIA AND INTERNATIONAL CONFLICT

EYTAN GILBOA

Bar-Ilan University, Israel

Fundamental interrelated changes in communication, politics, and international relations have altered the roles of mass communication in contemporary international conflicts (Gilboa, 2000, 2002a, 2002b, 2005a, 2005b). These changes include the revolution in communication technologies, the end of the Cold War, and changes in the nature of international conflicts and the use of force. The revolution in communication and information technologies, the capability to globally broadcast—often live—almost every significant development in world events, and the creation and expansion of the Internet, have all led to the globalization of electronic communication and to substantial growth in networks, stations, and communication consumers worldwide. Growing mass participation in political processes has transformed many societies from autocracies into democracies. Before the Cold War, authoritarian regimes controlled most of the countries in the world; after the war, democratic regimes replaced most of them.

The actors involved in international conflicts have changed. Until the end of the Cold War, most international conflicts occurred between and among states, but afterward they mostly occurred at the intrastate or global levels. Ethnic and civil wars erupted in Yugoslavia and the former Soviet Union, and they also exploded in Africa in places such as Rwanda, Somalia, Sudan, and Liberia. Civil wars in the Balkans and Africa created humanitarian disasters that only external military intervention could have stopped. The September 11, 2001, terrorist attacks on New York and Washington by Islamic fundamentalists, and subsequent attacks in Kenya, Indonesia, Bali, Turkey, Spain, Tunisia, Saudi Arabia, and Egypt, as well as the U.S.-led wars in Afghanistan and Iraq, represent international conflict at the global level.

States and other actors in international relations have been increasingly using "soft power" to achieve their goals. Nye and Owens (1996) defined soft power as

> the ability to achieve desired outcomes in international affairs through attraction rather than coercion. In a rapidly changing world information about what is occurring becomes a central commodity of international relations, just as the threat and use of military force was seen as the central power resource in an international system overshadowed by the potential clash of superpowers. (p. 24)

The mass media, global television in particular, have become a central source of information about world affairs. The images of leaders or nations and control of information flow determine their status in the international community as much as—and perhaps even more than—their military and economic power.

Politicians, journalists, and scholars have suggested that the convergence of the revolutions in communication, politics, and international relations has created a new media-dominated governing system and has altered the meaning of power in contemporary world politics. *Mediademocracy, medialism, mediapolitik, mediacracy,* and *teledemocracy* are but a few postmodern terms coined to describe the new media-dominated political system. Application of the same perception to foreign policy and international relations yielded similar terms and concepts, such as *telediplomacy* and the *CNN effect.*

During the Cold War the rival superpowers and their respective blocks used the mass media, particularly radio, to conduct worldwide public diplomacy campaigns (Siefert, 2003). The airwave battles were designed to win the minds and hearts of peoples around the world. To a much lesser extent, leaders and groups also used the media to promote diplomacy and better understating among rival nations. Studies mostly focused on coverage of international conflicts (e.g., Aronson, 1973; Bruck, 1989; Galtung & Ruge, 1965; Hallin, 1994), public diplomacy (e.g., Fortner, 1994; Malone, 1988), images of conflicts and enemies (e.g., Eldrige, 1979; Ottosen, 1995), and contributions to international negotiation and conflict resolution (e.g., Arno & Dissanayake, 1984; Davison, 1974; Korzenny & Ting-Toomey, 1990; Roach, 1993).

The Cold War provided a convenient context for the coverage of international conflict. All the important elements were clear and predictable: locations, characters, motivation, and strategies. The unpredictable post–Cold War era and the revolution in communication technologies have challenged the media (Freedom Forum, 1993). Until the early 1990s, books on international conflict included very few references to the media's roles, and journals only rarely published articles on this topic. During the past decade, however, the revolution in communication technologies and the changing nature of international conflicts inspired scholars and journalists to investigate the media's roles. Various organizations have initiated studies and programs for

media intervention in conflict management and resolution, including the Carnegie Commission on Preventing Deadly Conflict (1997); the Center for Peacebuilding at Swisspeace (Spurk, 2002); Common Ground (Melone, Terzis, & Beleli, 2002); the Institute for Media, Policy, and Civil Society (Howard, 2002, 2003); the United States Institute of Peace (Frohardt & Temin, 2003); and the Aspen Institute (Walton, 2004). Geelen (2002) listed 32 media projects in five conflict regions, including Africa, the Balkans and Eastern Europe, the Middle East, South America, and South and Southeast Asia. Institutes and organizations have also organized courses on international conflict for journalists and published handbooks and manuals (e.g., McGoldrick & Lynch, 2000; Rubenstein, Botes, Dukes, & Stephens, 1994).

When analyzing the media's roles in international conflict, it is necessary to distinguish among different types of media. In many studies authors write about "the media," but they refer only to the Western media. Davis (2000) and Spurk (2002) made a significant distinction between local media or media in conflict regions and the Western media. I suggest distinguishing among five levels of media by geopolitical criteria: local, national, regional, international, and global. Local media include newspapers and television and radio stations operating in a town, a city, or a district. National media include newspapers and electronic media operating within the boundaries of nation-states. Regional media include the Qatar-based Al-Jazeera and the Dubai-based Al-Arabia, which broadcast primarily to the Middle East, and SABC Africa, which serves Africa. International media include broadcast and print media used by states and public and private organizations to operate across international borders. International media include, for example, the government-owned Voice of America or Radio Beijing, and the privately owned *International Herald Tribune* or *The Economist.* The global media essentially include television networks such as CNN International and BBC World. While the international media primarily represent the perspectives of a particular state, the global media claim to represent no particular national viewpoint. Both CNN and BBC, for example, operate two separate broadcasting systems: CNN International is a global network while CNN-US is national, and BBC World is global while BBC-UK is national. There are differences in approach and content between the national and the global broadcasting of the same network, but very little research has been conducted to find how wide the differences are and their significance. For the purposes of this study it is important to distinguish between the local media in conflict regions and media that operate outside these regions. The latter are called here the external media.

This work critically examines basic and applied research on media coverage and intervention in international conflicts. It focuses on roles more than on coverage. It explores normative theories and empirical results, identifies strengths and weaknesses, and offers new approaches and a framework for future research. I argue that the conceptual and theoretical effort of Galtung (2002) and others to distinguish between war and peace journalism or between hate and peace media (Gardner, 2001), and the simplistic dividing of conflict to three phases—pre-conflict, conflict, and post-conflict—are inadequate. Instead, the analysis here views international conflict as a process moving through four phases characterized by a specific condition and goal: prevention, management, resolution, and reconciliation. This work includes three sections. The first critically examines the distinction between war and peace journalism, and explains the approach used in this work to analyze phases and concepts of international conflicts. The second section investigates actual and potential media roles in each phase. It shows that scholars and practicioners have used too many different approaches and concepts. Future research will have to be much more systematic and cumulative, and require one framework and identical or similar variables or categories for all the four phases. Therefore, the last section offers a proposal for a new research framework based on the integration of conflict theories and the functional theory of communication.

SECTION I: APPROACHES

War Versus Peace Journalism

Diamond and McDonald (1996) wrote, "Conflict and violence make news and peace doesn't. News is perceived as what's exciting and different. People living happily together are of no interest to the public. Violence is reportable; nonviolence is boring" (p. 124). Thus, the media emphasize violence and refrain from legitimizing nonviolence and conflict resolution. Journalists, scholars, and practitioners have criticized coverage of violence and offered alternative approaches. Several criticized coverage of warfare, while others offered broader criticism and suggested more comprehensive approaches needed to confront coverage of the conflicts' wider dimensions. Based on his experience in the Bosnia war, Martin Bell (1997) criticized war coverage by distinguishing between "bystanders' journalism" and "journalism of attachment." Galtung (1998, 2002) contrasted "war/violence journalism" and "peace/conflict journalism," and Kempf (2002a) distinguished between "escalation-oriented conflict coverage," which is similar to Galtung's war journalism, and "de-escalation–oriented conflict coverage," which represents a more critical version of peace journalism. Howard (2003) distinguished between "traditional journalism" and "conflict sensitive journalism."

Bell (1997) criticized media neutrality in war coverage. He explained that bystanders' journalism concerns itself more with the circumstance of war, such as military formations, weapons, strategies, maneuvers, and tactics, while journalism of attachment concerns itself more with people: those who provoke wars, those who fight them, and those who suffer from them. "Journalism of attachment," argued Bell, "cares as well as knows; is aware of its responsibilities; and will not stand neutral between good and evil, right and wrong, the victim and the oppressor" (p. 8). Bell's colleagues in Bosnia, Christiane Amanpour (1996) and Ed Vulliamy (1999), adopted a similar approach. Amanpour argued that journalists can be objective by giving all sides a fair hearing, but they do not have to be neutral and treat all sides equally. Vulliamy argued:

> In the examples of Bosnia, Rwanda, Cambodia, and elsewhere, the neutrality adopted by diplomats and the media is both dangerous and reprehensible. By remaining neutral, we reward the bullies of history . . . [and] create a mere intermission before the next round of atrocities. There are times when we as reporters have to cross the line. (p. 604)

Bell, Amanpour, and Vulliamy supported the Muslims, and vehemently advocated military intervention against the Serbs. A similar pattern surfaced in other conflicts, such as the Palestinian-Israeli conflict, where Western journalists perceived the Palestinians as victims and sided with them (Lederman, 1992; Muravchik, 2004).

News organizations, editors, and reporters often ignore the media campaigns on behalf of a particular side in an international conflict because it may question the standard the media claim for fair, balanced, and objective coverage. The Bosnia coverage, however, inspired a needed debate on journalism of attachment among journalists and scholars (McLaughlin, 2002). David Binder of *The New York Times* called Bell's argument against neutrality in warfare "a garbage argument," and insisted that "our job is to report from all sides, not to play favorites" (Ricchiardi, 1996, p. 27). Hume (1997) argued that journalism of attachment threatens good journalism because it neglects historical and political contexts of violence and causes journalists to set themselves up as judge and jury. Ward (1998) thought that Bell's concept of objectivity was too narrow and dangerous because journalists may "devolve into unsubstantiated journalism where bias parade as moral principles" (p. 124). Ward believed that journalists are already "attached" and helping society by being professional and objective reporters. When covering war, Ward explained, "Reporters can convey the evil they confront simply by letting the images speak for themselves, without adding heavy-handed editorial comment" (p. 124). Gjelten (2001) also warned against Bell's sacrificing of professional ethics and standards.

Weaver (1998) criticized journalism of attachment from another perspective. He pointed out that reporters covering warfare are bombarded by propaganda and often are unable to check the facts. They begin to identify with one party to the conflict simply because the weight of information they are receiving is so one-sided. Also, as opposed to facts and analysis, pictures of individual suffering make interesting television. "Those who suffer more receive more media attention, and this has a distorting effect" (p. 3). Gowing (1997) added that the attitude of Amanpour and her colleagues was neatly exploited by Bosnian ministers who "usually enjoyed a free ride, their increasingly exaggerated claims accepted as fact by callow interviewers and anchors in distant studios, who didn't have the knowledge or background briefings to know better" (pp. 21–22). Kempf (2002a, 2002b) also concluded that journalism of attachment replaced the rules of journalism with the rules of propaganda, and that in Bosnia journalists served their moral impetus by controlling information and fabricating news. Journalism of attachment is also problematic because it deals only with predominantly Western coverage and ignores other types of media, such as the local media. The division of people into aggressors and victims is highly simplistic because it ignores the possibility that people ruled by aggressor leaders could also be victims, not only those who are being attacked. Galtung (1998) implied that Bell's journalism of attachment is not a good alternative to war journalism because it ignores the wider dimensions of conflict.

Galtung and Kempf offered other alternatives to war journalism. Galtung (1998, 2002) argued that the media generally follow the "low road" of war journalism in reporting conflict: chasing wars, the elites that run them, and a win-lose outcome. His alternative approach, the "high road" of peace journalism, focuses on conflict formation, the people who suffer from violence, and a win-win solution. According to Galtung, war journalism focuses on who advances and who capitulates at what cost in human lives and material. This coverage polarizes and escalates because it calls for hatred and more violence to avenge or stop "them." It sees "them" as the problem and dehumanizes "them." War journalism is driven by propaganda and manipulation and is therefore biased and distorted. In contrast, Galtung wrote, peace journalism explores the reasons behind the violence and provides a voice to all parties, as well as empathy and understanding. It focuses on suffering all over and humanizes all sides. Peace journalism is more truthful and attempts to de-escalate violence by highlighting peace and conflict resolution as much as violence. While war journalism attaches only to "our side," peace journalism is a journalism of attachment to all actual and potential victims. Similarly, Howard (2003) explained: "traditional journalism" brings only "the bare facts," while "conflict sensitive journalism" goes beyond these facts and explores solutions, new ideas, and new voices (p. 15). According to Howard, traditional journalism presents only bad news, does not seek other sides or points of view, assigns blame, uses emotional language such as *terrorism* or *massacre,* and takes sides. On the other hand, conflict sensitive journalism presents balanced reports and only what is known, it uses words carefully and refrains from emotional terms, seeks explanation and comment from all sides, and looks for solutions.

Kempf (2002a) built his approach on Galtung's ideas, but suggested a more critical peace journalism, which he called "de-escalation-oriented conflict coverage" (DEOCC). This approach questions war and military logic, and respects and fairly covers the opponent's rights. At the same time, however, DEOCC has to be cautious and self-critical in order to avoid dissemination of "peace propaganda," which is as counterproductive as "war propaganda." DEOCC must maintain a critical distance from the belligerents and equally and forcefully criticize their actions.

Although two organizations, TRANSCEND (Galtung, Jacobsen, & Brand-Jacobsen, 2000) and Conflict and Peace Forums, attempted to translate Galtung's ideas into specific manuals and programs (e.g., McGoldrick & Lynch, 2000), very little empirical research has been conducted on his approach. In a unique piece, Hanitzsch (2004) criticized peace journalism and related approaches for being at odds with mass communication theory. Peace journalism is based on the assumption of powerful, casual, and linear media effects. Communication theory, however, has produced very little empirical support for this approach. Peace journalism looks at the audience as a single aggregate of dispersed individuals, but communication theory has identified pluralistic audiences with different characteristics. Peace journalism assumes that publishers and journalists, especially at the local media level, can disregard the interests of their specific audiences, but communication theory suggests that this assumption is unnatural and economically impossible. Peace journalism places responsibility on the media to prevent, manage, resolve, and transform conflicts, but communication theory does not recognize this role, and sociological system theory places responsibility for these functions on political institutions and leaders. I think that peace journalism has offered interesting insights into the deficiencies of media attitudes toward international conflict, but as a heuristic approach it suffers from several weaknesses. In the next sections, I suggest a different integrative approach that may yield better normative and empirical results.

Concepts and Phases

Scholars have employed a variety of confusing terms and concepts to analyze international conflict. Initially, they distinguished between *conflict management* and *conflict resolution,* using the first to describe efforts to limit warfare and violence, and using the second to describe efforts to end conflicts. Later, conflict management served as an umbrella term for dealing with almost all aspects and phases of conflict. More recently, researchers have employed concepts such as "conflict prevention" and "conflict transformation" to, respectively, analyze efforts to prevent violence and to transform relations between former enemies after warfare.

International conflict is a dynamic process. It begins and ends at a particular period of time. It is not always easy to pinpoint the exact beginning and ending of conflict, but scholars and practitioners have identified life cycles of conflicts and analyzed them in chronological terms (Galtung, 1996; Lederach, 1995, 2005; Lund, 1996). Many scholars and practitioners distinguished among three highly simplistic phases: pre-conflict, conflict, and post-conflict (Howard, 2002; Spurk 2002) or pre-violence, violence, and post-violence (Jakobsen, 2000). I think that we need meaningful concepts and not just time frames to describe the pre- and post-conflict phases, and I suggest distinguishing among four stages of international conflict, based on a critical condition and a principal intervention goal: onset-prevention, escalation-management, de-escalation-resolution, and termination-reconciliation. Each phase has distinctive characteristics and ends in specific outcomes.

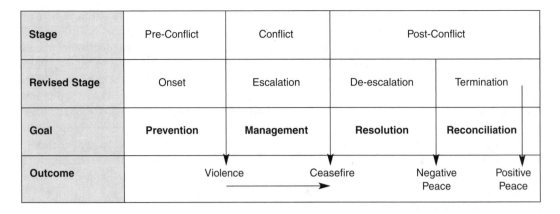

Stage	Pre-Conflict	Conflict	Post-Conflict	
Revised Stage	Onset	Escalation	De-escalation	Termination
Goal	**Prevention**	**Management**	**Resolution**	**Reconciliation**
Outcome		Violence	Ceasefire	Negative Peace	Positive Peace

Figure 22.1   Phases and Concepts

Prevention is characterized by the surfacing of conflict, the beginning of disagreements, and growth in verbal and behavioral hostile exchanges. At this stage, only effective prevention measures can stop the conflict from deteriorating into violence (Ackermann, 2003). If prevention succeeds, the conflict is peacefully settled and the conflict process temporarily or permanently terminates. If not, parties may escalate the conflict, believing they can impose a solution via violence. Uses of force include full-scale war, military intervention, terrorism and guerrilla warfare, firing across borders, and deployment of forces. Conflict management—limiting and halting violence to relatively tolerable levels—applies to the escalation-violence phase, which typically ends in a formal or informal ceasefire or an armistice.

I suggest that the post-conflict or post-violence phase should be divided into two separate stages: resolution and reconciliation. The difference between the two stems from the significant distinction Galtung (1969) made between "negative peace" and "positive peace." Negative peace refers only to the absence of violence, while positive peace refers to the building of new relations in many relevant areas between former enemies, including open borders, trade, tourism, and cultural ties. Other scholars made a similar distinction between "conflict resolution" and "conflict transformation" (Lederach, 1995, 1997). In the resolution phase, leaders attempt to negotiate an agreement to end violence. If they reach a formal agreement, it may end violence and facilitate transformation; if they do

not, they may resume violence or create a stalemate. According to Lederach, conflict transformation usually involves transforming perceptions of issues, actions, and other people or groups; the way conflict is expressed; and it must take place both at the personal and the systemic level.

The distinctions between resolution and transformation of conflicts are based on the assumption that even if the sides reach a peace agreement, it is only an agreement between leaders, not between peoples, and it has to be fully implemented and respected over time. Therefore, in the fourth and last stage, the parties attempt to move from negative peace to positive peace or from conflict resolution to conflict transformation. They try to engage their respective peoples fully and transform relations from hostility to amicability. Väyrynen (1999) raised questions about the meaning of transformation and placed the concept in a different context. To him transformation means a major change in a principal element of a conflict, including actors, issues, and rules, and therefore it may occur at any phase. He even argued that transformation must happen before resolution becomes possible. Given this approach and the different meanings applied to transformation, I searched for an alternative concept. The options were "peacebuilding" and "reconciliation." Several scholars equate the two (Jeong, 2002; Paris, 2004), but others (Howard, 2002; Lederach, 2005; Spurk, 2002) use peacebuilding as a general concept. I prefer reconciliation because it best captures the essence of the fourth phase (Bar-Siman-Tov,

2004; Brown & Poremski, 2005; Rothstein, 1999). Figure 22.1 describes the four suggested phases of conflict by stage, revised stage, goal, and outcome.

Each phase may end in outcomes different from those listed in Figure 22.1. For example, if prevention succeeds, the conflict does not become violent; if conflict resolution fails, the parties cannot sign a peace agreement. The listed outcomes typically occur when a conflict moves from one phase to another. An international conflict may not necessarily move linearly from one phase to another. A conflict may erratically move forward and backward, for example, from management to resolution and back to management. Phases of international conflict are often fluid. Events and processes, such as uses of force, negotiation, and mediation, may appear at more than one phase. Even when parties decide to seek resolution through negotiation, they may still use force to improve their bargaining power. Failure to reach an agreement may motivate parties to renew hostilities. Thus, force may be used in both the management and resolution phases. While the purpose of using force in the management phase is to impose a solution, the purpose of using force in the resolution phase is to affect negotiations. Uses of force in the two phases are also different: It is more massive and sustained in the management phase and more sporadic and limited in the resolution phase.

Similarly, negotiation and mediation occur during both prevention and resolution. Yet in the prevention phase the purpose of negotiations is to deal peacefully with the sources of conflict in order to prevent violence, while in the resolution phase, the purpose is to negotiate a peace agreement following the eruption of violence. Conflict resolution after war is both easier and more complicated. It is easier because parties may be ready to make concessions that, prior to the violent phase, they rejected; it is more complicated because the cost of violence in human and material resources becomes a significant constraining factor. This work suggests distinguishing among the phases through the principal condition, where force is dealt with in the management phase, and negotiation and mediation are dealt with in the resolution phase. The next section critically review research conducted on media

effects and intervention in each of the four conflict phases.

SECTION II: PHASES

Prevention

Scholars and practitioners have criticized all types of media—global, Western, and local—for their failures to promote prevention of international conflicts (Girardet, 1999). The Commission on Global Governance (1995), Jakobsen (2000), and Gowing (1997) all argued that the media become interested in conflicts only after they explode into violence, destruction, and death. Gowing concluded:

> Rarely is there media coverage of conflict that is about to explode. It is war, and the images of fighting, that catalyses television coverage, in particular, and not the vaguer possibility of a conflict breaking out at some indefinable moment. When it comes to prevention, media coverage is usually too late to help. (p. 3)

The reasons for this failure are ratings, conflict fatigue, the nature of conflict prevention, and professional journalism practices. "Since coverage of conflicts that *might* explode in violence is unlikely to boost ratings," wrote Jakobsen, "these conflicts are usually ignored" (p. 133). Commercial media claim that the public is mostly interested in local and national affairs, not in international events, and that this trend became even stronger after the end of the Cold War. The Western media cited declining public interest to justify substantial cuts in foreign affairs coverage and in foreign reporters and overseas bureaus. However, the Al-Qaida terrorist attacks in New York and Washington in 2001, and the U.S.-led wars in Afghanistan and Iraq, may have reversed this trend.

Vast amounts of vicious ongoing and potential conflicts in the world cause both the media and the public to lose interest in them. Conflict prevention is very slow, complicated, and mostly invisible. Moreover, successful conflict prevention is not attractive to the media because nothing happens. Finally, the media's standard operating procedures hinder the ability of journalists to fulfill useful roles in conflict prevention.

Reporters are assigned to the offices of presidents, prime ministers and ministries, and to parliaments and international organizations (O'Neill, 2000). Consequently, the news they gather and print comes primarily from secondary sources. Often, they learn about a conflict only after policy makers have told them it has grown to be a major crisis. In rare cases, even if media coverage happens to warn that violence is inevitable, as was the case in Bosnia, Rwanda, and Kosovo, policy makers tend to ignore it and avoid conflict prevention measures. They ignore warnings because they do not consider them sufficiently reliable, they may be occupied with other more pressing domestic or international problems, and, at this early stage, the public does not sufficiently support active engagement or intervention. The most useful way to review the media roles in prevention is to examine studies and approaches according to the distinction between local and external media and media-government relations.

Local media. The local media in conflict regions contribute more to escalation and violence than to prevention. This pattern happens more frequently in vulnerable societies where the media are susceptible to manipulation and abuse by those who wish to instigate violent conflict (Davis, 2000; Frohardt & Temin, 2003). Furthermore, the state of the media in these societies may indicate impending conflict, and intervention to alter the media's structure and content is necessary before they can be employed to prevent conflict. Vulnerable societies are those susceptible to movement toward civil conflict and/or repressive rule. They are mostly multi-ethnic societies in developing countries and in countries moving from authoritarian to democratic government. Structural and content media indicators may provide clues to violent conflict in these societies.

Structural indicators include media variety and plurality, media accessibility, degree of journalists' isolation from their domestic and international colleagues, and the legal environment for the media (Frohardt & Temin, 2003). The fact that the few existing media outlets are owned and controlled by the state, and media professionals belong to the ruling political movement and represent the government line, coupled with the lack of legal protection for the

freedom of the press, all indicate a potential for media manipulation by those interested in conflict escalation and violence. Content indicators include creating fear of an imminent attack by the other side based on past conflicts; manipulation of myths, stereotypes, and identities; and overemphasizing grievances, inequalities, or atrocities (Frohardt & Temin, 2003). Content indicators also include the creating of inevitability and resignation through the portrayal of conflict as an eternal process and discrediting of alternatives to conflict.

The best known and thoroughly researched case of leaders using local media to escalate a conflict is the role of radio in the Rwanda genocide. In 1994, *Radio-Television Libre des Milles Collins* (RTLM) played a major role in the slaughter of about 800,000 Tutsi and moderate Hutus in Rwanda. Extreme Hutu leaders, who took over the government, mobilized RTLM to help in the violent campaign against the Tutsis. Announcers on RTLM incited hatred and violence and called for a "final war" to exterminate the Tutsi "cockroaches" (Berkeley, 1994; Kellow & Steeves, 1998). They directed killers to particular places, targeted specific audiences, and used slogans such as "kill or be killed" to inspire mass murders. Due to RTLM's role in the Rwanda genocide, for the first time since the Nuremberg trials the directors of a station were charged and convicted of genocide in a special UN international court (LaFraniere, 2003). Scholars argued that had the international community taken measures against RTML's broadcasts, the tragedy would have been mitigated (Metzl, 1997; Nye & Owens, 1996).

A similar pattern of hate media appeared in the Bosnia and the Palestinian-Israeli conflicts. In Bosnia, the government-controlled media, such as Serb Radio Television, fomented violence and hatred (Buric, 2000). Ambassador Warren Zimmermann (1996) wrote,

> What we witnessed was violence-provoking nationalism from the top down, inculcated primarily through the medium of television. . . . The virus of television spread ethnic hatred like an epidemic throughout Yugoslavia. . . . An entire generation of Serbs, Croats, and Muslims were aroused by television to hate their neighbors. (pp. 151–153)

Similarly, the government-controlled Palestinian radio and television (Karsh, 2003; Nirenstein, 2001; Timmerman, 2003), and the Hezbollah's al-Manar radio and television in Lebanon (Torisch, 2004) have systematically incited for hatred, violence, and terrorism against Israelis and Jews. Unfortunately, these cases have not yet been sufficiently researched.

Gardner (2001) recommended several specific measures to stop hate media and promote peace, including legislation to prevent use of the media to incite violence, international sanctions against those using hate speech via the media, providing a forum for moderate voices, and tailoring of the media to local needs. Frohardt and Temin (2003) suggested a much more sophisticated approach that includes four possible types of media intervention at the local level: structural, content-specific, entertainment-oriented, and aggressive. Structural interventions are designed to reform the media in conflict regions and make them stronger, more independent, and more resistant to government pressure and manipulations. These include the strengthening of independent media, such as the strengthening of the anti-government Serbian radio station B92 during the Bosnia conflict; developing journalist competence, working with the legislature and the judiciary to protect free speech and independent media; promoting diversity in the journalist corps and media ownership; strengthening domestic and international networks in order to convince local journalists who operate in difficult circumstances that they are part of a larger community of journalists around the world; and media monitoring.

Content-specific interventions include "repersonalization" and "issue-oriented training" (Frohardt & Temin, 2003). The first calls for the portraying of people mostly as individuals. Pioneered by Internews, *Spacebridges* is an example of this strategy, as it allowed individuals from communities in conflict, such as Muslim, Serb, and Croat refugees from Bosnia, to conduct personal dialogues with each other over a live video feed. Issue-oriented training involves training of journalists on how to report on sensitive and explosive issues in a manner that would help, rather than hinder, conflict prevention. Entertainment-oriented programming is based on the assumption that all types of programs, not just news and documentaries, should be used to prevent or manage conflicts (Manoff, 1998). Common Ground, for example, established radio stations in Burundi, Liberia, and Sierra Leone that produced, among other programs, soap operas designed to encourage dialogue and discourage violence.

What do peoples in conflict regions think about the actual and potential media contributions to prevention? The Institute for War and Peace Reporting initiated and implemented a unique comparative study of local media behavior in four conflict areas—Georgia, Cambodia, Bosnia, and South Africa (Davis, 2000). Authors of the case studies employed the same methodology and applied the same questions. They interviewed journalists and generated public attitudes through focus groups. The 10 questions dealt with past and current performance and with desirable future performance. The first was seen in questions such as, "Has the way journalists reported conflicts improved the situation or made it worse?" Desirable performance was seen in questions such as, "Can or should journalists play a role in preventing conflicts, and if yes, how?" The study revealed both similarities and differences among the four conflicts. In all the cases, however, respondents blamed most of the media outlets for fomenting hatred and encouraging violence, but they attributed this behavior to the lack of democracy and freedom of the press. They called for the establishing of professional media and well-trained journalists, but were not sure how the reformed media could help conflict containment and resolution.

External media. Several studies, predominantly normative, suggested measures that the Western and the global media can take to help prevent conflicts from deteriorating to violence. Capitalizing on the idea of "preventive diplomacy," O'Neill (2000) argued for "preventive journalism," which he defined as "a systematic and continuing effort to patrol ahead for causes before they become results, to attack problems in the deepest recesses of society before they grow into political strife then explosions, and to reduce the incidents of folly and surprise" (p. 69). O'Neill believed that preventive journalism can produce early warning, which is a key element in conflict prevention. By detecting early signs of conflict and reporting them, the media could stir the public to force policy makers and "sluggish institutions" to note the emerging troubles and deal effectively with them sooner rather than later. Even if the media themselves could not detect early signs of emerging conflicts, they could still help conflict prevention through tacit collaboration with diplomats. The latter can use sophisticated conflict prevention techniques to detect emerging dangers early, and the media can then publicize them. O'Neill acknowledged that the structure and practices of contemporary journalism hinder preventive journalism. These include the entertainment element in news broadcasts, the absence of sufficient control of sources, the acute shortage of well-trained and qualified foreign correspondents, cost, and resistance to change. O'Neill ignores the current structure and conduct of contemporary diplomacy, which is also inadequate to support effective collaboration with journalists in prevention.

The Carnegie Commission (1997) called for measures that could strengthen the capability of the global and the Western media both to help conflict prevention through adequate coverage and to apply pressure on local media in conflict regions to refrain from instigating violence. The report asked major networks to expose "publics to the circumstances and issues that could give rise to mass violence through regular public service programming focusing on individual 'hot spots'" (pp. 121–122). It also recommended educating worldwide audiences on the advantages of peaceful resolution of conflicts through special media projects such as the 1995 Conflict Resolution Project of the Voice of America. For the local media, the report suggested the following measures: developing standards to ensure adequate coverage of efforts to defuse conflicts, and establishing an international press council, consisting of highly respected journalists, whose aim would be to monitor and enforce acceptable professional practices. This council would employ peer pressure and, if necessary, sanctions against editors in conflict areas responsible for dissemination of hate and violence messages.

Similarly, Metzl (1997) and Kaufman (2002) called for information intervention against local media that preach hate and encourage violence. Metzl argued that if the international community is unable or unwilling to intervene militarily in cases of human rights abuses, condemnations at international bodies, such as the UN, are impotent and insufficient. Based on experience in conflict areas such as Rwanda and Bosnia, he suggested a third option—"information intervention." Metzl offered two interrelated measures: jamming genocide broadcasts and replacing them with peace broadcasts, which would represent all the parties to a conflict and would promote conflict resolution rather than violence. Information intervention requires the constant monitoring, countering, and blocking of broadcasts that incite hatred and violence. It raises controversial questions about many issues: which body should monitor and counter genocide broadcasts and under what authority? Does information intervention infringe on the sovereignty of independent states? Does it constitute intervention in their internal affairs? And would it be a form of censorship and violation of the right for freedom of speech? So far, the UN and other international bodies have failed to adequately address the information intervention option and the questions it raises.

Apparently, writers on media and conflict prevention have not been aware of research conducted by political scientists who have argued that the media are already providing substantial clues to possible eruptions of conflict and violence. Hunt (1997) found that editorials constitute a leading indicator of conflictual events. He identified two types of editorials: analytic, in which foreign countries were calmly discussed, and critical, in which the prospects of violent conflict were raised. Analytic editorials were associated with diplomatic and economic conflict, while critical editorials appeared before escalation and violence. Hunt's study suggested that decoding editorials may predict violence and consequently may help initiate prevention efforts. Hunt suggested that governments must win sufficient public support before they can go to war, and that they use editorials to meet this condition. Further research should explore this hypothesis: If editorials were more independent and critical of government intentions, leaders would have to reconsider escalation and violence or use other communication channels to persuade the public to support their policy.

Authors who have advocated and prescribed roles for the media in the conflict prevention phase have often ignored several tough questions about the causes of international conflict and the determinants of media behavior. Scholars have oversimplified conflict causation upon which conflict prevention depends. The great number of variables at play makes it difficult to identify those responsible for a particular confrontation at a particular time. Furthermore, it is very difficult to predict when a conflict will become violent because actors may be engaged in conflict for a long period of time before they reach the violence phase. In addition, effective media contributions to prevention depend on substantial reforms in journalism and on a linear relationship between the media, the public, and policy makers. Researchers have underestimated the difficulties in reforming journalism practices and overestimated both the power of the media to shape public opinion and the power of the public to force policies on policy makers. The preceding survey of existing research reveals problematic prescriptions, such as preventive journalism and information intervention, as well as promising beginnings, such as the works of Davis (2000) and Frohardt and Temin (2003) on the roles of the local media.

Management

The media devote considerable attention to warfare and violence. Owners, editors, and reporters believe that war, terrorism, destruction, death, genocide, refugees, and ethnic cleansing attract wide circulation and high ratings. "Wars," wrote Taylor (2000), "produce a stream of human stories of tragedy and heroism . . . they invoke heightened emotions of patriotism, fear, anger and euphoria, and they involve winners and losers" (p. 183). The focus on violence and war, wrote Galtung (2002), dominated the media, which "view conflict as a sports arena and gladiator circus" (p. 259). There is substantial continuity in war coverage but also several significant changes (Kaplan, 2003). Coverage of war and violence since the 1991 Gulf War inspired new heated debates in professional and academic circles on the media's roles in warfare and conflict management. The debates focused on new phenomena such as "humanitarian military intervention" and "embedded journalism," and on new concepts such as "the CNN effect,"

"information management," "virtual wars," and "wars in time of peace."

Since the end of the Cold War, scholars analyzed violence coverage primarily via media-government relations. They used two diametrically opposing frameworks: "information management" and the "CNN effect." Information management, known also as "news management," refers to government's control of information and manipulation of the mass media as demonstrated in recent wars and military operations, from the 1991 Gulf War to the 2003 war in Iraq (Badsey, 2000; Bennett & Paletz, 1994; Hoskins, 2004; Tumber & Palmer, 2004). Information management means that the media primarily function as a tool in the hands of policy makers. Conversely, commentators and scholars employ the CNN effect to describe television coverage, primarily of horrific humanitarian disasters, that forces policy makers to take actions they otherwise would not have taken, such as military intervention (Gilboa 2005a; Robinson, 2002). This phenomenon means that the media determine the national interest and usurp policy-making from elected and appointed officials. Politicians, officials, journalists, and scholars have argued that the CNN effect caused the United States and Western humanitarian military interventions in Northern Iraq/Kurdistan (1991), Somalia (1992–1993), Bosnia (1992–1995), and Kosovo (1999).

Information management. The origins of the information management approach can be traced to the U.S. war in Vietnam (Carruthers, 2000; Taylor, 1997; Thrall, 2000). Although researchers have debated the media's effects on this war (Braestrup, 1977; Hallin, 1986), policy makers in liberal democracies have believed that the media were responsible for the U.S. defeat. The lesson was to view journalists as adversaries and to limit their access and ability to report from the battlefields. Britain employed a variety of measures to curtail media coverage of the war in the Falklands (1982), while the United States pursued a similar policy during the military interventions in Granada (1983) and Panama (1989). In the early 1990s, however, civilian and military leaders realized that controlling the media might not only block unfavorable reporting, but also provide them with tools to advance their goals. The United States and its allies were able to manage the news media in the 1991 Gulf War; in the humanitarian interventions in Bosnia, Somalia, Haiti, and Kosovo; in the United States immediately after the September 11 terrorist attacks; and in the wars in Afghanistan and Iraq.

The 2003 war in Iraq yielded innovative techniques of information management, predominantly "embedded journalism" (Katovsky & Carlson, 2003; Seib, 2004; Tumber & Palmer, 2004). Tumber (2004) showed that embedding was not entirely new and was used, for example, by the British government in the Falklands war. In the Falklands, journalists were embedded almost by accident whereas in the Iraq war they were deliberately embedded according to a carefully designed plan. Another difference is related to innovations in communication technologies, particularly in satellite phones and videophones. About 600 journalists from all over the world were assigned to accompany specific units and became an integral part of them (Chermak, Bailey, & Brown, 2003). They lived with soldiers, traveled with them, celebrated their victories, and shared their grief.

Embedding facilitated more information on the battlefield faster than ever before. Yet it also inevitably produced biased and distorted reporting (Ferrari & Tobin, 2003; Gitlin, 2003; Seib, 2004; Tumber & Palmer, 2004). First, embedded journalists completely depended on official sources for information. Second, each journalist witnessed only a small segment of the front. Only the supreme commanders saw the whole picture and chose what information to reveal and what to conceal. Third, embedding cancelled the distance journalists must maintain from the objects of their coverage. Too much identification created loyalty and commitment to the troops, as opposed to the truth. Embedded journalists had to consider the potential effects of reports on their own safety. Information that was potentially damaging to the units was also potentially damaging to the journalists.

Governments were able to manage information when certain conditions existed. First, leaders enjoyed a high degree of credibility, and the case they made for using force was persuasive. Second, the public supported limitations on the freedom of the press during warfare.

Third, the media collaborated with the government because they were reluctant to antagonize the public, fearing a negative response from their consumers that would translate into decreased ratings and circulation figures. The location of the battlefield was also a factor. The higher the isolation and difficulty to access, the easier it was for governments to manage the news. Control of the media was easier on islands such as the Falklands, Granada, and Haiti; in the desert between Iraq and Saudi Arabia and Kuwait; and in Afghanistan, and it was more difficult in places such as Panama and Bosnia.

Information management presents a dilemma to media professionals. Hess and Kalb (2003) described media-government relations in times of war as a "clash of responsibilities" (p. 10) that emerges from the conflicting requirements of waging and reporting war. On the one hand, journalists are citizens and are expected to provide for the common defense. On the other hand, they must fully expose and evaluate government policy and activities. During war, these two responsibilities often clash, and consequently journalists face a difficult dilemma (Cali, 2002). This is not a new problem, but in the global television age it has become more acute and more troubling. The military argues that media coverage of violence has tremendous effects on public opinion at home, on the soldiers at the front, and on the enemy. All combatants employ propaganda and psychological warfare and it would be more difficult and costlier to win a war if one side, particularly if it is democratic and liberal, allows free, complete, and uninterrupted coverage while the other side, particularly if it is authoritarian, fully controls and distorts coverage (Gruber, 2003). The right to win wars and to save human life, they said, is more important than the public right to know.

The effects and consequences of information management are highly controversial. Ignatieff (2000) criticized this technique for producing "virtual wars" that look like plays made for television or computer games. Warfare was sanitized. Reports from both the field and headquarters showed sophisticated, accurate weapons in action, but they did not show the bloody and horrific consequences of explosions. The pictures revealed violence with very few military and civilian casualties and little destruction. In addition, after September 11, the U.S. American media rallied around the president and became a "patriotic press" (Entman, 2004; Jamieson & Waldman, 2003). Patriotism was reflected on several planes: the pictures selected to encapsulate events, the stories that were not written, the extent to which the frames offered by the president were embraced by journalists, and the critiques that were suppressed. These symptoms were responsible for distorted coverage of major events and processes (Kellner, 2003). Studies (e.g., Pfau et al., 2004) showed that embedded journalists wrote reports more favorable to the coalition forces in Iraq and to U.S. policy than non-embedded journalists. Yet the question is not who files more favorable or less favorable reports on the military, but what kind of mix television audiences and newspapers readers receive from embedded and non-embedded sources. If the mix is balanced the distortion becomes minimal; if it is not, it becomes significant. Schechter (2003) argued that embedding free media in Europe provided much more accurate and balanced reporting on the war, but, as Hertoghe (2003) showed, this was not the case, at least not in France, where the media substantially distorted coverage of the war to fit with the critical stand of President Jacques Chirac.

Several newspapers and media executives have admitted professional and ethical failures in covering violence. In an editorial published on May 26, 2004, the *New York Times* acknowledged that coverage of whether or not Saddam Hussein had weapons of mass destruction "was not as rigorous as it should have been" and that "we wish we had been more aggressive in reexamining the claims as new evidence emerged— or failed to emerge" (p. A-10). Daniel Okrent (2004), the paper's public editor, also acknowledged deficiencies in the *New York Times* coverage of the case made by the Bush administration for an attack on Iraq. On the other hand, about a year earlier, CNN executive Eason Jordan (2003) acknowledged that his global network concealed information about atrocities committed by Saddam Hussein for more than a decade because it did not want to endanger the lives of Iraqis. His colleague, Peter Collins (2003), however, linked the cover-up to access conditions imposed by Hussein. The U.S. American media

expressed similar regrets after the 1991 Gulf War and promised to implement the appropriate lessons. Apparently, 10 years later the same breaches occurred.

Driving and constraining policy. The CNN effect has been one of the most interesting new hypotheses about the influence global television is having on military intervention in humanitarian crises. Politicians and officials from several countries testified that pictures of humanitarian crises forced them to intervene militarily in conflict regions to prevent genocide and ethnic cleansing. The effect has been the subject of many books, articles, and conferences and has drawn enormous attention. So far, however, scholars have not been able to validate the concept sufficiently (Gilboa, 2005a). Scholarly and professional studies of the CNN effect present mixed, contradictory, and confusing results. Studies of the humanitarian interventions in Kurdistan and Somalia demonstrate this record well. Shaw (1996) and Ammon (2001) argued that television coverage of Saddam Hussein's massacre of Kurds forced the governments of the United States and Britain to reverse their nonintervention policy, but Miller (2002) found exactly the opposite. Mandelbaum (1994), Shattuck (1996), and B. Cohen (1994) argued that television coverage forced the U.S. government into a policy of intervention in Somalia for humanitarian reasons. Mermin (1997, 1999), however, called this claim a myth, and Livingston and Eachus (1995) concluded that the U.S. decision "was the result of diplomatic and bureaucratic operations, with news coverage coming in response to those decisions" (p. 413). Robinson (2001) did not identify any CNN effect in Somalia, and Gibbs (2000) argued that policy makers employed humanitarian justification, but decided to intervene militarily in Somalia due to strategic and economic considerations.

A valid scientific approach to the study of the CNN effect requires two interrelated comparative analyses: (a) an assessment of global television's impact on a specific foreign policy decision in comparison to the relative impact of other factors; and (b) application of this procedure to several relevant case studies. Only a few researchers have systematically followed this procedure. Jakobsen (1996) examined the impact of the following factors on humanitarian intervention decisions: a clear humanitarian and/or legal case, national interest, chance of success, domestic support, and the CNN effect. He then examined the relative influence of these factors on decisions to intervene in several crises from the Gulf War to Haiti. He discovered that CNN's coverage was an important factor because it placed the crises on the agenda; however, the decision to intervene "was ultimately determined by the perceived chances of success" (p. 212).

Robinson (2000, 2002) developed a sophisticated policy-media interaction model that predicts that media influence is likely to occur when policy is uncertain, and media coverage is critically framed and empathizes with suffering people. When policy is certain, media influence is unlikely to occur. Robinson applied this model to the crises in Bosnia and Kosovo and found that U.S. policy defending the Gorazde "safe area" in Bosnia was influenced by the media because the policy of President Clinton was uncertain and the media strongly criticized him. In Kosovo, Clinton's air-war policy was clear, and consequently the media failed to expand the operation to include ground troops.

Investigations of the CNN effect reveal considerable debate and disagreement among scholars, officials, and journalists. The conclusions are that this effect has not dramatically changed media-government relations, does not exist, or has been highly exaggerated and may occur only in rare situations of extremely dramatic and persistent coverage, lack of leadership, and chaotic policymaking (Neuman, 1996; Seib, 2002). Several scholars (e.g., Gowing, 2003; Jakobsen, 2000; Natsios, 1996; Strobel, 1997) agreed that the CNN effect has been highly exaggerated.

Unfortunately, the focus on information management and the CNN effect, like most binaries, has obscured the widely varied subtleties around and between these poles of analysis, deflecting attention from more subtle effects of domestic and global media. Close examination of decision making reveals less visible but equally significant effects that exist between these polarities. Gilboa (2003, 2005b) suggested a third approach to media impact on policymaking

in international conflict: the constraining effect. Real-time television coverage is able to constrain the policy process in warfare and crisis situations primarily due to the high speed of broadcasting and transmission of information. Over the course of the 20th century, technology has reduced the time of information transmission from weeks to minutes. Major constraints of real-time coverage include shortening of the time available for policymaking and demanding immediate response to crises and events; excluding experts and diplomats; facilitating diplomatic manipulations; creating high expectations; broadcasting deficient reports; and making instant judgments.

The three major approaches to media and conflict management—information management, the CNN effect, and the constraining effect—have been developed in response to rapid changes in communication technologies and violence in the post–Cold War era. The convergence of access and satellite technology revolutionized the media's roles in conflict management. The debate on war versus peace journalism also deals primarily with coverage of violence. All the approaches have raised many questions about the real power of the media to affect the beginning, evolution, and termination of violence, and about professional and ethical issues. Many scholars and journalists have participated in the debates about the functions that the media should and are fulfilling in times of crises and violence (Zelizer & Allan, 2002). Authors have argued that the media have failed to meet their responsibilities in the new age of global terrorism and violence (Elliot, 2004), but others have asserted that it is difficult to imagine how the next war will be fought, much less how it will be covered by the media (Hall, 2004). Scholarship has been chasing the rapid new developments in violence and conflict management, but much more intellectual effort is needed to identify the appropriate questions and research them.

Resolution

The media perform several functions in conflict resolution, known mostly as "media diplomacy" (Y. Cohen, 1986; Gilboa, 1998a, 2002c). Politicians and policy makers use the media to advance negotiations, build confidence, and cultivate public support for negotiations and agreements. The media also function as an independent actor, initiating and facilitating negotiations and conducting mediation. Theories of international negotiation may help place the mediation roles of journalists in a proper context by emphasizing the significance of "pre-negotiation" stages, the role of "third parties," and "track-two diplomacy" (Zartman & Rasmussen, 1997). During the pre-negotiation stage, the sides explore the advantages and shortcomings of a specific negotiation process and make a decision—based on information received from the other party and domestic and external considerations—on whether or not they should enter formal negotiations (Saunders, 2001). At this stage, mediators attempt to persuade leaders to replace confrontation and violence with a commitment to peaceful resolution and negotiations. Frequently, parties to a conflict are unable to begin direct formal negotiations and need a third party to help. Third parties can be formal representatives of superpowers, neutral states, international or global organizations, or just ordinary individuals (Hampson, 2001). Third parties are particularly helpful in the pre-negotiation stage.

While "track-one diplomacy" refers to government-to-government, formal, and official interaction between representatives of sovereign states, "track-two diplomacy" refers to unofficial negotiators or mediators and informal forms of negotiation (McDonald & Bendahmane, 1995; Volkan, 1991). Gilboa (2005c) suggested that it is useful to view journalists acting independently as third parties, pursuing track-two diplomacy, particularly in pre-negotiation stages, and used the term "media-broker diplomacy" to define these roles. The models of media diplomacy and media-broker diplomacy will be used here to examine media involvement in conflict resolution.

Media diplomacy. Policy makers usually prefer secret negotiations, but in the absence of direct channels of communication, or when one side is unsure about how the other would react to conditions for negotiations or to proposals for conflict resolution, officials use the media, with or without attribution, to send signals and messages to leaders of rival states and non-state actors. Using the media for signaling purposes

has been known for many years (Jönsson, 1996). Using the media without attribution to sources is particularly efficient when policy makers wish to fly a "trial balloon." They can avoid embarrassment and disassociate themselves from an idea that may receive a negative response. Leaders use reliable third parties to secretly explore intentions of the other side, but sometimes they simultaneously use the media to support the secret exchanges and to further indicate their serious intentions.

After the 1973 Arab-Israeli war, Kissinger perfected the use of the media for the purposes of signaling and pressure during his famous and highly successful "shuttle diplomacy." He often gave senior diplomatic correspondents aboard his plane background reports, information, and leaks mostly intended to extract concessions from the negotiating parties and to break deadlocks (Isaacson, 1992; Kalb, Koppel, & Scali, 1982). During grave international crises, or when all diplomatic channels are severed, the media provide the only channel for communication and negotiation between the rival actors. During the first phase of the 1979–1981 Iranian Hostage crisis, the United States communicated with the terrorists holding the hostages exclusively through the media (Larson, 1986). A similar case occurred in the 1985 hijacking of a TWA jetliner to Beirut (Gilboa, 1990). During the 1991 Gulf War, George Bush and Saddam Hussein hurled messages back and forth via the global news networks, thus forming a "de facto hotline" between Washington and Baghdad (Newsom, 1996, p. 96). Sparre (2001) and Spencer (2004) argued that the parties to the conflict in Northern Ireland conducted dialogues and exchanged messages through the media because formal negotiations among them were neither possible nor desirable. The media dialogue helped the sides keep the peace process alive and exchange significant messages.

In recent years, leaders have been using global communication more frequently than traditional diplomatic channels to deliver messages intended to alter an image or to open a new page. U.S. State Department spokesperson Nicholas Burns (1996) admitted: "We use the briefings to send messages to foreign governments about our foreign policy. For example, I sometimes read carefully calibrated statements to communicate with the governments with which we have no diplomatic relations: Iraq, Iran, Libya and North Korea" (pp. 12–13). He explained that, "given the concentration of journalists in Washington and our position in the world, the United States is uniquely situated to use television to our best advantage, with our friends as well as with our adversaries." Leaders in other parts of the world employ the same technique. For example, in January 1998, the newly elected Iranian President Mohammed Khatami chose CNN to send a conciliatory message to the United States (Associated Press, January 8, 1998). CNN and the print media around the world alerted global audiences to the interview well in advance of the broadcast, and the interview was extensively discussed afterwards.

Sometimes attitudes toward journalists of the other side send an important signal. The Syrian leader Hafez Assad and his Foreign Minister Farouq al-Shara have accumulated an interesting record in approaching Israeli reporters (Gilboa, 2002c). In the 1991 Madrid Peace Conference, where Israeli and Syrian officials met for the first time in decades to explore conflict resolution, Shara's spokesman carefully picked out non-Israeli reporters to ask questions at a news conference. Israeli reporters were also excluded from a press conference held in January 1994 after a meeting between Clinton and Assad. Oddly enough, the main purpose of the meeting was to demonstrate Assad's interest in negotiations and peace. In September 1994, however, Shara answered for the first time a question by an Israeli reporter at a press conference in London, and later gave a first-ever interview to Israeli television (Rabinovich, 1998). Syria's new attitude toward Israeli journalists was seen as a possible attempt by Syria to build confidence required for peace with Israel. In July 2001, however, Shara refused to answer questions by an Israeli reporter, thus indicating the unwillingness of Syria to negotiate with Israel. Attitudes toward journalists of the other side have become a barometer of Syrian interest in conflict resolution.

Media-broker diplomacy. The communication and information revolution has inspired journalists to assume, directly and indirectly, mediation roles in complicated international conflicts.

While not new, international mediation by journalists seems to have been expanding in recent years. Larson (1988) observed: "television provides an interactive channel for diplomacy which is instantaneous or timely and in which journalists frequently assume an equal role with officials in the diplomatic dialogue" (p. 43). Gurevitch (1991) referred to journalists who directly intervene in diplomacy as "international political brokers" (pp. 187–188). Graber (2002) said they became "surrogates for public officials" by "actively participating in an evolving situation, such as a prison riot or a diplomatic impasse" (p. 171). The solution, she added, developed with journalists' assistance or at their initiative, "may then significantly shape subsequent government action" (p. 171). Journalists primarily pursue direct intervention, where they temporarily become mediators and specifically help parties to begin official negotiation; bridging, where they attempt to help parties realize the value of negotiation to resolve their conflict; and secret mediation, where they secretly explore a possible solution.

The direct intervention variant refers to situations where journalists are actively and directly engaged in international mediation. A journalist may initiate this role or may be asked by one or more parties to pursue it. In this variant, journalists talk to the two sides, transmit relevant information, and suggest detailed procedures, proposals, and ideas that may advance official negotiations. This format was seen in Walter Cronkite's (1996) mediation in 1977 between Egyptian President Anwar Sadat and Israeli Prime Minister Menachem Begin; in the attempt of the British correspondent Patrick Seale in 2000 to break the deadlock in Israeli-Syrian negotiations (Gilboa, 2002c); and the attempt in 2002 of Russian reporter Anna Politkovskaya (2002) to mediate between the Russian government and Chechen terrorists who held 700 hostages at the Moscow Theater.

Secret media-broker diplomacy appears to be a contradiction in terms (Gilboa, 1998b). The primary professional mission of journalists is to uncover events, not to conceal them: "Here we find a built-in conflict of interest. What one seeks to conceal the other seeks to reveal; and each is acting within the guiding principle of his vocation" (Eban, 1983, p. 347). Yet foreign affairs bureaucracies are known for rigidity and for resisting fundamental changes in relations with rival countries. Therefore, their personnel may leak information on negotiations, particularly if they oppose them. Thus, in certain sensitive cases, officials prefer outsiders, including reporters, to ensure secrecy (Ledeen, 1991). Secret media-broker diplomacy is rare. It happened during the Cold War and might have happened in the post–Cold War era. Information is not yet available on possible recent cases. One example of this variant concerns the role of Whitney Tower, the editor of *Sports Illustrated,* and Andre Laguerre, one of the magazine's chief correspondents, in the defection of Hungarian athletes during the 1956 Melbourne Olympic Games (Laguerre, 1956). A second example is of the mediation of John Scali (1995), diplomatic correspondent for ABC News, during the 1962 Cuban missile crisis.

In the critical pre-negotiation phase, journalists can unofficially promote and facilitate interaction among conflicted parties, and can improve communication and increase mutual understanding. The goal is to convince the sides that they should seriously consider negotiations as the preferred method for resolving their conflict. Bridging is more likely to happen when there is no formal third party helping enemies to engage in conflict resolution. It typically occurs when representatives of rival sides are brought together on air to discuss the issues dividing them. A well-known and respected journalist associated with a highly regarded program has a better chance of successfully performing this role. Bridging was seen in a series of special programs Ted Koppel broadcasted on *Nightline,* in 1988 and 2000, on the Palestinian-Israeli conflict, and in 1988 on the conflict in South Africa (Koppel & Gibson, 1996); the role of Thomas Friedman of *The New York Times* in initiating and promoting the 2002 Saudi Arabia plan for Arab-Israeli peace; and the role of Michael Gonzalez of *The Wall Street Journal* in 2003 in initiating and promoting a European alliance with the United States before the war in Iraq began (Gilboa, 2005c).

The thought of journalists' turning mediators in international conflicts is indeed intriguing. If parties to a conflict cannot make progress on their own, and if no third parties are around,

why should journalists be prevented from conducting mediation and constructive diplomacy? The frequent counterargument is that journalists are supposed to cover events, not create them. Gurevitch (1991) noted that "the active participation of journalists in the events they presumably 'cover' is often achieved at the cost of sacrificing traditional journalistic norms, such as editorial control" (p. 187). The journalists decide which actors, perspectives, and parts of the story to include and which to ignore. Furthermore, historically, journalists who have become players in a negotiation process have not suspended their professional reporting and coverage of the process. In fact, they have become players due to their professional standing and work. Therefore, journalists must be extremely cautious in using their profession to mediate in international conflicts, as should be policy makers who employ them for this purpose.

Reconciliation

Conflict resolution and peace agreements are significant but insufficient steps to reach "stable peace." Boulding (1978) defined stable peace as "a situation in which the probability of war is so small that it does not really enter the calculations of any of the people involved" (p. 13). International relations scholars believed that stable peace could be achieved and maintained via security, and economic and political cooperation (Kacowitz, Bar-Siman-Tov, Elgstrom, & Jerneck, 2000). More recently, however, they also became aware of the need to examine psychological dimensions of this phase (Crocker, Hampson, & Aall, 2001). Formal negotiations and peace agreements usually involve only leaders and certain elites who surround them. The public may reject both the process and the results of their efforts. Even if peoples accept a peace agreement, the grievances, mistrust, hostility, and fear they had accumulated during a protracted conflict may foil any progress toward true normalization and stable peace. Successful conflict resolution and peace agreements failed, for example, to produce normalization and stable peace in Angola and in Israeli-Egyptian relations.

Reconciliation goes beyond conflict resolution and peace agreements, and addresses psychological and cognitive barriers to stable peace

(Bar-Siman-Tov, 2004; Brown & Poremski, 2005; Helmick & Petersen, 2001; Rothstein, 1999). It moves from formal peace agreements to "changing the motivations, goals, beliefs, attitudes, and emotions of the great majority of the society members regarding the conflict, the nature of the relationship between the parties, and the parties themselves" (Bar-Tal & Bennink, 2004, p. 12). Reconciliation is both a process and an outcome. The outcome is friendship and harmony between former enemies (Ackermann, 1994; Kelman, 1999; Kemp & Fry, 2004).

Studies of reconciliation referred only briefly to the media and very few focused specifically on the media's roles (Chadha, 1995; Curtis, 2000). While discussing methods of reconciliation, Bar-Tal and Bennink (2004) demonstrated a typical highly simplistic assessment of potential media effects. The media's support for reconciliation is crucial, they wrote, because leaders can use the media to communicate messages about peace and reconciliation, and because the media frame the news and favorable framing can help reconciliation. Specific and more sophisticated studies reveal three approaches to media intervention in reconciliation. A few have criticized the media for doing nothing or very little to help move former enemies toward an era of reconciliation and positive peace. Others have criticized the media for doing exactly the opposite—exaggerating and inflating peace initiatives and peacemaking, which resulted in unrealistically high expectations and colossal disappointments. A third approach suggested that the local and international media were very helpful in changing the cultural norms and policy of actors in several major international conflicts.

Local media. The Gutierrez-Villalobos (2002) study is an excellent example of the first critical approach. She argued that the media failed to play a significant role in reconciliation efforts that emerged after the signing of regional and national accords in Central America. In 1987, the governments of El Salvador, Nicaragua, Honduras, Guatemala, and Costa Rica signed regional peace accords. Between 1987 and 1996, three of these countries that had been involved in war—Nicaragua, El Salvador, and Guatemala—also signed national peace agreements. Gutierrez-Villalobos claimed that the media failed to assist

reconciliation at both the national and the personal level where it meant, for example, demobilization and reintegration of ex-soldiers and ex-combatants. She wrote that the local media in each of the involved states could have contributed significantly to reconciliation, but failed to perform this task because the authors of the peace accords did not think the media were important actors in reconciliation. The accords provided for only free, independent, and more pluralistic mass communication systems, and assigned the media limited roles in covering first-time elections in former dictatorships. Freedom of the press and objective coverage of political events were new, important phenomena in Central America, but they did not contribute significantly to reconciliation.

Gutierrez-Villalobos (2002) provided examples of potential contributions that the media could have made to reconciliation in Central America. The media could have exploited the national election campaigns to explain the peace accords to the people and sponsor debates in each country on the short- and long-term advantages and risks of the accords for individuals and societies. Critics, including partisan mass media, described the accords as only "paper peace," but the mainstream media could have helped to legitimize the accords and make them more credible. Finally, the media could have demanded more accountability from those responsible for implementing the accords. Gutierrez-Villalobos offered a few lessons that can be learned from the experience in Central America, including adding specific articles to peace agreements on "peace communication." These articles would commit the parties to follow reconciliation discourse and the necessary steps needed to cultivate sensitivity and patience for new institutions and identities. Other lessons include training of media professionals and initiating specific reconciliation efforts among editors and reporters of former enemies.

Shinar's (2002) study of the Israeli media behavior during the Oslo peace process is an excellent example of the second critical approach, which blames the media for constructing a false reality of reconciliation. This dysfunction may happen in cases of protracted international conflicts deeply rooted in culture and identity. Anthropologists, political psychologists, and political scientists (e.g., Barber, 1995; Geertz, 1973; Huntington, 1996; Kelman, 1997) have defined cultural conflicts as deeply rooted in primordial affinities, identity, history, and religion. They are long lasting, total, and transcend territorial and national issues. Resolution or even reconciliation in territorial and national conflicts is possible; however, resolution, let alone reconciliation, in cultural conflicts is extremely difficult. Conflict management is the most appropriate concept and strategy to deal with cultural conflicts, not reconciliation. Leaders and the media have often ignored the deep cultural roots of international conflicts and instead have chosen to treat them as if they were merely territorial or national. The Arab-Israeli conflict, the conflict in Northern Ireland, and the Balkan conflicts are examples of cultural conflicts.

Shinar (2002) argued that from the beginning of the Israeli-Palestinian Oslo process in August 1993 until the eruption of the second *Intifada* (Palestinian campaign of violence against Israel) in September 2000, both the Western and the Israeli media primarily viewed the conflict as territorial and national. They adopted the reconciliation model, created high and unrealistic expectations in Israel and around the world for rapid reconciliation, and consequently contributed to confusion, frustration, and disillusionment. The Arab media, however, and the government-controlled Palestinian media in particular, adopted a different view that excluded reconciliation (Karsh, 2003). They interpreted events within a confrontational context over identity, religion, and history, not just over territory.

Western and Israeli media coverage of the Oslo process became problematic and confusing even during the governments of Yitzhak Rabin and Shimon Peres, the Israeli architects of the process. In 1995 and 1996, the media could not accept the idea of reconciliation with the continuing terrorism of the Palestinian Islamic organizations and the unwillingness of the Palestinian authority under Yasser Arafat to stop them (Shinar, 2002). The media ignored many signs of the parties' inability to reach reconciliation in the foreseeable future, and, caught by unwarranted peace euphoria, they misled the public and created exaggerated expectations that had no chance of being realized. Only after the eruption

of the second *Intifada,* in September 2000, did the Israeli and U.S. media learn the needed lessons: They abandoned the reconciliation model and returned to the conflict management model.

The third approach to media and reconciliation is more empirical and includes both single-country and comparative studies. Hagos (2001) investigated the impact of Studio Ijambo, a radio production program established in 1995, on reconciliation in Burundi. This excellent study found positive broad impact on five specific areas of reconciliation: inter-ethnic relations, social and political mobilization, political elite negotiations, public institutions, and mass or elite political behavior. The impact on the Burundian media culture and practice was the most definitive and visible. A comparative study (Gidron, Katz, & Hasenfeld, 2002) claimed that local media in three regions—Northern Ireland, Israel/Palestine, and South Africa—essentially collaborated with local peace and conflict resolution organizations (P/CROs) to advance conflict resolution and reconciliation. The study claimed that these organizations significantly altered the cultural norms surrounding the three conflicts, and that this success depended to a large degree on access to the media and on media acceptance of the alternative framing suggested by the P/CROs.

The study presented examples of successful innovative activities, which attracted considerable media attention in all the three conflicted regions. The conclusions, however, are somewhat problematic and confusing. The study claimed, for example, that the Palestinian P/CRO was very effective in getting the international media to publicize their views on human rights violations by the Israeli authorities, and "much less successful in gaining media access to publicize human rights abuses by the Palestinian Authority, due in part to the harassment journalists and reporters experienced when they attempted to provide such coverage" (Gidron et al., 2002, p. 219). In the study's own terms, The Palestinian P/CRO was supposed to change the cultural norms of the Palestinians, not the attitudes of the international media toward Israeli abuses. This organization failed to criticize the Palestinian abuses and did not change the cultural norms behind the hostile attitudes toward Israelis and Jews, but the study's authors still defined the media activities of P/CRO as successful.

A few empirical studies suggested detailed contingency plans for local media intervention in reconciliation. For example, the International Media Support (2003) initiated an interesting project for reconciliation in Sudan. Authors of the project explained that "the first year after a peace agreement is reached is critical to ensuring a sustainable peace" (p. 6). Dissemination of reliable and trustworthy information via the media is vital for reconciliation. The local media, then, should be given a key priority. The authors also added that conflicts are different, and transition from conflict resolution to reconciliation varies from one place to another. Therefore, applications of "ready-made package solutions" to the local media do not work. In anticipation of an agreement between the government of Sudan and the Sudan People's Liberation Movement, IMS prepared a well-researched and organized plan for media reforming and intervention. The work acknowledges many implementation difficulties and offers ways to counter them.

Media events. The media, particularly television, may contribute to reconciliation through media events—spectacular celebrations of peacemaking and peace agreements. Media events are broadcast live, organized outside the media, pre-planned, and presented with reverence and ceremony (Dayan & Katz, 1992). Live coverage of media events interrupts scheduled broadcasting and attracts wide audiences around the world. Diplomatic media events include summit meetings between rival powers, such as the United States and the Soviet Union during the Cold War, and celebrations of peace agreements signed between former enemies. Media events can be used at the onset of negotiations to build confidence and facilitate negotiations, or at the end of negotiations to mobilize public support for reconciliation. The reconciliation effect of media events gained vivid expression in chapters of U.S.-USSR "summit diplomacy" and in Arab-Israeli negotiations.

Gorbachev's summits with Presidents Reagan and Bush demonstrate how the two superpowers became adept at exploiting the media in the transition from the Cold War to the post–Cold War era. Their summits, above all, reflected the dramatic changes in superpower relations (Negrine, 1996). The climactic Gorbachev-Bush summit held in Washington in May 1990 officially ended the Cold War. Gorbachev, for his part, used the summits with Reagan and Bush to cultivate public support at home and abroad for his major political and economic reforms. Reagan, on the other hand, used the summits to legitimize the dramatic shift in his attitudes toward the Soviet Union, branded as "the evil empire" at the beginning of his presidency. Media events became increasingly popular and were frequently used in Arab-Israeli reconciliation efforts (Gilboa, 2002c). These include Sadat's historic visit to Jerusalem in November 1977 and the signing ceremonies of the Israeli-Egyptian Peace Treaty of March 1979, the PLO-Israel Declaration of Principles of September 1993, and the Israeli-Jordanian Peace Treaty of October 1994. Leaders consider media events to be an effective tool in building confidence and mobilizing domestic and global public support for difficult peacemaking processes and reconciliation. According to the typology of media events suggested by Dayan and Katz (1992), the U.S.-Soviet summit meetings and the Arab-Israeli media events belong to the category of conquests where a great leader, such as Gorbachev or Sadat, was able to overcome decades of hatred, conflict, and war and to replace them with negotiations, cooperation, and peace. However, media events become far less effective when employed too frequently, and the groundbreaking effect becomes diluted (Liebes & Katz, 1997).

Long and Brecke (2003) employed the term *reconciliation events* (p. 6) to assess reconciliation in civil and international conflicts. These are defined as turning points leading to improving relations and lessening the chance of a recurrence of violence. Reconciliation events include the following elements: direct physical contact or proximity between opponents, usually at a senior level; a public ceremony accompanied by substantial publicity or media attention that relays the event to the wider national society; and ritualistic or symbolic behavior that indicates the parties consider the dispute resolved and that more amicable relations are expected to follow. The authors argued that in both civil and international conflicts, reconciliation events are a valid proxy indicator of reconciliation. They found 11 cases of reconciliation events in civil conflicts and 21 cases in international conflicts in the 20th century. They offered two models of reconciliation: a forgiveness psychological model and a signaling rational choice model. The first is more useful in explaining reconciliation in civil conflicts, while the second is more useful in explaining reconciliation in international conflicts. The signaling model predicts that resumption of conflict after conflict resolution becomes less likely when reconciliation events are "part of a costly, novel, voluntary, and irrevocable concession in a negotiated bargain" (p. 3).

A reconciliation event in a civil conflict would be a peace agreement such as the 1992 Accords of Chapultepec signed between the government of El Salvador and the leftist guerrilla organization Farabundo Marti Front for National Liberation; or the establishment in 1995 of the Truce and Reconciliation Commission in South Africa. A reconciliation event in international conflicts would be a framework for peace such as the 1978 Israeli-Egyptian Camp David accords; the restoration of full diplomatic relations such as Great Britain and Argentina accomplished in 1990; or a formal peace agreement such as the agreement Vietnam and Cambodia signed in 1991. Long and Brecke (2003) concluded that emotion played a significant role in reconciliation, and that reconciliation events were associated with reductions in international conflict, de-escalated violence, and restored order. The problem with this study is the concept of a reconciliation event. The authors offered a highly simplistic definition of reconciliation and were probably unaware of the theory of media events that is very relevant for their study (Dayan & Katz, 1992). Despite these limitations, this study offers a media-dependent instrument that may help forecast chances for reconciliation in international conflict.

Shinar (2002) explained that the media prefer reconciliation over conflict management because it is simpler, clearer, and one dimensional. It deals with the present, demands little intellectual effort, and focuses on emotions. Reconciliation is very optimistic and is guided by clear and simple expectations for the end of conflict. Conflict management is much more complicated and open-ended; it deals with the present and the future, and requires substantial investment in historical understanding of cultural factors. Management focuses on dry rational calculations, collective identities, and abstract religious and other cultural symbols. It is pessimistic because it must always leave room for failure and resumption of violence. While confronting different conflict phases, the local media face a difficult dilemma. As citizens of societies engaged in conflict, they wish to pursue reconciliation, but as professional journalists they recognize a much more complex and difficult reality. Sometimes the temptation to confuse management with reconciliation is too high, as indeed happened to the Israeli media during the Oslo process.

SECTION III: A FRAMEWORK FOR FUTURE RESEARCH

Researchers have employed many different theories, methods, and concepts to analyze potential and actual media intervention in various phases of international conflict. These include normative and empirical approaches; war versus peace journalism; hate versus peace media; the roles of local and external media; media-government relations; and media strategies, messages, and effects. I think that future research has to be much more systematic and cumulative. Each of the different approaches, such as media-government relations, could serve as a focus for research on the media roles in all four of the conflict phases. However, I think that a more effective approach requires a multidisciplinary and multidimensional framework that could explore the four phases through several identical or similar categories. I suggest a framework that combines and integrates communication and conflict theories: the functional theory of communication and the life-cycle theory of conflicts. Sometimes a classic theory might help in guiding contemporary and future research. The functional theory is a classic communication theory anchored in sociological system theory, which views institutions, including the media, as performing roles designed to meet needs of individuals and societies (Merton, 1957).

The functional theory paved the way for several approaches and techniques in modern communication research including media effects, uses and gratifications, agenda-setting, framing, cultivation theory, and the spiral of silence theory (Boyd-Barrett & Newbold, 1995; Littlejohn, 1999; McLeod & Tichenor, 2003). Scholars have even described the functional theory as a paradigm—a master theory in control of most research in mass communication (McQuail, 2000).

Application of functionalism to mass communication developed over time through several stages. Lasswell (1948) first suggested three media functions: surveillance of the environment (news coverage); correlation of the parts of society (interpretation of news and information, commentary, and editorial opinion); and transmission of culture (history, values, religion, language, etc.). Wright (1960) added a fourth function: entertainment, and also distinguished between functions and dysfunctions, and constructed a framework for functional analysis. McQuail (1987) added a fifth function, mobilization: "the campaigning for societal objectives in the sphere of politics, war, economic development, work and sometimes religion" (p. 71). Mobilization exists in autocratic societies all the time, in the nation-building phase of new nations, and in democracies in times of crisis and warfare. Mobilization may result from a governmental initiative or from the media's own self-initiative. After the September 11 terror attacks, for example, American media self-mobilized and became a significant collaborating actor in the global war against terrorism.

Wright's (1960) important distinction between functions and dysfunctions is very pertinent to this study. Most approaches to media intervention in international conflict have ignored unintended consequences, be they positive or negative. The media may provide useful information to citizens who could be motivated to act against their own interests and the interests of their community. For example, when the media warn of an approaching storm, the purpose is not only to provide information but also to help citizens prepare for threats to life and property. A warning, however, could be dysfunctional if it caused panic and chaos and if everyone rushed to the roads and caused traffic jams. Similarly, the purpose of reporting on financial difficulties of a bank is positive—warning those who have accounts of a threat to their investments—but the result could be dysfunctional if all customers went to the bank, liquidated their assets, and drove the bank into bankruptcy.

Application of the Wright formula suggests that, even if the media are sincerely interested in positive contribution to prevent, manage, resolve, or reconcile international conflict, the results may backfire. Table 22.1 presents possible media functions and dysfunctions in coverage of international conflicts. For example, during the prevention phase, the media may wish to create awareness among the public for signs of an emerging conflict or possible violence. The result could be positive if awareness was created, or negative if the coverage produced apprehension leading to extreme policy. It is important to educate the public about the sources of conflict and the potential for violence or conflict resolution. If successful learning occurred, the coverage could be functional, but if preclusion occurred, the coverage could be dysfunctional. During the resolution phase, the media may wish to initiate a conflict resolution process and mobilize public support. If mobilization occurred, the coverage could be functional, but if coverage created stronger opposition leading to blocking of the initiative, the result could be counterproductive and dysfunctional. Similar dysfunctions could occur when the media attempt to legitimize conflict prevention or conflict resolution, build confidence, dramatize efforts to reduce violence and begin mediation, create realistic expectations, or present a positive balance of advantages and shortcomings of peace agreements.

Several functions and dysfunctions may appear at each of the four conflict phases, while others may be unique to each phase. In addition, functions and dysfunctions may vary for each of the five basic media functions, all of which are relevant to the study of media intervention in international conflict. Even entertainment may include implicit or explicit messages that may either help or hinder efforts to deal effectively with international conflicts (Baum, 2003). Substantial research is needed to explore functions and dysfunctions at each phase. Figure 22.2 describes the proposed framework for

Table 22.1   Functions and Dysfunctions

Functions	Dysfunctions
Awareness	Apprehension
Learning	Preclusion
Initiation	Blocking
Mobilization	Creating Opposition
Legitimacy	Illegitimacy
Confidence Building	Confidence Destruction
Dramatization	Over-Dramatization
Realistic Expectations	High Expectations
Positive Balance	Negative Balance

analysis. It shows how research can be organized to explore positive and negative contributions of the media by the five media functions and the four phases of international conflict. The framework is flexible and allows partial or selective applications. Researchers do not necessarily need to apply the whole framework to all the conflict phases. They may choose to investigate all the five functions in one phase; or one function, such as news, across all the four phases; or they can focus on one function in one phase, such as interpretation in reconciliation. They may also apply the framework to each of the five levels of media: local, national, regional, international, and global, or to a particular medium—newspaper, television, radio, or the Internet—in each category.

CONCLUSIONS

This work shows that, during the past decade, research on media and international conflict has grown substantially. The results, however, are somewhat disappointing because research has moved into very different directions, and findings have not yet been accumulated into a solid base of scientific knowledge. Based on normative approaches and theories, many studies only suggest what the media should or could do, not report what they actually do. There is also considerable confusion between normative and empirical studies. Moreover, most of the theoretical and applied studies have focused on intentional positive or negative consequences. The normative approaches mostly emphasize potential positive contributions, while empirical research mostly emphasizes negative effects, particularly during periods of violence. Many institutions sponsor programs designed to enhance constructive media effects on the life-cycle of international conflicts. The normative approaches, however, and the programs for media intervention are based on assumptions that communication theory does not necessarily support. Progress in this critical area of international behavior requires much more intensive and multidisciplinary empirical research aimed at verifying assumptions and evaluating the results of the diverse media programs.

Many authors assumed that the media are a powerful force in society capable of shaping public opinion and forcing policies on policy makers. A typical statement links media influence on policy to the impact of coverage on public opinion and to subsequent public pressure on leaders to adopt the policy advocated by the media. Authors of the Carnegie Commission Report (1997) wrote, "Across the spectrum of activities, from worldwide broadcasts of violence and misery to the local hate radio . . . the media's interpretative representation of violent events has a wide and powerful impact" (p. 121). Melone et al. (2002) stated: "[T]he media carry immense power in shaping the course of a conflict" (p. 1). Galtung (2002) even suggested that with more peace coverage "the conflict in and over Northern Ireland would have entered a more peaceful phase long ago" (p. 260). Empirical research, however, raises doubts about all these statements. Similarly, many researchers have used the CNN effect to specifically demonstrate how global television can enormously affect intervention in international conflicts, but this approach is also highly debatable. Other scholars adopted the opposite approach and claimed that the media serve only as tools in the hands of politicians and officials who manipulate information and cultivate public support for aggressive policy. To support this statement, they used the information

Function	Phase:	Prevention		Management		Resolution		Reconciliation	
	Contribution:	Function	Dysfunction	Function	Dysfunction	Function	Dysfunction	Function	Dysfunction
News									
Interpretation									
Cultural Transmission									
Entertainment									
Mobilization									

Figure 22.2 Functional Analysis Framework

management approach and control techniques such as embedded journalism.

The work shows that the media operate both as a tool in the hands of politicians and policy makers and as independent actors pursuing their own agenda and priorities. The media can help as well as hinder efforts to control and resolve international conflicts. The three major participants in international conflict policymaking— the government, the media, and the public—have not yet adapted to the media-rich political environments. We do not yet have an integrative theory of the triangular relationship that exists among these three key participants. Scholars have produced many good studies of the relationship existing between the media and public opinion and between the media and government, but very little research has been done to connect all the three. Entman's (2004) cascading activation model is the most promising, but it needs to be tested and applied to international conflicts. He suggests that several actors, including presidents and their chief advisers on defense and foreign affairs, other elites, and the media, are engaged in a battle to shape frames that reach the public through the media and greatly influence the formation of public opinion. His model explains how the "thoughts and feelings that support a frame extend down from the White House through the rest of the system— and who thus wins the framing contest and gains the upper hand politically" (p. 9). The model argues that some actors have more power than others to push frames down the road to the public and, therefore, could help identify when and how the media affect decision making during international conflicts.

Many authors have used terms such as *the media* or *the international community* without sufficiently explaining what they mean. As this work shows, several types of media tend to be directly involved, such as the media in conflict regions, and others tend to be indirectly involved, such as Western or global media. When analyzing "the media" in terms of problems and remedies, this distinction has to be carefully clarified. The same criticism applies to the term *international community*. Authors frequently have been telling this community to employ the media to promote peace, but whom exactly are they addressing: the United Nations,

the big powers, the Western world, or great moral leaders? Scholars and practitioners should either refrain from using these terms or explain them clearly.

This work also demonstrates substantial gaps in research on the media's roles in the four phases of international conflict. Scholars and practitioners have devoted much more attention to management and resolution and much less to prevention and reconciliation. Furthermore, the "new media"—the Internet, third- and fourth-generation mobile phones, digital radio, and interactive television—deal extensively with international conflicts, but very few studies have been conducted on their roles and effects (Kluver, 2002; Larson, 2004; Wall, 2002). The same critique applies to the rise of Netpolitik and e-images of countries and leaders (Bollier, 2003). Future research must be more balanced and, in the short run, may even have to focus more on the neglected phases and the new media.

Although the local media in conflict regions are much more important than the external media, scholars have conducted much more research on the latter. Future research should focus on the roles of the local media and evaluate the many programs for media intervention at the local level that many governments and organizations are pursuing around the world. Certain conflicts, such as the Palestinian-Israeli conflict or the Balkan conflicts, have received substantial attention in the Western and global media, while conflicts in other regions, such as the massacres in the Darfur region in Sudan, have received little attention (Hawkins, 2002; Ricchiardi, 2005). The main reasons cited for this imbalance include the presence or absence of cameras; the physical conditions on the ground; access restrictions; political, economic, and strategic interests of the world powers; and geopolitical proximity. If the media ignore a conflict, scholars do the same. They usually investigate what the media report, not what they miss. Scholars should look at omissions as much as they assess outputs.

Manoff (1998) argued that the best approach to developing effective media intervention in international conflict is not to ask "what the media can do" (p. 6), but to learn what conflict theories and practice say about needs, and then determine how the media may respond to them. "What the media can do" is a major field in contemporary communications studies. I suggest that many writers on media and international conflict have ignored communication theories and findings, and have not sufficiently used them in their research and programs. I also argue that the best way to move forward is to integrate and apply theories and approaches from both communication and conflict. The framework presented here could be a first step toward a new integrated, multidimensional, and multidisciplinary research effort.

REFERENCES

Ackermann, A. (1994). Reconciliation as a peace-building process in post-war Europe: The Franco-German case. *Peace and Change, 19,* 229–250.

Ackermann, A. (2003). The idea and practice of conflict prevention. *Journal of Peace Research, 40,* 339–347.

Amanpour, C. (1996). Television's role in foreign policy. *Quill, 84*(3), 16–17.

Ammon, R. (2001). *Global television and the shaping of world politics: CNN, telediplomacy, and foreign policy.* Jefferson, NC: McFarland.

Arno, A., & Dissanayake, W. (Eds.). (1984). *The news media in national and international conflict.* Boulder, CO: Westview.

Aronson, J. (1973). *The press and the Cold War.* Boston: Beacon.

Associated Press. (1998, January 8). Iranian president sends U.S. message. *International Herald Tribune,* p. 1.

Badsey, S. (Ed.). (2000). *The media and international security.* London: Cass.

Barber, B. R. (1995). *Jihad vs. McWorld.* New York: Times Books.

Bar-Siman-Tov, Y. (Ed.). (2004). *From conflict resolution to reconciliation.* New York: Oxford University Press.

Bar-Tal, D., & Bennink, G. (2004). The nature of reconciliation as an outcome and as a process. In Y. Bar-Siman-Tov (Ed.), *From conflict resolution to reconciliation* (pp. 11–38). New York: Oxford University Press.

Baum, M. (2003). *Soft news goes to war: Public opinion and American foreign policy in the media age.* Princeton, NJ: Princeton University Press.

Bell, M. (1997). TV news: How far should we go? *British Journalism Review, 8*(1), 7–16.

Bennett, W. L., & Paletz, D. (Eds.). (1994). *Taken by storm: The media, public opinion, and U.S. foreign policy in the Gulf War.* Chicago: University of Chicago Press.

Berkeley, B. (1994). Sounds of violence: Rwanda's killer radio. *New Republic, 21*(8–9), 18–19.

Bollier, D. (2003). *People/networks/power: Communication technologies and the new international politics.* Washington, DC: Aspen Institute, Communications & Society Program.

Boulding, K. (1978). *Stable peace.* Austin: University of Texas Press.

Boyd-Barrett, O., & Newbold, C. (Eds.). (1995). *Approaches to media.* London: Edward Arnold.

Braestrup, P. (1977). *Big story: How the American press and television reported and interpreted the crisis of Tet 1969 in Vietnam and Washington.* New Haven, CT: Yale University Press.

Brown, A., & Poremski, K. (Eds.). (2005). *Roads to reconciliation: Conflict and dialogue in the twenty-first century.* Armonk, NY: Sharpe.

Bruck, P. (1989). Strategies for peace, strategies for news research. *Journal of Communication, 39,* 108–127.

Buric, A. (2000). The media: War and peace in Bosnia. In A. Davis (Ed.), *Regional media in conflict: Case studies in local war reporting* (pp. 64–99). London: Institute for War and Peace Reporting.

Burns, N. (1996). Talking to the world about American foreign policy. *Harvard International Journal of Press/Politics, 1*(1), 10–14.

Carnegie Commission on Preventing Deadly Conflict. (1997). *Preventing deadly conflict: Final report.* Washington, DC: Carnegie Endowment for International Peace.

Carruthers, S. (2000). *The media at war.* New York: St. Martin's.

Cali, D. (2002). Journalism after September 11: Unity as moral imperative. *Journal of Mass Media Ethics, 17,* 290–303.

Chadha, N. (1995). Enemy images: The media and Indo-Pakistani tensions. In M. Krepon & A. Sevak (Eds.), *Crisis prevention, confidence building and reconciliation in South Asia* (pp. 171–198). New York: St. Martin's.

Chermak, S., Bailey, F., & Brown, M. (Eds.). (2003). *Media representation of September 11.* Westport, CT: Praeger.

Cohen, B. (1994). A view from the academy. In W. L. Bennett & D. Paletz (Eds.), *Taken by storm: The media, public opinion, and U.S. foreign policy in the Gulf War* (pp. 8–11). Chicago: University of Chicago Press.

Cohen, Y. (1986). *Media diplomacy.* London: Frank Cass.

Collins, P. (2003, April 15). Corruption at CNN: Network executives grovel before Saddam. *Washington Times,* p. A19.

Commission on Global Governance. (1995). *Our global neighborhood.* Oxford, UK: Oxford University Press.

Crocker, C., Hampson, F. O., & Aall, P. (Eds.). (2001). *Turbulent peace: The challenges of managing international conflict.* Washington, DC: United States Institute of Peace Press.

Cronkite, W. (1996). *A reporter's life.* New York: Random House.

Curtis, D. (2000). Broadcasting peace: An analysis of local media post-conflict peace-building projects in Rwanda and Bosnia. *Canadian Journal of Development Studies, 21,* 141–155.

Davis, A. (Ed.). (2000). *Regional media in conflict: Case studies in local war reporting.* London: Institute for War and Peace Reporting.

Davison, W. P. (1974). *Mass communication and conflict resolution.* New York: Praeger.

Dayan, D., & Katz, E. (1992). *Media events: The live broadcasting of history.* Cambridge, MA: Harvard University Press.

Diamond, L., & McDonald, J. (1996). *Multi-track diplomacy: A systems approach to peace* (3rd ed.). West Hartford, CT: Kumarian Press.

Eban, A. (1983). *The new diplomacy.* New York: Random House.

Eldrige, A. (1979). *Images of conflict.* New York: St. Martin's.

Elliot, D. (2004). Terrorism, global journalism, and the myth of the nation state. *Journal of Mass Media Ethics, 19,* 29–45.

Entman, R. (2004). *Projections of power: Framing news, public opinion, and U.S. foreign policy.* Chicago: University of Chicago Press.

Ferrari, M., & Tobin, J. (2003). *Reporting America at war.* New York: Hyperion.

Fortner, R. (1994). *Public diplomacy and international politics.* New York: Praeger.

Freedom Forum. (1993). *The media and foreign policy in the post–Cold War.* New York: Freedom Forum Media Studies Center.

Frohardt, M., & Temin, J. (2003). *Use and abuse of media in vulnerable societies* (Special Report No. 110). Washington, DC: United States Institute of Peace Press.

Galtung, J. (1969). Violence, peace, and peace research. *Journal of Peace Research, 6,* 167–191.

Galtung, J. (1996). *Peace by peaceful means: Peace and conflict, development and civilization.* London: Sage.

Galtung, J. (1998). High road, low road: Charting the course for peace journalism. *Track Two, 7.* Retrieved May 12, 2002, from http://ccrweb.ccr.uct.ac.za/archive/two

Galtung, J. (2002). Peace journalism—A challenge. In W. Kempf & H. Luostarinen (Eds.), *Journalism and the new world order: Studying war and the media* (pp. 259–272). Göteborg, Sweden: Nordicom.

Galtung, J., Jacobsen, C., & Brand-Jacobsen, K. (2000). *Searching for peace: The road to TRANSCEND.* London: Pluto.

Galtung, J., & Ruge , M. (1965). The structure of foreign news. *Journal of Peace Research, 1*(1), 64–90.

Gardner, E. (2001). The role of the media in conflicts. In L. Reychler & T. Paffenholtz (Eds.), *Peace-building: A field guide* (pp. 301–311). Boulder, CO: Lynne Rienner.

Geelen, M. (Ed.). (2002). *The role of the media in conflict prevention, conflict management and peace-building.* Amsterdam: Ministry of Foreign Affairs and the Netherlands Association of Journalists.

Geertz, C. (1973). *The interpretation of cultures: Selected essays.* New York: Basic Books.

Gibbs, D. (2000). *Realpolitik* and humanitarian intervention: The case of Somalia. *International Politics, 37,* 41–55.

Gidron, B., Katz, S., & Hasenfeld, Y. (Eds.). (2002). *Mobilizing for peace: Conflict resolution in Northern Ireland, Israel/Palestine and South Africa.* New York: Oxford University Press.

Gilboa, E. (1990). Effects of televised presidential addresses on public opinion: President Reagan and terrorism in the Middle East. *Presidential Studies Quarterly, 20,* 43–53.

Gilboa, E. (1998a). Media diplomacy: Conceptual divergence and applications. *Harvard International Journal of Press/Politics, 3*(3), 56–75.

Gilboa, E. (1998b). Secret diplomacy in the television age. *Gazette, 60,* 211–225.

Gilboa, E. (2000). Mass communication and diplomacy: A theoretical framework. *Communication Theory, 10,* 275–309.

Gilboa, E. (2002a). Global communication and foreign policy. *Journal of Communication, 52,* 731–748.

Gilboa, E. (Ed.). (2002b). *Media and conflict: Framing issues, making policy, shaping opinions.* Ardsley, NY: Transnational Publishers.

Gilboa, E. (2002c). Media diplomacy in the Arab-Israeli conflict. In E. Gilboa (Ed.), *Media and conflict: Framing issues, making policy, shaping opinions* (pp. 193–211). Ardsley, NY: Transnational Publishers.

Gilboa, E. (2003). Television news and U.S. foreign policy: Constraints of real-time coverage. *Harvard International Journal of Press/Politics, 8*(4), 97–113.

Gilboa, E. (2005a). The CNN effect: The search for a communication theory of international relations. *Political Communcation, 22*(1), 27–44.

Gilboa, E. (2005b). The effects of global television news on U.S. policy in international conflict. In P. Seib (Ed.), *Media and conflict in the 21st century* (pp. 1–31). New York: Palgrave.

Gilboa, E. (2005c). Media-broker diplomacy: When journalists become mediators. *Critical Studies in Media Communication, 22,* 99–120.

Girardet, E. (1999). Media intervention in conflict: So many missed opportunities. *Crosslines Global Report, 34.* Retrieved September 14, 2003, from http://www.nonlimit.ch/nsites/crosslines/34x/340eg/htm

Gitlin, T. (2003). Embed or in bed? The war, the media and the truth. *American Report, 14*(1), 42–43.

Gjelten, T. (2001). Finding the right "moral attitude": Journalists can best serve victims by balancing humanity and professionalism. *Media Studies Journal, 15*(Summer), 72–76.

Gowing, N. (1997). *Media coverage: Help or hindrance in conflict prevention?* Washington, DC: Carnegie Commission on Preventing Deadly Conflict.

Gowing, N. (2003). Real-time television coverage of armed conflicts and diplomatic crises: Does it pressure or distort foreign policy decisions? In N. Palmer (Ed.), *Terrorism, war and the press* (pp. 139–222). Cambridge, MA: Harvard University, Shorenstein Center on the Press, Politics and Public Policy.

Graber, D. (2002). *Mass media and American politics* (6th ed.). Washington, DC: Congressional Quarterly Press.

Gruber, D. (2003). Styles of image management during crises: Justifying press censorship. *Discourse & Society, 14,* 539–557.

Gurevitch, M. (1991). The globalization of electronic journalism. In J. Curran & M. Gurevitch (Eds.), *Mass media and society* (pp. 178–193). London: Edward Arnold.

Gutierrez-Villalobos, S. (2002). The media and reconciliation in Central America. In E. Gilboa (Ed.), *Media and conflict: Framing issues, making policy, shaping opinions* (pp. 295–309). Ardsley, NY: Transnational Publishers.

Hagos, A. (2001). *Media intervention in peacebuilding in Burundi: The Studio Ijambo experience and impact.* Washington, DC: Agency for International Development.

Hall, J. (2004). The fire next time: Fighting the next war. *Harvard International Journal of Press/Politics, 9*(3), 76–86.

Hallin, D. (1986). *The uncensored war.* Berkeley: University of California Press.

Hallin, D. (1994). *We keep America on top of the world.* London & New York: Routledge.

Hampson, F. O. (2001). Parent, midwife, or accidental executioner? The role of third parties in ending violent conflict. In C. Crocker, F. O. Hampson, & P. Aall (Eds.), *Turbulent peace: The challenges of managing international conflict* (pp. 387–406). Washington, DC: United States Institute of Peace Press.

Hanitzsch, T. (2004). Journalists as peacekeeping force? Peace journalism and mass communication theory. *Journalism Studies, 5,* 483–495.

Hawkins, V. (2002). The other side of the CNN factor: The media and conflict. *Journalism Studies, 3,* 225–240.

Helmick, R., & Petersen, R. (2001). *Forgiveness and reconciliation: Religion, public policy, and conflict transformation.* Philadelphia: Templeton Foundation.

Hertoghe, A. (2003). *La guerre à outrances: Comment la presse nous a désinformés sur L'Irak.* Paris: Kalman Levi.

Hess, S., & Kalb, M. (Eds.). (2003). *The media and the war on terrorism.* Washington, DC: Brookings Institution.

Hoskins, A. (2004). *Televising war: From Vietnam to Iraq.* London & New York: Continuum International Publishing.

Howard, R. (2002). *An operational framework for media and peacebuilding.* Vancouver, BC: Institute for Media, Policy, and Civil Society.

Howard, R. (2003). *Conflict sensitive journalism.* Vancouver, BC: Institute for Media, Policy, and Civil Society.

Hume, M. (1997). *Whose war is it anyway? The dangers of the journalism of attachment.* London: BM Inform.

Hunt, B. (1997). *Getting to war: Predicting international conflict with mass media indicators.* Ann Arbor: University of Michigan Press.

Huntington, S. (1996). *The clash of civilizations and the remaking of world order.* New York: Simon & Schuster.

Ignatieff, M. (2000). *Virtual war: Kosovo and beyond.* New York: Henry Holt.

International Media Support. (2003). *Media and peace in Sudan: Options for immediate action.* Copenhagen: Author.

Isaacson, W. (1992). *Kissinger: A biography.* New York: Simon & Schuster.

Jakobsen, P. (1996). National interest, humanitarianism or CNN: What triggers UN peace enforcement after the Cold War? *Journal of Peace Research, 33,* 205–215.

Jakobsen, P. (2000). Focus on the CNN effect misses the point: The real media impact on conflict management is invisible and indirect. *Journal of Peace Research, 37,* 131–143.

Jamieson, K. H., & Waldman, P. (2003). *The press effect.* New York: Oxford University Press.

Jeong, H. (Ed.). (2002). *Approaches to peacebuilding.* New York: Palgrave.

Jönsson, C. (1996). Diplomatic signaling in the television age. *Harvard International Journal of Press/Politics, 1*(3), 24–40.

Jordan, E. (2003, April 11). The news we kept for ourselves. *New York Times,* p. A25.

Kacowitz, A., Bar-Siman-Tov, Y., Elgstrom, O., & Jerneck, M. (Eds.). (2000). *Stable peace among nations.* Lanham, MD: Rowman & Littlefield.

Kalb, M., Koppel, T., & Scali, J. (1982). The networks and foreign news coverage. *Washington Quarterly, 5,* 39–51.

Kaplan, R. (2003). American journalism goes to war, 1898–2001: A manifesto in media and empire. *Media History, 9,* 209–220.

Karsh, E. (2003). *Arafat's war.* New York: Grove.

Katovsky, B., & Carlson, T. (Eds.). (2003). *Embedded: The media at war in Iraq.* Guilford, CT: Lyons Press.

Kaufman, E. (2002). A broadcasting strategy to win media wars. *Washington Quarterly, 25,* 115–127.

Kellner, D. (2003). *From 9/11 to terror war: The dangers of the Bush legacy.* Lanham, MD: Rowman & Littlefield.

Kellow, C., & Steeves, L. H. (1998). The role of radio in the Rwandan genocide. *Journal of Communication, 48,* 107–128.

Kelman, H. (1997). Social-psychological dimensions of international conflict. In I. W. Zartman & J. L. Rasmussen (Eds.), *Peacemaking in international conflict: Methods and techniques* (pp. 191–237). Washington, DC: United States Institute of Peace Press.

Kelman, H. (1999). Transforming the relationship between former enemies: A social-psychological analysis. In R. Rothstein (Ed.), *After the peace: Resistance and reconciliation* (pp. 193–205). Boulder, CO: Lynne Rienner.

Kemp, G., & Fry, D. (Eds.). (2004). *Keeping the peace: Conflict resolution and peaceful societies.* London & New York: Routledge.

Kempf, W. (2002a). Conflict coverage and conflict escalation. In W. Kempf & H. Luostarinen (Eds.), *Journalism and the new world order: Studying war and the media* (pp. 59–72). Göteborg, Sweden: Nordicom.

Kempf, W. (2002b). Escalating and deescalating aspects in the coverage of the Bosnia conflict: A comparative study. In W. Kempf & H. Luostarinen (Eds.), *Journalism and the new world order: Studying war and the media* (pp. 227–255). Göteborg, Sweden: Nordicom.

Kluver, A. (2002). The logic of new media in international relations. *New Media and Society, 4,* 499–517.

Koppel, T., & Gibson, K. (1996). *Nightline: History in the making and the making of television.* New York: Times Books.

Korzenny, F., & Ting-Toomey, S. (Eds.). (1990). *Communicating for peace: Diplomacy and negotiation.* London: Sage.

LaFraniere, S. (2003, December 4). Three convicted of genocide in Rwanda media. *International Herald Tribune,* p. 1.

Laguerre, A. (1956, December 17). Down a road called liberty. *Sports Illustrated, 5,* pp. 14–18.

Larson, J. (1986). Television and U.S. foreign policy: The case of the Iran hostage crisis. *Journal of Communication, 36,* 108–130.

Larson, J. (1988). *Global television and foreign policy* (Headline Series, No. 283). New York: Foreign Policy Association.

Larson, J. (2004). *The Internet and foreign policy* (Headline Series, No. 325). New York: Foreign Policy Association.

Lasswell, H. (1948). The structure and function of communication in society. In L. Bruson (Ed.), *The communication of ideas* (pp. 51–72). New York: Harper.

Ledeen, M. (1991). Secrets. In S. Serfaty (Ed.), *The media and foreign policy* (pp. 121–133). New York: St. Martin's.

Lederach, J. P. (1995). *Preparing for peace: Conflict transformation across cultures.* Syracuse, NY: Syracuse University Press.

Lederach, J. P. (1997). *Building peace: Sustainable reconciliation in divided societies.* Washington, DC: United States Institute of Peace Press.

Lederach, J. P. (2005). *The moral imagination: The art and soul of building peace.* New York: Oxford University Press.

Lederman, J. (1992). *Battle-lines: The American media and the Intifada.* New York: Henry Holt.

Liebes, T., & Katz, E. (1997). Staging peace: Televised ceremonies of reconciliation. *Communication Review, 2,* 235–257.

Littlejohn, S. (1999). *Theories of human communication* (6th ed.). Belmont, CA: Wadsworth.

Livingston, S., & Eachus, T. (1995). Humanitarian crises and U.S. foreign policy: Somalia and the CNN effect reconsidered. *Political Communication, 12,* 413–429.

Long, W., & Brecke, P. (2003). *War and reconciliation: Reason and emotion in conflict resolution.* Cambridge: MIT Press.

Lund, M. (1996). *Preventing violent conflicts: Strategy for preventive diplomacy.* Washington, DC: United States Institute of Peace Press.

Malone, D. (1988). *Political advocacy and cultural communication.* Lanham, MD: University Press of America.

Mandelbaum, M. (1994). The reluctance to intervene. *Foreign Policy, 95*(Summer), 3–8.

Manoff, R. (1998). Role plays: Potential media roles in conflict prevention and management. *Track Two, 7.* Retrieved May 12, 2002, from http://ccrweb.ccr.uct.ac.za/archive/two

McDonald, J., Jr., & Bendahmane, D. (Eds.). (1995). *Conflict resolution: Track two diplomacy.* Washington, DC: Institute for Multi-Track Diplomacy.

McGoldrick, A., & Lynch, J. (2000). *Peace journalism: How to do it?* Retrieved June 29, 2004, from www.transcend.org/

McLaughlin, G. (2002). *The war correspondent.* London: Pluto.

McLeod, D., & Tichenor, P. (2003). The logic of social and behavioral science. In G. Stempel, III, D. Weaver, & G. Wilhoit (Eds.), *Mass communication research and theory* (pp. 91–110). Boston: Allyn & Bacon.

McQuail, D. (1987). *Mass communication theory: An introduction* (2nd ed.). London, Sage.

McQuail, D. (2000). *McQuail's mass communication theory.* London: Sage.

Melone, S., Terzis, G., & Beleli, O. (2002). *Using the media for conflict transformation: The Common Ground experience.* Berlin: Berghof Research Center for Constructive Conflict Management.

Mermin, J. (1997). Television news and American intervention in Somalia: The myth of a media-driven foreign policy. *Political Science Quarterly, 112,* 385–403.

Mermin, J. (1999). *Debating war and peace: Media coverage of U.S. intervention in the post-Vietnam era.* Princeton, NJ: Princeton University Press.

Merton, R. K. (1957). *Social theory and social structure.* Glencoe, IL: Free Press.

Metzl, J. (1997). Information intervention: When switching channels isn't enough. *Foreign Affairs, 76*(6), 15–20.

Miller, D. (2002, March). *Measuring media pressure on security policy decision making in liberal states: The positioning hypothesis.* Paper presented at the annual convention of the International Studies Association, New Orleans.

Muravchik, J. (2004). *Covering the Intifada: How the media reported the Palestinian uprising.* Washington, DC: Washington Institute for Near East Policy.

Natsios, A. (1996). Illusions of influence: The CNN effect in complex emergencies. In R. Rotberg & T. Weiss (Eds.), *From massacres to genocide: The media, public policy, and humanitarian crises* (pp. 149–168). Cambridge, MA: World Peace Foundation.

Negrine, R. (1996). *The communication of politics.* London: Sage.

Neuman, J. (1996). *Lights, camera, war: Is media technology driving international politics?* New York: St. Martin's.

Newsom, D. (1996). *The public dimension of foreign policy.* Bloomington: Indiana University Press.

Nirenstein, F. (2001). How suicide bombers are made. *Commentary, 112,* 53–56.

Nye, J. S., Jr., & Owens, W. A. (1996). America's information edge. *Foreign Affairs, 75*(2), 20–36.

Okrent, D. (2004, May 30). Weapons of mass destruction? Or mass distraction? *New York Times,* p. 4/2.

O'Neill, M. (2000). Developing preventive journalism. In K. Cahill (Ed.), *Preventive diplomacy: Stopping wars before they start* (pp. 67–79). London & New York: Routledge.

Ottosen, R. (1995). Enemy images and the journalistic process. *Journal of Peace Research, 32,* 97–112.

Paris, R. (2004). *At war's end: Building peace after civil conflict.* Cambridge, UK: Cambridge University Press.

Pfau, M., Haigh, M., Gettle, M., Donnelly, M., Scott, G., Warr, D., & Wittenberg, E. (2004). Embedding journalists in military combat units: Impact on newspaper story frames and tone. *Journalism and Mass Communication Quarterly, 81,* 74–88.

Politkovskaya, A. (2002, October, 30). Inside story: I tried and failed. *The Guardian* (London), p. 6.

Rabinovich, I. (1998). *The brink of peace: The Israeli-Syria negotiations.* Princeton, NJ: Princeton University Press.

Ricchiardi, S. (1996, April). Over the line. *American Journalism Review, 18,* 25–30.

Ricchiardi, S. (2005, February-March). Déjà vu. *American Journalism Review, 27,* 35–41.

Roach, C. (Ed.). (1993). *Communication and culture in war and peace.* London: Sage.

Robinson, P. (2000). The policy-media interaction model: Measuring media power during humanitarian crisis. *Journal of Peace Research, 37,* 613–633.

Robinson, P. (2001). Operation Restore Hope and the illusion of a news media driven intervention. *Political Studies, 49,* 941–956.

Robinson, P. (2002). *The CNN effect: The myth of news, foreign policy and intervention.* London & New York: Routledge.

Rothstein, R. (Ed.). (1999). *After the peace: Resistance and reconciliation.* Boulder, CO: Lynne Rienner.

Rubenstein, R., Botes, J., Dukes, F., & Stephens, J. (1994). *Frameworks for interpreting conflict: A handbook for journalists.* Fairfax, VA: George Mason University, Institute for Conflict Analysis and Resolution.

Saunders, H. (2001). Prenegotiation and circum-negotiation: Arenas of the multilevel peace process. In C. Crocker, F. O. Hampson, & P. Aall (Eds.), *Turbulent peace: The challenges of managing international conflict* (pp. 483–496). Washington, DC: United States Institute of Peace Press.

Scali, J. (1995). Backstage mediation in the Cuban missile crisis. In J. McDonald, Jr., & D. Bendahmane (Eds.), *Conflict resolution: Track two diplomacy* (pp. 93–102). Washington, DC: Institute for Multi-Track Diplomacy.

Schechter, D. (2003). *Embedded: Weapons of mass deception. How the media failed to cover war on Iraq.* Amherst, NY: Prometheus.

Seib, P. (2002). *The global journalist: News and conscience in a world of conflict.* Lanham, MD: Rowman & Littlefield.

Seib, P. (2004). *Beyond the front lines.* New York: Palgrave.

Shattuck, J. (1996). Human rights and humanitarian crises: Policymaking and the media. In R. Rotberg & T. Weiss (Eds.), *From massacres to genocide: The media, public policy, and humanitarian crises* (pp. 169–175). Cambridge, MA: World Peace Foundation.

Shaw, M. (1996). *Civil society and media in global crises.* London: Pinter.

Shinar, D. (2002). Cultural conflict in the Middle East: The media as peacemakers. In E. Gilboa (Ed.), *Media and conflict: Framing issues, making policy, shaping opinions* (pp. 281–294). Ardsley, NY: Transnational Publishers.

Siefert, M. (2003). Radio diplomacy and the Cold War. *Journal of Communication, 53,* 365–373.

Sparre, K. (2001). Megaphone diplomacy in the Northern Irish peace process: Squaring the circle by talking to terrorists through journalists. *Harvard International Journal of Press/Politics, 6*(Summer), 88–104.

Spencer, G. (2004). The impact of television news on the Northern Ireland peace process. *Media, Culture & Society, 26,* 602–623.

Spurk, C. (2002). *Media and peacebuilding: Concepts, actors, and challenges* (Working Paper 1/2002). Bern, Switzerland: Swisspeace.

Strobel, W. (1997). *Late-breaking foreign policy: The news media's influence on peace operations.* Washington, DC: United States Institute of Peace Press.

Taylor, P. (1997). *Global communications, international affairs and the media since 1945.* London & New York: Routledge.

Taylor, P. (2000). The military and the media: Past, present and future. In S. Badsey (Ed.), *The media and international security* (pp. 177–202). London: Cass.

Thrall, A. T. (2000). *War in the media age.* Cresskill, NJ: Hampton Press.

Timmerman, K. (2003, January 6). Prime-time hate from Arafat TV. *Insight on the News,* p. 35.

Torisch, A. (2004). *Beacon of hatred: Inside Hizballah's al-Manar Television.* Washington, DC: Washington Institute for Near East Policy.

Tumber, H. (2004). Prisoners of news values? Journalists, professionalism, and identification in times of war. In S. Allen & B. Zelizer (Eds.), *Reporting war* (pp. 190–205). London & New York: Routledge.

Tumber, H., & Palmer, J. (2004). *Media at war: The Iraq crisis.* London: Sage.

Väyrynen, R. (1999). From conflict resolution to conflict transformation: A critical review. In H.-W. Jong (Ed.), *The new agenda for peace research* (pp. 135–160). Brookfield, VT: Ashgate.

Volkan, V. (1991). Official and unofficial diplomacy: An overview. In V. Volkan, J. Montville, & D. Julius (Eds.), *The psychodynamics of international relationships: Vol. II. Unofficial diplomacy at work* (pp. 1–16). Lexington, MA: Lexington Books.

Vulliamy, E. (1999). "Neutrality" and the absence of reckoning: A journalist's account. *Journal of International Affairs, 52,* 603–620.

Wall, M. (2002). The battle in Seattle: How NGOs used websites in their challenge to the WTO. In E. Gilboa (Ed.), *Media and conflict: Framing issues, making policy, shaping opinions* (pp. 25–43). Ardsley, NY: Transnational Publishers.

Walton, F. (2004). *In service of truth and the common good: The impact of media on global peace and conflict.* Washington, DC: Aspen Institute, Communications & Society Program.

Ward, S. (1998). An answer to Martin Bell: Objectivity and attachment in journalism. *Harvard International Journal of Press/Politics, 3*(3), 121–125.

Weaver, T. (1998). The end of war: Can television help stop it? *Track Two, 7.* Retrieved May 12, 2002, from http://ccrweb.ccr.uct.ac.za/archive/two

Wright, C. (1960). Functional analysis and mass communication. *Public Opinion Quarterly, 24,* 605–620.

Zartman, I. W., & Rasmussen, J. L. (Eds.). (1997). *Peacemaking in international conflict: Methods and techniques.* Washington, DC: United States Institute of Peace Press.

Zelizer, B., & Allan, S. (Eds.). (2002). *Journalism after September 11.* London & New York: Routledge.

Zimmermann, W. (1996). *Origins of a catastrophe: Yugoslavia and its destroyers.* New York: Times Books.

23

BUILDING PEACE
IN DIVIDED SOCIETIES

The Role of Intergroup Dialogue

BENJAMIN J. BROOME

Arizona State University

ANN-SOFI JAKOBSSON HATAY

Uppsala University

Dialogue, in a multitude of disguises, is a key feature of some of the most important political processes in today's world; namely, efforts to prevent or bring about an end to armed conflicts. A recent survey of conflicts around the world recorded (for 2004) a total of 30 ongoing armed conflicts.[1] The overwhelming majority of these conflicts were intrastate conflicts ("civil wars").[2] Media reports from places such as Burma/Myanmar, Burundi, Chechnya, Colombia, the Congo, Indonesia, Iraq, Israel/Palestine, Kashmir, Liberia, the Philippines, Sri Lanka, Sudan, and Uganda are testimonies of their legacy: human death and injury, displacement, serious economic harm, devastation of the social fabric, heavy damage to infrastructure, and irreparable destruction to historical treasures and fragile environments. Armed conflicts take a heavy toll on the psychological and physical health of individuals,

undermine democracy and democratization efforts, and leave behind a lasting negative effect on prospects for reconciliation. Those who bear the brunt of the damage are, of course, the affected local population, both in the immediate situation they face and in their prospects for the future. But armed conflicts invariably have negative effects also on regional stability, and often have far-reaching international implications. In short, the consequences are potentially catastrophic.

In this chapter, we examine some of the dialogic approaches that have emerged in response to the challenge of building peace in protracted intergroup conflict situations. A case study of peacebuilding dialogue initiatives in Cyprus serves the dual purpose of illustrating the diversity of dialogic approaches to peacebuilding, as well as their strengths and limitations. Our starting point is the need for an altogether wider notion of what a peace process entails, beyond that of reaching a negotiated settlement through inter-elite agreement. We agree with those who claim that the societal nature of contemporary conflicts calls for peace processes that are like-wise societal in nature (see, e.g., Lederach, 1997). Thus, what is required is a multi-level effort, involving not just the parties' respective leader-ships but society at large. We seek to contribute to the conceptualization of a peace process as a multi-track dialogue process that integrates an inclusive process of citizen peacebuilding with the inevitably more exclusive process of elite peacemaking and peace negotiations (see also Jakobsson Hatay, in press). We also point to the need to explore more systematically the linkages between different "peace tracks." We end the chapter with some recommendations for both research and practice concerned with dialogic approaches to peace.

As authors, we bring a "scholar-practitioner" perspective on intergroup dialogue as a peace-building tool in protracted conflict situations.[3] While we are both faculty members in univer-sity settings, we have each been involved for more than a decade in working with peacebuild-ing initiatives, in Cyprus and Northern Ireland in particular. We bring to our task different research emphases and backgrounds, drawing on the fields of communication studies and peace and conflict research. Together, we hope to provide for the reader a balanced and com-prehensive view of peacebuilding and dialogue that will be useful for those seeking to gain a better understanding of this complex phenome-non for their teaching, research, and practice. In order to set the context for our analysis, the fol-lowing section outlines the nature of contempo-rary conflicts and the challenges they pose.

PEACE AND CONFLICT: CONTEMPORARY DEVELOPMENTS AND CHALLENGES

A great many of today's conflicts are waged between parties identified along ethnic identity lines.[4] Many of these conflicts have a long history, not infrequently going back 25 years or more (Marshall & Gurr, 2003). Violence may not be a constant feature of these conflict situations, but even when subsided it often remains a latent possibility. Not infrequently the development of the conflict follows a pattern whereby periods of relative "peace" (or, more accurately, a truce) alternate with periods of open confrontation. Concerned communities are trapped in a vicious cycle, seemingly with no end in sight.

These conflicts are brought about by a diverse and complex set of forces, and their ever-changing dynamics are difficult for even the most seasoned conflict analyst or interna-tional relations expert to grasp. They have vari-ously been described as deeply rooted conflicts (Burton, 1987), protracted social conflicts (Azar, 1983, 1990; Azar & Farah, 1981), endur-ing rivalries (Goertz & Diehl, 1993), moral conflicts (Pearce & Littlejohn, 1997), and intractable conflicts (Kriesberg, 1998; Kriesberg, Northrup, & Thorson, 1989).

Civil wars, where neighbor fights neighbor, and even relatives may find themselves on dif-ferent sides of the conflict divide, understand-ably have particularly pernicious psychosocial effects. One of the more central issues is the *loss of trust* brought about through betrayal by the very people one knows and depends on in the immediate family and social network (Agger, 2001). The psychological effects are of course particularly serious for persons who themselves have suffered violent attacks. Survivors may be left with an enduring fear that their trauma may reoccur: a fear that undermines the possibil-ity of developing renewed trust and inhibits any (re)integration or even association with "them." *Intergenerational transmission of trauma and grievances* may entrap intergroup relations in vicious cycles of violence and revenge (Montville, 1993). In the former Yugoslavia, a "powerful reservoir of traumatic memory" of the atrocities committed during World War II, it has been suggested, added fuel to the recent wars (particularly so in relation to the Serb-Croat confrontation) (Denich, 1994). Protracted intergroup conflicts may also lock the parties into a relationship of *negative interdependence* such that assertion of each group's identity is seen to require the negation of the other group's identity (Kelman, 1987, 1999).[5] Violence leaves a legacy of *polarization:* social relations across group boundaries are loosened or severed in interpersonal relations; in organizational affilia-tion; and in the diverging of opinions, beliefs,

and ways of thinking (Ober... ...
weakening of ...
no
ren
des
(Sch
relat
acco
separ
(reinf
ther re

The
a societ
tion hav
the recou
offer may
by all se   ... vio-
lence, as   ...observed, is always in
some sense *extraordinary,* a departure from the
basic assumption of civil normality.

As their longevity shows, these conflicts
often defy traditional avenues for conflict
resolution. While domestic remedies—within
the framework of "normal politics"—may no
longer offer a way out, conflicts such as these
also pose particular challenges for international
diplomacy, notwithstanding the facts that state
boundaries have ceased to demarcate a no-go
area for international intervention and that the
balance between human rights and state sovereignty as guiding principles for international
behavior is shifting (Chandler, 2002). States no
longer enjoy immunity from interventions in
"domestic affairs"; and statesmen increasingly
face the risk of prosecution if they fail to uphold
agreed norms (Slobodan Milosevic set a prece-
dent by becoming the first head of state to
be indicted for war crimes against his own
citizens). After the ad hoc tribunals for war
crimes committed in Rwanda and the former
Yugoslavia, a permanent International Criminal
Court has been established.

Available diplomatic instruments for conflict
resolution are frequently too blunt to meet the
formidable challenges of ending violent conflict and building peace in divided societies.
Separating the parties into distinct polities is
generally not an option. Rarely, if ever, is the
population—also in divided societies—neatly
distributed along ethnic lines. At the same time,
the prospect of becoming a minority in a polity
dominated by "the other" is certain to trigger
fierce resistance. Moreover, the international
community remains firmly opposed to the idea of
re-drawing existing state boundaries (especially
it can be seen as condoning ethnic cleansing
operations).[6] Parties who may have been "killing
one another with considerable enthusiasm and
success," as Licklider (1993) wryly puts it, will
therefore in most cases have to find a way of
continuing to live and work together within the
framework of a common polity.

Other challenges relate to the fact that the
modus operandi of international diplomacy
developed in response to conflicts in which the
parties enjoy international recognition and where
their status as sovereign actors per se is not
disputed. In contemporary conflicts, however,
status and recognition tend to be major issues.
International organizations, including the only
"world organization," the United Nations, as well
as regional organizations such as the Association
of South-East Asian Nations (ASEAN), the
African Union (AU), the European Union (EU),
the Organization of American States (OAS), and
the Organization for Security and Co-operation
in Europe (OSCE) ultimately operate within
mandates set by their members states, represented as they are by governments. Status issues
coalesce with open opposition from parties to the
conflict who already enjoy international recognition (as heads of states or government representatives) to limit the access of substate actors to
international forums for conflict resolution, particularly if they want to challenge existing state
authorities. Meanwhile, parties who enjoy the
upper hand that comes with recognition are generally loath to engage with those who are not
("rebels") lest they confer legitimacy on the
demands of the other party and undermine their
own. The power to extend or withhold dialogue is
thus an important asset in many contemporary
conflicts, and one that frequently adds to existing
asymmetries between the parties.

Dialogue and negotiations between representatives of conflicting parties nevertheless remain
a central feature of peace processes in intra-state
conflicts as well. A peace agreement, voluntarily arrived at through a process of dialogue
and negotiation, constitutes a key piece of the
larger peace puzzle. Ideally, a peace agreement
signifies a mutual commitment to bringing

armed conflict to an end and to forfeiting the use of violence for political ends. A peace agreement (again ideally) provides a political framework for peaceful and cooperative intergroup relations to develop. Conversely, in the absence of a settlement to the conflict, the future is unpredictable and violence remains a distinct possibility. Uncertainty and insecurity in turn entrench positions, breed suspicion, and retain intergroup relations in a conflict mode: to progress toward reconciliation becomes difficult, if not impossible.

A peace agreement may—at best—offer a political framework for peaceful and cooperative intergroup relations to develop. Once it has been signed, however, in order to make the settlement "stick," further efforts are needed to nurture the new peaceful state of affairs (Hampson, 1996). While the increase in negotiated settlements in the immediate post–Cold War years gave ground for considerable optimism, we were also alerted to the many problems that might derail the peace process in the post-agreement period (Stedman, Rothchild, & Cousens, 2002). The post-agreement trials and tribulations encountered in contemporary peace processes in the Middle East after the 1993 Oslo Accords, in Bosnia and Herzegovina after the 1995 Dayton Agreement, and in Northern Ireland after the 1998 Belfast Agreement are but a few illustrations. A good many peace agreements—with estimations ranging from one third to more than half—are in fact never implemented (Licklider, 1995).

Against this rather gloomy background some positive developments are also worth noting. Although 22 countries experienced armed conflict in 2004 (which means that several countries had more than one ongoing conflict), the number of active armed conflicts in the world is actually at its lowest point since the early 1970s. Moreover, more conflicts than in the past end in a negotiated settlement, splitting the gains and losses between the parties, rather than in total victories and defeats. Data on armed conflicts since the end of the Cold War also tell us that armed conflict between states is becoming an increasingly rare phenomenon.[7]

In the remainder of this chapter, our focus is directed not so much at contemporary problems as at possible remedies. Based on a review of the literature we next discuss various approaches to the role of intergroup dialogue as a peacebuilding strategy. We then outline a framework for analyzing the impact of intergroup dialogue initiatives, noting the need for a multilevel approach. Thereafter we present a case study of intergroup dialogue as a peacebuilding strategy, focusing on initiatives undertaken to address the protracted conflict situation in Cyprus. We end the chapter with some recommendations for future research and practice. First, however, we introduce in the next section the two key concepts of our presentation: *dialogue* and *peacebuilding*.

KEY CONCEPTS: DIALOGUE AND PEACEBUILDING

The term *dialogue* is an ancient Greek word composed of *dia* (meaning "through" or "across") and *logos* (meaning "the word" or "reason"). Broken down into its linguistic roots, dialogue implies a sense of creating meaning through talking or reasoning together.

The modern emphasis on dialogue is often traced to Martin Buber, a Jewish philosopher who was also a theologian, playwright, educator, and advocate for peace and cooperation between Jews and Arabs in Palestine (and thus one of the first to bring together dialogue and peacebuilding). His seminal work *I and Thou*, first published in 1926, led to a shift in our thinking about communication, relationships, and the possibility for genuine human interaction (Buber, 1970). In his conceptualization of the "I–It" encounter, people are treated as if they were objects to be manipulated or changed in some way, while in the "I–Thou" relationship people are viewed as having unique histories that shape their beliefs, attitudes, and values. An I–Thou encounter is characterized by curiosity, discovery, and learning, rather than the persuasion, positioning, and argument that is typical of I–It encounters. In Buber's view, dialogue is a way of being with others, one that acknowledges the complexity of other people's experience and seeks understanding. Pearce and Littlejohn (1997) referred to this type of discourse as transformative, making it possible for participants to work through differences.

In addition to Buber, other influential theorists include Bohm (1996), whose work was applied in the "learning organization" concepts espoused by Senge (1990), Isaacs (1993), and Schein (1993). The concept of dialogue has gained attention in a multiplicity of disciplines in recent years, including anthropology, education, psychology and psychotherapy, sociology, management, political theory, philosophy, linguistics, and religion (Cissna & Anderson, 1998). In communication, dialogue has been a focus in a number of areas, including the study of rhetoric (Arnett, 1981; Johannesen, 1971; Poulakos, 1974), philosophy and communication (Stewart, 1978), interpersonal communication (Baxter & Montgomery, 1996), performance studies (Conquergood, 1988), organizational communication (Deetz, 1992; Eisenberg & Goodall, 1997), health communication (Geist & Dreyer, 1994), culture and communication (Philipsen, 1992), and conflict communication (Pearce & Littlejohn, 1997). Cissna and Anderson (1998, 2002) focused on dialogue by examining the Martin Buber–Carl Rogers relationship and their 1957 public conversation.

Approaches to intergroup dialogue in the field of conflict resolution are rooted in the contact hypothesis literature. Based on the early work of Gordon W. Allport, presented in *The Nature of Prejudice* (Allport, 1995), first published in 1958, and extended by, among others, Amir (1969) and Cook (1978), the contact hypothesis holds that under certain conditions intergroup contact can be effective in reducing prejudice. The four major conditions are (a) equal status of the contact groups, at least within the contact situation; (b) personal and sustained interactions between individuals from the two groups; (c) cooperative interdependence, where members of the contact groups engage in cooperative activities where they depend on one another's efforts to achieve superordinate goals; and (d) social norms favoring equality. Based on these foundations, the primary purposes of intergroup dialogue are (a) to open channels of communication, (b) to build trust, (c) to search for mutually acceptable outcomes, and (d) to encourage discourse as an alternative to violence. It is important to note that the contact hypothesis is not an unqualified prescription for *more* contact: rather, it suggests that contact should be encouraged when it can be expected to have "good" effects but minimized where it is likely to have "bad" effects; or, alternatively, that situations of contact to the extent possible should be changed into situations in which contact is assumed to have good effects.[8]

The concept of *peacebuilding* was introduced by Norwegian peace and conflict researcher Johan Galtung in the mid-1970s (Galtung, 1975). It was only when the concept reappeared as an element of the UN's overall strategy for dealing with conflict after the Cold War, however, that it received wider usage. In the 1992 *Agenda for Peace,* peacebuilding appeared along with the organization's more traditional instruments of preventive diplomacy: peacemaking and peacekeeping (Boutros-Ghali, 1992). Initially, the UN's vision of peacebuilding—*post-conflict peacebuilding*—was directed primarily toward efforts undertaken *after* a peace agreement to address the root causes and effects of conflict in order to improve the overall situation and build a more stable foundation for peace. In 2001, the UN Security Council adopted a revised definition that no longer relates the concept to a specific conflict phase. In its reconceptualized version, the "post-conflict" prefix has been abandoned, and the aim of peacebuilding is defined as "preventing the outbreak, the recurrence or continuation of armed conflict" (United Nations, 2001).

The peacebuilding concept has since come to be used for two very different strategies. The UN approach to peacebuilding is an interventionist, multi-dimensional effort that involves third-party assistance to reconciliation efforts, institution building, and political as well as economic transformation (Bertram, 1995; Jakobsson Hatay, 2005; Paris, 2004). This macro-level approach to peacebuilding coexists with micro-level approaches that link the concept to interactive, associational activities aiming at the improvement of relations between the parties and/or to contextual or cultural transformation. It is the latter that are the focus of our interest here. They both, however, share what Haugerudbraaten (2003), drawing on Galtung's (1996) notion of positive peace, identifies as the overall aim of peacebuilding, namely to create a "stable social equilibrium in which the surfacing of new disputes does not escalate into violence and war" (Haugerudbraaten, 2003, The Aim of Peacebuilding Section, para. 1).

APPROACHES TO INTERGROUP DIALOGUE: FROM INTERACTIVE WORKSHOPS TO INTEGRATED FRAMEWORKS

Beginning in the 1960s, a number of scholar-practitioners and former diplomats sought ways of creating a setting where political leaders, opinion leaders, and ordinary citizens could engage in discussions that focused on learning from each other through respectful inquiry. Thus, several initiatives were launched in which discussions were organized between unofficial representatives of groups from conflict zones. Carefully selected representatives from all sides of the conflict were brought together with a third-party "panel," which typically included conflict scholars, usually from different disciplines within academic institutions. Panelists, who came together with the participants for intensive discussions over a period of several days, sought to help the group analyze the sources of the conflict and develop possible solutions. These discussions became known as *problem-solving workshops*.

The primary purpose of problem-solving workshops is to open unofficial communication channels between the parties in preparation for and/or as a complement to official negotiations. They provide a low-risk, low-profile forum in which representatives of the parties can analyze their conflict and engage in problem solving. Meetings are often organized within an academic context, which imputes an appropriate atmosphere akin to that of academic deliberations and which allows participants to take part in discussions without the implication that they are recognizing or legitimizing the other. An attempt is made to shift the focus away from presenting and defending entrenched positions, and toward encouraging new ways of thinking about the conflict that induce the participants to approach it as a shared problem.

The person usually viewed as the initiator of the problem-solving approach is John W. Burton, a former Australian diplomat and founder in the 1960s of the Centre of the Analysis of Conflict at University College London. Following two workshops that he organized in London in the mid-1960s, one dealing with the Malaysia and Singapore conflict and the other with the Cyprus conflict, Burton developed a theory of practice that he termed *controlled communication* (Burton, 1969; Sandole, 2001). This term was selected in reference to the role of the panel, which he viewed as

> to control communication to create a nonthreatening atmosphere in which the participants can examine their perceptions and misperceptions about the conflict and about each other, and then jointly explore avenues for analyzing and resolving the conflict, partly through the development of common functional interests. (Fisher, 1997, p. 27)

Sessions often begin with a presentation by each party of its position on the conflict. The panelists then engage in directing the discussion by seeking clarifications, providing insights about the conflict, offering relevant perspectives from other conflict situations, questioning misperceptions they hear, and offering analytical frameworks for interpreting the conflict and the interaction occurring among the participants. Thus, the scholars bring knowledge from their different disciplines in an attempt to help the participants analyze the conflict and view it in terms of a problem that requires joint efforts in order to be solved. For Burton, a prime function of the controlled communication approach is to prepare the ground for more official negotiations by establishing the conditions under which these can be successful.

Burton brought the term *problem solving* into the lexicon of conflict resolution, using it to help distinguish his work from the process of diplomatic negotiation. Theoretically, he considered protracted conflicts as rooted in fundamental human needs. As these needs are not amenable to compromises, such conflicts are thus not negotiable in the traditional sense. Basic needs for security, recognition, justice, consistency, and sense of control instead require analysis that allows participants in conflicts to explore underlying motivations and ways to meet the needs of all involved parties (Burton, 1987, 1990). Burton saw traditional means of approaching conflict through negotiation and mediation as dealing primarily with surface interests rather than deeper motivations. He also believed that settlements brought about through persuasion, coercion, inducement, and application of international pressure are not only difficult to obtain, but they are unstable over time. Such agreements are often suboptimal, based on zero-sum assumptions that may fail to reflect opportunities for mutual gain that could be inherent in the conflict situation.

While Burton's approach can be considered predominantly analytical or rational, dealing primarily with the substance of the conflict, other scholar-practitioners organized intergroup dialogue projects that were typically less structured, often more informal efforts to ease tensions and improve relations in international conflicts. Bryant Wedge, a psychiatrist with an interest in international relations, is usually considered the pioneer of what is sometimes called the psychodynamic approach (see Volkan, Montville, & Julius, 1990, 1991). Wedge is the cofounder of the National Peace Academy Campaign, which led to the establishment of the United States Institute of Peace in 1984, and he was a primary force behind the creation of the Center for Conflict Resolution at George Mason University, which offered one of the first graduate degrees in the subject. Based on his intervention in the Dominican Republic in the mid-1960s, he believed that creating programs in which participants cooperated on superordinate goals could alter intergroup images in favorable directions, hopefully reducing the degree of violence between groups (Wedge, 1967, 1990).[9]

Two other academics, Vamik D. Volkan, also a psychiatrist, and Leonard W. Doob, a social psychologist, were also instrumental in the development of the psychodynamic approach. Volkan's work draws on psychoanalytic concepts and techniques of psychoanalytic therapy (Volkan, 1990, 1998). By bringing together politically influential citizens of opposing sides for a series of meetings to become acquainted, establish working relationships, and exchange ideas, he sought to humanize the "enemy," build confidence, and overcome hatred. His goal was to build an atmosphere in which the expression of emotions is acceptable, helping to reduce defense mechanisms such as externalization, projection, and identification that individuals often use as protective mechanisms in conflicts. He called his third-party team a *catalyst group.*

Volkan conducted workshops with Israelis and Egyptians, as well as with the Baltic Republics.

Doob adopted a sensitivity training model of intervention in which participants were engaged in learning about each other and their relations with each other, hopefully learning to communicate more effectively across the conflict divide and developing more creative solutions to their conflict. First working on issues in the Horn of Africa and later in Northern Ireland and Cyprus, Doob's attempts to apply a human relations training model (the Tavistock model) in sensitive conflict arenas were met with both skepticism and criticism by international relations specialists (Doob & Foltz, 1973, 1974; Doob, Foltz, & Stevens, 1969). However, based on his experiences, Doob (1981) concluded that human relations workshops can be useful as a precursor to negotiations, helping to uncover emotional issues that might otherwise affect the negotiations negatively.

Falling somewhere between the rational and psychodynamic approaches are those that give equal emphasis to both substance and relationship. Approaches developed by Herbert C. Kelman and Ronald J. Fisher, both social psychologists, and Edward E. Azar, a political scientist, fall into this category.

Kelman, who was one of the panelists in Burton's Cyprus workshop, emphasized equally the educational and the political aspects of the workshop, aiming to produce changes in the attitudes and perceptions of the participants (and ultimately also their behavior), while simultaneously transferring these changes to the political arena (Kelman, 1972, 2002; Kelman & Cohen, 1976). To Kelman, one of the main potential contributions of unofficial dialogue initiatives to an overall peace process is to help the parties overcome the psychological barriers for negotiations associated in particular with the early stages of a peace process: monolithic views of the enemy, lack of empathy, mutual denial and nonrecognition, and so on (Kelman, 1978, 1982, 1985, 1987). Overcoming these obstacles involves developing a more differentiated view of the enemy, and assisting the parties (or elements within them) "to persuade each other that there is someone to talk to and something to talk about" (Kelman, 1978, p. 179) and to understand that there are different groupings or political forces within each community (e.g., hawks and doves).[10] It is therefore crucial that participants in dialogue initiatives are selected from a broad political spectrum so as to enable exposure to different perspectives, viewpoints, and orientations from each "side." In later stages of the peace process, after the onset of negotiations, workshops can provide a forum for working out certain details during negotiations, or for discussing problems that deal with implementation of an agreement and long-term issues that have to be addressed once a political settlement has been reached.

Fisher developed a model of practice that he called third-party consultation in which he included concepts from the field of organizational psychology to further define the role of the third party (Fisher, 1972, 1980). With his colleague Loraleigh Keashly, he illuminated the consulting relationship of the third party with the actors in the conflict, emphasizing the need to gain trust, respect, and understanding in order to be effective (Keashly & Fisher, 1990). Fisher offered a number of workshops in Cyprus, Sri Lanka, and elsewhere, and he also played a key role in mapping the field of problem-solving approaches. His influential book *Interactive Conflict Resolution* (1997) provided a valuable state-of-the-art overview of both the pioneers in intergroup dialogue and the issues faced by the field.

Fisher (1993) presented a contingency model that integrates strategies for third-party intervention with stages of a conflict process (see also Fisher & Keashly, 1991; Keashly & Fisher, 1990). Peacebuilding—defined as "activities designed to improve the relationship and meet the basic needs of the parties, in order to de-escalate the conflict and render it amenable to peacemaking" (Fisher, 1993, p. 249)—performs a central role in this model where it is conceived as a bridge between peacekeeping and peacemaking.[11] Fisher argued that attempts at conflict resolution in protracted social conflicts frequently fail because they are immune to the dominant strategies of intervention, peacemaking, and peacekeeping, which do not address the underlying issues. Fisher's peacebuilding approach combines activities at the micro-level, such as interactive workshops, which address the subjective elements of conflict (attitudes and relationship between the parties), with macro-level

social change. Fisher argued that the improvement of relationships (as a result of peacebuilding) will put the parties in a better position to deal with their specific interest and positions, and eventually reach an agreement (through peacemaking).

Azar, who was a panelist in one of Kelman's early workshops and also collaborated with Burton, developed a model of protracted social conflict that moved away from the nation-state as the primary unit of analysis and instead emphasized the identity group, defined in racial, religious, ethnic, cultural, or other terms (Azar, 1983, 1986). He developed what he called the *problem-solving forum,* in which representatives of the parties to the conflict analyze their identity-related needs, helping participants recognize the legitimate needs and aspirations of the other. His experiences of working with the Lebanese conflict provide one of the most well-documented (and successful) examples of problem-solving workshops in practice (see Azar, 1990).

Another contributor to the field of intergroup dialogue is Jay Rothman, whose experiences include the Israeli-Palestinian conflict (focusing in particular on Jerusalem) and Cyprus (Rothman, 1991, 1992; Rothman, 1994). Rothman (1998) suggested that approaches to dialogue in intergroup conflict can be classified as (a) *human-relations dialogue,* in which work is focused primarily at the relational level, and in particular on the causes of misunderstandings and the stereotypes that typically arise between the parties, with objectives centered on mutual acknowledgment and increased respect by each party for the other; (b) *activist dialogue,* which centers on sorting and analyzing the issues separating the parties in order to identify common ground and/or to explore how the parties might contain their dispute through joint action; and (c) *problem-solving dialogue,* in which the disputants work systematically through the substance of their differences.[12]

Rothman (1997b) proposed a process for resolving identity-based conflicts called the ARIA (Antagonism-Resonance-Invention-Action) framework. He pointed out that in their beginning stages conflicts are usually framed in adversarial terms, with arguments over issues and the resources at stake, creating antagonism between the parties. He suggested that the use of a reflexive reframing process that focuses on the identity needs of the parties involved fosters resonance among the parties. Once the parties frame the conflict in similar terms, the stage is set for inventing integrative solutions. This allows agenda setting, which is the final step toward taking cooperative action. Together with Marc Howard Ross, Rothman also pioneered efforts to develop methods for the evaluation of peacebuilding interventions and initiatives, and introduced the concept of "action evaluation" (Ross & Rothman, 1999; Rothman, 1997a).

In addition to scholar-practitioners, a number of former diplomats also developed approaches to intergroup dialogue. Joseph V. Montville (1987), a former U.S. foreign service officer, coined the term *Track II diplomacy* to refer to unofficial, informal interaction between members of adversary groups or nations that aims to develop strategies, influence public opinion, and organize human and material resources in ways that might help resolve their conflict. Montville (1993) also explored psychological factors affecting reconciliation and conflict resolution. John W. McDonald, a former U.S. ambassador and career diplomat and the first president of the Iowa Peace Institute, and his colleague Louise Diamond, a human-relations trainer with NTL Institute, expanded the notion of tracks by proposing the concept of "multi-track diplomacy," which proposed nine additional tracks of unofficial diplomacy, ranging from analytical problem solving to educational exchange programs to cooperative business ventures (Diamond & McDonald, 1996; McDonald, 1991).

A key player in the group of former diplomats was Harold H. Saunders, who concluded his career as an assistant Secretary of State and was a member of the Camp David team that negotiated the peace treaty between Egypt and Israel (see Saunders, 1991). Saunders took part in workshops organized by Volkan and by Kelman and co-chaired (with former Russian diplomat Gennady I. Chufrin) the Dartmouth Conference, which for more than 45 years has brought together Soviet (and now Russian) and American foreign policy specialists for discussions about issues that concern the two nations (see Voorhees, 2002). In his work, Saunders has sought to provide a forum for conflicting groups

to probe the dynamics of their relationship, to think together about obstacles to changing it, and to design a sequence of interactive steps that might remove those obstacles. Chufrin and Saunders (1993) introduced the concept of a "public peace process" for "sustained action by citizens outside government to change the fundamental relationship between groups in conflict" (p. 156).

Saunders (1985) brought attention to what he considered a crucial but neglected phase of the peace process, namely, the phase that precedes the more visible negotiation phase. He called for "a larger theory of negotiation" that took into account also this pre-negotiation phase, and identified some of the tasks that need to be addressed *before* the onset of negotiations if they are to have a chance of being successful, such as to establish a shared or complementary definition of the problem and to develop a commitment to a negotiated settlement.

Saunders (1985, 1999b, 2003) proposed a framework for "sustained dialogue"—"a systematic, prolonged dialogue among small groups of representative citizens committed to changing conflictual relationships, ending conflict and building peace" (Saunders, 1999b, p. 12)—for the transformation of conflictual relationships. The framework consists of five phases: (a) defining the problem and deciding to engage; (b) mapping issues and relationships; (c) generating the will for a joint solution; (d) scenario building and negotiation; and (e) acting together to implement agreements.

The most well-publicized application of Saunders's dialogue approach is the Inter-Tajik Dialogue initiative (Iji, 2002; Saunders, 1999a, 2003; Slim & Saunders, 1996, 2001). The initiative began in 1996 and proceeded parallel with official peace negotiations that in 1997 produced a peace agreement, marking a formal end to the civil war in Tajikistan. After the peace agreement, participants in the dialogue initiative served in the Commission on National Reconciliation, tasked with overseeing the implementation of the agreement. In 2000, a peacebuilding NGO was formed: the Public Committee for Promoting Democratic Process in Tajikistan, under the auspices of which dialogue groups continue to work in six regions of the country.

Toward a Wider Conceptualization of a "Peace Process"

Most of the approaches described above focus on analyzing the causes and functions of the conflict and producing ideas that might feed into the official negotiations. Workshops usually involve influential, informal representatives of the parties to the conflict. The ambition is for participants to move away from an adversarial stance and toward a cooperative framework. Primary emphasis is given to transferring the workshop learnings into the political discourse and the policymaking process, either *directly* by involving some of the key players in the unofficial dialogue efforts or by injecting ideas from the dialogue sessions into the political arena, or *indirectly* by producing changes in the decision-making environment. Burton, Kelman, and other problem-solving workshop scholar-practitioners are primarily concerned with the impact of Track II dialogue initiatives on official, Track I negotiations. They see as the main purposes of such initiatives (a) to facilitate the initiation of official negotiations; (b) to assist in bringing these negotiations to a successful conclusion (i.e., an agreement); and (c) to underpin the implementation process in the later stages of a peace process.

In particular, informal workshops have been suggested as a means to alleviate two obstacles to engaging with the opposing side: the so-called entry and re-entry problems (Burton, 1986). The *entry problem* refers to obstacles for dialogue—including the onset of negotiations—that deter decision makers from engaging in what invariably is perceived as a "risky undertaking" (Zartman, 1989). The unofficial, often secret, character of the workshop permits the parties to make contact before they are ready to accept each other's legitimacy formally. By providing a "safe," low-risk (noncommittal) environment for conflict analysis, the problem-solving workshop aims at increasing the sense of opportunity and decreasing the sense of danger associated with negotiations (Kelman, 1982).

The *re-entry problem* refers to the post-workshop (or post-negotiation) situation when participants re-enter their home environment. The re-entry problem is complex: it involves issues such as the maintenance of credibility of the participants in the eyes of their constituencies,

the participants' maintenance of changes (of views and attitudes, etc.), and the transfer of the workshop experiences to the wider home environment. The challenges should not be underestimated. Participants returning to their home setting with new insights, increased understanding of and perhaps even empathy for the "enemy" are vulnerable to accusations of sellout and treachery from an environment where an antagonistic conflict mood prevails. The forces they are up against are powerful. As Forbes (1997) observed, "[F]riendship with outsiders will generally mean defection from the beliefs and practices of the in-group—or at least a more skeptical conformity with the demands of the group" (p. 167). This is likely to provoke negative reactions or sanctions against transgressors ("traitors") in an attempt to discourage further contact with out-group members. Such sanctions may range from normative resistance to social pressure, public denouncement and defamation (in the media, for example), to ostracism and physical danger.[13]

The problem-solving workshop approach to intergroup dialogue added a second subsidiary track (Track II) to diplomatic peace efforts (Track I). Other approaches to intergroup dialogue seek to incorporate considerations of other societal levels, as well, including citizens and civil society. They emphasize that negotiations between decision makers (Track I) and problem-solving workshops involving "influentials" (Track II) need to be embedded in a societal transformation process, involving not only political leaders but whole "policymaking" communities or societies. The introduction of the transformative approach is most closely linked to the work of John Paul Lederach (1985, 1995, 2003), but the later work of Harold H. Saunders (see, in particular, Saunders, 1999b) also falls into this category.

To Lederach, peacebuilding is a search for the values of peace and justice, truth and mercy, leading to the long-term transformation of a "war system" into a "peace system" characterized by political and economic participation, peaceful relationships, and social harmony (Lederach, 1999, 2003). Lederach (1995) presented a comprehensive framework that integrates peace initiatives at different levels with the aim of creating what he calls an *infrastructure for peace*. Lederach criticized the trickle-down approach that dominates international diplomacy and that assumes that the key to peace is negotiations at the top level. To him, peacemaking is not "a series of events or products, like achieving direct negotiations, ceasefires, and the signing of accords," but rather it is "embedded in the development and transformation of relationships over time" (p. 214). A peace process therefore, he argues, must simultaneously address—and involve—all the different levels of a society that have been affected by conflict: from the grassroots level (the vast majority), to national leaders (leaders from different sectors, regions, communities, or institutions), to the top level of military and political leadership (Lederach, 1997, 2001). In addition to the participants in negotiations or problems-solving workshops (top-level and middle-level leaders, respectively), Lederach emphasizes the need also to involve grassroots leaders and local communities, for example, within the framework of local peace commissions or initiatives for prejudice reduction, but he accords a key role to approaches directed at middle-range leaders (ethnic/religious leaders, leaders of NGOs, academics/intellectuals, among others). Literally located in the middle of Lederach's pyramidal framework, such leaders are strategically placed to influence and support changes both at the top leadership and societal levels.

Saunders's above-mentioned call for a wider notion of the negotiation process was followed by efforts to introduce a wider conceptualization of a peace process altogether. Saunders (1999b) conceptualized a peace process as a multi-level process that develops at multiple arenas.[14] His framework integrates four such "peace process arenas": *the official process* of (would-be) peace negotiations; *the quasi-official process,* made up of citizens outside government who consult with officials and feed them ideas or formulations; *a public peace process* involving dialogue between citizens outside government; and *civil society,* in particular civil society associations that span various ethnic, racial, religious, economic, social, and other dividing fault lines. Saunders (1996) maintained that:

> Crucial as it is, negotiation around the table is only a later part of larger political process in which conflicts are resolved by peaceful means. That larger political process is the peace process—a mixture of politics, diplomacy, changing relationships, negotiation, mediation, and dialogue in both official and unofficial arenas. (p. 419)

Saunders and his colleagues call this larger political process the *public peace process,* at the heart of which is "sustained action by citizens outside governments to change the fundamental relationship between groups in conflict" (Chufrin & Saunders, 1993, p. 156). Initiating sustained dialogue among citizens, they suggested, is a particularly important step for transforming conflictual relationships that are not yet ready for formal negotiation and mediation. In later stages, the public peace process can "complement, support or even energize the official peace process" (p. 9). Saunders's approach outlines a complementary division of labor between government and citizen initiatives. While governments negotiate around interests and issues, citizens play a crucial role in changing behavior and relationships, for "[i]t is in the public political arena . . . that issues are reframed, comparable interests recognized, perceptions changed, fears allayed, and choices among steps for changing relationships imagined" (Chufrin & Saunders, 1993, p. 158).[15]

Organizers and sponsors of intergroup dialogue activities are constantly looking for visible signs that their work has made a difference in the conflict situation. The theoretical and methodological challenges of evaluating individual initiatives or the cumulative impact of ongoing efforts are daunting; the problem is complex and the determinants multiple. The scholar-practitioner peacebuilding field is acutely aware of the need for further research and theorizing pertaining to such "peace impact." Nevertheless, the call has been answered by only a few. The next section reviews this rather weak state of the art when it comes to analyzing the impact of intergroup dialogue initiatives, but it also deduces from the literature some guidance for empirical analysis.

ANALYZING THE "PEACE IMPACT" OF INTERGROUP DIALOGUE INITIATIVES

There are numerous reasons why individuals in conflicted societies may opt to engage in dialogue.

It is our experience that many, when asked, profess initially to have been driven simply by a curiosity about the "other side," a desire to find out more about the "enemy." For some, the thrill of challenging the boundaries of the socially and politically permissible adds to the excitement. Opportunities for personal development and training often associated with the intergroup dialogue encounter in, for example, communication and/or negotiation skills may exert an additional pull. For some, of course, the decision to take part in dialogue is a political act or a political statement: The dialogue encounter is valued for the opportunity to "do something" about (or protest against) the existing political situation, whether that "something" is an opportunity to state one's case, persuade the other side about the rightfulness of one's cause, or explore and learn about the differences and generate ideas on how to advance peace, and the like. Third-party dialogue facilitators likewise are driven by a complex set of motivations, ranging from the personal (career advancement, research interests, financial remuneration, status, etc.) to the political. The motivations of participants and facilitators can thus be assumed to be both complex and varying. As a *peacebuilding strategy,* however, the ultimate aim of intergroup dialogue is to effect political change: to impact on the dynamics of the conflict in ways conducive to peace.

Efforts to identify peacebuilding impact mechanisms and linkages between different peace strategies are still at a very early stage. Kelman and Rouhana (Kelman, 1995, 1997, 1998; Rouhana, 2000; Rouhana & Kelman, 1994) have spearheaded efforts to identify linkages between Track I and Track II approaches (see also Lieberfeld, 2002; Richmond, 2001), while Jakobsson Hatay (in press) analyzed linkages between what she termed "citizen peacebuilding" (sometimes referred to as Track III) and "elite peacemaking" (Track I). Others have proposed more fine-grained frameworks that allow for an assessment of impact at several levels (Maiese, 2003; Ropers, 2003). A discussion of some of the proposed peace impact mechanisms and frameworks for analysis serve as a backdrop to our case study of peacebuilding dialogue initiatives in Cyprus.

Early in his work, Kelman (1972) identified linkages related to what has become known as the transfer problem; that is, how the changes and ideas generated in small intergroup encounters (in his case, problem-solving workshops) can influence official policy making. Kelman conceptualized this impact as a two-staged process in which the first stage consists of producing individual changes (improved attitudes, new orientations, etc.) within the confines of the workshop itself, and the second of the influence of these changes on the policy process. This conceptualization thus specifies two objectives for intergroup dialogue initiatives, both of which are required for the initiatives to have an impact on policy making, namely individual *learning* and *transfer* across levels.

In order to accomplish this dual purpose, the selection of workshop participants is of crucial importance. Ultimately, it is the participants who are the vehicles for transfer; they will have a major influence on the degree of transfer of outcomes to the wider relationship between the conflicted parties. To maximize the likelihood of both learning and transfer, Kelman (1972) suggested that the ideal participants are influential individuals at an intermediate distance from decision making but close enough to the centers of power to have some influence on decision makers, political elites, and public opinion. Rouhana and Kelman (1994) define the ideal participants as "influentials" or "pre-influentials" (i.e., people who are likely to become influentials in the future) and suggest that such individuals may be found in academia, the media, political parties, or social movements. Although the participation of decision makers themselves may increase the likelihood of transfer, decision makers at the same time are likely to be less amenable to learning due to the constraints they operate within (official positions, etc.). Kelman and Rouhana also presented a case for working with the same participants over a longer period of time—within the framework of a "continuing workshop"—in order to maximize political impact (Rouhana, 1995; Rouhana & Kelman, 1994).

Kelman and his colleagues, who have been organizing workshops with Israelis and Palestinians since the 1970s, claim that their work helped lay the groundwork for the successful negotiations preceding the Oslo Accords in the early 1990s. The breakthrough in negotiations in 1993 had been preceded by a series of workshops over a three-year period. According to Rouhana and Kelman (1994), their "continuing workshop" contributed to the Israeli-Palestinian peace process in the following ways: (a) most of the participants of the continuing workshop later played central roles, as negotiators and advisers, in the official peace talks; (b) the workshop produced new knowledge, understanding, and ideas that were fed into the peacemaking process; and (c) a new relationship between significant elements of the two communities evolved over the years. According to Kelman, the people involved in the workshops or similar activities over the years now constitute a significant proportion of the political elites of the two communities. His own impressionistic evaluation is that the cumulative effect of this range of activities helped to create a political atmosphere conducive to productive negotiations (Kelman, 1995, p. 20).

Kelman proposed that impact be conceived as a two-stage process whereby changes at the level of the individual participant within the confines of the dialogue initiative are also transferred to the decision-making level. Kelman and Rouhana developed the notion of transfer further, proposing several potential impact mechanisms whereby Track II dialogue initiatives can exert a political influence: (a) through the development of cadres and the transfer of individuals between levels, (b) through substantive inputs into the official decision making regarding negotiations, and (c) through effecting changes in the political context. They thus suggest that impact should be conceived of as being *direct* (a, b) as well as *indirect* (c).

The above discussion implies that the impact of dialogue initiatives cannot be assessed at a single level of analysis. Maiese (2003) suggests that possible dialogue outcomes can be classified at three different levels: (a) changes relating to the individual participants' attitudes and/or behavior, (b) changes relating to changes in intergroup relationships, and (c) changes relating to society as a whole. The *personal dimension* focuses on changes at the individual level. In most conflicts, there are deaths, rapes, missing persons, and other tragedies to overcome, and there is much psychological pain and suffering. Sometimes these lead to mental health problems, and people must confront fears, depression, guilt, and other forms of personal anxieties. In addition, the experience of violent conflict always involves challenges and changes to identity; because we define ourselves in relation to "the other," if that relationship changes, so does our identity. Peacebuilding must allow for personal healing, so that individual capacity for growth can be realized, and we can function as full members of a healthy society.

The *relational dimension* focuses on the repair and transformation of damaged relationships. An attempt is made to promote reconciliation by asking parties to acknowledge and take responsibility for their own role in creating and/or perpetuating the conflict. The aim is to help participants gain an appreciation for the perspectives of their adversaries and begin to see their grievances as having a legitimate basis. Peacebuilding activities focused on the relational dimension will often encourage parties to express sincere regret and remorse, perhaps acknowledging responsibility for what happened in the past. In turn, this leads to an effort to find ways to overcome the past, sometimes through compensation for loss. If such steps can be taken, the parties are in a better position to enter into a more productive working relationship.

The *structural dimension* of peacebuilding focuses on the systemic roots of the conflict, often rooted in complex social problems related to issues dealing with distribution of resources (e.g., land or territory) and power and political representation (e.g., unequal voice for nondominant groups). In order to establish sustainable peace, parties must analyze these structural causes and address them through economic and political changes and the strengthening of civil society.

These dimensions provide a framework for examining the larger impact of initiatives such as problem-solving workshops and other forms of intergroup dialogue. With the above discussion in mind, we now turn our attention to a specific case study in which we will draw upon our personal involvement in peacebuilding efforts on the eastern Mediterranean island of Cyprus.[16] We will illustrate and discuss the use of intergroup dialogue as a peacebuilding strategy in an inter-communal conflict, one that has eluded repeated attempts to reach an agreement that is acceptable to both sides in the conflict.

Conflict and Peacebuilding in Cyprus

To set the context for our discussion of inter-group dialogue efforts in Cyprus, we first outline some details about the conflict. Then we discuss the specific peacebuilding efforts that have been implemented in Cyprus and the outcomes of these efforts. Finally, we note some of the limitations of the peacebuilding activities, which, although they have accomplished much at the individual and interpersonal relationship levels, have failed to have much impact on the political process.

Background to the Cyprus Conflict[17]

The Cyprus conflict, which has divided the small eastern Mediterranean island into Greek-Cypriot and Turkish-Cypriot administered zones for more than 40 years, is viewed as one of the more intractable situations of modern times. Physically divided by war, it is also socially divided by differences in language, cultural heritage, religion, politics, view of the past, and vision of the future. Ethnically, approximately 80% of the population is Greek-speaking Orthodox Christian, and 18% is Turkish-speaking Sunni Muslim. There are also small communities of Maronites, Armenians, Latins (all groups that are today overwhelmingly Greek-speaking), and Roma. The island also hosts a large population of immigrants and foreign residents of diverse origin (e.g., Great Britain, the Philippines, Russia, Sri Lanka, and Turkey).

The Cyprus conflict has developed in three different phases (Jakobsson Hatay, 2004a). The first was the so-called Emergency during the last years of British rule (1955-1959). The second phase was the inter-communal troubles of the 1960s. The third and current phase came into play with the island's de facto partition in 1974 following the failed attempt by Greek ultra-nationalists to unite Cyprus with Greece, to which Turkey responded by launching a military intervention, seizing control of 37% of the island's territory.

In its early stages, the conflict manifested itself as a Greek-Cypriot anti-colonial revolt against Britain (1955-1959) with the concomitant demand for the unification of Cyprus with Greece (*enosis*). Due to Turkish-Cypriot (and Turkish) opposition to the Greek-Cypriot demands, to which later was added a counter-demand for the division of the island between Greece and Turkey (*taksim*), the conflict was never free of interethnic rivalry.[18] During the last year of the Greek-Cypriot revolt, interethnic violence escalated. This phase ended with an agreement between Greece and Turkey, signed also by Britain and representatives of the island's two contending communities, resulting in a settlement that ruled out ethno-nationalist demands and provided for the island's independence. Parts of the island's territory (158.5 square kilometers), hosting two military bases, remained under British sovereignty. Britain, Greece, and Turkey were designated co-guarantors of the settlement, bound to ensure the new republic's independence, security, and territorial integrity.

The second phase of the conflict began in December 1963 after only three years of independence. The breakdown of a precarious power-sharing arrangement—a cornerstone of the constitution—was followed by the outbreak of interethnic violence. The crisis left the Greek Cypriots in full control of the state machinery. The Turkish Cypriots moved on to establish a separate administration, a state-within-a-state, territorially anchored in patches of territory (enclaves) all over the island to which more than half of their numbers had taken refuge. In March 1964 a United Nations peacekeeping force was dispatched to the island (UNFICYP, United Nations Peace-Keeping Force in Cyprus). Low-level interethnic violence continued throughout the 1960s. The segregation process between the two communities was accentuated. Approximately of about 25,000 Turkish Cypriots (as well as a few hundred Greek Cypriots) were displaced. Greece dispatched troops to the island in reinforcement of Greek-Cypriot forces. For its part, Turkey threatened full-scale invasion and twice launched air attacks against Greek-Cypriot positions.

The third phase of the conflict began in July 1974 with the intervention of both Greece and Turkey. On July 15, the president of the Republic of Cyprus, Archbishop Makarios, was ousted in a Greek-supported coup aiming at uniting the island with Greece. Five days later, Turkey, citing her obligations as a guarantor power of the Republic of Cyprus and the precarious situation of the Turkish Cypriots amid the outbreak of intra-communal (Greek-Cypriot) violence in the wake of the coup, launched a military intervention that left the island divided. The intervention resulted in a large-scale exodus of Greek Cypriots (estimated 160,000) from the north. Almost all Turkish Cypriots in the southern part of the island (estimated 60,000) were relocated soon thereafter to areas under Turkish control, all but completing the island's ethno-territorial division. Altogether about one third of the Greek-Cypriot population and one half of the Turkish-Cypriot population were displaced as a result of the conflict. In 1983, a Turkish-Cypriot state—the Turkish Republic of Northern Cyprus—was declared, failing, however, to gain international recognition (except by Turkey). Although there has been no large-scale inter-communal violence since 1974, incidents along the UN-controlled buffer zone that separates the Greek-Cypriot and Turkish-Cypriot held areas have claimed occasional victims, most recently in 1996. The unresolved conflict has also remained a source of friction between Greece and Turkey. The island is heavily militarized, and Turkey retains a large troop presence in the northern part of the island.

Alongside the development toward increased ethnic and geographic separation, efforts have been undertaken with the aim of reuniting the two communities under one political administration. These efforts, carried out mostly under the auspices of the UN, have variously sought to bring about a comprehensive settlement in negotiations between the elite representatives of the two communities and, when this has proven difficult, engage the parties in confidence-building measures in order to prepare the ground for such a settlement. The results have so far been scant. In 1977, an agreement was reached to reunite the two administrations in a bi-communal, bi-zonal federation. However, disagreement pertaining to, among other issues, the degree of autonomy that should be accorded to the two zones—Turkish Cypriots pushing for a loose, decentralized structure and Greek Cypriots for a strong central government—has prevented its realization.

Although there has been minimal inter-communal violence since 1974, factors such as nationalist rhetoric and lack of appreciation for cultural differences (Anastasiou, 2002;

Anderson, 1995), combined with historical memory (Hadjipavlou-Trigeorgis, 1998), regional tensions (Bahcheli & Rizopoulos, 1996/1997; Joseph, 1997), major-power interference (O'Malley & Craig, 2001), and reluctance to change the status quo (Bölükbasi, 1998; Richmond, 1998) have prevented a negotiated settlement.

After the rejection in 1992 of a draft settlement proposal ("Set of Ideas") elaborated under the stewardship of UN Secretary General Boutros Boutros-Ghali, the two communities headed in opposite directions: the Greek Cypriots moving toward European integration and the Turkish Cypriots toward closer relations with Turkey. It was to take another decade before any substantive progress was made. A second UN draft proposal for a comprehensive settlement ("the Annan Plan"), presented to the parties in 2002, for the first time outlined in detail a political framework for reunification: a federation composed of two self-administered zones joined by a weak central government under a power-sharing regime. Parts of territory currently under Turkish-Cypriot administration were to be transferred to the Greek-Cypriot constituent state. A majority of those who had been displaced would gradually be able to return to their former residences and those who lost property as a result of the conflict were to have their property reinstated or be eligible for compensation. A major reduction of military forces and the establishment of a reconciliation commission also formed part of the proposal.

In April 2004, after a failure to enlist endorsement for the proposal from the leadership of either side, it was put to separate referenda and voted down by the Greek Cypriots, while being accepted by the Turkish Cypriots (Bahcheli, 2004; Heraclides, 2004; Jakobsson Hatay, 2004b). In May 2004, a divided Cyprus joined the European Union with the membership suspended for the Turkish-Cypriot northern zone.

The physical division of the island has affected nearly every aspect of people's lives, including the psychological condition of residents. Both communities carry a sense of injustice and victimization—for the Turkish Cypriots stemming from their experiences as a minority in a Greek-Cypriot dominated state in the 1960s, and for the Greek Cypriots from the events of 1974. The security guarantees they each have sought, including defense cooperation with Turkey and Greece, respectively, are for the other a source of insecurity.[19]

One of the most damaging aspects of the de facto ethnic partition of the island has been the cut-off of communication between ordinary citizens (Constantinou & Papadakis, 2001). After 1963, people no longer lived in mixed or adjacent villages, no longer encountered each other on a daily basis, and could not meet together or even exchange messages via telephone or mail service, accentuating the social divide that had always existed at some level between the two communities. Even before the inter-communal troubles there had never been close relationships between the two communities, but since the events of 1963–1964 and 1974 it has been impossible to form business partnerships, set up integrated classrooms, build joint community organizations, or establish interpersonal relationships. Until recently, when restrictions on freedom of movement were partially lifted (April 2003), not even casual encounters between members of the two communities took place without special arrangements.[20]

Although the separation of the two communities undoubtedly prevented inter-communal tension and violence, the lack of contact and communication also allowed each community to propagate myths and misconceptions more easily about the other community (Papadakis, 1998, 2005). Because of past actions by each side toward the other that brought disruption, displacement, loss of life, and other forms of suffering, both sides see themselves as victims of aggression, and neither side trusts the other. It is against this backdrop that intergroup dialogue efforts have been initiated and carried out in recent years.

Overview of Peacebuilding and Intergroup Dialogue Activities[21]

A substantial number of peacebuilding efforts involving intergroup dialogue have taken place in Cyprus over the years, starting as early as 1966 and becoming more intense in the early 1990s, when—encouraged also by the good-office mission of the United Nations Secretary General—a concerted effort was made by external third parties to promote cross-community dialogue. While much of the early peacebuilding work in Cyprus involved the assistance of outside third parties, it was usually a local initiative that was responsible for bringing in these experts from abroad.[22] There are still third parties involved with citizen peacebuilding work in Cyprus, but the preponderance of current activities are locally directed. In general, intergroup dialogue activities in Cyprus have taken the form of problem-solving workshops, conflict resolution training, interactive design sessions, and special seminars and dialogue groups.

Problem-solving workshops. The first problem-solving workshop directed toward the Cyprus conflict was held in 1966, when John Burton and his colleagues in London offered a five-day workshop in "controlled communication" (Burton, 1969). The workshop brought together high-level representatives from the two communities, resulting in an agreement in principle to return to negotiations that had stalled. It also communicated to the decision makers in each community insights that assisted in the resumption of settlement efforts (Mitchell, 1981). Some years later, in 1973, an informal seminar involving political leaders of the two communities was held in Rome (Talbot, 1977). Attempting to build on the success of this event, Lawrence Doob made plans to offer a workshop in Cyprus in July 1974, but the events of that period precluded such an activity (Doob, 1976, 1987). A locally organized workshop involving intellectuals, called Operation Locksmith, was held with Doob's participation in 1985. In 1979 and again in 1984, problem-solving workshops were conducted for community leaders by Kelman and his colleagues at Harvard University (Stoddard, 1986). Fisher held a series of four problem-solving workshops over a five-year period, with the two primary workshops focusing on the educational system in the two communities (Fisher, 1992, 1994, 1997).

The problem-solving workshops in Cyprus occurred in parallel with the growth of the field of conflict resolution, and they provided some of the case material that helped spawn the development of problem-solving methodologies. For the most part, these activities were periodic and small in number (fewer than 10 over a 25-year period). Nevertheless, they exposed a number of individuals in both communities to the notion of citizen peacebuilding, and thus they were important for future development of dialogue activities.

Conflict resolution training workshops. With impetus from the problem-solving workshops described above, a series of training workshops began in 1991 when Louise Diamond, a conflict resolution specialist from the Institute for Multi-Track Diplomacy (IMTD) in the United States, visited Cyprus at the invitation of members of the newly formed Peace Center in the Greek-Cypriot community. During this visit and on a subsequent trip later that year, Diamond met with members of both communities, as well as the international diplomatic community, to explore the need for training in conflict resolution and how funding could be secured for such efforts. Some of the people with whom she worked had taken part in the earlier problem-solving workshops conducted by Fisher. During follow-up visits, Diamond offered several public presentations, mini-workshops on conflict resolution, and eventually a full-day workshop in each community. A joint steering committee[23] was formed for purposes of promoting conflict resolution efforts in Cyprus, and plans were drawn up for offering more extensive training. Their plans were eventually realized in July 1993, when a group of 10 Greek Cypriots and 10 Turkish Cypriots went to Oxford, England, for a 10-day workshop facilitated by Louise Diamond and her associates (Diamond, 1997; Diamond & Fisher, 1995). This workshop proved to be pivotal in forming a strong and committed group of citizen peacebuilders who spanned the political spectrum in both communities and included people from various levels of society. Although its participants were subjected to widespread criticism and harsh personal attacks in the media, the event helped generate a sustained effort in peacebuilding activities that has continued to the present day.

Partly as a result of the success of this program, a number of training workshops were held in the summer of 1994, organized by the Cyprus Fulbright Commission (CFC) and conducted by the Cyprus Consortium, a group that consists of IMTD, the Conflict Management Group (CMG) of Harvard University, and National Training Laboratory (NTL) based in Virginia. Funded by the U.S. Agency for International Development and administered by CFC, several weeklong workshops were offered, including two that covered basic conflict resolution principles and skills and one that offered training for those interested in conducting local workshops. Additional workshops were held in the United States for policy leaders and for returning scholarship students. In subsequent years, more workshops conducted by the Cyprus Consortium were held in both Cyprus and in the United States, including an advanced training of trainers workshop and a bi-communal team that conducted an intractability study to examine why the conflict has been so difficult to resolve.

Interactive design sessions. An approach to intergroup dialogue that falls outside the conflict resolution mainstream has been applied in Cyprus over the past decade, starting in 1994 when one of the authors (Broome) held the position of Senior Fulbright Scholar in Cyprus. Initially, he carried out a series of planning and design workshops with a group of 30 Greek Cypriots and Turkish Cypriots, composed primarily of participants from the summer 1994 Cyprus Consortium workshops. Over a nine-month period Broome facilitated weekly sessions utilizing the Interactive Management (IM) design process (Broome & Keever, 1989). The IM design sessions focused on developing a strategy for peacebuilding efforts in Cyprus. During these sessions, the group progressed through three primary stages: (a) analysis of the current situation affecting peacebuilding activities in Cyprus, (b) building a collective vision for the future of peacebuilding efforts, and (c) developing a collaborative action agenda.[24]

Several important results emerged from this series of workshops. First, each community group produced a systems analysis of the obstacles to peacebuilding efforts in Cyprus. By exploring the relationships among various factors that inhibit efforts to build peace, the group was able to present a holistic picture of the situation confronting those who work for peace in each community. Their analyses were the source of much learning when the two community groups exchanged their products at their first bi-communal meeting, and they have been instructive to those outside the group interested in a deeper analysis of the situation. Second, the bi-communal group created a "collective vision statement" for future peacebuilding activities in Cyprus. They proposed goals for their efforts and explored the manner in which various goals support each other, resulting in a structure of goals that could guide their choices and their actions. They struggled together to understand and appreciate ideas that at first seemed incompatible with their own community's goals, and in the end they developed an inclusive product that addressed the needs and concerns of the collective whole. Third, the group developed a plan of activities that would guide their work during the next several years. They proposed a total of 242 separate possibilities for workshops, presentations, training programs, and other events that could make a difference in Cyprus. From this large set, they selected 15 projects for immediate implementation, holding a bi-communal *agora/bazaar* (activities fair) at which they recruited interested participants to join them in carrying out the selected projects.[25]

Special seminars and dialogue sessions. In addition to the workshops that employed the more structured dialogue methods utilized by problem-solving approaches, conflict resolution training, and interactive design sessions, there have been a number of less structured dialogue activities that focused on specific topics and issues. For example, several dialogue sessions held in the mid-1990s centered on the topic of federation. Participants were interested in learning more about various models of federal governing arrangements (e.g., the Belgian model or the Swiss model of federation) and in exchanging views about how federation might work in Cyprus. Later, as accession talks got under way for Cyprus's entry into the European Union, dialogue sessions were organized around the topic of EU membership and what this might mean for the future of the island and for the course of the conflict. Finally, Broome conducted, as part of his Fulbright residency, a series of dialogue sessions focused on the topic of "identity" in Cyprus. Participants identified and shared elements of the "Greek-Cypriot identity" and the "Turkish-Cypriot identity," and

they explored the ways in which identity issues both fuelled the conflict and offered potential for living together in the future (see Broome, 2004a).

Outcomes and Impact

As discussed earlier, evaluating individual initiatives or the cumulative impact of ongoing efforts like those in Cyprus is a complex endeavor, in part because of multiple determinants of the results. Since the mid-1990s, when the peacebuilding activities in Cyprus increased in scope and quantity, there have been significant changes at the political level, including several changes of leadership in both the Turkish-Cypriot and Greek-Cypriot communities, improvements in Turkish-Greek relations, and the recent (May 2004) entry of Cyprus into the European Union. Any progress (or lack thereof) on the peacebuilding front is affected by these and other factors, and they must be taken into consideration when discussing the overall contribution of intergroup dialogue initiatives.

With this in mind, we now turn our attention to identifying effects that can be attributed to peacebuilding initiatives in Cyprus (see Table 23.1).[26] As we will discuss below, while the impact of intergroup dialogue initiatives has occurred across all levels, the stronger influence has been at the *personal* and *relational* levels, where many of the individuals who took part in the dialogue activities were affected in significant and meaningful ways. The impact at the *societal* or *structural* level is weaker and less visible, due both to the influence of larger political and social forces and to the longer-term nature of change at this level.[27]

Providing opportunities for contact. As a starting point for our discussion, it should be noted that until the recent easing of restrictions on travel between north and south on the island (April 2003), the intergroup dialogue activities provided one of the only corridors through the physical barrier of the buffer zone. Without these activities, very little contact between ordinary citizens would have occurred across community lines over a 30-year period. This structural-level impact can be seen as one of the most tangible benefits of efforts to bring

Table 23.1   Outcomes and Impact of Intergroup Dialogue Initiatives in Cyprus

Personal Level	*Relational Level*	*Societal/Structural Level*
• Reducing the psychological burden from past events • Understanding the fears, hopes, and concerns of the other community	• Breaking the cycle of mutual blame and accusations • Creating a forum in which difficult issues can be discussed productively • Building potential for future partnerships	• Providing opportunities for contact • Providing a moderating voice in response to provocative events • Presenting an alternative scenario of the future • Influencing policymaking and the official peace process • Strengthening commitment of the international community to assist in brokering a settlement

individuals together across community lines. The contact made possible by organized dialogue sessions underpins the outcomes that we discuss next, starting with the personal-level impacts.

Reducing the psychological burden from past events. Memories of episodes that took place between 1955 and 1974 dominate the minds of many people in Cyprus. Those who lost family members; had to leave their homes and means of livelihood; witnessed massacres, bombings, rapes, and other acts of violence; or lived as refugees cannot easily lay aside mental images of these horrors. Even those of the younger generation, who did not directly experience such incidents, are confronted with them on a daily basis through stories from their parents; lessons in school; and constant renditions in the newspapers, radio programs, and television specials. The psychological burden imposed by images of the past weighs heavily on the minds of all Cypriots, creating a pathology that permeates society. The weight does not lessen with time, although it may take different forms. In addition, while the partition of the two communities in Cyprus brought a certain sense of safety and relief from the anxieties associated with cross-community contact (especially for the Turkish Cypriots, whose fewer numbers left them more vulnerable to discrimination and sometimes physical harm), it also created (for some) a sense of loss and incompleteness associated with the tear in the social fabric caused by the separation. The intergroup dialogue sessions provide one of the few means for healing the

chasm created by the ethnic division. The pain from past events cannot be erased, but perhaps it can be dealt with in a healthier manner by meeting individuals from the other community as fellow human beings and co-inhabitants of the island, by exchanging stories of the past and visions for the future, and by working together in building that future.

Understanding the fears, needs, and concerns of the other community. The buffer zone created both physical and psychological barriers between the two communities. Without contact, the fears, hopes, and concerns of each community are quickly lost to the other side. Intergroup dialogue opportunities provided a means to keep alive some understanding of the other community, opening for a small group of people a window into the world of the other. The insight that participants gain from such experiences might enable them to make more informed choices about the future, even if that future is "living together separately" on a divided island. In the absence of an agreed settlement, there may be no way to calm the fears of either side completely, but those involved in the intergroup dialogues personally were able to obtain a certain amount of relief through the human connections they made with the "enemy."

Breaking the cycle of mutual blame and accusations. One of the few places where the cycle of mutual blame and accusations that characterizes rhetoric across community lines has been broken in Cyprus is within some of the ongoing intergroup dialogue groups. These groups have encountered difficulties, at times experiencing the same mistrust that characterizes the larger society, but in many cases they have managed to work through their differences. Their work demonstrates that, if the proper setting is created and if individuals adopt a constructive attitude, it is possible to replace the cycle of blame and accusation with one that more closely resembles mutual trust, tolerance, and understanding. Showing that dialogue across the conflict divided is possible, these initiatives have thus set an example for others.

Creating a forum in which difficult issues can be discussed productively. No one would claim there is a shortage of discussions about political topics in Cyprus, but most of them tend to polarize the issues rather than help resolve them. When politicians, educators, journalists, church leaders, and taxi-drivers present their views on the core issues, their rhetoric is often positional posturing that elicits even stronger statements from the other side. Chances are small that any progress can be made in the general public's understanding of issues such as identity concerns, property matters, security, territorial adjustment and concomitant relocation, and the like—all of which need to be addressed in the framework of a political settlement—unless people have the chance to hear individuals from both sides talking *with* each other rather than *at* each other. The intergroup seminars that addressed these issues have shown that productive dialogue can occur on these topics, through which it is possible that progress might occur in identifying a set of options for dealing with concerns that drive the Cyprus problem.

Building potential for future partnerships. When in the future an agreement between the two communities is eventually signed and accepted by the people of Cyprus, opportunities will exist for business and institutional partnerships to be formed. Some cooperation, in the business sector for example, will be driven primarily by perceived potential for profit, but many of the efforts to develop relationships across community lines will require determined initiative by individuals who understand their importance, who are aware of the potential

difficulties, and who are committed to their success. Participants from the intergroup dialogues, especially those with significant experience over the years, may be the individuals best situated to promote true partnerships on the island. They have the necessary contacts with the other community, and they are at least minimally sensitive to the concerns of the other community. In addition, they are also aware of some of the issues that might cause misunderstanding and conflict, and they possess at least some of the skills for dealing with it. Intergroup dialogue initiatives have provided opportunities to learn to talk about divisive issues in ways that avoid unintentional provocation.[28]

Providing a moderating voice in response to provocative events. In August 1996, a series of violent clashes took place in the buffer zone in which Greek-Cypriot motorcyclists rallied under the cry "Ride to Kyrenia" (a picturesque harbor on the northern coast), resulting in the death of two Greek-Cypriot protestors. The events produced an outcry in both communities and the tension built rapidly, nearly leading to military clashes and possibly all-out war. The rhetoric on both sides was uncompromising. The peacebuilding network provided one of the few arenas where there were attempts to understand why the events had spiraled out of control, how they might be perceived by the other community, and how the one-sided rhetoric was hurting the cause of each side as well as the image of Cyprus in the outside world. Although these discussions could not take place in a bi-communal setting at that time, the individuals and groups with bi-communal experience met together within their own communities and provided a moderating voice in response to an otherwise extreme and narrow discussion of blame and accusations. Their voice was not one that received major coverage in the press, but in a small way it may have helped pull Cyprus back from a course toward possible war.

Presenting an alternative scenario of the future. A common theme in many discussions about the Cyprus conflict is fear of the future. Some of these fears center on concerns about the possibility for confrontations such as those that took place in 1996, others on the possibility of armed conflict between Greece and Turkey. For the Greek Cypriots, the presence on the island of Turkish troops constitutes a source of insecurity, while the island's partition is perceived as a violation of human rights. The large Greek-Cypriot military force is a source of concern for the Turkish Cypriots, as is the prospect of any solution that would reduce their self-determination and fail to acknowledge their equal status within a renewed partnership arrangement. The fact that a few people are meeting and working together across the divide holds out the potential that the coming years might bring a settlement that would prevent both another war and the domination of one side over the other. Although there is no hard evidence to support its validity, it seems reasonable to suggest that in addition to the effects on individuals participating in the dialogue sessions, the existence of such activities provides the larger population of Cyprus with an alternative future to consider. Exposure to the other side and insights thus gained also enable participants to challenge simplistic or erroneous notions about the other side, in this way contributing to a more informed debate on options for the organization of intergroup relations in the future, including political frameworks.[29]

Influencing policymaking and the official peace process. Although there is little hard evidence to support a claim that the dialogue groups have influenced policymaking and the official peace process in any significant ways, there are two ways in which such influence may have taken place. First, several of the participants in intergroup dialogue initiatives have come from or moved on to positions of political leadership. For political and community leaders the opportunity to engage in meaningful dialogue with their counterparts may have contributed to the confidence to make proposals for cooperation that went beyond what had been official policy for decades.[30] Second, some long-term participants in dialogue sessions contend that the recent UN draft proposal for a political settlement, referred to as the Annan Plan (United Nations, 2003), includes ideas that were often discussed in the intergroup seminars and workshops in which they took part. Some of the individuals who played a role in drafting the plan had attended one or more of these workshops,

and they had access to reports from other bi-communal groups. Although the ideas that found their way into the plan undoubtedly came from many sources, and we must interpret such claims with caution, it is possible that proposals developed in the dialogue groups over the years influenced the thinking of those who developed the United Nations plan for a settlement in Cyprus.

Strengthening commitment of the international community to assist in brokering a settlement. The lack of progress in negotiations in Cyprus over the years has left many members of the international community discouraged about prospects for settlement. As dozens of special delegations, special envoys, fact-finding trips, "final push" efforts, shuttle talks, proximity talks, secluded negotiations, and other attempts to bring the leaders of the two communities toward a settlement proved fruitless, many third-party negotiators and diplomatic personnel developed a sense of hopelessness about the possibility of reaching a viable agreement. Especially during the 1996–1997 period, when the number of people involved in various intercommunal events was at its height, the diplomatic community often talked about them as offering a "breath of fresh air" amid the seemingly unchanging rhetoric of the officials and the lack of movement within the official peace process. While the international commitment to negotiations in Cyprus is primarily a function of higher-level political and strategic forces, it can be argued that peacebuilding initiatives may have contributed in some small way to more positive assessments by locally stationed diplomats about the prospects for fruitful negotiations. To the extent that "reports from the field" by local diplomats were taken into account by U.S., UN, and EU policymakers, the peacebuilding work may have helped make possible continuing attempts by the international community to broker talks between the two sides.

Limitations

Although the experiences from Cyprus illustrate some of the roles that intergroup dialogue can play in creating conditions conducive for peacebuilding, they also serve to illustrate some of the limitations. Some of these limitations may be particular to the specific case of Cyprus and the ways in which intergroup dialogue approaches have been applied there. Due to the fact that the two communities have different mother tongues and very few people command the language of the other community, intergroup dialogue necessitates the use of a foreign language, usually English. Even though this may serve an equalizing function (and may thus be far preferable to the use of one or the other of the local languages) it also introduces a measure of awkwardness in the encounter. More important, it excludes from participation those whose command of the third language is inadequate. Although English is widely spoken in Cyprus, which in the past formed part of the British Empire, the language barrier limits participation by substantial sections of the communities.

A related aspect of the intergroup dialogue sessions in Cyprus is the important and at times dominant role played by third parties from English-speaking countries (the U.S. in particular) as organizers and facilitators of intergroup dialogue initiatives. Although the conditions for intergroup dialogue in Cyprus have been better than those in many conflict situations around the world, notably due to the absence of violence, they are also in some ways more challenging than those faced in other conflicts. The heavy restrictions imposed until recently on freedom of movement limited intergroup dialogue opportunities to *created*, and in some sense of the word, artificial contact situations; "bi-communal islets" were created, very different from and with limited interaction with the otherwise segregated communities. The partial lifting of the restrictions since 2003 has created a dramatically different environment for inter-group dialogue and for peacebuilding than that which existed when the above-discussed initiatives took place.

Other limitations encountered in Cyprus may have less to do with the particularities of the Cyprus case and may be of a more general nature. One example relates to difficulties pertaining to the transfer of change. The above analysis shows that individuals can engage in productive dialogue across conflict divide but also that changing relations at the community level may be a challenge of a different order.

Another, and related, example points to the political constraints that follow from a lack of progress in the official peace process and that also impose limitations on peacebuilding at the citizen level. In Cyprus, the effects of these constraints on peacebuilding initiatives have been very tangible indeed, manifested both in opposition from "outside" (from nonparticipants and from authorities) and in opposition from participants themselves to engage in activities that may have challenged too strongly the boundaries of the "officially" permissible.

Our case study suggests two lessons of general relevance: First, although intergroup dialogue, in our view, does have a role to play as a peacebuilding strategy in divided societies, it is important to bear in mind that such initiatives are not— and should not be, if they are to have any impact—isolated from the conflict dynamics at large. While the ultimate aim is to change these dynamics, the dynamics of the conflict will at the same time act as constraints and impose limitations on what is realistically feasible. Second, and related to the first point, the Cyprus experiences underscore the importance of simultaneous progress at the official peace-making level if peacebuilding is to have any impact on the overall situation. Until a decision has been taken at the official level to end the conflict, unofficial intergroup dialogue initiatives are likely to provoke opposition from "officials" unwilling to shed the prerogative of setting the agenda for dialogue across the divide for fear that their positions be undermined. In the absence of progress at the official dialogue arena, citizen dialogue initiatives may at best have only limited impact on the conflict situation, primarily restricted to participants themselves, and may at worst contribute to polarization between and/or within the parties.

DIRECTIONS FOR FUTURE RESEARCH AND PRACTICE

Important works in the field of conflict resolution over the recent 12-year period by scholars such as Sandole and van der Merwe (1993), Zartman and Rasmussen (1997), Deutsch and Coleman (2000), Kriesberg (2001), Cheldelin, Druckman, and Fast (2003), and Fisher (2005) show that the theory and practice of intergroup dialogue in protracted conflicts has matured in the four decades since Burton's introduction of his controlled communication problem-solving approach to third-party intervention. There is growing acknowledgment that various approaches to dialogue have an important role to play in the larger work of peacemaking (see Crocker, Hampson, & Aall, 1999). Nevertheless, our review in this chapter highlights the rather abstract nature of current work. There is a relative absence of empirical research, both in relation to individual initiatives and in relation to specific conflicts. The complexities involved, together with the need to take into account context-specific conditions, may never allow for a definite answer as to what works, when, and how. Our understanding of the role of intergroup dialogue as a peacebuilding strategy would nevertheless benefit from more systematic empirical studies, both in-depth case studies and/or comparative analysis of several instances (initiatives as well as conflict situations).

Empirical work however, requires theoretical guidance . Efforts to identify intergroup dialogue influence mechanisms and theoretical linkages between different approaches, and between dialogue at different levels, have only begun. While current work has provided us with an understanding of the challenges of peacebuilding in divided societies at a general level, we need to break the complexity down into manageable parts to examine it more closely. The aim is not to reduce the complexity but to improve our ability to address it; complexity, it has to be remembered, is partly conditional on the state of our theory. We believe there are three areas that are ripe for both theoretical and practical development: the *linkage* between intergroup dialogue practices and official diplomacy; the relation of *culture* and dialogue processes; and the role of *communication* in dialogue processes.

The *linkage* question is certainly not a new one, but it has become increasingly important as conflict resolution efforts have expanded. As discussed earlier, proponents of problem-solving workshops such as Kelman and Fisher have long made a strong case for the complementarity of unofficial interventions with formal peace processes, and contributions by Lederach and Saunders helped expand our understanding of

the need for a wider conceptualization of peace processes. No one makes the argument that citizen dialogue initiatives should substitute for official negotiations, but it is commonly understood (within the conflict resolution field) that such work supplements and in some cases is essential to the creation of a stable peace. While frameworks such as those provided by Lederach (1997) are helpful in understanding the need for all levels of society to be involved in peace processes, there are few specific recommendations for *how* to create and foster this linkage so that it is both functional and durable. As our case study indicates, the relationship between the different levels may also (in reality) be less harmonious than current approaches assume, particularly if they fail to progress in tandem. We need both further conceptual development in this area and specific research that will test the assumptions of the complementarity argument.

The *culture* question has also been considered by numerous scholars and practitioners. Widely recognized as a factor in conflict, cultural differences can play a dominant role in determining the course of the influence, and they can have an impact on interaction and perception in subtle ways. Michelle Lebaron (2003b) sums up the relationship between culture and conflict in the following way:

> Intractable conflicts like the Israeli-Palestinian conflict or the India-Pakistan conflict over Kashmir are not just about territorial, boundary, and sovereignty issues—they are also about acknowledgement, representation, and legitimization of different identities and ways of living, being, and making meaning. (Culture and Conflict section, para. 2)

While there are several books that deal with culture and conflict (Avruch, 1998; Avruch, Black, & Scimecca, 1998; Gudykunst, 2003; Ting-Toomey & Oetzel, 2001), there has historically been surprisingly little attention given to questions of culture by those who pioneered the problem-solving and other approaches to dialogue. Even though culture is dealt with more explicitly by contemporary scholars (e.g., Lederach, 1996), we believe there is still insufficient in-depth discussion of culture and conflict in our research, training, and curriculum.

There are two areas in particular where we need to give more attention to the question of culture. First, cultural assumptions of current practice need to be examined, as does the applicability of transfer of approaches across different cultural contexts. Until now, most dialogue methodologies applied in protracted conflicts have been developed in the United States or other Western countries. Third-party interventions, based on Western political experiences, are sometimes criticized as attempts to export communication values that promote a particular form of democratic input into decision making. The Western bias of negotiation and conflict resolution research has been recognized by a number of scholars (see Avruch, 1998; Cohen, 1991; Druckman, 1997; Kimmel, 1994; Lebaron, 2003a; Lederach, 1996; Ting-Toomey & Oetzel, 2001; Weldon & Jehn, 1995). The approaches that we have reviewed are notable for being in general consensual, both in their assumptions and in their prescriptions. The belief in the feasibility of win-win solutions and the ability of dialogue to produce consensual outcomes are but two examples. Such examinations are all the more important as the field has developed from within a very narrow cultural context, which is, moreover, not one of protracted intergroup conflict. It is not coincidental or the result of selectivity on our part that our review has identified the average intergroup dialogue scholar-practitioner as being a male, middle-aged, White Anglo-Saxon.

Second, and related to the above, is the need to examine a wider range of approaches to conflict resolution (see Oetzel, Arcos, Mabizela, Weinman, & Zhang, Chapter 20 in this volume). Most societies have developed methods of dialogue that were used traditionally for resolving disputes at the local level (see Augsburger, 1992), and while times and conditions have changed significantly, affecting their direct application to contemporary problems, recent research shows that much can be learned from studying traditional techniques for conflict resolution. Irani (2000), for example, explored non-Western modes and rituals of conflict reduction in Arab-Islamic societies, and Offiong (1997) analyzed the methods used by the Ibibio of Nigeria. Adeleke (2004) examined five Yorùbá myths that offer lessons that can be applied to the conflict resolution process in general. Other works, such as those by Abu-Nimer (1999) and Bar-On (2000), show how techniques like storytelling can be used as forms of dialogue. Zartman (2000), in an edited book, provided a number of case studies from various regions of Africa, examining both similarities and differences among these methods, and suggesting how they could be integrated within modern negotiation and diplomacy strategies.

While we need additional studies that examine indigenous approaches to dialogue and their application to protracted conflicts, we must steer clear of the tendency to romanticize traditional societies, and we must avoid promoting unrealistic expectations about the utilization of traditional practices within contemporary society. There are many difficulties and complexities inherent in attempts to transfer methods and techniques, whether the transfer is from Western society to other parts of the world or from indigenous approaches to Western political systems. The field is in need of more research and analysis that examines how traditional techniques can make a practical difference in peacebuilding.

The *communication* question is one that has not received as much attention in the field of conflict resolution, even though one of the core aims of intergroup dialogue is to promote more effective discourse among the participants. From a communication perspective, it is through interaction that human beings create their world (Berger & Luckmann, 1966; Pearce & Littlejohn, 1997), and when dialogue is examined from this perspective, how we communicate becomes especially significant. It is through the form of our dialogue with others that we create, as well as reflect, the differences and commonalities that exist within the conflict system, and communication becomes a form of action that separates or brings people together, that tears down relationships or builds coalitions, that magnifies differences or helps people discover common interests, that increases distrust or enhances confidence in one another, that furthers contempt or demonstrates respect, that polarizes the conversation or brings tolerance for diverse views. Communication is the medium through which participants create a common culture and shared understandings that go beyond simply understanding where the other is coming from or how the other views the situation (see Broome, 1993, for a discussion of relational empathy in conflict situations). Communication is the key to helping participants in dialogue groups create a collective vision or develop an agreeable plan of action. It is the mechanism through which participants create a peace culture within their group, as well as the primary instrument for transforming their society into a peace system that values dialogue (in its various cultural forms) as a means to settle disputes.

In part, the lack of attention to communication variables in conflict studies is due to the paucity of communication scholars with a focus on peacebuilding in the international context. Despite the impressively wide range of settings in which communication scholars conduct research (as evidenced by the chapters in this volume, which address interpersonal, family, organizational, community, environmental, media, crisis communication, and training and other settings), there is not an abundance of activity centered on protracted conflicts in international settings. While there are exceptions (Ellis & Maoz, 2002; Maoz & Ellis, 2001), our communication journals carry surprisingly few articles that address what we described at the beginning of this chapter as "some of the most important political processes in today's world; namely, efforts to prevent or bring about an end to armed conflicts." Yet, the study of communication is crucial to the study of conflict and its resolution, especially in the arena of intergroup dialogue. The challenge for communication scholars is to find ways to bring the insights we have gained from the study of other contexts into the examination of protracted conflicts.

CONCLUSION

In this chapter, we have outlined the development of approaches to intergroup dialogue as a peacebuilding strategy for divided societies and presented at least a glimpse into the diversity of approaches that exist. We have also discussed some problems associated with assessment of these initiatives, which, we noted, are undertaken, after all, with the assumption that they will promote peace. Our case study of intergroup dialogue initiatives in Cyprus enabled us to discuss and assess their role in a particular context, while also extracting some suggestions for the reverse relationship. Along the way we have noted some of the strengths and weaknesses of the field, both in terms of scholarship and in terms of practice, hopefully contributing to what has been an inherent objective of the field from the very beginning. Finally we have presented some suggestions for further development of the scholar-practitioner field of intergroup dialogue and peacebuilding.

Perhaps it goes without saying that protracted conflicts are complex phenomena. Incompatible values, incongruous assumptions, irreconcilable outlooks, and divergent perceptions can make conversation difficult in any situation, but when groups have been torn apart by conflict, it is even more problematical for them to discuss the issues that divide them. They have to deal with different interpretations of facts and events, widely varying views of history, feelings of injustice, and convictions that the other is to blame for the conflict. More often than not, discourse breaks down into destructive debate, characterized by defensive postures, failure to listen, personal attacks, accusations, and a focus on one's own status as a victim. Rhetoric is often directed toward making impassioned statements about the issues, and rarely does either side learn much about how the other sees the situation. The atmosphere is competitive, and effective communication is blocked by prejudice, misunderstanding, and fear. As a result, tension is heightened, positions become increasingly polarized, people are unreceptive to new ideas, and the relationship between the parties further deteriorates.

The methods of intergroup dialogue discussed in this chapter are, without doubt, important contributions to our continuing search for ways to deal effectively with the daunting situation described above. We have learned from past examples that official negotiations are usually not sufficient to produce a viable settlement that can be accepted by the people involved and implemented effectively, and those of us involved as third parties working with citizen peacebuilding groups are confident that intergroup dialogue is a necessary part of a comprehensive approach to transforming conflicts. At the same time, we must keep in mind, as Ropers (2003) reminds us, that the ultimate concerns of most disputes are conflicts of interest and the struggle for power and influence, rather than solely differences in perceptions, opinions, or cultural norms and values. Thus, we must view intergroup dialogue as more than a means for promoting improved communication. We must contextualize it as part of a larger peace process that requires sustained effort on multiple levels, affected by a wide array of political forces and strategic concerns, many of which are beyond our ability to impact, even with the most enlightened forms of dialogue.

NOTES

1. Unless otherwise stated, the conflict data are based on information from the Uppsala Conflict Data Program (UCDP) at the Department of Peace and Conflict Research, Uppsala University, Sweden. The project monitors the development of armed conflicts globally and presents its findings annually. The project registers only conflicts in which at least one party is the government of a state and where the use of force has resulted in at least 25 battle-related deaths in any single year. For some recent reports, see Eriksson and Wallensteen (2004) and Harbom (2004). The data are also available at http://www.pcr.uu.se.

2. Much against what conventional wisdom holds, the predominance of intra-state conflicts is not a recent phenomenon; this has been the case for the whole post–World War II period. Fearon and Laitin (2003) estimate that between 1945 and 1999 there were about five times as many civil wars as inter-state wars (25 compared to 127) that killed at least 1,000 people. In what they claim to be is a conservative estimate, civil wars also claimed about five times the death toll of inter-state wars: 16.2 million.

3. It should be noted that *intergroup* refers to the saliency of group identification in the encounter: An inter-personal encounter between two individuals can thus constitute an instance of intergroup contact (Sherif, 1966).

4. It would a mistake, however, to attribute the causes of these conflicts to ethnicity itself. *Ethnic conflicts* should be seen as a descriptive but not explanatory term; describing, that is, the characteristics along which political mobilization occurs. These characteristics may be only minor or even, as

constructivists propose, invented. Nevertheless, the process of (ethno)-political mobilization inevitably has the effect of solidifying intergroup boundaries, particularly if it leads to intergroup violence.

5. In Cyprus, for example, Greek Cypriots in the past justified aspirations for the island's unification with Greece with references to the "fact" that the Turkish Cypriots on the island were in reality Greeks, who in the past had been "Islamicized." Turkish Cypriots, for their part, used blood sample studies to "prove" that Greek Cypriots were not Greeks at all, as they themselves believed, but in reality of Anatolian descent—and hence "Turks." The assumption was that once these delusions were shed, and the "other" had been made to realize that they were not after all a distinct people, the conflict would cease to exist. More recently, DNA analysis has been used to underpin Greek-Cypriot arguments in support of the commonality between Greek Cypriots and Turkish Cypriots and their separateness from Greeks and Turks.

6. Long taboo also in academic circles, the idea of partition has in recent years been the focus of renewed interest. The arguments for partition as an option of last resort are laid by Kaufmann (1996, 1998) and countered by, for example, Kumar (1997), Kaufman (2001), and Sambanis (2000).

7. After Iraq's invasion of Kuwait in 1991, there was no other major interstate conflict until war broke out between Ethiopia and Eritrea in 1998. In 2003, there were only two interstate conflicts: the conflict between India and Pakistan over Kashmir and the U.S.-led coalition versus Iraq.

8. The contact hypothesis was developed within the context of race relations in the United States in the 1940s and 1950s where it played an important role in shaping desegregation policies (Brewer & Miller, 1984). It has also informed policies in other multi-ethnic societies, among them Israel (Amir, 1969) and Northern Ireland (Knox & Hughes, 1996), as well as numerous international exchange programs.

9. The cooperation hypothesis that forms the basis of Wedge's approach is usually attributed to a series of experiments by Sherif (1966), in which researchers introduced cooperative tasks involving superordinate goals, that is, goals that have "a compelling appeal for members of each group, but that neither group can achieve without participation of the other" (p. 89). While single incidents of cooperation proved insufficient to eliminate intergroup hostilities, the cumulative effects of a series of joint activities did have a significant influence on intergroup attitudes.

Sherif's results have been supported by others, which has led to suggestions that the contact hypothesis be renamed the cooperation hypothesis (van Oudenhoven, 1989).

10. It should be stressed, however, as Kelman (1993) reminds us, that these terms should not be conceived of as fixed groupings but rather as orientations whose actual base in reality may very well display a variation over time.

11. Fisher builds on Johan Galtung's (1975) three approaches to peace: peacemaking, peacebuilding, and peacekeeping.

12. Rothman also talks about "positional dialogue," where the parties articulate their respective views as positions and attitudes that merely require acknowledgment. As in a parliamentary debate, communication serves primarily to score points, as one argument is set against the other. This type of discussion is not considered part of the usual dialogue tradition.

13. In order to alleviate the re-entry problem, Burton once suggested that, "It is healthy if those opposite each other at the table leave with as much antagonism and prejudice as when they came! Agreement is then on some functional basis that satisfies the interests, needs and goals as perceived by the respective parties" (Burton, 1986, p. 108). An alternative approach to alleviating the re-entry problem is, of course, to prepare the ground for accommodation through the creation of a "peace constituency" (Jakobsson Hatay, in press; Lederach, 1995).

14. Saunders (2003), who himself takes credit for coining the "peace process" concept in the 1970s (Saunders, 1991), attributes the origin of the notion of a "multilevel peace process" to participants in the Inter-Tajik Dialogue (see below).

15. Saunders (1999b) cites two exceptions when top leaders/negotiators played a main role in actually changing relationships. The first is President Anwar al-Sadat's 1977 visit to Jerusalem, unprecedented for an Arab leader, where, in an address to the Knesset, he talked about the human dimensions of the relationship between the two peoples, identifying the "psychological barrier" as constituting 70% of the problem. The other is Mikhail Gorbachev's speech to the UN General Assembly in 1988 where he, with particular reference to the American people, endorsed "people's diplomacy" initiatives and their contributions to mutual understanding.

16. We have each been involved with the design and facilitation of dozens of dialogue initiatives in Cyprus over the past decade, and we have also co-facilitated several dialogue workshops involving Greek and Turkish Cypriots that took place outside Cyprus.

17. For overviews of the history of Cyprus and some important contributions to the vast literature on the Cyprus conflict, see Attalides (1979), Bahcheli (1990), Bryant (2004), Calotychos (1998), Crawshaw (1978), Denktash (1988), Ehrlich (1974), Gazioglu (1990), Joseph (1997), Markides (1977), Necatigil (1993), Patrick (1976), Richmond (1998), Volkan (1979), and Xydis (1973).

18. It is important to note that the conflict in all its phases also has had an element of intra-communal division and rivalry, particularly severe on the Greek-Cypriot side (Loizos, 1974; Mavratsas, 1997; Papadakis, 2003). In the Greek-Cypriot community, internal divisions based on an ideological cleavage between left- and right-wing elements, onto which was superimposed different notions of nationalism, on several occasions manifested themselves in violence, most notably during the anti-colonial struggle and in the early 1970s.

19. For overviews of the current situation, see Anastasiou (2000, 2002), Barkey and Gordon (2001/2002), Cockburn (2004), Savvides (2002), and Tocci (2004). A wealth of material can be found at www.cyprus-conflict.net. In Turkey, the Turkish Economic and Social Studies Foundation (TESEV), http://www.tesev.org.tr, publishes ongoing reports about Cyprus, while in Greece, the Hellenic Foundation for European and Foreign Policy (ELIAMEP), http://www.eliamep.gr, produces occasional papers about the Cyprus conflict.

20. The decision by the Turkish-Cypriot authorities to partially lift the restrictions on movement across the buffer zone greatly expanded the opportunity for visits, meetings, and other face-to-face communications. The effects of this move have not been adequately analyzed, and at the time of this writing it is too early to say how it will affect overall relations between the two communities.

21. This section is based on Broome (1998). It should be noted that this is not a comprehensive account of all peacebuilding activities in the Cyprus conflict, and that the overview focuses mainly on activities that have taken place in Cyprus itself. In addition, numerous peacebuilding initiatives involving Greek Cypriots and Turkish Cypriots have been organized in other countries, particularly, but not exclusively, during times when the political situation

has prevented on-the-island contacts across the divide.

22. A major player in sponsoring these initiatives, especially during the period 1990–1997, was the Cyprus Fulbright Commission, an American-based educational exchange program. Various diplomatic entities have also been instrumental in organizing and funding bi-communal programs, including the American Embassy, the British High Commissioner, the European Commission, the Slovak Embassy, and others, in particular the United Nations mission in Cyprus. In recent years, foreign academic institutions, such as the International Peace Research Institute, Oslo (PRIO), and the Department of Peace and Conflict Research, Uppsala University, have also been among the "third parties" involved. The main funders of cross-community projects has been the United States and the United Nations Office for Project Services (UNOPS). The European Commission has also provided funding for some projects, particularly in recent years.

23. This group later became known as the Bi-communal Steering Committee. It served in the capacity of advisor for development of further conflict resolution activities, and it eventually obtained an office in the buffer zone for its meetings. It was recognized in one UN report for the valuable role it played in promoting better relations between the two communities.

24. These activities are described more extensively in Broome (1997, 2004b).

25. A full report of these workshop activities is available, containing a copy of all the group products. Contact the Fulbright Commission in Nicosia, Cyprus, or online at http://www.fulbright.org.cy.

26. Portions of this section are adapted from Broome (in press).

27. It is important to keep in mind that transformative changes at the societal and structural levels are much more difficult and can sometimes take decades. It is probably unrealistic to expect major changes in the relatively short time period since dialogue activities became widespread in Cyprus (less than 10 years). Although it is difficult, at this point in time, to gauge the degree and depth of influence at the structural level, we believe that more should be done to strengthen this connection.

28. For an experience of the need in intergroup encounters to invent a "new language" in order to avoid the provocations triggered by the official rhetoric, see Papadakis (2005).

29. In one of the few assessments of the conflict resolution initiatives in Cyprus, Richmond (2004) argues that although there is no empirical evidence to indicate that conflict resolution processes have had a direct impact on developments in the official negotiation process, they have contributed in meaningful ways to the emergence of a peace process on the island. He suggests, for example, that the "debates" that take place between members of the two communities in workshop settings "have become part of the public consciousness and have played a role in developing an awareness that there may be alternative paths out of the conflict" (p. 210).

30. Personal communication with prominent representatives of the Turkish-Cypriot community indicates this to have been the case.

REFERENCES

Abu-Nimer, M. (1999). *Dialogue, conflict resolution, and change: Arab-Jewish encounters in Israel.* New York: State University of New York Press.

Adeleke, D. A. (2004). Lessons from Yorùbá mythology. *Journal of Asian and African Studies, 39*(3), 179–191.

Agger, I. (2001). Psychosocial assistance during ethnopolitical warfare in the former Yugoslavia. In D. Chirot & M. E. P. Seligman (Eds.), *Ethnopolitical warfare: Causes, consequences, and possible solutions* (pp. 305–318). Washington, DC: American Psychological Association.

Allport, G. (1995). *The nature of prejudice.* Reading, MA: Addison-Wesley.

Amir, Y. (1969). Contact hypothesis in ethnic relations. *Psychological Bulletin, 71*(5), 319–342.

Anastasiou, H. (2000). Negotiating the solution to the Cyprus problem: From impasse to post-Helsinki hope. *Cyprus Review, 12*(1), 11–33.

Anastasiou, H. (2002). Communication across conflict lines: The case of ethnically divided Cyprus. *Journal of Peace Research, 39*(5), 581–596.

Anderson, B. (1995). *Imagined communities: Reflection on the origin and spread of nationalism.* London: Verso.

Arnett, R. C. (1981). Toward a phenomenological dialogue. *Western Journal of Speech Communication, 45,* 201–212.

Attalides, M. A. (1979). *Cyprus: Nationalism and international politics.* Edinburgh: Q Press.

Augsburger, D. W. (1992). *Conflict mediation across cultures: Pathways and patterns*. Louisville, KY: Westminster/John Knox Press.

Avruch, K. (1998). *Culture and conflict resolution*. Washington: United States Institute of Peace Press.

Avruch, K., Black, P. W., & Scimecca, J. A. (Eds.). (1998). *Conflict resolution: Cross-cultural perspectives*. London: Praeger.

Azar, E. E. (1983). The theory of protracted social conflict and the challenge of transforming conflict situations. In D. A. Zinnes (Ed.), *Conflict processes and the breakdown of international systems* (Monograph Series in World Affairs, Vol. 20, pp. 81–99). Denver, CO: University of Denver, Graduate School of International Studies.

Azar, E. E. (1986). Protracted international conflicts: Ten propositions. In E. E. Azar & J. W. Burton (Eds.), *International conflict resolution. Theory and practice* (pp. 28–39). Sussex, UK: Wheatsheaf Books.

Azar, E. E. (1990). *The management of protracted social conflict: Theory and cases*. Aldershot, UK: Dartmouth.

Azar, E. E., & Farah, N. (1981). The structure of inequalities and protracted social conflict: A theoretical framework. *International Interactions, 7*(4), 317–335.

Bahcheli, T. (1990). *Greek-Turkish relations since 1955*. Boulder, CO: Westview.

Bahcheli, T. (2004). Saying yes to EU accession: Explaining the Turkish Cypriot referendum. *Cyprus Review, 16*(2), 55–65.

Bahcheli, T., & Rizopoulos, N. X. (1996/1997). The Cyprus impasse: What next? *World Policy Journal, 13*(4), 27–39.

Barkey, H. J., & Gordon, P. H. (2001/2002, Winter). Cyprus: The predictable crisis. *National Interest,* pp. 83–93.

Bar-On, D. (Ed.). (2000). *Bridging the gap: Storytelling as a way to work through political and collective hostilities*. Hamburg: Korber-Stiftung.

Baxter, L. A., & Montgomery, B. M. (1996). *Relating: Dialogues and dialectics*. New York: Guilford.

Berger, P., & Luckmann, T. (1966). *The social construction of reality: A treatise in the sociology of knowledge*. Garden City, NY: Doubleday.

Bertram, E. (1995). Reinventing governments: The promise and perils of United Nations peace building. *Journal of Conflict Resolution, 39*(5), 387–418.

Bohm, D. (1996). *On dialogue*. London: Routledge.

Bölükbasi, S. (1998). The Cyprus dispute and the United Nations: Peaceful non-settlement between 1954 and 1996. *International Journal of Middle East Studies, 30,* 411–434.

Boutros-Ghali, B. (1992). *An agenda for peace: Preventive diplomacy, peacemaking and peacekeeping, a/47/277–s/24111*. New York: United Nations.

Brewer, M. B., & Miller, N. (1984). Beyond the contact hypothesis: Theoretical perspectives on desegregation. In M. B. Brewer & N. Miller (Eds.), *Groups in contact: The psychology of desegregation* (pp. 281–302). Orlando, FL: Academic Press.

Broome, B. J. (1993). Managing differences in conflict resolution. In D. J. D. Sandole & H. van der Merwe (Eds.), *Conflict resolution theory and practice: Integration and application* (pp. 95–111). Manchester, UK: Manchester University Press.

Broome, B. J. (1997). Designing a collective approach to peace: Interactive design and problem-solving workshops with Greek Cypriot and Turkish Cypriot communities in Cyprus. *International Negotiation, 2*(3), 381–407.

Broome, B. J. (1998). Overview of conflict resolution activities in Cyprus: Their contribution to the peace process. *Cyprus Review, 10*(1), 47–66.

Broome, B. J. (2004a). Building a shared future across the divide: Identity and conflict in Cyprus. In M. Fong & R. Chuang (Eds.), *Communicating ethnic and cultural identity* (pp. 275–294). Lanham, MD: Rowman & Littlefield.

Broome, B. J. (2004b). Reaching across the dividing line: Building a collective vision for peace in Cyprus. *International Journal of Peace Research, 41*(2), 191–209.

Broome, B. J. (in press). *Building bridges across the Green Line: A guide to intercultural communication in Cyprus*. Nicosia, Cyprus: United Nations Bicommunal Development Program.

Broome, B. J., & Keever, D. B. (1989). Next generation group facilitation: Proposed principles. *Management Communication Quarterly, 3*(1), 107–127.

Bryant, R. (2004). *Imagining the modern: The cultures of nationalism in Cyprus*. London: I. B. Tauris.

Buber, M. (1970). *I and thou*. New York: Scribner.

Burton, J. W. (1969). *Conflict and communication: The use of controlled communication in international relations*. London: Macmillan.

Burton, J. W. (1986). The procedures of conflict resolution. In E. E. Azar & J. W. Burton (Eds.), *International conflict resolution: Theory and practice* (pp. 92–116). Sussex, UK: Wheatsheaf Books.

Burton, J. W. (1987). *Resolving deep-rooted conflict: A handbook*. Lanham, MD: University Press of America.

Burton, J. W. (1990). *Conflict: Resolution and provention*. London: Macmillan.

Calotychos, V. (Ed.). (1998). *Cyprus and its people: Nation, identity, and experience in an unimaginable community, 1955–1997*. Boulder, CO: Westview.

Chandler, D. (2002). *From Kosovo to Kabul: Human rights and international intervention*. London: Pluto.

Cheldelin, S., Druckman, D., & Fast, L. (Eds.). (2003). *Conflict: From analysis to intervention*. New York: Continuum.

Chufrin, G. I., & Saunders, H. H. (1993). A public peace process. *Negotiation Journal, 9*(2), 155–177.

Cissna, K. H., & Anderson, R. (1998). Theorizing about dialogic moment: The Buber-Rogers position and postmodern themes. *Communication Theory, 8,* 63–104.

Cissna, K. H., & Anderson, R. (2002). *Moments of meeting: Buber, Rogers, and the potential for public dialogue*. Albany: State University of New York Press.

Cockburn, C. (2004). *The line. Women, partition and the gender order in Cyprus*. London: Zed Books.

Cohen, R. (1991). *Negotiating across cultures: Communication obstacles in international diplomacy*. Washington, DC: United States Institute of Peace Press.

Conquergood, D. (1988). Health theater in a Hmong refugee camp. *Journal of Performance Studies, 32,* 171–208.

Constantinou, C. M., & Papadakis, Y. (2001). The Cypriot state(s) in situ: Cross-ethnic contact and the discourse of recognition. *Global Society, 15*(2), 125–148.

Cook, S. W. (1978). Interpersonal and attitudinal outcomes in cooperating interracial groups. *Journal of Research and Development in Education, 12,* 97–113.

Crawshaw, N. (1978). *The Cyprus revolt: An account of the struggle for union with Greece*. London: George Allen & Unwin.

Crocker, C. A., Hampson, F. O., & Aall, P. (Eds.). (1999). *Herding cats: Multiparty mediation in a complex world*. Washington, DC: United States Institute of Peace Press.

Deetz, S. (1992). *Democracy in an age of corporate colonization*. Albany: State University of New York Press.

Denich, B. (1994). Dismembering Yugoslavia: Nationalist ideologies and the symbolic revival of genocide. *American Ethnologist, 21,* 367–390.

Denktash, R. R. (1988). *The Cyprus triangle* (Rev. ed.). London: K. Rustem & Brother.

Deutsch, M., & Coleman, P. T. (Eds.). (2000). *The handbook of conflict resolution: Theory and practice*. San Francisco: Jossey-Bass.

Diamond, L. (1997). Training in conflict-habituated systems: Lessons from Cyprus. *International Negotiation, 2*(3), 353–380.

Diamond, L., & Fisher, R. J. (1995). Integrating conflict resolution training and consultation: A Cyprus example. *Negotiation Journal, 11*(3), 287–301.

Diamond, L., & McDonald, J. (1996). *Multi-track diplomacy: A systems approach to peace*. West Hartford, CT: Kumarian Press.

Doob, L. W. (1976). A Cyprus workshop: Intervention methodology during a continuing crisis. *Journal of Social Psychology, 98,* 143–144.

Doob, L. W. (1981). *The pursuit of peace*. Westport, CT: Greenwood.

Doob, L. W. (1987). Adieu to private intervention in political conflicts? *International Journal of Group Tensions, 17*(1–4), 15–27.

Doob, L. W., & Foltz, W. J. (1973). The Belfast Workshop: An application of group techniques to a destructive conflict. *Journal of Conflict Resolution, 18,* 489–512.

Doob, L. W., & Foltz, W. J. (1974). The impact of a workshop upon grass-roots leaders in Belfast. *Journal of Conflict Resolution, 18,* 237–256.

Doob, L. W., Foltz, W. J., & Stevens, R. B. (1969). The Fermeda Workshop: A different approach to border conflicts in eastern Africa. *Journal of Psychology, 73,* 249–266.

Druckman, D. (1997). Negotiating in the international context. In J. L. Rasmussen & I. W. Zartman (Eds.), *Peacemaking in international conflict: Methods and techniques*. Herndon, VA: USIP Press.

Ehrlich, T. (1974). *Cyprus 1958–1967. International crises and the role of law*. Oxford, UK: Oxford University Press.

Eisenberg, E. M., & Goodall, H. L. (1997). *Organizational communication: Balancing creativity and constraint* (2nd ed.). New York: St. Martin's.

Ellis, D. G., & Maoz, I. (2002). Cross-cultural argument interactions between Israeli-Jews and Palestinians. *Journal of Applied Communication Research, 30*, 181–194.

Eriksson, M., & Wallensteen, P. (2004). Armed conflict, 1989–2003. *Journal of Peace Research, 41*(5), 625–636.

Fearon, J. D., & Laitin, D. D. (2003). Ethnicity, insurgency, and civil war. *American Political Science Review, 97*(1), 75–90.

Fisher, R. J. (1972). Third party consultation: A method for the study and resolution of conflict. *Journal of Conflict Resolution, 16*, 67–94.

Fisher, R. J. (1980). A third-party consultation workshop on the India-Pakistan conflict. *Journal of Social Psychology, 112*, 191–206.

Fisher, R. J. (1992). *Peace building for Cyprus: Report on a conflict analysis workshop, June 1991*. Ottawa: Canadian Institute for International Peace and Security.

Fisher, R. J. (1993). The potential for peacebuilding: Forging a bridge from peacekeeping to peacemaking. *Peace and Change, 18*(3), 247–266.

Fisher, R. J. (1994). *Education and peacebuilding in Cyprus: A report on two conflict analysis workshops*. Ottawa: Canadian Institute for International Peace and Security.

Fisher, R. J. (1997). *Interactive conflict resolution*. Syracuse, NY: Syracuse University Press.

Fisher, R. J. (Ed.). (2005). *Paving the way: Contributions of interactive conflict resolution to peacemaking*. Lanham, MD: Lexington Books.

Fisher, R. J., & Keashly, L. (1991). The potential complementarity of mediation and consultation within a contingency model of third party intervention. *Journal of Peace Research, 28*(1), 29–42.

Forbes, H. D. (1997). *Ethnic conflict: Commerce, culture, and the contact hypothesis*. New Haven, CT: Yale University Press.

Galtung, J. (1975). Three approaches to peace. In J. Galtung (Ed.), *Essays in peace research* (Vol. 1, pp. 282–304). Copenhagen: Christian Ejlers.

Galtung, J. (1996). *Peace by peaceful means: Peace and conflict, development and civilization*. London/Oslo: Sage/PRIO.

Gazioglu, A. C. (1990). *The Turks in Cyprus. A province of the Ottoman Empire (1571–1878)*. London: K. Rustem & Brother.

Geist, P., & Dreyer, J. (1994). The demise of dialogue: A critique of the medial encounter. *Western Journal of Communication, 57*, 233–246.

Goertz, G., & Diehl, P. F. (1993). Enduring rivalries: Theoretical constructs and empirical patterns. *International Studies Quarterly, 27*, 147–171.

Gudykunst, W. B. (2003). *Bridging differences: Effective intergroup communication*. Thousand Oaks, CA: Sage.

Hadjipavlou-Trigeorgis, M. (1998). Different relationships to the land: Personal narratives, political implications and future possibilities in Cyprus. In V. Calotychos (Ed.), *Cyprus and its people: Nation, identity, and experience in an unimaginable community, 1955–1997* (pp. 251–276). Boulder, CO: Westview.

Hampson, F. O. (1996). *Nurturing peace: Why peace settlements succeed or fail*. Washington, DC: United States Institute of Peace Press.

Harbom, L. (Ed.). (2004). *States in armed conflict 2003*. Uppsala, Sweden: Uppsala University, Department of Peace and Conflict Research.

Haugerudbraaten, H. (2003). *Peacebuilding: Six dimensions and two concepts*. Institute for Security Studies. Retrieved August 14, 2004, from http://www.iss.co.za/Pubs/ASR/7No6/Peacebuilding.html

Heraclides, A. (2004). The Cyprus problem: An open or shut case? Probing the Greek Cypriot rejection of the Annan Plan. *Cyprus Review, 16*(2), 37–54.

Iji, T. (2002). Multiple mediation in Tajikistan: The 1997 peace agreement. *International Negotiation, 6*, 357–385.

Irani, G. E. (2000). *Islamic mediation techniques for Middle East conflicts*. Retrieved June 15, 2005, from http://www.mediate.com/articles/mideast.cfm

Isaacs, W. N. (1993). Taking fight: Dialogue, collective thinking, and organizational thinking. *Organizational Dynamics, 22*, 24–39.

Johannesen, R. L. (1971). The emerging concept of communication as dialogue. *Quarterly Journal of Speech, 57,* 373–382.

Jakobsson Hatay, A.-S. (2004a). Cyprus. In K. Kordell & S. Wolff (Eds.), *Ethnopolitical encyclopaedia of Europe* (pp. 519–538). London: Palgrave Macmillan.

Jakobsson Hatay, A.-S. (2004b, May 5 & May 6). Popular referenda and peace processes: The twin referenda on the Annan Plan for a reunited Cyprus put in perspective. *Turkish Daily News.*

Jakobsson Hatay, A.-S. (2005). *Peacebuilding and reconciliation in Bosnia and Herzegovina, Kosovo and Macedonia 1995–2004.* Uppsala, Sweden: Uppsala University, Department of Peace and Conflict Research.

Jakobsson Hatay, A.-S. (in press). *The struggle for hearts and minds: The political dynamics of peacebuilding and peacemaking in Northern Ireland and Cyprus.* Uppsala, Sweden: Uppsala University, Department of Peace and Conflict Research.

Joseph, J. S. (1997). *Cyprus. Ethnic conflict and international politics: From independence to the threshold of the European Union.* London: Macmillan.

Kaufman, S. J. (2001). *Modern hatreds: The symbolic politics of ethnic war.* Ithaca, NY: Cornell University Press.

Kaufmann, C. (1996). Possible and impossible solutions to ethnic civil wars. *International Security, 20*(4), 136–175.

Kaufmann, C. D. (1998). When all else fails: Ethnic population transfers and partitions in the twentieth century. *International Security, 23*(2), 120–156.

Keashly, L., & Fisher, R. J. (1990). Towards a contingency approach to third party intervention in regional conflict: A Cyprus illustration. *International Journal, 45*(2), 424–453.

Kelman, H. C. (1972). The problem-solving workshop in conflict resolution. In R. L. Merritt (Ed.), *Communication in international politics* (pp. 168–204). Urbana: University of Illinois Press.

Kelman, H. C. (1978). Israelis and Palestinians: Psychological prerequisites for mutual acceptance. *International Security, 3*(1), 162–186.

Kelman, H. C. (1982). Creating the conditions for Israeli-Palestinian negotiations. *Journal of Conflict Resolution, 26*(1), 39–75.

Kelman, H. C. (1985). Overcoming the psychological barrier: An analysis of the Egyptian-Israeli peace process. *Negotiation Journal, 1,* 213–234.

Kelman, H. C. (1987). The political psychology of the Israeli-Palestinian conflict: How can we overcome the barriers to a negotiated solution. *Political Psychology, 8*(3), 347–363.

Kelman, H. C. (1993). Coalitions across conflict lines: The interplay of conflicts within and between the Israeli and Palestinian communities. In S. Worchel & J. A. Simpson (Eds.), *Conflict between people and groups: Causes, processes, and resolutions* (pp. 236–294). Chicago: Nelson-Hall.

Kelman, H. C. (1995). Contributions of an unofficial conflict resolution effort to the Israeli-Palestinian breakthrough. *Negotiation Journal, 11,* 19–27.

Kelman, H. C. (1997). Some determinants of the Oslo breakthrough. *International Negotiation, 2*(2), 183–194.

Kelman, H. C. (1998). Social-psychological contributions to peacemaking and peacebuilding in the Middle East. *Applied Psychology, 47*(1), 5–28.

Kelman, H. C. (1999). Transforming the relationship between former enemies. In R. L. Rothstein (Ed.), *After the peace: Resistance and reconciliation* (pp. 193–205). Boulder, CO: Lynne Rienner.

Kelman, H. C. (2002). Interactive problem-solving: Informal mediation by the scholar-practitioner. In J. Bercovitch (Ed.), *Studies in international mediation* (pp. 167–193). London: Palgrave Macmillan.

Kelman, H. C., & Cohen, S. P. (1976). The problem-solving workshop: A social-psychological contribution to the resolution of international conflicts. *Journal of Peace Research, 13*(2), 79–90.

Kimmel, P. (1994). Cultural perspectives on international negotiations. *Journal of Social Issues, 50*(1), 179–196.

Knox, C., & Hughes, J. (1996). Crossing the divide: Community relations in Northern Ireland. *Journal of Peace Research, 22*(1), 83–98.

Kriesberg, L. (1998). Intractable conflict. In E. Weiner (Ed.), *The handbook of interethnic coexistence* (pp. 332–342). New York: Continuum.

Kriesberg, L. (2001). The growth of the conflict resolution field. In C. A. Crocker, F. O. Hampson, & P. Aall (Eds.), *Turbulent peace: The challenges of managing international conflict* (pp. 407–426). Washington, DC: United States Institute of Peace Press.

Kriesberg, L., Northrup, T. A., & Thorson, S. J. (Eds.). (1989). *Intractable conflicts and their transformation.* Syracuse, NY: Syracuse University Press.

Kumar, R. (1997). *Divide and fall? Bosnia in the annals of partition.* London: Verso.

Lebaron, M. D. (2003a). *Bridging cultural conflicts: New approaches for a changing world.* San Francisco: Jossey-Bass.

Lebaron, M. D. (2003b). Culture and conflict. *Intractable Conflict Knowledge Base Project.* Retrieved March 1, 2005, from http://www.beyondintractability.org/m/culture_conflict.jsp

Lederach, J. P. (1985). *Preparing for peace: Conflict transformation across cultures.* Syracuse, NY: Syracuse University Press.

Lederach, J. P. (1995). Conflict transformation in protracted internal conflicts: The case for a comprehensive framework. In K. Rupesinghe (Ed.), *Conflict transformation* (pp. 201–222). London: Macmillan.

Lederach, J. P. (1996). *Preparing for peace: Conflict transformation across cultures* (2nd ed.). Syracuse, NY: Syracuse University Press.

Lederach, J. P. (1997). *Building peace: Sustainable reconciliation in divided societies.* Washington, DC: United States Institute of Peace Press.

Lederach, J. P. (1999). *The journey toward reconciliation.* Scottsdale, AZ: Herald Press.

Lederach, J. P. (2001). Civil society and reconciliation. In C. A. Crocker, F. O. Hampson, & P. Aall (Eds.), *Turbulent peace: The challenges of managing international conflict* (pp. 841–854). Washington, DC: United States Institute of Peace Press.

Lederach, J. P. (2003). *The little book of conflict transformation.* Intercourse, PA: Good Books.

Licklider, R. (1993). What have we learned and where do we go from here? In R. Licklider (Ed.), *Stopping the killing: How civil wars end* (pp. 303–322). New York: New York University Press.

Licklider, R. (1995). The consequences of negotiated settlements in civil wars, 1945–1993. *American Political Science Review, 89*(3), 681–690.

Lieberfeld, D. (2002). Evaluating the contributions of track-two diplomacy to conflict termination in South Africa, 1984–90. *Journal of Peace Research, 39*(3), 355–372.

Loizos, P. (1974). The progress of Greek nationalism in Cyprus, 1878–1970. In J. Davis (Ed.), *Choice and change: Essays in honor of Lucy Mair* (pp. 114–133). London: Athlone Press.

Maiese, M. (2003). *Peacebuilding.* Retrieved August 14, 2004, from http://www.beyondintractability.org/m/peacebuilding.jsp

Maoz, I., & Ellis, D. G. (2001). Going to ground: Argument between Israeli-Jews and Palestinians. *Research on Language and Social Interaction, 4,* 399–419.

Markides, K. C. (1977). *The rise and fall of the Cyprus republic.* New Haven, CT: Yale University Press.

Marshall, M. G., & Gurr, T. R. (2003). *A global survey of armed conflicts, self-determination movements, and democracy.* College Park: University of Maryland, Center for International Development and Conflict Management.

Mavratsas, C. V. (1997). The ideological contest between Greek-Cypriot nationalism and Cypriotism 1974–1995: Politics, social memory and identity. *Ethnic and Racial Studies, 20*(4), 717–737.

McDonald, J. W. (1991). Further exploration of track two diplomacy. In L. Kriesberg & S. J. Thorson (Eds.), *Timing the de-escalation of international conflicts* (pp. 201–220). New York: Syracuse University Press.

Mitchell, C. R. (1981). *Peacemaking and the consultant's role.* New York: Nichols.

Montville, J. V. (1987). The arrow and the olive branch: A case for track two diplomacy. In J. W. McDonald, Jr., & D. Bendahmane, B. (Eds.), *Conflict resolution: Track two diplomacy* (pp. 5–20). Washington, DC: U.S. Department of State, Foreign Service Institute.

Montville, J. V. (1993). The healing function in political conflict resolution. In D. J. D. Sandole & H. van der Merwe (Eds.), *Conflict resolution theory and practice: Integration and application* (pp. 112–127). Manchester, UK: Manchester University Press.

Necatigil, Z. M. (1993). *The Cyprus question and the Turkish position in international law* (Rev. 2nd ed.). Oxford, UK: Oxford University Press.

Oberschall, A. (2001). From ethnic cooperation to violence and war in Yugoslavia. In D. Chirot & M. E. P. Seligman (Eds.), *Ethnopolitical warfare: Causes, consequences, and possible solutions* (pp. 119–150). Washington, DC: American Psychological Association.

Offiong, D. A. (1997). Conflict resolution among the Ibibio of Nigeria. *Journal of Anthropological Research, 53*(4), 423–442.

O'Malley, B., & Craig, I. (2001). *The Cyprus conspiracy: America, espionage and the Turkish invasion*. London: I. B. Tauris.

Papadakis, Y. (1998). Enosis and Turkish expansionism: Real myths or mythic realities? In V. Calotychos (Ed.), *Cyprus and its people: Nation, identity and experience in an unimaginable community, 1955–1997* (pp. 69–84). Boulder, CO: Westview.

Papadakis, Y. (2003). Nation, narrative and commemoration: Political ritual in divided Cyprus. *History and Anthropology, 14*(3), 253–270.

Papadakis, Y. (2005). *Echoes from the dead zone: Across the Cyprus divide*. London: I. B. Tauris.

Paris, R. (2004). *At war's end. Building peace after civil conflict*. Cambridge, UK: Cambridge University Press.

Patrick, R. A. (1976). *Political geography and the Cyprus conflict: 1963–1971*. Ontario, Canada: University of Waterloo, Department of Geography.

Pearce, W. B., & Littlejohn, S. W. (1997). *Moral conflict: When social worlds collide*. Thousand Oaks, CA: Sage.

Philipsen, G. (1992). *Speaking culturally: Explorations in social communication*. Albany: State University of New York Press.

Poulakos, J. (1974). The components of dialogue. *Western Speech, 38,* 199–212.

Richmond, O. P. (1998). *Mediating in Cyprus: The Cypriot communities and the United Nations*. London: Frank Cass.

Richmond, O. P. (2001). Rethinking conflict resolution: The linkage problematic between "Track I" and "Track II." *Journal of Conflict Studies, 22*(2), 109–131.

Richmond, O. P. (2004). The dilemmas of conflict resolution: A comparison of Sri Lanka and Cyprus. *Nationalism and Ethnic Politics, 10,* 185–219.

Ropers, N. (2003). Assessing the role and impact of dialogue projects. *Berghof handbook for conflict transformation*. Retrieved May 10, 2005, from http://www.berghof-handbook.net

Ross, M. H., & Rothman, J. (Eds.). (1999). *Theory and practice in ethnic conflict management: Theorizing success and failure*. London: Macmillan.

Rothman, J. (1991). Conflict research and resolution: Cyprus. *Annals of the American Academy of Political and Social Science, 518,* 95–108.

Rothman, J. (1992). *From confrontation to cooperation: Resolving ethnic and regional conflict*. London: Sage.

Rothman, J. (1997a). Action evaluation and conflict resolution training: Theory, method and case study. *International Negotiation, 2*(3), 451–470.

Rothman, J. (1997b). *Resolving identity-based conflict in nations, organizations, and communities*. San Francisco: Jossey-Bass.

Rothman, J. (1998). Dialogue in conflict: Past and future. In E. Weiner (Ed.), *The handbook of interethnic coexistence* (pp. 216–235). New York: Continuum.

Rothman, J. (with Land, R. J., & Twite, R.). (1994). *The Jerusalem peace initiative: Project on managing political disputes*. Jerusalem: Hebrew University of Jerusalem, Leonard Davis Institute for International Relations.

Rouhana, N. N. (1995). The dynamics of joint thinking between adversaries in international conflict: Phases of the continuing problem-solving workshop. *Political Psychology, 16*(2), 321–345.

Rouhana, N. N. (2000). Interactive conflict resolution: Issues in theory, methodology and evaluation. In P. C. Stern & D. Druckman (Eds.), *International conflict resolution after the cold war* (pp. 294–337). Washington, DC: National Academy Press.

Rouhana, N. N., & Kelman, H. C. (1994). Promoting joint thinking in international conflicts: An Israeli-Palestinian continuing workshop. *Journal of Social Issues, 50*(1), 157–178.

Rule, J. B. (1988). *Theories of civil violence*. Berkeley: University of California Press.

Sambanis, N. (2000). Partition as a solution to ethnic war: An empirical critique of the theoretical literature. *World Politics, 52,* 437–483.

Sandole, D. J. D. (2001). John Burton's contribution to conflict resolution theory and practice: A personal view. *International Journal of Peace Studies, 6*(1). Retrieved September 8, 2001, from http://www.gmu.edu/academic/ijps/vol6_1/Sandole.htm

Sandole, D. J. D., & van der Merwe, H. (1993). *Conflict resolution theory and practice: Integration and application*. Manchester, UK: Manchester University Press.

Saunders, H. H. (1985). We need a larger theory of negotiation: The importance of pre-negotiating phases. *Negotiation Journal, 1*(3), 249–262.

Saunders, H. H. (1991). *The other walls: The Arab-Israeli peace process in a global perspective* (Rev. ed.). Princeton, NJ: Princeton University Press.

Saunders, H. H. (1996). Prenegotiation and circum-negotiation: Arenas of the peace process. In C. A. Crocker & F. O. Hampson (Eds.), *Managing global chaos* (pp. 419–432). Washington, DC: United States Institute of Peace Press.

Saunders, H. H. (1999a). The multilevel peace process in Tajikistan. In C. A. Crocker, F. O. Hampson, & P. Aall (Eds.), *Herding cats: Multiparty mediation in a complex world* (pp. 159–179). Washington, DC: United States Institute of Peace Press.

Saunders, H. H. (1999b). *A public peace process: Sustained dialogue to transform racial and ethnic conflicts*. New York: St. Martin's.

Saunders, H. H. (2003, January). Sustained dialogue in managing intractable conflict. *Negotiation Journal, 19,* 85–95.

Savvides, P. K. (2002). *Cyprus at the gate of the European Union*. Athens: Hellenic Foundation for European and Foreign Policy.

Scheff, T. J. (1994). *Bloody revenge: Emotions, nationalism, and war*. Boulder, CO: Westview.

Schein, E. H. (1993). On dialogue, culture, and organizational learning. *Organizational Dynamics, 22*(40–51).

Senge, P. M. (1990). *The fifth discipline*. Garden City, NY: Doubleday.

Sherif, M. (1966). *Group conflict and co-operation: Their social psychology*. London: Routledge & Kegan Paul.

Slim, R. M., & Saunders, H. H. (1996, January). Managing conflict in divided societies. *Negotiation Journal*, pp. 31–46.

Slim, R. M., & Saunders, H. H. (2001). The inter-Tajik dialogue: From civil war towards civil society. In K. Abduallaev & C. Barnes (Issue Eds.), *Politics of compromise: The Tajikistan peace process. Accord, 10*. London: Conciliation Resources.

Stedman, S. J., Rothchild, D., & Cousens, E. M. (Eds.). (2002). *Ending civil wars: The implementation of peace agreements*. Boulder, CO: Lynne Rienner.

Stewart, J. (1978). Foundations of dialogic communication. *Quarterly Journal of Speech, 64,* 183–201.

Stoddard, P. H. (1986). An experiment in track two diplomacy. In D. B. Bendahmane & J. W. McDonald (Eds.), *Perspectives on negotiations* (pp. 139–143). Washington, DC: U.S. Department of State, Foreign Service Institute.

Talbot, P. (1977). The Cyprus seminar. In M. Berman & J. E. Johnson (Eds.), *Unofficial diplomats*. New York: Columbia University Press.

Ting-Toomey, S., & Oetzel, J. G. (2001). *Managing intercultural conflict effectively*. Thousand Oaks, CA: Sage.

Tocci, N. (2004). *EU accession dynamics and conflict resolution. Catalysing peace or consolidating partition?* Aldershot, UK: Ashgate.

United Nations. (2001). *Statement by the President of the Security Council, s/prst/2001/5*. Retrieved September 8, 2005, from http://daccess-ods.un.org/TMP/6326794.html

United Nations. (2003). *The Annan Plan for Cyprus*. Retrieved September 8, 2005, from http:// 82.138.229.164/cyprus_decides/English/Annan_ Plan/Foundation%20Agreement.htm

van Oudenhoven, J. P. (1989). Improving interethnic relationships: How effective is cooperation? In J. P. van Oudenhoven & T. M. Willemsen (Eds.), *Ethnic minorities: Social psychological perspectives*. Amsterdam: Swets & Zeitlinger.

Volkan, V. D. (1979). *Cyprus—War and adaptation: A psychoanalytic history of two ethnic groups in conflict*. Charlottesville: University Press of Virginia.

Volkan, V. D. (1990). An overview of psychological concepts pertinent to interethnic and/or international relationships. In V. D. Volkan, J. V. Montville, & D. A. Julius (Eds.), *The psychodynamics of international relationships: Vol. 1. Concepts and theories* (pp. 31–46). Lexington, MA: Lexington Books.

Volkan, V. D. (1998). Ethnicity and nationalism: A psychoanalytic perspective. *Applied Psychology, 47*(1), 45–57.

Volkan, V. D., Montville, J. V., & Julius, D. A. (Eds.). (1990). *The psychodynamics of international relationships: Vol. 1*. Lexington, MA: Lexington Books.

Volkan, V. D., Montville, J. V., & Julius, D. A. (Eds.). (1991). *The psychodynamics of international relationships: Vol. 2*. Lexington, MA: Lexington Books.

Voorhees, J. (2002). *Dialogue sustained. The multilevel peace process and the Dartmouth*

Conference. Washington, DC: United States Institute of Peace Press/Charles F. Kettering Foundation.

Wedge, B. (1967, July 21). Psychiatry and international affairs. Science, 157(3786), 281–285. Available online at http://links.jstor.org/sici?sici=0036-8075%2819670721%293%3A157%3A3786%3C281%3APAIA%3E2.0.CO%3B2-W

Wedge, B. (1990). The individual, the group and war. In J. Burton & F. Dukes (Eds.), *Conflict: Readings in management and resolution* (pp. 101–116). Houndmills, UK: Macmillan.

Weldon, E., & Jehn, K. A. (1995). Examining cross-cultural differences in conflict management behavior: A strategy for future research. *International Journal of Conflict Management, 6*(4), 387–403.

Woodward, S. L. (1995). *Balkan tragedy*. Washington, DC: Brookings Institution.

Xydis, S. G. (1973). *Cyprus: Reluctant republic*. The Hague: Mouton.

Zartman, I. W. (1989). Prenegotiation: Phases and functions. In J. G. Stein (Ed.), *Getting to the table: The processes of international prenegotiations* (pp. 1–17). Baltimore: Johns Hopkins University Press.

Zartman, I. W. (Ed.). (2000). *Traditional cures for modern conflicts, African conflict "medicine."* Boulder, CO: Lynne Rienner.

Zartman, I. W., & Rasmussen, J. L. (Eds.). (1997). *Peacemaking in international conflicts: Methods and techniques*. Washington, DC: United States Institute of Peace Press.

24

INTERNATIONAL/INTERCULTURAL CONFLICT RESOLUTION TRAINING

SUSAN W. COLEMAN

Coleman Raider International

ELLEN RAIDER

Coleman Raider International

For over a combined 40 years, we have been engaged in international/intercultural negotiation and conflict resolution training, delivering beginner to advanced programs in conflict resolution, collaborative negotiation skills, and mediation. Our core program has been collaborative negotiation skills. As practitioners, we have been fortunate to work with tens of thousands of people from different parts of the globe. Our varied assignments have been with large diplomatic organizations, inner-city schools, lawyers, doctors, activists, managers, and teachers. From all of those experiences, our understanding of conflict resolution and our training focus has evolved and sharpened.

Our intent here is to offer some of our insights about the cultural component of conflict and negotiation, especially within the context of training. The chapter is organized in eight sections. First, we begin with background information about ourselves, our work, and the contexts in which we have been training. Second, we discuss some of the philosophical principles that underlie our intercultural conflict training programs. Third, we review several customization methods of our conflict resolution course. Fourth, we outline a sample of our training objectives (i.e., knowledge, attitudes, and skills) and module contents. Fifth, we describe the ways that we infuse cross-cultural concepts into our conflict training modules and include some diverse training tools and delivery examples. Sixth, we explain why we believe that the culture of collaboration is most critical when considering intercultural conflict resolution training. Seventh, we focus on the issue of power in intergroup conflict training sessions and propose ten core principles that prompt the escalation of intergroup conflicts. Finally, while we have offered many insights and lessons learned throughout the chapter, we end by presenting some specific suggestions for future intercultural/intergroup practitioners.

CONFLICT TRAINERS: BACKGROUNDS AND PROFESSIONAL PATHS

Personal Backgrounds

Our backgrounds may help our readers understand better who we are and what we are trying to say. *Susan's* focus in college was on the political, economic, and cultural relationship between the "first" and "third" worlds, specifically, the United States and Latin America. She subsequently became a community activist, establishing the North Star Fund, a community foundation whose purpose was to support progressive grassroots social change in New York City. She went on to law school and practiced litigation. The focus was corporate, but she also did legal work for migrant farm workers and for Haitians seeking legal asylum. After three years, she attended the Kennedy School of Government at Harvard with the intent being to continue studying international development. Nonetheless, she was sidetracked by the field of negotiation—especially its interdisciplinary nature, incorporating law, international development, and social psychology. She became determined to do work in intercultural negotiation, but was told by her professors at the time that there was no such field. But then she met Ellen Raider.

Ellen received a Master's degree in educational psychology and group dynamics from Temple University. Subsequently, she spent many years as program director at International House, first at Berkeley, and then in New York City. At International House, she designed and conducted intercultural training workshops for U.S. American and foreign students from more than 80 countries, organized conferences on international economic development issues, and represented International House as an NGO at the United Nations. She then moved on to the human resources training department at a large brokerage firm in New York City where she conducted management training seminars. At a time of great tension between the United States and the then-USSR, she left that organization to become part of the US/USSR trade negotiation project sponsored by the U.S. National Science Foundation and the Soviet Academy of Foreign Trade. In this capacity, she developed the ability to teach people in high-tension intercultural situations to negotiate with one another. When the Soviets invaded Afghanistan, however, the project was dropped. Based on the training work she had been doing, she created her own company, *Ellen Raider International* and began working with many multinational and nonprofit clients including UNICEF, the European Economic Community, and the Committee for National Security.

Societal Backgrounds

Like all of us, our professional backgrounds tell only part of the story of how we came to our chosen directions. We came to this work as women growing up in times and environments where culture and conflict were dominant themes. Although we are 15 years apart in age, both of us were profoundly affected by the Vietnam War years. At Berkeley (in 1968), Ellen was surrounded by an intense antiwar environment. Students at International House had lively discussions about the issues of the day, while having to use discretion due to their visitor status to the country. Susan, an activist herself, was also profoundly affected by her sister's joining forces with an offshoot of the Weather Underground. She also lived and traveled in various parts of Latin America, where both U.S. influence and social injustice were glaring. Both of us became feminists, both became acutely aware of racism and its effect on every aspect of life. We read Malcolm X, we read Gandhi, Shulamith Firestone, Adrienne Rich, and Saul Alinsky. We both became interested in searching for nonviolent ways to move toward a more tolerant and equitable world.

Trainers in Collaboration

Ellen and Susan began their work together in 1987. Susan came to work for Ellen Raider International, while also working as a mediator with American Intermediation Service out of San Francisco. Together, they continued the training work Ellen had begun in multinationals. They also started working with school communities—training principles, teachers, and other school staff in negotiation and conflict resolution skills.

In 1988, Ellen joined forces with Mort Deutsch to found the International Center for Cooperation and Conflict Resolution (ICCCR) at Teacher's College, Columbia University. Ellen became the Training Director at the Center and sometime thereafter Susan became one of the first instructors. The Raider and Coleman Negotiation and Mediation programs became one of the core programs in what would later become a multi-offering certificate program in conflict resolution. Through the ICCCR, both of us started doing significant work in the New York City public schools—a hugely diverse educational system. For example, in the borough of Queens, alone, about 116 languages are spoken. Around the same time, Susan started doing a certain amount of diversity work in addition to training and mediation.

The work at Teachers College evolved slowly. However, starting in 1995, the program began to blossom with thousands of students of education and organization development being trained in conflict resolution skills. The certificate in conflict resolution that evolved included the basic programs in collaborative negotiation skills and mediation skills (using the Raider and Coleman methods and materials), and various advanced programs that included a course on conflict theory, a course titled "Rank, Power and Privilege," a course on designing conflict resolution systems, and others. In addition to training students, we also ran a number of "in-service" programs, including a training program for representatives of all New York City high schools, with the intent being to establish conflict resolution centers and expertise in all of those schools.

Meanwhile, our work outside of the ICCCR continued. Susan delivered training programs for multinational groups such as the World Trade Institute in New York City, the Port Authority of New York and New Jersey, the Colombian Government, and some corporate clients such as AT&T, Sterling Pharmaceuticals, and Citibank. In 1996, Susan was contacted by the U.N. Secretariat to run a pilot in collaborative negotiation skills and conflict resolution. After the success of that program, we began running larger contracts in conflict resolution for the Secretariat, through the auspices of the ICCCR, work that continued through 2004. Other engagements included creating a user-friendly program for UNICEF, programs in international trade negotiations for the U.S. Department of Agriculture, courses in intercultural conflict for unions of

nurses, as well as others. We were also both mediating—Susan in both legal and organizational contexts and Ellen often in the context of school disputes. Susan, in addition, was now doing a significant amount of culture-specific and diversity work.

From its inception, our training models have woven the topic of culture throughout the process of teaching and learning negotiation and mediation skills. Our original audiences were made up of managers from multinational organizations eager to learn how to negotiate across borders. Building on the work of Weiss and Stripp (1985), Hofstede (1980, 1991, 2001), Ting-Toomey (1994, 1999, 2004), and others, we facilitated the trainees' learning through readings, video clips (e.g., *Going International, Part Two,* Griggs, 1983; *The Multicultural Workplace,* Wurzel, 1990; *Cross-Cultural Conference Room,* Wurzel, 2002), and conducting role plays to understand and internalize cultural dimensions such as high or low power distance, high or low communication context, and collectivism or individualism.

While the marketplace defined culture in national terms, we, from the outset, saw it as something broader and more in keeping with Hofstede's (2001) definition: "the collective programming of the mind that distinguishes the members of one human group from another" (p. 9). For us, culture was to a group what personality was to an individual (Hofstede, 1980). We saw the same phenomenon of culture showing up in mediations between groups of U.S. residents in New York City and diversity issues inside local organizations as we did in the international training room. Thus, intercultural conflict was where conflict existed between individuals or groups where perceptions of worldview differences were present. This was often accompanied by perceived threats and attacks on the level of worldview. To be more specific, to us, the goals of intercultural conflict resolution were helping identity groups to understand the phenomenon of cultural and worldview differences, building awareness of different perspectives, reducing judgments that one view is better than another, and refocusing disputants' attention onto getting needs met rather than making worldview-laden and inflammatory accusations.

INTERCULTURAL CONFLICT TRAINING: PHILOSOPHICAL PRINCIPLES

In our training programs, we have never specifically laid out the set of values or philosophies that underlie our program models, although we have frequently discussed certain value principles with participants. Nonetheless, we think it is helpful to identify here the underlying values that have informed our work. When Ellen met Mort Deutsch, she also realized that there was great synchronicity between our value set and the value set he enumerated in his pioneering conflict writings (Deutsch, 2000).

The first value or principle is essentially what in the Western world is referred to as the Golden Rule—"Do unto others as you would have them do unto you," what Deutsch phrased as *"reciprocity"* (Deutsch, 2000). We understood that while this rule worked universally at the need and feeling level, it might better be phrased at the behavioral level as: "Do unto others as they would have you do unto them." This re-phrasing also echoes what Milton Bennett (1986; see also J. Bennett & M. Bennett, 2004) termed as the Platinum Rule ("Do unto others as they themselves would have done unto them") in conveying intercultural empathy. For instance, you might like a child to show respect to you by shaking hands with you and addressing you directly, but what do you think a child would prefer? He might prefer waving his hand and smiling. Or if the child is from a traditional Asian culture, she might prefer to look down and bow rather than shaking hands with you. As Deutsch (2000) elaborated:

> [This] requires each party to treat the other with the fairness that it would normatively expect if in the other's position. . . . The fairness in behavior, in process, and in outcomes. . . . As defined by one's culture, it is how the conflicting parties should or should not behave toward one another if they are, at a minimum, to avoid a destructive conflict or, more positively, to promote constructive management of their conflict. (p. 34)

The second principle is essentially about *human equality*—that, while human beings may have different degrees of education, wealth, and power, on a spiritual level all human life must be equally valued. Of course, this is the essence of collaboration, as it is based on getting people's commitments to constructive processes and outcomes rather than their compliance due to greater power. We also make it clear to all of our participants that, when looking at human needs and emotions, we all have the same set of deep-level needs and emotions regardless of the discrepancies in how they are met or in how they might manifest.

The third principle is *interdependence,* or what Deutsch (2000) has phrased *"shared community."* We tell people in our programs that collaboration (as opposed to competition) is best where there is interdependence. But the point we try to make them see is that there are few situations in life where there is not some form of interdependence. Or, in the words of the famous environmentalist John Muir (1911/1988), "When we try to pick out anything by itself, we find it hitched to everything else in the universe" (p. 110).

The fourth principle is the one that Deutsch (2000) has called "fallibility." This is essentially that everyone can be wrong, and that no one has a corner on the truth. This principle dispels the righteousness that is at the heart of all fundamentalist movements. It is also at the heart of what we might call "deep democracy." Many societies embrace hierarchical models of the world where, in the best sense, those on top are required to take care of those beneath them. But even with the most benign of rulers, it is difficult to see what the world looks like from others' standpoints or perspectives. For example, if wealthy, Western, White men make all the decisions, it is only human that they will not fully incorporate the interests of all the rest of us.

The fifth principle, related to the last, is participatory decision making; that those who are affected by decisions need to have a say in making them. We realized, in teaching the Hofstede principle of "power distance," that we were not being entirely honest in saying "one way of doing things is not necessarily better than the other. It is just different." The reality is that collaboration requires commitment to decisions, which requires some participation, which is anathema to power distance (see section on final recommendations for further discussion on rethinking power distance).

The last principle is nonviolence, of either the physical or psychological variety (e.g., humiliation) (Deutsch, 2000). We believe, for example, that when adults hit children to influence their behavior, they are only conveying that force is a useful method of getting one's way—a concept that later as adults the children pass on to others. While we are sympathetic to many people's movements where violence has been used as a means to balance power, we think that history has proven that nonviolent methods have been every bit as effective or more effective at changing society than aggressive, violent approaches (Schell, 2003).

INTERCULTURAL CONFLICT TRAINING PROGRAMS: AUDIENCE ASSESSMENTS AND COURSE CUSTOMIZATION

When teaching people about conflict or negotiation, we think it is critical to be on target with the particular contexts in which our audiences are working. Therefore, although the core of what we teach remains largely the same, the specifics of each training program can look very different. This is accomplished through selecting or creating case simulations, including previously recorded video examples of negotiations or mediations from our library, and prior assessments of the trainee group (see also Paige, 2004).

This pre-course assessment and customization is an important part of our work. During the assessment, the training team builds rapport with the client and discovers many of the conflicting issues currently in the client's system. This information enables the team to anticipate, recognize, and then incorporate relevant "teachable moments" during the training; that is, to link the training material to real concerns of the learner—as they emerge. By incorporating data from the client system in this way, we have been able to teach this course effectively to such diverse groups as school teachers in New York, Dallas, and Skopje; corporate executives from Buenos Aires, Paris, and Tokyo; grassroots community groups dealing with tenant organizing and environmental justice; diplomats from the Association of South-East Asian Nations and the European Economic Community, and the United Nations staff throughout the world. The

course has been taught over the past 12 years to about 10,000 people. The materials have been translated into French, Spanish, Portuguese, Japanese, Arabic, and Macedonian; and a book based on our manual has been published in Japanese.

Probably the most important customization method we use is case selection and preparation. We often use a generic conflict case for initial case role plays—specifically so that trainees do not get caught up in the details of their own issues, but rather, they can focus on the process. After that, however, we have almost always created customized conflict cases. The process of case development looks very similar to the typical data collection work of an organizational consultant. We first are connected with our internal liaison—typically someone in the human resources part of the organization. With their help, we identify employees of the organization to interview in order to identify typical conflict issues that require negotiation skills. Sometimes, we interview one or two persons, sometimes many. This is always dependent on budget and how lucky we are to zoom in on a problematic conflict episode that is workable. Once we have it, we write it up (and it's often a composite of issues) with enough fiction in it so that, while the episode will seem real to participants, no one can be obviously identified.

What has been interesting to us is that we do use these cases in other contexts and have found them relevant. For instance, we created a case that was pure fiction, about a company that wanted to come in and mine in a third world community and was opposed by the community and the environmentalists, only to have a number of participants in different settings express certainty that we were talking about a community in their country. Similarly, we created a case for a UN Peacekeeping mission only to hear from other peacekeeping missions that it was theirs that we were writing about. We wrote a case based on a situation that Ellen mediated in an inner-city school setting that had to do with representation and power sharing around race. We used it in one instance with a diplomatic organization only to be told that it felt very relevant to what goes on in high-level international bodies. Thus, what we have found is that, while the cases are customized, the intercultural or intergroup conflict issues are ones that reappear in many organizational systems and can feel familiar to many.

Another form of customization is the creation of conflict critical incidents. These are very short scenarios with a clash of positions and some indication as to underlying needs. We used to spend more time on this earlier in our work, but more recently, have tended to de-emphasize it as we became more interested in using participants' cases and issues. Nonetheless, a list of typical organizational critical incidents can be useful to jog people's memories about conflicts that have been real to them and that they would like to work on.

Videos are an important part of our training program. We have used these to model the skills that we are talking about as well as to demonstrate intercultural issues. We have used commercial videos, but mostly we have created our own. Our videos have always been simple and inexpensive, but always very effective as teaching tools. They also have allowed us to create as much cross-cultural variation as we can. The commercial videos used (e.g., *Going International Part 2: Managing the Overseas Assignment,* Griggs, 1983) have some excellent intercultural conflicts, but all involve at least one U.S. citizen. In our homemade videos, we have been able to "mix it up" and not always have the cross-cultural reference point be to the United States.

An important form of customization for programs in various countries of the world has been to make sure that the timing of the program is in sync with what is normative. For instance, in programs that we have done in Beirut, we have had to start our day much earlier, have many more breaks for people to pray, and have ended earlier so that people can go home to have lunch with their families. Still another way that we "customize" is to have people tape themselves negotiating. People are hearing different voices, different communication styles, and it sounds real, because it is. In most client systems, we are not able to do any significant pre- and post-course assessments. This is because most of our work is for in-service training with busy professionals who are not sure until the last minute if they can register for a training program. Another obstacle is that many clients do not want to pay for such assessments. We do, however, regularly send out a pre-course welcome letter to give participants a sense of the program as well as to get a sense of who will be joining us. In the letter, we suggest pre-reading, ask people to think through conflict issues that they might use in the training program, and ask them a series of questions such as the following:

1. Tell us briefly about yourself and your job responsibilities. Please include such facts as your gender, nationality, and length of time with this organization.

2. Identify what you would like to take away from this seminar on negotiation.

3. What types of issues do you negotiate most frequently and with whom do you negotiate? What types of professional conflicts or differences are typical at work?

4. Think of a conflict situation that has come up at work that was of moderate difficulty for you to handle. What did you want? What did the other person want (or say) that was in opposition to your preferred solution?

5. Have you ever taken a course or training program in negotiation or conflict resolution? If yes, please describe.

6. Are there diversity issues (e.g., gender, race, nationality, age, etc.) that cause difficulty for you either in your work or in the local environment? If yes, please explain.

Finally, we consider trainer selection to be an important form of customization. We have a team of about 15 trainers worldwide who are certified to deliver our program and who work with us regularly. We attempt always to staff the program with a training team that is as diverse as possible and the right kind of trainer for the particular client.

INTERCULTURAL CONFLICT TRAINING PROGRAMS: SAMPLE TRAINING OBJECTIVES AND MODULE CONTENTS

Conflict Resolution: Strategies for Collaborative Problem Solving is a highly interactive workshop typically conducted in a three-day or six-day format with varying teams of trainers. It is based on Raider's (1987) training manual, *A Guide to International Negotiation*. The three-day format is for groups requesting training in collaborative negotiation. The longer format includes an extensive three-day module on mediation. All participants receive a training manual, which is divided into sections corresponding to the seven course modules.

Module one presents an overview of conflict resolution, with emphasis on distinguishing between competitive and collaborative resolution strategies. *Module two* introduces a structural model, the elements of negotiation. In this module, we focus on the difference between positions and needs or interests, as well as the skill of *reframing* and the use of a pre-negotiation planning tool. *Module three* describes five communication behaviors or tactics that are typically used during negotiations—Attack, Evade, Inform, Open, and Unite. In this module, we emphasize the difference between the *intent* and the *impact* of any message. *Module four* describes how cultural differences affect the conflict resolution process. Combining the learning from all the previous modules, *module five* gives the learner a sense of the flow of a collaborative negotiation by introducing a stage model. *Module six* helps participants understand and deal with emotions, which typically arise during interpersonal and intercultural conflict. In its short form, *module seven* introduces mediation as an alternative if negotiation breaks down. The longer form teaches participants the skill and practice of mediation (for a more detailed description of our program, see Raider, Coleman, & Gerson, 2000).

All of the material covered in the training modules is coalesced in a training model that can be summarized in the following eight-point capsule:

1. Get agreement that you would like to negotiate, name the issue in a neutral way, and agree on a time and place.

2. Establish a collaborative climate by building rapport with the other, taking cultural differences into account.

3. Find out the other's preferred solution to the problem (their "negotiating position").

4. Pull out the need or interest underlying their position and reflect it back to them to confirm your accurate understanding. This must be done with an authentic desire to understand how their view makes sense.

5. State your underlying needs and, if necessary, your preferred solution (position).

6. Reframe the conflict by putting the underlying needs into a sentence like "how can we meet your need for _____ and my need for _____?"

7. Use creative brainstorming to explore solutions that meet the needs of both sides.

8. Choose the best possible packaging of solutions.

Like other educators, we find it useful to identify for ourselves specific knowledge, attitude, and skills objectives for what we hope trainees will get out of our training programs. We pay close attention to questions such as these: What do we want them to know leaving our programs? How would we like to have shifted their attitudes and awareness about themselves and the world around them? What do we want them to be able to do as a result of the program? Some of these objectives we spell out for participants; others we simply identify for our own clarity. Here are some examples of what we consider as sample objectives in each category and how they might inform what we actually do in the training room.

Knowledge Objectives

There are obviously many areas of academic inquiry that affect the study of conflict and its resolution, and it is difficult to cull those that should be included in an introductory experiential workshop. One that has been critical for us is the distinction between competitive and collaborative approaches to conflict resolution. Thus, we want participants to understand conceptually and experientially why and under what conditions cooperative conflict resolution processes such as collaborative negotiations and mediation are a better choice for individuals and society than are the commonly used strategies of competition and avoidance. Although we make it clear that we value cooperation, we also believe that we must not impose it in the training room. Our pedagogy encourages participants to "try on" this paradigm to see if it is useful. Ultimately, each participant must be self-motivated to make meaningful changes in his or her conflict-resolving behavior. We hope to provide information and experiences during our training that foster this exploration (Raider et al., 2000).

For example, at the very outset of our basic negotiations programs, we ask participants to negotiate a case first competitively and then collaboratively. After introducing the concepts and the types of behaviors that go with it, we have participants move from the conceptual and abstract to the concrete and listen to their recorded negotiations. The trainees form their own opinions from each other's reactions of whether they think the competitive or collaborative approach does a better job of achieving their conflict negotiation goals. We also make a point, throughout the program, of trying to compare and contrast the pros and cons of a competitive versus a collaborative approach, so that the participants develop a sense of the strengths and weaknesses of the two different approaches in different contexts. One of the ways of teaching the concepts is by modeling them. While we will express our opinion, we strive to have students develop their own based on their own experience and observation of their own, and others', behaviors together with the behavioral impacts.

Although specific knowledge objectives are associated with each module, there are some "global" knowledge objectives for the course:

> To develop understanding that conflict is a natural and necessary part of life, and that how one responds to conflict determines whether the outcomes are constructive or destructive

> To develop awareness that competition and collaboration are the two main strategies for negotiation and for resolving conflict

> To develop more self-awareness about how one thinks about and responds to conflict

> To become aware of key ways in which worldviews differ and how that can manifest into conflict

> To expand one's understanding that culture is broader than differences between national groups

> To become a better conflict manager—in other words, to know which conflict resolution method is best suited to a particular conflict problem (e.g., avoidance, negotiation, mediation, arbitration, litigation, or force)

> To become aware of how critical it is to the process of constructive conflict resolution to share information about one's own perspective without attacking the other, and to listen and work to understand the perspective of the other side

Attitude Objectives

The shifts in attitude and awareness that we hope to create are a little harder to enumerate succinctly. We hope the learners leave the program believing that collaborative conflict resolution skills are useful in their own lives. We hope that they commit to the larger goal of increasing the use of cooperative conflict resolution skills at all levels to create a more just and caring society. We want people to leave with a greater sense of "humility" or "conscious incompetence"—being aware that there is room for improvement of their conflict negotiation skills and that to improve will not only make their own lives better, but will improve the world around them. We want them to be aware of how pervasive the phenomenon of identity-based conflict is and to increase their own sense of humility to counter the self-righteousness and dangerous fundamentalism that has grown so exponentially in our time. We want them to leave owning their part.

In a similar vein, we want participants to leave with an appreciation of difference as a source of richness rather than a liability. We want them to be intrigued by the multiple perspectives that human beings from around the globe can have about the same event, and the multiple possibilities there are for misunderstanding. While we want to excite and motivate, we also want to avoid the Pollyanna effect with participants underestimating just how difficult it can be to use these skills. In most of our programs, participants are returning to systems that are not predominantly collaborative. They will likely encounter managers and colleagues who very well may not support them in their use of collaborative conflict management skills. We want them to leave ready and wanting to do the hard work, and to be realistic about how difficult it can be.

Skills Objectives

In our view, human beings learn something most completely by doing it. It is for this reason that the skills objectives are for us perhaps the most key to knowing that we have indeed transferred something and that people have it "in their bones." The most fundamental skills objectives of our training are the following:

To effectively distinguish positions from needs or interests

To reframe a conflict so that it can be seen as a mutual problem to be resolved collaboratively

To distinguish threats, justifications, positions, needs, and feelings and to be able to communicate one's perspective using these distinctions

To ask open-ended questions in a manner that elicits the needs, rather than the defenses, of the other and, by so doing, communicate a desire to engage in a process of mutual need satisfaction

To be able, when under attack, to listen to the other and reflect back the other's needs or interests behind the attack

To be able to listen when one's identity group is under attack and be able to avoid ethnocentric or identity-based responses

To create a collaborative climate through the use of *informing, opening,* and *uniting* behaviors

How do we help participants build skill in avoiding ethnocentric responses, for example? There are many techniques we use. One is to watch an intercultural video and slow the process down, message by message, using our behavioral model as a lens. Slowing the communication down helps people begin to see how they need to stay connected to themselves as well as the other in complicated interactions. We use a filter check model (see Figure 24.1) to help people notice when they feel internal discomfort.

We suggest that they use their discomfort as a signal that there might be an intercultural misunderstanding that they need to identify. We also coach people to understand that, while they may not always be able to acquire specific cross-cultural understanding, it makes a huge difference to simply avoid identity group insults and to convey an authentic sense of respect for the other in spite of difference.

While we can isolate knowledge, attitude, and skills objectives for our own clarity and for analysis, we find it less important in the context of delivering a training program. It is indeed useful to let clients know what the "take-aways" might be, and it is useful to spell out objectives for participants at the beginning of a training program and perhaps before a segment. But beyond that we find it best not to try to isolate but rather to integrate learning objectives in our cases, skill practice, and discussion. Our approach has been to use a case method of teaching these skills; with each case, many different learning objectives will show up. After the case processing, we may do a short lecture in which we talk about various knowledge objectives. We then may do some skill practice emanating from the case, and then end with debriefing that raises participants' awareness about what they have just learned and intuited.

The process is reiterative, as we add a piece each time, and knowledge, attitude, and skills build on each other with each round. In the delivery of the program, all of the objectives and others we have not mentioned are integrated and do not really stand alone. Through short essays in the training manual and mini-lectures, we then highlight in non-technical language key insights from the intercultural and conflict fields. In the graduate program at Columbia University, we have supplemented these essays and mini-lectures with additional assigned readings.

INFUSING CROSS-CULTURAL TRAINING INTO NEGOTIATION AND CONFLICT RESOLUTION TRAINING

Our programs are based on the premise that *all conflict and negotiation training is intercultural and should contain an intercultural component.* We have found this to be true regardless of the client system in which we are working. We address in this section how we have come to this point of view, how we infuse culture into our programs, how we work with culture-specific material, and what we think is most important with respect to intercultural conflict negotiation skills.

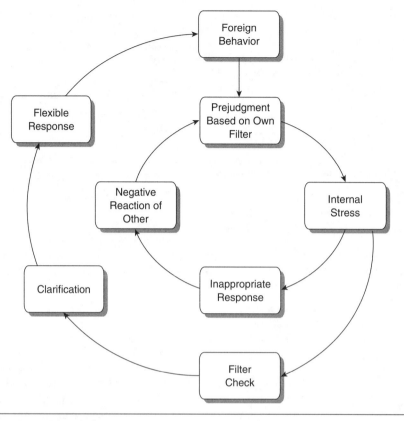

Figure 24.1   Filter Check Model

All Conflict Resolution Training Is "Cross-Cultural" and Should Integrate a Cross-Cultural Perspective

As stated above, we have worked in many different systems—inner-city schools in New York City, United Nations offices in various parts of the world, multinational corporations, and others. In all these groups, there is always a degree of diversity within the group. Nonetheless, what we have learned is that, when conflict exists, there is no group that we have worked with that is not, in some respects, "intercultural." We suspect that, in the vast majority of groups experiencing conflict, an intercultural element will inevitably manifest. When people are in adversarial conflict, a predictable recurring phenomenon is that they will blame their conflict on identity group differences. This blaming will happen whether they be Arabs and

Israelis, men and women, Black Americans and White Americans, or others.

For both of us, in our early work, intercultural training was something that was done internationally. Our focus and work was international—with large multinational U.S.-based corporations that often had difficulty doing their work because of "cultural" differences. What became clear to us was that the word *international* meant to our clients any nation other than the United States. This was a phenomenon similar to the use of the word *ethnic* to refer to anyone who is not White, Anglo-Saxon. In other words, these kinds of terms—*international, ethnic,* and even *cross-cultural*—could imply "the other" or "the stranger," at least for some individuals with a narrow mind-set. Another phenomenon we have noticed from our practice is the changing zeitgeist with respect to various terms used in the field. For instance, when we started our practice, the term *international* was most common. Over time, it seemed to evolve to either *global* or *cross-cultural* or *intercultural,* with the choice of word implying a different emphasis on what was being valued. At the time, *global* seemed to imply a new emerging culture of a corporate elite that transcended national cultural differences. *Cross-cultural* or *intercultural* seemed to imply the phenomenon of cultural difference was everywhere—much broader than international—and something that needed to be understood and appreciated.

As practitioners, we saw ourselves moving away from the term *international* because it stopped having much meaning for us. Indeed, international or cross-cultural or intercultural was, in our eyes, everywhere. What really mattered was whether an individual or group had a competitive or collaborative stance. And, if competitive, were people projecting negative stereotypes onto each other based on identity group differences? With a touch of humor, we began using the term *group-o-centric* (as opposed to the more limited ethnocentric) to describe how broad the phenomenon of ingroup/outgroup is in adversarial conflict, a point that we will discuss more fully later in this chapter.

Infusing Intercultural Training Into Negotiation and Conflict Resolution Components of Our Design

It is important to emphasize that our core training programs in negotiation and mediation have not started with "culture" as the lead topic. Instead, our main focus has been on building negotiation and conflict resolution skills, which includes cross-cultural awareness building. With more time, we have dedicated course hours specifically to culture, but rarely do we get more than three days of training time with a particular group (in our collaborative negotiation skills program). Nevertheless, as we have stated, our training models have always woven the topic of culture throughout the process of teaching and learning negotiation and mediation skills. No matter what we do, we have always made culture part of the equation, and all of our trainers are highly skilled in mining the intercultural "teachable moments," which always emerge. In addition, because we frequently have had multicultural audiences in the room, intercultural issues are typically abundant, with numerous consequent teachable moments for the group to explore and connect to what we are teaching in the course. In our core program, there are ways that we infuse skills that are critical to effective intercultural communication. We follow with a few examples.

Understanding the elements of the negotiation process is a core concept for us. Along with typical negotiation concepts like positions versus needs, we have always incorporated the concept of "worldview." We tell participants that worldview can come from one's life experience, one's personality type (e.g., Myers-Briggs Type Indicator; Myers and Briggs Foundation, 2005), or from one's culture. Very early in our training design, we typically show a video example of this. One of the classic video clips from *Going International Part Two: Managing the Overseas Assignment* (Griggs, 1983) shows a businessman from the United States (Mr. Thompson) waiting for his Mexican counterpart (Sr. Herrera) in an outdoor café in Mexico City. Mr. Thompson reacts negatively to the late arrival of Sr. Herrera (to whom he is trying to make a sale), apparently assuming the lateness is some form of disrespect or power play. The video captures elegantly and with humor how monochronic and polychronic[1] individuals can misunderstand each other, a good example of a worldview clash. Sr. Herrera, the polychronic of the two, is late because he is greeting important people along the way. He also does not want to get down to business until he has gotten to know something about the man with whom he is doing business. Mr. Thompson, though, is driven by the task, always looking at his watch and pushing to get the contract signed—so *then* he can go out and have a good time!

When presented, we explain to groups that neither way is the right way; they are just examples of the ways that negotiation counterparts experience worldviews differently. We also ask people, "What are the negative stereotypes that each will project on to the other" and "whether they do it vocally or not?" For the polychronic toward the monochronic, the group responses include "cold," "tight," "too task oriented," and so on. For the monochronic toward the polychronic, they might say "lazy," "not dependable," "unprofessional," and the like. We point out that this phenomenon—negative stereotyping around identity group differences—is predictable in conflict, can be very destructive, and is one that we will continue to explore throughout the course (see also Boyacigiller, Goodman, & Phillips, 2003, and Fowler & Blohm, 2004, for additional intercultural situations).

An example of how we infuse "culture" with audiences of educators, is our role-play simulation, "Melting Pot or Salad Bowl," which surfaces issues of race. The disputants in this case are two groups: the Black Teachers Caucus (BTC) and the predominately White school governance committee at an urban High School in New York City (Note: this case is based on a real conflict mediated by Raider). The BTC demands a Black seat on the governance committee, claiming that the student population is predominantly "of color." The governance committee rejects this demand for a "race-based" seat, countering that representation should be by academic department, not by racial or ethnic identity group. We help participants move from these potentially volatile negotiation positions to focus on the underlying needs, which include multicultural representation in policy making and curriculum development as well as some way to represent all fairly. We point out that, where worldview conflict is at issue, moving to a needs focus can help reduce or even dissipate the focus on worldview differences. This is a critical intercultural conflict skill.

For international audiences, we have frequently used a case called the "Ossipilla Community," a fictitious but true-to-life case. In the Ossipilla case, there are four groups: investors, government, environmentalists, and community representatives. The "investor group" has joined forces with the "government group" representatives to promote a mining project in the community of Ossipilla. The "community group" representatives oppose this project and are joined by "environmentalist group" representatives. Along with focusing on the underlying needs and interests of all sides, we are also able to talk about power as well as the worldview issues that emerge naturally as people stereotype all four groups.

One way we use this case is to divide a group of four into sides A and B. In *Round One* of the negotiation, each side presents its point of view while the other side tries hard to listen and paraphrase the underlying needs it is hearing. In *Round Two,* sides A and B switch and repeat the negotiation, following the model of academic controversy (Johnson & Johnson, 1987). This technique helps not only to move the conflict toward resolution but gets participants to realize how difficult it is to step into the shoes of the other side, a key intercultural negotiation skill.

Exploring Cultural Variables in a Dedicated Segment of a Negotiations Training

When we have more time, we will often dedicate a component of the program to the exploration of culture. What follows is a couple of examples of the kinds of discussions we might present and facilitate.

We often will start our exploration of culture with talking about the concept more generally or doing an intercultural experiential exercise. As we stated earlier, we often used Hofstede's definition of culture. We then go on to suggest that "personality is to an individual what culture is to a group." Culture is a group's personality. Inspired by our diversity work, we may ask folks what human groups they identify as being part of, and we generate a list of "categories of culture." It might include the following: (a) Nationality, (b) Ethnicity, (c) Age, (d) Gender, (e) Professional Status, (f) Sexual Orientation, (g) Education, (h) Language, (i) Religion, and (j) Social or Economic Class.

We remind people of the videotape we have seen earlier—of Mr. Thompson and Sr. Herrera—and the negative stereotypes that each could easily make of the other when in a destructive pattern of conflict. We point out that this can happen as easily in a non-international conflict situation; a husband and wife in a destructive conflict dialogue can easily find themselves using or thinking gender-related put-downs—with heightened frustrations perhaps culminating in "I hate women" or "These insensitive men!" Similar phenomena can happen with any individuals from different identity groups—for instance, a Pakistani in conflict with an Indian, a Haitian with a Black American, or a young person with an older person. We ask people to become aware of how much those stereotypes live in each one of us and how quickly they roll off our tongues. We suggest that one of the hallmarks of being collaborative is to avoid demonizing the other side around identity group differences when conflict becomes adversarial. While people can feel very justified when calling someone a name with an "ist" ending (e.g., racist, sexist), we suggest that identifying needs, avoiding assumptions, and thinking of the ways we prejudge can be far more useful than making claims that a person is a perpetuator of an unjust system. This is true whether the difference we are talking about is international, inter-gender, inter-race, or something else.

In training people about the ways that cultures differ, we have always worked to find fun and effective experiential exercises to counter what otherwise can be a didactic lecture. We might do something short and sweet like an exercise with different nonverbal instructions to different dyadic pairs and ask them to have a conversation with each other. Or, we might conduct a more complicated intercultural cocktail party where we divide trainees into groups and create "cultures" that they must interact. In a very short time, we can get the two groups to create lists of descriptions of the other that are very judgmental. We explain the difference between a description, an interpretation, and a judgment (Ting-Toomey, 1999) so that people can see how quickly they move to judgment while thinking they are just simply describing (see, e.g., "Alpha and Omega Intergroup Conflict Negotiation" simulation de-briefing, Ting-Toomey, 2004).

After talking about culture in general, we have often moved on to exploring all or some of Hofstede's (1991, 2001) value dimensions: power distance, collectivism/individualism, risk or uncertainty avoidance, and the masculine/ feminine dimension, which we have rephrased as "quality of life versus task orientation." We sometimes have participants come into class on the day we are going to explore culture having taken a questionnaire based on Hofstede's work. We then show a video clip that captures the Hofstede variables. For instance, to explore the concept of high/low power distance, we often have used a scenario from the movie *Praying With Anger* (M. Night Shyamalan, 1992)—a film

about an alienated, Americanized teenager of East Indian heritage who is sent back to India where he discovers not only his roots but a lot about himself. In the clip we show, the teenager is acting very "American" in the classroom: challenging the teacher's authority, wearing his baseball cap, not standing when he is called upon, and so on. The teacher is offended by the student's behavior, sends him out of the classroom, and tells him that he is "very close to suspension," much to the puzzlement of the student, who believes he is behaving appropriately. We ask the group, What are the assumptions that the teacher is making about teaching and learning? What are the assumptions that the student is making? Is either right? No, they are just different. Where did each of you fall on your questionnaire with respect to power distance? Does this make sense to you? What are the implications of this dimension for how you parent your children? What are the implications for how you manage people?

Video clips and exercises like this are debriefed by using our "filter check model" (see Figure 24.1). With the filter check chart as a focus, we explain that when one experiences behavior that feels foreign, judges it, and then feels stress, the stress should trigger a heightened desire to go into a collaborative mode to try to discover whether there is an intercultural or perceptual difference.

As stated above, when there is more limited time, we edit out course components dedicated exclusively to culture. We do this for a variety of reasons, two of which we will explain below. The main reason is that, in our experience, the skill set of collaborative negotiation is the core intercultural skill that transcends participants' learning any specific intercultural theory or information, and it can take all the time that we have to impart it effectively. In the past, we have delivered many briefing programs on specific cultures. What always struck us was that, while it was useful to acquire information about a specific culture, it could also be misleading. The world is changing at lightening speed and culture-specific information can set the participant up for making rigid assumptions. Following the traditional Chinese saying, quoted by Mao Zedong (Mao Tse-Tung), we thought it more useful to teach people how to fish, rather than to give them fish. This meant helping students truly master perspective-taking—a key skill in our collaborative negotiations sequence.

An additional reason has to do with our preference for interactive learning experiences rather than didactic lecture. Simply presenting intercultural theory and information can be very dry, but the most powerful intercultural/intergroup simulations we have created are lengthy to run and debrief.

THE "CULTURE" OF COMPETITION VERSUS COLLABORATION

After years of practice, we are both left with the perception that culture does matter, and cross-cultural sensitivity and understanding are very important. But they are secondary compared to the primary issue of whether the "culture" is competitive or collaborative. What we teach participants is that, if they are truly able to negotiate a situation collaboratively, they will find that the worldview issues (of which we define culture as being part) will become a non-issue. It is the competitive conflict that exacerbates cultural differences and makes situations more volatile. Our goal, therefore, is to teach our trainees that changing the climate to one of collaboration is their primary task. Trainees are encouraged to respect and understand cultural differences so they do not become the source of the conflict, but the main focus must be shifting from a competitive to a collaborative orientation.

How do we convey this more specifically? To elaborate, we will use examples from training segments of four distinct modules of our program—*The Elements of Negotiation, Behaviors in Negotiation, Emotions,* and *The Stages of Negotiation.*

The Elements of Negotiation

One of the skill sets we teach as part of our module *The Elements of Negotiation* is how to plan for an upcoming negotiation or discussion of a conflict issue. Our suggested method is to use a form to break the information down into several identified elements—*worldview, positions, needs, reframing,* and *alternative chips or chops* (Raider & Coleman, 1992, 1997, 2004). After presenting to participants about how we

suggest they plan, we give them a case so they can immediately apply the methodology. One case, which derives from a conflict in a multinational diplomatic organization, is called "A Mission Possible?" In this case, the Director of the Environmental Analysis Division, a man, wants his subordinate to spend her time doing administrative work. The subordinate, a young, bright, and well-connected woman "who just returned from a sabbatical at the Institute for Development Studies in Sussex, England," took the job thinking that she would be working on a newsletter. She is upset by her boss's orders and has complained to a number of people in the office that her boss is a "narrow-minded sexist who feels threatened by her." As participants analyze the information in the case, they see that the case could explode into adversarial accusations ending in some kind of discrimination charge. Instead, through the process of analyzing the needs underlying the positions, it becomes clear that what the subordinate really wants is meaningful work around environmental policy making. What the boss wants is to ensure that his office has a real impact on environmental policy making before he retires in three years. Once these needs are uncovered and reframed, and some common ground is recognized, there are many options for solution that meet both sides' concerns, and the discrimination charges become irrelevant. In other words, when parties' needs are met, the apparent worldview clash disappears.

In debriefing discussions of the exercise we might ask participants for examples of where they have seen similar phenomena in the world. One participant, for example, raised the "sale" of Manhattan Island by the Native Americans to the Dutch as a good case in point of the intercultural issue being secondary to whether the "culture" of the interaction was collaborative or competitive. In that instance, by trading land for corn and other goods, researchers now say the Native Americans believed that what they were trading was the right to *share* land since no one could own land in their culture. This, of course, conflicted with the European worldview of early capitalism and private property rights. Had the intent of the interaction been collaborative, when the misunderstanding became clear there would have been a resolution that met the needs of both sides. Instead, what happened was that the Europeans

Behaviors Used in Negotiation

A
Attack

Threats, hostile tones or gestures, insults, defending, criticizing, patronizing, stereotyping, blaming, discounting others' ideas, interrupting, counterattacks, asking leading judgmental questions.

E
Evade

Ignore, change subject, withdraw, postpone to get more information, confer with colleagues, or think.

I
Inform

State what you want and why; justify your position with facts or opinions; reveal your underlying needs or feelings.

O
Open

Ask nonjudgmental questions about the other's position, needs, or feelings; actively listen by paraphrasing; test understanding and summarize without necessarily agreeing.

U
Unite

Ritual sharing to build rapport, establish common ground, reframe the issue to meet both sides' needs, propose solutions that link expressed needs to bargaining chips.

Y
Yes

and sometimes

Split the difference or some form of integrative agreement that meets both sides' needs.

Figure 24.2   Behaviors Used in Negotiation: A.E.I.O.U. Model

SOURCE: Copyright © 1992, 1997, Ellen Raider International, Inc. and The Coleman Group International, Inc. Permission has been given for use in this chapter. Other use is prohibited without written permission of the copyright holder.

drove the Indians from the land, claiming that the land now belonged to them. Of course, that resulted in a great deal of conflict and bloodshed.

Behaviors in Conflict Negotiation

In our module on *Negotiation Behaviors* it becomes very clear how the choice of one's behavior can impact whether the communication moves toward competition or collaboration. It also becomes clear to most participants (regardless of nationality) how difficult it is to avoid getting into a competitive communication cycle with all of the associated ethnocentric and group-o-centric attacks and defensive moves.

First, we describe our conflict behavioral model in more detail. As stated above, we divide human communication in negotiation or conflict into five categories: *Attack, Evade, Inform,*

Open, and Unite (i.e., the A.E.I.O.U. acronym), which is represented in Figure 24.2.

In the first scenario, the actors use a competitive style that escalates to a place where they have moved the conflict to an issue of worldview or cultural difference. For example, let's say the boss is from Culture A (a dominant cultural group in the organization) and the subordinate from Culture B (a minority group in the organization that has a history of being discriminated against inside the organization and in the world).

Interaction Example 1:
Competitive conversation using
Attacking, Evading, and Informing behaviors.

Boss: I realize that you have plans to go on vacation as of tomorrow, but I need to ask you to postpone them. (*Inform*)

Subordinate: That's impossible! I can't do it. (*Inform,* or more likely *Attack*)

Boss: Well, I think you better think about how to do it. It seems you are not very serious about your work when we have so much on our plate and all you are thinking about is your vacation! (*Attack*)

Subordinate: Listen. I followed all the rules for putting in for my leave. If you stand in my way, I will have to grieve this. You can't discriminate against me like this. (*Attack*)

Now we model doing the interaction collaboratively—listening for needs, reframing, and then brainstorming what they can offer to each other to meet needs as opposed to positions.

Interaction Example 2:
Collaborative conversation using
Informing, Opening, and Uniting behaviors.

Boss: I realize that you have plans to go on vacation as of tomorrow, but I need to ask you to postpone them. (*Inform*)

Subordinate: That's difficult. (*Inform.*) Could you tell me more about what you need? (*Open*)

Boss: Yes. My boss has requested we get to her immediately the plan we have been developing for a redesign of the internal system of dispute resolution. It's particularly important that the plan reflect the results of the needs assessment that you did. (*Inform*)

Subordinate: So what you need from me is to make sure that the results of the needs assessment are reflected accurately in the report? (*Open*)

Boss: That's exactly it. (*Inform*)

Subordinate: I need to tell you that it's difficult for me to stay. The issue for me is that I have a nonrefundable ticket and I am also concerned that I will forfeit my leave altogether if I don't take it now. I am exhausted and I need a break. (*Inform*)

Boss: So you have two concerns: needing a rest and not losing the money you spent on the ticket? (*Open*)

Subordinate: That's right. With respect to the ticket, I spent $900 and I think I will only get $100 back if I don't use the ticket as planned . . . (*Inform*)

Subordinate (continuing): I think you know how much I share with you the need to present an excellent work product from this office as well as to create an effective internal system of resolving disputes. (Highlighting Common Ground—a form of *Uniting* behavior)

Subordinate (continuing): Is there a way to ensure that my knowledge of the needs assessment be reflected in our work product and ensure that I don't lose my vacation time and have a ticket when I get it? (Reframe—a form of *Uniting* behavior)

The parties then brainstorm solutions (or what we call *bargaining chips* that they can offer each other to meet needs) which include the following: From SUBORDINATE: staying, bringing laptop, and reviewing document by e-mail, and more; from BOSS: frequent flyer miles, assure future vacation time, and the like. They finally resolve to have the subordinate postpone his vacation for a week, and in exchange, get a guarantee of future vacation time with a few days added on, plus the chief offers to cover the cost of the air ticket with frequent flyer miles she has accumulated and which she is not going to use and that are about to expire.

We intentionally use an "out of the box" solution (e.g., boss offering frequent flyer miles) to get people to see that collaboration means being creative. We often cite Betty Reardon (1993) for the idea that the absence of peace stems from a failure of imagination. We hope the reader sees clearly how this example demonstrates why the culture of collaboration versus competition is ultimately more critical than culture itself.

Emotions

In the segment of our program where we explore emotions, we have experienced further evidence that the culture of "collaboration" is preeminent over any cultural differences we may encounter. One example of this is a listening exercise that we regularly use. Participants line up in two facing lines across from a counterpart with whom they will converse. In this exercise, we introduce a simple model of human emotions—mad, sad, glad, scared, loving. We also use Abraham Maslow's (Maslow & Murphy, 1954) hierarchy of needs as one model that identifies the range of human needs. Those include physical needs, security needs, belonging, recognition, and self-actualization. In this exercise, we also explore the cultural range of listening styles; for instance, physical proximity, direction of head shaking, use of touch, and others. We ask participants to explore a feeling state with their counterpart, for example, "a time when I was afraid." In the process of practicing listening skills, we ask people to think about the needs that are coming up around the feelings. We explain that feelings are information to us about needs that are either being met or being thwarted. We also point out that there are some real parallels between certain feelings that come up and different categories of need. For instance, when we ask, "What category of need was at issue around the feelings of fear?" The vast majority of the time the participants will talk about security needs. The same predictable connections occur between feelings of sadness and belonging needs, and feelings of anger and recognition needs.

We frequently have done this exercise with multinational audiences—people coming from every part of the globe—sometimes from countries we honestly have never heard of. What we feel tangibly in the room is that the categories of feelings and needs are universal to everyone and transcend any cultural differences that are coming up. Of course, for those whose cultural behavior is familiar, greater levels of rapport and trust may be possible, but the universality of feelings and needs trumps any cultural differences.

Again, we sometimes make a connection between what we are experiencing in the room and what is happening at the global level. For instance, we might talk about mothers in Israel and Palestine who have all lost sons and daughters and who are coming together—transcending identity group divides and connecting at a gut emotional level to talk about creating a world where people do not live in constant fear of losing their beloved (Families Forum, 2004).

Stages of Conflict Negotiation

Finally, we move to an example from our section titled the *Stages of Negotiation*. For us, the stages module represents the macro view of the negotiation process. In this module, we are trying to help participants "pull it all together" to understand the whole of what needs to exist in a collaborative negotiation. Our model consists of *Ritual Sharing* or *Setting the Climate, Identifying Positions and Needs, Reframing,* and *Exploring Alternatives* (Raider & Coleman, 1992, 1997, 2004).

We often use a fictitious video case study developed for UNICEF to depict the stage flow (Raider & Silverman, 1992). In this example, a donor country, Richland, wants UNICEF to provide quarterly instead of annual reports. UNICEF would like to stick with the status quo, which is the annual report. The needs underlying the positions are "more frequent information" on the part of Richland and "workload management" on the part of UNICEF. Moving from positions to needs, "reframing" the conflict, and then coming up with "chips" that they each can offer to link with needs—the collaborative approach—the role-players are able to work out a good agreement that works for both sides. Nonetheless, at one point the Richland representative does suggest that the reason she should have these quarterly reports is because they have made a "significant increase in contribution." In our language this is a "justification" in support of a position, which is used as part of a competitive, and not collaborative process. We point out how quickly this can escalate from justification to threat—for example, "We have other potential recipients of our money waiting in the wings, and if you don't do as we say, we will pull the plug." This is the language of intimidation and power used to resolve disputes. We make sure participants recognize it and then we typically give some examples that play out in the world, which are, unfortunately in our view, far too pervasive.

Cross-Cultural Understanding Contributes to Collaboration

While we believe the fundamental orientation of competition or collaboration is key, we certainly do not mean to suggest that increasing awareness of cross-cultural difference is not important. For years we have been saying to participants that if "worldview issues are not respected or understood, they will become the source of an impasse or conflict." We still believe this. One of the quickest ways to create a conflict and certainly to exacerbate one is to convey identity group disrespect. Conversely, educating a group about cross-cultural differences is a key ingredient in creating a collaborative atmosphere.

The more people learn about difference, the more they expand their worldview, and the more they expand their worldview, the more they become collaborative. For example, at the end of one of our courses in Malaysia, with a diverse group of participants, people came up to get a diploma and each used their culturally appropriate greeting and thanks. Some shook hands, some put hands together in prayer, some bowed, some used an *abrazo* [hug], and so forth. Everybody watched others being culturally appropriate. They were "in community." So, the increased cross-cultural awareness increased the sense of community and respect and greatly contributed to the sense of collaboration in the room. We believe our training program and others like it are small but powerful examples of forces that are teaching people the nuts and bolts of collaboration, and are moving the planet toward deeper democracy.

FROM INTERCULTURAL TO INTERGROUP CONFLICT TRAINING

It is clear from the discussion above that while understanding cultural differences is important, learning how to be collaborative is the key: If collaboration is the norm in an interaction, the potential for significant intercultural conflict is virtually obliterated. Having said that, we recognize that overcoming the pervasiveness of identity group competition—as it shows up in the training room and as it shows up in the world—is a huge challenge. As trainers, this is a phenomenon that, while difficult to impact in a time-bound training course, is an essential ingredient of one's awareness while doing intercultural training work. Thus, we would like to

explore the issues more fully below as well as describe some of the ways we address them in our programs.

Power, Culture, and Intergroup Conflict

As we have stated, a predictable recurring phenomenon of adversarial conflict is that people will blame their inability to reach a resolution on apparent identity group differences. This phenomenon becomes more problematic when we add the ingredient of social or economic power. The groups that have established themselves as the normative groups in terms of, for example, ethnicity, age, class, race, political ideology, or sexual orientation will use the power of that norm to resolve differences in their favor.

These types of examples range from the mundane to those events that take much of our global focus and resources. Scissors are generally made for right-handed people. In school curriculum, in spite of efforts to the contrary, there are hidden messages about which groups are more important than others. Indeed, what gets taught and is determined important typically emanates from the dominant culture. The words we use are defined by the dominant culture of the particular system we are in—for instance, whether someone is a "terrorist" or a "freedom fighter." The recent Kyoto Accords provided a good example of "a culture war" where the dominant culture's values (the U.S., in that instance) would win out with respect to the environment. Indeed, as the United States stands currently as the world's only superpower, it is in a position to impose its norms (cultural and otherwise) on the rest of the world.

Using dominance to resolve conflict. From our experience, if their frame is competitive, people will use the dominance of their identity group to resolve conflict in their favor. Perhaps to protect themselves from the injustice of their action, they go farther and use self-righteousness to justify what they have done. Throughout history, many have used this tactic to establish themselves as being on the side of morality and even God.

This happens in big and little ways all the time. If we are looking, we can all see regular, daily examples. For example, Susan recently took her then 8-year-old son, Jack, snowboarding. More than once, adult skiers or snowboarders reprimanded Jack for being in their way when, in fact, he was standing off to the side and they were skiing too fast down the side of the mountain. They were using the privilege of their adulthood to resolve the conflict in their favor, judging Jack to be in the wrong. When Jack spoke out about the injustice, Susan supported him. When kids are not supported, they internalize the injustice and then pass it on, perhaps in contexts much more damaging than a ski slope.

We recently observed an interesting example in the training room in a very hierarchical organization where the training group consisted of people from different parts of the hierarchy. We were doing what we call the "Berlin Wall" exercise. The group is split in half and lines up facing each other, with each participant facing one negotiation counterpart. They are asked to visualize an imaginary line between them and that "everything on your side of the line is your territory, and everything on the other's side of the line is theirs." Each pair is given one minute to "get their partner to come into their territory using whatever methodology you wish." The exercise is used to discuss possible outcomes in negotiation, from impasse to integrative solutions. What we observed in this instance, however, was that the group used the positional power from the organization to resolve the conflict. Positional power was completely irrelevant to our exercise, but the lower level staff people simply accommodated the senior folks in the room.

Dominance becomes oppression. One of the most insidious aspects of ingroup dominance is the way individuals from ingroups or outgroups internalize their respective dominance or oppression. For a time in graduate school, Susan had a roommate from Somalia, whom we will call Fatima, who had been circumcised. When sharing her experience with Susan, Fatima expressed distress at her mother's threat that if Fatima left her 6-year-old daughter alone with the grandmother, the grandmother would make sure her granddaughter was circumcised. The grandmother had swallowed whole the appropriateness of circumcision for all girls, in spite of all the physical and emotional scars it leaves

in its wake. How do we as trainers handle these very complicated issues in the course of a multiple-day training? We will discuss some of our training techniques and models and then some suggestions for the kinds of awareness that are necessary in doing this work.

We use the concepts of identity group differences mixed with power in our programs to help people understand the "isms"—how one group's worldview becomes normative or even institutionalized at the expense of other groups. This material can create a lot of discomfort in groups, and we often expect resistance from participants. Essentially, we are teaching nothing different from the kind of perspective taking that is needed in a cross-cultural interaction where power is equal. Nonetheless, the concept of "power over" and the privilege or lack of privilege that ensues have large sociopolitical implications that involve everyone.

The resistance can come from either side of the political spectrum. Those who are working within a hierarchical structure and who are either resigned to it or embrace it will complain that collaboration is not realistic. Similarly, political activists may say that, when in low power, negotiation is useless—that power must be taken and is never given away. In our workshops or classes, we deal with these observations either by talking conceptually or through experiential exercises, or both. For a short conceptual answer we might discuss process choice. For example, we might explain that every conflict has a needs analysis, a rights analysis, and a power analysis (Ury, Brett, & Goldberg, 1988). One must be aware of all three levels but be conscious of which channel one is choosing to deal with the issue. We might also get more refined (and certainly do in a course in mediation) and discuss conflict resolution methodologies—negotiation, mediation, arbitration, litigation, nonviolent civil disobedience, and war.

When we have the luxury of a longer program, such as the Rank, Power, and Privilege class described earlier, we might engage the group in an experiential exercise and then debrief it by exploring social psychological principles as described below. We recommend experiential exercises first, if possible, as they reduce the amount of resistance to the intellectual concepts that we may later present. In one experiential exercise, we ask participants to design a poster about power. We divide the group into multiple subgroups and give each increasingly fewer resources with which to create the poster. Group one, for instance, may get the poster board, some paints, some glue, different interesting magazine clippings, and so on. The last group may get a pencil with a broken tip and one uninteresting picture. Inevitably, what begins to occur is that the group with the limited resources ends up stealing from the groups with more. Discussions that follow help all participants widen their scope of justice by becoming more aware of the negative stereotypes and misperceptions that they have of those who have been deprived of their fair share of societal resources based on being consigned to a low rank in a competitive social order.

Another powerful experiential exercise we use is to line everyone up shoulder to shoulder in one line and holding hands. The facilitator leads the group through the exercise, asking everyone in the group to take a step forward if they have the privilege that the facilitator suggests. For instance, the facilitator may start with something that most people in the room will have, for example, two legs—and everyone will take a step forward. Increasingly, the facilitator will state things that fewer people are likely to have (e.g., a graduate degree). As this occurs, people will find that they move ahead or fall behind others in the group and eventually have to let go of their hand. The privilege or lack thereof experienced in the training environment among participants who have become friendly with one another in the course of the training allows heartfelt connections and dialogue.

These kinds of exercises move the group beyond the typical use of collaborative negotiation skills to a place where the focus is on deep listening and dialogue to replace stereotyping and prejudging. People connect on a human-to-human level to hear and understand how the different aspects of privilege and oppression have affected them on a personal level. We also use intellectual discussion around the social psychology of ingroup and outgroup relations to put some theory behind the experiences the group has just had (see Stephan, 1999; Stephan & Stephan, 2001). Ellen has frequently used the chart displayed in Table 24.1 to debrief experiential

exercises or guide a group through a discussion surrounding a keynote presentation. The kinds of discussions and exercises that ensue are described.

Human beings sort and categorize. We discuss how this is a perfectly natural phenomenon that all of us use to make meaning of our world. We might sort according to age, gender, race, professional interest, and so on. We all identify as belonging to a multiple of identity groups. For example, a young man in his 30s from the United States, who has never had use of his right arm, may identify as being part or all of the following human groups—men, U.S. nationals, generation Xers, activists, affluent, short, and physically challenged. Most people will have a relatively easy time understanding and accepting this concept.

To understand this sorting mechanism, we may do an exercise such as the following: We may ask everyone to pick from a pile of multicolored pieces of construction paper, each cut into a variety of shapes. We ask them to pin the paper on their chest and then, without further instruction, to form groups. Having no other information about criteria to use in forming groups, participants will often sort according to pieces of paper that are most similar to one another. We suspect this exercise is a derivative of what social psychologists call the "minimalist group experiment" (Tagfel, 1982) where it was demonstrated that within 30 minutes the subjects of the experiment would favor the group that was most like them. One person was given a red jacket and one a white jacket and then they were asked to distribute money to individuals who were brought into the room. If someone came in wearing a red jacket, the red-jacketed person would be likely to give more money to red-jacketed persons than to white-jacketed persons (a laboratory-created minimalist group). In our training, we discuss that if this phenomenon can be created in a laboratory setting within 30 minutes, imagine how pervasive this tendency is among human beings. We seem to want to be kind to the people who are like us, and that will affect whom we will side with and whom we think is trustworthy when we are part of a conflict (Tagfel, 1982).

So we discuss with audiences about how we sort people into groups and categories and favor those who are like us. But then, we ask them,

Table 24.1   10 Principles of Intergroup Conflict

1. Human minds inevitably sort people and things into categories or groups.

2. We each are identified or are classified by others into different groups.

3. We all have a fundamental need to belong. Groups we identify with are our "ingroups." Others are seen as the "outgroups."

4. Many societies socialize their members to rank groups and then disproportionately distribute resources by those ranks. This ranking is perceived as normal, natural, "the way things are" rather than human-made and changeable.

5. Groups ranked high are privileged, while groups ranked low are disadvantaged and are targets of individual and institutional discrimination.

6. From our "ingroup" perspective, when we are in a conflict where issues of rank, power and privilege are salient and we feel threatened by someone from an "outgroup," we perceive ourselves as right, moral and good. The other is assumed to be misguided at best; wrong or evil at worst.

7. If you belong to a group that is a target of discrimination and the group identity is important to you, you will likely respond to bias against you or your group. If you chose not to leave or can not leave your targeted group, either you will internalize the bias seeing yourselves as a victim, try to raise your group's status, or "change the rules of the game."

8. As a member of an advantaged group, you are likely to hold unexamined negative stereotypes of the disadvantaged group, be unaware of your privilege as well as the "uneven playing field" for members of the targeted group.

9. Whether you are a target of discrimination or privileged, because of the inherent unfairness in a system, you will have strong emotions, which you may need to deal with in order to protect your self esteem. The advantaged may have to cope with feelings of guilt and the fear of retaliation. The disadvantaged may have to cope with feelings such as shame, humiliation, rage and depression. Lack of awareness of these emotions can prevent you from trying to take control of those things in your personal and civic life which you might be able to change. This can leave you vulnerable to the manipulations of those who want to take advantage of intergroup conflict.

10. Intergroup relations often take a destructive course in a competitive context. By contrast, in a cooperative environment, diversity rather than a source of anxiety, tension and conflict, can be the source of personal and societal growth.

SOURCE: Copyright © 1999 Ellen Raider International, Inc., and may be used without permission.

is the opposite true? When dealing with people who are different, are we hardwired to do them harm? Some come to our course believing that is true. We hope participants leave having internalized through discussion and experiential exercises the concepts and ideas we provide that would suggest otherwise.

Ranking is learned behavior. We continue by exploring how many societies socialize their members to rank groups and then distribute resources disproportionately according to those ranks. The pernicious part of this ranking is that all social institutions, such as government, schools, and media, largely support the perception that this ranking is normal, natural, and "the way things are" rather than human-made and changeable. We explain to groups that this phenomenon of ranking is not hardwired, but rather is human made (Deutsch, 1985). It is important to separate the process of "sorting" and "ranking." Specifically, sorting by perceived differences may be innate, but ranking some people as more humanly valuable is socialized or learned. Ranking has a lot to do with a group-o-centric competitive mind-set. Human beings have both tendencies—they can rank and be competitive and they can be collaborative and get beyond surface differences.

Human beings have a collaborative past. To further emphasize that ranking is learned, participants find it interesting to learn that there is evidence that humans have not necessarily always been competitive (Ury, 1999). For instance, in her trailblazing book, *The Chalice and the Blade,* Rianne Eisler (1988) talks about the shifting in human history from partnership models to dominator models:

> [T]his cataclysmic turning point during the pre-history of Western civilization, when the direction of our cultural evolution was quite literally turned around . . . from societies that worshiped the life-generating and nurturing powers of the universe . . . [to] a very different form of social organization . . . [the] people who worshiped "the lethal power of the blade"—the power to take rather than give life that is the ultimate power to establish and enforce domination. (p. xvii)

We also see evidence that the species over time seems to be seeing the need for less ranking. For example, the creation of documents like the *Universal Declaration of Human Rights* is testament to the principle of human equality—but we clearly have a long way to go.

When ranking is institutionalized. There is nothing wrong with organizational hierarchy as a means of structuring work, or as a concept of respect in accordance with role prescriptions in a family system. Where we get into difficulty is when we make the "high-archy" more valuable than the "low-archy" ("He's my boss, he's a more valuable human being than I am"). What's especially problematic is when the ranking is institutionalized into the system and taught to our young (e.g., management is better than labor, Whites are better than Blacks, men are better than women, Western is better than Eastern, or whatever the hierarchies might be in the particular society or system in question). For

example, the "hidden curriculum" of our children's schools conveys the message that boys are better than girls at math and sports; the movie industry regularly reflects the standard of success and beauty by who it selects for fame. These are the kinds of discussions and presentation that happen around the ten principles of intergroup conflict.

The issue of imbalance of power at the interpersonal, intergroup, and global levels raises interesting pedagogical and professional issues for trainers of cross-cultural conflict or communication. Many of these questions are very tricky to raise in a classroom or training room setting, and it must be done with care. A pedagogical tool we have used with success is to talk about power dynamics and their interface to a culture farther from home for the target audience. For instance, in talking about race in the United States, a good starting point might be to show an intercultural interaction between someone from the United States and someone from India. The subsequent discussion would then pull from the audience their observations about the similarities and differences to identity group issues closer to home.

Is the cross-cultural research we present a product of colonialism or imperialism? We suspect that the cultural dimensions that have been identified in the literature are steeped in power dynamics and the history of colonialism throughout the world. Can "cultural" differences be identified without looking at the power dynamics that have framed the worldview of a particular group? For instance, in his research Hofstede (1980, 1991) focused on nation-states and not on indigenous groups. As nation-states are frequently creations of colonialism, what does that suggest about the cross-cultural comparisons that can be made? The ethnic tension that is experienced today between Arabs and the United States owes its origins in large part to the ways colonial powers divided the world into nation-states. So, is the high power distance in a British colony attributable to indigenous culture or something that came from colonial oppression? What is Iraqi culture, for instance, but an amalgamation of many cultures and subcultures? Or, for example, is Haitian patois a cultural variation, or is it simply a group's response to colonization? Many indigenous groups in Africa, Asia, and the Americas had collaborative cultures, at least internally. To understand their "culture" now, however, one would have to understand how colonialism has impacted them and shifted their worldview.

How Does Intergroup Dominance Impact the Training Itself?

The issue of power permeates the delivery of training in cross-cultural negotiation skills as well. People or organizations that can pay for in-service training are typically those with resources and power. Our early work in international negotiations was for multinational corporations and governmental elites. When we worked through negotiation issues with them, or replayed a negotiation that did not go well, for instance, our charge was to look at only the negotiation counterparts, not the negotiation stakeholders—most of whom were not at the table.

For instance, when we were doing a training program for participants from various developing nations, we invited some representatives of a few multinational corporations. There was a good interaction between the people in the room, and we were satisfied with our intervention. Our goal was to empower developing nations in their negotiations with multinational corporations. But what dawned on us was that all of those present in the room, diplomats and corporate representatives alike, were elites. Most of the people who would be affected by their negotiations were not at the table. Democracy requires representation, but as long as we are not in a collaborative world the people who have power will be the ones to come to the table and make decisions for everyone else.

We have trained administrators and teachers in collaborative negotiation skills, but those programs do not include other stakeholders like the parents or the students, who also have a huge stake in the outcome of any bargaining session. As trainers, we are not coming in as peaceworkers to identify who is not at the table. We typically do not have the power to bring in indigenous representatives, even if they are major stakeholders to a negotiation.[2] The tables are made by the powerful and, if the powerful do not want to play, negotiation alone will not

work. Thus, one needs to ask the question, What exactly does "international" or "cross-cultural" training mean, and what does it mean within the context of the power relationships in the world? Does it mean training to work in international settings? Does it mean training one cultural group to work with another? Is it about nationality, ethnicity, or what?

SOME FINAL RECOMMENDATIONS FOR THE FIELD

We have tried to give the reader a good sense of the work we have been doing and the conclusions we have drawn from it. What follows is some of our thinking for the future about some practical considerations that we think trainers must keep in mind in doing intercultural conflict resolution training.

Maintain a Diverse Training Team

In our practice, we have worked with trainers from all over the world and have gone to great pains to ensure as diverse a training team as possible. We suspect the importance of this is clear to any of our readers. The diversity of our training team has had a number of desired effects on our training. The first is our own learning from each other. Second, we have been able to model in front of the group the resolution of cross-cultural issues "live." Probably the most important impact on the training is that when a participant identifies with one of the trainers he or she is often more supported in taking risks, feeling empowered, and otherwise feeling a part of the program. The more we can create that effect, the more we have created the collaborative atmosphere we desire.

For instance, we have noted in a multinational group with the presence of a few Black Africans that the presence of an African American trainer, while a different nationality, was important to the Africans in the room. We have had similar observations of the impact on Asian participants when we use an Asian trainer. Indeed, the same can be said for having a trainer from any identity group, although it is most important to us when the group is traditionally less dominant, as they might be the participants that are more likely to hold back. We have to model what we seek to create.

Create More Global and Inclusive Training Materials and Videos

Increasing the availability of training materials that are more global and inclusive will aid in moving our profession forward. Training videos, for instance, are incredibly useful to demonstrate an intercultural interaction. As mentioned earlier, one of the most useful videos for us (though increasingly dated) has been *Going International: Managing the Overseas Assignment,* by Copeland Griggs (1983). We have used segments to demonstrate monochronic versus polychronic behavior, and individualism and collectivism value tendencies. We have also used another segment to demonstrate the unfortunate consequences of making cultural assumptions and coming across as *attacking,* and we have used small segments from movies as alternates to the above. While all of these videos have been invaluable, they all show interactions between an individual from the United States and someone from another nation. This is an ongoing source of frustration for us.

We think it is important to demonstrate a broad array of intercultural interaction that does not always include the United States as a point of reference. As a result, we have created this in some of our productions, but have been generally disappointed with what we have found commercially (but see Wurzel, 2002, for an exception). We understand that this is because videos are very expensive to produce. *Going International* was produced with U.S. multinationals in mind because they had the deep pockets required to pay for it. But we think a real addition to the field would be a much wider selection of videos from many different worldviews, in the broadest sense of that word.

Improve Intercultural Research

We have always used research to inform our participants about what has been learned about intercultural interactions. We have drawn from Geert Hofstede (1980, 1991, 2001), Trompenaars and Hampden-Turner (1998), Ting-Toomey (1994, 1999, 2004), Weiss and Stripp (1985), and Edward Hall (e.g., Hall & Hall, 1989), among others. While we originally tried to cover the breadth of cross-cultural dimensions, those

that have had most meaning for us and for our clients are small and large power distance, individualism and collectivism, and dimensions of time and space.

We have always worked to ensure that participants do not use the research to stereotype an individual. We have done that by showing the research, explaining its limitations, and drawing a bell curve on a flip chart to demonstrate that where a group falls on a particular cultural dimension has to do with the median of the group, and that individuals from that group may fall on either side of the bell curve with respect to a given dimension. We know for ourselves that, in spite of our extensive international experience, our views are culture bound and we suspect this is true of any researcher. We also understand that currently between 75% and 80% of intercultural research is coming from the United States, and most of the degrees in intercultural communication are from U.S. universities (personal communication, Stella Ting-Toomey, September 14, 2004). To advance our field, and increase our impact, intercultural researchers must come from a wide range of international and worldview perspectives.

Rethink Power Distance

For the longest time we introduced the variable of power distance without any judgment on our part about whether coming from a low/small power distance or high/large power distance was better or worse. Instead, we would ask a question something like the following: "What are the gifts/baggage of coming from a low/small versus a high/large power distance worldview?" We would also make distinctions between a functional versus non-functional large power distance situation. For instance, in a functional situation, the authority takes care of the people beneath him. Authority is respected, but authority also has responsibilities to take care of those in its care. On the other hand, a non-functional situation is where the authority abuses its power and uses its power for its own gain rather than to care for subordinates.

Over time, however, we have come to believe that the essence of collaboration (e.g., power holders table their authority in order to get commitment rather than compliance) more closely resembles a small power distance worldview. In fact, it seems to us that learning collaboration is the essence of deeper democracy and that deeper democracy and a large power distance worldview seem anathema to each other. Partially, our views have been influenced by how difficult it is to take a collaborative stance in a highly hierarchical organization. We recognize, nonetheless, that a benign authority can have a needs focus for its constituency and be a highly effective "mediator" of conflict.

MODEL COLLABORATION IN THE TRAINING ROOM AND IN THE WORLD

Our focus has been on teaching people collaborative negotiation skills and adaptive intercultural communication. Consequently, in the training room (as well as outside of it) it has been key to model collaboration ourselves and help participants do the same. What has been important for our group of trainers is to "walk the talk" when presenting the program. That means that when someone *attacks* us, we use *opening* (listening for underlying needs) behavior in response. There is nothing that discredits us more quickly than responding defensively in front of a group to which we are trying to teach collaborative skills. For instance, an occasional *attack* that we have experienced from a multinational diplomatic group is, "The course is too American." We often respond by saying, "Tell me more," an *open* response that attempts to understand the needs behind the "position" of the statement. Inevitably, what we will learn more about, for instance, is the frustration and hopelessness the participant feels from working in very hierarchical bureaucracies where differences are resolved through positional power and not through collaborative negotiation.

Be Clear About When Collaboration Will Not Work— But Exhaust Collaboration First

Even though we emphasize collaboration, we try to help participants in our programs understand where collaboration loses its usefulness as a process strategy. We would be naïve to assume that a concentration of power will shift through collaboration alone. This certainly would not have helped Gandhi or Nelson Mandela or Rosa Parks. Sometimes, with a long-range view of collaboration and democracy, one needs a short-term strategy to establish more democratic laws or otherwise tip the balance of power toward greater equity.

When this topic comes up in our programs, as it often does, we use a chart titled "Corrective Action." For instance, a participant who is working in a highly top-down organization may complain that there is no way that she can negotiate collaboratively with her superior, if she can negotiate at all. This may be compounded by where both parties fall on the power distance scale. When we are faced with this kind of situation, we will first explore the participant's skill set in collaborative negotiation. Many people will say that collaborative negotiation is not possible, but then discover that they simply do not know how to do it. If the subordinate uses competition in that kind of situation (e.g., "It's my right that I should be able to take my vacation at such and such a time"), a top-down boss from a more autocratic culture may distance him- or herself and use his or her power to resolve the conflict. In the interim, various intercultural slurs may swirl in the environment— around gender or race, for example. But if the subordinate does, in fact, have a high level of skill and still cannot negotiate up through the system in a collaborative way, then she might need to consider some form of "corrective action." She might sue her boss—a rights-based approach. She might take a longer view and sit on a committee whose charge it is to change the culture of the organization toward more participatory management.

In our programs, we have felt that it is important to keep the focus on collaboration. Sometimes participants want to learn more about competition or advocacy, but truly learning the skill of collaboration is hard enough in the short time we have. Besides, what we find with a majority of our clients is that they already have well-developed skills as advocates or competitive negotiators. As trainers, we must coach them to become acutely aware of which "channel" they are speaking on. Is it a channel of power, rights, needs/interests? (Ury, 1999). It is our observation that, if your goal is to be collaborative, you need to stay with the language of needs and interests. What does that mean exactly? It means helping people to avoid debate-style or rights-based language. Rights-based language can include "justice," "it's my right," and a number of advocacy-based approaches to communication. Of course we support talking about rights and justice in other forums, but participants must be aware that if their goal is to mindfully cultivate a collaborative resolution process and outcome, rights-based language will often backfire into debate-style polarized arguments. This is hard retraining for many.

Heighten Awareness of the Parallels Between Conflict Behavior in Small and Large Human Systems

Our work, like that of many practitioners, is informed by systems theory. We are fascinated by the idea that, in terms of conflict skill and approach, what goes on at the global level is paralleled and reflected at each smaller level of the system and vice versa. The system layers we are talking about might be international, intergroup, interpersonal, and even intra-psychic or within the body. Frequently in our training programs, we put a daily quote or idea on the wall that is relevant to the day's material. One of our favorites is that everyone understands authority, but democracy is a learned behavior (Lewin, 1948). We see this struggle at the global level, we see it mirrored inside large complex organizations, and we see it in the family systems of which we are part. When we work with individuals, we see the same challenges that are played out on the world stage, reflected in individual behavior.

This raises some interesting questions for trainers and consultants about where and how to intervene to have the desired impact on a complex system. Is it ultimately leadership that creates an environment where collaboration is possible? Is intercultural conflict training even helpful if the leadership is ethnocentric and competitive and does not see a need to change? If you impact the individuals at the middle or lower level, will the system change? What kind of a critical mass is needed to do that? Our practice has shown that progress can be made by training individuals even if the senior leadership

continues to embrace a more authoritarian approach. We have been involved in trainings for large numbers of middle-level managers, and we have seen shifts in the organization as a result. Nonetheless, we believe that making sure the senior leadership understands and can model a more collaborative approach is a significantly more efficient way to have greater impact throughout the system.

Conclusion

Understanding and respecting cultural differences is very important; if that does not occur, it can be a critical source of escalating conflict. In and of itself, understanding cultural differences can contribute to collaboration. Nonetheless, it is our view that cultural or identity group differences mostly become an issue in a competitive conflict climate. Indeed, it is the "culture" of competition or collaboration that is ultimately the most important factor in resolving conflict.

To conclude, we have focused our work on training people in intercultural collaborative negotiation skills at the intrapersonal, interpersonal, and intergroup level. Thankfully, many others have done the same. It is our hope that the value of our collective work lies in the changes that can ultimately occur when a critical mass of human beings have the awareness and skill to choose a collaborative way. The more people understand these concepts and can hold a collaborative vision, the more we and our institutions will shift in the direction of a more peaceful world.

Notes

1. A person with a polychronic orientation will prioritize relationships over tasks; a person with a monochronic orientation will get tasks done and then focus on the relationship. A monochronic orientation is characterized by tightly controlling time. A polychromic orientation is more loose with time. See, for example, Hall, 1959/1973, for further discussion of these cultural dimensions.

2. Pablo Restrepo, a colleague of ours in Colombia, was asked to assist in a difficult negotiation between an oil company and a local indigenous population, but only because the local population had

used both violent and nonviolent methods to get themselves a seat at the negotiating table.

REFERENCES

Bennett, J., & Bennett, M. (2004). Developing intercultural sensitivity: An integrative approach to global and domestic diversity. In D. Landis, J. Bennett, & M. Bennett (Eds.), *Handbook of intercultural training* (3rd ed., pp. 147–165). Thousand Oaks, CA: Sage.

Bennett, M. (1986). A developmental approach to training for intercultural sensitivity. *International Journal of Intercultural Relations, 10,* 179–196.

Boyacigiller, N., Goodman, R., & Phillips, M. (Eds.). (2003). *Crossing cultures: Insights from master teachers.* New York: Routledge.

Deutsch, M. (1985). *Distributive justice.* New Haven, CT: Yale University Press.

Deutsch, M. (2000). Cooperation and competition. In M. Deutsch & P. Coleman (Eds.), *The handbook of conflict resolution: Theory and practice* (pp. 34–45). San Francisco: Jossey-Bass.

Eisler, R. (1988). *The chalice and the blade.* San Francisco: Harper.

Families Forum. (2004). *Families forum: Bereaved families supporting peace, reconciliation, and tolerance.* Retrieved October 1, 2004, from the Parents' Circle Web site: http://www.theparents circle.org

Fowler, S., & Blohm, J. (2004). An analysis of methods for intercultural training. In D. Landis, J. Bennett, & M. Bennett (Eds.), *Handbook of intercultural training* (3rd ed., pp. 37–84). Thousand Oaks, CA: Sage.

Griggs, C. (Producer & Director). (1983). *Going international, part two: Managing the overseas assignment* [Videotape]. San Francisco: Griggs Production.

Hall, E. T. (1973). *The silent language.* Garden City, NY: Doubleday. (Original work published 1959)

Hall, E. T., & Hall, M. R. (1989). *Understanding cultural differences: Germans, French and Americans.* Yarmouth, ME: Intercultural Press.

Hofstede, G. (1980). *Culture's consequences: International differences in work-related values.* Beverly Hills, CA: Sage.

Hofstede, G. (1991). *Cultures and organizations: Software of the mind.* London: McGraw-Hill.

Hofstede, G. (2001). *Culture's consequences: Comparing values, behaviors, institutions, and organizations across nations* (2nd ed.). Thousand Oaks, CA: Sage.

Johnson, D. W., & Johnson, R. T. (1987). *Creative conflict.* Edina, MN: Interaction.

Lewin, K. (Ed.). (1948). *Resolving social conflicts: Selected papers in group dynamics.* New York: Harper & Row.

Maslow, A. H., & Murphy, G. (Eds.). (1954). *Motivation and personality.* New York: Harper & Row.

Muir, J. (1988). *My first summer in the Sierra* (Sierra Club Book). Boston: Houghton Mifflin. (Original work published 1911)

Myers and Briggs Foundation. (2005). *Myers and Briggs Foundation.* Retrieved March 3, 2005, from http://www.myersbriggs.org

Paige, M. (2004). Instrumentation in intercultural training. In D. Landis, J. Bennett, & M. Bennett (Eds.), *Handbook of intercultural training* (3rd ed., pp. 85–128). Thousand Oaks, CA: Sage.

Raider, E. (1987). *A guide to international negotiation.* Brooklyn, NY: Ellen Raider International.

Raider, E., & Coleman, S. (1992). *Conflict resolution: Strategies for collaborative problem solving.* New York: Coleman Raider International.

Raider, E., & Coleman, S. (1997). *Conflict resolution: Strategies for collaborative problem solving* (2nd ed.). New York: Coleman Raider International.

Raider, E., & Coleman, S. (2004). *Conflict resolution: Strategies for collaborative problem solving* (3rd ed.). New York: Coleman Raider International.

Raider, E., Coleman, S., & Gerson, J. (2000). Teaching conflict resolution skills in a workshop. In M. Deutsch & P. Coleman (Eds.), *The handbook of conflict resolution: Theory and practice* (pp. 499–521). San Francisco: Jossey-Bass.

Raider, E. (Producer), & Silverman, A. (Director). (1992). *Negotiating for UNICEF.* [Videotape]. New York, NY: Ellen Raider International and Alan Silverman and Shelly Productions.

Reardon, B. A. (1993). *Women and peace: Feminist visions of global security.* Albany: SUNY Press.

Schell, J., (2003, March). No more unto the breach: Why war is futile. *Harper's Magazine,* pp. 33–46.

Shyamalan, M. N. (Producer & Director). (1992). *Praying with anger* [Motion picture]. Northampton, MA: Northern Arts Entertainment.

Stephan, W. (1999). *Reducing prejudice and stereotyping in schools.* New York: Teachers College Press.

Stephan, W., & Stephan, C. (2001). *Improving intergroup relations.* Thousand Oaks, CA: Sage.

Tagfel, H. (1982). *Social identity and intergroup relations.* New York: Cambridge University Press.

Ting-Toomey, S. (1994). Managing intercultural conflict effectively. In L. A. Samovar & R. E. Porter (Eds.), *Intercultural communication: A reader* (7th ed., pp. 360–372). Belmont, CA: Wadsworth.

Ting-Toomey, S. (1999). *Communicating across cultures.* New York: Guilford.

Ting-Toomey, S. (2004). Translating conflict face-negotiation theory into practice. In D. Landis, J. Bennett, & M. Bennett (Eds.), *Handbook of intercultural training* (3rd ed., pp. 217–248). Thousand Oaks, CA: Sage.

Trompenaars, F., & Hampden-Turner, C. (1998). *Riding the waves of culture: Understanding diversity in global business* (2nd ed.). New York: McGraw-Hill.

Ury, W. (1999). *Getting to peace.* New York: Viking.

Ury, W., Brett, J., & Goldberg, B. (1988). *Getting disputes resolved.* San Francisco: Jossey-Bass.

Weiss, S. E., & Stripp, W. (1985). *Negotiating with foreign businesspersons: An introduction for Americans with propositions on six cultures.* Unpublished manuscript, International Business Department, Graduate School of Business Management, New York University.

Wurzel, J. (Producer). (1990). *The multicultural workplace* [Videotape]. Saint Louis, MO: Phoenix Learning Resources/MTI Films.

Wurzel, J. (Producer). (2002). *Cross-cultural conference room* [Videotape]. Newton, MA: Intercultural Resource Corporation.

25

EXPLAINING INTERCULTURAL CONFLICT

Promising Approaches and Directions

STELLA TING-TOOMEY

California State University at Fullerton

JIRO TAKAI

Nagoya University

Intercultural conflict takes place when visible or invisible cultural group membership factors shape a conflict communication exchange process between members of two or more different cultural communities. The cultural membership differences can include deep-level differences such as cultural worldviews and values. Concurrently, they can also include the mismatch of applying different expectations in a particular conflict scene. Conflict can be an emotionally threatening interaction process that entails perceived or actual incompatibility of values, norms, goals, face orientations, uneven power currencies, scarce resources, and/or conflict styles between two or more interdependent parties in a face-to-face or mediated situation (Ting-Toomey & Oetzel, 2001).

Culture is a learned system of meanings that fosters a particular sense of shared identity-hood and community-hood among its group members. It is a complex frame of reference that consists of patterns of traditions, beliefs, values, norms, symbols, and meanings that are shared to varying degrees by interacting members of an identity group (Ting-Toomey, 1999). "Intercultural" conflict takes place when our cultural group membership factors, to a certain extent, affect our conflict negotiation process on either a conscious or unconscious level. "Intergroup" conflict takes place when salient identity group factors (e.g., ethnic identity group membership, religious identity, language identity, or gender identity, to name a few) impact our conflict management or reconciliation process. However, we use these two terms loosely and interchangeably in this chapter.

This chapter opens with a summary review of various theories that we believe can deepen our understanding of the complex, multilayered "intercultural conflict" phenomenon. There are many reasons why it is important to use a theory to guide intercultural conflict research. First, a sound intercultural theory contains explanatory concepts that can be useful to explain in greater depth the interrelationship among relevant conflict concepts. Second, the use of a well-conceptualized theoretical frame can help to bring out further heuristic or inspirational ideas to advance the development of the intercultural conflict communication field. Third, in using an intercultural theory as a compass or a map, we can reflect more deeply the differences and similarities of specific conflict themes and issues across cultural and ethnic lines.

Likewise, depending on the particular training context and objectives, it is important to have several credible intercultural theories at the trainers' "finger tips" for the following reasons. First, a good theory can help with the general design of an intercultural conflict training program. Without a theory for training, concepts and activities may have no staying power. Second, a clear set of training objectives can be derived from the core assumptions of a well-researched intercultural or intergroup communication theory. By using a theory with some research backing, trainers can gain enhanced credibility as intercultural educators in the training arena. Third, with the aid of a good theory, trainers can pace the training program with well-sequenced activities that complement the knowledge base of the theory. Fourth, a good theory can serve as the springboard for generating a set of meaningful debriefing questions. Fifth, facilitators who are using a sound intercultural theory to train can role model some of the constructive behaviors or skills that are specified in the theory. Finally, in using a theory-based framework to design and conduct intercultural conflict training, clear assessment outcomes can be developed and measured.

In this chapter, we try to identify theories and concepts that can help you to gain entrance to analyzing intercultural/intergroup conflict process and also to apply some of the theoretical ideas for effective intercultural conflict training. The chapter is organized in three sections. The first section introduces relevant theories that hold promise for understanding intercultural and intergroup conflict. The second section summarizes some key research findings stemming from the conflict face-negotiation theory and extend the theory from a situational appraisal perspective. More specifically, the situational appraisal perspective includes integrating concepts of face threats, self-construal activation, relational distance, and status difference features in shaping face concerns and conflict styles. The third section provides specific recommendations for future theorizing, researching, and application efforts in explaining the intricate theme of intercultural conflict communication.

PROMISING THEORETICAL APPROACHES

After half of a decade of researching and theorizing about intercultural communication, many scholars have developed well-designed and well-tested theories to explain the differences and similarities of communication behavior across cultures and identity groups (see Gudykunst, 2003, 2005a; Bennett & Bennett, 2004; Milhouse, Asante, & Nwosu, 2001). For the purpose of this particular chapter and because of space limitations, we have selected several theories that we believe hold theoretical and research promise for studying intercultural and intergroup conflict for the next research generation.

The three criteria for our selection of theories or models include: (a) the theory covers some intriguing angle on intergroup or intercultural encounter and can be directly applied to the intercultural conflict field, (b) the theory can help us to enhance our understanding of intercultural conflict practice issues, and (c) the theory has heuristic function for both theorizing and training orientations in intercultural conflict management. We have selected the following four theories for a synoptic review and discussion in the first section: anxiety/uncertainty management theory and integrated threat theory, expectancy violations theory, and cultural values' dimensional grid.

The first two theories, the anxiety/uncertainty management theory (Gudykunst, 2005a) and the integrated threat theory (Stephan, 1999), are selected and presented in the particular order because when cultural strangers initially encounter one another, they often experience anxiety and uncertainty (Gudykunst, 2005a). Emotional anxiety and cognitive uncertainty oftentimes push individuals back to their habitual or stereotypic way of reacting (i.e., using their ethnocentric lens) in appraising a culture clash situation. Beyond the individual-level anxiety and uncertainty level, conflict does not happen in a vacuum. It always takes place in embedded situational and macro-level systems. Macro-level conditions and systems (e.g., prior intergroup conflict history), as illustrated in the integrated threat theory (Stephan, 1999), can further compound individuals' conflict lenses and biased attributions. We start our summary review of key concepts concerning the anxiety/uncertainty management theory and the integrated threat theory. We also urge readers to read the original versions of the richly textured intercultural communication theories for their specific understanding and application. We also draw out some relevant intercultural conflict implications based on our own interpretations of these theories.

Anxiety/Uncertainty Management Theory and Integrated Threat Theory

Anxiety/uncertainty management (AUM) theory. Intercultural or intergroup anxiety often arises because of the fear of the unfamiliar or unknown. Both anxiety/uncertainty management (AUM) theory and integrated threat (IT) theory deal with the experience of anxiety, vulnerability, fear, and, ultimately, perceived threats between ingroup and outgroup circles. Perceived threats can reinforce ethnocentrism, trigger polarized group-based evaluations, intensify negative intergroup stereotypes, and, ultimately, lead to intergroup prejudice and also vicious conflict cycles. From perceived intergroup threats come intergroup hostility and competition. One of the theories that has amassed a solid base of research findings and has undergone various stages of rigorous theoretical testing is the theory by the late Dr. William Gudykunst, the anxiety/uncertainty management theory. Although AUM theory has not been directly applied in the intercultural conflict communication field yet, we believe that the breadth and depth of the theory warrants attention from researchers and practitioners who are interested in greater explanatory depth of intercultural conflict encountering process.

Gudykunst's AUM theory (1995, 2005a) on effective communication across cultures focuses on the theme of stranger and the encountering of stranger. According to Gudykunst (2005a), when we encounter strangers or culturally dissimilar others, we experience both anxiety and uncertainty. Anxiety refers to a complex of feelings such as experiencing uneasiness, awkwardness, confusion, stress, or apprehensiveness about what might occur in the encounter. Uncertainty, on the other hand, is a cognitive phenomenon and involves both predictive uncertainty and explanatory uncertainty. While predictive uncertainty refers to our inability to predict strangers' attitudes, values, and behavior, explanatory uncertainty refers to our inability to make sense or come up with a coherent explanation for strangers' unfamiliar attitudes, values, language habits, and nonverbal behaviors. Furthermore, Gudykunst believed that people have minimum and maximum thresholds for anxiety and uncertainty and that either too much or too little anxiety and uncertainty hampers intercultural communication effectiveness. It is obvious to note that when anxiety or uncertainty is too high or too low, fight or flight (or indifferent) response will set in—in an initial intercultural conflict encounter process. Gudykunst (2005a) further observed that when emotional anxiety is too high, cultural strangers would tend to communicate on automatic pilot and interpret dissimilar others' behaviors using their own cultural frame of reference. Moreover, when cognitive uncertainty is too high, cultural strangers would not be able to accurately interpret each other's conflict messages and make accurate predictions. They would more than likely engage in communication misunderstandings, verbal and nonverbal clashes, and sometimes, fatal collusions.

The final version of Gudykunst's (2005a) AUM-based effective communication theory has 47 axioms and covers the relationship among seven antecedent factors (self-concept, motivation to interact, reactions to strangers, social categorization of strangers, situational processes, connections with strangers, and ethical interactions), two core causes (uncertainty management and anxiety management), one moderating process (mindfulness), and one outcome factor on communication effectiveness.

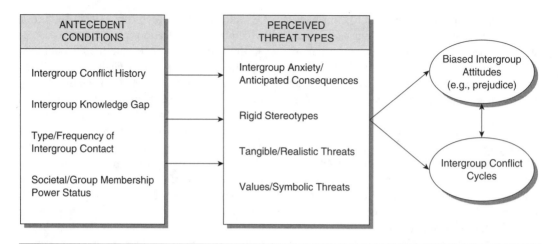

Figure 25.1   An Adaptive Model of Integrated Threat Theory

SOURCE: Adapted from W. Stephan (1999).

To illustrate the theory, four AUM axioms are provided: *Axiom 11:* An increase in the rigidity of our attitudes toward strangers will produce an increase in our anxiety and a decrease in our ability to predict their behavior accurately; *Axiom 20:* An increase in perceiving that we share superordinate ingroup identities with strangers will produce a decrease in our anxiety and an increase in our ability to predict their behavior accurately; *Axiom 33:* An increase in our respect for strangers will produce a decrease in our anxiety; and *Axiom 37:* An increase in our mindfulness of the process of our communication with strangers will produce an increase in our ability to manage anxiety and an increase in our ability to manage our uncertainty. Generally speaking, as anxiety and uncertainty increase in our interactions with unfamiliar others, the perceived threat levels especially when encountering members from historically hostile groups are also heightened and magnified.

Integrated threat (IT) theory. Throughout the years, Gudykunst and W. Stephan and C. Stephan (see Stephan, 1999; Stephan, Stephan, & Gudykunst, 1999) have collaborated closely together and influenced each others' ideas in their respective development of the AUM theory and the IT theory. IT theory (Stephan, 1999; C. W. Stephan & W. G. Stephan, 2003) integrates various affective theories in the social identity and prejudice literature and emphasizes one key

causal factor on prejudice, namely, feelings of fear or threat. Feelings of fear or threat are closely aligned with Gudykunst's (2005a) notion on anxiety management issues. Stephan (1999) proposes that there are four antecedent conditions that prime the various perceived threat types (see Figure 25.1). These conditions are: prior conflict history, ignorance or knowledge gap, contact, and status.

According to Stephan (1999), *intergroup conflict history* is "the single most important seedbed of prejudice" (p. 32). More important, past intergroup conflict history serves as a backdrop to current intergroup contact relations. The more damaging and protracted the past conflict, the more perceived threats and prejudiced attitudes exist in the intergroup relations. Second, *intergroup knowledge gap or ignorance* of the outgroup refers to the fact that when intergroup members know very little of each other or they think they know too much (i.e., based on their overgeneralized, stereotypic lens), they are likely to perceive the other group as threatening in the context of an intergroup hostility situation. Third, the *type* (positive vs. negative) *and frequency of intergroup contact* also affect feelings of security or insecurity, familiarity or unfamiliarity, trust or mistrust between members of different identity groups. The more positive and personalized the contact, the more likely members of both groups can see the "human face" beyond the broad-based identity group categories. The more negative and surface-level the contact, the greater the perceived negative stereotypes and prejudice justifications. Fourth, *societal/group membership power status* refers to both institutional power dominance/resistance issues and individual power perception issues. On the institutional level, dominant group members in a society can be perceived as controlling the key political, economic, and media functioning of a society. On the individual level, it can refer to how high-status group members view low-status group members in a society or in a particular institutional setting, and vice versa. Oftentimes, high-status members may want to reinforce their own power positions and not want to give up power resources or constantly worry about hostility or enviousness from low-status members. Low-status members, indeed, may resent the power resources or positions amassed by the high-status members. They feel the historical legacy of inequality, injustice, and unfair treatment weighing on them. Thus, they are constantly frustrated because of the uneven playing field. The wider the cultural knowledge schism and the wider the perceived power schism, the more misunderstanding or fear is being generated in the escalatory conflict cycles.

These antecedent conditions can either escalate or de-escalate the threat level in intergroup conflict. According to Stephan (1999), the four basic threat types that lead to escalatory prejudice and conflict cycles are intergroup anxiety, negative or rigid stereotypes, tangible/realistic threats, and value/symbolic threats. The theory also emphasizes *subjectively* perceived threats posed by the other, "enemy" group. The first type of threat, *intergroup anxiety/anticipated consequences,* often arises in unfamiliar intergroup encounter processes (Gudykunst, 1995). In intergroup encounters, people can be especially anxious about anticipated negative consequences such as negative psychological consequences (e.g., confusion, frustration, feeling incompetent), negative behavioral consequences (e.g., being exploited, harmed), and negative evaluations by outgroup members (e.g., rejection, or being identified with marginalized outgroup members). Individuals have anticipated intergroup anxiety because they are concerned about potential face threats or their identities being stigmatized, embarrassed, rejected, or even excluded in intergroup contact situations. Emotional fear or anxiety is usually heightened and intensified when there exist intergroup historical grievances, low or little prior intergroup contact, or when the contact is consistently antagonistic or reinforces existing negative stereotypes. The second type of threats, *rigid stereotypes or negative stereotypes,* poses as threats to ingroup (especially dominant ingroup) because ingroup members typically learn negative images and traits of outgroups through the mass media and second-hand sources. These negative images can generate negative self-fulfilling prophecies and expectations and, thus, arouse negative intergroup encountering processes and outcomes. We believe that rigid positive stereotypes can also be a perceived intergroup threat because of the fear that this particular group is taking over the educational system or the medical field or the technological system, and so on. Alternatively, members in this group do not conform to the preconceived "box," therefore posing disorientations or expectancy confusions. Overly positive and negative stereotypes can also prompt further majority-minority and minority-minority intergroup conflicts in a society. This rigid stereotypic mentality leads to a third type of threat.

The third type of threats, *tangible/realistic threats,* refers to perceived content threats from the outgroups such as a battle for territory, wealth, scarce resources, and natural resources and also the perceived threats and competitions of economic, housing, education placements, and/or political clout. The fourth type of threats, perceived *values/symbolic threats,* is founded in cultural/ethnic membership differences in morals, beliefs, values, norms, standards, and attitudes. These are threats to the "standard way of living" and the "standard way of behaving" of the dominant ingroup. Outgroups who hold worldviews and values that are different from the ingroup threaten the core value systems of the ingroup, which may then lead to fossilized ingroup ethnocentrism and outgroup avoidance to rejection (see Bennett & Bennett, 2004). According to Stephan (1999), values/symbolic threats can be experienced by minorities, disadvantaged groups, and subordinate groups, as well as by majority or dominant groups.

In sum, intergroup anxiety and fear can color our expectations and intensify our perceived threat levels in dealing with culturally dissimilar strangers or what we consider as our "enemies." Especially on the macro-level of analysis, if the backdrop of the intergroup relations has continuous, acrimonious tensions or hostilities, it is difficult for identity group members to come together with a clean slate.

Expectancy Violations Theory and Cultural Values Dimensional Grid

With historically tinted glasses, members from dominant and minority groups view each other with certain mistrust, suspicions, and negative expectancies. Burgoon (1995) and Burgoon and Ebesu Hubbard's (2005) expectancy violations theory and Ting-Toomey and Oetzel's (2001) cultural values dimensional grid may help to explain further how intercultural and intergroup conflicts get entangle in different expectancy webs and cultural values' collusion issues.

Expectancy violations theory (EVT). In any anticipated intercultural or intergroup contact process, people hold expectations of how the interaction scene should play out and how it should be handled. Expectations or normative anticipations are often learned within a cultural socialization process. As Burgoon and Ebesu Hubbard (2005) observed,

> [E]very culture has guidelines for human conduct that carry associated anticipations for how others will behave. Those guidelines and anticipations manifest in interactions between people. Intercultural communication, then, involves communicators adjusting and influencing the behaviors of each other, partly through the lens of expectations. (p. 149)

The focal constructs in the EVT that have relevance for intercultural conflict are communication expectancies, expectancy violations, communicator valence, and behavior valence (Burgoon, 1993, 1995; Burgoon & Ebesu Hubbard, 2005; Burgoon & Walther, 1990).

Communication expectancies in this context refer to verbal and nonverbal communication acts that are modal (most typical) in a given culture or subculture. Furthermore, there are two types of communication expectancies: prescriptive

and predictive. Prescriptive expectancy refers to socially normative patterns of behavior concerning "what should or should not happen" in a given cultural context and connotes general cultural community value-level knowledge. Thus, in a conflict situation, individuals hold certain cognitive schemata of what should or should not happen in a conflict scene. For example, if conflict is taking place between a manager and an employee in a collectivistic/large power distance workplace setting, a manager would expect that his or her employee would yield or accommodate to his or her conflict request. On the other hand, predictive expectancy refers to context-specific and person-specific knowledge and predictions of how the other person would typically act in a given communication or conflict situation. Thus, an individual has to be quite familiar with the other conflict party to engage in accurate predictive expectancy. Predictive expectancy in everyday conflict interaction is shaped by three classes of factors: (a) characteristics of individual communicators, (b) characteristics of the relationship between the sender and the receiver, and (c) features of the communication context itself (Burgoon & Ebesu Hubbard, 2005). These predictive expectancies, however, require constant culture-specific adjustment and reframing to get to the interaction adaptation stage. It goes without saying that when intercultural conflict is escalating between members of two contrastive identity groups and when both groups do not have accurate knowledge about each other, prescriptive and predictive expectancies would be low or expectancies would be violated because of the application of ethnocentric standards and worldviews.

The second EVT focal concept, *expectancy violations,* refers to actions sufficiently discrepant from the expectancy to be noticeable. Expectancy violations happen within and across cultures. However, since cultural difference takes place at the heterogeneous end of the homogeneity-heterogeneity spectrum, expectancy violations clashes—especially along the hidden value content dimensions (e.g., Triandis's, 1995, individualism-collectivism value dimension)—are often the prototypical cases. Burgoon and Ebesu Hubbard (2005) commented, "Fundamental differences in philosophies, values, and social organization, coupled with widespread ignorance about cultural differences, makes intercultural encounters prime candidates for colliding expectancies" (p. 154). When individuals' expectations are violated, they are emotionally alerted or aroused and they will redirect their attention to the violator and the violation act itself. The third EVT concept, *communicator valence,* refers to perceived physical attractiveness, task expertise and knowledge, socioeconomic status, appealing group identity or personal attributes, similarity, familiarity, and so on. On balance, when a communicator or identity group is deemed rewarding or attractive, individuals may reframe the violating act from a positive angle. When a communicator or identity group is deemed costly or power coercing or resisting, individuals will likely evaluate the situation as a negative expectancy violations incident. Repeated negative expectancy violations can further polarize the two or more identity groups in their conflict negotiation struggles or conflict competitive process.

In intercultural or intergroup conflict situations, when cultural ignorance is usually the key, individuals would most likely evaluate any conflict violation act from a negatively valenced angle. Thus, communicator valence or identity group valence has a moderating role between expectancy violations and behavior valence. The last concept, *behavior valence,* refers to the meaning associated with a given violation act (i.e., interpretation) and the act's positive or negative desirability (i.e., evaluation of good or bad). As mentioned previously, both the interpretation and the evaluation of the violation act are influenced by the knowledge of the context, communication expectancies, and the communicator valence calculations. According to Burgoon and Ebesu Hubbard (2005), while some human commonalities and meaning coordination efforts have to exist across diverse cultural groups, the *content* of each culture's interactional expectancies will vary substantially along such cultural value dimensions as "collectivism-individualism, uncertainty avoidance, power distance, masculinity-femininity, ascription versus achievement orientations, time and activity orientation, universalism-particularism, degree of face concern, and high-versus low-context communication" (p. 151). To echo the basic premise of expectancy violations theory, we now turn to the contents of cultural

expectancies that often create divergent cultural conflict lenses and expectancy dissonances. By helping you to understand some of the core cultural value differences that can create expectancy collisions and expectancy anxieties and threats, it is hoped that culture-based knowledge can provide some initial insights for competent conflict management.

Cultural values dimensional (CVD) grid. Drawing from some of the key ideas in the anxiety/uncertainty management theory, the integrated threat theory, and the expectancy violations theory, it is obvious that when individuals from diverse identity communities encounter each other, they often experience anxieties and expectancy violations because of unfamiliarity, fear, and emotional defense seizures. Thus, understanding the value patterns of individualism and collectivism can serve as an initial frame in explaining why individuals differ in their conflict expectations and conflict concerns. Intercultural researchers (Gelfand, Bhawuk, Nishi, & Bechtold, 2004; Gudykunst & Ting-Toomey, 1988; Hofstede, 1991, 2001; Triandis, 1995, 2002) in diverse disciplines have provided empirical evidence that the value spectrums of individualism and collectivism are indeed pervasive in a wide range of cultures. Indeed, the most recent GLOBE research project (House, Hanges, Javidan, Dorfman, & Gupta, 2004) provided additional evidence that the foundational constructs of individualism and collectivism permeate 62 countries (and with a sample size of 17,370 middle managers from three industries) at the societal, organizational, and individual levels of analysis.

Basically, *individualism* refers to the broad value tendencies of a culture to emphasize the importance of the "I" identity over the "we" identity, individual rights over group interests, and ego-focused emotions over social-focused emotions. In comparison, *collectivism* refers to the broad value tendencies of a culture to emphasize the importance of the "we" identity over the "I" identity, ingroup interests over individual wants, and other-face concerns over self-face concerns (Ting-Toomey, 1985, 1988). Individualistic and collectivistic value tendencies are manifested in everyday interpersonal, family, school, and workplace interactions.

While both sets of value tendencies can exist in the same culture or identity group and in each person, there are more situations in individualistic cultures that entail expectations for "I-identity" responses, and there are more situations in group-based cultures that call for "we-identity" reactions. Hofstede's (2001) and Triandis's (1995) research indicates that individualism is a cultural pattern found in most northern and western regions of Europe and in North America. Collectivism refers to a cultural pattern common in Asia, Africa, the Middle East, Central and South America, and the Pacific Islands. Within each culture, different ethnic communities can also display distinctive individualistic and collectivistic value patterns. Furthermore, distinctive forms and practice functions of individualism and collectivism also reside within each unique ethnic/cultural grouping (see Oetzel, Arcos, Mabizela, Weinman, & Zhang, Chapter 20 in this volume). Gelfand et al. (2004) concurred that individualism and collectivism are multidimensional constructs that can be conceptualized on the value level (e.g., "In this society, leaders *should* encourage group loyalty even if individual goal suffers") and the practice level (e.g., "In this organization, leaders encourage group loyalty even if individual goal suffers").

Beyond individualism-collectivism, another important value dimension we should take into consideration in explaining conflict communication differences is the dimension of power distance (Carl, Gupta, & Javidan, 2004; Hofstede, 1991, 2001). In fact, a conflict negotiation process often entails a complex power interplay between the conflict parties at different expectation levels of how respect and deference should be enacted. *Power distance*, from the cultural value analysis standpoint, refers to the way a culture deals with status differences and social hierarchies. Cultures differ in the extent to which they view status inequalities (e.g., family background, age, birth order, gender, caste, occupation, education, wealth, and personal achievements) as good or bad, fair or unfair. People in *small power distance* cultures tend to value equal power distributions, symmetrical relations, and equitable reward and cost distributions based on individual merits. People in *large power distance* cultures tend to accept unequal power distributions; asymmetrical relations; and rewards and sanctions based on rank, role, status, age, and perhaps even gender identity.

In small power distance work situations, power is, in an ideological sense, evenly distributed. When there are differences in opinions, subordinates expect to be consulted, and the ideal manager is a resourceful democrat. Comparatively, in large power distance work situations, the power of an organization is centralized in the upper management level. When there are conflicting viewpoints, subordinates often expect to be told what to do, and the ideal manager plays a benevolent autocratic role in making the final decision. Small power distance index values are found, for example, in Austria, Israel, Denmark, New Zealand, Ireland, Sweden, and Norway. Large power distance index values are found in Malaysia, Guatemala, Panama, the Philippines, Mexico, Venezuela, and Arab countries (Hofstede, 2001). While the United States scores on the low side of power distance, it is not extremely low. Hofstede (1991) explained that "U.S. leadership theories tend to be based on subordinates with medium-level dependence needs: not too high, not too low" (p. 42). Carl et al. (2004) concluded in the GLOBE project:

> Power distance is a cultural dimension that is relevant for both Eastern and Western societies. Within the high power distance cultures of the East, the stable distribution of power is expected to bring order to the society and to allow unambiguous allocation of roles. . . . In contrast, within the low power distance cultures of the West, the flexible distribution of power is expected to facilitate entrepreneurial innovation. . . . There are, however, significant variations in the practice and preference of power distance in both Eastern and Western societies, which indicates that the dominant expectations in these regions are largely historically derived. (p. 539)

In combining both individualism-collectivism and small/large power distance value patterns, we can discuss four predominant conflict approaches along the two grids of an individualism-collectivism continuum and a small-large power distance continuum in multicultural and global workplace settings: impartial, status-achievement, benevolent, and communal (Ting-Toomey & Oetzel, 2001). The *impartial*

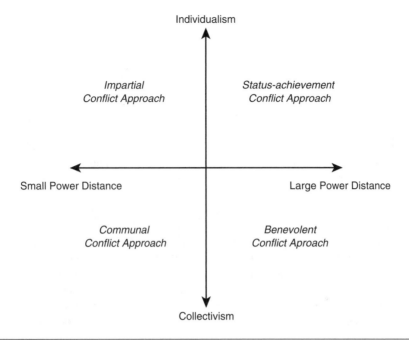

Individualism

Impartial
Conflict Approach

Status-achievement
Conflict Approach

Small Power Distance

Large Power Distance

Communal
Conflict Approach

Benevolent
Conflict Aproach

Collectivism

Figure 25.2   Cultural Values Dimensional Grid: Four Conflict Approaches

SOURCE: Adapted from Ting-Toomey and Oetzel (2001).

approach reflects a combination of an individualistic and small power distance value orientation; the *status-achievement approach* consists of a combination of an individualistic and large power distance value orientation; the *benevolent approach* reflects a combination of a collectivistic and large power distance value orientation; and the *communal approach* consists of a combination of collectivistic and small power distance value orientation (see Figure 25.2).

Thus, managers and employees around the world have different expectations of how a workplace conflict should be resolved and also the role of the manager in mediating or facilitating different-rank versus same-rank employee-to-employee workplace conflicts and tensions.

More specifically, in the *impartial approach* to workplace conflict, the predominant values are personal freedom and equality. Countries that predominantly reflect the impartial managerial approach include Australia, Canada, Northern European nations (Scandinavian and Germanic nations), Israel, the United States, and Great Britain. In addition, the United States and Great Britain also have tendencies that are reflective of the status-achievement approach,

especially in business settings (Smith, Dugan, Peterson, & Leung, 1998). From the impartial conflict approach lens, if an interpersonal conflict arises between a manager and an employee, the manager has a tendency to deal with the conflict in an upfront and direct manner. An employee is also expected to articulate his or her conflict concerns directly and to defend his or her viewpoints. In an equal-rank employee-employee conflict, the manager would generally play the role of "impartial" and "neutral" third party and would encourage the two employees to talk things over and find their own solution. Both the manager and the employees would tend to rely on the principle of fairness or objectivity and also use a fact-finding approach to resolve a conflict situation.

Alternatively, in a *status-achievement approach* to conflict the predominant values are personal freedom and earned inequality. Countries that predominantly reflect the status-achievement approach include some Latin European nations (e.g., France and Italy) and to a moderate extent the United States and Great Britain (Hofstede, 2001; Storti, 2001). For example, in France, employees often feel that they have the freedom to voice directly and complain about their managers in the workplace. Concurrently, they do not expect their managers to change much because they are their bosses and, thus, by virtue of their titles, hold certain rights and power resources. The managers, meanwhile, also expect conflict accommodations from their subordinates. When the conflict involves two same-rank coworkers, the use of a range of upfront conflict tactics to aggression tactics is a hallmark of the status-achievement approach. The aim is to achieve one's own individual conflict goals and wishes over someone else's conflict goals and interests. Ting-Toomey and Oetzel (2001) also observed that U.S. management style often follows a conjoint impartial approach and a status-achievement approach because the larger U.S. culture emphasizes that via hard work, personal ambition, and competitiveness, status can be earned and status cues can be displayed with credibility (e.g., by having the spacious corner office or the privileged parking space).

In comparison, many managers in other part of the globe tend to see themselves as interdependent and at a different status level from others. That is, these managers think of themselves as individuals with interlocking connections with others and as members of a hierarchical network. They practice the *benevolent approach* of management style. Two values that pervade this approach are obligation to others and inequality. Countries that predominantly reflect the benevolent approach include most Latin and South American nations (e.g., Mexico, Venezuela, Brazil, Chile), most Asian nations (e.g., India, Japan, China, South Korea), most Arab nations (e.g., Egypt, Saudi Arabia, Jordan), and most African nations (e.g., Nigeria, Uganda; Hofstede, 2001). Under the benevolent conflict approach, it is very rare that employees will directly challenge a manager's authority or face during a conflict interaction process in an upfront, assertive manner. However, they might opt for using passive aggressive or sabotage conflict strategies to deal with workplace tensions or frustrations. In dealing with low-premium conflicts, managers are supposed to consider the personal relationships and try to "smooth over" the conflict and maintain workplace relational harmony. Managers may also talk with each of the conflict employees separately, being careful not to directly challenge the

face of either party. However, in dealing with high-premium conflicts, benevolent managers often practice preferential treatment or particularism by treating members of ingroups better than members of outgroups, or by treating senior employees more favorably than junior employees. Thus, relational distance feature, status difference feature, and perceived conflict goals' importance are all critical factors in influencing how individuals from diverse organizational cultures handle a problematic conflict situation or crisis.

Lastly, the *communal approach* (a combination of both collectivism and small power distance value orientation) is the least common of the four conflict approaches (Ting-Toomey & Oetzel, 2001). The values that encompass this approach are the recognition of authentic interdependent connection to others and genuine equality. Costa Rica is the only country found to fit this approach (Hofstede, 2001). However, two other groups also fit this perspective: the kibbutz, and organizations built on feminist principles. A kibbutz is a communal settlement in Israel that emphasizes socialistic ideology and collectivistic values (Erez & Somech, 1996). Principles of kibbutz include communal, rather than hierarchical, decision making, and also direct democracy so that everyone has a say, and also taking turns in rotating leadership. Similarly, feminist principles include holistic and integrative problem solving, an emphasis on connectiveness between substantive and affective conflict data, and the importance of engaging in collaborative dialogue and culturally inclusive climate-building (Buzzanell, 1994). While there is limited research on conflict styles from the communal conflict lens approach, it is clear that managers are expected to emphasize common-interest superordinate goals during conflict and to resist using power as a means to settle differences. Managers and employees are considered to be co-equals and are expected to be expressive during conflict and to work together to develop mutually acceptable options, criteria, and doable solutions. They are also expected to share conflict feelings, metaphors, and narrative stories in conjunction with conflict substantive issues. Many nonprofit conflict mediation centers and mediation training/facilitation models also rely heavily on the collaborative, communal dialogue worldview (see, e.g., Donohue, Chapter 8; Littlejohn, Chapter 14; Barge, Chapter 19; and Broome & Jakobsson Hatay, Chapter 23; all in this volume).

Understanding the cultural, situational, and individual-based expectancies concerning conflict norms and conflict interaction styles can help individuals to manage conflict more mindfully in diverse cultural and organizational situations. The cultural values dimensional grid is one out of many theoretical and applied tools that conflict practitioners can use to cross-check expectations and expectancy violations between managers' and employees' viewpoints on how conflict should be approached and resolved in diverse global organizations. By probing "what is expected" on societal, organizational, and individual levels concerning conflict worldviews and beliefs, to "what is actually commonly practiced" in an organization, and to "what is actually preferred" by employees and managers in an organization, practitioners can gather multiple-level data using the expectancy violations theory and the cultural values dimensional model as two functional, applied conflict diagnostic tools.

Moving beyond the discussion on promising theoretical approaches, we now turn to a discussion of the core assumptions and the accompanying research findings of the conflict face-negotiation theory (Ting-Toomey, 1988, 2005). The face-negotiation theory has directly addressed salient issues in linking cultural value patterns, face concerns, and conflict styles for the past 18 years or so in a diverse range of cultures and ethnic identity groups.

CONFLICT FACE-NEGOTIATION THEORY: CORE ASSUMPTIONS AND EXTENSIONS

While face and facework are universal phenomena, how we "frame" or interpret the situated meaning of face and how we enact facework differ from one cultural community to the next. The concept of *face* is about identity respect and other-identity consideration issues within and beyond the actual encounter episode. *Face* is tied to the emotional significance and estimated calculations that we attach to our own social self-worth and that of the others' social self-worth. It is therefore a precious identity

resource in communication because it can be threatened, enhanced, undermined, and bargained over—on both emotional reactive level and cognitive appraisal level. *Facework* refers to the specific verbal and nonverbal behaviors that we engage in to maintain or restore face loss and to uphold and honor face gain. Face loss occurs when we are being treated in such a way that our expected identity claims in a conflict situation are challenged or ignored. A face threatening episode is, in short, an anxiety-provoking and identity expectancy violation episode.

According to the conflict face-negotiation theory (Ting-Toomey, 2005; Ting-Toomey & Kurogi, 1998), the *orientation of face* determines the focus to which the face negotiator will direct her or his attention and energy of the subsequent conflict messages. *Self-face* is the protective concern for one's own image when one's own face is threatened in the conflict situation. *Other-face* is the concern or consideration for the other conflict party's image in the conflict situation. *Mutual-face* is the concern for both parties' images and/or the "image" of the relationship. While individualists or independents tend to be more concerned with protecting or preserving self-face images during an ongoing conflict episode, collectivists or interdependents tend to be more concerned with either accommodating the other-face images or saving mutual-face images in a conflict. This line of reasoning is drawn from the value spectrums of individualism and collectivism. Cultural value dimensions provide the underlying interpretive logic or motivational bases in framing why people behave the way they do in a cultural scene. Relational and situational features also assert a strong influence in terms of the foci and movements of face concerns and face efforts.

In a nutshell, Ting-Toomey's (1988, 2005; Ting-Toomey & Kurogi, 1998) conflict face-negotiation theory assumes the following: *Assumption 1:* People in all cultures try to maintain and negotiate face in all communication situations; *Assumption 2:* The concept of face is especially problematic in emotionally threatening or identity vulnerable situations (such as embarrassment, request, or conflict situations) when the situated identities of the communicators are called into question; *Assumption 3:* The cultural value spectrums of individualism-collectivism and small/large power distance shape the orientations, movements, contents, and styles of facework; *Assumption 4:* Individualism and collectivism value patterns shape members' preferences for self-oriented facework versus other-oriented facework; *Assumption 5:* Small and large power distance value patterns shape members' preferences for horizontally based facework versus vertically based facework; *Assumption 6:* The cultural variability dimensions, in conjunction with individual (e.g., self-construal, personal goals/intentions, ethnic/cultural identification salience issues), relational (e.g., intimacy, status, ingroup/outgroup), and situational (e.g., competitive vs. cooperative task, heterogeneous vs. homogeneous teams) factors influence the use of particular facework behaviors in particular cultural scenes; and *Assumption 7:* Intercultural facework competence refers to the optimal integration of knowledge, mindfulness, and communication skills in managing vulnerable identity-based conflict situations appropriately, effectively, and adaptively.

Since the 1988 version (Ting-Toomey, 1988) and the 1998 version (Ting-Toomey & Kurogi, 1998), many more face-based conflict research studies have been conducted on the relationship between culture-level factors and face concerns, culture-level factors and conflict styles, individual-level factors and face concerns, and individual-level factors and conflict styles. Thus, based on existing research findings, the recent 2005 version of the face-negotiation theory (see Ting-Toomey, 2005) has altogether 24 revised theoretical propositions: 12 propositions on culture-level facework and conflict styles, 10 propositions on individual-level facework and conflict styles, and 2 propositions on situational-level face concerns. The 2005 version of the theory also added the following conflict face threat process (FTP) conditions: (a) the more important the culturally appropriate facework rule that is violated, the more severe the perceived FTP; (b) the larger the cultural distance between the conflict parties, the more mistrust or misunderstanding cumulate in the FTP; (c) the more important the conflict topic or imposition of the conflict demand, as interpreted from distinctive cultural angles, the more severe the perceived FTP; (d) the more power the conflict initiator has over the conflict recipient, the more

severe the perceived FTP by the recipient; (e) the more harm or hurt the FTP produces, the more time and effort is needed to repair the FTP; (f) the more the actor is perceived as directly responsible for initiating the conflict cycle, the more that person is held accountable for the FTP; and (g) the more the actor is viewed as an outgroup member, the more severe the perceived FTP.

Furthermore, individuals also engage in various *face movements* in a conflict negotiation process. Face movements refer to the various options that a conflict negotiator confronts when choosing whether to maintain, defend, and/or upgrade self-face versus other-face in a conflict episode. Based on the conceptual dimensions of concern for self-face (high vs. low) and concern for other-face (high vs. low), there are four possible conflict movement options: (a) mutual-face protection moves: high concern for self-face and high concern for other-face movements; (b) mutual-face obliteration moves: low concern for self-face and low concern for other-face movements; (c) self-face defensive moves: high concern for self-face and low concern for other-face movements; and (d) other-face upgrading moves: low concern for self-face and high concern for other-face movements (Ting-Toomey, 2005).

A problematic face issue becomes more noticeable when everyday face poise or face equilibrium is being threatened (e.g., in any frustrating conflict situations) or shattered (e.g., encountering racist or prejudice episodes) in diverse emotionally vulnerable situations. In almost all conflict situations, face-defending or face-saving strategies are needed when one's face is being threatened or attacked. When our face is under attack, emotional vulnerability or anxiety sets in, and associated emotions such as fear, anger, humiliation, guilt, shame, disgust, and contempt follow closely. The need to recoup face loss and face humiliation, and the need to restore face disequilibrium levels to an acceptable face equilibrium "respectful" level often underlie some of these identity-based, fragile emotions. Culture socialization, however, does profoundly influence the fluctuation range of face threat toleration and face threat restoration levels and the accompanying meanings and interpretations that constitute a severe or a minor face threat episode in a given conflict situation.

Thus, face concerns and face defensive movements (or protective issues) become incrementally more salient if several of the above face threat process (FTP) conditions are simultaneously present. From an individualistic cultural lens, the more severe the perceived FTP is in a conflict situation, the more likely the conflict communicators will engage in upfront, aggressive facework strategies to counter the direct face attacks. However, from a collectivistic cultural lens, the collectivistic communicators may opt to use high-context (Hall, 1959, 1976) avoidance strategies to wait for the conflict to simmer down and to buy time to recoup their hurt feelings. In addition, they may also turn to a third-party intermediary to mediate the conflict and avoid further head-on face-threatening clashes and embarrassments. A combination of some of the above FTP conditions, in conjunction with the situational face needs of the conflict negotiators, would determine the emotional tone, types, and particular strategies of facework management process in a conflict episode. The following sections review the literature about conflict and face at the cultural/ethnic-identity level, the individual level, and the situational level.

Culture-Level and Ethnic Identity-Level Research Findings

More specifically, in relating national cultures with face concerns, research reveals that while individualists (e.g., U.S. respondents) tend to use more direct, self-face concern conflict behaviors (e.g., dominating/competing style), collectivists (e.g., Taiwan and China respondents) tend to use more indirect, other-face concern conflict behaviors (e.g., avoiding and obliging styles). Males (from both Japan and the U.S.) also reported the use of more dominating or competing conflict behaviors than females (Cai & Fink, 2002; Cocroft & Ting-Toomey, 1994; Ting-Toomey et al., 1991; Trubisky, Ting-Toomey, & Lin, 1991). In addition, other-/mutual-face concern has been found to relate positively with integrating facework strategies and conflict styles (Oetzel & Ting-Toomey, 2003; Oetzel et al., 2001).

In an organizational facework study, Oetzel, Myers, Meares, and Lara (2004) examined face concerns and conflict styles in U.S. organizations.

They surveyed 184 managers and employees and asked them to describe their reactions to typical conflicts with either a peer or a person of different status. It was found that *self-face concern* was associated positively with dominating and emotionally expressive styles. *Other-face concern* was associated positively with integrating, obliging, and compromising styles. *Mutual-face concern* was associated positively with integrating, obliging, and compromising styles. In addition, inclusion of face concerns provided a better prediction of which conflict style would be utilized than other relevant variables for six out of the eight conflict styles considered.

More recently, in a direct empirical test of the conflict face-negotiation theory (Oetzel & Ting-Toomey, 2003), the objective of the study was to test the underlying assumption of the face-negotiation theory that face is an explanatory mechanism for culture's influence on conflict behavior. A questionnaire was administered to 768 participants in four national cultures (China, Germany, Japan, and the U.S.) in their respective languages asking them to recall and describe a recent interpersonal conflict. The major findings of the study were as follows: (a) cultural individualism-collectivism had direct effects on conflict styles, as well as mediated effects through self-construal and face concerns; (b) self-face concern was associated positively with dominating conflict styles and other-face concern was associated positively with avoiding and integrating conflict styles; and (c) face concerns accounted for all of the total variance explained in dominating, most of the total variance explained in integrating, and some of the total variance explained in avoiding when considering face concerns, cultural individualism-collectivism, and self-construals.

In another interesting cross-national conflict study, Ohbuchi (1993) compared cross-cultural differences of Japanese and U.S. Americans on different conflict strategies—based on the two dimensions of directness-indirectness, and unilateral-bilateral conflict tactics. According to this schema, *direct-bilateral strategies* include persuasion, exchange, and compromise; *direct-unilateral strategies* consist of requesting, pleading, asserting, blackmailing, and ordering. Furthermore, *indirect-bilateral strategies* included hinting, impression management, complimenting, deceiving, and harmonizing, and finally, *indirect-unilateral strategies* included criticism, avoidance, anger, ignoring, violence, crying, withdrawal, and third-person mediation. With regard to strategy use in conflict situations, the results showed that almost half of the Japanese respondents used no strategies at all, meaning that they typically let the conflict situation be. U.S. Americans, on the other hand, preferred to use direct-unilateral strategies the most, followed by direct-bilateral strategies. The two direct conflict strategies were also viewed as the most effective by U.S. Americans.

In attempting to understand ethnic diversity issues and conflict styles within the United States, Ting-Toomey et al. (2000) examined the influence of ethnic background and ethnic/cultural identity factors on conflict styles among African Americans, Asian Americans, European Americans, and Latino(a) Americans. Some of the major findings of the study included: (a) African Americans have a stronger ethnic-oriented identity and a weaker cultural identity (i.e., assimilated identity) than the other three U.S. ethnic groups, (b) European Americans have a weaker ethnic identity than the other three minority groups, (c) Asian and Latino(a) Americans tend to use avoiding and third-party conflict styles more than African Americans, (d) Asian Americans also tend to use more avoidance conflict tactics than European Americans; in addition, (e) individuals with strong ethnic identities (i.e., identifying with their ethnic ingroup memberships) tend to use integrating conflict styles more so than individuals with weak ethnic identities and (f) individuals with bicultural, ethnic, and assimilated identities tend to use more compromising and conflict tactics than individuals with marginal identities.

Individual-Level Research Findings

Assumption 6 of the face-negotiation theory posits that the cultural value dimensions in conjunction with individual factors influence the use of specific facework behaviors in particular cultural scenes. Self-construal is one of the major individual factors that focuses on individual variation within and between cultures. *Self-construal* is one's self-image and is composed of an independent and an interdependent self (Markus & Kitayama, 1991, 1998). The independent construal of self involves the view that an individual is a unique entity with an individuated repertoire of feelings, cognitions, and motivations. In contrast, the interdependent construal of self involves an emphasis on the importance of relational or ingroup connectedness.

Self-construal is the individual-level equivalent of the cultural variability dimension of individualism-collectivism. For example, Gudykunst, Matsumoto et al. (1996), Oetzel (1998a, 1998b, 1999), and Ting-Toomey, Oetzel, and Yee-Jung (2001) argued that independent self-construal is predominantly associated with people of individualistic cultures, while interdependent self-construal is predominantly associated with people of collectivistic cultures. However, both dimensions of self exist within each individual, regardless of cultural identity (Oetzel, 1998b). In individualistic cultural communities, there may be more conflict communication situations that evoke the need for independent-based decisions and behaviors. In collectivistic communities, there may be more conflict interaction situations that demand the sensitivity for interdependent-based decisions and actions. The manner in which individuals conceive of their self-images—independent versus interdependent selves—should have a profound influence on what types of facework they would use in a particular conflict episode. For example, in a cross-national study in four nations, Oetzel and Ting-Toomey (2003) found that independent self-construal is associated positively with self-face concern. Interdependent self-construal, on the other hand, is associated positively with other-face concern. Self-face concern is also found to relate positively with dominating/competing conflict tactics, while other-face concern is related positively with avoiding and integrating conflict tactics. Further, Oetzel (1998a), in comparing Japanese work groups to European American groups on conflict strategies, found that groups consisting of members characterized by interdependent self-construals are less likely to use competitive/dominating tactics and more likely to use cooperative/integrative tactics than those characterized by independent self-construals. From the above, it would appear that independent self-construal fosters the use of direct, upfront, and low-context assertive to aggressive conflict behaviors, while interdependent self-construal emphasizes indirect, circumspective, high-context, accommodating, passive aggressive, and nonconfrontational conflict behaviors. Dominating conflict style basically reflects the emphasis of promoting self-face interest above and beyond other-face or mutual-face interest. Avoiding style, on the other hand, from the face-negotiation perspective and the research findings across different cultures has been found to associate positively with other-face and mutual-face protection interest in the conflict interaction process (see Kim & Leung, 2000; Ting-Toomey, 1988). Moreover, integrative conflict style has been discovered to reflect a high concern for both other-face and mutual-face interest and to involve mutual respectful treatment in a cross-cultural or intercultural conflict episode.

In another interesting study (Ting-Toomey et al., 2001), the researchers examined the combination of the two self-construal dimensions that result in four self-construal types: biconstrual (high on both dimensions), independent orientation (high independent, low interdependent), interdependent orientation (low independent, high interdependent), and ambivalent (low on both orientations). They examined the self-construals and conflict styles of four ethnic groups in the United States who recalled an acquaintance conflict. The researchers found that (a) biconstruals use integrating and compromising conflict styles more than ambivalents; (b) biconstruals use an emotionally expressive style more than ambivalents; (c) biconstruals use a dominating/competing style more than ambivalents; (d) ambivalents use a third-party help style more than biconstruals; and (e) ambivalents use a neglecting (i.e., passive-aggressive) style more than biconstruals.

Overall, it seems that the biconstruals have a wide range of conflict repertoires for dealing with different conflict situations, whereas ambivalents prefer to use neglecting conflict style or complaining to third-party more than biconstruals, independents, and interdependents. It seems that if we train individuals to flex their mind-sets (i.e., to develop both independent and interdependent attributes) and to be willing to be more flexible and adaptive in their different conflict negotiation styles, the intercultural or intergroup conflict process can be less antagonistic and more collaborative. However, a flexible conflict style can be nurtured or fostered only in a respectful, shared-power workplace environment. Otherwise, minority group members may be the ones who have to do all the adapting and flexing, while the higher-status dominant group members may be oblivious to the adaptive efforts and the "muted voices" of the nondominant group members. Furthermore, perhaps the role of "third-party" help also needs to be further re-conceptualized in future conflict style research—whether disputants seek third-party help constructively or passive-aggressively may mean different things to different members in different speech communities. In sum, cultural individualism-collectivism has direct effects on conflict styles, as well as mediated effects through self-construals and face concern dimensions. Although Assumption 6 of the conflict face-negotiation theory emphasizes the importance of situational and relational features in the conflict face-negotiation theorizing process, no systematic discussion has been devoted to this particular emphasis yet in this chapter. We use the discussions that follow to launch a dialogue on a situational appraisal perspective on the activation of independent/interdependent self as moderated by factors such as perceived conflict face threat issues, divergent conflict goals, and different relational distance and status issues in cueing different face concerns in a particular conflict episode.

Self and a Situational Appraisal Perspective

To begin our discussion, in recent years much research on communication styles based on self-construal theory (Markus & Kitayama, 1991) has been generated. The basic themes of such research are rooted in the concern for communication outcome or concern for relationship process, and that of directness-indirectness communication styles. For example, Kim et al. (1996) discovered that in their Korean, Japanese, Hawaiian, and U.S. American comparisons of conversational styles, independent self-construal, are related positively to outcome-oriented concerns, while interdependent self-construal is associated positively with other-oriented relationship concerns. Gudykunst, Matsumoto et al. (1996) compared U.S. Americans, Japanese, Koreans, and Australians on communication styles, and found that independent self-construal is related negatively to indirect interaction style while interdependent self-construal is related positively to indirect communication style.

Thus, self-construal theory and the associated individualism-collectivism theoretical framework illustrate that individualists and those with independent self-construal would favor direct styles of communication, while collectivists and those with interdependent self-construal prefer indirect styles. This preconception, however, has often proven to hold inconsistent findings. For instance, Gudykunst, Matsumoto et al. (1996), in their four-nation study of communication styles, found that the Japanese sample, known to be collectivistic and interdependent, was the least able to interpret indirect, high-context communication style in comparison to the U.S. American sample. Takano and Osaka (1999), citing the example of inconsistent finding in studies involving Japanese, add that the changes in the social and global environment have caused a transition from collectivism to individualism in the Japanese culture. They suggest that historical developments have dissipated the need for Japanese to be collectivistic, and have encouraged individualism. Given that individual socialization is culturally conditioned or even "programmed," however, it would be difficult to conceive of globalization having such an immediate and sweeping impact on both cultural and individual level changes. We believe that perhaps for both individualists and collectivists (and maybe more so for collectivists or interdependent, high-context folks), their perceptions and assessments of situational factors in a particular communication or conflict episode strongly moderate their activation of an independent or interdependent self.

Regarding theoretical validity, Matsumoto (1999) suggested that cross-cultural theories, especially those concerning independent and interdependent self-construals, may be based upon assumptions that are inadequate to explain differences between certain cultures, particularly those theories that have yielded unexpected results. He also suggested that the scales utilized in measuring concepts intended for testing hypotheses based on this theory may be lacking in construct validity (see also Bresnahan et al.,

2005; Levine et al., 2003). More specifically, many scholars (Cross, Gore, & Morris, 2003; Endo, 2000; Gonclaves & Salgado, 2001; Wiemann, Takai, Ota, & Wiemann, 1997) also propose a relational or a malleable self viewpoint in connecting Japanese conception of self to a wide range of communication behaviors. Since the conflict face-negotiation theory posits that face is a situated identity construct and is closely tied to perceived identity threat or identity disrespect issues in a particular situation, we now turn to a more culture-specific discussion, especially concerning the meaning of "relational self" issues in the Japanese society as an illustration of the multilayered complexity of studying the interrelationship of self, situation, facework, and conflict styles.

Relational self in communication. Markus and Kitayama (1991) noted that, generally, individualistic, Western cultures tend to conceptualize the self as being bounded, unitary, and stable. On the other hand, they claim that collectivistic, Asian cultures or those with an interdependent self-construal tend to have variable selves. Kanagawa, Cross, and Markus (2001) argued that in the United States, in particular, the self is a "more or less integrated whole composed of abilities, values, personality attributes, preferences, feeling states, and attitudes" that are "not bound to particular situations or relationships but instead are seen as transcendent and enduring" (p. 91). In an empirical test of this notion, Suh (2002) found that individuals with consistent selves are evaluated more positively with regard to social skills and likeability in the United States, relative to South Korea.

In contrast, the notion of a relational self has been widely accepted in the Japanese culture. For example, Cousins (1989) revealed that in a Twenty Statements Test, Japanese respondents are not able to report on their inner attributes very well when provided no specific context, as compared to when a relational context is specified. Sakuma and Muto (2003) found that Japanese respondents are not only aware of the fluctuations of the self, but they also view such fluctuations much more positively and as more desirable than undesirable. This argument can be illustrated by the linguistic features of the contrasted cultures. Whereas English speakers are limited with

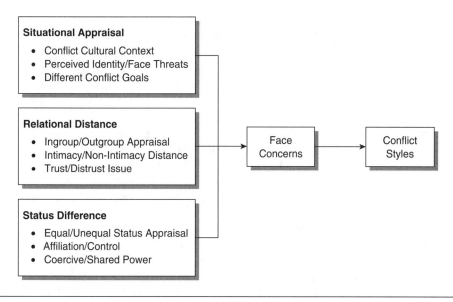

Figure 25.3   Situational Appraisal Factors and Relational Features on Face Concerns and Conflict Styles

respect to self-reference to "me, myself, and I," the Japanese language is equipped with various references to the self depending on the specific relational context of the interaction (Okabe, 1988). For example, in front of a higher status person, one would tend to refer to the self as *watakushi,* which reflects self-deference, while in front of a subordinate, the high-status confident *ore* might be used. Different modes of self-presentation accompany these linguistic self-references, and these modal differences may appear as multiple selves. From the above brief discussion, it would appear that face concern issues and conflict styles could also benefit from a situational appraisal, adaptive-self standpoint.

A situational appraisal perspective. Our working model of a situational appraisal perspective emphasizes the notions that culture-level factors (e.g., value patterns of individualism-collectivism and small/large power distance) do condition the development of various self-conceptions (e.g., independent and interdependent self) in a diverse range of cultures. Three of the possible factors that moderate the activation of an independent versus an interdependent self in a conflict interaction episode include a *specific situational appraisal process* in assessing (or emotionally reacting mindlessly) to the perceived face threat contents, the weighing of the

rewards/costs/alternatives of the different content, relational, and identity conflict goals, and where the conflict encounter is actually happening (e.g., what cultural setting, what specific situational context, etc.). Furthermore, whether we choose to assert self-face concern interest in the conflict process or extend consideration or respect to the other-face and mutual-face interest is highly dependent on *relational distance issues* (e.g., ingroup/outgroup consideration, degree of intimacy, and trust/distrust issues) and *status difference issues* (e.g., status appraisal calculations, affiliation/control issues, and perceived coercive vs. shared power issues) in a particular conflict setting (see Figure 25.3).

For example, emotional frustrations and aggravations are prevalent in conflict interaction in which diverse *face content needs* and different *conflict interaction goals* are unmet. According to Ting-Toomey (2005), individuals often have different face wants or face needs in a diverse range of identity-threat or identity-disrespectful situations. Against the backdrop of macro- and meso-level historical (e.g., competitive intergroup history) and organizational climate (e.g., exclusion vs. inclusion workplace practice) issues, some interpersonal face threat content domains include, but are not limited to, autonomy face, inclusion face, approval face, status face, competence face, and moral face

(Brown & Levinson, 1987; Lim, 1994; Ting-Toomey, 1994).

Autonomy face is concerned with our need for others to acknowledge our independence, self-sufficiency, privacy, boundary, non-imposition, control issues, and vice versa (i.e., our consideration for the face needs of the other on the autonomy face domain, etc.). *Inclusion face* (or fellowship face) is concerned with our need for others to recognize that we are worthy companions, likeable, agreeable, pleasant, friendly, and cooperative. *Status face* is concerned with our need for others to admire our tangible or intangible assets or resources such as appearance, social attractiveness, reputation, position, power, and material worth. *Reliability face* is concerned with our need for others to realize that we are trustworthy, dependable, reliable, loyal, and consistent in our words and actions. *Competence face* (as in "communication competence") is concerned with our need for others to recognize our qualities or social abilities such as intelligence, skills, expertise, leadership, team-building skills, networking skills, conflict mediation skills, facework skills, and problem-solving skills. *Moral face* is concerned with our need for others to respect our sense of integrity, dignity, honor, propriety, and moral uprightness.

The boundaries between face domains are permeable and overlapped such that in negotiating face reliability, we also need to tend to face competence. In dealing with face autonomy, we also need to tend to face fellowship or inclusion. Thus, the different face content domains exist in a three-dimensional, matrix-like space—in tight intersection with one another (Ting-Toomey, 2005). When the need or expectation for one face content domain is not met, there will be repercussions for other face content domains. Concurrently, in dealing competently with one face content domain, the satisfied face domain may also carry a ripple effect for other face content domains. Drawing from the self-construal theory, we can speculate that while independent selves would tend to emphasize the autonomy-face content domain, interdependent selves would tend to emphasize the inclusion-face domain. Moreover, independent selves or individualists would tend to emphasize more intrinsic emotions such as personal pride or anger, personal jealousy or aggravation, personal insult

or humiliation, individual fairness or unfairness, and individual justice or injustice issues. Interdependent selves or collectivists, on the other hand, would focus more on social-focused emotions such as family or community shame, public embarrassment, social humiliation, communal honor or dishonor, and social wrongdoing or ingroup-based injustice issues (Markus & Kitayama, 1991, 1998).

While both independent and interdependent selves may experience a wide range of conflict emotions, they may internalize certain types of self-conscious emotions (e.g., embarrassment, pride, shame, and guilt—the "big four" self-conscious emotions; see Lewis & Haviland-Jones, 2000; Shweder & Haidt, 2000) with varying intensity in responding to the different unmet face need domains. For example, an interdependent self might tend to experience a higher intensity of shame for the wrongdoings of a close relative than an independent self would on the fellowship face issue. Or an independent self might tend to locate the cause of a face loss situation from an individual accountability standpoint, while an interdependent self would locate the failure to the entire team or group. The more we hold a particular face content domain in high regard, the more emotionally vulnerable we are in that face content domain and the more we crave identity affirmation or respect in that domain. The more that competent facework negotiators understand their own face needs and desires, the more they can understand the "tipping points" that can trigger their face threat thresholds. The more they can work at understanding the face needs and the face desires (plus the underlying culture-based face meanings) of the other conflict parties, the more they can validate those valued face domains. The more severe the face-transgression in particular face domains, the more defensive the facework negotiators can become in their desire to save or protect the vulnerable identity spots in those valued assets.

Moreover, the perceived or actual conflict differences associated with our emotional frustrations often revolve around the following situational-based conflict goal issues: content, relational, and identity (Wilmot & Hocker, 1998). *Content conflict goals* refer to the substantive issues external to the individual involved. For example, intercultural business partners might argue about whether they should hold their business meetings in Mexico City or Los Angeles. Recurrent content conflict issues often go hand in hand with relational conflict goals. *Relational conflict goals* refer to how individuals define, or would like to define, the particular relationship in that particular conflict episode. Nonintimate-intimate and formal-informal are two ways individuals might relate to one another (for further discussions, see the "Relational distance features" and "Status difference features" sections). A business partner from the United States might opt to use short-hand e-mail message or abbreviated Internet language such as "BTW" ("By The Way") or "IMO" ("In My Opinion") or "BRB" ("Be Right Back") to communicate with his or her newly acquainted international partner from Japan. The latter might well view this short-hand or informal communication as a cavalier and unfriendly gesture. The Japanese partner may consequently perceive face disrespect and experience relationship distress. The U.S. business partner, however, may not even realize that sending a message in this offhand manner was a faux pas. The U.S. American perceived the informal note as signaling affiliation or friendliness to minimize the formal relationship distance. *Identity-based goals* revolve around issues of identity confirmation-rejection, respect-disrespect, and approval-disapproval of the individuals in the conflict situation. Embedded identity conflict goals are often at the heart of many unresolved intercultural conflicts (Rothman, 1997; Ting-Toomey, 1993). Identity conflict goals are directly linked to face-saving and face-honoring issues. A person whose face is threatened in a conflict episode is likely to feel stressed, humiliated, shamed, aggravated, or embarrassed.

Identity conflict goals are broadly linked to the underlying beliefs and value patterns of the culture and the individual (Ting-Toomey, 1993, 1999). Thus, to reject someone's proposal or idea in a conflict can mean rejecting that person's deeply held beliefs and convictions. As an example, when an interfaith couple is arguing about which religious faith they should instill in their children, they are, at the same time, assessing which religious faith is more or less "worthwhile"

in the family system. Likewise, in the case of deciding where the next Olympic Games should be held, the competing countries may be fighting over the merits and costs of a location site; however, they are also pushing and defending their national pride, honor, dignity, prestige, reputation, or *face* in the public arena. The decision to hold the Olympic Games in country X may be interpreted as enhanced power or increased status for the representatives of that country. In this way, identity goals are tied closely to culture-based face-orientation factors. Unresolved identity conflict needs often reside at the heart of many recurring conflict problems.

Beyond situational-based face content threat issues and different conflict goal considerations, there are other relational features at work in shaping the various face concerns and particular conflict styles (see Oetzel, Ting-Toomey, Yokochi, Masumoto, & Takai, 2000, and Ting-Toomey & Oetzel, 2002, for discussions of research findings on situational and relational features in moderating self-conception and face concerns and conflict styles). In addition, Oetzel's (1995, 2005) intercultural workgroup communication theory also contains specific assumptions and propositions (and situational workplace research findings) about group compositions, and also situational and relational factors shaping the decision-making processes and outcomes of culturally homogeneous versus culturally heterogeneous workgroups. We now turn to a culture-specific explication (i.e., the Japanese culture) in discussing the relational distance and status difference features of cross-cultural conflict communication process (see Figure 25.4). Behind the brief Japanese review is the premise that to conduct sound cross-cultural comparative research on face-sensitive issues and conflict style issues, intercultural theorists and researchers have to delve deeper into the linguistic and sociolinguistic (and also context-based nonverbal meanings, interpretations, and messages) features from an emic, insider viewpoint.

Relational distance features: Ingroup vs. outgroup. Perhaps the most complex factor influencing Japanese conflict communication style, for example, is the relational distance intimacy dimension. Through the Japanese communication

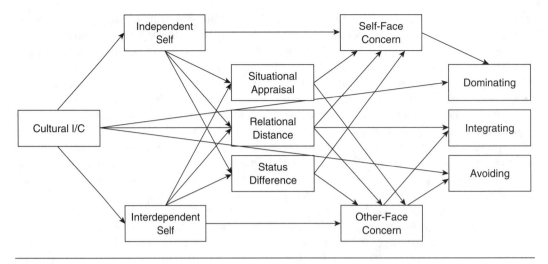

Figure 25.4   Understanding Intercultural Conflict: A Situational Appraisal Framework

lens, Midooka (1990) categorized four groups of relationships, the ingroup consisting of *kino-oke-nai-kankei* and *nakama,* and the outgroup consisting of *najimi-no-tanin* and *muen-no-kankei. Kino-okenai-kankei* ("intimate ingroups") consists of very intimate, or equal-status relationships in which communication is causal, open, and direct. Examples of such relationships are best friends, family/siblings, close relatives, childhood buddies, and intimate dating relationships. In these relationships, differences in age or seniority are superseded by intimacy, and no hierarchical rituals, especially in the "best friends" category, are heeded. *Nakama* ("familiar interactive ingroups"), on the other hand, are intimate ingroup relations especially in terms of everyday familiarity, yet not so much as to override status differences. These typically include everyday colleagues in the same workplace, where maximum care must be taken to perform proper ingroup role-based communication rituals to preserve relational harmony and trust. A certain level of appropriate decorum or formality is expected to be maintained and followed in the *nakama* category. In conflict disputes or skirmishes, individuals in the *nakama* circle would try to smooth over minor conflicts or use tolerance or forbearance in the hope that the conflict would go away. They might also seek out third-party help (especially a third party that both individuals respect and trust) to mediate the conflict behind the scenes. They might even appeal to the

reasoning that, for the third party's face, they would try to get along. They might even use apology rituals for bringing so much stress to their own ingroup or causing so much grief in their own workplace.

On the other hand, *Najimi-no-tanin* ("acquaintance interactive outgroups") refers to a less intimate, acquaintance relationship, characterized more as an outgroup rather than as an ingroup relationship. For example, acquaintance colleagues in other universities or friend of a close friend who needs a favor. While being *tanin,* or in this "acquaintanceship interactive outgroups" category, conflict communication behaviors toward this outgroup member would differ greatly depending on the perceived value or reward/cost appraisal of the relationship. Yet because Japan is overall a collectivistic society, interdependent social ties have interlocking importance and implications from one spectrum of the society to another. If the relationship poses a threat to one's public face (*sekentei*), one is still careful to observe appropriate interaction formality and interpersonal conflict rituals. Yoneyama (1983) contended that age, status, gender, roles, and conflict topics play important parts in determining specific conflict attitude and behavioral mode. Moreover, one misstep can also be costly and can be misunderstood easily in this acquaintance outgroup category. Finally, *muen-no-kankei* ("stranger outgroups") indicates a purely outgroup, stranger relationship with no relationship ties at all. According to Midooka (1990), "Japanese interact with [*muen-no-kankei*] others in an indifferent manner . . . often quite impolitely" (p. 481) because strangers are way beyond the bounds of established social or personalized ties. Often, in a head-on antagonistic collision or dispute, no *enryo* or any form of courtesy or considerate behavior needs to be exercised in this stranger-stranger conflict relationship context, as there are no preexisting emotional sentiments that bind the two people together. Individuals might use very low-context, direct, upfront, to aggressive conflict tactics in this relationship category.

The Japanese, thus, do not merely distinguish between broad-based ingroup and outgroup categories, as many of the cross-cultural studies indicated, but they actually use a differentiated system to subdivide ingroup and outgroup into more specific interaction layers. Thus, for example, direct and explicit self-face concern and conflict interaction style (e.g., dominating, competing, or even aggressive conflict tactics) can be employed toward the *muen-no-kankei* or "stranger outgroups," whereas, interestingly, greater flexibility and a diverse range of conflict styles (e.g., integrating and compromising to emotionally expressive conflict responses) can be used in the *kino-okenai-kankei* or "intimate ingroups" category—especially when the relationship ties are intimate and of equal status rankings. However, when dealing with the *nakama or* "familiar interactive ingroups" category, status difference is of paramount importance. The indirect/avoidance conflict style and accommodating/obliging conflict style would be two ideal styles to use toward the higher status *senpai* of the *nakama* ingroup. In addition, respectful other-face giving and diplomatic other-face honoring conflict styles should also be used toward the higher status *senpai* in the *najimi-no-tanin* relationship category (i.e., "acquaintance interactive outgroup") because of anticipated future interactions and the fear of anticipated future interaction costs.

From these elaborate relational categorization schemes, it appears that the simple dichotomy of ingroup and outgroup distinctions is insufficient to explain Japanese interpersonal conflict behavior and, of course, that of many other cultural communities, as well, on both domestic diversity and global diversity fronts. We believe that more interculturalists and sociolinguists should join hands in investigating the intricate, multidimensional "ingroup" and "outgroup" linguistic categories and the associated competent versus incompetent conflict behaviors in diverse cultural community systems. We further recommend here that a more in-depth understanding of the differentiated "ingroup" and "outgroup" linguistic categories and the conjoint sociolinguistic situations associated with various face concerns and face movements will greatly enhance our understanding of the complex intercultural conflict negotiation processes and the particular conflict competence or incompetence outcomes.

Status difference features. Furthermore, it is apparent that Japanese sociotypes and conflict styles are in operation within certain relationships on a general level, but not necessarily in particular relationship types. Another prime example of the importance of relational features in the Japanese society is definitely status difference. For example, the vast literature on *nihonjinron* (study of Japanese people) reveals three distinct themes: dependence on situation, sensitivity to seniority and status differences, and behavioral distinction between ingroup and outgroup (as discussed previously under "Relational Distance Features: Ingroup/Outgroup"). Hamaguchi (1977, 1983), for example, asserted that U.S. Americans follow rules and norms regardless of the situation, such as not parking in parking spaces marked by a wheelchair sign, while Japanese act according to current circumstances; thus they would occupy designated parking areas if nobody was using it and if they required only a short time to finish their business. Lebra (1975) called this behavioral pattern situational interaction. She elaborated that Japanese abide by behavioral standards consisting of *soto* and *uchi* (outgroup vs. ingroup), and *omote* and *ura* (front vs. back). While the *soto-omote* ("outgroup-front") situation relies on ritualistic interaction, the *soto-ura* ("outgroup-back") is an anomic/estranged situation. Moreover, while the *uchi-omote* ("ingroup front") situation is a courteous, pleasant one, the *uchi-ura* ("ingroup-back") situation follows flexible rules and diverse conflict interaction norms. Furthermore, Lebra characterized Japanese status orientation as consisting of sensitivity to rank order and of dichotomization of conflict communication behavior into up-faced (toward superior) and down-faced (toward subordinate), status motives (including status display, status elevation), status-based induced shame, and the strategic status assertion as a ploy. Given such status consciousness culture-based facework functions, various face maneuvers and conflict tactics, then, would differ significantly with regard to relational distance, status difference, intentions and motivations, and rank orderings of the other conflict parties in a particular "frontroom" (with witnessing audience being present) or "backroom" situation (without an audience) in the Japanese society.

In sum, we propose that the intersections between relational intimacy dimension (e.g., along ingroup/outgroup as a starting point) and relational status dimension (e.g., horizontal vs. vertical facework) on face concerns and conflict styles need to be further understood in a diverse range of cultural communities in future face-negotiation theorizing effort. Bilingual and multilingual researchers may further want to pay close attention to the functional equivalence (i.e., the cultural endorsement of the importance of the various research concepts) and construct (or conceptual) equivalence (i.e., the meaning similarity level of concepts within the cognitive interpretation schema of the members of the cultures being examined) issues in studying any conflict-related concepts. Common-usage conflict concepts such as a conflict "management," conflict "resolution," conflict "compromising," conflict "reconciliation," or conflict "transformation" process may carry different construct relevance or meanings for people in the local cultural scenes.

We have discussed an extension model on the conflict face-negotiation theory through the incorporation of perceived face threats in a conflict situation plus the addition of insights of an emic viewpoint in conceptualizing ingroup/outgroup dynamics and status-conscious upward/downward face issues in dealing with high-status versus low-status members in the Japanese society. We believe all cultural communities have their own lingoes and code words in dealing with different intergroup and intercultural

conflicts. The future development of the face-negotiation theory may need more insider cultural insights and narratives from diverse racial and ethnic groups within multiple spectrums of the larger society to express what they consider as "fair" and "just" face-identity treatments regarding interethnic and interracial conflict tensions and problems. We end the chapter with some recommendations for applications and research directions of the various theories discussed in the earlier sections.

UNDERSTANDING INTERCULTURAL CONFLICT: APPLICATIONS AND RESEARCH DIRECTIONS

Drawing from the ideas discussed previously, we map out some practical implications and doable research directions for researchers who are energized by the quest for clarification and explanation of the complex phenomenon of intercultural conflict communication. We start our recommendations with the anxiety/uncertainty management (AUM) theory and the integrated threat (IT) theory.

Anxiety/Uncertainty and Integrated Threat Theories

Applications. From Gudykunst's (2005a) viewpoint, effective intercultural communication involves the enactment of mindfulness—in

> creating new categories for strangers (e.g., looking for individuating information about strangers), be open to new information (e.g., things we do not know already about the strangers with whom we are communicating), and be aware of how strangers are interpreting incoming messages. (p. 313)

Gudykunst, Guzley, and Hammer (1996) mapped out a systematic effective intercultural communication training program based on the AUM theory and principles.

Basically, if we draw from the contents of the anxiety/uncertainty management theory, increased cultural and person-based knowledge can decrease cultural strangers' anxiety and uncertainty levels. Understanding strangers' language, metaphors, and nonverbal conflict habits can also greatly reduce interactive anxiety and uncertainty between two cultural strangers or two conflict negotiators from diverse cultural worlds. Reflecting about the sources of our anxiety and uncertainty and actively seeking out accurate information and knowledge about cultural strangers' conflict paradigms and preferences can also help to increase our ability to communicate competently with cultural strangers. More important, redirecting some of that anxious energy toward paying more focused attention to the conflict interaction process and conflict nuances may help to move the self-paralyzed state to a more alert conflict attentive process. Mindful deep breathing and meditation techniques to intentionally questioning whether the conflict still counts as an important conflict "three days down the road" or "three months from now" may also help to reset our priorities and loosen up personal anxieties and uncertainties.

On a macro-level of competent conflict interaction and training, C. W. Stephan and W. G. Stephan (2003) stated that some of the possible remedies to lighten the perceived emotional anxiety and threat loads are: (a) accurate knowledge of major value difference dimensions between cultures should increase mutual understanding and decrease mutual ignorance, (b) information about overriding human values (such as family security, respect, and compassion) common to all cultures should decrease prejudice based solely on values/symbolic threats and group membership contrasts, (c) accurate data concerning the exaggerated nature of people's beliefs relating to scarce resources should counteract the notion of perceived tangible/realistic threats, (d) the mindful creation of superordinate identities so that identity groups can realize the connected human souls that exist between them, and (e) reminding people of the multiple social categories or overlapping circles to which they belong would help to lower individuals' anxiety and perceived threat levels.

In addition, setting up opportunities for two or more identity groups to engage in cooperative learning techniques would help both groups to see the "human face" beyond the broad-based stereotypic group membership labels. Cooperative learning techniques include face-to-face active communication engagements between dominant group and minority groups in solving an interdependent problem and that the outcome also holds positive reward incentive. More important, both groups should be able to experience some concrete interdependent contributions to the problem-solving task. Cooperative learning techniques should also have built-in semi-structured time to promote friendships and a mutual personalized sharing process. Thus, the contact condition should allow individuals to get to know each other on a personalized, culture-sensitive sharing level as versus a superficial, stereotypic level (see Schneider, 2004, for his theoretical insights and systematic assessments on all the specific intergroup contact and prejudice reduction techniques that a practitioner or teacher can use in a learning environment). Lastly, the intergroup contact should be strongly supported or endorsed by key authority figures or change agents in the organization or the community and, it is hoped, with adequate resource funding and also open cooperative spaces for the different groups to work. In these cooperative settings, the *positive goal interdependence* of groups has been identified as the key causal factor in accomplishing positive interpersonal relationship and achievement outcome (W. G. Stephan & C. W. Stephan, 2001).

Furthermore, understanding and applying J. Bennett and Bennett's (2004) developmental model of intercultural sensitivity (DMIS) may also help practitioners to analyze the learning readiness of their intercultural trainees or learners and also understand the specific threats or anxieties they are experiencing. According to Bennett and Bennett (2004; see also M. Bennett, 1993), the DMIS is a framework through which one's experience of cultural difference becomes more sophisticated as one's competence in intercultural relations increases. There are six stages in the DMIS model, and each stage is a particular worldview configuration and creates certain kinds of attitudes and behaviors that are typically associated with that stage. The first set of three stages (denial, defense, minimization) of the DMIS framework is *ethnocentric,* meaning one's own cultural frame of reference is the central reality of one's existence. Briefly, in the ethnocentric "denial stage" individuals would deny that cultural difference exists or they might use the social Darwinism principle to justify the existence of "naturally superior people" who are either born into or achieve membership in the dominant group. On the other hand, in the "defense stage" individuals may object to generalizations about their own groups (e.g., "Each one of us is a unique individual"); however, they would continue to use a stereotypic lens to view outgroup members. Furthermore, the defense stage is cast in an us-versus-them mentality, and the prevailing attitude is one of being "under siege" or being "robbed." According to Bennett and Bennett (2004), from an outsider viewpoint,

> what members of the dominant group are defending is their cultural privilege, but of course, it is not experienced that way from the interior of the group. For nondominant groups, the siege attitude is similar, but the assumed attacker is different. People here are more likely to be protecting their cultural identities from the dominant group's pressure to assimilate. (p. 154)

Lastly, in the "minimization" ethnocentric stage, superficial cultural etiquette and other cultural customs are acknowledged, but an ethnocentric, surface assumption is made that "deep down, we are all the same."

Fortunately, Bennett and Bennett (2004) also provide some remedies to counteract the denial-defense-minimization ethnocentric continuum. The second set of three DMIS stages (acceptance, adaptation, integration) is *ethnorelative,* meaning one begins to make movement toward perspective-shift in viewing cultural strangers' behavior from an alternative cultural frame of reference. Briefly, in the "acceptance stage," individuals accept cultural differences on a cognitive level. Emotionally or behaviorally, however, they might not have the emotional resonance or the sophisticated competence skills to deal with identity diversities or racial/cultural diversity issues. In the "adaptation stage," individuals start to learn to cognitively shift their worldview perspective and begin to empathize with the cultural strangers' worldviews and values. They also start practicing some behavioral adaptation because "it feels right," and not because "that is how one is supposed to act." Lastly, in the ethnorelative "integration" stage, individuals have incorporated an enriched, multidimensional worldview and, at the meta-level, have a sense of identity coherence. On the cognitive,

affective, behavioral, and ethical levels, these learners have developed sophisticated intercultural sensitivity skills and are able to facilitate positive changes in diverse cultural contexts. Many successful intercultural conflict mediators or practitioners may be operating from this "integrative" ethnorelative stage. Understanding the various DMIS stages may help trainers and practitioners to design and develop their intercultural conflict training program based on the developmental DMIS stage-linked approach. J. Bennett (2003) has also presented a coherent set of training objectives and pedagogical strategies in her "Turning the Frogs Into Interculturalists" chapter.

Research directions. In terms of further expanding the heuristic value of the AUM theory (Gudykunst, 2005a), here are some interesting directions for future research: At what optimal anxiety/uncertainty developmental stage should mindfulness be introduced as a tool to counteract our fear of cultural strangers? Are individuals more strategic in their management of face threatening issues in the moderate range versus the maximum or minimum range of anxiety/uncertainty zones? How do anticipated positive or negative interaction consequences influence the selection of particular conflict strategies between two cultural strangers?

In terms of the IT theory (C. W. Stephan & W. G. Stephan, 2003; W. Stephan, 1999), the following research questions may help to clarify further the intergroup conflict negotiation process: How do the different threat types relate to the various enthnocentric stages (i.e., denial, defense, and minimization)? How do individuals actually approach intercultural or intergroup conflict at each stage of the ethnocentrism-ethnorelativism developmental model? What would an intergroup conflict scenario look like when one individual is at one stage of the ethnocentric continuum and another individual is coming from another ethnocentric or ethnorelative stage?

Expectancy Violations Theory and Cultural Values Dimensional Grid

Applications. In terms of conflict training issues, EVT lends itself especially to conflict training sessions on "de-stereotyping" exercises or activities. For example, by soliciting stereotypic categories and interpretations from trainees concerning anonymous faces or pictures (e.g., in reaction to a set of posters with faces from different racial/cultural or multiracial groups) and asking trainees a set of written questions (both positive and negative questions, such as professions or dream professions, families, hobbies, vanities, self-perceived flaws, being pulled over by police, etc.) about those faces, trainers can solicit some overgeneralized perceptions and impressions about those "poster faces." At times, the "stereotypes" can be on a totally wrong track. Sadly, there might be questions (e.g., which high school kid tends to be pulled over by the police more often than other kids) that the learners can guess accurately. Of course, an intercultural trainer has to conduct such de-stereotyping to stereotyping dialogue training with intercultural sensitivity and observant skills—being mindful that members of other racial and cultural groups are present and whose faces are represented on those posters. The skillful intercultural conflict trainer can use the focal concepts in the EVT to solicit the factors that shape the trainees' expectancies. They can also use the key themes from the theory to discuss positive versus negative expectancy violations. They can also debunk their learners' stereotypes by offering accurate information in the poster-faces exercise. In fact, this poster-faces exercise has actually been conducted successfully throughout the years by the California Orange County Human Relations Group (http://www.ochumanrelations.org). Often, when a trusting training climate is established, both adults and high school students can engage in a very insightful and open dialogue session, sharing their own past experiences of being stereotyped and the pain that was involved. When a trusting climate has been established, learners most likely would also share their own biased stereotypes and even prejudices against outgroup members—especially under the mindful guidance of a highly skilled facilitator or co-facilitators. The notions of positive versus negative expectancy violations can also be used as further debriefing questions based on the EVT lens. Again, effective intercultural conflict training sessions depend heavily on the competencies and the respectful stances that are being modeled by the intercultural trainers in the training room.

In terms of practical application of the CVD grid, we believe that a good starting point in any intercultural conflict training is to increase cultural self-awareness. Thus, using self-assessment tools to heighten trainees' sensitivity and their own awareness of their own cultural and personal value systems would be very useful. Furthermore, giving trainees enough time to process and understand the value patterns of diverse cultural trainees in the training setting (especially on multiple value levels such as society, workplace, family, and personal values) would be invaluable. Moreover, assessment tools can be used to measure different face concerns and conflict styles in particular conflict situations. Various wonderful international films and film clips can also be used to illustrate values and conflict style clashes (for a complete film listing, see the Instructor Manual that accompanies the basic intercultural text by Ting-Toomey & Chung, 2005). Specific concepts from the value grid (e.g., benevolent conflict approach or status-achievement approach) can be used as relevant and credible debriefing training tools. Furthermore, we have also used artwork projects or impressionistic postcards to generate conflict stories and cases by asking trainees to pick a postcard that resonates deeply with them. We have also used "sculpting-chair rotation" techniques in which trainees take time to tell their conflict stories from diverse cultural or personal value lenses.

Research directions. In terms of the EVT's (Burgoon & Ebesu Hubbard, 2005) future research directions, here are some researchable questions: How does expectancy violations work when cultural members use a different conflict style than stereotypically expected? How do the factors of individual communicators, relationship issues, and context issues serve as moderating factors between high and low communication expectancies along the different conflict reconciliation stages? Should conflict mediators hold realistic or idealistic communication expectancies when facilitating intergroup conflict dialogue processes? What constitutes a tolerable range of expectancy violations to instill changes and transformations in mediating a protracted conflict situation?

The CVD grid (Ting-Toomey & Oetzel, 2001) offers some intriguing research and also applied questions: When do individuals activate their culture-based conflict approach (e.g., impartial vs. benevolent), and what types of motivations are needed to train managers or employees to switch styles? How can members of different cultures learn to clarify their conflict expectations and at the same time stay true to their own conflict approaches in a constructive manner? Which conflict resolution mode should be the preferred "common space" conflict mode in a domestic diversity or global organization? How can we learn to pay more attention to other creative conflict worldviews and techniques without co-opting them into a preexisting theoretical framework?

Conflict Face-Negotiation Theory

Applications. According to Assumption 7 of the face-negotiation (FN) theory, intercultural facework competence refers to the optimal integration of knowledge, mindfulness, and communication skills in managing vulnerable identity-based interaction scenes appropriately, effectively, and adaptively. According to the FN theory, of all the components of facework competence, knowledge is the most important component because it underscores the other components of competence. Without culture-sensitive knowledge, disputants cannot learn to uncover the implicit "ethnocentric lenses" they use to evaluate behaviors in an intercultural conflict situation. Without knowledge, people cannot have an accurate perspective or reframe their interpretation of a conflict situation from the other's culture standpoint. Knowledge here refers to developing in-depth understanding of important facework concepts that can help to manage culture-based conflict competently.

Intercultural trainers can use the base of individualism-collectivism and small/large power distance as a twofold framework to explain a variety of face-based communication situations. They can also deepen the complexity of the trainees' learning by emphasizing the importance of understanding relational and situational features in shaping any facework behaviors in a conflict scene. They can also use some of the core facework taxonomies to process a case

study, a videotaped conflict interaction, and a team discussion session. The knowledge that we acquire about the other conflict parties, our willingness to be mindful of our own and the others' face concerns and needs, and the skills that we use to manage the conflict adaptively will dramatically influence the outcome dimension of the conflict.

In-depth cultural knowledge can lead to some truly "aha!" moments that illuminate conflict learning. These "aha!" moments coupled with mindful reflections can help an individual develop constructive conflict skills and build competent interaction habits. To be a mindful observer and interpreter of intercultural conflict, one must develop a holistic view of the critical factors that frame the interactive process of a conflict. *Mindfulness* means attending to one's internal assumptions, cognitions, and emotions and, at the same time, becoming attuned to the other's conflict assumptions, cognitions, and emotions (Thich, 1991; Ting-Toomey, 1999). Mindful reflexivity requires us to tune in to our own cultural and personal habitual assumptions in scanning a conflict interaction scene. The roots of mindfulness practice are in the contemplative practices common to both Eastern and Western spiritual traditions (Robins, Schmidt, & Linehan, 2004). Mindfulness is at once a spiritual, meditative, reflective, and applied way of conscious living. The same authors note that mindfulness, as a set of skills, is the "intentional process of observing, describing, and participating in reality nonjudgmentally, in the moment, and with effectiveness" (p. 37).

To be mindful of intercultural differences, we have to learn to see the unfamiliar behavior from a nonjudgmental angle. In the context of intercultural conflict, we have to deal with our own vulnerable emotions regarding face-threatening behaviors. Concurrently, we have to be responsive to new conflict interaction scripts. We also need to develop multiple lenses in understanding the culture-level and situational-level factors that shape the escalating conflict episode. When training trainees to develop a set of mindful attributes, an intercultural trainer can emphasize the following characteristics of "mindfulness": (a) learning to see behavior or information presented in the conflict situation as novel or fresh, (b) learning to view a conflict situation from several vantage points or perspectives, (c) learning to attend to the conflict context and the person in whom we are perceiving the behavior, and (d) learning to create new categories through which this new conflict behavior may be understood (Langer, 1989, 1997). It is hoped that through mindful training, trainees can learn to shift perspective and be able to understand and analyze a conflict episode from multiple cultural frames of reference. On a general level, we cannot suddenly learn to be mindful during a conflict episode. Mindfulness is a systematic way of cultivating a sense of exquisite attention and noticing of individuals, events, conflict stories, and evolving contexts around you and around your conflict partner on a day-to-day basis. Mindfulness is the mediating step in linking knowledge with intentional conflict competence practice.

In using the FN theory to conduct an intercultural conflict competence program, for example, we can role model, hold skill-practice training sessions, and conduct feedback coaching to guide the development of constructive conflict skills. Constructive conflict skills refer to our operational abilities to manage an intercultural conflict situation appropriately, effectively, and adaptively. Constructive conflict communicators use culture-sensitive interaction skills to manage the process of conflict adaptively and reach important goals for all parties amicably. Many conflict skills are useful in enhancing intercultural conflict competence. Of the many possible skill sets (see Ting-Toomey, 1997, 2004; Ting-Toomey & Chung, 2005; Ting-Toomey & Oetzel, 2001), we believe skills such as deep listening, mindful reframing, de-centering, and face-sensitive respectful dialogue competencies across cultural and racial lines can promote effective intergroup and intercultural conflict relations. According to Oetzel's (1995, 2005) intercultural workgroup communication theory and accompanying research findings, consensus decision making, cooperative conflict, and respectful communication are culturally appropriate communication behaviors in that they relate to both task and relational effectiveness. Oetzel's (2005) practical theory further emphasizes that the more members of a culturally diverse group who have other- or mutual-face concerns in the forefront, the more likely the multicultural team will engage in

effective conflict communication management and outcome.

Research directions. Gleaned from the existing findings and gaps in the conflict face-negotiation theory, the following four research areas hold promise and need future research attention: facework situations, facework emotions, facework movements, and facework competence. The study of face negotiation in conflict would definitely benefit from examining the relationship between *situations* and different face content domains or face movements. For example, questions such as the following need more systematic research investigations: Under what situational conditions would facework negotiators be more concerned with inclusion face issues versus autonomy face issues? Under what specific situational conditions would conflict disputants be more interested in mutual-face protection versus self-face protection? Under what triggering mechanisms would conflict negotiators be more concerned with mutual-face protection versus mutual-face obliteration? What are the necessary and sufficient conditions that can move the developmental trajectories of facework transformation from self-interest to mutual-interest to universal-interest concerns? If we dig deeper, we find face concerns are directly linked to affective-based identity issues in conflict. We need more systematic studies to understand the developmental ebbs and flows of *facework emotions* and facework emotional engagement. We need to understand the core metaphors, language, themes, psychosomatic change, conflict rhythms, conflict harmonic synchrony, and nonverbal signals that surround the onset of affective facework embarrassment and affective facework resolution. Furthermore, we need to design more multi-method studies on the affective aspects of respect, trust, dignity, honor, and forgiveness. For example, since "respect" is such an important concept in intercultural facework negotiation, we need to develop more complex models to systematically analyze the cognitive, affective, behavioral, and ethical dimensions of "facework respect" in different cultural communities. Furthermore, the emotions of pride, shame, guilt, and redemption are all powerful emotional concepts lacking sufficient treatment in the intercultural conflict literature. These are complex, affective responses generated and experienced in reaction to others and related to the cognitive appraisals of the worthiness of self-face and other-face issues. Facework emotional reactions and cognitive appraisals also prompt facework defensive or supportive conflict behaviors.

Facework movements and temporality are important dimensions for understanding how individuals complete the process of face-negotiation during and after the actual conflict negotiation process. The lack of investigation into face movements and temporality may be a byproduct of the methods utilized for the majority of research on cross-cultural conflict. The majority of the studies on conflict facework have relied heavily on self-report measures of face behavior in hypothetical or recalled conflicts. The use of these methods does not allow researchers to examine the developmental process of face-negotiation, making it particularly difficult to study temporality. More important, while we have accumulated research evidence on self-face and other-face conflict issues, the concept of "give-and-take negotiation" has not been addressed adequately. The study of conflict face-negotiation would benefit from examining actual interaction via procedures such as interaction analysis or discourse analysis or from the narrative paradigm approach. In addition, while many cross-cultural comparison studies have been conducted on the face strategy dimension, we need more "interracial" or "intercultural" face-to-face discourse or interactional or co-orientation studies to understand the diverse ways in which individuals defend and maintain face, as well as how they proactively or reactively manage identity-vulnerable face and conflict issues. We also need to address more fully the outcome dimensions of competent facework management and the accompanying culture-based meanings of terms such as *facework appropriateness, effectiveness, satisfaction, productivity,* or *transformation* (see Cupach & Canary, 1997). Finally, post-conflict interviews, in-depth case studies, or journal tracking can elicit the logic or narrative accounts that individuals use to justify their facework behaviors during and after an intergroup or interracial conflict.

Although the knowledge component has been emphasized as the most important area for intercultural conflict competence training (in comparison to the mindfulness and skills components), we need more empirical research to test this assertion. We also need to know how we can sequence *knowledge-mindfulness-skills* in an optimal manner in order to train effectively and competently. We also need more well-designed pretest and posttest research studies to understand the rate and quality of change in the knowledge, mindfulness, and skills domains as a direct result of an intercultural conflict training program. Moreover, we also need more follow-up studies to measure the subsequent retention and application of conflict management knowledge and skills in the trainees' everyday workplace performance.

Finally, another intriguing future direction for research is the concept of mindfulness training. Can we actually train people to be mindful with a three-day or a week-long intercultural workshop? Is mindfulness a trait or a state? Are there some individuals who are so hopelessly "mindless" that they are untrainable? What are the conceptual and operational factors of "mindfulness"? Is it possible to develop a culture-universal measure to assess "mindfulness," or do we need to develop a culture-specific measurement to research "mindfulness"? Better yet, do we need to develop a situational-based appraisal approach to conceptualize and operationalize "mindfulness"? Some individuals can be very "mindful" in certain situational domains and act totally "mindless" in other domains. Should we learn to honor and respect such different mindfulness capacities or should we engage in cross-situational research and training in the facilitation of a mindful consciousness and philosophy?

Mindfulness exists on philosophical, spiritual, meditative, cognitive, affective, behavioral, and ethical levels. At what level should we train and coach "mindfulness"? Ting-Toomey (1999), borrowing a schema explored by Howell (1982), has conceptualized "mindfulness" from a staircase developmental perspective. From this perspective, intercultural competence can be conceptualized along the stages of unconscious incompetence, conscious incompetence, conscious competence, and unconscious competence. The first stage basically refers to the *oblivious mindlessness stage* on the cognitive, affective, and behavioral levels. The second stage refers to the *semi-mindfulness stage,* when a learner actually "catches" himself or herself when making incompetent cultural mistakes. The third stage refers to the *full mindfulness stage,* when a learner is aware of his or her intercultural interaction mistakes and is committed to integrating the new knowledge, mind-set, and skills into competent practice. The fourth stage, the *mindlessly mindfulness stage,* refers to a dynamic consciousness in which the learner is able to communicate effortlessly and competently with locals in the new culture. Concurrently, this cultural transformer can communicate so adaptively in diverse cultural situations that it is possible to slip between mindless and mindful attentiveness without conscious processing. Thus, "mindlessness" can have two interpretations—it can be construed as an oblivious mindless attitude on the surface level, or it can be interpreted as a deep-level, dynamic looseness of learning. In slipping between the double loops of mindless and mindful consciousness, this cultural transformer is comfortable with polarities, ambiguities, and uncertainties. The learner is able to forge a sense of security and balance in moving back and forth between worldviews, values, and behaviors and is on a constant search for learning and relearning. These observations concerning the developmental stages from "total mindlessness" to "mindlessly mindful" stages await further model development, empirical testing, and conceptual refinement.

In conclusion, all human beings like to be respected and approved of—especially during vulnerable identity-threat situations. How diverse individuals protect and maintain self-face needs and, at the same time, learn to honor the face needs of the other conflict party very likely differ from one culture to the next, and differ from one conflict scene to the next. The study and the researching of intercultural conflict communication is a complex, multidimensional, and multilevel phenomenon. This chapter offers a beginning step to integrating in one chapter some of the heuristic theories and ideas for you to stretch your imagination and to invite you to "play" and "sample" for yourself some of the artfully designed theories in the exciting intercultural conflict communication field.

REFERENCES

Bennett, J. M. (2003). Turning frogs into interculturalists: A student-centered development approach to teaching intercultural communication. In N. Boyacigiller, R. Goodman, & M. Phillips (Eds.), *Crossing cultures: Insights from master teachers* (pp. 157–170). London: Routledge.

Bennett, J. M., & Bennett, M. J. (2004). Developing intercultural sensitivity: An integrative approach to global and domestic diversity. In D. Landis, J. Bennett, & M. Bennett (Eds.), *Handbook of intercultural training* (3rd ed., pp. 147–165). Thousand Oaks, CA: Sage.

Bennett, M. J. (1993). Toward ethnorelativism: A developmental model of intercultural sensitivity. In R. M. Paige (Ed.), *Education for the intercultural experience* (pp. 21–71). Yarmouth, ME: Intercultural Press.

Bresnahan, M., Levine, T., Shearman, S., Lee, S. Y., Park, C. Y., & Kiyomiya, T. (2005). A multimethod multitrait validity assessment of self-construals in Japan, Korea, and the United States. *Human Communication Research, 31,* 33–59.

Brown, P., & Levinson, S. (1987). *Politeness: Some universals in language usage.* Cambridge, UK: Cambridge University Press.

Burgoon, J. K. (1993). Interpersonal expectations, expectancy violations, and emotional communication. *Journal of Language and Social Psychology, 12,* 30–48.

Burgoon, J. K. (1995). Cross-cultural and intercultural applications of expectancy violations theory. In R. Wiseman (Ed.), *Intercultural communication theory* (pp. 194–214). Thousand Oaks, CA: Sage.

Burgoon, J. K., & Ebesu Hubbard, A. (2005). Cross-cultural and intercultural applications of expectancy violations and interaction adaptation theory. In W. B. Gudykunst (Ed.), *Theorizing about intercultural communication* (pp. 149–171). Thousand Oaks, CA: Sage.

Burgoon, J. K., & Walther, J. (1990). Nonverbal expectancies and the evaluative consequences of violations. *Human Communication Research, 17,* 232–265.

Buzzanell, P. (1994). Gaining a voice: Feminist organizational communication theorizing. *Management Communication Quarterly, 7,* 339–383.

Cai, D. A., & Fink, E. L. (2002). Conflict style differences between individualists and collectivists. *Communication Monographs, 69,* 67–87.

Carl, D., Gupta, V., & Javidan, M. (2004). Power distance. In R. House, P. Hanges, M. Javidan, P. Dorfman, & V. Gupta (Eds.), *Culture, leadership, and organizations: The GLOBE study of 62 societies* (pp. 513–563). Thousand Oaks, CA: Sage.

Cocroft, B., & Ting-Toomey, S. (1994). Facework in Japan and the United States. *International Journal of Intercultural Relations, 18,* 469–506.

Cousins, S. D. (1989). Culture and self-perception in Japan and the United States. *Journal of Personality and Social Psychology, 56,* 124–131.

Cross, S. E., Gore, J. S., & Morris, M. L. (2003). The relational interdependent self-construal, self-concept consistency, and well-being. *Journal of Personality and Social Psychology, 85,* 933–944.

Cupach, W. R., & Canary, D. J. (Eds.). (1997). *Competence in interpersonal conflict.* New York: McGraw-Hill.

Endo, Y. (2000). What is self-esteem? A review from an interpersonal perspective on self-esteem. *Japanese Journal of Experimental Social Psychology, 39,* 150–167.

Erez, M., & Somech, A. (1996). Is group productivity loss the rule or the exception? Effects of culture and group-based motivation. *Academy of Management Journal, 39,* 1513–1537.

Gelfand, M., Bhawuk, D., Nishi, L., & Bechtold, D. (2004). Individualism and collectivism. In R. House, P. Hanges, M. Javidan, P. Dorfman, & V. Gupta (Eds.), *Culture, leadership, and organizations: The GLOBE study of 62 societies* (pp. 438–512). Thousand Oaks, CA: Sage.

Gonclaves, M. M., & Salgado, J. (2001). Mapping the multiplicity of the self. *Culture and Psychology, 7,* 363–377.

Gudykunst, W. B. (1995). Anxiety/uncertainty management (AUM) theory: Current status. In R. Wiseman (Ed.), *Intercultural communication theory* (pp. 8–58). Thousand Oaks, CA: Sage.

Gudykunst, W. B. (Ed). (2003). *Cross-cultural and intercultural communication.* Thousand Oaks, CA: Sage.

Gudykunst, W. B. (2005a). An anxiety/uncertainty management (AUM) theory of effective communication: Making the mesh of the net finer. In W. B. Gudykunst (Ed.), *Theorizing about intercultural communication* (pp. 281–322). Thousand Oaks, CA: Sage.

Gudykunst, W. B. (Ed.). (2005b). *Theorizing about intercultural communication.* Thousand Oaks, CA: Sage.

Gudykunst, W. B., Guzley, R., & Hammer, M. (1996). Designing intercultural training. In D. Landis & R. Bhagat (Eds.), *Handbook of intercultural training* (2nd ed., pp. 61–80). Thousand Oaks, CA: Sage.

Gudykunst, W. B., Matsumoto, Y., Ting-Toomey, S., Nishida, T., Kim, K. S., & Heyman, S. (1996). The influence of cultural individualism-collectivism, self construals, and individual values on communication styles across cultures. *Human Communication Research, 22,* 510–543.

Gudykunst, W. B., & Ting-Toomey, S. (1988). *Culture and interpersonal communication.* Newbury Park, CA: Sage.

Hall, E. T. (1959). *The silent language.* New York: Doubleday.

Hall, E. T. (1976). *Beyond culture.* New York: Doubleday.

Hamaguchi, E. (1977). *Kanjinshugi no shakai nihon.* Tokyo: Toyo Keizai Shinposha.

Hamaguchi, E. (1983). *Nihon rashisa no sai hakken.* Tokyo: Nihon Keizai Shinbunsha.

Hofstede, G. (1991). *Culture and organizations: Software of the mind.* London: McGraw-Hill.

Hofstede, G. (2001). *Culture's consequences: Comparing values, behaviors, institutions, and organizations across cultures* (2nd ed.). Thousand Oaks, CA: Sage.

House, R., Hanges, P., Javidan, M., Dorfman, P., & Gupta, V. (Eds.). (2004). *Culture, leadership, and organizations: The GLOBE study of 62 societies.* Thousand Oaks, CA: Sage.

Howell, W. (1982). *The empathic communicator.* Belmont, CA: Wadsworth.

Kanagawa, C., Cross, S. E., & Markus, H. R. (2001). Who am I? The cultural psychology of the conceptual self. *Personality and Social Psychology Bulletin, 27,* 90–103.

Kim, M. S., Hunter, J., Miyahara, A., Horvath, A., Bresnahan, M., & Yoon, H. J. (1996). Individual vs. culture-level dimensions of individualism and collectivism: Effects on preferred conversational styles. *Communication Monographs, 63,* 29–49.

Kim, M. S., & Leung, T. (2000). A multicultural view of conflict management styles: Review and critical synthesis. In M. Roloff (Ed.), *Communication Yearbook 23* (pp. 227–269). Thousand Oaks, CA: Sage.

Langer, E. (1989). *Mindfulness*. Reading, MA: Addison-Wesley.

Langer, E. (1997). *The power of mindful learning*. Reading, MA: Addison-Wesley.

Lebra, T. S. (1975). *Japanese patterns of behavior*. Honolulu: University of Hawaii Press.

Levine, T., Bresnahan, M., Park, H. S., Lapinski, M., Wittenbaum, G., Shearman, S., Lee, S. Y., Chung, D., & Ohashi, R. (2003). Self-construal scales lack validity. *Human Communication Research, 29,* 210–252.

Lewis, M., & Haviland-Jones, J. (Eds.). (2000). *Handbook of emotions* (2nd ed.). New York: Guilford.

Lim, T.-S. (1994). Facework and interpersonal relationships. In S. Ting-Toomey (Ed.), *The challenge of facework* (pp. 209–229). Albany: State University of New York Press.

Markus, H. R., & Kitayama, S. (1991). Culture and self: Implication for cognition, emotion, and motivation. *Psychological Review, 98,* 224–253.

Markus, H. R., & Kitayama, S. (1998). The cultural psychology of personality. *Journal of Cross-Cultural Psychology, 29,* 63–87.

Matsumoto, D. (1999). Culture and self: An empirical assessment of Markus and Kitayama's theory of independent and interdependent self-construal. *Asian Journal of Social Psychology, 2,* 289–310.

Midooka, K. (1990). Characteristics of Japanese-style communication. *Media, Culture and Society, 12,* 477–489.

Milhouse, V., Asante, M., & Nwosu, P. (Eds.). (2001). *Transcultural realities: Interdisciplinary perspectives on cross-cultural relations*. Thousand Oaks, CA: Sage.

Oetzel, J. G. (1995). Intercultural small groups: An effective decision-making theory. In R. Wiseman (Ed.), *Intercultural communication theories* (pp. 247–270). Thousand Oaks, CA: Sage.

Oetzel, J. G. (1998a). Culturally homogeneous and heterogeneous groups: Explaining communication processes through individualism-collectivism and self-construal. *International Journal of Intercultural Relations, 22*(2), 135–161.

Oetzel, J. G. (1998b). The effects of self-construals and ethnicity on self-reported conflict styles. *Communication Reports, 11,* 133–144.

Oetzel, J. G. (1999). The influence of situational features on perceived conflict styles and self-construals in small groups. *International Journal of Intercultural Relations, 23,* 679–695.

Oetzel, J. G. (2005). Effective intercultural workgroup communication theory. In W. B. Gudykunst (Ed.), *Theorizing about intercultural communication* (pp. 351–371). Thousand Oaks, CA: Sage.

Oetzel, J. G., Myers, K., Meares, M., & Lara, E. (2004). Interpersonal conflict in organizations: Explaining conflict styles via face-negotiation theory. *Communication Research Reports, 20,* 106–115.

Oetzel, J. G., & Ting-Toomey, S. (2003). Face concerns in interpersonal conflict: A cross-cultural empirical test of the face-negotiation theory. *Communication Research, 30,* 599–624.

Oetzel, J. G., Ting-Toomey, S., Masumoto, T., Yokochi, Y., Pan, X., Takai, J., & Wilcox, R. (2001). Face behaviors in interpersonal conflicts: A cross-cultural comparison of Germany, Japan, China, and the United States. *Communication Monographs, 68,* 235–258.

Oetzel, J., Ting-Toomey, S., Yokochi, Y., Masumoto, T., & Takai, J. (2000). A typology of facework behaviors in conflicts with best friends and relative strangers. *Communication Quarterly, 48,* 397–419.

Ohbuchi, K. (1993). Interpersonal conflict of Japanese and Americans. In F. Watanabe & J. Takahashi (Eds.), *Chikiyu shakai jidai o dou toraeru ka* (pp. 18–37). Kyoto: Nakanishiya.

Okabe, R. (1988). Verbal and nonverbal messages. In G. Furuta (Ed.), *Intercultural communication: The requirements of the new international person* (pp. 81–100). Tokyo: Yuhikaku Press.

Robins, C., Schmidt, H., III, & Linehan, M. (2004). Dialectical behavior therapy: Synthesizing radical acceptance with skillful means. In S. Hayes, V. Follette, & M. Linehan (Eds.), *Mindfulness and acceptance: Expanding the cognitive-behavioral tradition* (pp. 30–44). New York: Guilford.

Rothman, J. (1997). *Resolving identity-based conflict in nations, organizations, and communities*. San Francisco: Jossey-Bass.

Sakuma, M., & Muto, T. (2003). Variability in the relational self and self-esteem: College students. *Japanese Journal of Educational Psychology, 51,* 33–42.

Schneider, D. J. (2004). *The psychology of stereotyping*. New York: Guilford.

Shweder, R., & Haidt, J. (2000). The cultural psychology of emotions: Ancient and new. In M. Lewis & J. Haviland-Jones (Eds.), *Handbook of emotions* (2nd ed., pp. 397–414). New York: Guilford.

Smith, P. B., Dugan, S., Peterson, M. F., & Leung, K. (1998). Individualism: Collectivism and the handling of disagreement: A 23 country study. *International Journal of Intercultural Relations, 22,* 351–367.

Stephan, C. W., & Stephan, W. G. (2003). Cognition and affect in cross-cultural relations. In W. B. Gudykunst (Ed.), *Cross-cultural and intercultural communication* (pp. 111–126). Thousand Oaks, CA: Sage.

Stephan, W. G. (1999). *Reducing prejudice and stereotyping in schools*. New York: Teachers College Press.

Stephan, W. G., & Stephan, C. W. (2001). *Improving intergroup relations*. Thousand Oaks, CA: Sage.

Stephan, W. G., Stephan, C. W., & Gudykunst, W. B. (1999). Anxiety in intergroup relations: A comparison of anxiety/uncertainty management theory and integrated threat theory. *International Journal of Intercultural Relations, 23,* 613–628.

Storti, C. (2001). *Old world/new world*. Yarmouth, ME: Intercultural Press.

Suh, E. M. (2002). Culture, identity consistency, and subjective well-being. *Journal of Personality and Social Psychology, 83,* 1378–1391.

Takano, Y., & Osaka, E. (1999). An unsupported common view: Comparing Japan and U.S. on individualism/collectivism. *Asian Journal of Social Psychology, 2,* 331–341.

Thich, N. H. (1991). *Peace is every step: The path of mindfulness in everyday life*. New York: Bantam Books.

Ting-Toomey, S. (1985). Toward a theory of conflict and culture. In W. Gudykunst, L. Stewart, & S. Ting-Toomey (Eds.), *Communication, culture, and organizational processes* (pp. 71–86). Beverly Hills, CA: Sage.

Ting-Toomey, S. (1988). Intercultural conflicts: A face-negotiation theory. In Y. Y. Kim & W. Gudykunst (Eds.), *Theories in intercultural communication* (pp. 213–235). Newbury Park, CA: Sage.

Ting-Toomey, S. (1993). Communicative resourcefulness: An identity negotiation perspective. In R. Wiseman & J. Koester (Eds.), *Intercultural communication competence* (pp. 72–111). Newbury Park, CA: Sage.

Ting-Toomey, S. (Ed.). (1994). *The challenge of facework: Cross-cultural and interpersonal issues*. New York: State University of New York Press.

Ting-Toomey, S. (1997). Intercultural conflict competence. In W. Cupach & D. Canary (Eds.), *Competence in interpersonal conflict* (pp. 120–147). New York: McGraw-Hill.

Ting-Toomey, S. (1999). *Communicating across cultures*. New York: Guilford.

Ting-Toomey, S. (2004). Translating conflict face-negotiation theory into practice. In D. Landis, J. Bennett, & M. Bennett (Eds.), *Handbook of intercultural training* (3rd ed., pp. 217–248). Thousand Oaks, CA: Sage.

Ting-Toomey, S. (2005). The matrix of face: An updated face-negotiation theory. In W. B. Gudykunst (Ed.), *Theorizing about intercultural communication* (pp. 71–92). Thousand Oaks, CA: Sage.

Ting-Toomey, S., & Chung, L. C. (2005). *Understanding intercultural communication*. Los Angeles, CA: Roxbury.

Ting-Toomey, S., Gao, G., Trubisky, P., Yang, Z., Kim, H. S., Lin, S. L., & Nishida, T. (1991). Culture, face maintenance, and styles of handling interpersonal conflict: A study in five cultures. *International Journal of Conflict Management, 2,* 275–296.

Ting-Toomey, S., & Kurogi, A. (1998). Facework competence in intercultural conflict: An updated face-negotiation theory. *International Journal of Intercultural Relations, 22,* 187–225.

Ting-Toomey, S., & Oetzel, J. G. (2001). *Managing intercultural conflict effectively*. Thousand Oaks, CA: Sage.

Ting-Toomey, S., & Oetzel, J. G. (2002). Cross-cultural face concerns and conflict styles: Current status and future directions. In W. Gudykunst & B. Mody (Eds.), *Handbook of international & intercultural communication* (2nd ed., pp. 143–163). Thousand Oaks, CA: Sage.

Ting-Toomey, S., Oetzel, J. G., & Yee-Jung, K. (2001). Self-construal types and conflict management styles. *Communication Reports, 14,* 87–104.

Ting-Toomey, S., Yee-Jung, K., Shapiro, R., Garcia, W., Wright, T., & Oetzel, J. G. (2000). Ethnic/cultural identity salience and conflict styles in four U.S. ethnic groups. *International Journal of Intercultural Relations, 24,* 47–81.

Triandis, H. C. (1995). *Individualism and collectivism.* Boulder, CO: Westview.

Triandis, H. C. (2002). Individualism and collectivism. In M. Gannon & K. Newman (Eds.), *Handbook of cross-cultural management* (pp. 16–45). New York: Lawrence Erlbaum.

Trubisky, P., Ting-Toomey, S., & Lin, S.-L. (1991). The influence of individualism-collectivism and self-monitoring on conflict styles. *International Journal of Intercultural Relations, 15,* 65–84.

Wiemann, J., Takai, J., Ota, H., & Wiemann, M. (1997). A relational model of communication competence. In B. Kovacics (Ed.), *Emerging theories of human communication* (pp. 25–44). Albany: State University of New York Press.

Wilmot, W., & Hocker, J. (1998). *Interpersonal conflict* (5th ed.). Boston: McGraw-Hill.

Yoneyama, T. (1983). *Nihonjin no nakama ishiki.* Tokyo: Kodansha.

CONCLUSION

26

CONFLICT COMMUNICATION IN CONTEXTS

A Social Ecological Perspective

JOHN G. OETZEL
University of New Mexico

STELLA TING-TOOMEY
California State University at Fullerton

SUSANA RINDERLE
University of New Mexico

Conflict communication affects, and is affected by, many factors at multiple levels or contexts. We organized this handbook in four specific contexts: interpersonal, organizational, community, and intercultural/international. The four contexts represent the predominant fields in which scholars and practitioners research and apply conflict communication theories and principles. The authors of this handbook have done an outstanding job of reviewing and synthesizing relevant theories and research on their topics within their contexts. These chapters represent the state of the art on each of these topics and should be very inspiring and relevant for future conflict communication research and practice.

Several themes emerge when reviewing the chapters of this volume: The important role of context in understanding conflict communication, the possibilities of integrative systems approaches, the blurring of essentialized categories, and the presence of change and movement on both macro and micro levels of conflict analysis. Convergence among many divergent perspectives, contexts, and topics suggests bountiful theorizing and applied opportunities for scholars and practitioners of conflict communication. While some authors do use contextual or situational features to frame their development of various conflict topics, the majority of the chapters do not necessarily cross domain boundaries (e.g., incorporating research studies from different disciplinary domains or applying conflict principles from contexts different from their particular analytical lens) or integrate other settings into their particular context (e.g., connecting community setting with interpersonal conflict context or vice versa). The objective of this chapter is to provide some connective fibers to hook the different levels or contexts of conflict communication together in a systematic fashion that we believe is beneficial for future theorizing, researching, and practicing of conflict communication.

Synthesizing such a diverse body of scholarship and practice can be a daunting task. Any attempt will, by necessity, focus on a slice of the "big picture." Our modest goal here is to provide an overarching framework that examines the intersections between and among different conflict topics and contexts—as promising avenues for future theorizing and practice. Specifically, we recommend a social ecological theoretical framework that examines conflict communication within and across contexts (we interchange the words *contexts* and *levels* within this chapter). We begin this chapter by first defining social ecological theory and what we mean by multiple levels or contexts. Second, we discuss the different types of relationships present in a social ecological model, using some of the chapters in this handbook to illustrate these interconnected relationships. Finally, we identify future research directions to advance multilevel theorizing and practical applications of conflict communication.

MULTILEVEL THEORIZING

While they are relatively new to the communication field, multilevel approaches such as meso-analysis and social ecological frameworks have been discussed in other fields, such as family systems (Bronfenbrenner, 1979, 1989), organizational behavior (e.g., Klein, Tosi, & Cannella, 1999; Rousseau & House, 1994), and public health (e.g., Little & Kaufman Kantor, 2002; McLeroy, Bibeau, Steckler, & Glanz, 1988; Oetzel & Duran, 2004; Stokols, 1996). In this section, we describe the benefits and challenges of multilevel theorizing and then describe their specific levels.

Benefits and Challenges of Multilevel Theorizing

There are a number of benefits of multilevel theorizing. Any research or practice that focuses on any single level will, by definition, underestimate the effects of other contexts (Klein et al., 1999; Rousseau & House, 1994; Stokols, 1996). The tendency in the conflict communication field in general is to focus the analysis on either micro (e.g., individual behavior) or macro (e.g., social structures and media) processes. In contrast, multilevel theorizing focuses on understanding concepts at multiple levels as well as between different levels. In this manner, multilevel models create a rich, layered picture of the phenomenon under study. Multilevel theorizing fosters synthesis and synergy, creates links and loops where there were none before, and also illuminates reciprocal contextual influences (Klein et al., 1999).

These benefits are illustrated in specific research contexts. For example, Rousseau and House (1994) suggested that a multilevel paradigm advances the field of organizational behavior because it is more realistic, expands units of study, and emphasizes "the distinctive nature of behavioral processes *in and of organizations*" (p. 16; emphasis in original). They stressed the importance of setting, and the interdependence of individual, group, and organizational levels that challenge the "self-contained" views of these various contexts that the micro-macro framework perpetuates. Similarly, McLeroy et al. (1988) identified four key benefits of adopting an ecological perspective within public health promotion: (a) recognizing the importance of environmental supports in delivering health services to individuals, (b) identifying how environment supports or inhibits behavior change in individuals, (c) noting the benefits and importance of evaluating health promotion efforts at multiple levels, and (d) removing some of the burden on individuals in claiming sole responsibility for their health.

In the same vein, conflict communication research and practice can benefit from multilevel perspectives. Multilevel perspectives provide the opportunity to understand (and possibly challenge) what are held as generally believed and practiced principles of conflict management. Multilevel research may illustrate that conflict management practice has consistencies and inconsistency when context is considered. In addition, multilevel perspectives help to illustrate the multitude of factors that shape individuals' conflict communication, as well as how individual conflict behaviors socially construct organizational, community, and cultural systems.

However, multilevel frameworks do pose simultaneous challenges and burdens centering on research concerns and practical applications. For example, when conducting multilevel conflict research, scholars need to be concerned with several factors: (a) the overwhelming amount of potentially relevant conflict concepts and variables, (b) the difficulty of determining the scope of multilevel theory that is not overly simple or overly complex, and (c) the difficulty of multilevel data collection and analysis (Klein et al., 1999; Stokols, 1996). In addition, multilevel research may be limited due to scholars' interests, values, academic training (Klein et al., 1999), and valuable journal space and page limitations for publication.

In terms of practical applications, Stokols (1996) cautioned that a social ecological perspective can require a great deal of close coordination and collaborative energy from multiple people, teams, and sectors, as well as integration of diverse knowledge and expertise. In addition, a social ecological approach may present an ethical dilemma in the form of subtle coercion. While such models may reduce incidences of "blaming the victim," they may simultaneously create more stressors or malcontents for individuals to cope with given the multitude of complex multiple systems and institutions that individual change is linked to (Stokols, 1999). Thus, multilevel frameworks have complexities that single-level approaches do not have. However, this complexity represents social reality and potentially provides rich theoretical and practical insight (Klein et al., 1999) into the layers of human cognition, affect, and behavior.

Levels in Multilevel Frameworks

There are many approaches to examine the specific levels in multilevel frameworks. We review three here. In the context of organizational behavior, Rousseau and House (1994) suggested "meso organizational" research as a third paradigm that challenges the traditional dichotomy of micro and macro perspectives. Using the term *meso* to imply "in between," they refer to "an integration of micro and macro theory in the study of processes specific to organizations which by their very nature are a synthesis of psychological and socioeconomic processes" (p. 14). Reminiscent of the Daoist philosophy of dialectical balance through the yin-yang complementary approach, a meso framework involves *simultaneous,* not separate, examination of processes at two or more levels. A meso approach considers the following four key issues: (a) the effects of context on individual behaviors, (b) the construction of context by individuals and social dynamics, (c) parallels *and* discontinuities in processes across contexts, and (d) expansion of units of study beyond concrete entities (that may have been falsely reified) to include more abstract processes (Klein et al., 1999; Rousseau & House, 1994).

In public health, different social ecological approaches are frequently used to understand and promote healthy behaviors. Scholars argue that most public health issues are too complex to be adequately addressed using single (usually micro) levels of analysis (Stokols, 1996); hence the rise of social ecological models. Social ecology refers to the study of relationships between organisms and their environment (Hawley, 1950). Social ecology is an interdisciplinary approach that gained momentum in the mid-1960s and early 1970s to better address the influences of social and cultural contexts on human behavior, as opposed to primarily biological and geographical influences (Bronfenbrenner, 1977, 1979; McLeroy et al., 1988; Stokols, 1996). In family communication, for example, Ihinger-Tallman and Cooney (2005) used the social ecological framework to discuss the family system as an institution and as small groups and how the study of family should be understood within the nested historical, social class, and racial contexts.

More specifically, Stokols (1996) described the social ecological perspective as rooted in five core principles. First, health outcomes are influenced by the cumulative effect of multiple physical, social, and cultural factors. Second, health outcomes are also affected by individual attributes and specific situations. Third, social ecology incorporates concepts from systems theory such as interdependence and homeostasis to understand the relationship between individuals and their broader contexts. Fourth, social ecology recognizes not only the interconnections among multiple settings, but also the interdependence of conditions within particular settings. Fifth, the social ecological perspective is interdisciplinary, involves multilevel domain analysis, and incorporates diverse methodologies. Many public health scholars utilize five distinct levels: (a) intrapersonal factors (individual psychological features and developmental history), (b) interpersonal processes and primary groups (formal and informal social networks), (c) institutional and organizational factors, (d) community factors (relationships among groups and organizations within a system; often defined in a physical space), and (e) public policy (laws regarding health behaviors).

In this volume and this chapter, we utilized four specific contexts (interpersonal, organizational, community, and intercultural/international) to discuss conflict communication. This approach most closely follows a third social ecological framework that Bronfenbrenner (1977, 1979) advanced, which divides environmental influences into four system levels: micro (face-to-face interactions in specific settings—interpersonal conflict), meso (interrelationships among various microsystems—organizational conflict), exo (forces within the larger social system—community conflict), and macro (cultural beliefs and values—intercultural/international conflict). A key feature of Bronfenbrenner's model is that these systems affect the individual, but also that these subsystems change due to changes in their constituent members. In referring to Bronfenbrenner's model, McLeroy et al. (1988) noted, "an ecological perspective implies reciprocal causation between the individual and the environment" (p. 354). They also asserted that while ecological models are systems models, they differ by viewing *patterned behaviors* (such as conflict communication) across time and life cycles, not merely system functioning or production, as the predominant outcomes of interest.

RELATIONSHIPS BETWEEN AND AMONG LEVELS IN CONFLICT COMMUNICATION

In examining the reciprocal causation between the individual and the environment (e.g., intergroup conflict in a community setting), we focus on two specific types of relationships between and among levels of analysis: (a) parallels (or isomorphisms) and discontinuities, and (b) cross-level effects (Klein et al., 1999; Rousseau & House, 1994). Figure 26.1 illustrates these relationships graphically. Specifically, the unidirectional arrows illustrate cross-level effects (e.g., bottom-up and top-down) while the circular arrows demonstrate parallel relationships (the absence of isomorphic relationships could be represented by the lack of parallel arrows). In the following sections, we describe these types of relationships and then provide illustrations of these relationships in conflict communication from the extant literature, especially the conflict chapters in this volume.

Parallels and Discontinuities

Isomorphic models posit that the relationship between and among variables at one level (e.g., interethnic team conflict) will be the same, or parallel, at another level (e.g., community-level conflict; Klein et al., 1999; Rousseau & House, 1994). In contrast, when different types of relationships are found among concepts or variables at different levels, these are described as discontinuities. Initial attempts to move from a single-level theory to a multilevel theory often involve simply adding a simplistic proposition at an additional level because isomorphic relationships are assumed. For example, Oetzel's (1995) theory of intercultural workgroups stated that the more collectivism in individuals, the more likely they would manage conflict with cooperative conflict strategies. He stated that, at a group level, the more individuals in a group who have collectivistic backgrounds, the more likely the group will manage conflict with cooperative strategies (Oetzel, 1998). Such simplistic propositions do little to help understand conflict communication at multiple levels, however, because they over-generalize from one level to another (Rousseau & House, 1994). In fact, Oetzel, Torres, and Sanchez (2004) recently found that certain types of group compositions (e.g., homogeneous or heterogeneous) have different effects on individuals' communication processes (specifics discussed under "Interactive Effects").

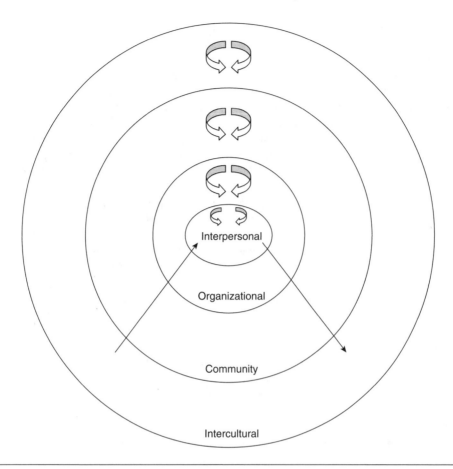

Figure 26.1   Social Ecological Model of Conflict Contexts

One isomorphic relationship that is often directly or indirectly stated in conflict communication research is that collaborative tactics (e.g., problem solving, dialogue, and cooperative conflict behaviors) have positive outcomes (e.g., satisfaction, peace, and relationship/community building). A quick review of the chapters in this volume demonstrates this assumption (although no single chapter directly states this relationship); for example, in interpersonal conflict, integrative problem solving is associated with more satisfactory marital and family relationships (Canary & Lakey, Chapter 7; Caughlin & Vangelisti, Chapter 5; Koerner & Fitzpatrick, Chapter 6); in organizational conflict, cooperation is associated with positive outcomes such as job satisfaction and lower incidents of violence in schools (Poole & Garner, Chapter 10; Jones, Chapter 9); in community conflicts, dialogue is heralded as a key consensus and

community building tool (Barge, Chapter 19; Littlejohn, Chapter 14); in intercultural conflicts, collaborative problem solving is critical to improved relationships among culturally diverse people (Coleman & Raider, Chapter 24; Ting-Toomey & Takai, Chapter 25). At first glance, this appears to be an isomorphic relationship. However, this assumption has not been directly tested. In fact, consensus building may have some negative impacts. Peterson and Franks in their environmental conflict chapter in this handbook (Chapter 15) note arguments about potential weaknesses of consensus building for environmental policy. Specifically, they identify scholars who believe that at times consensus building leads to conflict avoidance and inferior environmental policy (Gregory, McDaniels, & Fields, 2001; Poncelet, 2001). Whether isomorphic relationships exist at these multiple levels may be contingent on the type of outcome sought (e.g., relationship vs. substantive, satisfaction vs. compliance), but these need to be examined directly to improve theorizing about conflict communication.

When examining whether relationships among variables are characterized by parallels or discontinuities, conflict researchers and practitioners should consider two questions. First, do similar concepts mean the same thing at multiple levels? Patterns among variables are not parallel if concepts do not mean the same thing at each level. For example, conflict practitioners often advocate the use of dialogue as a productive, creative, and relationship-building tool to manage conflict. However, is dialogue when addressing moral conflict the same as dialogue between relational partners? Certainly there are shared characteristics (e.g., active listening and reframing), but surely there are key differences as well (e.g., active listening for developing understanding vs. intimacy, reframing for agenda-setting vs. relational empathy). Similarly, conflict competence is generally considered to be a positive characteristic at all levels. However, what it means to be competent likely involves a different set of behaviors and a different set of attunements at different levels (see Canary and Lakey's chapter on conflict competence and Guerrerro and La Valley's chapter on conflict emotions). For example, individuals who are competent at managing family conflicts may not be competent at intervening in racial conflicts. The former involves conflict behaviors such as holistic listening and constructive anger management tools, while the latter likely involves these characteristics, but also cultural sensitivity, ethnorelative perspective-taking, sharing power, a sense of social justice, and a sense of socio-historical relations (this is meant as an illustrative example and not as a full description of competence in these situations).

Second, is the nature of the relationships among variables and people consistent across levels? In an isomorphic relationship, the nature of the relationship at the community level, for example, should be consistent with the relationship at the interpersonal level. Donohue discusses different types of mediation at different levels (peer, divorce, environmental). Each of these contexts requires general mediation skills, but certainly there are unique qualities and factors

(enough differences to require specialized mediation training for each). Warfield discusses a number of cases where organizations intervened to address racial and/or ethnic hatred conflicts in several communities. His research and practice identified several key principles to help communities address these conflicts. However, did relationships between neighbors improve in the same way and to the same degree as they did at the community level? Similarly, Gilboa notes that when a peace accord is signed between geopolitical entities, interpersonal relationships among individuals from these communities do not necessarily improve. At a more micro level, Koerner and Fitzpatrick report that family conflict may have different impacts on parents than on children.

Multilevel theorizing can help provide a more multilayered understanding of how conflict affects relationships and outcomes (and vice versa) at multiple levels. Therefore, future research needs to consider carefully the meaning of concepts and the nature of relationships among people at different levels or contexts. These factors can help identify whether conflict patterns are isomorphic or discontinuous. Further, conflict theorists and practitioners can help build on each other's analytical lens in deepening their conceptualizations of the reciprocal causes and outcomes of conflict. In a general sense, the chapters in this handbook help to illustrate comprehensive research or application coverage on particular topics within each of these levels and demonstrate some of the parallels and discontinuities in the relationships among concepts in other levels in an implicit or explicit manner. We now turn to a specific discussion of the three types of cross-level effects: top-down effects, bottom-up effects, and interactive effects.

Cross-Level Effects

Single-level research often overestimates the importance of local effects and underestimates cross-level effects (Rousseau & House, 1994). For example, investigating interpersonal conflict will emphasize individual and relationship communication patterns, while lessening (and in some cases ignoring) the focus on societal and cultural factors. Studying conflict communication at any single level belies the fact that individuals, organizations, communities, and cultures are interconnected. Multilevel theorizing is influenced by general systems theory principles of interdependence and hierarchy (Rousseau & House, 1994). General systems theory emphasizes that levels are nested structures organized hierarchically. Given this assumption, three types of cross-level effects should be considered: (a) top-down effects, (b) bottom-up effects, and (c) interactive effects. Each is considered in turn and relevant chapters are noted.

Top-down effects. Research on social ecological models tends to emphasize top-down environmental effects (McLeroy et al., 1988; Stokols, 1996). In this context, individual behavior is shaped by the structures in which people are nested. A review of the chapters in this volume reveals that multiple authors in each of the four contexts emphasize some sort of top-down relationship. In the interpersonal context, Guerrero and La Valley explain that the conflict communication in an interpersonal relationship affects the emotions individuals express. In addition, Caughlin and Vangelisti explicitly hypothesize that various environmental features (e.g., temporal, social, etc.) affect interpersonal conflict communication. In the organizational context, Kirby, Wieland, and McBride report that work problems are often taken home and affect micro-level family relationships. Coming from a cultural/institutional level, Lipsky and Seeber note that the legal context in the United States encouraged the creation of dispute resolution systems in many organizations. In the community context, Peterson and Franks demonstrate that the societal/cultural context (i.e., legal components) contributed to the creation of public hearings for environmental conflict. Rogan and Hammer illustrate how community and organizational contexts frame individuals' management of crisis situations. In the intercultural context, Orbe and Everett discuss how ethnicity and historical relationships among ethnic groups shape individual conflict management approaches. Coleman and Raider (and Ting-Toomey & Takai) address how culture and institutional power imbalance issues influence intercultural conflict training and learning. Thus, there is no shortage of researchers and practitioners addressing top-down effects.

Bottom-up effects. Bottom-up effects focus on how lower levels (e.g., individuals and interpersonal relationships) affect higher levels (e.g., community and culture). These types of effects are not as prevalent in the literature as are top-down, but they are no less important. In this volume, several authors focus on these directly, while others consider them indirectly. In the interpersonal context, Guerrero and La Valley identify the causes of emotion (i.e., anger, hurt, jealousy, and guilt) in conflict interactions and how emotional distress signals occur because of external precipitating events and internal psychological and physiological upheavals. In their interpersonal conflict and cognition chapter, Roloff and Waite Miller describe how social knowledge and cognitive processes affect the way that individuals behave in interpersonal conflicts. Additionally, Koerner and Fitzpatrick discuss how adolescent conflict behaviors influence family conflict patterns and systems. In the organizational context, Jones illustrates that one goal of peer mediation is to reduce the overall prevalence of conflict and violence in schools. The research illustrates that teaching individual students conflict resolution skills results in a school climate that does not tolerate violence and destructive conflict. Poole and Garner note that individual conflict behaviors are constitutive of group climate and impact the group's effectiveness. Nicotera and Dorsey discuss the importance of conflict management training for its impact on individual relationships and organizational outcomes. At the community level, Rogan and Hammer use a social constructivist lens in connecting face-sensitive skills to hostage negotiation processes. Both Littlejohn and Barge imply that the use of dialogue by individuals will help community building efforts. Similarly, Warfield discusses the importance of individual efforts for addressing racial conflicts in the community. In the intercultural context, Broome and Jakobsson Hatay describe how the work of peacebuilders at a local level can influence larger peacebuilding efforts. In addition, Gilboa reviews research about peace journalism and how media coverage can influence policy makers.

Interactive effects. Interactive effects involve mutual and simultaneous effects at more than one level (Rousseau & House, 1994). In some cases, the effects of one level (e.g., culture) moderate the outcomes at another level (e.g., interpersonal). Interactive effects differ from top-down (or bottom-up) in that the former assumes simultaneous process effects or outcome effects at multiple levels while the latter assumes some sort of summative or cumulative effect passing down (or up) from one level to the next. We present several examples of interactive effects in the discussion that follows.

Culture often changes the nature of interpersonal and organizational behaviors. In culturally diverse workgroups, the type of composition (heterogeneous or homogeneous) affects the nature of conflict behaviors and group outcomes. For example, Oetzel et al. (2004) found that groups diverse in terms of sex were more likely to have negative group processes (including conflict processes) and outcomes than homogeneous groups. This study corroborated other research demonstrating that men (especially in male-dominated organizations) had a greater propensity to leave when they were in diverse groups than men in homogeneous groups (or women in diverse groups; Williams & O'Reilly, 1998). Culture also shapes interpersonal behavior, which impacts conflict practitioners. For example, Barge discusses expectations of mediation behavior between people of different cultures. Certain cultural group members expect mediation to be directive and performed by a respected elder, whereas other cultural group members expect mediation to be nondirective and performed by a neutral third party who does not determine the outcome. Thus, researchers who are interested in investigating the reciprocal relationship between cultural group and third-party help intervention need to check the "goodness of fit" or interaction effect between the cultural group traits, third-party help conflict expectations, and process versus outcome-based orientations. Likewise, conflict practitioners need to frame their language usage or intervention tools carefully when addressing the reciprocal concerns of the entry, process, and outcome cycles of a situational-based conflict case study and the conflict clients in the audience.

Furthermore, time is also a critical factor in the social ecological lens and can influence simultaneous effects at multiple levels. Gilboa

discusses four phases of international conflict: prevention, management, resolution, and reconciliation. While he notes the media have a role at each phase, individual behavior is much more important in the reconciliation phase than the other three phases. Thus, the development of the conflict over time changes the emphasis on necessary conflict behavior at different levels. Caughlin and Vangelisti also directly integrate time as a contextual feature for individual behavior. For example, they mention how a molar temporal perspective illustrates the impact of historical changes on marital conflict (e.g., the variation of privacy of intimate conflict in modern times compared to historical eras).

While theorizing about top-down and bottom-up effects is still in its nascency, theorizing about interactive effects is practically nonexistent. One reason is lack of empirical research identifying multilevel effects. In addition, the focus on a single level limits examining other levels as relevant. Future research efforts are needed for all three types of cross-level effects, as well as isomorphic effects. The next section considers possible future research directions and applications for conflict researchers and practitioners.

FUTURE DIRECTIONS: THEORIZING, RESEARCHING, AND PRACTICE

Using the social ecological lens, we identify some specific directions for future research and applied directions in each conflict context (in keeping with the design of this handbook) and in their overlapping ecological contexts. We organize this section from the top-down perspective.

Intercultural/International Conflict Context

Oetzel et al.'s chapter identified macro-level factors such as spiritual and political factors in shaping conflict attitudes and meanings in four collectivistic cultural groups (i.e., Muslim, Chinese, Colombian, and South African membership groups). While they have underscored the common themes of harmony and face as prevalent in all four groups, they also emphasize an emic view of how harmony and face are viewed within each distinctive sociocultural and sociopolitical environment. For example, in Colombia, conflict and violence occur with such frequency that individuals often compete to ensure that their needs (and their immediate family's needs) are taken care of despite their collectivistic communal tendency. In comparison, in South Africa conflict and apartheid have caused so many scars and wounds that individuals in that contemporary society seek reconciliations, redemptions, forgiveness, and harmonious resolutions to conflict. On the other hand, in the Muslim-Arab world, with the influence of the religious root of Islam, the restoration of justice and honor is of primary concern to facework negotiation process. Thus, the interpretation of justice or honor in the Muslim-Arab world is closely linked to restoring face imbalance or face shame issues. In comparison, however, in the Chinese culture, facework is often used as a proactive lubricant to build further trusting relationships or to circumvent anticipated face loss or face embarrassment.

As another illustrative example, Ting-Toomey and Oetzel (2001) proposed a culture-based situational model of conflict communication. With the culture-based situational conflict lens, they examined some of the cultural, personal, and situational factors that shape face-to-face intercultural conflict. Four clusters of factors in the situational model include: (a) primary orientation factors: cultural value patterns, personal attributes, conflict norms, and face concerns; (b) situational and relationship boundary features: ingroup/outgroup boundaries, relationship parameters, conflict goal assessments, and conflict intensity; (c) conflict communication process factors: conflict styles, facework strategies, emotional expressions, and conflict rhythms; and (d) conflict competence dimensions, criteria, and outcomes. Situational and relationship features are viewed as the mediating factors that link primary orientation factors and conflict communication process factors.

These are just two examples of theorizing that explains why and how top-down effects exist. Specific theorizing is indeed needed given particular conflict contexts, conflict topics, and conflict processes. However, future researchers and practitioners can also benefit from contemplating the ripple effect of a top-down approach.

Some future research and application directions can include the following questions: Who or which group sets the agenda for this particular set of values and norms as the predominant cultural values in this culture? Who or which group promotes or devalues this particular conflict practice? Who or which group endorses or resists this practice and with what reasons? Who is benefiting? Who is suffering—voluntarily or involuntarily?

On the exo-level (i.e., the community level) and the meso-level (i.e., the organization level), we can raise the following issues: How do the macro-level conflict worldviews (or peacebuilding worldviews), beliefs, and values trickle down to the community and the social agency level? What are the agencies' strategies for dealing with some of the top-down conflict issues and ethical dilemmas? What role do the media play in reinforcing existing social stereotypic images? How do individuals form alliances and build coalitions to counteract some of the top-down initiatives?

Community Conflict Context

To illustrate bottom-up effects, Barge's chapter on democracy-building and community conflict emphasizes the importance of dialogue as a form of communication that allows community members to work through conflicts and foster democratic practice. He summarizes the relationships among dialogue, conflict, and democratic practice within community settings and highlights three important movements that take these sets of interrelationships seriously: (a) community mediation, (b) public participation and dialogue, and (c) appreciative inquiry. The tensions of inclusion-exclusion, deliberative-relational, and macro-micro practices represent dilemmas in dialogical democratic practice that merit future theorizing and research. Thus, understanding how a small group of individuals uses dialogue to construct a peaceful climate (e.g., Barge; Broome & Jakobsson Hatay; Littlejohn) may provide insights into how to make peace work at a higher level (assuming there are isomorphic relationships).

Some future research questions to ponder from the exo-level can include: What are the conditions that make a small group or a critical mass of individuals ripe to promote constructive conflict changes at the macro level? How do community dialogues work to reflect fairly the competing interests of different stakeholders on the conflict issues on different levels? Should issues of justice and fairness be equally applied to all groups even when the playing field is uneven or tilted? What happens to groups that are "underprivileged" in the art of "verbal-based" dialogue? What are the ethical dilemmas we need to address when conflict transformation means diluting the traditional practices of indigenous cultures?

Community conflict practitioners may want to consider the following questions in their training or mediation practices: Where do they acquire their assumptions, worldviews, ideologies, or values in their conflict training or practice? Are the conflict facilitation concepts or tools they use culturally sensitive and culturally inclusive? Can they recognize the different transformative moments via the different clashing voices that are being expressed? Are they skilled enough to pay attention to both content and process issues that are being conveyed concerning the macro-, exo-, meso-, and micro-level conflict expectations? Should they pair with skilled insider facilitators to draw out the voices, metaphors, and silences that are being communicated in the community conversation forums? How might they work effectively with different stakeholders from within and beyond the communities to generate the best options that recognize the overlapping interdependent boundaries of conflict and reconciliation from a social ecological model?

Practitioners are encouraged to articulate their sensibility for both dialogue and silence as viable means to address conflict tensions in specific community situations and to ensure culture-sensitive coherence within their practice. Furthermore, another fruitful area to look at is how individuals utilize active resistance as a powerful strategy for creating new structures and forms in organizations and communities (e.g., Trethewey, 1997). Finally, future theorizing in this area likely should also emphasize coordination or synergistic efforts of individuals in the process of community building. Understanding how, at one level, a small group of individuals uses dialogue to construct a peaceful climate

(e.g., Barge; Broome & Jakobsson Hatay; Littlejohn) may provide insight into how to make peace work at a higher level (assuming there are isomorphic relationships).

Organizational Conflict Context

In the organizational context, Kirby, Wieland, and McBride report that work problems are often taken home and affect micro-level family relationships. The authors employ structuration theory as a conceptual framework for explaining how individuals construct (and reproduce) organizational policies. They review and synthesize interdisciplinary research on work/life conflict issues on four levels of analysis. At the intrapersonal micro-level, they describe in detail the antecedents and consequences of work/life conflict. At the interpersonal micro-level, they explore supervisory and coworker relationships as well as the intersecting relationships between family and personal relationships. At the meso-level of analysis, they analyze work/life policies, review their effects, and highlight the importance of organizational support in balancing work/life conflict tensions. Lastly, at the macro-societal level, they explain how historical/cultural and political/economic systems shape work/life internal and external struggles.

Thus, Kirby et al. use bottom-up effects in linking the hoops and loops from the ground-up level of intrapersonal conflict perspective to the "big picture" macro-level of cultural worldviews and resource distributions. Their structuration theory and bottom-up effects review may be fruitful in other conflict communication research contexts as well. Similar to top-down effects, explaining bottom-up effects also needs to move from descriptive to theoretical efforts. In general, bottom-up effects assume that individuals constitute groups, organizations, communities, and cultures.

On another level, the study of networks of conflict practitioners and organizations may provide insight as to how a well-coordinated effort holds the possibility for increasing productive synergy, stability-change balance, and constructive conflict changes at higher levels. The culture of a community or organization consists of norms, expectations, recurrent micro-events, and behaviors that reflect its core traditions and values. Thus, deep-level change in any organization that rocks its fundamental routines, habits, and interaction patterns is difficult to implement. In designing organizational conflict management system, Lipsky and Seeber's recommendations on the intentional design of multiple access points or portals for employees to voice their grievances, multiple options or paths (e.g., interest-based vs. rights-based options) to facilitate the conflict resolution processes and outcomes, and developing support structures (e.g., conflict skills' training for all social service agencies at different levels) and resources at each level of the organization can be very useful. Furthermore, the authors also mention coaching, mediation, problem solving, and collaborative negotiation skills as part of an important conflict competence training program.

Future researchers and practitioners can consider a variety of questions at the meso-level. These include top-down and bottom-up questions. For the top-down, they might consider: How do conflict training programs benefit the individuals in organizations? Are these benefits for the individuals or the organization? What historical and political issues affect the ways the organizations manage conflict? How can practitioners utilize cultural perspectives to teach without essentializing? What adaptations will conflict education programs in schools need to consider in multicultural communities? From the bottom-up, they might consider: How does organizational conflict management affect individuals in communities? Given the power of corporations, do the perspectives of organizations outweigh local entities? How do global corporations change the cultures in which they do business?

Interpersonal Conflict Context

As Caughlin and Vangelisti mention in their chapter, conflict in romantic relationships often has spillover effects for individuals beyond the interpersonal system. Marital conflict, for example, is an even more important predictor of negative outcomes for children than is parental divorce. In developing their chapter, they use part of Huston's (2000) social ecological model to analyze intimate conflicts. Following Huston, they focus on three interconnected levels of analysis: (a) the behavioral system of the relationship, which is composed partly of relational conflict behaviors and conflict patterns; (b) the individuals, including the enduring characteristics that individuals bring to their relationship and the attitudes and beliefs they develop during the relationship; and (c) the environment, which ranges from broad societal influences to a couple's specific social and physical context. One important aspect of this perspective is that it highlights the dynamic nature of the individuals, their interdependent conflict patterns, and their evolving interpersonal relationship.

Although Caughlin and Vangelisti use a bottom-up effects approach in organizing their chapter review, their concluding summary advocates a more top-down approach to hook macro-level cultural traditions and worldviews to micro-level interpersonal conflict encounters and behavioral patterns. In addition, the authors also directly integrate time as a contextual feature for individual behavior. For example, they mention how a molar temporal perspective illustrates the impact of historical changes on marital conflict (e.g., the variation of privacy of intimate conflict in modern times compared to historical eras). In fact, all three levels of social ecological analysis can be examined over different temporal periods. In the environment, one could take a molar temporal perspective and consider the impact of historical changes on marital conflict (one could also examine a shorter time frame). On the macro-level, for example, when a culture celebrates a holiday that often involves family gatherings (e.g., Thanksgiving in the U.S.), relational conflict may be affected (e.g., by highlighting an existing conflict pertaining to in-laws). Caughlin and Vangelisti explicitly hypothesize that various environmental features (e.g., temporal, cultural, social, etc.) affect interpersonal conflict communication.

Some relevant interaction-level effects research questions—in connecting macro-level, with meso- and micro-level effects—can be posed as follows: How do cultural changes (e.g., in the environmental/technological level) on the macro-level promote instantaneous interpersonal relationship formation or "sudden death" relationship termination? How do face-to-face interpersonal conflict relationship development cycles differ from online relationship development cycles? What impact does technology (e.g., PDAs, e-mail, cell phones) serve in exacerbating or alleviating interpersonal conflicts? Can we cross-compare the interaction effects between conflict style written messages (e.g., via e-mails or text messages) versus actual face-to-face conflict style patterns? To what extent are online mediations more effective or less effective in comparison to face-to-face mediation sessions? How do workplace stressors affect intimate relationship conflicts and vice versa? How do community disputes arouse family and relational conflicts? How are interracial-intimate conflicts and blended family conflicts being portrayed in the media and major television programs? How do interracial couples, gay and lesbian couples, or any individuals with visible to invisible membership identities go about demanding positive changes and representations in the media as versus the stereotypic images being reinforced one more time?

CONCLUSION

We believe future theorizing and researching effort should continue in order to understand the social ecological interaction-level effects, such as how to better analyze the reciprocal causations and influences between macro-level context (e.g., cultural worldviews, beliefs, values, historical, political, economic, social class, and spiritual systems) and exo-level context (e.g., peacebuiding at the community-level); between exo-level context and meso-level context (e.g., social agency or organizational policies); and lastly between meso-level context and micro-level context (e.g., individual employees demanding effective intergroup conflict training) and all the interconnective ripples between levels. Concurrently, with the promises and the collaboration of the interdisciplinary field of conflict communication, we believe that the bottom-up and interaction effects of the mindful conflict competence approach, dialogue approach, and constructive coalition building approach all have additive change value to foster positive change at a higher level of analysis.

Furthermore, we believe that it is not enough to merely include contextual features in conflict models. We need to understand and explain further the hows, the whys, and the whens that make bottom-up effects the most effective in cueing constructive peacebuilding processes and movements at the macro levels. Likewise, we also need a deeper understanding of the interaction effects on creating mass movements and changes at the macro-levels by paying close attention to the meso-level and exo-level of boundary stretching and conflict resolution success stories and case studies. Methodologically, since social ecological theorizing processes are still in their infancy in the conflict communication domain, we believe interpretive, critical, and quantitative methods are all well suited to address different levels of conflict analysis, pending the research questions asked. More important, a social ecological lens attempts to add breadth and depth of understanding to the multiple complexities of conflict communication from a kaleidoscopic viewpoint. It appears vital that collaborative research and practitioner teams from different levels or contexts of conflict analysis, from different academic boundaries, and from different ethnic and cultural regions come together to listen, to dialogue, to conflict, to resonate, and to come to some hybrid creativity and consensus in the study of conflict and peace-bridging for the 21st century.

REFERENCES

Bronfenbrenner, U. (1977). Toward an experimental ecology of human development. *American Psychologist, 32,* 513–531.

Bronfenbrenner, U. (1979). *The ecology of human development*. Cambridge, MA: Harvard University Press.

Bronfenbrenner, U. (1989). Ecological systems theory. *Annals of Child Development, 6,* 187–249.

Gregory, R., McDaniels, T., & Fields, D. (2001). Decision aiding, not dispute resolution: Creating insights through structured environmental decisions. *Journal of Policy Analysis and Management, 20,* 415–432.

Hawley, A. H. (1950). *Human ecology: A theory of community structure*. New York: Ronald Press.

Huston, T. L. (2000). The social ecology of marriage and other intimate unions. *Journal of Marriage and the Family, 62,* 298–320.

Ihinger-Tallman, M., & Cooney, T. (2005). *Families in context: An introduction.* Los Angeles: Roxbury.

Klein, K. J., Tosi, H., & Cannella, A. A. (1999). Multilevel theory building: Benefits, barriers, and new developments. *Academy of Management Review, 24,* 243–248.

Little, L., & Kaufman Kantor, G. (2002). Using ecological theory to understand intimate partner violence and child maltreatment. *Journal of Community Health Nursing, 19,* 133–145.

McLeroy, K. R., Bibeau, D., Steckler, A., & Glanz, K. (1988). An ecological perspective on health promotion programs. *Health Education Quarterly, 15,* 351–377.

Oetzel, J. G. (1995). Intercultural small groups: An effective decision-making theory. In R. L. Wiseman (Ed.), *Intercultural communication theories* (pp. 247–270). Thousand Oaks, CA: Sage.

Oetzel, J. G. (1998). Culturally homogeneous and heterogeneous groups: Explaining communication processes through individualism-collectivism and self-construal. *International Journal of Intercultural Relations, 22,* 135–161.

Oetzel, J. G., & Duran, B. (2004). Intimate partner violence in American Indian and/or Alaska Native communities: A social ecological framework of determinants and interventions. *American Indian and Alaska Native Mental Health Research: A Journal of the National Center, 11*(3), 49–68.

Oetzel, J. G., Torres, A. B., & Sanchez, C. (2004, November). *A multilevel analysis of process and performance in culturally diverse work groups.* Paper presented at the annual meeting of the National Communication Association, Chicago.

Poncelet, E. C. (2001). "A kiss here and a kiss there": Conflict and collaboration in environmental partnerships. *Environmental Management, 27,* 13–25.

Rousseau, D. M., & House, R. J. (1994). Meso organizational behavior: Avoiding three fundamental biases. In C. L. Cooper & D. M. Rousseau (Eds.), *Trends in organizational behavior* (Vol. 1, pp. 13–30). New York: John Wiley.

Stokols, D. (1996). Translating social ecological theory into guidelines for community health promotion. *American Journal of Health Promotion, 10,* 282–298.

Ting-Toomey, S., & Oetzel, J. (2001). *Managing intercultural conflict effectively.* Thousand Oaks, CA: Sage.

Trethewey, A. (1997). Resistance, identity, and empowerment: A postmodern feminist analysis of clients in a human service organization. *Communication Monographs, 64,* 281–301.

Williams, K. Y., & O'Reilly, C. A. (1998). Demography and diversity in organizations: A review of 40 years of research. In B. M. Staw & L. L. Cummings (Eds.), *Research in organizational behavior* (Vol. 20, pp. 77–140). Greenwich, CT: JAI.

AUTHOR INDEX

Subject Index

ABOUT THE EDITORS

John G. Oetzel (Ph.D., University of Iowa, 1995) is Associate Professor and Chair in the Department of Communication and Journalism at the University of New Mexico. In 2004, he was named Regents' Lecturer by the College of Arts and Sciences at the University of New Mexico. He teaches courses in intercultural, health, and organizational communication, as well as research methods. His research interests focus on culture and conflict communication in workgroups, organizations, and health settings. His work has appeared in journals such as *Human Communication Research, Communication Monographs, Communication Research, Management Communication Quarterly, Small Group Research, Communication Quarterly, Communication Reports,* and the *International Journal of Intercultural Relations.* He is coauthor (with Stella Ting-Toomey) of *Managing Intercultural Communication Effectively* (Sage, 2001). He serves on several editorial boards, including *Communication Education, International and Intercultural Communication Annual,* and *Western Journal of Communication.*

Stella Ting-Toomey is Professor of Human Communication Studies at California State University, Fullerton. Her research interests focus on fine-tuning the conflict face-negotiation theory and testing the impact of situational and ethnic identity factors on conflict styles. She also has a strong interest in linking intercultural communication theories with training practice. She has published more than 70 book chapters and articles in various academic journals, including *International Journal of Intercultural Relations, Human Communication Research, Communication Monographs,* and *Communication Research,* among others. She is also the author and editor of 15 books, most recently *Understanding Intercultural Communication* (with Leeva Chung), *Managing Intercultural Conflict Effectively* (with John Oetzel; Sage), *Communicating Effectively With the Chinese* (with Ge Gao; Sage), and *Communicating Across Cultures.* She has lectured widely throughout the United States, Asia, and Europe on the theme of mindful intercultural conflict competence.

ABOUT THE CONTRIBUTORS

Bibiana Arcos (B.A. in Architecture, Universidad Javeriana de Bogotá, Colombia) is an M.A. student in the Department of Communication and Journalism at the University of New Mexico. She has published articles and worked as a managing editor of an architecture magazine in Colombia, where she began her emphasis in organizational communication. Her academic interests include organizational and intercultural communication in intersection with discourses of place, belonging, and identity.

J. Kevin Barge (Ph.D., University of Kansas) is Associate Professor of Speech Communication at the University of Georgia. He is also a member of the Public Dialogue Consortium, a group of scholars and practitioners devoted to developing new forms of communicative practice that facilitate communities' working through polarized and polarizing issues. His major research interests center on developing a communication approach to management and leadership, and exploring the relationship between dialogue and public deliberation. His research has been published in *The Academy of Management Review, Management Communication Quarterly, Communication Theory, Communication Monographs, Journal of Applied Communication Research,* and *Journal of Conflict Resolution.* He has served on a number of national and international editorial boards for journals, such as *Communication Monographs, Management Communication Quarterly, Journal of Applied Communication Research,* and *Conflict Resolution Quarterly.* He is a former editor of *Communication Studies.*

Benjamin J. Broome is Professor in the Hugh Downs School of Human Communication at Arizona State University (ASU), where he teaches courses in intercultural communication, group facilitation, and conflict resolution. His research focuses on the third-party facilitator role in complex problem situations. His publications have appeared in journals such as *International Negotiation, Systems Research and Behavioral Science, International Journal of Intercultural Relations, Human Communication Research, Management Communication Quarterly, Journal of Conflict Resolution, Journal of Social Psychology, International Journal of Conflict Management, Small Group Research, American Indian Quarterly,* and *Communication Education.* Over the past decade, he has been involved with peacebuilding efforts in Cyprus, where he has worked closely with groups of Greek Cypriots and Turkish Cypriots in conflict resolution, problem solving, and interactive design. In addition he has worked with a number of government agencies, business organizations, professional associations, educational institutions, Native American Tribes, and community groups in the United States, Europe, and Mexico. He has a strong commitment to developing avenues for genuine dialogue that meaningfully addresses the increasingly complex and diverse issues facing our contemporary world.

Deborah A. Cai (Ph.D., Michigan State University, 1994) is Associate Professor in the Department of Communication at the University of Maryland. As an international researcher with ties to China, her scholarly interests center on intercultural communication, negotiation, and conflict management. Her research focuses on the interaction of contextual factors of conflict situations with the cultural orientations of those involved in affecting conflict outcomes and processes. Particular emphasis is given to the effect of cultural and religious values in Asian countries on communication processes. Her past works examine cultural differences in negotiation plans, enactment of face-management strategies, and the mediating effects of role on culture in business negotiation. Her research has been presented at national and international conferences and is published in places such as *Communication Monographs, Communication Yearbook, Human Communication Research, Journal of Applied Communication,* and the *Asian Journal of Communication.*

Daniel J. Canary is Professor in the Hugh Downs School of Human Communication at Arizona State University. He has authored or coauthored nine books and more than 50 articles and scholarly book chapters. A former President of the International Network on Personal Relationships, he has served on many editorial boards that publish research on the topic of interpersonal communication. He is current Editor of the *Western Journal of Communication.* He completed his Ph.D. from the University of Southern California in 1983. Contact information: Arizona State University, Tempe, AZ 85287–1205; e-mail: dan.canary@asu.edu; tel: 480–965–6650.

John P. Caughlin is Associate Professor of Speech Communication at the University of Illinois at Urbana-Champaign. His research examines communication in families and other close relationships, focusing on the causes and consequences of avoiding communication. Recent work has appeared in journals such as *Communication Monographs, Human Communication Research, Journal of Marriage and Family, Journal of Social and Personal Relationships, Journal of Personality and Social Psychology,* and *Personal Relationships.* One of his papers on the demand/withdraw pattern of communication in marriage won the Knower Outstanding Article Award from the Interpersonal Division of the National Communication Association. In 2004 he received the Miller Early Career Achievement Award from the International Association for Relationship Research.

Susan W. Coleman has worked as an international organizational consultant and trainer specializing in negotiation, cross-cultural communication, conflict resolution, and collaborative strategies to help people and systems deal more effectively with differences and find creative solutions since 1988. She has designed and implemented a worldwide conflict resolution program for the United Nations Secretariat and was also a key player in establishing a conflict resolution program at Teachers College, Columbia University, where she served as the Director of International Projects from 1997 to 2004. She has worked for a wide variety of diplomatic organizations, schools, global companies, governments, and nonprofits, and her training materials have been translated into many languages. She was published in *The Handbook of Conflict Resolution: Theory and Practice* (2000) and is currently working on a conflict skills book for the general public with an accompanying demonstration and skills practice CD-ROM. To order any of her manuals, videotapes, or other materials or for inquiries about her services, please go to her website at www.colemanraider.com or write to Coleman Raider International, 44 Travis Corners Road, Garrison, NY 10524; tel: 845-424-8300.

William A. Donohue is currently Distinguished Professor of Communication at Michigan State University. He received his Ph.D. in Communication in 1976 from The

Ohio State University. His work lies primarily in the areas of mediation and crisis negotiation. He has worked extensively with several state and federal agencies in both training and research activities related to violence prevention and hostage negotiation. He has more than 60 publications dealing with various communication and conflict issues and has won several awards for his scholarship from national and international professional associations. He is an active member of the International Association for Conflict Management, is on the editorial board of several journals in the areas of conflict management and communication, and is an evaluator for several federal grants. He has published in a variety of journals, including *International Negotiation, International Journal of Conflict Management,* and *Negotiation Journal.*

Laura Kathleen Dorsey (Ph.D., Howard University, 2000) is Assistant Professor of Speech Communication at Morgan State University in Baltimore, Maryland. Her areas of teaching and research expertise include organizational communication, small group communication, interpersonal communication, racial/ethnic relations, leadership development, unconscious group processes, and internalized oppression. She also has more than a decade of experience in organizational consultation and training, both nationally and internationally.

Melodi A. Everett (M.A., Western Michigan University, 2003) is an advertising account coordinator with BBDO Detroit. Her research interests include diversity in organizations, interracial conflict, and the impact of fatherlessness on the adult relationships of women of color.

Edward L. Fink is Professor and Chair of the Department of Communication, Affiliate Professor of Sociology, and Affiliate Professor of Psychology at the University of Maryland. His research involves attitude and belief change, communication theory, and research methods and statistics. He is a University of Maryland Distinguished Scholar-Teacher and recipient of the International Communication Association's B. Aubrey Fisher Mentorship Award. He coauthored *The Measurement of Communication Processes* and has published more than 50 articles, monographs, and chapters in the communication, sociology, psychology, criminology, and health education literatures. From 1991 to 1996 he served as Associate Editor of the *Journal of Communication,* and from 1998 to 2000 he was editor of *Human Communication Research.*

Mary Anne Fitzpatrick (Ph.D., Temple University) is founding Dean of the College of Arts and Sciences at the University of South Carolina and a Carolina Foundation Distinguished Professor of Psychology. The author of more than 100 articles, chapters, and books, she also is a past President of the International Communication Association and recipient of the ICA Career Productivity Award of 2001.

Rebecca Royer Franks is a doctoral candidate in communication at the University of Utah. She has an M.A. in Communication from Texas A&M University. She was a Dispute Resolution Specialist with the Bureau of Land Management before returning to graduate school to study environmental conflict. Her research examines the intersection of power, resistance, and identity in environmental conflicts.

Johny T. Garner is a doctoral candidate at Texas A&M University. He received his M.A. degree from Abilene Christian University in 2001. His research interests include dissent and resistance in organizations, coworker communication, and group dialectics.

Eytan Gilboa (Ph.D., Harvard University) is Professor of Communications and Government and senior researcher at the Begin-Sadat Center for Strategic Studies, at Bar-Ilan University in Israel, and is currently Visiting Professor at the University of

Southern California. His most recent works include an edited volume, *Media and Conflict: Framing Issues, Policy Making, Shaping Opinions* (2002) and articles published in the *Journal of Communication, Political Communication, Harvard International Journal of Press/Politics, Critical Studies in Media Communication,* and *Georgetown Journal of International Affairs.* He is the recipient of the 2001 Best Article Award of the International Communication Association.

Laura K. Guerrero (Ph.D., University of Arizona, 1994) is Professor in the Hugh Downs School of Human Communication at Arizona State University, where she specializes in relational and nonverbal communication. Her work on emotion focuses on communicative responses to jealousy, anger, sadness, and hurtful events. She also conducts research on conflict communication in both relational and task-oriented contexts. Her book credits include *The Handbook of Communication and Emotion* (coedited with Peter Andersen) and *Without Words: Nonverbal Communication in Close Relationships* (coauthored with Kory Floyd). She was awarded the Gerald R. Miller Early Achievement Award from the International Association for Relationship Research.

Mitchell R. Hammer, Ph.D., is Principal in *Hammer Consulting,* LLC, an intercultural consulting firm, and Professor of International Peace and Conflict Resolution at the American University in Washington, D.C. His work focuses on crisis and conflict dynamics across cultures and author identification. His 1997 book (coedited with R. G. Rogan & C. Van Zandt), *Dynamic Processes of Crisis Negotiation: Theory, Research and Practice,* was given the Outstanding Book Award in 1998 by the International Association of Conflict Management. He has published widely, and won awards for his scholarship from the Speech Communication Association, the Academy of Management, the International Communication Association, and the Society of Intercultural Education, Training and Research. In 1997, he advised the Japanese government on negotiation strategies concerning the hostage crisis in Peru, and in 1996 he and Randall G. Rogan identified a set of letters with the writing of the "Unabomber Manifesto," assisting the investigation that identified Ted Kaczynski as the "Unabomber."

Ann-Sofi Jakobsson Hatay (B.A., M.A., doctoral candidate) is a peace and conflict researcher and lecturer at Uppsala University, Sweden. Her research focuses on peace processes in intrastate conflicts, the role of civil society in peace and democratization processes, and reconciliation. For many years she conducted field research on the conflicts and peace processes in Northern Ireland and Cyprus. Her other research projects include an analysis of international assistance to democratization and reconciliation in Bosnia and Herzegovina, Kosovo, and Macedonia. Among her most recent publications are *The Political Dynamics of Peacebuilding and Peacemaking in Divided Societies: A Comparative Study of the Peace Processes in Northern Ireland and Cyprus* (in press) and *Macedonia: A Strategic Conflict Analysis* (2005). She is also the organizer and facilitator of numerous peacebuilding dialogue initiatives, and a consultant on peace and conflict related matters.

Tricia S. Jones is Professor in the Department of Psychological Studies in Education, Temple University. She has published more than 40 articles and book chapters on conflict, and coedited the volumes *New Directions on Mediation* (Sage, 1994), *Does It Work? The Case for Conflict Resolution Education in Our Nation's Schools* (2000), and *Kids Working It Out: Stories and Strategies for Making Peace in Our Schools* (2003). Her research in conflict resolution education has been funded by the William and Flora Hewlett Foundation, the Packard Foundation, the Surdna Foundation, the Pennsylvania Commission on Crime and Delinquency, the George Gund Foundation, and the United States Information Agency. Her current funded research from the U.S. Department of

Education's Fund for the Improvement of Postsecondary Education program is the Conflict Resolution Education in Teacher Education program, educating preservice teacher and counselor candidates in urban education environments about conflict resolution education. She is a past President (1996–1997) of the International Association of Conflict Management. She currently serves as the Editor-in-Chief of *Conflict Resolution Quarterly,* the scholarly journal of the Association for Conflict Resolution. She is the recipient of the 2004 Jeffrey Z. Rubin Theory to Practice Award from the International Association for Conflict Management.

Krishna Kandath is Assistant Professor in the Department of Communication and Journalism at the University of New Mexico. He received his Ph.D. from The Ohio University, Athens. His teaching and research interests are in history and philosophy of communication, theory, and critical/cultural inquiry.

Erika L. Kirby (Ph.D., University of Nebraska–Lincoln) is Associate Professor and Chair in the Department of Communication Studies at Creighton University. Her teaching and research interests include organizational, applied, and work-family/life communication and discourse as well as their intersections with gender and feminism. She has published articles in outlets such as the *Journal of Applied Communication Research, Management Communication Quarterly, Communication Yearbook,* and *Communication Studies,* and serves on the editorial boards of the *Journal of Applied Communication Research, Communication Studies,* and *Communication Teacher.*

Ascan F. Koerner (Ph.D., University of Wisconsin) is Associate Professor of Communication Studies at the University of Minnesota–Twin Cities. His research focuses on family communication and on the cognitive bases of relationships and their influence on interpersonal communication, including message production and message interpretation. He is a contributor to publications such as *The Handbook of Family Communication* and *The Handbook of Personal Relationships,* and journals such as *Communication Monographs, Communication Theory,* and *Human Communication Research.*

Sandra G. Lakey is Associate Professor at Pennsylvania College of Technology; she is also head of the Communication and Literature Department. She completed her Ph.D. from Pennsylvania State University in 2000. Working with Dan Canary, she focused her research on interpersonal goals, communication competence, and interpersonal conflict. Currently, she is working on a study of relationships between interpersonal goals and perceptions of effectiveness and appropriateness. In addition, her classroom experiences are creating an increasing interest in the ways students' mindless nonverbal behaviors in the classroom affect instructors' perceptions and behaviors. Contact information: Pennsylvania College of Technology, 1 College Ave., Williamsport, PA 17701; e-mail: slakey@pct.edu; tel: 570–326–3761.

Angela G. La Valley (M.A., University of Colorado–Boulder, 2003) is a doctoral student in the Hugh Downs School of Human Communication at Arizona State University, where she specializes in interpersonal and family communication. Her current research interests include the nonverbal communication of emotions and intergenerational family communication around issues related to care giving and support.

David B. Lipsky is Professor of Industrial and Labor Relations and Director of the Institute on Conflict Resolution at Cornell University. He is currently the President-Elect of the Labor and Employment Relations Association. He served as Dean of the School of Industrial and Labor Relations (ILR) at Cornell from 1988 until 1997 and has been a member of the Cornell faculty since 1969. He received his B.S. in 1961 from the

ILR at Cornell and his Ph.D. in Economics from MIT in 1967. He is the author of 53 articles and the author or editor of 15 books and monographs. He is the coauthor (with Ronald L. Seeber and Richard D. Fincher) of *Emerging Systems for Managing Workplace Conflict* (2003). He is also the coeditor (with Thomas A. Kochan) of *Negotiations and Change: From the Workplace to Society* (2003). He was a member of the inaugural class of the National Academy of Human Resources. In 1998 he received the Judge William B. Groat Alumni Award for professional accomplishment and service to the School of Industrial and Labor Relations. He received the General Mills Foundation Award for Achievement in Teaching from the ILR School in 2003.

Stephen W. Littlejohn is a partner in the communication consulting firm Domenici Littlejohn, Inc., and is a project manager for the Public Dialogue Consortium. Most recently, he helped to design and facilitate peace dialogues in Sri Lanka and Indonesia, and he currently facilitates institutional planning for U.S. tribal colleges. His work has taken him to Ireland, the United Kingdom, Argentina, and throughout the United States, helping groups and communities work collaboratively to resolve difficult issues. He has written widely on topics related to communication, conflict, and dialogue, including *Moral Conflict: When Social Worlds Collide* (Sage, 1997), *Engaging Communication in Conflict: Systemic Practice* (Sage, 2001), and *Mediation: Empowerment in Conflict Management* (2001). The eighth edition of his book *Theories of Human Communication* was recently published (2005), and he is working on two new books, *Communication, Conflict, and the Management of Difference* and *Communication and the Management of Face: From Theory to Practice,* both forthcoming in 2006. He received his Ph.D. in Communication from the University of Utah and was a professor of Speech Communication at Humboldt State University for 26 years. He now lives in Albuquerque, New Mexico. Additional information can be found at www.domenici-littlejohn.com.

Phola Mabizela (M.A., University of New Mexico, 2004) is a communication consultant, focusing on imparting "soft skills," in particular intercultural communication, cultural fluency, and interpersonal communication within the South African corporate environment. Her ongoing research is the construction of identity among women in multicultural, tradition-bound, and still-patriarchal societies.

M. Chad McBride (Ph.D., University of Nebraska–Lincoln) is Assistant Professor of Communication Studies at Creighton University. His research and teaching interests include communication in personal relationships, families, and social networks.

Courtney Waite Miller (Ph.D., Northwestern University, 2004) is an Assistant Professor in the Communication Arts and Sciences department at Elmhurst College. Her research is focused on interpersonal communication, specifically conflict in close relationships.

Anne Maydan Nicotera (Ph.D., Ohio University, 1990) is Associate Professor of Communication and Culture at Howard University. Her research focuses on culture and conflict in organizational and relational contexts, race and gender issues, diversity, and aggressive communication predispositions. She has published her research in numerous journals. She has also published four books and several chapters. Her consulting specialty is design and implementation of communication skills workshops and seminars.

Mark P. Orbe (Ph.D., Ohio University, 1993) is Professor of Communication and Diversity in the School of Communication at Western Michigan University, where he also holds a joint appointment in the Center for Women's Studies. His research and teaching interests center on exploring the inextricable relationship between culture and communication across multiple contexts.

Tarla Rai Peterson is Professor of Communication at University of Utah, and Adjunct Professor of Wildlife Sciences at Texas A&M University. Her research focuses on how rhetoric and dissent influence environmental policy within democratic systems. She has facilitated workshops to enhance understanding and management of environmental conflicts in the United States and Europe. She has authored more than 50 articles and book chapters, as well as a book titled *Sharing the Earth: The Rhetoric of Sustainable Development.*

Marshall Scott Poole is Professor of Communication and of Information and Operations Management at Texas A&M University. He received his Ph.D. in 1980 from the University of Wisconsin and taught at the Universities of Illinois and Minnesota before coming to Texas A&M. His research interests include group and organizational communication, information systems, conflict management, and organizational innovation. His articles have appeared in *Management Science, Organization Science, Information Systems Research, MIS Quarterly, Human Communication Research, Communication Monographs, Small Group Research,* and *Academy of Management Review.* He has coauthored or edited ten books, including *Communication and Group Decision-Making, Theories of Small Groups: Interdisciplinary Perspectives, Organizational Change and Innovation Processes: Theory and Methods for Research,* and *The Handbook of Organizational Change and Innovation.* He is a Fellow of the International Communication Association.

Linda L. Putnam (Ph.D., University of Minnesota, 1977) is George T. and Gladys H. Abell Professor in the Department of Communication at Texas A&M University and past Director of the Conflict and Dispute Resolution Program at the Bush School of Public Affairs. Her current research interests include negotiation and organizational conflict, environmental conflict, and language analysis in organizations. She is the coeditor of *The New Handbook of Organizational Communication* (2001), *Communication and Negotiation* (1992), and *Communication and Organization: An Interpretive Approach* (1983), and the *Handbook of Organizational Discourse* (2004). She is the 1993 recipient of the Charles H. Woolbert Research Award for innovative research in communication, the 1999 recipient of the Distinguished Scholar Award from the National Communication Association, the 2005 recipient of the Steven H. Chaffee Career Productivity Award, a Fellow and Past President of the International Communication Association, and Past President of the International Association for Conflict Management.

Ellen Raider (M.Ed., Temple University) is a mediator, trainer, and program developer whose training materials have been used by educational, business, and governmental organizations throughout the world. In partnership with Morton Deutsch, she launched the International Center for Cooperation and Conflict Resolution (ICCCR) and graduate studies in Conflict Studies at Teachers College at Columbia University. In collaboration with the New York City Board of Education she trained staff from 150 high schools, launching a major citywide effort to reduce school violence by increasing students' conflict resolution and mediation skills. In her own consulting practice, she has designed cross-cultural conflict resolution programs for the worldwide staff at UNICEF; the Committee for National Security; the American Friends Service Committee; and the U.S./USSR Trade Negotiation Project. She is currently a member of the Independent Commission on Public Education in New York City, a group whose mission is to bring about a human-rights based system of education in New York City.

Susana Rinderle (M.A., Communication, University of New Mexico; B.A., Sociology, UCLA) has a varied background as a social worker, journalist, social service/academic program manager, business consultant, professional trainer, mediator, performer, and university instructor. She studied at Universidad Nacional Autónoma de México (UNAM) in Mexico City and worked in Guadalajara, México. Her main research interests are identity and labels, intercultural conflict, the U.S. Latino experience, and Mexican-White U.S. American communication. She recently left teaching communication and sociology at UNM to become an Organizational Development consultant and trainer for UNM Hospitals. Her work is forthcoming in the *Journal of Communication Inquiry* and the *International and Intercultural Communication Annual.*

Randall G. Rogan (Ph.D., Michigan State University) is Professor and currently serves as Department Chair for the Department of Communication at Wake Forest University. His research is in forensic discourse analysis of crisis negotiations and author identification. In particular, his research focuses on the affective and framing features of conflict communication, for which he has received scholarly awards. In fact, his 1997 book (coedited with M. R. Hammer & C. Van Zandt), *Dynamic Processes of Crisis Negotiation: Theory, Research and Practice,* was awarded the Outstanding Book Award in 1998 by the International Association of Conflict Management. He is recognized as an international expert and leading researcher in crisis negotiation. He has consulted with various law enforcement agencies on crisis negotiation and threatening communication. Of particular note, his analysis of written documents assisted in the investigation that resulted in the arrest of the Unabomber.

Michael E. Roloff (Ph.D., Michigan State University, 1975) is Professor of Communication Studies at Northwestern University. His research interests include bargaining and negotiation, and conflict management. He is the author of *Interpersonal Communication: The Social Exchange Approach* and coeditor of *Persuasion: New Directions in Theory and Research, Interpersonal Processes: New Directions in Communication Research, Social Cognition and Communication,* and *Communication and Negotiation.* His work has been published in such journals as *Communication Monographs, Communication Research,* and *Human Communication Research.* He is Senior Associate Editor of the *International Journal of Conflict Management,* and he has served as editor of the *Communication Yearbook* and as coeditor of *Communication Research.*

Ronald L. Seeber is Professor and Associate Dean at the School of Industrial and Labor Relations at Cornell University. He is also Executive Director of the Cornell Institute on Conflict Resolution. He received his B.S. in Industrial Engineering at Iowa State University in 1975 and received his A.M. (1977) and Ph.D. (1981) degrees in labor and industrial relations from the University of Illinois. He has written on a wide range of topics in the field of labor-management relations and dispute resolution and has published extensively in academic journals. He has been an active participant in the professional meetings of the Labor and Employment Relations Association, the Association for Conflict Resolution, and the Academy of Management. He has coauthored or edited eight books on labor relations and dispute resolution topics, including (most recently) *Emerging Systems of Managing Workplace Conflict* with David B. Lipsky and Richard D. Fincher (2003). He has conducted numerous seminars and workshops on negotiations and dispute resolution for corporate, government, and union groups.

Jiro Takai is Associate Professor of Social and Cultural Psychology at the Department of Educational Psychology, Nagoya University, in Japan. He received his Ph.D. from the

Department of Communication at the University of California, Santa Barbara. His general research interests are in cross-cultural comparisons of interpersonal communication competence. His specific research interests are aimed at explaining diverse communication styles from a conception-of-self perspective. His publications include articles that have appeared in the *International Journal of Intercultural Relations, Communication Monographs,* and the *Japanese Journal of Experimental Social Psychology.*

Anita L. Vangelisti is interested in interpersonal communication among family members and between romantic partners. Her current work focuses how communication affects, and is affected by, emotions and interpretive processes such as attribution. She has published her research in journals such as *Communication Monographs, Human Communication Research, Journal of Personality and Social Psychology, Personal Relationships, Family Relations, Journal of Adolescent Research,* and *Journal of Social and Personal Relationships.* She is coeditor of the Cambridge University Press book series on *Advances in Personal Relationships,* was associate editor of *Personal Relationships,* edited the *ISSPR Bulletin,* and has served on the editorial boards of numerous journals. She has coauthored and edited several books and is presently working on two more volumes.

Qi Wang (M.A., Kent State University, 2000; B.A., Peking University, 1997) is a doctoral student in the Department of Communication at the University of Maryland. Her areas of interest include intercultural communication, negotiation and conflict management, social influence, and research methods.

Wallace Warfield is Associate Professor at the Institute for Conflict Analysis and Resolution, George Mason University in Fairfax, Virginia. In this capacity, he teaches laboratory-simulation and practicum courses, as well as theory courses. As a practitioner, he has done mediation, facilitation, training, and problem-solving workshops in community, interethnic, and organizational conflict in the United States and other countries. He is the author of a number of publications in the field of conflict analysis and resolution and has most recently been a member of a research team looking at conflict zones of peace in Colombia.

A. Michael Weinman is a doctoral candidate in the Department of Communication and Journalism at the University of New Mexico. After emigrating from Jerusalem to Taos, New Mexico, in 1972 and working as an electrical engineer and an educator, he entered the fields of intercultural communication and educational technologies in 1996 in order to promote communication among learners from different cultures. He received a Master's degree from UNM College of Education after completing research in Morocco concerning the use of distance education technologies in international intercultural education. His academic and civic interests are in introducing, promoting, and researching dialogic communication in American Muslim communities, community building through participative action research, mediation as community service, and conflict resolution.

Stacey M. Wieland (M.A., University of Southern California) is a doctoral student in the Department of Communication at the University of Colorado, Boulder. She studies organizational communication and is specifically interested in how individuals discursively construct the relationship between working life and private life. She considers how people (re)produce and shape structures and policies in ways that simultaneously enable and constrain them in relation to work and life. As such, she is specifically interested in the Swedish context for studying work/life and considering what organizations and individuals in the United States and Sweden can learn from one another about work/life issues.

Qin Zhang (Ph.D., University of New Mexico) is Assistant Professor in the Department of Communication at Fairfield University. Her research interests focus on intercultural communication in interpersonal and instructional contexts. She is particularly interested in intercultural conflict management and resolution and effective teacher communication behaviors across cultures. Her publications have appeared in the *International and Intercultural Communication Annual, Journal of Intercultural Communication Studies,* and *Journal of Intergroup Relations.*